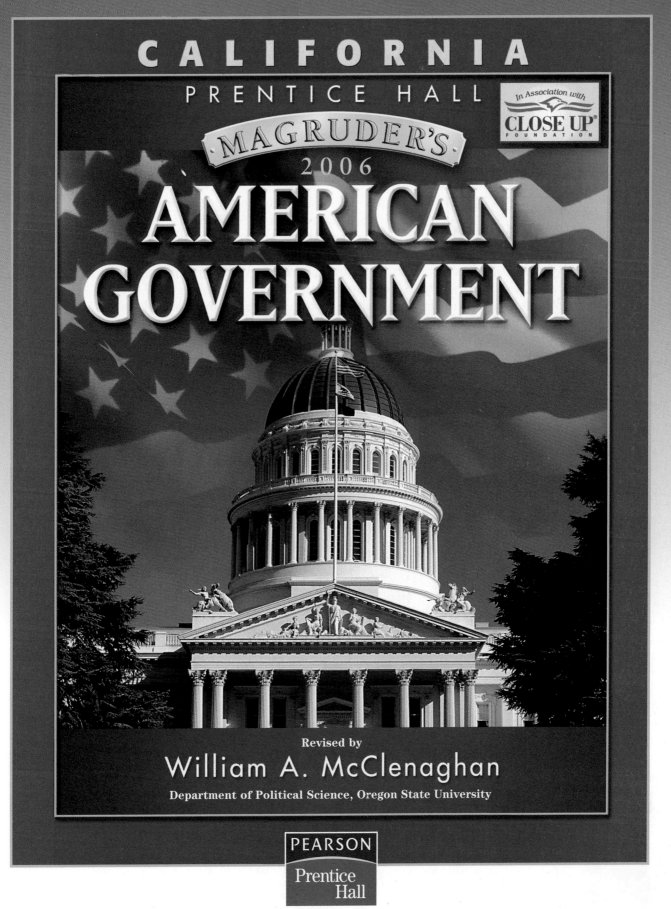

CALIFORNIA

PRENTICE HALL

In Association with CLOSE UP® FOUNDATION

·MAGRUDER'S·

2006

AMERICAN GOVERNMENT

Revised by

William A. McClenaghan

Department of Political Science, Oregon State University

PEARSON

Prentice Hall

Boston, Massachusetts
Upper Saddle River, New Jersey

Magruder's American Government,

first published in 1917 and revised annually, is an enduring symbol of the author's faith in American ideals and American institutions. The life of Frank Abbott Magruder (1882–1949) was an outstanding example of Americanism at its very best. His career as a teacher, author, and tireless worker in civic and religious undertakings remains an inspiring memory to all who knew him.

The Close Up Foundation is the nation's largest civic education organization. Since 1971, Close Up has been a leader in the social studies field, reaching millions of students, educators, and other adults. The Foundation's mission of informed participation in government and democracy drives its experiential civic education programs in Washington, D.C., for students and teachers, as well as its television programs on C-SPAN, and its award-winning publications and videos. Close Up's work represents a multidimensional approach to citizenship education by increasing community involvement and civic literacy—one student, one citizen, at a time.

Program Consultants

Constitution Consultant

Dr. Christine L. Compston
University of Massachusetts
Boston, Massachusetts

Reading Consultant

Dr. Bonnie Armbruster
University of Illinois at
Urbana-Champaign
Champaign, Illinois

Curriculum and Assessment Specialist

Jan Moberley
Dallas, Texas

Internet Consultant

Dr. Larry Elowitz
Professor of Political Science
Georgia College and State
University
Milledgeville, Georgia

Block Scheduling Consultant

Gwen L. Patterson
Marcus High School
Flower Mound, Texas

40000002550210

ISBN 0-13-133579-0
8 9 10 10 09 08

Program Reviewers

Comparative Government Consultant

Dr. Craig Arceneaux
California Polytechnic State University
San Luis Obispo, California

California Consultant

Jan E. Ebey
San Bernardino City Schools
San Bernardino, California

Teacher Reviewers

Elizabeth Battle
Aldine Independent School District
Houston, Texas

Sam Brewster
Shawnee Mission East High School
Shawnee Mission, Kansas

Judith Cannizzaro
Metro Nashville Public Schools
Nashville, Tennessee

Greg Clevenger
Adams High School
Rochester Hills, Michigan

Michael "Jerry" DaDurka
David Starr Jordan High School (LBUSD)
Long Beach, California

Mary Ellen Daneels
Community High School
West Chicago, Illinois

Les Fortune
Tallwood High School
Virginia Beach, Virginia

Rita Geiger
Norman Public Schools
Norman, Oklahoma

Margaret J. Jamison
Pasadena Independent School District
Pasadena, Texas

Mary Lynn Johnson
Spring Independent School District
Houston, Texas

Richard Kean
Central High School
Cheyenne, Wyoming

David Kenewell
Utica Schools
Sterling Heights, Michigan

Vicki Kuker
Bishop Dwenger High School
Fort Wayne, Indiana

Bridget Loft
Wakefield High School
Arlington, Virginia

Lawrence Moaton
Memphis City Schools
Memphis, Tennessee

Elizabeth Morrison
Parkway South High School
Manchester, Missouri

K. Chaka K. Nantambu
Central High School
Detroit, Michigan

Yoshi Negoro
St. Lucie West Centennial High School
Port St. Lucie, Florida

Carol Schroder
Decatur High School
Federal Way, Washington

Ninfa Sepúlveda
Stephen F. Austin High School
Houston, Texas

Kate Sintros
Concord Public Schools
Concord, New Hampshire

Bill Smiley
Leigh High School
San Jose, California

Barbara Maness Stafford
Central High School
Little Rock, Arkansas

Gerald A. Stupiansky
Lakewood High School
Lakewood, Ohio

Kristena M. Watson
Spring Woods High School
Houston, Texas

Student Reviewers

Brannen Bagley
Tallwood High School
Virginia Beach, Virginia

Rebekah Kaufman
Bishop Dwenger High School
Fort Wayne, Indiana

Andrew Kreamer
Leigh High School
San Jose, California

Chuyen Phan
Stephen F. Austin High School
Houston, Texas

Adam Valadez
Community High School
West Chicago, Illinois

Law and Goverment Reviewer

Greg I. Massing
Assistant District Attorney
Salem, Massachusetts

Program Advisors

Michal Howden
Social Studies Consultant
Zionsville, Indiana

Joe Wieczorek
Social Studies Consultant
Baltimore, Maryland

Table of Contents

UNIT 3

UNIT 4

The Executive Branch 350

Special Features

Close Up on the Supreme Court

Background information and key arguments on landmark Supreme Court Cases

Close Up on Primary Sources

Excerpted documents that highlight key issues

Government Online

Issues in government with links to www.phschool.com

SKILLS FOR LIFE

Step-by-step lessons to learn and practice important skills

Voices on Government

Opinions, views, and comments on the American political system

Madeleine M. Kunin

Frequently Asked Questions

Frequently Asked Questions—and their answers—about pertinent topics in American Government.

The Enduring Constitution

Time lines that show how the Constitution is an enduring document

Face the Issues

Debates on crucial issues facing Americans today

Political Cartoons

Maps, Graphs, Charts, Diagrams, Time Lines, and Tables

Maps

Graphs, Charts, Diagrams

Time Lines

Tables

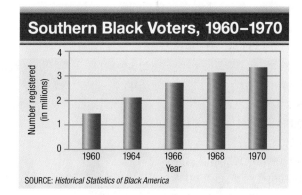

Southern Black Voters, 1960–1970

SOURCE: *Historical Statistics of Black America*

The Six Basic Principles of the Constitution

*T**he Constitution of the United States is built on six basic principles of government. The Framers of the Constitution drew on their knowledge and experience to craft a document that serves as "the supreme law of the land." The descriptions at the beginning of each unit will help you see how these six principles—and the Constitution itself—have proved an enduring yet flexible guide for governing the nation for over 200 years.*

Popular Sovereignty

The Preamble to the Constitution begins with this bold phrase: "We the people…" These words announce that in the United States, the people establish government and give it its power. The people are sovereign. Since the government receives its power from the people, it can govern only with their consent.

Limited Government

Because the people are the source of government power, the government has only as much authority as the people give it. Much of the Constitution, in fact, consists of specific limitations on government power. Limited government means that neither the government itself nor any government official is "above the law" and can overstep these constitutional bounds.

Separation of Powers

Government power is not only limited; it is also divided. The Constitution assigns specific powers to each of the three branches: the legislative (Congress), the executive (President), and the judicial (federal courts). This separation of powers is intended to prevent misuse of power by any of the three branches of government.

Checks and Balances

The system of checks and balances extends the restrictions established by the separation of powers. Each branch of government has the authority to restrain the actions of either of the other two branches. This system makes government less efficient but also prevents tyranny by one branch of government.

Judicial Review

Who decides whether an act of government oversteps the limits placed on it by the Constitution? Historically, the federal courts have done so. The principle of judicial review was established early in this nation's history. It means that federal courts have the power to review governmental actions and to nullify (cancel) any that are unconstitutional, any that violate some provision of the Constitution.

Federalism

A federal system divides power between a central government and several regional (local) governments. This sharing of power is intended to ensure that the central government is powerful enough to be effective, yet not so powerful as to threaten the existence of the regional governments or the rights of the people. It also allows individual States to deal with local problems as they choose—so long as their actions are constitutional.

Use This Book for Success

The American system of government's fundamental principles and its basic structure have remained constant over time. Many of its other characteristics, however, have changed. A number of the features in this book are designed to help you understand how our government works and to encourage you to be an active, participating citizen.

California Standards Preview

Every chapter begins with a correlation to California standards in government and a Chapter in Brief outline that can be used to preview the chapter content or to review for an exam.

Learn More Online

Government Online appears throughout your book. Use this feature to learn about issues of interest that you can explore online at **PHSchool.com**

Connect Government to Your Life

You Can Make a Difference activities at the end of every chapter suggest ways for you to take an active role in your community. The Why It Matters statement in every section preview helps you understand why government is important in your life.

Learn to Be an Active Citizen

The Skills for Life features teach important citizenship, critical thinking, technology, and chart and graph skills.

Learn About Important Supreme Court Cases

Close Up on the Supreme Court features in every chapter outline landmark cases in the California government standards and encourage you to evaluate the arguments of both sides.

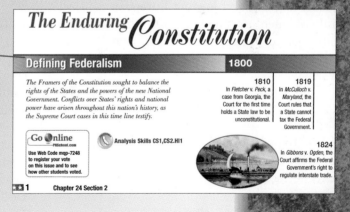

CLOSE UP FOUNDATION — on the Supreme Court

Can Groups' Liberties Be Limited During Wartime?

Analysis Skills HR4, HI3, HI4

Many difficult questions concerning personal freedoms arise during national emergencies. When the survival of the nation is threatened, strong government action may be necessary to confront the threat. Such action might harm individuals or groups. May government impose limits on civil rights in case of emergencies?

Korematsu v. United States (1944)

Japan's attack on Pearl Harbor, Hawaii, on December 7, 1941, prompted widespread fear that Japan might try to invade the West Coast, and that persons of Japanese ancestry living there might aid the invasion. At that time, about 120,000 persons of Japanese descent lived in the West Coast States; some 70,000 of these were *Nisei* (native-born American citizens).

On February 19, 1942, President Franklin Roosevelt issued Executive Order No. 9066 authorizing the military to designate military areas and to exclude "any or all persons" from them. This order was intended to help protect the country from espionage or sabotage. Congress then passed a law requiring that all persons excluded from those military areas be sent to "war relocation camps" outside the sensitive military areas.

On March 2, 1942, the general in charge of the West Coast Defense Command issued the first of a series of orders that identified the entire Pacific Coast as Military Area No. 1. Soon, all persons of Japanese descent were ordered out of that area.

Fred Korematsu, a native-born American citizen, refused to leave his home in San Leandro, across the bay from San Francisco. He was arrested, charged with failure to report for relocation, and convicted in federal district court. After losing in the court of appeals, he appealed to the Supreme Court.

Arguments for Korematsu

1. Executive Order 9066 denied Korematsu his liberty without due process of law, in violation of the 5th Amendment.

2. The military does not have the authority to regulate civilian conduct, and the President cannot delegate that power to the military when martial law has not been declared.

3. The order of exclusion created a classification based on race, in violation of the Constitution.

Arguments for the United States

1. Although the relocation would not be proper in peacetime, the danger of espionage and sabotage justified this denial of liberty to American citizens under wartime circumstances.

2. Because war had been declared, the President had the authority as commander in chief to issue such orders to the military.

3. The United States had been attacked by Japan, so it was logical that people of Japanese ancestry were suspect. The decision to relocate people from sensitive military areas was based on security concerns and not on racial prejudice.

Decide for Yourself

1. Review the constitutional grounds on which each side bases its arguments and the specific arguments each side presented.

2. Debate the opposing viewpoints presented in this case. Which viewpoint do you favor?

3. Predict the impact of the Court's decision on discrimination based on race and national ancestry in the United States. (To read a summary of the Court's decision, turn to pages 799–806.)

Go Online PHSchool.com Use Web Code mqp-4147 to register your vote on this issue and to see how other students voted.

The Federal Court System **527**

Face the Issues

Defending America

Background For more than 30 years now, the ranks of the nation's armed forces have been filled entirely by volunteers. Today, however, many worry that the continuing demands of wars in Iraq and Afghanistan threaten to stretch the capacities of the armed forces—in particular, the Army—to the breaking point. This has led some people to urge a return to the draft. Neither the President nor the Defense Department has supported that proposal.

A U.S. soldier returns from Iraq
Analysis Skills CS1, HI1

An All-Volunteer Military

This country has relied on voluntary military forces through much of its history-and for good reason, says noted military sociologist David Segal. "Americans have been willing . . . to volunteer when they felt that national security was threatened. We have been much less comfortable with involuntary servitude."

The American people have always been troubled by compulsory military service. Draft riots erupted during the Civil War and heated resistance to selective service arose during World War I. The existence of an all-volunteer military today is, in no small part, a reaction to the opposition to the draft in the Vietnam era. Gallup polls on the matter have put opposition to the reinstatement of the draft at more than 80 percent.

The stellar performance of the all-volunteer military in both wars in Iraq and in Afghanistan and elsewhere stand as the best evidence of the success of the current system. Volunteers are motivated and dedicated because they choose to serve in uniform, and they deserve the nation's full support.

Crisis Demands a Draft

The draft has served this nation well at various times in our history—most notably during World War II, when more than 10 million of the 16 million Americans who served in the armed forces were draftees.

We are at war again. Because we are, this should be a time of shared sacrifice by all of the people. Those who were in uniform in World War II represented a cross-section of the American people. Today we honor them as "the greatest generation" for their service and patriotism. The burdens of war are not shared generally today, however. They are, instead, borne mostly by the members of the active military and the National Guard and reservists—altogether, some two million people—and by their families.

Senator Chuck Hagel (R., Nebraska) says a draft "may become necessary" in the future. Another decorated combat veteran, Congressman Charles Rangel (D., New York) goes much further. He argues that a draft should be in place today—a move that he says would stimulate genuine patriotism and spread the burdens of military service fairly, across the entire population.

Exploring the Issues

1. Why do you think the Bush Administration has not supported calls for a new draft?

2. What effect might another military conflict—one with, for example, Iran or North Korea—have on the question of a draft?

To learn more about the debate over a draft, view "Defending America."

490 Chapter 17

Debate Current Issues

Face the Issues features challenge you to confront contemporary issues from new perspectives. Background information on each topic provides a starting point for debate and discussion.

Keep Up-to-Date

Learning about government means learning about change. The Enduring Constitution time lines show how the interpretation of the Constitution has developed over the years. In addition, you'll find key graphs, charts, and tables marked with the Internet Update logo. Updated versions of these illustrations along with the most recent election and other political data appear on the *Magruder's American Government* Web site at **PHSchool.com**

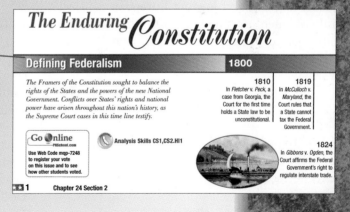

The Enduring Constitution

Defining Federalism	1800

The Framers of the Constitution sought to balance the rights of the States and the powers of the new National Government. Conflicts over States' rights and national power have arisen throughout this nation's history, as the Supreme Court cases in this time line testify.

Go Online PHSchool.com Use Web Code mqp-7248 to register your vote on this issue and to see how other students voted.

Analysis Skills CS1,CS2,HI1

1810 In *Fletcher* v. *Peck*, a case from Georgia, the Court for the first time holds a State law to be unconstitutional.

1819 In *McCulloch* v. *Maryland*, the Court rules that a State cannot tax the Federal Government.

1824 In *Gibbons* v. *Ogden*, the Court affirms the Federal Government's right to regulate interstate trade.

1 Chapter 24 Section 2

Go Online PHSchool.com

For: An activity on public policy issues
Web Code: mqd-2091

Go Online at PHSchool.com

Use the Web Code in each Go Online Box to access information or activities at PHSchool.com.

How to Use the Web Code:
1. Go to PHSchool.com
2. Enter the Web Code
3. Click Go!

Here is a complete list of the Grade 12 History-Social Science Standards for Government so that you know what you will learn this year.

CONTENT STANDARDS

12.1 Students explain the fundamental principles and moral values of American democracy as expressed in the U.S. Constitution and other essential documents of American democracy.

What It Means to You

The United States is a democracy, and in a democracy, the people govern. Democracies needs guidelines and principles in order to succeed. The U.S. Constitution sets the rules of American democracy and the principles that define our government. You will read the U.S. Constitution, the Declaration of Independence, and other important documents in order to understand why the United States was founded and how the ideals of the Founders guide our government today.

California Standard	What You Will Learn
12.1.1 Analyze the influence of ancient Greek, Roman, English, and leading European political thinkers such as John Locke, Charles-Louis Montesquieu, Niccolo Machiavelli, and William Blackstone on the development of American government.	You will learn how the origins of our democratic government can be traced to philosophers and writers who lived in Europe many centuries ago. You will learn how the ancient Greeks developed the idea of democracy and the ancient Romans created a system of law. You will read the words of John Locke, who taught that governments draw their power from the people.
12.1.2 Discuss the character of American democracy and its promise and perils as articulated by Alexis de Tocqueville.	Alexis de Tocqueville was a native of France who visited the United States in the 1830s and wrote about his experiences in Democracy in America. De Tocqueville admired the United States for the opportunity it provided its citizens to succeed and form strong, democratic communities. He praised American democracy, in contrast to European countries, and predicted that the United States would become a powerful country in the future.

Alexis de Tocqueville

California Standard	What You Will Learn
12.1.3 Explain how the U.S. Constitution reflects a balance between the classical republican concern with promotion of the public good and the classical liberal concern with protecting individual rights; and discuss how the basic premises of liberal constitutionalism and democracy are joined in the Declaration of Independence as "self-evident truths."	The Declaration of Independence describes what good governments must do and what rights individuals have under a government. Governments are expected to provide for the public good, which means acting on behalf of everyone in society, together. They must also respect the rights of individuals. Sometimes these two principles conflict.
12.1.4 Explain how the Founding Fathers' realistic view of human nature led directly to the establishment of a constitutional system that limited the power of the governors and the governed as articulated in the Federalist Papers.	The Founding Fathers recognized that in any government, some people will try to take too much power for themselves. Democracies must be protected from the threat of any single person gaining too much power and destroying the system. To protect democracy, the Founding Fathers planned a system of limited government defined by a constitution. Under this system, no single person or administration can grow stronger than the democratic system itself.
12.1.5 Describe the systems of separated and shared powers, the role of organized interests (Federalist Paper Number 10), checks and balances (Federalist Paper Number 51), the importance of an independent judiciary (Federalist Paper Number 78), enumerated powers, rule of law, federalism, and civilian control of the military.	You will read Federalist Papers Number 10, 51, and 78 to gain insight into the thoughts of the Founding Fathers as they wrote the U.S. Constitution. You will identify ideas in the Federalist Papers that were included in the U.S. Constitution and define the Federal Government's powers.
12.1.6 Understand that the Bill of Rights limits the powers of the federal government and state governments.	You will learn that the Bill of Rights recognizes many rights held by individuals. These rights prevent federal and State governments from passing laws that infringe too much on individual rights to self-expression, religion, and liberty. The also protect people accused of crimes from unfair treatment.

12.2 Students evaluate and take and defend positions on the scope and limits of rights and obligations as democratic citizens, the relationships among them, and how they are secured.

What It Means to You

The U.S. Constitution describes many of the rights Americans enjoy and how the Federal Government should protect those rights. However, even today, Americans disagree on the extent of those rights and what individuals should do to contribute to democracy. You will read the Constitution and other documents, including the Federalist Papers, to understand the ideas behind our constitutional rights. You will evaluate the degree to which Americans enjoy those rights today and learn to argue and defend your own point of view.

California Standard	What You Will Learn
12.2.1 Discuss the meaning and importance of each of the rights guaranteed under the Bill of Rights and how each is secured (e.g., freedom of religion, speech, press, assembly, petition, privacy).	The Bill of Rights guarantees the basic rights that all Americans enjoy. The 1st Amendment protects the right of individuals to say what they wish, to worship as they please, to meet peacefully, and to ask the government to address their concerns. The next seven amendments list additional rights guaranteed to the people, including the right to bear arms and the right to a fair trial. The 9th and 10th Amendments state that any rights not listed in the Bill of Rights are still held by the States or the people.
12.2.2 Explain how economic rights are secured and their importance to the individual and to society (e.g., the right to acquire, use, transfer, and dispose of property; right to choose one's work; right to join or not join labor unions; copyright and patent).	Not all rights are political. Americans enjoy economic rights that are recognized by the government and which are essential to our free enterprise system. For example, your property belongs to you and can not be taken away without a very compelling reason. The Constitution recognizes some economic rights, such as the right to earn money from books, pictures, and photographs you create.
12.2.3 Discuss the individual's legal obligations to obey the law, serve as a juror, and pay taxes.	Citizenship carries responsibilities as well as benefits. Individuals must contribute a share of their time and money in order for governments to carry out their obligations to people. By serving on a jury, you enable a person charged with a crime to enjoy his or her constitutional right to a full and fair trial. By paying taxes, you give the federal, State, and local governments the powers they need to protect Americans from harm and carry out their constitutional responsibilities.

California Standard

What You Will Learn

12.2.4 Understand the obligations of civic-mindedness, including voting, being informed on civic issues, volunteering and performing public service, and serving in the military or alternative service.

In addition to serving on a jury and paying taxes, citizens have other obligations that are not required by law but are nonetheless essential to keep American democracy strong and safe. You will learn why it is important to educate yourself about current events and to make your voice heard by voting. You will understand how contributing your time to public service or the defense of the United States strengthens our society and our institutions.

12.2.5 Describe the reciprocity between rights and obligations; that is, why enjoyment of one's rights entails respect for the rights of others.

You will learn about the importance of respecting the rights of others in order to preserve our free society. Individual rights are protected only when individuals respect one another and treat each other as equals under the law.

12.2.6 Explain how one becomes a citizen of the United States, including the process of naturalization (e.g., literacy, language, and other requirements).

The United States is a nation of immigrants. Each year, thousands of immigrants complete a difficult process to become citizens of the United States. You will study the steps of this process to learn what immigrants must do in order to earn U.S. citizenship.

12.3 Students evaluate, take, and defend positions on what the fundamental values and principles of civil society are (i.e., the autonomous sphere of voluntary personal, social, and economic relations that are not part of government), their interdependence, and the meaning and importance of those values and principles for a free society.

What It Means to You

Civil society describes the organizations, clubs, and religious groups people form outside of government. These organizations are as important to day-to-day life as the work of the government, and for many people, they are closer and more relevant. Civil society reflects the history, ideals, and morals of many Americans and carries these principles forward. You will read about some institutions that make up civil society in the United States and how they affect your life.

California Standard	What You Will Learn
12.3.1 Explain how civil society provides opportunities for individuals to associate for social, cultural, religious, economic, and political purposes.	Think of some of the clubs at your school: yearbook, athletic teams, language clubs, pre-professional groups like FHA-HERO, FFA, and FBLA. Outside of schools, Americans participate in a broad range of groups, including cultural heritage groups, sports clubs, and political associations. Like school clubs, these associations provide an outlet for people's interests and an opportunity to help.
12.3.2 Explain how civil society makes it possible for people, individually or in association with others, to bring their influence to bear on government in ways other than voting and elections.	When people bring their voices together and speak as one, they are more likely to be heard. Private groups and government officials can often work together to find solutions that meet everyone's needs.
12.3.3 Discuss the historical role of religion and religious diversity.	From the arrival of Catholic priests in New Spain, the United States has been home to vibrant and diverse religious traditions. You will learn about the role religion has played in the history of the United States and the development of our government institutions.
12.3.4 Compare the relationship of government and civil society in constitutional democracies to the relationship of government and civil society in authoritarian and totalitarian regimes.	You will learn how democratic governments flourish by stepping back and letting individuals develop a civil society. In contrast, dictatorships try to push into all areas of people's lives. They fear institutions that they do not control, so they discourage people from forming their own groups and making decisions that might oppose the government.

12.4 Students analyze the unique roles and responsibilities of the three branches of government as established by the U.S. Constitution.

What It Means to You

You will read the U.S. Constitution as a blueprint for the Federal Government. The Constitution describes, in detail, the powers and structure of the three branches of the Federal Government: the legislative branch, which writes laws; the executive branch, which enforces laws; and the judicial branch, which interprets laws. These branches have grown and changed since the Constitution was adopted. Some of these changes have been written into the Constitution.

California Standard	What You Will Learn
12.4.1 Discuss Article I of the Constitution as it relates to the legislative branch, including eligibility for office and lengths of terms of representatives and senators; election to office; the roles of the House and Senate in impeachment proceedings; the role of the vice president; the enumerated legislative powers; and the process by which a bill becomes a law.	Congress is sometimes known as the "first branch" of government. Composed of the House of Representatives and the Senate, Congress writes laws and controls spending for the Federal Government. Article I of the U.S. Constitution describes the qualifications for serving in Congress and how members of Congress are elected. The Constitution also includes broad outlines for how Congress should work.
12.4.2 Explain the process through which the Constitution can be amended.	You will learn the four methods for amending, or making changes to, the U.S. Constitution. Twenty-six of the 27 amendments to the Constitution were added using one of these methods. The most common way to amend the Constitution is for both houses of Congress to approve an amendment by a 2/3 majority and then send it to the States. When 3/4 of the States have ratified, or approved, the amendment, it is added to the Constitution.
12.4.3 Identify their current representatives in the legislative branch of the national government. 	You are represented in Congress by two senators, who are elected statewide, and one representative, who is elected to serve a small district within California. In 2006, Senator Barbara Boxer and Senator Dianne Feinstein, both Democrats, represented California in the United States Senate. California has 53 representatives in the House of Representatives, and each one is elected by a district with about 650,000 residents.

California Standard	What You Will Learn
12.4.4 Discuss Article II of the Constitution as it relates to the executive branch, including eligibility for office and length of term, election to and removal from of office, the oath office, and the enumerated executive powers.	You will learn how the U.S. Constitution defines the term and powers of the President of the United States. For example, the Constitution gives the President the power to command the armed forces, to make treaties, to nominate federal judges, and to pardon criminals. The Constitution limits the number of years a President may hold office.
12.4.5 Discuss Article III of the Constitution as it relates to judicial power, including the length of terms of judges and the jurisdiction of the Supreme Court.	You will learn how Article III of the U.S. Constitution sets the powers and responsibilities of the U.S. Supreme Court and other federal courts. The Constitution describes the types of cases that can be tried in federal courts. You will also learn how the Constitution grants federal judges the right to hold their offices for lifetime "during good behavior"
12.4.6 Explain the processes of selection and confirmation of Supreme Court justices.	You will understand that the President has the sole power to name people to serve as Supreme Court justices. The Senate may reject or accept the nomination. If a majority of senators vote to confirm, or accept, the nomination, the justice is appointed for a lifetime term. You will learn about recent appointments to the Supreme Court, including Chief Justice John Roberts, and how a President chooses judges.

12.5 Students summarize landmark U.S. Supreme Court interpretations of the Constitution and its amendments.

What It Means to You

The Supreme Court holds a unique power to interpret the Constitution. The Supreme Court judges whether laws follow the rules set out in the Constitution, and the Court may strike down those laws that violate the Constitution or its many amendments. You will study key Supreme Court cases in depth, including Marbury v. Madison, Brown v. Board of Education of Topeka, and United States v. Nixon.

California Standard	What You Will Learn
12.5.1 Understand the changing interpretations of the Bill of Rights over time, including interpretations of the basic freedoms (religion, speech, press, petition, and assembly) articulated in the First Amendment and the due process and equal-protection-of-the-law clauses of the Fourteenth Amendment.	Since the U.S. Constitution was written, the rights protected in the Bill of Rights have changed along with the country. For example, the 1st Amendment lists rights including freedom of the press, but how has that freedom changed with the invention of radio, television, and the Internet? Interpretations of the 5th Amendment and 14th Amendment have helped decide how far individual rights can be protected against the acts of the Federal Government and the States, respectively.
12.5.2 Analyze judicial activism and judicial restraint and the effects of each policy over the decades (e.g., the Warren and Rehnquist courts).	You will learn that Americans disagree on how judges should approach laws. Those who favor judicial restraint believe that judges should act conservatively and only consider the Constitution as it was originally written when weighing the constitutionality of a law. Others argue that judges should demonstrate judicial activism and consider the changing needs and beliefs of American society when making decisions.
12.5.3 Evaluate the effects of the Court's interpretations of the Constitution in Marbury v. Madison, McCulloch v. Maryland, and United States v. Nixon, with emphasis on the arguments espoused by each side in these cases.	You will read arguments on both sides of key Supreme Court cases that helped decide the balance of power in the Federal Government. Marbury v. Madison established the Supreme Court's right to review and overturn laws. In McCulloch v. Maryland, the Supreme Court ruled that Congress could do far more with its power than what was described, literally, in the Constitution. In U.S. v. Nixon, the Supreme Court asserted its authority over the President and ensured that no member of government was above the law.

California Standard	What You Will Learn

12.5.4 Explain the controversies that have resulted over changing interpretations of civil rights, including those in Plessy v. Ferguson, Brown v. Board of Education, Miranda v. Arizona, Regents of the University of California v. Bakke, Adarand Constructors, Inc. v. Pena, and United States v. Virginia (VMI).

The United States has struggled to overcome the legacy of centuries of slavery and discrimination. Enacted in laws and practiced by private businesses, discrimination closed off opportunities to minorities and held back America's potential. Historically, Supreme Court rulings contributed to discrimination. More recent rulings have removed many barriers of discrimination. In the courts, Americans continue to debate the best way to overcome discrimination.

12.6 Students evaluate issues regarding campaigns for national, state, and local elective offices.

What It Means to You

In the United States, most public officials are chosen in competitive elections. People who want to serve in government have to offer reasons why voters should choose them. Campaigns begin months, and sometimes years, before an election. You will learn about the issues driving today's campaigns for office so you will be able to make educated choices when you vote.

California Standard	What You Will Learn

12.6.1 Analyze the origin, development, and role of political parties, noting those occasional periods in which there was only one major party or were more than two major parties.

Many people are familiar with the idea of "red vs. blue." In 2000 and 2004, elections maps showed a country split almost evenly between the Democratic and Republican parties. These maps showed a division that changes from election to election and masks divisions within States, counties, towns, and even households. In some elections, America has voted for one party only; other presidential election maps need four colors to represent all parties.

California Standard	What You Will Learn
12.6.2 Discuss the history of the nomination process for presidential candidates and the increasing importance of primaries in general elections.	You will learn how presidential candidates from the two major parties must win two sets of elections: the primary elections within the parties, and the general election in November. You will read how elections are held in key States to shrink the number of candidates from each party down to one.
12.6.3 Evaluate the roles of polls, campaign advertising, and the controversies over campaign funding.	Modern candidates use sophisticated tools to understand their voters and win their support. They poll voters to understand what issues matter to them and what messages can bring them to the polls to vote. Campaign advertising on television and the radio plays an important role in defining a candidate and a race in the eyes of the voters. Television advertising is expensive, and the Federal Government closely tracks the money candidates raise to pay for commercials.
12.6.4 Describe the means that citizens use to participate in the political process (e.g., voting, campaigning, lobbying, filing a legal challenge, demonstrating, petitioning, picketing, running for political office).	You will learn how you can participate in the election process. There are many ways to help elect candidates you support, both through the political process and by expressing yourself in public. With enough experience, you may learn enough to run for office someday.
12.6.5 Discuss the features of direct democracy in numerous states (e.g., the process of referendums, recall elections).	In direct democracy, voters decide issues through elections instead of through their elected representatives. In California, citizens can vote on laws through the process of referendums. Voters may even have the opportunity to recall, or remove, an elected official from office. California voters did just that in 2003 when they voted to recall Governor Gray Davis and replace him with Arnold Schwarzenegger.

California Standard	What You Will Learn

12.6.6 Analyze trends in voter turnout; the causes and effects of reapportionment and redistricting, with special attention to spatial districting and the rights of minorities; and the function of the Electoral College.

Although the United States is a democracy, it is not a pure democracy. When voters are distributed unevenly among States or districts, the share of candidates elected from each party can look very different from the share of votes each party received. States must draw their districts to ensure that legislatures and Congress reflect America's ethnic and racial diversity. The electoral college, which elects the President, gives voters in smaller States a relatively larger say in the election than voters in populous states like California.

12.7 Students analyze and compare the powers and procedures of the national, state, tribal, and local governments.

What It Means to You

You will learn about the different levels of government that exist in the United States, in California, in your county and town, and within Native American nations. You will compare issues and ways of governing at different levels and contrast their strengths and weaknesses. You will learn how the different levels of government work with one another.

California Standard	What You Will Learn

12.7.1 Explain how conflicts between levels of government and branches of government are resolved.

Not surprisingly, when different levels of government hold sway over a common piece of land or population, they can disagree about how to share authority. States often fight with the Federal Government over the proper use of land within their borders; towns argue with State governments about funding for roads and schools. You will learn how our democracy resolves disagreements.

California Standard	What You Will Learn
12.7.2 Identify the major responsibilities and sources of revenue for state and local governments.	State and local governments need money to pay for schools, health care, crime prevention, and transportation. You will learn that State and local governments raise money chiefly through income taxes, property taxes, sales taxes, and other fees. Compared to other States, California raises relatively more money through income and sales taxes, and less through property taxes, for its State and local needs.
12.7.3 Discuss reserved powers and concurrent powers of state governments.	You will learn that concurrent powers are powers that both States and the Federal Government enjoy. Taxation is a concurrent power, as both the Federal Government and States can collect taxes. Reserved powers are powers that the Constitution, in the 10th Amendment, does not assign to the Federal Government and do not deny to the States. Reserved powers include much of what State and local governments do.
12.7.4 Discuss the Ninth and Tenth Amendments and interpretations of the extent of the federal government's power.	You will learn that citizens and States are not limited to the rights set out in the first eight amendments of the Bill of Rights. The final two amendments of the Bill of Rights state that all other rights not mentioned are still held by the people and by the States. These amendments limit the power of the Federal Government by placing all undetermined rights in the hands of the people and their chosen State governments.
12.7.5 Explain how public policy is formed, including the setting of the public agenda and implementation of it through regulations and executive orders.	Public policy is defined as everything that a government decides to do. You will learn how governments decide public policy and put those policies into effect.

California Standard	What You Will Learn
12.7.6 Compare the processes of lawmaking at each of the three levels of government, including the role of lobbying and the media.	You will learn how the Federal Government and California State and local governments pass laws that affect you. You will read about how voters and private groups try to influence legislatures to change the laws or write new ones.
12.7.7 Identify the organization and jurisdiction of federal, state, and local (e.g., California) courts and the interrelationships among them.	The courts interpret the laws and judge people who are accused of committing crimes. Like legislatures, courts exist at all levels of government. You will learn how responsibilities are divided up among the many levels of courts and how they interact with each other.
12.7.8 Understand the scope of presidential power and decision making through examination of case studies such as the Cuban Missile Crisis, passage of Great Society legislation, War Powers Act, Gulf War, and Bosnia.	As the chief executive of the United States, the President must make important decisions about how the United States deals with other countries. You will learn how past Presidents have made decisions in historic cases of domestic and foreign policy, including the decision to go to war.

12.8 Students evaluate and take and defend positions on the influence of the media on American political life.

What It Means to You

"The media" include the newspapers, television shows, radio broadcasts, and Web sites. The media communicate information, news, and entertainment in thousands of ways to millions of people. Politics is no exception; the media have an important role in how modern politicians do their jobs. You will analyze the role of the media in politics today and criticize or defend what they do.

California Standard	What You Will Learn
12.8.1 Discuss the meaning and importance of a free and responsible press.	Freedom of the press is so important that the Founding Fathers protected it in the 1st Amendment. Today, "the press" has grown to include radio, television, and Internet news outlets. A free press can spread new ideas, give potential leaders a voice, and prevent governments from misleading the people.
12.8.2 Describe the roles of broadcast, print, and electronic media, including the Internet, as means of communication in American politics.	You will learn that the rise in the number of voters has made it impossible for candidates to interact with them face-to-face. As a result, the media have become more important than ever in defining the key issues of a campaign and communicating candidates' messages to the public.
12.8.3 Explain how public officials use the media to communicate with the citizenry and to shape public opinion.	You will learn how public officials recognize the importance of the media and use the media to talk to voters. By choosing which issues to discuss and how to discuss them, officials can shape public debates. Many public officials have staff members whose sole job is to work with the media to get their message out.

12.9 Students analyze the origins, characteristics, and development of different political systems across time, with emphasis on the quest for political democracy, its advances, and its obstacles.

What It Means to You

The United States has been fortunate to have enjoyed two centuries of democratic government. Just as the government of the United States has become more democratic over time, other countries have moved toward democracy. You will learn how countries evolve into democracies. You will read about the challenges they face and study the experiences of specific countries who have worked to become more democratic.

California Standard	What You Will Learn
12.9.1 Explain how the different philosophies and structures of feudalism, mercantilism, socialism, fascism, communism, monarchies, parliamentary systems, and constitutional liberal democracies influence economic policies, social welfare policies, and human rights practices.	You will trace the roots of the modern democratic state to the feudal system of the Middle Ages and the kingdoms of Spain, France, and England. You will learn how popular sovereignty—the idea that governments rule in the name of the people—changed how governments worked and how they treated their subjects.
12.9.2 Compare the various ways in which power is distributed, shared, and limited in systems of shared powers and in parliamentary systems, including the influence and role of parliamentary leaders (e.g., William Gladstone, Margaret Thatcher).	You will study the parliamentary system of government in Britain and Japan in contrast to our own presidential system. You will learn how the parliamentary system combines executive and legislative power in a single branch of government, led by a Prime Minister.
12.9.3 Discuss the advantages and disadvantages of federal, confederal, and unitary systems of government.	You will learn how nations divide power according to geography. Unitary states have very strong central governments and weak local governments. Confederal states bring together strong, nearly independent states in a weak association. Federal governments, including the government of the United States, balance between the two extremes.
12.9.4 Describe for at least two countries the consequences of conditions that gave rise to tyrannies during certain periods (e.g., Italy, Japan, Haiti, Nigeria, Cambodia).	You will read how governments can turn into tyrannies, taking away the rights of people to choose their own leaders. You will study the experiences of Japan, Haiti, and Nigeria to learn how democracies can break down and give way to dictatorships.

California Standard	What You Will Learn
12.9.5 Identify the forms of illegitimate power that twentieth-century African, Asian, and Latin American dictators used to gain and hold office and the conditions and interests that supported them.	You will learn how tyrants keep control over their people and identify groups that have supported tyrannies in certain countries.
12.9.6 Identify the ideologies, causes, stages, and outcomes of major Mexican, Central American, and South American revolutions in the nineteenth and twentieth centuries.	You will study revolutions in Mexico, Central America, and South America to learn why people rebelled and how they changed their governments. You will learn about the important role the military played in revolutions.
12.9.7 Describe the ideologies that give rise to Communism, methods of maintaining control, and the movements to overthrow such governments in Czechoslovakia, Hungary, and Poland, including the roles of individuals (e.g., Alexander Solzhenitsyn, Pope John Paul II, Lech Walesa, Vaclav Havel).	You will read how communist governments ruled half of Europe for nearly 50 years under the leadership of the Soviet Union. You will learn how courageous individuals such as Lech Walesa and Vaclav Havel helped overthrow their countries' communist governments.
12.9.8 Identify the successes of relatively new democracies in Africa, Asia, and Latin America and the ideas, leaders, and general societal conditions that have launched and sustained, or failed to sustain, them.	You will read about countries in Africa, Asia, and the Americas that have held free elections. You will learn the important steps countries must complete to build a democratic society that can last through crises and challenges.

12.10 Students formulate questions about and defend their analyses of tensions within our constitutional democracy and the importance of maintaining a balance between the following concepts: majority rule and individual rights; liberty and equality; state and national authority in a federal system; civil disobedience and the rule of law; freedom of the press and the right to a fair trial; the relationship of religion and government.

What It Means to You

To study government is to ask questions about the rights you have, as a citizen and an American, and the proper role of the government. The U.S. Constitution provides some answers to these questions by defining the most important rights you hold and the shape of the Federal Government. As you get older, you will have a chance to make changes to government, whether it is at a local, State, or federal level. You will need to study debates Americans have had in the past about key principles of government—and prepare yourself for the choices of the future.

HISTORICAL AND SOCIAL SCIENCES ANALYSIS SKILLS
Chronological and Spatial Thinking

California Standard	What You Will Learn
CS1 Students compare the present with the past, evaluating the consequences of past events and decisions and determining the lessons that were learned.	You will look at events from the past and compare them to similar events today. You'll also look for long-term consequences of events from the past on the government today.
CS2 Students analyze how change happens at different rates at different times; understand that some aspects can change while others remain the same; and understand that change is complicated and affects not only technology and politics but also values and beliefs.	You will look at examples of political, social, and economic changes that have taken place throughout history. You'll examine the complex impact of these changes on people's lives.
CS3 Students use a variety of maps and documents to interpret human movement, including major patterns of domestic and international migration, changing environmental preferences and settlement patterns, the frictions that develop between population groups, and the diffusion of ideas, technological innovations, and goods.	You will examine movements of people from one region of the country to another as well as the impact such movement has on the government of the United States.
CS4 Students relate current events to the physical and human characteristics of places and regions.	You will examine events taking place in the world today by looking at the physical and human context in which they occur.

Historical Research, Evidence, and Point of View

California Standard	What You Will Learn
HR1 Students distinguish valid arguments from fallacious arguments in historical interpretations.	You will learn to read history closely and judge the arguments that historians use.
HR2 Students identify bias and prejudice in historical interpretations.	You will look for signs of a historian's point of view when reading historical writing.
HR3 Students evaluate major debates among historians concerning alternative interpretations of the past, including an analysis of authors' use of evidence and the distinctions between sound generalizations and misleading oversimplifications.	You will compare arguments by different historians and learn how to choose which explanation best fits the evidence you have read. You will learn to look for words and phrases that can mislead readers.

California Standard	What You Will Learn
HR4 Students construct and test hypotheses; collect, evaluate, and employ information from multiple primary and secondary sources; and apply it in oral and written presentations.	You will learn to gather information and bring facts and evidence together to explain what happened in the past. You will learn how to share your findings with others by writing or speaking.

Historical Interpretation

California Standard	What You Will Learn
H1 Students show the connections, causal and otherwise, between particular historical events and larger social, economic, and political trends and developments.	You will learn to make connections between specific historical events and larger issues. These connections will help you see how themes and trends reoccur throughout history.
H2 Students recognize the complexity of historical causes and effects, including the limitations on determining cause and effect.	You will learn that historical events have complex causes and effects that can be difficult to determine.
H3 Students interpret past events and issues within the context in which an event unfolded rather than solely in terms of present-day norms and values.	You will learn to understand events as the people who lived through them understood them, rather than only from the viewpoint of today's expectations.
H4 Students understand the meaning, implication, and impact of historical events and recognize that events could have taken other directions.	You will learn how to interpret the significance and influence of historical events and understand the implications of these events. You will be able to see how events could have happened differently.
H5 Students analyze human modifications of landscapes and examine the resulting environmental policy issues.	You will learn how to evaluate changes that humans have made to the environment and to study the issues that these changes have created.
H6 Students conduct cost-benefit analyses and apply basic economic indicators to analyze the aggregate economic behavior of the U.S. economy.	You will consider the costs and rewards of different choices. You will learn how to compare costs and rewards to help make decisions for an individual or a country.

Recognizing Propaganda

 **Analysis Skill HR1**

The term *propaganda* is highly charged. People tend to think of it as deceptive information, but in fact the term has a broader meaning.

Propaganda is information—either true or false—intended to persuade people to think or act in a certain way. True or not, propaganda is usually a one-sided explanation or opinion. Some typical propaganda techniques are shown at right.

Propaganda can be a powerful tool for promoting or destroying attitudes, beliefs, and values. In the 1930s, Adolf Hitler rose to power in part through his skillful use of propaganda to whip up hatred toward various minority groups. To counter Nazi propaganda, in 1942 the United States created a radio network called the Voice of America (VOA) to broadcast propaganda about American ideals, values, and democracy.

For much of the twentieth century, the United States engaged in a propaganda war with its chief rival for power, the Soviet Union. One of the chief targets of American propaganda was Soviet leader Josef Stalin, who boldly predicted that communism would ultimately spread throughout the world. Stalin is depicted in the pamphlet at right. Use these steps to evaluate the content on the cover:

1. Determine whether the item constitutes propaganda. Which of the propaganda techniques listed here are used in the pamphlet? Explain.

2. Analyze the purpose of the propaganda. This pamphlet was published in the United States in 1938. (a) Who is it intended to influence? (b) What beliefs or behavior are people being urged to follow?

3. Draw conclusions. How and why might this propaganda have been effective in influencing Americans' beliefs about communism?

Test for Success

Complete one of the following activities: (a) Find a political cartoon in this book that uses propaganda techniques. List the techniques and explain how they are used. (b) Create a fictitious political poster that uses at least two propaganda techniques.

Propaganda Techniques

Most Americans encounter propaganda during political campaigns, when candidates try to sway voters.

Celebrity Testimonials Using endorsements from famous people—from actors to sports figures—to try to persuade you: *Mr. Action Hero says, "Vote for X. He's my choice."*

Multiple Identities Claiming to be just like you, no matter who you are: *"I'm one of you. I share your beliefs and concerns."*

The Bandwagon Argument Urging you to follow the crowd, the majority: *"A is voting for me. So are B, C, and D. Why not you, too?"*

Name Calling Attacking and labeling the opposition instead of discussing issues: *"My opponent is un-American."*

Scare Tactics Using words or pictures to persuade people to act out of fear of consequences, real or perceived: *"A vote for my opponent will destroy our children's future."*

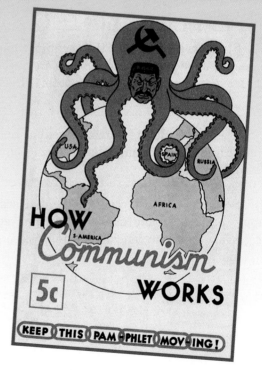

Skills for Life

Making Comparisons

 Analysis Skill HR4

You've probably been making comparisons ever since you first tasted food. Making comparisons means examining two or more ideas, objects, events, or people to find out how they are either similar or different. In the study of government, you will often use this skill to evaluate differing proposals on public issues. To make valid comparisons, use these steps:

1. Identify the basis of comparison. Comparing two or more items works only when the items have some attribute in common. Consider the Virginia Plan and the New Jersey Plan, discussed on page 51. Both plans put forth models for creating a new government. What else did they have in common?

2. Identify the attributes of each item to be compared. An easy way to compare complex items is to create a list or chart of their key attributes. The charts at right summarize the main features of the Virginia and New Jersey Plans.

3. Find ways in which the items are similar. Once you put the attributes in a chart, it becomes easy to identify similarities. Study the charts. Then list the similarities of the Virginia Plan and the New Jersey Plan.

4. Find ways in which the items are different. The two Constitution plans differ not only in what they offer, but also in what they do not offer. List the differences.

5. Summarize and evaluate your comparison. Decide whether the two items you are comparing are mostly similar or mostly different, and analyze why. Write a sentence or two summarizing the main differences between the Virginia Plan and the New Jersey Plan.

Test for Success

Controversy over the size and powers of the Federal Government is as lively today as ever. Find two sources of opinion on this issue and write a brief comparison of them.

Virginia Plan

- Branches of government: legislative, executive, judicial
- Structure of legislative branch: bicameral, with a lower house, the House of Representatives, and an upper house, the Senate
- How representation is apportioned: by population or by amount of money contributed to the National Government
- Congress retains powers given to it under the Articles of Confederation: Yes.
- National powers vs. State powers: strong
- Structure of executive branch: single executive who executes national laws
- How executive is chosen: by Congress
- Structure of judicial branch: one or more supreme courts with lower courts
- How judiciary is chosen: by Congress

New Jersey Plan

- Branches of government: legislative, executive, judicial
- Structure of legislative branch: unicameral Congress of the Confederation
- How representation is apportioned: equal number of votes for every State
- Congress retains powers given to it under the Articles of Confederation: Yes.
- National powers vs. State powers: weak
- Structure of executive branch: plural executive (more than one person)
- How executive is chosen: by Congress
- Structure of judicial branch: single supreme court
- How judiciary is chosen: by the executive

Expressing Problems Clearly

To express a problem clearly means to describe the nature of an issue that is difficult, puzzling, or open to debate. Expressing a problem clearly is the first step in solving it.

1. Gather information. When you are confronted with a problem, gather information on the topic. For example, in *McCulloch* v. *Maryland* (1819), Chief Justice John Marshall addressed questions about the relationship between the Federal Government and the States. Reread the passage about *McCulloch* v. *Maryland* on page 95. Then read the excerpt below.

2. Identify the basic concepts involved. Specific problems often relate to a general principle. For example, the Supreme Court often chooses to rule on a specific case that illustrates a broad principle that can be applied to similar cases. To identify the problem in *McCulloch* v. *Maryland*, state what each side wants to achieve.

3. Identify supporting details or arguments. In the *McCulloch* excerpt, find the arguments that support the plaintiffs' view and the defendants' view.

4. Express the problem clearly. Now that you have identified the main area of dispute and stripped away details, you're ready to express the problem clearly. In your own words, state the nature of the problem that the Supreme Court addressed in 1819.

Test for Success

Find a newspaper editorial in print or on the Internet. Analyze the editorial using the steps listed above to express the problem or controversy in a clear and concise way.

How does each side make its case?

What are the arguments for and against the bank?

What's the main issue in this case?

How can I summarize the case?

"In the case now to be determined, the defendant, a sovereign State [Maryland], denies the obligation of a law enacted by [Congress], and the plaintiff [the National Bank] contests the validity of an act which has been passed by the legislature of that State. . . .

In discussing this question, the counsel for the State of Maryland have deemed it of some importance . . . to consider [the U.S. Constitution] not as emanating from the people, but as the act of sovereign and independent States. The powers of the [national] government, it has been said, are delegated by the States . . . and must be exercised in subordination to the States, who alone possess supreme dominion. . . .

It being the opinion of the Court, that the act incorporating the bank is constitutional . . . we proceed to inquire . . . [w]hether the State of Maryland may, without violating the constitution, tax that branch [the branch in Maryland]?

That the power of taxation is . . . retained by the States; that it is not [reduced] by the grant of a similar power to the government of the Union . . . are truths which have never been denied. But . . . States are expressly forbidden to lay any duties on imports or exports . . . . If [this limitation on States' power to tax] must be conceded, the same [principle] would seem to restrain . . . a State from such other exercise of this power. . . . On this ground the counsel for the bank place its claim to be exempted from the power of a State to tax its operations."

—*Chief Justice John Marshall*, McCulloch v. Maryland, *1819*

Skills for Life

Identifying Political Roots and Attitudes

Analysis Skill CS3

As a voter, how will you evaluate political parties and candidates and make voting decisions? Will you vote the way your friends are voting? The better way of making voting decisions is to analyze the political traditions that have shaped the candidates' views, and then make a decision based on your own values.

Identifying political traditions will help you understand the shorthand that politicians often use. For instance, if a candidate says she's a "pro-labor Democrat" or a "religious conservative," these labels imply a whole set of beliefs with deep roots in American politics and culture. With no historical frame of reference, you would have difficulty interpreting what these labels really mean and what policies a candidate or party supports.

Whether you're examining your own political roots or someone else's, try these steps:

1. Learn about political traditions. You read in this section that American politics has long been dominated by two political parties, Republican and Democrat. A basic knowledge of the origins and history of these parties is necessary in order to understand most political dialogue in this country. (a) What specific policies or goals do many Republicans favor? (b) What do many Democrats favor?

2. Identify major cultural influences. Our beliefs can be influenced by several factors: education, occupation, location, ethnic and religious ties, and the types of activities we pursue.

While being careful not to stereotype people, we can often predict the political views of many people based on such cultural factors. For example, in areas where Christian groups are politically active, you might find strong support for prayer in public schools. What political views might you expect to be held by people who (a) like to hunt; (b) have a college degree; (c) are Native American; (d) work in a factory?

3. Analyze the effects of personal experience. People and events in our lives can have a powerful effect,

positive or negative, on our political views. During the 2004 presidential campaign, both George W. Bush and John Kerry said their political careers were inspired by family members. Arizona Senator John McCain, a former prisoner of war in Vietnam who sought the Republican nomination in 2000, favored a strong military. Some candidates base their political ideals on their religious beliefs. Have your political views been influenced by your personal experiences? Explain.

Finding Your Political Roots

1 What is the first political event you can recall? How did you and others around you react to it?

2 If you have politically active family members or friends, to what political party do they belong?

3 If you discuss politics with family or friends, how have they influenced your thinking, if at all?

4 Where do you get information about politics—newspapers, television, the Internet? Are you influenced most by what you read or see or hear?

5 How would you describe your political attitudes? Do you lean toward a particular political party? Are your views mostly liberal, mostly conservative, or a mixture of both? Explain.

Test for Success

(a) Use the questionnaire above and the steps outlined above to describe how political traditions influenced your political attitudes.
(b) Interview a friend or family member. Write a paragraph summarizing his or her political roots and attitudes.

Skills for Life

Predicting Consequences

Analysis Skill HI4

The Motor Voter Law requires States to allow people to register to vote when they apply for a driver's license. Several other of its provisions also make voter registration a more convenient process (see page 155).

The law became effective in 1995, and many predicted that it would reverse the downward trend in voter turnout. They were wrong. Voter registrations did reach record levels for the presidential elections of 1996 and 2000. But voter turnout in both elections fell well short of what it had been in 1992 until the 2004 election.

Consider another example. Many who fail to vote say that they are too busy—at work, at school, and so on—to take the time to go to the polls. Some suggest that this problem can be met by allowing both registration and voting via the Internet. To predict the consequences of Internet voting, follow these steps:

1. Identify the problem, cause, or decision. Begin by writing a question that summarizes and clarifies what you're trying to predict. What question might summarize issues involved in voting on the Internet?

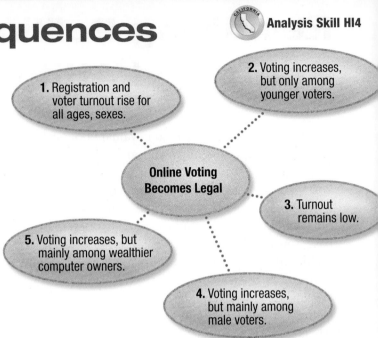

1. Registration and voter turnout rise for all ages, sexes.

2. Voting increases, but only among younger voters.

3. Turnout remains low.

4. Voting increases, but mainly among male voters.

5. Voting increases, but mainly among wealthier computer owners.

Online Voting Becomes Legal

2. Brainstorm and chart possible outcomes. Jot down all the possible consequences, good and bad, that you think could occur. At first, don't rule out any possibilities. Create a web diagram like the one above to display all the possibilities.

3. Apply prior knowledge or new information. To rule out some of the possible consequences, you probably need to apply existing or new knowledge about voting behavior. Policymakers often look for a historical *precedent*—a similar situation in the past. They also rely on their own intuition and experience. There is no precedent for Internet voting. But which prediction might you favor if you read about (a) a new study showing that most computer users are women, or (b) a new poll showing overwhelming voter disinterest in the election?

4. Make a prediction. State your prediction about the results of Internet voting in a way that makes your reasoning clear.

Voting Booth
Information Voting Booth (IVB)

Photo	Candidate	Click To Vote	Attendence At Last Post	% Money From Companies & Orgainizations	Largest Single Contribution From A Company	% Money From Individuals	Largest Single Contribution From An Individual	Educational Qualifications	Stand On Issues	Champaign Web Site
	Wilson Henry		50%	70%	40,000	30%	$100			
	Silvia Jones		75%	65%	25,000	35%	5000			
	Henry Oscar		98%	20%	400	80%	150			
	Fritz Hertz		20%	79%	5,000,000	21%	50			

◄ Back   ▲ Up   ► Next

Efforts are underway in several States to allow voting on the Internet. Here is one mock-up of what an online ballot might look like.

Test for Success

Use the steps above and the following facts to make a prediction about voting patterns: (1) Voter participation tends to be highest among older Americans. (2) The "baby boom" population is entering into its 50s and beyond.

Recognizing Bias

 **Analysis Skills HR1, HR2**

When you're doing research—for instance, trying to become informed on a ballot issue—you need to know whether the information you find is biased or unbiased. Why? Information that is biased reflects a particular point of view. It might exclude, intentionally or not, other legitimate views, or present them in an unfavorable way.

Recognizing bias is especially important now that so much information is available on anonymous Web sites across the Internet. The following steps will help you to identify biased information when you encounter it:

1. Identify the source. Who provided the information? Some interest groups choose names that do not truly disclose who they represent. They may use names that are designed to appeal to your beliefs or values. Be on the lookout for names that sound vague, often patriotic. Read the fictitious press release at right. (a) Identify the source of the "facts." (b) Who might this group represent?

2. Identify the purpose. Determine whether the information is intended to inform or to persuade. An item designed to persuade might leave out information that does not support the author's viewpoint. What is the purpose of this press release?

3. Read carefully for evidence of bias. Use the checklist (at upper right) to evaluate the item.

4. Decide if the item is biased. Remember, a biased account is not necessarily deceptive or bad. It might in fact reflect a worthy yet one-sided account. If you are looking for a balanced account of an issue, you should find one that avoids the pitfalls explained here. Is the press release shown here biased? If so, note the language that indicates the bias.

A BIAS TEST

- Does it present a single viewpoint, or more than one view?
- Is the conclusion supported by verifiable, relevant facts?
- Does the item contain opinion disguised as fact?
- Is it based on valid assumptions?
- Does it include stereotypes or generalizations?
- Does it exclude important information?

Study Says

Pastries Are Health Food

NEW YORK: The Society for Better Living today released a new study showing conclusively that certain types of pastries actually help reduce heart attacks. The study tracked the incidence of heart attacks in consumers of Creampuff Healthy Pastries and found that most consumers felt "completely healthy."

"We're pleased with the results," a Creampuff spokesman said today. "We think our customers are smart enough to assess the state of their own health. In the interest of free enterprise and free choice, we demand that the government stop forcing pastry manufacturers to list the amount of calories and fat in their products."

Test for Success

Find a report or a quotation in the news that reflects bias. What items in the Bias Test (upper right) does it violate?

Skills for Life

Making Decisions

 Analysis Skills HR4, HI4

In 1962, U.S. intelligence reports revealed that the Soviet Union was building missile bases in Cuba. An infuriated President John F. Kennedy had to decide how to respond to this new nuclear threat in America's backyard.

President Kennedy summoned his top national security and military advisors to discuss the crisis. What followed is an example of the decision-making process:

1. Identify the issue to be decided. The first step in good decision making is to figure out *whether* a decision is needed and to clarify *what* ultimately needs to be decided. Reports of the Soviet activity in Cuba immediately raised two questions:

(a) Should the United States respond?

(b) If so, how can the Soviet Union be made to withdraw its arsenal without triggering a catastrophic nuclear war?

The two superpowers already had scores of long-range nuclear weapons aimed at each other's cities. Yet Kennedy felt that the Cuba buildup required a swift response. Why do you think he felt that strong action was needed?

2. Gather information. In a memo, National Security Advisor McGeorge Bundy outlined President Kennedy's orders on how to proceed. Read the excerpts from the memo, above right. What part instructs the staff to collect more information on the situation?

3. Identify options. A decision requires choosing among two or more options. What part of the memo concerns identifying options?

4. Predict consequences. What part of the memo concerns predicting consequences of various courses of action?

5. Make a decision. On October 22, President Kennedy announced his decision to launch a naval blockade of Cuba to prevent more missiles from reaching the island. Tense days followed, as the

---

THE WHITE HOUSE
WASHINGTON

TOP SECRET AND SENSITIVE

August 23, 1962

NATIONAL SECURITY ACTION MEMORANDUM NO. 181

To: Secretary of State / Secretary of Defense / Attorney General / Acting Director, CIA / General Taylor

The President has directed that the following actions and studies be undertaken in the light of the new . . . activity in Cuba. . . .

5. An analysis should be prepared of the probable military, political, and psychological impact of the establishment in Cuba of either surface-to-air missiles or surface-to-surface missiles which could reach the U.S.

6. A study should be made of the advantages and disadvantages of making a statement that the U.S. would not tolerate the establishment of military forces . . . which might launch a nuclear attack from Cuba against the U.S.

7. A study should be made of the various military alternatives which might be adopted in executing a decision to eliminate any installations in Cuba. . . . What would be the pros and cons, for example of pinpoint attack, general counter-force attack, and outright invasion.

8. A study should be made of the advantages and disadvantages of action to liberate Cuba by blockade or invasion or other action . . . .

—Memo from National Security Advisor McGeorge Bundy

---

superpowers came to the brink of nuclear war. In the end, the Soviets backed down, called back their ships, and dismantled the Cuban bases. Why do you think the President chose the option of blockading Cuba?

Test for Success

Make a decision-making chart on the Cuban Missile Crisis. Identify two or more courses of action that President Kennedy could have taken, and describe the possible consequences (pro and con) of each course of action.

Skills for Life

Understanding Point of View

An old saying advises you to "walk a mile in your neighbor's shoes." That is, when you're evaluating or contradicting someone's opinion, think about how the issue looks from that person's perspective, or point of view. It might make you more tolerant of the other opinion, or it might help you strengthen your own argument.

Many factors can shape someone's perspective. Here are some guidelines for understanding point of view:

1. Identify the source. Find out whatever you can about the person whose views you are evaluating. Who are the sources of the excerpts below?

2. Identify the view being presented. In the excerpts below, the senators discuss different ways of dealing with the hostility between the North and the South over slavery. To preserve the Union, Senator John C. Calhoun favored nullification, giving Southern States the right to refuse to carry out federal laws that they opposed. Senator Jefferson Davis spoke nearly a decade later, advocating secession, withdrawal from the Union. (a) Summarize the main idea of each quotation. (b) Identify the intended audience for each speech. (c) Identify the purpose of each.

3. List attributes that might influence the source's point of view. Consider factors such as the person's origins, age, sex, ethnic group, education, socioeconomic group, personal experiences, lifestyle, values, and priorities.

Test for Success

Find background information on Calhoun and Davis. Compare and contrast the two points of view on the topic of *nullification* vs. *secession*.

" . . . [W]hen the Constitution was ratified and the Government put in action, there was nearly a perfect equilibrium between the [North and South], which afforded ample means to each to protect itself against the aggression of the other; but, as it now stands, [the North] has the exclusive power of controlling the Government, which leaves [the South] without any adequate means of protecting itself against its encroachment and oppression. . . . How can the Union be saved? . . . [B]y adopting such measures as will satisfy the [Southern States] that they can remain in the Union consistently with their honor and their safety. "

—*South Carolina Senator John C. Calhoun, "Proposal to Preserve the Union," Senate speech, 1850*

" It was because of his deep-seated attachment to the Union . . . that Mr. Calhoun advocated the doctrine of nullification, which he proclaimed to be peaceful, to be within the limits of State power, not to disturb the Union. . . . Secession belongs to a different class of remedies. It is to be justified upon the basis that the states are sovereign. There was a time when none denied it. I hope the time may come again when a better comprehension of the theory of our Government, and the inalienable rights of the people of the States, will prevent any one from denying that each State is a sovereign, and thus may reclaim the [agreements] which it has made to any [other government] whomsoever. "

—*Mississippi Senator Jefferson Davis, Farewell speech to the Senate, 1861*

Determining Cause and Effect

 Analysis Skills HI1, HI2

Remembering individual facts, dates, and events might help you on a game show or test. But finding out why events happen helps you understand specific events in history and politics. To answer the question *Why?*, try these steps:

1. Identify possible causes and effects. A cause is an event or action that brings about an effect. For that reason, the cause must occur before the effect. Yet an event that precedes another does not necessarily cause it. Words such as *because, due to,* and *on account of* signal causes. Words such as *so, therefore,* and *as a result* signal effects. Which of these sentences describe a cause-effect relationship? (a) *Soviet aggression in the postwar era led to the cold war.* (b) *Within a short time, the United States was transformed into the world's mightiest military power.* (c) *Nixon's visit to China paved the way to further contacts and, finally, to formal diplomatic ties between the United States and China.* (d) *The growth of U.S.-Soviet tensions was due in part to the opposing post war goals of the two superpowers.*

2. Diagram the cause-effect relationship. Diagrams can help you analyze relationships among events. Diagrams can also help you identify multiple causes. Several causes can combine to create one effect, just as one cause can bring about several effects. What does Diagram A show?

3. Diagram a chain of events. A single event can be both a cause and an effect. Causes and effects can form a chain of events that continue over a period of time. How is Diagram B a chain of events?

4. Draw conclusions based on your analysis. What general statements can you make based on this analysis of cause and effect? Look for connected ideas and trends.

Test for Success

Read the paragraphs about the Korean War on pages 486–487. Using the steps above, diagram the causes and effects of the war. Make sure that the events are truly causes, not just a series of events.

Diagram A

Cause/Effect: The Cold War

CAUSES

Soviets impose communism in Eastern Europe
Soviets try to seize Iranian oil fields
Soviets demand seaport in Turkey

EFFECT

U.S. and U.S.S.R. engage in the cold war

Diagram B

Cause/Effect: The Cold War

CAUSES

Soviets impose communism in Eastern Europe
Soviets try to seize Iranian oil fields
Soviets demand seaport in Turkey

EFFECT

U.S. and U.S.S.R. engage in the cold war

EFFECTS

Truman Doctrine
Containment policy
Berlin blockade
Cuban missile crisis
Wars in Korea and Vietnam

Drawing Conclusions

A caravan of police cars converges on a Chicago neighborhood known for illegal drug trafficking. A man sees the police and flees the scene. Suspicious, the police chase him down and "frisk" him for weapons. They find a handgun. They arrest him.

Was this a legal search and seizure? The 4th Amendment to the Constitution protects U.S. citizens from "unreasonable searches and seizures." Did the police officers have sufficient reason to suspect that the fleeing man had committed a crime, even though they did not see him do anything wrong? In *Wardlow v. Illinois*, 2000, the Supreme Court ruled that the police acted legally when they drew this conclusion.

Drawing a conclusion means arriving at an idea or opinion that is suggested, indirectly, from given information. How did the officers reach their conclusion? Instinctively, within seconds, they used a process like this:

1. Assess information. Analyze a fact or set of facts to see if they suggest other ideas. Sometimes a given piece of information may imply a cause-effect relationship. In the Chicago case, what did police actually observe when they arrived on scene?

2. Apply prior knowledge. To come to a conclusion, you usually combine new information with facts you already know. What relevant information did the police already know when they arrived on scene?

3. Reach a conclusion. Often a conclusion can be stated in this form: *X, therefore Y*. Use this format to state the conclusion that the police drew from the scene.

4. Test your conclusion. It's possible to draw the wrong conclusion from a set of facts. Always test the validity of your conclusion by considering whether any other conclusion is possible from the information given. Is there another possible explanation for what the Chicago police saw? If so, is it a likely explanation? Explain.

What did the Supreme Court think of the police officers' conclusions? In a ruling in early 2000, the Court said that "An individual's presence in a 'high crime area,' standing alone, is not enough to support a reasonable, particularized suspicion of criminal activity," but the man's "nervous, evasive behavior" and "unprovoked flight" were "sufficiently suspicious to warrant further investigation." The officers' conclusions, the Court found, were sufficiently valid to justify their actions.

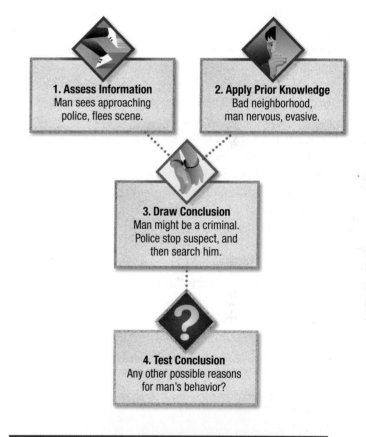

1. Assess Information
Man sees approaching police, flees scene.

2. Apply Prior Knowledge
Bad neighborhood, man nervous, evasive.

3. Draw Conclusion
Man might be a criminal. Police stop suspect, and then search him.

4. Test Conclusion
Any other possible reasons for man's behavior?

Test for Success

Use the steps above and the facts in the following paragraph to draw a conclusion about *Plessy* v. *Ferguson*. State your conclusion as *X, therefore Y*.

In Plessy *v.* Ferguson *(1896) the Supreme Court ruled that racially segregated facilities were constitutional as long as the facilities were "separate but equal." In 1954 the Court overturned* Plessy *in* Brown *v.* Board of Education.

Reading Tables and Analyzing Statistics

People have been collecting and analyzing statistics for a long time. For instance, the census—the practice of counting people—dates back at least to ancient Egypt. In our electronic age, collecting and storing data are becoming easier all the time. Therefore, reading and analyzing statistics are now much-needed skills. Use the steps below to help you interpret data tables:

1. Determine the source of the information and decide if the source is reliable. Faulty data produce faulty conclusions, so make sure your sources are accurate, complete, and trustworthy. A disreputable source might be sloppy in its data-gathering procedures, or it might edit out data that doesn't suit its purposes. Published government data are usually considered reliable. Be skeptical about information with an unfamiliar source or no source at all. (a) What is the source of the information in the table below? (b) Is the source reliable?

2. Study the table to determine its purpose. Information is collected for a variety of purposes: to compare and contrast, to show proportions, or to identify trends over time. What is the purpose of the table below?

3. Identify relationships among the data. Figure out percentage increases and decreases over time. (a) What ethnic group is expected to have the biggest percentage increase in population from 2000 to 2030? (b) Is the population of any ethnic group projected to decrease during that time?

4. Draw conclusions. The ethnic groups appear in order from the largest population (white) to the smallest (other) in 2000. (a) Is this ranking expected to change by 2030? (b) From this fact, state a one- or two-sentence conclusion.

Test for Success

The number of Hispanic Americans is expected to surpass the number of African Americans within several years, making Hispanics the largest minority in the country. Given this fact, and using information from the table, what can you conclude about the size of households of these two groups?

U.S. Population, by Race and Hispanic Origin: 2000 to 2030				
Ethnic Group	**2000**	**2010†**	**2020†**	**2030†**
White	228,548,000	244,995,000	260,629,000	275,731,000
Black	35,818,000	40,454,000	45,365,000	50,422,000
Hispanic Origin*	35,622,000	47,756,000	59,756,000	73,055,000
Asian American	10,684,000	14,241,000	17,988,000	22,580,000
Other**	7,075,000	9,246,000	11,822,000	14,831,000
Total	282,125,000	308,936,000	335,805,000	363,584,000

*Persons of Hispanic Origin may be of any race. **Includes American Indian and Alaskan Native, Native Hawaiian and Other Pacific Islander, and Two or More Races. †Projected

SOURCE: U.S. Census Bureau

Drawing Inferences

Drawing inferences means reading between the lines; that is, forming conclusions that are not stated directly but are suggested by other facts. For instance, the Queen of England appoints several officials of the Church of England. Knowing that in the United States, Congress and the President have no such powers, you can infer that British tradition does not separate the functions of church and state the way the United States Constitution requires.

Use the following steps to practice drawing inferences from what you read:

1. Find the main idea in a sentence or passage. To find information that is suggested but unstated in a passage, you have to understand the stated content of the passage. Read the subsection entitled "The Monarchy," on page 627. You can state the main idea of the passage by answering these questions:
(a) In earlier times, what was the role of the monarchy in Britain?
(b) What is the role of the monarchy today?

2. Apply other facts or prior knowledge. You also read that opponents of the monarchy periodically try to have it abolished. You probably know that the monarchy has lasted for more than 1,000 years. This combination of facts should suggest to you certain inferences. What other facts do you know about the popularity of the monarchy that might help you draw inferences?

3. Decide whether the information suggests an unstated fact or conclusion. When you integrate, or combine, this series of facts, it's possible to infer that the majority of Britons still support the monarchy. What can you infer about the role of the monarchy in national unity and stability? Explain.

◄ At left, Britain's Queen Elizabeth II waves to crowds from her carriage during the celebration of her 60th birthday, in 1986. Below, the nation celebrates the Queen's Silver Anniversary, the 25th year of her reign, in 1977.

Test for Success

If you were to read in the news that Britain's government had fallen, what might you be able to infer? Use the knowledge you gain by reading about British elections on page 629.

Skills for Life

Using Time Lines

 Analysis Skills CS1, CS2

Even if you have a fantastic memory, it's difficult to keep a lot of dates in your head in the right order. A time line lets you visualize a sequence of events so that you can see relationships among dates and events. Often a time line reveals causes and effects as well as events that recur in time.

The time line below presents key events in the presidency of Richard Nixon. Use the steps below to analyze the time line:

1. Identify the time period covered by the time line. The upper time line shown here spans the years of Richard Nixon's presidency, from his first election in 1968 to his resignation in 1974. (a) How many years does the upper time line cover? A secondary time line appears to pop out from the upper line. This lower time line magnifies in detail the events on a certain segment of the upper time line. (b) How many years does the lower time line cover?

2. Determine how the time line is divided. Most time lines are divided into equal periods, or increments, of time: years, decades, or centuries. (a) What increments of time are used in the upper line? (b) What increments are used in the lower line?

3. Study the time line to see how events are related. (a) State what content is shown in the upper time line. (b) State the content of the lower time line.

4. Use the time line to help you draw conclusions about the period you are studying. What do you think happened to Nixon's popularity between his landslide reelection and his resignation? Explain.

Test for Success

Construct a time line of your life or the life of someone you know. Make a secondary time line of a particular year or grade in school that shows some details from that period.

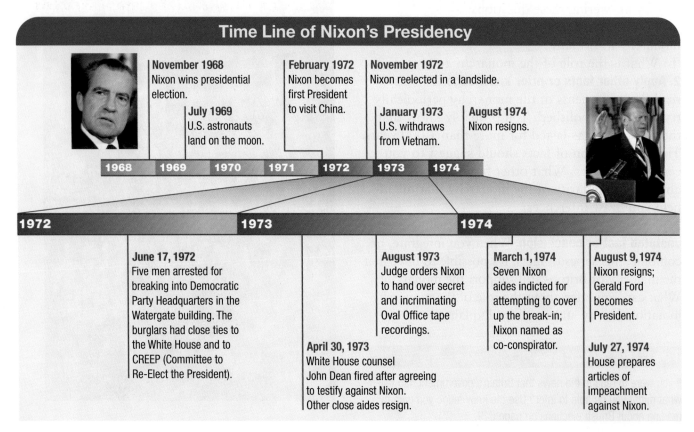

Time Line of Nixon's Presidency

November 1968
Nixon wins presidential election.

July 1969
U.S. astronauts land on the moon.

February 1972
Nixon becomes first President to visit China.

November 1972
Nixon reelected in a landslide.

January 1973
U.S. withdraws from Vietnam.

August 1974
Nixon resigns.

1968 | 1969 | 1970 | 1971 | 1972 | 1973 | 1974

1972 | 1973 | 1974

June 17, 1972
Five men arrested for breaking into Democratic Party Headquarters in the Watergate building. The burglars had close ties to the White House and to CREEP (Committee to Re-Elect the President).

August 1973
Judge orders Nixon to hand over secret and incriminating Oval Office tape recordings.

April 30, 1973
White House counsel John Dean fired after agreeing to testify against Nixon. Other close aides resign.

March 1, 1974
Seven Nixon aides indicted for attempting to cover up the break-in; Nixon named as co-conspirator.

August 9, 1974
Nixon resigns; Gerald Ford becomes President.

July 27, 1974
House prepares articles of impeachment against Nixon.

Skills for Life

Interpreting Line Graphs

Throughout the 1990s, the world's oil consumers enjoyed low petroleum prices. In fact, in the late 1990s, prices when adjusted for inflation plunged to their lowest levels in decades. Major oil producers in the Middle East and elsewhere suffered severely from the loss of revenues. In 1999, the producers were finally able to agree on large cuts in oil production. Read about supply and demand on page 661 and use the steps below to interpret the information in Graph A.

1. Identify the type of information presented on the graph. The graph title and the labels on the *x* axis and *y* axis tell the meanings of the points and lines on the graph. Look at Graph A and answer these questions: (a) What do the numbers on the *x* axis (horizontal) and the *y* axis (vertical) represent? (b) What relationship does the line graph describe?

2. Read the data on the graph. Before studying overall patterns, look at specific elements of the graph.

For example: (a) What is the maximum cost per barrel of oil that can be shown on this graph? (b) How many years does the graph cover? (c) Why were these dates chosen?

3. Study the data on the graph to draw conclusions. You already know that U.S. oil supplies dropped sharply in the late 1990s. In Chapter 21, you can learn what happens to prices when supplies of a product are reduced. Use this knowledge to draw a conclusion from Graph A. State your conclusion in a sentence or two.

Test for Success

In our free-enterprise economy, wages are usually determined not by the government but by what the free market will pay for labor. Wages also follow the laws of supply and demand for labor. Use this knowledge to draw conclusions from Graph B.

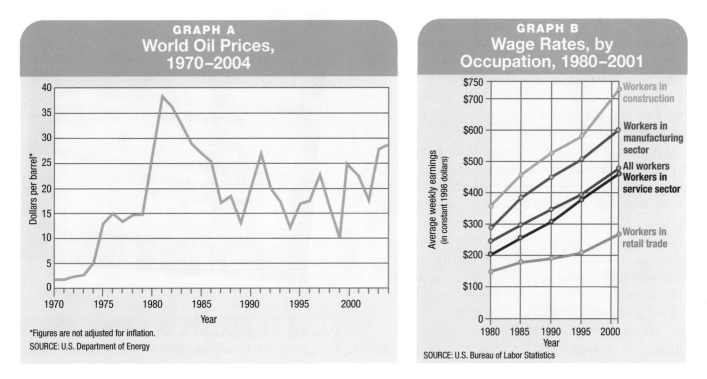

GRAPH A
World Oil Prices, 1970–2004

Dollars per barrel*

*Figures are not adjusted for inflation.
SOURCE: U.S. Department of Energy

GRAPH B
Wage Rates, by Occupation, 1980–2001

Average weekly earnings (in constant 1998 dollars)

Workers in construction
Workers in manufacturing sector
All workers
Workers in service sector
Workers in retail trade

SOURCE: U.S. Bureau of Labor Statistics

Creating a Multimedia Presentation

Maps help to orient your audience

Use written text for lengthy, complex topics

Add realism with audio/video passages

Create a Web site with quizzes and links

Photographs add visual interest

As chalkboards and typewriters make way for computer and TV monitors, there are many new ways to tell a story. A "report" can include written text, maps, charts, photographs, video clips, audio segments, and Web pages. Use these steps to create an exciting presentation:

1. Define your topic. This step determines the success of your project. Multimedia presentations lend themselves to topics that have a variety of aspects or subtopics. Choose carefully. A topic that's too broad—say, "Civil Liberties"—is difficult to cover thoroughly. How might you narrow that topic?

2. Make a "blueprint"—a plan—for your project. Create a blueprint by brainstorming ideas for covering your topic in various media. First, find out what media are available to you. Then make a detailed plan for how you want to tell your "story." Use the form at right as a model. Assign roles to others involved in the project, if needed. Set a deadline for each main task. Why do you think a blueprint is especially helpful for a multimedia presentation?

3. Develop your presentation. Carry out your project plan by doing research, writing scripts, and gathering materials. You may want to collect more material than you'll use. This gives you flexibility in editing and assembling your work. Aim for an accurate, lively, and logical flow of ideas with coordinated visual and audio content.

4. Present your work. The best presentations are interactive in some way. Try to involve your audience in the presentation.

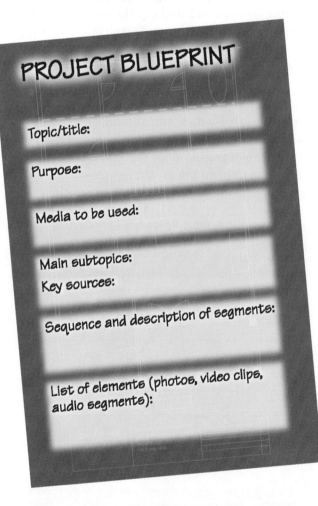

PROJECT BLUEPRINT

Topic/title:

Purpose:

Media to be used:

Main subtopics:

Key sources:

Sequence and description of segments:

List of elements (photos, video clips, audio segments):

Test for Success

Choose a possible topic for a multimedia presentation, and create a project blueprint.

Skills for Life

Analyzing Maps

 **Analysis Skill CS3**

Maps bring information to life in a way that words alone cannot. Maps are particularly useful to people who grasp concepts better when they are illustrated. To analyze a map and draw information from it, try these steps:

1. Identify the purpose of the map. The map shown here is a cartogram. It is a special-purpose map used to present statistics geographically. Here, the original 13 States are shown not in proportion to their land area, but according to the relative sizes of their populations in 1770. The cartogram intentionally distorts the sizes and shapes of territories in order to compare them visually. Compare this map with the one on page 31. (a) Which States had a large population for their small physical size? (b) Which States had a rather small population for their large size?

2. Apply prior knowledge to draw conclusions from the map. You may read on page 263 about the debate, ongoing since the nation's founding, over whether to have equal representation in the Senate for every State, regardless of its size or population.

Knowing this, study the cartogram again. (a) At the nation's founding, which States stood to gain from having equal representation? (b) Which would gain from having representation tied to population? (c) How did the Constitution reconcile this problem?

Test for Success

In the library or on the Internet, find a present-day population map of the United States. (a) List three States that would be awarded a large number of senators if they were apportioned according to population size, as in the House of Representatives. (b) List at least three States that would fare poorly with representation by population in the Senate.

▲ Above, engraving of a map of the United States; at right, cartogram of the colonies

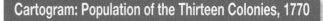
Cartogram: Population of the Thirteen Colonies, 1770

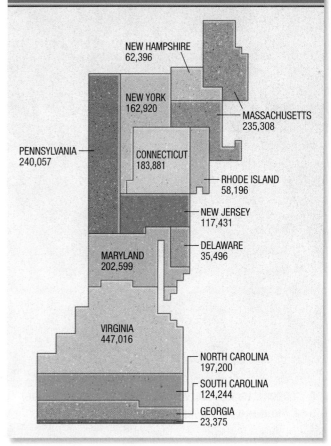

NEW HAMPSHIRE
62,396

NEW YORK
162,920

MASSACHUSETTS
235,308

PENNSYLVANIA
240,057

CONNECTICUT
183,881

RHODE ISLAND
58,196

NEW JERSEY
117,431

DELAWARE
35,496

MARYLAND
202,599

VIRGINIA
447,016

NORTH CAROLINA
197,200

SOUTH CAROLINA
124,244

GEORGIA
23,375

◆ **Conservators preserving the Star Spangled Banner
at the National Museum of American History**

Foundations of American Government

CONSTITUTIONAL PRINCIPLES

Popular Sovereignty The Declaration of Independence embraced the theory that people form governments to protect their natural rights, and that the powers of government must be based on the consent of the governed. In doing so, the document justified the colonies' split from Great Britain and established precedent for a government that is responsible to its people.

Separation of Powers The Constitution gives certain powers to each branch of government. Distributing government's powers among the executive, legislative, and judicial branches prevents any one branch from exercising too much authority.

Federalism In the United States, powers are divided between the National Government and the State governments. Thus, the Constitution helps to ensure the National Government's strength, while protecting the uniqueness of State governments.

The Impact on You

Both separation of powers and federalism involve the dividing of governmental power. The Framers of the Constitution provided for that fragmentation of power in order to limit the ability of government to exercise its powers—and so to protect you, and all of the people, from the abuse of governmental power.

Principles of Government

❝The way of democracy is both frustrating and invigorating. It lacks the orderly directives of dictatorship, and instead relies on millions to demonstrate self-discipline and enlightened concern for the common good.❞
—Nancy Landon Kassebaum (1996)

Here, Senator Kassebaum tells us that a democracy—which insists on the importance of each and every person and, at the same time, insists on the equality of *all* persons—inevitably produces a political climate "both frustrating and invigorating."

◆ New Americans celebrate taking the oath of citizenship.

Standards Preview

H-SS 12.1.1 Analyze the influence of ancient Greek, Roman, English, and leading European political thinkers such as John Locke, Charles-Louis Montesquieu, Niccolo` Machiavelli, and William Blackstone on the development of American government.

H-SS 12.1.3 Explain how the U.S. Constitution reflects a balance between the classical republican concern with promotion of the public good and the classical liberal concern with protecting individual rights; and discuss how the basic premises of liberal constitutionalism and democracy are joined in the Declaration of Independence as "self-evident truths."

H-SS 12.2.2 Explain how economic rights are secured and their importance to the individual and to society (e.g., the right to acquire, use, transfer, and dispose of property; right to choose one's work; right to join or not join labor unions; copyright and patent).

H-SS 12.2.4 Understand the obligations of civic-mindedness, including voting, being informed on civic issues, volunteering and performing public service, and serving in the military or alternative service.

H-SS 12.2.5 Describe the reciprocity between rights and obligations; that is, why enjoyment of one's rights entails respect for the rights of others.

H-SS 12.3.4 Compare the relationship of government and civil society in constitutional democracies to the relationship of government and civil society in authoritarian and totalitarian regimes.

H-SS 12.7.5 Explain how public policy is formed, including the setting of the public agenda and implementation of it through regulations and executive orders.

H-SS 12.8.2 Describe the roles of broadcast, print, and electronic media, including the Internet, as means of communication in American politics.

H-SS 12.9.1 Explain how the different philosophies and structures of feudalism, mercantilism, socialism, fascism, communism, monarchies, parliamentary systems, and constitutional liberal democracies influence economic policies, social welfare policies, and human rights practices.

H-SS 12.9.3 Discuss the advantages and disadvantages of federal, confederal, and unitary systems of government.

H-SS 12.10 Students formulate questions about and defend their analyses of tensions within our constitutional democracy and the importance of maintaining a balance between the following concepts: majority rule and individual rights; liberty and equality; state and national authority in a federal system; civil disobedience and the rule of law; freedom of the press and the right to a fair trial; the relationship of religion and government.

SECTION 1

Government and the State (pp. 4–10)

★ Government enables a society to protect the peace and carry out its policies.

★ A state, not to be confused with one of the fifty States of the United States, is a land with people, a defined territory, and a sovereign government.

★ Several theories attempt to explain the origin of the state.

★ Among these theories, the political philosophy of John Locke had the most profound impact on the Declaration of Independence and the United States Constitution.

★ The goals of the Federal Government are described in the Preamble to the Constitution.

SECTION 2

Forms of Government (pp. 12–16)

★ Each government is unique, but governments can be grouped into categories according to three sets of characteristics.

★ Democratic governments rely on the participation of the people, while dictatorships concentrate power in the hands of a few.

★ The distribution of power between local governments and a central government determines whether a government is unitary, federal, or confederate.

★ Presidential governments divide power among several branches of government, while parliamentary governments focus power in one dominant branch.

SECTION 3

Basic Concepts of Democracy (pp. 18–22)

★ Democracy is built upon five principles: respect for the individual, equality of all persons, acceptance of majority rule and minority rights, compromise, and protection of individual freedoms.

★ The free enterprise system of the United States, like democracy, relies on individual freedoms.

★ In a mixed economy, the government plays a role in the economy.

★ The Internet has opened up new opportunities for democracy, but users must carefully evaluate the information that they find.

Go Online
PHSchool.com

For: Current Data
Web Code: mqg-1015

For: Close Up Foundation debates
Web Code: mqh-1018

① Government and the State

OBJECTIVES

1. **Define** government and the basic powers every government holds.
2. **Describe** the four defining characteristics of the state.
3. **Identify** four theories that attempt to explain the origin of the state.
4. **Understand** the purpose of government in the United States and other countries.

WHY IT MATTERS

Government is essential to the existence of human beings in a civilized society. What any particular government is like and what that government does have an extraordinary impact on the lives of all people who live within its reach.

POLITICAL DICTIONARY

★ government
★ public policy
★ legislative power
★ executive power
★ judicial power
★ constitution
★ dictatorship
★ democracy
★ state
★ sovereign

This is a book about government—and, more particularly, about government in the United States. Why should you read it? Why should you study government? These are legitimate questions, and they can be answered in several different ways—as you will see throughout the pages of this book. But, for now, consider this response: you should know as much as you possibly can about government because government affects *you* in an uncountable number of very important ways. It does so today, it did so yesterday, it will tomorrow, and it will do so every day for the rest of your life.

Think of our point here in this light: What would your life be like *without* government? Who would protect you, and all of the rest of us, against the attacks of terrorists and against other threats from abroad? Who would provide for education, guard the public's health, and protect the environment? Who would pave the streets, regulate traffic, punish criminals, and respond to fires and other human-made and natural disasters? Who would protect civil rights and care for the elderly and the poor? Who would protect consumers and property owners?

Government does all of these things, of course—and much more. In short, if government did not exist, we would have to invent it.

What Is Government?

Government is the institution through which a society makes and enforces its public policies. Government is made up of those people who exercise its powers, all those who have authority and control over people.

The **public policies** of a government are, in short, all of those things a government decides to do. Public policies cover matters ranging from taxation, defense, education, crime, and health care to transportation, the environment, civil rights, and working conditions. The list of public policy issues is nearly endless.

Governments must have power in order to make and carry out public policies. Power is the ability to command or prevent action, the ability to achieve a desired end.

Every government has and exercises three basic kinds of power: (1) **legislative power**—the power to make law and to frame public policies; (2) **executive power**—the power to execute, enforce, and administer law; and (3) **judicial power**—the power to interpret laws, to determine their meaning, and to settle disputes that arise within the society. These powers of government are often outlined in a country's constitution. A **constitution** is the body of fundamental laws setting out the principles, structures, and processes of a government.

The ultimate responsibility for the exercise of these powers may be held by a single person or by a small group, as in a **dictatorship.** In this form of government, those who rule cannot be held responsible to the will of the people. When the responsibility for the exercise of these powers rests with a majority of the people, that form of government is known as a **democracy.** In a democracy, supreme authority rests with the people.

Government is among the oldest of all human inventions. Its origins are lost in the mists of time. But, clearly, government first appeared when human beings realized that they could not survive without some way to regulate both their own and their neighbors' behavior.

The earliest known evidences of government date from ancient Egypt. More than 2,300 years ago, the Greek philosopher Aristotle observed that "man is by nature a political animal."[1] As he wrote those words, Aristotle was only recording a fact that, even then, had been obvious for thousands of years.

What did Aristotle mean by "political"? That is to say, what is "politics"? Although people often equate the two, politics and government are very different things. Politics is a process, while government is an institution.

More specifically, politics is the process by which a society decides how power and resources will be distributed within that society. Politics enables a society to decide who will reap the benefits, and who will pay the costs, of its public policies.

The word *politics* is sometimes used in a way that suggests that it is somehow immoral or something to be avoided. But, again, politics is a *process,* the means by which government is conducted. It is neither "good" nor "bad," but it is necessary. Indeed, it is impossible to conceive of government without politics.

The State

Over the course of human history, the state has emerged as the dominant political unit in the world. The **state** can be defined as a body of people, living in a defined territory, organized politically (that is, with a government), and with the power to make and enforce law without the consent of any higher authority.

▲ *Patriotism in a Time of Crisis* Americans showed their pride in their country and support for their government in the wake of the terrorist attacks on the World Trade Center and the Pentagon. **H-SS 12.2.4**

There are more than 190 states in the world today. They vary greatly in size, military power, natural resources, and economic importance. Still, each of them possesses all four characteristics of a state: population, territory, sovereignty, and government.

Note that the state is a legal entity. In popular usage, a state is often called a "nation" or a "country." In a strict sense, however, the word *nation* is an ethnic term, referring to races or other large groups of people. The word *country* is a geographic term, referring to a particular place, region, or area of land.

Population

Clearly, a state must have people—a population. The size of that population, however, has nothing directly to do with the existence of a state. One of the world's smallest states, in population terms, is San Marino. Bounded on all sides by Italy, it has only some 27,000

---

[1] In most of the world's written political record, the words *man* and *men* have been widely used to refer to all of humankind. This text follows that form when presenting excerpts from historical writings or documents and in references to them.

The Four Characteristics of the State

Population **Territory** **Sovereignty** **Government**

Interpreting Charts To be considered a state, a group of people must have a defined body of land and an independent, sovereign government. ***Does your school qualify as a state? If not, which requirements does it lack?***

people. The People's Republic of China is the world's most populous state with more than 1.3 *billion* people—just about one fifth of the world's population. The nearly 300 million who live in the United States make it the world's third most populous, after China and India.

The people who make up a state may or may not be *homogeneous*. The adjective homogeneous describes members of a group who share customs, a common language, and ethnic background. Today, the population of the United States includes people from a wide variety of backgrounds. Still, most Americans think of themselves as exactly that: Americans.

Territory

Just as a state cannot exist without people, so it must have land—territory, with known and recognized boundaries. The states in today's world vary as widely in terms of territory as they do in population. Here, too, San Marino ranks among the world's smallest states. It covers less than 24 square miles—smaller than thousands of cities and towns in the United States.[2]

Russia, the world's largest state, stretches across some 6.6 million square miles. The total area of the United States is 3,787,425 square miles.

Sovereignty

Every state is **sovereign**—it has supreme and absolute power within its own territory and can decide its own foreign and domestic policies. It is neither subordinate nor responsible to any other authority.

Thus, as a sovereign state, the United States can determine its form of government. Like any other state in the world, it can frame its economic system and shape its own foreign policies. Sovereignty is the one characteristic that distinguishes the state from all other, lesser political units.

The States within the United States are not sovereign and so are not states in the international, legal sense. Each State is subordinate to the Constitution of the United States.[3]

Government

Every state is politically organized. That is, every state has a government. Recall, a government is the institution through which society makes and

---

[2]The United States also recognizes the State of Vatican City, with a permanent population of some 900 persons and a roughly triangular area of only 109 acres. The Vatican is wholly surrounded by the City of Rome. American recognition of the Vatican, which had been withdrawn in 1867, was renewed in 1984.

[3]In this book, state printed with a small "s" denotes a state in the family of nations, such as the United States, Great Britain, and Mexico. State printed with a capital "S" refers to a State in the American union.

enforces its public policies. A government is the agency through which the state exerts its will and works to accomplish its goals. Government includes the machinery and the personnel by which the state is ruled.

Government is necessary to avoid what the English philosopher Thomas Hobbes (1588–1679) called "the war of every man against every man." Without government, said Hobbes, there would be "continual fear and danger of violent death and life [would be] solitary, poor, nasty, brutish, and short." The world has seen a number of examples over recent years of what happens when a government disappears: In Lebanon, Bosnia, Somalia, and many other places, life became "nasty, brutish, and short."

Major Political Ideas

For centuries, historians, philosophers, and others have pondered the question of the origin of the state. What set of circumstances first brought it into being?

Over time, many different answers have been offered, but history provides no conclusive evidence to support any of them. However, four theories have emerged as the most widely accepted explanations for the origin of the state.

The Force Theory Many scholars have long believed that the state was born of force. They hold that one person or a small group claimed control over an area and forced all within it to submit to that person's or group's rule. When that rule was established, all the basic elements of the state—population, territory, sovereignty, and government—were present.

The Evolutionary Theory Others claim that the state developed naturally out of the early family. They hold that the primitive family, of which one person was the head and thus the "government," was the first stage in political development. Over countless years the original family became a network of related families, a clan. In time the clan became a tribe. When the tribe first turned to agriculture and gave up its nomadic ways, tying itself to the land, the state was born.

The Divine Right Theory The theory of divine right was widely accepted in much of the Western world from the fifteenth through the eighteenth centuries. It held that God created the state and that God had given those of royal birth a "divine right" to rule. The people were bound to obey their ruler as they would God; opposition to "the divine right of kings" was both treason and mortal sin.

During the seventeenth century, philosophers began to question this theory. Much of the thought upon which present-day democracies rest began as a challenge to the theory of divine right.

Force

Evolutionary

Divine Right

Social Contract

◀ Different explanations have been offered for the origin of the state. Pharoah Akhenaten of Egypt (middle) believed that power flowed from Aten, the god of the sun disk. *Critical Thinking Can more than one of these theories accurately explain the origin of the state? Explain why or why not.* H-SS 12.1.1

The notion of divine right was not unique to European history. The rulers of many ancient civilizations, including the Chinese, Egyptian, Aztec, and Mayan civilizations, were held to be gods or to have been chosen by the gods. The Japanese emperor, the *mikado*, governed by divine right until 1945.

The Social Contract Theory In terms of the American political system, the most significant of the theories of the origin of the state is that of the "social contract." Philosophers such as Thomas Hobbes, James Harrington (1611–1677), and John Locke (1632–1704) in England and Jean Jacques Rousseau (1712–1778) in France developed this theory in the seventeenth and eighteenth centuries.

Hobbes wrote that in earliest history humans lived in unbridled freedom, in a "state of nature," in which no government existed and no person was subject to any superior power. That which people could take by force belonged to them. However, all people were similarly free in this state of nature. No authority existed to protect one person from the aggressive actions of another. Thus, individuals were only as safe as their own physical strength and intelligence could make them.

Human beings overcame their unpleasant condition, says the social contract theory, by agreeing with one another to create a state. By contract, people within a given area agreed to give up to the state as much power as was needed to promote the safety and well-being of all. In the contract (that is, through a constitution), the members of the state created a government to exercise the powers they had voluntarily given to the state.

In short, the social contract theory argues that the state arose out of a voluntary act of free people. It holds that the state exists only to serve the will of the people, that they are the sole source of political power, and that they are free to give or to withhold that power as they choose. The theory may seem far-fetched today. The great concepts that this theory promoted, however—popular sovereignty, limited government, and individual rights—were immensely important to the shaping of the American governmental system.

The Declaration of Independence (see pages 40–43) justified its revolution through the social contract theory, arguing that King George III and his ministers had violated the contract. Thomas Jefferson called the document "pure Locke."

The Purpose of Government

What does government do? You can find a very meaningful answer to that question in the Constitution of the United States. The American system of government was created to serve the purposes set out there.

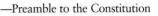

FROM THE Constitution *"We the People of the United States, in Order to form a more perfect Union, establish Justice, insure domestic Tranquility, provide for the common defence, promote the general Welfare, and secure the Blessings of Liberty to ourselves and our Posterity, do ordain and establish this Constitution for the United States of America."*
—Preamble to the Constitution

Reproduced by permission of Johnny Hart and Field Enterprises

Interpreting Political Cartoons American government was influenced strongly by the social contract theory. *How does this cartoon poke fun at that theory?*

Form a More Perfect Union

The United States, which had just won its independence from Great Britain, faced an altogether uncertain future in the postwar 1780s. In 1781, the Articles of Confederation, the nation's first constitution, created "a firm league of friendship" among the 13 States. That league soon proved to be neither very firm nor very friendly. The government created by the Articles was powerless to overcome the intense rivalries and jealousies among the States that marked the time.

The Constitution of today was written in 1787. The original States adopted it in order to link them, and the American people, more closely together. That Constitution was built in the belief that in union there is strength.

Establish Justice

To provide justice, said Thomas Jefferson, is "the most sacred of the duties of government." No purpose, no goal of public policy, can be of greater importance in a democracy.

But what, precisely, is justice? The term is difficult to define, for justice is a concept—an idea, an invention of the human mind. Like other concepts such as truth, liberty, and fairness, justice means what people make it mean.

As the concept of justice has developed over time in American thought and practice, it has come to mean this: The law, in both its content and its administration, must be reasonable, fair, and impartial. Those standards of justice have not always been met in this country. We have not attained our professed goal of "equal justice for all." However, this, too, must be said: The history of this country can be told largely in terms of our continuing attempts to reach that goal.

"Injustice anywhere," said Martin Luther King, Jr., "is a threat to justice everywhere." You will encounter this idea again and again in this book.

Insure Domestic Tranquility

Order is essential to the well-being of any society, and keeping the peace at home has always been a prime function of government. Most people can only imagine what it would be like to live in a state of anarchy—without government, law, or order. In fact, people do live that way in some parts of the world today. For

years now, Somalia, which is located on the eastern tip of Africa, has not had a functioning government; rival warlords control different parts of the country.

In *The Federalist* No. 51, James Madison observed: "If men were angels, no government would be necessary." Madison, who was perhaps the most thoughtful of the Framers of the Constitution, knew that most human beings fall far short of this standard.

Provide for the Common Defense

Defending the nation against foreign enemies has always been one of government's major responsibilities. You can see its importance in the fact that defense is mentioned far more often in the Constitution than any of the other functions of the government. The nation's defense and its foreign policies are but two sides of the same coin: the security of the United States.

The United States has become the world's most powerful nation, but the world remains a dangerous place. The United States must maintain its vigilance and its armed strength. Just a glance at today's newspaper or at one of this evening's television news programs will furnish abundant proof of that fact.

Promote the General Welfare

Few people realize the extent to which government acts as the servant of its citizens, yet you can see examples everywhere. Public schools are one illustration of government's work to promote the general welfare. So, too, are government's efforts to protect the quality of the air you breathe, the water you drink, and the food you eat. The list of tasks government performs for your benefit goes on and on.

Some governmental functions that are common in other countries—operating steel mills, airlines, and coal mines, for example—are not carried out by government in this country. In general, the services that government provides in the United States are those that benefit all or most people. These are the services that are not very likely to be provided by the voluntary acts of private individuals or groups.

Secure the Blessings of Liberty

This nation was founded by those who loved liberty and prized it above all earthly possessions. They believed with Thomas Jefferson that "the God who gave us life gave us liberty at the same time." They subscribed to Benjamin Franklin's maxim: "They that can give up essential liberty to obtain a little temporary safety deserve neither liberty nor safety."

The American dedication to freedom for the individual recognizes that liberty cannot be absolute. It is, instead, a relative matter. No one can be free to do whatever he or she pleases, for that behavior would interfere with the freedoms of others. As Clarence Darrow, the great defense lawyer, once said: "You can only be free if I am free."

Both the Federal Constitution and the State constitutions set out many guarantees of rights and liberties for the individual in this country. That does not mean that those guarantees are so firmly established that they exist forever, however. To preserve and protect them, each generation must learn and understand them anew, and be willing to stand up for them when necessary.

For many people, the inspiration to protect our rights and liberties arises from deep feelings of patriotism. Patriotism is the love of one's country; the passion which aims to serve one's country, either in defending it from invasion, or by protecting its rights and maintaining its laws and institutions in vigor and purity. Patriotism is the characteristic of a good citizen, the noblest passion that animates a man or woman in the character of a citizen. As a citizen, you, too, must agree with Jefferson: "Eternal vigilance is the price of liberty."

Second Treatise of Government

Analysis Skills HR4, HI3, H-SS 12.1.1

In 1690, English philosopher John Locke produced two treatises (essays) on government. In his second treatise, he discussed the responsibilities of a government and claimed that the people have the right to overthrow an unjust government. Locke's ideas greatly influenced Thomas Jefferson and other supporters of the American Revolution. In this selection, Locke explains why people form governments.

John Locke
1632–1704

To understand political power aright . . . we must consider what estate all men are naturally in, and that is, a state of perfect freedom to order their actions, and dispose of their possessions and persons as they think fit, within the bounds of the law of nature, without asking leave or depending upon the will of any other man. . . .

Men being . . . by nature, all free, equal and independent, no one can be put out of this estate and subjected to the political power of another without his own consent, which is done by agreeing with other men, to join and unite into a community for their comfortable, safe and peaceable living, one amongst another, in a secure enjoyment of their properties, and a greater security against any that are not of it. . . .

When any number of men have, by the consent of every individual, made a community, they have thereby made that community one body, with a power to act as one body, which is only by the will and determination of the majority. . . . And thus every man, by consenting with others to make one body politic under one government, puts himself under an obligation to every one in that society to submit to the determination [decision] of the majority, and to be concluded by it. . . .

If man in the state of nature . . . be absolute lord of his own person and possessions, equal to the greatest and subject to nobody, why will he part with his freedom, this empire, and subject himself to the dominion [authority] and control of any other power? . . . It is obvious to answer that though in the state of nature he hath such a right, yet the enjoyment of it is very uncertain and constantly exposed to the invasion of others; for all being kings as much as he, every man his equal, . . . the enjoyment of the property he has in this state is very unsafe, very insecure. This makes him willing to quit this condition which, however free, is full of fears and continual dangers; and it is not without reason that he seeks out and is willing to join in society with others . . . for the mutual preservation of their lives, liberties and estates, which I call by the general name—property.

The great and chief end, therefore, of men uniting into commonwealths, and putting themselves under government, is the preservation of their property. . . .

Analyzing Primary Sources

1. According to Locke, what freedoms did people have before the founding of governments?
2. What are the potential dangers of a person living in what Locke called "perfect freedom"?
3. According to Locke, how are governments formed?
4. What trade-off does Locke say occurs when people live under governments?

2 Forms of Government

Section Preview

OBJECTIVES

1. **Classify** governments according to three sets of characteristics.
2. **Define** systems of government based on who can participate.
3. **Identify** different ways that power can be distributed, geographically, within a state.
4. **Describe** a government by how power is distributed between the executive branch and legislative branch.

WHY IT MATTERS

Governments come in many different forms—democratic or dictatorial, unitary or federal or confederate, presidential or parliamentary. But, whatever its form, government has an impact on nearly every moment and nearly every aspect of your life.

POLITICAL DICTIONARY

★ **autocracy**
★ **oligarchy**
★ **unitary government**
★ **federal government**
★ **division of powers**
★ **confederation**
★ **presidential government**
★ **parliamentary government**

Does the form a government takes, the way in which it is structured, have any importance? Political scientists, historians, and other social commentators have long argued that question. The English poet Alexander Pope weighed in with this couplet in 1733:

PRIMARY Sources

> "*For Forms of Government let fools contest; Whate'er is best adminster'd is best. . . .*"
>
> —*Essay on Man*

Was Pope right? Does it matter what form a government takes? Pope thought not, but you can form your own opinion as you read this section.

Classifying Governments

No two governments are, or ever have been, exactly alike, for governments are the products of human needs and experiences. All governments can be classified according to one or more of their basic features, however. Over time, political scientists have developed many bases upon which to classify (and so to describe, compare, and analyze) governments.

Three of those classifications are especially important and useful. These are classifications according to (1) who can participate in the governing process, (2) the geographic distribution of governmental power within the state, and (3) the relationship between the legislative (lawmaking) and the executive (law-executing) branches of the government.[4]

Who Can Participate

To many people, the most meaningful of these classifications is the one that depends on the number of persons who can take part in the governing process. Here there are two basic forms to consider: democracies and dictatorships.

Democracy

In a democracy, supreme political authority rests with the people. The people hold the sovereign power, and government is conducted only by and with the consent of the people.[5]

Abraham Lincoln gave immortality to this definition of democracy in his Gettysburg Address in 1863: "government of the people, by the people, for the people." Nowhere is there a better, more concise statement of the American understanding of democracy.

A democracy can be either direct or indirect in form. A direct democracy, also called a pure democracy, exists where the will of the people

---

[4]Note that these classifications are not mutually exclusive. Each of them can be used to describe any national government in the world today.

[5]The word *democracy* is derived from the Greek words *dēmos* meaning "the people" and *kratia* meaning "rule" or "authority." The Greek word *dēmokratia* means "rule by the people."

is translated into public policy (law) directly by the people themselves, in mass meetings. Clearly, direct democracy can work only in small communities, where the citizenry can meet in a central place, and where the problems of government are few and relatively simple.

Direct democracy does not exist at the national level anywhere in the world today. However, the New England town meeting, which you will read about in Chapter 25, and the *Landsgemeinde* in a few of the smaller Swiss cantons are excellent examples of direct democracy in action.[6]

Americans are more familiar with the indirect form of democracy—that is, with representative democracy. In a representative democracy, a small group of persons, chosen by the people to act as their representatives, expresses the popular will. These agents of the people are responsible for carrying out the day-to-day conduct of government—the making and executing of laws and so on. They are held accountable to the people for that conduct, especially at periodic elections.

At these elections, the people have an opportunity to express their approval or disapproval of their representatives by casting ballots for or against them. To put it another way, representative democracy is government by popular consent—government with the consent of the governed.

Some people insist that the United States is more properly called a republic rather than a democracy. They hold that in a republic the sovereign power is held by those eligible to vote, while the political power is exercised by representatives chosen by and held responsible to those citizens. For them, democracy can be defined only in terms of direct democracy.

Many Americans use the terms *democracy, republic, representative democracy,* and *republican form of government* interchangeably, although they are not the same things. Whatever the terms used, remember that in a democracy the people are sovereign. They are the only source for any and all of government's power. In other words, the people rule.

▲ **Direct Democracy Today** At this town meeting in New Hampshire, every adult citizen in the town enjoys the right to speak out and vote on issues. *Critical Thinking **Why are town meetings impractical in large cities?*** H-SS 12.2.4

Dictatorship

A dictatorship exists where those who rule cannot be held responsible to the will of the people. The government is not accountable for its policies, nor for how they are carried out. Dictatorship is probably the oldest, and it is certainly the most common, form of government known to history.[7]

Dictatorships are sometimes identified as either autocracies or oligarchies. An **autocracy** is a government in which a single person holds unlimited political power. An **oligarchy** is a government in which the power to rule is held by a small, usually self-appointed elite.

All dictatorships are authoritarian—those in power hold absolute and unchallengeable authority over the people. Modern dictatorships have tended to be totalitarian, as well. That is, they exercise complete power over nearly every aspect of human affairs. Their power embraces all matters of human concern.

The leading examples of dictatorship in the modern era have been those in Fascist Italy (from 1922 to 1943), in Nazi Germany (from 1933 to 1945), in the Soviet Union (from 1917

---

[6]The *Landsgemeinde,* like the original New England town meeting, is an assembly open to all local citizens qualified to vote. In a more limited sense, lawmaking by initiative petition is also an example of direct democracy; see Chapter 24.

[7]The word *dictatorship* comes from the Latin *dictare,* meaning to dictate, issue orders, give authoritative commands. *Dictator* was the ancient Roman republic's title for the leader who was given extraordinary powers in times of crisis. Julius Caesar (100–44 B.C.) was the last of the Roman dictators.

until the late 1980s), and one that still exists in the People's Republic of China (where the present regime came to power in 1949).

Although they do exist, one-person dictatorships are not at all common today. A few close approaches to such a regime can now be found in Libya, which has been dominated by Muammar al-Qaddafi since 1969, and in some other Arab and African states.

Most present-day dictatorships are not nearly so absolutely controlled by a single person or by a small group as may appear to be the case. Outward appearances may hide the fact that several groups—the army, religious leaders, industrialists, and others—compete for power in the political system.

Dictatorships often present the outward appearance of control by the people. The people often vote in popular elections; but the vote is closely controlled, and ballots usually contain the candidates of but one political party. An elected legislative body often exists, but only to rubber-stamp the policies of the dictatorship.

Typically, dictatorial regimes are militaristic in character. They usually gain power by force. The military holds many of the major posts in the government. After crushing all effective opposition at home, these regimes may turn to foreign aggression to enhance the country's military power and prestige.

▲ **Dictatorship and Democracy in Germany** Today, the Federal Republic of Germany is a vigorous democracy. It was born out of the defeat of Adolf Hitler's Nazi dictatorship in World War II. **H-SS 12.3.4**

Geographic Distribution of Power

In every system of government the power to govern is located in one or more places, geographically. From this standpoint, three basic forms of government exist: unitary, federal, and confederate governments.

Unitary Government

A **unitary government** is often described as a centralized government. All powers held by the government belong to a single, central agency. The central (national) government creates local units of government for its own convenience. Those local governments have only those powers that the central government chooses to give them.

Most governments in the world are unitary in form. Great Britain is a classic illustration. A single central organization, the Parliament, holds all of the government's power. Local governments exist solely to relieve Parliament of burdens it could perform only with difficulty and inconvenience. Though unlikely, Parliament could do away with these and other agencies of local government at any time.

Be careful not to confuse the unitary form of government with a dictatorship. In the unitary form, all of the powers held by the government are concentrated in the central government. That government might not have *all* power, however. In Great Britain, for example, the powers held by the government are limited. British government is unitary and, at the same time, democratic.

Federal Government

A **federal government** is one in which the powers of government are divided between a central government and several local governments. An authority superior to both the central and local governments makes this **division of powers** on a geographic basis; and that division cannot be changed by either the local or national level acting alone. Both levels of government act directly on the people through their own sets of laws, officials, and agencies.

In the United States, for example, the National Government has certain powers and the 50 States have others. This division of powers is set out in the Constitution of the United States. The Constitution stands above both levels of government; and it cannot be changed unless the people, acting through both the National Government and the States, agree to that change.

Australia, Canada, Mexico, Switzerland, Germany, India, and some 20 other states also have federal forms of government today. In the United States, the phrase "the Federal Government" is often used to identify the National Government, the government headquartered in Washington, D.C. Note, however, that each of the 50 State governments in this country is unitary, not federal, in form.

Confederate Government

A **confederation** is an alliance of independent states. A central organization, the confederate government, has the power to handle only those matters that the member states have assigned to it. Typically, confederate governments have had limited powers and only in such fields as defense and foreign affairs.

Most often, they have not had the power to make laws that apply directly to individuals, at least not without some further action by the member states. A confederate structure makes it possible for the several states to cooperate in matters of common concern and, at the same time, retain their separate identities.

Confederations have been rare in the modern world. The European Union (EU) is the closest approach to one today. The EU, formed by 11 countries in 1993, has established free trade among its now 25 member-nations, launched a common currency, and seeks to coordinate its members' foreign and defense policies.

In our own history, the United States under the Articles of Confederation (1781 to 1789) and the Confederate States of America (1861 to 1865) are also examples of this form of government.

Relationship Between Legislative and Executive Branches

Political scientists also classify governments based on the relationship between their legislative and executive agencies. This grouping yields two basic forms of government: presidential and parliamentary.

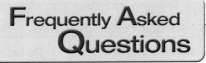

Frequently Asked Questions

Government

Why do we have a federal system of government?
The Framers of the Constitution had to deal with several critical matters as they drafted a new fundamental law for the United States. Not the least: How could they possibly design a strong and effective central government for the nation and, at the same time, preserve the existing States? Their solution: Federalism—an arrangement in which the powers of government would be divided between the new National Government on the one hand, and the States on the other.

Why not a unitary system?
None of the Framers favored a strong central government based on the British (unitary) model. The revolutionary war had been fought in the name of local self-government, and the Framers were determined to preserve that cherished principle.

Any Questions?
What else would you like to know about United States government? Brainstorm two new questions and exchange them with a classmate. What did you learn?

Presidential Government

A **presidential government** features a separation of powers between the executive and the legislative branches of the government. The two branches are independent of one another and coequal. The chief executive (the president) is chosen independently of the legislature, holds office for a fixed term, and has a number of significant powers that are not subject to the direct control of the legislative branch.

The details of this separation of the powers of these two branches are almost always spelled out in a written constitution—as they are in the United States. Each of the branches is regularly given several powers with which it can block actions of the other branch.

The United States is the world's leading example of presidential government. In fact, the United States invented the form. Most of the other presidential systems in the world today are also found in thr Western Hemisphere.

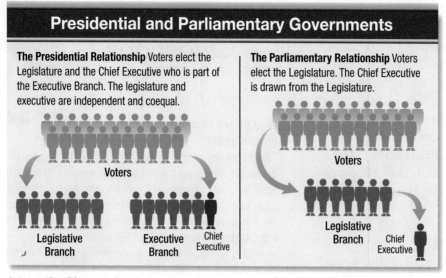

Presidential and Parliamentary Governments

The Presidential Relationship Voters elect the Legislature and the Chief Executive who is part of the Executive Branch. The legislature and executive are independent and coequal.

Voters

Legislative Branch

Executive Branch

Chief Executive

The Parliamentary Relationship Voters elect the Legislature. The Chief Executive is drawn from the Legislature.

Voters

Legislative Branch

Chief Executive

Interpreting Diagrams Compare presidential and parliamentary forms of government. ***In which form of government is the chief executive both elected from and part of the legislature?***

Parliamentary Government

In **parliamentary government**, the executive is made up of the prime minister or premier, and that official's cabinet. The prime minister and cabinet themselves are members of the legislative branch, the parliament. The prime minister is the leader of the majority party or of a likeminded group of parties in parliament and is chosen by that body. With parliament's approval, the prime minister selects the members of the cabinet from among the members of parliament. The executive is thus chosen by the legislature, is a part of it, and is subject to its direct control.

The prime minister and the cabinet (often called "the government") remain in office only as long as their policies and administration have the support of a majority in parliament. If the parliament defeats the prime minister and cabinet on an important matter, the government may receive a "vote of no confidence," and the prime minister and his cabinet must resign from office. Then a new government must be formed. Either parliament chooses a new prime minister or, as often happens, all the seats of parliament go before the voters in a general election.

A majority of the governmental systems in the world today are parliamentary, not presidential, in form—and they are by a wide margin. Parliamentary government avoids one of the major problems of the presidential form: prolonged conflict and sometimes deadlock between the executive and legislative branches. On the other hand, it should be noted that the checks and balances of presidential government are not a part of the parliamentary system.

Section 2 Assessment

Key Terms and Main Ideas

1. What defines a **unitary government**?
2. How is power distributed in a **federal government**?
3. Who holds power in an **oligarchy**?
4. What specific trait gives the United States a **presidential system** of government?

Critical Thinking

5. **Making Comparisons** In a democracy, those who are responsible for the day-to-day conduct of government are accountable to the people for what is done in their name. Which form of government, presidential or parliamentary, do you think comes closer to this ideal? Why?

Standards Monitoring *Online*
For: Self-Quiz and vocabulary practice
Web Code: mqa-1012

6. **Drawing Inferences** More than a century ago, British prime minister Benjamin Disraeli (1804–1881) declared: "I must follow the people. Am I not their leader?" What do you think he meant when he made that comment?

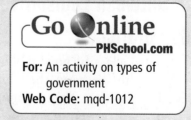

Go Online
PHSchool.com
For: An activity on types of government
Web Code: mqd-1012

Face the
Issues

The Future of the State

Background *The place of the state as the basic political unit in the world has been challenged in recent decades by the emergence of several regional, multinational organizations. The European Union, today a coalition of 25 member-nations with some 460 million people, is the prime example of this development. The EU is a potent economic and political entity, but member-nations must negotiate and compromise on many aspects of policy in ways that the United States, as an independent power, does not.*

EU flags before the European Parliament in Strasbourg, France

Analysis Skills CS1, CS3, CS4

Work Together Across Borders

Europe emerged from World War II in ruins from years of war and occupation. Nowadays, when European countries come into conflict, their weapons of choice are words. Many Europeans believe that an EU super-state represents their last, best chance for lasting peace and prosperity at home and greater influence abroad. The EU has created a huge free-trade market among 25 once separate and bickering countries. The citizens of any one of these countries can now live and work anywhere in the EU with little difficulty. And many foresee ever closer political ties among the EU's members.

A larger force is at work helping to erase old borders—globalization. Technology, human mobility, and the free flow of capital are all converging to make nations more interdependent than ever. As a result, nations are losing some of their powers. Multinational corporations make products in one country, process them in another, while selling to consumers the world over. The movement of products, money, and people within the EU has increased the exchange of ideas and made Europe more peaceful and powerful.

Nation-States Function Best

Reality check: Europeans still identify as citizens of Italy, Ireland, or Poland, not the European Union. Britain refuses to adopt the EU's euro as its currency. French farmers and Belgian truck drivers stage riots against EU agricultural policies. Germany's Prime Minister wins re-election by stressing Germany's economic needs over Europe's.

International cooperation has brought peace and a high standard of living to Europe. Yet the European Union pushes boundaries too far by taking powers long held by nation-states. Should a world committee tell Americans how much we should tax ourselves, what environmental laws we must pass, or even how to define "chocolate"? The EU government has taken all of these powers from member states in a process many call undemocratic. Many EU leaders are appointed, not elected. They cannot be voted out.

The United States has enjoyed unparalleled success with an independent, democratic approach to its economy and government. Americans should treasure their control over their own destiny.

Exploring the Issues

1. Many Europeans urge a common military force for the EU. Offer one major argument for and one major argument against the creation of such a force.

2. Should the United States promote a strong, economically robust EU? Why or why not?

For more information on international organizations, view "The Future of the State."

Face the **Issues** Video Collection

3 Basic Concepts of Democracy

Section Preview

OBJECTIVES

1. **Understand** the foundations of democracy.
2. **Analyze** the connections between democracy and the free enterprise system.
3. **Identify** the role of the Internet in a democracy.

WHY IT MATTERS

Democracy insists on the fundamental importance of each and every individual. The free enterprise system is a natural counterpart to democracy—for it, too, is built on the concept of individualism.

POLITICAL DICTIONARY

★ **compromise**
★ **free enterprise system**
★ **law of supply and demand**
★ **mixed economy**

What do you make of James Bryce's assessment of democracy? "No government demands so much from the citizen as Democracy, and none gives so much back." What does democratic government demand from you? What does it give you in return?

Foundations

Democracy is not inevitable. It does not exist in the United States simply because Americans regard it as the best of all possible political systems. Rather, democracy exists in this country because the American people believe in its basic

concepts. It will continue to exist only for as long as we, the people, continue to subscribe to and practice those concepts.

Winston Churchill (1874–1965) once argued for democracy this way: "No one pretends that democracy is perfect or all-wise. Indeed, it has been said that democracy is the worst form of government except all those other forms that have been tried from time to time."

The American concept of democracy rests on these basic notions:

(1) A recognition of the fundamental worth and dignity of every person;

(2) A respect for the equality of all persons;

(3) A faith in majority rule and an insistence upon minority rights;

(4) An acceptance of the necessity of compromise; and

(5) An insistence upon the widest possible degree of individual freedom.

Of course, these ideas can be worded in other ways. No matter what the wording, however, they form the very minimum that anyone who professes to believe in democracy must agree to.

Worth of the Individual

Democracy is firmly based upon a belief in the fundamental importance of the individual. Each individual, no matter what his or her station in life, is a separate and distinct being.

This concept of the dignity and worth of the individual is of overriding importance in democratic thought. At various times, of course, the welfare of one or a few individuals

▲ At Gettysburg, Pennsylvania, Abraham Lincoln declared that the United States was "conceived in liberty, and dedicated to the proposition that all men are created equal." *Critical Thinking Which of the five foundations of democracy are best described by this quote?*

is subordinated to the interests of the many in a democracy. People can be forced to do certain things whether they want to or not. Examples range from paying taxes to registering for the draft to stopping at a stop sign.

When a democratic society forces people to pay a tax or obey traffic signals, it is serving the interests of the many. However, it is *not* simply serving the interests of a mass of people who happen to outnumber the few. Rather, it is serving the many who, as individuals, together make up that society.

Equality of All Persons

Hand-in-hand with the belief in the worth of the individual, democracy stresses the equality of all individuals. It holds, with Jefferson, that "all men are created equal."

Certainly, democracy does *not* insist on an equality of condition for all persons. Thus, it does not claim that all are born with the same mental or physical abilities. Nor does it argue that all persons have a right to an equal share of worldly goods.

Rather, the democratic concept of equality insists that all are entitled to (1) equality of opportunity and (2) equality before the law. That is, the democratic concept of equality holds that no person should be held back for any such arbitrary reasons as those based on race, color, religion, or gender. The concept holds that each person must be free to develop himself or herself as fully as he or she can (or cares to), and that each person should be treated as the equal of all other persons by the law.

We have come a great distance toward the goal of equality for all in this country. It is clear, however, that the journey is far from over.

Majority Rule, Minority Rights

In a democracy, the will of the people and not the dictate of the ruling few determines public policy. But what is the popular will, and how is it determined? Some device must exist by which these crucial questions can be answered. The only satisfactory device democracy knows is that of majority rule. Democracy argues that a majority of the people will be right more often than they will be wrong, and that the majority will also be right more often than will any one person or small group.

▲ *Equality of Opportunity* Under Title IX of the Educational Amendments of 1972, women must have the same athletic opportunities as men in schools and colleges. **H-SS 12.7.5**

Democracy can be described as an experiment or a trial-and-error process designed to find satisfactory ways to order human relations. Democracy does *not* say that the majority will always arrive at the best decisions on public matters. In fact, the democratic process does not intend to come up with "right" or "best" answers. Rather, the democratic process searches for *satisfactory* solutions to public problems.

Of course, democracy insists that the majority's decisions will usually be more, rather than less, satisfactory. Democracy does admit the possibility of mistakes; it acknowledges the possibility that "wrong" or less satisfactory answers will sometimes be found. Democracy also recognizes that seldom is any solution to a public problem so satisfactory that it cannot be improved upon, and that circumstances can change over time. So, the process of experimentation, of seeking answers to public questions, is never-ending.

Certainly, a democracy cannot work without the principle of majority rule. Unchecked, however, a majority could destroy its opposition and, in the process, destroy democracy as well. Thus, democracy insists upon majority rule restrained by minority rights. The majority must always recognize the right of any minority to become, by fair and lawful means, the majority. The majority must always be willing to listen to a minority's argument, to hear its objections, to bear its criticisms, and to welcome its suggestions.

Necessity of Compromise

In a democracy, public decision making must be largely a matter of give-and-take among the various competing interests. It is a matter of **compromise** in order to find the position most acceptable to the largest number. Compromise is the process of blending and adjusting competing views and interests.

Compromise is an essential part of the democratic concept for two major reasons. First, remember that democracy puts the individual first and, at the same time, insists that each individual is the equal of all others. In a democratic society made up of many individuals and groups with many different opinions and interests, how can the people make public decisions except by compromise?

Second, few public questions have only two sides. Most can be answered in several ways. Take the apparently simple question of how a city should pay for the paving of a public street. Should it charge those who own property along the street? Or should the costs be paid from the city's general treasury? Or should the city and the adjacent property owners share the costs? What about those who will use the street but do not live in the city? Should they have to pay a toll?

Remember, compromise is a process, a way of achieving majority agreement. It is never an end in itself. Not all compromises are good, and not all are necessary.

Individual Freedom

It should be clear by this point that democracy can thrive only in an atmosphere of individual freedom. However, democracy does not and cannot insist on *complete* freedom for the individual. Absolute freedom can exist only in a state of anarchy—the total absence of government. Anarchy can only lead, inevitably and quickly, to rule by the strong and ruthless.

Democracy does insist, however, that each individual must be as free to do as he or she pleases as far as the freedom of all will allow. Justice Oliver Wendell Holmes once had this to say about the relative nature of each individual's rights: "The right to swing my fist ends where the other man's nose begins."

Drawing the line between the rights of one individual and those of another is far from easy. Still, the drawing of that line is a continuous and vitally important function of democratic government. As John F. Kennedy put it: "The rights of every man are diminished when the rights of one man are threatened."

Striking the proper balance between freedom for the individual and the rights of society as a whole is similarly difficult—and vital. Abraham Lincoln once stated democracy's problem in these words:

> **PRIMARY Sources** *"Must a government of necessity be too strong for the liberties of its own people, or too weak to maintain its own existence?"*
> —*Response to a Serenade*, November 10, 1864

Human beings desire both liberty and authority. Democratic government must work constantly to strike the proper balance between the two. The authority of government must be adequate to the needs of society. At the same time, that authority must never be allowed to become so great that it restricts the individual beyond necessity.

Democracy and the Free Enterprise System

The American commitment to freedom for the individual is deep-rooted, and it is as evident in the nation's economic system as it is in the political system. The American economic system is often called the **free enterprise system.**

Interpreting Political Cartoons **If the two chefs represent lawmakers in a democracy, what might the stew represent?**

★★★ **20** Chapter 1 Section 3

It is an economic system characterized by the private ownership of capital goods, investments made by private decision, not by government directive, and success or failure determined by competition in the marketplace. The free enterprise system is based on four fundamental factors: private ownership, individual initiative, profit, and competition.

How the System Works

The free enterprise system is often called capitalism, and it is also known as the private enterprise system and as a market-based system. It does not rely on government to decide what items are to be produced, how much of any particular item should be produced, or how much any item is to sell for. Rather, those decisions are to be made by the market, through the **law of supply and demand.** That law states that when supplies of goods and services become plentiful, prices tend to drop. When supplies become scarcer, prices tend to rise.

Democracy and the free enterprise system are not the same thing. One is a political system, and the other is an economic system. However, both are firmly based on the concept of individual freedom. America's experience with both systems clearly suggests that the two reinforce one another in practice.

Government and the Free Enterprise System

The basis of the American economic system is the free market. However, government plays a role in the American economy, and always has. An economy in which private enterprise exists in combination with a considerable amount of government regulation and promotion is called a **mixed economy.** Government's participation in the economy serves a twofold purpose: to protect the public and to preserve private enterprise.

Government's participation in the economy can be seen at every level in this country: national, State, and local. Here are but a few examples: Economic activities are *regulated* by government through antitrust laws, pure food and drug laws, anti-pollution standards, and city and county zoning ordinances and building codes.

The nation's economic life is *promoted* in a great number of public ways. The government

▲ Entrepreneurs are the foundation of the American system of free enterprise. Businesses like this pastry shop help consumers find the items they need at market prices. *Critical Thinking What qualities define an entrepreneur?* H-SS 12.2.2

grants money for transportation systems, scientific research, and the growing of particular food crops; builds roads and operates public schools; provides services such as the postal system, weather reports, and a national currency; and much more.

Thus some activities that might be carried out privately are in fact conducted by government. Public education, the postal system, local fire departments, city bus systems, and road building are examples of long standing.

How much should government participate, regulate and promote, police and serve? Many of the most heated debates in American politics center on that question, and we are often reminded of Abraham Lincoln's advice:

PRIMARY Sources ❝The legitimate object of government, is to do for a community of people, whatever they need to have done, but can not do, at all, or can not, so well do, for themselves—in their separate, and individual capacities. ❞

—Abraham Lincoln, July 1, 1854

Most Americans believe that a well-regulated free enterprise system—one of free choice, individual initiative, private enterprise—is the best guarantee of a better life for everyone.

Government Online

Online Campaigning As it has just about everywhere else, the Internet has rapidly transformed electoral politics. How rapidly? Consider that the Democratic National Party didn't erect its first Web site until June 1995 (with the Republicans following days later).

The first major election in which the Internet made the difference was professional wrestler Jesse Ventura's upset victory in the 1998 Minnesota governor's race. Ventura's cash-strapped, third party campaign created a fresh, interactive Web site that allowed him to spread his message quickly and cheaply. By gathering visitors' email addresses, he was also able to recruit volunteers, raise money, and mobilize his voters on election day.

Web sites were a campaign staple by the 2000 presidential election, providing voters access to the candidates' detailed positions on the issues. After his victory in the New Hampshire Republican primary, Arizona Senator John McCain noted that his Web site helped him enlist thousands of new volunteers and raise millions of dollars.

That year, Web White & Blue, a nonprofit Web site, also hosted the first online presidential debate. It lasted 38 days and featured daily exchanges between the candidates, and their answers to questions from Internet users.

> **Go Online**
> PHSchool.com
>
> Use Web Code mqd-1016 to find out more about campaigning online and for help in answering the following question:
> *What are the advantages and disadvantages of online campaigning for candidates and voters?*

Democracy and the Internet

At least 180 million Americans can now log on to the Internet to send and receive e-mail, to buy or sell practically anything, to entertain themselves, to inform themselves, and to do any number of other things. It is clear that cyberspace has become a major marketplace and an important channel of communication.

Democracy demands that the people be widely informed about the government. Thus, democracy and the Internet would seem to be made for one another. Internet users can check out the Web sites of political candidates, discover what's happening in Congress, read the most recent Supreme Court decisions, and do much else. Theoretically, this makes knowledgeable participation in the democratic process easier than ever before.

However, the speed with which and the quantity in which information can be found on the World Wide Web does *not* guarantee the reliability of that data. There is a vast amount of unverified, often unverifiable, and frequently false information and biased analysis in cyberspace.

Some argue that elections should be held online. In fact, some cyber votes were cast in the Democratic Party's presidential primary in Arizona in 2000 and, most recently, in that party's presidential primary in Michigan in 2004. The Defense Department conducted a very small online voting project in connection with the presidential election in 2000, but cancelled plans for a much larger project in 2004 because it could find no way to guarantee the absolute integrity of an online voting system. A leap to online elections appears unlikely, however—at least in the near term, as you will see when we turn to the electoral process in Chapter 7 (page 194).

Section 3 Assessment

Key Terms and Main Ideas

1. Why is **compromise** an important part of democracy?
2. List three characteristics of the **free enterprise system.**
3. How does the **law of supply and demand** help determine the price of an item?
4. What is the role of government in a **mixed economy?**

Critical Thinking

5. **Recognizing Cause and Effect** List three examples of governmental actions that tend to promote the free market and three examples of governmental actions that might interfere with the free market.
6. **Drawing Inferences** Describe, in your own words, the responsibilities of the majority in a system of "majority rules, minority rights."

> **Standards Monitoring Online**
> For: Self-Quiz and vocabulary practice
> Web Code: mqa-1013

7. **Predicting Consequences (a)** How might the growth of the Internet affect the relationship between government and the people? **(b)** What are some possible advantages and disadvantages of Internet voting?

> **Go Online**
> PHSchool.com
> **For:** An activity on the American economy
> **Web Code:** mqd-1013

May Congress Limit Access to the Internet in Public Libraries?

Analysis Skills HR4, HI3, HI4

Two federal programs provide public libraries with money for computers and Internet services. As it often does when making monetary grants, Congress required libraries to meet certain conditions to receive the funds. Can Congress impose conditions that restrict library users' access to certain Internet sites?

United States v. American Library Association (2003)

Under the Library Services and Technology Act (LSTA), Congress provides grants to libraries to buy computers, install them, and link them to the Internet. Under Congress's "E-rate" program, libraries are able to purchase Internet access at a discount. Today, with the help of these programs, nearly all libraries in the United States provide public Internet access.

Unfortunately, some citizens have used library Internet services to obtain pornographic or obscene materials. Congress became concerned that children using libraries were being exposed to these materials—sometimes by accident, sometimes intentionally.

To address this problem, Congress passed the Children's Internet Protection Act. This law requires any library receiving LSTA grants or participating in the E-rate program to install filters to block sites that contain obscenity or images harmful to minors.

These filters do not work perfectly. Sometimes they fail to block sites containing harmful materials. Other times they block perfectly innocent or informative sites, such as medical sites with images of the human body. The statute allows libraries to disable the filters on request.

The American Library Association filed a lawsuit claiming that the Act was unconstitutional. A special three-judge district court panel held that the Act violated the 1st Amendment rights of the libraries and their users. The government appealed to the Supreme Court.

Arguments for the United States

1. The 1st Amendment's guarantee of free speech does not prevent public libraries from voluntarily installing filters on their computers. Public libraries are not required to provide everything their patrons want.
2. Adults who require access to blocked sites can simply ask for the filter to be disabled, and this is no more difficult or embarrassing than asking to put a book on hold or requesting an inter-library loan.
3. Libraries that want to provide unfiltered Internet access are free to do so with their own money.

Arguments for American Library Association

1. Congress would violate freedom of speech if it commanded libraries not to carry certain books because of their political viewpoint. The mandatory installation of filters interferes with citizen's access to information in a similar way.
2. The Act interferes with libraries' free decisions regarding the materials they choose to provide.
3. By forcing users to ask permission to view certain Internet sites, the Act burdens citizens' access to information they have every right to obtain.

Decide for Yourself

1. Review the constitutional grounds on which each side based its arguments and the specific arguments each side presented.
2. Debate the opposing viewpoints presented in this case. Which viewpoint do you favor?
3. Predict how the Court's decision will affect the availability of Internet access in libraries. (To read a summary of the Court's decision, turn to pages 799–806.)

Go Online
PHSchool.com
Use Web Code mqp-1017 to register your vote on this issue and to see how other students voted.

Political Dictionary

government (p. 4), public policy (p. 4), legislative power (p. 4), executive power (p. 4), judicial power (p. 4), constitution (p. 5), dictatorship (p. 5), democracy (p. 5), state (p. 5), sovereign (p. 6), autocracy (p. 13), oligarchy (p. 13), unitary government (p. 14), federal government (p. 14), division of powers (p. 14), confederation (p. 15), presidential government (p. 15), parliamentary government (p. 16), compromise (p. 20), free enterprise system (p. 20), law of supply and demand (p. 21), mixed economy (p. 21)

Standards Review

H-SS 12.1.1 Analyze the influence of ancient Greek, Roman, English, and leading European political thinkers such as John Locke, Charles-Louis Montesquieu, Niccolo` Machiavelli, and William Blackstone on the development of American government.

H-SS 12.1.3 Explain how the U.S. Constitution reflects a balance between the classical republican concern with promotion of the public good and the classical liberal concern with protecting individual rights; and discuss how the basic premises of liberal constitutionalism and democracy are joined in the Declaration of Independence as "self-evident truths."

H-SS 12.2.2 Explain how economic rights are secured and their importance to the individual and to society (e.g., the right to acquire, use, transfer, and dispose of property; right to choose one's work; right to join or not join labor unions; copyright and patent).

H-SS 12.2.4 Understand the obligations of civic-mindedness, including voting, being informed on civic issues, volunteering and performing public service, and serving in the military or alternative service.

H-SS 12.2.5 Describe the reciprocity between rights and obligations; that is, why enjoyment of one's rights entails respect for the rights of others.

H-SS 12.3.4 Compare the relationship of government and civil society in constitutional democracies to the relationship of government and civil society in authoritarian and totalitarian regimes.

H-SS 12.7.5 Explain how public policy is formed, including the setting of the public agenda and implementation of it through regulations and executive orders.

H-SS 12.8.2 Describe the roles of broadcast, print, and electronic media, including the Internet, as means of communication in American politics.

H-SS 12.9.1 Explain how the different philosophies and structures of feudalism, mercantilism, socialism, fascism, communism, monarchies, parliamentary systems, and constitutional liberal democracies influence economic policies, social welfare policies, and human rights practices.

H-SS 12.9.3 Discuss the advantages and disadvantages of federal, confederal, and unitary systems of government.

H-SS 12.10 Students formulate questions about and defend their analyses of tensions within our constitutional democracy and the importance of maintaining a balance between the following concepts: majority rule and individual rights; liberty and equality; state and national authority in a federal system; civil disobedience and the rule of law; freedom of the press and the right to a fair trial; the relationship of religion and government.

Practicing the Vocabulary

Matching *Choose a term from the list above that best matches each description.*

1. Describes a state that has supreme power within its territory
2. The institution through which society makes and enforces its policies
3. That which a government decides to do
4. A form of government that is often totalitarian and authoritarian; can be led by one person or many people

Fill in the Blank *Choose a term from the list above that best completes the sentence.*

5. In a _____, the executive branch of government is led by members of the legislative branch.
6. A _____ is also known as a centralized government.
7. _____ is the power to write new laws.
8. Government regulates and promotes businesses in a _____.

Reviewing Main Ideas

Section 1

9. What characteristics define a state?
10. Briefly describe the four most widely held theories that attempt to explain the origin of the state.
11. For what reasons do people form governments?
12. Describe briefly the purposes of government set out in the Preamble to the Constitution.

Section 2

13. List the three questions that can be used to classify governments.
14. What is the difference between an autocracy and an oligarchy?

15. Name and briefly describe the three forms of government that can result depending on how governmental power is distributed geographically.
16. Explain how power is distributed in a presidential government.

Section 3

17. Briefly describe the five basic concepts of democracy.
18. Describe the relationship between the rights of the individual and the rights of the overall society.
19. (a) What is the free enterprise system? (b) How does it differ from a mixed economy?
20. List one benefit and one drawback of using the Internet for research.

Critical Thinking Skills

Analysis Skills HR3, HR4

21. *Face the Issues* Stephen D. Krasner wrote, "For many states, there is no longer a sharp distinction between citizens and noncitizens. Permanent residents, guest workers, refugees, and undocumented immigrants are entitled to some bundle of rights even if they cannot vote. [This is due to] ease of travel and the desire of many countries to attract either capital or skilled workers." How would supporters of international organizations respond to this statement?

22. *Recognizing Point of View* Consider Martin Luther King, Jr.'s statement that "injustice anywhere is a threat to justice everywhere." (a) What is your understanding of that statement? (b) Why is such a belief necessary to maintain a democratic society?

23. *Drawing Inferences* Review the discussion of Thomas Hobbes' views. (a) How did did Hobbes describe the conditions under which human beings lived in the "state of nature"? (b) How does he say human beings overcame those conditions? Does this seem to you a reasonable explanation of the origin of the state? Why or why not?

24. *Making Comparisons* The equality of all persons is a basic democratic concept. (a) Can a democracy possibly exist without both equality of opportunity and equality before the law? (b) Is an equality of conditions (in income, housing, and the like) a necessary ingredient of democracy?

Analyzing Political Cartoons

Using your knowledge of government and this cartoon, answer the questions below.

"The Athenians are here, Sire, with an offer to back us with ships, money, arms, and men—and of course, their usual lectures about democracy."

25. What form of government is represented by the King in this cartoon?

26. What does this cartoon imply about the origins of democracy?

Participation Activities

Analysis Skills CS1, CS4, HR4, HI1

27. *Current Events Watch* Separatist movements—efforts to win the independence of some region in a country—can be found in many places in the world today. Select one of them—for example, the *Parti Québecois* in Canada or the Basques in Spain. Learn as much as you can about that movement from current news reports and other sources. By what means, peaceful or violent, do the separatists pursue their goal? How do you rate their chances for success?

28. *Time Line Activity* Identify a country that has become a functioning democracy within the span of your lifetime. Discover the political events that highlighted that country's transition from dictatorship to democracy. Then construct a time line that includes those events and shows the length of time it took for the transition to occur.

29. *It's Your Turn* Write your own "social contract" in which you express your feelings about what should be required of members of a political society, and what government should provide the people. Start by creating a chart with two columns. In one column, list the responsibilities of the citizens in your proposed social contract. In the other column, list what you feel government should provide its citizens. Then detail your ideas for the contract. Proofread and revise for corrections. Then, prepare a final copy. **(Creating a Chart)**

Standards Monitoring *Online*

For: Chapter 1 Self-Test **Visit:** PHSchool.com
Web Code: mqa-1014

As a final review, take the Magruder's Chapter 1 Self-Test and receive immediate feedback on your answers.
The test consists of 20 multiple-choice questions designed to test your understanding of the chapter content.

CHAPTER 2

Origins of American Government

"It is, Sir, the people's Constitution, the people's government, made for the people, made by the people, and answerable to the people."

—Daniel Webster (1830)

The Constitution grew out of a long heritage of law and politics. Before Americans could create their new government, they endured years of turmoil and revolution. In writing the Constitution, the Framers had to consider the rights and interests of many factions. Two hundred years later, Americans still seek and debate their rights.

◆ Independence Hall, Philadelphia, Pennsylvania

Go Online
PHSchool.com

For: Current Data
Web Code: mqg-1027

For: Close Up Foundation debates
Web Code: mqh-1029

SECTION 1

Our Political Beginnings *(pp. 28–32)*

★ American colonists benefited from a developing English tradition of ordered, limited, and representative government.

★ This tradition was based on landmark documents, including the Magna Carta, the Petition of Right, and the English Bill of Rights.

★ The English established three types of colonial governments, all of which provided training for the colonists in the art of government.

SECTION 2

The Coming of Independence *(pp. 34–39)*

★ Great Britain became more involved with the colonies in the 1760s.

★ The colonists reacted to the changes in British policies by taking small steps toward unity.

★ Twelve of the 13 colonies joined in the First Continental Congress to plan opposition to the British policies.

★ In May of 1775, the Second Continental Congress began. It became the government of the new United States and produced the Declaration of Independence.

★ The newly formed States wrote constitutions that would later influence the making of the U.S. Constitution.

SECTION 3

The Critical Period *(pp. 44–47)*

★ To provide a more lasting plan of government, the Second Continental Congress created the Articles of Confederation.

★ The Articles contained many weaknesses and led to bickering among the States.

★ The chaos of this critical period led to a movement for change toward a more powerful central government at the Constitutional Convention in May 1787.

SECTION 4

Creating the Constitution *(pp. 48–54)*

★ The Constitutional Convention in Philadelphia involved delegates from every State but Rhode Island.

★ The Virginia and New Jersey Plans each offered ways to organize the new government.

★ The delegates agreed to compromises that allowed them to agree on the configuration of Congress and other issues.

SECTION 5

Ratifying the Constitution *(pp. 56–58)*

★ The Federalists promoted the Constitution.

★ The Anti-Federalists attacked the document out of fear of the plan's strong central government and because it lacked a bill of rights.

★ The new Congress convened in March 1789 in what was then the capital, New York City. On April 30, 1789, George Washington was inaugurated as the nation's first President.

Section Preview

OBJECTIVES

1. **Identify** the three basic concepts of government that influenced government in the English colonies.
2. **Explain** the significance of the following landmark English documents: the Magna Carta, the Petition of Right, the English Bill of Rights.
3. **Describe** the three types of colonies that the English established in North America.

WHY IT MATTERS

Our system of government has its origins in the concepts and political ideas that English colonists brought with them when they settled North America. The colonies served as a school for learning about government.

POLITICAL DICTIONARY

★ **limited government**
★ **representative government**
★ **Magna Carta**
★ **Petition of Right**
★ **English Bill of Rights**
★ **charter**
★ **bicameral**
★ **proprietary**
★ **unicameral**

The American system of government did not suddenly spring into being with the signing of the Declaration of Independence in 1776. Nor was it suddenly created by the Framers of the Constitution in 1787.

The beginnings of what was to become the United States can be found in the mid-sixteenth century when explorers, traders, and settlers first made their way to North America. The French, Dutch, Spanish, Swedes, and others contributed to the European domination of this continent—and to the domination of those Native Americans who were here for centuries before the first Europeans arrived. It was the English, however, who came in the largest numbers. And it was the English who soon controlled the 13 colonies that stretched for some 1,300 miles along the Atlantic coast.

◀ English settlers brought to North America a political system as well as the skills needed to create household items, such as this carved Hadley chest.

Basic Concepts of Government

The earliest English settlers brought with them knowledge of a political system—established laws, customs, practices, and institutions—that had been developing for centuries.

The political system they knew was that of England, of course. But some aspects of that structure had come to England from other times and places. For example, the concept of the rule of law that influenced English political ideas had roots in the early river civilizations of Africa and Asia.[1] More directly, the ancient Romans who occupied much of England from A.D. 43 to 410 left behind a legacy of law, religion, and custom to the people. From this rich political history, the English colonists brought to North America three ideas that were to loom large in the shaping of government in the United States.

---

[1] For example, King Hammurabi of Babylonia developed a codified system of laws known as Hammurabi's Code around 1750 B.C. Its 282 laws covered real estate, trade, and business transactions, as well as criminal law. The code distinguished between major and minor offenses, established the state as the authority that would enforce the law, and tried to guarantee social justice. Because of the Babylonians' close contact with the Hebrews, many of their laws became part of the Hebrew law and thus later a part of the Old Testament of the Bible—for example, "An eye for an eye." The English and the English colonists were familiar with and devoutly attracted to this Biblical concept of the rule of law.

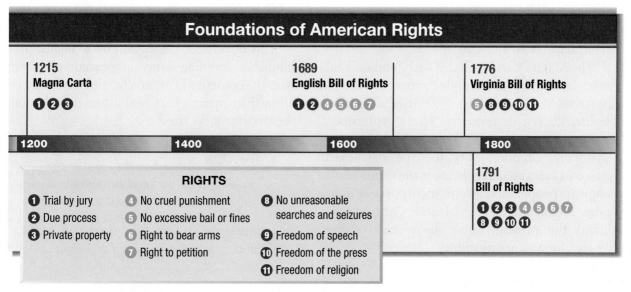

Foundations of American Rights

1215	1689	1776
Magna Carta	**English Bill of Rights**	**Virginia Bill of Rights**
❶❷❸	❶❷❹❺❻❼	❺❽❾❿⓫

```
1200          1400          1600          1800
```

1791
Bill of Rights
❶❷❸❹❺❻❼
❽❾❿⓫

RIGHTS

❶ Trial by jury
❷ Due process
❸ Private property
❹ No cruel punishment
❺ No excessive bail or fines
❻ Right to bear arms
❼ Right to petition
❽ No unreasonable searches and seizures
❾ Freedom of speech
❿ Freedom of the press
⓫ Freedom of religion

Interpreting Charts The rights established in these landmark documents were revolutionary in their day. They did not, however, extend to all people when first granted. Over the years, these rights have influenced systems of government in many countries. ***How might the right to petition, first granted in the English Bill of Rights, prevent abuse of power by a monarch?*** **H-SS 12.1.1**

Ordered Government

Those first English colonists saw the need for an orderly regulation of their relationships with one another—that is, for government. They created local governments, based on those they had known in England. Many of the offices and units of government they established are still with us today: the offices of sheriff, coroner, assessor, and justice of the peace, the grand jury, counties, townships, and several others.

Limited Government

The colonists also brought with them the idea that government is not all-powerful. That is, government is restricted in what it may do, and each individual has certain rights that government cannot take away.

This concept is called **limited government,** and it was deeply rooted in English belief and practice by the time the first English ships reached the Americas. It had been planted in England centuries earlier, and it had been developing there for nearly 400 years before Jamestown was settled in 1607.

Representative Government

The early English settlers also carried another important concept to America: **representative government.** This idea that government should serve the will of the people had also been developing in England for centuries. With it had come a growing insistence that the people should have a voice in deciding what government should and should not do. As with the concept of limited government, this notion of "government of, by, and for the people" found fertile soil in America, and it flourished here.

Landmark English Documents

These basic notions of ordered government, of limited government, and of representative government can be traced to several landmark documents in English history.

The Magna Carta

A group of determined barons forced King John to sign the **Magna Carta**— the Great Charter—at Runnymede in 1215. Weary of John's military campaigns and heavy taxes, the

▶ King John's conflicts with English nobles led to the signing of the Magna Carta.
Critical Thinking Could the basic notions of ordered, limited, and representative government have developed without the signing of the Magna Carta? Explain your answer.
H-SS 12.1.1

barons who developed the Magna Carta were seeking protection against heavy-handed and arbitrary acts by the king.

The Magna Carta included such fundamental rights as trial by jury and due process of law—protection against the arbitrary taking of life, liberty, or property. These protections against the absolute power of the king were originally intended only for the privileged classes. Over time, they became the rights of all English people and were incorporated into other documents. The Magna Carta established the principle that the power of the monarchy was not absolute.

The Petition of Right

The Magna Carta was respected by some monarchs and ignored by others for 400 years. During this time, England's Parliament, a representative body with the power to make laws, slowly grew in influence. In 1628, when Charles I asked Parliament for more money in taxes, Parliament refused until he signed the **Petition of Right.**

The Petition of Right limited the king's power in several ways. Most importantly, the document demanded that the king no longer imprison or otherwise punish any person but by the lawful judgment of his peers, or by the law of the land. It also insisted that the king not impose martial law (rule by the military) in time of peace, or require homeowners to shelter the king's troops without their consent. In addition, the Petition stated that no man should be:

PRIMARY Sources *compelled to make or yield any gift, loan, benevolence, tax, or such like charge, without common consent by act of parliament.*
—X, Petition of Right

The Petition challenged the idea of the divine right of kings, declaring that even a monarch must obey the law of the land.

The Bill of Rights

In 1688, after years of revolt and turmoil, Parliament offered the crown to William and Mary of Orange. The events surrounding their ascent to the throne are known in English history as the Glorious Revolution. To prevent abuse of power by William and Mary and all future monarchs, Parliament, in 1689, drew up a list of provisions to which William and Mary had to agree.

This document, the **English Bill of Rights,** prohibited a standing army in peacetime, except with the consent of Parliament, and required that all parliamentary elections be free. In addition, the document declared

PRIMARY Sources *that the pretended power of suspending the laws, or the execution of laws, by regal authority, without consent of Parliament is illegal . . . .*

that levying money for or to the use of the Crown . . . without grant of Parliament . . . is illegal . . .

that it is the right of the subjects to petition the king . . . and that prosecutions for such petitioning are illegal . . .
—English Bill of Rights

The English Bill of Rights also included such guarantees as the right to a fair trial, and freedom from excessive bail and from cruel and unusual punishment.

Our nation has built on, changed, and added to those ideas and institutions that settlers brought here from England. Still, much in American government and politics today is based on these early English ideas.

The English Colonies

England's colonies in North America have been described as "13 schools of government." The colonies were the settings in which Americans first began to learn the difficult art of government.[2]

The 13 colonies were established separately, over a span of some 125 years. During that long period, outlying trading posts and isolated farm settlements developed into organized

---

[2]The Europeans who came to the Americas brought with them their own views of government, but this does not mean that they brought the idea of government to the Americas. Native Americans had governments. They had political institutions that worked to accomplish the goals of the state; they had political leaders; and they had policies toward other states.

Some Native American political organizations were very complex. For example, five Native American tribes in present-day New York State—the Seneca, Cayuga, Oneida, Onondaga, and Mohawk—formed a confederation known as the Iroquois League. The League was set up to end conflicts among the tribes, but it was so successful as a form of government that it lasted for over 200 years.

communities. The first colony, Virginia, was founded with the first permanent English settlement in North America at Jamestown in 1607.[3] Georgia was the last to be formed, with the settlement of Savannah in 1733.

Each of the colonies was born out of a particular set of circumstances, and so each had its own character. Virginia was originally organized as a commercial venture. Its first colonists were employees of the Virginia Company, a private trading corporation. Massachusetts was first settled by people who came to North America in search of greater personal and religious freedom. Georgia was founded largely as a haven for debtors, a refuge for the victims of England's harsh poor laws.

But the differences between and among the colonies are really of little importance. Of much greater significance is the fact that all of them were shaped by their English origins. The many similarities among all 13 colonies far outweighed the differences.

Each colony was established on the basis of a **charter,** a written grant of authority from the king. Over time, these instruments of government led to the development of three different kinds of colonies: royal, proprietary, and charter.

Royal Colonies

The royal colonies were subject to the direct control of the Crown. On the eve of the American Revolution in 1775, there were eight: New Hampshire, Massachusetts, New York, New Jersey, Virginia, North Carolina, South Carolina, and Georgia.

The Virginia colony did not enjoy the quick success its sponsors had promised. So, in 1624, the king revoked the London Company's charter, and Virginia became the first royal colony. Later, as the original charters of other colonies

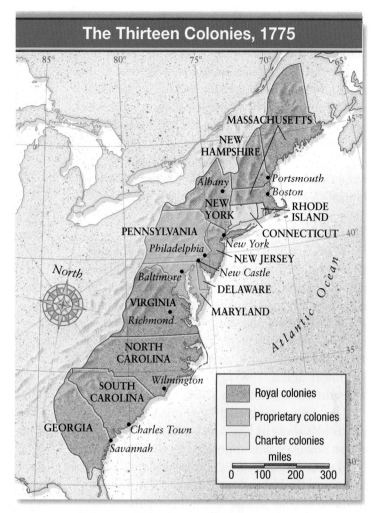

The Thirteen Colonies, 1775

Royal colonies
Proprietary colonies
Charter colonies
miles
0   100   200   300

Interpreting Maps Despite the different circumstances surrounding the settlement of each colony, they all shared a common English background. **How were royal colonies governed?**

were canceled or withdrawn for a variety of reasons, they became royal colonies.

A pattern of government gradually emerged for each of the royal colonies. The king named a governor to serve as the colony's chief executive. A council, also named by the king, served as an advisory body to the royal governor. In time, the governor's council became the upper house of the colonial legislature. It also became the highest court in the colony. The lower house of a **bicameral** (two-house) legislature was elected by those property owners qualified to vote.[4] It

---

[3]St. Augustine, Florida, is the oldest continuously populated European settlement in what is now the United States. St. Augustine was founded by Pedro Menéndez in 1565 to establish Spanish authority in the region.

---

[4]The Virginia legislature held its first meeting in the church at Jamestown on July 30, 1619, and was the first representative body to meet in the North American English colonies. It was made up of burgesses—that is, representatives—elected from each settlement in the colony. Virginia called the lower house of its colonial legislature the House of Burgesses; South Carolina, the House of Commons; Massachusetts, the House of Representatives.

owed much of its influence to the fact that it shared with the governor and his council the power of the purse—that is, the power to tax and spend. The governor, advised by the council, appointed the judges for the colony's courts.

The laws passed by the legislature had to be approved by the governor and the Crown. Royal governors often ruled with a stern hand, following instructions from London. Much of the resentment that finally flared into revolution was fanned by their actions.

The Proprietary Colonies

By 1775, there were three **proprietary** colonies: Maryland, Pennsylvania, and Delaware.[5] These colonies were organized by a proprietor, a person to whom the king had made a grant of land. By charter, that land could be settled and governed much as the proprietor (owner) chose. In 1632 the king had granted Maryland to Lord Baltimore and in 1681, Pennsylvania to William Penn. In 1682 Penn also acquired Delaware.

The governments of these three colonies were much like those in the royal colonies. The governor, however, was appointed by the proprietor. In Maryland and Delaware, the legislatures were bicameral. In Pennsylvania, the legislature was a **unicameral** (one-house) body. There, the governor's council did not act as one house of the

---

[5]New York, New Jersey, North Carolina, South Carolina, and Georgia also began as proprietary colonies. Each later became a royal colony.

legislature. As in the royal colonies, appeals from the decisions of the proprietary colonies could be carried to the king in London.

The Charter Colonies

Connecticut and Rhode Island were charter colonies. They were based on charters granted in 1662 and 1663, respectively, to the colonists themselves.[6] They were largely self-governing.

The governors of Connecticut and Rhode Island were elected each year by the white, male property owners in each colony. Although the king's approval was required before the governor could take office, it was not often asked. Laws made by their bicameral legislatures were not subject to the governor's veto nor was the Crown's approval needed. Judges in charter colonies were appointed by the legislature, but appeals could be taken from the colonial courts to the king.

The Connecticut and the Rhode Island charters were so liberal for their time that, with independence, they were kept with only minor changes as State constitutions—until 1818 and 1843, respectively. In fact, many historians say that had Britain allowed the other colonies the same freedoms and self-government, the Revolution might never have occurred.

---

[6]The Massachusetts Bay Colony was established as the first charter colony in 1629. Its charter was later revoked and Massachusetts became a royal colony in 1691. Religious dissidents from Massachusetts founded Connecticut in 1633 and Rhode Island in 1636.

Section 1 Assessment

Key Terms and Main Ideas

1. Explain the concepts of ordered government, **limited government,** and **representative government.**
2. What were some of the fundamental rights and principles established in the **Magna Carta,** the **Petition of Right,** and the **English Bill of Rights?**
3. Identify and describe the three types of government in the English colonies.
4. Explain the difference between a **bicameral** and a **unicameral** legislative body.

Critical Thinking

5. **Testing Conclusions** "Had Britain given each colony the degree of self-government found in Connecticut and Rhode

Standards Monitoring *Online*
For: Self-Quiz and vocabulary practice
Web Code: mqa-1021

Island, the Revolution might never have occurred." Do you agree or disagree? Explain.

6. **Making Comparisons** In what ways were the colonial governments similar? How did they differ?

Go Online
PHSchool.com
For: An activity on colonial charters
Web Code: mqd-1021

on Primary Sources

The Magna Carta

Analysis Skills HR4, HI3

Signed by England's King John in 1215, the Magna Carta (Great Charter) was the first document to limit the power of England's monarchs. The result of tough negotiations between the king and rebellious nobles, the Magna Carta established the principle that rulers are subject to law—a major step toward constitutional government.

W e . . . by this our present Charter, have confirmed, for us and our heirs forever: —

1. That the English Church shall be free and shall have her whole rights and her liberties inviolable [secure from harm]. . . .

9. Neither we nor our bailiffs shall seize any land or rent for any debt while the chattels [possessions] of the debtor are sufficient for the payment of the debt. . . .

12. No scutage [tax] or aid [subsidy] shall be imposed in our kingdom, unless by the common counsel of our kingdom. . . .

14. And also to have the common council of the kingdom to assess and aid, . . . and for the assessing of scutages, we will cause to be summoned the archbishops, bishops, abbots, earls, and great barons, . . . And besides, we will cause to be summoned . . . all those who hold of us in chief, at a certain day . . . and to a certain place; and in all the letters of summons, we will express the cause of the summons; and the summons being thus made, the business shall proceed on the day appointed, according to the counsel of those who shall be present, although all who have been summoned have not come. . . .

39. No free-man shall be seized, or imprisoned, or dispossessed, or outlawed, or in any way destroyed; nor will we condemn him, nor will we commit him to prison, excepting by the legal judgment of his peers, or by the laws of the land.

40. To none will we sell, to none will we deny, to none will we delay right or justice.

King John signs the Magna Carta.

41. All merchants shall have safety and security in coming into England, and going out of England, and in staying and in traveling through England . . . to buy and sell, . . . excepting in the time of war, and if they be of a country at war against us. . . .

42. It shall be lawful to any person . . . to go out of our kingdom, and to return safely and securely, by land or by water, saving his allegiance to us, unless it be in time of war, for some short space, for the common good of the kingdom. . . .

52. If any have been disseised [deprived] or dispossessed by us, without a legal verdict of their peers, of their lands, castles, liberties, or rights, we will immediately restore these things to them. . . .

63. Wherefore our will is . . . that the men in our kingdom have and hold the aforesaid liberties, rights, and concessions . . . fully and entirely, to them and their heirs, . . . in all things and places forever.

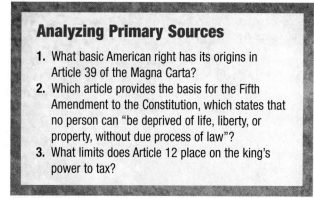

Analyzing Primary Sources

1. What basic American right has its origins in Article 39 of the Magna Carta?
2. Which article provides the basis for the Fifth Amendment to the Constitution, which states that no person can "be deprived of life, liberty, or property, without due process of law"?
3. What limits does Article 12 place on the king's power to tax?

·2· The Coming of Independence

Section Preview

OBJECTIVES

1. **Explain** how Britain's colonial policies contributed to the growth of self-government in the colonies.
2. **Identify** some of the steps that led to growing feelings of colonial unity.
3. **Compare** the outcomes of the First and Second Continental Congresses.
4. **Analyze** the ideas in the Declaration of Independence.
5. **Describe** the drafting of the first State constitutions and summarize the constitutions' common features.

WHY IT MATTERS

Changes in British colonial policies led to resentment in the colonies and eventually to the American Revolution. Ideas expressed in the early State constitutions influenced the development of the governmental system under which we live today.

POLITICAL DICTIONARY

★ **confederation**
★ **Albany Plan of Union**
★ **delegate**
★ **boycott**
★ **repeal**
★ **popular sovereignty**

"**W**e must all hang together, or assuredly we shall all hang separately." Benjamin Franklin is said to have spoken these words on July 4, 1776, as he and the other members of the Second Continental Congress approved the Declaration of Independence. Those who heard him may have chuckled. But they also may have felt a shiver, for Franklin's humor carried a deadly serious message.

In this section, you will follow the events that led to the momentous decision to break with Great Britain.[7] You will also consider the new State governments that were established with the coming of Independence.

▲ Colonists who made their tea in this pot voiced their opposition to the Stamp Act.

Britain's Colonial Policies

The 13 colonies, which had been separately established, were separately controlled under the king, largely through the Privy Council and the Board of Trade in London. Parliament took little part in the management of the colonies. Although it did become more and more interested in matters of trade, it left matters of colonial administration almost entirely to the Crown.[8]

Over the century and a half that followed the first settlement at Jamestown, the colonies developed within that framework of royal control. In theory, they were governed in all important matters from London. But London was more than 3,000 miles away, and it took nearly two months to sail that distance across a peril-filled Atlantic. So, in practice, the colonists became used to a large measure of self-government.

Each colonial legislature began to assume broad lawmaking powers. Many found the power of the purse to be very effective. They often bent a royal governor to their will by not voting the money for his salary until he came to terms with them. As one member of New Jersey's Assembly put it: "Let us keep the dogges poore, and we'll make them do as we please."

---

[7]England became Great Britain by the Act of Union with Scotland in 1707.

[8]Much of English political history can be told in terms of the centuries-long struggle for supremacy between monarch and Parliament. That conflict was largely settled by England's Glorious Revolution of 1688, but it did continue through the American colonial period and into the nineteenth century. However, Parliament paid little attention to the American colonies until very late in the colonial period.

By the mid-1700s, the relationship between Britain and the colonies had become, in fact if not in form, federal. This meant that the central government in London was responsible for colonial defense and for foreign affairs. It also provided a uniform system of money and credit and a common market for colonial trade. Beyond that, the colonies were allowed a fairly wide amount of self-rule. Little was taken from them in direct taxes to pay for the central government. The few regulations set by Parliament, mostly about trade, were largely ignored.

This was soon to change. Shortly after George III came to the throne in 1760, Britain began to deal more firmly with the colonies. Restrictive trading acts were expanded and enforced. New taxes were imposed, mostly to support British troops in North America.

Many colonists took strong exception to these moves. They objected to taxes imposed on them from afar. This arrangement, they claimed, was "taxation without representation." They saw little need for the costly presence of British troops on North American soil, since the French had been defeated and their power broken in the French and Indian War (1754–1763).

The colonists considered themselves British subjects loyal to the Crown. They refused, however, to accept Parliament's claim that it had a right to control their local affairs.

The king's ministers were poorly informed and stubborn. They pushed ahead with their policies, despite the resentments they stirred in America. Within a few years, the colonists faced a fateful choice: to submit or to revolt.

Growing Colonial Unity

A decision to revolt was not one to be taken lightly—or alone. The colonies would need to learn to work together if they wanted to succeed. Indeed long before the 1770s, several attempts had been made to promote cooperation among the colonies.

Early Attempts

In 1643 the Massachusetts Bay, Plymouth, New Haven, and Connecticut settlements formed the New England Confederation. A **confederation** is a joining of several groups for a common purpose. In the New England Confederation, the

Benjamin Franklin dedicated years to public service, including time as a delegate to the Second Continental Congress, a commissioner to France during the War for Independence, and a member of the Constitutional Convention. Franklin proposed the Albany Plan of Union to provide for the defense of the American colonies. In his autobiography, he spoke of its defeat and defended his plan:

❝ *The different and contrary Reasons of dislike to my Plan, makes me suspect that it was really the true Medium; and I am still of Opinion it would have been happy for both Sides the Water if it had been adopted. The Colonies so united would have been sufficiently strong to have defended themselves; there would then have been no need of Troops from England; of course the subsequent Pretence for Taxing America, and the bloody Contest it occasioned, would have been avoided.* ❞

Evaluating the Quotation

What did Franklin see as the ultimate result of the failure to adopt the Albany Plan of Union? Do you think this was a reasonable conclusion?

settlements formed a "league of friendship" for defense against the Native Americans. As the danger from Native Americans passed and friction among the settlements grew, the confederation lost importance and finally dissolved in 1684.

In 1696 William Penn offered an elaborate plan for intercolonial cooperation, largely in trade, defense, and criminal matters. It received little attention and was soon forgotten.

The Albany Plan

In 1754 the British Board of Trade called a meeting of seven of the northern colonies at Albany: Connecticut, Maryland, Massachusetts, New Hampshire, New York, Pennsylvania, and Rhode Island. The main purpose of the meeting was to discuss the problems of colonial trade and the danger of attacks by the French and their Native American allies. Here, Benjamin Franklin offered what came to be known as the **Albany Plan of Union.**

In his plan, Franklin proposed the formation of an annual congress of **delegates** (representatives) from each of the 13 colonies. That body would have the power to raise military and naval forces, make war and peace with the Native Americans, regulate trade with them, tax, and collect customs duties.

Franklin's plan was ahead of its time. It was agreed to by the representatives attending the Albany meeting, but it was turned down by the colonies and by the Crown. Franklin's plan was to be remembered later.

The Stamp Act Congress

Britain's harsh tax and trade policies of the 1760s fanned resentment in the colonies. Parliament had passed a number of new laws, among them the Stamp Act of 1765. That law required the use of tax stamps on all legal documents, on certain business agreements, and on newspapers.

The new taxes were widely denounced, in part because the rates were perceived as severe, but largely because they amounted to "taxation without representation." In October of 1765, nine colonies—all except Georgia, New Hampshire, North Carolina, and Virginia—sent delegates to the Stamp Act Congress in New York. They prepared a strong protest, called the Declaration of Rights and Grievances, against the new British policies and sent it to the king. These actions marked the first time a significant number of the colonies had joined to oppose the British government.

Parliament repealed the Stamp Act, but frictions mounted. New laws were passed and new policies were made to tie the colonies more closely to London. Colonists showed their resentment and anger in wholesale evasion of the laws. Mob violence erupted at several ports, and many colonists supported a **boycott** of English goods. A boycott is a refusal to buy or sell certain products or services. On March 5, 1770, British troops in Boston fired on a jeering crowd, killing five, in what came to be known as the Boston Massacre.

Organized resistance was carried on through Committees of Correspondence, which had grown out of a group formed by Samuel Adams in Boston in 1772. These committees soon spread throughout the colonies, providing a network for cooperation and the exchange of information among the patriots.

Protests multiplied. The famous Boston Tea Party took place on December 16, 1773. A group of men, disguised as Native Americans, boarded three tea ships in Boston harbor and dumped the cargo into the sea to protest British control of the tea trade.

The First Continental Congress

In the spring of 1774, Parliament passed yet another set of laws, this time to punish the colonists for the troubles in Boston and elsewhere. These new laws, denounced in America as the Intolerable Acts, prompted widespread calls for a meeting of all the colonies.

Delegates from every colony except Georgia met in Philadelphia on September 5, 1774. Many of the ablest men of the day were there: Samuel Adams and John Adams of Massachusetts; Roger Sherman of Connecticut; Stephen Hopkins of Rhode Island; John Dickinson and Joseph Galloway of Pennsylvania; John Jay and Philip Livingston of New York; George Washington, Richard Henry Lee, and Patrick Henry of Virginia; and John Rutledge of South Carolina.

For nearly two months the members of that First Continental

▲ This colored engraving, printed in 1793, is the earliest known American depiction of the Boston Tea Party. *Critical Thinking **What did the colonists hope to accomplish by destroying the cargo of tea?*** H-SS 12.10

▲ Washington once complained that his soldiers were forced to "eat every kind of horse food but hay." He won the respect of the men who served under his command when he demanded that Congress provide better treatment for the army. *Critical Thinking How does this nineteenth-century engraving of Washington and his troops welcoming a train of supplies reinforce Washington's image as a strong leader?*

Congress discussed the worsening situation and debated plans for action. They sent a Declaration of Rights, protesting Britain's colonial policies, to King George III. The delegates urged each of the colonies to refuse all trade with England until the hated taxes and trade regulations were **repealed** (withdrawn, cancelled). The delegates also called for the creation of local committees to enforce that boycott.

The meeting adjourned on October 26, with a call for a second congress to be convened the following May. Over the next several months, all the colonial legislatures, including Georgia's, gave their support to the actions of the First Continental Congress.

The Second Continental Congress

During the fall and winter of 1774–1775, the British government continued to refuse to compromise, let alone reverse, its colonial policies. It reacted to the Declaration of Rights as it had to other expressions of colonial discontent—with even stricter and more repressive measures.

The Second Continental Congress met in Philadelphia on May 10, 1775. By then, the Revolution had begun. The "shot heard 'round the world" had been fired. The battles of Lexington and Concord had been fought three weeks earlier, on April 19.

Representatives

Each of the 13 colonies sent representatives to the Congress. Most of those who had attended the First Continental Congress were again present. Most notable among the newcomers were Benjamin Franklin of Pennsylvania and John Hancock of Massachusetts.

Hancock was chosen president of the Congress.[9] Almost at once, a continental army was created, and George Washington was appointed its commander in chief. Thomas Jefferson then took Washington's place in the Virginia delegation.

Our First National Government

The Second Continental Congress became, by force of circumstance, the nation's first national government. However, it rested on no constitutional base. It was condemned by the British as an unlawful assembly and a den of traitors. But it was supported by the force of public opinion and practical necessity.

The Second Continental Congress served as the first government of the United States for five fateful years, from the formal adoption of the

---

[9]Peyton Randolph, who had also served as president of the First Continental Congress, was originally chosen for the office. He resigned on May 24, however, because the Virginia House of Burgesses, of which he was the speaker, had been called into session. Hancock was then elected to succeed him.

Declaration of Independence in July 1776 until the Articles of Confederation went into effect on March 1, 1781. During that time the Second Continental Congress fought a war, raised armies and a navy, borrowed funds, bought supplies, created a money system, made treaties with foreign powers, and did those other things that any government would have had to do in the circumstances.

The unicameral Congress exercised both legislative and executive powers. In legislative matters, each colony—later, State—had one vote. Executive functions were handled by committees of delegates.

The Declaration of Independence

Slightly more than a year after the Revolution began, Richard Henry Lee of Virginia proposed to the Congress:

PRIMARY *Sources* **"**Resolved, *That these United Colonies are, and of right ought to be, free and independent States, that they are absolved from all allegiance to the British Crown, and that all political connection between them and the State of Great Britain is, and ought to be, totally dissolved.* **"**

—Resolution of June 7, 1776

Congress named a committee of five—Benjamin Franklin, John Adams, Roger Sherman, Robert Livingston, and Thomas Jefferson—to prepare a proclamation of independence. Their momentous product, the Declaration of Independence, was very largely the work of Jefferson.

On July 2, the final break came. The delegates agreed to Lee's resolution—but only after spirited debate, for many of the delegates had serious doubts about the wisdom of a complete separation from England. Two days later, on July 4, 1776, they adopted the Declaration of Independence, proclaiming the existence of the new nation.

The Declaration announces the independence of the United States in its first paragraph. Much of the balance of the document—nearly two thirds of it—speaks of "the repeated injuries and usurpations" that led the colonists to revolt. At its heart, the Declaration proclaims:

PRIMARY *Sources* **"***We hold these truths to be self-evident, that all men are created equal, that they are endowed by their Creator with certain unalienable Rights, that among these are Life, Liberty and the pursuit of Happiness. That to secure these rights, Governments are instituted among Men, deriving their just powers from the consent of the governed; That whenever any Form of Government becomes destructive of these ends it is the Right of the People to alter or to abolish it, and to institute new Government, laying its foundations on such principles and organizing its powers in such form, as to them shall seem most likely to effect their Safety and Happiness.* **"**

—The Unanimous Declaration of the
Thirteen United States of America

With these brave words, the United States of America was born. The 13 colonies became free and independent States. The 56 men who signed the Declaration sealed it with this final sentence:

"*And for the support of this Declaration, with a firm reliance on the protection of Divine Providence, we mutually pledge to each other, our lives, our Fortunes, and our sacred Honor.* **"**

The First State Constitutions

In January 1776, New Hampshire adopted a constitution to replace its royal charter. Less than three months later, South Carolina followed suit. Then, on May 10, nearly two months before the adoption of the Declaration of Independence, the Congress urged each of the colonies to adopt: "such governments as shall, in the opinion of the representatives of the people, best conduce to the happiness and safety of their constituents."

Drafting State Constitutions

In 1776 and 1777, most of the States adopted written constitutions—bodies of fundamental laws setting out the principles, structures, and processes of their governments. Assemblies or conventions were commonly used to draft and then adopt these new documents.

Massachusetts set a lasting example in the constitution-making process. There, a convention submitted its work to the voters for ratification. The Massachusetts constitution of 1780 is the oldest of the present-day State constitutions. In fact, it is the oldest written constitution in force anywhere in the world today.[10]

Common Features

The first State constitutions differed, sometimes widely, in detail. Yet they shared many similar features. The most common features were the principles of **popular sovereignty** (government can exist only with the consent of the governed), limited government, civil rights and liberties, and separation of powers and checks and balances. These principles are outlined in detail in the table at right.

The new State constitutions were rather brief documents. For the most part, they were declarations of principle and statements of limitation on governmental power. Memories of the royal governors were fresh, and the new State governors were given little real power. Most of the authority that was granted to State government was placed in the legislature. Elective terms of office were made purposely short, seldom more than one or two years. The right to vote was limited to those adult white males who could meet rigid qualifications, including property ownership.

---

[10]From independence until that constitution became effective in 1780, Massachusetts relied on its colonial charter, in force prior to 1691, as its fundamental law.

Common Features of State Constitutions	
POPULAR SOVEREIGNTY	The principle of popular sovereignty was the basis for every new State constitution. That principle says that government can exist and function only with the consent of the governed. The people hold power and the people are sovereign.
LIMITED GOVERNMENT	The concept of limited government was a major feature of each State constitution. The powers delegated to government were granted reluctantly and hedged with many restrictions.
CIVIL RIGHTS AND LIBERTIES	In every State it was made clear that the sovereign people held certain rights that the government must respect at all times. Seven of the new constitutions contained a bill of rights, setting out the "unalienable rights" held by the people.
SEPARATION OF POWERS AND CHECKS AND BALANCES	The powers granted to the new State governments were purposely divided among three branches: executive, legislative, and judicial. Each branch was given powers with which to check (restrain the actions of) the other branches of the government.

Interpreting Tables Most of the newly created States adopted written constitutions in the two years following the Declaration of Independence. **Why did the first State constitutions share several common features?** H-SS 12.10

We shall return to the subject of State constitutions later, in Chapter 24. For now, note this very important point: The earliest of these documents were, within a very few years, to have a marked impact on the drafting of the Constitution of the United States.

Section 2 Assessment

Key Terms and Main Ideas

1. Why did some colonists support a **boycott** of English goods?
2. What was the **Albany Plan of Union** and how was it received by the colonies and by the Crown?
3. Explain the concept of **popular sovereignty.**
4. What was the outcome of the First Continental Congress?
5. In what ways did the Second Continental Congress serve as the first national government?

Critical Thinking

6. **Distinguishing Fact from Opinion** The Declaration of Independence states that all men are endowed "with

Standards Monitoring *Online*
For: Self-Quiz and vocabulary practice
Web Code: mqa-1022

certain unalienable Rights, that among these are Life, Liberty and the pursuit of Happiness." Is this statement a fact or opinion? Explain your answer.
7. **Expressing Problems Clearly** What problems arose from changes in British policy toward the colonies in the 1760s?

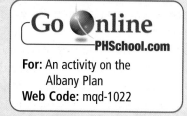

For: An activity on the Albany Plan
Web Code: mqd-1022

The Declaration of Independence

The Unanimous Declaration of the Thirteen United States of America

▲ The Declaration of Independence was largely the work of Thomas Jefferson, who chaired the five-person committee assigned to the task.

When in the Course of human events, it becomes necessary for one people to dissolve the political bands which have connected them with another, and to assume among the powers of the earth, the separate and equal station to which the Laws of nature and of Nature's God entitle them, a decent respect to the opinions of mankind requires that they should declare the causes which impel them to the separation.

We hold these truths to be self-evident, that all men are created equal, that they are endowed by their Creator with certain unalienable Rights, that among these are Life, Liberty and the pursuit of Happiness. That to secure these rights, Governments are instituted among Men, deriving their just powers from the consent of the governed; That whenever any Form of Government becomes destructive of these ends it is the Right of the People to alter or to abolish it, and to institute new Government, laying its foundation on such principles and organizing its powers in such form, as to them shall seem most likely to effect their Safety and Happiness. Prudence, indeed, will dictate that Governments long established should not be changed for light and transient causes; and accordingly all experience hath shown, that mankind are more disposed to suffer, while evils are sufferable, than to right themselves by abolishing the forms to which they are accustomed. But when a long train of abuses and usurpations, pursuing invariably the same Object evinces a design to reduce them under absolute Despotism, it is their right, it is their duty, to throw off such Government, and to provide new Guards for their future security.

Such has been the patient sufferance of these Colonies; and such is now the necessity which constrains them to alter their former Systems of Government. The history of the present King of Great Britain is a history of repeated injuries and usurpations, all having in direct object the establishment of an absolute Tyranny over these States. To prove this, let Facts be submitted to a candid world.

He has refused his Assent to Laws, the most wholesome and necessary for the public good.

He has forbidden his Governors to pass Laws of immediate and pressing importance, unless suspended in their operation till his Assent should be obtained; and when so suspended, he has utterly neglected to attend to them.

He has refused to pass other Laws for the accommodation of large districts of people, unless those people would relinquish the right of Representation in the Legislature, a right inestimable to them and formidable to tyrants only.

He has called together legislative bodies at places unusual, uncomfortable, and distant from the depository of their Public Records, for the sole purpose of fatiguing them into compliance with his measures.

He has dissolved Representative Houses repeatedly, for opposing with manly firmness his invasions on the rights of the people.

He has refused for a long time, after such dissolutions, to cause others to be elected; whereby the Legislative powers, incapable of Annihilation, have returned to the People at large for their exercise; the State remaining in the mean time exposed to all the dangers of invasions from without, and convulsions within.

He has endeavored to prevent the population of these States; for that purpose obstructing the Laws for Naturalization of Foreigners; refusing to pass others to encourage their migration hither, and raising the conditions of new Appropriations of Lands.

He has obstructed the Administration of Justice, by refusing his Assent to Laws for establishing Judiciary powers.

He has made Judges dependent on his Will alone for the tenure of their offices, and the amount and payment of their salaries.

He has erected a multitude of New Offices, and sent hither swarms of Officers to harass our people and eat out their substance.

He has kept among us in time of peace, Standing Armies, without the Consent of our legislatures.

He has affected to render the Military independent of, and superior to, the Civil Power.

He has combined with others to subject us to a jurisdiction foreign to our constitutions, and unacknowledged by our laws; giving his Assent to their Acts of pretended Legislation:

For quartering large bodies of armed troops among us;

For protecting them, by a mock Trial, from punishment for any Murders which they should commit on the Inhabitants of these States;

For cutting off our Trade with all parts of the world;

For imposing Taxes on us without our Consent;

For depriving us, in many cases, of the benefits of Trial by Jury;

For transporting us beyond Seas to be tried for pretended offenses;

For abolishing the free System of English Laws in a neighboring Province, establishing therein an Arbitrary government, and enlarging

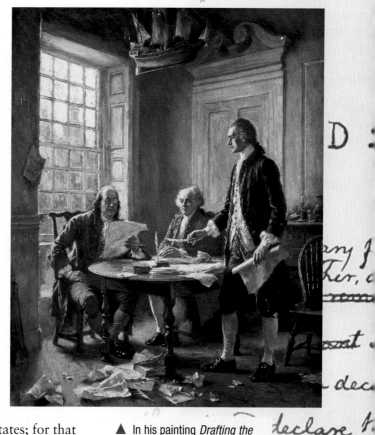

▲ In his painting *Drafting the Declaration of Independence,* artist Jean Leon Gerome Ferris (1888–1930) shows members of the committee reviewing Jefferson's proposed Declaration.

▲ This hand-colored woodcut shows the scene at the signing of the Declaration of Independence.

▼ John Hancock (below), President of the Continental Congress from 1775 to 1777, was the first to sign the Declaration of Independence.

its Boundaries so as to render it at once an example and fit instrument for introducing the same absolute rule into these Colonies;

For taking away our Charters, abolishing our most valuable Laws, and altering fundamentally the Forms of our Governments;

For suspending our own Legislatures, and declaring themselves invested with Power to legislate for us in all cases whatsoever.

He has abdicated Government here, by declaring us out of his Protection, and waging War against us.

He has plundered our seas, ravaged our Coasts, burned our towns, and destroyed the lives of our people.

He is at this time transporting large Armies of foreign mercenaries to complete the works of death, desolation and tyranny, already begun with circumstances of Cruelty and perfidy scarcely paralleled in the most barbarous ages, and totally unworthy the Head of a civilized nation.

He has constrained our fellow Citizens taken Captive on the high Seas to bear Arms against their Country, to become the executioners of their friends and Brethren, or to fall themselves by their Hands.

He has excited domestic insurrections amongst us, and has endeavored to bring on the inhabitants of our frontiers the merciless Indian Savages whose known rule of warfare, is an undistinguished destruction of all ages, sexes, and conditions.

In every stage of these Oppressions We have Petitioned for Redress in the most humble terms. Our repeated Petitions have been answered only by repeated injury. A Prince, whose character is thus marked by every act which may define a Tyrant, is unfit to be the ruler of a free People.

Nor have We been wanting in attentions to our British brethren. We have warned them from time to time of attempts by their legislature to extend an unwarrantable jurisdiction over us. We have reminded them of the circumstances of our emigration and settlement here. We have appealed to their native justice and magnanimity, and we have conjured them by the ties of our common kindred to disavow these usurpations, which, would inevitably interrupt our connections and correspondence. They too have been deaf to the voice of justice and of consanguinity. We must, therefore, acquiesce in the necessity, which denounces our Separation, and hold them, as we hold the rest of mankind, Enemies in War, in Peace Friends.

We, therefore, the Representatives of the United States of America, in General Congress, Assembled, appealing to the Supreme Judge of the world for the rectitude of our intentions, do, in the Name, and by the Authority of the good People of these Colonies, solemnly publish and declare, That these United Colonies are, and of right ought to be Free and Independent States; that they are Absolved from all Allegiance to the British Crown, and that all political connection between them and the State of Great Britain, is and ought to be totally dissolved, and that as Free and Independent States, they have full Power to levy

War, conclude Peace, contract Alliances, establish Commerce, and to do all other Acts and Things which Independent States may of right do. And for the support of this Declaration, with a firm reliance on the protection of Divine Providence, we mutually pledge to each other our Lives, our Fortunes and our sacred Honor.

John Hancock

New Hampshire
Josiah Bartlett
William Whipple
Mathew Thornton

Massachusetts Bay
Samuel Adams
John Adams
Robert Treat Paine
Elbridge Gerry

Rhode Island
Stephan Hopkins
William Ellery

Connecticut
Roger Sherman
Samuel Huntington
William Williams
Oliver Wolcott

New York
William Floyd
Philip Livingston
Francis Lewis
Lewis Morris

New Jersey
Richard Stockton
John Witherspoon
Francis Hopkinson
John Hart
Abraham Clark

Delaware
Caesar Rodney
George Read
Thomas M'Kean

Maryland
Samuel Chase
William Paca
Thomas Stone
Charles Carroll of
  Carrollton

Virginia
George Wythe
Richard Henry Lee
Thomas Jefferson
Benjamin Harrison
Thomas Nelson, Jr.
Francis Lightfoot Lee
Carter Braxton

Pennsylvania
Robert Morris
Benjamin Rush
Benjamin Franklin
John Morton
George Clymer
James Smith
George Taylor
James Wilson
George Ross

North Carolina
William Hooper
Joseph Hewes
John Penn

South Carolina
Edward Rutledge
Thomas Heyward, Jr.
Thomas Lynch, Jr.
Arthur Middleton

Georgia
Button Gwinnett
Lyman Hall
George Walton

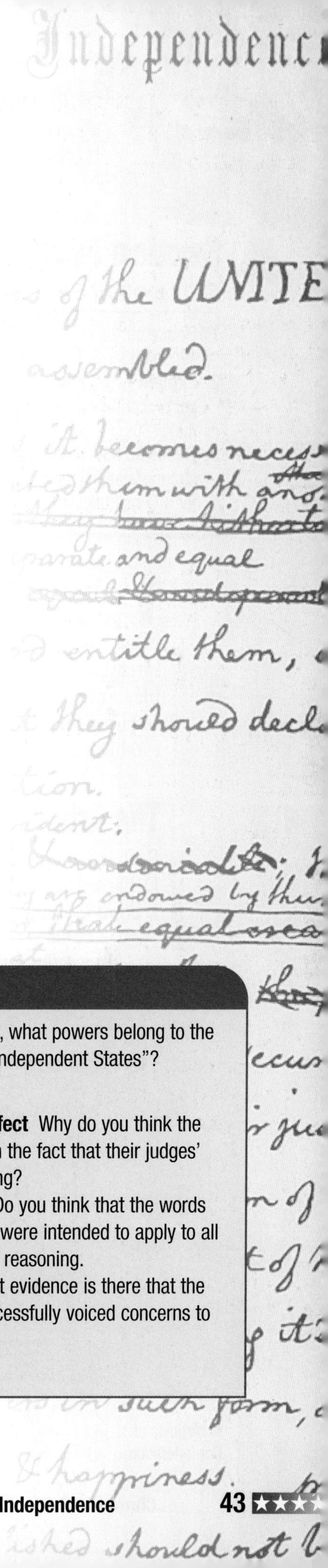

Reviewing the Declaration

Vocabulary
Choose ten words in the Declaration with which you are unfamiliar. Look them up in the dictionary. Then, on a piece of paper, copy the sentence in the Declaration in which each unfamiliar word is used. After the sentence, write the definition of the unfamiliar word.

Comprehension
1. Which truths in the second paragraph are "self-evident"?
2. Name the three unalienable rights listed in the Declaration.
3. From what source do governments derive their "just powers"?
4. In the series of paragraphs beginning, "He has refused his Assent," to whom does the word "He" refer?

5. According to the Declaration, what powers belong to the United States "as Free and Independent States"?

Critical Thinking
6. **Recognizing Cause and Effect** Why do you think the colonists were unhappy with the fact that their judges' salaries were paid by the king?
7. **Identifying Assumptions** Do you think that the words "all men are created equal" were intended to apply to all human beings? Explain your reasoning.
8. **Drawing Conclusions** What evidence is there that the colonists had already unsuccessfully voiced concerns to the king?

The Critical Period

Section Preview

OBJECTIVES

1. **Describe** the structure of the government set up under the Articles of Confederation.
2. **Explain** why the weaknesses of the Articles led to a critical period for the government in the 1780s.
3. **Describe** how a growing need for a stronger national government led to plans for a Constitutional Convention.

WHY IT MATTERS

The Articles of Confederation established a fairly weak central government, which led to conflicts among the States. The turmoil of the Critical Period of the 1780s led to the creation of a stronger National Government.

POLITICAL DICTIONARY

★ **Articles of Confederation**
★ **ratification**
★ **presiding officer**

The First and Second Continental Congresses rested on no legal base. They were called in haste to meet an emergency, and they were intended to be temporary. Something more regular and permanent was clearly needed. In this section, you will look at the first attempt to establish a lasting government for the new nation.

The Articles of Confederation

Richard Henry Lee's resolution leading to the Declaration of Independence also called on the Second Continental Congress to propose "a plan

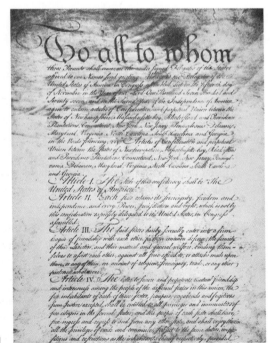

► Articles of Confederation

of confederation" to the States. Off and on, for 17 months, Congress considered the problem of uniting the former colonies. Finally, on November 15, 1777, the **Articles of Confederation** were approved.

The Articles of Confederation established "a firm league of friendship" among the States. Each State kept "its sovereignty, freedom, and independence, and every Power, Jurisdiction, and right . . . not . . . expressly delegated to the United States, in Congress assembled." The States came together "for their common defense, the security of their Liberties, and their mutual and general welfare. . . ."

The Articles did not go into effect immediately, however. The **ratification,** or formal approval, of each of the 13 States was needed first. Eleven States agreed to the document within a year. Delaware added its approval in February 1779. But Maryland did not ratify until March 1, 1781, and the Second Continental Congress declared the Articles effective on that date.

Governmental Structure

The government set up by the Articles was simple indeed. A Congress was the sole body created. It was unicameral, made up of delegates chosen yearly by the States in whatever way their legislatures might direct. Each State had one vote in the Congress, whatever its population or wealth.

The Articles established no executive or judicial branch. These functions were to be handled by committees of the Congress. Each year the

Congress would choose one of its members as its president. That person would be its **presiding officer** (chair), but not the president of the United States. Civil officers such as postmasters were to be appointed by the Congress.

Powers of Congress

Several important powers were given to the Congress. It could make war and peace; send and receive ambassadors; make treaties; borrow money; set up a money system; establish post offices; build a navy; raise an army by asking the States for troops; fix uniform standards of weights and measures; and settle disputes among the States.

State Obligations

By agreeing to the Articles, the States pledged to obey the Articles and acts of the Congress. They would provide the funds and troops requested by the Congress; treat citizens of other States fairly and equally with their own; and give full faith and credit to the public acts, records, and judicial proceedings of every other State. In addition, the States agreed to surrender fugitives from justice to one another; submit their disputes to Congress for settlement; and allow open travel and trade between and among the States.

Beyond these few obligations, the States retained those powers not explicitly given to the Congress. They, not the Congress, were primarily responsible for protecting life and property. States were also accountable for promoting the general welfare of the people.

Weaknesses

The powers of the Congress appear, at first glance, to have been considerable. Several important powers were missing, however. Their omission, together with other weaknesses, soon proved the Articles inadequate to the needs of the time.

The Congress did not have the power to tax. It could raise money only by borrowing and by asking the States for funds. Borrowing was, at best, a poor source. The Second Continental Congress had borrowed heavily to support the costs of fighting the Revolution, and many of those debts had not been paid. And, while the Articles remained in force, not one State came close to meeting the financial requests made by the Congress.

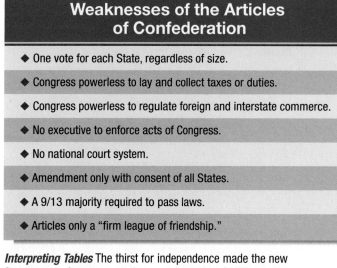

Weaknesses of the Articles of Confederation

◆ One vote for each State, regardless of size.

◆ Congress powerless to lay and collect taxes or duties.

◆ Congress powerless to regulate foreign and interstate commerce.

◆ No executive to enforce acts of Congress.

◆ No national court system.

◆ Amendment only with consent of all States.

◆ A 9/13 majority required to pass laws.

◆ Articles only a "firm league of friendship."

Interpreting Tables The thirst for independence made the new States wary of strong central government. ***How is this caution reflected in the weaknesses built into the Articles of Confederation?***

Nor did the Congress have the power to regulate trade between the States. This lack of a central mechanism to regulate the young nation's commerce was one of the major factors that led to the adoption of the Constitution.

The Congress was further limited by a lack of power to make the States obey the Articles of Confederation or the laws it made. Congress could exercise the powers it did have only with the consent of 9 of the 13 State delegations. Finally, the Articles themselves could be changed only with the consent of all 13 of the State legislatures. This procedure proved an impossible task; not one amendment was ever added to the Articles of Confederation.

The Critical Period, the 1780s

The long Revolutionary War finally ended on October 19, 1781. America's victory was confirmed by the signing of the Treaty of Paris in 1783. Peace, however, brought the new nation's economic and political problems into sharp focus. Problems, caused by the weaknesses of the Articles of Confederation, soon surfaced.

With a central government unable to act, the States bickered among themselves and grew increasingly jealous and suspicious of one another. They often refused to support the new central government, financially and in almost every other way. Several of them made agreements with foreign governments without the approval of the

Congress, even though that was forbidden by the Articles. Most even organized their own military forces. George Washington complained, "We are one nation today and 13 tomorrow. Who will treat with us on such terms?"

The States taxed one another's goods and even banned some trade. They printed their own money, often with little backing. Economic chaos spread throughout the colonies as prices soared and sound credit vanished. Debts, public and private, went unpaid. Violence broke out in a number of places as a result of the economic chaos.

The most spectacular of these events played out in western Massachusetts in a series of incidents that came to be known as Shays' Rebellion. As economic conditions worsened, property holders, many of them small farmers, began to lose their land and possessions for lack of payment on taxes and other debts. In the fall of 1786, Daniel Shays, who had served as an officer in the War for Independence, led an armed uprising that forced several State judges to close their courts. Early the next year, Shays mounted an

▲ **Shays' Rebellion** Following the series of incidents known as Shays' Rebellion, the Supreme Judicial Court of Massachusetts condemned Daniel Shays and about a dozen others to death. Shays petitioned for and received a pardon in 1788. **H-SS 12.10**

unsuccessful attack on the federal arsenal at Springfield. State forces finally moved to quiet the rebellion and Shays fled to Vermont. In response to the violence, the Massachusetts legislature eventually passed laws to ease the burden of debtors.

A Need for Stronger Government

The Articles had created a government unable to deal with the nation's troubles. Inevitably, demand grew for a stronger, more effective national government. Those who were most threatened by economic and political instability —large property owners, merchants, traders, and other creditors—soon took the lead in efforts to that end. The movement for change began to take concrete form in 1785.

Mount Vernon

Maryland and Virginia, plagued by bitter trade disputes, took the first step in the movement for change. Ignoring the Congress, the two States agreed to a conference on their trade problems. Representatives from the two States met at Alexandria, Virginia, in March 1785. At George Washington's invitation, they moved their sessions to his home at nearby Mount Vernon.

Their negotiations proved so successful that on January 21, 1786, the Virginia General Assembly called for "a joint meeting of [all of] the States to recommend a federal plan for regulating commerce."

Annapolis

That joint meeting opened at Annapolis, Maryland, on September 11, 1786. Turnout was poor, with representatives from only five of the 13 States attending.[11] Disappointed, but still hopeful, the convention called for yet another meeting of the States

 at Philadelphia on the second Monday in May next, to take into consideration the situation of the United States, to devise such further provisions as

---

[11]New York, New Jersey, Pennsylvania, Delaware, and Virginia. Although New Hampshire, Massachusetts, Rhode Island, and North Carolina had appointed delegates, none attended the Annapolis meeting.

▲ **Mount Vernon** George Washington's graceful home overlooking the Potomac River served as the location for trade talks between Maryland and Virginia. The success of that meeting caused some to move for further steps toward a stronger federal government.

shall appear to them necessary to render the constitution of the Federal Government adequate to the exigencies of the Union. "

—Call of the Annapolis Convention

By mid-February of 1787, seven of the States had named delegates to the Philadelphia meeting. These were Delaware, Georgia, New Hampshire, New Jersey, North Carolina, Pennsylvania, and Virginia. Then on February 21, the Congress, which had been hesitating, also called upon the States to send delegates to Philadelphia

PRIMARY Sources " *for the sole and express purpose of revising the Articles of Confederation and reporting to Congress and the several legislatures such alterations and provisions therein as shall when agreed to in Congress and confirmed by the States render the [Articles] adequate to the exigencies of Government and the preservation of the Union.* "

—The United States in Congress Assembled, February 21, 1787

That Philadelphia meeting became the Constitutional Convention.

Section 3 Assessment

Standards Monitoring *Online*

For: Self-Quiz and vocabulary practice
Web Code: mqa-1023

Key Terms and Main Ideas

1. What were the **Articles of Confederation** and what powers did they grant to Congress?
2. Before the Articles of Confederation could go into effect, how many States were needed for **ratification?**
3. Identify at least three weaknesses of the government under the Articles of Confederation.
4. What was the result of the meetings at Mount Vernon and Annapolis in 1785 and 1786?

Critical Thinking

5. **Identifying Central Issues** The Articles of Confederation contained several weaknesses. Why would the States purposefully create a weak government under the Articles?

6. **Drawing Conclusions** For what reasons is the period during which the Articles were in force called the Critical Period in American history?

Go Online
PHSchool.com

For: An activity on the origins of the U.S. government
Web Code: mqd-1023

Section Preview

OBJECTIVES

1. **Identify** the Framers of the Constitution and discuss how the delegates organized the proceedings at the Philadelphia Convention.
2. **Compare** and contrast the Virginia Plan and the New Jersey Plan for a new constitution.
3. **Summarize** the major compromises that the delegates agreed to make and the effects of those compromises.
4. **Identify** some of the sources from which the Framers of the Constitution drew inspiration.
5. **Describe** the delegates' reactions to the Constitution as they completed their work.

WHY IT MATTERS

The Framers of the Constitution created a document that addressed the major concerns of the States attending the Philadelphia Convention. By reaching compromise on items about which they disagreed, the Framers created a new National Government capable of handling the nation's problems.

POLITICAL DICTIONARY

★ **Framers**
★ **Virginia Plan**
★ **New Jersey Plan**
★ **Connecticut Compromise**
★ **Three-Fifths Compromise**
★ **Commerce and Slave Trade Compromise**

Picture this scene. It's hot—sweltering, in fact. Yet the windows are all closed to discourage eavesdroppers. Outside, soldiers keep interested onlookers at a distance. Inside, the atmosphere is tense as men exchange their views. Indeed, some become so angry that they threaten to leave the hall. A few carry out their threats.

This was the scene throughout much of the Philadelphia meeting that began on Friday, May 25, 1787.[12] Over the long summer months, the participants labored to build a new government that would best meet the needs of the nation. In this section, you will consider that meeting and its work.

▶ Delegates to the Constitutional Convention gathered in Independence Hall.

The Framers

Twelve of the 13 States, all but Rhode Island, sent delegates to Philadelphia.[13] In total, 74 delegates were chosen by the legislatures in those 12 states. For a number of reasons, however, only 55 of them actually attended the convention.

Of that 55, this much can be said: Never, before or since, has so remarkable a group been brought together in this country. Thomas Jefferson, who was not among them, later called the delegates "an assembly of demi-gods."

The group of delegates who attended the Philadelphia Convention, known as the **Framers** of the Constitution, included many outstanding individuals. These were men of wide knowledge and public experience, of wealth and prestige. Their collective record of public service was truly impressive. Many of them had fought in the Revolution; 39 had been members of the Continental Congress or the Congress of the

---

[12]Not enough States were represented on the date Congress had set, Monday, May 14, to begin the meeting. The delegates who were present met and adjourned each day until Friday the 25th, when a quorum (in this case, a majority) of the States was on hand.

[13]The Rhode Island legislature was controlled by the soft-money forces, mostly debtors and small farmers who were helped by inflation and so were against a stronger central government. The New Hampshire delegation, delayed mostly by lack of funds, did not reach Philadelphia until late July.

Selected Framers of the Constitution

Name	State	Background
George Washington	Virginia	Planter, commander of the Continental Army
James Madison	Virginia	Legislator, major figure in movement to replace Articles
Edmund Randolph	Virginia	Lawyer, governor of Virginia
George Mason	Virginia	Planter, author of Virginia's Declaration of Rights
Benjamin Franklin	Pennsylvania	Writer, printer, inventor, legislator, diplomat
Gouverneur Morris	Pennsylvania	Lawyer, merchant, legislator
Robert Morris	Pennsylvania	Merchant, major financier of the Revolution
James Wilson	Pennsylvania	Lawyer, legislator, close student of politics, history
Alexander Hamilton	New York	Lawyer, legislator, champion of stronger central government
William Paterson	New Jersey	Lawyer, legislator, attorney general of New Jersey
Elbridge Gerry	Massachusetts	Merchant, legislator, major investor in land, government securities
Rufus King	Massachusetts	Legislator, opponent of extensive changes to Articles
Luther Martin	Maryland	Lawyer, legislator, attorney general of Maryland
Oliver Ellsworth	Connecticut	Lawyer, legislator, judge, theologian
Roger Sherman	Connecticut	Merchant, mayor of New Haven, legislator, judge
John Dickinson	Delaware	Lawyer, historian, major advocate of independence
John Rutledge	South Carolina	Lawyer, legislator, principal author of South Carolina's constitution
Charles Pinckney	South Carolina	Lawyer, legislator, leader in move to replace Articles

Interpreting Tables In reference to creating the Constitution, James Madison noted that considering "the natural diversity of human opinions on all new and complicated subjects, it is impossible to consider the degree of concord which ultimately prevailed as less than a miracle." ***What similarities and differences can you see in the Framers' backgrounds? Do you think their personal experiences helped or hurt their ability to draft the Constitution?*** **H-SS 12.1.4**

Confederation, or both. Eight had served in constitutional conventions in their own States, and seven had been State governors. Eight had signed the Declaration of Independence. Thirty-one of the delegates had attended college in a day when there were but a few colleges in the land, and their number also included two college presidents and three professors. Two were to become Presidents of the United States, and one a Vice President. Seventeen later served in the Senate and eleven in the House of Representatives.

Is it any wonder that the product of such a gathering was described by the English statesman William E. Gladstone, nearly a century later, as "the most wonderful work ever struck off at a given time by the brain and purpose of man"?

Remarkably, the average age of the delegates was only 42, and nearly half were only in their 30s. Indeed, most of the real leaders were in that age group—James Madison was 36, Gouverneur Morris 35, Edmund Randolph 34, and Alexander Hamilton 32. At 81, Benjamin Franklin was the oldest. His health

was failing, however, and he was not able to attend many of the meetings. George Washington, at 55, was one of the few older members who played a key role in the making of the Constitution.

By and large, the Framers of the Constitution were of a new generation in American politics. Several of the better-known leaders of the Revolutionary period were not in Philadelphia. Patrick Henry said he "smelt a rat" and refused to attend. Samuel Adams, John Hancock, and Richard Henry Lee were not selected as delegates by their States. Thomas Paine was in Paris. So, too, was Thomas Jefferson, as American minister to France. John Adams was our envoy to England and Holland at the time.

Organization and Procedure

The Framers met that summer in Philadelphia's Independence Hall, probably in the same room in which the Declaration of Independence had been signed 11 years earlier.

► This nineteenth-century engraving shows George Washington presiding over the Constitutional Convention in 1787. *Critical Thinking What impressions did the artist try to convey about this historic gathering?* **H-SS 12.1.4**

They organized immediately on May 25, unanimously electing George Washington president of the convention.[14] Then, and at the second session on Monday, May 28, they adopted several rules of procedure. A majority of the States would be needed to conduct business. Each State delegation was to have one vote on all matters, and a majority of the votes cast would carry any proposal.

Working in Secrecy

The delegates also decided to keep their deliberations secret. The convention had drawn much public attention and speculation. So, to protect themselves from outside pressures, the delegates adopted a rule of secrecy. On the whole, the rule was well kept.

A secretary, William Jackson, and other minor, nonmember officials were appointed. Jackson kept the convention's *Journal*. That official record, however, was quite sketchy. It was mostly a listing of members present, motions put forth, and votes taken; and it was not always accurate at that.

Fortunately, several delegates kept their own accounts of the proceedings. Most of what is known of the work of the convention comes from James Madison's voluminous *Notes*. His brilliance and depth of knowledge led his

[14]Twenty-nine delegates from seven States were present on that first day. The full number of 55 was not reached until August 6, when John Francis Mercer of Maryland arrived. In the meantime, some delegates had departed, and others were absent from time to time. Some 40 members attended most of the daily sessions of the convention.

colleagues to hold him in great respect. Quickly, he became the convention's floor leader. Madison contributed more to the Constitution than did any of the others, and still he was able to keep a close record of its work. Certainly, he deserves the title "Father of the Constitution."

The Framers met on 89 of the 116 days from May 25 through their final meeting on September 17. They did most of their work on the floor of the convention. They handled some matters in committees, but the full body ultimately settled all questions.

A Momentous Decision

The Philadelphia Convention was called to recommend revisions in the Articles of Confederation. However, almost at once the delegates agreed that they were, in fact, meeting to create a *new* government for the United States. On May 30 they adopted this proposal:

PRIMARY Sources ❝*Resolved, . . . that a national Government ought to be established consisting of a supreme Legislative, Executive and Judiciary.*❞
–Edmund Randolph, Delegate from Virginia

With this momentous decision, the Framers redefined the purpose of the convention. From that point on, they set about the writing of a new constitution. This new constitution was intended to replace the Articles of Confederation. Their debates were spirited, even bitter. At times the convention seemed near collapse. Once they had passed Randolph's resolution, however, the goal of a majority of the convention never changed.

The Virginia Plan

No State had more to do with the calling of the convention than Virginia did. It was not surprising, then, that its delegates should offer the first plan for a new constitution. On May 29 the **Virginia Plan,** largely the work of Madison, was presented by Randolph.

The Virginia Plan called for a new government with three separate branches: legislative, executive, and judicial. The legislature—Congress—would be bicameral. Representation in each house was to be based either upon each State's population or upon the amount of money it gave for the support of the central government. The members of the lower house, the House of Representatives, were to be popularly elected in each State. Those of the upper house, the Senate, were to be chosen by the House from lists of persons nominated by the State legislatures.

Congress was to be given all of the powers it held under the Articles. In addition, it was to have the power "to legislate in all cases to which the separate States are incompetent" to act, to veto any State law in conflict with national law, and to use force if necessary to make a State obey national law.

Under the proposed Virginia Plan, Congress would choose a "National Executive" and a "National Judiciary." Together, these two branches would form a "Council of revision." They could veto acts passed by Congress, but a veto could be overridden by the two houses. The executive would have "a general authority to execute the National laws." The judiciary would "consist of one or more supreme tribunals [courts], and of inferior tribunals."

The Virginia Plan also provided that all State officers should take an oath to support the Union, and that each State be guaranteed a republican form of government. Under the plan, Congress would have the exclusive power to admit new States to the Union.

The Virginia Plan, then, would create a new constitution by thoroughly revising the Articles. Its goal was the creation of a truly national government with greatly expanded powers and, importantly, the power to enforce its decisions.

The Virginia Plan set the agenda for much of the convention's work. But some delegates—especially those from the smaller States of Delaware, Maryland, and New Jersey, and from New York—found it too radical.[15] Soon they developed their counterproposals. On June 15 William Paterson of New Jersey presented the position of the small States.

The New Jersey Plan

Paterson and his colleagues offered several amendments to the Articles, but not nearly so thorough a revision as that proposed by the Virginia Plan. The **New Jersey Plan** retained the unicameral Congress of the Confederation, with each of the States equally represented. To those powers Congress already had, would be added closely limited powers to tax and to regulate trade between the States.

The New Jersey Plan also called for a "federal executive" of more than one person. This plural executive would be chosen by Congress and could be removed by it at the request of a majority of the States' governors. The "federal judiciary" would be composed of a single "supreme Tribunal," appointed by the executive.

Among their several differences, the major point of disagreement between the two plans centered on this question: How should the States be represented in Congress? Would it be on the basis of their populations or financial contributions, as in the Virginia Plan? Or would it be on the basis of State equality, as in the Articles and the New Jersey Plan?

For weeks the delegates returned to this conflict, debating the matter again and again. The lines were sharply drawn. Several delegates, on both sides of the issue, threatened to withdraw. Finally, the dispute was settled by one of the key compromises the Framers were to make as they built the Constitution.

Compromises

The disagreement over representation in Congress was critical. The large States expected to dominate the new government. The small

---

[15]The Virginia Plan's major support came from the three largest States: Virginia, Pennsylvania, and Massachusetts. New York was then only the fifth largest State. Alexander Hamilton, the convention's most outspoken champion of a stronger central government, was regularly outvoted by his fellow delegates from New York.

Slavery in the United States, 1790

State	Total Population	Slave Population	Percent Slave Population
Connecticut	238,000	2,648	1.11
Delaware	59,000	8,887	15.06
Georgia	83,000	29,264	35.26
Maryland	320,000	103,036	32.20
Massachusetts	476,000	0	0.0
New Hampshire	142,000	157	0.11
New Jersey	184,000	11,423	6.21
New York	340,000	21,193	6.23
North Carolina	394,000	100,783	25.58
Pennsylvania	434,000	3,707	0.85
Rhode Island	69,000	958	1.39
South Carolina	249,000	107,094	43.01
Virginia	692,000	292,627	42.29

SOURCES: *Historical Statistics of Black America;*
Historical Statistics of the United States, Colonial Times to 1970

Interpreting Tables The agricultural economy of the southern States relied on slave labor to produce cotton, tobacco, and other crops. *Why did the southern States want slaves counted in their States' total population?*

States feared that they would not be able to protect their interests. Tempers flared on both sides. The debate became so intense that Benjamin Franklin suggested that "henceforth prayers imploring the assistance of Heaven . . . be held in this Assembly every morning before we proceed to business."

The Connecticut Compromise

The conflict was finally settled by a compromise suggested by the Connecticut delegation. Under the **Connecticut Compromise**, it was agreed that Congress should be composed of two houses. In the smaller Senate, the States would be represented equally. In the House, the representation of each State would be based upon its population.

Thus, by combining basic features of the rival Virginia and New Jersey Plans, the convention's most serious dispute was resolved. The agreement satisfied the smaller States in particular, and it made it possible for them to support the creation of a strong central government.

The Connecticut Compromise was so pivotal to the writing of the Constitution that it has often been called the Great Compromise.

The Three-Fifths Compromise

Once it had been agreed to base the seats in the House on each State's population, this question

arose: Should slaves be counted in the populations of the southern States?

Again debate was fierce. Most delegates from the southern States argued that slaves should be counted. Most of the northerners took the opposing view. The table on this page shows the significant percentage of slaves among the populations of the southern States.

Finally, the Framers agreed to the **Three-Fifths Compromise.** It provided that all "free persons" should be counted, and so, too, should "three-fifths of all other persons." (Article I, Section 2, Clause 3. For "all other persons" read "slaves.") For the three-fifths won by the southerners, the northerners exacted a price. That formula was also to be used in fixing the amount of money to be raised in each State by any direct tax levied by Congress. In short, the southerners could count their slaves, but they would have to pay for them.

This odd compromise disappeared from the Constitution with the adoption of the 13th Amendment, which abolished slavery, in 1865. For 140 years now, there have been no "all other persons" in this country.

The Commerce and Slave Trade Compromise

The convention agreed that Congress had to have the power to regulate foreign and interstate trade. To many southerners that power carried a real danger, however. They worried that Congress, likely to be controlled by northern commercial interests, would act against the interests of the agricultural South.

They were particularly fearful that Congress would try to pay for the new government out of export duties, and southern tobacco was the major American export of the time. They also feared that Congress would interfere with the slave trade.

Before they would agree to the commerce power, the southerners insisted on certain protections. So, according to the **Commerce and Slave Trade Compromise,** Congress was forbidden the power to tax the export of goods from any State. It was also forbidden the power to act on the slave trade for a period of at least 20 years. It could not interfere with "the migration or importation of such persons as any State now existing shall think proper to admit," except for a small head tax, at least until the year 1808.[16]

A "Bundle of Compromises"

The convention spent much of its time, said Franklin, "sawing boards to make them fit." The Constitution drafted at Philadelphia has often been called a "bundle of compromises." These descriptions are apt, if they are properly understood.

There were differences of opinion among the delegates, certainly. After all, the delegates came from 12 different States that were widely separated in geographic and economic terms. The delegates often reflected the interests of their States. Bringing these interests together did require compromise. Indeed, final decisions on issues such as selection of the President, the treaty-making process, the structure of the national court system, and the amendment process were reached as a result of compromise.

But by no means did all, or even most, of what shaped the document come from compromises. The Framers agreed on many of the basic issues they faced. Thus, nearly all the delegates were convinced that a new *national* government, a federal government, had to be created, and had to

---

[16]Article I, Section 9, Clause 1. Congress promptly banned the importation of slaves in 1808, and in 1820 it declared the slave trade to be piracy. The smuggling of the enslaved into this country continued until the outbreak of the Civil War, however.

have the powers necessary to deal with the nation's grave social and economic problems. The Framers were also dedicated to the concepts of popular sovereignty and of limited government. None questioned for a moment the wisdom of representative government. The principles of separation of powers and of checks and balances were accepted almost as a matter of course.

Many disputes did occur, and the compromises by which they were resolved came only after hours and days and even weeks of heated debate. The point here, however, is that the differences were not over the most fundamental of questions. They involved, instead, such vital but lesser points as these: the details of the structure of Congress, the method by which the President was to be chosen, and the practical limits that should be put on the several powers to be given to the new central government.

Sources of the Constitution

The Framers were well educated and widely read. They were familiar with the governments of ancient Greece and Rome and those of contemporary Great Britain and Europe. They knew the political writings of their time, of such works as William Blackstone's *Commentaries on the Laws of England,* the Baron de Montesquieu's *The Spirit of the Laws,* Jean Jacques Rousseau's *Social Contract,* John Locke's *Two Treatises of Government,* and many others.

More immediately, the Framers drew on their own experiences. Remember, they were familiar with the Second Continental Congress, the Articles of Confederation, and their own State governments. Much that went into the Constitution came directly, sometimes word for word, from the Articles. A number of provisions were drawn from the several State constitutions, as well.

The Convention Completes Its Work

For several weeks, through the hot Philadelphia summer, the delegates took up resolution after resolution. Finally, on September 8, a committee was named "to revise the stile of and arrange the articles which had been agreed to" by the

▲ Detail from Washington's chair at the Constitutional Convention.

convention. That group, the Committee of Stile and Arrangement headed by Gouverneur Morris, put the Constitution in its final form.

Then, on September 17, the convention approved its work and 39 names were placed on the finished document.[17] Perhaps none of the Framers were completely satisfied with their work. Nevertheless, wise old Benjamin Franklin put into words what many of the Framers must have thought on that final day:

> **PRIMARY Sources** *"Sir, I agree with this Constitution to all its faults, if they are such; because I think a general Government necessary for us . . . I doubt . . . whether any other Convention we can obtain, may be able to make a better Constitution. For when you assemble a number of men to have the advantage of their joint wisdom, you inevitably assemble with those men, all their prejudices, their passions, their errors of opinion, their local interests, and their selfish views. From such an assembly can a perfect production be*

expected? It therefore astonishes me, Sir, to find this system approaching so near to perfection as it does . . ."
—*Notes* of Debates in the Federal Convention of 1787, James Madison

On Franklin's motion, the Constitution was signed. Madison tells us that

> **PRIMARY Sources** *". . . Doctor Franklin, looking toward the President's chair, at the back of which a rising sun happened to be painted, observed to a few members near him, that Painters had found it difficult to distinguish in their art a rising from a setting sun. I have, said he, often and often in the course of the Session . . . looked at that behind the President without being able to tell whether it was rising or setting. But now at length I have the happiness to know that it is a rising and not a setting sun."*
—*Notes* of Debates in the Federal Convention of 1787, James Madison

---

[17]Three of the 41 delegates present on that last day refused to sign the proposed Constitution: Edmund Randolph of Virginia, who later did support ratification and served as Attorney General and then Secretary of State under President Washington; Elbridge Gerry of Massachusetts, who later became Vice President under Madison; and George Mason of Virginia, who continued to oppose the Constitution until his death in 1792. George Read of Delaware signed both for himself and for his absent colleague John Dickinson.

Section 4 Assessment

Key Terms and Main Ideas

1. Identify the **Framers** of the Constitution and describe, in general, their backgrounds and experiences.
2. What momentous decision did the Framers make at the beginning of the Philadelphia Convention?
3. Why did the delegates from the smaller States object to the **Virginia Plan?**
4. What was agreed to under the **Connecticut Compromise?**
5. What sources influenced the Framers in writing the Constitution?

Critical Thinking

6. **Making Comparisons** Compare and contrast the Virginia Plan and the New Jersey Plan.
7. **Determining Relevance** The Three-Fifths Compromise and the Commerce and Slave Trade Compromise were included

Standards Monitoring *Online*
For: Self-Quiz and vocabulary practice
Web Code: mqa-1024

in the Constitution at the insistence of the southern States. Why did States in the South think these items were important and what price, if any, did southern States pay for their inclusion?

8. **Drawing Conclusions** The Constitution has been called a "bundle of compromises." Is this an accurate description of the document? Explain your answer.

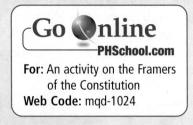

Go **Online**
PHSchool.com

For: An activity on the Framers of the Constitution
Web Code: mqd-1024

Skills for Life

Participating in Public Debates

 Analysis Skill HR4

The process of debating public issues has never been more "transparent" than it is today. That is, the process is more open to public scrutiny. The increase in media outlets, such as cable TV and the Internet, has created opportunities for people to register their opinions. Use your opportunities to voice your opinions by following these steps:

1. Identify the issue(s) of concern to you. Get in the habit of looking at the morning newspaper or the evening news. If you see something of interest, study the topic further rather than basing your opinions on short TV sound bites. What public issue is of most interest to you?

2. Find out whom to contact. Your opinion counts most when you express it to those people who have some authority or influence on the issue. That could be a government official, a private lobbying group, or a media outlet that reaches many voters. Who might you contact to express your views on your topic? Why?

3. Decide on a strategy for publicizing your opinions. Decide on the best way to get your ideas across. Consider your communications skills—do you express yourself better through speaking or through writing? Which of the strategies in the box at right would be best for you?

4. Present your ideas. Generally, a battle to win the hearts and minds of your fellow citizens is won on the strength of good ideas well presented. What short-term and long-term goals might you seek through participating in public debates?

Indiana teenager Ryan White became a nationally known political activist, speaking and lobbying on behalf of the rights of AIDS patients, prior to his death from AIDS in 1990, at age 19.

Test for Success

Choose an issue that is being publicly debated right now. Follow the steps listed here to develop a strategy for airing your views about it. Write a brief letter to the editor or a newsgroup posting, or prepare an oral argument on the issue.

Make Your Opinions Known

▶ Write a letter to the editor. Your letter should be brief, quickly stating the issue, your opinion, and facts to support your opinion. Letters that are well-reasoned may have more influence than hostile or insulting prose.

▶ Contact a government official or agency. Find out who the decision makers are on your issue.

▶ Join a public interest group or other lobbying organization. You might want to work for a cause you believe in. Find out if there are any requirements for joining, such as fees.

▶ Join an Internet chatroom or newsgroup. Live, "real time" chatrooms let you participate in actual conversations and debates. Consult with your teacher about appropriate groups.

▶ Address a government hearing on an issue of concern to you. Come prepared with facts and a few specific points to make. Be prepared to rebut any opposing arguments.

▶ Participate in a public protest or demonstration of support. Coming together with other activists to rally support and send a loud message can be an exciting way to participate in public debate, if the event is legal and orderly.

▶ Participate in a petition drive. A great way to register grassroots support for an issue or a specific bill is to gather signatures for a petition. You'll learn more about petitions in Chapter 24.

Section Preview

OBJECTIVES

1. **Identify** the opposing sides in the fight for ratification and describe the major arguments for and against the Constitution.
2. **Describe** the inauguration of the new government of the United States of America.

WHY IT MATTERS

The Constitution could not take effect until it had been ratified by nine States. The battle between those who supported and those who opposed the Constitution was hard fought in all the States.

POLITICAL DICTIONARY

★ **Federalists**
★ **Anti-Federalists**
★ **quorum**

oday, the Constitution of the United States is the object of extraordinary respect and admiration, both here and abroad. But in 1787 and 1788, it was widely criticized, and in every State there were many who opposed its adoption. The battle over the ratification of the Constitution was not easily decided.

The Fight for Ratification

Remember, the Articles of Confederation provided that changes could be made to them only if all of the State legislatures agreed. But the new Constitution was intended to replace, not amend, the Articles. The Framers had seen how crippling the unanimity requirement could be. So, the new Constitution provided that

FROM THE *Constitution* **"** *The ratification of the conventions of nine States shall be sufficient for the establishment of this Constitution between the States so ratifying the same.* **"**

—Article VII

The Congress of the Confederation agreed to this irregular procedure. After a short debate, it sent copies of the new document to the States on September 28, 1787.

Federalists and Anti-Federalists

The Constitution was printed, circulated, and debated vigorously. Two groups quickly emerged in each of the States: the **Federalists,** who favored ratification, and the **Anti-Federalists,** who opposed it.

The Federalists were led by many of those who had attended the Philadelphia Convention. Among them, the most active and the most effective were James Madison and Alexander Hamilton. Their opposition was headed by such well-known Revolutionary War figures as Patrick Henry, Richard Henry Lee, John Hancock, and Samuel Adams.

The Federalists stressed the weaknesses of the Articles. They argued that the many difficulties facing the Republic could be overcome only by a new government based on the proposed Constitution.

The Anti-Federalists attacked nearly every part of the new document. Many objected to the ratification process, to the absence of any mention of God, to the denial to the States of

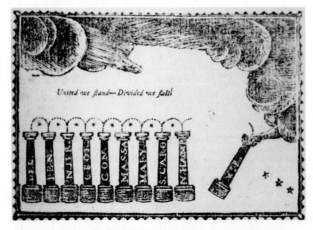

United we stand—Divided we fall!

▲ *Interpreting Political Cartoons* This cartoon, printed in the New Hampshire *Gazette* on June 26, 1788, shows the States as pillars, with nine upright and a tenth being raised. *What is the message of the words in the cartoon?*

a power to print money, and to many other features of the Framers' proposals.

Two major features of the proposed Constitution drew the heaviest fire: (1) the greatly increased powers of the central government and (2) the lack of a bill of rights. The proposed document did not provide for such basic liberties as freedom of speech, press, and religion, nor for the rights of fair trial. At Virginia's ratifying convention, Patrick Henry said of the proposed Constitution, "I look upon that paper as the most fatal plan that could possibly be conceived to enslave a free people."

Nine States Ratify

The contest for ratification was close in several States, but the Federalists finally won in all of them. Delaware was the first State to ratify. On June 21, 1788, New Hampshire brought the number of ratifying States to nine.

Under Article VII, New Hampshire's ratification should have brought the Constitution into effect, but it did not. Neither Virginia nor New York had yet ratified, and without either of these key States the new government could not hope to succeed.

Virginia's Ratification

Virginia's vote for ratification followed New Hampshire's by just four days. The brilliant debates in its convention were followed closely throughout the State. The Federalists were led by Madison, the young John Marshall, and Governor Edmund Randolph (even though he had refused to sign the Constitution at Philadelphia). Patrick Henry, leading the opposition, was joined by such outstanding Virginians as James Monroe, Richard Henry Lee, and George Mason (another of the non-signers).

Although George Washington was not one of the delegates to Virginia's convention, his strong support for ratification proved vital. With Madison, he was able to get a reluctant Jefferson to support the document. Had Jefferson fought as did other Anti-Federalists, Virginia might never have ratified the Constitution.

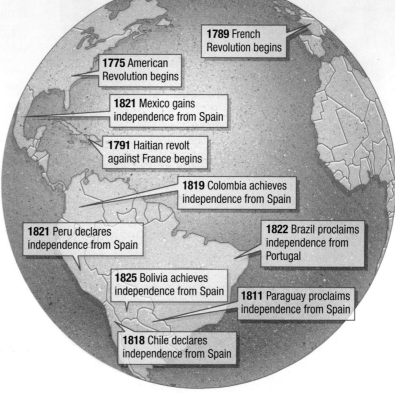

1789 French Revolution begins

1775 American Revolution begins

1821 Mexico gains independence from Spain

1791 Haitian revolt against France begins

1819 Colombia achieves independence from Spain

1821 Peru declares independence from Spain

1822 Brazil proclaims independence from Portugal

1825 Bolivia achieves independence from Spain

1811 Paraguay proclaims independence from Spain

1818 Chile declares independence from Spain

Interpreting Maps The American Revolution was one of many struggles for independence that took place around the world between 1775 and 1825. **Do you think this global turmoil was coincidence, or were the events in various countries somehow connected?**

Ratification of the Constitution

State	Date	Vote
Delaware	December 7, 1787	30–0
Pennsylvania	December 12, 1787	46–23
New Jersey	December 18, 1787	38–0
Georgia	January 2, 1788	26–0
Connecticut	January 9, 1788	128–40
Massachusetts	February 6, 1788	187–168
Maryland	April 28, 1788	63–11
South Carolina	May 23, 1788	149–73
New Hampshire	June 21, 1788	57–46
Virginia	June 25, 1788	89–79
New York	July 26, 1788	30–27
North Carolina	November 21, 1789*	195–77
Rhode Island	May 29, 1790	34–32

*Second vote; ratification was originally defeated on August 4, 1788, by a vote of 184–84.

Interpreting Tables Virginia's ratification came only after a long struggle. **In what other States was ratification won by only a narrow margin?**

▲ **Defending the Constitution** All the essays in *The Federalist* were signed with the pen name Publius. Modern scholars attribute fifty-one to Hamilton (right), five to Jay (left), and twenty-nine to Madison. **H-SS 12.1.4**

New York, The Last Key State

A narrow vote in the New York convention brought the number of States to 11, on July 26. New York ratified only after a long battle. The Anti-Federalists were led by Governor George Clinton and by two of the State's three delegates to the Philadelphia Convention.[18]

The contest in New York gave rise to a remarkable campaign document: *The Federalist.* It was a collection of 85 essays supporting the Constitution written by Alexander Hamilton, James Madison, and John Jay. Those essays were first published as letters to the people in various newspapers of the State and soon were collected in book form. Though written in haste, they remain an excellent commentary on the Constitution, and are among the best political writings in the English language.

Inaugurating the Government

On September 13, 1788, with 11 of the 13 States "under the federal roof," the Congress of the Confederation paved the way for its successor.[19] It chose New York as the temporary capital.[20] It set the first Wednesday in January as the date on which the States would choose presidential electors. The first Wednesday in February was set as the date on which those electors would vote, and the first Wednesday in March as the date for the inauguration of the new government.

The new Congress convened on March 4, 1789. It met in Federal Hall, on Wall Street in New York City. But because it lacked a **quorum** (majority), it could not count the electoral votes until April 6. Finally, on that day, it found that George Washington had been elected President by a unanimous vote. John Adams was elected Vice President with a substantial majority.

On April 30, after an historic trip from Mount Vernon to New York, Washington took the oath of office as the first President of the United States.

---

[18]Robert Yates and John Lansing had quit Philadelphia in July, arguing that the convention had gone beyond its authority. Like many other Anti-Federalist leaders, Governor Clinton later supported the Constitution.

[19]Neither North Carolina nor Rhode Island had ratified the new Constitution before it became effective. As you can see in the table on page 57, the Constitution failed in a first convention in North Carolina and was finally approved by a second one in late November of 1789. Rhode Island did not hold a ratifying convention until May of 1790, more than a year after Washington's inauguration.

[20]The District of Columbia did not become the nation's capital until 1800. Congress moved its sessions from New York to Philadelphia in December 1790. It held its first meeting in the new "federal city," Washington, D.C., on November 17, 1800.

Section 5 Assessment

Key Terms and Main Ideas

1. What was the **Federalist** position on the adoption of the Constitution? Why did they feel that way?
2. Who were the **Anti-Federalists**?
3. What was "irregular" about the ratification of the Constitution?

Critical Thinking

4. **Expressing Problems Clearly** Why might the failure of New York and Virginia to ratify have doomed the Constitution?
5. **Understanding Point of View** The Anti-Federalists were greatly concerned that the proposed Constitution increased the powers of the central government and lacked a bill of rights. Why would these specific issues have been important to them?

Standards Monitoring *Online*

For: Self-Quiz and vocabulary practice
Web Code: mqa-1025

Go Online
PHSchool.com

For: An activity on the Federalist Papers
Web Code: mqd-1025

Is Flag-Burning "Free Speech"?

Analysis Skills HR4, HI3, HI4

Free speech, one of Americans' most cherished freedoms, is commonly thought of in terms of spoken or printed words. Yet speech also can take the form of a symbolic action, like the burning of an American flag. Does the reverence with which most Americans regard the flag override our commitment to free speech? In other words, can the government restrict the ways in which national symbols such as the flag can be used in protests?

United States v. Eichman (1990)

In the 1989 case *Texas* v. *Johnson*, the Supreme Court struck down a State law that forbade the destruction of the United States flag. That law, ruled the Court, violated the 1st Amendment guarantee of free expression. Congress reacted to the decision by passing the Flag Protection Act of 1989, which stated that anyone who "knowingly mutilates, defaces, physically defiles, burns, maintains on the floor or ground, or tramples upon" a United States flag can be prosecuted. (Disposing of worn or soiled flags was permitted under the law.) Violators could be fined or imprisoned for up to one year.

The United States prosecuted Eichman and others for knowingly setting fire to several American flags. These flag-burnings took place both on the steps of the Capitol (to protest certain government policies) and in Seattle (to protest the passage of the Flag Protection Act itself).

The defendants asked the courts to dismiss the charges on the grounds that the Act violated the 1st Amendment. They cited *Texas* v. *Johnson* as giving 1st Amendment protection to flag-burning as a means of expression. Federal courts in Washington State and the District of Columbia both ruled that the Act was unconstitutional. The Federal Government then appealed these decisions to the Supreme Court.

Arguments for the United States

1. The Flag Protection Act does not outlaw flag-burning in order to prevent the expression of a particular point of view. Rather, it prohibits mistreatment of the flag for any reason in order to protect the flag's identity as a national symbol.

2. Desecration (abuse) of the flag is deeply offensive to many Americans. The government should have the right to protect its national symbols against mistreatment.

3. Protection of the flag would not interfere with protesters' ability to express their opinions by other means.

Arguments for Eichman

1. The government's effort to protect the flag limits the free expression of opposition to government policies.

2. The destruction of a flag does not diminish the flag's importance as a symbol of this country.

3. Although many people are offended by flag desecration, the government cannot prohibit expression of ideas simply because the ideas may be offensive or disagreeable to many people.

Decide for Yourself

1. Review the constitutional grounds on which each side based its arguments and the specific arguments each side presented.

2. Debate the opposing viewpoints presented in this case. Which viewpoint do you favor?

3. Predict the impact of the Court's decision on ways in which people may choose to protest government policies. (To read a summary of the Court's decision, turn to pages 799–806.)

Go Online
PHSchool.com
Use Web Code mqp-1028 to register your vote on this issue and to see how other students voted.

limited government (p. 29), representative government (p. 29), Magna Carta (p. 29), Petition of Right (p. 30), English Bill of Rights (p. 30), charter (p. 31), bicameral (p. 31), proprietary (p. 32), unicameral (p. 32), confederation (p. 35), Albany Plan of Union (p. 35), delegate (p. 36), boycott (p. 36), repeal (p. 37), popular sovereignty (p. 39), Articles of Confederation (p. 44), ratification (p. 44), presiding officer (p. 45), Framers (p. 48), Virginia Plan (p. 51), New Jersey Plan (p. 51), Connecticut Compromise (p. 52), Three-Fifths Compromise (p. 52), Commerce and Slave Trade Compromise (p. 53), Federalists (p. 56), Anti-Federalists (p. 56), quorum (p. 58)

Standards Review

H-SS 12.1.1 Analyze the influence of ancient Greek, Roman, English, and leading European political thinkers such as John Locke, Charles-Louis Montesquieu, Niccolo` Machiavelli, and William Blackstone on the development of American government.

H-SS 12.1.3 Explain how the U.S. Constitution reflects a balance between the classical republican concern with promotion of the public good and the classical liberal concern with protecting individual rights; and discuss how the basic premises of liberal constitutionalism and democracy are joined in the Declaration of Independence as "self-evident truths."

H-SS 12.1.4 Explain how the Founding Fathers' realistic view of human nature led directly to the establishment of a constitutional system that limited the power of the governors and the governed as articulated in the *Federalist Papers*.

H-SS 12.1.6 Understand that the Bill of Rights limits the powers of the federal government and state governments.

H-SS 12.3.3 Discuss the historical role of religion and religious diversity.

H-SS 12.4.1 Discuss Article I of the Constitution as it relates to the legislative branch, including eligibility for office and lengths of terms of representatives and senators; election to office; the roles of the House and Senate in impeachment proceedings; the role of the vice president; the enumerated legislative powers; and the process by which a bill becomes a law.

H-SS 12.7.1 Explain how conflicts between levels of government and branches of government are resolved.

H-SS 12.10 Students formulate questions about and defend their analyses of tensions within our constitutional democracy and the importance of maintaining a balance between the following concepts: majority rule and individual rights; liberty and equality; state and national authority in a federal system; civil disobedience and the rule of law; freedom of the press and the right to a fair trial; the relationship of religion and government.

Practicing the Vocabulary

Using Words in Context *For each of the terms below, write a sentence that shows how it relates to this chapter.*

1. Articles of Confederation
2. Three-Fifths Compromise
3. charter
4. boycott
5. bicameral
6. ratification
7. proprietary
8. Commerce and Slave Trade Compromise

Word Relationships *Three of the terms in each of the following sets of terms are related. Choose the term that does not belong and explain why it does not belong.*

9. (a) Magna Carta (b) Albany Plan of Union (c) English Bill of Rights (d) Petition of Right
10. (a) Articles of Confederation (b) Virginia Plan (c) New Jersey Plan (d) Connecticut Compromise
11. (a) Framers (b) Federalists (c) Anti-Federalists (d) boycott
12. (a) limited government (b) popular sovereignty (c) ratification (d) representative government

Reviewing Main Ideas

Section 1

13. What three ideas about government did the colonists bring with them from England?
14. How was the development of English government affected by (a) the Magna Carta? (b) The Petition of Right? (c) The English Bill of Rights?
15. Outline the development of colonial government.

Section 2

16. Describe how the British governed the colonies (a) before 1760. (b) After 1760.
17. (a) Who wrote the Declaration of Independence? (b) What rights are outlined in the document? (c) How did they signify the colonists' relationship to Britain?
18. Describe the common features of the first State constitutions.

Section 3

19. What were the major characteristics of the Articles of Confederation?
20. How did the States respond to the weaknesses of the Articles of Confederation?

Section 4

21. Explain the New Jersey Plan. Why was it introduced?
22. What major issues did the Framers disagree upon and what, if any, compromises did they reach?

Section 5

23. Why did the Federalists want to replace the Articles?
24. What were the main arguments used by the Anti-Federalists?
25. Why was ratification by Virginia and New York essential for the success of the Constitution?

Critical Thinking Skills

Analysis Skills HR4, HI4, HI6

26. ***Applying the Chapter Skill*** There are a number of interest groups that focus on 1st Amendment issues. Contact a group that takes a stand on an issue that interests you, and find out what its position is, how it goes about promoting its cause, and how successful the group has been. Summarize this information, and state whether you think the group is one that you might wish to join.

27. ***Recognizing Ideologies*** The Second Continental Congress became, in effect, this country's first national government. **(a)** Why did the British condemn it as an unlawful assembly and a den of traitors? **(b)** How might the king and his ministers have avoided the Revolution?

28. ***Formulating Questions*** Weaknesses in the Articles of Confederation surfaced during the Critical Period in American history. Write three questions that will help you understand why many leaders of the day urged a stronger national government, and how they could achieve this.

29. ***Checking Consistency*** How does the history of America from the 1600s to 1789 demonstrate that "questions of politics and economics are, in fact, inseparable"?

Analyzing Political Cartoons

Using your knowledge of American government and this cartoon, answer the questions below.

30. This cartoon, originally published by Benjamin Franklin in 1754, appeared in several versions during the American Revolution. **(a)** What do the segments of the snake represent? **(b)** How do you know?

31. **(a)** What is the message of the cartoon? **(b)** In your opinion, is this cartoon an effective means of persuasion? Why or why not?

★ You Can Make a Difference

Is there a particular issue that you feel is not being properly handled in your school or community, such as a safety problem, an issue of privacy, or a dispute between groups of students? Who is responsible for dealing with the matter—a school official, a student organization, or some other person or group? Write a letter to your school's newspaper in which you **(a)** describe the matter that concerns you and **(b)** suggest steps that could be taken to resolve it.

Participation Activities

Analysis Skills CS1, HR1, HI1

32. ***Current Events Watch*** The Framers drew on their skills, knowledge, and experience in creating the Constitution. What kinds of experience and training do political leaders draw on today? Select a current political leader—a member of Congress or the governor of your State, for example—and write a brief biography of this person. Your biographical sketch should identify the skills, knowledge, and experience that person draws upon in his or her current position.

33. ***Time Line Activity*** Using information from the chapter, create a time line showing the steps that led to the ratification of the Constitution. Include at least eight entries in your time line. You might begin with the First Continental Congress of 1774. What, in your opinion, was the most important step in the process? Why?

34. ***It's Your Turn*** It is 1788. Write a letter to the editor of your local paper in which you express your opinion on whether or not the Constitution should be ratified. First, create a list of what you see as the positive aspects of the document. Then, list the negative features. Note any suggestions you have for improvements. Next, write a draft of the letter in which you politely offer your ideas. Revise your letter, making certain that each idea is clearly explained. Proofread your letter and draft a final copy. **(Writing a Letter)**

Standards Monitoring *Online*

For: Chapter 2 Self-Test **Visit:** PHSchool.com
Web Code: mqa-1026

As a final review, take the Magruder's Chapter 2 Self-Test and receive immediate feedback on your answers. The test consists of 20 multiple-choice questions designed to test your understanding of the chapter content.

CHAPTER 3

The Constitution

"These principles form the bright constellation which has gone before us and guided our steps through an age of revolution and reformation."
—Thomas Jefferson (1801)

The Constitution rests on a set of basic principles that make the government of this country unique in the history of the world. Those basic principles have endured and they are intact today—despite the fact that the Constitution has been changed in various ways over the course of the past 200 years.

◆ George Washington presiding over the Constitutional Convention

Standards Preview

H-SS 12.1.4 Explain how the Founding Fathers' realistic view of human nature led directly to the establishment of a constitutional system that limited the power of the governors and the governed as articulated in the *Federalist Papers*.

H-SS 12.1.5 Describe the systems of separated and shared powers, the role of organized interests (*Federalist Paper Number 10*), checks and balances (*Federalist Paper Number 51*), the importance of an independent judiciary (*Federalist Paper Number 78*), enumerated powers, rule of law, federalism, and civilian control of the military.

H-SS 12.1.6 Understand that the Bill of Rights limits the powers of the federal government and state governments.

H-SS 12.4.2 Explain the process through which the Constitution can be amended.

H-SS 12.6.1 Analyze the origin, development, and role of political parties, noting those occasional periods in which there was only one major party or were more than two major parties.

H-SS 12.7.1 Explain how conflicts between levels of government and branches of government are resolved.

H-SS 12.10 Students formulate questions about and defend their analyses of tensions within our constitutional democracy and the importance of maintaining a balance between the following concepts: majority rule and individual rights; liberty and equality; state and national authority in a federal system; civil disobedience and the rule of law; freedom of the press and the right to a fair trial; the relationship of religion and government.

SECTION 1

The Six Basic Principles (pp. 64–70)

★ The Constitution sets out the six basic principles and the framework of government in the United States.

★ In this country, the people are sovereign and government is limited, not all-powerful.

★ The Constitution distributes powers among three separate branches of government: legislative, executive, and judicial.

★ Each of those branches has powers with which it can check the operations of the other two branches.

★ The Constitution also distributes governmental powers on a geographic basis, in a federal system.

SECTION 2

Formal Amendment (pp. 72–77)

★ Since 1789, 27 amendments have been added to the Constitution.

★ The formal amendment process reflects both federalism and popular sovereignty.

★ The first ten amendments, known as the Bill of Rights, guarantee several basic freedoms.

★ Formal amendments may be added through four different methods.

SECTION 3

Constitutional Change by Other Means (pp. 79–82)

★ Over time, many changes have been made in the Constitution by means other than formal amendment.

★ Those changes have not involved any changes in the written words of the Constitution.

★ The major agents of those changes have been Congress, various Presidents, the courts, political parties, and custom.

1 The Six Basic Principles

Section Preview

OBJECTIVES

1. **Outline** the important elements of the Constitution.
2. **List** the six basic principles of the Constitution.

WHY IT MATTERS

The Constitution is a brief, straightforward document that has guided American government for over 200 years. Its authors wrote the Constitution based on the principles that political power resides with the people, and that the National Government should be limited and divided into three branches to limit the power of any one of those three branches.

POLITICAL DICTIONARY

★ **Preamble**
★ **articles**
★ **constitutionalism**
★ **rule of law**
★ **separation of powers**
★ **checks and balances**
★ **veto**
★ **judicial review**
★ **unconstitutional**
★ **federalism**

The Constitution of the United States dates from the latter part of the eighteenth century. It was written in 1787, and took effect in 1789. The fact that the Constitution is more than 200 years old does *not* mean, however, that now, in the twenty-first century, it is only an interesting historical artifact, fit for museums and dusty shelves. On the contrary, it remains a vitally important and vibrant document.

The Constitution is this nation's fundamental law. It is, by its own terms, "the supreme Law of the Land"—the highest form of law in the United States.

An Outline of the Constitution

The Constitution sets out the basic principles upon which government in the United States was built and operates today. The document lays out the basic framework and procedures of our government, and sets out the limits within which that government must conduct itself.

The Constitution is a fairly brief document. Its little more than 7,000 words can be read in half an hour. You will find the text of the Constitution beginning on page 758. As you read it, remember that this brief document has successfully guided this nation through two centuries of tremendous growth and change. One of the Constitution's greatest strengths is that it deals largely with matters of basic principle. Unlike most other constitutions—those of the 50 States and those of most other nations—the Constitution of the United States is not weighted down with detailed and cumbersome provisions.

As you read the Constitution, you will also see that it is organized in a simple and straightforward way. It begins with a short, noteworthy

► Although the members of the Federal Government are continually changing, from leaders of the past like Senator Henry Cabot Lodge (R., Massachusetts) to contemporary lawmakers such as Senator Mary Landrieu (D., Louisiana), the Constitution provides a lasting link between the past and present.

introduction, the **Preamble,** and the balance of the original document is divided into seven numbered sections called **articles.** The first three articles deal with the three branches of the National Government: Congress, the presidency, and the federal court system. These articles outline the basic organization and powers of each branch and the methods by which the members of Congress, the President and Vice President, and federal judges are chosen. Article IV deals mostly with the place of the States in the American Union and with their relationship with the National Government and with one another. Article V explains how formal amendments may be added to the document. Article VI declares that the Constitution is the nation's supreme law; Article VII provided for the ratification of the Constitution.

The seven articles of the original document are followed by 27 amendments, printed in the order in which they were adopted.

The Basic Principles

The Constitution is built around six basic principles: popular sovereignty, limited government, separation of powers, checks and balances, judicial review, and federalism.

Popular Sovereignty

In the United States, all political power resides in the people. The people are sovereign. They are the *only* source for any and all governmental power. Government can govern only with the consent of the governed.

The principle of popular sovereignty, so boldly proclaimed by the Declaration of Independence, is

Articles of the Constitution	
Section	**Subject**
Preamble	States the purpose of the Constitution
Article I	Legislative branch
Article II	Executive branch
Article III	Judicial branch
Article IV	Relations among the States
Article V	Amending the Constitution
Article VI	National debts, supremacy of national law, and oaths of office
Article VII	Ratifying the Constitution

Interpreting Tables The Constitution sets up the basic structure of our Federal Government. ***How do the first three articles differ from those that follow?***

woven throughout the Constitution. In its very opening words, in the Preamble, the Constitution declares: "We the People of the United States . . . do ordain and establish this Constitution for the United States of America."

In essence, the National Government draws its power from the people of the United States, and the people have given their government the power that it has through the Constitution. Similarly, each one of the State governments draws its authority from the people of that State, through that State's constitution.

Limited Government

The principle of limited government holds that no government is all-powerful, that a government may do *only* those things that the people have given it the power to do.

In effect, the principle of limited government is the other side of the coin of popular sovereignty. It is that principle stated the other way around: The people are the only source of any and all of government's authority; and government has only that authority the people have given to it.

The concept of limited government can be expressed another way: Government must obey the law. Stated this way, the principle is often called **constitutionalism**—that is, that government must be conducted according to constitutional

▲ **The Rule of Law** During the Watergate scandal prosecutors accused many of President Richard Nixon's closest advisers of breaking the law. This poster implies that Nixon shared their guilt and would soon be exposed. **H-SS 12.10**

principles. The concept of limited government is also described as the **rule of law,** which holds that government and its officers are always subject to—never above—the law.

In large part, the Constitution is a statement of limited government. Much of it reads as clear prohibitions of power to government.[1] For example, notice the Constitution's guarantees of freedom of expression. Those great guarantees—of freedom of religion, of speech, of press, of assembly, and of petition—are vital to democratic government. They are set out in the First Amendment, which begins with the words: "Congress shall make no law. . . ."

Separation of Powers

Recall the brief discussion of the parliamentary and the presidential forms of government in

---

[1]See, especially, Article I, Sections 9 and 10; the 1st through the 10th amendments; and the 13th, 14th, 15th, 19th, 24th, and 26th amendments.

Section 2 of Chapter 1. In a parliamentary system the legislative, executive, and judicial powers of government are all gathered in the hands of a single agency. British government is a leading example. In a presidential system, these basic powers are distributed—separated—among three distinct and independent branches of the government.

This concept is known as **separation of powers.** The idea had been written into each of the State constitutions adopted during the Revolution. A classic expression of the doctrine can be found in the Massachusetts constitution of 1780:

PRIMARY Sources *"In the government of this commonwealth, the legislative department shall never exercise the executive and judicial powers, or either of them: The executive shall never exercise the legislative and judicial powers, or either of them: The judicial shall never exercise the legislative and executive powers, or either of them: to the end it may be a government of laws and not of men. "*

—Part the First, Article XXX

The Constitution of the United States distributes the powers of the National Government among the Congress (the legislative branch), the President (the executive branch), and the courts (the judicial branch). This separation of powers is clearly set forth in the opening words of each of the first three Articles of the Constitution.

Article I, Section 1 declares: "All legislative Powers herein granted shall be vested in a Congress of the United States. . . ." Thus, Congress is the lawmaking branch of the National Government.

Article II, Section 1 declares: "The executive Power shall be vested in a President of the United States of America." Thus, the President is given the law-executing, law-enforcing, law-administering powers of the National Government.

Article III, Section 1 declares: "The judicial Power of the United States shall be vested in one supreme Court, and in such inferior Courts as the Congress may from time to time ordain and establish." Thus, the federal courts, and most importantly the Supreme Court, interpret and apply the laws of the United States in cases brought before them.

Remember, the Framers of the Constitution intended to create a stronger government for the United States. Yet they also intended to limit the powers of that government. The doctrine of separation of powers was designed to that end.

Defending this arrangement, James Madison wrote:

PRIMARY Sources *"The accumulation of all powers, legislative, executive, and judiciary, in the same hands, whether of one, a few, or many . . . may justly be pronounced the very definition of tyranny."*
—The Federalist No. 47

Checks and Balances

The National Government is organized around three separate branches. As you have just seen, the Constitution gives to each branch its own field of governmental authority: legislative, executive, and judicial.

These three branches are not entirely separated nor completely independent of one another. Rather, they are tied together by a complex system of **checks and balances.** This means that each branch is subject to a number of constitutional checks (restraints) by the other branches. In other words, each branch has certain powers with which it can check the operations of the other two.

The chart on the next page describes the major features of the check-and-balance arrangement. As you can see, the Congress has the power to make law, but the President may **veto** (reject) any act of Congress. In its turn, Congress can override a presidential veto by a two-thirds vote in each house. Congress can refuse to provide funds requested by the President, or the Senate may refuse to approve a treaty or an appointment made by the President. The President is the commander in chief of the armed forces, but Congress provides that military force; and so on.

The chart also shows how the system of checks and balances links the judicial branch to the legislative and the executive branches. The President has the power to name all federal judges. Each appointment, however, must be approved by a majority vote in the Senate. At the same time, the courts have the power to determine the constitutionality of acts of Congress and of presidential actions, and to strike down those they find unconstitutional.

Head-on clashes between the branches do not often happen. The checks-and-balances system operates all the time, however, and in routine fashion. The very fact that it exists—that each branch has its several checks—affects much of what happens in Washington, D.C.

For example, when the President picks someone to serve in some important office in the executive branch—as, say, secretary of state or director of the Central Intelligence Agency (CIA)—the President is quite aware that the Senate must confirm that appointment. So, the President is apt to pick someone who very likely will be approved by the Senate. In a similar sense, when Congress makes law, it does so with a careful eye on both the President's veto power and the power of the courts to review its actions.

Spectacular clashes—direct applications of the check-and-balance system—do sometimes occur, of course. The President does veto some acts of Congress. On rare occasion, Congress does override one of those vetoes. And, even

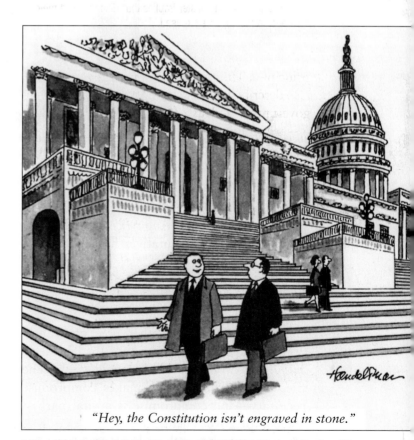

"Hey, the Constitution isn't engraved in stone."

Interpreting Political Cartoons Is the Constitution "carved in stone"? Why or why not?

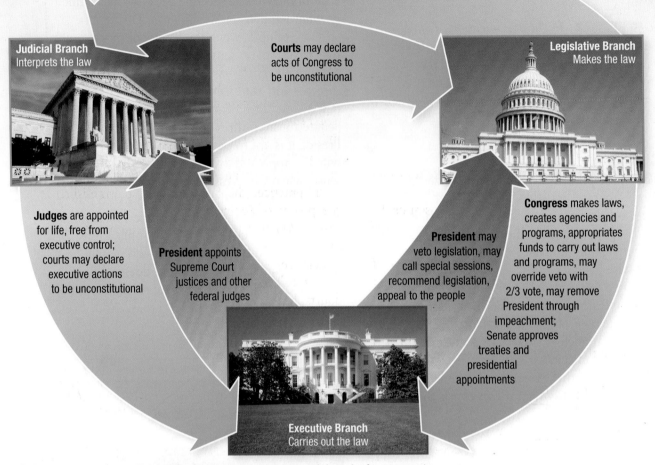

Congress creates lower courts, may remove judges through impeachment; Senate approves or rejects appointment of judges

Judicial Branch Interprets the law

Courts may declare acts of Congress to be unconstitutional

Legislative Branch Makes the law

Judges are appointed for life, free from executive control; courts may declare executive actions to be unconstitutional

President appoints Supreme Court justices and other federal judges

President may veto legislation, may call special sessions, recommend legislation, appeal to the people

Congress makes laws, creates agencies and programs, appropriates funds to carry out laws and programs, may override veto with 2/3 vote, may remove President through impeachment; Senate approves treaties and presidential appointments

Executive Branch Carries out the law

Interpreting Diagrams Under the system of checks and balances, each branch of government can check the actions of the others. *In what way can the power of the judiciary be checked by the other branches?* **H-SS 12.1.5**

more rarely, the Senate does reject one of the President's appointees. And twice in our history, the House of Representatives has impeached, or brought charges against, a President—Andrew Johnson in 1868 and Bill Clinton in 1998—although on both occasions the President was acquitted by the Senate.

But, again, these and other direct confrontations are not common. Congress, the President, and even the courts try to avoid them. The check-and-balance system makes compromise necessary—and compromise is a vital part of democratic government.

Over time, the check-and-balance system has worked quite well. It has done what the Framers

intended it to do. It has prevented "an unjust combination of the majority." At the same time, the system of checks and balances has not often forestalled a close working relationship between the executive and legislative branches of the Federal Government.

Note, however, that that working relationship runs more smoothly when the President and a majority in both houses of Congress have been of the same political party. When the other party controls one or both houses, partisan friction and conflict play a larger than usual part in that relationship.

Through most of our history, the President and a majority of the members of both houses of

Congress have been of the same party. Over the past 50 years or so, however, the American people have become quite familiar with divided government—that is, with split control, with a political environment in which one of the major parties occupies the White House and the other controls Congress.

That is not the situation today. The Republican Party has firm control of both the executive and legislative branches of the National Government—and it strengthened that dominant position with decisive victories in both the presidential and the congressional elections of 2004.

Judicial Review

One aspect of the principle of checks and balances is of such overriding importance in the American constitutional system that it stands, by itself, as one of that system's basic principles: judicial review.

The power of **judicial review** is the power of courts to determine whether what government does is in accord with what the Constitution provides. More precisely, judicial review may be defined this way: It is the power of a court to determine the constitutionality of a governmental action.

In part, then, judicial review is the power to declare **unconstitutional**—to declare illegal, null and void, of no force and effect—a governmental action found to violate some provision in the Constitution. The power of judicial review is held by all federal courts and by most State courts, as well.[2]

The Constitution does not provide for judicial review in so many words. Yet it seems clear that the Framers intended that the federal courts, and in particular the Supreme Court, should have that power. In *The Federalist* No. 78 Alexander Hamilton wrote that "independent judges" would prove to be "an essential safeguard against the effects of occasional ill humors in society." In *The Federalist* No. 51 James Madison called the judicial power one of the "auxiliary precautions" against the possible dominance of one branch of government over another.

In practice, the Supreme Court established the power of judicial review in the landmark case of *Marbury* v. *Madison* in 1803. (We shall take a close look at that case and the doctrine of judicial review in Chapter 18.) Since *Marbury*, the Supreme Court and other federal and State courts have used the power in thousands of cases. For the most part, the courts have

---

[2]Generally, the power is held by all courts of record. These are courts that keep a record of their proceedings and have the power to punish for contempt. Usually, only the lowest courts in a State—justice of the peace courts, for example—are not courts of record.

▲ The Supreme Court has struck down federal laws that regulated child labor and outlawed the burning of the United States flag. *Critical Thinking What characteristic of a law can lead the Supreme Court to overturn it?*

upheld challenged governmental actions. That is, in most cases in which the power of judicial review is exercised, the actions of government are found to be constitutional.

That is not always the case. To date, the Supreme Court has decided some 150 cases in which it has found an act or some part of an act of Congress to be unconstitutional. It has struck down several presidential and other executive branch actions as well. The Court has also voided hundreds of actions of the States and their local governments, including more than 1,100 State laws.

Federalism

As you know, the American governmental system is federal in form. The powers held by government are distributed on a territorial basis. The National Government holds some of those powers, and others belong to the 50 States.

The principle of **federalism**—the division of power among a central government and several regional governments—came to the Constitution out of both experience and

▲ This statue in Concord, Massachusetts, pays tribute to the Minutemen who fought British troops to protect self-government.

necessity. In Philadelphia, the Framers faced a number of difficult problems, not the least of them: How to build a new, stronger, more effective National Government while preserving the existing States and the concept of local self-government.

The colonists had rebelled against the harsh rule of a powerful and distant central government. They had fought for the right to manage their local affairs without the meddling and dictation of the king and his ministers in far-off London. Surely, they would not now agree to another such government.

The Framers found their solution in federalism. In short, they constructed the federal arrangement, with its division of powers, as a compromise. It was an alternative to the system of nearly independent States, loosely tied to one another in the weak Articles of Confederation, and a much feared, too powerful central government. We shall explore the federal system at length in the next chapter.

Section 1 Assessment

Key Terms and Main Ideas

1. What is the purpose of the **Preamble** to the Constitution?
2. List two examples of how **checks and balances** work in the Federal Government.
3. What is the immediate effect if a law is declared **unconstitutional?**
4. Explain **federalism** in your own words.

Critical Thinking

5. **Making Comparisons** What are the different roles of the executive branch, legislative branch, and judicial branch?
6. **Understanding Point of View** Why were the Framers of the Constitution careful to limit the powers of the Federal Government?

Standards Monitoring *Online*
For: Self-Quiz and vocabulary practice
Web Code: mqa-1031

7. **Drawing Conclusions** Some people consider the judicial branch the least democratic of the three branches of the government because federal judges are not elected and cannot be easily removed. How can voters and their elected representatives check the power of the judicial branch?

Go Online
PHSchool.com
For: An activity on the separation of powers
Web Code: mqd-1031

Face the
Issues

The 2nd Amendment

Background *The 2nd Amendment to the Constitution states: "A well-regulated militia being necessary to the security of a free state, the right of the people to keep and bear arms shall not be infringed." The Framers considered the "right to bear arms" one of the basic rights of a free people. For years, Americans have disagreed over how to interpret the Second Amendment. Look over the arguments below. What do you think?*

Citizens rally for gun ownership rights

Analysis Skill HR3

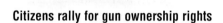

Control Guns in America	**Respect the Right to Bear Arms**

The first part of the amendment states: "A well-regulated militia being necessary to the security of a free state . . ." The Framers of the Constitution clearly intended to guarantee each State the right to maintain armed militia—today's national guard. This was a right that the British had tried to deny the American colonies. The 2nd Amendment was meant to protect the state militias from being disarmed by a despotic central government.

The Supreme Court has agreed with this reading of the Constitution in its few 2nd Amendment cases. In the most important of them, it upheld an act of Congress that requires the owners of certain weapons to register them with the government and pay a $200 license fee. The Court has never found that the 2nd Amendment restricts the ability of States to regulate weapons.

The Framers could not have foreseen the weapons available today. For public safety, gun ownership may be limited according to the wishes of the people by their elected representatives.

The 2nd Amendment clearly spells out an individual's right to own guns. The amendment's main clause says: "[T]he right of the people to keep and bear arms shall not be infringed." The 2nd Amendment is meant to protect individuals from being disarmed today as the colonists were in the 1770s.

The right to own arms, like much in the Constitution, has its roots in English law. The English Bill of Rights (1689) allowed Protestants to own arms for their own defense. Moreover, several early colonial laws went so far as to require civilians to own guns.

The leaders of the Revolution were enthusiastic proponents of widespread gun ownership as a protection against despotic government. "Unfortunately, nothing will preserve [the public liberty] but downright force," said Patrick Henry, "the great object is that every man be armed."

Constitutional rights must be respected by legislators and the courts. Gun ownership, like freedom of religion and the press, is a fundamental right of all law-abiding Americans.

Exploring the Issues

1. Why do supporters of gun rights often point to early English law to support their arguments?

2. Is public safety a sound reason for limiting constitutional rights? Why or why not?

For more information on the right to bear arms, view "Gun Ownership."

Face the
Issues
Video Collection

Formal Amendment

Section Preview

OBJECTIVES

1. **Identify** the four different ways by which the Constitution may be formally changed.
2. **Explain** how the formal amendment process illustrates the principles of federalism and popular sovereignty.
3. **Outline** the 27 amendments that have been added to the Constitution.

WHY IT MATTERS

The Framers of the Constitution realized that, inevitably, changes would have to be made in the document they wrote. Article V provides for the process of formal amendment. To this point, 27 amendments have been added to the Constitution.

POLITICAL DICTIONARY

★ **amendment**
★ **formal amendment**
★ **Bill of Rights**

The Constitution of the United States has now been in force for more than 200 years—longer, by far, than the written constitution of any other nation in the world.[3]

When the Constitution became effective in 1789, the United States was a small agricultural nation of fewer than four million people. That population was scattered for some 1,300 miles along the eastern edge of the continent. Travel and communications among the 13 States were limited to horseback and sailing ships. The new States struggled to stay alive in a generally hostile world.

Today, nearly 300 million people live in the United States. The now 50 States stretch across the continent and beyond, and the country also has many far-flung commitments. The United States is today the most powerful nation on Earth, and its modern, highly industrialized and technological society has produced a standard of living that has long been the envy of the rest of the world.

How has the Constitution, written in 1787, endured and kept up with that astounding change and growth? The answer lies in this highly important fact: The United States Constitution of today *is*, and at the same time *is not*, the document of 1787. Many of its words are the same, and much of their meaning remains the same. But some of its words have been changed, some have been eliminated, and some have been added. And, very importantly, the meanings of many of its provisions have been modified as well.

This process of constitutional change, of modification and growth, has come about in two basic ways: (1) by formal amendment and (2) by other, informal means. In this section, you will look at the first of them: the addition of formal amendments to the Constitution.

Formal Amendment Process

The Framers knew that even the wisest of constitution makers cannot build for all time. Thus, the Constitution provides for its own **amendment**—that is, for changes in its written words.

Article V sets out two methods for the proposal and two methods for the ratification of constitutional amendments. So, there are four

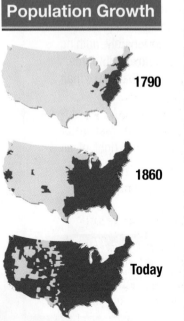

Population Growth

1790

1860

Today

◀ The United States population has grown and expanded across the continent since the Constitution was adopted. The Constitution has been amended to meet the changing needs of the country.

---

[3]The British constitution dates from well before the Norman Conquest of 1066, but it is not a single, written document. Rather, it is an "unwritten constitution," a collection of principles, customs, traditions, and significant parliamentary acts that guide British government and practice. Israel, which has existed only since 1948, is the only other state in the world without a written constitution.

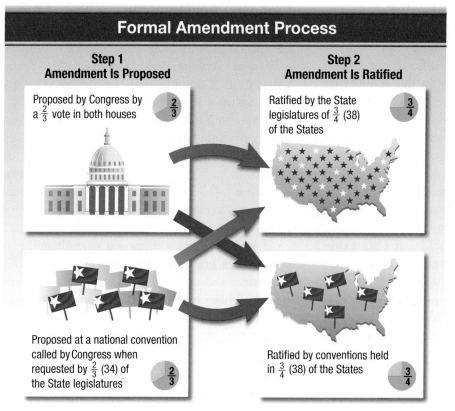

Formal Amendment Process

Step 1
Amendment Is Proposed

Proposed by Congress by a $\frac{2}{3}$ vote in both houses $\frac{2}{3}$

Proposed at a national convention called by Congress when requested by $\frac{2}{3}$ (34) of the State legislatures $\frac{2}{3}$

Step 2
Amendment Is Ratified

Ratified by the State legislatures of $\frac{3}{4}$ (38) of the States $\frac{3}{4}$

Ratified by conventions held in $\frac{3}{4}$ (38) of the States $\frac{3}{4}$

Interpreting Diagrams The four different ways in which amendments may be added to the Constitution are shown here. All but one of the 27 amendments were proposed in Congress and then ratified by the State legislatures. *How does the formal amendment process illustrate federalism?* H-SS 12.4.2

possible methods of **formal amendment**—changes or additions that become part of the written language of the Constitution itself. The diagram above sets out these four methods.

First Method An amendment may be proposed by a two-thirds vote in each house of Congress and be ratified by three fourths of the State legislatures. Today, 38 State legislatures must approve an amendment for it to become a part of the Constitution. Twenty-six of the Constitution's 27 amendments were adopted in this manner.

Second Method An amendment may be proposed by Congress and then ratified by conventions, called for that purpose, in three fourths of the States. Only the 21st Amendment (1933), was adopted in this way. Conventions were used to ratify the 21st Amendment largely because Congress felt that the conventions' popularly elected delegates would be more likely to reflect public opinion on the question of the repeal of nationwide prohibition than would State legislators.

Third Method An amendment may be proposed by a national convention, called by Congress at the request of two thirds of the State legislatures—today, 34. As you can see in the diagram, it must then be ratified by three fourths of the State legislatures. To this point, Congress has not called such a convention.[4]

Fourth Method An amendment may be proposed by a national convention and ratified by conventions in three fourths of the States. Remember that the Constitution itself was adopted in much this same way.

Federalism and Popular Sovereignty

Note that the formal amendment process emphasizes the federal character of the governmental system. Proposal takes place at the national level and ratification is a State-by-State matter. Also note that when the Constitution is amended, that action represents the expression of the people's sovereign will. The people have spoken.

Some criticize the practice of sending proposed amendments to the State legislatures rather than to ratifying conventions, especially

---

[4]The calling of a convention was a near thing twice over the past 40 years. Between 1963 and 1969, 33 State legislatures, one short of the necessary two thirds, sought an amendment to erase the Supreme Court's "one-person, one-vote" decisions; see Chapter 24. Also, between 1975 and 1983, 32 States asked for a convention to propose an amendment that would require that the federal budget be balanced each year, except in time of war or other national emergency.

because it permits a constitutional change without a clear-cut expression by the people. The critics point out that State legislators, who do the ratifying, are elected to office for a mix of reasons: party membership; name familiarity; their stands on such matters as taxes, schools, welfare programs; and a host of other things. They are almost never chosen because of their stand on a proposed amendment to the federal Constitution. On the other hand, the delegates to a ratifying convention would be chosen by the people on the basis of only one factor: a yes-or-no stand on the proposed amendment.

The Supreme Court has held that a State cannot require an amendment proposed by Congress to be approved by a vote of the people of the State before it can be ratified by the State legislature. It made that ruling in *Hawke* v. *Smith* in 1920. However, a state legislature can call for an advisory vote by the people before it acts, as the Court most recently held in *Kimble* v. *Swackhamer* in 1978.

Proposed Amendments

The Constitution places only one restriction on the subjects with which a proposed amendment may deal. Article V declares that "no State, without its Consent, shall be deprived of its equal Suffrage in the Senate."

When both houses of Congress pass a resolution proposing an amendment, Congress does not send it to the President to be signed or vetoed, though the Constitution would seem to require it.[5] This is because when Congress proposes an amendment, it is not making law (not legislating).

If a State rejects a proposed amendment, it is not forever bound by that action. It may later reconsider and ratify the proposal. Most constitutional scholars agree that the reverse is not true,

---

[5]See Article I, Section 7, Clause 3. This practice of not submitting proposed amendments to the President is an example of the many changes in the Constitution that have been made by means other than formal amendment, a matter we shall turn to shortly.

The Enduring *Constitution*

Changing Views of Free Speech

1800

1925

The guarantees of freedom of speech and press, set out in the 1st Amendment, have produced controversy for more than 200 years now.

Go Online
PHSchool.com
Use Web Code mqp-1036 to access an interactive time line.

1798 Sedition Act makes it a crime to criticize the government in speech or writing. The law is not renewed after the election of 1800.

1918 Sedition Act, added to Espionage Act of 1917, passed; prohibits speech, writing, or publishing critical of the form of government in the U.S.

1919 Supreme Court rules that sending written material to eligible men urging them to resist the draft is unlawful because it creates a "clear and present danger" to national security. (*Schenck* v. *United States*)

1925 Supreme Court r that 14th Amendment's D Process Clause incorpora 1st Amendment's guaran freedom of speech and p (*Gitlow* v. *New York*)

Analysis Skills CS1, CS2, HI1

however. Once a State has approved an amendment, that action is final and unchangeable.

Nearly 15,000 joint resolutions calling for amendments to the Constitution have been proposed in Congress since 1789. Only 33 of them have been sent on to the States. Of those, only 27 have been finally ratified. One of the unratified amendments had been offered by Congress in 1789—along with 10 other proposals that became the Bill of Rights in 1791, and another that became the 27th Amendment in 1992. The unratified amendment of 1789 dealt with the distribution of seats in the House of Representatives. A second amendment, proposed in 1810, would have voided the citizenship of anyone accepting any foreign title or other honor. Another, in 1861, would have prohibited forever any amendment relating to slavery. A fourth, in 1924, was intended to empower Congress to regulate child labor. A fifth one, proclaiming the equal rights of women (ERA), was proposed by Congress in 1972; it fell three States short of ratification and died in 1982. An amendment to give the District of Columbia seats in Congress was proposed in 1978; it died in 1985. Congress can place "a reasonable time limit" on the ratification process, *Dillon* v. *Gloss*, 1921. When Congress proposed the 18th Amendment (in 1917), it set a seven-year deadline for its ratification. It has set a similar deadline for the ratification of each of the amendments (except the 19th) it has proposed since, although Congress granted the ERA a three-year extension in 1979.

The 27 Amendments

The Constitution's 27 amendments are described in the table on the next page. As you review the amendments, note this important fact: As significant as they are, these 27 amendments have not in fact been responsible for the extraordinary vitality of the Constitution. That is to say, they

1969 Supreme Court decides that the Constitution protects students who wear armbands in school to protest the Vietnam War. (*Tinker* v. *Des Moines School District*)

1989 Supreme Court rules that burning an American flag as a political protest is "symbolic speech," protected by the 1st and 14th amendments. (*Texas* v. *Johnson*)

1950 | 1975 | 2000

1951 Supreme Court upholds the Smith Act of 1940 and rejects challenge by 11 Communist Party leaders convicted of conspiring to teach and advocate violent overthrow of government. (*Dennis* v. *United States*)

1971 Government tries to stop the *New York Times* publication of the "Pentagon Papers" about the Vietnam War. The Supreme Court upholds the paper's right to do so. (*New York Times* v. *United States*)

2003 Supreme Court rules that Congress can require public libraries that receive federal funds to use filters that block access to Internet pornography. (*United States* v. *American Library Association*)

Analyzing Time Lines

1. What was the Court's reason for protecting a protester who burned an American flag?
2. Both the *Schenck* case (1919) and the *Tinker* case (1969) involved antiwar protests. How would you explain the difference between the Supreme Court decisions?

have *not* been a major part of the process by which the Constitution has kept pace with more than two centuries of far-reaching change.

The Bill of Rights

The first ten amendments were added to the Constitution less than three years after it became effective. They were proposed by the first session of the First Congress in 1789 and were ratified by the States in late 1791. Each of these amendments arose out of the controversy surrounding the ratification of the Constitution itself. Many people, including Thomas Jefferson, had agreed to support the Constitution only if a listing of the basic rights held by the people were added to it immediately.

Collectively, the first ten amendments are known as the **Bill of Rights.** They set out the great constitutional guarantees of freedom of belief and expression, of freedom and security of the person, and of fair and equal treatment before the law. We shall consider these guarantees at some length in Chapters 19 and 20. The 10th Amendment does not deal with civil rights as such. Rather, it spells out the concept of reserved powers in the federal system.

The Later Amendments

Each of the other amendments that have been added to the Constitution over the past 200 years also grew out of some particular, and often interesting, set of circumstances. For example, the 11th Amendment declares that no State may be sued in the federal courts by a citizen of another State or by a citizen of any foreign state. It was proposed by Congress in 1794 and ratified in 1795, after the State of Georgia had lost its case in the United States Supreme Court. The case (*Chisholm* v. *Georgia*, decided by the Court in 1793) had been brought to the brand new federal court system by a man who lived in South Carolina.

Amendments to the Constitution

Amendment	Subject	Year	Time Required for Ratification
1st–10th	Bill of Rights	1791	2 years, 2 months, 20 days
11th	Immunity of States from certain lawsuits	1795	11 months, 3 days
12th	Changes in electoral college procedures	1804	6 months, 6 days
13th	Abolition of slavery	1865	10 months, 6 days
14th	Citizenship, due process, equal protection	1868	2 years, 26 days
15th	No denial of vote because of race, color, or previous enslavement	1870	11 months, 8 days
16th	Power of Congress to tax incomes	1913	3 years, 6 months, 22 days
17th	Popular election of U.S. Senators	1913	10 months, 26 days
18th	Prohibition of alcohol	1919	1 year, 29 days
19th	Woman suffrage	1920	1 year, 2 months, 14 days
20th	Change of dates for start of presidential and Congressional terms	1933	10 months, 21 days
21st	Repeal of Prohibition (18th Amendment)	1933	9 months, 15 days
22nd	Limit on presidential terms	1951	3 years, 11 months, 6 days
23rd	District of Columbia vote in presidential elections	1961	9 months, 13 days
24th	Ban of tax payment as voter qualification	1964	1 year, 4 months, 27 days
25th	Presidential succession, vice presidential vacancy, and presidential disability	1967	1 year, 7 months, 4 days
26th	Voting age of 18	1971	3 months, 8 days
27th	Congressional pay	1992	202 years, 7 months, 12 days

Interpreting Tables These 27 amendments have been added to the Constitution since it became effective in 1789. *Which amendment was adopted in the shortest time? Which one took the most time to ratify?*

The 12th Amendment was added to the Constitution in 1804 after the electoral college had failed to produce a winner in the presidential election of 1800. Thomas Jefferson became the third President of the United States in 1801, but only after a long, bitter fight in the House of Representatives.

The 13th Amendment, added in 1865, provides another example. It abolished slavery in the United States and was a direct result of the Civil War. So, too, were the 14th Amendment on citizenship (in 1868) and the 15th Amendment on the right to vote (in 1870).

As you can see in the table on page 76, the 18th Amendment, establishing a nationwide prohibition of alcohol, was ratified in 1919. What came to be known as "the noble experiment" lasted fewer than 14 years. The 18th Amendment was repealed by the 21st in 1933.

The 22nd Amendment (1951) was proposed in 1947, soon after the Republican Party had gained control of Congress for the first time in 16 years. Over that period, Franklin D. Roosevelt, a Democrat, had won the presidency four times.

The 26th Amendment was added in 1971. It lowered the voting age to 18 in all elections in the United States. Many of those who backed the amendment began to work for its passage during World War II, with the argument "Old enough to fight, old enough to vote." Its ratification was spurred by the war in Vietnam.

▲ **Two ERA Supporters** People fought unsuccessfully in the 1970s and 1980s to add the Equal Rights Amendment to the Constitution. **H-SS 12.4.2**

The most recent amendment, the 27th, was among the first to be offered by Congress. This amendment forbids members of Congress from raising their own pay during that term. It was proposed in 1789 and ratified nearly 203 years later, in 1992.

Section 2 Assessment

Key Terms and Main Ideas

1. How many **amendments** were added to the Constitution in the twentieth century?
2. Describe the four possible methods of **formal amendment.**
3. In your own words, describe three freedoms protected by the **Bill of Rights.**

Critical Thinking

4. **Drawing Conclusions** Why does the Constitution provide that *both* houses of Congress must agree to the proposal of an amendment?
5. **Determining Cause and Effect** Cite three events or controversies that led to amendments to the Constitution,

and explain how each of these amendments settled a particular question.

6. **Drawing Inferences** Why does the Constitution require an extraordinary majority for the ratification of amendments to the Constitution?

Letters of Liberty

Analysis Skills HR4, HI3

Thomas Jefferson and James Madison enjoyed a lifelong friendship. While Jefferson served in Paris as United States Minister to France (1785 to 1789), he and Madison exchanged several letters. Their correspondence included the letters below, in which they discuss the addition of a bill of rights to the recently drafted Constitution.

James Madison
1751–1836

JEFFERSON TO MADISON
December 20, 1787

I will now add what I do not like [about the Constitution]. First the omission of a bill of rights providing clearly . . . for freedom of religion, freedom of the press, protection against standing armies, restriction against monopolies, . . . and trials by jury in all matters of fact triable by the laws of the land. . . . Let me add that a bill of rights is what the people are entitled to against every government on earth, general or particular, and what no just government should refuse, or rest on inference. . . .

MADISON TO JEFFERSON
October 17, 1788

. . . My own opinion has always been in favor of a bill of rights, provided it be so framed as to not imply powers not meant to be included. . . . At the same time, I have never thought the omission a material defect. . . . I have favored it because I supposed it might be of use, and if properly executed could not be of disservice. . . .

Experience proves the [ineffectiveness] of a bill of rights on those occasions when its control is most needed. Repeated violations of these parchment barriers have been committed by overbearing majorities in every state. In Virginia I have seen the [state constitution's] bill of rights violated in every instance where it has been opposed to a popular current. . . . Wherever the real power in a government lies, there is the danger of oppression. In our government, the real power lies in the majority of the community, and the invasion of privacy rights is chiefly to be [feared], not from acts of government contrary to the sense of its constituents, but from acts in which the government is the mere instrument of the major number of constituents. . . .

JEFFERSON TO MADISON
March 15, 1789

. . . In the arguments in favor of a declaration of rights, you omit one which has great weight with me, the legal check which it puts into the hands of the judiciary. This is a body, which if rendered independent, and kept strictly to their own department merits great confidence for their learning and integrity. . . .

. . . Experience proves the [ineffectiveness] of a bill of rights. True. But [though] it is not absolutely [effective] under all circumstances, it is of great potency always. . . .

Analyzing Primary Sources

1. Why did Jefferson want a bill of rights added to the Constitution?
2. According to Madison, from where did the greatest danger to individual rights come?
3. What did Madison mean when he referred to a bill of rights as a "parchment barrier"?
4. Why, as Jefferson states, would a bill of rights strengthen the judicial branch of government?

Constitutional Change by Other Means

Section Preview

OBJECTIVES

1. **Identify** how basic legislation has changed the Constitution over time.
2. **Describe** the ways in which the Constitution has been altered by executive and judicial actions.
3. **Analyze** the role of party practices and custom in shaping the Constitution.

WHY IT MATTERS

The 27 formal amendments to the Constitution have *not* been a major part of the process by which that document has kept pace with more than 200 years of far-reaching change in this country. Rather, constitutional change has more often occurred as a result of the day-to-day, year-to-year workings of government.

POLITICAL DICTIONARY

★ **executive agreement**
★ **treaty**
★ **electoral college**
★ **Cabinet**
★ **senatorial courtesy**

The Constitution is a comparatively short document. Much of it is devoted to matters of principle and of basic organization, structure, and process. Most of its sections are brief, even skeletal in nature. For this reason, to understand the Constitution and the process of constitutional change, you must grasp this key point: There is much—in fact, a great deal—in the Constitution that cannot be seen with the naked eye. Much has been put there not by formal amendment, but, rather, by the day-to-day, year-to-year experiences of government under the Constitution.

To put this essential point another way: Over time, many changes have been made in the Constitution which have not involved any changes in its written words. This vital process of constitutional change by means other than formal amendment has taken place—and continues to occur—in five basic ways: through (1) the passage of basic legislation by Congress; (2) actions taken by the President; (3) key decisions of the Supreme Court; (4) the activities of political parties; and (5) custom.

Basic Legislation

Congress has been a major agent of constitutional change in two important ways. First, it has passed a number of laws to spell out several of the Constitution's brief provisions. That is, Congress has added flesh to the bones of those sections of the Constitution that the Framers left purposely skeletal—provisions they left for Congress to detail as circumstances required.

Take the structure of the federal court system as an example. In Article III, Section 1, the Constitution provides for "one supreme Court, and . . . such inferior Courts as the Congress may from time to time ordain and establish." Beginning with the Judiciary Act of 1789, all of the federal courts, except the Supreme Court, have been set up by acts of Congress. Or, similarly, Article II creates only the offices of President and Vice President. The many departments, agencies,

▲ *National Convention* Political parties are a basic feature of American government, but they are not mentioned in the Constitution. **H-SS 12.6.1**

▲ *Across the Border* Congress can pass laws under its constitutional power to regulate interstate commerce, or trade that crosses State boundaries.

and offices in the now huge executive branch have been created by acts of Congress.

As another example, the Constitution deals with the matter of presidential succession, but only up to a point. The 25th Amendment says that if the presidency becomes vacant, the Vice President automatically succeeds to the office. Who becomes President if both the presidency and the vice presidency are vacant? The Constitution leaves the answer to that question to Congress and its lawmaking power.

Second, Congress has added to the Constitution by the way in which it has used many of its powers. The Constitution gives to Congress the expressed power to regulate

▲ President Bush used his power as commander in chief to commit troops to combat in Iraq. Here, a soldier examines an Iraqi driver's papers at a checkpoint in Baghdad. *Critical Thinking Should the President be able to make war without a declaration of war by Congress?*

foreign and interstate commerce.[6] But what is "foreign commerce"? What is "interstate commerce"? What, exactly, does Congress have the power to regulate? The Constitution does not say. Congress has done much to define those words, however, by exercising its commerce power with the passage of literally thousands of laws. As it has done so, Congress has, in a very real sense, added to the Constitution.

Executive Action

The manner in which various Presidents have used their powers has also contributed to the growth of the Constitution. For example, the document says that only Congress can declare war.[7] But the Constitution also makes the President the commander in chief of the nation's armed forces.[8] Acting under that authority, several Presidents have made war without a declaration of war by Congress. In fact, Presidents have used the armed forces abroad in combat without such a declaration on several hundred occasions in our history.

Take the use of executive agreements in the conduct of foreign affairs as another example here. An **executive agreement** is a pact made by the President directly with the head of a foreign state. A **treaty,** on the other hand, is a formal agreement between two or more sovereign states. The principal difference between these agreements and treaties is that executive agreements need not be approved by the Senate. They are as legally binding as treaties, however. Recent Presidents have often used them in our dealings with other countries, instead of the much more cumbersome treaty-making process outlined in Article II, Section 2 of the Constitution.

Court Decisions

The nation's courts, most tellingly the United States Supreme Court, interpret and apply the Constitution in many

---

[6]Article I, Section 8, Clause 3.
[7]Article I, Section 8, Clause 11.
[8]Article II, Section 2, Clause 1.

cases they hear. You have already seen several of these instances of constitutional interpretation—that is, constitutional amplification—by the Court, such as in *Marbury* v. *Madison,* 1803. You will encounter more of these landmark cases on through this book, for the Supreme Court is, as Woodrow Wilson once put it, "a constitutional convention in continuous session."

Party Practices

The nation's political parties have also been a major source of constitutional change over the course of our political history, despite the fact that the Constitution makes no mention of political parties. In fact, most of the Framers were opposed to their growth. In his Farewell Address in 1796, George Washington warned the people against what he called "the baneful effects of the spirit of party." Washington feared the divisive effect of party politics. Yet, even as he spoke, parties were developing. They have played a major role in the shaping of government and its processes ever since. Illustrations of that point are almost without number.

Neither the Constitution nor any law provides for the nomination of candidates for the presidency. From the 1830s on, however, the major parties have held national conventions to do just that. The parties have converted the **electoral college,** the group that makes the formal selection of the nation's President, from what the Framers intended into a "rubber stamp" for each State's popular vote in presidential elections (see pages 365–367). Both houses of Congress are organized and conduct much of their business on the basis of party. The President makes appointments to office with an eye to party politics. In short, government in the United States is in many ways government through party.

Custom

Unwritten custom may be as strong as written law, and many customs have developed in our governmental system. Again, there are many examples. By custom, not because the Constitution says so, the heads of the 15 executive departments make up the **Cabinet,** an advisory body to the President.

On each of the eight occasions when a President died in office, the Vice President succeeded to that office—most recently Lyndon Johnson, following John Kennedy's assassination in 1963. Yet, the written words of the Constitution did not provide for this practice until the adoption of the 25th Amendment in 1967. Until then, the Constitution said only that the powers and duties of the presidency—but *not* the office itself—should be transferred to the Vice President.[9]

It is a long-established custom that the Senate will approve only those presidential appointees who are acceptable to the senator or senators of the President's party from the State involved, for example, a federal judge or a United States marshal. This practice is known as **senatorial courtesy,** and it amounts to an unwritten rule that is closely followed in the Senate. Notice that its practical effect is to shift

---

[9]Read, carefully, Article II, Section 1, Clause 6, and then Section 1 of the 25th Amendment.

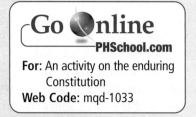

▲ The tradition of limiting Presidents to two terms became a major issue in the presidential campaign of 1940 and again in 1944. *Critical Thinking Why did Roosevelt's reelection lead supporters of the "no-third-term" tradition to push for a constitutional amendment?* **H-SS 12.4.2**

a portion of the appointing power from the President, where the formal wording of the Constitution puts it, to certain members of the Senate.

Both the strength and the importance of unwritten customs can be seen in the reaction to the rare circumstances in which one of them has not been observed. For nearly 150 years, the "no-third-term tradition" was a closely followed rule in presidential politics. The tradition began

in 1796, when George Washington refused to seek a third term as President, and several later Presidents followed that lead. In 1940, and again in 1944, however, Franklin Roosevelt broke the no-third-term custom. He sought and won a third and then a fourth term in the White House. As a direct result, the 22nd Amendment was added to the Constitution in 1951. What had been an unwritten custom, an informal rule, became part of the written Constitution itself.

Section 3 Assessment

Standards Monitoring *Online*
For: Self-Quiz and vocabulary practice
Web Code: mqa-1033

Key Terms and Main Ideas

1. By what means other than **formal amendment** has constitutional change occurred?
2. What role does the **Cabinet** play in government?
3. What is the current role of the **electoral college?**
4. What is an **executive agreement?**

Critical Thinking

5. **Drawing Conclusions** Why has it been necessary to make changes in the Constitution by methods in addition to formal amendment?

6. **Determining Cause and Effect** What do you think would happen in this situation: The President insists on making an appointment, despite the fact that a key senator has invoked the rule of senatorial courtesy against that appointment?

Go Online
PHSchool.com

For: An activity on the enduring Constitution
Web Code: mqd-1033

May States Impose Terms Limits for Members of Congress?

Analysis Skills HR4, HI3, HI4

The Constitution sets age, citizenship, and residence requirements for members of Congress. Can the States set additional qualifications for their senators and representatives, or can the additional qualifications be imposed only by constitutional amendment?

U.S. Term Limits, Inc. v. Thornton (1995)

According to a 1992 amendment to the Arkansas constitution, any person who had served three or more terms as a member of the U.S. House of Representatives from Arkansas, or two or more terms as one of its U.S. senators, could not have his or her name placed on the ballot again for that office. The amendment did not prevent any such person from campaigning as a write-in candidate.

A number of Arkansas citizens filed a lawsuit to have this term-limit amendment declared unconstitutional. U.S. Term Limits, Inc., a national organization formed to promote term limits for elected officials, and the State of Arkansas joined the lawsuit to defend the amendment. Ray Thornton, then serving his fourth term as one of Arkansas' House members, joined the lawsuit opposing the amendment because it would prevent his name from appearing on the ballot again.

The Arkansas supreme court held that the amendment violated the Constitution. The State of Arkansas and U.S. Term Limits appealed to the Supreme Court of the United States.

Arguments for U.S. Term Limits

1. Elected officials who remain in office for long periods lose touch with the people they represent, and the fact of incumbency gives them an unfair advantage in running for re-election.
2. The Constitution does not specify the number of terms a senator or representative may serve. Because all powers not specifically assigned to the National Government are reserved to the States, the States have the authority to act where the Constitution is silent.

3. Even if the Constitution is the only instrument that may set requirements for members of Congress, the Arkansas amendment does not prevent anyone from running for office; it only restricts their access to the State ballot.

Arguments for Thornton

1. The Constitution is the exclusive source of qualifications for membership in Congress, and the same qualifications must apply in each State to insure uniformity. A constitutional amendment is necessary to change or add to the qualifications.
2. The States never had the power to set the qualifications of the members of the national legislature. Accordingly, the States cannot exercise a reserved power they never had.
3. Even if the Arkansas amendment does not technically create term limits for national office, the chances of succeeding as a write-in candidate are so slim that the amendment has the same effect as a term limit.

Decide for Yourself

1. Review the constitutional grounds on which each side based its arguments and the specific arguments each side presented.
2. Debate the opposing viewpoints presented in this case. Which viewpoint do you favor?
3. How will the Court's decision affect the States' ability to choose their own representatives? (To read a summary of the Court's decision, turn to pages 799–806.)

Go Online PHSchool.com

Use Web Code mqp-1037 to register your vote on this issue and to see how other students voted.

Political Dictionary

Preamble (p. 65), articles (p. 65), constitutionalism (p. 65), rule of law (p. 66), separation of powers (p. 66), checks and balances (p. 67), veto (p. 67), judicial review (p. 69), unconstitutional (p. 69), federalism (p. 70), amendment (p. 72), formal amendment (p. 73), Bill of Rights (p. 76), executive agreement (p. 80), treaty (p. 80), electoral college (p. 81), Cabinet (p. 81), senatorial courtesy (p. 81)

Standards Review

H-SS 12.1.4 Explain how the Founding Fathers' realistic view of human nature led directly to the establishment of a constitutional system that limited the power of the governors and the governed as articulated in the *Federalist Papers*.

H-SS 12.1.5 Describe the systems of separated and shared powers, the role of organized interests (*Federalist Paper Number 10*), checks and balances (*Federalist Paper Number 51*), the importance of an independent judiciary (*Federalist Paper Number 78*), enumerated powers, rule of law, federalism, and civilian control of the military.

H-SS 12.1.6 Understand that the Bill of Rights limits the powers of the federal government and state governments.

H-SS 12.4.2 Explain the process through which the Constitution can be amended.

H-SS 12.6.1 Analyze the origin, development, and role of political parties, noting those occasional periods in which there was only one major party or were more than two major parties.

H-SS 12.7.1 Explain how conflicts between levels of government and branches of government are resolved.

H-SS 12.10 Students formulate questions about and defend their analyses of tensions within our constitutional democracy and the importance of maintaining a balance between the following concepts: majority rule and individual rights; liberty and equality; state and national authority in a federal system; civil disobedience and the rule of law; freedom of the press and the right to a fair trial; the relationship of religion and government.

Practicing the Vocabulary

Matching *Choose a term from the list above that best matches each description.*

1. A governmental system in which the powers of government are divided on a geographic basis
2. The idea that government must conduct itself in accordance with the principles of the Constitution
3. The power of courts to determine the constitutionality of a law or other governmental action
4. A system by which one branch of government can be restrained by one or both of the other branches

Fill in the Blank *Choose a term from the list above that best completes each sentence below.*

5. Under the principle of _____ , the Federal Government has three equal branches.
6. The Constitution is divided into seven major sections, called _____.
7. The first ten amendments to the United States Constitution are known as the _____.
8. _____ results in changes to the written words of the Constitution.

Reviewing Main Ideas

Section 1
9. How is the text of the Constitution organized?
10 What are the six basic principles of the Constitution?
11. **(a)** How are popular sovereignty and limited government related? **(b)** Why were these principles important to the Framers of the Constitution?
12. What is the purpose of checks and balances?
13. **(a)** How can the judicial branch check the legislative branch? **(b)** How can the executive branch check the legislative branch?

Section 2
14. How many amendments have been formally added to the Constitution?
15. **(a)** What has been the most common method for adding an amendment to the Constitution? **(b)** Which method has been used only once?

16. **(a)** Which amendment required the longest amount of time to ratify? **(b)** How long did it take?
17. How does the formal amendment process reflect federalism?
18. What event led to the 13th, 14th, and 15th amendments?

Section 3
19. By what five ways has the Constitution been changed other than by formal amendment?
20. How has Congress contributed to the process of constitutional change and development?
21. Cite two examples of the exercise of presidential power that illustrate the process of constitutional change by other than formal amendment.
22. How does the presidential nominating process illustrate the process of constitutional change and development?
23. What is the role of custom in government?

Critical Thinking Skills

Analysis Skills CS3, HR3, HR4

24. ***Face the Issues*** John Adams spoke in favor of "arms in the hands of citizens, to be used at individual discretion . . . in private self-defense." **(a)** Which side of the gun control debate is more likely to cite this quote? **(b)** How might individuals on the other side respond?

25. ***Drawing Conclusions*** The Preamble to the Constitution begins with the words "We the People." **(a)** Was every person living in the United States in 1789 included in that collective "We"? **(b)** Which, if any, of the 27 amendments to the Constitution corrected that situation?

26. ***Demonstrating Reasoned Judgment*** James Madison defended the concepts of separation of powers and checks and balances in *The Federalist* No. 51. What did he mean when he wrote that, to guard against a concentration of power in one of the branches of government, "ambition must be made to counteract ambition"?

27. ***Testing Conclusions*** The text says that the United States Constitution is a flexible document. Find evidence from the text that you believe supports that conclusion.

Analyzing Political Cartoons

Using your knowledge of American government and this cartoon, answer the questions below.

28. What point is the cartoonist trying to make about the ease or difficulty of proposing constitutional amendments?

29. Based on your reading, do you agree or disagree with the cartoonist's opinion? Explain your answer.

Participation Activities

Analysis Skills CS1, HR4, HI1

30. ***Current Events Watch*** The Constitution gives the President the power to appoint all federal judges. However, it also gives the Senate the power to confirm or reject those appointments by majority vote. Research the recent appointment of a federal judge and write a brief report on his or her background and how senators from the opposing party responded to the President's nomination.

31. ***Time Line Activity*** Create a time line of the Equal Rights Amendment, beginning with its proposal in 1972 and ending with its failure to be ratified ten years later. List the number of States that voted to ratify it each year and include the three-year extension to the time limit passed in 1979. Compare this time line to the table on page 76. What does your time line tell you about the ratification process? Do you think the ten-year time limit was fair? Explain your answer.

32. ***It's Your Turn*** You are a newspaper editor in the late 1700s. Alexander Hamilton has just referred to democracy as "mobocracy." Write an editorial in response to Hamilton's view. Define the position that you want to take in the editorial. Next, list your arguments. As you revise your editorial, make certain that your arguments are persuasive. Finally, proofread and make a final copy.

Standards Monitoring *Online*

For: Chapter 3 Self-Test   **Visit:** PHSchool.com
Web Code: mqa-1034

As a final review, take the Magruder's Chapter 3 Self-Test and receive immediate feedback on your answers.
The test consists of 20 multiple-choice questions designed to test your understanding of the chapter content.

CHAPTER 4

Federalism

"The true 'essence' of federalism is that the States as States have legitimate interests which the National Government is bound to respect even though its laws are supreme."

—Justice Sandra Day O'Connor (1985)

The federal system divides power between the National Government and the States. In this way, federalism ensures that the National Government is strong enough to meet the nation's needs. At the same time, federalism preserves the strength and uniqueness of the individual States.

◆ National and State flags

SECTION 1

Federalism: The Division of Power (pp. 88–95)

★ The Framers sought to create a central government strong enough to meet the nation's needs and still preserve the strength of the States.

★ The National Government has only those powers delegated to it by the Constitution.

★ The States are governments of reserved powers—powers that the Constitution does not grant to the National Government or deny to the States.

★ Most of the powers of the National Government are exercised by the National Government alone.

★ The concurrent powers are possessed by both the National Government and the States.

★ Local governments exist only as parts of their parent State.

★ The Constitution stands above all other forms of law in the United States.

SECTION 2

The National Government and the 50 States (pp. 97–103)

★ The National Government guarantees the States a representative form of government, protection against invasion and internal disorder, and respect for their territorial integrity.

★ Congress has the power to admit new States.

★ The American federal system involves a broad range of powers shared between the National Government and the States.

SECTION 3

Interstate Relations (pp. 105–108)

★ The States can make interstate compacts that enable them to cooperate on matters of mutual concern.

★ The Constitution requires each State to respect the laws, official records, and court actions of other States.

★ The Constitution requires each State to return fugitives to the State from which they fled.

★ No State can draw unreasonable distinctions between its own residents and residents of other States.

Go Online
PHSchool.com

For: Current Data
Web Code: mqg-1045

For: Close Up Foundation debates
Web Code: mqh-1047

Federalism: The Division of Power

1

Section Preview

OBJECTIVES

1. **Define** federalism and explain why the Framers chose this system of government.
2. **Identify** powers delegated to and denied to the National Government, and powers reserved for and denied to the States.
3. **Understand** that the National Government holds exclusive powers; it also holds concurrent powers with the States.
4. **Explain** the place of local governments in the federal system.
5. **Examine** how the Constitution functions as "the supreme Law of the Land."

WHY IT MATTERS

The federal system divides government power in order to prevent its abuse. There are two basic levels of government in the federal system—National and State. The Supreme Court settles disputes between the two.

POLITICAL DICTIONARY

★ **federalism**
★ **division of powers**
★ **delegated powers**
★ **expressed powers**
★ **implied powers**
★ **inherent powers**
★ **reserved powers**
★ **exclusive powers**
★ **concurrent powers**

You know that federal law requires young men to register for military service at age 18; that most employers must pay their workers at least $5.15 an hour and time-and-a-half for overtime; and that no person can be denied a job on the basis of his or her race or ethnicity.

You also know that State law says that you must have a driver's license in order to drive a car; that it is illegal for anyone under 21 to buy alcoholic beverages, or for anyone under 18 to buy cigarettes or other tobacco products; and that only those persons who can satisfy certain requirements can buy or own firearms.

These examples illustrate a very complex system: the division of governmental power in the United States between National and State governments. This section will help you better understand that complicated arrangement.

▲ State laws forbid the sale of cigarettes to minors.

Why Federalism?

When the Framers of the Constitution met at Philadelphia in 1787, they faced a number of difficult issues. Not the least of them: How

could they possibly create a new central government that would be strong enough to meet the nation's needs and, at the same time, preserve the strength of the existing States?

Few of the Framers favored a strong central government based on the British model; and all of them knew that the Revolution had been fought in the name of self-government. Yet they also knew that the government under the Articles of Confederation had proved too weak to deal with the nation's many problems.

Remember, most of the Framers were dedicated to the concept of limited government. They were convinced (1) that governmental power poses a threat to individual liberty, (2) that therefore the exercise of governmental power must be restrained, and (3) that to divide governmental power, as federalism does, is to curb it and so prevent its abuse.

Federalism Defined

Federalism is a system of government in which a written constitution divides the powers of government on a territorial basis between a central, or national, government and several regional governments, usually called states or provinces. Each of these levels of government has its own substantial set of powers. Neither level, acting alone, can change the basic division of powers the constitution has created. In addition, each level of government operates through its own agencies and acts directly through its own officials and laws.

The American system of government stands as a prime example of federalism. The basic design of this system is set out in the Constitution. This document provides for a **division of powers** between the National Government and the States. That is, it assigns certain powers to the National Government and certain powers to the States. This division of powers was implied in the original Constitution and then spelled out in the Bill of Rights:

FROM THE Constitution **❝**The powers not delegated to the United States by the Constitution, nor prohibited by it to the States, are reserved to the States respectively, or to the people.**❞**

—10th Amendment

In effect, federalism produces a dual system of government. That is, it provides for two basic levels of government, each with its own area of authority. Each operates over the same people and the same territory at the same time.

Federalism's major strength is that it allows local action in matters of local concern, and national action in matters of wider concern. Local traditions, needs, and desires vary from one State to another, and federalism allows for this very significant fact.

Illustrations of this point are nearly endless. For example, a third of the States are directly involved in the liquor business, operating it as a public monopoly; elsewhere private enterprise is the rule. In 48 States many gas stations are self-service; in New Jersey and Oregon, the law forbids motorists to pump their own gas. Only one State—North Dakota—does not require voters to register in order to cast their ballots. Only Nebraska has a unicameral (one-house) legislature. Oregon is the only State that has legalized physician-assisted suicide. Only five States—Alaska, Delaware, New Hampshire, Montana, and Oregon—do not impose a general sales tax.

While federalism allows individual States to handle State and local matters, it also provides for the strength that comes from union.

▲ The National Government provides protection from harm for the entire country. State governments provide protection from harm within State borders. *Critical Thinking How do these photos illustrate the federal system?*

National defense and foreign affairs offer useful illustrations of this point. So, too, do domestic affairs. Take, for example, a natural disaster. When a flood, drought, winter storm, or other catastrophe hits a particular State, the resources of the National Government and all of the other States may be mobilized to aid the stricken area.

Powers of the National Government

The National Government is a government of **delegated powers.** That is, it has only those powers delegated (granted) to it in the Constitution. There are three distinct types of delegated powers: expressed, implied, and inherent.

The Expressed Powers

The **expressed powers** are delegated to the National Government in so many words—spelled out, expressly, in the Constitution. These powers are also sometimes called the "enumerated powers."

You can find most of the expressed powers in Article I, Section 8. There, in 18 clauses, the Constitution expressly gives 27 powers to Congress. They include the power to lay and collect taxes, to coin money, to regulate foreign

Expressed Power   Implied Power   Inherent Power

▲ The powers delegated to the National Government include the power to coin money, to pro-hibit race-based discrimination, and to conduct foreign relations. In 1971, Richard Nixon (right) became the first American President to visit China; his historic trip led to United States recognition of the government of the People's Republic of China. *Critical Thinking Why is establishing diplomatic relations considered an inherent power?*

and interstate commerce, to raise and maintain armed forces, to declare war, to fix standards of weights and measures, to grant patents and copyrights, and to do many other things.

Several other expressed powers are set out elsewhere in the Constitution. Article II, Section 2 gives several powers to the President. They include the power to act as commander in chief of the armed forces, to grant reprieves and pardons, to make treaties, and to appoint major federal officials. Article III grants "the judicial Power of the United States" to the Supreme Court and other courts in the federal judiciary. Finally, several expressed powers are found in various amendments to the Constitution; thus, the 16th Amendment gives Congress the power to levy an income tax.

The Implied Powers

The **implied powers** are not expressly stated in the Constitution but are reasonably suggested—implied—by the expressed powers. The constitutional basis for the implied powers is found in one of the expressed powers. Article I, Section 8, Clause 18 gives Congress the "necessary and proper power." The Necessary and Proper Clause says that Congress has the power

FROM THE Constitution *"to make all Laws which shall be necessary and proper for carrying into Execution the foregoing Powers and all other Powers vested by this Constitution in the Government of the United States, or in any Department or Officer thereof. "*

—Article I, Section 8, Clause 18

Through congressional and court interpretation, the words *necessary and proper* have come to mean, in effect, "convenient and useful." Indeed, the Necessary and Proper Clause is sometimes called the Elastic Clause, because, over time, it has been stretched to cover so many situations.

Here are but a few of the thousands of examples of the exercise of implied powers. Congress has provided for the regulation of labor-management relations, the building of hydro-electric power dams, and the building of the 42,000-mile interstate highway system. It has made federal crimes of such acts as moving stolen goods, gambling devices, and kidnapped persons across State lines. It has prohibited racial discrimination in granting access to such places as restaurants, theaters, hotels, and motels.

Congress has taken these actions, and many more, because the power to do so is reasonably implied by just one of the expressed powers: the power to regulate interstate commerce.[1]

The Inherent Powers

The **inherent powers** belong to the National Government because it is the national government of a sovereign state in the world community. Although the Constitution does not expressly provide for them, they are powers that, over time, all national governments have possessed. It stands to reason that the Framers of the Constitution intended the National Government they created to hold these powers.

The inherent powers are few in number. The major ones include the power to regulate immigration, to deport undocumented aliens, to acquire territory, to grant diplomatic recognition to other states, and to protect the nation against rebellion or other attempts to overthrow the government by force or violence.

One can argue that most of the inherent powers are implied by one or more of the expressed powers. For example, the power to regulate immigration is suggested by the expressed power to regulate foreign trade. The power to acquire territory can be drawn from the treaty-making power and the several war powers. But the doctrine of inherent powers holds that it is not necessary to go to these lengths to find these powers in the Constitution. In short, these powers exist because the United States exists.

Powers Denied to the National Government

Although the Constitution delegates certain powers to the National Government, it also denies the National Government certain powers. It does so in three distinct ways.

First, the Constitution denies some powers to the National Government in so many words—expressly.[2] Among them are the powers to levy duties on exports; to prohibit freedom of reli-

---

[1] Article I, Section 8, Clause 3. The doctrine of implied powers is treated in greater detail in Chapter 11.

[2] Most of the expressed denials of power are found in Article I, Section 9 and in the 1st through the 8th amendments.

Voices on Government

President Ronald Reagan (1911–2004) was 69 years old when he took office in 1981. During his two terms, President Reagan made it a priority to give power back to the States. The excerpt below comes from his first inaugural address.

❝It is my intention to curb the size and influence of the Federal establishment and to demand recognition of the distinction between the powers granted to the Federal Government and those reserved to the States or to the people. All of us need to be reminded that the Federal Government did not create the States; the States created the Federal Government.❞

Evaluating the Quotation

What does President Reagan mean when he notes that "the Federal Government did not create the States; the States created the Federal Government"?

gion, speech, press, or assembly; to conduct illegal searches or seizures; and to deny to any person accused of a crime a speedy and public trial or a trial by jury.

Second, several powers are denied to the National Government because of the silence of the Constitution. Recall that the National Government is a government of delegated powers; it has only those powers the Constitution gives to it.

Among the many powers not granted to the National Government are the powers to create a public school system for the nation, to enact uniform marriage and divorce laws, and to set up units of local government. The Constitution says nothing about these matters. It says nothing that would give the National Government the power to do any of these things, expressly, implicitly, or inherently. In short, the lack of any such provision—the silence of the Constitution—denies power to the National Government.

Third, some powers are denied to the National Government because of the federal system itself.

Clearly the Constitution does not intend that the National Government should have any power to take action that would threaten the existence of that system. For example, in the exercise of its power to tax, Congress cannot tax any of the States or their local units in the carrying out of their governmental functions. If it could, it would have the power to destroy—tax out of existence—one or more, or all, of the States.[3]

The States

The 50 States are the other half of the very complicated equation we call federalism. Their role in the American federal system is no less important than the role of the National Government.

Powers Reserved to the States

As you recall, the 10th Amendment declares that the States are governments of reserved powers. (See page 89.) The **reserved powers** are those powers that the Constitution does not grant to the National Government and does not, at the same time, deny to the States.

Thus, any State can forbid persons under 18 to marry without parental consent, or those under 21 to buy liquor. It can ban the sale of pornography, outlaw prostitution, and permit some forms of gambling and prohibit others. A State can require that doctors, lawyers, hairdressers, and plumbers be licensed in order to practice in the State. It can confiscate automobiles and other property used in connection with such illicit activities as illegal drug trafficking or prostitution. It can establish public schools, enact land use laws, regulate the services and restrict the profits of such public utilities as natural gas, oil, electric power, and telephone companies, and do much, much more.

In short, the sphere of powers held by each State—the scope of the reserved powers—is huge. The States can do all of those things just mentioned, and much more, because (1) the Constitution does not give the National Government the power to take these actions and (2) it does not deny the States the power to take them.

How broad the reserved powers really are can be understood from this fact: Most of what government does in this country today is done by the States (and their local governments), not by the National Government. The point can also be seen from this fact: The reserved powers include the vitally important police power—the power of a State to protect and promote the public health, the public morals, the public safety, and the general welfare.

The Constitution does not grant expressed powers to the States, with one exception. Section 2 of the 21st Amendment gives the States a virtually unlimited power to regulate the manufacture, sale, and consumption of alcoholic beverages.

Powers Denied to the States

Just as the Constitution denies many powers to the National Government, it also denies many powers to the States. Some of these powers are denied to the States in so many words.[4] For example, no State can enter into any treaty, alliance, or confederation. Nor can a State print or coin money or deprive any person of life, liberty, or property without due process of law.

Some powers are denied to the States inherently—that is, by the existence of the federal system. Thus, no State (and no local government)

▲ *Land Use* Enacting land use laws in order to preserve open spaces is one of many powers reserved to the States. **H-SS 12.7.3**

---

[3]But note that when a State, or one of its local units, performs a so-called nongovernmental function—for example, maintains liquor stores, runs a bus system, or operates a farmers market—it is liable to federal taxation. We shall come back to this point later, in Chapter 25.

[4]Most of these expressed prohibitions of power to the States (and so, too, to their local governments) are found in Article I, Section 10 and in the 13th, 14th, 15th, 19th, 24th, and 26th Amendments.

can tax any of the agencies or functions of the National Government. Remember, too, each State has its own constitution. That document also denies many powers to the State.[5]

The Exclusive and the Concurrent Powers

Most of the powers that the Constitution delegates to the National Government are **exclusive powers.** These powers can be exercised by the National Government alone. They cannot be exercised by the States under any circumstances.

Some of these powers are expressly denied to the States. Examples include the power to coin money, to make treaties with foreign states, and to lay duties (taxes) on imports. Some powers are not expressly denied to the States but are, nonetheless, among the exclusive powers of the Federal Government because of the nature of the particular power involved. The power to regulate interstate commerce is a leading example of this point. If the States could exercise that power, trade between and among the States would be at best chaotic and at worst impossible.[6]

Some of the powers delegated to the National Government are **concurrent powers.** The concurrent powers are those powers that both the National Government and the States possess and exercise. They include, for example, the power to levy and collect taxes, to define crimes and set punishments for them, and to condemn (take) private property for public use.

The concurrent powers are held and exercised separately and simultaneously by the two basic levels of government. That is, the concurrent powers are those powers that the Constitution does not grant exclusively to the National Government and that, at the same

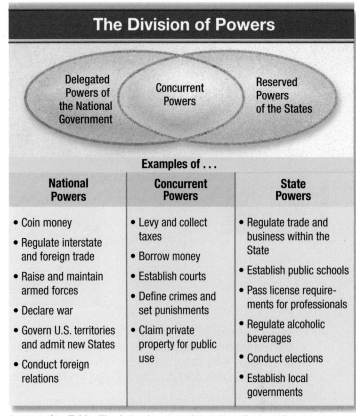

The Division of Powers

Delegated Powers of the National Government — Concurrent Powers — Reserved Powers of the States

Examples of . . .		
National Powers	**Concurrent Powers**	**State Powers**
• Coin money	• Levy and collect taxes	• Regulate trade and business within the State
• Regulate interstate and foreign trade	• Borrow money	• Establish public schools
• Raise and maintain armed forces	• Establish courts	• Pass license requirements for professionals
• Declare war	• Define crimes and set punishments	• Regulate alcoholic beverages
• Govern U.S. territories and admit new States	• Claim private property for public use	• Conduct elections
• Conduct foreign relations		• Establish local governments

Interpreting Tables The federal system determines the way that powers are divided and shared between the National and the State governments. *Name one national, one State, and one concurrent power.*

time, does not deny to the States. The concurrent powers, in short, are those powers that make it possible for a federal system of government to function.

The Federal System and Local Governments

Government in the United States is often discussed in terms of three levels: national, State, and local. However convenient this view may be, it is at best misleading. Recall that there are only two basic levels in the federal system: the National Government and the State governments.

Governments do exist at the local level all across the country, of course. In fact, there are more than 87,000 units of local government in the United States today. You will take a look at them later in this book. For now, keep this important point in mind: All of these thousands of local governments are parts—subunits—of the various State governments.

Each of these local units is located within one of the 50 States. In its constitution and in its laws,

---

[5]Study your own State's constitution on the powers denied to the States. As you do, note the significance of the words "or to the people" in the 10th Amendment in the Federal Constitution. We shall look at State constitutions later, and in more detail, in Chapter 24.

[6]The States cannot regulate interstate commerce as such, but they can and do affect it. For example, in regulating highway speeds, the States regulate vehicles not only operating wholly within the State, but also those operating from State to State. Generally, the States can affect interstate commerce, but they may not impose an unreasonable burden on it.

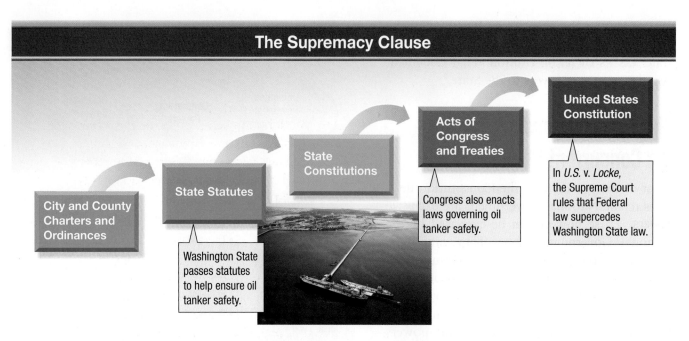

Interpreting Charts The Supremacy Clause creates a hierarchy of laws. Local law (city and county charters and ordinances) must yield to State law. State law must yield to federal law. At the top of the hierarchy is the United States Constitution, which stands above all other forms of law in the United States. ***How does the case of* United States v. Locke *illustrate this hierarchy of laws?*** **H-SS 12.7.1**

each State has created these units. None exists apart from its parent State. Local government can provide services, regulate activities, collect taxes, and do many other things. It can do these things, however, only because the State has established and given it the power to do so. In short, when local governments exercise their powers, they are actually exercising State powers.

Another way of putting all of this is to remind you of a point that was first made in Chapter 1. Each of the 50 States has a unitary form of government—a central government that creates local units of government for its own convenience.

The Supreme Law of the Land

As you have just seen, the division of powers in the American federal system produces a dual system of government, one in which two basic levels of government operate over the same territory and the same people at the same time.

Such an arrangement is bound to result in conflicts between national law and State law.

The Supremacy Clause

The Framers anticipated these conflicts—and so they wrote the Supremacy Clause into the Constitution. That provision declares that

FROM THE *Constitution* *❝ This Constitution, and the Laws of the United States which shall be made in Pursuance thereof; and all Treaties made, or which shall be made, under the Authority of the United States, shall be the supreme Law of the Land; and the Judges in every State shall be bound thereby, any Thing in the Constitution or Laws of any state to the Contrary notwithstanding. ❞*

—Article VI, Section 2

As you can see from the chart above, the Constitution and the laws and treaties of the United States are "the supreme Law of the Land." This means that the Constitution stands above all other forms of law in the United States. Acts of Congress and treaties stand immediately beneath the Constitution.[7]

The Supremacy Clause has been called the "linchpin of the Constitution" because it joins the National Government and the States into a

---

[7]Acts of Congress and treaties stand on equal planes with one another. Neither can conflict with any provision in the Constitution. In the rare case of conflict between the provisions of an act and those of a treaty, the one more recently adopted takes precedence—as the latest expression of the sovereign people's will. The Supreme Court has regularly held to that position from the first cases it decided on the point, *The Head Money Cases,* 1884.

single governmental unit, a federal government. In other words, the Supremacy Clause holds together the complex structure that is the American federal system.

The Supreme Court and Federalism

The Supreme Court is the umpire in the federal system. One of its chief duties is to apply the Supremacy Clause to the conflicts that the dual system of government inevitably produces.

The Court was first called to settle a clash between a national and a State law in 1819. The case, *McCulloch* v. *Maryland*, involved the controversial Second Bank of the United States. The bank had been chartered by Congress in 1816. In 1818, the Maryland legislature, hoping to cripple the bank, placed a tax on all notes issued by its Baltimore branch. James McCulloch, the branch cashier, refused to pay the tax, and the Maryland courts convicted him for that refusal.

The Supreme Court unanimously reversed the Maryland courts. Speaking for the Court, Chief Justice John Marshall based the decision squarely on the Constitution's Supremacy Clause:

PRIMARY Sources " *[If] any one proposition could command the universal assent of mankind, we might expect it would be this—that the government of the Union, though limited in its powers, is supreme within its sphere of action . . . . [T]he states have no power . . . to retard, impede,*

burden, or in any manner control, the operations of the constitutional laws enacted by Congress. . . . " [8]

—*McCulloch* v. *Maryland*, Opinion of the Court

Since this landmark case, it has been impossible to overstate the significance of the Court's function as the umpire of the federal system. Had the Court not taken this role, the federal system and probably the United States itself could not have survived its early years. Justice Oliver Wendell Holmes once made the point in these words:

PRIMARY Sources " *I do not think the United States would come to an end if we [the Court] lost our power to declare an Act of Congress void. I do think the Union would be imperiled if we could not make that declaration as to the laws of the several States.* "

—Collected Legal Papers[9]

---

[8] The case is also critically important in the development of the constitutional system because in deciding it, the Court for the first time upheld the doctrine of implied powers. It also held the National Government to be immune from any form of State taxation.

[9] The Supreme Court first held a State law unconstitutional in a case from Georgia, *Fletcher* v. *Peck*, 1810. The Court found that a Georgia law of 1795 making a grant of land to John Peck amounted to a contract between the State and Peck. It ruled that the legislature's later repeal of that law violated the Constitution's Contract Clause (Article I, Section 10, Clause 1). Since then, the Court has found more than 1,100 State laws unconstitutional (and has upheld the constitutionality of thousands of others).

Section 1 Assessment

Key Terms and Main Ideas

1. Why did the Framers settle on **federalism** as the system of government for the new nation?
2. Explain each of the following: **expressed powers, implied powers,** and **inherent powers.**
3. Do local governments have powers other than those granted to them by their State? Explain your answer.
4. What is the significance of *McCulloch* v. *Maryland* in the development of the federal system?

Critical Thinking

5. **Drawing Conclusions** Identify several public issues in your community that you think are best handled locally, not by the Federal Government.

Standards Monitoring *Online*
For: Self-quiz with vocabulary practice
Web Code: mqa-1041

6. **Determining Relevance** In *Texas* v. *White*, 1869, Chief Justice Salmon P. Chase declared: "The Constitution, in all its provisions, looks to an indestructible Union, composed of indestructible States." Identify three specific provisions in the Constitution that indicate "an indestructible Union" and three that point to "indestructible States."

For: An activity on federalism
Web Code: mqd-1041

on Primary Sources

More Power to the States

Analysis Skills HR4, HI3

Linda Chavez is the president of the Center for Equal Opportunity in Washington, D.C. She served as White House Director of Public Liaison in the Reagan administration. Here, Ms. Chavez argues that shifting responsibility for many social programs back to the States keeps power closer to the people.

One of the things the Founders of our nation most feared was centralized government power. Indeed, our Constitution and our Bill of Rights were written explicitly to ensure that power rested with the people and that no single branch of government—whether the executive, legislative, or judicial—gains a monopoly of power.

The Tenth Amendment to the Constitution also guaranteed that powers not specifically delegated to the federal government or prohibited to the states by the Constitution be retained by the states or the people.

Despite the intent of the founders, the history of our government, particularly in the last half of the twentieth century, has been one of growing federal power. Some of this has been accomplished directly by the government taking over certain functions; some has come indirectly, especially by the "power of the purse strings."

Whenever the federal government gives money to the states or to local governments or agencies, certain obligations or rules follow. . . . [T]he federal government gives billions of dollars a year to support public elementary and secondary schools, and along with the money comes federal dictates about exactly how the money can be spent. . . .

For a limited number of functions—national defense being the most obvious—the federal government is clearly the only institution that can properly manage and fund the necessary programs. . . . But many other functions that the

The United States flag and the Wisconsin State flag fly at Wisconsin's State capitol in Madison.

federal government performs, and taxes citizens to pay for, would be better decided on and funded at the local or state level, where people can keep track of what is being done and how much it costs. . . .

Efficiency and accountability are two reasons why state and local governments are better equipped to undertake certain tasks, but another . . . is flexibility. Some social problems are particularly difficult to solve, and what may work in one community may not be appropriate for another. . . .

Unfortunately, the federal government's involvement sometimes makes matters worse. It takes the decision making out of the hands of elected officials closest to the people and puts it in the hands of unelected bureaucrats in Washington. The founders of our nation anticipated the problems of centralized power and established constitutional guarantees to safeguard against it, but the people must make sure those guarantees are enforced.

Analyzing Primary Sources

1. According to Chavez, how has the Federal Government extended its power over the States?
2. Why is Chavez concerned about the growing power of the Federal Government?
3. Why does Chavez believe States are better able to handle local problems?

The National Government and the 50 States

Section Preview

OBJECTIVES

1. **Summarize** the obligations that the Constitution places on the nation for the benefit of the States.
2. **Explain** the process for admitting new States to the Union.
3. **Examine** the many and growing areas of cooperative federalism.

WHY IT MATTERS

In this country, the power to govern is shared by the National Government and each of the 50 States (including their thousands of local governments). Given this fact, conflicts are inevitable—and cooperation is absolutely necessary.

POLITICAL

DICTIONARY

★ enabling act
★ act of admission
★ grants-in-aid program
★ revenue sharing
★ categorical grant
★ block grant
★ project grant

Have you ever really focused on the words *United States?* The United States is a union of States, the several States joined together, the States united.

The Constitution created and is intended to preserve that union. To that end, the Constitution (1) requires the National Government to guarantee certain things to the States and (2) makes it possible for the National Government to do certain things for the States.

The Nation's Obligations to the States

The Constitution places several obligations on the National Government for the benefit of the States. Most of them are found in Article IV.

Republican Form of Government

The Constitution requires the National Government to "guarantee to every State in this Union a Republican Form of Government."[10] The Constitution does not define "Republican Form of Government," and the Supreme Court has regularly refused to do so. The term is generally understood to mean a "representative government."

The Supreme Court has held that the question of whether a State has a republican form of government is a political question. That is, it is one to be decided by the political branches of the government—the President and Congress—and not by the courts.[11]

---

[10]Article IV, Section 4.

[11]The leading case here is *Luther* v. *Borden,* 1849. This case grew out of Dorr's Rebellion, a revolt led by Thomas W. Dorr against the State of Rhode Island in 1841–1842. Dorr and his followers had written and proclaimed a new constitution for the State. When they tried to put the new document into operation, however, the governor in office under the original constitution declared martial law, or temporary rule by military authorities. The governor also called on the Federal Government for help. President John Tyler took steps to put down the revolt, and it quickly collapsed. Although the question of which of the competing governments was the legitimate one was a major issue in *Luther* v. *Borden,* the Supreme Court refused to decide the matter.

▲ After the Civil War, the "Republican Form of Government" figured prominently as laws were broadened to help recognize African American voting rights.

The Major Disaster Process

STEP 1	**Local Government Responds**. If overwhelmed, turns to the State for assistance.
STEP 2	**The State Responds** with State resources, such as the National Guard and State agencies.
STEP 3	**Damage Assessment** by local, State, Federal, and volunteer organizations.
STEP 4	**A Major Disaster Declaration** is requested by the governor, based on damage assessment.
STEP 5	**FEMA Evaluates** the request and recommends action to the White House.
STEP 6	**The President Approves** the request or FEMA informs the governor it has been denied.

SOURCE: Federal Emergency Management Agency

Interpreting Tables The Federal Emergency Management Agency (FEMA) helps State and local governments in the case of a natural disaster such as a hurricane. Coast Guard helicopters (above) rescued civilians trapped by flooding following Hurricane Katrina in 2005. *Explain the steps that lead to a community receiving federal disaster aid. How does this process illustrate federalism?* **H-SS 12.1.5**

The only extensive use ever made of the republican-form guarantee came in the years immediately following the Civil War. Congress declared that several southern States did not have governments of a republican form. It refused to admit senators and representatives from those States until the States had ratified the 13th, 14th, and 15th amendments and broadened their laws to recognize the voting and other rights of African Americans.

Invasion and Internal Disorder

The Constitution states that the National Government must also

FROM THE Constitution *"protect each of them [States] against Invasion; and on Application of the Legislature, or of the Executive (when the Legislature cannot be convened) against domestic Violence. "*
—Article IV, Section 4

Today it is clear that an invasion of any one of the 50 States would be met as an attack on the United States itself. This constitutional guarantee is therefore now of little, if any, significance.

That was not the case in the late 1780s. During that time, it was not at all certain that all 13 States would stand together if a foreign power attacked one of them. So, before the 13 States agreed to give up their war-making powers, each demanded an ironclad pledge that an attack on any single State would be met as an attack on all States.

The federal system assumes that each of the 50 States will keep the peace within its own borders. Thus, the primary responsibility for curbing insurrection, riot, or other internal disorder rests with the individual States. However, the Constitution does accept that a State might not be able to control some situations. It therefore guarantees protection against internal disorder, or what the Constitution calls "domestic Violence," in each of them.

The use of federal force to restore order within a State has historically been a rare event. Several instances did occur in the 1960s, however. When racial unrest exploded into violence in Detroit during the "long, hot summer" of 1967, President Lyndon Johnson ordered units of the United States Army into the city. He acted at the request of the governor of Michigan, George Romney, and only after Detroit's police and firefighters, supported by State Police and National Guard units, could not control riots, arson, and looting in the city. In 1968, again at the request of the governors involved, federal troops were sent into Chicago and Baltimore to help put down the violence that erupted following the assassination of Martin Luther King, Jr.

Normally, a President has sent troops into a State only in answer to a request from its governor or legislature. If national laws are being broken, national functions interfered with, or national property endangered, however, a President does not need to wait for such a plea.[12]

The ravages of nature—storms, floods, drought, forest fires, and such—can be more destructive than human violence. Here, too, acting to protect the States against "domestic Violence," the Federal Government stands ready to aid stricken areas.

Respect for Territorial Integrity

The National Government is constitutionally bound to respect the territorial integrity of each of the States. That is, the National Government must recognize the legal existence and the physical boundaries of each State.

The basic scheme of the Constitution imposes this obligation. Several of its provisions do so, as well. For example, Congress must include, in both of its houses, members chosen in each one of the States.[13] Recall, too, that Article V of the Constitution declares that no State can be deprived of its equal representation in the United States Senate without its own consent.

Admitting New States

Only Congress has the power to admit new States to the Union. As part of the National Government's guarantee of respect for each State's territorial integrity, the Constitution places only

California became the 31st State on September 9, 1850, two years after being ceded by Mexico.

one restriction on that power. A new State cannot be created by taking territory from one or more of the existing States without the consent of the legislature(s) of the State(s) involved.[14]

Congress has admitted 37 States since the original 13 formed the Union, as the map on the next page shows. Five States (Vermont, Kentucky, Tennessee, Maine, and West Virginia) were created from parts of already existing States. Texas was an independent republic before admission. California was admitted shortly after being ceded to the United States by Mexico. Each of the other 30 States entered the Union only after a longer period of time, frequently more than 15 years, as an organized territory.

Admission Procedure

The process of admission to the Union is usually fairly simple. The area desiring Statehood first asks Congress for admission. If and when Congress chooses, it passes an **enabling act,** an act directing the people of the territory to frame a proposed State constitution. A convention prepares the constitution, which is then put to a popular vote in the proposed State. If the voters

---

[12]President Grover Cleveland ordered federal troops to put an end to rioting in the Chicago rail yard during the Pullman Strike in 1894 despite the objections of Governor William Altgeld of Illinois. The Supreme Court upheld his actions in *In re Debs,* 1895. The Court found that rioters had threatened federal property and impeded the flow of the mails and interstate commerce. Thus, more than "domestic Violence" was involved. Since then, several Presidents have acted without a request from the State involved. Most recently, President Dwight Eisenhower did so at Little Rock, Arkansas, in 1957, and President John Kennedy did so at the University of Mississippi in 1962 and at the University of Alabama in 1963. In each of those instances, the President acted to halt the unlawful obstruction of school integration orders issued by the federal courts.

---

[13]In the House, Article I, Section 2, Clause 1; in the Senate, Article I, Section 3, Clause 1 and the 17th Amendment.

[14]Article IV, Section 3, Clause 1. Some argue that this provision was violated with West Virginia's admission in 1863. That State was formed from the 40 western counties that had broken away from Virginia over the issue of secession from the Union. The consent required by the Constitution was given by a minority of the members of the Virginia legislature—those who represented the 40 western counties. Congress accepted their action, holding that they were the only group legally capable of acting as the Virginia legislature at the time.

approve the constitution, it is submitted to Congress for its consideration. If Congress still agrees to Statehood after reviewing the document, it passes an **act of admission,** an act creating the new State. If the President signs the act, the new State enters the Union.

The two newest States, Alaska and Hawaii, shortened the usual process of gaining admission to the Union. Each adopted a proposed constitution without waiting for an enabling act, Hawaii in 1950 and Alaska in 1956. Both became States in 1959.

Conditions for Admission

Before finally admitting a new State, Congress has often set certain conditions. For example, in 1896, Utah was admitted on condition that its constitution outlaw polygamy, the practice of having more than one spouse at a time. In the act admitting Alaska to the Union as the 49th State, Congress forever prohibited that State from claiming title to any lands legally held by any Native American.

Each State enters the Union on an equal footing with each of the other States. Thus,

although Congress can set certain conditions like those just described, it cannot impose conditions of a political nature on the States. For example, when Oklahoma was admitted to the Union in 1907, Congress said the State could not remove its capital from Guthrie to any other place before 1913. In 1910, however, the Oklahoma legislature moved the State's capital to Oklahoma City. When this step was challenged, the United States Supreme Court held, in *Coyle* v. *Smith,* 1911, that Congress can set conditions for a prospective State's admission. But the Court also held that the conditions cannot be enforced when they compromise the independence of a State to manage its own internal affairs.

Consider one more example: President William Howard Taft vetoed a resolution to admit Arizona to the Union in 1911. He did so because Arizona's proposed constitution provided that members of the State's judiciary could be recalled (removed from office) by popular vote. This provision meant, said Taft, that a judge would have to keep one eye on the law and the other on public opinion. In

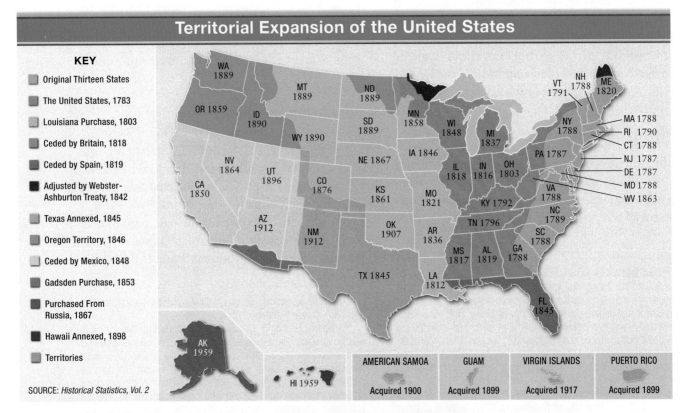

Territorial Expansion of the United States

KEY

- Original Thirteen States
- The United States, 1783
- Louisiana Purchase, 1803
- Ceded by Britain, 1818
- Ceded by Spain, 1819
- Adjusted by Webster-Ashburton Treaty, 1842
- Texas Annexed, 1845
- Oregon Territory, 1846
- Ceded by Mexico, 1848
- Gadsden Purchase, 1853
- Purchased From Russia, 1867
- Hawaii Annexed, 1898
- Territories

SOURCE: *Historical Statistics, Vol. 2*

WA 1889 · MT 1889 · ND 1889 · VT 1791 · NH 1788 · ME 1820 · OR 1859 · ID 1890 · MN 1858 · WI 1848 · NY 1788 · MA 1788 · RI 1790 · CT 1788 · WY 1890 · SD 1889 · MI 1837 · NJ 1787 · DE 1787 · MD 1788 · WV 1863 · NV 1864 · UT 1896 · NE 1867 · IA 1846 · PA 1787 · CA 1850 · CO 1876 · KS 1861 · IL 1818 · IN 1816 · OH 1803 · VA 1788 · MO 1821 · KY 1792 · NC 1789 · AZ 1912 · NM 1912 · OK 1907 · AR 1836 · TN 1796 · SC 1788 · TX 1845 · MS 1817 · AL 1819 · GA 1788 · LA 1812 · FL 1845 · AK 1959 · HI 1959

AMERICAN SAMOA	GUAM	VIRGIN ISLANDS	PUERTO RICO
Acquired 1900	Acquired 1899	Acquired 1917	Acquired 1899

Interpreting Maps Thirty-seven States have joined the original 13. *When did your State join the Union? How much of the nation's present area did the United States cover at that time?*

response to Taft's concern, Arizona removed the recall section from the document. In 1912 Congress passed, and the President signed, another act of admission for Arizona. Almost immediately after admission, however, the new State amended its new constitution to provide for the recall of judges. That provision remains a valid part of Arizona's constitution today.

Cooperative Federalism

Remember, federalism produces a dual system of government, one in which two basic levels operate over the same people and the same territory at the same time. As a result of this complex arrangement, competition, tensions, and conflict are a regular and ongoing part of American federalism. In short, the American governmental system is much like a tug-of-war, a continuing power struggle between the National Government and the several States.

The American federal system also involves a broad area of *shared* powers. That is, in addition to the two separate spheres of power held and exercised by the two basic levels of government, there are large and growing areas of cooperation between them. These areas include the funds that the Federal Government grants to the States as well as the various services that the States perform for the Federal Government.

Federal Grants-in-Aid

Perhaps the best-known examples of this intergovernmental cooperation are the many federal **grants-in-aid programs**—grants of federal money or other resources to the States and/or their cities, counties, and other local units. Many of these governments are regularly strapped for funds; these grants often help them perform a large share of their everyday functions.

The history of grants-in-aid programs goes back more than 200 years, to the period before the Constitution. In the Northwest Ordinance of 1787, the Congress under the Articles of Confederation provided for the government of the territory beyond the Ohio River. Looking forward to the existence of new States on that frontier, the Congress set aside sections of land for the support of public education in those future States. On

The Massachusetts Central Artery project, known as the "Big Dig," was the largest, most complex, and technologically challenging public works project to date in American history. *Critical Thinking How does this project illustrate cooperative federalism?* H-SS 12.1.5

Federal funding 58.5%

State and local funding 41.5%

through the nineteenth century, States received grants of federal lands for a number of purposes: schools and colleges, roads and canals, flood control work, and several others. A large number of the major State universities, for example, were founded as land-grant colleges. These schools were built with money obtained from the sale of public lands given to the States by the Morrill Act of 1862.

Congress began to make grants of federal money quite early, too. In 1808, it gave the States $200,000 to support the militia. Cash grants did not come to play a large role, however, until the Depression years of the 1930s. Many of the New Deal programs aimed at bringing the nation out of its economic crisis were built around grants of money.

Since then, Congress has set up hundreds of grants-in-aid programs. In fact, more than 500 are now in operation. Dozens of programs function in a variety of areas: in education, mass transit, highway construction, health care, on-the-job training, and many others.

▲ Federal monies help fund school lunch programs in schools across the country.
Critical Thinking *What examples of cooperative federalism affect your own life?*

Grants-in-aid are based on the National Government's taxing power. The Constitution gives Congress that power in order

FROM THE *Constitution* **"***to pay the Debts and provide for the common Defense and general Welfare of the United States. . . .***"**
—Article I, Section 8, Clause 1

Today, these grants total some $275 billion, and account for about 25 percent of all State and local government spending each year.

In effect, grants-in-aid blur the division of powers line in the federal system. They make it possible for the Federal Government to operate in many policy areas in which it would otherwise have no constitutional authority—for example, in such fields as education, low-income housing, local law enforcement, and mental health.

Critics of grants-in-aid have long made this point. They also argue that the grants often give Washington a major—and they say an unwarranted—voice in making public policy at the State and local levels.

Revenue Sharing

A quite different form of federal monetary aid, known as **revenue sharing,** was in place from 1972 to 1987. Under this program, Congress gave an annual share of the huge federal tax revenue to the States and their cities, counties, and townships. Altogether, those "shared revenues" amounted to more than $83 billion over the years the program was in force.

Virtually no strings were attached to this money. In fact, Congress placed only one major restriction on the use of the funds. The money could not be spent for any program in which discrimination on the basis of race, sex, national origin, age, religious belief, or physical disability was evident. Otherwise, the "shared revenues" could be used very largely as the States and their local units chose to spend them.

Needless to say, revenue sharing was quite popular with and strongly supported by many governors, mayors, and other State and local officials. It was opposed by the Reagan Administration, however, and fell victim to the financial needs of the deficit-ridden National Government. Various efforts to revive revenue sharing to help today's cash-strapped State and local governments have not won significant support in Congress, at least to this point in time.

Types of Federal Grants

Today, Congress appropriates money for three types of grants-in-aid. These include categorical grants, block grants, and project grants.

Over time, most grants have been categorical. **Categorical grants** are made for some specific, closely defined purpose: for school lunches or for the construction of airports or wastewater treatment plants, for example. Categorical grants are usually made with conditions attached. These "strings" require the State to (1) use the federal monies only for the specific purpose involved, (2) make its own monetary contribution, often a matching amount but sometimes much less, (3) provide an agency to administer the grant, and (4) obey a set of guidelines tailored to the particular purpose for which the monies are given.

Block grants have come into wide use over the last several years. They are made for much more broadly defined purposes than are categorical grants, such as health care, social services, or welfare. They are also made with fewer strings attached, so State and local governments have much greater freedom in deciding just how and on what to spend block grant dollars. Beginning in the Reagan years, from the 1980s on, many programs once supported by separate and fragmented categorical grants have been merged into broader block grants.

Congress also provides money for **project grants.** These are grants made to States, localities, and sometimes private agencies that apply for them. The Department of Health and Human Services makes many project grants—through its National Institutes of Health, for example, to support scientists engaged in research on cancer, diabetes, neurological disease, and other medical issues. Many State and local governments also apply for these grants to fund their job training and employment programs.

Other Forms of Federal Aid
The National Government aids the States in several other important ways. For example, the FBI gives extensive help to State and local police. The army and the air force equip and train each State's National Guard units. The Census Bureau's data are essential to State and local school, housing, and transportation officials as they plan for the future.

Many other forms of aid are not nearly so visible. "Lulu payments," for example, are federal monies that go to local governments in those areas in which there are large federal landholdings. These direct payments are made in lieu of—to take the place of—the property taxes that those local governments cannot collect from the National Government.

State Aid to the National Government
Intergovernmental cooperation is a two-way street. That is, the States and their local units of government also aid the National Government in many ways.

Thus, State and local election officials conduct national elections in each State. These elections are financed with State and local funds, and they are regulated largely by State laws. The legal process by which aliens can become citizens, called naturalization, takes place most often in State, not federal, courts. Those who commit federal crimes and are sought by the FBI and other federal law enforcement agencies are often picked up by State and local police officers and then held in local jails. And the examples go on and on.

Section 2 Assessment

Standards Monitoring *Online*
For: Self-quiz with vocabulary practice
Web Code: mqa-1042

Key Terms and Main Ideas
1. What are three obligations that the Constitution places on the National Government for the benefit of the States?
2. Explain the difference between an **enabling act** and an **act of admission.**
3. (a) What is a **block grant?**
   (b) How do block grants reflect cooperative federalism?
4. In what ways do the States aid the National Government?

Critical Thinking
5. **Recognizing Ideologies** If the Framers had been alive, how do you think they might have reacted when, only a few years ago, several States had to raise the legal drinking age to avoid losing a substantial portion of their federal grants for highway construction? Explain your answer.

6. **Making Comparisons** Suppose your State is to receive increased federal funding for a program to provide day care for the children of some working parents. Would this funding likely come as a categorical grant, a block grant, or a project grant? Why?
7. **Expressing Problems Clearly** In what type of situation would your State be most likely to need federal protection against "domestic Violence?" Explain your answer.

Go Online
PHSchool.com
For: An activity on Statehood
Web Code: mqd-1042

Face the
Issues

Public Lands

Background *In early 2001, President Bill Clinton issued an executive order prohibiting road-building on 58.8 million acres of national forest lands. The area involved, most of it in the West, contains nearly all of the nation's remaining old-growth forests. In 2005, President George W. Bush rewrote the Clinton order. Now each State's governor can petition the Secretary of Agriculture, designating the forest lands he or she thinks should be opened or remain closed to new road construction.*

**Logging in Alaska's
Tongass National Forest**

Analysis Skill HI5

Federalism in Action

The Bush policy is rooted in federalism. It gives the States a major role in deciding whether—and, if so, which—federal forest lands are to be developed. The Secretary of Agriculture has the final word, but a governor's recommendation will carry great weight.

Opening selected areas to logging, mining, and other commercial endeavors can provide jobs and spur local economies throughout the West. Modern-day road-building, logging, and mining techniques mean that environmental damage will be minimal.

John Bennet, who heads a major timber company in Idaho, says: "It is a step in the right direction to identify those lands that are suitable [for logging] . . . instead of putting a big lock on them." Barry Russell, president of the Independent Petroleum Association of America, agrees. The Bush approach, he says, helps "eliminate government obstacles and regulatory [barriers] so that our natural resources can be produced and provide the enormous amounts of energy" this nation needs.

Block the New Rule

The Bush administration has gutted the original rule, with a new policy that will do major and irreversible damage to national lands. The Clinton rule was the product of years of study and more than 600 public hearings. As one environmental group put it, the Clinton policy "protected untouched lands and cold, pure rivers that give many Americans their cleanest sources of drinking water, and preserved much of the little that remains of the old-growth forests that once blanketed this country."

Officials in California, New Mexico, and Oregon have filed a lawsuit to block the new rule. Several governors complain that they do not have the staff or money for the petition process, which requires mapping, estimates of effects on wildlife and public safety, and assessments of the likelihood of forest fires.

California's attorney general Bill Lockyer says the new policy "simply paves the way for logging, mining, and other kinds of mineral extraction" on public lands.

Exploring the Issues

1. Identify three major goals that you think should guide the management of the nation's public lands.?

2. Why do you think federal officials often weigh environmental and economic costs differently than local officials do?

For more information on state and federal disputes, view "Public Lands."

Face the **Issues** Video Collection

③ *Interstate Relations*

Section Preview

OBJECTIVES

1. **Explain** why States make interstate compacts.
2. **Understand** the purpose of the Full Faith and Credit Clause.
3. **Define** *extradition* and explain its purpose.
4. **Discuss** the purpose of the Privileges and Immunities Clause.

WHY IT MATTERS

What if Texas citizens were not allowed to travel into Oklahoma, or needed a special passport to do so? What if your North Carolina driver's license were not valid when you drove through Ohio? Fortunately, several key provisions in the Constitution promote cooperation between and among the States.

POLITICAL DICTIONARY

★ **interstate compact**
★ **Full Faith and Credit Clause**
★ **extradition**
★ **Privileges and Immunities Clause**

As you know, conflict among the States was a major reason for the writing and adoption of the Constitution. The fact that the new document strengthened the hand of the National Government, especially regarding commerce, lessened many of those frictions. So, too, did several of the Constitution's provisions that deal directly with the States' relationships with one another. This section is concerned with those provisions.

Interstate Compacts

No State can enter into any treaty, alliance, or confederation. However, the States may, with the consent of Congress, enter into **interstate compacts**—agreements among themselves and with foreign states.[15]

By 1920, the States had made only 26 compacts. Since then, the number of interstate compacts has been growing. New York and New Jersey led the way in 1921 with a compact creating what is now the Port Authority of New York and New Jersey to manage and develop the harbor facilities bordering both States. More than 200 compacts are now in force, and many involve several States. In fact, all 50 States have joined in two of them: the Compact for the Supervision of Parolees and Probationers and the Compact on Juveniles. These two compacts enable States to share important law-enforcement data. Other agreements cover a widening range of subjects. They include, for example, compacts designed to coordinate the development and conservation of such resources as water, oil, wildlife, and fish; prevent forest fires; combat stream and harbor pollution; provide for tax collections; promote motor vehicle safety; facilitate the licensing of drivers; and encourage the cooperative use of public universities.

▲ Seven western States belong to the Colorado River Compact, which apportions the waters of the Colorado River Basin. **H-SS 12.7.2**

---

[15]Article I, Section 10, Clause 3. The Supreme Court has held that Congressional consent is not needed for compacts that do not tend to increase the political power of the States, *Virginia* v. *Tennessee*, 1893. But it is often difficult to decide whether an agreement is political or nonpolitical. So, most interstate agreements are submitted to Congress as a matter of course.

Full Faith and Credit

The Constitution commands that

FROM THE Constitution *"Full Faith and Credit shall be given in each State to the public Acts, Records, and judicial Proceedings of every other State. "*
—Article IV, Section 1

The term *public acts* refers to the laws of a State. *Records* refers to such documents as birth certificates, marriage licenses, deeds to property, car registrations, and the like. The words *judicial proceedings* relate to the outcome of court actions: damage awards, the probating (proving) of wills, divorce decrees, and so forth.

The **Full Faith and Credit Clause** most often comes into play in court matters. Take this example: Allen sues Bill in Florida, and the Florida court awards Allen $50,000 in damages. Bill cannot escape payment of the damages by moving to Georgia, because Allen could simply ask the Georgia courts to enforce the damage award. Neither would the case have to be retried in Georgia. Instead, the Georgia courts would have to give full faith and credit to—recognize and respect the validity of—the judgment made by the Florida court.

▲ **Full Faith and Credit** The Full Faith and Credit Clause ensures that records such as birth certificates and marriage licenses are recognized in all 50 States. **H-SS 12.7.1**

In a similar vein, a person can prove age, place of birth, marital status, title to property, and similar facts by securing the necessary documents from the State where the record was made. The validity of these documents will be recognized in each of the 50 States.

Exceptions

The Full Faith and Credit Clause is regularly observed and usually operates routinely between and among the States. This rule has two exceptions, however. First, it applies only to civil, not criminal, matters. One State cannot enforce another State's criminal law. Second, full faith and credit need not be given to certain divorces granted by one State to residents of another State.

On the second exception, the key question is always this: Was the person who obtained the divorce in fact a resident of the State that granted it? If so, the divorce will be accorded full faith and credit in other States. If not, then the State granting the divorce did not have the authority to do so, and another State can refuse to recognize it.

Williams v. North Carolina

The matter of interstate "quickie" divorces has been troublesome for years, especially since the Supreme Court's decision in a 1945 case, *Williams* v. *North Carolina.* In that case, a man and a woman had traveled to Nevada, where each wanted to obtain a divorce so they could marry each other. They lived in Las Vegas for six weeks, the minimum period of State residence required by Nevada's divorce law. The couple received their divorces, were married, and soon after returned to North Carolina. Problems arose when that State's authorities refused to recognize their Nevada divorces. North Carolina brought the couple to trial and a jury convicted each of them of the crime of bigamous cohabitation (marrying and living together while a previous marriage is still legally in effect).

On appeal, the Supreme Court upheld North Carolina's denial of full faith and credit to the Nevada divorces. It ruled that the couple had not in fact established bona fide—good faith, valid—residence in Nevada. Rather, the Court held that

▲ Each State requires that those who operate motor vehicles be licensed to do so. **Critical Thinking** *Why is it possible to drive across the country without having to obtain a driver's license in each State along the way?*

the couple had remained legal residents of North Carolina. In short, it found that Nevada lacked the authority to grant their divorces.

A divorce granted by a State court to a *bona fide* resident of that State must be given full faith and credit in all other States. To become a legal resident of a State, a person must intend to reside there permanently, or at least indefinitely. Clearly, the Williamses had not intended to do so.

The *Williams* case, and later ones like it, cast dark clouds of doubt over the validity of thousands of other interstate divorces. The later marriages of people involved in these divorces, and the frequently tangled estate problems produced by their deaths, suggest the confused and serious nature of the matter.[16]

Extradition

According to the Constitution

> **FROM THE Constitution** *" A Person charged in any State with Treason, Felony, or other Crime, who shall flee from Justice, and be found in another State, shall on Demand of the executive Authority of the State from which he fled, be delivered up, to be removed to the State having Jurisdiction of the Crime. "*
>
> — Article IV, Section 2, Clause 2

This clause refers to **extradition,** the legal process by which a fugitive from justice in one State can be returned to that State. Extradition is designed to prevent a person from escaping justice by fleeing a State.

The return of a fugitive from justice is usually a routine matter; governors regularly approve the extradition requests they receive from other States' chief executives. Some of those requests, however, are contested. This is especially true in cases with strong racial or political overtones, and in cases of parental kidnapping of children involved in custody disputes.

Until the 1980s, governors could, and on occasion did, refuse to return fugitives. In *Kentucky* v. *Dennison,* 1861, the Supreme Court held that the Constitution did not give the Federal Government any power with which to compel a governor to act in an extradition case. So, for more than a century, the Constitution's word *shall* in the Extradition Clause had to be read as "may."

The Court overturned this ruling in 1987, however. In *Puerto Rico* v. *Branstad,* a unanimous Court held that the federal courts can indeed order an unwilling governor to extradite a fugitive.

Privileges and Immunities

The Constitution also provides that

> **FROM THE Constitution** *" The Citizens of each State shall be entitled to all Privileges and Immunities of Citizens in the several States. "*
>
> —Article IV, Section 2, Clause 1[17]

This clause, known as the **Privileges and Immunities Clause,** means that no State can draw unreasonable distinctions between its own residents and those persons who happen to live in other States.

Each State must recognize the right of any American to travel in or become a resident of that State. It must also allow any citizen, no matter where he or she lives, to use its courts and make contracts; buy, own, rent, or sell property; or marry within its borders.

---

[16]The Defense of Marriage Act, passed in 1996, declares that no State is required to recognize a same-sex marriage performed in another State. Its constitutionality has not been resolved in court.
[17]The provision is reinforced in the 14th Amendment.

Under the Privileges and Immunities Clause, public colleges and universities often charge higher rates for nonresidents than residents. The University of California, Los Angeles, for example, charged residents tuition and fees of $7,062 and nonresidents $24,882 in 2005–2006. **Critical Thinking** *Do you think that this practice is justified? Explain your answer.*

At the same time, a State cannot do such things as try to relieve its unemployment problems by requiring employers to give a hiring preference to in-State residents. Thus, the Supreme Court struck down a law in which the State of Alaska directed employers to prefer Alaskans in the hiring of workers to construct that State's oil and gas pipelines, *Hicklin* v. *Orbeck,* 1978. And the Court has overturned a California law that set the welfare benefits paid to newly arrived residents at a lower level than those paid to long-term residents, *Saenz* v. *Roe,* 1999.

However, the Privileges and Immunities Clause does allow States to draw reasonable distinctions between its own residents and those of other States. Thus, any State can require that a person live within the State for some time before he or she can vote or hold public office. It also can require some period of residence before one can be licensed to practice law, medicine, dentistry, and so on.

In another example, the wild fish and game in a State are considered to be the common property of the people of that State. So, a State can require nonresidents to pay higher fees for fishing or hunting licenses than those paid by residents—who pay taxes to provide fish hatcheries, enforce game laws, and so on. By the same token, State colleges and universities regularly set higher tuition rates for students from out-of-State than those they charge residents of the State.

Section 3 Assessment

Key Terms and Main Ideas

1. What agreements does the Constitution prohibit the States from making?
2. What is the meaning of the **Full Faith and Credit Clause?**
3. What is the purpose of **extradition?**
4. **(a)** Give at least two examples of actions protected under the **Privileges and Immunities Clause. (b)** What types of actions are not protected by this clause?

Critical Thinking

5. **Predicting Consequences** What difficulties might result if each State were not required to give full faith and credit to the public acts, records, and judicial proceedings of other States? Provide at least two examples to support your conclusion.

6. **Drawing Inferences** Provide at least two examples of how the Privileges and Immunities Clause has affected your life or might do so in the future.

on the Supreme Court

Should States Be Required to Enforce Federal Laws?

Analysis Skills HR4, HI3, HI4

States are required to obey the federal Constitution and federal laws and treaties. Can Congress require State officials to help enforce federal laws and regulations?

Printz v. United States (1997)

The Gun Control Act of 1968 outlined rules for the distribution of firearms. Dealers were prohibited from selling guns to persons under 21, out-of-state residents, and convicted felons and fugitives. The Brady Act, a 1993 amendment to that law, required the attorney general to establish by 1998 a national system for conducting instant background checks on prospective handgun buyers.

The Brady Act also created a temporary background check system. Before selling a handgun, a firearms dealer was required to obtain identification from the purchaser, and to forward that information to the "chief law enforcement officer" (CLEO) of the purchaser's residence. The Brady Act required CLEOs to make a reasonable effort to determine within the five business days whether the purchaser may lawfully possess a gun.

Jay Printz and Richard Mack, sheriffs serving as CLEOs in counties in Montana and Arizona, respectively, challenged the Brady Act in federal district court. They argued that the provisions requiring them to perform federal functions and execute federal laws were unconstitutional. The district court agreed with their argument, but the court of appeals found the entire Act constitutional, and the case went to the Supreme Court for review.

Arguments for Printz

1. The balance of power between Federal and State governments would be disrupted if the Federal Government could force the States to implement federal laws, especially if the States had to pay the implementation costs.
2. Under the Constitution, executing the laws of the United States is the function of the President.

The Brady Act would transfer part of this function to State and local officials, over whom the President has no meaningful control.
3. The Framers of the Constitution rejected the idea of having the central government act through the States in favor of a federal system of government.

Arguments for the United States

1. Congress has the expressed power to regulate commerce among the States. The Brady Act provisions are "necessary and proper" to carry out this power and thus are a lawful exercise of the power.
2. The burden imposed by the Brady Act on State or local officials is small, and therefore does not threaten the balance of power between States and the Federal Government.
3. Congress found that there is an "epidemic" of gun violence, and it can lawfully require State and local officials to help deal with emergency situations on a temporary basis.

Decide for Yourself

1. Review the constitutional grounds on which each side based its arguments and the specific arguments each side presented.
2. Debate the opposing viewpoints presented in this case. Which viewpoint do you favor?
3. Predict the impact of the Court's decision on federal programs that require local enforcement. (To read a summary of the Court's decision, turn to pages 799–806.)

Go Online
PHSchool.com

Use Web Code mqp-1046 to register your vote on this issue and to see how other students voted.

Political Dictionary

federalism (p. 88), division of powers (p. 89), delegated powers (p. 89), expressed powers (p. 89), implied powers (p. 90), inherent powers (p. 91), reserved powers (p. 92), exclusive powers (p. 93), concurrent powers (p. 93), enabling act (p. 99), act of admission (p. 100), grants-in-aid program (p. 101), revenue sharing (p. 102), categorical grant (p. 102), block grant (p. 103), project grant (p. 103), interstate compact (p. 105), Full Faith and Credit Clause (p. 106), extradition (p. 107), Privileges and Immunities Clause (p. 107)

Standards Review

H-SS 12.1.5 Describe the systems of separated and shared powers, the role of organized interests (*Federalist Paper Number 10*), checks and balances (*Federalist Paper Number 51*), the importance of an independent judiciary (*Federalist Paper Number 78*), enumerated powers, rule of law, federalism, and civilian control of the military.

H-SS 12.2.1 Discuss the meaning and importance of each of the rights guaranteed under the Bill of rights and how each is secured (e.g., freedom of religion, speech, press, assembly, petition, privacy).

H-SS 12.7.1 Explain how conflicts between levels of government and branches of government are resolved.

H-SS 12.7.3 Discuss reserved powers and concurrent powers of state governments.

H-SS 12.7.2 Identify the major responsibilities and sources of revenue for state and local governments.

H-SS 12.7.4 Discuss the Ninth and Tenth Amendments and interpretations of the extent of the federal government's power.

H-SS 12.10 Students formulate questions about and defend their analyses of tensions within our constitutional democracy and the importance of maintaining a balance between the following concepts: majority rule and individual rights; liberty and equality; state and national authority in a federal system; civil disobedience and the rule of law; freedom of the press and the right to a fair trial; the relationship of religion and government.

Practicing the Vocabulary

Matching *Choose a term from the list above that best matches each description.*

1. The powers that the Constitution grants to the National Government in so many words
2. Congressional measure admitting a United States territory into the Union as a State
3. A type of federal grant-in-aid that is used for a specific, narrowly defined purpose
4. A system of government in which a constitution divides the powers of government between a National Government and several regional governments
5. Agreements made by the States among themselves and with foreign powers

Fill in the Blank *Choose a term from the list above that best completes the sentence.*

6. _____ are those powers held by the States in the federal system.
7. _____ are those powers granted to the National Government in the Constitution.
8. Some people have questioned whether the _____ gives the National Government too much say in matters of State and local concern.
9. Congress directs a territory desiring Statehood to frame a proposed State constitution in a(n) _____ .
10. Those powers that can only be exercised by the National Government are called _____ .

Reviewing Main Ideas

Section 1

11. How did the principle of federalism enable the Framers to solve the problems they faced in 1787?
12. Briefly describe the powers the Constitution gives to the National Government.
13. **(a)** In what three ways does the Constitution deny powers to the National Government? **(b)** Give at least one example of each.
14. How does the Constitution provide for the powers of the States in the federal system?
15. What is the role of the Supreme Court in the federal system?

Section 2

16. According to the Constitution, what are the National Government's obligations to the States?
17. Outline the steps Congress has usually taken in admitting new States to the Union.

18. What is cooperative federalism?
19. Give at least three examples of cooperative federalism at work.
20. **(a)** What is a block grant? **(b)** Give an example of a program that a State might fund using block grant money.

Section 3

21. List at least three examples of the kinds of interstate compacts that exist today.
22. Under what circumstances can a State deny full faith and credit to a law, a public record, or the outcome of a court case in another State?
23. Explain the purpose of the Privileges and Immunities Clause.
24. What is the significance of the Supreme Court's decision in *Williams* v. *North Carolina?*
25. Can governors refuse to return fugitives from justice to the State from which they fled? Explain your answer.

Critical Thinking Skills

Analysis Skills HR4, HI1, HI5

26. **Applying the Chapter Skill** In your opinion, who should have final say over lands currently under federal control, the States or the Federal Government? Explain your reasoning.

27. **Drawing Conclusions** Why might a governor be reluctant to call for federal troops to combat domestic violence in a city in his or her State?

28. **Expressing Problems Clearly** Why did the Framers create a government that is federal rather than unitary?

29. **Drawing Conclusions** Why do you think the Framers thought it necessary to include the Supremacy Clause in the Constitution? Why was the 10th Amendment added?

Analyzing Political Cartoons

Using your knowledge of American government and this cartoon, answer the questions below.

LEVELS OF CONSCIOUSNESS

FEDERAL
STATE
LOCAL

30. What does the cartoon suggest about the relative importance of local government?

31. The cartoon portrays three levels of government—Federal, State, and local. From what you have read about the federal system, is this portrayal entirely accurate? Explain your answer.

Participation Activities

Analysis Skills CS1, HR4, HI1

32. **Current Events Watch** Find three to five examples in the news that illustrate a power of the National Government, such as sending troops abroad or regulating immigration. Do the same for powers reserved to the States, such as establishing and regulating public schools. Prepare an oral presentation explaining how the State and national powers that you have chosen affect you and your community.

33. **Time Line Activity** Research how your State (or another State of your choosing) became a State. Then create a time line in which you explain your findings. Illustrate main events in your time line with drawings or copies of photos. Be sure to point out anything unique about the process by which your selected State entered the Union.

34. **It's Your Turn** When a person moves from one State to another, he or she must do such things as obtain a new driver's license and change his or her automobile and voter registrations. Create a newsletter to advise persons moving to your State how they can accomplish these tasks. **(Writing a Newsletter)**

Standards Monitoring *Online*

For: Chapter 4 Self-Test   **Visit:** PHSchool.com
Web Code: mqa-1044

As a final review, take the Magruder's Chapter 4 Self-Test and receive immediate feedback on your answers.
The test consists of 20 multiple-choice questions designed to test your understanding of the chapter content.

◆ **Americans expressing their patriotism**

Political Behavior: Government By the People

CONSTITUTIONAL PRINCIPLES

Popular Sovereignty When the voters go to the polls in this country, they reaffirm the principle of popular sovereignty. When they vote, they choose those public officeholders who will represent them in the day-to-day conduct of their government. In short, the people rule, the people are sovereign.

Federalism The voters elect more than half-a-million public officeholders in this country today—at the national, the State, and the local levels. They fill offices from the presidency down to, literally, in some places today, dogcatchers.

Judicial Review The right to vote is protected by the Federal Constitution—and these protections are backed by the power of the courts to strike down any governmental action that interferes with the exercise of that right.

The Impact on You

Why vote? Because those whom the voters choose decide dozens upon hundreds of vital public policy questions at every level of government. They decide on matters that range from environmental protection and civil rights to public education, transportation, and communication—and much more. In short, those whom the voters choose have a major impact on your every waking and sleeping moment.

CHAPTER 5

Political Parties

"A party of order or stability, and a party of progress or reform, are both necessary elements of a healthy state of political life."

—John Stuart Mill (1859)

John Stuart Mill, a British philosopher, noted the benefits of two competing political parties. In this country, the balance of power has historically switched between two broad-based parties. Our major parties choose candidates and play important roles in government. Minor parties have challenged, but never really changed, this two-party system.

◆ A political party holds its national convention.

Go Online
PHSchool.com

For: Current Data
Web Code: mqg-2057

For: Close Up Foundation debates
Web Code: mqh-2050

SECTION 1

Parties and What They Do (pp. 116–118)

★ The primary purpose of the two major American political parties is to control government through winning election to public office.

★ Political parties nominate candidates, rally their supporters, participate in government, act as a "bonding agent" for their own officeholders, and act as a watchdog over the other party.

SECTION 2

The Two-Party System (pp. 119–124)

★ The two-party system is a product of our history and tradition, the electoral system, and the American ideological consensus.

★ Multiparty systems provide more choice for the electorate but a less stable government. In one-party systems only the ruling party can participate in elections.

★ While the two major parties are broadly based, each party does tend to attract certain segments of the electorate.

SECTION 3

The Two-Party System in American History (pp. 126–131)

★ The first American parties originated in the battle over ratifying the Constitution.

★ There have been three eras of single-party domination in U.S. history from 1800–1968.

★ An era of divided government—with neither major party consistently in power—began in 1968 and continues to this day.

SECTION 4

The Minor Parties (pp. 132–135)

★ Minor parties in the United States include ideological parties, single-issue parties, economic protest parties, and splinter parties.

★ Even though they do not win national elections, minor parties play an important role as critics and innovators.

★ Strong third-party candidacies can influence elections.

SECTION 5

Party Organization (pp. 137–142)

★ The major parties have a decentralized structure because of federalism and the sometimes divisive nominating process.

★ At the national level, the four basic elements of both major parties are the national convention, the national committee, the national chairperson, and the congressional campaign committee.

★ At the State level, the party is organized around a State central committee headed by a State chairperson, while local organizations vary widely.

★ Party structure can also be viewed as made up of the party organization, or machinery; the people who usually vote the party ticket; and the party's officeholders.

★ Parties are currently in decline: fewer people identify themselves as major party members, and many people vote a split ticket.

Parties and What They Do

OBJECTIVES

1. **Define** a political party.
2. **Describe** the major functions of political parties.

WHY IT MATTERS

Political parties are essential to democratic government. In the United States, political parties have shaped the way the government works. Today, the major parties perform several important functions without which our government could not function.

POLITICAL DICTIONARY

★ **political party**
★ **major parties**
★ **partisanship**
★ **party in power**

"Winning isn't everything; it's the only thing." So said legendary football coach Vince Lombardi. Lombardi was talking about teams in the National Football League. His words, however, could also be used to describe the Republican and Democratic parties. They, too, are in the business of competing and winning.

What Is a Party?

A **political party** is a group of persons who seek to control government through the winning of elections and the holding of public office. This definition of a political party is broad enough to fit any political party. It certainly describes the two **major parties** in American politics, the Republican and the Democratic parties.

Another, more specific definition can be used to describe most political parties, both here and abroad. That is, a political party is a group of persons, joined together on the basis of common principles, who seek to control government in order to affect certain public policies and programs.

This definition, with its emphasis on principles and public policy positions, will not fit the two major American parties, however. The Republican and Democratic parties are not primarily principle- or issue-oriented. They are, instead, election-oriented.

What Do Parties Do?

It is clear from American history, as well as from the histories of other peoples, that political parties are essential to democratic government. Parties are the major mechanisms behind the development of broad policy and leadership choices; they are the medium through which those options are presented to the people.

Political parties are a vital link between the people and their government; that is, between the governed and those who govern. Many observers argue that political parties are the principal means by which the will of the people is made known to government and by which government is held accountable to the people.

Parties serve the democratic ideal in another important way. They work to blunt conflict; they are "power brokers." Political parties bring conflicting groups together. They modify and encourage compromise among the contending views of different interests and groups, and so help to unify, rather than divide, the American people. They soften the impact of extremists at both ends of the political spectrum.

Again, political parties are indispensable to American government. This fact is underscored by the major functions they perform.

▲ Bumper stickers reveal party loyalty.

Nominating Candidates

The major function of a political party is to nominate—name—candidates for public office. That is, the parties select candidates and then present them to the voters. Then the parties work to help their candidates win elections.

To have a functioning democracy, there must be a procedure for finding (recruiting and choosing) candidates for office. There must also be a mechanism for gathering support (votes) for these candidates. Parties are the best device yet found to do those jobs.

The nominating function is almost exclusively a party function in the United States.[1] It is the one activity that most clearly sets political parties apart from all of the other groups in politics.

Informing and Activating Supporters

Parties inform the people, and inspire and activate their interest and participation in public affairs. Other groups also perform this function—in particular, the news media and interest groups.

Parties try to inform and inspire voters in several ways. Primarily, they campaign for their candidates, take stands on issues, and criticize the candidates and the positions of their opponents.

Each party tries to inform the people as it thinks they should be informed—to its own advantage. For example, a party selects information in order to present its own positions and candidates in the best possible light. It conducts this "educational" process through pamphlets, signs, buttons, and stickers; with advertisements in newspapers and magazines and on radio, television, and the Internet; in speeches, rallies, and conventions; and in many other ways.

Remember, both parties want to win elections, and that consideration has much to do with the stands they take on most issues. Both parties try to shape positions that will attract as many voters as possible—and that will, at the same time, offend as few voters as possible.

The Bonding Agent Function

In business, a bond is an agreement that protects a person or company against loss caused by a third party. In politics, a political party

▲ *Campaign Fundraiser* Candidates rely on the money raised at political party fundraisers to help pay for their campaigns. Here President G. W. Bush waves from the podium at a fundraiser for his reelection campaign in Ft. Lauderdale, Florida. **H-SS 12.6.1**

acts as a "bonding agent," to ensure the good performance of its candidates and officeholders. In choosing its candidates, the party tries to make sure that they are men and women who are both qualified and of good character—or, at least, that they are not unqualified for the offices they seek.

The party also prompts its successful candidates to perform well in office. The democratic process imposes this bonding agent function on a party, whether the party really wants to perform it or not. If it fails to assume this responsibility, both the party and its candidates may suffer the consequences in future elections.

Governing

In several respects, government in the United States is government by party. For example, public officeholders—those who govern—are regularly chosen on the basis of party. Congress and the State legislatures are organized on party lines, and they conduct much of their business on the basis of **partisanship**—the strong support of their party and its policy stands. In addition, most appointments to executive offices, at both the federal and State levels, are made with an eye to party considerations.

---

[1] The exceptions are in nonpartisan elections and in those rare instances in which an independent candidate enters a partisan contest. Nominations are covered at length in Chapter 7.

▲ From left to right: Democratic presidential hopefuls Senator John Kerry of Massachusetts and former Vermont governor Howard Dean shake hands; Senate Majority Leader Bill Frist (R.-Tenn.) discusses passage of Medicare prescription drug legislation; the powerful House Ways and Means Committee holds a hearing. *Critical Thinking What party functions are represented by these three photos?* H-SS 12.1.5

In yet another sense, parties provide a basis for the conduct of government. In the complicated separation of powers arrangement, the executive and legislative branches must cooperate with one another if government is to accomplish anything. It is political parties that regularly provide the channels through which these two branches are able to work together.

Political parties have played a significant role in the process of constitutional change. Consider this important example: The Constitution's cumbersome system for electing the President works principally because political parties reshaped it in its early years and have made it work ever since.

Acting as Watchdog

Parties act as watchdogs over the conduct of the public's business. This is particularly true of the party out of power. It plays this role as it criticizes the policies and behavior of the **party in power.**

In American politics the party in power is the party that controls the executive branch of government—the presidency at the national level or the governorship at the State level.

In effect, the party out of power attempts to convince the voters that they should "throw the rascals out," that the "outs" should become the "ins" and the "ins" the "outs." The scrutiny and criticism by the "out" party tends to make the "rascals" more careful of their public charge and more responsive to the wishes and concerns of the people. In short, the party out of power plays the important role of "the loyal opposition"—opposed to the party in power but loyal to the people and the nation.

Section 1 Assessment

Key Terms and Main Ideas

1. What is a **political party**?
2. Identify two functions of political parties.
3. In what ways is American government conducted on the basis of **partisanship**?
4. **(a)** At this time, which is the **party in power** in your State? **(b)** In the nation?

Critical Thinking

5. **Analyzing Information** In what ways do political parties tend to unify, rather than divide, the American people?

6. **Drawing Conclusions** The party out of power serves an important function in American government. Explain that function.

Section Preview

OBJECTIVES

1. **Identify** the reasons why the United States has a two-party system.
2. **Understand** multiparty and one-party systems and how they affect the functioning of government.
3. **Describe** party membership patterns in the United States.

WHY IT MATTERS

The two-party system in the United States is a product of historical forces, our electoral system, and the ideological consensus of the American people. It provides more political stability than a multiparty system and more choice than a one-party system.

POLITICAL DICTIONARY

★ **minor party**
★ **two-party system**
★ **single-member district**
★ **plurality**
★ **bipartisan**
★ **pluralistic society**
★ **consensus**
★ **multiparty**
★ **coalition**
★ **one-party system**

Does the name Earl Dodge mean anything to you? Probably not. Yet Mr. Dodge has run for President of the United States six times. He was the presidential candidate of the Prohibition Party in 1984, 1988, 1992, 1996, 2000, and most recently, 2004.

One reason Mr. Dodge is not very well known is that he belongs to a **minor party,** one of the many political parties without wide voter support in this country. Two major parties, the Republicans and the Democrats, dominate American politics. That is to say, this country has a **two-party system.** In a typical election, only the Republican or the Democratic Party's candidates have a reasonable chance of winning public office.

Why a Two-Party System?

In some States, and in many local communities, one of the two major parties may be overwhelmingly dominant. And it may remain so for a long time—as, for example, the Democrats were throughout the South from the post-Civil War years to the 1960s. But, on the whole, and through most of our history, the United States has been a two-party nation.

A number of factors help to explain why America has had and continues to have a two-party system. No one reason alone offers a wholly satisfactory explanation for the phenomenon. Taken together, however, several reasons do add up to a quite persuasive answer.

The Historical Basis

The two-party system is rooted in the beginnings of the nation itself. The Framers of the Constitution were opposed to political parties. As you saw in Chapter 2, the ratification of the Constitution saw the birth of America's first two parties: the Federalists, led by Alexander Hamilton, and the Anti-Federalists, who followed Thomas Jefferson. In short, the American party system *began* as a two-party system.

The Framers hoped to create a unified country; they sought to bring order out of

► The symbols of the political parties turn up in many forms—especially in an election year.

Mary Matalin is a leading Republican campaign consultant. She worked in the Bush campaign in 2000 and 2004. She was an Assistant to the President and Counselor to the Vice President from 2001 to 2003. Here, she comments on political campaigns from the inside:

❝ *Politics is about winning. . . . Participating in a presidential campaign full-time, as a professional, is very emotional and very draining. You don't want to put that much effort into a race unless you have a real chance. . . . In the culture of campaigns it's not ideological. Most of us have a philosophical grounding—we're working for Republicans only—but in terms of issues the differences between candidates are often pretty small.* ❞

Evaluating the Quotation

How does Matalin's view of political campaigns fit in with what you have read about the two major parties?

the chaos of the Critical Period of the 1780s. To most of the Framers, parties were "factions," and therefore agents of divisiveness and disunity. George Washington reflected this view when, in his Farewell Address in 1796, he warned the new nation against "the baneful effects of the spirit of party."

In this light, it is hardly surprising that the Constitution made no provision for political parties. The Framers could not foresee the ways in which the governmental system they set up would develop. Thus, they could not possibly know that two major parties would emerge as prime instruments of government in the United States. Nor could they know that those two major parties would tend to be moderate, to choose middle-of-the-road positions, and so help to unify rather than divide the nation.

The Force of Tradition

Once established, human institutions are likely to become self-perpetuating. So it has been with the two-party system. The very fact that the

nation began with a two-party system has been a leading reason for the retention of a two-party system. Over time, it has become an increasingly important, self-reinforcing reason.

The point can be made this way: Most Americans accept the idea of a two-party system simply because there has always been one. This inbred support for the arrangement is a principal reason why challenges to the system—by minor parties, for example—have made so little headway. In other words, America has a two-party system *because* America has a two-party system.

The Electoral System

Several features of the American electoral system tend to promote the existence of but two major parties. That is to say, the basic shape, and many of the details, of the election process work in that direction.

The prevalence of **single-member districts** is one of the most important of these features. Nearly all of the elections held in this country— from the presidential contest on down to those at the local levels—are single-member district elections. That is, they are contests in which only one candidate is elected to each office on the ballot. They are winner-take-all elections. The winning candidate is the one who receives a **plurality,** or the largest number of votes cast for the office. Note that a plurality need not be a majority, which is more than half of all votes cast.

The single-member district pattern works to discourage minor parties. Because only one winner can come out of each contest, voters usually face only two viable choices: They can vote for the candidate of the party holding the office, or they can vote for the candidate of the party with the best chance of replacing the current officeholder. In short, most voters think of a vote for a minor party candidate as a "wasted vote."

Another important aspect of the electoral system works to the same end. Much of American election law is purposely written to discourage non-major party candidates.[2] Republicans and Democrats regularly act in a **bipartisan** way in

---

[2]Nearly all election law in this country is State, not federal, law— a point discussed at length in the next two chapters. But, here, note this very important point: Nearly all of the nearly 7,400 State legislators—nearly all of those persons who make State law—are either Democrats or Republicans. Only a handful of minor party members or independents now sit, or have ever sat, in State legislatures.

this matter. That is, the two major parties find common ground and work together here.

They deliberately shape election laws to preserve, protect, and defend the two major parties and the two-party system, and thus to frustrate the minor parties. In most States it is far more difficult for minor parties and independent groups to get their candidates listed on the ballot than for the major parties to do so.

The 2004 presidential election offered a striking illustration of the point. George W. Bush and John Kerry were on the ballots of all 50 States and the District of Columbia. None of the several other serious presidential hopefuls made the ballot everywhere in 2004.

To this point, non-major party candidates have made it to the ballot everywhere in only seven presidential elections. The Socialist Party's Eugene V. Debs was the first to do so, in 1912. The Socialist candidate in 1916, Allan L. Benson, also appeared on the ballots of all of the then 48 States. In 1980 Ed Clark, the Libertarian nominee, and independent John Anderson, and in 1988 Lenora Fulani of the New Alliance Party made the ballots of all 50 States and the District of Columbia. So, too, did Libertarian Andre Marrou and independent Ross Perot in 1992. Every ballot contained the names of Libertarian Harry Browne and the Reform Party's Ross Perot in 1996.

In 2004 Libertarian Michael Badnarik was on the ballot in 48 States and the District of Columbia. Michael Peroutka of the Constitution Party was listed in 38 States, and the Green Party's nominee, David Cobb, in 28. All of the other minor party aspirants fell far short of those totals, however. (Independent candidate Ralph Nader made it to the ballots of 34 States in 2004.)

The American Ideological Consensus

Americans are, on the whole, an ideologically homogeneous people. That is, over time, the American people have shared many of the same ideals, the same basic principles, and the same patterns of belief.

This is not to say that Americans are all alike. Clearly, this is not the case. The United States is a **pluralistic society**—one consisting of several distinct cultures and groups. Increasingly, the members of various ethnic, racial, religious, and other

Interpreting Political Cartoons **What does the cartoon imply about what parties—and candidates—stand for?**

social groups compete for and share in the exercise of political power in this country. Still, there is a broad **consensus**—a general agreement among various groups—on fundamental matters.

Nor is it to say that Americans have always agreed with one another in all matters. Far from it. The nation has been deeply divided at times: during the Civil War and in the years of the Great Depression, for example, and over such critical issues as racial discrimination, the war in Vietnam, and abortion.

Still, note this very important point: this nation has not been regularly plagued by sharp and unbridgeable political divisions.

▲ Alabama Senator Richard Shelby was elected as a Democrat in 1986 and reelected in 1992. He became a Republican in 1995 and was easily reelected in 1998 and 2004. *Critical Thinking What might cause a politician to switch parties?* **H-SS 12.6.4**

▲ **Multiparty System** Like many European countries, Italy has a multi-party system. Prime Minister Silvio Berlusconi (right) heads Italy's center-right coalition government.

The United States has been free of long-standing, bitter disputes based on such factors as economic class, social status, religious beliefs, or national origin.

Those conditions that could produce several strong rival parties simply do not exist in this country. In this way, the United States differs from most other democracies. In short, the realities of American society and politics simply do not permit more than two major parties.

This ideological consensus has had another very important impact on American parties. It has given the nation two major parties that look very much alike. Both tend to be moderate. Both are built on compromise and regularly try to occupy "the middle of the road." Both parties seek the same prize: the votes of a majority of the electorate. To do so, they must win over essentially the same people. Inevitably, each party takes policy positions that do not differ a great deal from those of the other major party.

This is not to say that there are no significant differences between the two major parties today. There are. For example, the Democratic Party, and those who usually vote for its candidates, are more likely to support such things as social welfare programs, government regulation of business practices, and efforts to improve the status of minorities. On the other hand, the Republican Party and its adherents are much more likely to favor the play of private market forces in the economy and to argue that the Federal Government should be less extensively involved in social welfare programs.

Multiparty Systems

Some critics argue that the American two-party system should be scrapped. They would replace it with a **multiparty** arrangement, a system in which several major and many lesser parties exist, seriously compete for, and actually win, public offices. Multiparty systems have long been a feature of most European democracies, and they are now found in many other democratic societies elsewhere in the world.

In the typical multiparty system, the various parties are each based on a particular interest, such as economic class, religious belief, sectional attachment, or political ideology. Those who favor such an arrangement for this country say that it would provide for a broader representation of the electorate and be more responsive to the will of the people. They claim that a multiparty system would give voters a much more meaningful choice among candidates and policy alternatives than the present two-party system does.

Clearly, multiparty systems do tend to produce a broader, more diverse representation of the electorate. At the same time, that strength is also a major weakness of a multiparty system. It often leads to instability in government. One party is often unable to win the support of a majority of the voters. As a result, the power to govern must be shared by a number of parties, in a **coalition**. A coalition is a temporary alliance of several groups who come together to form a working majority and so to control a government.

Several of the multiparty nations of Western Europe have long been plagued by governmental crises. They have experienced frequent changes in party control as coalitions shift and dissolve. Italy furnishes an almost nightmarish example: It has had a new government on the average of once every year ever since the end of World War II.

Historically, the American people have shunned a multiparty approach to politics. They have refused to give substantial support to any but the two major parties and their candidates. Two of the factors mentioned above—single-member districts and the American ideological consensus—seem to make the multiparty approach impossible in the United States.

One-Party Systems

In nearly all dictatorships today, only one political party is allowed. That party is the party of the ruling clique. For all practical purposes, it is quite accurate to say that in those circumstances the resulting **one-party system** is really a "no-party" system.

In quite another sense, this country has had several States and many local areas that can be described in one-party terms. Until the late 1950s, the Democrats dominated the politics of the South. The Republican Party was almost always the winner in New England and in the upper Midwest.

Effective two-party competition has spread fairly rapidly in the past 30 years or so. Democrats have won many offices in every northern State. Republican candidates have become more and more successful throughout the once "Solid South." Nevertheless, about a third of the States can still be said to have a modified one-party system. That is, one of the major parties regularly wins most elections in those States. Also, while most States may have vigorous two-party competition at the Statewide level, within most of them are many areas dominated by a single party.

Party Membership Patterns

Membership in a party is purely voluntary. A person is a Republican or a Democrat, or belongs to a minor party, or is an independent—belonging to no organized party—because that is what he or she chooses to be.[3]

Remember, the two major parties are broadly based. In order to gain more votes than their opponents, they must attract as much support as they possibly can. Each party has always been composed, in greater or lesser degree, of a cross section of the nation's population. Each is made up of Protestants, Catholics, and Jews; whites, African Americans, Latinos, and other minorities; professionals, farmers, and union members. Each party includes the young, the middle-aged,

▲ Dictator Joseph Stalin, who was both leader of the Communist Party and premier of the Soviet Union, ruthlessly crushed all political opposition. *Critical Thinking Why might silencing other political points of view be a disadvantage to a government?*

and the elderly; city-dwellers, suburbanites, and rural residents among its members.

It is true that the members of certain segments of the electorate tend to be aligned more solidly with one or the other of the major parties, at least for a time. Thus, in recent decades, African Americans, Catholics and Jews, and union members have voted more often for Democrats. In the same way, white males, Protestants, and the business community have been inclined to back the GOP.[4] Yet, never have all members of any group tied themselves permanently to either party.

Individuals identify themselves with a party for many reasons. Family is almost certainly the most important among them. Studies show that nearly two out of every three Americans follow the party allegiance of their parents.

---

[3]In most States a person must declare a preference for a particular party in order to vote in that party's primary election. That declaration is usually made as a part of the voter registration process, and it is often said to make one "a registered Republican (or Democrat)." The requirement is only a procedural one, however, and wholly a matter of individual choice.

[4]GOP is common shorthand for the Republican Party. The initials stand for Grand Old Party, a nickname acquired in the latter part of the 19th century. The nickname may owe its origins to British politics. Prime Minister William Gladstone was dubbed "the Grand Old Man," often abbreviated "GOM," by the English press in 1882. Soon after, "GOP" appeared in headlines in the *New York Tribune,* the *Boston Post,* and other American papers.

Political Party Contacts

MAJOR POLITICAL PARTIES

Republican Party
310 First St. SE, Washington, DC 20003
http://www.rnc.org

Democratic Party
430 So. Capitol St. SE, Washington, DC 20003
http://www.democrats.org

SIGNIFICANT MINOR PARTIES

Libertarian Party (Founded 1971)
2600 Virginia Ave., N.W., Washington, DC 20037 http://www.lp.org
Stresses individual liberty; opposes taxes, foreign involvements, government intrusion into private lives.

America First Party (Founded 2002)
1630-A 30th St., Boulder, CO 80301 http://www.americafirstparty.org
Splinter from Reform Party; promotes Christian beliefs and originalist interpretation of the Constitution; opposes immigration, free trade, UN.

Reform Party (Founded 1995)
Box 126437, Forth Worth, TX 76126 http://www.reformparty.org
Formed by Ross Perot; advocates trade agreements to protect American jobs, balanced budget, tax and electoral reforms, term limits.

Green Party of the United States (Founded 1996)
1700 Connecticut Ave., N.W., Washington, D.C. 20009 http://www.gp.org
Committed to "environmentalism, nonviolence, social justice, and grass-roots democracy."

Constitution Party (Founded 1992)
23 North Lime St., Lancaster, PA 17602 http://www.constitutionparty.org
Anti-tax party; strongly pro-life; pro-school prayer; opposes gun control, immigration, free trade, UN, gay rights.

Socialist Labor Party (Founded 1891)
P.O. Box 218, Mountain View, CA 94042 http://www.slp.org
Marxist party; seeks "a classless society based on collectivist ownership of industries and social services."

Communist Party USA (Founded 1919)
235 West 23rd St., New York, NY 10011 http://www.cpusa.org
Promotes Communist ideology; seeks complete restructuring of American political and economic institutions.

Socialist Party USA (Founded 1900)
339 Lafayette St., New York, NY 10012 http://www.sp-usa.org
Staunchly anti-Communist; advocates democratic socialism; seeks "a non-racist, classless, feminist, socialist society."

Interpreting Tables **Which of the minor parties shown in the table has the most specific platform?** **H-SS 12.1.5**

Major events can also have a decided influence on the party affiliation of voters. Of these, the Civil War and the Depression of the 1930s have been the most significant in American political history.

Economic status also influences party choice, although generalizations are quite risky. Historically though, those in higher income groups are more likely to be Republicans, while those with lower incomes tend to be Democrats.

Several other factors also affect both party choice and voting behavior, including age, place of residence, level of education, and work environment. Some of those factors may conflict with one another in the case of a particular individual—and they often do. Therefore, predicting how a person or group will vote in any given election is a risky business, which keeps the pollsters and the analysts busy until the votes are counted.

Section 2 Assessment

Key Terms and Main Ideas

1. Briefly explain four reasons why the United States has a **two-party system.**
2. How do the terms **pluralistic** and **consensus** both apply to American society?
3. **(a)** What is a **multiparty system? (b)** Why do some people favor it for the United States?
4. Many factors tend to influence party choice. Name four.

Critical Thinking

5. **Synthesizing Information** What does the fact that the major parties cooperate to discourage minor parties and yet compete vigorously against each other during elections tell you about party politics in the United States?

Standards Monitoring *Online*
For: Self-quiz with vocabulary practice
Web Code: mqa-2052

6. **Recognizing Ideologies** You are campaigning for one of the two major parties. Create a short political advertisement to appeal to large numbers of voters and to distinguish your party from the other major party.

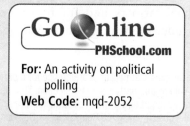

Go Online
PHSchool.com

For: An activity on political polling
Web Code: mqd-2052

Face the
Issues

Open Debates

Background *The Commission on Presidential Debates, an independent, nonpartisan group, sets strict rules to determine who may take part in the debates. Only candidates who score an average of at least 15 percent support in five national polls are invited. Candidates also must have qualified to appear on ballots in States that, taken together, add up to the 270 electoral votes necessary to win the presidency. In 2004, several minor party candidates, led by Ralph Nader, sued unsuccessfully to demand new rules.*

Ross Perot (center)

Analysis Skill HI1

Let Minor Party Candidates Debate

The Commission on Presidential Debates is staffed and run by Republicans and Democrats. Not surprisingly, since the commission was created in 1987, only one non-major party candidate, has qualified—Ross Perot in 1992.

Minor parties have promoted ideas that have radically changed American life. Women's right to vote, Social Security, child labor laws, and the 40-hour work week were all championed by minor parties before becoming law. The debates provide a forum for introducing new ideas.

The 1992 presidential campaign offers an important example. The three-way debates featuring President George H. W. Bush, Bill Clinton, and Ross Perot that year electrified voters and attracted almost 70 million viewers, well above the average. Perot forced the candidates to discuss the budget deficit and the costs of free trade. He won nearly 20 percent of the vote in November. But could he have gotten his message out without a debate seat? Our democracy is poorer when new voices cannot be heard.

Serious Contenders Only

The two-party system has been an enduring feature of American politics since the 1860s. Democrats and Republicans have maintained a stable government and presided over orderly transfers of power. The two parties offer constructive ways to improve America. By working within a party, an activist can introduce new ideas and programs and hope to get things done.

Only the two major parties have the popular support, the track record, and the alliances to get their message out, election after election. The major parties have a valuable brand that motivates voters.

Minor party candidates may have great ideas and high energy, but they often fail to get many votes on Election Day. Unlike major party nominees, failed minor party candidates usually leave no significant party or movement to continue to promote their ideas.

Debates offer voters a chance to learn about the candidates who might become the next president. Devoting scarce minutes of debate time to candidates who have no hope of winning only distracts voters and defeats the purpose of the debate.

Exploring the Issues

1. Did Ralph Nader have a right to participate in the 2004 debates? Why or why not?

2. Should Congress set the qualifications for participation in the Presidential debates? Why or why not?

For more information on minor parties, view "Open Debates."

Face the **Issues** Video Collection

The Two-Party System in American History

OBJECTIVES

1. **Understand** the origins of political parties in the United States.
2. **Identify** and describe the three major periods of single-party domination and describe the current era of divided government.

WHY IT MATTERS

The origins and history of political parties in the United States help explain how the two major parties work today and how they affect American government.

POLITICAL DICTIONARY

★ **incumbent**
★ **faction**
★ **electorate**
★ **sectionalism**

Henry Ford, the great auto maker, once said that all history is "bunk." Ford knew a great deal about automobiles and mass production, but he did not know much about history or its importance.

Listen, instead, to Shakespeare: "The past is prologue." Today is the product of yesterday. You are what you are today because of your history. Therefore, the more you know about your past, the better prepared you are for today, and for tomorrow.

Much the same can be said about the two-party system in American politics. The more you know about its past, the better you will understand its workings today.

The Nation's First Parties

The beginnings of the American two-party system can be traced to the battle over the ratification of the Constitution. The conflicts of the time, centering on the proper form and role of government in the United States, were not stilled by the adoption of the Constitution. Rather, those conflicts were carried over into the early years of the Republic. They led directly to the formation of the nation's first full-blown political parties.

The Federalist Party was the first to appear. It formed around Alexander Hamilton, who served as secretary of the treasury in the new government organized by George Washington. The Federalists were, by and large, the party of "the rich and the well-born." Most of them had supported the Constitution.

Led by Hamilton, the Federalists worked to create a stronger national government. They favored vigorous executive leadership and a set of policies designed to correct the nation's economic ills. The Federalists' program appealed to financial, manufacturing, and commercial interests. To reach their goals, they urged a liberal interpretation of the Constitution.

Thomas Jefferson, the nation's first secretary of state, led the opposition to the Federalists.[5] Jefferson and his followers were more sympathetic to the "common man" than were the Federalists. They favored a very limited role for the new government created by the Constitution. In their view, Congress should dominate that new government, and its policies should help the nation's small shopkeepers, laborers, farmers, and planters. The Jeffersonians insisted on a strict construction of the provisions of the Constitution.

▲ This ticket provided admission to the convention that nominated President Roosevelt for a second term.

[5]As you recall, George Washington was opposed to political parties. As President, he named arch foes Hamilton and Jefferson to his new Cabinet to get them to work together—in an unsuccessful attempt to avoid the creation of formally organized and opposing groups.

Jefferson resigned from Washington's Cabinet in 1793 to concentrate on organizing his party. Originally, the new party took the name Anti-Federalist. Later it became known as the Jeffersonian Republicans or the Democratic-Republicans. Finally, by 1828, it became the Democratic Party.

These two parties first clashed in the election of 1796. John Adams, the Federalists' candidate to succeed Washington as President, defeated Jefferson by just three votes in the electoral college. Over the next four years, Jefferson and James Madison worked tirelessly to build the Democratic-Republican Party. Their efforts paid off in the election of 1800. Jefferson defeated the **incumbent,** or current officeholder, President Adams; Jefferson's party also won control of Congress. The Federalists never returned to power.

American Parties: Four Major Eras

The history of the American party system since 1800 can be divided into four major periods. Through the first three of these periods, one or the other of the two major parties was dominant, regularly holding the presidency and usually both houses of Congress. The nation is now in a fourth period, much of it marked by divided government.

In the first of these periods, from 1800 to 1860, the Democrats won 13 of 15 presidential elections. They lost the office only in the elections of 1840 and 1848. In the second era, from 1860 to 1932, the Republicans won 14 of 18 elections, losing only in 1884, 1892, 1912, and 1916.

The third period, from 1932 to 1968, began with the Democrats' return to power and Franklin Roosevelt's first election to the presidency. The Democrats won seven of the nine presidential elections, losing only in 1952 and 1956. Through the fourth and current period, which began in 1968, the Republicans have won seven of ten presidential elections, and they hold the White House today. But the Democrats have controlled both houses of Congress over much of this most recent period—although they do not do so today.

The Era of the Democrats, 1800–1860

Thomas Jefferson's election in 1800 marked the beginning of a period of Democratic domination that was to last until the Civil War. As the time line on pages 128–129 shows, the Federalists, soundly defeated in 1800, had disappeared altogether by 1816.

For a time, through the Era of Good Feeling, the Democratic-Republicans were unopposed in national politics. However, by the mid-1820s, they had split into **factions,** or conflicting groups.

Interpreting Political Cartoons Political cartoonist Thomas Nast is credited with popularizing the party symbols in his 1874 cartoons for *Harper's Weekly.* At left, the Republican elephant trumpets Democratic Party defeats. At right, the Democratic donkey kicks Lincoln's Secretary of War. *What characteristics of the elephant and the donkey do you think Nast wanted to associate with each party?* H-SS 12.6.1

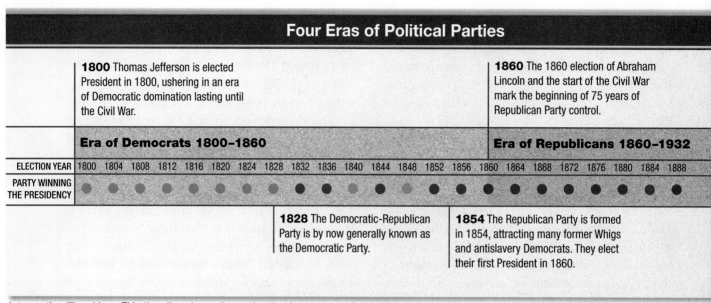

Four Eras of Political Parties

1800 Thomas Jefferson is elected President in 1800, ushering in an era of Democratic domination lasting until the Civil War.

1860 The 1860 election of Abraham Lincoln and the start of the Civil War mark the beginning of 75 years of Republican Party control.

Era of Democrats 1800–1860

Era of Republicans 1860–1932

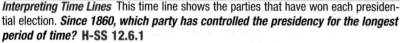

ELECTION YEAR	1800	1804	1808	1812	1816	1820	1824	1828	1832	1836	1840	1844	1848	1852	1856	1860	1864	1868	1872	1876	1880	1884	1888

PARTY WINNING THE PRESIDENCY

1828 The Democratic-Republican Party is by now generally known as the Democratic Party.

1854 The Republican Party is formed in 1854, attracting many former Whigs and antislavery Democrats. They elect their first President in 1860.

Interpreting Time Lines This time line shows the parties that have won each presidential election. *Since 1860, which party has controlled the presidency for the longest period of time?* H-SS 12.6.1

By the time of Andrew Jackson's administration (1829–1837), a potent National Republican (Whig) Party had arisen to challenge the Democrats. The major issues of the day—conflicts over public lands, the Second Bank of the United States, high tariffs, and slavery—all had made new party alignments inevitable.

The Democrats, led by Jackson, were a coalition of small farmers, debtors, frontier pioneers, and slaveholders. They drew much of their support from the South and West. The years of Jacksonian democracy produced three fundamental changes in the nation's political landscape: (1) voting rights for all white males, (2) a huge increase in the number of elected offices around the country, and (3) the spread of the spoils system—the practice of awarding public offices, contracts, and other governmental favors to those who supported the party in power.

The Whig Party was led by the widely popular Henry Clay and the great orator, Daniel Webster. The party consisted of a loose coalition of eastern bankers, merchants and industrialists, and many owners of large southern plantations. The Whigs were opposed to the tenets of Jacksonian democracy and strongly supported a high tariff. However, the Whigs' victories were few. Although they were the other major party from the mid-1830s to the 1850s, the Whigs were able to elect only two Presidents, both of

them war heroes: William Henry Harrison in 1840 and Zachary Taylor in 1848.

By the 1850s, the growing crisis over slavery split both major parties. Left leaderless by the deaths of Clay and Webster, the Whigs fell apart. Meanwhile, the Democrats split into two sharply divided camps, North and South. During this decade, the nation drifted toward civil war.

Of the several groupings that arose to compete for supporters among the former Whigs and the fragmented Democrats, the Republican Party was the most successful. Founded in 1854, it drew many Whigs and antislavery Democrats. The Republicans nominated their first presidential candidate, John C. Frémont, in 1856; they elected their first President, Abraham Lincoln, in 1860.

With Lincoln's election, the Republican Party became the only party in the history of American politics to make the jump from third-party to major-party status. As you will see, even greater things were in store for the Republicans.

The Era of the Republicans, 1860–1932
The Civil War signaled the beginning of the second era of one-party domination. For nearly 75 years, the Republicans dominated the national scene. They were supported by business and financial interests, and by farmers, laborers, and newly freed African Americans.

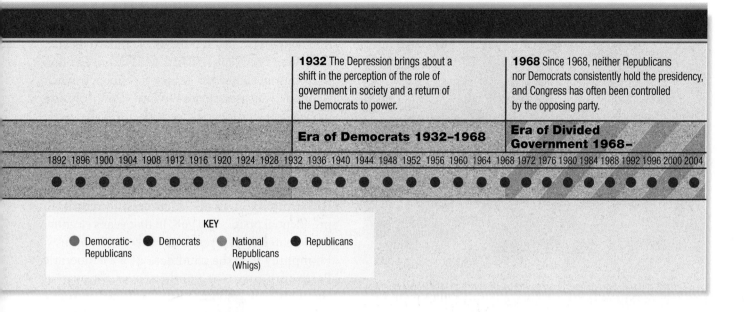

1932 The Depression brings about a shift in the perception of the role of government in society and a return of the Democrats to power.

1968 Since 1968, neither Republicans nor Democrats consistently hold the presidency, and Congress has often been controlled by the opposing party.

Era of Democrats 1932–1968

Era of Divided Government 1968–

1892 1896 1900 1904 1908 1912 1916 1920 1924 1928 1932 1936 1940 1944 1948 1952 1956 1960 1964 1968 1972 1976 1980 1984 1988 1992 1996 2000 2004

KEY

● Democratic-Republicans
● Democrats
● National Republicans (Whigs)
● Republicans

The Democrats, crippled by the war, were able to survive mainly through their hold on the "Solid South," after the era of Reconstruction came to a close in the mid-1870s. For the balance of the century, they slowly rebuilt their electoral base. In all that time, they were able to place only one candidate in the White House: Grover Cleveland in 1884 and again in 1892. Those elections marked only short breaks in Republican supremacy. Riding the crest of popular acceptance and unprecedented prosperity, the GOP remained the dominant party well into the twentieth century.

The election of 1896 was especially critical in the development of the two-party system. It climaxed years of protest by small business owners, farmers, and the emerging labor unions against big business, financial monopolies, and the railroads. The Republican Party nominated William McKinley and supported the gold standard. The Democratic candidate was William Jennings Bryan, a supporter of free silver, who was also endorsed by the Populist Party.

With McKinley's victory in 1896, the Republicans regained the presidency. In doing so, they drew a response from a broader range of the **electorate**—the people eligible to vote. This new strength allowed the Republicans to maintain their role as the dominant party in national politics for another three decades.

The Democratic Party lost the election of 1896, but it won on another score. Bryan, its young, dynamic presidential nominee, campaigned throughout the country as the champion of the "little man." He helped to push the nation's party politics back toward the economic arena, and away from the divisions of **sectionalism** that had plagued the nation for so many years. Sectionalism emphasizes a devotion to the interests of a particular region.

The Republicans suffered their worst setback of the era in 1912, when they renominated incumbent President William Howard Taft. Former President Theodore Roosevelt, denied the nomination of his party, left the Republicans to become the candidate of his "Bull Moose" Progressive Party. Traditional Republican support was divided between Taft and Roosevelt. As a result, the Democratic nominee, Woodrow Wilson, was able to capture the presidency. Four years later, Wilson was reelected by a narrow margin.

Again, however, the Democratic successes of 1912 and 1916 proved only a brief interlude. The GOP reasserted its control of the nation's politics by winning each of the next three presidential elections: Warren Harding won in 1920, Calvin Coolidge in 1924, and Herbert Hoover in 1928.

The Return of the Democrats, 1932–1968

The Great Depression, which began in 1929, had a massive impact on nearly all aspects of American life. Its effect on the American political landscape was considerable indeed. The landmark election of 1932 brought Franklin Roosevelt to the presidency and the Democrats back to power at the

▲ This 1900 campaign poster uses powerful imagery to win Republican votes. *Critical Thinking* *How does the poster contrast Republican achievements since 1896 with earlier conditions when the Democrats were in power?*

national level. Also, and of fundamental importance, that election marked a basic shift in the public's attitude toward the proper role of government in the nation's social and economic life.

Franklin Roosevelt and the Democrats engineered their victory in 1932 with a new electoral base. It was built largely of southerners, small farmers, organized labor, and big-city political organizations. Roosevelt's revolutionary economic and social welfare programs, which formed the heart of the New Deal of the 1930s, further strengthened that coalition. It also brought increasing support from African Americans and other minorities to the Democrats.

President Roosevelt won reelection in 1936. He secured an unprecedented third term in 1940 and yet another term in 1944, each time by heavy majorities. Roosevelt's Vice President, Harry S Truman, completed the fourth term following FDR's death in 1945. Truman was elected to a full term of his own in 1948, when he turned back the GOP challenge led by Governor Thomas E. Dewey of New York.

The Republicans did manage to regain the White House in 1952, and they kept it in 1956. World War II hero Dwight Eisenhower led the Republicans to victory in these elections. Both times, Eisenhower defeated the Democratic nominee, Governor Adlai Stevenson of Illinois.

The Republicans' return to power was short-lived, however. Senator John F. Kennedy of Massachusetts recaptured the White House for the Democrats in 1960. He did so with a razor-thin win over the Republican standard bearer, then Vice President Richard M. Nixon. Lyndon B. Johnson succeeded to the presidency when Kennedy was assassinated in late 1963. Johnson won a full presidential term in 1964, by overwhelming his Republican opponent, Senator Barry Goldwater of Arizona.

The Start of a New Era

Richard Nixon made a successful return to presidential politics in 1968. In that year's election, he defeated Vice President Hubert Humphrey. Humphrey was the candidate of a Democratic Party torn apart by conflicts over the war in Vietnam, civil rights, and a variety of social welfare issues. Nixon also faced a strong third-party effort by the American Independent Party nominee, Governor George Wallace of Alabama. The Republicans won with only a bare plurality over Humphrey and Wallace.

In 1972, President Nixon retained the White House when he routed the choice of the still-divided Democrats, Senator George McGovern of South Dakota. However, Nixon's role in the Watergate scandal forced him from office in 1974.

Vice President Gerald Ford then became President and filled out the balance of Nixon's second term. Beset by problems in the economy, by the continuing effects of Watergate, and by his pardon of former President Nixon, Ford lost the presidency in 1976. The former governor of Georgia, Jimmy Carter, and the resurgent Democrats gained the White House that year.

A steadily worsening economy, political fallout from the Iranian hostage crisis, and his own inability to establish himself as an effective President spelled defeat for Jimmy Carter in 1980. Led by Ronald Reagan, the former governor of California, the Republicans scored an impressive victory that year. Reagan won a second term by a landslide in 1984, overwhelming a Democratic ticket headed by former Vice President Walter Mondale.

The GOP kept the White House with a third straight win in 1988. Their candidate, George H.W. Bush, had served as Vice President through the Reagan years. He led a successful campaign against the Democrats and their nominee, Governor Michael Dukakis of Massachusetts.

The Reagan and Bush victories of the 1980s triggered wide-ranging efforts to alter many of the nation's foreign and domestic policies. President George H.W. Bush lost his bid for another term in 1992, however. Democrat Bill Clinton, then the governor of Arkansas, defeated him and also turned back an independent challenge by Texas billionaire Ross Perot. Mr. Clinton won a second term in 1996—defeating the Republican candidate, long-time senator from Kansas, Bob Dole, and, at the same time, thwarting a third-party effort by Mr. Perot.

The GOP regained the White House in the very close presidential contest of 2000. Their candidate, George W. Bush, was then the governor of Texas, and is the son of the former Republican President. Mr. Bush failed to win the popular vote contest in 2000, but he did capture a bare majority of the electoral votes and so the White House. His Democratic opponent, Vice President Al Gore, became the first presidential nominee since 1888 to win the popular vote and yet fail to win the presidency; see pages 379–381.

The years since Richard Nixon's election in 1968 have been marked by divided government. Through much of the period, Republicans have occupied the White House while the Democrats have usually controlled Congress.[6] That situation was reversed in the midst of President Clinton's first term, however. The GOP took control of both houses of Congress in 1994, and they kept their hold on Capitol Hill on through the elections of 2000.

Historically, a newly elected President has almost always swept many of his party's candidates into office with him. But the victories of several recent Presidents—most recently, George W. Bush in 2000—have not carried that kind of coattail effect.

The Republicans lost seats in the House and Senate in 2000. They did manage to keep a narrow hold on both chambers, however—by a nine-seat margin in the House and by virtue of a 50-50 split in the Senate. But the Democrats reclaimed the upper house in mid-2001, when Senator James Jeffords of Vermont bolted the Republican Party and became an independent.

Sparked by the prodigious campaign efforts of President Bush, the Republicans won back the Senate and padded their slim majority in the House in the off-year congressional elections of 2002. The GOP had not picked up seats in both houses of Congress in a midterm election with a Republican in the White House in 100 years—not since Theodore Roosevelt's first term, in 1902.

The Republicans continued their winning ways in 2004. Mr. Bush defeated his Democratic opponent, Senator John F. Kerry of Massachusetts, in a bruising campaign—and, this time, he won a clear majority of the popular vote. The President also led his party to substantial gains in both the House and Senate. Has the era of divided government that began in 1968 now come to an end? Only time will tell.

---

[6] The Democrats held almost uninterrupted control of Congress from 1933 to 1995. Over those years, the Republicans controlled both houses of Congress for only two two-year periods—first, after the congressional elections of 1946 and then after those of 1952. The GOP did win control of the Senate (but not the House) in 1980; the Democrats recaptured the upper chamber in 1986.

Section 3 Assessment

Key Terms and Main Ideas

1. When did the American two-party system begin to emerge?
2. Why would the development of **factions** within a political party hurt that party's chances for success?
3. Explain how **sectionalism** played an important role in party politics during at least one period of American history.
4. Describe one period of single-party domination.

Critical Thinking

5. **Drawing Conclusions** To which of the major parties of today do you think Thomas Jefferson would belong? Alexander Hamilton? Explain your reasoning.

Standards Monitoring Online
For: Self-Quiz and vocabulary practice
Web Code: mqa-2053

6. **Predicting Consequences** Do you think that the GOP's decisive victories in 2004 signal the end of the fourth era in the history of the two-party system? Why or why not?

For: An activity on comparing political parties
Web Code: mqd-2053

The Minor Parties

Section Preview

OBJECTIVES

1. **Identify** the types of minor parties that have been active in American politics.
2. **Understand** why minor parties are important despite the fact that none has ever won the presidency.

WHY IT MATTERS

Many minor parties have played important roles in American politics. They have provided alternatives to the positions of the major parties, and sometimes have affected particular elections and shaped public policies.

POLITICAL DICTIONARY

★ **ideological parties**
★ **single-issue parties**
★ **economic protest parties**
★ **splinter parties**

Libertarian, Reform, Socialist, Prohibition, Natural Law, Communist, American Independent, Green, Constitution—these are only some of the many parties that fielded presidential candidates in 2004. You know that none of these parties or their candidates had any real chance of winning the presidency. But this is not to say that minor parties are unimportant. The bright light created by the two major parties too often blinds us to the vital role several minor parties have played in American politics.

Minor Parties in the United States

Their number and variety make minor parties difficult to describe and classify. Some have limited their efforts to a particular locale, others to

▲ Earl Dodge has been the nominee of the Prohibition Party in every presidential election since 1984.

a single State, and some to one region of the country. Still others have tried to woo the entire nation. Most have been short-lived, but a few have existed for decades. And, while most have lived mothlike around the flame of a single idea, some have had a broader, more practical base.

Still, four distinct types of minor parties can be identified:

1. The **ideological parties** are those based on a particular set of beliefs—a comprehensive view of social, economic, and political matters. Most of these minor parties have been built on some shade of Marxist thought; examples include the Socialist, Socialist Labor, Socialist Worker, and Communist parties.

A few ideological parties have had a quite different approach, however—especially the Libertarian Party of today, which emphasizes individualism and calls for doing away with most of government's present functions and programs. The ideological parties have seldom been able to win many votes. As a rule, however, they have been long-lived.

2. The **single-issue parties** focus on only one public-policy matter. Their names have usually indicated their primary concern. For example, the Free Soil Party opposed the spread of slavery in the 1840s and 1850s; the American Party, also called the "Know Nothings," opposed Irish-Catholic immigration in the 1850s; and the Right to Life Party opposes abortion today.

Most of the single-issue parties have faded into history. They died away as events have

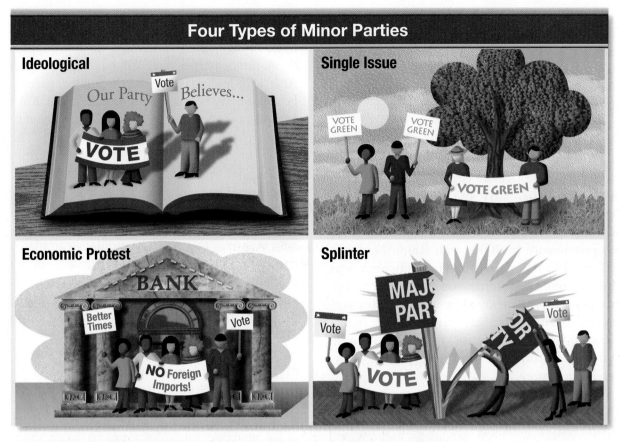

Four Types of Minor Parties

Ideological

Our Party Vote Believes...

VOTE

Single Issue

VOTE GREEN   VOTE GREEN

VOTE GREEN

Economic Protest

BANK

Better Times   Vote

NO Foreign Imports!

Splinter

Vote   MAJ PAR

Vote   VOTE

Interpreting Charts (a) According to the chart, which type of minor party is the most closely related to a major party? (b) Which type is likely to be the most cohesive and united?

passed them by, as their themes have failed to attract voters, or as one or both of the major parties have taken their key issues as their own.

3. The **economic protest parties** have been rooted in periods of economic discontent. Unlike the socialist parties, these groups have not had any clear-cut ideological base. Rather, they have proclaimed their disgust with the major parties and demanded better times, and have focused their anger on such real or imagined enemies as the monetary system, "Wall Street bankers," the railroads, or foreign imports.

Most often, they have been sectional parties, drawing their strength from the agricultural South and West. The Greenback Party, for example, tried to take advantage of agrarian discontent from 1876 through 1884. It appealed to struggling farmers by calling for the free coinage of silver, federal regulation of the railroads, an income tax, and labor legislation. A descendant of the Greenbacks, the Populist Party of the 1890s also demanded public ownership of railroads, telephone and telegraph

companies, lower tariffs, and the adoption of the initiative and referendum.

Each of these economic protest parties has disappeared as the nation has climbed out of the difficult economic period in which that party arose.

4. **Splinter parties** are those that have split away from one of the major parties. Most of the more important minor parties in our politics have been splinter parties. Among the leading groups that have split away from the Republicans are Theodore Roosevelt's "Bull Moose" Progressive Party of 1912, and Robert La Follette's Progressive Party of 1924. From the Democrats have come Henry Wallace's Progressive Party and the States' Rights (Dixiecrat) Party, both of 1948, and George Wallace's American Independent Party of 1968.

Most splinter parties have formed around a strong personality—most often someone who has failed to win his major party's presidential nomination. These parties have faded or collapsed when that leader has stepped aside. Thus, the Bull Moose Progressive Party passed away when Theodore Roosevelt returned to the Republican fold after the election of 1912. Similarly, the American Independent Party lost nearly all of its brief strength when Governor George Wallace rejoined the Democratic Party after his strong showing in the 1968 election.

The Green Party, founded in 1996, points up the difficulties of classifying minor parties in American politics. The Greens began as a classic single-issue party but, as the party has evolved, it simply will not fit into any of the categories set out here. The Green Party came to prominence in 2000, with Ralph Nader as its presidential nominee. His campaign was built around a smorgasbord of issues—environmental protection, of course, but also universal health care, gay and lesbian rights, restraints on corporate power, campaign finance reform, opposition to global free trade, and much more.

The Greens refused to renominate Ralph Nader in 2004. They chose, instead, David Cobb—who built his presidential campaign around most of the positions the Greens had supported in 2000.

Why Minor Parties Are Important

Even though most Americans do not support them, minor parties have still had an impact on American politics and on the major parties. For example, it was a minor party, the Anti-Masons, that first used a national convention to nominate a presidential candidate in 1831. The Whigs and then the Democrats followed suit in 1832. Ever since, national conventions have been used by both the Democrats and the Republicans to pick their presidential tickets.

Minor parties can have an impact in another way. A strong third-party candidacy can play a decisive role—often a "spoiler role"—in an election. Even if a minor party does not win any electoral votes, it can pull votes from one of the major parties, as the Green Party did in 2000. This spoiler effect can be felt in national, State, or local contests, especially where the two major parties compete on roughly equal terms.

The 1912 election dramatically illustrated this point. A split in the Republican Party and Roosevelt's resulting third-party candidacy produced the results shown below. Almost certainly, had Roosevelt not quit the Republican

The 1912 Presidential Election

The nickname for the Progressives was the Bull Moose Party.

Woodrow Wilson
Democrat
Popular Vote
6,296,547
41.87%
Electoral Vote
435

Theodore Roosevelt
Progressive
Popular Vote
4,118,571
27.39%
Electoral Vote
88

William H. Taft
Republican
Popular Vote
3,486,720
23.19%
Electoral Vote
8

Eugene V. Debs
Socialist
Popular Vote
900,672
5.9%
Electoral Vote
0

Eugene Chafin
Prohibition
Popular Vote
206,275
1.37%
Electoral Vote
0

Interpreting Graphs This bar graph shows the votes received by the major and the minor parties in 1912. *(a) Which party "came in second"? (b) Even though the Bull Moose Progressives were a minor party, how did they help determine which major party won the election?* H-SS 12.6.1

Party, Taft would have enjoyed a better showing, and Wilson would not have become President.

Historically, however, the minor parties have been most important in their roles of critic and innovator. Unlike the major parties, the minor parties have been ready, willing, and able to take quite clear-cut stands on controversial issues. Minor-party stands have often drawn attention to some issue that the major parties have preferred to ignore or straddle.

Over the years, many of the more important issues of American politics were first brought to the public's attention by a minor party. Examples include the progressive income tax, woman suffrage, railroad and banking regulation, and old-age pensions.

Oddly enough, this very important innovator role of the minor parties has also been a major source of their frustration. When their proposals have gained any real degree of popular support, one and sometimes both of the major parties have taken over those ideas and then presented the policies as their own. The late Norman Thomas, who was the Socialist Party's candidate for President six times, complained that "the major parties are stealing from my platform."

Seventeen minor party presidential candidates, some of them nominated by more than one party, appeared on the ballots of at least one State in 2004. The most visible minor-party presidential campaigns in 2004 were those of the Libertarian, Constitution, and Socialist parties. More than a thousand candidates from a wide variety of minor parties also sought seats in Congress or ran for various State and local offices around the country.

Significant Minor Parties in Presidential Elections, 1880–2004*

Year	Party	Candidate	% Popular Vote	Electoral Vote
1880	Greenback	James B. Weaver	3.36	—
1888	Prohibition	Clinton B. Fisk	2.19	—
1892	Populist	James B. Weaver	8.54	22
	Prohibition	John Bidwell	2.19	—
1904	Socialist	Eugene V. Debs	2.98	—
1908	Socialist	Eugene V. Debs	2.82	—
1912	Progressive (Bull Moose)	Theodore Roosevelt	27.39	88
	Socialist	Eugene V. Debs	5.99	—
1916	Socialist	Allan L. Benson	3.17	—
1920	Socialist	Eugene V. Debs	3.45	—
1924	Progressive	Robert M. La Follette	16.61	13
1932	Socialist	Norman M. Thomas	2.22	—
1948	States' Rights (Dixiecrat)	Strom Thurmond	2.41	39
	Progressive	Henry A. Wallace	2.37	—
1968	American Independent	George C. Wallace	13.53	46
1996	Reform	Ross Perot	8.40	—
2000	Green	Ralph Nader	2.74	—

*Includes all minor parties that polled at least 2% of the popular vote
Source: *Historical Statistics of the United States, Colonial Times to 1970*; Federal Election Commission

Interpreting Tables Which of these minor-party presidential candidates played a spoiler role? H-SS 12.6.1

Section 4 Assessment

Key Terms and Main Ideas

1. Why do **single-issue parties** tend to be short-lived?
2. (a) What are **economic protest parties?** (b) Why are they formed in times of economic distress?
3. Most of the more important minor parties in our history have been of which type? Explain the effect of one such party.
4. Why is the innovator role a source of frustration to minor parties?

Critical Thinking

5. **Expressing Problems Clearly** Suppose you are considering voting for a presidential candidate from a minor party. Explain the benefits and drawbacks of casting your vote that way.

Standards Monitoring *Online*
For: Self-Quiz and vocabulary practice
Web Code: mqa-2054

6. **Predicting Consequences** Minor parties usually are willing to take definite stands on controversial issues. How might voters react to this tendency?

Go Online
PHSchool.com
For: An activity on minor parties
Web Code: mqd-2054

The Republican Campaign

 Analysis Skills HR4, HI3

As Chairman of the Republican National Committee, Ed Gillespie led the Republican Party's efforts to win the presidency and congressional elections in 2004. During the campaign, Mr. Gillespie spoke to party members at the West Virginia State Convention to spell out his party's message and drive Republicans to work hard for the election.

Ed Gillespie

This presidential election presents the clearest choices we've seen in 20 years—since Ronald Reagan ran for re-election against Walter Mondale in 1984.

Let's talk a little about these choices that are before us.

The President's economic growth policies are working. Our economy is strong, and getting stronger.

Economic growth over the last year has been the fastest in nearly 20 years. . . . Employment over the last year was up in 44 of the 50 States and the unemployment rate was down in all regions and in 47 of the 50 States. . . .

The President's critics act as if none of these positive developments ever occurred. They long ago came to the cynical conclusion that what's worst for the American people is what's best for them politically. . . .

While we are seeing positive results, we have much more to do. The President, Republicans in Congress, and Republican Governors are committed to making sure that every American who wants a job can find a job. . . .

John Kerry has a different plan: one that calls for higher taxes, more regulation, and more litigation [law suits] that would kill jobs and derail our recovery. . . . Senator Kerry favors policies from a retired playbook, one that has failed many class warfare candidates in the past.

John Kerry voted for higher taxes. . . .

In these challenging times we cannot hope that magic is real; we need steady leadership.

The President's decision to put more money in the pockets of America's families has laid the foundation for growth and job creation for years to come.

When it comes to national security, when it comes to homeland security, when it comes to creating jobs, and when it comes to who shares our values, President Bush is right, his opponent is wrong, and we are going to prove it come November. It is for reasons like this our Party is united under George W. Bush in a way I have not seen since it was under President Reagan.

Our Party is growing. . . .We are successful when, at the grassroots, people are energized, and we're a bottom up Party. And our supporters are talking to one another after religious services, at soccer games, in grocery store aisles.

Every dollar you donate, every phone you call, every e-mail you forward, every door you knock, every neighborhood you walk, every yard sign you post, every bumper sticker you stick—matters!

Analyzing Primary Sources

1. According to Mr. Gillespie, why should Americans vote for his candidate, George W. Bush?
2. What words and phrases does Mr. Gillespie use to describe Bush's opponent, Senator John Kerry? Why does he describe Kerry in these terms?
3. Would you label this speech propaganda? Why or why not?

5 Party Organization

Section Preview

OBJECTIVES

1. **Understand** why the major parties have a decentralized structure.
2. **Describe** the national party machinery and how parties are organized at the State and local levels.
3. **Identify** the three components of the parties.
4. **Examine** the future of the major parties.

WHY IT MATTERS

The major parties of the United States have a decentralized structure, and the different parts and elements work together primarily during national elections. The parties themselves have been in decline, or losing influence, since the 1960s.

POLITICAL DICTIONARY

★ ward
★ precinct
★ split-ticket voting

How strong, how active, and how well organized are the Republican and Democratic parties in your community? Contact the county chairperson or another official in one or both of the major parties. They are usually not very difficult to find. For starters, try the telephone directory.

The Decentralized Nature of the Parties

The two major parties are often described as though they were highly organized, close-knit, well-disciplined groups. However, neither party is anything of the kind. Rather, both are highly decentralized, fragmented, disjointed, and often beset by factions and internal squabbling.

Neither party has a chain of command running from the national through the State to the local level. Each of the State party organizations is only loosely tied to the party's national structure. By the same token, local party organizations are often quite independent of their parent State organizations. These various party units usually cooperate with one another, of course—but that is not always the case.

---

[7]The party does have a temporary leader for a brief time every fourth year: its presidential candidate, from nomination to election day. A defeated presidential candidate is often called the party's "titular leader"—a leader in title, by custom, but not in fact. What's more, if he lost by a wide margin, the defeated candidate's leadership may be largely discredited.

The Role of the Presidency

The President's party is usually more solidly united and more cohesively organized than the opposing party. The President is automatically the party leader. He asserts that leadership with such tools as his access to the media, his popularity, and his power to make appointments to federal office and to dispense other favors.

The other party has no one in an even faintly comparable position. Indeed, in the American party system, there is seldom any one person in the opposition party who can truly be called its leader. Rather, a number of personalities, frequently in competition with one another, form a loosely identifiable leadership group in the party out of power.[7]

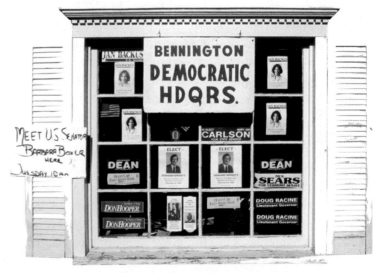

▲ The parties have many local headquarters, such as this one in Bennington, Vermont.

Taking the Public Pulse "When I die, I want to come back with real power—I want to come back as a member of a focus group," a powerful campaign strategist once said. Joking aside, the strategist was attesting to the growing influence of focus groups on who gets elected in this country, and who doesn't.

Focus groups were first used by businesses to test consumer products. Used as part of a political campaign, these groups can vary in number from 10 to as many as 30 or more people, typically members of the general public. They usually meet in two-to-three-hour sessions. Guided by trained monitors, their discussions help candidates identify issues that are important to voters. Focus groups are also used to test reactions to political commercials, speeches, and debates. They can be employed to probe opponents for weaknesses, as well.

Focus groups have had an important place in presidential campaigns since at least 1988. That year, they helped the Republican candidate George H. W. Bush defeat his Democratic opponent, Governor Michael Dukakis of Massachusetts, by identifying several weaknesses in the Dukakis campaign.

Use Web Code mqd-2058 to find out more about the use of focus groups in political campaigns and for help in answering the following question: *What kinds of issues might a campaign strategist address in order to find out about the opposition's weaknesses?*

The Impact of Federalism

Federalism is one major reason for the decentralized nature of the two major political parties. Remember, the basic goal of the major parties is to gain control of government by winning elective offices.

Today there are more than half a million elective offices in the United States. In the American federal system, those offices are widely distributed at the national, the State, and the local levels. In short, because the governmental system is highly decentralized, so too are the major parties that serve it.

The Role of the Nominating Process

The nominating process is also a major cause of party decentralization. Recall, from page 117, that the nominating process has a central role in the life of political parties. You will consider the selection of candidates at some length in Chapter 7, but, for now, look at two related aspects of that process.

First, candidate selection is an intraparty process. That is, nominations are made *within*

the party. Second, the nominating process can be, and often is, a divisive one. Where there is a fight over a nomination, that contest pits members of the same party against one another: Republicans fight Republicans; Democrats battle Democrats. In short, the prime function of the major parties—the making of nominations—is also a prime cause of their highly fragmented character.

National Party Machinery

The structure of both major parties at the national level has four basic elements. These elements are the national convention, the national committee, the national chairperson, and the congressional campaign committees.

The National Convention

The national convention, often described as the party's national voice, meets in the summer of every presidential election year to pick the party's presidential and vice-presidential candidates. It also performs some other functions, including the adoption of the party's rules and the writing of its platform.

Beyond that, the convention has little authority. It has no control over the selection of the party's candidates for other offices nor over the policy stands those nominees take. You will take a longer look at both parties' national nominating conventions in Chapter 13.

The National Committee

Between conventions, the party's affairs are handled, at least in theory, by the national committee and by the national chairperson. For years, each party's national committee was composed of a committeeman and a committeewoman from each State and several of the territories. They were chosen by the State's party organization. However, in recent years, both parties have expanded the committee's membership.

Today, the Republican National Committee (RNC) also seats the party chairperson from each State in which the GOP has recently had a winning record and members from the District of Columbia, Guam, American Samoa, Puerto Rico, and the Virgin Islands. Representatives of such GOP-related groups as the National Federation of Republican Women also serve on the RNC.

▲ **Step Right Up** Volunteers of all ages help their parties in national, State, and local races.

▲ **Madam Chairperson** Mary Louise Smith was national chairperson of the Republican Party in the 1970s.

The Democratic National Committee (DNC) is an even larger body. In addition to the committeeman and -woman from each State, it now includes the party's chairperson and vice-chairperson from every State and the several territories. It also includes additional members from the party organizations of the larger States, and up to 75 at-large members chosen by the DNC itself. Several members of Congress, as well as governors, mayors, and Young Democrats, also have seats.

On paper, the national committee appears to be a powerful organization loaded with many of the party's leading figures. In fact, it does not have a great deal of clout. Most of its work centers on staging the party's national convention every four years.

The National Chairperson

In each party, the national chairperson is the leader of the national committee. In form, he or she is chosen to a four-year term by the national committee, at a meeting held right after the national convention. In fact, the choice is made by the just-nominated presidential candidate and is then ratified by the national committee.

Only two women have ever held that top party post. Jean Westwood of Utah chaired the DNC from her party's 1972 convention until early 1973; and Mary Louise Smith of Iowa headed the RNC from 1974 until early 1977. Each lost her post soon after her party lost a presidential election. Ron Brown, the Democrats' National Chairman from 1989 to 1993, is the only African American ever to have held the office of national chairperson in either major party.

The national chairperson directs the work of the party's headquarters and its small staff in Washington. In presidential election years, the committee's attention is focused on the national convention and then the campaign. In between presidential elections, the chairperson and the committee work to strengthen the party and its fortunes. They do so by promoting party unity, raising money, recruiting new voters, and otherwise preparing for the next presidential season.

The Congressional Campaign Committees

Each party also has a campaign committee in each house of Congress.[8] These committees work to reelect incumbents and to make sure that seats given up by retiring party members remain in the party. The committees also take a hand in selected campaigns to unseat incumbents in the other party, at least in those House or Senate races where the chances for success seem to justify such efforts.

In both parties and in both houses, the members of these campaign committees are chosen by their colleagues. They serve for two years—that is, for a term of Congress.

State and Local Party Machinery

National party organization is largely the product of custom and of the rules adopted by the national conventions. At the State and

---

[8]They are the National Republican Campaign Committee and the Democratic Congressional Campaign Committee in the House; in the Senate, they are the National Republican Senatorial Committee and the Democratic Senatorial Campaign Committee.

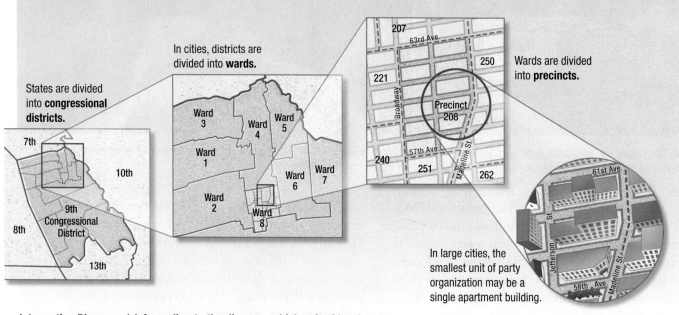

States are divided into **congressional districts**.

In cities, districts are divided into **wards**.

Wards are divided into **precincts**.

In large cities, the smallest unit of party organization may be a single apartment building.

Interpreting Diagrams (a) According to the diagram, which unit of local party organization is the largest in a State? (b) Which is the smallest?

local levels, however, party structure is largely set by State law.

The State Organization

At the State level, party machinery is built around a State central committee, headed by a State chairperson.

The chairperson may be an important political figure in his or her own right. More often than not, however, the chairperson fronts for the governor, a U.S. senator, or some other powerful leader or group in the politics of the State.

Together, the chairperson and the central committee work to further the party's interests in the State. Most of the time, they attempt to do this by building an effective organization and party unity, finding candidates and campaign funds, and so on. Remember, however, both major parties are highly decentralized, fragmented, and sometimes torn by struggles for power. This can complicate the chairperson's and the committee's job.

Local Organization

Local party structures vary so widely that they nearly defy even a brief description. Generally, they follow the electoral map of the State, with a party unit for each district in which elective offices are to be filled: congressional and legislative districts, counties, cities and towns, wards, and precincts. A **ward** is a unit into which cities are often divided for the election of city council members. A **precinct** is the smallest unit of election administration; the voters in each precinct report to one polling place.

In most larger cities, a party's organization is further broken down by residential blocks and sometimes even by apartment buildings. In some places, local party organizations are active year-round, but most often they are inactive except for those few hectic months before an election.

The Three Components of the Party

You have just looked at the makeup of the Republican and Democratic parties from an organizational standpoint. The two major parties can also be examined from a social standpoint—that is, in terms of the various roles played by their members. From this perspective, the two major parties are composed of three basic and closely interrelated components.

1. *The party organization.* These are the party's leaders, its activists, and its hangers-on—"all those who give their time, money, and

skills to the party, whether as leaders or followers."[9]

2. *The party in the electorate.* This component includes the party's loyalists who regularly vote the straight party ticket, and those other voters who call themselves party members and who usually vote for its candidates.

3. *The party in government.* These are the party's officeholders, those who hold elective and appointive offices in the executive, legislative, and judicial branches at the federal, State, and local levels of government.

You have taken a quick look at the party as an organization here. You will consider the party in the electorate in the next chapter, and the party in government in several later chapters.

▲ *Direct Access* Voters can judge the candidates for themselves by watching televised events such as this Democratic debate during the 2004 presidential primary campaign. From left to right: Florida Senator Bob Graham, Missouri Representative Dick Gephardt, former Illinois Senator Carol Mosley Braun, Massachusetts Senator John Kerry, Ohio Representative Dennis Kucinich, North Carolina Senator John Edwards, Connecticut Senator Joe Lieberman, and former Vermont Governor Howard Dean. **H-SS 12.8.2**

The Future of the Major Parties

Political parties have never been very popular in this country. Rather, over time, most Americans have had very mixed feelings about them. Most of us have accepted parties as necessary institutions, but, at the same time, we have felt that they should be closely watched and controlled. To many, political parties have seemed little better than necessary evils.

Political parties have been in a period of decline since at least the late 1960s. Their decline has led some analysts to conclude that the parties not only are in serious trouble, but that the party system itself may be on the point of collapse.

The present, weakened state of the parties can be traced to several factors. They include:

1. A sharp drop in the number of voters willing to identify themselves as Republicans or Democrats, and a growing number who regard themselves as independents.

2. A big increase in **split-ticket voting**—voting for candidates of different parties for different offices at the same election.

3. Various structural changes and reforms that have made the parties more "open," but have also led to greater internal conflict and disorganization. These changes range from the introduction of the direct primary in the early 1900s to the more recent and far-reaching changes in campaign finance laws.

4. Changes in the technology of campaigning for office—especially the heavy use of television and of the Internet, professional campaign managers, and direct-mail advertising. These changes

"I beg your pardon," said Alice, "but which of you is the Democrat?"

Interpreting Political Cartoons The two major political parties have been criticized as failing to distinguish themselves from one another. ***Do you agree with the point of view presented in the cartoon? Explain your answer using specific current issues.***

---

[9]Frank J. Sorauf and Paul Beck, *Party Politics in America,* 6th ed.

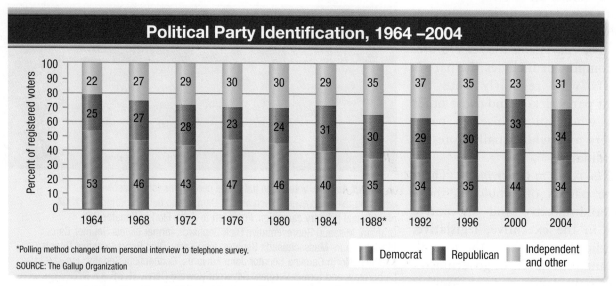

Political Party Identification, 1964–2004

Year	Democrat	Republican	Independent and other
1964	53	25	22
1968	46	27	27
1972	43	28	29
1976	47	23	30
1980	46	24	30
1984	40	31	29
1988*	35	30	35
1992	34	29	37
1996	35	30	35
2000	44	33	23
2004	34	34	31

*Polling method changed from personal interview to telephone survey.

SOURCE: The Gallup Organization

Interpreting Graphs This graph shows the percentage of voters who identify with the two major parties and the percentage of independents. *(a) Which group shows the biggest gain in support between 1964 and 2004? (b) Which group lost the most support during that time?* H-SS 12.3.1

in campaign technology have made candidates much less dependent on party organizations since, in many cases, they can now "speak" directly to the electorate.

5. The growth, in both numbers and impact, of single-issue organizations in our politics. These groups support (or more often, oppose) candidates on the basis of the group's own closely defined views in some specific area of public policy—for example, the environment, gun control, or abortion—rather than on a candidate's stands on the full range of public policy questions.

You will look at these and several other matters affecting the condition of the parties over the next four chapters. As you do so, remember these points: Political parties are indispensable to democratic government—and so, then, to American government. Our two major parties have existed far longer than has any other party anywhere in the world. And, as you have seen, they perform a number of quite necessary functions. In short, the reports of their passing may not only be premature, they might in fact be quite farfetched.

Section 5 Assessment

Key Terms and Main Ideas

1. What are the major causes of the decentralized nature of political parties?
2. What are the four main elements of major party organization at the national level?
3. Describe how **wards** and **precincts** are part of the local party organization.
4. (a) What is **split-ticket voting?** (b) How has its increase contributed to the weakened state of the two major parties?

Critical Thinking

5. **Drawing Conclusions** Based on what you know about parties, their goals, and the American people, why do you think local party organizations vary so widely?
6. **Formulating Questions** A growing number of voters consider themselves to be independents. Compose three questions that a pollster might ask in an attempt to learn why this is the case.
7. **Predicting Consequences** Do you think the major parties will survive and emerge from their current period of decline? Why or why not?

Standards Monitoring *Online*
For: Self-quiz with vocabulary practice
Web Code: mqa-2055

Go Online
PHSchool.com
For: An activity on State-level political parties
Web Code: mqd-2055

Can Judicial Candidates State Legal Views?

The 1st Amendment gives Americans the right to express freely their opinions on matters of public concern. But should the government be able to restrict free speech to protect other important governmental interests? For example, should judges who may have to decide a particular legal issue be free to tell the public in advance how they would decide?

Analysis Skills HR4, HI3, HI4

Republican Party of Minnesota v. *White* (2002)

A Minnesota Supreme Court rule said that lawyers running for judgeships could not announce their views on any legal matter that might come before their court if they were elected. This rule was intended to keep judges impartial and to maintain for the public a sense of judicial impartiality. Candidates could discuss their judicial philosophy in the abstract, but could not say what they believed about concrete issues that they might later decide or vote on.

In 1996, Attorney Gregory Wersal was running for associate justice of the Minnesota Supreme Court. As part of his campaign, he wrote and distributed documents criticizing several of that court's controversial decisions. He withdrew from the race after being accused of an ethical violation, but ran again in 1998. This time he sued the officers of the Lawyer's Professional Responsibility Board and the Minnesota Board of Judicial Standards, chaired by Suzanne White, in U.S. District Court. Wersal claimed that the rule prevented him from telling voters his positions on matters of public importance. The Minnesota Republican Party joined the suit, saying that the rule prevented them from learning Wersal's views, so they could not decide whether to support his candidacy.

Arguments for Wersal and the Republican Party

1. The constitutional right of free speech applies to candidates for elected office, and a candidate may not be prevented from expressing those beliefs during the campaign.

2. Minnesota cannot show that the restriction on free speech is necessary to protect important governmental interests.

3. Judges do not give up their impartiality just because they have opinions on controversial topics, and voters should be able to know what those opinions are.

Arguments for White

1. Judicial impartiality and the public's perception of impartial justice will be harmed if prospective judges publicly discuss their views on matters that may come before their courts.

2. Judicial decision-making will be harmed if judges have previously stated public opinions on important topics, because then judges will feel obligated to decide cases according to their prior statements rather than on the merits of the particular case.

3. The parties to a case would be denied fair judicial process if the judge had previously announced his or her view on the case.

Decide for Yourself

1. Review the constitutional grounds upon which each side based its arguments and the specific arguments each side presented.

2. Debate the opposing viewpoints presented in this case. Which viewpoint did you favor?

3. Predict the impact of the Court's decision on States' attempts to restrict the speech of public officials in other contexts. (To read a summary of the Court's decision, turn to pages 799–806.)

Go Online PHSchool.com Use Web Code mqp-2059 to register your vote on this issue and to see how other students voted.

Political Dictionary

political party (p. 116), major parties (p. 116), partisanship (p. 117), party in power (p. 118), minor party (p. 119), two-party system (p. 119), single-member district (p. 120), plurality (p. 120), bipartisan (p. 120), pluralistic society (p. 121), consensus (p. 121), multiparty (p. 122), coalition (p. 122), one-party system (p. 123), incumbent (p. 127), faction (p. 127), electorate (p. 129), sectionalism (p. 129), ideological parties (p. 132), single-issue parties (p. 132), economic protest parties (p. 133), splinter parties (p. 133), ward (p. 140), precinct (p. 140), split-ticket voting (p. 141)

Standards Review

H-SS 12.1.5 Describe the systems of separated and shared powers, the role of organized interests (*Federalist Paper Number 10*), checks and balances (*Federalist Paper Number 51*), the importance of an independent judiciary (*Federalist Paper Number 78*), enumerated powers, rule of law, federalism, and civilian control of the military.

H-SS 12.3.1 Explain how civil society provides opportunities for individuals to associate for social, cultural, religious, economic, and political purposes.

H-SS 12.6.1 Analyze the origin, development, and role of political parties, noting those occasional periods in which there was only one major party or were more than two major parties.

H-SS 12.6.4 Describe the means that citizens use to participate in the political process (e.g., voting, campaigning, lobbying, filing a legal challenge, demonstrating, petitioning, picketing, running for political office).

H-SS 12.7.5 Explain how public policy is formed, including the setting of the public agenda and implementation of it through regulations and executive orders.

H-SS 12.8.2 Describe the roles of broadcast, print, and electronic media, including the Internet, as means of communication in American politics.

Practicing the Vocabulary

Using Words in Context *For each of the terms below, write a sentence that shows how it relates to this chapter.*

1. multiparty
2. pluralistic society
3. party in power
4. minor party
5. split-ticket voting
6. one-party system
7. consensus
8. splinter parties
9. single-member district
10. two-party system

True/False *Determine whether each of the following statements is true or false. If it is true, write "true." If it is false, rewrite the sentence to make it true.*

11. A plurality is more than half the votes cast.
12. A ward is a unit into which cities are often divided for the election of city council members.
13. An ideological party arises over a particular issue or crisis and soon fades away.
14. Partisanship means membership in one of the major parties.

Reviewing Main Ideas

Section 1

15. What is the major function of a political party?
16. Which term better describes political parties in American politics: *divisive* or *unifying?* Why?
17. Cite two examples that show why American government may be described as government by party.

Section 2

18. In what two ways does the American electoral system tend to promote a two-party system?
19. How can the diversity of views represented in a multiparty system be seen as both a strength and a weakness?
20. How is the ideological consensus of the American electorate reflected in the membership of the major parties?

Section 3

21. **(a)** Which political party was the first to appear in the new United States? **(b)** Who was its leader and what type of government did it favor?

22. **(a)** How did the Republican Party begin? **(b)** How was its development unique in American politics?
23. What effect did the Great Depression have on American political parties?
24. What unusual feature characterizes the present era of American two-party history?

Section 4

25. Briefly describe the four types of minor parties.
26. Historically, what have been the most important roles of minor parties? Briefly explain one of these roles.

Section 5

27. Why is the party in power more cohesive than the opposition party?
28. Describe the role of the national chairperson.
29. List and explain four factors that have contributed to the present weakened state of the major parties.

Critical Thinking Skills

Analysis Skills CS1, CS2, HR1, HI2, HI4

30. *Face the Issues* Study the role of minor party candidates in the most recent presidential election. In your opinion, would including these candidates in the debates have changed the outcome of the election? Explain.

31. *Determining Relevance* If there had not been a group opposed to the adoption of the Constitution in the 1780s, do you think a strong two-party system would have developed in the United States? Why or why not?

32. *Distinguishing Fact from Opinion* Explain why you agree or disagree with this statement: "A vote for a minor party candidate is a vote wasted."

33. *Recognizing Cause and Effect* **(a)** How has television affected the state of the two-party system? **(b)** How has the Internet impacted the two-party system?

Analyzing Political Cartoons

Using your knowledge of American government and this cartoon, answer the questions below.

34. What does the cartoonist imply about the relationship between the two major parties? Explain how he conveys this idea.
35. Does the cartoonist regard the minor parties as a serious threat to the status quo? How do the major parties react to this threat?

Participation Activities

Analysis Skills CS1, HR4, HI1

36. *Current Events Watch* Look in newspapers or news magazines for a local or national issue on which there is public disagreement. See if the two major parties have taken stands on the issue. If not, look for the positions taken by elected officials and other representatives of the major parties. Using the information you have found, prepare a report telling whether each party is united or divided in its response to the issue and whether the two major parties oppose each other on this issue. Support your conclusions with examples.

37. *Time Line Activity* Using information from the chapter, create a time line showing the major political events of the current era of divided government. Include at least ten entries in your time line. You might begin with Richard Nixon's election to the presidency in 1968. So far, which party has held the White House more frequently during this era?

38. *It's Your Turn* Election law in this country is often written to discourage minor party candidates. Draw a political cartoon in which you comment on this situation. Take either the pro or the con position in your cartoon. **(Drawing a Cartoon)**

Standards Monitoring *Online*

For: Chapter 5 Self-Test **Visit:** PHSchool.com
Web Code: mqa-2056

As a final review, take the Magruder's Chapter 5 Self-Test and receive immediate feedback on your answers. The test consists of 20 multiple-choice questions designed to test your understanding of the chapter content.

CHAPTER 6

Voters and Voter Behavior

> "*It is not enough that people have the right to vote. . . . People must have the reason to vote as well.*"
> —Jesse Jackson (1988)

People who have struggled to win the right to vote know how important it is. Although, since 1789, suffrage has expanded to include many more people—notably African Americans and women—many Americans do not exercise this important right. A variety of factors influence whether and how people vote.

◆ *Stump Speaking*, a hand-colored engraving by Louis-Adolphe Gautier, 1856, shows a candidate addressing voters.

Standards Preview

H-SS 12.2.4 Understand the obligations of civic-mindedness, including voting, being informed on civic issues, volunteering and performing public service, and serving in the military or alternative service.

H-SS 12.5.4 Explain the controversies that have resulted over changing interpretations of civil rights, including those in *Plessy* v. *Ferguson, Brown* v. *Board of Education, Miranda* v. *Arizona, Regents of the University of California* v. *Bakke, Adarand Constructors, Inc.* v. *Pena,* and *United States* v. *Virginia* (VMI).

H-SS 12.6.4 Describe the means that citizens use to participate in the political process (e.g., voting, campaigning, lobbying, filing a legal challenge, demonstrating, petitioning, picketing, running for political office).

H-SS 12.6.6 Analyze trends in voter turnout; the causes and effects of reapportionment and redistricting, with special attention to spatial districting and the rights of minorities; and the function of the Electoral College.

SECTION 1

The Right to Vote (pp. 148–150)

★ The history of the expansion of the right to vote in the United States can be divided into five distinct steps.

★ The Constitution places five restrictions on the States' power to set voting qualifications.

SECTION 2

Voter Qualifications (pp.152–157)

★ All of the States set citizenship, residence, and age requirements for voting.

★ Other voting qualifications have been imposed by various States over time. Literacy tests and tax payment have been eliminated; registration is required in all but one State today.

SECTION 3

Suffrage and Civil Rights (pp. 159–163)

★ The 15th Amendment, ratified in 1870, declared that the right to vote cannot be denied to a citizen because of race.

★ Southern States used a variety of devices to circumvent the 15th Amendment and deny African Americans the vote. These tactics included literacy tests, white primaries, and gerrymandering.

★ Congress finally took action to protect minority voting rights in the Civil Rights Acts of 1957, 1960, and 1964.

★ The Voting Rights Act of 1965 and its later amendments finally ensured African American suffrage.

SECTION 4

Voter Behavior (pp. 164–172)

★ Millions of Americans who are qualified to vote do not do so.

★ Those who choose not to vote often lack a feeling of political efficacy. Age, education, income, and geography also affect whether a person is likely to vote or not.

★ Sociological factors—such as occupation, gender, and ethnic background—influence a person's voting choices.

★ Psychological factors—including party identification and perception of the candidates and issues—also contribute to voter behavior.

Go Online
PHSchool.com

For: Current Data
Web Code: mqg-2066

For: Close Up Foundation debates
Web Code: mqh-2069

The Right to Vote

OBJECTIVES

1. **Summarize** the history of voting rights in the United States.
2. **Identify and explain** constitutional restrictions on the States' power to set voting qualifications.

WHY IT MATTERS

Democratic government can succeed only if its citizens are willing to vote. The history of the United States has been marked by a steady expansion of the electorate through the elimination of restrictions on voting qualifications.

POLITICAL DICTIONARY

★ **suffrage**
★ **franchise**
★ **electorate**

Soon, you will be eligible to vote—but will you exercise that right? The record suggests that while *you* may do so, many of your friends will not, at least not for some time. The record also suggests that some of your friends will never vote. Yet, clearly, the success of democratic government depends on popular participation, and, in particular, on the regular and informed exercise of the right to vote.

The History of Voting Rights

The Framers of the Constitution purposely left the power to set suffrage qualifications to each State. **Suffrage** means the right to vote. **Franchise** is another term with the same meaning.[1]

▲ These historical flags (left to right: pre-1777, c. 1820, c. 1865) illustrate the expansion of the nation and growth of the electorate.

Expansion of the Electorate

When the Constitution went into effect in 1789, the right to vote in the United States was restricted to white male property owners. In fact, probably not one in fifteen adult white males could vote in elections in the different States. Benjamin Franklin often lampooned this situation. He told of a man whose only property was a jackass and noted that the man would lose the right to vote if his jackass died. "Now," asked Franklin, "in whom is the right of suffrage? In the man or the jackass?"

Today, the size of the American **electorate**— the potential voting population—is truly impressive. Some 220 million people, nearly all citizens who are at least 18 years of age, can now qualify to vote. That huge number is a direct result of the legal definition of suffrage. In other words, it is the result of those laws that determine who can and cannot vote. It is also the result of some 200 years of continuing, often bitter, and sometimes violent struggle.

The history of American suffrage since 1789 has been marked by two long-term trends. First, the nation has experienced the gradual elimination of several restrictions on the right to vote. These restrictions were based on such factors as

---

[1]Originally, the Constitution had only two suffrage provisions. Article I, Section 2, Clause 1 requires each State to allow anyone qualified to vote for members of "the most numerous Branch" of its own legislature to vote as well for members of the national House of Representatives. Article II, Section 1, Clause 2 provides that presidential electors be chosen in each State "in such Manner as the Legislature thereof may direct."

religious belief, property ownership, tax payment, race, and sex. Second, a significant share of what was originally the States' power over the right to vote has gradually been assumed by the Federal Government.

Extending Suffrage: The Five Stages

The growth of the American electorate to its present size and shape has come in five fairly distinct stages. The two trends described above—elimination of voting restrictions and growing federal control over voting—are woven through those stages. You will see several illustrations of both of these trends over the course of this chapter.

1. The first stage of the struggle to extend voting rights came in the early 1800s. Religious qualifications, instituted in colonial days, quickly disappeared. No State has had a religious test for voting since 1810. Then, one by one, States began to eliminate property ownership and tax payment qualifications. By mid-century, almost all white adult males could vote in every State.

2. The second major effort to broaden the electorate followed the Civil War. The 15th Amendment, ratified in 1870, was intended to protect any citizen from being denied the right to vote because of race or color. Still, for nearly another century, African Americans were systematically prevented from voting, and they remained the largest group of disenfranchised citizens in the nation's population.

3. The 19th Amendment prohibited the denial of the right to vote because of sex. Its ratification in 1920 completed the third expansion

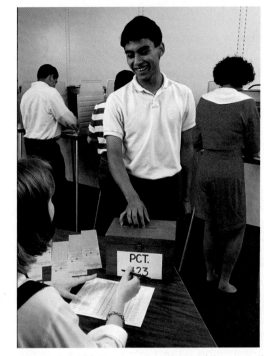

◀ This 18-year-old is casting a vote for the first time.
Critical Thinking
Do you think 18 is the right minimum age for voting? Why or why not?
H-SS 12.2.4

of suffrage. Wyoming, while still a territory, had given women the vote in 1869. By 1920 more than half of the States had followed that lead.

4. A fourth major extension took place during the 1960s. During that time, federal legislation and court decisions focused on securing African Americans a full role in the electoral process in all States. With the passage and vigorous enforcement of a number of civil rights acts, especially the Voting Rights Act of 1965 and its later extensions, racial equality finally became fact in polling booths throughout the country.

The 23rd Amendment, passed in 1961, added the voters of the District of Columbia to the presidential electorate. The 24th Amendment, ratified in 1964, eliminated the poll tax

◀ *Suffragist Struggle*
American suffragists first demanded the right to vote in 1848 at a meeting in Seneca Falls, New York. It took until 1920 to achieve ratification of the 19th Amendment, extending the vote to women in every State in the country.
H-SS 12.5.4

(as well as any other tax) as a condition for voting in any federal election.

5. The fifth and latest expansion of the electorate came with the adoption of the 26th Amendment in 1971. It provides that no State can set the minimum age for voting at more than 18 years of age. In other words, those 18 and over were given the right to vote by this amendment.

The Power to Set Voting Qualifications

The Constitution does not give the Federal Government the power to set suffrage qualifications. Rather, that matter is reserved to the States. The Constitution does, however, place five restrictions on how the States use that power.

1. Any person whom a State allows to vote for members of the "most numerous branch" of its own legislature must also be allowed to vote for representatives and senators in Congress.[2] This restriction is of little real meaning today. With only minor exceptions, each of the States allows the same voters to vote in all elections within the State.

2. No State can deprive any person of the right to vote "on account of race, color, or previous condition of servitude" (15th Amendment).[3]

3. No State can deprive any person of the right to vote on account of sex (19th Amendment).[4]

4. No State can require payment of any tax as a condition for taking part in the nomination or election of any federal officeholder. That is, no State can levy any tax in connection with the selection of the President, the Vice President, or members of Congress (24th Amendment).

5. No State can deprive any person who is at least 18 years of age of the right to vote because of age (26th Amendment).[5]

Beyond these five restrictions, remember that no State can violate any other provision in the Constitution in the setting of suffrage qualifications—or in anything else that it does. A case decided by the Supreme Court in 1975, *Hill* v. *Stone,* illustrates this point.

The Court struck down a section of the Texas constitution that declared that only those persons who owned taxable property could vote in city bond elections. The Court found the drawing of such a distinction for voting purposes—between those who do and those who do not own taxable property—to be an unreasonable classification, prohibited by the 14th Amendment's Equal Protection Clause.

---

[2]Article I, Section 2, Clause 1; the 17th Amendment extended the "most numerous branch" provision to the election of senators.

[3]The phrase "previous condition of servitude" refers to slavery. This amendment does not guarantee the right to vote to African Americans, or to anyone else. Instead, it forbids discrimination on these grounds when the States set suffrage qualifications.

[4]This amendment does not guarantee the right to vote to women as such. Technically, it forbids States the power to discriminate against males or females in establishing suffrage qualifications.

[5]This amendment does not prevent any State from allowing persons younger than age 18 to vote. It does prohibit a State from setting a maximum age for voting.

Section 1 Assessment

Key Terms and Main Ideas

1. Describe two long-term trends that have characterized the history of **suffrage** in the United States.
2. Describe five distinct stages in the growth of the American **electorate.**
3. Who exercises the **franchise?**
4. What restrictions does the Constitution place on the States in setting suffrage qualifications?

Critical Thinking

5. **Demonstrating Reasoned Judgment** It is the year 1970. Suppose that you are a young adult testifying before Congress in favor of granting the vote to 18-year-olds. What arguments would you present in order to make your case?

6. **Drawing Inferences** Why do you think the Federal Government took more and more control over the setting of voter qualifications? Why could the States not have accomplished the same ends?

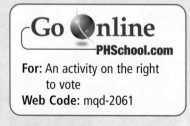

Casting Your Vote

 H-SS 12.6.4

Why have people risked their lives to get and keep the right to vote? In the United States, we tend to take this right for granted. Yet if we were ever deprived of it, we would surely come to recognize its great value.

The voting process may vary slightly from place to place, but in general, these steps apply:

1. Determine if you are eligible to vote. To qualify to vote, you must be an American citizen at least 18 years of age and a resident of the State in which you vote.

2. Register to vote. In every State except North Dakota, you must register to vote. You can register locally, usually at city hall or the county courthouse. Registration tables are often set up in shopping malls, supermarkets, libraries, and fire stations before an election. You can register by mail, and in many places, via the Internet. To register you will need proof of your age, such as a birth certificate.

3. Study the candidates and issues. Identify the candidates for each office and the duties of the office. Then research the candidates' views on major issues. Besides voting for candidates for office, voters often have the opportunity to directly approve or reject proposed State and local

laws. Don't wait until you are in the voting booth to become familiar with these issues.

4. Go to your polling place. In many States, voters receive a voter registration card identifying their precinct and polling place. Newspapers often publish lists of polling places prior to an election. Polls are usually open from 7:00 or 8:00 A.M. to 7:00 or 8:00 P.M. At the polling place, your name will be checked against a list of registered voters to make sure you are eligible to vote. A growing number of States now require all voters to show some proof of their identity, such as a driver's license, passport, or birth certificate. You will be directed to a booth with some type of voting device, or you will be given a paper ballot and directed to a voting booth.

5. Cast your vote. Follow the instructions on the voting device or ballot, so your vote will be counted properly. Do not feel rushed. If you have a question, ask an official. Make sure you've made a choice in every contest in which you wish to vote.

Test for Success

(a) Brainstorm at least three possible sources of voter information for voters in your area. (b) What sources would you consider most reliable?

Section Preview

OBJECTIVES

1. **Identify** the universal requirements for voting in the United States.
2. **Explain** the other requirements that States have used or still use as voting qualifications.

WHY IT MATTERS

All States have citizenship, residence, and age requirements for voting. Other voting qualifications differ from State to State. Some requirements—especially those that were used to disenfranchise certain groups—have been eliminated over time.

POLITICAL DICTIONARY

★ transient
★ registration
★ purge
★ poll books
★ literacy
★ poll tax

Are you qualified to vote? Probably not—at least not yet. Do you know why? In this section, you will see how the States, including yours, determine who can vote. You will also see that the various qualifications they set are not very difficult to meet.

Universal Requirements

Today, every State requires that any person who wants to vote must be able to satisfy qualifications based on three factors: (1) citizenship, (2) residence, and (3) age. The States have some leeway in shaping the details of the first two of these factors; they have almost no discretion with regard to the third one.

Citizenship

Aliens—foreign-born residents who have not become citizens—are generally denied the right

to vote in the United States. Still, nothing in the Constitution says that aliens cannot vote, and any State could allow them to do so if it chose. At one time about a fourth of the States permitted those aliens who had applied for naturalization to vote. Typically, the western States did so to help attract settlers.[6]

Only two States now draw any distinction between native-born and naturalized citizens with regard to suffrage. The Minnesota constitution requires a person to have been an American citizen for at least three months before he or she can vote in elections there. And the Pennsylvania constitution says that one must have become a citizen at least one month before an election in order to vote in that State.

Residence

In order to vote in this country today, one must be a legal resident of the State in which he or she wishes to cast a ballot. In most States a person must have lived in the State for at least a certain period of time before he or she can vote.

The States adopted residence requirements for two reasons: (1) to keep a political machine from importing (bribing) enough outsiders to affect the outcome of local elections (a once common practice), and (2) to allow new voters

▲ These people are participating in a ceremony making them American citizens—one qualification for voting.

[6]Arkansas, the last State in which aliens could vote, adopted a citizenship requirement in 1926. In a few States, local governments can permit noncitizens to vote in local contests—e.g., city council elections—and a handful do.

at least some time to become familiar with the candidates and issues in an election.

For decades, every State imposed a fairly lengthy residence requirement—typically, a year in the State, 60 or 90 days in the county, and 30 days in the local precinct or ward.[7] The requirement was a longer one in some southern States—for example, one year in the State, six months in the county, and three months in the precinct in Alabama, Louisiana, and South Carolina, and a year in the State, a year in the county, and six months in the precinct in Mississippi.

Residence requirements are not nearly so long today. In fact, most States now require that a voter be a legal resident but attach *no* time period to that qualification. About a fourth of them say that a voter must have lived in a State for at least 30 days. In a few, the period is somewhat shorter—for example, 29 days in Arizona, 28 in Kentucky, 20 in Minnesota, and 10 in Wisconsin.[8]

Today's much shorter requirements are a direct result of a 1970 law and a 1972 Supreme Court decision. In the Voting Rights Act Amendments of 1970, Congress banned any requirement of longer than 30 days for voting in presidential elections.[9] In *Dunn* v. *Blumstein*, 1972, the Supreme Court found Tennessee's requirement—at the time, a year in the State and 90 days in the county—unconstitutional. The Court held such a lengthy requirement to be an unsupportable discrimination against new residents and so in conflict with the 14th Amendment's Equal Protection Clause. The Supreme Court said that "30 days appears to be an ample period of time." Election law and practice among the States quickly accepted that standard.

Nearly every State does prohibit **transients,** persons living in the State for only a short time, from gaining a legal residence there. Thus, a traveling sales agent, a member of the armed services, or a college student usually cannot vote in a State where he or she has only a temporary physical

"THAT'S WHAT'S THE MATTER."
BOSS TWEED. "As long as I count the votes, what are you going to do about it? say?"

Interpreting Political Cartoons This 1870 cartoon depicts the "boss" of a corrupt New York City political "machine." *How do you think a dishonest administration might arrange to "count the votes" to its own advantage?*

residence. In several States, however, the courts have held that college students who claim the campus community as their legal residence can vote there.

Age

The 26th Amendment, added to the Constitution in 1971, declares:

FROM THE *Constitution* **"**The right of citizens of the United States, who are eighteen years of age or older, to vote shall not be denied or abridged by the United States or by any State on account of age. **"**
—26th Amendment

Thus, no State may set the minimum age for voting in any election at more than 18. In other words, the amendment extends suffrage to citizens who are at least 18 years of age. Notice, however, that any State could set the age at less than 18, if it chose to do so.

Until the 26th Amendment was adopted, the generally accepted age requirement for voting was 21. In fact, up to 1970, only four States had put the age under 21. Georgia was the first State to allow 18-year-olds to vote; it did so in 1943, in the midst of World War II. Kentucky followed suit in 1955. Alaska entered the Union in 1959 with the

---

[7]Recall, the precinct is the smallest unit of election administration; see page 140. The ward is a unit into which cities are often divided for the election of members of the city council.

[8]Until recently, Arizona imposed a 50-day requirement period. The Supreme Court upheld Arizona's residence law in *Marston* v. *Lewis* in 1973, but it also declared that that law "approaches the outer constitutional limits."

[9]The Supreme Court upheld this in *Oregon* v. *Mitchell* in 1970.

Interpreting Political Cartoons (a) What attitudes make this cartoon character a nonvoter? (b) What is the cartoonist's opinion of these attitudes?

Those States allow anyone whose 18th birthday falls after the primary but before the general election to vote in the primary election.

One State, Nebraska, has come very close to effectively lowering the voting age to 17 for all elections. There, any person who will be 18 by the Tuesday following the first Monday in November can qualify to vote in any election held during that calendar year.

Other Qualifications

The States have imposed a number of other qualifications over time—notably, requirements based on literacy, tax payment, and registration. Only registration has survived as a significant requirement.

Registration

Forty-nine States—all except North Dakota—require that most or all voters be registered to vote. **Registration** is a procedure of voter identification intended to prevent fraudulent voting. It gives election officials a list of those persons who are qualified to vote in an election. Several States also use voter registration to identify voters in terms of their party preference and, thus, their eligibility to take part in closed primaries.

Voter registration became a common feature of State election law in the early 1900s. Today, most States require all voters to register in order to vote in any election held within the State. A few do not impose the requirement for all elections, however. In Wisconsin, for example, only those in urban areas must register to vote.[10]

Typically, a prospective voter must register his or her name, age, place of birth, present address, length of residence, and similar facts. The information is logged by a local official, usually a registrar of elections or the county clerk. A voter typically remains registered unless or until he or she moves, dies, is convicted of a serious crime, or is committed to a mental institution.

State law directs local election officials to review the lists of registered voters and to remove the names of those who are no longer eligible to

voting age set at 19, and Hawaii became a State later that same year with a voting age of 20.

Both Alaska and Hawaii set the age above 18 but below 21 to avoid potential problems caused by high school students voting in local school-district elections. Whatever the fears at the time, there have been no such problems in any State since the passage of the 26th Amendment.

Efforts to lower the voting age to 18 nationwide began in the 1940s, during World War II. These efforts were capped by the adoption of the 26th Amendment in 1971, during the war in Vietnam. That amendment was ratified more quickly than any other amendment to the Constitution. This fact is testament to the emotional weight of the principal argument in its favor: "Old enough to fight, old enough to vote."

How have 18-to-20-year-olds responded to the 26th Amendment? In short, not very well. In election after election, young voters are much less likely to vote than any other age group in the electorate. In 1972, 48 percent of the 18-to-20 age group voted, but by 2000 that figure had plummeted to 28 percent. It did rise in 2004, and substantially—to nearly 38 percent. But contrast that figure with the turnout of Americans 65 and older. Despite the infirmities that may accompany their age, their rate regularly exceeds 60 percent, and it did so again in 2004.

In a growing number of States, some 17-year-olds can now cast ballots in primary elections.

---

[10]Wisconsin does not require registration by voters who live in rural areas or in cities with populations of less than 10,000.

vote. This process is known as **purging,** and it is usually supposed to be done every two or four years. Unfortunately, the requirement is often ignored. Where it is, the **poll books** (the official lists of qualified voters in each precinct) soon become clogged with the names of a great many people who, for one reason or another, are no longer eligible to vote.

There are some who think that the registration requirement should be abolished, everywhere. They see the qualification as a bar to voting, especially by the poor and less educated.

Those critics buttress their case by noting that voter turnout began to decline in the early 1900s, just after most States adopted a registration requirement. They also point to the fact that voter turnout is much higher in most European democracies than in the United States. In those countries voter registration is not a matter of individual choice; by law, public officials must enter the names of all eligible citizens on registration lists. The United States is the only democratic country

in which each person decides whether or not he or she will register to vote.

Most people who have studied the problem favor keeping the registration requirement as a necessary defense against fraud. However, they also favor making the process a more convenient one. In short, they see the problem in these terms: Where is the line between making it so easy to vote that fraud is encouraged, and making it so difficult that legitimate voting is discouraged?

Most States have eased the registration process over the last several years, and in 1993 Congress passed a law that required every State (but North Dakota) to do so. That law, dubbed the "Motor Voter Law," became effective in 1995. It directs every State to (1) allow all eligible citizens to register to vote when they apply for or renew a driver's license; (2) provide for voter registration by mail; and (3) make registration forms available at the local offices of State employment, welfare, and other social service agencies. The Federal Election Commission reports that by 2000 some

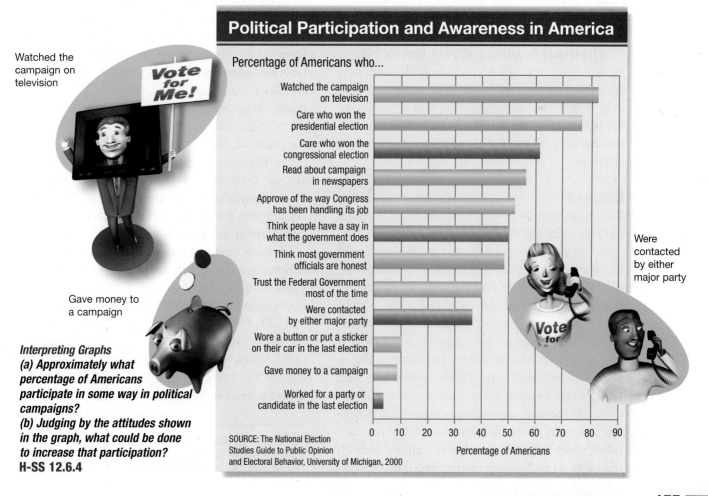

Watched the campaign on television

Gave money to a campaign

Were contacted by either major party

Political Participation and Awareness in America

Percentage of Americans who...

- Watched the campaign on television
- Care who won the presidential election
- Care who won the congressional election
- Read about campaign in newspapers
- Approve of the way Congress has been handling its job
- Think people have a say in what the government does
- Think most government officials are honest
- Trust the Federal Government most of the time
- Were contacted by either major party
- Wore a button or put a sticker on their car in the last election
- Gave money to a campaign
- Worked for a party or candidate in the last election

SOURCE: The National Election Studies Guide to Public Opinion and Electoral Behavior, University of Michigan, 2000

Percentage of Americans

Interpreting Graphs
(a) Approximately what percentage of Americans participate in some way in political campaigns?
(b) Judging by the attitudes shown in the graph, what could be done to increase that participation?
H-SS 12.6.4

"By th' way, what's that big word?"

8 million persons had registered to vote as a direct result of the Motor Voter Law.

The law also requires every State to mail a questionnaire to each of its registered voters every four years, so that the poll books can be purged for deaths and changes of residence. It also forbids the States to purge for any other reason, including failure to vote.

Maine and Wisconsin allow voters to register at any time, up to and including election day. Elsewhere a voter must be registered by some date before an election, often 20 or 30 days beforehand.[11] That cutoff gives election officials time to prepare the poll books for an upcoming election.

Literacy

Today, no State has a suffrage qualification based on voter **literacy**—a person's ability to read or write. At one time, the literacy requirement could be, and in many places was, used to make sure that a qualified voter had the capacity to cast an informed ballot. It also was used unfairly in many places to prevent or discourage certain groups from voting. For many years, it was a device to keep African Americans from voting in parts of the South, and Native Americans and Latinos from voting in the West and Southwest.

Some literacy requirements called for potential voters to prove they had the ability to read; other States required proof of the ability to both read and write. Still others required the ability to read, write, and "understand" some printed material, usually a passage taken from the State or Federal Constitution. Often, whites were asked to "understand" short, plainly worded passages; African Americans were faced with long and highly complex passages.

Connecticut adopted the first literacy qualifications in 1855. Massachusetts followed in 1857. Both of these States were trying to limit voting by Irish Catholic immigrants. Mississippi adopted a literacy requirement in 1890, and shortly, most of the other southern States followed suit. Southern literacy qualifications usually included an "understanding clause"— again, requiring potential voters to demonstrate comprehension of some printed material.

While those qualifications had been aimed at disenfranchising African Americans, they sometimes had unintended effects. Several States soon found that they needed to adjust their voting requirements by adding so-called "grandfather clauses" to their constitutions. These grandfather clauses were designed to enfranchise those white males who were unintentionally disqualified by their failure to meet the literacy or taxpaying requirements.

A grandfather clause was added to the Louisiana constitution in 1895; Alabama, Georgia, Maryland, North Carolina, Oklahoma, and Virginia soon added them as well. These clauses stated that any man, or his male descendants, who had voted in the State before the adoption of the 15th Amendment (1870) could become a legal voter without regard to any literacy or taxpaying qualifications. The Supreme Court found the Oklahoma provision, the last to be adopted (in 1910), in conflict with the 15th Amendment in *Guinn* v. *United States* in 1915.

A number of States outside the South also adopted literacy qualifications: Wyoming in 1889, California in 1894, Washington in 1896, New Hampshire in 1902, Arizona in 1913, New York in 1921, Oregon in 1924, and Alaska in 1949. Its unfair use finally led Congress to eliminate literacy as a suffrage qualification in the Voting Rights Act Amendments of 1970. The Supreme Court agreed in *Oregon* v. *Mitchell,* 1970:

---

[11]In Idaho, Minnesota, New Hampshire, and Wyoming, a person who is qualified to vote but misses the deadline can register (and then vote) on election day.

❝*In enacting the literacy test ban . . . Congress had before it a long history of the discriminatory use of literacy tests to disfranchise voters on account of their race.*❞

—Justice Hugo Black, Opinion of the Court

At the time Congress banned literacy tests, 18 States had some form of literacy requirement.

Tax Payment

Property ownership, proved by the payment of property taxes, was once a very common suffrage qualification. For decades several States also demanded the payment of a special tax, called the **poll tax,** as a condition for voting. Those requirements and others that called for the payment of a tax in order to vote have disappeared.

The poll tax was once found throughout the South. Beginning with Florida in 1889, each of the 11 southern States adopted the poll tax as part of their effort to discourage voting by African Americans. The device proved to be of only limited effectiveness, however. That fact, and opposition to the use of the poll tax from within the South as well as elsewhere, led most of those States to abandon it. By 1966, the poll tax was still in use only in Alabama, Mississippi, Texas, and Virginia.[12]

The 24th Amendment, ratified in 1964, outlawed the poll tax, or any other tax, as a condition for voting in any federal election. The Supreme Court finally eliminated the poll tax as a qualification for voting in all elections in 1966. In *Harper* v. *Virginia Board of Elections,* the Court held the Virginia poll tax to be in conflict with the 14th Amendment's Equal Protection

▲ This photo was taken in Mississippi, in 1978, when African American suffrage was supposed to be assured. *Critical Thinking What tactics does the sign use to intimidate African Americans who want to register to vote?* H-SS 12.5.4

Clause. The Court could find no reasonable relationship between the act of voting on the one hand and the payment of a tax on the other.

Persons Denied the Vote

Clearly, democratic government can exist only where the right to vote is very widely held. Still, every State does purposely deny the vote to certain persons. For example, none of the 50 States allows people in mental institutions, or any other persons who have been legally found to be mentally incompetent, to vote. A fourth of the States still prohibit anyone who commits a serious crime from ever gaining or regaining the right to vote. A few States also do not allow anyone dishonorably discharged from the armed forces to cast a ballot.

---

[12]By that time, the poll tax had been abolished in North Carolina (1924), Louisiana (1934), Florida (1937), Georgia (1945), South Carolina (1950), Tennessee (1951), and Arkansas (1964).

Section 2 Assessment

Key Terms and Main Ideas

1. For what reasons do most States require voter **registration**?
2. What is the Motor Voter Law? What is its purpose?
3. **(a)** Why do election officials keep **poll books**? **(b)** Why is it a good idea to **purge** them every few years?
4. How was the **poll tax** used as a voting qualification?

Critical Thinking

5. **Drawing Conclusions (a)** Do you think that one must be able to read in order to be a well-informed voter? Why or why not? **(b)** Do you think literacy is more or less important now than it was 100 years ago?

6. **Recognizing Bias** What were grandfather clauses? How did they discriminate against African Americans?

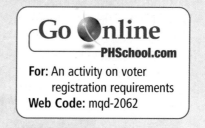

The Dangers of Voter Apathy

Analysis Skills HR4, HI3

Curtis Gans directs the Committee for the Study of the American Electorate, a non-partisan research organization that studies the causes of declining voter participation and looks for solutions. Here, Gans discusses low voter turnout and what can be done to reverse the trend.

Over [recent decades], the percentage of eligible Americans who vote has declined by 20 percent in both presidential and off-year elections. More than 20 million Americans who used to vote frequently have ceased participating altogether. The United States—with voter turnouts of around 50 percent in presidential elections and 35 percent in off-year elections—now has the lowest rate of voter participation of any democracy in the world.

More than half of America's nonparticipants are chronic nonvoters: people who have never voted or hardly ever vote, whose families have never voted, and who are poorer, less-educated, and less-involved participants in American society. But a growing number of Americans are simply dropping out of the political process—many of whom are educated, white-collar professionals. In addition, a growing number of younger Americans are failing to enter the political process. Both of these trends constitute a major national concern, for there is a very real danger that the habits of good citizenship will die and that government of the people, for the people, and by the people will become government of, for, and by the few. . . .

The scars of the Vietnam War and the Watergate scandal run deep. To many Americans, politics seem to be characterized by poor public leadership, increasingly complex issues, and ever-growing and inflexible government with few successes in meeting public needs. . . .

SON, IN A DICTATORSHIP THE PEOPLE VOTE BUT THEY DON'T HAVE A CHOICE

OH, I SEE... AND IN A DEMOCRACY THE PEOPLE HAVE A CHOICE BUT THEY DON'T VOTE

What does the cartoon suggest about voter apathy?

Sadly, for the average citizen, nonparticipation is becoming an increasingly rational act. Reversing this trend and instilling both hope and vigor among American voters will not be an easy task. But I think a few steps will improve participation in America. For example, we need to increase the amount and sophistication of civic education in our homes and schools. We must also develop policies that address the central concerns of the electorate, while realigning and strengthening the two-party system. . . . It is important for us to instill in our young people a sense of values that emphasizes something larger than the self.

In the end, voting is a religious act. Each citizen must come to believe that—despite the thousands of elections that are not decided by one vote—his or her vote *does* make a difference. It is that faith that needs to be restored.

Analyzing Primary Sources

1. How much has voter participation declined in recent decades?
2. What reasons does Gans give to explain the decline in voter participation?
3. What suggestions does Gans give for increasing voter participation?
4. Why should we be concerned about the declining rate of voter participation in the United States?

Suffrage and Civil Rights

Section Preview

OBJECTIVES

1. **Describe** the 15th Amendment and the tactics used to circumvent it in an effort to deny African Americans the vote.
2. **Explain** the significance of the early civil rights legislation passed in 1957, 1960, and 1964.
3. **Analyze** the provisions and effects of the Voting Rights Act of 1965.

WHY IT MATTERS

The 15th Amendment declared that the right to vote cannot be denied on account of race. Nevertheless, a variety of tactics were used in southern States to disenfranchise African Americans. The Supreme Court struck down a number of these efforts, and, beginning in the 1950s, Congress passed laws to protect minority voting rights.

POLITICAL DICTIONARY

★ **gerrymandering**
★ **injunction**
★ **preclearance**

How important is the right to vote? For those who do not have it, that right can seem as important as life itself. Indeed, in the Deep South of the 1960s, civil rights workers suffered arrest, beatings, shocks with electric cattle prods, even death—all in the name of the right to vote. Their efforts inspired the nation and led to large-scale federal efforts to secure suffrage for African Americans and other minority groups in the United States.

The Fifteenth Amendment

The effort to extend the franchise to African Americans began with the 15th Amendment, which was ratified in 1870. It declares that the right to vote cannot be denied to any citizen of the United States because of race, color, or previous condition of servitude. The amendment was plainly intended to ensure that African American men, nearly all of them former slaves and nearly all of them living in the South, could vote.

The 15th Amendment is not self-executing, however. In other words, simply stating a general principle without providing for a means to enforce implementation was not enough to carry out the intention of the amendment. To make it effective, Congress had to act. Yet for almost 90 years the Federal Government paid little attention to voting rights for African Americans.

During that period, African Americans were generally and systematically kept from the polls in much of the South. White supremacists employed a number of tactics to that end. Their major weapon was violence. Other tactics included more subtle threats and social pressures, such as firing an African American man who tried to register or vote, or denying his family credit at local stores.

More formal "legal" devices were used, as well. The most effective were literacy tests. White officials regularly manipulated these tests to disenfranchise African American citizens.

Registration laws served the same end. As written, they applied to all potential voters. In practice, however, they were often administered to keep African Americans from qualifying to vote. Poll taxes, "white primaries," gerrymandering, and several other devices were also regularly used to disenfranchise African Americans. **Gerrymandering** is the practice of drawing electoral district lines (the boundaries of the geographic area from which a candidate is elected to a public office) in order to limit the voting strength of a particular group or party.

The white primary arose out of the decades-long Democratic domination of politics in the South. It was almost a given that the Democratic candidate for an

▶ An African American woman registers to vote.

office would be elected. Therefore, almost always, it was only the Democrats who nominated candidates, generally in primaries. In several southern States, political parties were defined by law as "private associations." As such, they could exclude whomever they chose, and the Democrats regularly refused to admit African Americans. Because only party members could vote in the party's primary, African Americans were then excluded from a critical step in the public election process.

The Supreme Court finally outlawed the white primary in a case from Texas, *Smith* v. *Allwright*, 1944. The Court held that nominations are an integral part of the election process. Consequently, when a political party holds a primary it is performing a public function and it is, therefore, bound by the terms of the 15th Amendment.

The Supreme Court outlawed gerrymandering when used for purposes of racial discrimination in a case from Alabama, *Gomillion* v. *Lightfoot*, in 1960. In this case, the Alabama legislature had redrawn the electoral district boundaries of Tuskegee, effectively excluding all blacks from the city limits. The Court ruled that the legislature's act violated the 15th Amendment because the irregularly shaped district clearly was created to deprive blacks of political power.

Led by these decisions of the Supreme Court, the lower federal courts struck down many of the practices designed to disenfranchise African Americans in the 1940s and 1950s. Still, the courts could act only when those who claimed to be victims of discrimination sued. That case-by-case method was, at best, agonizingly slow.

Finally, and largely in response to the civil rights movement led by Dr. Martin Luther King, Jr., Congress was moved to act. It has passed several civil rights laws since the late 1950s. Those statutes contain a number of sections specifically intended to implement the 15th Amendment.

Early Civil Rights Legislation

The first law passed by Congress to implement the 15th Amendment was the Civil Rights Act of 1957, which set up the United States Civil Rights Commission. One of the Commission's major duties is to inquire into claims of voter discrimination. The Commission reports its findings to Congress and the President and, through the media, to the public. The Act also gave the attorney general the power to seek federal court orders to prevent interference with any person's right to vote in any federal election.

The Enduring Constitution

When the Constitution was written, only white male property owners could vote. Over time, the United States has become more and more democratic. The major features of that evolution are chronicled in this time line.

1870
15th Amendment—designed mainly to give former slaves the right to vote—protects the voting right of adult male citizens of every race.

1913
17th Amendment calls for members of the U.S. Senate to be elected directly by the people instead of by State legislatures.

Go Online
PHSchool.com

Use Web Code mqp-2067 to register your vote on this issue and to see how other students voted.

 Analysis Skills CS1, CS2, HI1

The Civil Rights Act of 1960 added an additional safeguard. It provided for the appointment of federal voting referees. These officers were to serve anywhere a federal court found voter discrimination. They were given the power to help qualified persons to register and vote in federal elections.

The Civil Rights Act of 1964

The Civil Rights Act of 1964 is much broader and much more effective than either of the two earlier measures. It outlaws discrimination in several areas, especially in job-related matters. With regard to voting rights, its most important section forbids the use of any voter registration or literacy requirement in an unfair or discriminatory manner.

The 1964 law continued a pattern set in the earlier laws. In major part, it relied on judicial action to overcome racial barriers and emphasized the use of federal court orders called injunctions. An **injunction** is a court order that either compels (forces) or restrains (limits) the performance of some act by a private individual or by a public official. The violation of an injunction amounts to contempt of court, a crime punishable by fine and/or imprisonment.

Dramatic events in Selma, Alabama, soon pointed up the shortcomings of this approach. Dr. King mounted a voter registration drive in that city in early 1965. He and his supporters hoped that they could focus national attention on the issue of African American voting rights—and they most certainly did.

Their registration efforts were met with insults and violence by local white civilians, by city and county police, and then by State troopers. Two civil rights workers were murdered, and many were beaten when they attempted a peaceful march to the State capitol. The nation saw much of the drama on television and was shocked. An outraged President Lyndon Johnson urged Congress to pass new and stronger legislation to ensure the voting rights of African Americans. Congress responded quickly.

The Voting Rights Act of 1965

The Voting Rights Act of 1965 made the 15th Amendment, at long last, a truly effective part of the Constitution. Unlike its predecessors, this act applied to *all* elections held anywhere in this country—State and local, as well as federal.

Originally, the Voting Rights Act was to be in effect for a period of five years. Congress has

1924
Indian Citizenship Act grants all Native Americans the rights of citizenship, including the right to vote in federal elections.

1964
24th Amendment bans poll tax as requirement for voting in federal elections.

1995
Federal "Motor Voter Law" takes effect, making it easier to register to vote.

1925　　**1950**　　**1975**　　**2000**

1920
19th Amendment guarantees American women the right to vote in all elections.

1965
Voting Rights Act protects the rights of minority voters and eliminates voting barriers such as the literacy test. Expanded and renewed in 1970, 1975, and 1982.

1971
26th Amendment sets the minimum voting age at 18.

2003
Federal Voting Standards and Procedures Act requires States to streamline registration, voting, and other election procedures.

Analyzing Time Lines

1. Which amendments have granted voting rights to specific groups of people?
2. What has been the general trend of constitutional changes related to voting?

Voters and Voter Behavior 161

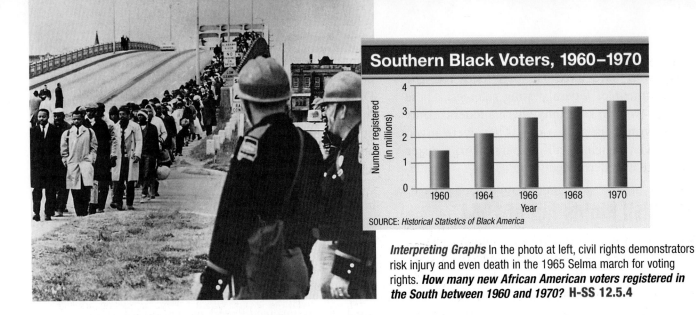

Southern Black Voters, 1960–1970

SOURCE: *Historical Statistics of Black America*

Interpreting Graphs In the photo at left, civil rights demonstrators risk injury and even death in the 1965 Selma march for voting rights. *How many new African American voters registered in the South between 1960 and 1970?* **H-SS 12.5.4**

extended its life three times, in the Voting Rights Act Amendments of 1970, 1975, and most recently 1982. The present version of the law was made effective for 25 years; its provisions are scheduled to expire in 2007.

The 1965 law directed the attorney general to challenge the constitutionality of the remaining State poll-tax laws in the federal courts. That provision led directly to *Harper* v. *Virginia Board of Elections,* in 1966 (see page 157).

The law also suspended the use of any literacy test or similar device in any State or county where less than half of the electorate had been registered or had voted in the 1964 presidential election. The law authorized the attorney general to appoint voting examiners to serve in any of those States or counties. It also gave these federal officers the power to register voters and otherwise oversee the conduct of elections in those areas.

Preclearance

The Voting Rights Act of 1965 created a further restriction on those States where a majority of the electorate had not voted in 1964. The act declared that no new election laws, and no changes in existing election laws, could go into effect in any of those States unless first approved —given **preclearance**—by the Department of Justice. Only those new or revised laws that do not "dilute" (weaken) the voting rights of minority groups can survive the preclearance process.

The preclearance hurdle has produced a large number of court cases since the passage of the law. Those cases show that the laws most likely to run afoul of the preclearance requirement are those that make these kinds of changes:

(1) the location of polling places;
(2) the boundaries of election districts;
(3) deadlines in the election process;
(4) from ward or district election to at-large elections;
(5) the qualifications candidates must meet in order to run for office.

Any State or county subject to the voter-examiner and preclearance provisions can be removed from the law's coverage through a "bail-out" process. That relief can come if the State can show the United States District Court in the District of Columbia that it has not applied any voting procedures in a discriminatory way for at least 10 years.

The voter-examiner and preclearance provisions of the 1965 Voting Rights Act originally applied to six entire States: Alabama, Georgia, Louisiana, Mississippi, South Carolina, and Virginia. The act also applied to 40 North Carolina counties.

The Supreme Court upheld the Voting Rights Act in 1966. In the case of *South Carolina* v. *Katzenbach,* a unanimous Court found the law to be a proper exercise of the power granted to Congress in Section 2 of the 15th Amendment. That provision authorizes Congress to use 'appropriate' measures to enforce the constitutional prohibition against racial discrimination in voting.

Amendments to the Act

The 1970 amendments extended the law for another five years. The 1968 elections were added to the law's triggering formula; the result was that a number of counties in six more States (Alaska, Arizona, California, Idaho, New Mexico, and Oregon) were added to the law's coverage.

The 1970 law also provided that, for five years, no State could use literacy as the basis for any voting requirement. That temporary ban as well as residence provisions outlined in the law were upheld by the Supreme Court in *Oregon* v. *Mitchell* in 1970.

In 1975, the law was extended again, this time for seven years, and the five-year ban on literacy tests was made permanent. Since 1975, no State has been able to apply any sort of literacy qualification to any aspect of the election process.

The law's voter-examiner and preclearance provisions were also broadened in 1975. Since then they have also covered any State or county where more than 5 percent of the voting-age population belongs to certain "language minorities." These groups are defined to include all persons of Spanish heritage, Native Americans, Asian Americans, and Alaskan Natives.

This addition expanded the law's coverage to all of Alaska and Texas and to several counties in 24 other States, as well. In these areas, all ballots and other official election materials must be printed both in English and in the language of the minority, or minorities, involved.

The 1982 amendments extended the basic features of the act for another 25 years. In 1992 the law's language-minority provisions

▲ *I Have a Dream* This famous speech, delivered by civil rights leader Martin Luther King, Jr., was a highlight of the 1963 March on Washington, which drew more than 200,000 people. **H-SS 12.5.4**

were revised: they now apply to any community that has a minority-language population of 10,000 or more persons.

Over the years, several States and a handful of counties in a few other States have been removed from the law's coverage, through the "bail-out" process. Today, eight entire States remain subject to the Voting Rights Act: Alabama, Alaska, Arizona, Georgia, Louisiana, Mississippi, South Carolina, and Texas. At least some counties in eight other States are also covered by the statute: California, Florida, Michigan, New Hampshire, New York, North Carolina, South Dakota, and Virginia.

Section 3 Assessment

Key Terms and Main Ideas

1. What is **gerrymandering?** What other devices were used to disenfranchise African Americans?
2. What part do **injunctions** play in the Civil Rights Act of 1964?
3. What is **preclearance?** How can a State "bail out" of the preclearance provisions of the Voting Rights Act of 1965?
4. **(a)** Identify the major civil rights laws enacted since 1950. **(b)** Describe voting rights provisions in these laws.

Critical Thinking

5. **Drawing Conclusions** Even after the ratification of the 15th Amendment, African Americans in the South were denied the right to vote because the amendment was not implemented. **(a)** What does that tell you about American attitudes from 1870 until the 1950s? **(b)** Why did those attitudes change?

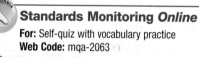

Standards Monitoring *Online*
For: Self-quiz with vocabulary practice
Web Code: mqa-2063

6. **Recognizing Cause and Effect (a)** How do you think the historical denial of voting rights to African Americans affected the makeup of Congress and many State legislatures? **(b)** How did that result, in turn, affect the likelihood that these legislatures would pass civil rights laws?

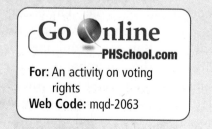

Go **O**nline
PHSchool.com

For: An activity on voting rights
Web Code: mqd-2063

4 Voter Behavior

Section Preview

OBJECTIVES

1. **Examine** the problem of nonvoting in this country, and describe the size of the problem.
2. **Identify** people who do not vote.
3. **Examine** the behavior of those who vote and those who do not.
4. **Understand** the sociological and psychological factors that affect voting and how they work together to influence voter behavior.

WHY IT MATTERS

Low voter turnout is a serious problem in this country. Among those who do vote, sociological and psychological factors work together to influence voter behavior over time and in particular elections.

POLITICAL DICTIONARY

★ off-year election
★ political efficacy
★ political socialization
★ gender gap
★ party identification
★ straight-ticket voting
★ split-ticket voting
★ independent

"Your vote is your voice. Use it." That's the advice of Rock the Vote, an organization that encourages young voters ages 18–25 to participate in the election process. In the United States, and in other democratic countries, we believe in all voices being heard. That is, we believe in voting.

Over the next several pages you will look at voter behavior in this country—at who votes and who does not, and at why those people who do vote, vote as they do.

Nonvoters

The word *idiot* came to our language from the Greek. In ancient Athens, idiots *(idiotes)* were those citizens who did not vote or otherwise take part in public life.

Tens of millions of Americans vote in presidential and congressional elections; in State elections; and in city, county, and other public elections. Still, there are many millions of other Americans who, for one reason or another, do not vote. There are some quite legitimate reasons for not voting, as you will see. But this troubling fact remains: Most of the millions of Americans who could—but do not—go to the polls cannot claim any of those justifications. Indeed, they would have been called idiots in the Greece of 2000 years ago.

The Size of the Problem

The table on page 165 lays out the major facts of the nonvoter problem in American elections. Notice that on election day in 2004 there were an estimated 215.7 million persons of voting age in the United States. Yet only some 122.3 million of them—only 56.7 percent—actually voted in the presidential election. Nearly 95 million persons who might have voted did not.

In 2004 some 114 million votes were cast in the elections held across the country to fill the 435 seats in the House of Representatives. That means that only 53 percent of the electorate voted in those congressional elections. (Notice the even lower rates of turnout in the **off-year elections**—that is, in the congressional elections held in the even-numbered years between presidential elections.)

Several facets of the nonvoter problem are not very widely known. Take, for example, this striking fact: There are millions of nonvoters *among those who vote.* Look again at the 2004 figures on page 165. Nearly eight million persons who voted in the last presidential election could also have voted for a congressional candidate, but they did not choose to do so.

"Nonvoting voters" are not limited to federal elections. In fact, they are much more common in State and local elections. As a general rule, the farther down the ballot an office is, the fewer the number of votes that will be cast for it. This phenomenon is sometimes called "ballot fatigue." The expression suggests that many voters exhaust their patience and/or their knowledge as they work their way down the ballot.

Some quick examples illustrate the phenomenon of ballot fatigue: In every State, more votes are regularly cast in the presidential election than in the gubernatorial election. More votes are generally cast for the governorship than for other Statewide offices, such as lieutenant governor or secretary of state. More voters in a county usually vote in the races for Statewide offices than vote in the contests for such county offices as sheriff, county clerk, or district attorney, and so on.

There are other little-recognized facets of the nonvoter problem, too. For example, the table on this page shows that turnout in congressional elections is consistently higher in presidential years than it is in off-year elections. That same pattern holds among the States in terms of the types of elections; more people vote in general elections than in either primary or special elections.

Why People Do Not Vote

Why do we have so many nonvoters? Why, even in a presidential election, do as many as half of those who could vote stay away from the polls?

Clearly, the time that it takes to vote should not be a significant part of the answer. For most people, it takes more time to go to a video store and pick out a movie than it does to go to their neighborhood polling place and cast a ballot. So we must look elsewhere for answers.

"Cannot-Voters"

To begin with, look at another of those little-recognized aspects of the nonvoter problem. Several million persons who are regularly identified as nonvoters can be much more accurately described as "cannot-voters." That is, although it is true that they do not vote, the fact is that they cannot do so.

The 2004 data support the point. Included in that figure of nearly 95 million who did not vote in the last presidential election are at least 10 million who are resident aliens. Remember, they are barred from the polls in every State.

Voter Turnout, 1968–2004					
Year	Population of Voting Age[1]	Votes Cast for President		Votes Cast for U.S. Representatives	
	(in millions)	(in millions)	(percent)	(in millions)	(percent)
1968	120.285	73.212	60.9	66.288	55.1
1970	124.498	—	—	54.173	43.5
1972	140.777	77.719	55.2	71.430	50.7
1974	146.388	—	—	52.495	35.9
1976	152.308	81.556	53.5	74.422	48.9
1978	158.369	—	—	55.332	34.9
1980	163.945	86.515	52.8	77.995	47.6
1982	169.643	—	—	64.514	38.0
1984	173.995	92.653	53.3	83.231	47.8
1986	177.922	—	—	59.619	33.5
1988	181.956	91.595	50.3	81.786	44.9
1990	185.812	—	—	61.513	33.1
1992	189.524	104.425	55.1	96.239	50.8
1994	193.650	—	—	70.781	36.6
1996	196.507	96.278	49.0	89.863	45.8
1998	200.929	—	—	66.033	33.9
2000	205.813	105.397	51.2	99.457	48.4
2002	210.321	—	—	73.844	35.2
2004	215.694	122.295	56.7	114.414	53.0

[1]As estimated by Census Bureau. Population 18 years of age and over since ratification of 26th Amendment in 1971; prior to 1971, 21 years and over in all States, except: 18 years and over in Georgia since 1943 and Kentucky since 1955, 19 years and over in Alaska and 20 and over in Hawaii since 1959.

SOURCES: *Statistical Abstract of the United States*; Federal Election Commission

Interpreting Tables This table shows voter turnout two ways: total numbers and percent of eligible voters. *(a) In what year shown did voting percentage peak for presidential races? (b) In what year did voting peak for congressional races?* **H-SS 12.6.6**

Another 5 to 6 million citizens were so ill or otherwise physically disabled that they simply could not vote in an election. An additional 2 or 3 million persons were traveling suddenly and unexpectedly, and so could not vote.

Other groups of cannot-voters can be discovered in the nonvoting group. They include some 500,000 persons in mental health care facilities or under some other form of legal restraint because of their mental condition; more than two million adults in jails and prisons; and perhaps as many as 100,000 who do not (cannot) vote because of their religious beliefs (for example, those who believe that acts such as voting amount to idolatry).

Interpreting Political Cartoons What does the "weight" of the nonvoters tell you about the kind of difference they are making?

Racial, religious, and other biases still play a part here, too—despite the many laws, court decisions, and enforcement actions of the past several years aimed at eliminating such discrimination in the political process. An unknown but certainly significant number of people could not vote in 2004 because of (1) the purposeful administration of election laws to keep them from doing so and/or (2) various "informal" local pressures applied to that same end.

Actual Nonvoters

Even so, there are millions of actual nonvoters in the United States. Thus, in 2004 more than 80 million Americans who could have voted in the presidential election did not.

There are any number of reasons for that behavior. As a leading example: Many who could go to the polls do not because they are convinced that it makes little real difference who wins a particular election.

That fairly large group includes two very different groups of nonvoters. On the one hand, it includes many who generally approve of the way the public's business is being managed—that is, many who believe that no matter who wins an election, things will continue to go well for themselves and for the country.

On the other hand, that group also includes many people who feel alienated—many who deliberately refuse to vote because they don't trust political institutions and processes. They

either fear or scorn "the system." To them, elections are meaningless, choiceless exercises.

Another large group of nonvoters is composed of people who have no sense of **political efficacy.** They lack any feeling of influence or effectiveness in politics. They do not believe that they or their votes can have any real impact on what government does.

Other Factors Affecting Turnout

Other factors also affect whether voters show up at the polls. Cumbersome election procedures—for example, inconvenient registration requirements, long ballots, and long lines at polling places—discourage voters from turning out on election day. Bad weather also tends to discourage turnout.

Another possible, though hotly debated, factor is the so-called "time-zone fallout" problem. This refers to the fact that, in presidential elections, polls in States in the Eastern and Central time zones close before polls in States in the Mountain and Pacific time zones. Based on early returns from the East and Midwest, the news media often project the outcome of the presidential contest before all the voters in the West have gone to the polls. Some people fear that such reports have discouraged western voters from casting their ballots.

Of all the reasons that may be cited, however, the chief cause for nonvoting is, purely and simply, a lack of interest. Those who lack sufficient interest, who are indifferent and apathetic, and who just cannot be bothered are usually woefully uninformed. Most often, they do not know even the simplest facts about the candidates and issues involved in an election.

Comparing Voters and Nonvoters

One useful way to get a handle on the problem of nonvoting is to contrast those persons who tend to go to the polls regularly with those who do not. There are many differences between them.

The people most likely to vote display such characteristics as higher levels of income, education, and occupational status. They are usually well integrated into community life. They tend to be long-time residents who are active in or at least comfortable with their surroundings. They are likely to have a strong sense of party identification and to believe

Voting by Groups in Presidential Elections, 1972–2004* (By Percentage of Votes Reported Cast)

	1972		1976		1980			1984		1988		1992			1996			2000			2004*	
	D	R	D	R	D	R	I	D	R	D	R	D	R	I	D	R	P	D	R	G	D	R
National Vote	37.5	60.7	50	48	41	50.7	6.6	41	59	46	54	43.2	37.8	19	49.2	40.7	8.4	48.7	48.6	2.7	48.5	51.5
Sex																						
Men	37	63	53	45	38	53	7	36	64	44	56	41	37	22	45	44	11	43	52	3	44	56
Women	38	62	48	51	44	49	6	45	55	48	52	46	38	16	54	39	7	53	45	2	52	48
Race																						
White	32	68	46	52	36	56	7	34	66	41	59	39	41	20	46	45	9	43	55	3	43	57
Nonwhite	87	13	85	15	86	10	2	87	13	82	18	77	11	12	82	12	6	87	9	4	83	17
Education																						
College	37	63	42	55	35	53	10	39	61	42	58	43	40	17	47	45	8	46	51	3	42	58
High school	34	66	54	46	43	51	5	43	57	46	54	40	38	22	52	34	14	52	46	2	54	46
Grade school	49	51	58	41	54	42	3	51	49	55	45	56	28	16	58	27	15	55	42	3	–	–
Age																						
Under 30	48	52	53	45	47	41	11	40	60	37	63	40	37	23	54	30	16	47	47	6	60	40
30–49	33	67	48	49	38	52	8	40	60	45	55	42	37	21	49	41	10	45	53	2	43	57
50 and older	36	64	52	48	41	54	4	41	59	49	51	46	39	15	50	45	5	53	45	2	49	51
Religion																						
Protestant	30	70	46	53	39	54	6	39	61	42	58	41	41	18	44	50	6	42	55	3	38	62
Catholic	48	52	57	41	46	47	6	39	61	51	49	47	35	18	55	35	10	52	46	2	52	48
Politics																						
Republican	5	95	9	91	8	86	5	4	96	7	93	7	77	16	10	85	5	7	92	1	6	93
Democrat	67	33	82	18	69	26	4	79	21	85	15	82	8	10	90	6	4	89	10	2	91	7
Independent	31	69	38	57	29	55	14	33	67	43	57	39	30	31	48	33	19	44	49	7	48	40
Region																						
East	42	58	51	47	43	47	9	46	54	51	49	47	35	18	60	31	9	55	42	3	56	39
Midwest	40	60	48	50	41	51	7	42	58	47	53	44	34	22	46	45	9	48	49	3	48	45
South	29	71	54	45	44	52	3	37	63	40	60	38	45	17	44	46	10	45	54	1	45	51
West	41	59	46	51	35	54	9	40	60	46	54	45	35	20	51	43	6	48	47	5	47	49

D = Democratic candidate; R = Republican candidate; I = Independent candidate (John B. Anderson, 1980; Ross Perot, 1992); P = Reform Party candidate (Ross Perot, 1996); G = Green Party candidate (Ralph Nader, 2000). Figures do not add to 100% in some groups because of rounding and/or minor party votes.
SOURCE: The Gallup Organization. *For preliminary 2004 election results, see Stop the Presses, pages 843–844.

Interpreting Tables Some groups of voters have favored one or the other major party over time. *In this table, which group most clearly demonstrates that point?* H-SS 12.6.6

that voting is an important act. They also are likely to live in those areas where laws, customs, and competition between the parties all promote turnout.

The opposite characteristics produce a profile of those less likely to vote. Nonvoters are likely to be younger than age 35, unmarried, and unskilled. More nonvoters live in the South and in rural, rather than urban or suburban, locales. Today, women are more likely to vote than men. This fact of political life has been apparent since the presidential elections of the 1980s and was reconfirmed in 2004.

A few of the factors that help determine whether or not a person will vote are so important that they influence turnout even when they are not supported by, or are in conflict with, other factors. Thus, those persons with a high sense of political efficacy are likely to vote—no matter what their income, education, age, race, and so on.

The degree of two-party competition has much the same kind of general, across-the-board effect. It, too, has an extraordinary impact on participation. Thus, the greater the competition between candidates, the more likely people will be to go to the polls, regardless of other factors.

Despite the greater weight of some of these factors, however, note this point: It is the combined presence of several factors, not the influence of one of them alone, that tends to determine whether a person will vote or not.

Voters and Voting Behavior

As you have just seen, tens of millions of potential voters do not go to the polls in this country. But many millions more do. How do those who do vote behave? What prompts many to vote most often for Republicans and many others to support the Democratic Party?

Answers to these questions are not as hard to find as you might think. Voting has been studied more closely than any other form of political participation in the United States. This is due partly to the importance of the topic and partly to the almost unlimited amount of data available. (There have been innumerable elections in which millions of voters have cast billions of votes over time.) That research has produced a huge amount of information about why people tend to vote as they do.

Studying Voting Behavior

Most of what is known about voter behavior comes from three sources.

1. *The results of particular elections.* Of course, how individuals vote in a given election is secret in the United States. However careful study of the returns from areas populated largely by African Americans or by Catholics or by high-income families will indicate how those groups voted in a given election.

2. *The field of survey research.* The polling of scientifically determined cross sections of the population is the method by which public opinion is most often identified and measured. The Gallup Organization conducts perhaps the best known of these polls today.

3. *Studies of **political socialization**.* This is the process by which people gain their political attitudes and opinions. That complex process begins in early childhood and continues through each person's life. Political socialization involves all of the experiences and relationships that lead people to see the political world, and to act in it, as they do.

In the rest of this chapter, you will consider voter behavior—how and why people vote as they do. In Chapter 8, you will take a closer look at public opinion, at the techniques of survey research, and the process of political socialization.

Factors That Influence Voters

Observers still have much to learn about voter behavior, but many sociological and psychological factors clearly influence the way people vote. Sociology is the study of groups and how people behave within groups. The sociological factors affecting voter behavior are really the many pieces of a voter's social and economic life. Those pieces are of two broad kinds: (1) a voter's personal characteristics—age, race, income, occupation, education, religion, and so on; and (2) a voter's group affiliations—family, co-workers, friends, and the like.

Frequently Asked Questions

Voting

How many choices does a voter have in a typical election contest?
Most elections in the United States are two-candidate contests. That is, they are elections in which two candidates run against one another for each office listed on the ballot. Candidate A versus Candidate B for this office, Candidate C versus Candidate D for that office, and so on down the ballot.

In any two-candidate race, a voter has not just two but, in fact, *five* options. He or she can:

1) vote FOR Candidate A
2) vote FOR Candidate B
3) vote AGAINST Candidate A (by marking the ballot for Candidate B)
4) vote AGAINST Candidate B (by marking the ballot for Candidate A)
5) decide not to vote for either candidate

Remember, the fifth choice, not voting, might very well be the result of a reasoned decision.

Any Questions?
What would you like to know about voting? Brainstorm two new questions and exchange them with a classmate. What did you learn?

Psychology is the study of the mind and of individual behavior. The psychological factors that influence voter behavior are a voter's perceptions of politics, that is, how the voter sees the parties, the candidates, and the issues in an election.

The differences between these two kinds of influences are not nearly so great as they might seem. In fact, they are closely related and they constantly interact with one another. How voters look at parties, candidates, or issues is often shaped by their own social and economic backgrounds.

Sociological Factors

From the table on page 167, you can draw a composite picture of the American voter in terms of a number of sociological factors. A word of caution here: Do not make too much of any one of these factors. As you examine the data, keep this point in mind: The table reports how voters, identified by a *single* characteristic, voted in each presidential election from 1976 through 2004. Remember, however, that each voter possesses not just one but *several* of the characteristics shown in the table.

To illustrate the point: College graduates are more likely to vote Republican. So are persons over age 50. African Americans, on the other hand, are more likely to vote for Democrats. So are members of labor unions. How, then, would a 55-year-old, college-educated African American who belongs to the AFL-CIO vote?

Income, Occupation

Voters in lower income brackets are more likely to be Democrats. Voters with higher incomes tend to be Republicans. This pattern has held up over time, no matter whether a particular election was a cliff-hanger or a blow-out. In 2004, voters with incomes below $15,000 a year backed Democrat John Kerry by a 3 to 2 margin, as did those making between $15,000 and $29,999. Voters who made $30,000 to $49,999 split their votes almost exactly evenly between the senator and President Bush.

Voters in higher income groups supported the President by wide margins. Thus, among those making more than $100,000 a year, Mr. Bush had a 3 to 2 advantage.

▲ *Worth the Wait* Blacks in South Africa fought for many years to gain the right to vote. In the first multiracial elections, held in 1994, many people stood in long lines for hours in order to exercise this hard-won right.

Most often, how much one earns and what one does for a living are closely related. Professional and business people, and others with higher incomes, tend to vote for Republican candidates. Manual workers, and others in lower income groups, usually vote for Democrats. Thus, with the single exception of 1964, professional and business people have voted heavily Republican in every presidential election in the modern era, including 2004.

Education

Studies of voter behavior reveal that there is also a close relationship between the level of a voter's education and how he or she votes. College graduates vote for Republicans in higher percentages than do high-school graduates; and high-school graduates vote Republican more often than do those who have only gone through grade school.

Gender, Age

There are often measurable differences between the partisan choices of men and women today. This phenomenon is known as the **gender gap,** and it first appeared in the 1980s. Women generally tend to favor the Democrats by a margin of five to ten percent, and men often give the GOP a similar edge. The gender gap was less apparent in 2004 than in previous presidential elections. President Bush won 48 percent of all of the votes cast by women in that election.

A number of studies show that men and women are most likely to vote differently when such issues as abortion, health care or other social welfare matters, or military involvements abroad are prominent in an election.

Traditionally, younger voters have been more likely to be Democrats than Republicans. Older voters are likely to find the GOP and its candidates more attractive. Thus, in every presidential election from 1960 through 1980, the Democrats won a larger percentage of the votes of the under-30 age group than of the 50-and-over age bracket. That long-standing pattern was broken by Ronald Reagan's appeal to younger voters in 1984, and by George Bush in 1988. However, Bill Clinton restored the Democrats' claim to those voters in 1992 and 1996. In 2000, Al Gore won 47 percent of the under-30 vote, George W. Bush received 47 percent, and most of the balance (6 percent) went to the Green Party's Ralph Nader. John Kerry won the major slice of the votes of that age group—54 percent—in 2004.

Religious, Ethnic Background

Historically, a majority of Protestants have most often preferred the GOP. Catholics and Jews have been much more likely to be Democrats.

President Bush won 62 percent of the votes cast by all Protestants and 67 percent of those cast by white Protestants in 2004. A larger-than-usual percentage of Catholics—48 percent—also backed the President. He won only 25 percent of the ballots cast by Jewish voters, however.

Moral issues—in particular, same-sex marriage—were unusually prominent in 2004. And church attendance has lately emerged as a significant indicator of partisan preference. Sixty-three percent of voters who go to church at least once a week marked their ballots for Mr. Bush in 2004.

For decades now, African Americans have supported the Democratic Party, consistently and massively. They form the only group that has given the Democratic candidate a clear majority in every presidential election since 1952. There are now more than 40 million African Americans, and they make up the second largest minority in the country.

---

[14]In 1960, John F. Kennedy became the first Roman Catholic President. His election marked a sharper split between Catholic and Protestant voters than that found in any of the elections covered by the table on page 167.

In the North, African Americans generally voted Republican until the 1930s, but then moved away from the party of Abraham Lincoln with the coming of the New Deal. The civil rights movement of the 1960s led to greater African American participation in the South. Today, African Americans vote overwhelmingly Democratic in that region, too.

The United States is now home to more than 42 million Latinos, people with Spanish-speaking backgrounds. Until now, Latinos have tended to favor Democratic candidates. Note, however, that the label "Latino" conceals differences among Cuban Americans, who most often vote Republican, and Mexican Americans and Puerto Ricans, who are strongly Democratic. The rate of turnout among Latinos is comparatively low—less than 40 percent in 2004.

Geography

Geography—the part of the country, the State, and/or the locale in which a person lives—also has an impact on voter behavior. After the Civil War, the States of the old Confederacy voted so consistently Democratic that the southeast quarter of the nation became known as the Solid South. For more than a century, most Southerners, regardless of any other factor, identified with the Democratic Party.

The Solid South is now a thing of the past. Republican candidates have been increasingly successful throughout the region over the past 40 years or so. This has been true in presidential elections and at the State and the local levels, as well. Historically, the States that have supported the Republicans most consistently are Maine and Vermont in the Northeast and Kansas, Nebraska, and the Dakotas in the Midwest.

Voters' attitudes also vary in terms of the size of the communities in which they live. Generally, the Democrats draw strength from the big cities of the North and East. Many white Democrats have moved from the central cities and taken their political preferences with them, but Republican voters still dominate much of suburban America. Voters in smaller cities and rural areas are also likely to be Republicans.

Family and Other Groups

To this point, you have seen the American voter sketched in terms of several broad social and economic characteristics. The picture can also be drawn on the basis of much smaller and more personal groupings, especially such primary groups as family, friends, and co-workers.

Typically, the members of a family vote in strikingly similar ways. Nine out of ten married couples share the same partisan leanings. As many as two out of every three voters follow the political attachments of their parents. Those who work together and circles of friends also tend to vote very much alike.

This like-mindedness is hardly surprising. People of similar social and economic backgrounds tend to associate with one another. In short, a person's group associations usually reinforce the opinions he or she already holds.

Psychological Factors

Although they are certainly important, it would be wrong to give too much weight to the sociological factors in the voting mix. For one thing, these factors are fairly static. That is, they tend to change only gradually and over time. To understand voter behavior, you must look beyond such factors as occupation, education, ethnic background, and place of residence. You must also take into account a number of psychological factors. That is, you must look at the voters' *perceptions* of politics: how they see and react to the parties, the candidates, and the issues in an election.

Party Identification

A majority of Americans identify themselves with one or the other of the major parties early in life. Many never change. They support that party, election after election, with little or no regard for either the candidates or the issues.

The hefty impact of **party identification,** or the loyalty of people to a particular political party, is the single most significant and lasting predictor of how a person will vote. A person who is a Democrat or a Republican will, for that reason, very likely vote for all or most of that party's candidates in any given

election. The practice of voting for candidates of only one party in an election is called **straight-ticket voting.**

Party identification is, therefore, a key factor in American politics. Among many other things, it means that each of the major parties can regularly count on the votes of millions of faithful supporters in every election.

Several signs suggest that, while it remains a major factor, party identification has lost some of its impact in recent years. One of those signs is the weakened condition of the parties themselves. Another is the marked increase in **split-ticket voting**—the practice of voting for the candidates of more than one party in an election. That behavior, which began to increase in the 1960s, is fairly common today.

Another telling sign is the large number of voters who now call themselves **independents.** This term is regularly used to identify those people who have no party affiliation. It includes voters who are independent of both the Republicans and the Democrats (and of any minor party, as well). "Independent" is a tricky term, however.[15] Many who claim to be independents actually support one or the other of the major parties quite regularly.

The loose nature of party membership makes it difficult to determine just what proportion of the electorate is independent. The best guesses put the number of independents at somewhere between a fourth and a third of all voters today. The role that these independent voters play is especially critical in those elections where the opposing major party candidates are more or less evenly matched.

Until recently, the typical independent was less concerned, less well informed, and less active in politics than those voters who identified themselves as Republicans or Democrats. That description still fits many independents.

However, a new breed of independent voter appeared in the 1960s and 1970s, and their ranks have grown over the years. Largely because of the political events and personalities of that period, these "new" independents preferred not to join either major party. Today, these independents are often young and above average in education, income, and job status.

---

[15]Note that the term "independent" is sometimes mistakenly used to suggest that independents form a more or less cohesive group that can be readily compared with Republicans and Democrats. (Although the Gallup Poll data on page 142 do not intend such comparisons, they can be misread to that effect.) In short, independents in American politics are not only independent of Republicans and Democrats; each of them is also independent of all other independents.

Candidates and Issues

Party identification is a long-term factor. While most voters identify with one or the other of the major parties and most often support its candidates, they do not always vote that way. One or more short-term factors can cause them to switch sides in a particular election, or at least vote a split ticket. Thus, in 2004, exit polls indicate that 5 percent of those persons who usually vote Republican voted for John Kerry for President, and 7 percent of those who normally support Democratic candidates marked their ballots for the President.

The most important of these short-term factors are the candidates and the issues in an election. Clearly, the impression a candidate makes on the voters can have an impact on how they vote. What image does a candidate project? How is he or she seen in terms of personality, character, style, appearance, past record, abilities, and so on?

Just as clearly, issues can also have a large impact on voter behavior. The role of issues varies, however, depending on such things as the emotional content of the issues themselves, the voters' awareness of them, and the ways in which they are presented to the electorate.

Issues have become increasingly important to voters over the past 40 years or so. The tumultuous nature of politics over the period—highlighted by the civil rights movement, the Vietnam War, the feminist movement, the Watergate scandal, and economic problems—is likely responsible for this heightened concern.

Section 4 Assessment

Standards Monitoring *Online*
For: Self-quiz with vocabulary practice
Web Code: mqa-2064

Key Terms and Main Ideas

1. How does a person's sense of **political efficacy** affect his or her voting behavior?
2. What is the **gender gap**?
3. How are **party identification** and **straight-ticket voting** related?
4. List three sociological factors that affect voting behavior.

Critical Thinking

5. **Predicting Consequences** What might be the results for the nation if all eligible voters were required to cast ballots? Why?

6. **Formulating Questions** Suppose you are a pollster. List three questions you would ask to determine if someone will vote in the next election, and three questions to find out what party he or she would be likely to support.

Go Online
PHSchool.com

For: An activity on voter participation
Web Code: mqd-2064

Who Decides Who May Vote?

Analysis Skills HR4, HI3, HI4

The Constitution gives States authority to set voting qualifications. In the past, some States purposely used that power to exclude certain groups—most notably African Americans—from the electoral process. Does Congress have the authority to limit the power of States to set voter qualifications?

Oregon v. Mitchell (1970)

In 1970, the States of Oregon, Texas, and Idaho sued the Federal Government (specifically, Attorney General John Mitchell) to challenge four provisions of the Voting Rights Act Amendments passed by Congress that year. One provision lowered the minimum voting age to 18 in all elections in the United States—federal, State, and local. Another barred the use of any literacy test in any election in this country for a five-year period. A third provision prohibits the States from setting residence requirements for voting in presidential elections at more than 30 days. The final provision established national rules for absentee voting in presidential elections. (Absentee voting allows people unable to go to their polling places on election day to receive and mark their ballots, and return them—usually by mail—before or no later than election day.) These provisions were clearly intended to allow more people to participate in the electoral process.

The case was heard by the Supreme Court in its original jurisdiction. (In other words, the case was not appealed to the Court from a lower court.) Fifteen States, though not part of the suit, filed briefs (written arguments) with the Court in the case. The American Civil Liberties Union, the NAACP, the Democratic National Committee, and various other groups also filed briefs.

Arguments for Oregon

1. Only the States have the power to set voting qualifications for State and local elections. Congress has no authority to require the States to allow persons between 18 and 21 to vote in State and local elections.

2. The Constitution does not give Congress the right to require the States to use different qualifications for voting in federal elections than those States adopt for their own elections.
3. States have the authority to set standards for voters, such as a minimum level of literacy or a minimum period of residence in the State.

Arguments for Mitchell

1. Congress may set standards for voter qualifications in federal elections.
2. Congress may prevent the States from excluding certain groups of citizens from the voting rolls for State elections, if the exclusion tends to discriminate against people based on characteristics such as race or national origin. (Such discrimination by States violates the 14th Amendment's Equal Protection Clause.)
3. Congress may prevent States from imposing a residency requirement that makes it impossible for people who have recently moved to vote in presidential elections.

Decide for Yourself

1. Review the constitutional grounds on which each side based its arguments and the specific arguments each side presented.
2. Debate the opposing viewpoints presented in this case. Which viewpoint do you favor?
3. Predict the impact of the Court's decision on changes in voter eligibility and voter participation in the United States. (To read a summary of the Court's decision, turn to pages 799–806.)

Go Online PHSchool.com Use Web Code mqp-2068 to register your vote on this issue and to see how other students voted.

Political Dictionary

suffrage (p. 148), franchise (p. 148), electorate (p. 148), transient (p. 153), registration (p. 154), purge (p. 155), poll books (p. 155), literacy (p. 156), poll tax (p. 157), gerrymandering (p. 159), injunction (p. 161), preclearance (p. 162), off-year election (p. 164), political efficacy (p. 166), political socialization (p. 168), gender gap (p. 169), party identification (p. 171), straight-ticket voting (p. 171), split-ticket voting (p. 171), independent (p. 171)

Standards Review

H-SS 12.2.4 Understand the obligations of civic-mindedness, including voting, being informed on civic issues, volunteering and performing public service, and serving in the military or alternative service.

H-SS 12.5.4 Explain the controversies that have resulted over changing interpretations of civil rights, including those in *Plessy* v. *Ferguson*, *Brown* v. *Board of Education*, *Miranda* v. *Arizona*, *Regents of the University of California* v. *Bakke*, *Adarand Constructors, Inc.* v. *Pena*, and *United States* v. *Virginia* (VMI).

H-SS 12.6.4 Describe the means that citizens use to participate in the political process (e.g., voting, campaigning, lobbying, filing a legal challenge, demonstrating, petitioning, picketing, running for political office).

H-SS 12.6.6 Analyze trends in voter turnout; the causes and effects of reapportionment and redistricting, with special attention to spatial districting and the rights of minorities; and the function of the Electoral College.

Practicing the Vocabulary

Using Words in Context *For each of the terms below, write a sentence that shows how it relates to this chapter.*

1. suffrage
2. electorate
3. registration
4. poll tax
5. injunction
6. off-year election
7. political efficacy
8. political socialization
9. straight-ticket voting
10. independents

Fill in the Blank *Choose a term from the list above that best completes the sentence.*

11. Suffrage and _____ mean approximately the same thing.
12. A(n) _____ is a court order that can be used to compel a public official to carry out a law.
13. Some people do not have a sense of _____ and therefore do not bother to vote.
14. Voters with a strong allegiance to a party often engage in _____ when they go to the polls.

Reviewing Main Ideas

Section 1

15. What two long-term trends mark the expansion of the American electorate?
16. What are the five stages of the extension of suffrage?
17. What are the constitutional restrictions on the power of the States to set voting qualifications?

Section 2

18. List the three factors that all 50 states use to set voter qualifications.
19. For what two reasons did States adopt residence requirements for voting?
20. What is a literacy requirement for voting, and how was it used to deny suffrage to certain groups?
21. What is a grandfather clause, and what was its purpose with respect to literacy tests?
22. How did Congress require States to ease their registration requirements in 1993?

Section 3

23. **(a)** What was the purpose of the 15th Amendment? **(b)** List three ways that some southern States tried to circumvent the 15th Amendment.
24. To whom does the Civil Rights Commission report its findings?
25. How did Dr. Martin Luther King, Jr.'s voter registration drive affect the passage of national civil rights legislation?
26. Explain two key provisions of the Voting Rights Act of 1965.

Section 4

27. **(a)** What is a nonvoting voter? **(b)** How is this phenomenon related to so-called "ballot fatigue"?
28. Describe three differences between voters and nonvoters.
29. Explain how income, education, and age usually affect party affiliation.
30. Explain how party identification develops, and how it affects the way individuals vote.

Critical Thinking

Analysis Skills CS1, CS4, HR1, HI1

31. *Applying the Chapter Skill* What criteria would you use in deciding for whom to vote in an election?

32. *Identifying Central Issues* What does the record of the expansion of suffrage tell you about trends in the United States from 1789 to the present?

33. *Demonstrating Reasoned Judgment* Do you think that resident aliens, those who have summer homes in a town, and other tax-paying transients should be allowed to vote in elections that determine how their taxes will be spent? Explain the reasons for your answer.

34. *Testing Conclusions* Some people suggest that we should not try to increase voter turnout in this country because that would only encourage uninformed voting and result in bad choices made for the wrong reasons. Do you agree or disagree? Why?

Analyzing Political Cartoons

Use your knowledge of American history and government and this cartoon to answer the questions below.

35. Many factors affect voter behavior. At which factor is the cartoonist poking fun?

36. What do you think the cartoonist thinks of the way the American electorate chooses its leaders today versus 150 years ago?

Participation Activities

Analysis Skills CS1, CS4, HR4

37. *Current Events Watch* There are still places in the world where people are struggling to achieve the right to choose the leaders who govern them. Select one such country, and read about recent efforts to gain or expand suffrage there. Write a brief report on the struggle. Conclude by predicting whether and/or when the struggle for suffrage will succeed.

38. *Time Line Activity* Using information from the chapter, make a time line of the federal laws (including constitutional amendments) that were designed to ensure the suffrage of African Americans. Which, in your opinion, was the most important law? Why?

39. *It's Your Turn* You have been hired to increase voter turnout in local elections in your community. Review the causes for low voter turnout and determine how they might apply to various groups in your community. Prepare a proposal to the election committee. Describe three tactics you would use to increase local voter turnout and explain why they might work. **(Writing a Proposal)**

Standards Monitoring *Online*

For: Chapter 6 Self-Test **Visit:** PHSchool.com
Web Code: mqa-2065

As a final review, take the Magruder's Chapter 6 Self-Test and receive immediate feedback on your answers. The test consists of 20 multiple-choice questions designed to test your understanding of the chapter content.

CHAPTER 7

The Electoral Process

"Any American who cannot bother to vote and who thinks that a single vote does not matter is letting America down."
—Marian Wright Edelman (1992)

Democracy relies on the willingness of the people to participate—and to participate intelligently—in every aspect of the electoral process.

◆ Presidential national convention delegates

Standards Preview

H-SS 12.2.4 Understand the obligations of civic-mindedness, including voting, being informed on civic issues, volunteering and performing public service, and serving in the military or alternative service.

H-SS 12.3.1 Explain how civil society provides opportunities for individuals to associate for social, cultural, religious, economic, and political purposes.

H-SS 12.6.1 Analyze the origin, development, and role of political parties, noting those occasional periods in which there was only one major party or were more than two major parties.

H-SS 12.6.2 Discuss the history of the nomination process for presidential candidates and the increasing importance of primaries in general elections.

H-SS 12.6.3 Evaluate the roles of polls, campaign advertising, and the controversies over campaign funding.

H-SS 12.6.4 Describe the means that citizens use to participate in the political process (e.g., voting, campaigning, lobbying, filing a legal challenge, demonstrating, petitioning, picketing, running for political office).

SECTION 1

The Nominating Process *(pp.178–186)*

★ The nominating process is critically important to democratic government.

★ Five major nominating methods are used in American politics.

★ The most widely used nominating method today is the direct primary.

SECTION 2

Elections *(pp.188–194)*

★ The election process is regulated mostly by State law.

★ Most ballots are cast at polling places in thousands of precincts around the country. However, absentee voting, early voting, and vote-by-mail are becoming increasingly common.

★ Every State now uses the Australian ballot, which is of either the party-column or the office-group type.

★ Various types of electronic voting and/or vote-counting devices are rapidly replacing both lever-operated voting machines and punch-card ballot devices in most States today.

SECTION 3

Money and Elections *(pp.196–202)*

★ Money plays a key role in politics but presents serious problems to democratic government.

★ Most campaign money comes from private sources, including political action committees (PACs).

★ Federal campaign laws are administered by the Federal Election Commission (FEC).

★ Loopholes in campaign finance laws allow candidates and contributors to evade some regulations.

Go Online
PHSchool.com

For: Current Data
Web Code: mqg-2075

For: Close Up Foundation debates
Web Code: mqh-2077

The Nominating Process

Section Preview

OBJECTIVES

1. **Explain** why the nominating process is a critical first step in the election process.
2. **Describe** self-announcement, the caucus, and the convention as nominating methods.
3. **Discuss** the direct primary as the principal nominating method used in the United States today.
4. **Understand** why some candidates use the petition as a nominating device.

WHY IT MATTERS

The nominating process narrows the field of possible candidates for office. It is thus an essential part of an election. The caucus and convention were important nominating methods in the past. The direct primary has largely replaced them. Self-announcement and petitions are also used today as nominating devices.

POLITICAL DICTIONARY

★ **nomination**
★ **general election**
★ **caucus**
★ **direct primary**
★ **closed primary**
★ **open primary**
★ **blanket primary**
★ **runoff primary**
★ **nonpartisan election**

Suppose your teacher stood in front of the class and said: "Here's a $1,000 bill. Who'd like to have it?" You, and everyone else in the room, would promptly say, or at least think: "Me!" Suppose the teacher then said: "Okay, we'll hold an election. The person who wins the most votes gets the money."

What would happen? If the election were held immediately, it is likely that each member of the class would vote for himself or herself. A few might vote for a friend. Almost certainly, however, the election would end in a tie. No one would win the money.

But suppose the teacher said: "We'll hold the election tomorrow." What do you think

▶ Campaign signs urging voters to support particular candidates appear in towns and cities across the country before elections.

would happen then? As you think about the answer to that question, you begin to get a sense of the practical importance of the nominating process—the first step in the process of electing candidates to office.

A Critical First Step

The nominating process is the process of candidate selection. **Nomination**—the naming of those who will seek office—is a critically important step in the election process.

You have already seen two major illustrations of the significance of the nomination process. In Chapter 5, you read about the making of nominations (1) as a prime function of political parties in the United States, and (2) as a leading reason for the decentralized character of the two major parties.

The nominating process also has a very real impact on the exercise of the right to vote. In the typical election in this country, voters can make only one of two choices for each office on the ballot. They can vote for the Republican or they can vote for the Democratic candidate.[1]

---

[1]Other choices are sometimes listed, of course—minor party or independent nominees. These are not often meaningful alternatives, however; most voters choose not to "waste" their votes on candidates who cannot win. Also, nonpartisan elections are an exception to this statement since candidates are not identified by party labels.

George Wallace
Four-time Democratic governor of Alabama, Wallace won 13% of the popular vote in 1968 as the populist candidate of the newly formed American Independent Party.

Eugene McCarthy
A representative and senator from Minnesota (1949–1971), McCarthy sought the Democratic nomination for President in 1968 as a critic of the Vietnam War. He ran in 1976 as an independent, winning 0.9% of the popular vote.

John Anderson
A Republican representative from Illinois (1961–1981), Anderson ran for President as an independent in 1980, winning 6.7% of the popular vote.

Ross Perot
Business executive and billionaire Ross Perot ran as an independent for President in 1992, winning 19% of the popular vote. (In 1996, Perot received 8% of the popular vote as the Reform Party nominee.)

Interpreting Charts These presidential candidates made use of self-announcement as a nominating device. *(a) Why do some candidates choose self-announcement as a method for getting on the ballot? (b) How might a self-announced candidate affect the ultimate outcome of an election?* **H-SS 12.6.4**

This is another way of saying that we have a two-party system in the United States. It is also another way to say that the nominating stage is a critically important part of the electoral process. Those who make nominations place real, very practical limits on the choices that voters can make in an election.

In one-party constituencies (those areas where one party regularly wins elections), the nominating process is usually the only point at which there is any real contest for a public office. Once the dominant party has made its nomination, the general election is little more than a formality.

Dictatorial regimes point up the importance of the nominating process. Many of them hold **general elections**—regularly scheduled elections at which voters make the final selection of officeholders—much as democracies do. But typically, the ballots used in those elections list only one candiate for each office—the candidate of the ruling clique; and those candidates regularly win with majorities approaching 100 percent.

There are five ways in which nominations are made in the United States. They include (1) self-announcement, (2) caucus, (3) convention, (4) direct primary, and (5) petition.

Self-Announcement

Self-announcement is the oldest form of the nominating process in American politics. First used in colonial times, it is still often found at the small-town and rural levels in many parts of the country.

The method is quite simple. A person who wants to run for office simply announces that fact. Modesty or local custom may dictate that someone else make the candidate's announcement, but, still, the process amounts to the same thing.

Self-announcement is sometimes used by someone who failed to win a regular party nomination or by someone unhappy with the party's choice. Note that whenever a write-in candidate appears in an election, the self-announcement process has been used. In recent history, four prominent presidential contenders have made

Nominating and Electing a Candidate

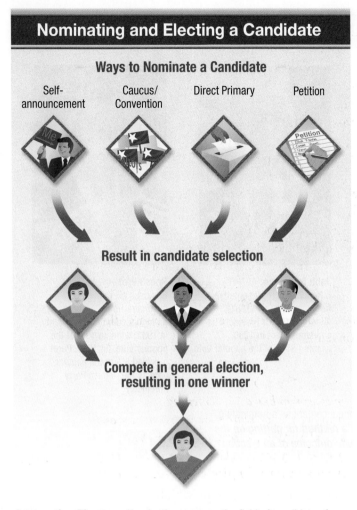

Ways to Nominate a Candidate

Self-announcement | Caucus/Convention | Direct Primary | Petition

Result in candidate selection

Compete in general election, resulting in one winner

Interpreting Diagrams Nominations narrow the field of candidates for the general election. **Why should voters participate in the nominating process?** H-SS 12.6.2

use of the process: George Wallace, who declared himself to be the American Independent Party's nominee in 1968; and independent candidates Eugene McCarthy in 1976; John Anderson in 1980; and Ross Perot in 1992. And all of the 135 candidates who sought to replace Governor Gray Davis of California in that State's recall election in 2003—including the winner, Arnold Schwarzenegger—were self-starters.

The Caucus

As a nominating device, a **caucus** is a group of like-minded people who meet to select the candidates they will support in an upcoming election. The first caucus nominations were made during the later colonial period, probably in Boston in the 1720s.[2] John Adams described the caucus this way in 1763:

PRIMARY Sources *"This day learned that the Caucus Club meets at certain Times in the Garret of Tom Dawes, the Adjutant of the Boston Regiment. He has a large House, and he has a moveable Partition in his Garret, which he takes down, and the whole Club meets in one Room. There they smoke tobacco till you cannot see from one End of the Garret to the other. There they drink flip I suppose, and they choose a Moderator, who puts Questions to the Vote regularly, and select Men, Assessors, Collectors, Wardens, Fire Wards, and Representatives are Regularly chosen before they are chosen in the Town."*

—Charles Francis Adams (ed.),
The Works of John Adams (1856)

Originally the caucus was a private meeting consisting of a few influential figures in the community. As political parties appeared in the late 1700s, they soon took over the device and began to broaden the membership of the caucus.

The coming of independence brought the need to nominate candidates for State offices: governor, lieutenant governor, and others above the local level. The legislative caucus—a meeting of a party's members in the State legislature—took on the job. At the national level, both the Federalists and the Democratic-Republicans in Congress were, by 1800, choosing their presidential and vice-presidential candidates through the congressional caucus.

The legislative and congressional caucuses were quite practical in their day. Transportation and communication were difficult at best. Since legislators already gathered regularly in a central place, it made sense for them to take on the nominating responsibility. The spread of democracy, especially in the newer States on the frontier, spurred opposition to caucuses, however. More and more, people condemned them for their closed, unrepresentative character.

Criticism of the caucus reached its peak in the early 1820s. The supporters of three of the

---

[2]The origin of the term *caucus* is not clear. Most authorities suggest that it comes from the word *caulkers,* because the Boston Caucus Club met at times in a room formerly used as a meeting place by caulkers in Boston's shipyards. (Caulkers made ships watertight by filling seams or cracks in the hulls of sailing vessels with tar or oakum.)

leading contenders for the presidency in 1824—Andrew Jackson, Henry Clay, and John Quincy Adams—boycotted the Democratic-Republicans' congressional caucus that year. In fact, Jackson and his supporters made "King Caucus" a leading campaign issue. The other major aspirant, William H. Crawford of Georgia, became the caucus nominee at a meeting attended by fewer than one third of the Democratic-Republican Party's members in Congress.

Crawford ran a poor third in the electoral college balloting in 1824, and the reign of King Caucus at the national level was ended. With its death in presidential politics, the caucus system soon withered at the State and local levels, as well.

The caucus is still used to make local nominations in some places, especially in New England. There, a caucus is open to all members of a party, and it only faintly resembles the original closed and private process.

The Convention

As the caucus method collapsed, the convention system took its place. The first national convention to nominate a presidential candidate was held by a minor party, the Anti-Masons, in Baltimore in 1831. The newly formed National Republican (soon to become Whig) Party also held a convention later that same year. The Democrats picked up the practice in 1832. All major-party presidential nominees have been chosen by conventions ever since. By the 1840s, conventions had become the principal means for making nominations at every level in American politics.

On paper, the convention process seems perfectly suited to representative government. A party's members meet in a local caucus to pick candidates for local offices and, at the same time, to select delegates to represent them at a county convention.[3]

At the county convention, the delegates nominate candidates for county offices and select delegates to the next rung on the convention ladder, usually the State convention. There, the delegates from the county conventions pick the party's nominees for governor and other State-wide offices. State conventions also send delegates to the party's national convention, where the party selects its presidential and vice-presidential candidates.

In theory, the will of the party's rank and file membership is passed up through each of its representative levels. Practice soon pointed up the weaknesses of the theory, however, as party bosses found ways to manipulate the process. By playing with the selection of delegates, usually at the local levels, they soon dominated the entire system.

As a result, the caliber of most conventions declined at all levels, especially during the late 1800s. How low some of them fell can be seen in this description of a Cook County, Illinois, convention in 1896:

PRIMARY Sources *"Of [723] delegates, those who had been on trial for murder numbered 17; sentenced to the penitentiary for murder or manslaughter and served sentence, 7; served terms in the penitentiary for burglary, 36; served terms in the penitentiary for picking pockets, 2; served*

◄ *Campaign Ribbons* These precursors of today's political buttons were widely used in the 1840s to 1890s.

---

[3]The meetings at which delegates to local conventions are chosen are still often called *caucuses*. Earlier, they were also known as primaries—that is, first meetings. The use of that name gave rise to the term *direct primary*, to distinguish that newer nominating method from the convention process.

terms in the penitentiary for arson, 1; . . .
jailbirds identified by detectives, 84; keepers
of gambling houses, 7; keepers of houses of
ill-fame, 2; convicted of mayhem, 3; ex-prize
fighters, 11; poolroom proprietors, 2; saloon
keepers, 265; . . . political employees, 148;
no occupation, 71; . . . **"**

—R.M. Easley, "The Sine qua Non of Caucus
Reform," *Review of Reviews* (Sept. 1897)

Many people had hailed the change from caucus to convention as a major change for the better in American politics. The abuses of the new device soon dashed their hopes. By the 1870s, the convention system was itself under attack as a major source of evil in American politics. By the 1910s, the direct primary had replaced the convention in most States as the principal nominating method in American politics.

Conventions still play a major role in the nominating process in some States—notably, Connecticut, Michigan, South Dakota, Utah, and Virginia. And, as you will see, no adequate substitute for the device has yet been found at the presidential level.

The Direct Primary

A **direct primary** is an intra-party election. It is held within a party to pick that party's candidates for the general election. Wisconsin adopted the first State-wide direct primary law in 1903; several other States soon followed its lead. Every State now makes at least some provision for its use.

In most States, State law requires that the major parties use the primary to choose their candidates for the United States Senate and House of Representatives, for the governorship and all other State offices, and for most local offices as well. In a few States, however, different combinations of convention and primary are used to pick candidates for the top offices.

In Michigan, for example, the major parties choose their candidates for the U.S. Senate and House, the governorship, and the State legislature in primaries. Nominees for lieutenant governor, secretary of state, and attorney general are picked by conventions.[4]

Although the primaries are party-nominating elections, they are closely regulated by law in most States. The State usually sets the dates on which primaries are held, and it regularly conducts them, too. The State, not the parties, provides polling places and election officials, registration lists and ballots, and otherwise polices the process.

Two basic forms of the direct primary are in use today: (1) the closed primary and (2) the open primary. The major difference between the two lies in the answer to this question: Who can vote in a party's primary—only qualified voters who are party members, or *any* qualified voter?

The Closed Primary

Today, 24 States provide for the **closed primary**—a party's nominating election in which only declared party members can vote. The party's primary is closed to all but those party members.[5]

In most of the closed primary States, party membership is established by registration; see page 154. When voters appear at their polling

Interpreting Political Cartoons What aspect of primary campaigning does this cartoon suggest?

"MY FORMER OPPONENT IS SUPPORTING ME IN THE GENERAL ELECTION. PLEASE DISREGARD ALL THE THINGS I HAVE SAID ABOUT HIM IN THE PRIMARY."

---

[4]In most States, minor parties are required to make their nominations by other, more difficult processes, usually in conventions or by petition. For the significance of this point, see Chapter 5.

[5]The Supreme Court has held that a State's closed primary law cannot forbid a party to allow independent voters to participate in its primary if the party itself chooses to do so. In *Tashjian* v. *Republican Party of Connecticut*, 1986, the Court struck down such a State law. Note that the Court did not outlaw the closed primary in this case, nor did it hold that a political party *must* allow Independents to vote in its primary. The Court found that the Connecticut law violated the 1st and 14th Amendment guarantees of the right of association—here the right of Connecticut Republicans to associate with Independents (invite Independents to join them) in making GOP nominations.

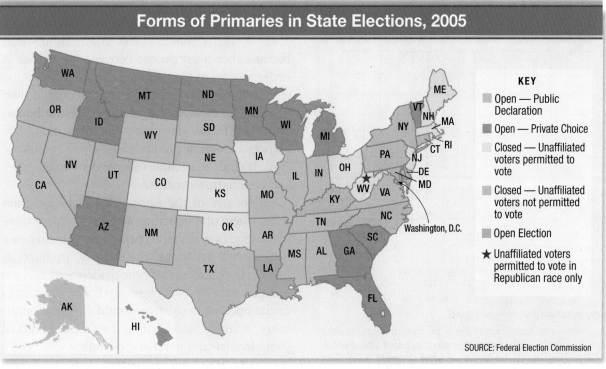

Forms of Primaries in State Elections, 2005

KEY

- Open — Public Declaration
- Open — Private Choice
- Closed — Unaffiliated voters permitted to vote
- Closed — Unaffiliated voters not permitted to vote
- Open Election
- ★ Unaffiliated voters permitted to vote in Republican race only

SOURCE: Federal Election Commission

Interpreting Maps **What form of the primary is used in your State?** H-SS 12.6.2

places on primary election day, their names are checked against the poll books and each voter is handed the primary ballot of the party in which he or she is registered. The voter can mark *only* that party's ballot; he or she can vote only in that party's primary.

In some of the closed primary States, however, a voter can change his or her party registration on election day. In those States, then, the primary is not as completely "closed" as it is elsewhere.

The Open Primary

The **open primary** is a party's nominating election in which *any* qualified voter can cast a ballot. Although it is the form in which the direct primary first appeared, it is now found in only 26 States.

When voters go to the polls in some open primary States, they are handed a ballot of each party holding a primary. Usually, they receive two ballots, those of the Republican and the Democratic parties. Then, in the privacy of the voting booth, each voter marks the ballot of the party in whose primary he or she chooses to vote. In other open primary States, a voter must ask for the ballot of the party in

whose primary he or she wants to vote. That is, each voter must make a *public* choice of party in order to vote in the primary.

Through 2000, three States used a different version of the open primary—the **blanket primary,** sometimes called the "wide-open primary." Washington adopted the first blanket primary law in 1935. Alaska followed suit in 1970, and California did so in 1996. In a blanket primary, every voter received the same ballot—a long one that listed *every* candidate, regardless of party, for every nomination to be made at the primary. Voters could participate however they chose. They could confine themselves to one party's primary; or they could switch back and forth between the parties' primaries, voting to nominate a Democrat for one office, a Republican for another, and so on down the ballot.

The Supreme Court found California's version of the blanket primary unconstitutional in 2000, however. In *California Democratic Party* v. *Jones,* the High Court held that that process violated the 1st and 14th amendments' guarantees of the right of association. It ruled that a State cannot force a political party to associate with outsiders—that is, with members of other

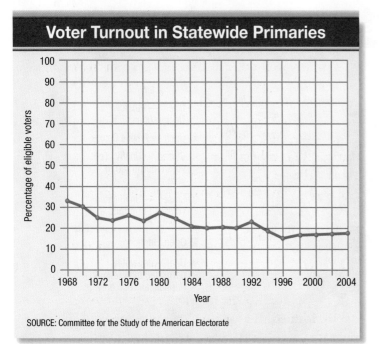

Voter Turnout in Statewide Primaries

Percentage of eligible voters

100
90
80
70
60
50
40
30
20
10
0

1968 1972 1976 1980 1984 1988 1992 1996 2000 2004

Year

SOURCE: Committee for the Study of the American Electorate

Interpreting Graphs *What does this chart suggest about voter interest in statewide primaries from 1968 to 2004?*

parties or with independents—when it picks its candidates for public office.

As a result, the blanket primary is a thing of the past. Alaska, California, and Washington now provide for the more traditional form of the open primary.

Louisiana has yet another form of the open primary, which was not affected by the Court's decision in *Jones*. Its unique "open-election law" provides for what amounts to a combination primary and election. The names of all the people who seek nominations are listed by office on a single primary ballot, regardless of party. A contender who wins more than 50 percent of the primary votes wins the office. In these cases, the primary becomes the election. In contests where there is no majority winner, the two top vote-getters, again regardless of party, face off in the general election.

Closed vs. Open Primary

The two basic forms of the primary have caused arguments for decades. Those who favor the closed primary regularly make three arguments in support of it:

1. It prevents one party from "raiding" the other's primary in the hope of nominating weaker candidates in the other party.

2. It helps make candidates more responsive to the party, its platform, and its members.

3. It helps make voters more thoughtful, because they must choose between the parties in order to vote in the primaries.

The critics of the closed primary contend that:

1. It compromises the secrecy of the ballot, because it forces voters to make their party preferences known in public, and

2. It tends to exclude independent voters from the nomination process.[6]

Advocates of the open primary believe that their system of nominating addresses both of these criticisms. In many open primaries, (1) voters are not forced to make their party preferences known in public, and (2) the tendency to exclude independent voters is eliminated. The opponents of the open primary insist that it (1) permits primary "raiding" and (2) undercuts the concepts of party loyalty and party responsibility.

The Runoff Primary

In most States, candidates need to win only a plurality of the votes cast in the primary to win their party's nomination.[7] (Remember, a *plurality* is the greatest number of votes won by any candidate, whether a *majority* or not.) In 10 States,[8] however, an absolute majority is needed to carry a primary. If no one wins a majority in a race, a **runoff primary** is held a few weeks later. In that runoff, the two top vote-getters in the first party primary face one another for the party's nomination, and the winner of that vote becomes the nominee.

The Nonpartisan Primary

In most States all or nearly all of the elected school and municipal offices are filled in **nonpartisan elections.** These are elections in which candidates

---

[6]See the discussion of *Tashjian* v. *Republican Party of Connecticut,* 1986, in footnote 5. The closed primary States have now amended their primary laws to comply with that decision.

[7]In Iowa, if no candidate wins at least 35 percent of the votes in a primary, the party must then nominate its candidate for that office by convention.

[8]Alabama, Arizona, Arkansas, Georgia, Kentucky, Mississippi, Oklahoma, South Carolina, Texas—and Louisiana under its unique "open election" law. In North Carolina a runoff is held when no candidate wins 40 percent of the primary vote. In South Dakota, if no one who seeks a party's nomination for governor, U.S. senator, or U.S. representative wins at least 35 percent, the party's candidate for that office must be picked in a runoff primary two weeks later.

are not identified by party labels. About half of all State judges are chosen on nonpartisan ballots, as well. The nomination of candidates for these offices takes place on a nonpartisan basis, too, often in nonpartisan primaries.

Typically, a contender who wins a clear majority in a nonpartisan primary then runs unopposed in the general election, subject only to write-in opposition. In many States, however, a candidate who wins a majority in the primary is declared elected at that point. If there is no majority winner, the names of the two top contenders are placed on the general election ballot.

The primary first appeared as a partisan nominating device. Many have long argued that it is not well suited for use in nonpartisan elections. Instead, they favor the petition method, which you will consider later in this section.

Evaluation of the Primary

The direct primary, whether open or closed, is an *intra*party nominating election. It came to American politics as a reform of the boss-dominated convention system. It was intended to take the nominating function away from the party organization and put it in the hands of the party's membership.

The basic facts about the primary have never been very well understood by most voters, however. So, in closed primary States, many voters resent having to declare their party preference. And, in both open and closed primary States, many are upset because they cannot express their support for candidates in more than one party. Many are also annoyed by the "bed-sheet ballots" they regularly see in primary elections—not realizing that the use of the direct primary almost automatically means a long ballot. And some are concerned because the primary (and, in particular, its closed form) tends to exclude independents from the nominating process.

These factors, combined with a lack of appreciation of the importance of primaries, result in this unfortunate fact: Nearly everywhere, voter turnout in primary elections is usually less than half what it is in general elections.

Primary campaigns can be quite costly. The fact that the successful contenders must then wage—and finance—a general election campaign adds to the money problems that bedevil American politics. Unfortunately, the financial facts of political life in the United States mean that some well-qualified people do not seek public office simply because they cannot muster the necessary funds.

The nominating process, whatever its form, can also have a very divisive effect on a party. Remember, the process takes place *within* the party—so, when there is a contest for a nomination, that is where the contest occurs. A bitter fight in the primaries can so wound and divide a party that it cannot recover in time to present a united front for the general election. Many a primary fight has cost a party an election.

Finally, because many voters are not very well informed, the primary places a premium on name familiarity. That is, it often gives an edge to a contender who has a well-known name or a name that sounds like that of some well-known person. But, notice, name familiarity in and of itself has little or nothing to do with a candidate's qualifications for office.

Obviously, the primary is not without its problems, nor is any other nominating device. Still, the primary does give a party's members the opportunity to participate at the very core of the political process.

Interpreting Political Cartoons **What aspect of the primary process does this cartoon critique?**

▲ *Getting on the Ballot* Petitions are widely used as nominating devices, particularly in nonpartisan elections at the local level.

The Presidential Primary

The presidential primary developed as an offshoot of the direct primary. It is not a nominating device, however. Rather, the presidential primary is an election that is held as one part of the process by which presidential candidates are chosen.

The presidential primary is a very complex process. It is one or both of two things, depending on the State involved. It is a process in which a party's voters elect some or all of a State party organization's delegates to that party's national convention; and/or it is a preference election in which voters can choose (vote their preference) among various contenders for a party's presidential nomination. Much of what happens in presidential politics in the early months of every fourth year centers on this very complicated process. (See Chapter 13 for an extended discussion of the presidential primary.)

Petition

One other nominating method is used fairly widely at the local level in American politics today—nomination by petition. Where this process is used, candidates for public office are nominated by means of petitions signed by a certain required number of qualified voters in the election district.[9]

Nomination by petition is found most widely at the local level, chiefly for nonpartisan school posts and municipal offices in medium-sized and smaller communities. It is also the process usually required by State law for nominating minor party and independent candidates. (Remember, the States often purposely make the process of getting on the ballot difficult for those candidates.)

The details of the petition process vary widely from State to State, and even from one city to the next. Usually, however, the higher the office and/or the larger the constituency represented by the office, the greater the number of signatures needed for nomination.

---

[9]The petition device is also an important part of the recall and the initiative and referendum processes; see Chapter 24.

Section 1 Assessment

Key Terms and Main Ideas

1. For what reasons is the making of **nominations** so important in the electoral process?
2. Explain the difference between a **closed primary** and an **open primary.**
3. What is a **nonpartisan election**?
4. What is a **caucus,** and what events led to its demise as a method for nominating candidates?

Critical Thinking

5. **Making Decisions** You read in this section that voter turnout in primaries is usually less than half of what it is in general elections. What steps could you take in your community to increase voter turnout in primary elections?

Standards Monitoring *Online*
For: Self-quiz with vocabulary practice
Web Code: mqa-2071

6. **Identifying Central Issues** Explain why the nominating process is a vital first step in the electoral process.

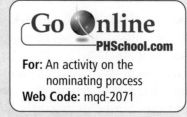
For: An activity on the nominating process
Web Code: mqd-2071

on Primary Sources

Establishing Primary Elections

CALIFORNIA

Analysis Skills HR4, HI3

In a 1901 speech to the Wisconsin legislature, Governor Robert La Follette called for an end to caucus and convention nominations and for the nomination of each party's candidates directly by the voters. Shortly thereafter, Wisconsin became the first State to establish Statewide primary elections.

Governor Robert La Follette
1855–1925

It is a fundamental principle of this republic that each citizen should have equal voice in government. This is recognized and guaranteed to him through the ballot. . . . Since government, with us, is conducted by the representatives of some political party, the citizen's voice in making and administering the laws is expressed through his party ballot. This privilege is vital. . . . It is here government begins. . . . Control lost at this point is never regained. . . .

For many years the evils of the caucus and convention system have multiplied. . . . The system in all its details is inherently bad. It not only favors, but . . . produces manipulation, scheming, trickery, fraud and corruption. The delegate elected in caucus is nominally [supposedly] the agent of the voter to act for him in convention. Too frequently . . . he acts not for the voter, but serves his own purpose instead. This fact in itself taints the trust from the outset, and poisons the system at its very source. No legitimate business could survive under a system where authority to transact its vital matters were delegated and re-delegated to agents and sub-agents, who controlled their own selection . . . and were responsible to nobody. . . .

The officials nominated by the [party] machine become its faithful servants and surrender judgment to its will. This they must do in self-preservation or they are retired to public life. Wielding a power

substantially independent of the voter, it is quite unnecessary to regard him as an important factor in government . . . .

It is of primary importance that the public official should hold himself directly accountable to the citizen. This he will do only when he owes his nomination directly to the citizen. If between the citizen and the official there is a complicated system of caucuses and conventions, by the easy manipulation of which the selection of candidates is controlled by some other agency or power, then the official will so render his services as to have the approval of such agency or power. The overwhelming demand of the people of this state, whom you represent, is that such intervening power and authority, and the complicated system which sustains it, shall be torn down and cast aside. . . .

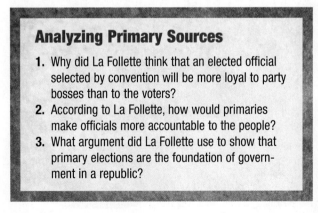

Analyzing Primary Sources

1. Why did La Follette think that an elected official selected by convention will be more loyal to party bosses than to the voters?
2. According to La Follette, how would primaries make officials more accountable to the people?
3. What argument did La Follette use to show that primary elections are the foundation of government in a republic?

Elections

Section Preview

OBJECTIVES

1. **Analyze** how the administration of elections in the United States helps make democracy work.
2. **Define** the role of precincts and polling places in the election process.
3. **Describe** the various ways in which voters can cast their ballots.
4. **Outline** the role that voting devices play in the election process.

WHY IT MATTERS

The election process lies at the very heart of the democratic concept. Indeed, it is impossible to picture a democratic government in which popular elections are not held.

POLITICAL DICTIONARY

★ absentee voting
★ coattail effect
★ precinct
★ polling place
★ ballot

Many high school students are not old enough to vote. In some parts of the country, however, high school students can serve on local election boards. First in Hawaii and Oregon and now in several States, 16- and 17-year-olds can become full-fledged members of the panels that administer elections.

Americans hold more elections and vote more often than most people realize. Indeed, Sundays and holidays are about the only days of the year on which people do not go to the polls somewhere in the United States. Americans also elect far more officeholders than most people realize—in fact, more than 500,000 of them.

▲ *Election Observers* In many parts of the world, election observers are needed to ensure that elections are free and fair. Here, former President Jimmy Carter monitors an election in Haiti.

The Administration of Elections

Democratic government cannot succeed unless elections are free, honest, and accurate. Many people see the details of the election process as too complicated, too legalistic, too dry and boring to worry about. Those who do miss the vital part those details play in making democracy work. *How* something can be done very often shapes what is in fact done—and that fact is as true in politics as it is in other matters. The often lengthy and closely detailed provisions of election law are meant to protect the integrity of the electoral process. And those provisions often have a telling effect on the outcome of elections. You saw how important the details of election law can be when you looked at voter qualifications and voter registration in the last chapter and again just a few pages ago when you considered the complexities of the direct primary.

Extent of Federal Control

Nearly all elections in the United States are held to choose the more than 500,000 persons who hold elective office in the more than 87,000 units of government at the State and local levels. It is quite understandable, then, that most election law in the United States is *State*—not federal—law.

Despite this fact, a body of federal election law does exist. The Constitution gives

Congress the power to fix "[t]he Times, Places, and Manner of holding Elections" of members of Congress.[10] Congress also has the power to set the time for choosing presidential electors, to set the date for casting the electoral votes, and to regulate other aspects of the presidential election process.[11]

Congress has set the date for holding congressional elections as the first Tuesday following the first Monday in November of every even-numbered year. It has set the same date every fourth year for the presidential election.[12] Thus, the next congressional elections will be held on November 7, 2006; and the next presidential election falls on November 4, 2008.

Congress has required the use of secret ballots and allowed the use of voting machines in federal elections. It has also acted to protect the right to vote, as you saw in Chapter 6; and it has prohibited various corrupt practices and regulated the financing of campaigns for federal office, as you will see in the pages ahead.

Congress expanded the body of federal election law with the passage of the Help America Vote Act of 2002. That law came in response to the many ballot and voter registration problems that plagued several States in the presidential election in 2000 (see pages 380–381).

In its major provisions, the new law requires the States to

• replace all their lever-operated and punch-card voting devices by 2006—a deadline that, in fact, most States failed to meet;

• upgrade their administration of elections, especially through the better training of local election officials and of those (mostly low-paid workers and volunteers) who work in precinct polling places on election day;

• centralize and computerize their voter registration systems, to facilitate the identification of qualified voters on election day and so minimize fraudulent voting;

---

[10]Article I, Section 4, Clause 1; 17th Amendment; see pages 276 and 277.
[11]Article II, Section 1, Clause 4; 12th Amendment; see pages 378 and 379.
[12]Congress has made an exception for Alaska. Because of the possibility of severe weather in much of Alaska in early November, that State may, if it chooses, elect its congressional delegation and cast its presidential vote in October. So far, however, Alaska has used the November date.

• provide for provisional voting, so a person whose eligibility to vote has been challenged can cast a ballot that will be counted if it is later found that he or she, is in fact, qualified to vote.

State law deals with all other matters relating to national elections—and with all of the details of State and local elections, as well.

Election Day

Most States hold their elections to fill State offices on the same date Congress has set for national elections: in November of every even-numbered year. The "Tuesday-after-the-first-Monday" formula prevents election day from falling on (1) Sundays (to maintain the principle of separation of church and state) and (2) the first day of the month, which is often payday and therefore peculiarly subject to campaign pressures.

Some States do fix other dates for some offices, however. Louisiana, Mississippi, New Jersey, and Virginia elect the governor, other executive officers, and State legislators in November of odd-numbered years. In Kentucky, the governor and other executive officers are chosen in odd-numbered years, but legislators are elected in even-numbered years. City, county, and other local election dates vary from State to State. When those elections are not held in November, they generally take place in the spring.

Early Voting

Millions of Americans cast their ballots before election day. Indeed, some 20 million did so in 2004, many of them by **absentee voting**—a process by which they could vote without actually going to their polling places on election day. Almost everywhere, voters can apply for an absentee ballot some weeks before an election, then mark those ballots and return them to the local election office, usually by mail and before election day.

Absentee voting was originally intended to serve a relatively small group of voters, especially the ill or disabled and those who expected to be away from home on election day. Most States have broadened their laws over recent years, however—to the point where, in most of them, any qualified voter can now cast an absentee ballot.

More than half the States now also provide for another form of early voting. They allow voters to cast their ballots at any time over a period of several days before an election—not as an absentee ballot but as though they were voting on election day itself.

The Coattail Effect

The **coattail effect** occurs when a strong candidate running for an office at the top of the ballot helps attract voters to other candidates on the party's ticket. In effect, the lesser-known office seeker "rides the coattails" of the more prestigious personality. In 1980 and 1984, for example, Ronald Reagan's coattails helped many Republican candidates win office. The coattail effect is usually most apparent in presidential elections. However, a popular candidate for senator or governor can have the same kind of pulling power.

A reverse coattail effect can occur, too. This happens when a candidate for some major office is less than popular with many voters—for example, Barry Goldwater as the Republican presidential nominee in 1964, and George McGovern for the Democrats in 1972. President Jimmy Carter's coattails were also of the reverse variety in 1980.

Some people have long argued that all State and local elections should be held on dates other than those set for federal elections. This, they say, would help voters pay more attention to State and local candidates and issues and lessen the coattail effects of presidential contests.

Precincts and Polling Places

A **precinct** is a voting district. Precincts are the smallest geographic units for the conduct of elections. State law regularly restricts their size, generally to an area with no more than 500 to 1,000 or so qualified voters. A **polling place**— the place where the voters who live in a precinct actually vote—is located somewhere in or near each precinct.

A precinct election board supervises the polling place and the voting process in each precinct. Typically, the county clerk or county board of elections draws precinct lines, fixes the location of each polling place, and picks the members of the precinct boards.

The precinct board opens and closes the polls at the times set by State law. In most States, the polls are open from 7:00 or 8:00 A.M. to 7:00 or 8:00 P.M. The precinct election board must also see that the ballots and the ballot boxes or voting machines are available. It must make certain that only qualified voters cast ballots in the precinct. Often the board also counts the votes cast in the precinct and then sends the results to the proper place, usually to the county clerk or county board of elections.

Poll watchers, one from each party, are allowed at each polling place. They may challenge any person they believe is not qualified to vote, check to be sure that their own party's supporters do vote, and monitor the whole process, including the counting of the ballots.

Casting the Ballot

A **ballot** is the device by which a voter registers a choice in an election.[15] It can take a number of different forms. Whatever its form, however, it is clearly an important and sensitive part of the election process.

Each State now provides for a secret ballot. That is, State law requires that ballots be cast in such manner that others cannot know how a person has voted.

Voting was a public process through much of the nation's earlier history, however. Paper ballots were used in some colonial elections, but voting was more commonly *viva voce*—by voice. Voters simply stated their choices to an election board. With suffrage limited to the privileged few, many people defended oral voting as the only "manly" way in which to participate. Whatever the merits of that view, the expansion of the electorate brought with it a marked increase in intimidation, vote buying, and other corruptions of the voting process.

Paper ballots were in general use by the mid-1800s. The first ones were unofficial— slips of paper that voters prepared themselves and dropped in the ballot box. Soon candidates and parties began to prepare ballots and hand them to voters to cast, sometimes paying them to do so. Those party ballots were often printed on distinctively colored paper, and

---

[15]The word comes from the Italian *ballotta,* "little ball," and reflects the practice of dropping black or white balls into a box to indicate a choice. The term *blackball* comes from the same practice.

OFFICE-GROUP BALLOT

Voters select each candidate by marking an X in the square

Candidates are grouped by office

Names are listed in random order

OFFICIAL BALLOT, GENERAL ELECTION

President and Vice President of the United States ☒
Four year term. Vote for one only.

BADNARIK, Michael/CAMPAGNA, Richard
Libertarian ☐

KERRY, John/EDWARDS, John
Democratic ☐

BUSH, George W./CHENEY, Dick
Republican ☐

COBB, David/LAMARCHE, Patricia
Green ☐

Office of the United States Senate

Six year term. Vote for one only.

HOLDEN, Bob
Democrat ☐

MACY, Elgar
Republican ☐

KLINE, Richard
Reform ☐

PARTY-COLUMN BALLOT

Party symbol and name at the top of the column that lists all of the party's candidates running for office

OFFICIAL BALLOT, GENERAL ELECTION

REPUBLICAN	DEMOCRATIC	LIBERTARIAN	GREEN
For President of the United States GEORGE W. BUSH	For President of the United States JOHN KERRY	For President of the United States MICHAEL BADNARIK	For President of the United States DAVID COBB
For Vice President of the United States DICK CHENEY	For Vice President of the United States JOHN EDWARDS	For Vice President of the United States RICHARD CAMPAGNA	For Vice President of the United States PATRICIA LAMARCHE
For United States Senator ELGAR MACY	For United States Senator BOB HOLDEN	For United States Senator RICHARD KLINE	

To vote for candidates of different parties, voters mark an X in the square next to the chosen candidate or candidates

Interpreting Diagrams By highlighting the office, rather than the party, an office-group ballot encourages split-ticket voting. ***How does a party-column ballot encourage voters to vote along party lines?*** H-SS 12.6.1

anyone watching could tell for whom voters were voting.

Political machines—local party organizations capable of mobilizing or "manufacturing" large numbers of votes on behalf of candidates for political office—flourished in many places in the latter 1800s. They fought all attempts to make voting a more dependably fair and honest process. The political corruption of the post-Civil War years brought widespread demand for ballot reforms.

The Australian Ballot

A new voting arrangement was devised in Australia, where it was first used in an election in Victoria in 1856. Its successes there led to its use in other countries. By 1900 nearly all of the States were using it, and it remains the basic form of the ballot in this country today.

The Australian Ballot has four essential features:

1. It is printed at public expense;
2. It lists the names of all candidates in an election;

3. It is given out only at the polls, one to each qualified voter; and
4. It is marked in secret.

Two basic varieties of the Australian ballot have developed over the years. Most States now use the office-group ballot. Only a handful of States use the party-column ballot.

The Office-Group Ballot

The office-group ballot is the original form of the Australian ballot. It is also sometimes called the Massachusetts ballot because of its early (1888) use there. On the office-group ballot, the candidates for an office are grouped together under the title of that office. Because the names of the candidates thus appear as a block, the form is also sometimes called the office-block ballot.

At first, the names of the candidates were listed in alphabetical order. Most States using the form now rotate the names—so that each candidate will have whatever psychological advantage there may be in having his or her name at the top of the list of candidates.

The Party-Column Ballot

The party-column ballot is also known as the Indiana ballot, from its early (1889) use in that State. It lists each party's candidates in a column under the party's name.

Professional politicians tend to favor the party-column ballot. It encourages straight-ticket voting, especially if the party has a strong candidate at the head of the ticket. Most students of the political process favor the office-group form because it encourages voter judgment and split-ticket voting.

Sample Ballots

Sample ballots, clearly marked as such, are available in most States before an election. In some States they are mailed to all voters, and they appear in most newspapers. They cannot be cast, but they can help voters prepare for an election.

First in Oregon (1907), and now in several States, an official voter's pamphlet is mailed to voters before every election. It lists all candidates and measures that will appear on the ballot. In Oregon, each candidate is allowed space to present his or her qualifications and position on the issues. Supporters and opponents of ballot measures are allowed space to present their arguments as well.

Bedsheet Ballots

The ballot in a typical American election is lengthy, often and aptly called a "bedsheet" ballot. It frequently lists so many offices, candidates, and ballot measures that even the most well-informed voters have a difficult time marking it intelligently.

The long ballot came to American politics in the era of Jacksonian Democracy in the 1830s. Many held the view at the time that the greater the number of elective offices, the more democratic the governmental system. The idea remains widely accepted today.

Generally, the longest ballots are found at the local level, especially among the nation's 3,000-odd counties. The list of elected offices is likely to include several commissioners, a clerk, a sheriff, one or more judges, a prosecutor, coroner, treasurer, assessor, surveyor, school superintendent, engineer, sanitarian, and even the proverbial dogcatcher.

Critics of the bed-sheet ballot reject the notion that the more people you elect, the more democratic you are. Instead, they say, the fewer the offices voters have to fill, the better they can know the candidates and their qualifications. Those critics often point to the factor of "ballot fatigue"— that is, to the drop-off in voting that can run as high as 20 to 30 percent at or near the bottom of the typical (lengthy) ballot.

There seems little, if any, good reason to elect such local officials as clerks, coroners, surveyors, and engineers. Their jobs do not carry basic policy-making responsibilities. Rather, they carry out policies made by others. Many believe that to shorten the ballot and promote good government, the rule should be: Elect those who make public policies; appoint those whose job it is to administer those policies.

Automated Voting

Well over half the votes now cast in national elections are cast on some type of voting machine—and, increasingly, on some type of electronic voting device.

Thomas Edison patented the first voting machine—the first mechanical device for the casting and counting of votes—in 1868, and his invention was first used in a public election in Locksport, New York, in 1892. The use of similar but much-improved devices soon spread to polling places across the country.

For the better part of a century, most voting machines were lever-operated, and quite cumbersome. Voters had to pull various levers in order to cast their ballots—one lever to open (unlock) the machine, others to indicate their choices of candidates, and yet another to close (lock) the machine and record their votes.

Those lever-operated machines did speed up the voting process; and they reduced both fraud and counting errors. The machines were quite expensive, however, and they also posed major

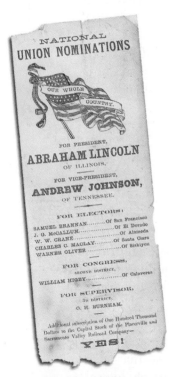

▲ **Campaign Ticket, 1864**
Sometimes tickets such as these were cast as ballots.

storage and transport problems from one election to the next.

Electronic Vote Counting

Electronic data processing (EDP) techniques were first applied to the voting process in the 1960s. California and Oregon led the way and EDP is now a vital part of that process in nearly every State.

For some years, the most widely used adaptations of EDP involved punch-card ballots, counted by computers. But punch-card ballots often produced problems—most frequently because voters failed to make clean punches. Their incomplete perforations left "hanging chads" that made the cards difficult or impossible for computers to read.

Punch-card ballots played a major role in the disputed presidential election vote count in Florida in 2000 (see pages 380–381); and that fiasco led to the passage of the Help America Vote Act of 2002. As we noted on page 189, that law requires the elimination of all punch-card voting devices (and all lever-operated voting machines, as well).

Most States are now turning to two other EDP-based voting systems. One of them involves paper ballots marked by voters and then counted by high-speed optical scanners. The other utilizes a touch-screen. See the illustration on this page for one version of touch-screen voting.

Vote-by-Mail Elections

A number of States conduct some elections by mail. Voters receive a ballot in the mail, make their choices, then mail the ballot back to election officials. The first such election was held in Monterey County, California, in 1977; and the first large-scale use of mail-in ballots took place in San Diego in 1981.

Usually, vote-by-mail elections have been confined to the local level and to voting on city or county measures, not on candidates for local offices. A few States do choose local officials by mail-in ballots, however. In addition, vote-by-mail is an integral part of the absentee voting process, and absentee voting is becoming an increasingly common practice in many places.

In fact, Oregon now holds all of its elections by mail and has done so since 1998. The State

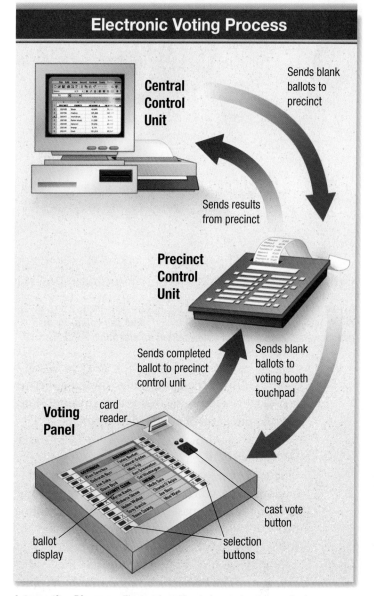

Electronic Voting Process

Central Control Unit

Sends blank ballots to precinct

Sends results from precinct

Precinct Control Unit

Sends completed ballot to precinct control unit

Sends blank ballots to voting booth touchpad

Voting Panel

card reader

cast vote button

ballot display

selection buttons

Interpreting Diagrams Electronic voting is becoming increasingly common, replacing mechanical voting machines. Here, voters make their choices on a touchpad similar to that on an automated teller machine. ***How are votes counted in an electronic voting system?***

held the first-ever all-mail primary election and the first-ever all-mail general election (including the presidential election) in 2000.

Vote-by-mail elections have stirred controversy, of course. Critics fear that the process threatens the principle of the secret ballot. They worry about fraud, especially the possibility that some voters may be subjected to undue pressures when they mark their ballots at home or any place other than within the security of a voting booth.

Supporters, on the other hand, say that vote-by-mail elections can be as fraud-proof as any other method of voting. They also cite this fact:

▲ This photo shows the mail-in ballot used by Oregon voters, who now vote by mail in all elections. *Critical Thinking How can voting by mail help increase the number of votes cast in an election?* **H-SS 12.6.4**

1997. In that year, election officials in Harris County, Texas, permitted astronaut David Wolf to vote in Houston's city election by e-mail from the space station *Mir*.

The first public elections in which some votes were cast by computer were held in 2000. In Arizona, some of the ballots cast in the Democratic Party's presidential primary in March were cast online. And, for the general election in November, the Defense Department ran a very limited project in which 84 members of the military stationed abroad voted. As noted earlier, however, DOD abandoned plans for a much larger project in 2004. Some 46,000 voters (28 percent of the total turnout) did vote by computer in the Democratic Party's presidential caucuses in Michigan in February of 2004.

A number of public officials in several States and a number of dot.com companies promote online voting. These supporters claim that it will make participation much more convenient, increase voter turnout, and reduce the costs of conducting elections.

Many skeptics believe that the electronic infrastructure is not ready for e-voting. Some fear digital disaster: jammed phone lines, blocked access, hackers, viruses, denials of service attacks, fraudulent vote counts, and violations of voter secrecy. Critics also point out that because not everyone can afford home computers, online voting could undermine basic American principles of equality.

The mail-in process usually increases voter turnout in elections and, at the same time, reduces the costs of conducting them.

Online Voting

Online voting—casting ballots via the Internet—has attracted considerable attention (and some support) in the past few years. Will e-voting become widespread—even commonplace, as some predict? Clearly, only time will tell.

Online voting is not an entirely new phenomenon. The first e-vote was cast in November

---

Section 2 Assessment

Key Terms and Main Ideas

1. What is the purpose of **absentee voting** laws?
2. How can the **coattail effect** influence election results?
3. What factor determines the location of each voter's **polling place**?
4. (a) What is a **ballot**? (b) What different forms does it take in the United States?

Critical Thinking

5. **Predicting Consequences** Consider elections held in your school for class president and student council. How might the absence of secret ballots affect these elections?

Standards Monitoring *Online*
For: Self-quiz with vocabulary practice
Web Code: mqa-2072

6. **Expressing Problems Clearly (a)** What are the advantages and disadvantages of voting by mail and voting online? **(b)** Do you support either of these voting methods? Explain your answer.

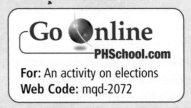

Go Online
PHSchool.com
For: An activity on elections
Web Code: mqd-2072

Face the
Issues

Electronic Voting

Background *The Help America Vote Act, passed by Congress in 2002, effectively prohibits the use of lever-operated voting machines or punch-card voting devices in any primary or general election. In response to the law, most States have now either adopted direct response electronic voting machines (DREs) or are in the process of doing so. DREs work much like ATMs. Voters make their choices by pushing buttons or touching a screen, and their votes then are recorded electronically. The adoption of these electronic voting systems has sparked controversy.*

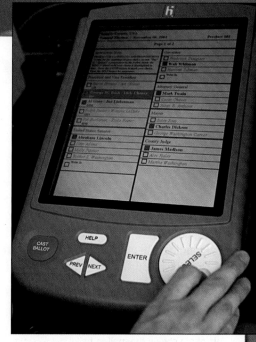

A voting terminal

Analysis Skills CS2, HI1

A Major Improvement

These computerized voting systems are easy to use. Among their several advantages, DREs make it impossible for a voter to make more than one choice in a given race. Thus, they reduce the number of spoiled ballots in an election—that is, the number of ballots that cannot be counted because of some voter-made error.

Unlike other voting systems, DREs can be made fully accessible to disabled persons, including those who are visually impaired. This means that, for many of those voters, they can cast ballots that are truly cast in secret. DREs also have the capacity to provide ballots in an unlimited number of languages, and so promote voter turnout among language minorities.

Finally, several studies show that, due to voter error, the ballots cast by minority voters are less likely to be counted where paper ballots are used. E-voting virtually eliminates that problem.

Beware of Electronic Voting

Many computer scientists see a number of flaws in the DREs currently available. Several of them are most concerned about source code, the language of the software. It is altogether possible, they say, that those who program a system, or hackers who gain access to it, can manipulate the outcome of an election.

Many also worry about the transmission of voter totals to central locations. Those results are not usually sent via the Internet. They may be transmitted by a direct modem connection, however, and intercepted by a hacker.

E-voting systems should provide a "paper trail," but most DREs now in use do not. They should be required to produce paper audit trails. These receipts, printed records of how ballots were marked, are critical to check for accuracy or tampering and provide a record when recounts are necessary. Most DREs do not yet produce these receipts. We require a receipt when we use a bank machine. Why not when we cast a vote?

Exploring the Issues

1. Why are people concerned about electronic voting?
2. List two advantages and two disadvantages of electronic voting. Which factors are more important to you, and why?

For more information on trends in voting, view "Electronic Voting."

Face the **Issues** Video Collection

Section Preview

OBJECTIVES

1. **Explain** the issues raised by campaign spending.
2. **Describe** the various sources of funding for campaign spending.
3. **Examine** federal laws that regulate campaign finance.
4. **Outline** the role of the Federal Election Commission in enforcing campaign finance laws.
5. **Describe** hard money and soft money.

WHY IT MATTERS

Money is an indispensable campaign resource. Yet money also poses a variety of problems in the election process. That's why the use of money is regulated in today's elections.

POLITICAL DICTIONARY

★ **political action committee (PAC)**
★ **subsidy**
★ **soft money**
★ **hard money**

▲ Seal of the Federal Election Commission, which administers federal law dealing with campaign finance.

Running for public office costs money, and often a lot of it. That fact creates some difficult problems in American politics. It leaves open the possibility that candidates will try to buy their way into public office. It also makes it possible for special interests to try to buy favors from those who are in office.

Clearly, government by the people must be protected from these dangers. But how? Parties and candidates must have money. Without it, they cannot campaign or do any of the many things they must do to win elections.

In short, dollars are an absolutely necessary campaign resource. Yet, the getting and spending of campaign funds can corrupt the entire political process.

Campaign Spending

No one really knows how much money is spent on elections in the United States. Reliable estimates of total spending in recent presidential election years—including nominations and elections at all levels—can be seen in the table on the next page.

The presidential election eats up by far the largest share of campaign dollars. For 2004, total spending for all of the major and minor party presidential efforts—for primaries, conventions, campaigns, for everything—reached a mind-boggling $2 billion.

The vast sums spent on congressional campaigns also continue to climb, election after election. Spending in all the Senate and House races around the country totaled a stupendous amount, more than one billion dollars in 2004. Spending will almost certainly exceed even that huge sum in 2006.

Radio and television time, professional campaign managers and consultants, newspaper advertisements, pamphlets, buttons, posters and bumper stickers, office rent, polls, data processing, mass mailings, Web sites, travel—these and a host of other items make up the huge sums spent in campaigns. Television ads are far and away the largest item in most campaign budgets today, even at the local level. As Will Rogers put it years ago, "You have to be loaded just to get beat."

The total amount spent in particular races varies widely, of course. How much depends on several things: the office involved, the candidate and whether he or she is the incumbent, the opposition, and, not least, the availability of campaign funds.

Sources of Funding

Parties and their candidates draw their money from two basic sources: private contributors and the public treasury.

Private and Public Sources

Private givers have always been the major source of campaign funds in American politics, and they come in various shapes and sizes:

1. Small contributors—those who give $5 or $10 or so, and only occasionally. Only about 10 percent of people of voting age ever make campaign contributions; so parties and candidates must look to other places for much of their funding.

2. Wealthy individuals and families—the "fat cats," who can make large donations and find it in their best interest to make them.

3. Candidates—both incumbents and challengers, their families, and, importantly, people who hold and want to keep appointive public offices. Ross Perot holds the all-time record in this category. He spent some $65 million of his own money on his independent bid for the presidency in 1992.

4. Various nonparty groups—especially **political action committees (PACs)**. Political action committees are the political arms of special-interest and other organizations with a stake in electoral politics.

5. Temporary organizations—groups formed for the immediate purposes of a campaign, including fund-raising. Hundreds of these short-lived units spring up every two years, and at every level in American politics.

Then, too, parties and their candidates often hold fund-raisers of various sorts. The most common are $100-, $500-, and $1,000-a-plate luncheons, dinners, picnics, receptions, and similar gatherings. Some of these events now reach the $100,000-or-more level in presidential campaigns. Direct mail requests, telethons, and Internet solicitations are also among the oft-used tools of those who raise campaign money.

Public funds—subsidies from the federal and some State treasuries—are now another prime source of campaign money. A **subsidy** is a grant of money, usually from a government. Subsidies have so far been most important at the presidential level, as you will see shortly.[13]

Why People Give

Campaign donations are a form of political participation. Those who make them do so for a number of reasons. Many small donors give simply because they believe in a party or in a

Total Campaign Spending, 1960–2004			
Year	Estimated spending	Voter turnout*	Spending per voter
1960	$175 million	68.8 million	$2.54
1964	$200 million	70.6 million	$2.83
1968	$300 million	73.2 million	$4.10
1972	$425 million	77.7 million	$5.47
1976	$540 million	81.6 million	$6.62
1980	$1.2 billion	86.6 million	$13.87
1984	$1.8 billion	92.7 million	$19.42
1988	$2.7 billion	91.6 million	$29.48
1992	$3.2 billion	104.4 million	$30.65
1996	$4.0 billion	96.5 million	$41.45
2000	$5.1 billion	105.4 million	$48.39
2004	$6.0 billion	120.2 million	$49.92

*Presidential elections

SOURCES: Federal Election Commission; Herbert E. Alexander, *Financing Politics*

Interpreting Tables Total campaign spending has risen dramatically in recent elections. **What factors may account for this rise?** H-SS 12.6.3

candidate. Many of those who give, however, want something in return. They want access to government, and hope to get it by helping their "friends" win elections. And, notice, some contributors give to both sides in a contest: Heads they win and tails they still win.

Some big donors want appointments to public office, and others want to keep the ones they have. Some long for social recognition. For them, dinner at the White House, meeting with a Cabinet official, or knowing the governor on a first-name basis may be enough. Organized labor, business, professional, and various other groups have particular policy aims. They want certain laws passed, changed, or repealed, or certain administrative actions taken.

Regulating Campaign Finance

Congress first began to regulate the use of money in federal elections in 1907. In that year, it became unlawful for any corporation or national bank to make "a money contribution in

---

[13]Public funds for presidential campaigns come from the federal treasury. Several States now also have some form of public financing for parties and/or candidates at the State and even the local level.

Senator Maria Cantwell (D., Washington) was elected to the United States Senate in 2000 after a campaign in which she refused to accept contributions from special interests. Later, as the Senate debated campaign finance reform legislation, she had this to say:

❝ *The only way we have to truly level the playing field, both between candidates and parties of opposing ideologies, and more importantly, between new candidates and incumbents, is to commit the resources to the process of getting people elected. Not until we create a campaign system with a shorter and more intensive campaign period—something I think the public would truly applaud—funded with finite and equal resources available to all candidates, will we be able to really listen carefully to what the people want.* **❞**

Evaluating the Quotation

What advantages and disadvantages are there—for both voters and candidates—of "a shorter and more intensive campaign period . . . funded with finite and equal resources available to all candidates"?

any election" to candidates for federal office. Since then, Congress has passed several laws to regulate the use of money in presidential and congressional campaigns. Today, these regulations are found in four detailed laws: the Federal Election Campaign Act (FECA) of 1971, the FECA Amendments of 1974 and of 1976, and the Bipartisan Campaign Reform Act of 2002.

The earliest federal laws were loosely drawn, not often obeyed, and almost never enforced. The 1971 law replaced them. The 1974 law was the major legislative response to the Watergate scandal of the Nixon years. The 1976 law was passed in response to a landmark Supreme Court decision, *Buckley* v. *Valeo,* in 1976. The 2002 law attempted to close the "soft-money" loophole in the 1974 and 1976 statutes; it was upheld by the High Court in *McConnell* v. *FEC* in 2003.

---

[14]State funding laws are summarized in *The Book of the States,* an annual publication of the Council of State Governments.

Congress does not have the power to regulate the use of money in State and local elections. Every State now regulates at least some aspects of campaign finance, however—some of them more effectively than others.[14]

The Federal Election Commission

The Federal Election Commission (FEC) administers all federal law dealing with campaign finance. Set up by Congress in 1974, the FEC is an independent agency in the executive branch. Its six members are appointed by the President, with Senate confirmation.

Federal campaign finance laws are both strongly worded and closely detailed. But they are not very well enforced. In large part this is because the FEC has been both underfunded and understaffed. That is to say, members of Congress—who, remember, raise and spend campaign money—have made it practically impossible for the FEC to do an effective job. In short, the FEC finds itself in a situation much like that of the chickens who must guard the fox house.

The laws that the FEC is supposed to enforce cover four broad areas. They (1) require the timely disclosure of campaign finance data, (2) place limits on campaign contributions, (3) place limits on campaign expenditures, and (4) provide public funding for several parts of the presidential election process.

Disclosure Requirements

Congress first required the reporting of certain campaign finance information in 1910. Today, the disclosure requirements are intended to spotlight the place of money in federal campaigns. Those requirements are so detailed that most candidates for federal office now include at least one certified public accountant in their campaign organization.

No individual or group can make a contribution in the name of another. Cash gifts of more than $100 are prohibited. So, too, are contributions from any foreign source.

All contributions to a candidate for federal office must be made through a single campaign committee. Only that committee can spend that candidate's campaign money. All contributions and spending must be closely accounted for by that one committee. Any contribution or loan of more than $200 must be identified by source and by date. Any spending over $200 must also be identified by the name of the person or firm to whom payment was made, by date, and by purpose.

Any contribution of more than $5,000 must be reported to the FEC no later than 48 hours after it is received. So, too, must any sum of $1,000 or more that is received in the last 20 days of a campaign.

Limits on Contributions

Congress first began to regulate campaign contributions in 1907, when it outlawed donations by corporations and national banks. A similar ban was first applied to labor unions in 1943. Individual contributions became subject to regulation in 1939.

Today, no person can give more than $2,100 to any federal candidate in a primary election, and no more than $2,100 to any federal candidate's general election campaign. Also, no person can give more than $5,000 in any year to a political action committee, or $26,700 to a national party committee. The total of any person's contributions to federal candidates and committees now must be limited to no more than $101,400 in an election cycle (the two years from one general election to the next one).

Those limits may seem generous; in fact, they are very tight. Before limits were imposed in 1974, many wealthy individuals gave far larger amounts. In 1972, for example, W. Clement Stone, a Chicago insurance executive, contributed more than $2 million to President Richard Nixon's reelection campaign.

PAC Contributions

Neither corporations nor labor unions can contribute to any candidate running for a federal office. Their political action committees, however, can and do.

Political action committees (PACs) seek to affect the making of public policy and, especially, the outcome of elections in the United States. More than 4,000 PACs are active today, and they are of two distinct types:

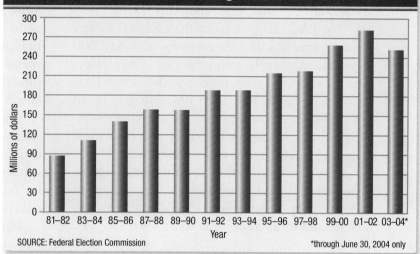

PAC Contributions to Congressional Candidates

SOURCE: Federal Election Commission   *through June 30, 2004 only

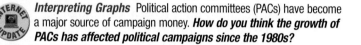

Interpreting Graphs Political action committees (PACs) have become a major source of campaign money. ***How do you think the growth of PACs has affected political campaigns since the 1980s?***

• Most PACs are the political arms of special interest groups—and especially of business associations, labor unions, and professional organizations. These groups are known as "segregated fund committees." They can raise funds *only* from their members—from the employees and stockholders of a corporation, from the members of a labor union, and so on. They *cannot* seek contributions from the general public. Each of these PACs is a part of its parent organization.

Leading examples of these groups include BIPAC (the Business-Industry Political Action Committee) and COPE (the AFL-CIO's Committee on Political Education).

• A few hundred PACs are "unconnected committees." Each of them was established as an independent entity, not as a unit in some larger organization. Many are ideologically based. These PACs can raise money from the public at large. One major example is EMILY's List, which recruits and funds pro-choice women as Democratic candidates. (The group takes its name from this political maxim: Early Money Is Like Yeast, it makes the dough rise.)

PACs fill their war chests with contributions from the members of the PAC's parent organization or with the dollars they raise from the public. PACs "bundle" the money they gather into a single large fund. Then they distribute that money to those candidates who (1) are sympathetic to the PAC's policy goals, and (2) have a reasonable chance of winning their races.

No PAC can give more than $5,000 to any one federal candidate in an election, or $10,000 per election cycle (primary and general election). However, there is no overall limit on PAC giving to candidates. Each PAC can give up to $5,000 per election to each of as many candidates as it chooses. A PAC may also contribute up to $15,000 a year to a political party.

PACs put more than $600 million into the presidential and congressional campaigns in 2004. They funneled untold other millions into State and local contests as well.

Limits on Expenditures

Congress first began to limit federal campaign spending in 1925. Most of the limits now on the books apply only to presidential (not congressional) elections. This fact is due mostly to the Supreme Court's decision in *Buckley* v. *Valeo*, 1976.

In *Buckley*, the High Court struck down several spending limits set by the FECA Amendments of 1974. It held each of those restrictions to be contrary to the 1st Amendment's guarantees of freedom of expression. In effect, said the Court, in politics "money is speech."

The most important of the provisions the Court threw out (1) limited campaign expenditures by candidates running for seats in the House or Senate, (2) limited how much of their own money candidates could put into their own campaigns, and (3) said that no person or group could spend more than $1,000 on behalf of any federal candidate without that candidate's permission.

The Court did recognize one exception to the ban on spending limits. It held that the money spent by those presidential contenders who accept FEC subsidies *can* be regulated. Candidates do not have to take the FEC money; but if they do they must accept spending limits as part of the deal.[15]

---

[15]To this point, only five major party aspirants (three Republicans and two Democrats) have not taken the public money—all five in the preconvention period and two of them twice. The three Republicans: John Connally in 1980, Steve Forbes in 1996 and 2000, and George W. Bush in 2000 and 2004. The Democrats: Howard Dean and John Kerry in 2004. (Mr. Bush did accept FEC funding for his general election campaigns in 2000 and 2004, as did Mr. Kerry in 2004.)

For 2004, those major party contenders who accepted the federal funds could spend no more than $37.3 million in the preconvention period. (President Bush, who did not take the FEC money for that period, was on track to spend more than five times that amount by the time the GOP convention met in New York in late August.)

After the conventions, in the general election campaign, each of the major party nominees could spend no more than $74.6 million. And neither major party's national committee could lay out more than $15 million for its presidential campaign efforts.

Minor party candidates can also qualify for FEC money. Only a few have been able to do so, however—most recently, the Reform Party's nominee, Pat Buchanan in 2000.

Public Funding of Presidential Campaigns

Congress first began to provide for the public funding of presidential campaigns in the Revenue Act of 1971. It broadened sections of that law in 1974 and again in 1976.

The 1971 law set up the Presidential Election Campaign Fund. Every person who files a federal income tax return can "check off" (assign) three dollars of his or her tax payment (six dollars on a joint return) to the fund. The monies in the fund are used every four years to finance (1) preconvention campaigns, (2) national conventions, and (3) presidential election campaigns. The FEC administers the public subsidy process.

1. *Preconvention Campaigns.* Presidential primary and caucus campaigns are supported by the private contributions a candidate raises plus the public money he or she receives from the FEC. To be eligible for public funds, a contender must raise at least $100,000 in contributions from individuals (not organizations). That amount must be gathered in $5,000 lots in each of at least 20 States, with each of those lots built from individual donations of not more than $250. This convoluted requirement is meant to discourage frivolous candidates.

For each presidential hopeful who passes this test, the FEC will match the first $250 of each individual's donation to that candidate, up to a total of half of the overall limit on primary spending. So, in 2004, the FEC could give a contender as much as $18.65 million, because the ceiling was $37.3 million. The FEC does not match contributions from PACs or other political organizations.

For 2004, all the major party presidential hopefuls combined spent nearly $250 million on their preconvention campaigns. This figure included some $28.5 million in matching funds from the FEC.

2. *National Conventions.* If a major party applies for the money, it automatically receives a grant to help pay for its national convention. The FEC paid the Republicans and the Democrats $14.6 million each for that purpose in 2004.

3. *Presidential Election Campaigns.* Every major party nominee automatically qualifies for a public subsidy to cover the costs of the general election campaign. For the 2004 election, that subsidy amounted to $74.6 million. A candidate can refuse that money, of course. Should that ever happen, the candidate would be free to raise however much he or she could from private sources.

So far (from 1976 through 2004), the nominees of both major parties have taken the public money each time. Because they did so, each automatically (1) could spend no more than the amount of the subsidy, and (2) could not accept campaign funds from any other source.

A minor party candidate can also qualify for public funding, but not automatically. To be eligible, the minor party must either (1) have won at least five percent of the popular vote in the last presidential election, or (2) win at least that much of the total vote in the current election.

In the latter case, the public money is received *after* the election and so could not possibly help the candidate in that election. (Remember, many provisions of both federal and State election law are purposely drawn to discourage minor party and independent efforts and thus help strengthen the two-party system.)

Except for Ross Perot in 1996, few minor party candidates have come even remotely close to winning five percent of the popular vote in any election since the subsidy arrangement was put in place. Over that period (1976 through 2004), however, two independent candidates did exceed the five-percent threshold.

John Anderson received 6.7 percent of the popular vote in 1980. He therefore received

Interpreting Political Cartoons *(a) Explain the difference between "hard" and "soft" money. (b) How does the cartoon help make that difference clear?* H-SS 12.6.3

$4.2 million from the FEC after that election. Ross Perot won 19 percent of the vote in 1992. Thus, the FEC ruled that he was eligible to receive $29.2 million from the Presidential Election Campaign Fund to finance his Reform Party candidacy in 1996. Perot won 8 percent of the popular vote in 1996, and so the Reform Party's candidate, Pat Buchanan, qualified for the federal subsidy in 2000.

Hard Money, Soft Money

Nearly 40 years ago, President Lyndon Johnson described the then-current body of federal campaign finance law as "more loophole than law." Over recent years, we have come very close to the point where LBJ's comment could be applied to federal election money statutes today—particularly because of soft money.

For over 30 years now, federal campaign finance laws have placed limits on **hard money**—that is, on money raised and spent to elect candidates for Congress and the White House. But, until 2002, those laws did *not* limit **soft money**—funds given to party organizations for such "party-building activities" as candidate recruitment, voter registration and get-out-the-vote drives, and similar efforts.

Both major parties began to raise soft money (began to exploit the soft-money loophole) in

"I may be awhile. I'm soliciting funds for my reëlection campaign."

Interpreting Political Cartoons *From what sources might this candidate solicit funds?*

the 1980s, and they intensified those efforts in the 1990s. The Republican and Democratic National Committees and their House and Senate campaign committees gathered millions of unregulated dollars from wealthy individuals, labor unions, corporations, and other interest groups. Officially, those funds were raised for party-building purposes, but both parties found it easy to filter them into their presidential and congressional campaigns.

The torrent of money rushing through the soft-money loophole rose from about $19 million in 1980 to more than $260 million by 1996 and to some $500 million in 2000. Look again at the figures on page 196 and at those in

the table on page 197. Those huge numbers, fueled in no small part by soft money, have convinced a great many people that the nation's campaign finance laws are in serious need of reform. As a step in that direction, Congress—after years of debate and delay—finally enacted the Bipartisan Campaign Reform Act (the BCRA) of 2002.

The new measure became law largely because of years of unremitting effort by its chief sponsors: Senators John McCain (R., Arizona) and Russ Feingold (D., Wisconsin) and Representatives Christopher Shays (R., Connecticut) and Martin Meehan (D., Massachusetts).

The BCRA's major provisions are aimed at the soft-money problem. They ban soft-money contributions to political parties. But the law does not say that other political groups cannot raise and spend those dollars. Almost immediately, a number of independent groups—groups with no formal ties to any party—emerged to do just that. In short, creative minds in both major parties found a way to skirt the ban on soft money. Some $200 million poured through that loophole in 2004.

The most prominent of those groups in the last presidential election included America Coming Together, MoveOn.org, and the Media Fund; all three supported John Kerry and other Democrats. The Program for America Voters Fund was the most visible independent group backing President Bush and other Republicans.

Section 3 Assessment

Key Terms and Main Ideas

1. What are **political action committees (PACs)**?
2. **(a)** What is a **subsidy**? **(b)** At what level in the election process are campaign subsidies most important?
3. How did **soft money** create a loophole in federal election-finance law?
4. How do soft money and **hard money** differ?

Critical Thinking

5. **Distinguishing Fact From Opinion** Explain why you agree or disagree with this statement: "Democracy would be best served if campaigns were entirely supported by the small contributions of millions of American voters."

Standards Monitoring *Online*
For: Self-quiz with vocabulary practice
Web Code: mqa-2073

6. **Drawing Conclusions** How might the electoral process be changed if there were no limits on campaign spending?

Go Online
PHSchool.com

For: An activity on funding political campaigns
Web Code: mqd-2073

Can States Limit Campaign Contributions?

Campaign finance laws attempt to prevent wealthy individuals and organizations from exercising undue influence in elections and on public officeholders. However, in Buckley v. Valeo, *1976, the Supreme Court struck down several limits on campaign contributions as violations of the 1st Amendment's guarantee of freedom of speech. Does that decision mean that States cannot limit campaign contributions?*

Analysis Skills HR4, HI3, HI4

Nixon v. Shrink Missouri Government PAC (2000)

In 1994, Missouri passed a law limiting the amount of money that individuals and organizations could give to political candidates. The specific limits depended on the particular office and were changed periodically to reflect changes in the cost of living. The Shrink Missouri Government Political Action Committee and Zev David Fredman, a candidate for State office, filed suit against Jeremiah J. Nixon, the Missouri attorney general, charging that the contribution limits violated their 1st Amendment rights. Shrink Missouri stated that it would have given more money to Fredman if the law had not prevented it, and Fredman argued that he could not campaign effectively without larger contributions.

The federal district court upheld the law. It held that the law supported the government's aim of increasing citizens' trust in government by reducing public fears that wealthy campaign donors had too much influence over government. The court of appeals reversed that decision, finding in part that the State legislature had not proven that large campaign contributions had caused actual corruption. Nixon then sought review by the Supreme Court.

Arguments for Nixon

1. The State has a legitimate interest in preventing corruption and the appearance of corruption that large campaign contributions can create.
2. The contribution limits imposed by Missouri were not unreasonably low. They did not prevent candidates from raising enough money to run effective campaigns.

3. Money is property; it is not speech. The "right" to contribute money is not entitled to the same high level of protection as is freedom of speech.

Arguments for Shrink Missouri

1. Missouri did not present actual evidence showing that large campaign contributions were creating corruption or even the appearance of corruption. Without such evidence, the abstract concern about the effect of large contributions does not justify restricting citizens' right to contribute.
2. Limits on campaign contributions make it more difficult for outside candidates who do not have the support of the media and of established political interests to conduct effective campaigns.
3. Campaign contributions are entitled to strong 1st Amendment protection, not because they themselves are speech but because they enable donors to promote the speech of candidates who share their views.

Decide for Yourself

1. Review the constitutional grounds on which each side based its arguments and the specific arguments each side presented.
2. Debate the opposing viewpoints presented in this case. Which viewpoint do you favor?
3. Predict the impact of the Court's decision on ways in which States may seek to regulate campaign financing in the future. (To read a summary of the Court's decision, turn to pages 799–806.)

Go Online PHSchool.com Use Web Code mqp-2076 to register your vote on this issue and to see how other students voted.

Political Dictionary

nomination (p. 178), **general election** (p. 179), **cau-cus** (p. 180), **direct primary** (p. 182), **closed prima-ry** (p. 182), **open primary** (p. 183), **blanket primary** (p. 183), **runoff primary** (p. 184), **nonpartisan elec-tion** (p. 184), **absentee voting** (p. 189), **coattail effect** (p. 190), **precinct** (p. 190), **polling place** (p. 190), **ballot** (p. 190), **political action committee (PAC)** (p. 197), **subsidy** (p. 197), **soft money** (p. 201), **hard money** (p. 202)

Standards Review

H-SS 12.2.4 Understand the obligations of civic-mindedness, including voting, being informed on civic issues, volunteering and performing public service, and serving in the military or alternative ser-vice.

H-SS 12.3.1 Explain how civil society provides opportunities for individuals to associate for social, cultural, religious, economic, and political purposes.

H-SS 12.6.1 Analyze the origin, development, and role of political parties, noting those occasional periods in which there was only one major party or were more than two major parties.

H-SS 12.6.2 Discuss the history of the nomination process for presidential candidates and the increasing importance of primaries in general elections.

H-SS 12.6.3 Evaluate the roles of polls, campaign advertising, and the controversies over campaign funding.

H-SS 12.6.4 Describe the means that citizens use to participate in the political process (e.g., vot-ing, campaigning, lobbying, filing a legal challenge, demonstrating, petitioning, picketing, running for political office).

Practicing the Vocabulary

Matching *Choose a term from the list above that best matches each description.*

1. A group of like-minded people who meet to choose candidates for office
2. The political arm of a special-interest group
3. An election held within a political party at which the voters choose candidates who will appear on the ballot in an upcoming general election
4. The place where voters go to cast their ballots
5. The device by which voters register their choices in an election

Fill in the Blank *Choose a term from the list above that best completes the sentence.*

6. In a _____, voters must choose between the two top finishers in an earlier primary election.
7. Because of the _____, candidates can benefit from the popularity of another candidate on the ballot from their party.
8. _____ is given to State and local party organizations for "party-building activities."
9. One commonly heard criticism of the _____ is that it encourages "raiding."
10. Each _____ has one polling place.

Reviewing Main Ideas

Section 1

11. You have read that the nominating process has "a very real impact on the exercise of the right to vote." Explain this state-ment in your own words.
12. What are the five broad categories that describe the way in which nominations are made?
13. How has the nominating process in American politics changed over time?
14. At which level is the convention still a major nominating device in American politics?
15. Describe the differences between the open and the closed pri-mary.

Section 2

16. What is the overall purpose and importance of election law in the American political process?
17. To what extent are the States involved in regulating the electoral process?
18. (a) To what extent is the Federal Government involved in the regulation of elections? (b) Give at least three examples of fed-eral laws that regulate elections.

19. (a) Describe the basic difference between the office-group ballot and the party-column ballot. (b) What are the advantages of each?
20. Why did Congress force the States to abandon the use of punch-card ballots?

Section 3

21. Briefly describe the role and importance of money in the election process.
22. (a) Identify five types of private donors to political campaigns. (b) Why might these individuals and groups wish to contribute money to candidates?
23. Outline the limitations placed on individual and PAC contributions to federal candidates and political parties.
24. (a) How does a presidential contender qualify for public funding in the pre-convention period? (b) Has any aspirant ever declined public money in the pre-convention period? If so, who?
25. What was the major purpose of the Bipartisan Campaign Reform Act of 2002?

Critical Thinking Skills

Analysis Skills HR4, HI1

26. *Face the Issues* Research the success of electronic voting in the 2004 Presidential election. Does the experience of this election strengthen or weaken the argument for electronic voting?

27. *Drawing Conclusions* Use what you have read in this chapter to make an argument for or against the following statement: *In some circumstances, the nomination of candidates is a more meaningful step in the electoral process than is the general election period.*

28. *Expressing Problems Clearly* Which offices in your State, city, and county are now filled by popular vote? Do you think that any of those posts should be filled instead by appointment? If so, which one(s) and why? If not, why not?

29. *Identifying Alternatives* What are the different types of primaries that a State may decide to use? What are the advantages and disadvantages of each type?

Analyzing Political Cartoons

Using your knowledge of American government and this cartoon, answer the questions below.

30. **(a)** Who are the characters in the cartoon? **(b)** Why are two of them covered in mud?

31. What can be the effect of a divisive primary on a political party?

★ You Can Make a Difference

Create an unbiased information sheet on political candidates. Obtain a list of candidates in a forthcoming local or State election—for example, people running for the State legislature. Start with a brief biography of each candidate. Include the person's personal and political history, stands he or she has taken on issues, and other relevant information. Use the back files of local newspapers as well as the Internet, the library, and other sources. Write your findings as a voters' guide.

Participation Activities

Analysis Skills CS4, HR4

32. *Current Events Watch* Keep track of stories in the news about money spent on election campaigns and about campaign finance reform. Then use what you have learned to write an essay explaining why you would favor or oppose legislation that limits the amount of money candidates can spend on campaigns.

33. *Chart Activity* Create a chart or calendar for the current election cycle in your State. The calendar should list the date of the next primary and general election, candidate filing deadlines, voter registration deadlines, and any other important dates. (Since in most States the secretary of state administers the election laws, that office is a good source for election information.)

34. *It's Your Turn* Write an editorial in which you probe this comment by Mark Hanna: "There are two things that are important in politics. The first is money, and I can't remember what the second one is." Find out who Mark Hanna was and include this information in your editorial. Do you think that he was expressing a cynical view or, instead, was trying to emphasize a point? **(Writing an Editorial)**

Standards Monitoring *Online*

For: Chapter 7 Self-Test **Visit:** PHSchool.com
Web Code: mqa-2074

As a final review, take the Magruder's Chapter 7 Self-Test and receive immediate feedback on your answers. The test consists of 20 multiple-choice questions designed to test your understanding of the chapter content.

CHAPTER 8

Mass Media and Public Opinion

"The hand that rules the press, the radio, the screen, and the far-spread magazine rules the country."

—Judge Learned Hand (1942)

Since Judge Hand made this observation, new types of media have emerged, but the power of the media remains strong. The media, along with influences such as family and education, help shape our opinions about politics and many other aspects of our lives.

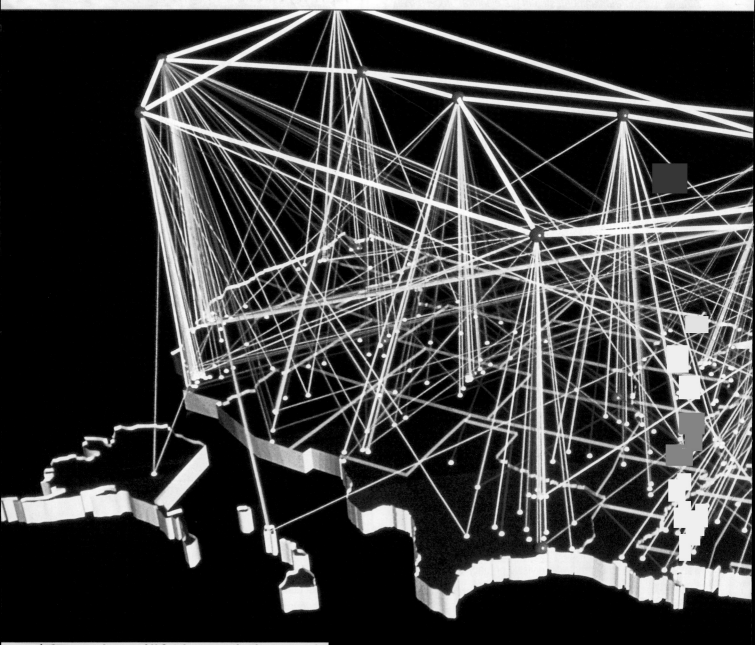

◆ **Computer image of U.S. telecommunications network**

Go Online
PHSchool.com

For: Current Data
Web Code: mqg-2085

For: Close Up Foundation debates
Web Code: mqh-2087

SECTION 1

The Formation of Public Opinion (pp. 208–213)

★ Public opinion refers to the attitudes of a significant number of people on matters of government and politics.

★ Family and education are two of the most important factors in shaping public opinion.

★ Additional factors that shape public opinion include peer groups, opinion leaders, historic events, and mass media.

SECTION 2

Measuring Public Opinion
(pp. 215–221)

★ Public opinion can be determined to some extent through elections, interest groups, the media, and personal contacts.

★ The best way to measure public opinion is through opinion polls.

★ The complex process of scientific polling results in the most reliable poll data.

★ Although it is important to measure public opinion, public opinion is only one of many factors that shape public policy.

SECTION 3

The Mass Media (pp. 223–230)

★ The American public gets information on public issues through several forms of mass media, especially through television.

★ The media influence American politics by helping to set the public agenda and by playing a central role in electoral politics.

★ The influence of the media is limited, in part because many people use mass media as sources of entertainment rather than information.

The Formation of Public Opinion

OBJECTIVES

1. **Examine** the term *public opinion* and understand why it is difficult to define.
2. **Analyze** how family and education shape public opinion.
3. **Describe** four additional factors that shape public opinion.

WHY IT MATTERS

You no doubt have opinions on a variety of issues, from school prayer to which political party should be in power. Several factors help shape your opinions. The two most important factors are family and education.

POLITICAL DICTIONARY

★ **public affairs**
★ **public opinion**
★ **mass media**
★ **peer group**
★ **opinion leader**

Do you like broccoli? Blue fingernail polish? Hard rock? What about sports? Old cars? Country music?

You almost certainly have an opinion on each of those things. On some of them, you may hold strong opinions, and those opinions may be very important to you. Still, each of those opinions is your own view, your *private* opinion. None of them qualifies as *public* opinion.

What Is Public Opinion?

Few terms in American politics are more widely used, and less well understood, than the term *public opinion*. It appears regularly in newspapers and magazines, and you hear it frequently on radio and television.

Quite often, the phrase is used to suggest that all or most of the American people hold the same view on some public issue, such as global warming or deficit spending. Thus, time and again, politicians say that "the people" want such and such, television commentators tell us that "the public" favors this or opposes that, and so on.

In fact, there are very few matters about which all or nearly all of "the people" think alike. "The public" holds many different and often conflicting views on nearly every public issue.

To understand what public opinion is, you must recognize this important point: Public opinion is a complex collection of the opinions of many different people. It is the sum of all of their views. It is *not* the single and undivided view of some mass mind.

Different Publics

Many publics exist in the United States—in fact, too many to be counted. Each public is made up of all those individuals who hold the same view on some particular public issue. Each group of people with a differing point of view is a separate public with regard to that issue.

For example, the people who think that Congress should establish a national health insurance program belong to the public that holds that view. People who believe that the President is doing an excellent job as chief executive, or that capital punishment should be abolished, or that prayers should be permitted in the public schools are members of separate publics with those particular opinions. Clearly, many people belong to more than one of those publics; but almost certainly only a very few belong to all four of them.

Notice this important point: Not many issues capture the attention of all—or even nearly all—Americans. In fact, those that do are few and far between. Instead, most public issues attract the interest of *some* people (and sometimes millions of them), but those same issues are of little or no interest to many (and sometimes millions of) other people.

This point is crucial, too: In its proper sense, public opinion includes only those views that relate to **public affairs**. Public affairs include politics, public issues, and the making of public policies—those events and issues that concern the people at large. To be a public opinion, a view must involve something of general concern

The Political Spectrum

LEFT ◄――――――――――――――――――――――――――――――― **CENTER** ――――――――――――――――――――――――――――――――► **RIGHT**

Radical	**Liberal**	**Moderate**	**Conservative**	**Reactionary**
Favors extreme change to create an altered or entirely new social system.	Believes that government must take action to change economic, political, and ideological policies thought to be unfair.	Holds beliefs that fall between liberal and conservative views, usually including some of both.	Seeks to keep in place the economic, political, and social structures of society.	Favors extreme change to restore society to an earlier, more conservative state.

Interpreting Diagrams People who have similar opinions on political issues are generally grouped according to whether they are "left," "right," or "center" on the political spectrum. The general range, or spectrum, of political opinions is shown here. *(a) How might a liberal and a conservative differ on an issue such as expanding social welfare programs? (b) Where do your views fall on the political spectrum?*

and of interest to a significant portion of the people as a whole.

Of course, the American people as a whole are interested in many things—rock groups and symphony orchestras, the New York Yankees and the Dallas Cowboys, candy bars and green vegetables, and a great deal more. Many people have opinions on each of these things, views that are sometimes loosely called "public opinion." But, again, in its proper sense, public opinion involves only those views that people hold on such things as parties and candidates, taxes, unemployment, welfare programs, national defense, foreign policy, and so on.

Definition

Clearly, public opinion is so complex that it cannot be readily defined. From what has been said about it to this point, however, **public opinion** can be described this way: those attitudes held by a significant number of people on matters of government and politics.

As we have suggested, you can better understand the term in the plural—that is, as public opinions, the opinions of different publics. Or, to put it another way, public opinion is made up of expressed group attitudes.

A view must be expressed in order to be an opinion in the public sense. Otherwise, it cannot be identified with any public. That expression need not be oral (spoken). It can take any number of other forms, as well: a protest demonstration, a film, a billboard, a vote for or against a candidate, and so on. The essential point is that a person's private thoughts on an issue enter the stream of

public opinion only when those thoughts are expressed publicly.

Family and Education

No one is born with a set of attitudes about government and politics. Instead, each of us learns our political opinions, and we do so in a lifelong "classroom" and from many different "teachers." In other words, public opinion is formed out of a very complex process. The factors involved in it are almost infinite.

You have already considered much of this in Chapter 6. In effect, that detailed look at why people vote as they do amounted to an extensive look at how public opinion is formed.

"Harold, would you say you are left of center, right of center, center, left of left, right of left, left of right, or right of right, or what?"

Interpreting Political Cartoons **What does the cartoon suggest about the political spectrum?**

In Chapter 6, remember, we described the process by which each person acquires political opinions—the process of political socialization. That complex process begins in early childhood and continues through a person's lifetime. It involves all of the experiences and relationships that lead us to see the political world and to act in it as we do.[1]

There are many different agents of political socialization at work in the opinion-shaping process. Again, you looked at these agents in Chapter 6: age, race, income, occupation, residence, group affiliations, and many others. Here, look again at two of them, the family and education. These have such a vital impact that they deserve another and slightly different discussion here.

The Family

Most parents do not think of themselves as agents of political socialization, nor do the other

members of most families. Parents and other family members are, nonetheless, very important factors in this process.

Children first see the political world from within the family and through the family's eyes. They begin to learn about politics much as they begin to learn about most other things. Children learn from what their parents have to say, from the stories that their older brothers and sisters bring home from school, from watching television with the family, and so on.

Most of what smaller children learn in the family setting are not really political opinions. Clearly, toddlers are not concerned with the wisdom of spending billions of dollars on an anti-missile defense system or the pros and cons of the monetary policies of the Federal Reserve Board.

Young children do pick up some fundamental attitudes, however. With those attitudes, they acquire a basic slant toward such things as authority and rules of behavior, property, neighbors, people of other racial or religious groups, and the like. In short, children lay some important foundations on which they will later build their political opinions.

---

[1]The concept of socialization comes from the fields of sociology and psychology. There, it is used to describe all of the ways in which a society transforms individuals into members of that society. To put this another way: Socialization is the multi-sided, lifelong process in which people come to know, accept, and follow the beliefs and practices of their society. *Political socialization* is a part of that much broader process.

▲ Family and education are the primary factors that shape one's values and opinions. These photos show a preschooler, whose opinions are largely shaped by family (left); school-age children practicing American values by reciting the Pledge of Allegiance (center); and a young adult putting her values to work through community service (right). *Critical Thinking How have your family and education shaped your own opinions and values?* H-SS 12.3.1

A large number of scholarly studies report what common sense also suggests. The strong influence the family has on the development of political opinions is largely a result of the near monopoly the family has on the child in his or her earliest, most impressionable years. Those studies also show that

PRIMARY Sources *"Children tend to absorb the political views of parents and other caregivers, perhaps without realizing it. . . . Children raised in households in which the primary caregivers are Democrats tend to become Democrats themselves, whereas children raised in homes where their caregivers are Republican tend to favor the GOP."*
—Benjamin Ginsberg, Theodore Lowi, and Margaret Weir, *We the People*

The Schools

The start of formal schooling marks the initial break in the influence of the family. For the first time, children become regularly involved in activities outside the home.

From the first day, schools teach children the values of the American political system. They work to indoctrinate the young, to instill in them loyalty to a particular cause or idea. In fact, training students to become good citizens is an important part of our educational system.

Schoolchildren salute the flag, recite the Pledge of Allegiance, and sing patriotic songs. They learn about George Washington, Abraham Lincoln, Susan B. Anthony, Martin Luther King, Jr., and other great Americans. From the early grades on, they pick up growing amounts of specific political knowledge, and they begin to form political opinions. In high school, they are often required to take a course in American government and even to read books such as this one.

School involves much more than books and classes, of course. It is a complex bundle of experiences and a place where a good deal of informal learning occurs—about the similarities and differences among individuals and groups, about the various ways in which decisions can be made, and about the process of compromise that must often occur in order for ideas to move forward.

Once again, the family and education are *not* the only forces at work in the process by which opinions are formed. A number of other influences are part of the mix. These two factors are singled out here to underscore their leading roles in that process.

Other Factors

No factor, by itself, shapes a person's opinion on any single issue. Some factors do play a larger role than others, however. Thus, in addition to family and education, occupation and race are usually much more significant than, say, gender or place of residence.

For example, on the question of national health insurance, the particular job a person has—how well-paying it is, whether its benefits include coverage by a private health-insurance plan, and so on—will almost certainly have a greater impact on that person's views than his or her gender or place of residence. On the other hand, the relative weight of each factor that influences public opinion also depends on the issue in question. If the issue involves, say, equal pay for women or the restoration of Lake Michigan, then gender or where one lives will almost certainly loom larger in the opinion-making mix.

Besides family, education, and such factors as occupation and race, four other factors have a major place in the opinion-making process. They are the mass media, peer groups, opinion leaders, and historic events.

Mass Media

The **mass media** include those means of communication that reach large, widely dispersed audiences (masses of people) simultaneously. No one needs to be told that the mass media, including newspapers, magazines, radio, the Internet, and in particular television, have a huge effect on the formation of public opinion.

Take this as but one indication of that fact: The Census Bureau reports that there is at least one television set in 98 percent of the nation's 110 million households. There are two or more sets in more than 40 million homes and millions more in many other places. Most of those sets are turned on for at least seven hours a day, for a mind-boggling total of more than a billion hours a day.

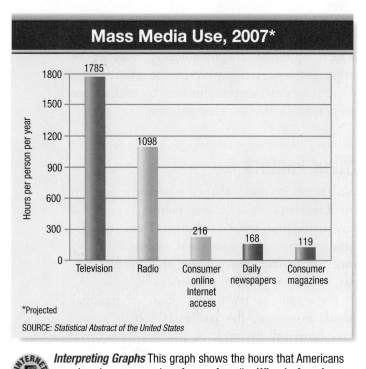

Mass Media Use, 2007*

Hours per person per year

- Television: 1785
- Radio: 1098
- Consumer online Internet access: 216
- Daily newspapers: 168
- Consumer magazines: 119

*Projected

SOURCE: *Statistical Abstract of the United States*

Interpreting Graphs This graph shows the hours that Americans spend each year on various forms of media. *Why do Americans spend more time watching television than on other forms of media?* H-SS 12.8.2

The chart above shows how much time Americans spend on various types of mass media. You will take a longer look at the influence of the mass media later in this chapter.

Peer Groups

Peer groups are made up of the people with whom one regularly associates, including friends, classmates, neighbors, and co-workers. When a child enters school, friends and classmates become an important factor in shaping his or her attitudes and behavior. The influence of peer groups continues on through adulthood.

Belonging to a peer group usually reinforces what a person has already come to believe. One obvious reason for this is that most people trust the views of their friends. Another is that the members of a peer group have shared many of the same socializing experiences, and so tend to think along the same lines.

To put this observation another way, contradictory or other unsettling opinions are not often heard within a peer group. Most people want to be liked by their friends and associates. As a result, they are usually reluctant to stray too far from what their peers think and how their peers behave.

Opinion Leaders

The views expressed by **opinion leaders** also bear heavily on public opinion. An opinion leader is any person who, for any reason, has an unusually strong influence on the views of others. These opinion shapers are a distinct minority in the total population, of course, but they are found everywhere.

Many opinion leaders hold public office. Some write for newspapers or magazines, or broadcast their opinions on radio or television. Others are prominent in business, labor, agriculture, and civic organizations. Many are professionals—doctors, lawyers, teachers, ministers, and rabbis—and have contact with large numbers of people on a regular basis. Many others are active members of their neighborhood or church, or have leadership roles in their local communities.

Whoever they may be—the President of the United States, a network television commentator, the governor, the head of a local citizens committee, or even a local talk-show host—these opinion leaders are people to whom others listen and from whom others draw ideas and convictions. Whatever their political, economic, or social standing or outlook may be, opinion leaders play a significant role in the formation of public opinion.

Historic Events

Historic events can have a major impact on the views of large numbers of people—and so have a major impact on the content and direction of public policy. Our history affords many examples of this point, not the least of them the Great Depression. This period began in 1929 and lasted for the better part of a decade.

The Depression was a shattering national experience. Almost overnight, need and poverty became massive national problems. Millions of Americans—one out of every four in the labor force—lost their jobs. Millions more were impoverished. Hunger and despair stalked the land. In 1929, some two million people were unemployed in the United States. By just four years later, that number had climbed to 13.5 million. In 1935, some 18 million men, women, and children were wholly dependent on public emergency relief programs. Some 10 million workers had no employment other than that provided by temporary public projects.

All of this changed the way millions of people viewed the proper place of government in the United States. The Depression persuaded a large majority of Americans to support a much larger role for government—and, in particular, for the National Government—in the nation's economic and social life.

The Great Depression also prompted a majority of Americans to shift their political loyalties from the Republican to the Democratic Party. As you know, the Republicans had dominated the national political scene from Abraham Lincoln's election in 1860 to the onset of the Depression. That situation changed quite abruptly, however, when Franklin D. Roosevelt's landslide victory in 1932 began nearly 40 years of Democratic domination.

The turbulent politics of the 1960s and early 1970s furnish another example of the way in which significant occurrences can impact and shape opinions. The American people had emerged from World War II and the prosperity of the 1950s with a largely optimistic view of the future

▲ During the Great Depression, millions of Americans were out of work.

and of the United States' place in the world. That rose-colored outlook was reflected in a generally favorable, even respectful, attitude toward government in this country.

The 1960s and early 1970s changed all that. Those years were highlighted by a number of traumatic events. Of special note were the assassinations of President John Kennedy in 1963 and of the Reverend Martin Luther King, Jr., and Senator Robert Kennedy in 1968. This period also included the civil rights movement and the Vietnam War, with all of the protests, violence, and strong emotions that accompanied both of those chapters in this nation's life. The era ended with the Watergate Scandal and the near-impeachment and subsequent resignation of President Richard Nixon in 1974.

Those years of turmoil and divisiveness produced a dramatic decline in the American people's estimate of their government—and most especially their evaluation of its trustworthiness. Evidences of that decline are still apparent in the United States of today.

Section 1 Assessment

Key Terms and Main Ideas

1. What is **public opinion,** and what factors shape it?
2. Give three examples of an **opinion leader.**
3. Describe the political socialization of a young child.
4. **(a)** What are the **mass media? (b)** What evidence can you give that the mass media influence public opinion?

Critical Thinking

5. **Drawing Conclusions** Is it likely that interaction with one's peer group would prompt one to switch his or her allegiance from one major party to the other? Why or why not?

6. **Synthesizing Information** Why is it so difficult to define public opinion?

The Latino Media Story

Analysis Skills HR4, HI3

With the rise in the Latino population of the United States, the demand for Spanish-language newspapers, radio, and other media has grown. In this article from **The Christian Science Monitor,** *staff writer Kim Campbell reports on how Latino media are scrambling to meet the new demand.*

Martin Berlanga, of Spanish-language network Univisión, prepares for a live shot in Austin, Texas.

Rural Georgia is not the place you'd expect to find a boom in Spanish-language media. But Dalton, a small town in the north, is now home to three Spanish-language newspapers and a Spanish-language pop radio station.

Hispanic media have grown in the past decade—newspapers alone have increased 55 percent—and with the news . . . from the [2000] census that Hispanics are the largest U.S. minority, more attention is being paid to how to reach this group that has a purchasing power of more than $490 billion a year. . . .

With the demand for more media has come a need for bilingual journalists. Some are being wooed away from mainstream media by Spanish-language publications and networks. Those who do the hiring say it can be tough to find staff who can speak and write well in both languages. Some Latinos, for example, don't speak Spanish; others have strong Spanish skills but can't do interviews in English or translate written reports.

Those who do cross over say there are advantages to working in Spanish-language media, including the opportunity to advance into management, to work with colleagues who understand the needs of the Hispanic community, and to practice advocacy-based journalism in which the target audience is clear. "There is this sense that you are really doing something to help the community," says Angelo Figueroa, editor of the monthly *People*

en Español. . . .

Spanish-language media often take a different approach from mainstream outlets—focusing, not surprisingly, on issues of importance to their audience. . . . In Miami, *The Miami Herald* and its Spanish-language sister paper, *El Nuevo Herald,* often take different approaches to the same issue. . . . "People pick up *El Nuevo Herald* not only because it's in Spanish, but because it speaks to them," says Barbara Gutiérrez, a reader representative for both papers, who points out that *El Nuevo Herald* has shorter articles and is more opinionated. "It's just a different kind of style, and closer, I think, to what many Hispanics are used to."

The census took some people by surprise, but Ms. Gutiérrez says she and her colleagues could see what was coming. She looks forward to what happens next: "The next 10 years are going to be very exciting."

Analyzing Primary Sources

1. Why is the growth of the U.S. Latino population an important consideration to the media?
2. How might the rise in the Latino population affect the formation of public opinion?
3. If you were planning on a career in the media, how might the information in this article affect you?

2 Measuring Public Opinion

Section Preview

OBJECTIVES

1. **Describe** the challenges involved in measuring public opinion.
2. **Explain** why scientific opinion polls are the best measure of public opinion.
3. **Identify** five steps in the polling process.
4. **Understand** the challenges of evaluating polls.
5. **Recognize** the limits on the impact of public opinion in a democracy.

WHY IT MATTERS

Have you ever responded to a poll? Taken a poll yourself? Scientific polls are the most effective means for measuring public opinion. Other measures include election returns, the activities of interest groups, and direct personal contact.

POLITICAL DICTIONARY

- **mandate**
- **interest group**
- **public opinion poll**
- **straw vote**
- **sample**
- **random sample**
- **quota sample**

How many times have you heard this phrase: "According to a recent poll . . ."? Probably more than you can count, especially in the months leading up to an important election. Polls are one of the most common means of gauging public opinion.

If public policy is to reflect public opinion, one needs to be able to find the answers to these questions: What are people's opinions on a particular issue? How many people share a given view on that issue? How firmly do they hold that view? In other words, there must be a way to "measure" public opinion.

Measuring Public Opinion

The general shape of public opinion on an issue can be found through a variety of means. These include voting; lobbying; books; pamphlets; magazine and newspaper articles; editorial comments in the press and on radio, television, and the Internet; paid advertising; letters to editors and public officials, and so on.

These and other means of expression are the devices through which the general direction of public opinion becomes known. Usually though, the means by which a view is expressed tells little—and often nothing reliable—about the size of the group that holds that opinion or how strongly it is held. In the American political system, this information is vital. To find it, some effort must be made to measure public

opinion. Elections, interest groups, the media, and personal contacts with the public all—at least to some degree—provide the means of measurement.

Elections

In a democracy, the voice of the people is supposed to express itself through the ballot box. Election results are thus very often said to be indicators of public opinion. The votes cast for the various candidates are regularly taken as evidence of the people's approval or rejection of the stands taken by those candidates and their parties.

▲ The AIDS Memorial Quilt is a unique expression of public opinion. Here the quilt is laid out in front of the Washington Monument.

▲ Senator Barbara Boxer (D.,California) discusses high gasoline prices in Los Angeles. *Critical Thinking What kinds of information can officials learn from meeting directly with the public?*

As a result, a party and its victorious candidates regularly claim to have received a **mandate** to carry out their campaign promises. In American politics a mandate refers to the instructions or commands a constituency gives to its elected officials.[2]

In reality, however, election results are seldom an accurate measure of public opinion. Voters make choices in elections for any of several reasons, as you have seen. Very often, those choices have little or nothing to do with the candidates' stands on public questions. And, as you know, candidates often disagree with some of the planks of their party's platform. In addition, candidates and parties often express their positions in broad, generalized terms.

In short, much of what you have read about voting behavior, and about the nature of parties, adds up to this: Elections are, at best, only useful indicators of public opinion. To call the typical election a mandate for much of anything other than a general direction in public policy is to be on very shaky ground.

Interest Groups

Interest groups are private organizations whose members share certain views and objectives and work to shape the making and the content of public policy. These organizations are also very aptly known as pressure groups and special-interest groups.

---

[2]The term *mandate* comes from the Latin *mandatum,* meaning a command.

Interest groups are a chief means by which public opinion is made known. They present their views (exert their pressures) through their lobbyists, by letters and telephone calls, in political campaigns, and by a number of other methods. In dealing with them, however, public officials often have difficulty determining two things: How many people does an interest group really represent? And just how strongly do those people hold the views that an organization says they hold?

The Media

Earlier you read some very impressive numbers about television. Those huge numbers help describe the place of the media in the opinion process; you will read more of those numbers later. Here, recognize this point: The media are also a gauge for assessing public opinion.

The media are frequently described as "mirrors" as well as "molders" of opinion. It is often said that the views expressed in newspaper editorials, syndicated columns, news magazines, television commentaries, and blogs are fairly good indicators of public opinion. In fact, however, the media are not very accurate mirrors of public opinion, often reflecting only the views of a vocal minority.

Personal Contacts

Most public officials have frequent and wide-ranging contacts in many different forms with large numbers of people. In each of these contacts, they try to read the public's mind. Indeed, their jobs demand that they do so.

Members of Congress receive bags of mail and hundreds of phone calls and e-mails everyday. Many of them make frequent trips "to keep in touch with the folks back home." Top administration figures are often on the road, too, selling the President's programs and gauging the people's reactions. Even the President does some of this, with speaking trips to different parts of the country.

Governors, State legislators, mayors, and other officials also have any number of contacts with the public. These officials encounter the public in their offices, in public meetings, at social gatherings, and even at ball games.

Can public officials find "the voice of the people" in all of those contacts? Many can and do, and often with surprising accuracy. But some public officials cannot. They fall into an ever-present trap: They find only what they want to find, only those views that support and agree with their own.

Polls—The Best Measure

Public opinion is best measured by **public opinion polls,** devices that attempt to collect information by asking people questions.[3] The more accurate polls are based on scientific polling techniques.

Straw Votes

Public opinion polls have existed in this country for more than a century. Until the 1930s, however, they were far from scientific. Most earlier polling efforts were of the **straw vote** variety. That is, they were polls that sought to read the public's mind simply by asking the same question of a large number of people. Straw votes are still fairly common. Many radio talk show hosts pose questions that listeners can respond to by telephone, and television personalities regularly invite responses by e-mail.

The straw-vote technique is highly unreliable, however. It rests on the false assumption that a relatively large number of responses will provide a fairly accurate picture of the public's views on a given question. The problem is this: Nothing in the process ensures that those who respond will represent a reasonably accurate cross section of the total population. The straw vote emphasizes the quantity rather than the quality of the sample to which its question is posed.

The most famous of all straw-polling mishaps took place in 1936. A periodical called the *Literary Digest* mailed postcard ballots to more than 10 million people and received answers from more than 2,376,000 of them. Based on that huge return, the magazine confidently predicted the outcome of the presidential election that year. It said that Governor Alfred Landon, the Republican nominee, would easily defeat incumbent Franklin Roosevelt. Instead, Roosevelt won in a landslide. He captured more than 60 percent of the popular vote and carried every State but Maine and Vermont.

The *Digest* had drawn its sample on an altogether faulty basis: from automobile registration lists and telephone directories. The *Digest* had failed to consider that in the mid-Depression year of 1936, millions of people could not afford to own cars or have private telephones.

The *Digest* poll failed to reach most of the vast pool of the poor and unemployed, millions of blue-collar workers, and most of the ethnic minorities in the country. Those were the very segments of the population from which Roosevelt and the Democrats drew their greatest support. The magazine had predicted the winner of each of the three previous presidential elections, but its failure to do so in 1936 was so colossal that it ceased publication not long thereafter.

Scientific Polling

Serious efforts to take the public's pulse on a scientific basis date from the mid-1930s. Attempts began with the work of such early pollsters as George Gallup and Elmo Roper. The techniques that they and others have developed since then have reached a highly sophisticated level.

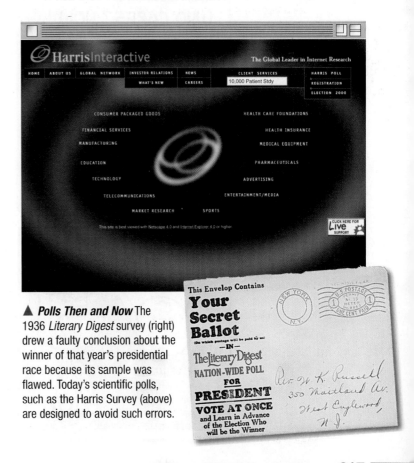

▲ **Polls Then and Now** The 1936 *Literary Digest* survey (right) drew a faulty conclusion about the winner of that year's presidential race because its sample was flawed. Today's scientific polls, such as the Harris Survey (above) are designed to avoid such errors.

---

[3] *Poll* comes from the old Teutonic word *polle,* meaning the top or crown of the head, the part that shows when heads are counted.

Interpreting Political Cartoons (a) According to the cartoon, how seriously should we view the answers to opinion polls? (b) Does the text agree or disagree with this assessment?
H-SS 12.6.3

There are now more than 1,000 national and regional polling organizations in this country. Many of them do mostly commercial work. That is, they tap the public's preferences on everything from toothpastes and headache remedies to television shows and thousands of other things. However, at least 200 of these polling organizations also poll the political preferences of the American people. Among the best known of the national pollsters today are the Gallup Organization (the Gallup Poll) and Louis Harris and Associates (the Harris Survey).

The Polling Process

Scientific poll-taking is an extremely complex process that can best be described in five basic steps. In their efforts to discover and report public opinion, pollsters must (1) define the universe to be surveyed; (2) construct a sample; (3) prepare valid questions; (4) select and control how the poll will be taken; and (5) analyze and report their findings to the public.

Defining the Universe

The *universe* is a term that means the whole population that the poll aims to measure. It is the group whose opinions the poll will seek to discover. That universe can be all voters in Chicago, or every high school student in Texas, or all Republicans in New England, or all Democrats in Georgia, or all Catholic women over age 35 in the United States, and so on.

Constructing a Sample

If a poll's universe is very small—say, the 25 members of a high school class—the best way to find out what that universe thinks about some issue would be to poll every one of them. In most cases, however, it is not possible to interview a complete universe. This is certainly true in matters of public policy that affect all the people in the nation. There are simply too many people in that universe to talk to. So the pollster must select a **sample,** a representative slice of the total universe.

Most professional pollsters draw a **random sample,** also called a probability sample. In a random sample, the pollster interviews a certain number of randomly selected people who live in a certain number of randomly selected places. A random sample is thus a sample in

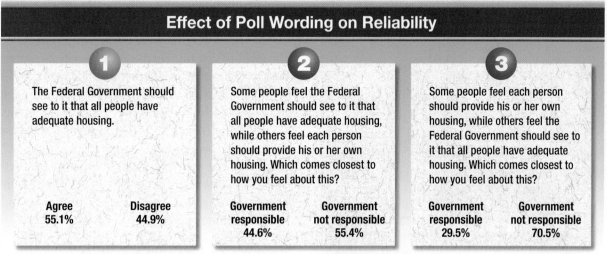

Effect of Poll Wording on Reliability

1

The Federal Government should see to it that all people have adequate housing.

Agree	Disagree
55.1%	44.9%

2

Some people feel the Federal Government should see to it that all people have adequate housing, while others feel each person should provide his or her own housing. Which comes closest to how you feel about this?

Government responsible	Government not responsible
44.6%	55.4%

3

Some people feel each person should provide his or her own housing, while others feel the Federal Government should see to it that all people have adequate housing. Which comes closest to how you feel about this?

Government responsible	Government not responsible
29.5%	70.5%

SOURCE: *Questions and Answers in Attitude Surveys*, 1981

Interpreting Charts This chart demonstrates the importance of carefully wording each question in a poll. ***(a) Which question is worded in the least biased manner? (b) How do you know?***

which each member of the universe and each geographic area within it have a mathematically equal chance of being included.

Each major national poll usually interviews just over 1,500 people to represent the universe of the nation's entire adult population (just over 200 million people today). How can the views of so few people represent the opinions of so many?

The answer to that question lies in the mathematical law of probability. Flip a coin 1,000 times. The law of probability says that, given an honest coin and an honest flip, heads will come up 500 times. Furthermore, the law states that the results of this test will be the same no matter how often you perform it, and no matter what kind of coin you use.

The law of probability is regularly applied in a great many situations. It is used by insurance companies to compute life expectancies, by food inspectors to check the quality of a farmer's truckload of beans, and by others who "play the odds," including pollsters who draw random samples.

In short, if the sample is of sufficient size and is properly selected at random from the entire universe, the law of probability says that the result will be accurate to within a small and predictable margin of error. Mathematicians tell us that a properly drawn random sample of some 1,500 people will reflect the opinions of the nation's entire adult population and will be accurate to within a margin of plus or minus (±) 3 percent.

Pollsters acknowledge that it is impossible to construct a sample that would be an absolutely accurate reflection of a large universe. Hence, the allowance for error. A margin of ±3 percent means a spread of 6 percentage points, of course. To reduce the sampling error from ±3 percent to ±1 percent, the size of the sample would have to be 9,500 people. The time and money needed to interview so big a sample make that a practical impossibility.

Some pollsters use a less complicated, but less reliable, sampling method. They draw a **quota sample,** a sample deliberately constructed to reflect several of the major characteristics of a given universe.

For example, if 51.3 percent of a universe is female, 17.5 percent of it is African American, and so on, then the quota sample will be made up of 51.3 percent females, 17.5 percent African Americans, and so on. Of course, most of the people in the sample will belong to more than one category. This fact is a major reason why such a sample is less reliable than random samples.

Preparing Valid Questions

The way in which questions are worded is very important. Wording can affect the reliability of any poll. For example, most people will probably say "yes" to this question put this way: "Should local taxes be reduced?" Many of those same people will also answer "yes" to this question: "Should the city's police force be increased to

▲ *A Famous Polling Failure* An elated Harry S Truman holds up a newspaper headline wrongly announcing his defeat in 1948. Pollsters and others had predicted an easy victory for Thomas E. Dewey in that election. **H-SS 12.6.3**

fight the rising tide of crime in our community?" Yet, expanding the police force almost certainly would require more local tax dollars.

Responsible pollsters acknowledge these issues and thus phrase their questions very carefully. They purposely try not to use "loaded," emotionally charged words, or terms that are difficult to understand. They also try to avoid questions that are worded in a way that will tend to shape the answers that are given to them.

Interviewing

How pollsters communicate with respondents can also affect accuracy. For decades, most polls were conducted door-to-door, face-to-face. That is, the interviewer questioned the respondent in person. Today, however, most pollsters do their work by telephone, with a sample selected by *random digit dialing*. Calls are placed to randomly chosen numbers within randomly chosen area codes around the country.

Telephone surveys are less labor intensive and less expensive than door-to-door polling. Still, most professional pollsters see advantages and drawbacks to each approach. But they all agree that only one technique, not a combination of the two, should be used in any given poll.

The interview itself, whether by phone or in person, is a very sensitive point in the process. An interviewer's tone of voice or the emphasis he or she gives to certain words can influence a respondent's replies and so affect the validity of a poll.

If the questions are not carefully worded, some of the respondent's replies may be snap judgments or emotional reactions. Others may be answers that the person being interviewed thinks "ought" to be given; or they may be replies that the respondent thinks will please—or offend—the interviewer. Thus, polling organizations try to hire and train their interviewing staffs very carefully.

Analyze and Report Findings

Polls, whether scientific or not, try to measure people's attitudes. To be of any real value, however, someone must analyze and report the results. Scientific polling organizations today collect huge amounts of raw data. In order to handle these data, computers and other electronic hardware have become routine parts of the process. Pollsters use these technologies to tabulate and interpret their data, draw their conclusions, and then publish their findings.

Evaluating Polls

How good are polls? On balance, the major national polls are fairly reliable. So, too, are most of the regional surveys around the country. Still, they are far from perfect. Fortunately, most responsible pollsters themselves are quite aware of that fact and readily acknowledge the limits of their polls. Many of them are involved in continuing efforts to refine every aspect of the polling process.

Pollsters know that they have difficulty measuring the intensity, stability, and relevance of the opinions they report. *Intensity* is the strength of feeling with which an opinion is held. *Stability* (or fluidity) is the relative permanence or changeableness of an opinion. *Relevance* (or salience) is how important a particular opinion is to the person who holds it.

Polls and pollsters are sometimes said to shape the opinions they are supposed to measure. Some critics of polls say that in an election, for example, pollsters often create a "bandwagon effect." That is, some voters, wanting to be with the winner, jump on the bandwagon of the candidate who is ahead in the polls.

In spite of these criticisms, it is clear that scientific polls are the most useful tools there are for the difficult task of measuring public opinion. Although they may not be always or precisely accurate, they do offer reasonably reliable guides to public thought. Moreover, they help to focus attention on public questions and to stimulate discussion of them.

Limits on the Impact of Public Opinion

More than a century ago, the Englishman Lord Bryce described government in the United States as "government by public opinion." Clearly, the energy devoted to measuring public opinion in this country suggests something of its powerful role in American politics. However, Lord Bryce's observation is true only if it is understood to mean that public opinion is the major, but by no means the only, influence on public policy in this country. Its force is tempered by a number of other factors—for example, by interest groups.

Most importantly, however, remember that our system of constitutional government is not designed to give free, unrestricted play to public opinion—and especially not to majority opinion. In particular, the doctrines of separation of powers and of checks and balances, and the constitutional guarantees of civil rights and liberties are intended to protect minority interests against the excesses of majority views and actions.

Interpreting Political Cartoons (a) What is the cartoon's message?(b) Does the text support this message?

Finally, polls are not elections, nor are they substitutes for elections. It is when faced with a ballot that voters must decide what is important and what is not. Voters must be able to tell the difference between opinions and concrete information, and should know the difference between personalities and platforms.

Democracy is more than a simple measurement of opinion. Democracy is about making careful choices among leaders and their positions on issues, and among the governmental actions that may follow. Ideally, democracy is the thoughtful participation of citizens in the political process.

Section 2 Assessment

Key Terms and Main Ideas

1. Why are **interest groups** uncertain gauges for measuring public opinion?
2. What is the major problem with the **straw vote** polling technique?
3. How is it that a **random sample** gives a fairly accurate representation of public opinion?
4. For what reasons is public opinion measured?

Critical Thinking

5. **Determining Relevance** List two good reasons for following polls during a presidential campaign.
6. **Understanding Point of View** How might the Framers of the Constitution have viewed public opinion polls?

7. **Predicting Consequences** What positive and/or negative effects might there be if polls were taken among student voters before a student government election?

Taking a Poll

 Analysis Skill HR4

Politicians have a love/hate relationship with public opinion polls. When a poll shows them gaining public approval, they hail the results as an endorsement of their views. When it shows their popularity slipping, many claim that they never pay attention to polls!

Indeed, a poorly constructed survey can deliver invalid information that can mislead decision makers or can be used to make false claims. Whether a poll is nationwide or within your classroom, certain standards of poll-taking apply. For instance:

1. Define the population to be polled. Decide what group you need to poll in order to find the answer to your question. For example, if you want to learn what percentage of registered voters in Fresno, California, voted in the last election, then it would not make sense to poll people who had not registered to vote.

2. Construct a sample. Within the group that you're polling, you can take a random sample—people chosen purely by chance. Or you can take a quota sample—a representative number of people from each subgroup in your survey.

3. Prepare valid questions. Ask objective questions rather than ones that lead the subject toward a particular answer. Try to ask questions that can be answered in one word, so your results will be easy to tally. Avoid wording that is difficult to understand, especially if your subjects are young or not fluent in English.

4. Select and control the means by which the poll will be taken. Decide whether you will conduct an in-person interview, a telephone interview, a mail interview, or an online interview. Be sure to interview all members of a group in the same manner. Choose interviewers who are careful not to influence the responses by their dress, attitude, or tone of voice.

5. Report your findings. Make a table of the responses to your poll. Analyze the results and draw conclusions based on that information.

Test for Success

Work individually or in small groups to design, conduct, and present the findings from a poll of your class. Create a topic, or choose from one of the following: (a) television viewing habits; (b) career plans; (c) consumption of genetically engineered foods.

▲ Above, a student conducts a survey. At right is the Web site of a major national polling service, the Gallup Organization.

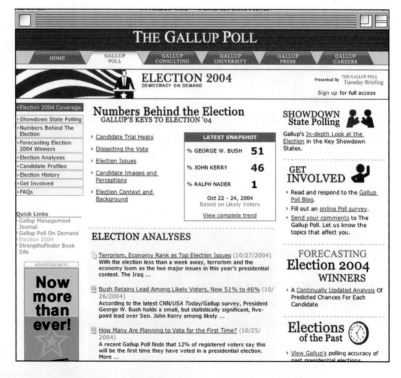

3 The Mass Media

Section Preview

OBJECTIVES

1. **Examine** the role of the mass media in providing the public with political information.
2. **Explain** how the mass media influence politics.
3. **Understand** the factors that limit the influence of the media.

WHY IT MATTERS

How often do you watch television, read a newspaper or magazine, listen to the radio? While these media provide entertainment, they are also our most important sources of political information.

POLITICAL DICTIONARY

★ **medium**
★ **public agenda**
★ **sound bite**

How much television do you watch each day? Little or none? Two hours a day? Three hours? More? However much you watch, you no doubt know that your peers spend a great deal of time in front of the TV. Studies show that by the time the average person graduates from high school today, he or she has spent nearly 11,000 hours in classrooms and nearly 14,000 hours watching television.

Television has an extraordinary impact on the lives of everyone in this country. As you will see in this section, so do the other elements of the mass media.

The Role of Mass Media

A **medium** is a means of communication; it transmits some kind of information. *Media* is the plural of medium. As you have read, the mass media include those means of communication that can reach large, widely dispersed audiences simultaneously.

Four major mass media are particularly important in American politics. Ranked in terms of impact, they are television, newspapers, radio, and magazines. Other media—books, films, and audio- and videocassettes, for example—play a lesser role. So, too, does the Internet, though its communicating capabilities are becoming increasingly important.

The mass media are not a part of government. Unlike political parties and interest groups, they do not exist primarily to influence government. They are, nonetheless, an important force in politics.

Besides providing entertainment, the media present people with political information. They do so directly when they report the news, in a newscast or in the news columns of a newspaper, for example. The media also provide a large amount of political information less directly—for example, in radio and television programs, newspaper stories, and magazine articles. These venues often deal with such public topics as crime, health care, or some aspect of American foreign policy. Either way, people acquire most of the information they know about government and politics from the various forms of media.

Television

Politics and television have gone hand in hand since the technology first appeared. The first public demonstration of television occurred at the New York World's Fair in 1939. President Franklin Roosevelt opened the fair on camera,

◀ *The "Wireless Web"* Some mobile phones provide access to the Internet, an increasingly important form of mass media.

and local viewers watched him on tiny five- and seven-inch screens.

World War II interrupted the development of the new medium, but it began to become generally available in the late 1940s. Television boomed in the 1950s. The first transcontinental broadcast came in 1951, when President Harry Truman, speaking in Washington, addressed the delegates attending the Japanese Peace Treaty Conference in San Francisco.

Today, television is all-pervasive. As you read earlier, there is at least one television set in 98 percent of the nation's 110 million households. In fact, there are more homes in this country today with a television set than with indoor plumbing facilities!

Television replaced newspapers as the principal source of political information for a majority of Americans in the early 1960s. Today, television is the principal source of news for an estimated 80 percent of the population.

The more than 1,700 television stations in this country include more than 1,400 commercial outlets and over 300 public broadcasters. Three major national networks have dominated television from its infancy: the Columbia Broadcasting System (CBS), the American Broadcasting Company (ABC), and the National Broadcasting Company (NBC). Those three giants furnish about 90 percent of the programming for some 700 local stations. That programming accounts for about 45 percent of all television viewing time today.

The major networks' audience share has been declining in recent years, however. The main challenges to their domination have come from three sources: (1) several independent broadcasting groups—for example, the Fox Network; (2) cable broadcasters[4]—for example, Turner Broadcasting, and especially its Cable News Network (CNN); and (3) the Public Broadcasting System (PBS) and its more than 350 local stations.

Some of the most highly touted presentations on television—a Super Bowl game, for example, or a debate between the major presidential candidates—are seen by as many as 100 million people. From 15 to 40 million watch the more popular sitcoms. Each of the three major network's nightly news programs draws 7 to 10 million viewers. In addition, more than 80 million places, including nearly three fourths of the nation's households, are now hooked up to cable systems.

---

[4]C-SPAN, the Cable-Satellite Public Affairs Network, is sponsored by the cable industry. C-SPAN, C-SPAN2, and C-SPAN3 cover a broad range of public events—including major floor debates and committee hearings in Congress, presidential and other press conferences, and speeches by notable public figures.

▲ *Shaping Public Opinion* West Berlin mayor Willy Brandt is interviewed in 1961 on *Meet the Press,* television's first and longest running talk show (left). On *Larry King Live* Larry King speaks with Attorney General John Ashcroft about the September 11, 2001 terrorist attacks (right).

Newspapers

The first regularly published newspaper in America, the *Boston News-Letter,* appeared in 1704.[5] Other papers soon followed, in Boston and then in Philadelphia, New York, Annapolis, and elsewhere. By 1775, 37 newspapers were being published in the colonies. All of them were weekly papers, and they were printed on one sheet that was usually folded to make four pages. The nation's first daily newspaper, the *Pennsylvania Evening Post and Daily Advertiser,* began publication in 1783.

Those first papers regularly carried political news. Several spurred the colonists to revolution, carrying the news of independence and the text of the Declaration to people throughout the colonies. Thomas Jefferson marked the vital role of the press in the earliest years of the nation when, in 1787, he wrote to a friend:

> **PRIMARY Sources** *" . . . were it left to me to decide whether we should have a government without newspapers or newspapers without a government, I should not hesitate a moment to prefer the latter."*
> —Letter to Colonel Edward Carrington, January 16, 1787

The 1st Amendment, added to the Constitution in 1791, made the same point regarding the importance of newspapers with its guarantee of the freedom of the press.

Today, more than 10,000 newspapers are published in the United States, including almost 1,450 dailies, more than 7,200 weeklies, some 550 semi-weeklies, and several hundred foreign-language papers. Those publications have a combined circulation of about 150 million copies per issue. About 45 percent of the nation's adult population read a newspaper every day, and they spend, on average, a half hour doing so.

The number of daily newspapers has been declining for decades, however, from more than 2,000 in 1920 to 1,745 in 1980 and to not quite 1,450 today. Radio and television, and more

---

[5]The world's first newspaper was almost certainly the *Acta Diurna,* a daily gazette in Rome dating from 59 B.C. Another very early forerunner of today's newspapers was *Tsing Pao,* a court journal in Beijing. Press historians believe that its first issues, printed from stone blocks, were published beginning in A.D. 618; its last issue appeared in 1911.

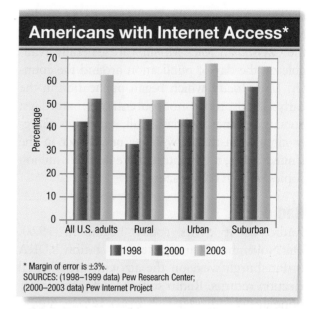

Americans with Internet Access*

* Margin of error is ±3%.
SOURCES: (1998–1999 data) Pew Research Center;
(2000–2003 data) Pew Internet Project

 Interpreting Graphs Internet use has jumped dramatically, and with it the number of people who turn to the Internet for daily news. *Might the Internet eventually replace television and newspapers as a source of news? Why or why not?* **H-SS 12.8.2**

recently the Internet, have been major factors in that downward trend.

So, too, have been the battles over readers and advertisers that competing papers have fought in many places nationwide. Often, those struggles have left only one survivor. Competing daily papers exist in fewer than 50 cities today. This represents a major change from only a few decades ago, when at least two and sometimes three, four, or five newspapers existed in most major cities.

Nevertheless, newspapers rank second only to television as the public's primary source of information about government and politics. Most newspapers cover stories in greater depth than television does, and many try to present various points of view in their editorial sections. Those newspapers that have the most substantial reputations and national influence today include the *New York Times,* the *Washington Post,* the *Chicago Tribune,* the *Los Angeles Times,* the *Wall Street Journal, USA Today,* and the *Christian Science Monitor.*

Most newspapers are local papers. That is, most of their readers live in or near the communities in which they are published. While local papers do carry some national and international news, most focus on their own locales.

Advances in telecommunications and computerized operations are changing that basic fact, however. Now, each day's editions of *USA Today*, the *New York Times*, the *Wall Street Journal*, and the *Christian Science Monitor* are generally available on the day of publication around the country. *USA Today*, which began publication in the early 1980s, does not publish on Saturdays, Sundays, or most holidays. Still, it now has a larger circulation than any other newspaper in the United States; it distributes more than 2.1 million copies of each day's paper.

Radio

Radio as it exists today began in 1920. On November 2nd of that year, station KDKA in Pittsburgh went on the air with presidential election returns. Radio soon became immensely popular.

By 1927, 733 commercial stations were on the air, Americans owned more than seven million radio sets, and two national networks were in operation. NBC was established in 1926 and CBS in 1927. The Mutual Broadcasting System was formed in 1934, and ABC was formed in 1943. The advent of networks made it possible

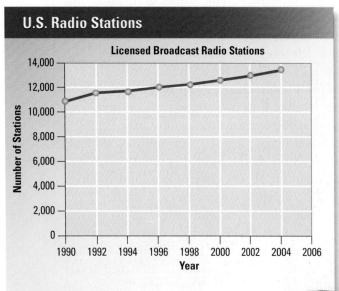

U.S. Radio Stations

Licensed Broadcast Radio Stations

Number of Stations (y-axis: 0 to 14,000)
Year (x-axis: 1990 to 2006)

Source: Federal Communications Commission

Interpreting Graphs The number of radio stations increased fairly steadily in recent years. ***How might this trend affect the quality and/or type of local radio programming?***

for broadcasters to present their programs and advertising messages to millions of people all over the country.

By the 1930s, radio had assumed much of the role in American society that television has today. It was a major entertainment medium, and millions of people planned their daily schedules around their favorite programs. The networks also provided the nation with dramatic coverage of important events, and radio exposed the American people to national and international politics as never before.

President Franklin Roosevelt was the first major public figure to use radio effectively. Author David Halberstam has described the impact of FDR's famous fireside chats:

PRIMARY Sources *"He was the first great American radio voice. For most Americans of [that] generation, their first memory of politics would be of sitting by a radio and hearing that voice, strong, confident, totally at ease. . . . Most Americans in the previous 160 years had never even seen a President; now almost all of them were hearing him, in their own homes. It was literally and figuratively electrifying."*
—David Halberstam, *The Powers That Be*

Many people thought that the arrival of television would bring the end of radio as a major medium. Radio has survived, however, in large part because it is so conveniently available. People can hear music, news, sports, and other radio programs in many places where they cannot watch television—in their cars, at work, in the country, and in a number of other places and situations.

Radio remains a major source of news and other political information. The average person hears 20 hours of radio each week. No one knows how many radios there are in this country—in homes, offices, cars, backpacks, and a great many other places. Those radios can pick up some 10,000 stations on the AM and FM dials.

Many AM stations are affiliated with one or another of the national networks. Unlike television, however, most radio programming is local. There are also some 700 public radio stations, most of them on the FM dial. These noncommercial outlets are part of National Public Radio (NPR), which is radio's counterpart of television's PBS.

Most radio stations spend little time on public affairs today. Many of them do devote a few minutes every hour to "the news"—really, to a series of headlines. All-news stations are now found in most of the larger and many medium-sized communities. They are usually on the air 24 hours a day, and they do provide somewhat more extensive coverage of the day's events. A growing number of stations now serve the preferences of Latino Americans, African Americans, and other minority listeners.

Over recent years, talk radio has become an important source of political comment. The opinions and analyses offered by a number of talk show hosts can be found on hundreds of stations across the country. Among the most prominent talk broadcasters today are conservatives Rush Limbaugh, Sean Hannity, and Bill O'Reilly and liberal Al Franken. Their programs air nationally and attract millions of listeners every weekday.

Many local radio stations now feature their own talk shows. Most of them focus on matters of local interest and their hosts regularly invite listeners to chime in by telephone and e-mail.

Magazines

Several magazines were published in colonial America. Benjamin Franklin began one of the very first, his *General Magazine,* in Philadelphia in 1741. On into the early 1900s, most magazines published in the United States were generally devoted to literature and the social graces. The first political magazines—among them, *Harper's Weekly* and the *Atlantic Monthly*—appeared in the mid-1800s.

The progressive reform period in the early 1900s spawned several journals of opinion, including a number that featured articles by the day's leading muckrakers.[6] For decades before radio and television, magazines constituted the only national medium.

Some 12,000 magazines are published in the United States today. Most are trade publications, such as Veterinary Forum and the Automotive Executive, or periodicals that target some special personal interest, such as Golf Digest, Teen, and American Rifleman. Among magazines with the highest circulation today: *AARP the Magazine, Reader's Digest,* and *National Geographic*. They each sell some 10 to 20 million or more copies per issue.

Three news magazines, *Time, Newsweek,* and *U.S. News & World Report,* rank in the top

Frequently Asked Questions

The Media

An uninformed public: the media's fault?

Any number of studies demonstrate this point: Overall, the American people are not very well informed about politics and public affairs. Some analysts claim that the media are largely responsible for this regrettable fact—because, they say, the media are much more interested in entertaining their audiences than they are in informing them. Most critics also note that "the news" tends to be negative in tone. That is, bad news regularly crowds out good news—and this, they say, leads many people to ignore, or at least fail to appreciate, the significance of news reports about public affairs.

. . . Or the public's fault?

Other observers argue that the public itself is to blame for its lack of knowledge and awareness. They say that virtually every aspect of public affairs is covered by the news media, on an ongoing basis. The problem here is that, by and large, most people don't play close attention to the news about public affairs—that is, don't bother to inform themselves.

Any Questions?

What would you like to know about the mass media? Brainstorm two new questions and exchange them with a classmate. What did you learn?

---

[6]The muckrakers were journalists who exposed wrongdoing in politics, business, and industry. The term was coined by Theodore Roosevelt in 1906 and is derived from the raking of muck—that is, manure and other barnyard debris. The muckrakers set the pattern for what is now called investigative reporting.

35 periodicals in terms of circulation. They have a combined circulation of nearly 10 million copies a week, and they are important sources of political news and comment. There are several other magazines devoted to public affairs, most of them vehicles of opinion, including the *Nation,* the *New Republic,* the *National Review,* and the *Weekly Standard.*

The Media and Politics

Clearly, the media play a significant role in American politics. Just how significant that role is, and just how much influence the media have, is the subject of a long, still unsettled debate.

Whatever its weight, the media's influence can be seen in any number of situations. It is most visible in two areas: (1) the public agenda and (2) electoral politics.

The Public Agenda

The media play a very large role in shaping the **public agenda,** the societal problems that the nation's political leaders and the general public agree need government attention. As they report and comment on events, issues, policies, and personalities, the media determine to a very large

▲ *Power of the Press* The media transmit information across the country instantly. They thus help to shape the public agenda and affect the outcome of elections. Shown here is a CNN newsroom. **H-SS 12.8.1**

extent what public matters the people will think and talk about—and, so, those matters that public-policy makers will be concerned about.

To put the point another way, the media have the power to focus the public's attention on a particular issue. They do so by emphasizing some things and ignoring or downplaying others. For example, they feature certain items on the front page or at the top of the newscast and bury others.

It is not correct to say that the media tell the people *what* to think; but it is clear that they tell the people what to think *about.* A look at any issue of a daily newspaper or a quick review of the content of any television news program will demonstrate that point. Remember, people rely on the media for most of the information they receive on public issues.

The mass media also has a direct impact on the nation's leaders. Some years ago, Stephen Hess, a widely respected authority on the media, identified several news organizations that form the "inner ring" of influence in Washington, D.C. He cited the three major television networks, CBS, ABC, and NBC; three newspapers, the *New York Times,* the *Washington Post,* and the *Wall Street Journal;* the leading news wire service, the Associated Press (AP); and the three major news weeklies, *Time, Newsweek,* and *U.S. News & World Report.* CNN, MSNBC, Fox News, Reuters and *USA Today* have since joined that select group.

Top political figures in and out of government pay close and continuing attention to these sources. In fact, the President receives a daily digest of the news reports, analyses, and editorial comments that these and other sources broadcast and publish.

Electoral Politics

You have seen several illustrations of the media's importance in electoral politics as you have read this book. Recall, for example, the fact that the media, and in particular television, have contributed to a decline in the place of parties in American politics.

Television has made candidates far less dependent on party organizations than they once were. Before television, the major parties generally dominated the election process. They recruited most candidates who ran for office, and they ran those candidates' campaigns. The candidates depended on party organizations in order to reach the voters.

Now, television allows candidates to appeal directly to the people, without the help of a party organization. Candidates for major office need not be experienced politicians who have worked their way up a party's political ladder over the course of several elections. Today it is not at all unusual for candidates to assemble their own campaign organizations and operate with only loose connections to their political parties.

Remember, too, that how voters see a candidate—the impressions they have of that candidate's personality, character, abilities, and so on—is one of the major factors that influence voting behavior. Candidates and professional campaign managers are quite aware of this fact. They know that the kind of "image" a candidate projects in the media can have a telling effect on the outcome of an election.

Candidates regularly try to manipulate media coverage to their advantage. Campaign strategists understand that most people learn almost everything they know about a candidate from television. They therefore plan campaigns that emphasize television exposure. Such technical considerations as timing, location, lighting, and camera angles loom large, often at the expense of such substantive matters as the issues involved in an election or a candidate's qualifications for public office.

Good campaign managers also know that most television news programs are built out of stories that (1) take no more than a minute or two of air time, and (2) show people doing something interesting or exciting. Newscasts seldom feature "talking heads," speakers who drone on and on about some complex issue.

Instead, newscasts featuring candidates are usually short, sharply focused **sound bites**—snappy reports that can be aired in 30 or 45 seconds or so. Staged and carefully orchestrated visits to historic sites, factory gates, toxic-waste dumps, football games, and the like have become a standard part of the electoral scene.

Limits on Media Influence

Having said all this, it is all too easy to overstate the media's role in American politics. A number of built-in factors work to limit the media's impact on the behavior of the American voting public.

Voices on Government

Joseph Turow, a professor at the Annenberg School of Communications, studies the ways in which the media influence our political perspectives. Turow examines the mass media—from radio to the Internet—and their impact on people.

❝ *We have to make people a little more sophisticated about video images. . . . News and entertainment are, essentially, a battle over the definition of the world. You've got various sources in public relations, and interest groups and political organizations are always maneuvering to have a reporter write this or that, and we don't know, for example, why this person is on this television show. One of the things I tell my students is to interrogate the newspaper, interrogate the television show.* ❞

Evaluating the Quotation

What do you think Turow means by "interrogating" a newspaper or a television news program? How would following his advice change you as a "consumer" of the news?

For one thing, few people follow international, national, or even local political events very closely. Many studies of voting behavior show that in the typical election, only about 10 percent of those who can vote and only about 15 percent of those who do vote are well informed on the many candidates and issues under consideration in that election. In short, only a small part of the public actually takes in and understands much of what the media have to say about public affairs.

Moreover, most people who do pay some attention to politics are likely to be selective about it. That is, they most often watch, listen to, and read those sources that generally agree with their own viewpoints. They regularly ignore those sources with which they disagree. Thus, for example, many Democrats do not watch the televised campaign appearances of Republican candidates. Nor do many Republicans read newspaper stories about the campaign efforts of Democratic candidates.

Another important limit on the media's impact is the content the media carries. This is especially true of radio and television. Most television programs, for example, have little or nothing to do with public affairs, at least not directly. (A number of popular programs do relate to public affairs in an indirect way, however. Thus, many are "crime shows," and crime is certainly a matter of public concern. Many also carry a political message—for example, that the police are hard-working public servants.)

Advertisers who pay the high costs of television air time want to reach the largest possible audiences. Because most people are more interested in being entertained than in being informed about public issues, few public-affairs programs air in prime time. There are exceptions, however, such as *60 Minutes*, *20/20*, *Dateline*, and *News Night*.

Radio and television mostly "skim" the news. They report only what their news editors judge to be the most important and/or the most interesting stories of the day. Even on widely watched evening news programs, most reports are presented in 60- to 90-second time

▲ **News or Entertainment?** Newspapers offer a variety of information, much of it not about politics, in order to appeal to the widest possible audience.

slots. In short, the broadcast media seldom give the kind of in-depth coverage that a good newspaper can supply.

Newspapers are not as hampered as many other media in their ability to cover public affairs. Still, much of the content of most newspapers is nonpolitical. Like nearly all of television and radio, newspapers depend on their advertising revenues, which in turn depend on producing a product with the widest possible appeal. Newspaper readers are often more interested in the sports pages and the social, travel, advertising, and entertainment sections of a newspaper than they are in its news and editorial pages.

In-depth coverage of public affairs is available in the media to those who want it and will seek it out. There are a number of good newspapers around the country. In-depth coverage can also be found in several magazines and on a number of radio and television stations, including public broadcast outlets. Remember, however, that there is nothing about democracy that guarantees an alert and informed public. Like voting and other forms of political participation, being an informed citizen requires some effort.

Section 3 Assessment

Key Terms and Main Ideas

1. Why is the Internet considered a **medium**?
2. How do the media influence the **public agenda**?
3. What limits are there on media influence?
4. Why has radio survived despite television's enormous appeal?

Critical Thinking

5. **Making Comparisons** Through which medium—newspapers, television, or the Internet—can the American people become best informed about public affairs today? Why?

Standards Monitoring *Online*
For: Self-quiz with vocabulary practice
Web Code: mqa-2083

6. **Understanding Point of View** Nicholas Johnson, former chair of the Federal Communications Commission, said "All television is educational television. The only question is, what is it teaching." Do you agree or disagree? Explain.

Go Online
PHSchool.com
For: An activity on the media's role in public opinion
Web Code: mqd-2083

on the Supreme Court

Can Religious Solicitation Be Regulated?

Jehovah's Witnesses follow the biblical command to "go ye into all the world, and preach the gospel to every creature." Their ability to fulfill this command has been thwarted by municipal regulations restricting or regulating door-to-door solicitation, however. As a result, the Supreme Court has periodically struggled with the balance between a municipality's right to limit solicitation and the Jehovah's Witnesses's religious requirement to advocate for their religion door-to-door.

Analysis Skills
HR4, HI3, HI4

Watchtower Bible & Tract Society of N.Y., Inc. v. *Village of Stratton* (2001)

The Village of Stratton, Ohio, passed an ordinance requiring all "canvassers" to get a Solicitation Permit from the mayor's office before going onto private residential property to promote any "cause." Applicants had to fill out a detailed Solicitor's Registration Form but did not have to pay any fee. The Solicitation Permit listed the name of the approved solicitor, who was required to show the permit whenever a police officer or homeowner requested. Violation of the ordinance was a misdemeanor.

A group of Jehovah's Witnesses that published and distributed religious materials sued the Village in Federal Court. They claimed that the ordinance violated their 1st Amendment rights of religion, free speech, and freedom of the press.

The District Court upheld the ordinance except in certain small respects. The Sixth Circuit affirmed, finding that the ordinance did not single out religious solicitation and was a legitimate attempt to protect Village residents from annoyance and to prevent criminals from posing as canvassers in order to defraud residents. The U.S. Supreme Court agreed to consider whether the permit requirement was constitutional, and whether religious or political solicitors have the right to advocate their beliefs without having to disclose their names.

Arguments for Watchtower Bible & Tract Society

1. The ordinance impermissibly restricts the right to distribute religious publications and discuss religious doctrine with residents of the Village.
2. Requiring solicitation permits does not realistically reduce the amount of crime in a municipality. Residents can post "no solicitation" signs if they do not wish to be disturbed.
3. Advocates for idealistic causes should not have to get advance permission or disclose their identities in order to present their views.

Arguments for Village of Stratton

1. The Village has a legitimate interest in preventing fraud and crime, and in protecting the privacy of its residents.
2. The ordinance is applied evenhandedly to all solicitors and does not unconstitutionally discriminate against religious advocates.
3. Requiring solicitors to disclose their names helps discourage solicitors from fraudulent or dishonest activities.

Decide for Yourself

1. Review the constitutional grounds upon which each side based its arguments and the specific arguments each side presented.
2. Debate the opposing viewpoints presented in this case. Which viewpoint did you favor?
3. Predict the impact of the Court's decision on other municipal efforts to regulate religious and commercial solicitations. (To read a summary of the Court's decision, turn to pages 799–806.)

Go Online
PHSchool.com

Use Web Code mqp-2086 to register your vote on this issue and to see how other students voted.

Political Dictionary

public affairs (p. 208), public opinion (p. 209), mass media (p. 211), peer group (p. 212), opinion leader (p. 212), mandate (p. 216), interest group (p. 216), public opinion poll (p. 217), straw vote (p. 217), sample (p. 218), random sample (p. 218), quota sample (p. 219), medium (p. 223), public agenda (p. 228), sound bite (p. 229)

Standards Review

H-SS 12.3.1 Explain how civil society provides opportunities for individuals to associate for social, cultural, religious, economic, and political purposes.

H-SS 12.3.2 Explain how civil society makes it possible for people, individually or in association with others, to bring their influence to bear on government in ways other than voting and elections.

H-SS 12.6.3 Evaluate the roles of polls, campaign advertising, and the controversies over campaign funding.

H-SS 12.7.5 Explain how public policy is formed, including the setting of the public agenda and implementation of it through regulations and executive orders.

H-SS 12.7.6 Compare the processes of lawmaking at each of the three levels of government, including the role of lobbying and the media.

H-SS 12.8.1 Discuss the meaning and importance of a free and responsible press.

H-SS 12.8.2 Describe the roles of broadcast, print, and electronic media, including the Internet, as means of communication in American politics.

H-SS 12.8.3 Explain how public officials use the media to communicate with the citizenry and to shape public opinion.

Practicing the Vocabulary

Matching *Choose a term from the list above that best matches each description.*

1. The people with whom one usually associates
2. A means of communication
3. The attitudes held by a significant number of people on matters of government and politics
4. A person who has an unusual amount of influence on the views held by other people
5. News reports that are brief and sharply focused
6. An organization that tries to influence public policy

Fill in the Blank *Choose a term from the list above that best completes each sentence.*

7. A type of sample that is carefully constructed to reflect the major characteristics of a particular universe is called a _____.
8. Winners of elections often claim that their victories at the polls represent a _____ to carry out their proposed programs.
9. A _____ is a type of sample in which each member of the sample universe has a mathematically equal chance of being included.
10. _____ are those means of communication that can reach large numbers of people.

Reviewing Main Ideas

Section 1

11. Why is it incorrect to say that public opinion represents the single, undivided view of the American people?
12. Why are the influences of education and family so powerful in the development of political attitudes?
13. Besides education and family, what forces help influence public opinion in American society?
14. Name at least three ways in which public opinion can be expressed.
15. **(a)** Why is your opinion about a rock group not a public opinion? **(b)** Give at least three examples of topics on which a group of people may have a public opinion.

Section 2

16. Elections, interest groups, the media, and personal contacts all are means of measuring public opinion. **(a)** Describe how each is used to measure public opinion. **(b)** What are the limitations of each?

17. What is the most reliable means of measuring public opinion? Explain your answer.
18. Why is it only partly correct to say that government in the United States is "government by public opinion"?
19. How does a straw vote differ from a scientific poll?
20. What factors can make a public opinion poll less than completely accurate?

Section 3

21. **(a)** What are the four major sources of political information in the United States? **(b)** List at least one advantage of each source.
22. Name two reasons for the decline in the number of daily newspapers in the United States.
23. Explain the impact of the mass media on the public agenda.
24. What is the impact of the mass media on electoral politics?
25. What factors limit the impact of the mass media on American politics?

Critical Thinking Skills

Analysis Skills HR3, HR4

26. *Applying the Chapter Skill* Write five questions that you would ask if you were conducting a poll on the significance of mass media in the lives of American voters.

27. *Drawing Inferences* Political scientist V. O. Key, Jr., once described public opinion as those expressions that governments "find it prudent to heed." Do you agree with Key's definition? Explain your answer.

28. *Expressing Problems Clearly* You have read that schools are key agents of political socialization. What are the most important elements of citizenship in American society that you think students ought to learn in school?

29. *Distinguishing False From Accurate Images* In spite of its powerful and important role in American society, television is often criticized for its lack of content on important issues. **(a)** Considering what you have read in this chapter, do you feel that it is accurate to characterize television as lacking in real content? **(b)** If so, what do you think is to blame for the quality of television programming?

Analyzing Political Cartoons

Using your knowledge of American government and this cartoon, answer the questions below.

The Great American Debate

30. Who are the characters in the cartoon intended to represent?
31. What does the cartoon suggest about television coverage of candidate debates?

Participation Activities

Analysis Skills CS1, HR4, HI1

32. *Current Events Watch* Choose a current topic, such as the death penalty or prayer in public schools, and find two newspaper reports about it. One should be a factual report, and one should be an editorial. Summarize the main points of each report. Then contrast the language, selection of details, and point of view of the two reports to explain how an editorial differs from a news story.

33. *Time Line Activity* Create a time line showing events in the development of television, newspaper, radio, magazine, and Internet news and information reporting. Include a summary of the trends in the roles of the various media that your time line illustrates.

34. *It's Your Turn* Create a poster that urges students to spend more time educating themselves about public issues. As you plan your poster, remember that the purpose of your poster is to encourage good citizenship. Show reasons why you think students should become more involved and suggest ways in which they might do so. Display your class's posters throughout the school. **(Creating a Poster)**

Standards Monitoring *Online*

For: Chapter 8 Self-Test **Visit:** PHSchool.com
Web Code: mqa-2084

As a final review, take the Magruder's Chapter 8 Self-Test and receive immediate feedback on your answers. The test consists of 20 multiple-choice questions designed to test your understanding of the chapter content.

CHAPTER 9

Interest Groups

"We are a nation of communities, of tens and tens of thousands of ethnic, religious, social, business, labor union, neighborhood, regional and other organizations, all of them varied, voluntary, and unique. . . ."
—George H.W. Bush (1988)

Do you think that interest groups represent only people with money, power, and influence? On the contrary, many interest groups serve as the voice of ordinary people who care passionately about a cause or policy. They represent the diversity of Americans and their opinions about issues.

◆ Minnesota farmers' protest

Standards Preview

H-SS 12.1.2 Discuss the character of American democracy and its promise and perils as articulated by Alexis de Tocqueville.

H-SS 12.1.5 Describe the systems of separated and shared powers, the role of organized interests (*Federalist Paper Number 10*), checks and balances (*Federalist Paper Number 51*), the importance of an independent judiciary (*Federalist Paper Number 78*), enumerated powers, rule of law, federalism, and civilian control of the military.

H-SS 12.2.2 Explain how economic rights are secured and their importance to the individual and to society (e.g., the right to acquire, use, transfer, and dispose of property; right to choose one's work; right to join or not join labor unions; copyright and patent).

H-SS 12.2.4 Understand the obligations of civic-mindedness, including voting, being informed on civic issues, volunteering and performing public service, and serving in the military or alternative service.

H-SS 12.3.1 Explain how civil society provides opportunities for individuals to associate for social, cultural, religious, economic, and political purposes.

H-SS 12.3.2 Explain how civil society makes it possible for people, individually or in association with others, to bring their influence to bear on government in ways other than voting and elections.

H-SS 12.6.4 Describe the means that citizens use to participate in the political process (e.g., voting, campaigning, lobbying, filing a legal challenge, demonstrating, petitioning, picketing, running for political office).

H-SS 12.7.5 Explain how public policy is formed, including the setting of the public agenda and implementation of it through regulations and executive orders.

H-SS 12.7.6 Compare the processes of lawmaking at each of the three levels of government, including the role of lobbying and the media.

SECTION 1

The Nature of Interest Groups (pp. 236–240)

★ Interest groups are private organizations that try to persuade public officials to respond to the shared attitudes of their members.

★ Unlike political parties, interest groups do not nominate candidates, focus on winning elections, or concern themselves with a broad range of issues.

★ Among their positive benefits, interest groups stimulate interest in public affairs and serve as a vehicle for participation in the political process.

★ Interest groups have been criticized for having influence disproportionate to their size and occasionally using unethical tactics.

SECTION 2

Types of Interest Groups (pp. 242–247)

★ Most people belong to several organizations that meet the definition of an interest group.

★ Most interest groups represent economic interests such as business, labor, agriculture, and certain professions.

★ Some interest groups are devoted to specific political and social causes, religious interests, or the welfare of a certain segment of the population.

★ Public-interest groups work for some aspect of the public good.

SECTION 3

Interest Groups at Work (pp. 249–254)

★ Interest groups supply the public with information favorable to the group's cause, work to build a positive image for the group, and promote the group's policies.

★ Interest groups frequently use propaganda to achieve their goals.

★ While most interest groups take a balanced approach to affecting public policy, single-interest groups focus on an individual issue and fight for this issue aggressively.

★ Lobbyists use a variety of techniques to try to persuade policy makers to share an interest group's point of view.

Go Online
PHSchool.com

For: Current Data
Web Code: mqg-2095

For: Close Up Foundation debates
Web Code: mqh-2097

Section Preview

OBJECTIVES

1. **Describe** the role of interest groups in influencing public policy.
2. **Compare and Contrast** political parties and interest groups.
3. **Explain** why people see interest groups as both good and bad for American politics.

WHY IT MATTERS

Aware of it or not, you almost certainly belong to at least one interest group today. And, knowingly or not, you will join several more of these groups over coming years.

POLITICAL DICTIONARY

★ **public policy**
★ **public affairs**

An interest group is a private organization that tries to persuade public officials to respond to the shared attitudes of its members. You may not think that you belong to any interest groups, but as you read this section, you may well discover that you do. In fact, you might even belong to several of them. You will probably also realize that you will become a part of many more of these organizations in the years to come—because interest groups provide one of

the most effective means by which Americans try to get government to respond to their wants and needs.

The Role of Interest Groups

Where do you stand on the question of gun control? What about prayer in public schools? Abortion? An increase in the minimum wage? What can you do to lend support to your views on these and other issues? How can you increase the chance that your position on these issues will carry the day?

Joining with others who share your views is both practical and democratic. Organized efforts to protect group interests are a fundamental part of the democratic process. Moreover, the right to do so is protected by the Constitution. Remember that the 1st Amendment guarantees "the right of the people peaceably to assemble, and to petition the Government for a redress of grievances."

Interest groups are sometimes called "pressure groups" and often "special interests" or "organized interests." They give themselves a variety of labels: leagues, clubs, federations, unions, committees, associations, and so on. But, whatever they call themselves, every interest group seeks to influence the making and content of **public policy**. Used in this general sense, public policy includes all of the goals that a government pursues in the many areas of human affairs in which it is involved—everything from seat belts, speed limits, and zoning

▲ Interest groups often send members items such as buttons and bumper stickers to help publicize their causes.

▲ Americans participate in a wide variety of interest groups. Families USA advocates for family health care (left). Students from the Texas School for the Deaf acted as members of an interest group when they marched on their State capitol to protest funding cuts that affected their school (right). **Critical Thinking** *What do these groups have in common?*

to flood control, old-age pensions, and the use of military force in international affairs.

Because interest groups exist to shape public policy, they operate wherever those policies are made or can be influenced. They also function at every level of government—on Capitol Hill and elsewhere in Washington, D.C., in every one of the 50 State capitals, in thousands of city halls and county courthouses, and in many other places at the local level all across the country. In short, as diplomat and historian Lord Bryce put it somewhat indelicately more than a century ago: "Where the body is, there will the vultures be gathered."

Remember, our society is a pluralistic one. It is not dominated by any single elite. It is, instead, composed of a number of distinct cultures and groups. Increasingly, the members of various ethnic, racial, religious, and other groups compete for and share in the exercise of political power in this country.

Political Parties and Interest Groups

Interest groups are made up of people who unite for some political purpose. So, too, are political parties. These two types of political organizations necessarily overlap in a number of ways. However, they differ from one another in three striking respects: (1) in the making of nominations, (2) in their primary focus, and (3) in the scope of their interests.

First, parties nominate candidates for public office; interest groups do not. Remember, making nominations is a major function of political parties. If an interest group were to nominate candidates, it would, in effect, become a political party.

Interest groups do, of course, try to affect the outcomes of primaries and other nominating contests. However, interest groups do not themselves pick candidates who then run under their labels. It may be widely known that a particular interest group actively supports a candidate, but that candidate seeks votes as a Republican or Democrat.[1]

Second, political parties are chiefly interested in winning elections and controlling government. Interest groups are chiefly concerned with controlling or influencing the *policies* of government. Unlike parties, interest groups do not face the problems involved in trying to appeal to the largest possible number of people. In short, political parties are mostly interested in the *who*,

---

[1]Note that this discussion centers on the differences between interest groups and major parties. There are some striking parallels between interest groups and most minor parties—for example, in terms of their scope of interest.

and interest groups are mostly concerned with the *what,* of government. To put it another way, political parties focus mostly on the candidate, while interest groups focus mostly on an issue such as environmental protection or gun control.

Third, political parties are necessarily concerned with the whole range of public affairs, with everything of concern to voters. Interest groups almost always concentrate only on those issues that most directly affect the interests of their members.

In addition, interest groups are private organizations. Unlike political parties, they are not accountable to the public. Their members, not the voters, pass judgment on their performance.

Interest Groups: Good or Bad?

Do interest groups pose a threat to the well-being of the American political system? Or, on the contrary, are they a valuable part of that system? The argument over the merit of interest groups goes back to the beginnings of the Republic.

Two Early Views

Many people have long viewed interest groups with deep suspicion. In 1787, James Madison warned the new nation against the dangers of what he called "factions." He made his view of those groups clear when he defined a faction as

PRIMARY Sources *"a number of citizens, whether amounting to a majority or minority of the whole, who are united and actuated by some common impulse of passion, or of interest, adverse to the rights of other citizens, or to the permanent and aggregate interests of the community. "*

— *The Federalist* No. 10[2]

Despite his mistrust, Madison thought that factions were inevitable in human society, and he was opposed to any attempt to abolish them. A society could only eliminate factions, he said, by eliminating freedom. Instead, wrote Madison, it was necessary to moderate the potential extremism of factions with a balance of powers; that is, with the governmental system set out in the proposed Constitution. The separations of power in that system would mean, said Madison, that factions would tend to counteract and balance each others' power. Thus, none could become a dominating influence.

Nearly fifty years later, Alexis de Tocqueville was deeply impressed by the vast number of organizations he found in the United States. Tocqueville was a Frenchman who toured much

---

[2] The text of *The Federalist* No. 10 appears in the historic documents section that begins on page 780.

▶ These photos show a vacant lot in Berkeley, California, being turned into a park by community activists. Many such activists belong to interest groups that work to persuade local governments to clean up and improve unused land in towns and cities throughout the United States. *Critical Thinking What are the advantages to an individual citizen of joining an interest group?* H-SS 12.2.4, 12.3.2

of this country in the early 1830s. In *Democracy in America* he wrote that

" *In no country in the world has the principle of association been more successfully used, or more unsparingly applied to a multitude of different objects, than in America.* **"**
— *Alexis de Tocqueville*

In a similar vein, he also observed that

"*Americans of all ages, all conditions, and all dispositions, constantly form associations . . . not only commercial and manufacturing . . . but . . . of a thousand other kinds—religious, moral, serious, futile, extensive or restricted, enormous or diminutive.* **"**

Are interest groups "good" or "bad"? To determine the answer, you must weigh, on the one hand, the functions those groups perform in American politics and, on the other, the various criticisms that are often leveled at them.

Valuable Functions of Interest Groups

First, among their several valuable functions, interest groups help to stimulate interest in **public affairs.** Public affairs are those issues and events that concern the people at large. Interest groups raise awareness of public affairs mostly by developing and promoting those policies they

favor and by opposing those policies they see as threats to their interests.

Second, interest groups represent their members on the basis of shared attitudes rather than on the basis of geography—by what their members think as opposed to where they happen to live. Public officials are elected from districts drawn on maps. But many of the issues that concern and unite people today have less to do with *where* they live than with, say, *how* they make a living. A labor union member who lives in Chicago may have much more in common with someone who does the same kind of work in Seattle than he or she does with someone who owns a business in Chicago or runs a farm in another part of Illinois.

Third, organized interests often provide useful, specialized, and detailed information to government—for example, on employment, price levels, or the sales of new and existing homes. These data are important to the making of public policy, and government officials often cannot obtain them from any other source. This flow of information works both ways, as well. Interest groups frequently get information from public agencies and pass it along to their members.

Fourth, interest groups are vehicles for political participation. They are a means through which like-minded citizens can pool their resources and channel their energies into collective political action. One mother concerned about drunk driving cannot accomplish very much acting alone. Thousands of people joined in an organization like MADD (Mothers Against Drunk Driving) certainly can.

Fifth, interest groups add another element to the checks-and-balances feature of the political process. Many of them keep close tabs on the work of various public agencies and officials and thus help to make sure that they perform their tasks in responsible and effective ways.

Finally, interest groups regularly compete with one another in the public arena. That competition places a very real limit on the lengths to which some groups might otherwise go as they seek to advance their own interests. For example, the automotive industry may work to weaken or postpone auto emission standards imposed under the Clean Air Act. Their efforts may be opposed—and to some

Interpreting Political Cartoons *What does the cartoon suggest about the relationship between interest groups and Congress?* **H-SS 12.1.5**

extent counterbalanced—by environmental and health-related organizations.

Criticisms

All of what has just been said is not meant to suggest that interest groups are above reproach. On the contrary, they can be, and often are, criticized on several counts.

The potential "bad" side of interest groups is sometimes all too apparent. Many of them push

their own special interests which, despite their claims to the contrary, are not always in the best interests of other Americans. Their critics often make these more specific charges:

1. Some interest groups have an influence far out of proportion to their size, or, for that matter, to their importance or contribution to the public good. Thus, the contest over "who gets what, when, and how" is not always a fair fight. The more highly organized and better-financed groups often have a decided advantage in that struggle.

2. It is sometimes hard to tell just who or how many people a group really represents. Many groups have titles that suggest that they have thousands—even millions—of dedicated members. Some organizations that call themselves such things as "The American Citizens Committee for . . ." or "People United Against . . ." are, in fact, only "fronts" for a very few people with very narrow interests.

3. Many groups do not in fact represent the views of all of the people for whom they claim to speak. Very often, both in and out of politics, an organization is dominated by an active minority who conduct the group's affairs and make its policy decisions.

4. Finally, some groups use tactics that, if they were to become widespread, would undermine the whole political system. These practices include bribery and other heavy-handed uses of money, overt threats of revenge, and so on. They are not altogether common, but the danger is certainly there.

Section 1 Assessment

Key Terms and Main Ideas

1. What is **public policy**?
2. List and describe the three main areas in which political parties and interest groups differ.
3. **(a)** How do interest groups stimulate interest in **public affairs**? **(b)** Name at least three additional functions of interest groups.
4. On what bases are interest groups often criticized?

Critical Thinking

5. **Demonstrating Reasoned Judgment** Suppose that you want to form a group in your school to combat racial discrimination. Which of the functions of interest groups described in this section would your group most likely fulfill? Explain your answer.

6. **Making Decisions** Suppose that you are asked to contribute money to an interest group that calls itself "Citizens for Better Schools." What information would you want to find out about this group before making a contribution?

Skills for Life

Using the Internet for Research

 Analysis Skill HR4

The Internet is a network of computers that links governments, organizations, and individuals around the world. The World Wide Web is one part of the Internet. Since the Internet has no central organization, finding the information you need can be difficult. To focus your search you can use search engines, the databases that track thousands of Web pages by subject.

Congress uses the Internet to communicate with the public. Congressional Web sites provide general information about legislators, committees, and hearings. These sites also provide information on proposed legislation. Use the steps below to locate and track the progress of a bill in Congress.

1. Plan the scope of your search. Choose a research topic that is not too vague. Searching for a broad subject can yield thousands of results that would be impossible to sift through. Try to state your research topic as a specific question. Then think of search terms that might return answers to your question. For example, rather than searching for broad terms such as *Congress* or *legislation,* identify a public issue that Congress is working on, such as *funding for disaster relief.* Then do a search on that topic.

2. Refine your search. Your first set of results usually includes Web sites that do not contain the information you need. Many search engines offer an advanced search option that allows you to narrow your search. You might decide to make your search terms more specific; for instance, *disaster relief AND earthquakes.* Or you might exclude unwanted information, as in *disaster relief NOT hurricanes.*

3. Navigate the sites. Once you find a site that meets your needs, explore its home page to determine how to find the information you need. Does the information in the site fully answer your question? Does the site have its own search tool to explore information contained in the site? Does it provide links to other Web sites that might better aid your research? To whom does the site belong, and is it a reliable source? (The Social Studies area at the following Web site has many useful research links: **www.phschool.com**)

For example, if your search led you to the Web site of the Federal Emergency Management Agency (FEMA), you might search within the site for *budget AND earthquakes* to find out how much funding FEMA has requested to cover damage from a particular earthquake. Then you might go to a congressional site to find out the status of the budget request for FEMA.

Test for Success

Conduct Internet research on an important public issue that is currently being debated in Congress. Find out what legislation is being proposed on this topic. Check the status of the legislation. Has it been proposed in both houses of Congress? At what stage is the bill in each house?

▶ Aftermath of the October 1989 earthquake in Oakland, California

Section Preview

OBJECTIVES

1. **Explain** how the American tradition of joining organizations has resulted in a wide range of interest groups.
2. **Describe** four categories of groups based on economic interests.
3. **Outline** the reasons why other interest groups have been created.
4. **Identify** the purpose of public-interest groups.

WHY IT MATTERS

America is "a nation of joiners"— including joiners of interest groups. Some of these groups are based on economic interests, some on other issues. Some are public-interest groups, which seek to benefit all Americans.

POLITICAL DICTIONARY

★ trade association
★ labor union
★ public-interest group

"**E**verything from A to Z." That expression can be aptly applied to the many interest groups in this country. These organizations include, among thousands of others, the American Association of Advertising Agencies, the American Legion, Amnesty International, the Association on American Indian Affairs, the Amateur Athletic Union of the United States, the Zionist Organization of America, and the American Zoo and Aquarium Association. All of these thousands of organizations can be more or less readily classified and, so, usefully described, as interest groups.

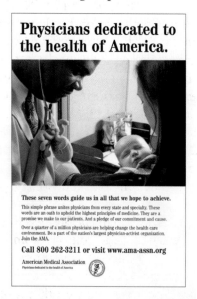

▲ American Medical Association This interest group represents the concerns of medical doctors to government officials and the public.

An American Tradition

The United States has often been called "a nation of joiners." Recall Alexis de Tocqueville's observations cited in the previous section. Tocqueville's comments, true when he made them, have become even more accurate over time.

No one really knows how many associations exist in the United States today. There are thousands upon thousands of them, however, and at every level in society. Each one is an interest group whenever it tries to influence the actions of government in order to promote its own goals and special interests.

Interest groups come in all shapes and sizes. They may have thousands or even millions of members, or only a handful. They may be well- or little-known, long-established or new and even temporary, highly structured or quite loose and informal, wealthy or with few resources. No matter what their characteristics, they are found in every field of human activity in this country.

The largest number of interest groups have been founded on the basis of an economic interest, especially on the bases of business, labor, agricultural, and professional interests. Some groups are grounded in a geographic area, such as the South, the Columbia River Basin, or the State of Indiana.

Other groups have been born out of a cause or an idea, such as prohibition of alcohol, environmental protection, or gun control. Still other interest groups exist to promote the welfare of certain groups of people—veterans, senior citizens, a racial minority, the homeless, women, people with disabilities and so on.

Many people belong to a number of interest groups. A car dealer, for example, may belong to the local Chamber of Commerce, a car dealers' association, the American Legion, a local taxpayers' league, a garden club, a church, the PTA, the American Cancer Society, the National Wildlife Federation, and several other local, regional, or national groups. All of these are, to one degree or another, interest groups—including the church and the garden club, even though the car dealer may never think of these groups in that light.[3]

Many people may belong to groups that take conflicting stands on political issues. For example, a program to improve the city's streets may be supported by the local Chamber of Commerce and the car dealers' association but opposed by the taxpayers' league. The taxpayers' league may endorse a plan to eliminate plantings in traffic islands while the garden club wants to keep the plantings.

Groups Based on Economic Interests

Most interest groups are formed on the basis of economic interests. That is, they are based on the manner in which people make their living. Among these groups, the most active—and certainly the most effective—are those representing business, labor, agriculture, and certain professions.

Business Groups

Business has long looked to government to promote and protect its interests. Recall that merchants, creditors, and property owners were the people most responsible for calling the Constitutional Convention in 1787. In the early years of the Republic, business interests fought

▲ Like Chambers of Commerce throughout the country, this Santa Monica, California, Chamber of Commerce supports local businesses. *Critical Thinking Why do most small businesses join not just one, but several, interest groups?* H-SS 12.3.1

for and won the protective tariff. Along with organized labor, many of them continue to work to maintain it, even now.

The United States Brewers' Association, the oldest organized interest group at work in national politics today, was born in 1862 when Congress first levied a tax on beer. The association's purpose was to assure the brewing trade that its interests would be "vigorously prosecuted before the legislative and executive departments."

Hundreds of business groups now operate in Washington, D.C., in the 50 State capitals, and at the local level across the country. The two best-known business organizations are the National Association of Manufacturers (NAM) and the Chamber of Commerce of the United States.

Formed in 1895, NAM now represents some 14,000 firms. It generally speaks for "big business" in public affairs. The Chamber of Commerce was founded in 1912. Over the years, it has become a major voice for the nation's thousands of smaller businesses. It has some 2,800 local chambers and now counts more than 3 million business and professional firms and some 5 million individuals among its members.

Another major group, the Business Roundtable, has also taken a large role in promoting and defending the business community in recent years. Begun in 1972, the Roundtable is composed of the chief executive officers of 150 of the nation's largest, most prestigious, and most influential corporations.

---

[3]Churches often take stands on such public issues as drinking, curfew ordinances, and legalized gambling, and they often try to influence public policy in those matters. Garden clubs often try to persuade cities to do such things as improve public parks and beautify downtown areas. Not every group to which people belong can properly be called an interest group, of course. But the point is that many groups that are not often thought to be interest groups in fact are.

Membership in Labor Unions

Percent of U.S. workers (y-axis: 0, 5, 10, 15, 20, 25, 30, 35)

Year (x-axis: 1930, 1940, 1950, 1960, 1970, 1980, 1990, 2000, 2010)

Note: Statistics are for nonfarm employees. Released Jan. 2004.

SOURCE: AFL-CIO, U.S. Department of Labor

Interpreting Graphs Although membership in labor unions has declined, organized labor remains a powerful force. **(a) In what years did union membership peak? (b) What factors might account for this peak and subsequent decline?** H-SS 12.2.2

Most segments of the business community also have their own interest groups, often called **trade associations.** They number in the hundreds and include the American Trucking Association, the Association of American Railroads, the American Bankers Association, the National Restaurant Association, and many more.

Despite their common goal of promoting business interests, business groups do not always present a solid front. In fact, they often disagree, and sometimes fight, among themselves. The trucking industry, for example, does its best to get as much federal aid as possible for highway construction. The railroads, however, are unhappy with what they see as "special favors" for their competition. At the same time, the railroads see federal taxes on gasoline, oil, tires, and other "highway users fees" as legitimate and necessary sources of federal income. The truckers take quite another view.

Labor Groups

A **labor union** is an organization of workers who share the same type of job or who work in the same industry. Labor unions press for government policies that will benefit their members.

The strength and clout of organized labor have ebbed over the past several years. Some 16 million Americans, less than 13.5 percent of the nation's labor force, belong to labor unions today. In the 1940s and 1950s, as many as a

third of all working Americans were union members; and as recently as 1975, union membership accounted for fully a fourth of the labor force. In spite of recent declines in union membership, however, labor unions remain a powerful force in American politics.

A host of groups represent the interests of organized labor. The largest, in both size and political power, is the AFL-CIO (the American Federation of Labor-Congress of Industrial Organizations). It is now made up of some 100 separate unions, such as the Retail Clerks International Union, the International Association of Machinists and Aerospace Workers, and the American Federation of State, County, and Municipal Employees. With all its unions, the AFL-CIO has about 13 million members. Each union, like the AFL-CIO itself, is organized on a national, State, and local basis.[4]

There are also a number of independent unions, that is, unions not affiliated with the AFL-CIO. The largest and most powerful of them include such groups as the Fraternal Order of Police, the National Treasury Employees Union, and the International Longshore and Warehouse Union.

Organized labor generally speaks with one voice on such social welfare and job-related matters as Social Security programs, minimum wages, and unemployment. Labor sometimes opposes labor, however. White-collar and blue-collar workers, for example, do not always share the same economic interests. Then, too, such factors as sectional interests (East-West, North-South, urban-rural, and so on) sometimes divide labor's forces. Production and transportation

---

[4]The AFL was formed in 1886 as a federation of craft unions. A craft union is made up of those workers who have the same craft or skill—for example, carpenters, plumbers, or electricians. The growth of mass-production industries created a large class of workers not skilled in any particular craft, however. The AFL found it difficult to organize these workers. Many of its craft unions opposed the admission of unions of unskilled workers to the AFL. In 1935, after years of bitter fighting, a group led by John L. Lewis of the United Mine Workers was expelled from the AFL. That group formed the CIO in 1938. The rivalries between these two major national unions eased to the point where a merger took place in 1955, creating the AFL-CIO.

interests (trucks versus railroads versus airplanes, for example) may create divisions, as well.

Agricultural Groups

For much of our history, most Americans lived in the country, and most of them lived on farms. The First Census, taken in 1790, set the nation's population at 3,929,214 persons. It found that nearly all the Americans of that day—94.9 percent of them—lived outside any city or town.

The nation's population has increased dramatically since 1790, of course—to more than 290 million today. Over that period the nation's farm population has plummeted. Fewer than five million people—less than two percent of the population—live on farms in this country today. Still, farmers' influence on the government's agricultural policies is and has been enormous. Several powerful associations serve the interests of agriculture. They include several broad-based farm groups and a larger number of groups that represent farmers who raise particular commodities.

The most prominent farm groups are the National Grange, the American Farm Bureau Federation, and the National Farmers Union. The Grange, established in 1867, is the oldest and generally the most conservative of these groups. Over the years, it has been as much a social as a political organization, concerned about the welfare of farm families. Some 300,000 farm families are now members, and much of the Grange's strength is centered in the Northeast and the Mid-Atlantic States.

The Farm Bureau is the largest and generally most effective of the three agricultural groups. Formed in 1919, it now claims over five million farm-family members and is especially strong in the Midwest. The Farm Bureau generally supports federal programs to promote agriculture. However, it opposes most government regulation and favors the free market economy.

The National Farmers Union draws its strength from smaller and less prosperous farmers. It now has some 250,000 farm-family members, most of them in the upper Midwest and West. The National Farmers Union often calls itself the champion of the dirt farmer, and frequently disagrees with the other two major organizations. It regularly argues for increased federal aid to the nation's family-sized farms.

Many other groups speak for the producers of specific farm commodities, such as dairy products, grain, fruit, peanuts, livestock, cotton, wool, corn, and soybeans. They include the National Association of Wheat Growers, the American Meat Institute, the National Cattlemen's Beef Association, the National Cotton Council, and many others.

Like business and labor groups, farm organizations sometimes find themselves at odds with one another. Thus, dairy, corn, soybean, and cotton groups compete as each of them tries to influence State laws regulating the production and sale of such products as margarine and yogurt. California and Florida citrus growers, each with their own groups, are sometimes pitted against one another, and so on.

Professional Groups

The professions are generally defined as those occupations that require extensive and specialized training, such as medicine, law, and teaching. These groups also maintain organizations to protect and promote their interests. Most professional groups are not nearly as large, well-organized, well-financed, or effective as most business, labor, and farm groups.

Three major professional groups are exceptions to the rule, however: the American

▲ **Farming of the Future** The potential risks and benefits of biotechnology are of keen interest to agricultural groups. This scientist is studying bioengineered sunflowers.

General Colin Powell retired from the Army in 1993 after 35 years of service. The son of Jamaican immigrants, he rose through the military ranks, and headed the Joint Chiefs of Staff during the Gulf War. He served as Secretary of State from 2001 to 2005. Before that, he led America's Promise—The Alliance for Youth, a national organization whose mission is to build the character and competence of our nation's youth. Of the group's mission, he stated:

" *Reclaiming the next generation of Americans is a national challenge that requires a national response. That response is America's Promise. It calls on all Americans to scale up their investment in our youth; to challenge young people by having high expectations of them; and to engage youth with opportunities to realize those expectations through constructive, character-building activities.* "

Evaluating the Quotation

Based on what you have read in this chapter, how do the ideals of a group like America's Promise compare with the goals of other types of interest groups?

Medical Association (the AMA, to which some 250,000 physicians belong), the American Bar Association (the ABA, with more than 400,000 lawyers as members), and the National Education Association (the NEA, with more than 2.7 million teachers on its membership rolls). Each of these organizations has a very real impact on public policies, and at every level of government.

There are hundreds of less well-known and less politically active professional organizations: the American Society of Civil Engineers, the American Library Association, the American Political Science Association, and many more. Much of their effort centers on such matters as the standards of the profession, the holding of professional meetings, and the publication of scholarly journals. Still, each acts in some ways as an interest group, bent on influencing government policies for the welfare of the profession and its members.

Other Interest Groups

Most interest groups are based on economic concerns, but hundreds have been formed for other reasons. Many of these other groups have a good deal of political clout.

Groups That Promote Causes

A large number of groups exist to promote a cause or an idea. It would take several pages just to list them here, and so what follows is only a sampling of the more important ones.

The American Civil Liberties Union was born in 1920. The ACLU now has some 400,000 members. It fights in and out of court to protect civil and political rights. Common Cause dates from 1970, and its membership now exceeds 210,000. It calls itself "the citizen's lobby" and works for major reforms in the political process. The League of Women Voters of the United States and its many local leagues have been dedicated to stimulating participation in and greater knowledge about public affairs since 1920. The League now has more than 130,000 members.

The list of groups devoted to causes goes on and on. Many groups—such as the National Women's Political Caucus and several others—carry the women's rights banner. Many other groups, including the National Wildlife Federation, the Sierra Club, the Wilderness Society, the Audubon Society, and Friends of the Earth, are pledged to conservation and environmental protection.

Some groups are devoted to opposing certain causes. Others support those same causes. The National Right-to-Life Committee, Women Exploited by Abortion, and other groups oppose abortion. They are countered by the National Abortion and Reproduction Rights Action League, Planned Parenthood, and their allies. Similarly, the National Rifle Association fights most forms of gun control; Handgun Control, Inc. works for it.

Organizations That Promote the Welfare of Certain Groups

A number of interest groups seek to promote the welfare of certain segments of the population. Among the best known and most powerful are the American Legion and the Veterans of Foreign Wars, which work to advance the interests of the country's veterans. Groups like Older Americans, Inc. and AARP are very active in such areas as pensions and medical care for senior citizens.

Several organizations—notably the National Association for the Advancement of Colored People (NAACP), the National Urban League, and People United to Save Humanity (PUSH)—are concerned with public policies affecting African Americans. Other organizations, such as the Japanese American Citizens League, the Mexican American Legal Defense Fund, and the National Association of Arab Americans, support the country's many ethnic groups.

Religious Organizations

Religious organizations also try to influence public policy in several important areas. Many Protestants and their local and national churches do so through the National Council of Churches. Other Protestants belong to such groups as Christian Voice and the Christian Coalition.

The National Catholic Welfare Council represents the interests of Roman Catholics. The American Jewish Congress and B'nai B'rith's Anti-Defamation League represent the interests of the Jewish community.

Public-Interest Groups

Recall that interest groups seek public policies of special benefit to their members—business, labor, agriculture, veterans, teachers, environmentalists and so on—and they work against policies that threaten their members' interests. Some groups, often called public-interest groups, have a broader goal. They work for the "public good." That is, a **public-interest group** is an interest group that seeks to institute certain public policies of benefit to all or most people in this country, whether or not they belong to or support that organization.[5]

Unlike most interest groups, public-interest groups focus on the roles that all Americans share. That is, they represent people as citizens, as consumers, as breathers of air, as drinkers of water, and so on.

Public-interest groups have become quite visible over the past 30 years or so. Among the best known and most active are Common Cause and the several organizations that make up Ralph Nader's Public Citizen, Inc. Some have existed for a much longer time—for example, the League of Women Voters, which has roots that reach deep into the history of woman suffrage.

---

[5]Of course, nearly all interest groups claim that they work for the "public good." Thus, the National Association of Manufacturers (NAM) says that lower taxes on business will stimulate the economy and so help everyone. The AFL-CIO says the same thing about spending more public dollars for more public works programs. But, as a general rule, most interest groups support or oppose public policies on a much narrower basis: on what they see to be the best interests of their own members.

Section 2 Assessment

Key Terms and Main Ideas

1. At what point does an organization become an interest group?
2. (a) What are the four major types of economically based interest groups? (b) List an example of each major type. (c) How does a **trade association** differ from a **labor union**?
3. For what reasons, other than economic ones, are interest groups created?
4. (a) What is a **public-interest group**? (b) How does it differ from other interest groups?

Critical Thinking

5. **Predicting Consequences** You have read that interest groups can disagree over certain issues, such as land use or taxes. Choose two groups mentioned in this section and create a scenario in which these groups conflict.

Standards Monitoring Online

For: Self-quiz with vocabulary practice
Web Code: mqa-2092

6. **Understanding Point of View** To which of the interest groups mentioned in this section might these persons belong: (a) Maria, an attorney in a city with a large minority population; (b) Bill, a retired midwestern soybean farmer? (c) To which groups might they both belong?

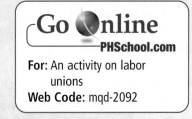

Go Online
PHSchool.com

For: An activity on labor unions
Web Code: mqd-2092

Destination: The American Dream

Analysis Skills CS3, HR4, HI3

The National Urban League was founded in 1910 to help African Americans arriving in northern cities from the southeast. Today, the National Urban League continues to represent African Americans with branches in 34 States and the District of Columbia. At a recent national convention, President Hugh B. Price offered a plan to bridge the economic gap between poor Americans of color and the rest of the nation.

Hugh B. Price

There are regions of America where all that folks know of the economic boom is what they see on the evening news.

Everyone says we should depend less on government largesse and start our own businesses like everybody else. That sounds fine.

But the truth is that even to this day, according to a study just published by the Federal Reserve Board, black entrepreneurs seeking small business loans are rejected twice as much as whites with the same credit rating. . . .

There won't be One America until the gulf that divides minorities from mainstream America disappears once and for all. . . .

The National Urban League is proposing Ten Opportunity Commandments for the 21st Century. . . . I'm not talking about dead-end expenditures that don't pay off. These investments are proven winners. They'll pay handsome dividends to society for generations to come. . . .

1. Offer quality pre-school education to every child whose parents cannot afford it.

2. Provide affordable health care for the 41 million Americans who are uninsured.

3. Ensure that every public school serving poor children equips them for self-reliance.

4. Vastly increase support for proven programs that get the estimated 15 million high school dropouts back on track.

5. Guarantee universal access to affordable higher education.

6. Maintain national economic policies that promote high employment and economic growth in communities that have missed out on the good times.

7. Eliminate the digital divide by making the acquisition of computers and use of the Internet affordable for everyone.

8. Assure full participation of minorities in higher education, employment and contracting. There must be no retreat to tokenism.

9. Eradicate the homeownership gap along ethnic lines by providing 100 percent mortgage guarantees for credit-worthy, working class minority families.

10. Equalize access to capital by totally eliminating discriminatory business loan practices, so that minority entrepreneurs can join the chorus in proclaiming that the business of America is business.

Analyzing Primary Sources

1. What problem is Price seeking to solve in this speech?
2. (a) How many of Price's proposals are directly related to education? (b) Why might the National Urban League place such a great emphasis on education?
3. Name three institutions that could help solve the problems described by Price, and explain what specific steps they should take.

③ Interest Groups at Work

Section Preview

OBJECTIVES

1. **Explain** interest groups' three major goals in influencing public opinion.
2. **Describe** how interest groups use propaganda to persuade people to their point of view.
3. **Analyze** how interest groups try to influence political parties and elections.
4. **Examine** how lobbying brings group pressures to bear on the process of making public policy.

WHY IT MATTERS

Flip through a newspaper or surf television or the Internet and you will no doubt see examples of interest groups at work—that is, using propaganda aimed at influencing public attitudes. Interest groups also work through political action committees and lobbyists to influence political parties and public policy.

POLITICAL DICTIONARY

★ propaganda
★ single-interest group
★ lobbying
★ grass roots

Interest groups exist to influence public policies. That is why they are good illustrations of the saying that politics is all about "who gets what, when, and how." Today, most interest groups use a wide variety of techniques as they try to influence public opinion, work to affect the outcome of elections, and lobby those who make public policy.

Influencing Public Opinion

Public opinion is the most significant long-term force in American politics. It is abundantly clear that, over the long run, no public policy can be followed successfully without the support of a sizeable portion of the population—and interest groups know this.

Interest groups regularly reach out to the public to accomplish one or all of three major goals:

1. To supply the public with information an organization thinks the people should have. This information is presented to support that group's interests, of course. Thus, Handgun Control, Inc. often runs full-page magazine ads keyed to one fact: the number of Americans who are killed by handguns each year.

2. To build a positive image for a group. Thus, the National Rifle Association frequently runs ads

that feature the NRA's gun-safety programs and the many shooting tournaments it sponsors.

3. To promote a particular public policy. This, of course, is the purpose of most interest groups' efforts.

Propaganda

Interest groups try to create the public attitudes they want by using **propaganda.**[6] Propaganda is a technique of persuasion aimed at influencing individual or group behaviors. Its goal is to create a particular belief. That belief may be completely true or false, or it may lie somewhere

▲ Like the advocacy group Friends of the River, many interest groups reach out to supporters on the Internet.

---

[6]The term comes from the Latin *propagare*—to propagate, to spread, to disseminate. It has been a part of the American political vocabulary since the 1930s.

between those extremes. Today, people tend to think of propaganda as a form of lying and deception. As a technique, however, propaganda is neither moral nor immoral; it is, instead, amoral.

Propaganda does not use objective logic. Rather, it begins with a conclusion. Then it brings together any evidence that will support that conclusion and disregards information that will not. Propagandists are advertisers, persuaders—and occasionally even brainwashers—who are interested in influencing others to agree with their point of view.

The development of the mass media in this country encouraged the use of propaganda, first in the field of commercial advertising, and then in politics. To be successful, propaganda must be presented in simple, interesting, and credible terms. Talented propagandists almost never attack the logic of a policy they oppose. Instead, they often attack it with name-calling. That is, they attach such labels as "communist" or "fascist." Other labels include "ultraliberal," "ultraconservative," "pie-in-the-sky," or "greedy." Or, they try to discredit a policy or person by card-stacking; that is, presenting only one side of the issue.

Policies that propagandists support receive labels that will produce favorable reactions. They use such glittering generalities as "American," "sound," "fair," and "just." Symbols are often used to elicit those reactions, too: Uncle Sam and the flag are favorites. So, too, are testimonials—endorsements, or supporting statements, from such well-known personalities as television stars or professional athletes. The bandwagon approach, which urges people to follow the crowd, is another favorite technique. The plain-folks approach, in which the propagandist pretends to be one of the common people, gets heavy use, too.

Propaganda is spread through newspapers, radio, television, the Internet, movies, billboards, books, magazines, pamphlets, posters, speeches—in fact, through every form of mass communication. The more controversial or less popular a group's position, the more necessary the propaganda campaign becomes.

Influencing Parties and Elections

As you know, interest groups and political parties are very different creatures. They exist in the same environment, however, and their paths often cross.

For their part, leaders of interest groups know that political parties play a central role in selecting those people who make public-policy decisions. They are quite aware, too, that much of the government's policy-making machinery is organized by and through political parties.

Interest groups thus try to influence the behavior of political parties, and they do so in a number of ways. Some groups keep close ties with one or the other of the major parties. Most hope to secure the support of both of them. Several urge their members to become active in party affairs and try to win posts in party organizations.

An interest group's election tactics often have to involve some very finely tuned decisions. The group must consider how its actions on behalf of or against a candidate might affect its overall goal of influencing policy.

▲ Democratic presidential nominee John Kerry receives the endorsement of the International Association of Firefighters in 2004. *Critical Thinking Why are interest group endorsements significant to political candidates?*

Growth of PACs

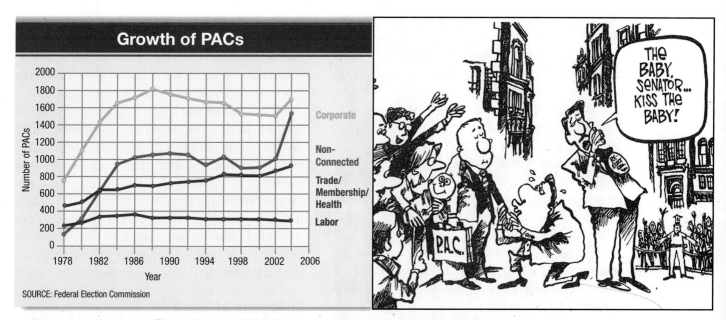

Number of PACs (y-axis: 0, 200, 400, 600, 800, 1000, 1200, 1400, 1600, 1800, 2000)

Year (x-axis: 1978, 1982, 1986, 1990, 1994, 1998, 2002, 2006)

Corporate

Non-Connected

Trade/Membership/Health

Labor

SOURCE: Federal Election Commission

THE BABY SENATOR... KISS THE BABY!

P.A.C.

Interpreting Graphs The total number of PACs has increased dramatically since the 1970s. *(a) How would you describe the growth of PACs during the 1990s? (b) What does the growth of PACs suggest about the way political campaigns are financed?* H-SS 12.3.2

If, for example, a group supports the Democratic candidate for a seat in the U.S. Senate, it may not want to help that candidate by attacking the Republican nominee in the race, especially if the Republican has some chance of winning. If the Republican does win the race, the group will not only have failed to advance its cause, but likely will have created an enemy. The interest group might also be concerned that another Republican candidate who wins some other office might be offended by attacks on a party colleague, even if he or she agrees with the group's policy aims.

Campaigns for public office cost a great deal of money. Interest groups are quite aware of this fact, and they are a major source of campaign funds today. Much of their financial help now goes to parties and their candidates through political action committees (PACs). As you know, PACs raise and distribute money to candidates who will further their goals. (See Chapter 7, page 199.)

The number of PACs has grown dramatically over the past 30 years or so. One particular variety, often called **single-interest groups,** has grown most rapidly. These organizations are PACs that concentrate their efforts on one issue, such as abortion, gun control, or health care. They work for or, more often, against a candidate solely on the basis of that candidate's stand on that one issue. For them, all other considerations—the candidate's record on other questions, his or her party identification or political experience, and so on—are of little or no importance.

Most interest groups focus on the public policy-making process. Any part they play in the electoral process is an offshoot of that primary concern. The efforts of single-interest groups stand as a notable exception to that rule.

Lobbying

Lobbying is usually defined as those activities by which group pressures are brought to bear on legislators and the legislative process. Certainly, it is that, but it is also much more. Realistically, lobbying includes all of the methods by which group pressures are brought to bear on all aspects of the public policy-making process.

What happens in a legislative body is often of deep concern to several different, and competing, interests. A bill to regulate the sale of firearms, for example, excites the interest of many individuals and groups. Those companies that make guns, those that sell them, and those that produce or sell ammunition, targets, scopes, hunting jackets, sleeping bags, and related products have a clear stake in that bill's contents and its fate. So, too, do law-enforcement agencies, hunters, wildlife conservationists, such groups

▲ **Making Their Views Known** Lobbyists make their interests known in a variety of ways, including direct contact with legislators (top). The League of Women Voters, which often works at the grassroots level, promotes active participation in government (bottom). **H-SS 12.6.4**

interest groups often have to carry their lobbying efforts beyond the legislative arena. Lobbying is thus also often brought into one and sometimes several agencies in the executive branch and sometimes into the courts, as well.

Nearly all of the more important organized interests in the country—business groups, labor unions, farm organizations, the professions, veterans, churches, and many more—maintain lobbyists in Washington. Most estimates put the number of people who earn at least part of their living by lobbying Congress at no fewer than 20,000. Lobbyists are also stationed in the 50 State capitals, and their number grows whenever the State's legislature is in session.[7]

Lobbyists at Work

Lobbyists themselves often prefer to be known by some other title—"legislative counsel" or "public representative," for example. Whatever they call themselves, their major task is to work for those matters that benefit their clients and against those that may harm them.

A lobbyist's effectiveness depends in large part on his or her knowledge of the political system. The competent lobbyist is thoroughly familiar with government and its procedures, with the facts of current political life, and with the techniques of "polite" persuasion. Some have been members of Congress or the State legislature. They know the "legislative ropes" and have many close contacts among present-day members. Many others are lawyers, former journalists, or men and women who have come into lobbying from the closely related field of public relations.

Lobbyists at work use a number of techniques as they try to persuade legislators and other policy makers to share their points of view. They see that articles, reports, and all sorts of other information favorable to their causes reach those officeholders. Many testify before legislative committees. If the House Committee on the Judiciary is considering a

as the National Rifle Association and the American Civil Liberties Union, and many others. These groups all seek to influence legislators as they consider the passage of that bill.

Public policy is made by much more than the words in a statute, however. What happens after a law has been passed is often of real concern to organized interests, too. How is the law interpreted? How vigorously is it applied by the agency that enforces it? What position will the courts take if the law is challenged on some legal ground? These questions point to the fact that

---

[7]The "lobby" is actually an outer room or main corridor or some other part of a capitol building to which the general public is admitted. The term *lobby-agent* was being used to identify favor-seekers at sessions of the New York State legislature in Albany by the late 1820s. By the 1830s the term had been shortened to lobbyist and was in wide use in Washington and elsewhere.

gun control bill, for example, representatives of all those groups with an interest in firearms mentioned earlier are certain to be invited, or to ask for the opportunity, to present their views. The testimony that lobbyists give is usually "expert," but, of course, it is also couched in terms favorable to the interests they represent.

Most lobbyists also know how to bring "grass-roots" pressures to bear. **Grass roots** means of or from the people, the average voters. The groups that the lobbyists speak for can mount campaigns by e-mail, letter, postcard, and phone from "the folks back home"—and often on short notice. The good lobbyist's arsenal of publicity includes any number of other weapons: favorable news stories, magazine articles, advertisements, radio and television appeals, and endorsements by noted personalities.

Several interest groups now publish ratings of members of Congress. These rankings are based on the votes cast on measures that those groups regard as crucial to their interests. Among the most prominent of the many organizations that now compile and publish such ratings are the Americans for Democratic Action (ADA), the American Civil Liberties Union (ACLU), the various State Public Interest Research Groups (PIRG), the American Conservative Union (ACU), the National Tax Limitation Committee (NTLC), and the Chamber of Commerce of the United States.

Each of these groups selects a number of key measures and then rates each member on the basis of his or her votes on those bills. In the usual rating scheme, each senator or representative is given a score that reflects how often he or she voted in accordance with the views of the interest group.

Interest groups see to it that the mass media publicize these ratings. They also distribute the ratings to the group's membership. Their ultimate objective is twofold: either to persuade unfriendly legislators to change their voting behavior or to help bring about their defeat in future elections.

The typical lobbyist of today is a far cry from those of an earlier day, and from many of the fictitious ones still found on television and in novels and the movies. The once fairly common practice of bribery and the widespread use of unethical practices are almost unknown. Most present-day lobbyists work openly, and their major techniques come under the headings of friendliness, persuasion, and helpfulness.

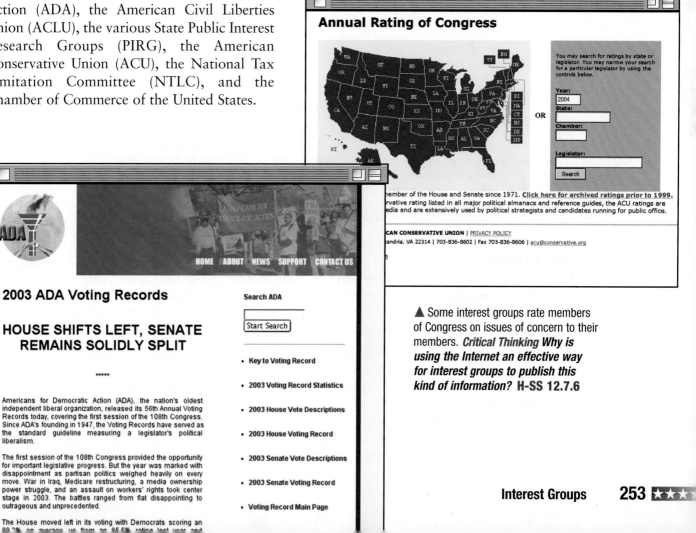

▲ Some interest groups rate members of Congress on issues of concern to their members. *Critical Thinking Why is using the Internet an effective way for interest groups to publish this kind of information?* H-SS 12.7.6

Lobbyists are ready to make campaign contributions, provide information, write speeches, and even draft legislation. The contributions are welcome, the information usually quite accurate, the speeches forceful, and the bills well-drawn. Most lobbyists know that if they behaved otherwise (gave false information, for example) they would damage, if not destroy, their credibility and thus their overall effectiveness.

Lobbyists work hard to influence committee action, floor debate, and the final vote in a legislative body. If they fail in one house, they carry their fight to the other. If they lose there too, they may turn to the executive branch and perhaps to the courts, as well.[8]

Lobby Regulation

Lobbying abuses do occur now and then, of course. False or misleading testimony, bribery, and other unethical pressures are not common, but they do happen. The first major attempt to corral lobbying came in 1946 when Congress passed the Federal Regulation of Lobbying Act. This law required lobbyists to register with the clerk of the House and the secretary of the Senate. More specifically, it required the registration of those individuals and groups who collected or spent money for the "principal purpose" of influencing legislation.

That vague phrase "principal purpose" proved to be a huge loophole through which many very active groups avoided registration. The 1946 law was also ineffective because its provisions applied only to lobbying efforts aimed at members of Congress, not at congressional staff members or at officials in the executive branch.

Congress finally responded to years of criticism of the 1946 law with a much tighter statute, the Lobbying Disclosure Act of 1995. That law eliminates the "principal purpose" standard. It requires registration by all individual lobbyists and organizations that seek to influence members of Congress, their staffers, or any policy-making official in the executive branch, from the President on down. Those who must register are required to supply such basic information as name, address, and principal place of business, plus a general description of their activities. They must also furnish similar information about their clients and describe in detail their lobbying activities in semiannual reports.

Each State also has its own law or laws regulating lobbying activities. The variations among them are extreme, however. Although most States have laws that are weaker than the federal statute, a few States have fairly rigorous laws. On the other hand, a few States condone virtually anything a lobbyist chooses to do.

---

[8]Notice that various government agencies often act much like interest groups in their relations with Congress or with a State's legislature—for example, when they seek funds or when they offer testimony for or against a bill in committee.

Section 3 Assessment

Key Terms and Main Ideas

1. For what three reasons do interest groups reach out to the public?
2. (a) Why do interest groups use **propaganda?** (b) Identify at least three major propaganda techniques.
3. (a) Why do interest groups try to influence political parties? (b) What is a **single-interest group?**
4. How is **lobbying** used to influence public policy?

Critical Thinking

5. **Expressing Problems Clearly** Create a "Help Wanted" ad for a lobbyist. Include a job description as well as the preferred professional experience and abilities that a candidate should bring to the position.

Standards Monitoring *Online*
For: Self-quiz with vocabulary practice
Web Code: mqa-2093

6. **Recognizing Propaganda** Choose an issue of particular interest to students, such as year-round schooling or censorship of school publications. Then write a paragraph in which you use at least two of the propaganda techniques described in this section to persuade your audience to support your point of view.

Go Online
PHSchool.com
For: An activity on PACs
Web Code: mqd-2093

May Taxpayers Challenge Federal Spending Laws?

Analysis Skills HR4, HI3, HI4

The federal courts possess the power of judicial review, but they can exercise that power only in those cases properly brought to them. May anyone who questions the constitutionality of a federal law challenge that law in court?

Flast v. *Cohen* (1968)

Flast was one of a group of seven taxpayers who objected to the use of federal funds to help support religious schools under the Elementary and Secondary Education Act of 1965. The group believed that public funding of these schools violated the First Amendment in two ways. First, such aid constituted an "establishment of religion." Second, by forcing the group to pay taxes to support religious activities, such aid interfered with the free exercise of their own religion. The group sued Secretary of Health, Education and Welfare Wilbur J. Cohen and other federal officials whose job it was to implement the Act.

The majority of a special three-judge federal court ruled that the Flast group did not have "standing" to proceed with the suit. "Standing" is a legal requirement under which a person can file a suit only if he or she has a personal stake in the outcome of the case. The court ruled that the plaintiffs' only stake in the outcome of the case was in their capacity as taxpayers, and this was not enough to give them standing. (In 1923, in the case of *Frothingham* v. *Mellon,* the Supreme Court had ruled that an individual could not challenge an act of Congress simply because that act affected the individual's tax bill.) The plaintiffs appealed to the Supreme Court, which considered whether its decision in *Frothingham* barred their suit.

Arguments for Flast

1. The *Frothingham* decision does not mean that a taxpayer may never challenge the constitutionality of an act of Congress. It merely means that a person's status as a taxpayer does not, by itself, give him or her standing to pose such a challenge. The plaintiffs in this case have a personal stake in the outcome of the case and should be allowed to proceed.

2. There is a connection between the plaintiffs' status as taxpayers and their claims in this case. The 1st Amendment's Establishment Clause limits Congress's power to collect taxes in support of religion. Thus the plaintiffs' role as taxpayers gives them a direct and concrete interest in the outcome of the case.

Arguments for Cohen

1. Federal courts already have a high caseload. The requirement that plaintiffs have sufficient standing helps prevent unnecessary lawsuits by ensuring that only those with a serious stake in the outcome bring cases.

2. People with no special interest in a controversy besides the tiny amount of their taxes that may be involved should not be allowed to sue in federal court.

Decide for Yourself

1. Review the constitutional grounds on which each side based its arguments and the specific arguments each side presented.
2. Debate the opposing viewpoints presented in this case. Which viewpoint do you favor?
3. Predict the impact of the Court's decision on other potential taxpayer suits challenging federal laws. (To read a summary of the Court's decision, turn to pages 799–806.)

Go Online
PHSchool.com

Use Web Code mqp-2096 to register your vote on this issue and to see how other students voted.

Political Dictionary

public policy (p. 236), public affairs (p. 239), trade association (p. 244), labor union (p. 244), public-interest group (p. 247), propaganda (p. 249), single-interest group (p. 251), lobbying (p. 251), grass roots (p. 253)

Standards Review

H-SS 12.1.2 Discuss the character of American democracy and its promise and perils as articulated by Alexis de Tocqueville.

H-SS 12.1.5 Describe the systems of separated and shared powers, the role of organized interests (*Federalist Paper Number 10*), checks and balances (*Federalist Paper Number 51*), the importance of an independent judiciary (*Federalist Paper Number 78*), enumerated powers, rule of law, federalism, and civilian control of the military.

H-SS 12.2.2 Explain how economic rights are secured and their importance to the individual and to society (e.g., the right to acquire, use, transfer, and dispose of property; right to choose one's work; right to join or not join labor unions; copyright and patent).

H-SS 12.2.4 Understand the obligations of civic-mindedness, including voting, being informed on civic issues, volunteering and performing public service, and serving in the military or alternative service.

H-SS 12.3.1 Explain how civil society provides opportunities for individuals to associate for social, cultural, religious, economic, and political purposes.

H-SS 12.3.2 Explain how civil society makes it possible for people, individually or in association with others, to bring their influence to bear on government in ways other than voting and elections.

H-SS 12.6.4 Describe the means that citizens use to participate in the political process (e.g., voting, campaigning, lobbying, filing a legal challenge, demonstrating, petitioning, picketing, running for political office).

H-SS 12.7.5 Explain how public policy is formed, including the setting of the public agenda and implementation of it through regulations and executive orders.

H-SS 12.7.6 Compare the processes of lawmaking at each of the three levels of government, including the role of lobbying and the media.

Practicing the Vocabulary

Matching *Choose a term from the list above that best matches each description.*

1. A type of interest group that represents business interests
2. The events and issues of concern to all the people in a society
3. Political action committee devoted to one issue
4. A type of interest group that works for the public good
5. The means by which group pressures are brought to bear on all aspects of the policy-making process
6. Of or from the common people, the average voters

Word Recognition *Replace the underlined definition with the correct term from the list above.*

7. Interest groups exist for the purpose of influencing <u>all of the many goals that a government pursues in all of the many areas of human affairs in which it is involved.</u>
8. In many industries workers have formed <u>organizations of those who share the type of job or who work in the same industry.</u>
9. One type of interest group is a(n) <u>organization devoted to the interests of all the people.</u>
10. Interest groups help to stimulate interest in <u>the events and issues that concern people at large.</u>

Reviewing Main Ideas

Section 1

11. Why are interest groups sometimes called "pressure groups" or "special interests"?
12. At what levels of government can you find interest groups operating?
13. In what ways are interest groups both similar to and different from political parties?
14. Summarize the debate over the role of interest groups in the American political system.
15. How do interest groups add an element to the checks-and-balances feature of the political process?

Section 2

16. For what reason has the United States often been called "a nation of joiners"?
17. What is the difference between private and public-interest groups?

18. **(a)** On what kinds of issues do labor groups generally agree? **(b)** On what kinds of issues might labor interests have different points of view?
19. **(a)** Describe three types of interest groups that are not based on economic interests. **(b)** List at least one example of each type of group.

Section 3

20. **(a)** For what reason must interest groups be concerned with public opinion? **(b)** For what purposes do interest groups appeal to public opinion?
21. What are the goals of a propagandist?
22. **(a)** To what extent are most interest groups concerned about elections? **(b)** What groups provide an exception to this rule?
23. At what stages of policymaking must lobbyists be involved? Explain your answer.
24. The Lobbying Disclosure Act requires registration by all those individuals and organizations that do what?

Critical Thinking Skills

Analysis Skill HR4

25. *Applying the Chapter Skill* Use the Internet to find three recent proposed amendments to the Constitution. Who is promoting these amendments, and why?

26. *Demonstrating Reasoned Judgment* You have read that forming interest groups is "both practical and democratic." **(a)** Explain your understanding of this statement. **(b)** What issues in your school or community might usefully be addressed by forming interest groups?

27. *Drawing Conclusions* Consider the discussion of the functions and criticisms of interest groups in Section 1. Based on this information, discuss your opinion about whether or not interest groups are positive or negative influences on the American political process.

Analyzing Political Cartoons

Using your knowledge of American government and this cartoon, answer the questions below.

28. (a) What does the building in the cartoon represent?
(b) What is the source of the words on the building?

29. What is the cartoon saying about the influence of special-interest groups on the political process?

★ You Can Make a Difference

With a group of friends, think of a policy issue on which you have a definite opinion. Then outline a plan for a group that would lobby for your side of that issue. Use the following suggestions for starting a local interest group.

(1) Find a faculty sponsor.
(2) Have a kickoff meeting.
(3) Gain attention and publicity in a variety of ways—tell your friends, announce your group on the PA system, write an editorial, put up fliers, speak to existing school clubs.

Participation Activities

Analysis Skills CS4, HR4

30. *Current Events Watch* Scan recent newspapers and magazines to find a reference to an interest group at work. Then answer the following questions: What is the interest group? What appears to be its goal? How is it attempting to reach that goal? Share your findings with those of your classmates. Of the interest groups you and your classmates have found, which seem to be the most powerful? Why?

31. *Chart Activity* Create a chart that summarizes the types of interest groups mentioned in Section 2. Use the headings in blue as your categories, and list up to five examples in each category. Then choose one of these groups and find out more about it: the issues it follows, how it attempts to influence public policy, its history, the groups from which it draws its membership, and its success rate in reaching its goals.

32. *It's Your Turn* Conduct a survey to discover the interest groups people in your community belong to and why. Before you begin your interviews, frame the questions you wish to ask. Be sure that groups not commonly thought of as interest groups, such as church clubs, are included in your survey. Plan to interview at least ten people. What conclusions do your interviews suggest? **(Conducting a Survey)**

Standards Monitoring *Online*

For: Chapter 9 Self-Test **Visit:** PHSchool.com
Web Code: mqa-2094

As a final review, take the Magruder's Chapter 9 Self-Test and receive immediate feedback on your answers.
The test consists of 20 multiple-choice questions designed to test your understanding of the chapter content.

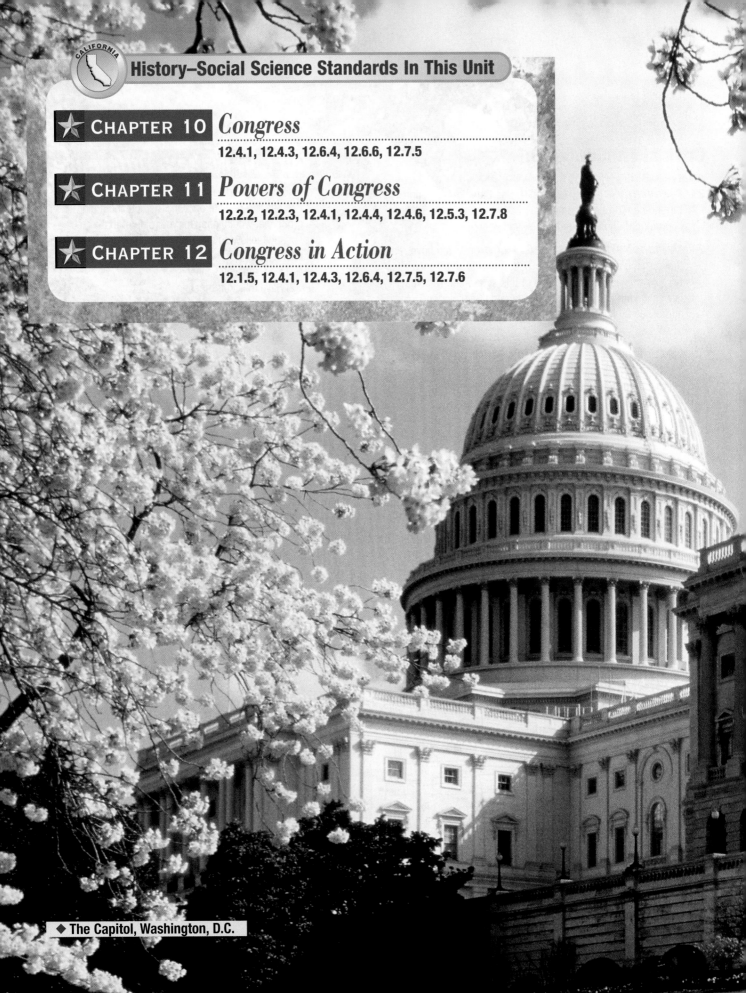

◆ The Capitol, Washington, D.C.

UNIT 3

The Legislative Branch

CONSTITUTIONAL PRINCIPLES

Separation of Powers The Constitution gives Congress the power to make laws. Separating the power to make laws from the power to enforce and the power to review them prevents the misuse of governmental authority.

Checks and Balances The Constitution gives Congress a number of powers with which it can check the actions of the executive and the judicial branches.

Limited Government Congress can exercise only those powers given to it by the Constitution—and, in doing so, it cannot violate any provision in the Constitution.

The Impact on You

What Congress does has an effect on you, quite directly—when it sets the minimum wage, for example, and when it decides how much tax you will pay on your wages. Among many other examples: Congress has decreed that all public high schools must allow student religious groups to meet in the school, on the same terms that other student groups may do so.

CHAPTER 10

Congress

"*Any one who is unfamiliar with what Congress actually does and how it does it, with all its duties and all its occupations, . . . is very far from a knowledge of the constitutional system under which we live.*"

—Woodrow Wilson (1885)

Wilson saw Congress, the legislative branch, as the most basic part of a democratic, constitutional government. The men and women elected to the House and Senate give the people a voice in setting public policy and making laws.

◆ **Representatives and aides outside the Capitol**

Standards Preview

H-SS 12.4.1 Discuss Article I of the Constitution as it relates to the legislative branch, including eligibility for office and lengths of terms of representatives and senators; election to office; the roles of the House and Senate in impeachment proceedings; the role of the vice president; the enumerated legislative powers; and the process by which a bill becomes a law.

H-SS 12.4.3 Identify their current representatives in the legislative branch of the national government.

H-SS 12.6.4 Describe the means that citizens use to participate in the political process (e.g., voting, campaigning, lobbying, filing a legal challenge, demonstrating, petitioning, picketing, running for political office).

H-SS 12.6.6 Analyze trends in voter turnout; the causes and effects of reapportionment and redistricting, with special attention to spatial districting and the rights of minorities; and the function of the Electoral College.

H-SS 12.7.5 Explain how public policy is formed, including the setting of the public agenda and implementation of it through regulations and executive orders.

SECTION 1

The National Legislature (pp. 262–265)

★ Congress is bicameral, or divided into two houses.
★ In the House of Representatives, States are represented according to population.
★ Each State has two members in the Senate.
★ Congress meets for two-year terms, divided into two one-year sessions.

SECTION 2

The House of Representatives (pp. 267–273)

★ Each member of the House of Representatives represents a district of roughly equal population and is up for reelection every two years.
★ After each census, seats in the House are redistributed among the States, and districts are redrawn to reflect changes in population.
★ Congressional districts are often gerrymandered by the dominant party in a State's legislature.

SECTION 3

The Senate (pp. 275–278)

★ The Senate includes 100 members, two from each State, who are elected to six-year terms.
★ Senators usually have more experience, power, and prestige than their colleagues in the House.
★ Senators are protected from some political pressures because they serve for a long period between elections.

SECTION 4

The Members of Congress (pp. 279–284)

★ Members of Congress are likely to be older and wealthier than the average American, and most members are men.
★ Members bring a variety of viewpoints and career backgrounds to Congress.
★ Members of Congress juggle a number of roles by working as lawmakers, party members, and servants of their constituents.
★ Congress sets its own pay and other compensations—and that fact poses peculiar problems for its members.

Go Online
PHSchool.com

For: Current Data
Web Code: mqg-3106

For: Close Up Foundation debates
Web Code: mqh-3109

Section Preview

OBJECTIVES

1. **Explain** why the Constitution provides for a bicameral Congress.
2. **Describe** a term of Congress.
3. **Summarize** how sessions of Congress have changed over time.

WHY IT MATTERS

The Framers of the Constitution created a Congress with two bodies: a small Senate and a much larger House of Representatives. Each Congress since 1789 has met for a term of two years; those terms are now divided into two one-year sessions.

POLITICAL DICTIONARY

★ **term**
★ **session**
★ **adjourn**
★ **prorogue**
★ **special session**

You know that you live in a democracy, and in a democracy, the people rule. But what does that really mean? You are one of "the people," but you do not rule, at least not in the hands-on sense. You do not make laws, collect taxes, arrest criminals, or decide court cases.

You do not do those or all of the other things that government does because you live in a *representative* democracy. Here, it is the representatives of the people who are responsible for the day-to-day work of government.

Congress stands as a leading example of that fact. It is the legislative branch of the National Government. Congress, then, is charged with the most basic governmental function in a democratic society—that of translating the public will into public policy in the form of law.

James Madison called Congress "the first branch" of the National Government. Just how profoundly important he and the other Framers thought Congress to be can be seen in this fact: the very first and longest of the articles of the Constitution is devoted to it.

 FROM THE Constitution *"All legislative Powers herein granted shall be vested in a Congress of the United States, which shall consist of a Senate and House of Representatives."*

—Article I, Section 1

A Bicameral Congress

As you have just seen, the Constitution immediately establishes a bicameral legislature—that is, one made up of two houses. It does so for historical, practical, and theoretical reasons.

1. **Historical** The British Parliament had consisted of two houses since the 1300s. The Framers and most other Americans knew the British system of bicameralism quite well. Most of the colonial assemblies and, in 1787, all but two of the new State legislatures were also bicameral. Among the original thirteen colonies, only

▲ *Party Leaders* Senator Bill Frist (R., Tennessee) is the Senate's majority leader today, and Representative Nancy Pelosi (D., California) serves as the minority leader in the House. **H-SS 12.4.1**

Georgia and Pennsylvania had unicameral colonial and then State legislatures. Georgia's legislature became bicameral in 1789 and Pennsylvania's in 1790 (Only one State, Nebraska, has a unicameral legislature today.)

2. **Practical** The Framers had to create a two-chambered body to settle the conflict between the Virginia and the New Jersey Plans at Philadelphia in 1787. As you have read in Chapter 2, the most populous States wanted to distribute the seats in Congress in proportion to the population of each State, while the smaller States demanded an equal voice in Congress. Bicameralism is a reflection of federalism. Each of the States is equally represented in the Senate and each is represented in line with its population in the House.

3. **Theoretical** The Framers favored a bicameral Congress in order that one house might act as a check on the other.

A leading constitutional historian recounts a breakfast-table conversation between Thomas Jefferson and George Washington. Jefferson, who had just returned from France, told Washington that he was opposed to a two-chambered legislature. As he made his point, he poured his coffee into his saucer, and Washington asked him why he did so. "To cool it," replied Jefferson. "Even so," said Washington, "we pour legislation into the senatorial saucer to cool it."[1]

The Framers were generally convinced that Congress would dominate the new National Government. As Madison observed,

PRIMARY Sources *"In a republican government, the legislative authority necessarily predominates. The remedy for this inconveniency is to divide the legislature into different branches."*
—*The Federalist* No. 51

The Framers saw bicameralism as a way to diffuse the power of Congress and so prevent it from overwhelming the other two branches of government.

For more than 200 years now, some people have argued that equal representation of the

---
[1] Max Farrand, *The Framing of the Constitution* (1913).
[2] There is not the remotest chance that that would ever be done. Recall, the Constitution provides in Article V that "no State, without its Consent, shall be deprived of its equal Suffrage in the Senate."

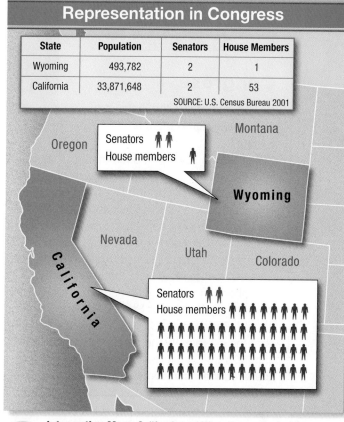

Representation in Congress

State	Population	Senators	House Members
Wyoming	493,782	2	1
California	33,871,648	2	53

SOURCE: U.S. Census Bureau 2001

Interpreting Maps California and Wyoming each elect two senators, despite a huge difference in their populations. *How does the distribution of Senate seats among the States illustrate the principle of federalism?* **H-SS 12.4.1**

States in the Senate is undemocratic and should be eliminated.[2] They often point to the two extremes to make their case. The State with the least population, Wyoming, has only some 500,000 residents. The largest State, California, now has a population of more than 35 million. Yet each of these States has two senators.

Those who argue against State equality in the Senate ignore a vital fact. The Senate was purposely created as a body in which the States would be represented as coequal members and partners in the Union. Remember, had the States not been equally represented in the Senate, there might never have been a Constitution.

Terms and Sessions

One woman, incensed at something her senator had done, said "You know, 535 of you people in Congress meet every two years. There are some of us who think that it would be much better if just two of you met every 535 years."

Frequently Asked Questions

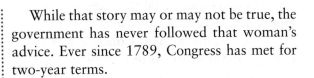

Congress

Does it matter that the States are not equally represented in the Senate?

Many people say that it does matter. They note that the Senate is the only legislative body in the United States that is not built on the principle of representation according to population. Most senators represent constituencies that are more white, rural, and conservative than would be the case if seats were allocated by population. The Senate's critics often note that many of the chamber's most powerful members regularly come from the smaller States. The late Senator Daniel P. Moynihan (D., NY), who knew firsthand that the interests of the residents of some States fare less well in the Senate than they might, declared that "sometime [soon] the United

States is going to have to address the question of apportionment in the Senate."

Is there any chance that the way in which seats in the Senate are distributed will ever be changed?

The short answer: No. The Constitution declares, in Article V, that "no State, without its Consent shall be deprived of its equal Suffrage in the Senate." Three-quarters of States would need to ratify a constitutional amendment to change the distribution of senators, and a great many people are satisfied with the current arrangement.

Any Questions?

What would you like to know about the United States Congress? Brainstorm two new questions and exchange them with a classmate. What did you learn?

While that story may or may not be true, the government has never followed that woman's advice. Ever since 1789, Congress has met for two-year terms.

Terms of Congress

Each **term** of Congress lasts for two years, and each term is numbered consecutively.[3] Congress began its first term on March 4, 1789, and that term ended two years later, on March 4, 1791.

The date for the start of each new term was changed by the 20th Amendment in 1933. In an earlier day, the several months from election to March 4 allowed for delays in communicating election results. This gave newly chosen lawmakers time to arrange their affairs and travel to Washington. The March date gave Congress less time to accomplish its work each year, however, and by the 1930s travel and communications were no longer an issue. The start of each new two-year term is now "noon of the 3d day of January" of every odd-numbered

year. So the term of the 109th Congress began on January 3, 2005, and it will end at noon on January 3, 2007.

Sessions

A **session** of Congress is that period of time during which, each year, Congress assembles and conducts business. There are two sessions to each term of Congress—one session each year. The Constitution provides

 The Congress shall assemble at least once in every year, and such meeting shall begin at noon on the 3d day of January, unless they shall by law appoint a different day.

—20th Amendment, Section 2

In fact, Congress often does "appoint a different day." The second session of each two-year term frequently begins a few days or even two or three weeks after the third of January.

Congress **adjourns,** or suspends until the next session, each regular session as it sees fit. Until World War II, the nation's lawmakers typically met for four or five months each year. Today, the many pressing issues facing Congress force it to remain in session through most of each

---

[3]Article I, Section 2, Clause 1 dictates a two-year term for Congress by providing that members of the House "shall be . . . chosen every second Year."

★★★★ **264**   Chapter 10 Section 1

year. Both houses do recess for several short periods during a session, however.

Neither house may adjourn *sine die* (finally, ending a session) without the consent of the other. The Constitution provides that

FROM THE **Constitution** *"Neither House . . . shall, without the Consent of the other, adjourn for more than three days, nor to any other Place than that in which the two Houses shall be sitting."*

—Article I, Section 5, Clause 4

Article II, Section 3 of the Constitution does give the President the power to **prorogue**—end, discontinue—a session, but only when the two houses cannot agree on a date for adjournment. No President has ever had to use that power.

Special Sessions

Only the President may call Congress into **special session**—a meeting to deal with some emergency situation.[4] Only 26 special sessions of Congress have ever been held. President Harry Truman called the most recent one in 1948, to consider anti-inflation and welfare measures in the aftermath of World War II.

Note that the President can call Congress *or* either of its houses into a special session. The Senate has been called into special session alone

---

[4]Article II, Section 3 says that the President "may, on extraordinary Occasions, convene both Houses, or either of them. . . ."

▲ *Outside Washington* Members of Congress have many responsibilities outside the regular legislative session in Washington. California Congressman Jim Costa (left) is shown here meeting with a constituent.

on 46 occasions, to consider treaties or presidential appointments, but not since 1933. The House has never been called alone.

Of course, the fact that Congress now meets nearly year-round reduces the likelihood of special sessions. That fact also lessens the importance of the President's power to call one. Still, as Congress nears the end of a session, the President sometimes finds it useful to *threaten* a special session if the two chambers do not act on some measure high on his legislative agenda.

Section 1 Assessment

Key Terms and Main Ideas

1. How long does a **term** of Congress last?
2. How does a **special session** differ from a regular session of Congress?
3. When does Congress **adjourn**?
4. Who has the power to **prorogue** a session of Congress?

Critical Thinking

5. **Determining Cause and Effect** What are the historical, practical, and theoretical reasons for bicameralism in Congress?
6. **Expressing Problems Clearly** Why do some people believe the Senate is undemocratic?

7. **Making Comparisons** The Articles of Confederation provided for a Congress that met for one-year terms. Why do you suppose the Framers of the Constitution created a Congress that meets for a term of two years?

Go Online
PHSchool.com

For: An activity on the national legislature
Web Code: mqd-3101

Face the
Issues

Health Care Reform

Background *The U.S. health care system is in crisis. Some 45 million Americans under 65 have no health insurance at all, and that number is growing. Meanwhile, the cost of Medicare, the government-funded health care system for retired people, skyrockets each year. Many are openly questioning whether the Federal Government should spend so much money in health care—or whether it should extend health coverage to everyone. What do you think?*

Prescription medications: a rising expense

Analysis Skill HR4

A Free-Market Solution

The root of our health care crisis is runaway spending. Any attempt by the government to extend health insurance in its current form to those without coverage will only make matters worse.

Most patients are spending someone else's money when they purchase health care services. That creates an incentive for wasteful spending. High spending makes insurance more expensive, so fewer workers can afford it. While workers are less able to afford insurance for themselves, they must pay higher taxes to cover rising Medicare costs for seniors.

We need to put responsibility for spending back in the hands of the patient. People could make deposits into tax-free Medical Savings Accounts (MSAs) to pay for expenses. Workers without insurance could put savings from lower taxes into their MSAs. Employers, who currently must pay rising insurance costs for their workers, could make deposits to employees' MSA accounts instead. Affordable insurance would still cover costs of catastrophic illness. When consumers pay their own health care bills, they will make smarter choices with their own dollars.

Let Governments Provide

We cannot fix our health care system without tackling runaway inflation among prescription drugs and medical services. Price hikes by drug manufacturers are endangering Medicare's future. The government must negotiate lower prices for Medicare prescriptions and doctor visits to reduce costs.

High-quality health care should be a right, not a privilege. All Americans should have access to government-funded health care. The solution to rising costs and lack of insurance among those under 65 is to extend Medicare to every American. Medicare is actually more efficient than private health insurance and spends less on bureaucrats and paperwork.

Our current system links health care to jobs. The unemployed and many minimum-wage workers are left out. People who are too sick to work run the risk of losing their insurance when they need it most. This system is unfair and hurts the most vulnerable members of our society. The Federal Government is the only institution big enough to provide inexpensive, effective health care to all citizens, working or unemployed. Medicare is the model.

Exploring the Issues

1. Both sides agree that higher costs for Medicare are a problem. Who is responsible for this spending according to each article?

2. Identify one reason why Medical Savings Accounts might not help every working American.

For more information about trends in the United States health care system, view "Health Care Reform."

Face the **Issues** Video Collection

Section Preview

OBJECTIVES

1. **Describe** the size and the elective terms of the members of the House.
2. **Explain** how House seats are reapportioned among the States after each census.
3. **Describe** a typical congressional election and congressional district.
4. **Analyze** the formal and informal qualifications for election to the House.

WHY IT MATTERS

The 435 members of the House of Representatives represent districts of roughly equal populations but very different characteristics. House members can serve an unlimited number of two-year terms. The House is often described as the branch of Congress closest to the people because of the short terms and relatively small districts of members.

POLITICAL DICTIONARY

★ apportion
★ reapportion
★ off-year election
★ single-member district
★ at-large
★ gerrymander

Every other autumn, all across the country, hundreds of men and women seek election to the House of Representatives. Most of them try to attract supporters and win votes with banners and posters, yard signs, billboards, flyers, buttons, and other eye-catching campaign materials. Nearly all of them make their "pitches" with radio and television spots, newspaper ads, and now in cyberspace. In this section, you will discover the general shape of the office that all of those candidates so eagerly pursue.

Size and Terms

The exact size of the House of Representatives—today, 435 members—is not fixed by the Constitution. Rather, it is set by Congress. The Constitution provides that the total number of seats in the House of Representatives shall be **apportioned** (distributed) among the States on the basis of their respective populations.[5]

Each State is guaranteed at least one seat in the House, no matter what its population. Today, seven States—Alaska, Delaware, Montana, North Dakota, South Dakota, Vermont, and Wyoming—have only one representative apiece.

The District of Columbia, Guam, the Virgin Islands, and American Samoa each elect a delegate to represent them in the House and Puerto Rico chooses a resident commissioner. Those

officials are not, however, full-fledged members of the House of Representatives.

Article I, Section 2, Clause 1 of the Constitution provides that "Representatives shall be . . . chosen every second Year"—that is, for two-year terms. This rather short term means that, for House members, the next election is always just around the corner. That fact tends to make them pay close attention to "the folks back home."

There is no constitutional limit on the number of terms any member of Congress may serve. In the 1990s, people tried to persuade Congress to offer a constitutional amendment to limit congressional terms. Most versions of such an amendment would put a three- or four-term limit (six or eight years) on service in the House and a two-term limit (twelve years) for the Senate.[6]

Reapportionment

Article I of the Constitution directs Congress to **reapportion**—redistribute—the seats in the House after each decennial census.[7] Until a first census could be taken, the Constitution set the size of the House at 65 seats. That many members served in the First and Second Congresses (1789–1793). The census of 1790 showed a national population of 3,929,214 persons;

---

[5]Article I, Section 2, Clause 3.

[6]The States do not have the power to limit the number of terms their members of Congress may serve, *United States* v. *Thornton,* 1995.

[7]Article I, Section 2, Clause 3. A decennial census is one taken every ten years.

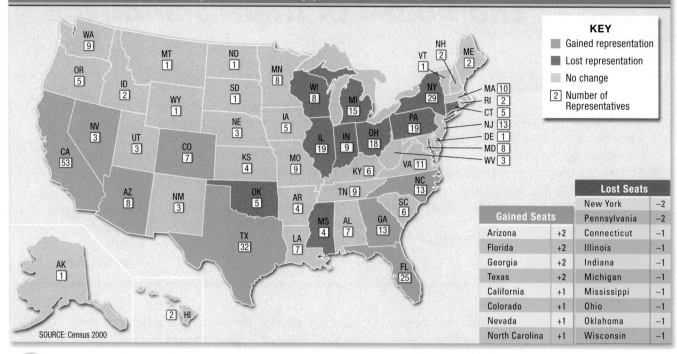

Congressional Apportionment, 2003–2013

KEY
- Gained representation
- Lost representation
- No change
- ☐2 Number of Representatives

SOURCE: Census 2000

Gained Seats

Arizona	+2
Florida	+2
Georgia	+2
Texas	+2
California	+1
Colorado	+1
Nevada	+1
North Carolina	+1

Lost Seats

New York	–2
Pennsylvania	–2
Connecticut	–1
Illinois	–1
Indiana	–1
Michigan	–1
Mississippi	–1
Ohio	–1
Oklahoma	–1
Wisconsin	–1

Interpreting Maps This map shows the changes in State representation due to the reapportionment of the House after the 2000 Census, and in effect from January 3, 2003 to January 3, 2013. The next reapportionment will be based on the census to be taken in 2010. ***What general trend in population growth around the country does this map show?*** H-SS 12.6.6

thus, in 1792 Congress increased the number of House seats by 41, to 106.

A Growing Nation

As the nation's population grew, and as the number of States increased, so did the size of the House. It went to 142 seats after the census of 1800, to 186 seats 10 years later, and so on.[8] By 1912, following the census of 1910 and the admission of Arizona and New Mexico, the House had grown to 435 seats.

With the census of 1920, Congress found itself in a painfully difficult political position. The House had long since grown too large for effective floor action. To reapportion without adding more seats to the House, however, would mean that some States would have to lose seats if every State were to be represented according to its population.

Congress met the problem by doing nothing. So, despite the Constitution's command, there

was no reapportionment on the basis of the 1920 census.

The Reapportionment Act of 1929

Faced with the 1930 census, Congress avoided repeating its earlier lapse by passing the Reapportionment Act of 1929. That law, still on the books, sets up what is often called an "automatic reapportionment." It provides:

(1) The "permanent" size of the House is 435 members. Of course, that figure is permanent only so long as Congress does not decide to change it. Congress did enlarge the House temporarily in 1959 when Alaska and then Hawaii became States. Today each of the 435 seats in the House represents an average of some 650,000 persons.

(2) Following each census, the Census Bureau is to determine the number of seats each State should have.

(3) When the Bureau's plan is ready, the President must send it to Congress.

(4) If, within 60 days of receiving it, neither house rejects the Census Bureau's plan, it becomes effective.

---

[8]Once, following the census of 1840, the size of the House was reduced from 242 to 232 seats.

The plan set out in the 1929 law has worked quite well through now eight reapportionments. The law leaves to Congress its constitutional responsibility to reapportion the House, but it gives to the Census Bureau the mechanical chores (and political "heat") that go with that task.

Congressional Elections

According to the Constitution, any person whom a State allows to vote for members of "the most numerous Branch" of its own legislature is qualified to vote in congressional elections.[9] The Constitution also provides that

> FROM THE Constitution **"**The Times, Places and Manner of holding [Congressional] Elections . . . shall be prescribed in each State by the Legislature thereof; but the Congress may at any time by Law make or alter such Regulations. . . .**"**[10]
> —Article I, Section 4, Clause 1

Date

Congressional elections are held on the same day in every State. Since 1872 Congress has required that those elections be held on the Tuesday following the first Monday in November of each even-numbered year. Congress has made an

[9]Article I, Section 2, Clause 1.
[10]The Constitution allows only one method for filling a vacancy in the House—by a special election, which may be called only by the governor of the State involved; Article I, Section 2, Clause 4.

exception for Alaska, which may hold its election in October. To date, however, Alaskans have chosen to use the November date.

In that same 1872 law, Congress directed that representatives be chosen by written or printed ballots. The use of voting machines was approved in 1899, and today, most votes cast in congressional elections are cast on some type of (usually electronic) voting machine.

Off-Year Elections

Those congressional elections that occur in the nonpresidential years—that is, between presidential elections—are called **off-year elections.** The most recent ones were held in 2002, and the next ones are due in 2006.

Far more often than not, the party in power—the party that holds the presidency—loses seats in the off-year elections. The time line below illustrates that point. The President's party did particularly poorly in 1974, after President Nixon resigned due to the Watergate Scandal, and in 1994, during President Clinton's first term. The 1998 off-year elections were an exception to the rule. That summer and fall, the Republican Congress held hearings to prepare to impeach President Clinton. Public opinion polls showed weak support for the impeachment, and many believe the hearings prompted significant support for Democratic candidates for Congress. And, recall, the elections of 2002 were also a departure, as we noted on page 131.

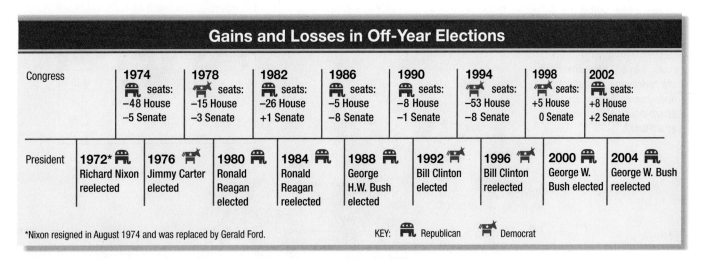

Gains and Losses in Off-Year Elections

Congress	1974 seats: −48 House −5 Senate	1978 seats: −15 House −3 Senate	1982 seats: −26 House +1 Senate	1986 seats: −5 House −8 Senate	1990 seats: −8 House −1 Senate	1994 seats: −53 House −8 Senate	1998 seats: +5 House 0 Senate	2002 seats: +8 House +2 Senate
President	1972* Richard Nixon reelected	1976 Jimmy Carter elected	1980 Ronald Reagan elected	1984 Ronald Reagan reelected	1988 George H.W. Bush elected	1992 Bill Clinton elected	1996 Bill Clinton reelected	2000 George W. Bush elected	2004 George W. Bush reelected

*Nixon resigned in August 1974 and was replaced by Gerald Ford.

KEY: Republican   Democrat

Interpreting Time Lines The President's party frequently loses seats in the House and Senate in an off-year election. *In which two election years above did the President's party lose the most seats in the House?*

Districts

The 435 members of the House are chosen by the voters in 435 separate congressional districts across the country. Recall that seven States now each have only one seat in the House of Representatives. There are, then, 428 congressional districts within the other 43 States.

The Constitution makes no mention of congressional districts. For more than half a century, Congress allowed each State to decide whether to elect its members by a general ticket system or on a single-member district basis. Under the **single-member district** arrangement, the voters in each district elect one of the State's representatives from among a field of candidates running for a seat in the House from that district.

Most States quickly set up single-member districts. Several States used the general ticket system, however. Under that arrangement, all of the State's seats were filled **at-large**—that is, elected from the State as a whole, rather than from a particular district. Every voter could vote for a candidate for each one of the State's seats in the House.

At-large elections proved grossly unfair. A party with even a very small plurality of voters Statewide could win all of a State's seats in the House. Congress finally did away with the general ticket system in 1842. Thereafter, all of the seats in the House were to be filled from single-member districts in each State. Since the seven States with the fewest residents each have only one representative in the House, these representatives are said to be elected "at-large." Although each representative represents a single-member district, that district covers the entire State.

The 1842 law made each State legislature responsible for drawing any congressional districts within its own State. It also required that each congressional district be made up of "contiguous territory," meaning that it must be all one piece. In 1872 Congress added the command that the districts within each State have "as nearly as practicable an equal number of inhabitants." In 1901 it further directed that all the districts be of "compact territory"—in other words, a comparatively small area.

These requirements of contiguity, population equality, and compactness were often disregarded by State legislatures, and Congress made no real effort to enforce them. The requirements were left out of the Reapportionment Act of 1929. In 1932 the Supreme Court held (in *Wood* v. *Broom*) that they had therefore been repealed. Over time, then, and most notably since 1929, the State legislatures have drawn many districts

Interpreting Maps
California gained one seat in the House after the 2000 Census. State legislators drew a map that realigned existing districts and created a new seat in the southern Central Valley. Districts in California are numbered from north to south, 1 to 53. *Why does the redrawing of district lines regularly produce sharp political conflicts in a State?* H-SS 12.6.6

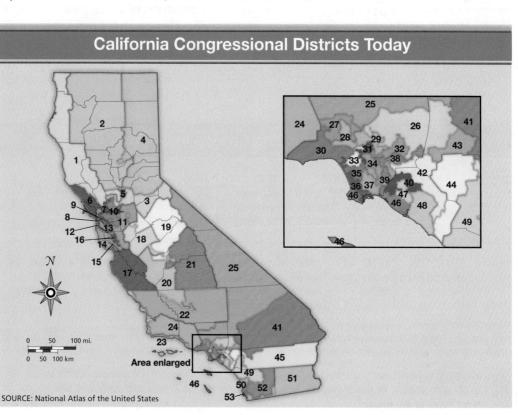

California Congressional Districts Today

Area enlarged

0   50   100 mi.
0   50 100 km

SOURCE: National Atlas of the United States

with very peculiar geographic shapes. Moreover, until fairly recently, many districts were also of widely varying populations.

Gerrymandering

Congressional district maps in several States show one and sometimes several districts of very odd shapes. Some look like the letters S or Y, some bear a resemblance to a dumbbell or a squiggly piece of spaghetti, and some defy description. Those districts have usually been **gerrymandered.** That is, they have been drawn to the advantage of the political party that controls the State's legislature.

Gerrymandering is widespread today—and not just at the congressional district level. Districts for the election of State legislators are regularly drawn for partisan advantage. In fact, gerrymandering can be found in most places where lines are drawn for the election of public officeholders—in cities, counties, school districts, and elsewhere.

Most often gerrymandering takes one of two forms. The lines are drawn either (1) to concentrate the opposition's voters in one or a few districts, thus leaving the other districts comfortably safe for the dominant party; or (2) to spread the opposition as thinly as possible among several districts, limiting the opposition's ability to win anywhere in the region. Gerrymandering's main goal is to create as many "safe" districts as possible—districts almost certain to be won by the party in control of the line-drawing process. And the computer-driven map-making techniques of today make the practice more effective than ever in its storied past.

For decades, gerrymandering produced congressional districts that differed widely in the number of people they included. State legislatures were responsible for this situation. A number of them regularly drew district lines on a partisan basis—with the Republicans gouging the Democrats in those States where the GOP controls the legislature, and the

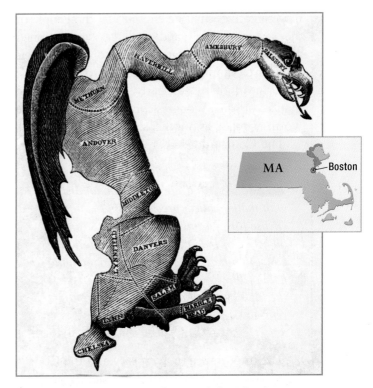

▲ **The original Gerrymander** Gerrymandering takes its name from Governor Elbridge Gerry of Massachusetts, who in 1812 drew the State's legislative districts to favor the Democratic-Republicans. It is said that the painter Gilbert Stuart added a head, wings, and claws on a district map hanging over the desk of a Federalist newspaper editor. "That," he said, "will do for a salamander." "Better say Gerrymander," growled the editor.

Democrats doing the same thing to the Republicans where they hold sway. In fact, that circumstance exists in several States today. Historically, most States were carved up on a rural versus urban as well as a partisan basis—because, through much of history, the typical State legislature was dominated by the less-populated (and over-represented) rural areas of the State.[11]

Wesberry v. Sanders, 1964

Suddenly, and quite dramatically, these long-standing patterns of wide population variations among House districts and of rural over-representation in the chamber came to an end in the mid- to late 1960s. These abrupt changes were the direct result of a historic decision by the Supreme Court in 1964. In *Wesberry* v. *Sanders*, the Court held that the population differences among Georgia's congressional districts were so great as to violate the Constitution.

In reaching its landmark decision, the Supreme Court noted that Article I, Section 2 declares that

[11]The pattern of rural over-representation in the State legislatures has now all but disappeared as a consequence of the Supreme Court's several "one-person, one-vote" decisions of the 1960s and 1970s. In the leading case, *Reynolds* v. *Sims,* 1964, the Court held that the 14th Amendment's Equal Protection Clause commands that the seats in both houses of a State's legislature must be apportioned on the basis of population equality.

representatives shall be chosen "by the People of the several States" and shall be "apportioned among the several States . . . according to their respective Numbers. . . ." These words, the Court held, mean that "as nearly as practicable one man's vote in a congressional election is to be worth as much as another's."

The Court added that

PRIMARY Sources *❝While it may not be possible to draw congressional districts with mathematical precision, that is no excuse for ignoring our Constitution's plain objective of making equal representation for equal numbers of people the fundamental goal of the House of Representatives. That is the high standard of justice and common sense which the Founders set for us. ❞*
—Justice Black, *Opinion of the Court*

The importance of *Wesberry* and the Court's later "one person, one vote" decisions cannot be overstated. They had an extraordinary impact on the makeup of the House, on the content of public policy, and on electoral politics in general. The nation's cities and suburbs now speak with a much larger voice in Congress than ever before. Notice, however, that it is quite possible

to draw congressional (or any other) district lines in accord with the "one person, one vote" rule and, at the same time, to gerrymander them.

Gerrymandering based solely on race, however, is a violation of the 15th Amendment, *Gomillion* v. *Lightfoot*, 1960. So-called "majority-minority districts" were drawn in some States following the census in 1990 and again in 2000—districts crafted to include a majority of African Americans and/or Latinos and so likely to send African Americans and Latinos to Congress. The Supreme Court struck down those race-based districts in several cases—most notably, in a case from Texas, *Bush* v. *Vera*, 1996. But, most recently, the Court has held this: while race cannot be the controlling factor in drawing district lines, race can be one of the mix of factors that shape that process. It did so in a case from North Carolina, *Hunt* v. *Cromartie*, in 2001.

Qualifications for House Members

You know that there are 435 members of the House of Representatives, and that each one of them had to win an election to get there. Each one of them also had to meet two quite different sets of qualifications to win office: the formal qualifications for membership in the House set out in the Constitution and a number of informal qualifications imposed by the realities of politics.

Formal Qualifications

The Constitution says that a member of the House
    (1) must be at least 25 years of age,
    (2) must have been a citizen of the United States for at least seven years, and
    (3) must be an inhabitant of the State from which he or she is elected.[12]

Longstanding custom, not the Constitution, also requires that a representative must live in the district he or she represents. The custom is based on the belief that the legislator should be closely familiar with the locale he or she represents, its people, and its problems. Rarely, then, does a district choose an outsider to represent it.

HOUSE	SENATE
Larger body (435 members)	Smaller body (100 members)
Shorter term (2 years)	Longer term (6 years)
Smaller constituencies (elected from districts within States)	Larger constituencies (elected from entire State)
Younger membership	Older membership
Less prestige	More prestige
Lower visibility in the news media	Higher visibility in the news media
Strict rules, limited debate	Flexible rules, nearly unlimited debate
Most work is done in committees, not on the floor	Work is split more evenly between committees and the floor
No power over treaties and presidential appointments	Approves or rejects treaties and presidential appointments

Major Differences Between the House and Senate

Interpreting Tables Members of the House and Senate work under very different rules and conditions. *Why do House members debate most bills in committees before bringing them to the House floor?*

[12]Article I, Section 2, Clause 2; see also Article I, Section 6, Clause 2.
[13]Article I, Section 5, Clause 1.
[14]Article I, Section 5, Clause 2.

The Constitution makes the House "the Judge of the Elections, Returns and Qualifications of its own Members."[13] Thus, when the right of a member-elect to be seated is challenged, the House has the power to decide the matter. Challenges are rarely successful.

The House may refuse to seat a member-elect by majority vote. It may also "punish its Members for disorderly Behavior" by majority vote, and "with the Concurrence of two thirds, expel a Member."[14]

Historically, the House viewed its power to judge the qualifications of members-elect as the power to impose additional standards. It did so several times. In 1900 it refused to seat Brigham H. Roberts of Utah because he was a polygamist—that is, he had more than one wife. In *Powell* v. *McCormack*, 1969, however, the Supreme Court held that the House could not exclude a member-elect who meets the Constitution's standards of age, citizenship, and residence. The House has not excluded anyone since that decision.

Over more than 200 years, the House has expelled only five members. Three were ousted in 1861 for their "support of rebellion." Michael Myers (D., Pennsylvania) was expelled in 1980 for corruption. Myers had been caught up in the Abscam probe, an undercover FBI investigation of corruption. Most recently, the House ejected James Traficant (D., Ohio) in 2002. Mr. Traficant had earlier been convicted of several counts of bribery, fraud, and tax evasion. Over time, a few members have resigned to avoid almost certain expulsion.

The House has not often punished a member for "disorderly Behavior," but such actions are not nearly so rare as expulsions. Most recently, the House voted to "reprimand" Barney Frank (D., Massachusetts) in 1990 for conduct stemming from his relationship with a male prostitute. Mr. Frank, an avowed homosexual, has been easily reelected by the voters in his congressional district every two years since then.

The Speaker of the House left Congress under a cloud in 1989. Jim Wright (D., Texas) resigned his seat after the House Ethics Committee charged him with a number of violations of House rules. Most of those allegations centered around Mr. Wright's financial dealings with individuals and companies with an interest in legislation before the House.

Informal Qualifications

The realities of politics produce a number of informal qualifications for membership in the House—beyond those qualifications set out in the Constitution. These additional qualifications vary somewhat from time to time and from State to State, and sometimes from one congressional district to another within the same State.

Informal qualifications have to do with a candidate's vote-getting abilities. They include such factors as party identification, name familiarity, gender, ethnic characteristics, and political experience. The "right" combination of these factors will help a candidate win nomination and then election to the House. The "wrong" ones, however, will almost certainly spell defeat.

Section 2 Assessment

Key Terms and Main Ideas

1. How are the seats in the House of Representatives **apportioned**?
2. When will the next two **off-year elections** occur?
3. Explain the difference between a **single-member district** seat and an **at-large** seat.
4. Why do politicians **gerrymander** districts?

Critical Thinking

5. **Drawing Inferences** How did *Wesberry* v. *Sanders* change the makeup of Congress?
6. **Predicting Consequences** Since 1910, the average number of people in a congressional district has tripled from 210,000 to well over 650,000. How might this have affected the ability of members of Congress to represent their constituents?

Standards Monitoring *Online*
For: Self-quiz with vocabulary practice
Web Code: mqa-3102

Go Online
PHSchool.com

For: An activity on gerrymandering
Web Code: mqd-3102

on Primary Sources

Redistricting and Race

Analysis Skills CS3, HR4, HI3

African Americans and Latinos have historically been underrepresented in the House of Representatives. As a result, several States designated "majority-minority" congressional districts to elect more minority members to Congress. Although the Supreme Court had previously rejected one such district, North Carolina's 12th, in 1993 and 1996, it reversed itself in **Hunt v. Cromartie (2001)** *as explained by commentator Richard A. Zitrin.*

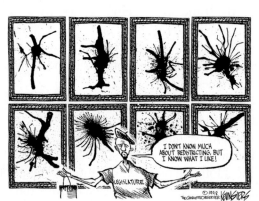

What does the cartoon suggest about the process of redistricting?

The U.S. Supreme Court has ruled 5–4 that race was not proven to be the predominant factor in the creation of a highly contested North Carolina congressional district. . . .

The decision upholds the legality of North Carolina's 12th Congressional District, currently represented by Democrat Melvin Watt, one of two black representatives from the state. . .

The court's ruling reversed a federal district court decision that the North Carolina legislature violated the equal protection clause of the 14th Amendment by using "facially race-driven" criteria in changing the 12th district's boundaries.

The 12th district is about 47 percent African-American. It is a long narrow district that stretches 71 miles and includes the cities of Greensboro, Winston-Salem and Charlotte.

In defending the district, the state said it was drawn for political considerations because North Carolina wanted to maintain an even split between Republicans and Democrats in its congressional delegation.

Writing for the Supreme Court majority, Justice Breyer said that in cases "where majority-minority districts (or the approximate equivalent) are at issue and where racial identification correlates highly with political affiliation, the party attacking the legislatively drawn boundaries must show at least that

the legislature could have achieved its legitimate political objectives in alternative ways that are comparable (and) consistent with traditional districting principles. That party must also show that those districting alternatives would have brought about significantly greater racial balance."

In a dissenting opinion, Justice Clarence Thomas wrote that the Supreme Court should have deferred to the trier of fact [the federal district court].

"The only question that this Court should decide is whether the District Court's finding of racial predominance was clearly erroneous," Thomas wrote. "In light of the direct evidence of racial motive and the inferences that may be drawn from the circumstantial evidence, I am satisfied that the District Court's finding was permissible, even if not compelled by the record."

Analyzing Primary Sources

1. What is the main issue in *Hunt* v. *Cromartie*?
2. On what grounds did the Court reverse itself in *Hunt* v. *Cromartie*?
3. The Supreme Court has ruled that States can group voters into districts by party, but not by race. Do you agree or disagree with that decision? Give reasons for your position.

Section Preview

OBJECTIVES

1. **Compare** the size of the Senate to the size of the House of Representatives.
2. **Describe** how States have elected senators in the past and present.
3. **Explain** how and why a senator's term differs from a representative's term.
4. **Identify** the qualifications for serving in the Senate.

WHY IT MATTERS

Each State has two seats in the Senate, the smaller and more prestigious house of Congress. Senators are generally older and more experienced than representatives, and their longer terms offer some protection against political pressures.

POLITICAL DICTIONARY

★ continuous body
★ constituency

You should not be very much surprised by these facts: Nearly a third of the present members of the Senate once served in the House of Representatives; none of the current members of the House has ever served in the Senate. Indeed, many of the men and women who now serve in the House look forward to the day when, they hope, they will sit in the Senate. As you read this section, you will come to see why the Senate is often called the "upper house."

Size, Election, and Terms

Why are there 100 members of the United States Senate? Have the members of the Senate always been elected by the voters of their States? Why do senators serve six-year terms? The organization of the Senate has changed some over time, but it remains a vital part of our government.

Size

The Constitution says that the Senate "shall be composed of two Senators from each State," and so the Senate is a much smaller body than the House of Representatives.[15] The Senate had only 22 members when it held its first session in March of 1789, and 26 members by the end of the First Congress in 1791. Like the House, the size of the upper chamber has grown with the country. Today 100 senators represent the 50 States.

---

[15]Article I, Section 3, Clause 1 and the 17th Amendment.

The Framers hoped that the smaller Senate would be a more enlightened and responsible body than the House. Many of them thought that the House would be too often swayed by the immediate impact of events and by the passions of the moment. The Framers reinforced that hope by giving senators a longer term and by setting the qualifications for membership in the Senate a cut above those they set for the House.

James Madison saw those provisions as "a necessary fence" against the "fickleness and passion" of the House of Representatives. Nearly a century later, Woodrow Wilson agreed with Madison:

▲ Senator Blanche K. Bruce (R., Mississippi) was one of the first two African Americans to serve in the Senate. He served one term from 1875 to 1881.

PRIMARY Sources *" It is indispensable that besides the House of Representatives which runs on all fours with popular sentiment, we should have a body like the Senate which may refuse to run with it at all when it seems to be wrong—a body which has time and security enough to keep its head, if only now and then and but for a little while, till other people have had time to think. "*

—Woodrow Wilson, *Congressional Government*

Choose a method. You can write to your representative's local address or to their Washington address. Check your telephone directory's blue pages to find local addresses. Letters can be sent to representatives in Washington at the following addresses:

Representative _____
House Office Building
Washington, D.C. 20515

Senator _____
Senate Office Building
Washington, D.C. 20510

Write while your issue is still current. Don't wait until a bill is out of the committee or has passed the House (or Senate).

Be specific. Identify the issue that prompted you to write, preferably in your first paragraph. Give the bill number or mention its popular title - e.g. the Minimum Wage Bill, the Child Care Bill.

Be brief, but give the reasons for your position. Avoid these don'ts:
- Don't make threats or promises.
- Don't berate your lawmaker.
- Don't pretend to wield vast political power.
- Don't try to instruct your lawmaker on every issue.

9 Robin Court
New Carrollton, MD 20784
September 17, 2001

Rep. Albert Wynn
House Office Building
Washington, D.C. 20515

Dear Mr. Wynn:

I am writing to express my support for H.R. 113, which would provide $14.2 billion to public high schools for repairs and construction. Since H.R. 113 will be debated next month, I would like to explain why I believe this bill is important to my school and others in the 4th district.

I am a junior at Stevens High School, a public high school in New Carrollton. Like many schools in the United States, Stevens High School was built more than forty years ago and needs major repairs. This year the entire heating system had to be replaced, the roof is in poor condition, and the science laboratories are outdated. Our district simply does not have the money to make all of the repairs that are needed. As you can understand, students find it difficult to learn in this environment.

I understand that lawmakers must make difficult decisions about the federal budget. However, I believe that school funding is crucial and I encourage you to vote "Yes" on H.R. 113.

Sincerely,

Ethan Locker
Ethan Locker

SOURCE: *Congressional Quarterly*

Interpreting Diagrams These guidelines were suggested by former Representative Morris Udall (D., Arizona).
Why is it important to write while a bill is still in committee? H-SS 12.6.4

Members of the Senate represent entire States. So nearly all of them represent a larger, more diverse population and a broader range of interests than do the representatives from their State. If you look at your own State—at the size, diversity, and major characteristics of its population and at its history, geography, and economy—you will see the point.

Election

Originally, the Constitution provided that the members of the Senate were to be chosen by the State legislatures. Since the ratification of the 17th Amendment in 1913, however, senators have been picked by the voters in each State at the regular November elections. Only one senator is elected from a State in any given election, except when the other seat has been vacated by death, resignation, or expulsion.[16]

Before the coming of popular election, the State legislatures often picked popular and qualified senators. On other occasions, however, their choice was the result of maneuvering and in-fighting among the leaders of various factions in the State. These leaders all spent a great deal of energy trying to gain (and sometimes buy) enough legislators' votes to win a seat in the United States Senate. By the late 1800s, the Senate was often called the "Millionaires' Club," because so many wealthy party and business leaders sat in that chamber.

The Senate twice defeated House-passed amendments to provide for popular election. In 1912, it finally bowed to public opinion and agreed to what became the 17th Amendment. The Senate was also persuaded by the fact that several States had already devised ways to ensure that their legislatures would choose senators who were supported by the people of the State.

---

[16]The 17th Amendment gives each State a choice of methods for filling a Senate vacancy. A State may (1) fill the seat at a special election called by the governor, or (2) allow the governor to appoint someone to serve until the voters fill the vacancy at such a special election or at the next regular (November) election. Most States use the appointment-special election method.

Each senator is elected from the State at-large. The 17th Amendment declares that all persons whom the State allows to vote for members of "the most numerous Branch" of its legislature are qualified to vote for candidates for the United States Senate.

Term

Senators serve for six-year terms, three times the length of those for which members of the House are chosen.[17] Senators may be elected to any number of terms. The late Strom Thurmond (R., South Carolina) set the all-time record. Senator Thurmond was elected to the Senate nine times, and he served there for nearly 50 years. He was first elected to fill a vacancy in 1954 and won a full term in 1956. First elected as a Democrat, he became a Republican in 1964 and finally retired in 2003 at the age of 100.

Senators' terms are staggered. Only a third of them—33 or 34 terms—expire every two years. The Senate is, then, a **continuous body.** That is, all of its seats are never up for election at the same time.

The six-year term gives senators a somewhat greater degree of job security than members of the lower house have. Those six years give senators some insulation from the rough-and-tumble of day-to-day politics. The six-year term also tends to make senators less subject to the pressures of public opinion and less susceptible to the pleas of special interests than are members of the House.

The larger size and the geographic scope of their **constituencies**—the people and interests the senators represent—are designed to have much the same effect. In other words, senators are supposed to be less concerned with the interests of a specific small locality and more focused on the "big picture" of the national interest. Indeed, senators are in general more likely to be regarded as national political leaders than most House members.

The large size of the House generally prevents representatives from gaining as much notice and public exposure as members of the Senate attract. Senators, and especially those who have presidential ambitions, are better able to capture national media attention. Over the past several elections, the Senate has emerged as a prime source of contenders for the presidential nomination in both parties. Senators also find it easier to establish themselves as the champions of public policies that appeal to large segments of the American people—for example, social security or national health care.

Senators are also more likely to be covered by the media in their States. They tend to have more clout in their State's politics than that enjoyed by members of the lower house.

Qualifications for Senators

A senator must meet a higher level of qualifications than those the Constitution sets for a member of the House. A senator must be at least 30 years of age, must have been a citizen of the United States for at least nine years, and must be an inhabitant of the State from which he or she is elected.[18]

---

[18]Article I, Section 3, Clause 3. Under the inhabitant qualification, a senator need not have lived in the State for any particular period of time. Most often, of course, senators have been longtime residents of their States.

Government Online

The Senate Oral History Program What was it like to be a reporter covering the Senate? What happened when an African American staff member challenged de facto segregation of the Senate cafeteria in the early 1950s? What preparations were made in the Senate for Richard Nixon's impeachment?

You can find the answers to these questions and many others through the Senate's Oral History program. The Senate Historical Office has been interviewing retired Senate staff members since 1976. These personal recollections provide behind-the-scene views of the Senate. They include the observations of former Senate pages, Capitol police officers, Senate aides and assistants, and members of the press.

The Historical Office concentrates on staff members with more than 20 years of service in the Senate. Their interviews are in-depth. (A typical interview totals 10 to 12 hours, over 6 to 8 sessions.) They are available in several national archives, including the manuscript division of the Library of Congress. The Senate Historical Office has begun publishing the interviews online, as well.

Go Online
PHSchool.com
Use Web Code mqd-3107 to find out more about the Senate Oral History Program and for help in answering the following question: *Christine S. McCreary was on the staff of two senators (Symington and Glenn). Why might an historian be interested in her recollections about helping to desegregate the Senate staff cafeterias?*

---

[17]Article I, Section 3, Clause 1.

Interpreting Political Cartoons This 1890 cartoon depicts a candidate for the Senate. *Why does the candidate deposit his money in a box labeled "State Legislature"?* **H-SS 12.4.1**

"THE WAY WE BECOME SENATORS NOWADAYS"

The Senate, like the House, judges the qualifications of its members, and it may exclude a member by a majority vote.[19] As has the House, the Senate has at times refused to seat a member-elect. The Senate may also "punish its Members for disorderly Behavior" by majority vote and "with the Concurrence of two thirds, expel a Member."[20]

Fifteen members of the Senate have been expelled by that body, one in 1797 and 14 during

[19]Article I, Section 5, Clause 1.
[20]Article I, Section 5, Clause 2.

the Civil War. Senator William Blount of Tennessee was expelled in 1797 for conspiring to lead two Native American tribes, supported by British warships, in attacks on Spanish Florida and Louisiana. The 14 senators ousted in 1861 and 1862 were all from States of the Confederacy and were expelled for supporting secession.

Since the country was founded, a few senators have resigned in the face of almost certain expulsion. Most recently, the Senate's Ethics Committee had recommended that Senator Bob Packwood (R., Oregon) be expelled from the Senate because of several episodes of sexual harassment and other personal misconduct. Packwood, in his fifth term in the upper house, had fought the charges for years. But the Ethics Committee's chairman, Senator Mitch McConnell (R., Kentucky), noted that lengthy committee investigations had shown "a habitual pattern of aggressive, blatantly sexual advances." Such behavior, McConnell declared, "cannot be tolerated in the United States Senate." Senator Packwood resigned effective October 1, 1995.

The punishing of a senator for "disorderly Behavior" has also been rare. In the most recent case, in 1990, the Senate formally "denounced" Senator David Durenberger (R., Minnesota). The Ethics Committee had found him guilty on several counts of financial misconduct. The Senate called Durenberger's conduct "reprehensible" and declared that he had "brought the Senate into dishonor and disrepute." Senator Durenberger chose not to seek reelection to a third term in 1994.

Section 3 Assessment

Standards Monitoring *Online*
For: Self-quiz with vocabulary practice
Web Code: mqa-3103

Key Terms and Main Ideas

1. Why is the Senate called a **continuous body**?
2. How does a typical senator's **constituency** differ from that of a typical representative in the House?
3. Why do most senators receive more public attention than their colleagues in the House of Representatives?

Critical Thinking

4. **Determining Cause and Effect** Why did the 17th Amendment change the way that senators are chosen?
5. **Making Comparisons** Why did the Framers set each senator's term at six years instead of two years?

6. **Drawing Inferences** In order to expel a senator from the Senate, two thirds of the Senate must agree. Why do you think the Constitution sets such a high requirement?

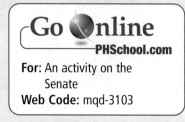

Go Online
PHSchool.com

For: An activity on the Senate
Web Code: mqd-3103

4 The Members of Congress

Section Preview

OBJECTIVES

1. **Identify** the personal and political backgrounds of the current members of Congress.
2. **Describe** the duties performed by those who serve in Congress.
3. **Describe** the compensation and privileges of members of Congress.

WHY IT MATTERS

Members of Congress must fill several roles as lawmakers, politicians, and servants of their constituents. For their work, they receive fairly generous pay and benefits.

POLITICAL DICTIONARY

★ **trustee**
★ **partisan**
★ **politico**
★ **oversight function**
★ **franking privilege**

Can you name your two senators? Your representative? Regrettably, most Americans cannot—let alone tell you much about their backgrounds, qualifications, or voting records.

Personal and Political Backgrounds

Whatever else they may be, the 535 members of Congress are *not* a representative cross section of the American people. Rather, the "average" member is a white male in his early 50s. The median age of the members of the House is just over 56 and of the Senate, 61.

There are more women in Congress today than ever—70 in the House and 14 in the Senate—and they are moving into positions of leadership. Nancy Pelosi (D., California) is now the House Minority Leader; Deborah Pryce (R., Ohio) heads the GOP's caucus in the House; and Maine's two Republican senators, Susan Collins and Olympia Snowe, now chair committees in the upper house.

There are now 42 African Americans, 24 Hispanics, five Asian Americans, and one Native American in the House. One African American, two Hispanics, one Asian American, and one Native Hawaiian sit in the Senate. Representative David Wu (D., Oregon), first elected in 1998, is the first-ever Chinese American to sit in either house. Senator Barack Obama (D., Illinois), elected in 2004, is only the fifth African American ever elected to the Senate.

Nearly all members are married, a few are divorced, and they have, on the average, two children. Only a few members say they have no religious affiliation. Just about 60 percent are Protestants, 30 percent are Roman Catholics, and some 6 percent are Jewish.

Well over a third of the members of the House and well over half the senators are lawyers. Nearly all went to college. More than four out of five have a college degree and most, in fact, have advanced degrees.

Most senators and representatives were born in the States they represent. Only a handful were born outside the United States. Sprinkled among the members of Congress are several millionaires. A surprisingly large number of the men and women who sit in the House depend on their congressional salaries as their major source of income, however.

Most members of Congress have had considerable political experience. The average senator is serving a second term, and the typical representative has served four terms. Nearly a third of the senators once sat in the House. Several senators are former governors. A few senators have held Cabinet seats or other high posts in the executive branch of

▲ Senator Barack Obama (D., Illinois) served as a State senator before his election to the U.S. Senate in 2004.

the Federal Government. The House has a large number of former State legislators and prosecuting attorneys among its members.

Again, Congress is not an accurate cross section of the nation's population. Rather, it is made up of upper-middle-class Americans, who are, on the whole, quite able and hard-working people.

The Job

One leading commentary on American politics describes Congress and the job of a member of Congress this way:

 " *Congress has a split personality. On the one hand, it is a lawmaking institution and makes policy for the entire nation. In this capacity, all the members are expected to set aside their personal ambitions and perhaps even the concerns of their constituencies. Yet Congress is also a representative assembly, made up of 535 elected officials who serve as links between their constituents and the National Government. The dual roles of making laws and responding to constituents' demands forces members to balance national concerns against the specific interests of their States or districts.* **"**

—Burns, et al., *Government by the People*

Members of Congress play five major roles. They are most importantly (1) legislators and (2) representatives of their constituents. Beyond these roles, they are also (3) committee members, (4) servants of their constituents, and (5) politicians. You will take a close look at their lawmaking function in the next two chapters. Here, we consider their representative, committee member, and servant functions.

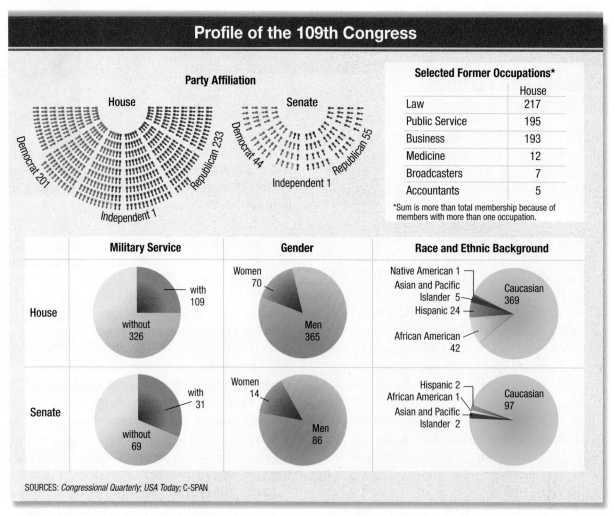

Profile of the 109th Congress

Party Affiliation

House
Democrat 201
Republican 233
Independent 1

Senate
Democrat 44
Republican 55
Independent 1

Selected Former Occupations*

	House
Law	217
Public Service	195
Business	193
Medicine	12
Broadcasters	7
Accountants	5

*Sum is more than total membership because of members with more than one occupation.

Military Service

House
with 109
without 326

Senate
with 31
without 69

Gender

House
Women 70
Men 365

Senate
Women 14
Men 86

Race and Ethnic Background

House
Native American 1
Asian and Pacific Islander 5
Hispanic 24
African American 42
Caucasian 369

Senate
Hispanic 2
African American 1
Asian and Pacific Islander 2
Caucasian 97

SOURCES: *Congressional Quarterly; USA Today;* C-SPAN

 Interpreting Graphs Members of Congress come to Washington, D.C., with a wide variety of backgrounds. ***How does racial and ethnic diversity differ between the House and the Senate?*** H-SS 12.4.3

Representatives of the People

Senators and representatives are elected to represent people. But what does that really mean? They cast hundreds of votes during each session of Congress. Many of those votes involve quite routine, relatively unimportant matters; for example, a bill to designate a week in May as National Wild Flower Week. But many of those votes, including some on matters of organization and procedure, are cast on matters of far-reaching import.

So, no questions about the lawmaking branch can be more vital than these: How do the people's representatives represent the people? On what basis do they cast their votes?

In broad terms, each lawmaker has four voting options. He or she can vote as a trustee, as a delegate, as a partisan, or as a politico.

Trustees believe that each question they face must be decided on its merits. Conscience and independent judgment are their guides. Trustees call issues as they see them, regardless of the views held by their constituents or by any of the other groups that seek to influence their decisions.

Delegates see themselves as the agents of those who elected them. They believe that they should vote the way they think "the folks back home" would want. They are willing to suppress their own views, ignore those of their party's leaders, and turn a deaf ear to the arguments of colleagues and of special interests from outside their constituencies.

Those lawmakers who owe their first allegiance to their political party are **partisans**. They feel duty-bound to vote in line with the party platform and the wishes of their party's leaders. Most studies of legislators' voting behavior show that partisanship is the leading factor influencing their votes on most important measures.

Politicos attempt to combine the basic elements of the trustee, delegate, and partisan roles. They try to balance these often conflicting factors: their own views of what is best for their constituents and/or the nation as a whole, the political facts of life, and the peculiar pressures of the moment.

Committee Members

In every session of Congress, proposed laws (bills) are referred to committees in each chamber. As committee members, senators and

representatives must screen those proposals. They decide which will go on to floor consideration—that is, be considered and acted upon by the full membership of the House or Senate.

Another vital part of their committee work involves the **oversight function.** Oversight is the process by which Congress, through its committees, checks to see that the various agencies in the executive branch are working effectively and acting in line with the policies that Congress has set by law.

Servants

Members of the House and Senate also act as servants of their constituents. Most often, they do this as they (and, more particularly, their staff aides) try to help people who have various problems with the federal bureaucracy. Those problems may involve a Social Security benefit, a passport application, a small business loan, or any one of a thousand other issues.

Some of "the folks back home" believe that members of Congress are in Washington

▲ Representative Ileana Ros-Lehtinen (R., Florida) must balance several different roles. Her jobs include publicizing important issues, meeting with constituents, and working with her fellow lawmakers in Washington. *Critical Thinking Why is it important for a representative to speak often with constituents?* H-SS 12.4.1

primarily to do favors for them. Most members are swamped with constituent requests from the moment they take office. The range of these requests is almost without limit—everything from help in securing a government contract or an appointment to a military academy, to asking for a free sightseeing tour of Washington or even a personal loan. Consider this job description offered only half-jokingly by a former representative:

PRIMARY Sources ❝ *A Congressman has become an expanded messenger boy, an employment agency, getter-outer of the Navy, Army, Marines, ward heeler, wound healer, trouble shooter, law explainer, bill finder, issue translator, resolution interpreter, controversy oil pourer, gladhand extender, business promoter, convention goer, civil ills skirmisher, veterans' affairs adjuster, ex-serviceman's champion, watchdog for the underdog, sympathizer with the upper dog, namer and kisser of babies, recoverer of lost luggage, soberer of delegates, adjuster for traffic violators, voters straying into Washington and into toils of the law, binder up of broken hearts, financial wet nurse, Good Samaritan, contributor to good causes—there are so many good causes—cornerstone layer, public building and bridge dedicator, ship christener—to be sure he does get in a little flag waving—and a little constitutional hoisting and*

spread-eagle work, but it is getting harder every day to find time to properly study legislation—the very business we are primarily here to discharge, and that must be done above all things. ❞
—Rep. Luther Patrick (D., Alabama)

Most members of Congress know that to deny or fail to respond to these requests would mean to lose votes in the next election. This is a key fact, for all of the roles a member of Congress plays—legislator, representative, committee member, constituent servant, and politician—are related, at least in part, to their efforts to win reelection.

Compensation

The Constitution says that members of Congress "shall receive a Compensation for their Services, to be ascertained by Law. . . ."[21] That is, the Constitution says that Congress fixes that "Compensation."

Salary

Today, senators and representatives are paid a salary of $162,000 a year. A few members are paid somewhat more. The Speaker of the

---

[21] Article I, Section 6, Clause 1. The 27th Amendment modified this pay-setting authority. It provides that no increase in members' pay can take effect until after the next congressional election—that is, not until the voters have had an opportunity to react to the pay raise.

House makes $208,100 a year, the same salary that Congress has set for the Vice President. The Senate's president *pro tem* and the majority and minority floor leaders in both houses receive $180,100 a year.

Nonsalary Compensation

Each member receives a number of "fringe benefits," some of which are quite substantial. For example, each member has a special tax deduction, not available to any other federal income tax payer. That deduction is designed to help members who must maintain two residences, one in his or her home State and another in Washington.

Generous travel allowances offset the costs of several round trips each year between home and Washington. Members pay relatively small amounts for life and health insurance and for outpatient care by a medical staff on Capitol Hill; they can get full medical care, at very low rates, at any military hospital. They also have a generous retirement plan, to which they contribute. The plan pays a pension based on years of service in Congress, and longtime members can retire with an income of $150,000 or more a year. Members of Congress are also covered by Social Security's retirement and medicare programs.

Members are also provided with offices in one of the several Senate and House office buildings near the Capitol and allowances for offices in their home State or district. Each member is given funds for hiring staff and for operation costs related to running those offices. The **franking privilege** is a well-known benefit that allows them to mail letters and other materials postage-free by substituting their facsimile signature (frank) for the postage.

Congress has also provided its members with the free printing—and through franking, the free distribution—of speeches, newsletters, and the like. Radio and television tapes can be produced at very low cost. Each member can choose among several fine restaurants in the Capitol. There are also two first-rate gymnasiums, with swimming pools, exercise rooms, and saunas. Members receive still more privileges, including such things as the help of the excellent services of the Library of Congress and free parking in spaces reserved for them at the Capitol and also at Washington's major airports.[22]

The Politics of Pay

There are only two real limits on the level of congressional pay. One is the President's veto power. The other and more potent limit is the fear of voter backlash, an angry reaction by constituents at the ballot box. That fear of election-day fallout has always made most members reluctant to vote to raise their own salaries.

Congress has often tried to skirt the troublesome and politically sensitive pay question. It has done so by providing for such fringe benefits as a special tax break, a liberal pension plan, more office and travel funds, and other perquisites, or "perks"—items of value that are much less apparent to "the folks back home."

The debate over congressional pay is not likely to end soon—at least not as long as the current method of establishing salaries remains in effect. All sides of the issue present reasonable arguments.

[22]For decades, many members of Congress supplemented their salaries with honoraria—speaking fees and similar payments from private sources, mainly special interest groups. Critics long attacked that widespread practice as at least unseemly and, at its worst, a form of legalized bribery. The House finally prohibited its members from accepting honoraria in 1989, and the Senate did so in 1991.

"Congratulations on your raise, sir."

Interpreting Political Cartoons The salaries and benefits enjoyed by members of Congress have long been a sensitive political issue. ***Why are voters reluctant to see members of Congress increase their benefits and pay?***

Clearly, decent salaries—pay in line with the responsibilities of the job—will not automatically bring the most able men and women to Congress, or to any other public office. But certainly, decent salaries can make public service much more appealing to qualified people.

Membership Privileges

Beyond the matter of their salaries and other compensation, members of Congress enjoy several privileges. The Constitution commands that senators and representatives

> **FROM THE Constitution** *"shall in all Cases, except Treason, Felony and Breach of the Peace, be privileged from Arrest during their Attendance at the Session of their respective Houses, and in going to and returning from the same. . . ."*
> —Article I, Section 6, Clause 1

The provision dates from English and colonial practice, when the king's officers often harassed legislators on petty grounds. It has been of little importance in our national history, however.[23]

Another much more important privilege is set out in the same place in the Constitution. The Speech or Debate Clause of Article I, Section 6, Clause 1 declares ". . . for any Speech or Debate in either House, they shall not be questioned in any other Place." The words "any other Place" refer particularly to the courts.

The privilege is intended to "throw a cloak of legislative immunity" around members of Congress. The clause protects representatives and senators from suits for libel or slander arising out of their official conduct. The Supreme Court has held that the immunity applies "to things generally done in a session of the House [or Senate] by one of its members in relation to the business before it."[24] The protection goes, then, beyond floor debate, to include work in committees and all other things generally done by members of Congress in relation to congressional business.

The important and necessary goal of this provision of the Constitution is to protect freedom of legislative debate. Clearly, members must not feel restrained in their vigorous discussion of the sometimes contentious issues of the day. However, this provision is not designed to give members unbridled freedom to attack others verbally or in writing. Thus, a member is not free to defame another person in a public speech, an article, a conversation, or otherwise.

---

[23]The courts have regularly held that the words "Breach of the Peace" cover all criminal offenses. So the protection covers only arrest for civil (noncriminal) offenses while engaged in congressional business.

[24]The leading case is *Kilbourn* v. *Thompson,* 1881. The holding has been affirmed many times since. In *Hutchinson* v. *Proxmire,* 1979, however, the Court held that members of Congress may be sued for libel for statements they make in news releases or in newsletters.

Section 4 Assessment

Key Terms and Main Ideas

1. What does a **trustee** value most when deciding how to vote on a bill?
2. What does a **partisan** value most when deciding how to vote on a bill?
3. How does the **franking privilege** help members of Congress?
4. What is the **oversight function**?

Critical Thinking

5. **Drawing Conclusions** What are the different roles that a member of Congress plays?
6. **Determining Cause and Effect** Why are members of Congress reluctant to pass laws that give them new benefits or higher pay?

7. **Drawing Inferences** Look again at the diagram on page 276. Why might it not be a good idea for a letter writer to berate his or her lawmaker?

May Congresspersons Be Sued for Their Statements?

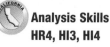

Analysis Skills
HR4, HI3, HI4

The "Speech or Debate Clause" in Article I, Section 6 of the Constitution provides that senators and representatives "shall not be questioned in any other place" over "any speech or debate in either House." This has been interpreted to mean that they cannot be sued for anything they say in their legislative chambers. How far does this protection extend?

Hutchinson v. Proxmire (1979)

Senator William Proxmire of Wisconsin invented the "Golden Fleece of the Month Award" to publicize what he saw as examples of wasteful government spending. In 1975 he gave awards to various federal agencies for spending almost half a million dollars to fund Professor Ronald Hutchinson's research on emotional behavior. Hutchinson was trying to develop an objective measure of aggression, and his research focused on certain behavior patterns, such as clenching of the jaw.

In an "awards speech" to the Senate, Proxmire stated: "In view of the transparent worthlessness of Hutchinson's study of jaw-grinding and biting by angry . . . monkeys, it is time we put a stop to the bite [that] Hutchinson and the bureaucrats who fund him have been taking of the taxpayer." His remarks were published in the *Congressional Record* and in a press release and in various newsletters.

Hutchinson sued Proxmire, saying his professional reputation had been damaged. Proxmire responded that his remarks were protected by the Speech or Debate Clause and by the First Amendment. The district court and court of appeals ruled in favor of Proxmire, and the case went to the Supreme Court for review.

Arguments for Hutchinson

1. The Speech or Debate Clause should not extend protection to comments that are made outside of the Senate chamber or are not part of the legislative function of the Senate.
2. The newsletters and press release about the Golden Fleece Award were aimed at persons outside Congress and thus are not part of the senator's official duties.
3. Since Professor Hutchinson is not a public figure, he does not have to prove as part of his lawsuit that the senator's remarks were made with actual malice (desire to harm).

Arguments for Proxmire

1. The senator's comments in the Senate about matters of national importance were protected by the Speech or Debate Clause; the use of these comments in a press release and newsletters describing the Senate speech were part of the senator's official duty to inform the public about his activities.
2. The senator's criticisms of wasteful spending of public funds were also privileged under the Free Speech Clause of the First Amendment.
3. Professor Hutchinson is a public figure; therefore, he must prove as part of his suit that Proxmire acted with actual malice.

Decide for Yourself

1. Review the constitutional grounds on which each side based its arguments and the specific arguments each side presented.
2. Debate the opposing viewpoints presented in this case. Which viewpoint do you favor?
3. Predict the impact of the Court's decision on activities and statements by members of Congress outside the House and Senate chambers. (To read a summary of the Court's decision, turn to pages 799–806.)

Go Online
PHSchool.com

Use Web Code mqp-3108 to register your vote on this issue and to see how other students voted.

Political Dictionary

term (p. 264), session (p. 264), adjourn (p. 264), prorogue (p. 265), special session (p. 265), apportion (p. 267), reapportion (p. 267), off-year election (p. 269), single-member district (p. 270), at-large (p. 270), gerrymander (p. 271), continuous body (p. 277), constituency (p. 277), trustee (p. 281), partisan (p. 281), politico (p. 281), oversight function (p. 281), franking privilege (p. 283)

Standards Review

H-SS 12.4.1 Discuss Article I of the Constitution as it relates to the legislative branch, including eligibility for office and lengths of terms of representatives and senators; election to office; the roles of the House and Senate in impeachment proceedings; the role of the vice president; the enumerated legislative powers; and the process by which a bill becomes a law.

H-SS 12.4.3 Identify their current representatives in the legislative branch of the national government.

H-SS 12.6.4 Describe the means that citizens use to participate in the political process (e.g., voting, campaigning, lobbying, filing a legal challenge, demonstrating, petitioning, picketing, running for political office).

H-SS 12.6.6 Analyze trends in voter turnout; the causes and effects of reapportionment and redistricting, with special attention to spatial districting and the rights of minorities; and the function of the Electoral College.

H-SS 12.7.5 Explain how public policy is formed, including the setting of the public agenda and implementation of it through regulations and executive orders.

Practicing the Vocabulary

Matching *Choose a term from the list above that best matches each description.*

1. What happens to the seats in the House of Representatives every decade

2. What the President can do if the two houses of Congress cannot agree on a date to adjourn

3. The right of members of Congress to send mail postage-free by using a signature in place of a stamp

4. The function Congress is performing when it checks on the programs of the executive branch

5. How you might describe a congressional district that has been drawn by a legislature in a very odd shape

Fill in the Blank *Choose a term from the list above that best completes the sentence.*

6. Congress can _____, or suspend its meeting, whenever it chooses.

7. Each member of the House represents a _____ of about 630,000 people.

8. A member of the House of Representatives is elected for a two-year _____.

9. In States with a low population, members of the House of Representatives are chosen in _____ districts.

10. A _____ is a member of Congress who votes primarily according to the wishes of his or her party.

Reviewing Main Ideas

Section 1

11. How does bicameralism in Congress reflect the principle of federalism?

12. (a) How are States represented in the House of Representatives? (b) How are States represented in the Senate?

13. (a) What is a special session? (b) Why have special sessions lost their importance?

Section 2

14. For what reasons must seats in Congress be reapportioned every 10 years?

15. In what ways has the redistricting of House seats been used for the political gain of certain groups and parties in the various States?

16. (a) What are the constitutional qualifications that all members of the House must meet? (b) What are the informal qualifications that members of the House should meet?

Section 3

17. How do senators differ from their colleagues in the House of Representatives?

18. (a) How do constituencies vary within the Senate? (b) Which State's senators have the largest constituency?

19. (a) In what ways does the long six-year term affect how senators vote? (b) How does this confirm the Framers' intentions for the Senate?

20. The Constitution sets up what formal qualifications for membership in the Senate?

Section 4

21. (a) Do the members of Congress reflect a cross section of the American people? (b) Why or why not?

22. (a) When deciding how to vote, what does a delegate consider? (b) When deciding how to vote, what does a politico consider?

23. How are members of Congress compensated for their work? List several examples.

Critical Thinking Skills

Analysis Skills HR1, HR4

24. *Face the Issues* Do American citizens have a right to government-funded health care? Explain your answer with reference to the U.S. Constitution.

25. *Predicting Consequences* Reread the conversation between Thomas Jefferson and George Washington on page 263. Why did Washington think the Congress should be bicameral rather than unicameral?

26. *Understanding Point of View* Congress is a frequent target of criticism in the media and elsewhere. Yet the text says that the members of Congress are on the whole hard-working and able people. How can you explain the existence of these two opposing viewpoints?

27. *Expressing Problems Clearly* Why would you favor or oppose **(a)** a constitutional amendment to lengthen the elected terms of members of the House and **(b)** an amendment that would shorten the terms of members of the Senate?

Analyzing Political Cartoons

Using your knowledge of American government and this cartoon, answer the questions below.

MEASURING POLITICAL CANDIDATES

28. According to this cartoonist, what factor plays an important role in determining who runs for office?

29. Based on your reading in this chapter, is the cartoonist correct? Explain your answer.

Participation Activities

Analysis Skills HR4, HI1

30. *Current Events Watch* Find a recent news account of a vote cast by one of the members of your State's congressional delegation. Why was that vote newsworthy? Would you have voted that way if you were a member of the House (or Senate)? Why?

31. *Graphing Activity* Turn to the map on page 268 and find the ten States with the greatest number of representatives in the House. Create a circle graph showing each State's representatives as a percentage of the 435 members of the House of Representatives. Remember to label the part of the circle graph that represents the other 40 States. What does this graph tell you about the influence of these States in the House of Representatives?

32. *It's Your Turn* Write a newspaper editorial expressing your views on the qualifications for membership in Congress. List the formal qualifications and those informal ones that you think members should satisfy. Suggest changes (if any) that you would make in those qualifications. Indicate why you think each of the informal qualifications you cite is important. Read your draft for clarity and revise it. Then proofread and draft a final copy. **(Writing an Editorial)**

Standards Monitoring *Online*

For: Chapter 10 Self-Test **Visit:** PHSchool.com
Web Code: mqa-3105

As a final review, take the Magruder's Chapter 10 Self-Test and receive immediate feedback on your answers.
The test consists of 20 multiple-choice questions designed to test your understanding of the chapter content.

CHAPTER 11

Powers of Congress

"The range of issues that come before the United States Senate is infinite: from ratifying treaties, to confirming federal judges, . . . to appropriating the federal dollars that fund the programs upon which we all rely."

— Senator Susan Collins (R.) of Maine (2000)

As Senator Collins points out, members of Congress must consider an amazing array of issues as part of their lawmaking duties. How far the powers of Congress should extend has been a source of debate and controversy throughout the history of the nation.

◆ **Floor of the United States House**

Standards Preview

H-SS 12.2.2 Explain how economic rights are secured and their importance to the individual and to society (e.g., the right to acquire, use, transfer, and dispose of property; right to choose one's work; right to join or not join labor unions; copyright and patent).

H-SS 12.2.3 Discuss the individual's legal obligations to obey the law, serve as a juror, and pay taxes.

H-SS 12.4.1 Discuss Article I of the Constitution as it relates to the legislative branch, including eligibility for office and lengths of terms of representatives and senators; election to office; the roles of the House and Senate in impeachment proceedings; the role of the vice president; the enumerated legislative powers; and the process by which a bill becomes a law.

H-SS 12.4.4 Discuss Article II of the Constitution as it relates to the executive branch, including eligibility for office and length of term, election to and removal from office, the oath of office, and the enumerated executive powers.

H-SS 12.4.6 Explain the processes of selection and confirmation of Supreme Court justices.

H-SS 12.5.3 Evaluate the effects of the Court's interpretations of the Constitution in *Marbury* v. *Madison*, *McCulloch* v. *Maryland*, and *United States* v. *Nixon*, with emphasis on the arguments espoused by each side in these cases.

H-SS 12.7.8 Understand the scope of presidential power and decision making through examination of case studies such as the Cuban Missile Crisis, passage of Great Society legislation, War Powers Act, Gulf War, and Bosnia.

SECTION 1

The Scope of Congressional Powers
(pp. 290–292)

★ Congress has only those powers delegated (granted) to it by the Constitution.

★ How those powers should be interpreted and applied—whether strictly or liberally—has been sharply debated throughout our history.

SECTION 2

The Expressed Powers of Money and Commerce (pp. 294–300)

★ The Framers gave Congress the taxing power and the commerce power—two hugely important powers that it did not have under the Articles of Confederation.

★ Congress has the vital power to borrow money and to create a monetary system for the country.

SECTION 3

Other Expressed Powers (pp. 301–304)

★ Congress shares power with the President in both defense and foreign affairs.

★ Congress regulates several matters that affect everyday life—including such things as mail, weights and measures, and copyrights and patents.

SECTION 4

The Implied Powers (pp. 305–308)

★ Congress has a number of important powers not set out in so many words in the Constitution.

★ What Congress can and cannot do in the exercise of its implied powers has been and remains a subject of intense debate.

SECTION 5

The Nonlegislative Powers (pp. 310–314)

★ Congress may propose amendments to the Constitution with a two-thirds vote in each house.

★ The House of Representatives decides a presidential election if no candidate wins a majority of electoral votes.

★ The House has the power to impeach (accuse) the President and the Senate may convict (remove) an impeached President. The House has impeached two Presidents—Andrew Johnson and Bill Clinton; neither was convicted by the Senate.

★ The Senate has the power to confirm or reject major presidential appointments and to approve or reject treaties.

★ Congress may investigate any matter that falls within the scope of its legislative powers.

Go Online
PHSchool.com

For: Current Data
Web Code: mqg-3117

For: Close Up Foundation debates
Web Code: mqh-3110

The Scope of Congressional Powers

Section Preview

OBJECTIVES

1. **Identify** the three types of congressional power.
2. **Compare** the strict construction and liberal construction positions on the scope of congressional power.

WHY IT MATTERS

The Constitution makes Congress the lawmaking branch—the basic policy-making branch of the National Government. The powers of Congress are limited, yes—but those powers are many, and they are also far-reaching.

POLITICAL DICTIONARY

★ **expressed powers**
★ **implied powers**
★ **inherent powers**
★ **strict constructionist**
★ **liberal constructionist**
★ **consensus**

A typical day in either chamber of Congress might suggest that there is no limit to what Congress can do. On any given day, the House might consider bills dealing with such varying matters as the interstate highway system, an increase in the minimum wage, and grazing on public lands. Meanwhile, the Senate might be considering aid to a famine-stricken country in Africa, the President's nomination of someone to fill a vacancy on the Supreme Court, or any number of other matters.

Still, remember that there are very real limits on what Congress can do. Recall that (1) the government in the United States is limited government, and (2) the American system of government is federal in form. These two fundamental facts work both to shape and to limit the powers of Congress.

Congressional Power

Remember, Congress has only those powers delegated (granted, given) to it by the Constitution. Large areas of power are denied to Congress in so many words in the Constitution, by the Constitution's silence on many matters, and because the Constitution creates a federal system.

There is much that Congress cannot do. It cannot create a national public school system, require people to vote or attend church, or set a minimum age for marriage or drivers' licenses. It cannot abolish jury trials, confiscate all handguns, or censor the content of newspaper columns or radio or television broadcasts. Congress cannot do these and a great many other things because the Constitution does not allow it to do so.

Still, Congress *does* have the power to do many things. The Constitution grants it a number of specific powers—and, recall, it does so in three different ways: (1) explicitly, in its specific wording—the **expressed powers;** (2) by reasonable deduction from the expressed powers—the **implied powers;** and (3) by creating a national government for the United States—the **inherent powers.**

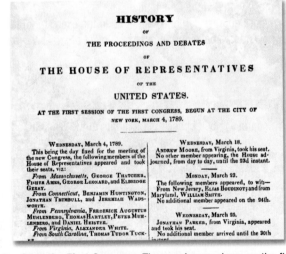

▲ **Notes from the First Congress** The gavel came down on the first session of the House of Representatives on March 4, 1789, but the body lacked a quorum and had to adjourn every day until April 1, when enough members finally made it to New York City. The first order of business was to elect a Speaker. **H-SS 12.4.1**

Strict Versus Liberal Construction

The Framers of the Constitution intended to create a new and stronger National Government. The ratification of their plan was opposed by many, and that opposition was not stilled by the adoption of the Constitution. Rather, the conflict between the Federalists and the Anti-Federalists continued into the early years of the Republic. Much of that conflict centered on the powers of Congress. Just how broad, in fact, were those powers?

The **strict constructionists,** led by Thomas Jefferson, continued to argue the Anti-Federalist position from the ratification period. They insisted that Congress should be able to exercise only (1) its expressed powers and (2) those implied powers absolutely necessary to carry out those expressed powers. They wanted the States to keep as much power as possible. They agreed with Jefferson that "that government is best which governs least."

Most of these Jeffersonians did acknowledge a need to protect interstate trade, and they recognized the need for a strong national defense. At the same time, they feared the consequences of a strong National Government. They believed, for instance, that the interests of the people of Connecticut were not the same as those of South Carolinians or Marylanders or Pennsylvanians. They argued that only the States—not the far-off National Government—could protect and preserve those differing interests.

Voices on Government

Xavier Becerra (D., California), who represents part of Los Angeles in the House, is an active member of the Congressional Hispanic Caucus. Improving education, especially for Hispanic students, is a major focus of his efforts in Congress.

❝ *Talk is not enough when the future of our children is at stake. We must end politics at the schoolhouse door. I urge Congress to work on [an] education . . . plan [that] would reduce class size to a national average of 18, modernize 5,000 schools nationwide, and make the needed investments to provide schools and students with after-school programs, technology and other tools to bring our schools into the 21st century.* ❞

Evaluating the Quotation
What does Becerra mean when he says "We must end politics at the schoolhouse door"?

The **liberal constructionists,** led by Alexander Hamilton, had led the fight to adopt the Constitution. Now they favored a liberal interpretation of the Constitution, a broad construction of the powers given to Congress.

Interpreting Illustrations The debate over the scope of the powers of the Federal Government is as heated today as it was in early America. *What techniques does this illustration use to depict the conflict?* **H-SS 12.4.1**

Liberal Constructionists from Hamilton's time to today have favored a strong Federal Government...

while Strict Constructionists in the tradition of Jefferson have sought to limit the powers of the Federal Government.

How much pruning can we do and still get apples?

Interpreting Political Cartoons *What point is the cartoonist making about the big government/small government debate? What details in the drawing help to make the point?*

They believed that the country needed, as Hamilton put it, "an energetic government."

The liberal constructionists won that conflict in the early years of the Republic, as you will see. Their victory set a pattern that, in general, has been followed ever since. Over the years, the powers wielded by the National Government have grown to a point that even the most

ardent supporters of liberal construction could not have imagined.

Several factors, working together with the liberal construction of the Constitution, have been responsible for that marked growth in national power. They have included wars, economic crises, and other national emergencies. Spectacular advances, especially in transportation and communication, have also had a real impact on the size and the scope of government. Equally important have been the demands of the people for more and more services from government.

Congress has been led by these and other factors to view its powers in broader and broader terms. Most Presidents have regarded their powers in like fashion. The Supreme Court has generally taken a similar position in its decisions in cases involving the powers of the National Government.

Moreover, the American people have generally agreed with a broader rather than a narrow reading of the Constitution. This **consensus,** this general agreement, has prevailed even though our political history has been marked, and still is, by controversies over the proper limits of national power.

Section 1 Assessment

Key Terms and Main Ideas

1. Explain the differences among Congress's **expressed powers, implied powers,** and **inherent powers.**
2. Compare the views of a **strict constructionist** and a **liberal constructionist.**
3. Give three examples of laws that Congress can enact under the Constitution and three examples of laws that Congress cannot enact.
4. Explain this sentence: *Historically, there has been a* ***consensus*** *in this country with regard to a broad rather than a narrow construction of the Constitution.*

Critical Thinking

5. **Understanding Point of View** Why might Alexander Hamilton, a supporter of a strong National Government, be

 Standards Monitoring *Online*
For: Self-quiz with vocabulary practice
Web Code: mqa-3111

surprised at the scope of the powers of the National Government today?

6. **Making Comparisons** Explain why these two seemingly contradictory statements are both true: **(a)** Most Americans agree with a broad reading of the Constitution. **(b)** The issue of the extent of the Federal Government's power is hotly debated today.

For: An activity on the Framers
Web Code: mqd-3111

Paying Your Taxes

 H-SS 12.2.3

To some people, they are the three most dreaded letters in the English language: IRS—the Internal Revenue Service. The IRS, an agency within the Treasury Department, enforces tax laws made by Congress and collects federal income taxes.

Uncle Sam has been taking a bite out of Americans' paychecks since 1914, when the 16th Amendment took effect. Every year of your working life you will probably file a federal tax return, the form on which you calculate how much tax you owe.

The federal tax system includes tax deductions for taxpayers with certain financial burdens, such as mortgages, college loans, or high medical bills. Such tax breaks can save you hundreds of dollars a year.

People in many places must pay federal, State, and local taxes. It is important, then, to prepare for tax time. For most people, these are the steps to follow:

1. Fill out a W-4 form. When you start a new job, the employer will give you IRS Form W-4, which you use to calculate how much of your pay you wish to have withheld for taxes. Tax laws require most people to have a certain minimum percentage withheld. At the end of the year, you figure out the amount of tax you owe. If you had too much money withheld, the Treasury gives that surplus back to you as a tax refund. If you did not have enough money withheld during the year, you must pay the balance you owe.

Fill out a W-4 and return it to your employer. If you need help, call the IRS or check out the "W-4 Calculator" on the IRS Web site.

Tax Help

The IRS Web site is friendly and helpful, with loads of information. Try out TaxInteractive, an online information service. http://www.irs.ustreas.gov

Call the IRS toll-free at 1-800-829-1040. You can get help over the telephone, schedule an appointment, or use a walk-in service at some locations. Tax preparation services and tax accountants will prepare your tax return for a fee. They provide forms, make suggestions, and answer questions. Many will file your return for you.

2. Collect important documents. In January or early February you should receive IRS Form W-2, from your employer(s). That form shows how much you earned in the prior year and the taxes withheld from that period. If you have an interest-bearing account at a bank or other institution, you'll also receive a statement of interest you earned, which counts as income. Save these documents! Your W-2s must be attached to your tax return when you file.

3. Calculate your taxes. The tax "season" runs from January to April 15. During that time, you need to fill out and file your tax return. Tax forms and instruction booklets are free. You'll find them at most post offices, public libraries, and banks. You can download forms at the IRS Web site, or get them via the IRS TaxFax Service.

Follow the directions on your tax form to calculate how much tax you owe, or how much should be refunded to you. Never put false information on a tax form. If the IRS suspects you've cheated on your taxes, you'll be called in for an audit, a detailed review of your finances. Penalties for tax fraud or nonpayment are severe.

4. Get help, if needed. Each tax form has step-by-step instructions, but if you have questions, don't guess. Get help from one of the sources shown at left.

5. File your tax return. Your federal tax return must be postmarked by midnight on April 15. Late filers receive penalties and interest charges. If you prepare your return on paper, send it to an IRS Service Center listed in the instruction booklets and at the IRS Web site. To get a fast tax refund, file online. If you owe money, you can pay by check or credit card.

Test for Success

What types of documents should you save to help you prepare your tax return?

The Expressed Powers of Money and Commerce

Section Preview

OBJECTIVES

1. **Summarize** key points relating to Congress's power to tax.
2. **Describe** how Congress uses its power to borrow money.
3. **Analyze** the importance of Congress's commerce power.
4. **Identify** the reasons that the Framers gave Congress the power to issue currency.
5. **Explain** how the bankruptcy power works.

WHY IT MATTERS

Its powers to tax and to regulate both interstate and foreign trade give Congress a critical role in the nation's economy. Neither its taxing power nor its commerce power are unlimited, however.

POLITICAL DICTIONARY

★ **tax**
★ **direct tax**
★ **indirect tax**
★ **deficit financing**
★ **public debt**
★ **commerce power**
★ **legal tender**
★ **bankruptcy**

Most, but not all, of the expressed powers of Congress are found in Article I, Section 8 of the Constitution. There, in 18 separate clauses, 27 different powers are explicitly given to Congress.[1]

These grants of power are brief. What they do and do not allow Congress to do often cannot be discovered by merely reading the few words involved. Rather, their meaning is found in the ways in which Congress has exercised its powers since 1789, and in scores of Supreme Court cases arising out of the actions taken by Congress.

As a case in point, take the Commerce Clause, which gives to Congress the power

FROM THE *Constitution* ❝*To regulate Commerce with foreign Nations, and among the several States, and with the Indian Tribes.*❞

—Article I, Section 8, Clause 3

What do these words mean? Congress and the Court have had to answer hundreds of questions about the scope of the Commerce Clause. Here are but a few examples: Does "commerce" include people crossing State lines or entering or leaving the country? What about business practices?

Working conditions? Radio and television broadcasts? The Internet? Does the Commerce Clause give Congress the power to ban the shipment of certain goods from one State to another? To prohibit discrimination? To regulate the Internet? What trade is "foreign" and what is "interstate"? What trade is neither?

In answering these and dozens upon dozens of other questions arising out of this one provision, Congress and the Court have defined—and are still defining—the meaning of the Commerce Clause. So it is with most of the other constitutional grants of power to Congress.

The Power to Tax

The Constitution gives Congress the power

FROM THE *Constitution* ❝*To lay and collect Taxes, Duties, Imposts and Excises, to pay the Debts and provide for the common Defense and general Welfare of the United States. . . .*❞

—Article I, Section 8, Clause 1

---

[1]Several of the expressed powers of Congress are set out elsewhere in the Constitution. Thus, Article IV, Section 3 grants Congress the power to admit new States to the Union (Clause 1) and to manage and dispose of federal territory and other property (Clause 2). The 16th Amendment gives Congress the power to levy an income tax. The 13th, 14th, 15th, 19th, 24th, and 26th amendments grant Congress the "power to enforce" the provisions of the amendments "by appropriate legislation."

▲ When they wrote the Commerce Clause, the Framers could not have envisioned this: a warehouse worker in Massachusetts filling orders for an online grocery service.

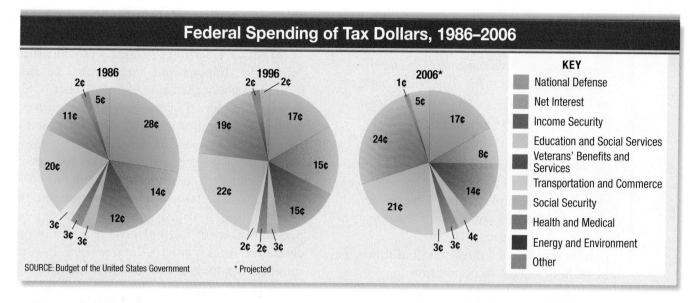

Federal Spending of Tax Dollars, 1986–2006

1986
2¢
5¢
11¢
28¢
20¢
14¢
3¢ 3¢ 3¢
12¢

1996
2¢ 2¢
19¢
17¢
15¢
22¢
15¢
2¢ 2¢ 3¢

2006*
1¢
5¢
24¢
17¢
8¢
21¢
14¢
3¢ 3¢ 4¢

KEY
- National Defense
- Net Interest
- Income Security
- Education and Social Services
- Veterans' Benefits and Services
- Transportation and Commerce
- Social Security
- Health and Medical
- Energy and Environment
- Other

SOURCE: Budget of the United States Government   * Projected

Interpreting Graphs Congress's priorities can be seen in the way it spends tax revenues. These graphs show what proportions of a tax dollar were spent on what federal programs. **What major shifts in federal spending occurred (a) between 1986 and 1996 and (b) between 1996 and 2006? H-SS 12.4.1**

Recall that the Articles of Confederation had not given Congress the power to tax. Congress did have the power to requisition (request) funds from the States; that is, Congress could ask (in reality, beg) each of the thirteen States for money. But, through the 1780s, not a single State came even remotely close to meeting the requisitions Congress made, and some States paid nothing at all. The government was impotent, and the lack of a power to tax was a leading cause for the creation of the Constitution.

The Purpose of Taxes

We shall take another and longer look at the taxing power in Chapter 16. But, here, a number of important points: The Federal Government will take in some $2.3 trillion in fiscal year 2006, and almost certainly an even larger sum in 2007. Most of that money—well over 95 percent of it—will come from the various taxes levied by Congress.

A **tax** is a charge levied by government on persons or property to raise money to meet public needs. But notice, Congress does sometimes impose taxes for other purposes as well. The protective tariff is perhaps the oldest example of this point. Although it does bring in some revenue every year, its real goal is to "protect" domestic industry against foreign competition by increasing the cost of foreign goods.

Taxes are also sometimes levied to protect the public health and safety. The Federal Government's regulation of narcotics is a case in point. Only those who have a proper federal license can legally manufacture, sell, or deal in those drugs—and licensing is a form of taxation.

Limits on the Taxing Power

Congress does not have an unlimited power to tax. As with all other powers, the taxing power must be used in accord with all other provisions of the Constitution. Thus, Congress cannot lay a tax on church services, for example—because such a tax would violate the 1st Amendment. Nor could it lay a poll tax as a condition for voting in federal elections—for that would violate the 24th Amendment.

More specifically, the Constitution places four explicit limitations on the taxing power:

(1) Congress may tax only for public purposes, not for private benefit. Article I, Section 8, Clause 1 says that taxes may be levied only "to pay the Debts and provide for the common Defense and general Welfare of the United States. . . ."

(2) Congress may not tax exports. Article I, Section 9, Clause 5 declares "[n]o Tax or Duty shall be laid on Articles exported from any State." Thus, customs duties (tariffs), which are taxes, can be levied only on goods brought into the country (imports), not on those sent abroad (exports).

(3) Direct taxes must be apportioned among the States, according to their populations:

> **FROM THE Constitution**
> "No Capitation, or other direct, Tax shall be laid, unless in Proportion to the Census of Enumeration herein before directed to be taken."
> —Article I, Section 9, Clause 4

A **direct tax** is one that must be paid directly to the government by the person on whom it is imposed—for example, a tax on the ownership of land or buildings, or a capitation (head or poll) tax.

An income tax is a direct tax, but it may be laid without regard to population:

> **FROM THE Constitution**
> "The Congress shall have power to lay and collect taxes on incomes, from whatever source derived, without apportionment among the several States, and without regard to any census or enumeration."
> —16th Amendment

Wealth (which translates to the ability to pay taxes) is not evenly distributed among the States. So, a direct tax levied in proportion to population would fall more heavily on the residents of some States than it would on others—and would, therefore, be grossly unfair. Consequently, Congress has not levied any

direct tax—except for the income tax—outside the District of Columbia since 1861.

(4) Article I, Section 8, Clause 1 provides that "all Duties, Imposts and Excises, shall be uniform throughout the United States." That is, all indirect taxes levied by the Federal Government must be levied at the same rate in every part of the country. These include the federal taxes on gasoline, alcoholic beverages and tobacco products.

As a general rule an **indirect tax** is one first paid by one person but then passed on to another. It is indirectly paid by that second person. Take, for example, the federal tax on cigarettes. It is paid to the Treasury by the tobacco company, but is then passed on through the wholesaler and retailer to the person who finally buys the cigarettes.

The Borrowing Power

Article I, Section 8, Clause 2 gives Congress the power "[t]o borrow Money on the credit of the United States." There are no constitutional limits on the amount of money that Congress may borrow, and no restriction on the purposes for which the borrowing can be done.

Congress has put a statutory ceiling on the public debt, however. The **public debt** is all of the money borrowed by the Federal Government over the years and not yet repaid, plus the accumulated interest on that money. That legal limit has never amounted to much more than a political gesture, however. Congress has always raised the ceiling whenever the debt has threatened to exceed it. The public debt is now (2006) more than $8.5 trillion.

For decades, the Federal Government has practiced **deficit financing**. That is, it regularly spends more than it takes in each year—and then borrows to make up the difference. Thus, the government relied on deficit financing, or borrowing to deal with the Depression of the 1930s, to meet the huge costs of World War II, and to fund wars and social programs over the next several decades.

In fact, the government's books showed a deficit in all but seven years from 1931 to 1969. And they were in the red *every* year from 1969 to 1998. As a result, the public debt climbed over those years—to more than $5.5 trillion at the beginning of fiscal year 1998.

Interpreting Political Cartoons Paying taxes often requires following complicated instructions. *According to this cartoon, how successful have been repeated efforts to simplify federal income tax forms?*

In the Balanced Budget Act of 1997, Congress and President Clinton vowed to eliminate deficit financing by 2002. Their goal was realized much sooner than that, however. The nation's economy was so robust at the time that the government's income rose dramatically—and the Treasury reported a modest surplus for fiscal year 1998, and somewhat larger ones for 1999, 2000, and 2001.

Deficits are once again the order of the day, however. Three major factors combined to make those four years of budget surpluses only a brief interlude: (1) a sharp downturn in the nation's economy; (2) several major tax cuts pushed by President Bush and enacted by Congress in 2001, 2002, 2003, and 2004; (3) the onset of the global war on terrorism in 2001 and the ongoing conflicts in Afghanistan and Iraq.

The Treasury has reported a deficit for each fiscal year since 2001. The shortfall topped $318 billion in 2005, and it will almost certainly exceed that stupendous sum in fiscal year 2006.

The interest the Federal Government pays out cannot be taxed by the States. That fact makes the Federal Government's notes and bonds quite attractive to investors.

The Commerce Power

The **commerce power**—the power of Congress to regulate interstate and foreign trade—is as vital to the welfare of the nation as is the taxing power. As you know, the commerce power played a major role in the formation of the Union. The weak Congress created under the Articles of Confederation had no power to regulate interstate trade and little authority over foreign commerce. The Critical Period of the 1780s was marked by intense commercial rivalries and bickering among the States. High trade barriers and spiteful State laws created chaos and confusion in much of the country.

Consequently, the Framers wrote the Commerce Clause. It gives Congress the power

FROM THE **Constitution** *❝ To regulate Commerce with foreign Nations, and among the several States, and with the Indian Tribes. ❞*

—Article I, Section 8, Clause 3

▲ This engraving from the 1830s shows Robert Fulton's steamboat, the *Clermont*. **Critical Thinking** *If Fulton had held on to his riverboat monopoly in New York, what might have been the effects on interstate commerce?*

The Commerce Clause proved to be more responsible for the building of a strong and *United* States out of a weak confederation than any other provision in the Constitution. Its few words have prompted the growth in this country of the greatest open market in the world.

Gibbons v. Ogden, 1824

The first case involving the Commerce Clause to reach the Supreme Court was *Gibbons* v. *Ogden,* decided in 1824. The case arose out of a clash over the regulation of steamboats by the State of New York, on the one hand, and the Federal Government, on the other. In 1807 Robert Fulton's steamboat, the *Clermont,* had made its first successful run up the Hudson River, from New York City to Albany. The State legislature then gave Fulton an exclusive, long-term grant to navigate the waters of the State by steamboat. Fulton's monopoly then gave Aaron Ogden a permit for steamboat navigation between New York City and New Jersey.

Thomas Gibbons, operating with a coasting license from the Federal Government, began to carry passengers on a line that competed with Ogden. Ogden sued him, and the New York courts held that Gibbons could not sail by steam in New York waters.

Gibbons appealed that ruling to the Supreme Court. He claimed that the New York grant conflicted with the congressional power to regulate commerce. The Court agreed. It rejected Ogden's argument that "commerce" should be defined narrowly, as simply "traffic" or the mere buying and selling of goods. Instead, it read the Commerce Clause in very broad terms:

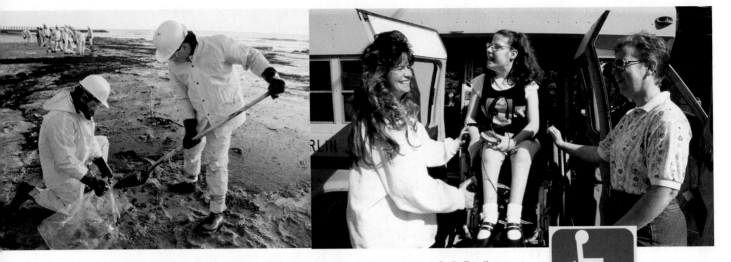

▲ Congress's commerce power affects the daily lives of all Americans—including these workers cleaning up after an oil spill and this student on a school bus wheelchair lift in Berlin, Maryland. *Critical Thinking* **How might the Commerce Clause affect these people?**

PRIMARY Sources **“***Commerce undoubtedly is traffic, but it is something more—it is intercourse. It describes the commercial intercourse between nations, and parts of nations, in all its branches, and is regulated by prescribing rules for carrying on that intercourse.* **”**

—Chief Justice John Marshall

The Court's ruling was widely popular at the time because it dealt a death blow to steamboat monopolies. Freed from restrictive State regulation, many new steamboat companies came into existence. As a result, steam navigation developed rapidly. Within a few years, the railroads, similarly freed, revolutionized transportation within the United States.

Over the decades, the Court's sweeping definition of commerce has brought an extension of federal authority into many areas of American life—a reach of federal power beyond anything the Framers could have imagined. As another of the many examples of the point, note this: It is on the basis of the commerce power that the Civil Rights Act of 1964 prohibits discrimination in access to or service in hotels, motels, theaters, restaurants, and in other public accommodations on grounds of race, color, religion, or national origin.[2]

Based on the expressed powers to regulate commerce and to tax, Congress and the courts have built nearly all of the implied powers.

Most of what the Federal Government does, day to day and year to year, it does as the result of legislation passed by Congress in the exercise of these two powers.

Limits on the Commerce Power

Like Congress's taxing power, its commerce power is not unlimited. It, too, must be exercised in accord with all other provisions in the Constitution. Thus, the Supreme Court struck down the Gun-Free School Zone Act of 1990 in *United States* v. *Lopez,* 1995. That act had made it a federal crime for anyone other than a police officer to possess a firearm in or around a school. The Court could find no useful connection between interstate commerce and guns at school, and it held that Congress in this case had invaded the reserved powers of the States.

In more specific terms, the Constitution places four explicit limits on the use of the commerce power. Congress

(1) cannot tax exports, Article I, Section 9, Clause 5;

(2) cannot favor the ports of one State over those of any other in the regulation of trade, Article I, Section 9, Clause 6;

---

[2]The Supreme Court upheld this use of the commerce power in *Heart of Atlanta Motel* v. *United States* in 1964. The unanimous Court noted that there was "overwhelming evidence of the disruptive effect of racial discrimination on commercial intercourse." You will look at this case again in Chapter 21.

(3) cannot require that "Vessels bound to, or from, one State, be obliged to enter, clear or pay Duties in another," Article I, Section 9, Clause 6; and, finally,

(4) could not interfere with the slave trade, at least not until the year 1808, Article I, Section 9, Clause 1. This last limitation, part of the curious slave-trade compromise at the Constitutional Convention, has been a dead letter for nearly two centuries now.

The Currency Power

Article I, Section 8, Clause 5 gives Congress the power "[t]o coin Money [and] regulate the Value thereof." The States are denied that power.[3]

Until the Revolution, the English money system, built on the shilling and the pound, was in general use in the colonies. With independence, that stable currency system collapsed. The Second Continental Congress and then the Congress under the Articles issued paper money. Without sound backing, and with no taxing power behind it, however, the money was practically worthless. Each of the 13 States also issued its own currency.

---

[3]Article I, Section 10, Clause 1 forbids the States the power to coin money, issue bills of credit (paper money), or make anything but gold and silver legal tender.

In several States, this amounted to little more than the State's printing its name on paper and calling it money. Adding to the confusion, people still used English coins, and Spanish money circulated freely in the southern States.

Nearly all the Framers agreed on the need for a single, national system of "hard" money. So the Constitution gave the currency power to Congress, and it all but excluded the States from that field. From 1789 on, among the most important of all of the many tasks performed by the Federal Government has been that of providing the nation with a uniform, stable monetary system.

From the beginning, the United States has issued coins—in gold, silver, and other metals. Congress chartered the first Bank of the United States in 1791 and gave it the power to issue bank notes—that is, paper money. Those notes were not legal tender, however. **Legal tender** is any kind of money that a creditor must by law accept in payment for debts. Congress did not create a national paper currency, and make it legal tender, until 1863.

The new national notes, known as Greenbacks, had to compete with other paper currencies already in the marketplace. Although the States could not issue paper money themselves, State governments chartered (licensed) private banks, whose notes did circulate as

The Development of a National Currency

CONTINENTAL CURRENCY

One third dollar, 1776
This "Continental" note, engraved by Benjamin Franklin, was issued to finance the American Revolution.

U.S. COINAGE

United States half cent, 1834 On the face of this early American coin is a woman representing Liberty; on the reverse is a laurel wreath.

DEMAND CURRENCY

$10 demand note, 1861
With metal badly needed for the Civil War, Congress issued this "Greenback," the first paper currency since the Continental. Congress made these notes legal tender in 1863.

STATE CURRENCY

$5 Louisiana state bank note, 1862 From 1837 to 1863, just about anyone could issue currency—from States to stores to individuals— creating economic chaos.

SILVER CERTIFICATE

$1 silver certificates, 1896
George Washington was not the only member of his family to have his face on a bill; this note, redeemable for silver, features his wife, Martha.

SOURCE: Federal Reserve Bank of San Francisco

Interpreting Charts The colonies, the States, and the young United States experimented with a variety of coins and paper notes in the effort to build a stable currency. For a long time, people trusted coins more than paper. ***Why do you think some forms of currency succeeded while others failed?***

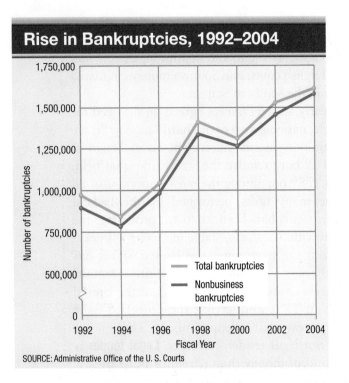

Rise in Bankruptcies, 1992–2004

Number of bankruptcies

1,750,000
1,500,000
1,250,000
1,000,000
750,000
500,000
0

1992 1994 1996 1998 2000 2002 2004

Fiscal Year

Total bankruptcies
Nonbusiness bankruptcies

SOURCE: Administrative Office of the U. S. Courts

Interpreting Graphs Congress, along with the States, has the power to set bankruptcy laws. ***Describe the change in nonbusiness bankruptcies from 1992 to 2004 as shown in the graph.*** **H-SS 12.4.1**

money. When those private bank notes interfered with the new national currency, Congress (in 1865) set a ten percent tax on their production. The private bank notes soon disappeared. The Supreme Court upheld the 1865 law as a proper exercise of the taxing power in *Veazie Bank* v. *Fenno*, 1869.

At first, the Greenbacks could not be redeemed for gold or silver. Their worth fell to less than half their face value. Then, in 1870, the Supreme Court held their issuance to be unconstitutional. In *Hepburn* v. *Griswold* it said "to coin" meant to stamp metal and so the Constitution did not authorize paper money.

The Court soon changed its mind, however, in the *Legal Tender Cases* in 1871 and again in *Juliard* v. *Greenman* in 1884. In both cases it held the issuing of paper money as legal tender to be a proper use of the currency power. The Court also declared this a power properly implied from the borrowing and the war powers.

The Bankruptcy Power

Article I, Section 8, Clause 4 gives Congress the power "[t]o establish . . . uniform Laws on the subject of Bankruptcies throughout the United States." A bankrupt individual or company or other organization is one a court has found to be insolvent—that is, unable to pay debts in full. **Bankruptcy** is the legal proceeding in which the bankrupt's assets—however much or little they may be—are distributed among those to whom a debt is owed. That proceeding frees the bankrupt from legal responsibility for debts acquired before bankruptcy.

The States and the National Government have concurrent power to regulate bankruptcy. Today federal bankruptcy law is so broad that it all but excludes the States from the field. Nearly all bankruptcy cases are heard now in federal district courts.

Section 2 Assessment

Key Terms and Main Ideas

1. Explain the difference between a **direct tax** and an **indirect tax,** and give examples of each.
2. What three factors brought about the recent return to **deficit financing** at the federal level?
3. Give three examples of how Congress uses its **commerce power.**
4. What problems led the Framers to give Congress the power to coin money and make it **legal tender?**

Critical Thinking

5. **Making Inferences** Reread the four ways that the Constitution limits Congress' power to tax (pages 295–296). What can you infer about the Framers' reasons for limiting this power?

6. **Expressing Problems Clearly** This issue is hotly debated today: Should Congress regulate the Internet—for example, to ban false advertising? Do you think the Commerce Clause gives Congress the power to regulate Internet activity? Explain your reasoning.

Other Expressed Powers

Section Preview

OBJECTIVES

1. **Identify** the key sources of Congress's foreign relations powers.
2. **Describe** the power-sharing arrangement between Congress and the President on the issues of war and national defense.
3. **List** other key powers exercised by Congress.

WHY IT MATTERS

The Constitution gives Congress several other expressed powers—powers that cover matters that range from foreign affairs and national security to the mail you send and receive and the copyrights on your CDs and DVDs.

POLITICAL DICTIONARY

★ **naturalization**
★ **copyright**
★ **patent**
★ **eminent domain**

We have just reviewed the several expressed powers that Congress has with regard to money and to foreign and interstate commerce. The Constitution grants a number of other very important powers to Congress, and they are the focus of this section.

Foreign Relations Powers

The National Government has greater powers in the field of foreign affairs than in any other area. Congress shares power in this field with the President, who is primarily responsible for the conduct of our relations with other nations. Because the States in the Union are not sovereign, they have no standing in international law. The Constitution does not allow them to take part in foreign relations.[4]

The foreign relations powers of Congress come from two sources: (1) from various expressed powers, espccially the war powers and the power to regulate foreign commerce, and (2) from the fact that the United States is a sovereign state in the world community. As the nation's lawmaking body, Congress has the inherent power to act on matters affecting the security of the nation—for example, the regulation of immigration and measures to combat terrorism here and abroad. You will explore this vitally important subject at much greater length in Chapter 17.

---

[4]See Article I, Section 10, Clauses 1 and 3.

War Powers

Eight of the expressed powers given to Congress in Article I, Section 8 deal with war and national defense.[5] Here, too, Congress shares power with the chief executive. The Constitution makes the President the commander in chief of the nation's armed forces,[6] and, as such, the President dominates the field.

The congressional war powers, however, are extensive and substantial. Only Congress may declare war. It has the power to raise and support armies, to provide and maintain a navy, and to make rules pertaining to the governing of land and naval forces. Congress also has the power to provide for "calling forth the Militia" and for the organizing, arming, and disciplining of it. Congress has the power to grant letters of marque and reprisal[7] and to make rules concerning captures on land and water.

With the passage of the War Powers Resolution of 1973, Congress claimed the power to restrict the use of American forces in

---

[5]The war powers of Congress are set out in Clauses 11 through 16.

[6]Article II, Section 2, Clause 1.

[7]A few of the expressed powers are of little importance today. Thus, Congress has the power to grant letters of marque and reprisal, Article I, Section 8, Clause 11, and the States are denied the power to issue them, Article I, Section 10, Clause 1. Letters of marque and reprisal are written grants of power authorizing private persons to outfit vessels to capture and destroy enemy vessels in time of war. In effect, they authorize a form of legalized piracy. Letters of marque and reprisal are forbidden by international law by the Declaration of Paris, 1856, and the United States honors the rule.

combat in areas where a state of war does not exist; see Chapters 14 and 17.

Other Expressed Powers

The Constitution sets out a number of other expressed powers. Many of these powers have a direct influence on the daily lives of Americans.

Naturalization

The process by which citizens of one country become citizens of another is called **naturalization.** Article I, Section 8, Clause 4 gives Congress the exclusive power "[t]o establish an uniform Rule of Naturalization." Today, our population includes more than 11 million naturalized citizens; we shall return to this matter in Chapter 21.

The Postal Power

Article I, Section 8, Clause 7 says that Congress has the power "[t]o establish Post Offices and post Roads." Post roads are all postal routes, including railroads, airways, and waters within the United States, during the time that mail is being carried on them.

The United States Postal Service traces its history back to the early colonial period. Benjamin Franklin is generally credited as the founder of the present-day postal system. Today some 38,000 post offices, branches, stations, and community post offices serve the nation. The Postal Service and its some 750,000 employees handle more than 200 billion pieces of mail a year.

Congress has established a number of crimes based on the postal power. Thus, it is a federal crime for anyone to obstruct the mails, to use the mails to commit any fraud, or to use the mails in the committing of any other crime.

Congress has also prohibited the mailing of many items. Any articles prohibited by a State's laws—for example, firecrackers or switchblade knives—cannot be sent into that State by mail. A great many other items, including chain letters and obscene materials, cannot be sent through the mails.

The States and their local governments cannot interfere with the mails unreasonably. Nor can they require licenses for Postal Service vehicles or tax the gas they use, or tax post offices or any other property of the United States Postal Service.

Congressional Powers Expressed in Article 1, Section 8

PEACETIME POWERS		WAR POWERS	
Clause	Provision	Clause	Provision
1	To impose and collect taxes, duties, and excises	11	To declare war; to make laws regarding captures on land and water
2	To borrow money		
3	To regulate foreign and interstate commerce	12	To raise and support armies
4	To provide for naturalization; to create bankruptcy laws	13	To provide and maintain a navy
5	To coin money and regulate its value; to regulate weights and measures	14	To make laws governing land and naval forces
6	To punish counterfeiters of federal money and securities	15	To provide for summoning the militia to execute federal laws, suppress uprisings, and repel invasions
7	To establish post offices and post roads		
8	To grant patents and copyrights		
9	To create courts inferior to the Supreme Court		
10	To define and punish crimes at sea and violations of international law	16	To provide for organizing, arming, and disciplining the militia and governing it when in the service of the Union
17	To exercise exclusive jurisdiction over the District of Columbia and other federal properties		
18	To make all laws necessary and proper to the execution of any of the other expressed powers		

Interpreting Tables This table sets out the expressed powers of Congress. *Choose two war powers and two peacetime powers and explain why you think the Framers felt it important to give these powers to Congress.* H-SS 12.4.1

Copyrights and Patents

The Constitution gives Congress the power

 "To promote the Progress of Science and useful Arts, by securing for limited Times to Authors and Inventors the exclusive Right to their respective Writings and Discoveries.**"**
—Article I, Section 8, Clause 8

A **copyright** is the exclusive right of an author to reproduce, publish, and sell his or her creative work. That right may be assigned —transferred by contract—to

Types of Intellectual Property

Utility patents protect useful processes, machines, articles of manufacture, and compositions of matter. Examples: fiber optics, computer hardware, medications.

Design patents prohibit the unauthorized use of new, original, and ornamental designs for manufactured articles. Examples: the look of an athletic shoe, a bicycle helmet, Star Wars characters.

Plant patents protect certain invented or discovered plant varieties. Examples: hybrid tea roses, Silver Queen corn, Better Boy tomatoes.

Copyrights protect works of authorship, such as writings, music, and works of art that have been "tangibly expressed"—that is, in some way published, written, recorded, or made. Examples: *Gone With the Wind* (book and film), Beatles recordings, video games.

Trademarks protect words, names, symbols, sounds, or colors that distinguish goods and services. Trademarks, unlike patents, can be renewed forever, as long as they are being used in business. Examples: the roar of the lion in MGM movies, the pink of the Owens-Corning Pink Panther, the word "three-peat"—coined by former Los Angeles Lakers basketball coach Pat Riley in 1989 in reference to record-setting three-in-a-row NBA championship victories.

Trade secrets are information that companies keep secret to give them an advantage over their competitors. Examples: the recipe for Coca-Cola, the recipe for Kentucky Fried Chicken.

SOURCE: United States Patent and Trademark Museum

Interpreting Charts In 2000, the government created a stir by granting an Internet store, Amazon.com, a patent on the structure of its Web page, which links to other merchants. *(a) Which type of patent listed above might have been given to Amazon.com? (b) Why do you think the granting of this patent was controversial?* H-SS 12.2.2

another, as to a publishing firm by mutual agreement between the author and the other party.

Copyrights are registered by the Copyright Office in the Library of Congress. Under present law they are good for the life of the author plus 70 years. They cover a wide range of creative efforts: books, magazines, newspapers, musical compositions and lyrics, dramatic works, paintings, sculptures, cartoons, maps, photographs, motion pictures, sound recordings, and much more.[8]

The Copyright Office does not enforce the protections of a copyright. If a copyright is infringed or violated, the owner of the right may sue for damages in the federal courts.

A **patent** grants a person the sole right to manufacture, use, or sell "any new and useful art, machine, manufacture, or composition of matter, or any new and useful improvement thereof." A patent is good for up to 20 years. The term of a patent may be extended only by a special act of Congress. The Patent and Trademark Office in the Department of Commerce administers patent laws.[9]

Weights and Measures

Article I, Section 8, Clause 5 gives Congress the power to "fix the Standard of Weights and Measures" throughout the United States. The power reflects the absolute need for accurate, uniform gauges of time, distance, area, weight, volume, and the like.

In 1838 Congress set the English system of pound, ounce, mile, foot, gallon, quart, and so on, as the legal standards of weights and measures in this country. In 1866 Congress also legalized the use of the metric system of gram, meter, kilometer, liter, and so on.

In 1901, Congress created the National Bureau of Standards in the Commerce Department. Now known as the National Institute of Standards and Technology, the agency keeps the original standards for the United States. It is these standards by which all other measures in the United States are tested and corrected.

---

[8]Not all publications can be protected by copyright. Thus, the Supreme Court has held that such "factual compilations" as telephone directories "lack the requisite originality" for copyright protection, *Feist Publications, Inc.,* v. *Rural Telephone Service Co.,* 1991.

[9]The power to protect trademarks is an implied power, drawn from the commerce power. A trademark is some distinctive word, name, symbol, or device used by a manufacturer or merchant to identify his goods or services and distinguish them from those made or sold by others. A trademark need not be original, merely distinctive. The registration of a trademark carries the right to its exclusive use in interstate commerce for 10 years. The right may be renewed an unlimited number of times.

Federal Land in the Western United States*

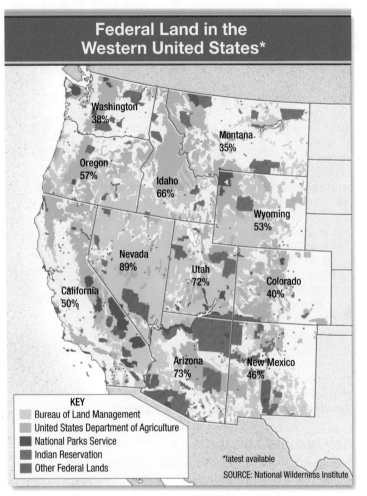

KEY
- Bureau of Land Management
- United States Department of Agriculture
- National Parks Service
- Indian Reservation
- Other Federal Lands

*latest available
SOURCE: National Wilderness Institute

Washington 38%
Oregon 57%
Montana 35%
Idaho 66%
Wyoming 53%
Nevada 89%
Utah 72%
California 50%
Colorado 40%
Arizona 73%
New Mexico 46%

Interpreting Maps The Federal Government owns vast areas of the West. **(a) In which States is most of the land owned by the Federal Government? (b) Why do certain agencies own so much land?**

Power Over Territories and Other Areas

Article I, Section 8, Clause 17 and Article IV, Section 3, Clause 2 give Congress the power to acquire, manage, and dispose of various federal areas. That power relates to the District of Columbia and to the several federal territories, including Puerto Rico, Guam, and the Virgin Islands. It also covers hundreds of military and naval installations, arsenals, dockyards, post offices, prisons, parks and forest preserves, and many other federal holdings.

The Federal Government may acquire property by purchase or gift. It may also do so through the exercise of **eminent domain,** the inherent power to take private property for public use.[10] Territory may also be acquired from a foreign state based on the power to admit new States, on the war powers, and on the President's treaty-making power.

Judicial Powers

As a part of the system of checks and balances, Congress has several judicial powers. These include the expressed power to create all of the federal courts below the Supreme Court and to structure the federal judiciary.

Congress also has the power to define federal crimes and set punishment for violators of federal law. The Constitution mentions only four. Three are found in Article I, Section 8: counterfeiting, piracies and felonies on the high seas, and offenses against international law. Treason is listed in Article III, Section 3. Congress has used its implied powers to establish more than one hundred other federal crimes.

---

[10]The 5th Amendment restricts the government's use of the power with these words: "nor shall private property be taken for public use, without just compensation."

Section 3 Assessment

Key Terms and Main Ideas

1. Explain how Congress and the President share power in the fields of foreign relations and defense.
2. Where does Congress get its power to regulate **naturalization**?
3. How does a **copyright** differ from a **patent**?

Critical Thinking

4. **Drawing Inferences** Choose three congressional powers discussed in this section and indicate why the Framers gave these powers to Congress rather than to the States.
5. **Making Decisions** Some people suggest that the U.S. Postal Service be abolished because they say today's for-profit mail companies could operate more efficiently, effectively, and economically. Do you agree? Explain.

Standards Monitoring *Online*
For: Self-quiz with vocabulary practice
Web Code: mqa-3113

Go Online
PHSchool.com

For: An activity on the U.S. Postal Service
Web Code: mqd-3113

4 The Implied Powers

Section Preview

OBJECTIVES

1. **Explain** how the Necessary and Proper Clause gives Congress flexibility in lawmaking.
2. **Summarize** the key developments in the battle over the implied powers of Congress.

WHY IT MATTERS

The Necessary and Proper Clause sparked an early battle over the extent of the powers granted to Congress by the Constitution, and that debate has continued for more than two centuries.

POLITICAL DICTIONARY

★ appropriate
★ Necessary and Proper Clause
★ doctrine

What does the Constitution say about education? Nothing, not a word. Still, Congress **appropriates**—assigns to a particular use—more than $60 billion a year for the U.S. Department of Education to spend in various ways throughout the country. Look around you. What evidence of these federal dollars can you find in your school? If you attend a public school anywhere in the United States, those indications should not be hard to see.

How can this be? You know that Congress has only those powers delegated to it by the Constitution, and the Constitution says nothing about education. The answer lies in the implied powers of Congress.

The Necessary and Proper Clause

Remember that the implied powers are those powers that are not set out in so many words in the Constitution but are implied by those that are. The constitutional basis for the implied powers is found in one of the expressed powers. The **Necessary and Proper Clause** gives to Congress the expressed power

FROM THE Constitution **❝**To make all Laws which shall be necessary and proper for carrying into Execution the foregoing Powers and all other Powers vested by this Constitution in the Government of the United States, or in any Department or Officer thereof.**❞**

—Article I, Section 8, Clause 18

Much of the vitality and adaptability of the United States Constitution can be traced directly to this provision—and even more so to the ways both Congress and the Supreme Court have interpreted and applied it over the years. For good reason, the Necessary and Proper Clause has often been called the "Elastic Clause," because it has been stretched so far and made to cover so much over the years.

The Battle Over Implied Powers

The Constitution had barely come into force when the meaning of the Necessary and Proper Clause was called into question. In 1790

Interpreting Political Cartoons This cartoon depicts New York State's ratification of the Constitution in 1788. *(a) What does the ship represent? (b) What does the cartoon imply about the Federal Government? (c) Was the cartoonist a Federalist or an Anti-Federalist?*

Alexander Hamilton, as Secretary of the Treasury, urged Congress to set up a national bank. That proposal touched off one of the most important disputes in all of American political history.

The opponents of Hamilton's plan insisted that nowhere did the Constitution give to Congress the power to establish such a bank. Remember, those strict constructionists, led by Thomas Jefferson, believed that the new government had only (1) those powers expressly granted to it by the Constitution, and (2) those few other powers *absolutely* necessary to carrying out the expressed powers.

Hamilton and other liberal constructionists looked to the Necessary and Proper Clause. They said that it gave Congress the power to do anything that was reasonably related to the exercise of the expressed powers. As for the national bank, they argued that its creation was clearly related to the execution of the taxing, borrowing, commerce, and currency powers.

The strict constructionists were sorely troubled by that broad view of the powers of Congress. They were sure that it would give the new government almost unlimited authority and all but destroy the reserved powers of the States.[11]

Reason and practical necessity carried the day for Hamilton and his side. Congress established the Bank of the United States in 1791. Its charter (the act creating it) was to expire in 1811. During those 20 years, the constitutionality of both the bank and the concept of implied powers went unchallenged in the courts.

McCulloch v. Maryland, 1819

In 1816 Congress created the Second Bank of the United States. Its charter came only after

---

[11]In 1801 a bill was introduced in Congress to incorporate a company to mine copper. As Vice President, Jefferson ridiculed that measure with this comment: "Congress is authorized to defend the nation. Ships are necessary for defense; copper is necessary for ships; mines necessary for copper; a company necessary to work the mines; and who can doubt this reasoning who has ever played at 'This Is the House that Jack Built'?" While Jefferson himself was President (1801–1809), he and his party were many times forced to reverse their earlier stand. Thus, for example, it was only on the basis of the implied powers doctrine that the Louisiana Purchase in 1803 and the embargo on foreign trade in 1807 could be justified.

The Enduring Constitution

Congressional Power	1825	1875	1925

The concept of implied powers has been a major factor in the growth and development of the powers of Congress—and so of the National Government— over the past two centuries.

Go Online
PHSchool.com
Use Web Code mqp-3118 to access an interactive time line.

Analysis Skills CS1, CS2, HI1

1819 Supreme Court upholds the concept of implied powers, declaring that the powers to tax, borrow, and regulate commerce give Congress the power to establish a national bank.

1871 Supreme Court holds that the issuing of paper money is a proper excercise of the currency power. (*Legal Tender Cases*)

1849 Supreme Court rejects State efforts to regulate immigration, declaring it a Congressional issue. (*Passenger Cases*)

1890 Sherman Antitrust Act, based on the commerce power, regulates monopolies and other practices that limit competition.

★★★ **306** **Chapter 11 Section 4**

another hard-fought battle over the extent of the powers of Congress.

Having lost in Congress, opponents of the new bank now tried to persuade several State legislatures to cripple its operations. In 1818 Maryland placed a tax on all notes issued by any bank doing business in the State but not chartered by the State legislature. The tax was aimed directly at the Second Bank's branch in Baltimore. James McCulloch, the bank's cashier, purposely issued notes on which no tax had been paid. The State won a judgment against him in its own courts. Acting for McCulloch, the United States then appealed to the Supreme Court.

Maryland took the strict-construction position before the Court. It argued that the creation of the bank had been unconstitutional. The United States defended the concept of implied powers, and also argued that no State could lawfully tax any agency of the Federal Government.

In one of its most important decisions, the Court unanimously reversed the Maryland courts. It held that the Constitution need not expressly empower Congress to create a bank.

The creation of the Second Bank, said the Court, was "necessary and proper" to the execution of four of the expressed powers of Congress: the taxing, borrowing, currency, and commerce powers. In short, the Court gave sweeping approval to the concept of implied powers.[12]

Chief Justice John Marshall wrote the Court's opinion in the case. For the Court, he said:

> **PRIMARY Sources** *We admit, as all must admit, that the powers of the government are limited, and that its limits are not to be transcended. But we think the sound construction of the Constitution must allow to the national legislature that discretion, with respect to the means by which the powers it confers are to be carried into execution, which will enable that body to perform the high duties assigned to it, in the manner most beneficial to the people.*
> —*McCulloch* v. *Maryland*, Opinion of the Court

[12]The Court also invalidated the Maryland tax. Because, said the Court, "the power to tax involves the power to destroy," no State may tax the United States or any of its agencies or functions.

1937 Supreme Court upholds the Social Security Act of 1935, as a proper exercise of the powers to tax and provide for the general welfare. (*Steward Machine Co.* v. *Davis*; *Helvering* v. *Davis*)

1964 Supreme Court upholds the public accommodations provisions of the Civil Rights Act of 1964, as a valid exercise of the commerce power. (*Heart of Atlanta Motel* v. *United States*)

1950   **1975**   **2000**

1935 Wagner Act, based on the commerce power, recognizes labor's right to organize and bargain collectively.

1956 Interstate and National Defense Highway Act, based on the commerce and war powers, provides for a national interstate highway system.

1965 Congress amends the Social Security Act of 1935 to create Medicare, to cover most hospital and other health-care costs of the elderly.

1990 The Americans with Disabilities Act, based on the commerce power, prohibits discrimination against the physically impaired.

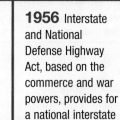

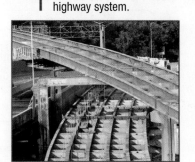

Analyzing Time Lines

1. Which expressed power has been the basis for most of the expansion of Congress's powers? Why do you think this is so?
2. According to this time line, through what means has congressional power expanded over time?

The Implied Powers of Congress

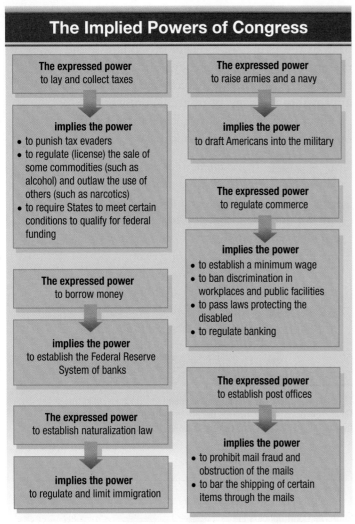

The expressed power to lay and collect taxes	The expressed power to raise armies and a navy
implies the power • to punish tax evaders • to regulate (license) the sale of some commodities (such as alcohol) and outlaw the use of others (such as narcotics) • to require States to meet certain conditions to qualify for federal funding	**implies the power** to draft Americans into the military

The expressed power to borrow money	The expressed power to regulate commerce
implies the power to establish the Federal Reserve System of banks	**implies the power** • to establish a minimum wage • to ban discrimination in workplaces and public facilities • to pass laws protecting the disabled • to regulate banking

The expressed power to establish naturalization law	The expressed power to establish post offices
implies the power to regulate and limit immigration	**implies the power** • to prohibit mail fraud and obstruction of the mails • to bar the shipping of certain items through the mails

Interpreting Charts This chart indicates the sources of several implied powers, those that are not specifically spelled out in the Constitution but can be reasonably assumed. ***Choose three of the implied powers listed above and explain specifically why we can assume that these powers belong to Congress.*** H-SS 12.5.3

Then he penned these deathless words:

"Let the end be legitimate, let it be within the scope of the Constitution, and all means which are appropriate, which are plainly adapted to that end, which are not prohibited, but consist with the letter and spirit of the Constitution, are constitutional."

—*McCulloch* v. *Maryland*, Opinion of the Court

This broad interpretation of the powers granted to Congress has become firmly fixed in our constitutional system. Indeed, it is impossible to see how the United States could have developed as it has under the Constitution without the principle established by *McCulloch*.

The Doctrine in Practice

A **doctrine** is a principle or fundamental policy. The doctrine of implied powers has been applied in instances almost too numerous to count. The way Congress has looked at and used its powers, along with the supporting decisions of the Supreme Court, have made Article I, Section 8, Clause 18 truly the Elastic Clause. Today the words "necessary and proper" really read "convenient and useful."

This is most especially true when applied to the power to regulate interstate commerce and the power to tax. Yet, recall, Congress cannot do something merely because it seems to promote the "general welfare" or be in the "public interest."

Section 4 Assessment

Key Terms and Main Ideas

1. Explain what it means to **appropriate** funds.
2. **(a)** What is the **Necessary and Proper Clause** sometimes called? **(b)** How did it get that name?
3. What is the **doctrine** of implied powers?

Critical Thinking

4. **Expressing Problems Clearly (a)** Write a one-sentence summary of the central dispute in the case of *McCulloch* v. *Maryland*. **(b)** Identify the key individuals and institutions involved in the case. **(c)** Summarize the outcome of the case. **(d)** Explain the long-term consequences of the decision.
5. **Evaluating the Quotation** Restate the first quotation from the *McCulloch* v. *Maryland* decision on page 307 in your own words.
6. **Drawing Conclusions** If the strict constructionists had won their battle to limit Congress's implied powers, how might our government be different today?

Standards Monitoring *Online*
For: Self-quiz with vocabulary practice
Web Code: mqa-3114

Go Online
PHSchool.com
For: An activity on strict and liberal construction
Web Code: mqd-3114

on Primary Sources

Reining in Congress

Analysis Skills HR4, HI3

Over recent years, the Supreme Court has appeared more willing to overturn federal laws when it felt that Congress had exceeded its authority. In this selection, Court observer Dan Carney discusses this trend and how it may impact the way in which Congress exercises its powers in the future.

James Brady (right) and his allies speak in favor of gun control before the Supreme Court building.

In early December [1996], Acting Solicitor General Walter E. Dellinger III argued before the U.S. Supreme Court on the merits of the Brady Act, which allows a police background check on people seeking to buy handguns. Almost in passing, he mentioned that the vast majority of sheriffs and police chiefs support the legislation.

This struck a raw nerve with Chief Justice William H. Rehnquist, who curtly informed Dellinger that the Supreme Court of the United States did not base its rulings on straw polls. If a person's constitutional rights are being violated by a popular statute, Rehnquist reasoned, the Court is not going to say: "Gee, plenty of other people obey this law and here you are complaining about it."

Under normal circumstances, this kind of statement might be dismissed as offhand. But in light of the Court's recent decisions—and cases it is now hearing—the remark illustrates the Court's growing willingness to strike down federal statutes on the grounds that Congress has overstepped its power.

The Supreme Court has undertaken a re-evaluation of Congress's legislative authority. . . .

The chief question in these cases is if Congress has ventured into areas where it has no right to be. . . . All of these cases involve limits to federal power, and most are likely to turn on interpretation of the 10th Amendment, which restricts the Federal Government to those powers specifically enumerated in the Constitution. For Congress, this is not some arcane legal debate taking place at the

Court. It could have a dramatic effect on the type of legislation Congress can enact, and the way that it does it. "There are enough cases now where I think Congress ought to think of it as a wake-up call," says A. E. Dick Howard, a law professor at the University of Virginia. "Surely all this adds up to changing the way Congress does its business." . . . Orrin G. Hatch (R., Utah), chairman of the Senate Judiciary Committee, said he is "very happy with these decisions" because they indicate that "we have a Congress that operates under limited and enumerated powers."

At the very least, the Supreme Court's renewed interest in the 10th Amendment will likely mean more legislation based on the interstate commerce clause in Article I of the Constitution. Congress's authority to regulate such commerce is arguably its broadest and hardest-to-define power.

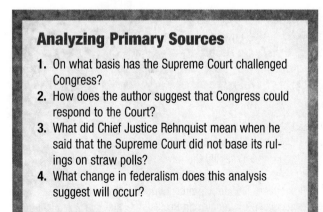

Analyzing Primary Sources

1. On what basis has the Supreme Court challenged Congress?
2. How does the author suggest that Congress could respond to the Court?
3. What did Chief Justice Rehnquist mean when he said that the Supreme Court did not base its rulings on straw polls?
4. What change in federalism does this analysis suggest will occur?

Section Preview

OBJECTIVES

1. **Describe** Congress's role in amending the Constitution and in deciding elections.
2. **Describe** Congress's power to impeach, and summarize presidential impeachment cases.
3. **Identify** Congress's executive powers.
4. **Describe** Congress's investigatory power.

WHY IT MATTERS

Impeachment trials, close elections, far-reaching constitutional change, congressional committee investigations, presidential appointments—Congress has often captured the undivided attention of the American people as it has exercised one of its several non-legislative powers.

POLITICAL DICTIONARY

★ successor
★ impeach
★ acquit
★ perjury
★ censure
★ subpoena

Congress is a legislative body; its primary function is to make law. But the Constitution does give it some other chores—several nonlegislative duties—to perform as well.

Constitutional Amendments

Article V says that Congress may propose amendments by a two-thirds vote in each house. It has done so 33 times. Article V also provides that Congress may call a national convention of delegates from each of the States to propose an amendment—but only if requested to do so by at

▲ Suffragettes celebrate passage of the 19th Amendment, giving women the right to vote. In 1972, Congress proposed an Equal Rights Amendment (ERA), but after a long, divisive battle, the effort to win ratification failed. *Critical Thinking* **Why did the Framers make the amendment process difficult, requiring State ratification in addition to congressional approval?**

least two thirds (34) of the State legislatures. No such convention has ever been called.

In recent years several State legislatures have petitioned Congress for amendments—among them measures that would require Congress to balance the federal budget each year, prohibit flag burning, permit prayer in the public schools, outlaw abortions, impose term limits on members of Congress, and prohibit same-sex marriages.

Electoral Duties

The Constitution gives certain electoral duties to Congress. But they are to be exercised only in very unusual circumstances.

The House may be called on to elect a President. The 12th Amendment says that if no one receives a majority of the electoral votes for President, the House, voting by States, is to decide the issue. It must choose from among the three highest contenders in the electoral college balloting. Each State has but one vote to cast, and a majority of the States is necessary for election.

Similarly, the Senate must choose a Vice President if no candidate wins a majority of the electoral votes for that office. In that situation, the vote is not by States but by individual senators, with a majority of the full Senate necessary for election.[13]

---

[13]Notice that the 12th Amendment makes it possible for the President to be of one party and the Vice President another.

The House has twice chosen a President: Thomas Jefferson in 1801 and John Quincy Adams in 1825. The Senate has had to pick a Vice President only once: Richard M. Johnson in 1837.

Remember, too, that the 25th Amendment provides for the filling of a vacancy in the vice presidency. When one occurs, the President nominates a **successor**—a replacement, someone to fill the vacancy, subject to a majority vote in both houses of Congress. That process has been used twice: Gerald Ford was confirmed as Vice President in 1973 and Nelson Rockefeller in 1974.

Impeachment

The Constitution provides that the President, Vice President, and all civil officers of the United States may "be removed from Office on Impeachment for and Conviction of, Treason, Bribery, or other high Crimes and Misdemeanors."[14] The House has the sole power to **impeach**—to accuse, bring charges. The Senate has the sole power to try—to judge, sit as a court—in impeachment cases.[15]

Impeachment requires only a majority vote in the House; conviction requires a two-thirds vote in the Senate. The Chief Justice presides over the Senate when a President is to be tried. The penalty for conviction is removal from office. The Senate may also prohibit a convicted person from ever holding federal office again; and he or she can be tried in the regular courts for any crime involved in the events that led to the impeachment. To date, there have been 17 impeachments and seven convictions; all seven persons removed by the Senate were federal judges.[16]

Two Presidents have been impeached by the House: Andrew Johnson in 1868 and Bill Clinton in 1998. The Senate voted to **acquit** both men— that is, it found them not guilty.

---

[14]Article II, Section 4. Military officers are not considered "civil officers," nor are members of Congress.

[15]Article I, Section 2, Clause 5; Section 3, Clause 6.

[16]Four other federal judges were impeached by the House but later acquitted by the Senate. Two federal judges impeached by the House resigned before the Senate could act in their cases. One of the seven judges removed from office was later elected to Congress. The only other federal officer ever impeached was William W. Bellknap, President Grant's Secretary of War. Bellknap had been accused of accepting bribes and, although he had resigned from office, was impeached by the House in 1876. He was then tried by the Senate and found not guilty.

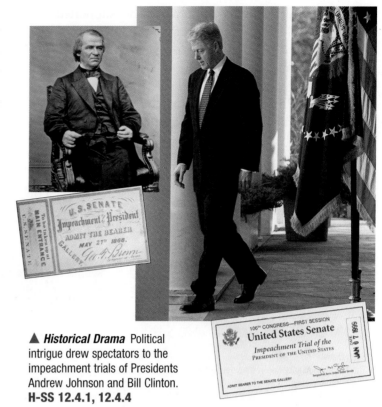

▲ **Historical Drama** Political intrigue drew spectators to the impeachment trials of Presidents Andrew Johnson and Bill Clinton. **H-SS 12.4.1, 12.4.4**

Andrew Johnson

Andrew Johnson became the nation's 17th President when Abraham Lincoln was assassinated in 1865. Johnson soon became enmeshed in disputes with the Radical Republicans who controlled Congress. Many of those disagreements centered on the treatment of the defeated Southern States in the immediate post–Civil War period.

Matters came to a head when Congress passed the Tenure of Office Act, over the President's veto, in 1867. President Johnson's deliberate violation of that law triggered his impeachment by a House bent on political revenge. The table on the next page summarizes the episode.

Bill Clinton

Bill Clinton was impeached by the House in 1998. In proceedings steeped in partisanship, the House voted two articles of impeachment against him on December 19. Both articles arose out of the President's admitted "inappropriate relationship" with a White House intern. As you can see in the table on the next page, the first article charged the President with **perjury,** or lying under oath. The second article accused him of obstruction of justice because he withheld information about his affair with the intern.

Members of the House who supported the articles of impeachment contended that lying under oath and withholding evidence were within the meaning of the Constitution's phrase "other high Crimes and Misdemeanors," and justified the President's immediate removal from office.

Their opponents argued that the facts involved in the case did not justify either charge. They insisted that, while the President's conduct was deplorable and should be condemned, that conduct did not rise to the level of an impeachable offense. Many of them pressed for a resolution to censure the President—that is, for a formal condemnation of his behavior.

The Senate received the articles of impeachment when the new Congress convened in 1999, and it began to sit in judgment of the President on January 7. The Senate trial and its outcome are summarized in the table below.

Richard Nixon

A few officeholders have resigned in the face of almost certain impeachment—most notably, Richard Nixon, who resigned the presidency in 1974. Nixon's second term in office was cut short by the Watergate scandal.

The Impeachment Process

THE PROCESS	PRESIDENT ANDREW JOHNSON IMPEACHMENT 1868	PRESIDENT BILL CLINTON IMPEACHMENT 1998–1999
Step One The House Judiciary Committee debates charges against the accused and votes on whether to send articles of impeachment to the full House. A simple majority vote is needed to start the process.	**Feb. 22, 1868** House committee votes to send to the full House articles of impeachment against Johnson for having violated the Tenure of Office Act, by firing Secretary of War Edwin Stanton.	**Dec. 11–12, 1998** After three months of hearings, the House Judiciary Committee approves four articles of impeachment against Clinton: two counts of perjury, obstruction of justice, and making false statements relating to his relations with a White House intern.
Step Two Acting much like a grand jury, the House considers the charge(s) brought by the Judiciary Committee. It can subpoena witnesses and evidence. It hears and debates arguments.	**Feb. 22–24, 1868** The House, led by the Radical Republicans, holds a raucous debate on charges against Johnson, a Democrat. The outcome is never in doubt.	**Dec. 18–19, 1998** The House holds 13 hours of bitter, partisan debate, in which more than 200 House members speak. Democrats briefly walk out to protest Republican leaders' refusal to consider the lesser punishment of censure.
Step Three The House votes on each article. If any article is approved by a majority vote, the official is impeached, which is similar to being indicted. The House sends the article(s) of impeachment to the Senate.	**Feb. 24, 1868** The House votes 126 to 47 to impeach. It drafts 11 articles of impeachment, including violation of the Tenure of Office Act and attempting to bring disgrace upon Congress.	**Dec. 19, 1998** The House votes to impeach Clinton on two counts. The votes are 228–206 on one count of perjury and 221–212 on obstruction of justice. Voting is mostly along party lines.
Step Four The Senate tries the case. If the President is to be tried, the Chief Justice of the United States presides. Selected members of the House act as managers (prosecutors).	**March 30, 1868** Opening statements begin in the Senate trial with Chief Justice Salmon P. Chase presiding. Johnson does not attend, but the gallery is packed with observers.	**January 7, 1999** Chief Justice William Rehnquist opens a televised trial. Rep. Henry Hyde of Illinois leads a team of 13 House managers. White House Counsel Charles Ruff leads Clinton defense.
Step Five Senators hear testimony and evidence. House prosecutors and lawyers for both sides present their cases. Additional witnesses may be called. Senators may also vote to curb testimony.	**March 30–May 15, 1868** The trial yields little new evidence. Votes are known from the start. The outcome rests on one swing vote, an undecided Republican, who is offered bribes by both sides.	**Jan. 7–Feb. 11, 1999** With public distaste for impeachment growing, the Senate limits testimony to four witnesses, the intern not among them. Closing arguments follow. For three days, the Senate deliberates in secret (despite Democrats' objections).
Step Six The Senate debates the articles, publicly or privately. It need not render a verdict. It could, for example, vote to drop the case or censure the official. A two-thirds vote is required for conviction.	**May 16, May 26, 1868** In voting on two days, 35 Republicans vote to convict, one vote short of two thirds. Twelve Democrats and seven Republicans, including the swing vote, support acquittal.	**Feb. 12, 1999** In a televised session, the Senate acquits Clinton on both charges, falling well short of the two-thirds vote needed for conviction. On perjury, 45 Democrats and 10 Republicans vote not guilty. On obstruction, the vote splits 50–50.

Interpreting Tables This table details the complex process of impeaching a President.
(a) What measures did the Framers build into the impeachment process to try to make it fair?
(b) Why do you think both attempts to remove U.S. Presidents resulted in failure? H-SS 12.4.1, 12.4.4

The term *Watergate* comes from a June 1972 attempt by Republican operatives to break into the Democratic Party's national headquarters in the Watergate office complex in Washington, D.C. The investigation of that incident, by the *Washington Post* and then by other media, led to official investigations by the Department of Justice and by the Senate's Select Committee on Presidential Campaign Activities, popularly known as the Senate Watergate Committee.

The probes unearthed a long list of illegal acts, including bribery, perjury, income tax fraud, and illegal campaign contributions. They also revealed the use of the Federal Bureau of Investigation, the Internal Revenue Service, and other government agencies for personal and partisan purposes.

The House Judiciary Committee voted three articles of impeachment against President Nixon in late July 1974. He was charged with obstruction of justice, abuse of power, and failure to respond to the committee's subpoenas. A **subpoena** is a legal order directing one to appear in court and/or to produce certain evidence. Mr. Nixon had ignored the committee's subpoena of several tape recordings of Watergate-related conversations in the Oval Office.

It was quite apparent that the full House would impeach the President and that the Senate would convict him. Those facts prompted Mr. Nixon to resign the presidency on August 9, 1974.

Beyond doubt, the Watergate scandal involved the most extensive and the most serious violations of public trust in the nation's history. Among its other consequences, several Cabinet officers, presidential assistants, and others were convicted of various felonies and misdemeanors—and many of them served jail time.

Executive Powers

The Constitution gives two executive powers to the Senate. One of those powers has to do with appointments to office, and the other with treaties made by the President.[17]

Appointments

All major appointments made by the President must be confirmed by the Senate by majority vote.

◀ *A Final Farewell* The threat of impeachment drove President Richard Nixon from office in 1974. He resigned the presidency on August 9, 1974, giving a final wave from his helicopter as he left the White House for the last time.

Each of the President's nominations is referred to the appropriate standing committee of the Senate. That committee may then hold hearings to decide whether or not to make a favorable recommendation to the full Senate for that appointment. When the committee's recommendation is brought to the floor of the Senate, it may be, but seldom is, considered in executive (secret) session.

The appointment of a Cabinet officer or of some other top member of the President's "official family" is rarely turned down by the Senate. To this point, only 12 of now more than 600 Cabinet appointments have been rejected.[18]

It is with the President's appointment of federal officers who serve in the various States (for example, U.S. attorneys and federal marshals) that the unwritten rule of "senatorial courtesy" comes into play. The Senate will turn down such a presidential appointment if it is opposed by a senator of the President's party from the State involved. The Senate's observance of this unwritten rule has a significant impact on the President's exercise of the power of appointment; in effect, this rule means that some senators virtually dictate certain presidential appointments.

---

[17]Article II, Section 2, Clause 2.

[18]The first was Roger B. Taney, Andrew Jackson's choice for Secretary of the Treasury. Jackson later named Taney Chief Justice. The most recent rejection came in 1989, when the Senate refused President George H.W. Bush's nomination of John Tower as Secretary of Defense.

▲ Teenagers testify in Congress about fatal shootings that took place at West Paducah High School in Kentucky. Congress launched an investigation of school gun violence after a series of mass murders in public schools around the country. *Critical Thinking* ***What purpose do congressional investigations serve?***

Treaties

The President makes treaties "by and with the Advice and Consent of the Senate, . . . provided two thirds of the Senators present concur."[19] For a time after the adoption of the Constitution, the President asked the advice of the Senate when a treaty was being negotiated and prepared. Now the President most often consults the members of the Senate Foreign Relations Committee and other influential senators of both parties.

The Senate may accept or reject a treaty as it stands, or it may decide to offer amendments, reservations, or understandings to it. Treaties are sometimes considered in executive session. Because the House has a hold on the public purse strings, influential members of that body are often consulted in the treaty-making process, too.

Investigatory Power

Congress has the power to investigate any matter that falls within the scope of its legislative powers. Congress exercises this authority through its standing committees, and their subcommittees, and often through special committees, as well.

Congress may choose to conduct investigations for several reasons. Most often, those inquiries are held to (1) gather information useful to Congress in the making of some legislation; (2) oversee the operations of various executive branch agencies; (3) focus public attention on a particular subject, from the drug war to movie violence; (4) expose the questionable activities of public officials or private persons; and/or (5) promote the particular interests of some members of Congress.

---

[19]Article II, Section 2, Clause 2. It is often said that the Senate "ratifies" a treaty. It does not. The Senate may give or withhold its "advice and consent" to a treaty made by the President. Once the Senate has consented to a treaty, the President ratifies it by exchanging "instruments of ratification" with other parties to the agreement.

Section 5 Assessment

Key Terms and Main Ideas

1. If the vice presidency becomes vacant, how is a **successor** chosen?
2. **(a)** What public officers can the House **impeach?**
   (b) Which two Presidents were impeached by the House?
   (c) Describe the outcomes of their trials.
3. Why did some Clinton supporters want to **censure** him during his impeachment?
4. What did the House Judiciary Committee seek in the **subpoenas** it served on President Nixon?

Critical Thinking

5. **Making Inferences** Why does the Chief Justice—not the President of the Senate—preside over the impeachment trial of a President?

Standards Monitoring *Online*
For: Self-quiz with vocabulary practice
Web Code: mqa-3115

6. **Recognizing Bias** During the Clinton impeachment hearings and trial, members of Congress from both parties were accused of excessive partisanship. **(a)** Explain this accusation. **(b)** What evidence might support this claim?

Go Online
PHSchool.com
For: An activity on impeachment
Web Code: mqd-3115

Can Congress Prohibit Discrimination by Private Businesses?

Analysis Skills HR4, HI3, HI4

The 14th Amendment guarantees each individual the equal protection of the laws. It has been interpreted to prohibit various forms of discrimination by the government, but it does not deal with discrimination by private firms. Do other parts of the Constitution give Congress the authority to prohibit such forms of discrimination?

Heart of Atlanta Motel, Inc. v. United States (1964)

A provision of the Civil Rights Act of 1964 makes it unlawful for hotels, motels, restaurants, or any other place of "public accommodation" to discriminate in granting access or providing service because of a customer's race, sex, color, religion, or national origin. Congress passed the law after hearing testimony on the growing number of people of all races who were traveling from State to State and on African Americans' difficulties in finding accommodations in many parts of the country.

The Heart of Atlanta Motel was one facility that had regularly refused to rent rooms to African Americans. The motel was located in downtown Atlanta, Georgia, close to two State highways and two interstate freeways. It advertised in national media, and about 75 percent of its registered guests came from out of State.

The motel's owner filed suit in federal district court, claiming that the public accommodation provisions were unconstitutional. The court decided that the law was an acceptable use of Congress's power to regulate interstate commerce. The owner then appealed to the Supreme Court.

Arguments for the Heart of Atlanta Motel, Inc.

1. The operation of privately-owned hotels, motels, and restaurants is essentially local. Therefore, Congress may not regulate these firms on the basis of its authority to regulate interstate commerce.
2. The Civil Rights Act prevents the motel owner from operating his business as he wishes. Thus it deprives him of his liberty and propert without due process, and takes his property without just compensation.
3. By requiring the motel owner to rent rooms to anyone against his will, Congress is subjecting him to involuntary servitude in violation of the 13th Amendment.

Arguments for the United States

1. The lack of adequate accommodations for African American travelers interferes significantly with interstate travel. Congress has the authority under the Commerce Clause to pass laws that correct that problem.
2. The 5th Amendment prohibits the "taking" of property without just compensation, but does not prohibit reasonable regulations that affect the ways in which an owner may use his or her property.
3. The regulations do not constitute involuntary servitude under the 13th Amendment.

Decide for Yourself

1. Review the constitutional grounds on which each side based its arguments and the specific arguments each side presented.
2. Debate the opposing viewpoints presented in this case. Which viewpoint do you favor?
3. Predict the impact of the Court's decision on efforts to reduce discrimination in the United States. (To read a summary of the Court's decision, turn to pages 799–806.)

Go Online
PHSchool.com
Use Web Code mqp-3119 to register your vote on this issue and to see how other students voted.

Political Dictionary

expressed powers (p. 290), implied powers (p. 290), inherent powers (p. 290), strict constructionist (p. 291), liberal constructionist (p. 291), consensus (p. 292), tax (p. 295), direct tax (p. 296), indirect tax (p. 296), deficit financing (p. 296), public debt (p. 296), commerce power (p. 297), legal tender (p. 299), bankruptcy (p. 300), naturalization (p. 302), copyright (p. 302), patent (p. 303), eminent domain (p. 304), appropriate (p. 305), Necessary and Proper Clause (p. 305), doctrine (p. 308), successor (p. 311), impeach (p. 311), acquit (p. 311), perjury (p. 311), censure (p. 312), subpoena (p. 313)

Standards Review

H-SS 12.2.2 Explain how economic rights are secured and their importance to the individual and to society (e.g., the right to acquire, use, transfer, and dispose of property; right to choose one's work; right to join or not join labor unions; copyright and patent).

H-SS 12.2.3 Discuss the individual's legal obligations to obey the law, serve as a juror, and pay taxes.

H-SS 12.4.1 Discuss Article I of the Constitution as it relates to the legislative branch, including eligibility for office and lengths of terms of representatives and senators; election to office; the roles of the House and Senate in impeachment proceedings; the role of the vice president; the enumerated legislative powers; and the process by which a bill becomes a law.

H-SS 12.4.4 Discuss Article II of the Constitution as it relates to the executive branch, including eligibility for office and length of term, election to and removal from office, the oath of office, and the enumerated executive powers.

H-SS 12.4.6 Explain the processes of selection and confirmation of Supreme Court justices.

H-SS 12.5.3 Evaluate the effects of the Court's interpretations of the Constitution in *Marbury* v. *Madison*, *McCulloch* v. *Maryland*, and *United States* v. *Nixon*, with emphasis on the arguments espoused by each side in these cases.

H-SS 12.7.8 Understand the scope of presidential power and decision making through examination of case studies such as the Cuban Missile Crisis, passage of Great Society legislation, War Powers Act, Gulf War, and Bosnia.

Practicing the Vocabulary

Matching Choose a term from the list above that best matches each description.

1. To assign money to a particular purpose
2. The money owed by the Federal Government to its creditors
3. A principle
4. Powers of Congress that are specifically spelled out in the Constitution
5. A general agreement
6. The sole right to sell an invention for a certain period of time
7. A charge levied by government on persons or property to meet public needs

Using Words in Context For each of the terms below, write a sentence that shows how it relates to this chapter.

8. direct tax
9. naturalization
10. Necessary and Proper Clause
11. implied powers
12. impeach
13. liberal constructionist
14. eminent domain

Reviewing Main Ideas

Section 1

15. Give an example of the **(a)** expressed powers; **(b)** implied powers of Congress.
16. Was Thomas Jefferson a strict constructionist or a liberal constructionist? Explain.
17. In what ways does the Constitution limit Congress's power?

Section 2

18. Give three examples of Congress's expressed powers relating to money and commerce.
19. The Articles of Confederation did not give Congress the power to tax. Why did the Framers of the Constitution decide to grant Congress this power?
20. Explain the difference between a direct tax and an indirect tax.
21. How does deficit financing add to the public debt?

Section 3

22. What powers does Congress have in the areas of foreign policy and defense?

23. What judicial powers does the Constitution give to Congress?
24. Give three examples of Congress's territorial powers.

Section 4

25. Has the Necessary and Proper Clause been used to expand or limit congressional power? Explain.
26. What were the long-term consequences of the ruling in *McCulloch* v. *Maryland?*
27. Why is Congress's power to appropriate funds so important?

Section 5

28. What particular officeholders have most often been impeached and removed by Congress?
29. **(a)** What body votes on impeachment? **(b)** What body conducts an impeachment trial? **(c)** Who presides at the trial of a President?
30. Under what circumstances must Congress choose a President? Vice President?
31. Why did Richard Nixon resign the presidency?

Critical Thinking Skills

Analysis Skill HR4

32. ***Applying the Chapter Skill*** Find a blank income tax form and review the questions asked. List ten pieces of information that a taxpayer would need in order to complete the form properly.

33. ***Expressing Problems Clearly*** How does each of the nonlegislative powers of Congress illustrate the system of checks and balances?

34. ***Evaluating the Quotation*** Reread the quotation from Article I, Section 9, Clause 4 on page 296 and the quotation from the 16th Amendment on the same page. Restate each passage in your own words and explain the difference between them.

Analyzing Political Cartoons

Using your knowledge of American government and this cartoon, answer the questions below.

"THAT LAST ONE DIDN'T FLY AT ALL"

35. **(a)** In the cartoon above, why did the cartoonist choose to represent tax cuts as kites? **(b)** What does the caption at the top of the cartoon mean?

36. What is the central message of the cartoon?

Participation Activities

Analysis Skills HR4, HI3

37. ***Current Events Watch*** Scan news reports to find at least three stories about legislation that Congress is considering or has recently passed. **(a)** Summarize the key facts about each measure. **(b)** Identify the specific congressional power involved in each piece of legislation. **(c)** Identify each as an example of either expressed or implied powers.

38. ***It's Your Turn*** The year is 1790. Alexander Hamilton has just made his proposal that Congress set up a national bank. Write an address to your colleagues in Congress, arguing for or against the proposal. Begin by summarizing the debate, explaining its importance to the country. Put forth your views on strict construction vs. liberal construction. Then make your specific arguments about the bank plan. Write a conclusion that you hope will rally support to your side.

39. ***Creating a Chart*** Expand the chart on page 302 to include all of the other expressed powers that the Constitution gives to Congress. Create another column in which, for each of the expressed powers, you attempt to provide an example of the exercise by Congress of the implied powers.

Congress in Action

"It is very easy to defeat a bill in Congress. It is much more difficult to pass one."

—John F. Kennedy (1962)

Making the nation's laws is the main job of Congress. Yet, as President Kennedy recognized, that is not an easy task. In trying to reach consensus, members of Congress draw on their own knowledge and experience. They also listen to other points of view, from both experts and ordinary citizens.

◆ House Judiciary Committee

Standards Preview

H-SS 12.1.5 Describe the systems of separated and shared powers, the role of organized interests (*Federalist Paper Number 10*), checks and balances (*Federalist Paper Number 51*), the importance of an independent judiciary (*Federalist Paper Number 78*), enumerated powers, rule of law, federalism, and civilian control of the military.

H-SS 12.4.1 Discuss Article I of the Constitution as it relates to the legislative branch, including eligibility for office and lengths of terms of representatives and senators; election to office; the roles of the House and Senate in impeachment proceedings; the role of the vice president; the enumerated legislative powers; and the process by which a bill becomes a law.

H-SS 12.4.3 Identify their current representatives in the legislative branch of the national government.

H-SS 12.6.4 Describe the means that citizens use to participate in the political process (e.g., voting, campaigning, lobbying, filing a legal challenge, demonstrating, petitioning, picketing, running for political office).

H-SS 12.7.5 Explain how public policy is formed, including the setting of the public agenda and implementation of it through regulations and executive orders.

H-SS 12.7.6 Compare the processes of lawmaking at each of the three levels of government, including the role of lobbying and the media.

SECTION 1

Congress Organizes (pp. 320–327)

★ Congress begins each new term on January 3 of every odd-numbered year; each new term follows the general election in November.

★ The Speaker of the House, usually the leader of the majority party, controls the agenda in the House of Representatives, while the Vice President and an experienced senator serve as largely ceremonial presidents in the Senate.

★ After the Speaker, the floor leaders and their whips in both houses are the most powerful members of Congress.

★ Committee chairmen, potent in their own domain, are chosen according to the seniority rule.

SECTION 2

Committees in Congress (pp. 329–333)

★ Most work in Congress is divided among committees that focus on special areas like national defense, the budget, agriculture, and the like.

★ The powerful House Rules Committee can speed, delay, or even prevent House action on a bill.

★ Both houses may create select committees, which are special, often temporary, bodies.

★ Joint committees are composed of members of both houses.

SECTION 3

How a Bill Becomes a Law: The House (pp. 334–340)

★ Only a member can introduce a bill in either house.

★ Bills are referred to standing committees, and are usually considered in subcommittees.

★ Bills approved by the appropriate committee and the Rules Committee are given floor consideration by the House.

★ Measures that win House approval are sent to the Senate.

SECTION 4

The Bill in the Senate (pp. 342–346)

★ Debate in the Senate is largely unrestricted.

★ The Senate's dedication to free debate gives rise to the filibuster—the tactic of "talking a bill to death."

★ After both houses approve a bill, it is sent to the President.

★ The President can sign the bill, allow it to become law without his signature, veto it, or apply a pocket veto.

Go Online
PHSchool.com

For: Current Data
Web Code: mqg-3126

For: Close Up Foundation debates
Web Code: mqh-3129

1 Congress Organizes

Section Preview

OBJECTIVES

1. **Describe** how and when Congress convenes.
2. **Compare** the roles of the presiding officers in the Senate and the House.
3. **Identify** the duties of the party officers in Congress.
4. **Describe** how committee chairmen are chosen and explain their role in the legislative process.

WHY IT MATTERS

How Congress is organized, and how its leaders are chosen and who they are, plays a large part in determining what the nation's lawmakers can and will do.

POLITICAL DICTIONARY

★ **Speaker of the House**
★ **president of the Senate**
★ **president *pro tempore***
★ **party caucus**
★ **floor leader**
★ **whip**
★ **committee chairman**
★ **seniority rule**

What comes to mind when you hear the word *Congress?* The imposing Capitol? Some particular bill? Those senators and representatives you often see on the evening news? Of course, you know that Congress is much more than that. It is in fact a very complex enterprise, and much larger than most people realize.

Some 30,000 men and women work for the legislative branch; and Congress appropriates some $4 billion every year to finance its own many-sided operations.[1] Given the large size and complexity of Congress, it must be well organized to conduct its business.

▲ Seal of Congress

Congress Convenes

Congress convenes—begins a new term—every two years, on January 3 of every odd-numbered year. Each new term follows the general elections in November.

[1] More than 15,000 of those who work in the legislative branch have jobs in the House or Senate—in members' offices, as committee staff, or in some part of the congressional administrative organization. The other 15,000 or so work in the various agencies Congress has, over time, established within the legislative branch—the Library of Congress, the Government Printing Office, the Congressional Budget Office, and the Government Accountability Office.

Opening Day in the House

Every other January, the 435 men and women who have been elected to the House come together at the Capitol to begin a new term. At that point, they are, in effect, just so many representatives-elect. Because all 435 of its seats are up for election every two years, the House technically has no sworn members, no rules, and no organization until its opening-day ceremonies are held.

Representative Sherrod Brown (D., Ohio) remembers his first opening day, in 1993, this way:

PRIMARY Sources *"My first day on the House floor was thrilling—and a little scary. . . . Walking around the chamber . . . I was awed and nervous. . . . Questions gnawed at me when I walked into that august [majestic] room, when I met several members about whom I had read and whom I had seen on television. And then I thought about the President of the United States coming in to address us—'Do I deserve to be here with all these people? How did I get here? Will I measure up? How was I chosen for this privilege?'"*

—Sherrod Brown, *Congress From the Inside*

The clerk of the House in the preceding term presides, or chairs, at the beginning of the first

▲ Opening day in the House of Representatives follows a traditional routine of votes and speeches. The House chooses its Speaker and other officers for the coming term. *Critical Thinking* *Why are most of the votes on opening day only formalities?*

day's session.[2] The clerk calls the chamber to order and checks the roll of representatives-elect. Those members-to-be then choose a Speaker as their permanent presiding officer. By custom, the Speaker is a long-standing member of the majority party, and election on the floor is only a formality. The majority party's members in the House have settled the matter beforehand.

The Speaker then takes the oath of office. It is administered by the Dean of the House, the member-elect with the longest record of service in the House of Representatives.[3] With that accomplished, the Speaker swears in the rest of the members as a body. The Democrats take their seats to the right of the center aisle; the Republicans, to the left.

Next, the House elects its clerk, sergeant at arms, chief administrative officer, and chaplain. None of these people are members of the House, and the elections are also a formality. The majority party has already decided who these nonmember officers will be.

---

[2]The clerk, a nonmember officer of the House, is picked by the majority party and usually keeps the post until that party loses control of the chamber.

[3]Today, John D. Dingell (D., Michigan), who became a member of the House on December 13, 1955.

Then, the House adopts the rules that will govern its proceedings through the term. The rules of the House have been developing for over 200 years, and they are contained in a volume of about 400 pages. They are readopted, most often with little or no change, at the beginning of each term.

Finally, members of the 19 permanent committees of the House are appointed by a floor vote. With that, the House is organized.

Opening Day in the Senate

The Senate is a continuous body. It has been organized without interruption since its first session in 1789. Recall that only one third of the seats are up for election every two years. From one term to the next, two thirds of the Senate's membership is carried over. As a result, the Senate does not face large organizational problems at the beginning of a term. Its first-day session is nearly always short and routine, even when the elections have brought a change in the majority party. Newly elected and reelected members must be sworn in, vacancies in Senate organization and on committees must be filled, and a few other details attended to.

"Let's run through this once more—and, remember, you choke up at Paragraph Three and brush away the tear at Paragraph Five."

Interpreting Political Cartoons What does this cartoon say about the art of delivering speeches—including the President's State of the Union address?

State of the Union Message

When the Senate is notified that the House of Representatives is organized, a joint committee of the two chambers is appointed and instructed "to wait upon the President of the United States and inform him that a quorum of each House is assembled and that the Congress is ready to receive any communication he may be pleased to make."

Within a few weeks—in late January or early February—the President delivers his annual State of the Union message to a joint session of Congress. The speech is a major political event based on this constitutional command:

FROM THE Constitution ❝*He shall from time to time give to the Congress Information on the State of the Union, and recommend to their Consideration such Measures as he shall judge necessary and expedient . . .*❞
—Article II, Section 3

From Woodrow Wilson's first message in 1913, the President has almost always presented his annual assessment in person. The members of both houses, together with the members of the Cabinet, the justices of the Supreme Court, the foreign diplomatic corps, and other dignitaries, assemble in the House chamber to hear him.

In his address, the President reports on the state of the nation as he sees it, in both domestic and foreign policy terms. The message is televised live, and it is followed very closely, both here and abroad. In fact, the President's speech is as much a message to the American people, and to the world, as it is an address to Congress. In it, the President lays out the broad shape of the policies his administration will follow and the course he has charted for the nation. His message regularly includes a number of specific legislative recommendations. It is soon followed by scores of bills drawn up in the executive branch and introduced in the House and Senate by various members of the President's party.

With the conclusion of the President's speech, the joint session is adjourned. Each house turns to the legislative business before it.

The Presiding Officers

The Constitution provides for the presiding officers of each house—the Speaker of the House and the president of the Senate. Article I, Section 2, Clause 5 says "The House of Representatives shall choose their Speaker and other Officers. . . ." And Article I, Section 3, Clause 4 declares: "The Vice President of the United States shall be President of the Senate. . . ."

The Speaker of the House

Of the two positions, the **Speaker of the House** is by far the more important and more powerful within the halls of Congress. This is particularly so because the Speaker is both the elected presiding officer of the House and the acknowledged leader of its majority party.

Although neither the Constitution nor its own rules require it, the House has always chosen the Speaker from among its own members. Today, the post is held by Dennis Hastert (R., Illinois). He was first elected to the House in 1986, and he became Speaker in 1999.[4]

The Speaker is expected to preside in a fair and judicious manner, and he regularly does. He is also expected to aid the fortunes of his party and its legislative goals, and he regularly does that, too.

Nearly all of the Speaker's powers revolve around two duties: to preside and to keep order. The Speaker presides over most sessions of the House, but occasionally appoints another member as temporary presiding officer. No member may speak until he or she is recognized by the Speaker. He interprets and applies the rules, refers bills to committee, rules on points of order (questions of procedure raised by members), puts motions to a vote, and also decides the outcome of most votes taken on the floor of the House. (The Speaker can be overridden by a vote of the House, but that almost never happens.) Importantly, the Speaker also names the members of all select and conference committees and he must sign all bills and resolutions passed by the House.

As a member, the Speaker may debate and vote on any matter before the House. If he chooses to do so, however, he must appoint a temporary presiding officer and that member then occupies the Speaker's chair. The Speaker does not often vote, and the House rules say only that he must vote to break a tie. Notice then, that because a tie vote defeats a question, the Speaker occasionally votes to cause a tie and so defeat a proposal.

The Speaker of the House follows the Vice President in the line of succession to the presidency. That fact is a considerable testimony to the power and importance of both the office and the person who holds it.

The President of the Senate

The Constitution makes the Vice President the **president of the Senate,** the Senate's presiding officer. This fact means that (1) unlike the House, the Senate does not choose its own presiding officer and (2) unlike the Speaker of the House, the Senate's presiding officer is not in fact a member of the body over which he presides. Indeed, the Vice President might not even be a member of the party that controls the Senate.

All of this adds up to the major reason why the Vice President plays a much less powerful role in the Senate than that played by the

▲ Dennis Hastert (R., Illinois), who became Speaker of the House in 1999, has maintained a relatively low profile in public. *Critical Thinking How does the role of the Speaker differ from the role of the president of the Senate?*

Speaker of the House. Also note this important point: the Vice President's career path, the route he has traveled to his current post, is a much different path than the one the Speaker has followed. In short, the Vice President has not become the Senate's presiding officer out of long service in that body. He has, instead, come to the post out of a much different process—as you will see when we take a longer look at the vice presidency in Chapter 13.

The president of the Senate does have the usual powers of a presiding officer: to recognize members, put questions to a vote, and so on. However, the Vice President cannot take the floor to speak or debate and may vote *only* to break a tie.

Any influence a Vice President may have in the Senate is largely the result of personal abilities and relationships. Several of the more recent Vice Presidents came to that office from the Senate: Harry Truman, Alben Barkley, Richard Nixon, Lyndon Johnson, Hubert Humphrey, Walter Mondale, Dan Quayle, and Al Gore. Each of them was able to build at least some power into the position out of that earlier experience.

The Senate does have another presiding officer, the **president *pro tempore,*** who serves in the Vice President's absence. The president *pro tempore,* or president *pro tem* for short, is elected by the Senate itself and is always a leading member of the majority party—usually its longest serving member. Today, the post is occupied by

<hr>

[4]Speaker Hastert is the 51st person to hold the post. The first Speaker, elected by the House in 1789, was Frederick A. C. Muhlenburg, a Federalist from Pennsylvania. Sam Rayburn (D., Texas) held the office for a record 17 years, 62 days in the period from 1940 to 1961. Mr. Hastert succeeded Newt Gingrich (R., Georgia) whose tenure (1995–1999) marked the first time a Republican had held the post in more than 40 years.

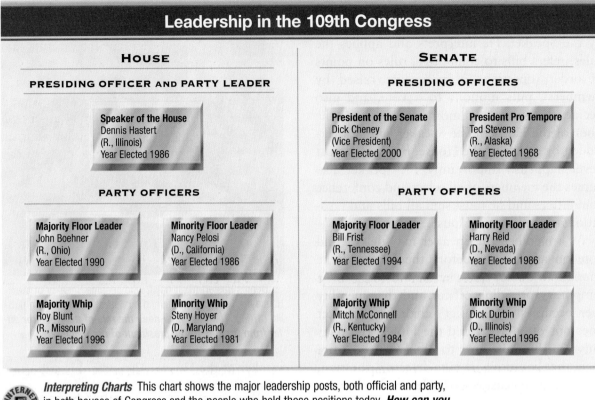

Leadership in the 109th Congress

HOUSE

PRESIDING OFFICER AND PARTY LEADER

Speaker of the House
Dennis Hastert
(R., Illinois)
Year Elected 1986

PARTY OFFICERS

Majority Floor Leader
John Boehner
(R., Ohio)
Year Elected 1990

Minority Floor Leader
Nancy Pelosi
(D., California)
Year Elected 1986

Majority Whip
Roy Blunt
(R., Missouri)
Year Elected 1996

Minority Whip
Steny Hoyer
(D., Maryland)
Year Elected 1981

SENATE

PRESIDING OFFICERS

President of the Senate
Dick Cheney
(Vice President)
Year Elected 2000

President Pro Tempore
Ted Stevens
(R., Alaska)
Year Elected 1968

PARTY OFFICERS

Majority Floor Leader
Bill Frist
(R., Tennessee)
Year Elected 1994

Minority Floor Leader
Harry Reid
(D., Nevada)
Year Elected 1986

Majority Whip
Mitch McConnell
(R., Kentucky)
Year Elected 1984

Minority Whip
Dick Durbin
(D., Illinois)
Year Elected 1996

Interpreting Charts This chart shows the major leadership posts, both official and party, in both houses of Congress and the people who hold these positions today. *How can you tell which party holds power in the Senate?* H-SS 12.4.1

Senator Ted Stevens (R., Alaska). Senator Stevens, who was elected to his first term in the upper house in 1968, became president *pro tem* in 2003.

The president *pro tem* follows the Speaker in the line of presidential succession. Other senators occasionally preside over the Senate, on a temporary basis; newly elected members regularly do so early in their terms.

Party Officers

Congress is a political body. This is so for two leading reasons: (1) because Congress is the nation's central policy-making body, and (2) because of its partisan makeup. Reflecting its political complexion, both houses of Congress are organized along party lines. This organization creates some very powerful positions.

The Party Caucus

The **party caucus** is a closed meeting of the members of each party in each house. It meets just before Congress convenes in January and occasionally during a session. In recent years the Republicans have called their caucus in each

house the party conference, and the Democrats now use this term in the Senate, too.

The caucus deals mostly with matters of party organization, such as the selection of the party's floor leaders and questions of committee membership. It sometimes takes stands on particular bills, but neither party tries to force its members to follow its caucus decisions, nor can it.[5]

The policy committee, composed of the party's top leadership, acts as an executive committee for the caucus. Strictly speaking, that body is known as the policy committee in each party's structure in the Senate and in the Republicans' organization in the House. However, it is called the steering and policy committee by the Democrats in the lower chamber.

The Floor Leaders

Next to the Speaker, the majority and minority **floor leaders** in the House and Senate are the most important officers in Congress. They do

---

[5]A number of informal groupings of members of Congress meet to discuss matters of mutual interest. Some are partisan, others are bipartisan, and several use the word *caucus* in their titles. Some of these informal groups include, for example, the Congressional Black Caucus, the House Republican Study Committee, the Pro-Life Caucus, and the Congressional Hispanic Caucus.

not hold official positions in either chamber. Rather, they are party officers, picked for their posts by their party colleagues.

The floor leaders are legislative strategists. They try to carry out the decisions of their parties' caucuses and steer floor action to their parties' benefit. Each of them is also the chief spokesman for his party in his chamber. All of that calls for political skills of a high order.

The majority leader's post is the more powerful in each house—for the obvious reason that the majority party has more seats (more votes) than the other party has. And, the majority leader very largely controls the order of business on the floor in his chamber.

The two floor leaders in each house are assisted by party **whips.** The majority whip and the minority whip are, in effect, assistant floor leaders. Each of them is chosen by the party caucus, almost always at the floor leader's recommendation. A number of assistant whips serve in the House, and the floor leaders in both houses have a paid staff.

Whips serve as a liaison—a two-way link—between the party's leadership and its rank-and-file members.[6] The whips check with party members and tell the floor leader which members,

and how many votes, can be counted on in any particular matter. The whips also see that all members of the party are present for important votes and that they vote with the party leadership. If a member must be absent for some reason, a whip sees that that member is paired with a member of the other party who will also be absent that day or who agrees not to vote on certain measures at that day's session—so one nonvote cancels out another.

Committee Chairmen

The bulk of the work of Congress, especially in the House, is really done in committee. Thus, **committee chairmen**—those members who head the standing committees in each chamber—also hold strategic posts. The chairman[7] of each of

---

[6]The term was borrowed from British politics. There, it came from the "whipper-in" in a fox hunt, the rider who is supposed to keep the hounds bunched in a pack.

[7]The title *chairman* is used here because this is the form used in both houses of Congress, both officially and informally. Only eight women (three in the Senate, five in the House) have ever chaired a standing committee. Only two do so today, both in the upper house, and both became chairman in 2003: Susan Collins (R., Maine), who chairs the Senate's Committee on Governmental Affairs, and Olympia Snowe (R., Maine), who chairs the Committee on Small Business and Entrepreneurship.

Party Strength (at beginning of term)

HOUSE 435 MEMBERS			Years	SENATE 100 MEMBERS		
292	143		1977 – 1979	61	38	1
277	158		1979 – 1981	58	41	1
242	192	1	1981 – 1983	46	53	1
269	166		1983 – 1985	46	54	
253	182		1985 – 1987	47	53	
258	177		1987 – 1989	55	45	
260	175		1989 – 1991	55	45	
267	167	1	1991 – 1993	56	44	
258	176	1	1993 – 1995	57	43	
204	230	1	1995 – 1997	48	52	
207	227	1	1997 – 1999	45	55	
211	223	1	1999 – 2001	45	55	
212	221	2	2001 – 2003*	50	50	
205	229	1	2003 – 2005	48	51	1
202	232	1	2005 – 2007	44	55	1

SOURCES: Clerk of the House; *Congressional Quarterly*

*Democrats gained control of the Senate (50 Democrats, 49 Republicans, 1 Independent) in July 2001.

KEY ■ Democrat ■ Republican ■ Other

Interpreting Graphs This graph indicates party strength in Congress over recent years. *Which party controlled the House of Representatives for most of the 1980s? Which party controlled the House of Representatives for the second half of the 1990s?*

these permanent committees is chosen from the majority party by the majority party caucus. Committee chairmen decide when their committees will meet, which bills they will take up, whether they will hold public hearings, and what witnesses the committee should call. When a committee's bill has been reported to the floor, the chairman usually manages the debate and tries to steer it to final passage.

You will take a closer look at committees and their chairs in a moment. But, first, consider the fabled seniority rule.

Seniority Rule

The **seniority rule** is, in fact, an unwritten custom. It dates from the late 1800s, and is still closely followed in both houses today. The seniority rule provides that the most important posts, in both the formal and the party organization, will be held by those party members with the longest records of service in Congress.

The rule is applied most strictly to the choice of committee chairmen. The head of each committee is almost always the longest-serving majority party member of that committee.

Representation by State, 109th Congress

	House D	House R	Senate D	Senate R		House D	House R	Senate D	Senate R		House D	House R	Senate D	Senate R
Alabama	2	5	0	2	Louisiana	2	5	1	1	Ohio	6	12	0	2
Alaska	0	1	0	2	Maine	2	0	0	2	Oklahoma	1	4	0	2
Arizona	2	6	0	2	Maryland	6	2	2	0	Oregon	4	1	1	1
Arkansas	3	1	2	0	Massachusetts	10	0	2	0	Pennsylvania	7	12	0	2
California	33	20	2	0	Michigan	6	9	2	0	Rhode Island	2	0	1	1
Colorado	3	4	1	1	Minnesota	4	4	1	1	South Carolina	2	4	0	2
Connecticut	2	3	2	0	Mississippi	2	2	0	2	South Dakota	1	0	1	1
Delaware	0	1	2	0	Missouri	4	5	0	2	Tennessee	5	4	0	2
Florida	7	18	1	1	Montana	0	1	1	1	Texas	11	21	0	2
Georgia	6	7	0	2	Nebraska	0	3	1	1	Utah	1	2	0	2
Hawaii	2	0	2	0	Nevada	1	2	1	1	Vermont	0 *	0	1 *	0
Idaho	0	2	0	2	New Hampshire	0	2	0	2	Virginia	3	8	0	2
Illinois	10	9	2	0	New Jersey	7	6	2	0	Washington	6	3	2	0
Indiana	2	7	1	1	New Mexico	1	2	1	1	West Virginia	2	1	2	0
Iowa	1	4	1	1	New York	20	9	2	0	Wisconsin	4	4	2	0
Kansas	1	3	0	2	North Carolina	6	7	1	1	Wyoming	0	1	0	2
Kentucky	1	5	0	2	North Dakota	1	0	2	0					

* 1 Independent

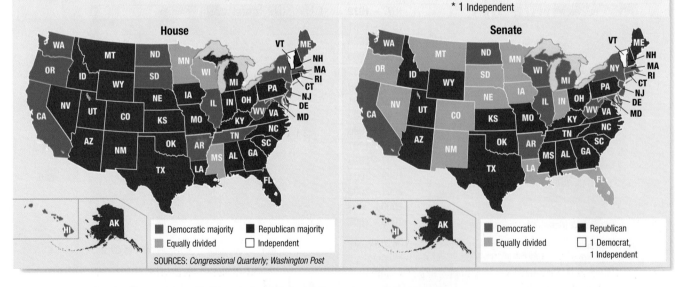

House

■ Democratic majority ■ Republican majority
■ Equally divided □ Independent

Senate

■ Democratic ■ Republican
■ Equally divided □ 1 Democrat, 1 Independent

SOURCES: *Congressional Quarterly; Washington Post*

Interpreting Maps The map and the chart show State-by-State representation in the House and Senate. *Identify five States that regularly send (a) a majority of Republicans and (b) a majority of Democrats to both houses of Congress.* H-SS 12.4.3

◄ John Conyers, Jr. (D., Michigan) has been a member of the House since 1965 and has now served for a longer time in public office than any other African American in the nation's history. Mr. Conyers is the second-most senior member of the House and the ranking Democratic member of the House Judiciary Committee. He served on that committee during both the 1974 hearings on the Watergate scandal and the 1998 impeachment of President Clinton. *Critical Thinking* **What are the benefits and drawbacks of the seniority rule?**

Criticism of the Seniority Rule

Critics of the seniority rule are many, and they do make a strong case. They insist that the seniority system ignores ability, rewards mere length of service, and works to discourage younger members. Critics also note that the rule means that a committee head often comes from a "safe" constituency—a State or district in which, election after election, one party regularly wins the seat. With no play of fresh and conflicting forces in those places, critics claim, the chairman of a committee is often out of touch with current public opinion.

Defenders of the seniority rule argue that it ensures that a powerful and experienced member will head each committee. They also note that the rule is easy to apply, and that it very nearly eliminates the possibility of fights within the party.

Opponents of the rule have gained some ground in recent years. Thus, the House Republican Conference (caucus) now picks several GOP members of House committees by secret ballot. House Democrats use secret ballots to choose a committee chairman whenever 20 percent of their caucus requests that procedure.

House Republicans forged a major change in the seniority rule when they took control of the lower chamber in 1995. They adopted a party rule that limits the tenure of their committee chairmen. Now, no GOP chairman can serve more than six years (three terms of Congress) in his or her post. The Republicans have now controlled the House for more than a decade and the rule has meant a much larger than usual turnover in chairmanships at the beginning of each new term of Congress. Whatever the arguments against the seniority rule, it is unlikely to be eliminated. Those members with the real power to abolish it are also the ones who reap the largest benefits from it.

Section 1 Assessment

Key Terms and Main Ideas

1. What role does the **Speaker of the House** play?
2. What role does the **president of the Senate** play?
3. What are the duties of the party **whips**?
4. Identify the purpose of a **party caucus.**

Critical Thinking

5. **Making Comparisons** Compare the organizational structures of both houses of Congress. Create a Venn diagram showing similarities and differences between the two houses.
6. **Synthesizing Information** What factors make committee chairmen so influential?

7. **Predicting Consequences** What might happen if the president of the Senate were given the same powers as the Speaker of the House? What problems could arise?

Organizing Congressional Committees

Pat Schroeder retired from public office in 1997, after 12 terms in Congress. In her memoir, 24 Years of House Work . . . and the Place Is Still a Mess, *she relates her experiences in the House of Representatives. In this excerpt, Schroeder recalls her appointment, as a newly elected representative and a woman, to the powerful House Armed Services Committee.*

**Analysis Skills
HR4, HI3**

In a setup typical of Congress, where everything is done by committee, there is a committee to decide committee assignments for incoming freshmen. In 1973 it was headed by Representative Wilbur Mills of Arkansas. . . .

Considering that no senior member was going to fall on his sword for me, I expected to be assigned to something like Merchant Marine and Fisheries. Since my Denver district is landlocked . . . it would have meant sudden death for a new congressional career. I wanted to be on the Armed Services Committee. I wanted to be part of the committee that controlled approximately sixty-five cents out of every dollar allocated to Congress. . . .

The Armed Services chairman, F. Edward Hébert, was a seventy-two-year-old Louisiana Democrat who was dead set against my appointment. . . . Even though Mills chaired the [assignments] committee, I couldn't understand why he would override Hébert's veto. There was an unspoken rule that old congressional barons never cross each other. . . . Unbeknownst to me, Mills' wife had taken an interest in my career and apparently kept telling her husband that he should do whatever he could to help me. . . . Mills . . . performed the necessary arm-twisting.

Although I was [put] on the committee, I did not get a seat. Hébert was patronizingly contemptuous [lacking respect] of women in politics. . . . He also objected to the appointment of Congressman Ron

Pat Schroeder, former Democratic representative from Colorado

Dellums (Democrat from California). Ron had been in the House only one term when it was decided that it was time for an African-American to be on the Armed Services Committee. Hébert didn't appreciate the idea of a girl and a black forced on him. He was outraged that for the first time a chairman's veto of potential members was ignored. He announced that while he might not be able to control the makeup of the committee, he could . . . control the number of chairs in his hearing room, where he was enthroned on a carpet of stars, surrounded by military flags. He said that women and blacks were worth only half of one "regular" member, so he added only one seat to the committee room and made me and Ron share it. Nobody else objected, and nobody offered to scrounge up another chair. . . .

Ron and I had two choices: to go ballistic or to hang in. We decided to hang [in].

Analyzing Primary Sources

1. Why did Schroeder want to serve on the Armed Services Committee?
2. What difficulties did Schroeder face and why?
3. How and why did Hébert embarrass Schroeder?
4. Aside from her gender, why is it surprising that Schroeder was assigned to the Armed Services Committee?

② Committees in Congress

Section Preview

OBJECTIVES

1. **Explain** how the standing committees function.
2. **Describe** the duties and responsibilities of the House Rules Committee.
3. **Compare** the functions of joint and conference committees.

WHY IT MATTERS

The lawmaking process in both houses is built around committees, and these bodies play a major role in shaping the public policies of the United States.

POLITICAL DICTIONARY

★ standing committee
★ select committee
★ joint committee
★ conference committee

Do you know the phrase "a division of labor"? Roughly explained, it means dividing the work to be done, assigning the several parts of the overall task to various members of the group.

The House and the Senate are both so large, and the business they each face is so great, that both chambers must rely on a division of labor. That is to say, much of the work that Congress does is in fact done by committees. Indeed, Representative Clem Miller (D., Calif.) once described Congress as "a collection of committees that comes together periodically to approve one another's actions."

Standing Committees

In 1789 the House and Senate each adopted the practice of naming a special committee to consider each bill as it was introduced. By 1794 there were more than 300 committees in each chamber. Each house then began to set up permanent panels, known as **standing committees,** to which all similar bills could be sent.

Committee Assignments

The number of these committees has varied over the years. The graphic on page 330 lists the 20 standing committees in the House and the 17 in the Senate today. Each House committee has from 10 to as many as 75 members, and each Senate committee has from 14 to 28. Representatives are normally assigned to one or two standing committees and senators to three

or four. The pivotal role these committees play in the lawmaking process cannot be overstated. Most bills receive their most thorough consideration in these bodies. Members of both houses regularly respect the decisions and follow the recommendations they make. Thus, the fate of most bills is decided in the various standing committees, not on the floor of either house. More than a century ago, Woodrow Wilson described "Congress in its committee rooms" as "Congress at work," and that remains the fact of the matter today.

Some panels are more prominent and more influential than others. As you would expect, most members try to win assignments to these important panels. The leading committees in the House are the Rules, Ways and Means, Appropriations, Armed Services, Judiciary, International Relations, and Agriculture committees. In the Senate, senators usually compete for places on the Foreign Relations, Appropriations, Finance, Judiciary, Armed Services, and Banking, Housing, and Urban Affairs committees. Of course, some of the other committees are particularly attractive to some members. Thus, a representative whose district lies wholly within a major city might want to sit on the

▶ The House Committee on Banking and Financial Services considers bills that affect finance, including the proposal that led to the golden dollar coin.

Permanent Committees of Congress

HOUSE STANDING COMMITTEES	JOINT COMMITTEES OF CONGRESS	SENATE STANDING COMMITTEES
Agriculture	Economic	Agriculture, Nutrition, and Forestry
Appropriations	The Library	Appropriations
Armed Services	Printing	Armed Services
Budget	Taxation	Banking, Housing, and Urban Affairs
Education and the Workforce		Budget
Energy and Commerce		Commerce, Science, and Transportation
Financial Services		Energy and Natural Resouces
Government Reform		Environment and Public Works
Homeland Security		Finance
House Administration		Foreign Relations
International Relations		Homeland Security and Governmental Affairs
Judiciary		Indian Affairs
Resources		Judiciary
Rules		Health, Education, Labor and Pensions
Science		Rules and Administration
Small Business		Small Business and Entrepreneurship
Standards of Official Conduct		Veterans' Affairs
Transportation and Infrastructure		
Veterans' Affairs		
Ways and Means		

Interpreting Tables Most legislation is considered in standing committees, and party politics can shape those panels. *What considerations might lead a member of Congress to want to serve on a particular committee?* **H-SS 12.7.5**

House Committee on Education and the Workforce. A senator from one of the western States might angle for assignment to the Senate's Committee on Energy and Natural Resources.

Most of the standing committees handle bills dealing with particular policy matters, such as veterans' affairs. There are three standing committees that do not operate as subject-matter bodies, however: in the House the Rules Committee and the Committee on Standards of Official Conduct, and in the Senate the Committee on Rules and Administration.

When a bill is introduced in either house, the Speaker or the president of the Senate refers the measure to the appropriate standing committee. Thus, the Speaker sends all tax measures to the House Ways and Means Committee; in the Senate tax measures go to the Finance Committee. A bill dealing with, say, enlistments in the armed forces goes to the Armed Services Committee in the House and to the Armed Services Committee in the Senate.

Recall that the chairman of each of the standing committees is chosen according to the seniority rule. To see the point, look at the tables on pages 331 and 332. Notice that most committee chairmen have served in Congress for at least 12 years and some much longer. The seniority rule is also applied closely in each house when it elects the other members of each of its committees.

The members of each standing committee are formally elected by a floor vote at the beginning of each term of Congress. In fact, each party has already drawn up its own committee roster before the vote, and the floor vote merely ratifies those party choices.

The majority party always holds a majority of the seats on each standing committee.[8] The other party is well represented, however.

---

[8]The only exception is the House Committee on Standards of Official Conduct, with five Democrats and five Republicans. Often called the House Ethics Committee, it investigates allegations of misconduct by House members. In the Senate, a six-member bipartisan Select Committee on Ethics plays a similar role.

Most standing committees are divided into subcommittees, and each subcommittee is responsible for a particular slice of the committee's overall workload. There are now some 150 subcommittees in the two houses; nearly 70 in the Senate and 80 in the House.

To illustrate, the Senate's 24-member Committee on Armed Services does much of its work in six subcommittees. Each member serves on at least two of them, and the subcommittee titles generally describe their focus: the Subcommittee on Emerging Threats and Capabilities; the Subcommittee on Airland Forces; the Subcommittee on Personnel; the Subcommittee on Readiness and Management Support; the Subcommittee on Seapower; and the Subcommittee on Strategic Forces.

The House Rules Committee

The House Committee on Rules is sometimes called the "traffic cop" in the lower house. So many measures are introduced in the House each term that some sort of screening is necessary.

Most bills die in the committees to which they are referred. Still, several hundred are reported out every year. So, before most of these bills can reach the floor of the House, they must also clear the Rules Committee.

Normally, a bill gets to the floor only if it has been granted a rule—been scheduled for floor consideration—by the Rules Committee. The committee decides whether and under what conditions the full House will consider a measure. As you will see, this means that the potent 13-member Rules Committee can speed, delay, or even prevent House action on a measure.

In the Senate, where the process is not so closely regulated, the majority floor leader controls the appearance of bills on the floor.

Select Committees

At times, each house finds need for a **select committee.** These groups are sometimes called special committees; they are panels set up for some specific purpose and, most often, for a

House Committee Chairs, 2006

Committee	Name	Age*	Year Elected to House	Party Affiliation and State
Agriculture	Bob Goodlatte	60	1992	R., Virginia
Appropriations	Jerry Lewis	72	1978	R., California
Armed Services	Duncan Hunter	58	1980	R., California
Budget	Jim Nussle	46	1990	R., Iowa
Education and the Workforce	John Boehner	57	1990	R., Ohio
Energy and Commerce	Joe Barton	57	1984	R., Texas
Financial Services	Michael G. Oxley	62	1981	R., Ohio
Government Reform	Tom Davis	57	1994	R., Virginia
Homeland Security	Peter King	62	1992	R., New York
House Administration	Robert W. Ney	52	1994	R., Ohio
International Relations	Henry J. Hyde	82	1974	R., Illinois
Judiciary	F. James Sensenbrenner, Jr.	63	1978	R., Wisconsin
Resources	Richard Pombo	45	1992	R., California
Rules	David Dreier	54	1980	R., California
Science	Sherwood L. Boehlert	70	1982	R., New York
Small Business	Donald A. Manzullo	62	1992	R., Illinois
Standards of Official Conduct	Doc Hastings	65	1994	R., Washington
Transportation and Infrastructure	Don Young	73	1973	R., Alaska
Veterans' Affairs	Steve Buyer	48	1992	R., Indiana
Ways and Means	Bill Thomas	65	1978	R., California

SOURCES: *Congressional Directory* and the Clerk of the House   *As of birth date in 2006.

Interpreting Tables Committee chairs have what amounts to life-or-death power over bills referred to their committee. *What do the data in this table tell you about the post each of these members holds?* H-SS 12.7.6

limited time. The Speaker of the House or the president of the Senate appoints the members of these special committees, with the advice of the majority and minority leaders.

Most select committees are formed to investigate a current matter. The congressional power to investigate is an essential part of the lawmaking function. Congress must decide on the need for new laws and gauge the adequacy of those already on the books. It also must exercise its vital oversight function, to ensure that federal agencies are following the laws it has already passed. At times, too, a committee may conduct an investigation of an issue—for example, the threat of domestic terrorism—in order to focus public attention on that matter.

Most investigations are conducted by standing committees or by their subcommittees. Select committees occasionally do that work, however. Thus, the Senate's Special Committee on Aging conducts an ongoing study of the elderly. It holds hearings in Washington and around the country, issues reports and press releases, and otherwise tries to bring greater public and governmental attention to the problems facing older Americans.

At times, a select committee becomes a spectacularly important body. This happened, for example, with the Senate's Select Committee on Presidential Campaign Activities, popularly known as the Senate Watergate Committee. As the Watergate scandal began to unfold in 1973, the Senate created that committee. Chaired by Senator Sam Ervin (D., North Carolina), its job was to investigate "the extent, if any, to which illegal, improper, or unethical activities were engaged in by any persons . . . in the presidential election of 1972." Its sensational hearings riveted the nation for months. Eventually, they formed a key link in the chain of events that led to President Richard Nixon's resignation from office in 1974.

Since then, the most notable instance came in 1987, with the work of two panels: the Senate's Select Committee on Secret Military Assistance to Iran and the Nicaraguan Opposition, and the House Select Committee to Investigate Covert Arms Transactions with Iran. These twin committees, often referred to as the Iran-Contra Committee, probed the Reagan administration's conduct of two highly secret projects abroad:

Senate Committee Chairs, 2006

Committee	Name	Age*	Year Elected to Senate†	Party Affiliation and State
Agriculture, Nutrition, and Forestry	Saxby Chambliss	63	2002 (4)	R., Georgia
Appropriations	Thad Cochran	69	1978 (3)	R., Mississippi
Armed Services	John Warner	79	1978	R., Virginia
Banking, Housing, and Urban Affairs	Richard C. Shelby, Jr.	72	1986 (4)	R., Alabama
Budget	Judd Gregg	59	1992 (4)	R., New Hampshire
Commerce, Science, and Transportation	Ted Stevens	84	1968	R., Alaska
Energy and Natural Resources	Pete Domenici	74	1972	R., New Mexico
Environment and Public Works	James M. Inhofe	72	1994 (4)	R., Oklahoma
Finance	Charles E. Grassley	73	1980 (3)	R., Iowa
Foreign Relations	Richard G. Lugar	74	1976	R., Indiana
Governmental Affairs	Susan Collins	54	1996	R., Maine
Health, Education, Labor, and Pensions	Mike Enzi	62	1996	R., Wyoming
Homeland Security	Susan Collins	54	1996	R., Maine
Indian Affairs	John McCain	70	1986 (3)	R., Arizona
Judiciary	Arlen Specter	76	1980	R., Pennsylvania
Rules and Administration	Trent Lott	65	1988 (8)	R., Mississippi
Small Business and Entrepreneurship	Olympia Snowe	59	1994 (8)	R., Maine
Veterans' Affairs	Larry Craig	61	1990 (5)	R., Idaho

SOURCES: *Congressional Directory* and Secretary of the Senate   * As of birthdate in 2006   † Number in parentheses indicates terms served in House.

Interpreting Tables Critics complain that the seniority system discourages younger members of Congress. ***How does this table demonstrate the importance of seniority in the United States Senate?*** **H-SS 12.7.6**

the covert sale of arms to Iran and clandestine efforts to give military aid to the Contra rebels in Nicaragua. The operation in Iran was intended, at least in part, as an arms-for-hostages deal, and it failed. The aid to the Contras was funded in part with money from the Iranian arms sales, despite an act of Congress that expressly prohibited such aid by the United States.

Most congressional investigations are not nearly so visible, nor so historic. Their more usual shape can be seen when, for example, the House Committee on Agriculture looks at the spruce budworm problem, an infestation affecting trees in the Pacific Northwest.

Joint and Conference Committees

A **joint committee** is one composed of members of both houses. You may recall them from the chart on page 330. Some are select committees set up to serve some temporary purpose. Most are permanent groups that serve on a regular basis. Because the standing committees of the two houses often duplicate one another's work, many have long urged that Congress make much greater use of the joint committee device.

Some joint committees are investigative in nature and issue periodic reports to the House and Senate—for example, the Joint Economic Committee. Most often they perform more routine duties, however—for example, the Joint Committee on Printing and the Joint Committee on the Library of Congress.

Before a bill may be sent to the President, each house must pass it in identical form. Sometimes, the two houses pass differing versions, and the first house will not agree to the changes the other has made. When this happens, a **conference committee**—a temporary, joint body—is created to iron out the differences in the bill. Its job is to produce a compromise bill that both houses will accept—as you will see shortly.

Government Online

The Library of Congress Picture 530 miles of bookshelves—roughly the distance between St. Louis and Atlanta. That's what it takes to hold the 18 million books, 54 million manuscripts, 12 million photos, 4.5 million maps, and 2.5 million recordings on store at the world's largest library, the Library of Congress.

The library was founded in 1800 and is housed today in three buildings on Capitol Hill, in Washington, DC. Its basic job is to do research for Congress. Each year, it answers a half million questions and produces about 1,000 reports for its members and their various committees. Over time, though, it has also become America's library, welcoming scholars, scientists, teachers, and students.

Among its many attractions: the private papers and letters of 23 U.S. Presidents and thousands of famous Americans, and the maps and atlases used by explorers to chart the earth and outer space. You will find everything from the earliest movies to the latest databases—from the 2,100 early (1887–1914) baseball cards donated by the poet Carl Sandburg, to a joking letter sent to Alexander Graham Bell's father-in-law by Mark Twain, complaining about his telephone service.

Go Online PHSchool.com
Use Web Code mqd-3127 to find out more about the Library of Congress and for help in answering the following question:
The Library of Congress houses a variety of correspondence to Alexander Graham Bell. How do such materials enhance the library?

Standards Monitoring Online
For: Self-quiz with vocabulary practice
Web Code: mqa-3122

Section 2 Assessment

Key Terms and Main Ideas

1. What is a **standing committee** and why are such committees called "subject-matter" committees?
2. What is the usual role of **select committees** in the House and Senate?
3. How do **joint committees** differ from **conference committees**?

Critical Thinking

4. **Testing Conclusions** Explain why you agree or disagree with the following statement: The Committee on Rules is the most powerful committee in the House.

5. **Drawing Conclusions** Woodrow Wilson once noted that Congress in its committee rooms is Congress at work. Explain the meaning of this statement in your own words.
6. **Recognizing Cause and Effect** How does the majority party manage to control all the committees in its house, and why does it do so?

Go Online PHSchool.com
For: An activity on congressional committees
Web Code: mqd-3122

How a Bill Becomes a Law: The House

Section Preview

OBJECTIVES

1. **List** the first steps in the introduction of a bill to the House.
2. **Describe** what happens to a bill once it is referred to a committee.
3. **Explain** how House leaders schedule debate on a bill.
4. **Explain** what happens to a bill on the House floor, and identify the final step in the passage of a bill in the House.

WHY IT MATTERS

The lawmaking process is quite complicated—indeed, it may be likened to a very difficult obstacle course. Only a small fraction of the bills introduced in either House survive that course.

POLITICAL DICTIONARY

★ **bill**
★ **joint resolution**
★ **concurrent resolution**
★ **resolution**
★ **rider**
★ **discharge petition**
★ **subcommittee**
★ **Committee of the Whole**
★ **quorum**
★ **engrossed**

These numbers may surprise you: As many as 10,000 measures are introduced in the House and Senate during a term of Congress. Fewer than 10 percent ever become law. Where do all those measures come from? Why are so few of them passed? By what process does Congress make law?

The First Steps

A **bill** is a proposed law presented to the House or Senate for consideration. Most bills introduced in either house do not originate with members of Congress themselves. Instead, most bills—the important as well as the routine—are born somewhere in the executive branch. Business, labor, agriculture, and other special interest groups often draft measures as well. Some bills, or at least the ideas for them, come from private citizens who think "there ought to be a law . . . ." Many others are born in the standing committees of Congress.

◄ A bill introduced in the House must be placed in the hopper.

According to the Constitution:

FROM THE Constitution *❝All Bills for raising Revenue shall originate in the House of Representatives; but the Senate may propose or concur with amendments as on other Bills. ❞*

—Article I, Section 7, Clause 1

Measures dealing with any other matter may be introduced in either chamber. Only members can introduce bills in the House, and they do so by dropping them into the "hopper," a box hanging on the edge of the clerk's desk. [9]

Types of Bills and Resolutions

The thousands of measures—bills and resolutions—Congress considers at each session take several forms. To begin with, there are two types of bills: public bills and private bills.

Public bills are measures applying to the nation as a whole—for example, a tax measure or an amendment to the copyright laws. Private bills are measures that apply to certain persons or places

---

[9]Puerto Rico's resident commissioner and the delegates from the District of Columbia, Guam, the Virgin Islands, and American Samoa also may introduce measures in the House. Only a senator may introduce a measure in the upper house. He or she does so by addressing the chair.

rather than to the entire nation. As an example, Congress recently passed an act to give an Idaho sheep rancher $85,000 for his losses resulting from attacks by grizzly bears, which had been moved from Yellowstone National Park onto nearby public lands on which he grazed his flock.

Joint resolutions are similar to bills, and when passed have the force of law. Joint resolutions most often deal with unusual or temporary matters. For example, they may be used to appropriate money for the presidential inauguration ceremonies or to correct an error in a statute already passed. Joint resolutions also are used to propose constitutional amendments and they have been used to annex territories.

Concurrent resolutions deal with matters in which the House and Senate must act jointly. However, they do not have the force of law and do not require the President's signature. Concurrent resolutions are used most often by Congress to state a position on some matter—for example, in foreign affairs.

Resolutions deal with matters concerning either house alone and are taken up only by that house. They are regularly used for such things as the adoption of a new rule of procedure or the amendment of some existing rule. Like concurrent resolutions, a resolution does not have the force of law and is not sent to the President for approval.

A bill or resolution usually deals with a single subject, but sometimes a **rider** dealing with an unrelated matter is included. A rider is a provision not likely to pass on its own merit that is attached to an important measure certain to pass. Its sponsors hope that it will "ride" through the legislative process on the strength of the main measure.

Most riders are tacked onto appropriations measures, those in which Congress provides the money to pay for something. In fact, some money bills are hung with so many riders that they are called "Christmas trees." The opponents of those "decorations" and the President are almost always forced to accept them if they want the bill's major provisions to become law.

The First Reading

The clerk of the House numbers each bill as it is introduced. Thus, H.R. 3410 would be the 3,410th measure introduced in the House during the congressional term. Bills originating in the Senate receive the prefix S.—such as S. 210.

Types of Bills and Resolutions	
BILL	A proposed law; a public bill applies to the entire nation; a private bill applies only to certain people or places
JOINT RESOLUTION	A proposal for some action that has the force of law when passed; usually deals with special circumstances or temporary matters
CONCURRENT RESOLUTION	A statement of position on an issue, adopted by the House and Senate acting jointly; does not have the force of law; does not require the President's signature
RESOLUTION	A measure dealing with some matter in one house; does not have the force of law; does not require the President's signature

Interpreting Charts To be considered by Congress, a measure must be introduced in either the House or the Senate in one of the above formats. *In what ways do joint resolutions and concurrent resolutions differ?* H-SS 12.4.1

Resolutions are similarly identified in each house in the order of their introduction.[10]

The clerk also gives each bill a short title—a brief summary of its principal contents. Having received its number and title, the bill is then entered in the House *Journal* and in the *Congressional Record* for the day.

The *Journal* contains the minutes, the official record, of the daily proceedings in the House or Senate. The *Congressional Record* is a voluminous account of the daily proceedings (speeches, debates, other comments, votes, motions, etc.) in each house. The *Record* is not quite a word-for-word account, however. Members have five days in which to make changes in each temporary edition. They often insert speeches that were in fact never made, reconstruct "debates," and revise thoughtless or inaccurate remarks.

With these actions the bill has received its first reading. All bills are printed immediately after introduction and distributed to the members.

---

[10] Thus, H.J. Res. 12 would be the 12th joint resolution introduced in the House during the term, and similarly in the Senate, S.J. Res. 19. Concurrent resolutions are identified as H. or S. Con. Res. 4, and simple resolutions as H. or S. Res. 166.

▲ **Testifying Before Congress** Committees often call upon citizens to give testimony at public hearings. Actor Michael J. Fox appeared before the Senate Appropriations Committee to discuss Parkinson's disease, a progressive disease with which he has been diagnosed. **H-SS 12.4.1**

Each bill that is finally passed in either house is given three readings along the legislative route. In the House, second reading comes during floor consideration, if the measure gets that far. Third reading takes place just before the final vote on the measure. Each reading is usually by number and title only: "H.R. 3410, A bill to provide. . . ." However, the more important or controversial bills are read in full and taken up line by line, section by section, at second reading.

The three readings, an ancient parliamentary practice, are intended to ensure careful consideration of bills. Today, the readings are little more than way stations along the legislative route. They were quite important in the early history of Congress, however, when some members could not read.

After the first reading, the Speaker refers the bill to the appropriate standing committee. That is, the proposal is sent to the committee that has jurisdiction over its subject matter.

The Bill in Committee

The Constitution makes no mention of standing committees. These bodies play an absolutely essential role in the lawmaking process, however—and in both houses of Congress. Indeed, their place is so pivotal that they are sometimes called "little legislatures."

The standing committees act as sieves. They sift through all of the many bills referred to them—rejecting most, considering and reporting only those they find to be worthy of floor consideration. In short, the fate of most bills is decided in these committees rather than on the floor of either house of Congress.

Most of the thousands of bills introduced in each session are pigeonholed.[11] That is, they are buried, they die in committee. They are simply put away, never to be acted upon.

Most pigeonholed bills deserve their fate. On occasion, however, a committee buries a measure that a majority of the House wants to consider. When that happens, the bill can be blasted out of the committee with a discharge petition.

A **discharge petition** enables members to force a bill that has remained in committee 30 days (7 in the Rules Committee) onto the floor for consideration. Any member may file a discharge motion. If that motion is signed by a majority (218) of House members, the committee has seven days to report the bill. If it does not, any member who signed the motion may, on the second and fourth Mondays of each month, move that the bill be discharged from the committee—that is, sent to the floor. If the motion carries, the rules require the House to consider the bill at once. This maneuver is not often tried, and it seldom succeeds.

The process was most recently successful in 2002, however. What went on to become the Bipartisan Campaign Reform Act of 2002 was blasted out of the Committee on House Administration—where the House leadership had managed to bury it for several years. That measure marked the first significant changes in federal campaign finance law in 25 years.

---

[11]The term comes from the old-fashioned rolltop desks with pigeonholes—slots into which papers were put and often soon forgotten. Most "by request" bills are routinely pigeonholed; they are the measures that members introduce but only because some constituent or some interest group has asked them to do so.

Gathering Information

Those bills that a committee, or at least its chairman, does wish to consider are discussed at times chosen by the chairman. Today, most committees do most of their work through their several **subcommittees**—divisions of existing committees formed to address specific issues. There are now some 80 of these committees within committees in the House, and nearly 70 in the Senate.

Where an important or controversial bill is involved, a committee, or more often one of its subcommittees, holds public hearings on the measure. Interested persons, special interest groups, and government officials are invited to testify at these information-gathering sessions.[12] If necessary, a committee can issue a subpoena, forcing a witness to testify under threat of imprisonment.

Occasionally, a subcommittee will make a junket (trip) to locations affected by a measure. Thus, several members of the House Judiciary Committee's Subcommittee on Africa, Global Human Rights and International Operations may take a firsthand look at conditions in famine-stricken Niger. Or, a few members of the Public Lands and Forests Subcommittee of the Senate's Energy & Natural Resources Committee may spend a few days in northern California to study a proposal to establish a new national wildlife refuge there.

These junkets are made at public expense, and members of Congress are sometimes criticized for taking them. Some junkets deserve criticism. But an on-the-spot investigation often proves to be the best way a committee can inform itself.

Committee Actions

When a subcommittee has completed its work on a bill, the measure goes to the full committee. That body may do one of several things. It may:

1. Report the bill favorably, with a "do pass" recommendation. It is then the chairman's job to steer the bill through debate on the floor.

2. Refuse to report the bill—that is, pigeonhole it. Again, this is the fate suffered by most measures in both houses.

3. Report the bill in amended form. Many bills are changed in committee, and several bills on the same subject may be combined into a single measure.

4. Report the bill with an unfavorable recommendation. This does not often happen. Occasionally, however, a committee feels that the full House should have a chance to consider a bill or does not want to take the responsibility for killing it.

5. Report a committee bill. This is an entirely new bill that the committee has substituted for one or several bills referred to it.

Scheduling Floor Debate

Before it goes to the floor for consideration, a bill reported by a standing committee is placed on one of several calendars. A calendar is a schedule of the order in which bills will be taken up on the floor.

Calendars

There are five calendars in the House:

(1) The Calendar of the Committee of the Whole House on the State of the Union, commonly known as the Union Calendar,

▲ Members of the House of Representatives joined the Iraqi Foreign Minister at a press conference following a meeting. *Critical Thinking Which House committee would have been most likely to hear these representatives' testimony?*

---

[12] If necessary, a committee may subpoena witnesses. A subpoena is an order compelling one to appear. Failure to obey a subpoena may lead the House or Senate to pass a resolution citing the offender for contempt of Congress—a federal crime punishable by fine and/or imprisonment.

Interpreting Political Cartoons *What does this cartoon imply about political debate?*

for all bills having to do with revenues, appropriations, or government property.

(2) The House Calendar, for all other public bills.

(3) The Private Calendar, for all private bills.

(4) The Corrections Calendar, for all bills from the Union or House Calendar taken out of order by unanimous consent of the House of Representatives. These are most often minor bills to which there is no opposition.

(5) The Discharge Calendar, for petitions to discharge bills from committee.

Under the rules of the House, bills are taken from each of these calendars for consideration on a regularly scheduled basis. For example, bills from the Corrections Calendar are supposed to be considered on the second and fourth Tuesdays of each month. Measures relating to the District of Columbia can be taken up on the second and fourth Mondays, and private bills on the first and third Tuesdays. On "Calendar Wednesdays," the various committee chairmen may each call up one bill from the House or Union calendars that has cleared their committees.

Rules

None of these arrangements is followed too closely, however. What often happens is even more complicated. First, remember that the Rules Committee plays a critical role in the legislative process of the House. It must grant a rule before most bills can in fact reach the floor. That is, before most measures can be taken from a calendar, the Rules Committee must approve that step and set a time for its appearance on the floor.

By not granting a rule for a bill, the Rules Committee can effectively kill it. Or, when the Rules Committee does grant a rule, it may be a special rule—one setting conditions under which the members of the House will consider the measure. A special rule regularly sets a time limit on floor debate. It may even prohibit amendments to certain, or even to any, of the bill's provisions.

Then, too, certain bills are privileged. They may be called up at almost any time, ahead of any other business before the House. The most highly privileged measures include major appropriations (spending) and general revenue (tax) bills, conference committee reports, and special rules from the Rules Committee.

On certain days, usually the first and third Mondays and Tuesdays, the House may suspend its rules. A motion to that effect must be approved by a two-thirds vote of the members present. When that happens, as it sometimes does, the House moves so far away from its established operating procedures that a measure can go through all the many steps necessary to enactment in a single day.

All of these—the calendars, the role of the Rules Committee, and the other complex procedures—have developed over time and for several reasons. In major part, they have developed because of the large size of the House and the sheer number and variety of bills its members introduce. In their own ways, the calendars, rules, and other complex procedures have developed to help members of the House manage their heavy workload. Without such help, no one member could possibly know the contents, let alone the merits, of every bill on which he or she has to vote.

The Bill on the Floor

If a bill finally reaches the floor, it receives its second reading in the House. Many bills the House passes are minor ones, with little or no opposition. Most minor bills are called from the

Corrections Calendar, get their second reading by title only, and are quickly disposed of.

Nearly all the more important measures are dealt with in a much different manner, however. They are considered in the **Committee of the Whole,** an old parliamentary device for speeding business on the floor.

The Committee of the Whole includes all the members of the House. However, they sit as one large committee of the House, not as the House itself. The rules of the Committee of the Whole are much less strict than the rules of the House, and floor action moves along at a faster pace. For example, a **quorum,** or majority of the full membership (218), must be present in order for the House to do business. However, only 100 members need be present in the Committee of the Whole.

When the House resolves itself into the Committee of the Whole, the Speaker steps down because the full House of Representatives is no longer in session. Another member presides. General debate begins, and the bill receives its second reading, section by section. As each section is read, amendments may be offered. Under the five-minute rule, supporters and opponents of each amendment have just that many minutes to make their cases. Votes are taken on each section and its amendment as the reading proceeds.

When the bill has been gone through—and many run to dozens and sometimes hundreds of pages—the Committee of the Whole has completed its work. It then rises, that is, dissolves itself. The House is now back in session. The Speaker resumes the chair, and the House formally adopts the committee's work.

Debate

Its large size has long since forced the House to impose severe limits on floor debate. A rule first adopted in 1841 forbids any member from holding the floor for more than one hour without unanimous consent to speak for a longer time. Since 1880 the Speaker has had the power to force any member who strays from the subject at hand to give up the floor.

The majority and minority floor leaders generally decide in advance how they will split the time to be spent on a bill. But at any time, any member may "move the previous question."

Voices on Government

Carolyn Cheeks Kilpatrick (D., Michigan) was first elected to the House of Representatives in 1996. She believes "America's problems are all in [Detroit's] 15th Congressional District" and is more interested in finding solutions than focusing on politics. "The best public policy is bipartisan," she says. These beliefs are displayed in Representative Kilpatrick's attitude toward floor debate.

❝ *When I speak during floor debate on a bill, I feel an awesome responsibility to make an accurate and cogent argument. I know that my words will reach millions of Americans. I also know that I may persuade one or more of my colleagues to take a second look at a position that they may have never considered. Floor debate is an exhilarating experience and an important duty.* ❞

Evaluating the Quotation

For what reasons does Representative Kilpatrick find floor debate "exhilarating" and "an important duty"?

That is, any member may demand a vote on the issue before the House. If that motion is adopted, debate ends. An up-or-down vote must be taken. This device is the only motion that can be used in the House to close (end) debate, but it can be a very effective one.

Voting

A bill may be the subject of several votes on the floor. If amendments are offered, as they frequently are, members must vote on each of them. Then, too, a number of procedural motions may be offered, for example, one to table the bill (lay it aside), another for the previous question, and so on. The members must vote on each of these motions. These several other votes are very often a better guide to a bill's friends and foes than is the final vote itself. Sometimes, a member votes for a bill that is now certain to pass, even though he or she had supported amendments to it that, had they been adopted, would have scuttled the measure.

The House uses four different methods for taking floor votes:

1. Voice votes are the most common. The Speaker calls for the "ayes" and then the "noes," the members answer in chorus, and the Speaker announces the result.

2. If any member thinks the Speaker has erred in judging a voice vote, he or she may demand a standing vote, also known as a division of the House. All in favor, and then all opposed, stand and are counted by the clerk.

3. One fifth of a quorum (44 members in the House or 20 in the Committee of the Whole) can demand a teller vote. When this happens, the Speaker names two tellers, one from each party. The members pass between the tellers and are counted, for and against. Teller votes are rare today. The practice has been replaced by electronic voting, as you will see below.

4. A roll-call vote, also known as a record vote, may be demanded by one fifth of the members present.[13]

In 1973, the House installed a computerized voting system for all quorum calls and record votes to replace the roll call by the clerk. Members now vote at any of the 48 stations on the floor by inserting a personalized plastic card in a box and then pushing one of three buttons: "Yea," "Nay," or "Present." The "Present" button is most often used for a quorum call—a check to make sure that a quorum of the members is in fact present. Otherwise, it is used when a member does not wish to vote on a question but still wants to be recorded as present.[14]

A large master board above the Speaker's chair shows instantly how each member has voted. The House rules allow the members 15 minutes to answer quorum calls or cast record votes. Voting ends when the Speaker pushes a button to lock the electronic system, producing a permanent record of the vote at the same time. Under the former roll-call process, it took the clerk up to 45 minutes to call each member's name and record his or her vote. Before 1973, roll calls took up about three months of House floor time each session.

Voting procedures are much the same in the Senate. The upper house uses voice, standing, and roll-call votes, but does not take teller votes or use an electronic voting process. Only six or seven minutes are needed for a roll-call vote in the upper chamber.

Final Steps

Once a bill has been approved at second reading, it is **engrossed.** This means the bill is printed in its final form. Then it is read a third time, by title, and a final vote is taken. If the bill is approved at third reading, the Speaker signs it. A page—a legislative aide—then carries it to the Senate and places it on the Senate president's desk.

---

[13]The Constitution (Article I, Section 7, Clause 2) requires a record vote on the question of overriding a presidential veto. No record votes are taken in the Committee of the Whole.

[14]A "present" vote is not allowed on some questions—for example, a vote to override a veto.

Section 3 Assessment

Standards Monitoring Online
For: Self-quiz with vocabulary practice
Web Code: mqa-3123

Key Terms and Main Ideas

1. Explain the difference between the two types of **bills.**
2. Why do members of Congress attach **riders** to bills that are almost certain to pass?
3. Why does the House often use the **Committee of the Whole** to consider important measures?
4. What is the purpose of a **discharge petition?**

Critical Thinking

5. **Predicting Consequences** What might happen if all proposed bills were sent directly to the full House for a vote? Cite the pros and cons of such an arrangement.

6. **Understanding Point of View** Why might members of a House committee choose to report a bill with an unfavorable recommendation rather than pigeonhole it?

Go Online PHSchool.com

For: An activity on how a bill becomes a law
Web Code: mqd-3123

Face the Issues

Divided Government

Background *Divided government exists when one political party occupies the White House and the other party holds a majority of the seats in one or both houses of Congress. Through much of our history, from 1789 to the mid-1950s, the same party almost always held both the presidency and Congress. That has not been the case over much of the period since then, however. Does divided government reflect a weakness in our political system, or, instead, the strength of that system?*

Democrats and Republicans often share power in Washington

 **Analysis Skill HR3**

Same-Party Control Is Best

The Constitution gives a sizable share of the power to govern to the President and, at the same time, a sizable share of that power to Congress. Given that complex arrangement, conflict between the executive and legislative branches has been inevitable. Historically, the two major parties have been the principal agents through which that conflict has been moderated and compromises reached. Clearly, conflicts can most easily be settled when the same party controls both ends of Pennsylvania Avenue.

Same-party control means that the voters can more readily assign credit or blame (hold the party in power accountable) on election day. In short, same-party control means greater accountability and, therefore, better government.

Divided government intensifies partisan bickering and can lead to gridlock—to a situation in which government is incapable of acting as it should. In fact, divided government led to a nearly complete shutdown of the Federal Government for several weeks in late 1995 and early 1996.

Divided Government Is Best

The Framers of the Constitution designed a system of government in which the power to govern is both shared and divided. They very purposefully created that complicated system in order to make it difficult for government to take "hasty and ill-considered actions." Indeed, it can be argued that the Framers believed that there are worse fates for a government than gridlock. Gridlock, says Sarah Binder in the *Brookings Review,* is "the natural consequence of separated institutions sharing and competing for power."

Both the financial markets and the electorate seem to prefer divided government. The *Wall Street Journal* has found that, over the years since 1896, the stock market has recorded its highest returns when there was a Democrat in the White House and the Republican Party controlled at least one house of Congress. And, for more than 20 years now, public opinion polls have regularly shown that a majority of the American people believe that divided government, not same-party control, is best for the country.

Exploring the Issues

1. Why did the Framers design a governmental system in which the executive branch and legislative branch were likely to conflict?

2. Why do you think a majority of the people seem to prefer divided to same-party control of government?

For more information about partisan division in the Federal Government, view "Divided Government."

The Bill in the Senate

Section Preview

OBJECTIVES

1. **Explain** how a bill is introduced in the Senate.
2. **Compare** the Senate's rules for debate with those in the House.
3. **Describe** the role of conference committees in the legislative process.
4. **Evaluate** the actions the President can take after both houses have passed a bill.

WHY IT MATTERS

A bill that survives the legislative obstacle course in one house must still be passed in the other chamber—and face yet more hurdles before it can become law.

POLITICAL DICTIONARY

★ **filibuster**
★ **cloture**
★ **veto**
★ **pocket veto**

The basic steps in the lawmaking process are much the same in the House and the Senate. There are a few critical differences, as you can see in the chart on page 345. Given the many similarities, there is no need here to trace a bill step-by-step through the Senate. However, it is important to look at those differences, and then at what happens to bills once they have passed in each house.

Introducing the Bill

Bills are introduced by senators, who are formally recognized for that purpose. A measure is then given a number and short title, read twice, and referred to committee, where bills are dealt with much as they are in the House.

All in all, the Senate's proceedings are less formal and its rules less strict than those of the much larger House. For example, the Senate has only one calendar for all bills reported out by its committees. Bills are called to the floor at the discretion of the majority floor leader.[15]

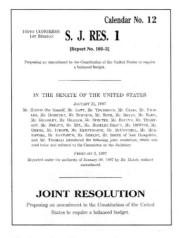

Calendar No. 12

105TH CONGRESS
1ST SESSION

S. J. RES. 1

[Report No. 105–3]

Proposing an amendment to the Constitution of the United States to require a balanced budget.

IN THE SENATE OF THE UNITED STATES

JANUARY 21, 1997

Mr. HATCH (for himself, Mr. LOTT, Mr. THURMOND, Mr. CRAIG, Mr. NICKLES, Mr. DOMENICI, Mr. STEVENS, Mr. ROTH, Mr. BRYAN, Mr. KOHL, Mr. GRASSLEY, Mr. GRAHAM, Mr. SPECTER, Mr. BAUCUS, Mr. THOMPSON, Mr. BREAUX, Mr. KYL, Ms. MOSELEY-BRAUN, Mr. DEWINE, Mr. GREGG, Mr. INHOFE, Mr. KEMPTHORNE, Mr. McCONNELL, Mr. MURKOWSKI, Mr. SANTORUM, Mr. SHELBY, Mr. SMITH of New Hampshire, and Mr. THOMAS) introduced the following joint resolution; which was read twice and referred to the Committee on the Judiciary

FEBRUARY 3, 1997

Reported under the authority of January 30, 1997 by Mr. Hatch, without amendment

JOINT RESOLUTION

Proposing an amendment to the Constitution of the United States to require a balanced budget.

▲ Senate bill

[15]The Senate does have another, nonlegislative calendar, the Executive Calendar, for treaties and appointments made by the President and awaiting Senate approval or, rarely, rejection. The majority leader controls that schedule, too.

Rules for Debate

The major differences between House and Senate procedures involve debate. Floor debate is strictly limited in the House, but almost unrestrained in the Senate. In fact, most senators are intensely proud of belonging to what has often been called "the greatest deliberative body in the world."

As a general matter, senators may speak on the floor for as long as they please. Unlike the House, the Senate has no rule that requires a senator to speak only to the measure before the chamber; and the Senate's rules do not allow any member to move the previous question.

The Senate's consideration of most bills is brought to a close by unanimous consent agreements. That is, discussion ends and the chamber votes at a time previously agreed to by the majority and minority floor leaders. But if any senator objects—and so prevents unanimous consent—the procedure fails.

The Senate does have a "two-speech rule." Under this rule, no senator may speak more than twice on a given question on the same legislative day. By recessing—temporarily interrupting—rather than adjourning a day's session, the Senate can prolong a "legislative day" indefinitely. Thus, the two-speech rule can successfully limit the amount of time the Senate spends on some matters on its agenda.

The Senate's dedication to freedom of debate is almost unique among modern legislative bodies. That freedom is intended to encourage the fullest possible discussion of matters on the floor. But, notice, the great latitude it allows also gives rise to the filibuster.

The Filibuster

Essentially, a **filibuster** is an attempt to "talk a bill to death." It is a stalling tactic, a process in which a minority of senators seeks to delay or prevent Senate action on a measure. The filibusters try to so monopolize the Senate floor and its time that the Senate must either drop the bill or change it in some manner acceptable to the minority.

Talk—and more talk—is the filibusterers' major weapon. In addition, senators may use time-killing motions, quorum calls, and other parliamentary maneuvers. Indeed, anything to delay or obstruct is grist for the minority's mill as it works to block a bill that would very likely pass if brought to a vote.

Among the many better known filibusterers, Senator Huey Long (D., Louisiana) spoke for more than 15 hours in 1935. He stalled by reading from the Washington telephone directory and giving his colleagues his recipes for "potlikker," corn bread, and turnip greens. In 1947, Glen Taylor (D., Idaho) used more than eight hours of floor time talking of his children, Wall Street, baptism, and fishing. Senator Strom Thurmond (R., South Carolina) set the current filibuster record. He held the floor for 24 hours and 18 minutes in an unsuccessful, one-person effort against what later became the Civil Rights Act of 1957.

No later efforts have come close to matching that one. Still, the practice is often used and to great effect in the Senate. Over the past century and more, well over 200 measures have been killed by filibusters. Just the *threat* of a filibuster alone has resulted in the Senate's failure to consider a number of bills and the amending of many more.

The Senate often tries to beat off a filibuster with lengthy, even day-and-night, sessions to wear down the participants. At times, some little-observed rules are quite strictly enforced. Among them are the requirements that senators stand—not sit, lean on their desks, or walk about—as they speak and that they not use "unparliamentary language." These counter-measures seldom work, however.

▲ Senators rest on cots set up in the old Supreme Court Chamber during the filibuster that attempted to prevent passage of the Civil Rights Act of 1957. *Critical Thinking Why is a filibuster an effective way to kill legislation?*

The Cloture Rule

The Senate's real check on the filibuster is its Cloture Rule, Rule XXII in the Standing Rules of the Senate. It was first adopted in 1917, after one of the most notable of all filibusters in Senate history. That filibuster lasted for three weeks, and took place less than two months before the United States entered World War I on April 6, 1917.

German submarines had renewed their attacks on shipping in the North Atlantic, so President Wilson asked Congress for legislation to permit the arming of American merchant vessels. The bill, widely supported in the country, was quickly passed by the House by a vote of 403–12. The measure died in the Senate, however, because twelve senators filibustered it until the end of the congressional term on March 4th.

The public was outraged. President Wilson declared: "A little group of willful men, representing no opinion but their own, has rendered the great Government of the United States helpless

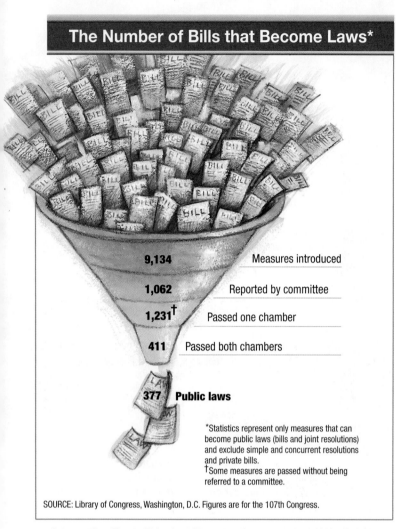

The Number of Bills that Become Laws*

9,134   Measures introduced

1,062   Reported by committee

1,231†   Passed one chamber

411   Passed both chambers

377   **Public laws**

*Statistics represent only measures that can become public laws (bills and joint resolutions) and exclude simple and concurrent resolutions and private bills.
†Some measures are passed without being referred to a committee.

SOURCE: Library of Congress, Washington, D.C. Figures are for the 107th Congress.

Interpreting Charts This chart illustrates the many stages through which a bill must pass before it becomes a law. **After which step do most bills "die"?** H-SS 12.4.1

and contemptible." The Senate passed the Cloture Rule at its next session, later that same year.

Rule XXII provides for **cloture**—limiting debate. The rule is not in regular, continuing force; it can be brought into play only by a special procedure. A vote to invoke the rule must be taken two days after a petition calling for that action has been submitted by at least 16 members of the Senate. If at least 60 senators—three fifths of the full Senate—then vote for the motion, the rule becomes effective. From that point, no more than another 30 hours of floor time may be spent on the measure. Then it *must* be brought to a final vote.

Invoking the rule is no easy matter. So far, more than 400 attempts have been made to invoke the rule, and only about one third have succeeded. Many senators hesitate to support cloture motions for two reasons: (1) their

dedication to the Senate's tradition of free debate, and (2) their practical worry that the frequent use of cloture will undercut the value of the filibuster that they may some day want to use.

Conference Committees

If you have ever watched a marathon, you know that no matter how well a runner covers the first 25 miles or so, he or she still has some distance to go in order to finish the race. So it is for bills in the legislative process. Even those that survive the long route through committees and rules and the floor in both houses still face some important steps before they can finally become law. Some of those final steps can be very difficult.

Any measure enacted by Congress *must* have been passed by both houses in identical form. Most often, a bill passed by one house and then approved by the other is not amended in the second chamber. When the House and Senate do pass different versions of the same bill, the first house usually concurs in the other's amendments, and congressional action is completed.

There are times when the House or the Senate will not accept the other's version of a bill. When this happens, the measure is turned over to a conference committee, a temporary joint committee of the two houses. It seeks to iron out the differences and come up with a compromise bill.

The conferees—managers—are named by the respective presiding officers. Mostly, they are leading members of the standing committee that first handled the measure in each house.

Both the House and Senate rules restrict a conference committee to the consideration of those points in a bill on which the two houses disagree. The committee cannot include any new material in its compromise version. In practice, however, the conferees often make changes that were not even considered in either house.

Once the conferees agree, their report, the compromise bill, is submitted to both houses. It must be accepted or rejected without amendment. Only rarely does either house turn down a conference committee's work. This is not surprising, for two major reasons: (1) the powerful membership of the typical conference committee, and (2) the fact that its report usually comes in

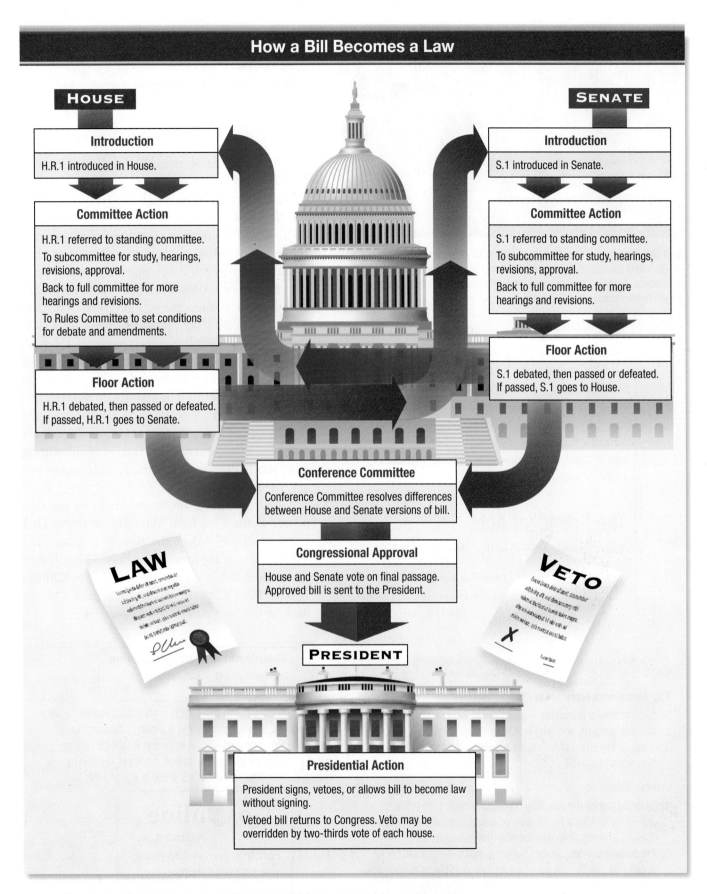

How a Bill Becomes a Law

HOUSE

Introduction

H.R.1 introduced in House.

Committee Action

H.R.1 referred to standing committee.

To subcommittee for study, hearings, revisions, approval.

Back to full committee for more hearings and revisions.

To Rules Committee to set conditions for debate and amendments.

Floor Action

H.R.1 debated, then passed or defeated. If passed, H.R.1 goes to Senate.

SENATE

Introduction

S.1 introduced in Senate.

Committee Action

S.1 referred to standing committee.

To subcommittee for study, hearings, revisions, approval.

Back to full committee for more hearings and revisions.

Floor Action

S.1 debated, then passed or defeated. If passed, S.1 goes to House.

Conference Committee

Conference Committee resolves differences between House and Senate versions of bill.

Congressional Approval

House and Senate vote on final passage. Approved bill is sent to the President.

LAW

VETO

PRESIDENT

Presidential Action

President signs, vetoes, or allows bill to become law without signing.

Vetoed bill returns to Congress. Veto may be overridden by two-thirds vote of each house.

Interpreting Charts A typical bill may be introduced in either house. It must be passed by each house before going to the President. *In what way does the process of moving a bill through the House differ from the process in the Senate?* H-SS 12.4.1

▲ **A Bill Becomes a Law** President George W. Bush signs the Keeping Children and Families Safe Act, reauthorizing programs that help prevent child abuse. Flanking him are a coalition of child safety advocates and government officials. **H-SS 12.4.1**

the midst of the rush to adjournment at the end of a congressional session.

The conference committee stage is a most strategic step in the legislative process. A number of major legislative decisions and compromises are often made at that point. Indeed, the late Senator George Norris (R., Nebraska) once quite aptly described conference committees as "the third house of Congress."

The President Acts

The Constitution requires that

FROM THE *Constitution* ❝*Every Bill which shall have passed the House of Representatives and the Senate, . . . [and] Every Order,*

Resolution, or Vote to which the Concurrence of the Senate and House of Representatives may be necessary (except on a question of Adjournment) shall be presented to the President. . . .❞
—Article I, Section 7, Clauses 2 and 3

The Constitution presents the President with four options at this point:

1. The President may sign the bill, and it then becomes law.

2. The President may **veto**—refuse to sign the bill. The measure must then be returned to the house in which it originated, together with the President's objections (a veto message). Although it seldom does, Congress may then pass the bill over the President's veto, by a two-thirds vote of the full membership of each house.

3. The President may allow the bill to become law without signing it—by not acting on it within 10 days, not counting Sundays, of receiving it.

4. The fourth option is a variation of the third, called the **pocket veto.** If Congress adjourns its session within 10 days of submitting a bill to the President, and the President does not act, the measure dies.

Congress added another element to the veto power in the Line Item Veto Act of 1996. That law gave the President the power to reject individual items in appropriations bills. The Supreme Court held the law unconstitutional, in *Clinton v. New York City,* 1998. You will take a closer look at the veto power in Chapter 14.

Section **4** Assessment

Key Terms and Main Ideas

1. Explain how a **filibuster** is designed to work.
2. What is **cloture,** and why is it hard to achieve?
3. What is the effect of a President's **veto,** and how can Congress respond?

Critical Thinking

4. **Making Comparisons** Why do the Senate's rules allow individual senators much greater freedom to affect the law-making process than members of the House have?
5. **Predicting Consequences** Suppose that there is a bill up for debate on the Senate floor, but a small number of determined members oppose it. Would it be easier or harder for a

majority of senators to pass such a bill than it would be for a majority of House members in a similar situation? Why?

6. **Drawing Conclusions** If you were the President, under what circumstances might you use a pocket veto? Why might you let a bill become law without signing it?

on the Supreme Court

How Broad Is Congress's Power to Investigate?

Analysis Skills HR4, HI3, HI4

Congress has broad authority to conduct investigations as part of the legislative process. Through investigations, Congress can evaluate existing laws and determine whether new laws are needed. How far can Congress go in these investigations?

Watkins v. *United States* (1957)

During the 1950s, the House Un-American Activities Committee (HUAC) investigated possible communist activities and influence in various areas of American life. John Watkins, a leader in the labor movement, was called to testify before a subcommittee of HUAC. In response to questions, he described his background in union activities and his connections with the Communist Party.

A lawyer for the committee then read a list of names to Watkins and asked him to identify the ones he knew to have been members of the Communist Party. Watkins stated that he was willing to answer questions about people who he believed were currently party members, but that he would not identify or answer questions about those who he believed had withdrawn from party membership.

The House requested that the United States attorney prosecute Watkins for his refusal to answer these questions. He was tried, found guilty, and fined $1000. His prison sentence (one year) was suspended and he was placed on probation. A three-judge panel of the court of appeals reversed the conviction, but the full court of appeals later approved the conviction. The case then went to the Supreme Court.

Arguments for Watkins

1. Congressional investigations must relate to legitimate subjects of legislative concern. Congress may not force witnesses to testify merely to embarrass or punish people whose beliefs may be unpopular.
2. The questions to Watkins interfered with his 1st Amendment rights of speech, political belief, and association.

3. The subject matter of a congressional investigation must be stated so that witnesses can decide whether the questions posed to them are relevant to the investigation.

Arguments for the United States

1. Congress has broad authority to investigate matters of national concern, and may require citizens to provide information that may be relevant to these investigations. The Court may not dictate the manner in which Congress conducts its investigations.
2. The questions Watkins refused to answer were sufficiently related to the subject of communist influence in labor organizations. Witnesses should not be permitted to pick and choose which questions they will answer.
3. Although some individuals may be "exposed" as a result of witness testimony, there is no violation of 1st Amendment rights when Congress has a legitimate reason to ask its questions.

Decide for Yourself

1. Review the constitutional grounds on which each side based its arguments and the specific arguments each side presented.
2. Debate the opposing viewpoints presented in this case. Which viewpoint do you favor?
3. Predict the impact of the Court's decision on other types of congressional investigations. (To read a summary of the Court's decision, turn to pages 799–806.)

Go Online
PHSchool.com
Use Web Code mqp-3128 to register your vote on this issue and to see how other students voted.

Political Dictionary

Speaker of the House (p. 322), president of the Senate (p. 323), president *pro tempore* (p. 323), party caucus (p. 324), floor leader (p. 324), whip (p. 325), committee chairman (p. 325), seniority rule (p. 326), standing committee (p. 329), select committee (p. 331), joint committee (p. 333), conference committee (p. 333), bill (p. 334), joint resolution (p. 335), concurrent resolution (p. 335), resolution (p. 335), rider (p. 335), discharge petition (p. 336), subcommittee (p. 336), Committee of the Whole (p. 339), quorum (p. 339), engrossed (p. 340), filibuster (p. 343), cloture (p. 344), veto (p. 346), pocket veto (p. 346)

Standards Review

H-SS 12.1.5 Describe the systems of separated and shared powers, the role of organized interests (*Federalist Paper Number 10*), checks and balances (*Federalist Paper Number 51*), the importance of an independent judiciary (*Federalist Paper Number 78*), enumerated powers, rule of law, federalism, and civilian control of the military.

H-SS 12.4.1 Discuss Article I of the Constitution as it relates to the legislative branch, including eligibility for office and lengths of terms of representatives and senators; election to office; the roles of the House and Senate in impeachment proceedings; the role of the vice president; the enumerated legislative powers; and the process by which a bill becomes a law.

H-SS 12.4.3 Identify their current representatives in the legislative branch of the national government.

H-SS 12.6.4 Describe the means that citizens use to participate in the political process (e.g., voting, campaigning, lobbying, filing a legal challenge, demonstrating, petitioning, picketing, running for political office).

H-SS 12.7.5 Explain how public policy is formed, including the setting of the public agenda and implementation of it through regulations and executive orders.

H-SS 12.7.6 Compare the processes of lawmaking at each of the three levels of government, including the role of lobbying and the media.

Practicing the Vocabulary

Matching *Choose a term from the list above that best matches each description.*

1. Selects the party's leaders in each house of Congress
2. Can force a committee to bring a bill to the floor of the House or Senate
3. The minimum number of legislators needed to conduct official business
4. A provision added to a popular bill because it is unlikely to succeed on its own
5. A legislative committee created for a limited time and specific purpose

Word Relationships *Three of the terms in each of the following sets are related. Choose the term that does not belong and explain why it does not.*

6. (a) committee chairman (b) seniority rule (c) party caucus (d) resolution
7. (a) filibuster (b) whip (c) cloture (d) discharge petition
8. (a) Speaker of the House (b) president of the Senate (c) president *pro tempore* (d) committee chairman
9. (a) discharge petition (b) resolution (c) bill (d) concurrent resolution
10. (a) rider (b) bill (c) quorum (d) resolution

Reviewing Main Ideas

Section 1

11. Why is the opening session of the House each term quite different from the opening session of the Senate?
12. What are the duties of the presiding officers in the House and Senate?
13. (a) How does the seniority rule function? (b) What are two criticisms of the seniority rule?

Section 2

14. What role do committees play in turning bills into laws?
15. (a) What are the different types of committees? (b) What are the duties of each type of committee?
16. What are the sources of the bills introduced into Congress?

Section 3

17. What happens to a bill immediately after its introduction in the House?
18. (a) How is a resolution different from a bill? (b) Describe the different types of resolutions.
19. What options does a committee have when reviewing a bill?
20. (a) How have debate and voting rules in the House changed in the past two centuries? (b) What are the benefits of these changes?

Section 4

21. (a) What is the usual purpose of a filibuster? (b) How can the Senate defeat a filibuster?
22. What is the purpose of a conference committee?
23. What are the President's options when he receives a bill from Congress?

Critical Thinking Skills

24. *Face the Issues* Federal spending usually increases faster during times of unified government, such as the Johnson and George W. Bush administrations, than under times of divided government, as in the mid-1990s. Why is divided government likely to lead to lower federal spending?

25. *Drawing Inferences* Why does the President's State of the Union address play an important part in each congressional session? What are some possible ways that Congress can react to the speech?

26. *Expressing Problems Clearly* Why do you think the lawmaking process in both houses of Congress should (or should not) be simplified?

27. *Identifying Assumptions* The *Congressional Record* reports the way in which each member of the House and Senate responds to roll-call votes. Why might a member not want to vote on certain roll calls?

Analyzing Political Cartoons

Using your knowledge of American government and this cartoon, answer the questions below.

28. (a) If the flowers and gift represent new legislation, what might the pigs represent? **(b)** What legislative practice is represented by tying the pigs to the flowers and the gift?

29. How might a representative respond to the cartoonist to defend this legislative practice?

Participation Activities

30. *Current Events Watch* Scan news reports for examples of two of the following: a bill that dies in Congress, a bill that passes Congress but is vetoed by the President, and a bill that passes Congress and is signed by the President. Clip two articles and create a wall chart with each class member's contributions.

31. *Graphing Activity* Create a circle graph showing the percentage of bills introduced that actually became laws during the last session of Congress. Then create a second graph showing the same information from the 106th Congress, when a Democratic President governed with a Republican Congress, and the 103rd Congress, when a Democratic President governed with a Democratic Congress. Who controls these branches today, and how do the rates of passage compare?

32. *It's Your Turn* You have recently been elected to the House of Representatives from your home district. Write a letter to your local newspaper in which you talk about the bills you would like to see Congress pass and what steps you will take to make that happen. Also, describe the committees on which you would like to serve, and how these committees fit the needs of your district and your own interests. Conclude your letter by listing three challenges you expect to encounter in the House. Proofread and revise to correct errors. Then draft a final copy. **(Writing a Letter)**

◆ **The White House, Washington, D.C.**

The Executive Branch

CONSTITUTIONAL PRINCIPLES

Limited Government The presidency is often called "the most powerful office in the world." The President is not all-powerful, however. The Constitution puts a number of restrictions on his ability to act.

Separation of Powers The system of separation of powers means that the President must share the power to govern with both the legislative and the judicial branches of the National Government.

Checks and Balances Congress has several powers with which it can limit the President's ability to act. The courts, with the power of judicial review, can also curb the exercise of presidential power.

The Impact on You

While the President is not all-powerful, his powers are nonetheless many and extraordinary. What he says and what he does very largely set the nation's agenda—shape what government, the media, and the people are most concerned about. And it is to the President that the media and the people regularly turn when anything significant occurs, at home or abroad.

CHAPTER 13

The Presidency

"The presidency has made every man who occupied it, no matter how small, bigger than he was, and no matter how big, not big enough for its demands."
—Lyndon B. Johnson (1972)

As President Johnson knew, the responsibilities of the presidency can be overwhelming. The President not only leads the government and the nation, but also heads a political party. Even before he or she reaches the White House, the long and arduous campaign process tests the President's mettle.

◆ **Air Force One in South Korea**

SECTION 1

The President's Job Description (pp. 354–358)

★ The President has eight major roles, which are exercised simultaneously.
★ The Constitution outlines the formal qualifications for the presidency.
★ Presidents are limited to two four-year terms.
★ Congress determines the President's salary.

SECTION 2

Presidential Succession and the Vice Presidency (pp. 359–363)

★ The Constitution provides for an orderly succession of power if the President dies or leaves office.
★ The Constitution provides for the transfer of power should the President become disabled.
★ Although the vice presidency is often belittled, the Vice President is "a heartbeat away" from becoming President.

SECTION 3

Presidential Selection: The Framers' Plan (pp. 365–367)

★ The Framers created the electoral college for choosing the President and Vice President.
★ With the election of 1800, political parties began to control the nominating process.

SECTION 4

Presidential Nominations (pp. 368–375)

★ National conventions play a key role in the presidential nominating process.
★ Most States hold presidential primaries to determine convention delegates.
★ A few States select delegates through the caucus-convention process.
★ National conventions follow a schedule, culminating in the candidate's acceptance speech.
★ The candidate who is considered most electable usually wins the nomination.

SECTION 5

The Election (pp. 377–384)

★ Presidential electors today mainly "rubber-stamp" their party's candidate.
★ The electoral college is plagued by three major flaws.
★ Critics of the electoral college have proposed a variety of reforms.

① The President's Job Description

Section Preview

OBJECTIVES

1. **Identify** the President's many roles.
2. **Understand** the formal qualifications necessary to become President.
3. **Discuss** issues involving the length of the President's term.
4. **Describe** the President's pay and benefits.

WHY IT MATTERS

The American people elect a President every four years. Soon, you and your friends will be able to participate in that process—if, in fact, you have not already done so. Before your first vote, you will want to know as much as you can about the office and all it involves.

POLITICAL DICTIONARY

★ chief of state
★ chief executive
★ chief administrator
★ chief diplomat
★ commander in chief
★ chief legislator
★ chief of party
★ chief citizen

Do you know who was the youngest person ever to be President? The oldest? Who held the presidency for the longest time? How long a person must live in the United States in order to run for President? You will find the answers to these questions and many more in this section, which provides a basic overview of the presidential office.

The President's Roles

At any given time, of course, only one person is President of the United States. The office, with all of its powers and duties, belongs to that one individual. Whoever that person may be, he—and

▶ These cowboy boots, a gift to President Eisenhower, are an example of the many gifts that a President receives.

most likely someday she[1]—must fill a number of different roles, and all of them at the same time. The President is simultaneously (1) chief of state, (2) chief executive, (3) chief administrator, (4) chief diplomat, (5) commander in chief, (6) chief legislator, (7) party chief, and (8) chief citizen.

1. To begin with, the President is **chief of state.** This means he is the ceremonial head of the government of the United States, the symbol of all the people of the nation. He is, in President William Howard Taft's words, "the personal embodiment and representative of their dignity and majesty."

In many countries, the chief of state reigns but does not rule. That is certainly true of the queens of England and Denmark, the emperor of Japan, the kings of Norway and Sweden, and the presidents of Italy and Germany. It is most certainly not true of the President of the United States, who both reigns and rules.

2. The President is the nation's **chief executive;** he is vested by the Constitution with "the executive Power" of the United States. That power is immensely broad in both domestic and foreign affairs. Indeed, the American presidency is often described as "the most powerful office in the world."

---

[1]To this point all of the Presidents have been men, but nothing in the Constitution prevents the election of a woman to that office.

But remember, the President is not *all-powerful*. He lives in an environment filled with checks and balances and in which there are other practical limits on what he can and cannot do.

3. The President is also the **chief administrator,** the director of the huge executive branch of the Federal Government. He heads one of the largest governmental machines the world has known. Today, the President directs an administration that employs more than 2.7 million civilians and spends some $2.5 trillion a year.

Managing the sprawling executive branch is, in itself, a full-time job. Yet it is only *one* of the several jobs the President has. Harry Truman complained that he had to spend too much of his time "flattering, kissing, and kicking people to get them to do what they were supposed to do anyway."

4. The President is also the nation's **chief diplomat,** the main architect of American foreign policy and the nation's chief spokesperson to the rest of the world. "I make foreign policy," President Truman once said—and he did. What the President says and does is carefully followed in this country and abroad.

5. In close concert with the President's role in foreign affairs, the Constitution also makes the President the **commander in chief** of the nation's armed forces. The 1.4 million men and women in uniform and the nation's entire military arsenal are subject to the President's direct and immediate control. The Constitution gives Congress some power over foreign affairs and the military, but the President has long since become dominant in both fields.

6. The President is also the nation's **chief legislator,** the main architect of its public policies. Most often it is the President who sets the overall shape of the congressional agenda. As chief legislator, the President initiates, suggests, requests, insists, and demands that Congress enact much of its major legislation.

The President does sometimes clash with Congress, and he does not always get his way on Capitol Hill. Still, working with Congress is a major part of the President's job.

These six presidential roles all come directly from the Constitution. Yet they do not complete the list. The President must fill still other vital roles.

Voices on Government

Robert Reich was a professor at Harvard's John F. Kennedy School of Government before he became President Clinton's Secretary of Labor in 1993. As a member of the Cabinet for four years, Reich was in a good position to observe the presidency:

"Unlike Britain and other democratic monarchies, we ask our country's leader to do two jobs simultaneously, to act both as head of government and as the symbol of the nation. It's a hard act. Governing involves tough compromises and gritty reality. Symbolism requires nobility and grandeur. We demand a street-smart wheeler-dealer, but we also want a king and a royal family."

Evaluating the Quotation

What other jobs do Americans expect the President to do? Use Reich's observation and what you read in this chapter to compile a full "job description."

7. The President acts as the **chief of party,** the acknowledged leader of the political party that controls the executive branch. As you know, parties are not mentioned in the Constitution, yet they have a vital place in the workings of the American governmental system. Thus, much of the real power and influence wielded by the President depends on the manner in which he plays this critical role.

8. The office also automatically makes its occupant the nation's **chief citizen.** The President is expected to be "the representative of all the people." As chief citizen, the President is expected to work for and represent the public interest against the many different and competing private interests. "The presidency," said Franklin Roosevelt, "is not merely an administrative office. That is the least of it. It is preeminently a place of moral leadership."

Listing the President's several roles is a very useful way to describe the President's job. But, remember, the President must play all of these roles simultaneously, and they are all interre-

John F. Kennedy was the youngest person elected President. He is shown here with his son, John F. Kennedy, Jr. *Critical Thinking Why do you think that the Framers required that a President be at least 35 years old?* H-SS 12.4.1

lated. None of them can be performed in isolation. The manner in which a President plays any one role can have a powerful effect on his ability to play the others.

As two illustrations, take the experiences of Presidents Lyndon Johnson and Richard Nixon. Each was a strong and relatively effective President during his first years in office. Johnson's actions as commander in chief during the agonizing and increasingly unpopular war in Vietnam seriously damaged his effectiveness in the White House. In fact the damage was so great that it persuaded the President not to run for reelection in 1968.

The many-sided, sordid Watergate scandal proved to be President Nixon's downfall. The manner in which he filled the roles of party leader and chief citizen so destroyed Mr. Nixon's presidency that he was forced to leave office in disgrace in 1974.

---

[2]Article II, Section 1, Clause 5.

[3]Martin Van Buren, who was born December 5, 1782, was the first President actually born in the United States. His seven predecessors (and his immediate successor) were each born in the colonies, before the Revolution—that is, before there was a United States. But notice that the Constitution anticipated that situation with these words: "or a citizen of the United States at the time of the adoption of this Constitution."

Formal Qualifications

Whatever else a President must be, the Constitution says that he—and, certainly, one day she—must meet three formal qualifications for office.[2] The President must:

1. Be "a natural born Citizen . . . of the United States." A person born abroad to American citizen parents is legally an American citizen at birth. That fact leads many to argue that a person born in a foreign country may become President if his or her parents are citizens. Some dispute that view, however. The question of what the Constitution means here cannot be answered until someone born a citizen, but born abroad, does in fact become President.[3]

2. Be at least 35 years of age. John F. Kennedy, at 43, was the youngest person ever to be elected President. Theodore Roosevelt reached the presidency by succession at age 42. Only five others took the oath of office before age 50: James K. Polk, Franklin Pierce, Ulysses Grant, James Garfield, and Grover Cleveland.

Ronald Reagan, who was 69 when he was first elected in 1980, was the oldest man ever elected to the office; and, when he completed

▲ This poster urged President Roosevelt to run for his third term. F.D.R. was the only President to serve more than two terms in office. *Critical Thinking Do you agree that a President should serve for no more than two terms? Explain your answer.* H-SS 12.8.2

his second term eight years later, he was the oldest person ever to hold the post. Most Presidents, though, have been in their 50s when they reached the White House. George W. Bush was 54 when he became President in 2001.

3. "[H]ave been fourteen years a Resident within the United States.[4]" Given the elections of Herbert Hoover (1928) and Dwight Eisenhower (1952), we know that here the Constitution means any 14 years in a person's life. Both Hoover and Eisenhower spent several years outside the country before they won the White House.

While these formal qualifications do have some importance, they are really not very difficult to meet. In fact, more than 100 million people in this country today do so. There are other and much more telling *informal* qualifications for the presidency—as you will soon see.

---

[4]Article II, Section 1, Clause 1.

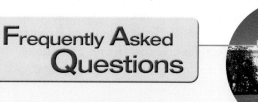

Frequently Asked Questions

The Presidency

What role should the First Lady play?
Historically, each "first spouse" has shaped her own answer to this question. Almost certainly, one day a "first spouse" will provide *his* answer, too. Some presidential wives have been quite visible, and they have significantly influenced the way in which their husbands conducted the presidency—among them, Dolley Madison, Edith Wilson, and Eleanor Roosevelt. Others have preferred to remain in the background, such as Bess Truman and Pat Nixon. Some, like Lady Bird Johnson, Betty Ford, and Rosalynn Carter, devoted themselves to projects of special interest to them.

Hillary Rodham Clinton was for eight years a close and influential advisor to her husband. Laura Bush, on the other hand, has preferred a lower profile, purposely refusing to become involved in policy matters. A one-time school librarian, she has a keen interest in promoting reading and in celebrating books and their authors.

Any Questions?
What would you like to know about the presidency? Brainstorm two new questions and exchange them with a classmate. What did you learn?

The President's Term

The Framers considered a number of different limits on the length of the presidential term. Most of their debate centered on a four-year term, with the President eligible for reelection, versus a single six-year or seven-year term. They finally settled on a four-year term.[4] They agreed, as Alexander Hamilton wrote in *The Federalist* No. 71, that four years was a long enough period for a President to have gained experience, demonstrated his abilities, and established stable policies.

Until 1951, the Constitution placed no limit on the number of terms a President might serve. Several Presidents, beginning with George Washington, refused to seek more than two terms, however. Soon, the "no-third-term tradition" became an unwritten rule.

Franklin D. Roosevelt broke the tradition by seeking and winning a third term in 1940, and then a fourth in 1944. To prevent future Presidents from following this precedent, the 22nd Amendment made the unwritten custom limiting presidential terms a part of the written Constitution. This amendment, adopted in 1951, reads in part:

FROM THE Constitution " *No person shall be elected to the office of the President more than twice, and no person who has held the office of President, or acted as President, for more than two years of a term to which some other person was elected President shall be elected to the office of the President more than once.* "
—22nd Amendment

As a general rule, then, each President may now serve a maximum of two full terms—eight years—in office. A President who succeeds to the office after the midpoint in a term could possibly serve for more than eight years. In that circumstance, the President may finish out the predecessor's term and then seek two full terms of his or her own. However, no President may serve more than 10 years in the office.

Many people, including Presidents Truman, Eisenhower, and Reagan, have called for the repeal of the 22nd Amendment and its limit on presidential

▲ **Benefits of the Presidency** President Jimmy Carter and his wife, Rosalynn, enjoying the White House and its grounds.

service. They argue that the two-term rule is undemocratic because it places an arbitrary limit on the right of the people to decide who should be President. Some critics also say that the amendment undercuts the authority of a two-term President, especially in the latter part of his second term. Supporters of the amendment defend it as a reasonable safeguard against "executive tyranny."

Several Presidents have urged a single six-year term. They and others have argued that a single, nonrenewable term would free a President from the pressures of a campaign for a second term—and so would allow the chief executive to focus on the pressing demands of the office.

Pay and Benefits

Congress determines the President's salary. It can neither be increased nor decreased during a presidential term.[5] The President's pay was first set at $25,000 a year, in 1789. It is now $400,000 a year. Congress set that figure in 1999, and it became effective on January 20, 2001.

Congress has also provided the President with a $50,000-a-year expense allowance. That money may be spent however the President chooses; it is, in effect, a part of his pay, and it is taxed as part of his income.

The Constitution forbids the President "any other emolument from the United States, or any of them." This clause does not prevent the President from being provided with a great many benefits, however. These include the White House, a magnificent 132-room mansion set on an 18.3-acre estate in the heart of the nation's capital; a sizable suite of offices and a large staff; a fleet of automobiles, the lavishly fitted *Air Force One* and several other planes and helicopters; Camp David, the resort hideaway in the Catoctin Mountains in Maryland; the finest medical, dental, and other health care available; generous travel and entertainment funds; and many other fringe benefits.

---

[5]Article II, Section 1, Clause 7. At Philadelphia, Benjamin Franklin argued that, as money and power might corrupt a man, the President ought to receive nothing beyond his expenses; his suggestion was not put to a vote at the Convention.

Section 1 Assessment

Standards Monitoring *Online*
For: Self-quiz with vocabulary practice
Web Code: mqa-4131

Key Terms and Main Ideas

1. Explain the President's role as **chief of state.**
2. How does the President function as **chief of party** and **chief citizen?**
3. What are the three formal qualifications necessary to become President?
4. What is the purpose of the 22nd Amendment?

Critical Thinking

5. **Synthesizing Information** Admiral George Dewey once said, "the office of President is not such a very difficult one to fill, his duties being mainly to execute the laws of Congress." Do you agree or disagree with this statement? Explain why.
6. **Demonstrating Reasoned Judgment** List five informal qualifications you think one should have in order to be seriously considered for the presidency. Explain your choices.
7. **Making Decisions** At $400,000 a year, the President's salary is far more than that of the average citizen, yet less than the yearly income of many wealthy Americans. Do you think the President is fairly compensated? Why or why not?

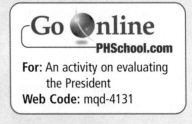

Go Online
PHSchool.com

For: An activity on evaluating the President
Web Code: mqd-4131

2 Presidential Succession and the Vice Presidency

Section Preview

OBJECTIVES

1. **Explain** how the Constitution provides for presidential succession.
2. **Understand** the constitutional provisions relating to presidential disability.
3. **Describe** the role of the Vice President.

WHY IT MATTERS

Should the President die, be removed from office, or resign, the Vice President succeeds to the presidency. The Vice President is, indeed, just a heartbeat away from the President.

POLITICAL DICTIONARY

★ **presidential succession**
★ **Presidential Succession Act of 1947**
★ **balance the ticket**

Consider these facts. Forty-six men have served as Vice President.[7] Fourteen of them later reached the White House—most recently, George H. W. Bush in 1989. Indeed, five of our last eleven Presidents were once Vice President.

The Constitution and Succession

Presidential succession is the scheme by which a presidential vacancy is filled. If a President dies, resigns, or is removed from office by impeachment, the Vice President succeeds to the office.

Originally, the Constitution did not provide for the succession of the Vice President. Rather, it declared that "the powers and duties" of the office—not the office itself—were to "devolve on [transfer to] the Vice President."[8]

In practice the Vice President did succeed to the office when it became vacant. Vice President John Tyler set this precedent in 1841 when he succeeded President William Henry Harrison, who died of pneumonia just one month after taking office. What had been practice became a part of the written Constitution with the adoption of the 25th Amendment in 1967:

 FROM THE Constitution *"In case of the removal of the President from office or of his death or resignation, the Vice President shall become President. "*

—25th Amendment, Section 1

---

[7]No woman has yet held the office, but nothing in the Constitution bars that possibility.
[8]Article II, Section 1, Clause 6.

Presidential Succession

1	Vice President
2	Speaker of the House
3	President *pro tempore* of the Senate
4	Secretary of State
5	Secretary of the Treasury
6	Secretary of Defense
7	Attorney General
8	Secretary of the Interior
9	Secretary of Agriculture
10	Secretary of Commerce
11	Secretary of Labor
12	Secretary of Health and Human Services
13	Secretary of Housing and Urban Development
14	Secretary of Transportation
15	Secretary of Energy
16	Secretary of Education
17	Secretary of Veterans Affairs
18	Secretary of Homeland Security

Interpreting Charts The Vice President is first in line to succeed to the presidency should the office become vacant. Such was the case when Lyndon Johnson took the oath of office aboard *Air Force One* after the assassination of President Kennedy in 1963. **How does the chart demonstrate the importance of the position of Speaker of the House?** H-SS 12.4.1

Congress fixes the order of succession following the Vice President.[9] The present law on the matter is the **Presidential Succession Act of 1947.** By its terms, the Speaker of the House and then the President *pro tem* of the Senate are next in line. They are followed, in turn, by the secretary of state and then by each of the other 14 heads of the Cabinet departments, in order of precedence—the order in which the offices were created by Congress.[10]

Presidential Disability

Before the passage of the 25th Amendment, there were serious gaps in the arrangement for presidential succession. Neither the Constitution nor Congress had made any provision for deciding when a President was disabled. Nor was there anything to indicate by whom such a decision was to be made.

For nearly 180 years, then, the nation played with fate. President Eisenhower suffered three serious but temporary illnesses while in office: a heart attack in 1955, ileitis in 1956,

and a mild stroke in 1957. Two other Presidents were disabled for much longer periods. James Garfield lingered for 80 days before he died from an assassin's bullet in 1881. Woodrow Wilson suffered a paralytic stroke in 1919 and was an invalid for the rest of his second term. He was so ill that he could not meet with his Cabinet for seven months after his stroke.

Sections 3 and 4 of the 25th Amendment fill the disability gap, and in detail. The Vice President is to become Acting President if (1) the President informs Congress, in writing, "that he is unable to discharge the powers and duties of his office," or (2) the Vice President and a majority of the members of the Cabinet inform

---

[9]Article II, Section 1, Clause 6. On removal of the President by impeachment, see Chapter 11, pages 311–313.

[10]A Cabinet member is to serve only until a Speaker or a president *pro tem* is available and qualified. Notice that the 25th Amendment also provides for the filling of any vacancy in the vice presidency. In effect, that provision makes the Presidential Succession Act a law with little real significance—except in the highly unlikely event of simultaneous vacancies in the presidency and vice presidency.

The Enduring *Constitution*

Analysis Skills CS1, CS2, HI1

Changes in the Presidency

| | 1800 | | 1900 |

Over more than two centuries now, many events have contributed to the ever-evolving shape of the presidential office. The most important of them are displayed in this time line.

Go Online
PHSchool.com
Use Web Code mqp-4137 to access an interactive time line.

1796 George Washington does not run for a third term, setting the precedent of a two-term limit.

1800 Political parties begin to transform the electoral college system by choosing elector candidates.

1804 12th Amendment requires separate ballots for President and Vice President.

1831 Anti-Masonic Party holds first national convention to nominate a presidential candidate.

1841 After William Henry Harrison dies in office, Vice Pesident John Tyler sets a precedent by succeeding to the presidency.

1905 Wisconsin adopts the nation's first presidential primary law.

Congress, in writing, that the President is so incapacitated.[11]

In either case, the President may resume the powers and duties of the office by informing Congress that no inability exists. However, the Vice President and a majority of the Cabinet may challenge the President on this score. If they do, Congress then has 21 days in which to decide the matter.

To this point, the disability provisions of the 25th Amendment have come into play twice. On the first occasion, in 1985, Ronald Reagan transferred the powers of the presidency to Vice President George H.W. Bush for a period of nearly eight hours, while surgeons removed a tumor from Mr. Reagan's large intestine. And, in 2002, George W. Bush conveyed his powers to Vice President Dick Cheney for two hours, while Mr. Bush was anesthetized during a routine medical procedure.

---

[11]The 25th Amendment gives this authority to the Vice President and the Cabinet or to "such other body as Congress may by law provide." To date, no "such other body" has been established.

The Vice Presidency

"I am Vice President. In this I am nothing, but I may be everything." So said John Adams, the nation's first Vice President. Those words could have been repeated, very appropriately, by each of the 45 Vice Presidents who have followed him in that office.

Importance of the Office

The Constitution pays little attention to the office of the Vice President. It assigns the position only two formal duties: (1) to preside over the Senate[12] and (2) to help decide the question of presidential disability.[13] Beyond those duties, the Constitution makes the Vice President a "President-in-waiting."

Through much of the nation's history, in fact, the vice presidency was treated as an office of little real consequence and, often, as the butt of jokes. Indeed, many Vice Presidents themselves have

---

[12]Article I, Section 3, Clause 4; see Chapter 12, page 323.
[13]25th Amendment, Sections 3 and 4.

1944 FDR wins a fourth term; Congress later acts (1947) to limit a President to two terms in office (22nd Amendment, ratified in 1951).

1947 Presidential Succession Act lists officials who would succeed to the presidency after the Vice President.

1967 25th Amendment sets up procedures to follow when a President is disabled or vice presidency is vacant.

1985 Disability provision of the 25th Amendment first used when Vice President Bush becomes Acting President while President Reagan is in surgery.

1925   **1950**   **1975**   **2000**

1933 20th Amendment moves President's inauguration from March to January.

The Inaugural Ball 1957

1973 President Nixon, following the 25th Amendment, nominates Gerald Ford to replace Vice President Agnew, who had resigned.

1974 The 25th Amendment is invoked again as President Ford nominates Nelson Rockefeller as his successor in the vice presidency.

2000 Supreme Court finds vote recount in Florida unconstitutional, and so effectively decides the presidential election. (*Bush* v. *Gore*)

Analyzing Time Lines

1. Which amendment deals with a vacancy in the office of Vice President? When and why was this provision first used?
2. For what reason do you think the 20th Amendment was passed?

It worries me that he just wants to be vice president when he grows up.

Interpreting Political Cartoons *What does the cartoon suggest about the still all-too-common perception of the vice presidency?*

Vice Presidents Who Succeeded to the Presidency

Successor	Reason for Succession
John Tyler	Death (pneumonia) of William Henry Harrison, April 4, 1841
Millard Fillmore	Death (gastroenteritis) of Zachary Taylor, July 9, 1850
Andrew Johnson	Death (assassination) of Abraham Lincoln, April 15, 1865
Chester A. Arthur	Death (assassination) of James A. Garfield, September 19, 1881
Theodore Roosevelt	Death (assassination) of William McKinley, September 14, 1901
Calvin Coolidge	Death (undisclosed illness) of Warren G. Harding, August 2, 1923
Harry S Truman	Death (cerebral hemorrhage) of Franklin D. Roosevelt, April 12, 1945
Lyndon B. Johnson	Death (assassination) of John F. Kennedy, November 22, 1963
Gerald R. Ford	Resignation of Richard M. Nixon, August 9, 1974

Interpreting Tables Eight Presidents have died in office, and one was forced to resign. In each case, the Vice President succeeded to the office. *What circumstances, other than the death or resignation of the President, may lead to the Vice President succeeding to the presidency?*

had a hand in this. John Adams described his post as "the most insignificant office that ever the invention of man contrived or his imagination conceived." Thomas Jefferson, who followed him, found the office "honorable and easy" and "tranquil and unoffending."

Theodore Roosevelt, who reached the White House from the vice presidency in 1901, was annoyed by the tinkling of the prisms of a chandelier in the presidential study. He ordered it removed, saying: "Take it to the office of the Vice President. He doesn't have anything to do. It will keep him awake." The fixture has been in the Vice President's office just off the Senate floor ever since.

John Nance Garner, who served for two terms as Franklin D. Roosevelt's Vice President (1933–1941), once declared: "The vice presidency isn't worth a warm pitcher of spit." Alben Barkley, who served during Harry Truman's second term, often told the story of a woman who had two sons. One of them, Barkley said, went away to sea and the other one became Vice President, "and neither of them was ever heard from again."

Despite these and a great many other unkind comments, the office is clearly an important one. Its occupant is literally "only a heartbeat away from the presidency." Remember, eight Presidents have died in office, and one, Richard M. Nixon, was forced to resign.

Much of the blame for the low status of the vice presidency can be laid on the two major parties and the way they choose their candidates for the office. Traditionally, each national convention names the hand-picked choice of its presidential candidate. Usually, the presidential candidate picks someone who will **"balance the ticket."** That is, the presidential candidate chooses a running mate who can strengthen his chance of being elected by virtue of certain ideological, geographic, racial, ethnic, gender, or other characteristics. In short, fate—presidential succession—does not very often have a high priority in the vice presidential candidate selection process.

---

[14] John C. Calhoun resigned to become a senator from South Carolina in 1832. Spiro T. Agnew resigned in 1973, after a conviction for income tax evasion and in the face of other charges. The seven who died in office were: George Clinton (1812), Elbridge Gerry (1814), William R. King (1853), Henry Wilson (1875), Thomas A. Hendricks (1885), Garret A. Hobart (1899), and James S. Sherman (1912).

Vice Presidential Vacancy

The vice presidency has been vacant 18 times thus far: nine times by succession to the presidency, twice by resignation, and seven times by death.[14] Yet, not until 1967 and the 25th Amendment did the Constitution deal with the matter. The amendment provides, in part:

FROM THE Constitution *“Whenever there is a vacancy in the office of the Vice President, the President shall nominate a Vice President who shall take office upon confirmation by a majority vote of both Houses of Congress.”*
—25th Amendment, Section 2

This provision was first implemented in 1973. In that year, President Richard Nixon selected and Congress confirmed Gerald R. Ford to succeed Spiro Agnew as Vice President. It came into play again in 1974 when, following Mr. Nixon's resignation, President Ford named and Congress approved Nelson Rockefeller.

The Vice President Today

Vice President Dick Cheney is widely seen as the most influential Vice President in the nation's history. He came to the office with an impressive public resumé, and he works very closely with President George W. Bush. Mr. Cheney was President Gerald Ford's White House Chief of Staff (1975–1977), a member of the House (from Wyoming, 1979–1989) and one of the

▲ *An Active Vice President* Vice President Dick Cheney (right) meets with Mexican President Vicente Fox. **H-SS 12.4.1**

leaders of the GOP in that body, and later Secretary of Defense in the administration of President George H.W. Bush (1989–1993).

Still, even with the elevation of the office in recent years, no President has been willing to make his Vice President a true "Assistant President." The major reason: Of all the President's official family, only the Vice President is not subject to the ultimate discipline of removal from office by the President. No matter what the circumstances, the President cannot fire the Vice President.

Section 2 Assessment

Key Terms and Main Ideas

1. What is the purpose of the **Presidential Succession Act of 1947**?
2. How is presidential disability to be determined?
3. Why are vice presidential candidates often chosen to **balance the ticket**?
4. **(a)** What official duties does the Constitution assign to the Vice President? **(b)** How has the role of the Vice President changed in recent years?

Critical Thinking

5. **Formulating Questions** Suppose you have just been offered the vice-presidential nomination. Make a list of questions that will help you decide whether to accept or reject the offer.

Standards Monitoring *Online*
For: Self-quiz with vocabulary practice
Web Code: mqa-4132

6. **Predicting Consequences** You have read that no matter what the circumstances, the President cannot fire the Vice President. **(a)** Why is this the case? **(b)** What might be the consequences if this were not the case?

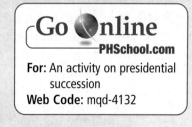
Go Online PHSchool.com
For: An activity on presidential succession
Web Code: mqd-4132

Choosing the Vice President

Analysis Skills HR4, HI3

How many of the nation's Vice Presidents can you name? For many political figures, the vice presidency has been a forgettable final stop in their careers. Eminent historian John A. Garraty argues that the method for selecting the Vice President is illogical and undemocratic, and has led to the office's unimpressive history.

California Ronald Reagan chose Texan George Bush as his running mate in 1980, thus geographically "balancing the ticket."

When the Founding Fathers created the office of president . . . they had little to say about the vice presidency. . . . They saw the vice president as a kind of understudy . . . in case the star should, as the Constitution explains, die, become incapacitated, resign, or be found guilty of treason, bribery, or "other high Crimes and Misdemeanors." . . .

Yet time after time, both parties [have] selected their vice-presidential candidates with little or no thought of how effective they would be should the single heart between them and the White House cease to beat. Preserving party unity and adding strength to the ticket in a particular state or region . . . , not the ability of the person selected, continued to be the determining factors in nearly every case. Still more disturbing, since television and the increase in the number of presidential primaries have diminished the role of national conventions in the selection of candidates, the choice of a running mate has become a prerogative of the person who wins the presidential nomination.

Presidential candidates have nearly always had a hand in choosing their running mates. But until the decline of the conventions' importance, they had to give some thought to how the delegates would react to their selection. . . .

Leaving the choice to the head of the ticket has not changed the reasons particular candidates are chosen. But despite all their hoopla and sordid dealing, the old-fashioned nominating conventions gave substance to the idea that the people, through their chosen delegates, were deciding who the party standard-bearers should be.

The primary system is undoubtedly a more effective way of discovering which candidates for president the voters prefer. The primaries practically compel candidates to describe what they intend to do if nominated, but they studiously avoid committing themselves as to whom they want as running mates. And there are no vice-presidential primaries.

Given the frequency with which fate has turned vice presidents into instant presidents, this is disturbing. That presidents should be able to pick their successors is undemocratic. It is also illogical. Since they must be dead, incompetent, or disgraced before the occasion can arise, they are the last persons who should have that power.

Analyzing Primary Sources

1. According to Garraty, for what reasons are most Vice Presidents selected?
2. Why, according to Garraty, has the growth of presidential primaries made the selection of the Vice President less democratic?
3. What positive aspect of the primary system does Professor Garraty describe?

Presidential Selection: The Framers' Plan

Section Preview

OBJECTIVES

1. **Explain** the Framers' original provisions for choosing the President.
2. **Outline** how the rise of political parties changed the original process set out in the Constitution.

WHY IT MATTERS

Selecting the President is a complex process that many Americans do not fully grasp. Understanding the Framers' plan for choosing the President will help you understand this complicated process.

POLITICAL DICTIONARY

★ **presidential electors**
★ **electoral votes**
★ **electoral college**

In formal terms, the President is chosen according to the provisions of the Constitution.[15] In practice, however, the President is elected through an altogether extraordinary process that is not very well understood by most Americans. That process is a combination of constitutional provisions, State and federal laws, and, in largest measure, a number of practices born of the nation's political parties. To make sense of this very complex system, you must first understand what the Framers had in mind when they designed the presidential election process.

Original Provisions

The Framers gave more time to the method for choosing the President than to any other matter. It was, said James Wilson of Pennsylvania, "the most difficult of all on which we have had to decide." The difficulty arose largely because most of the Framers were against selecting the President by either of the obvious ways: by Congress or by a direct vote of the people.

Early in the Convention, most of the delegates favored selection by Congress. Later, nearly all delegates came to believe that congressional selection would, as Alexander Hamilton said, put the President "too much under the legislative thumb."

Only a few of the Framers favored choosing the President by popular vote. Nearly all agreed that such a process would lead to "tumult and disorder." Most delegates felt, too, that the people, scattered over so wide an area, could not possibly know enough about the available candidates to make wise, informed choices. George Mason of Virginia spoke for most of his colleagues at the convention: "The extent of the Country renders it impossible that the people can have the requisite capacity to judge of the respective pretensions of the Candidates."

After weeks of debate, the Framers finally agreed on a plan first put forward by Hamilton. Under it, the President and Vice President were to be chosen by a special body of **presidential electors**. These electors would each cast two **electoral votes**, each for a different candidate. The candidate with the most votes would become President. The person with the second

▲ George Washington's inauguration was commemorated by objects such as these. The brass coat buttons are precursors of today's campaign buttons.

---

[15]The Constitution deals with the process of presidential selection in several places: Article II, Section 1, Clauses 2, 3, and 4, and the 12th, 20th, and 23rd Amendments.

The Framers' Plan for the Electoral College

1. Each State would have as many presidential electors as it has senators and representatives in Congress.

2. These electors would be chosen in each State in a manner the State legislature directed.

3. The electors, meeting in their own States, would each cast two votes—each for a different person for President.

4. These electoral votes from the States would be opened and counted before a joint session of Congress.

5. The person receiving the largest number of electoral votes, provided that total was a majority of all the electors, would become President.

6. The person with the second highest number of electoral votes would become Vice President.

7. If a tie occurred, or if no one received the votes of a majority of the electors, the President would be chosen by the House of Representatives, voting by States.

8. If a tie occurred for the second spot, the Vice President would be chosen by the Senate.

Interpreting Charts The Framers' Plan for the electoral college provided for a group of presidential electors to choose the President. **How was the Vice President to be chosen?** H-SS 12.6.2

most votes would become Vice President. The chart above details the Framers' plan.[16]

The Framers intended the electors to be "the most enlightened and respectable citizens" from each State. They were to be "free agents" in choosing the people best qualified to fill the nation's two highest offices.

The Rise of Parties

The **electoral college,** then, is the group of people (electors) chosen from each State and the District of Columbia to formally select the President and Vice President. The original version of the electoral college worked as the Framers intended only as long as George Washington was willing to seek and hold the presidency. He did so twice, and was unanimously elected President, in 1789 and again in 1792.

Flaws began to appear in the system in 1796, however, with the rise of political parties. John Adams, the Federalist candidate, was elected to the presidency. Thomas Jefferson, an arch-rival and Democratic-Republican, lost to Adams by just three votes in the electoral balloting. Jefferson then became Adams' Vice President.

The Election of 1800

The system broke down in the election of 1800. By then there were two well-defined parties: the Federalists, led by Adams and Hamilton, and the Democratic-Republicans, headed by Jefferson. Each of these parties nominated presidential and vice-presidential candidates. They also nominated candidates to serve as presidential electors in the several States. Those elector-candidates were picked with the clear understanding that, if elected, they would vote for their party's presidential and vice-presidential nominees.

---

[16]Remember, these were the original provisions, in Article II, Sections 2, 3, and 4; they were modified by the 12th Amendment.

Elections Leading to the 12th Amendment

1789 and 1792 George Washington is unanimously elected President.

1796 John Adams (Federalist) is elected President. Thomas Jefferson (Democratic-Republican), losing to Adams by three electoral votes, becomes Vice President.

1800 After 36 ballots, the House finally breaks the tie between Jefferson and Aaron Burr in 1801. Jefferson becomes President, Burr Vice President.

1804 The 12th Amendment separates the presidential and vice presidential choices in the electoral college and almost certainly guarantees that the President and Vice President will be of the same party.

Interpreting Charts After the elections of 1789 and 1792, the Framers' plan for the electoral college broke down. **How did the election of 1800 show the need for the 12th Amendment?** H-SS 12.6.2

Each of the 73 Democratic-Republicans who won posts as electors voted for his party's nominees: Jefferson and Aaron Burr. In doing so, they produced a tie for the presidency. Remember that the Constitution gave each elector two votes, each to be cast for a different person, but each to be cast for someone as President. Popular opinion clearly favored Jefferson for the presidency, and the party had intended Burr for the vice presidency. Still, in 1801, the House of Representatives had to take 36 separate ballots before it finally chose Jefferson.

The spectacular election of 1800 marked the introduction of three new elements into the process of selecting a President: (1) party nominations for the presidency and vice presidency, (2) the nomination of candidates for presidential electors pledged to vote for their party's presidential ticket, and (3) the automatic casting of the electoral votes in line with those pledges. Gone forever was the notion that the electors would act as "free agents" in the process.

The 12th Amendment

The election of 1800 produced another notable result: the 12th Amendment. This amendment was added to the Constitution in 1804 to make certain there would never be another such fiasco. The amendment is lengthy, but it made only one major change in the electoral college system. It separated the presidential and vice-presidential elections: "The Electors . . . shall name in their ballots the person voted for as President, and in distinct ballots the person voted for as Vice-President. . . ."[17]

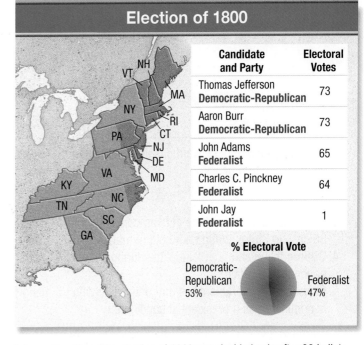

Election of 1800

Candidate and Party	Electoral Votes
Thomas Jefferson Democratic-Republican	73
Aaron Burr Democratic-Republican	73
John Adams Federalist	65
Charles C. Pinckney Federalist	64
John Jay Federalist	1

% Electoral Vote

Democratic-Republican 53% Federalist 47%

Interpreting Maps The election of 1800 was decided only after 36 ballots in the House of Representatives. *How does the map show the political divisions in the country in 1800?*

With the appearance of parties, the election of 1800, and the 12th Amendment, the constitutional framework was laid for the presidential selection system as it exists today. That system is, indeed, a far cry from what was agreed to in 1787, as you will see in the sections ahead.

[17]Not only does the amendment mean there cannot be a repeat of the circumstances that produced a tie in 1800, it almost certainly guarantees that the President and Vice President will be of the same party.

Section 3 Assessment

Key Terms and Main Ideas

1. Why were most of the Framers opposed to choosing the President by popular vote? By Congress?
2. (a) Outline the original provisions for the **electoral college.** (b) How did the Framers expect the **presidential electors** to vote?
3. In what three ways did the presidential election process change as a result of the election of 1800?

Critical Thinking

4. **Recognizing Ideologies** The Framers intended the presidential electors to be "the most enlightened and respectable

Standards Monitoring *Online*
For: Self-quiz with vocabulary practice
Web Code: mqa-4133

citizens" in each State. What does this statement suggest about their definition of good citizenship?
5. **Recognizing Cause and Effect** How did the rise of political parties change the way the electoral college functions?

Go Online
PHSchool.com

For: An activity on the electoral college
Web Code: mqd-4133

Presidential Nominations

The Constitution makes no provision for the nomination of candidates for the presidency. Rather, as you have just seen, the Framers designed a system in which presidential electors would, out of their own knowledge, select the "wisest and best man" to be President. Later, the rise of parties altered that system dramatically.

The Role of Conventions

The first method the parties developed to nominate their presidential candidates was the congressional caucus. As you may recall from Chapter 7, that method was regularly used in the elections of 1800 to 1824. However, the closed, nonrepresentative character of this system led to its downfall in the mid-1820s. For the election of 1832, both major parties turned to the national convention as their nominating device, and it has continued to serve them ever since.

Convention Arrangements

Not only does the Constitution say nothing about presidential nominations; there is, as well, almost no federal or State statutory law on the matter. The convention system has been built almost entirely by the two major parties in American politics.

In both parties, the national committee makes the arrangements for the party's convention. The committee sets the date and picks the place

for that meeting. Over recent elections, the party out of power has held its convention first, usually in July, and the President's party has met some weeks later, in August.

Many of the nation's largest cities bid for the honor—and the financial return to local business—of hosting a convention. The map on the next page shows where the major parties' conventions have been held over time. As you can see, the Democrats picked Boston for their quadrennial meeting in 2004, and the Republicans opted for New York City.

The Apportionment of Delegates

With the date and the location set, the national committee issues its "call" for the convention. That formal announcement names the time and place. It also tells the party's organization in each State how many delegates it may send to the national gathering.

By tradition, both parties give each State party a certain number of delegates based on that State's electoral vote. Over the past several conventions, both parties have developed complicated formulas that also award bonus delegates to those States that have supported the party's candidates in recent elections.

For 2004, the Republicans' formula produced a convention of 2,509 delegates. The Democrats' more complex plan called for 4,353. Given

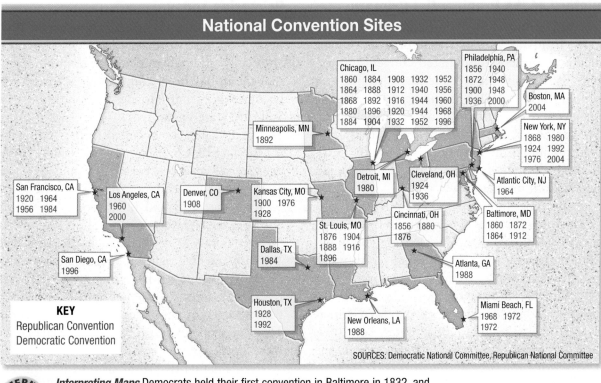

National Convention Sites

Philadelphia, PA
1856 1940
1872 1948
1900 1948
1936 2000

Boston, MA
2004

Chicago, IL
1860 1884 1908 1932 1952
1864 1888 1912 1940 1956
1868 1892 1916 1944 1960
1880 1896 1920 1944 1968
1884 1904 1932 1952 1996

New York, NY
1868 1980
1924 1992
1976 2004

Minneapolis, MN
1892

Detroit, MI
1980

Cleveland, OH
1924
1936

Atlantic City, NJ
1964

San Francisco, CA
1920 1964
1956 1984

Los Angeles, CA
1960
2000

Denver, CO
1908

Kansas City, MO
1900 1976
1928

St. Louis, MO
1876 1904
1888 1916
1896

Cincinnati, OH
1856 1880
1876

Baltimore, MD
1860 1872
1864 1912

San Diego, CA
1996

Dallas, TX
1984

Atlanta, GA
1988

Houston, TX
1928
1992

New Orleans, LA
1988

Miami Beach, FL
1968 1972
1972

KEY
Republican Convention
Democratic Convention

SOURCES: Democratic National Committee, Republican National Committee

Interpreting Maps Democrats held their first convention in Baltimore in 1832, and met there through 1852. The Republicans held their first convention in Philadelphia in 1856. ***How can you explain the popularity of such cities as Chicago, New York, and Philadelphia as convention sites?***

those large numbers, it should be fairly clear that neither party's national convention can be called "a deliberative body" able to give each of its decisions thoughtful consideration.

Selection of Delegates

There are really *two* campaigns for the presidency. One is the contest between the Republican and Democratic candidates in the fall. The other is earlier and quite different. It takes place *within* each party: the struggle for convention delegates.

State laws and/or party rules fix the procedures for picking delegates in each State. That fact is a reflection of federalism, and it has produced a jigsaw puzzle of presidential primaries, conventions, and caucuses among the 50 States.

To a large extent, the Republican Party leaves the matter of delegate selection to its State organizations and to State law. The Democratic Party, on the other hand, has adopted several national rules to govern the process. Most of those rules reflect attempts to broaden participation in the delegate selection process, especially by the young, African Americans, other minorities, and women.

Presidential Primaries

More than three fourths of all the delegates to both parties' conventions come from States that hold presidential primaries. Many of those primaries are major media events. Serious contenders in both parties must make the best possible showing in at least most of them.

Depending on the State, a **presidential primary** is an election in which a party's voters (1) choose some or all of a State party organization's delegates to their party's national convention, and/or (2) express a preference among various contenders for their party's presidential nomination.

---

[18]Both parties allot delegates to the District of Columbia, Puerto Rico, the Virgin Islands, Guam, and American Samoa; the Democrats also provide for delegates who represent Democrats Abroad. The Democratic convention also includes a large number of "superdelegates"—mostly party officers and Democrats who hold major elective offices. They are automatically members of their respective State delegations. More than 750 superdelegates were seated at the 2004 Democratic convention; their number included all of the members of the Democratic National Committee, all Democratic State governors, and nearly all of the Democratic members of the House and Senate.

History of the Presidential Primary

The presidential primary first appeared in the early 1900s as part of the reform movement aimed at the boss-dominated convention system. Wisconsin passed the first presidential primary law in 1905, providing for the popular election of national convention delegates. Several States soon followed that lead, and Oregon added the preference feature in 1910. By 1916 nearly half the States had adopted presidential primary laws.

For a time, the primary system fell into disfavor so that by 1968, primaries were found in only 16 States and the District of Columbia. Efforts to reform the national convention process, especially in the Democratic Party, reversed that downward trend in the 1970s, however. Some form of the presidential primary can now be found in most States. For 2004, the device was in place in 36 States, and in the District of Columbia and Puerto Rico.[18]

---

[18]Presidential primaries were not held in 14 States: Alaska, Colorado, Hawaii, Idaho, Iowa, Maine, Michigan, Minnesota, Nevada, New Mexico, North Carolina, North Dakota, Washington, and Wyoming. In some States, the law permits but does not require a major party to hold a primary. In South Carolina the presidential primary is a product of party rules, not State law.

◀ *Campaigning Then and Now*
Campaigning for the presidency has changed dramatically since Harry S Truman's 1948 whistle-stop train tours were one of the best ways to reach voters. Today's candidates make wide use of the Internet to do so. **H-SS 12.8.2**

Primaries Today

Again, a presidential primary is either or both of two things: a delegate-selection process and/or a candidate preference election. Once that much has been said, however, the system becomes very hard to describe, except on a State-by-State basis.

The difficulty comes largely from two sources: (1) the fact that in each State the details of the delegate-selection process are determined by that State's own law—and those details vary from one State to the next, and (2) the ongoing reform efforts in the Democratic Party. Since 1968, when the Democrats were shattered by disputes over Vietnam and civil rights policies, the Democratic National Committee has written and rewritten the party's rules to promote greater grassroots participation in the delegate-selection process. Those new rules have prompted many changes in most States' election laws.

Even a matter that seems as simple as the date for the primary illustrates the crazy-quilt pattern of State laws. New Hampshire holds the first of the presidential primaries every four years, and it has done so since 1940. New Hampshire guards its first-in-the-nation title with a law that sets the date for its primary as the Tuesday of the week before the date on which any other State schedules its contest. For 2004, the New Hampshire primary was held on January 27, and all of the others were held at various times over the next five months.

Most States prefer an early date, and so the primary schedule has become heavily "front-loaded." More than half of the primaries, including the contests in most of the larger States, now come in March and early April.

Name recognition and money have always been important factors in the presidential primary process, and front-loading has multiplied their significance. Until lately, a candidate who was not very well known nationally could hope to build a following from primary to primary—as, for example, Bill Clinton did in 1992. The process leaves little or no time for that strategy

today, however. Candidates now have to mount (and pay for) campaigns in a number of widely separated States that hold their primaries fairly early and often on the same day or within a few days of one another.

Proportional Representation

Until fairly recently, most primaries were both delegate-selection and preference exercises. Several primaries were also **winner-take-all** contests. That is, the candidate who won the preference vote automatically won the support of all delegates chosen at the primary.

Winner-take-all primaries have now all but disappeared. The Democratic Party rules now prohibit them. Instead, the Democrats have a complex **proportional representation** rule. Any candidate who wins at least 15 percent of the votes cast in a primary gets the number of that State's Democratic convention delegates that corresponds to his or her share of that primary vote. Take, for example, a State that has 40 convention delegates. If a candidate wins 45 percent of the primary vote, he automatically gains the support of at least 18 of the delegates.

Most States had to change their primary laws to account for the Democrats' proportional representation rule. So in many States, Republican delegates are also chosen on a proportional representation basis. Still, a few States do permit winner-take-all primaries, and the Republicans hold them where they can.

The Democrats' proportional representation rule had yet another major impact on the shape of presidential primaries. It led several States—among them Oregon and Wisconsin, the States that had pioneered the presidential primary—to give up the popular selection of delegates.

More than half of the presidential primary States now hold only a preference primary. The delegates themselves are chosen later, at party conventions. In most of these States, the delegates must be picked in line with the results of the preference primary—for example, for the Democrats in 2004, so many delegates for John Kerry, so many for Wesley Clark, so many for Howard Dean, and so on. In some States, however, the preference vote does not govern the choice of the delegates. In those States, the preference primary is often called a "beauty contest."

▲ *Getting a Head Start* Because the New Hampshire primaries are an early indicator of future success, presidential hopefuls spend time and money in New Hampshire early in their candidacies. Here Senator John Kerry (D., Mass.) rallies with supporters in Manchester, New Hampshire, months before the 2004 primary. **H-SS 12.6.2**

Most of the preference contests are also "all-candidate" primaries. That is, they are contests in which all generally recognized contenders for a party's presidential nomination must be listed on that party's preference ballot.

Evaluation of the Primary

No one who surveys the presidential primary system needs to be told that it is complicated, nor that it is filled with confusing variations. Still, these primaries are vital. For half a century now, they have played *the* major part in deciding the presidential nominating contests in both parties—especially the party out of power.

Presidential primaries tend to democratize the delegate-selection process. And, importantly, they force would-be nominees to test their candidacies in actual political combat. For the party out of power, especially, the primaries are often "knock-down, drag-out" battles. Without the unifying force of the President as party leader, several leaders and factions in the party vie with one another, vigorously, for the presidential nomination. Here, a key function of the presidential primary can be seen: the screening out of the lesser possibilities to the point where only one or a few contenders for the nomination remain.

Such hard-fought contests occur but are not common in the party in power. This tends to be true either because the President (1) is himself seeking reelection, or (2) has given his backing to someone he favors for the nomination. In either case the President regularly gets his way.

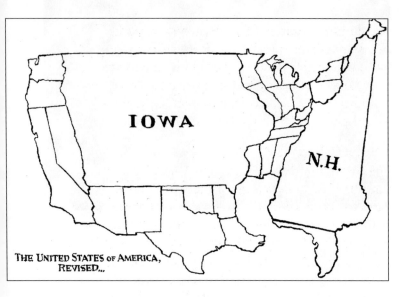

IOWA

N.H.

THE UNITED STATES OF AMERICA, REVISED...

Interpreting Political Cartoons *What does the cartoon suggest about the significance of the Iowa caucuses and the New Hampshire primary?*

There are exceptions, of course. Ronald Reagan made a stiff run at President Ford in the Republican Party in 1976; and Senator Edward Kennedy gave President Carter a real fight in the Democratic Party in 1980. The 2000 election provided another exception: Former Senator Bill Bradley's heated battle with President Clinton's choice for the Democratic nod, Vice President Al Gore.

Reform Proposals

The fact that so many States now hold presidential primaries places great demands on candidates in terms of time, effort, money, scheduling, and fatigue. The primary season also tests the public's endurance.

For these and other reasons, many critics of the current system think that each of the major parties should hold a single, nationwide presidential primary. Some critics would have both parties nominate their presidential candidates in those contests. They would do away with conventions, except perhaps to pick vice-presidential nominees and/or to write platforms.

Other critics favor a series of regional primaries, held at two- or three-week intervals in groups of States across the country. Hope for any of these plans is dim at best—each would require joint action by Congress, the States, and both major parties.

The Caucus-Convention Process

In those States that do not hold presidential primaries, delegates to the national conventions are chosen in a system of caucuses and conventions. The process works basically as described here, although the details differ from State to State.

The party's voters meet in local caucuses, generally at the precinct level. There they choose delegates to a local or district convention, where delegates to the State convention are picked. At the State level, and sometimes in the district conventions, delegates to the national convention are chosen.

The caucus-convention process is the oldest method for picking national convention delegates. Its use has declined significantly over the years, however. In 2004, less than one fourth of all delegates to either party's convention came from those States that still use the caucus-convention process.

The Iowa caucuses generally get the most attention, largely because they are now the first delegate-selection event held in every presidential election season. Iowa purposely schedules the start of its caucus process early. In 2004 the event took place on January 19, five days before New Hampshire held its first-in-the-nation presidential primary.

The National Convention

Once all of the primaries and caucuses have been held and all of the delegates have been chosen, another event looms large. The two major parties hold their **national conventions,** the meetings at which the delegates vote to pick their presidential and vice-presidential candidates.

For a century and more, those gatherings were highly dramatic, often chaotic and even stormy affairs at which, after days of heated bargaining, the party would finally nominate its presidential and vice presidential candidates. Both parties' meetings have become much tamer in recent years—largely because there is now little doubt about who will win the party's grand prize. Regularly, the leading contender has won enough delegates in the primaries and caucuses to lock up the nomination before the convention meets.

Each party's convention remains a major event, nonetheless. Each of them seeks three major goals: (1) naming the party's presidential and vice-presidential candidates, (2) bringing the various factions and the leading personalities in the party together in one place for a common purpose, and (3) adopting the party's **platform**— its formal statement of basic principles, stands on major policy matters, and objectives for the campaign and beyond.

If the meeting is successful, the convention also does several other things. It promotes party unity, mobilizes support for the party ticket, and captures the interest and attention of the country.

The First Two Days

Each party's convention now meets in one or two daily sessions over four days. Each of those sessions is tightly scheduled and closely scripted. In short, they are made for television.

The first day is dedicated to welcoming the delegates and organizi ng the convention, and to dozens of short speeches by an array of party figures. The second day sees a continuing parade of speakers but is highlighted by two major events: the adoption of the party's platform and the delivery of the keynote address.

The platform comes to the convention floor as a report by the committee on platform and resolutions. In fact, it has been drawn up by the party's leadership beforehand. Platform-writing is a fine art. Recall, the platform is a statement of party principles and stands on policy matters. But it is also an important campaign document aimed at appealing to as many people and as many groups as possible. So, both parties tend to produce somewhat generalized comments on some of the hard questions of the day. Platforms are regularly criticized for blandness. Listen to this comment, made by the Republican presidential nominee in 1964:

PRIMARY Sources *"Platforms are written to be ignored and forgotten. . . . Like Jell-O shimmering on a dessert plate, there is usually little substance and nothing you can get your teeth into. "*

—Barry Goldwater

Still, the platforms are important. They *do* set out a number of hard and fast stands in many policy areas. They also reflect the compromise nature of American politics and of the two major parties.

The **keynote address** is usually a barn-burner, delivered by one of the party's most accomplished orators. The keynoter's remarks, like nearly all the speeches the delegates hear, follow a predictable pattern. They glorify the party, its history, its leaders, and its programs, blister the other party, and predict a resounding victory for the party and its candidates in November.

The Last Two Days

The convention turns to its chief task on the third day: the nomination of the party's candidates for President and Vice President. The delegates turn first to the vice-presidential choice. Historically, that task often involved some suspense and a good deal of bargaining among party factions. Nowadays, however, the soon-to-be nominated presidential candidate announces his choice of a running mate before the convention meets—and the delegates ratify that choice with little or no dissent.

The vice-presidential candidate then delivers his or her acceptance speech—another effort to fire up the party faithful and appeal to as many other voters as possible.

The third day's session culminates with the selection of the party's presidential candidate. The names of several contenders may be offered, especially in the party out of power.[19] Once the

---

[19]Most of them have no real chance of becoming the party's nominee, but they are put forward for some other reason. Thus a "favorite son" may be touted because a State delegation wants to honor one of its own.

▲ *A Hard-to-Get Ticket* Each party's convention reaches a climax with the just-nominated presidential candidate's acceptance speech. The holder of this ticket heard John F. Kennedy accept the Democratic Party's nomination at the party's convention in Los Angeles in 1960. **H-SS 12.6.4**

Sound Bites Sound bites are brief, often snappy remarks made by candidates and used by TV news people to help encapsulate the day's events on the campaign trail. As such, they are decried by critics for reducing complex political issues to simplistic slogans.

The length of sound bites has shrunk over the years. According to one study, candidates in 1968 got an average of 42 seconds to make their point on the evening news. By 1992, they were getting just 8.5 seconds. Various remedies have been suggested, such as giving candidates two to five minutes of free air time each night to say their piece. These ideas, however, have usually been deemed impractical.

John Kerry and George W. Bush debate in 2004

Sounds bites can make or break a candidate. "Are you better off today than you were four years ago?" Ronald Reagan asked during the 1980 presidential debate, crystallizing widespread voter dissatisfaction with Jimmy Carter. Similarly, in 1988, George H. W. Bush galvanized a Republican majority when he said, "Read my lips: No new taxes!"

Go Online
PHSchool.com
Use Web Code mqd-4138 to find out more about sound bites and political campaigns and for help in answering the following question: *What is the danger of relying on sound bites for information?*

nominating (and several seconding) speeches are made, the delegates vote. The convention secretary calls the States in alphabetical order, and the chair of each State delegation announces how that delegation's votes are cast. Each complete roll call is known as a ballot, and the balloting continues until one of the contenders wins a majority of the delegates' votes.

Most often, the first ballot produces a winner. Over the now 27 conventions held by each party from 1900 through 2004, the Republicans made a first ballot choice 23 times and the Democrats 22 times. Indeed, the GOP has not had to take a second ballot since 1948, and the Democrats not since 1952.[20]

With its candidates named, the convention comes to the final major item on its agenda: the presidential candidate's acceptance speech. That speech caps the convention and launches the general election campaign.

Who Is Nominated?

If an incumbent President wants another term, the convention's choice of a nominee is easy. The President is almost certain to get the nomination, and usually with no real opposition from within the party. The President's advantages are immense: the majesty and publicity of the office and close control of the party's machinery.[21]

When the President is not in the field, up to a dozen or so contenders may surface in the preconvention period. At most, two or three of them may survive to contest the prize at the convention.

Political Experience

Who among the contenders will win the nomination? The historical record argues this answer: the one who is, in the jargon of politics, the most available—that is, the most electable. Conventions want to pick candidates who can win, those with the broadest possible appeal within the party and to the electorate.

Most presidential candidates come to their nominations with substantial and well-known records in public office. But those records have to be free of controversies that could have antagonized important elements within the party or among the voting public. Generally, presidential candidates have served in elective office, where they have shown vote-getting ability. Seldom does a candidate step from the business world or from the military directly into the role of candidate, as did Wendell Willkie in 1940 or Dwight Eisenhower in 1952.

Historically, the governorships of larger States have produced the largest number of presidential candidacies. Of the 20 men nominated by the two

---

[20] A convention can become deadlocked, unable to make a choice between the top contenders. In that case, a "dark horse"—that is someone who did not seem a likely choice before the convention—may finally emerge as the nominee. The most spectacular deadlock in convention history occurred at the Democratic convention in New York in 1924. That convention took 103 ballots before John W. Davis of West Virginia won the nomination.

[21] In fact, only four sitting Presidents have ever been denied nomination: John Tyler by the Whigs in 1844; Millard Fillmore by the Whigs in 1852; Franklin Pierce by the Democrats in 1856; and Chester Arthur by the Republicans in 1884.

major parties between 1900 and 1956, eleven were either then serving or had once served as a governor.

For a time the Senate became the prime source of major party presidential candidates. In the four elections from 1960 through 1972, each major party nominee had been a senator. None had ever been a governor.

More recently, however, the old pattern has been restored. Jimmy Carter, the former governor of Georgia, was nominated by the Democrats in 1976 and 1980. Ronald Reagan, former governor of California, was the GOP choice in 1980 and again in 1984. The Democrats nominated the governor of Massachusetts, Michael Dukakis, in 1988, and they picked Governor Bill Clinton of Arkansas in 1992 and renominated him in 1996. The Republicans went with then-Governor George W. Bush of Texas in 2000 and stayed with him in 2004.

Other Characteristics

Most leading contenders for presidential nominations have been Protestants. The most notable exceptions, all Democrats and all Catholics, are Alfred E. Smith in 1928, John F. Kennedy in 1960, Eugene McCarthy and Robert F. Kennedy in 1968, Michael Dukakis (Eastern Orthodox) in 1988, and John Kerry in 2004.

Most presidential candidates have come from the larger States. Thus, hopefuls from such pivotal States as New York, Ohio, Illinois, Texas, and California have an advantage.

Television has reshaped this matter over the past several elections, however. The Republicans picked Barry Goldwater of Arizona in 1964 and Bob Dole of Kansas in 1996. And the Democrats nominated George McGovern of South Dakota in 1972, Jimmy Carter of Georgia in 1976, and Bill Clinton of Arkansas in 1992.

Both parties' nominees usually have a pleasant and healthy appearance, seem to be happily married, and have an attractive (and exploitable) family. To this point, only four nominees have been divorced: Adlai Stevenson, the Democratic nominee in 1952 and 1956; Ronald Reagan, the Republican candidate in 1980 and 1984; Bob Dole, the Republicans' choice in 1996; and John Kerry, the Democrats' standard bearer in 2004.

A well-developed speaking ability has always been a plus in American politics. Of course, being able to project well over television has long since become a must, as well.

Neither party has, to this point, seriously considered a woman as its candidate for the presidency—or, until 1984 with the Democratic Party's nomination of Geraldine Ferraro, for the vice presidency. Nor has either party yet nominated a member of any minority group for President, although the Democrats nominated an Orthodox Jew, Senator Joseph Lieberman of Connecticut, for Vice President in 2000.

Section 4 Assessment

Key Terms and Main Ideas

1. What are the two major processes used to select delegates to **national conventions**?
2. How does **proportional representation** differ from the **winner-take-all** system?
3. Why are hard-fought **presidential primaries** fairly common in the party out of power and rare for the President's party?

Critical Thinking

4. **Expressing Problems Clearly** As you have read, some critics of the current primary system favor a series of regional primaries held at two- or three-week intervals. What might be the advantages and disadvantages of such a system?

5. **Demonstrating Reasoned Judgment** Presidential contender Adlai Stevenson once said "The hardest thing about any political campaign is how to win without proving that you are unworthy of winning." What do you think he meant?

Skills for Life

Evaluating Leadership

When you participate in representative government, you choose people to make decisions for you. What kind of person do you want representing you? Do you want someone who is full of new ideas? Who knows how to get things done? Who has experience? Which qualities are most important to you?

In an election, candidates compete to convince you that they have the stuff of leadership. Examine their claims carefully. Otherwise you'll be basing your decisions on criteria such as "She's really cool" or "He looks like my cousin."

Whether you're evaluating a candidate for President of the United States or for student council president, consider these steps:

1. Establish your criteria for evaluating a leader. Most people would agree on certain qualities that make a good leader, such as honesty and commitment to duty. Other characteristics may vary widely. Some jobs demand a person with a great deal of experience. Other positions are less dependent on experience, but require creative ideas. Are you looking for a "hands-on" leader (who personally gets things done) or a skilled manager who inspires others to work productively? Make a list of criteria *you* look for in a leader. The table below lists some possible characteristics.

2. Rate your subject. Using the leadership criteria you've established, rate the person you are evaluating on a scale of 0 to 5 (with 5 being the highest), as shown in the table.

3. Compare or contrast your subject with other leaders. Use your checklist to compare candidates' leadership attributes. That might mean doing a little homework, such as calling campaign offices or doing other research on the candidates' views.

4. Summarize your opinion. When you finish, you should be able to say, "So-and-so would make a good leader <u>because</u> . . . ." If you *still* can't think of a reason, perhaps you should vote for somebody else.

Test for Success

Choose someone in a leadership position or someone you think might make a good leader. Evaluate that person, and summarize your findings in a paragraph.

Rating Sheet: Qualities of a Leader

Qualities	Rating
Has fresh ideas	4
Has experience	2
Is honest	5
Takes charge	5
Encourages team building, cooperation	3
Is dynamic	5
Has strong sense of duty	4
Inspires others to excel	3
Is good decision maker	4
Shows political courage	4
Has steady personality, is dependable	2
Keeps promises	4

5 The Election

Section Preview

OBJECTIVES

1. **Understand** the function of the electoral college today.
2. **Describe** the flaws in the electoral college.
3. **Outline** the advantages and disadvantages of proposed reforms of the electoral college.

WHY IT MATTERS

Most people do not understand the workings of the electoral college system. They do not understand that, no matter what the popular vote results may be, the electoral votes determine the outcome of a presidential election.

POLITICAL DICTIONARY

★ **district plan**
★ **proportional plan**
★ **direct popular election**
★ **electorate**
★ **national bonus plan**

The presidential campaign—the all-out effort to win the votes of the people—begins soon after the conventions. Each candidate's campaign organization works to present its candidate in the best possible light. Voters are bombarded by radio and television speeches; "whistle-stop" tours; press conferences and press releases; public rallies; party dinners; newspaper, radio, and television advertisements; stickers and buttons; placards and pamphlets; billboards and match-covers; Web sites and e-mail. The candidates pose for hundreds of photographs and shake thousands of hands as each of them tries to convince the people that he is best for the country.

The presidential campaign ends on election day. Millions of voters go to the polls in all 50 States and the District of Columbia. But the President, whoever that is to be, is not formally elected until the presidential electors' votes are cast and counted, several weeks later.

The Electoral College Today

You have arrived at one of the least understood parts of the American political process. As the people vote in the presidential election, they do not cast a vote directly for one of the contenders for the presidency. Instead, they vote to elect presidential electors.

Remember, the Constitution provides for the election of the President by the electoral college, in which each State has as many electors as it has members of Congress. The Framers expected the electors to use their own judgment in selecting a President. But today the electors, once chosen, are really just "rubber stamps." They are expected to vote automatically for their party's candidates for President and Vice President. In short, the electors go through the form set out in the Constitution in order to meet the letter of the Constitution, but their behavior is a far cry from its original intent.

▲ New York's then-Governor Franklin Roosevelt autographed this electoral college ballot not long after it was cast by a presidential elector at the State Capitol in Albany in 1932. The electoral college vote concludes more than a year of campaigning.

Choosing Electors

The electors are chosen by popular vote in every State[22] and on the same day everywhere: the Tuesday after the first Monday in November every fourth year. So the next presidential election will be held on November 4, 2008. In every State except Maine and Nebraska, the electors are chosen at-large.[23] That is, they are chosen on a winner-take-all basis. The presidential candidate—technically, the slate of elector-candidates nominated by his party—receiving the largest popular vote in a State regularly wins all of that State's electoral votes.

Today, the names of the individual elector-candidates appear on the ballot in only a handful of States. In most States, only the names of the presidential and vice-presidential candidates are listed. They stand as "shorthand" for the elector slates.

[22]The Constitution (Article II, Section 1, Clause 2) says that the electors are to be chosen in each State "in such Manner as the Legislature thereof may direct." In several States the legislatures themselves chose the electors in the first several elections. By 1832, however, every State except South Carolina had provided for popular election. The electors were picked by the legislature in South Carolina through the elections of 1860. Since then, all presidential electors have been chosen by popular vote in every State, with two exceptions. The State legislatures chose the electors in Florida in 1868 and in Colorado in 1876.

Counting Electoral Votes

The Constitution provides that the date Congress sets for the electors to meet "shall be the same throughout the United States."[24] The 12th Amendment provides that "the electors shall meet in their respective states." The electors thus meet at their State capitol on the date set by Congress, now the Monday after the second Wednesday in December. There they each cast their electoral votes, one for President and one for Vice President. The electors' ballots, signed and sealed, are sent by registered mail to the president of the Senate in Washington.

Which party has won a majority of the electoral votes, and who then will be the next President of the United States, is usually known by midnight of election day, more than a month before the electors cast their ballots. But the

[23]Maine (beginning in 1972) and Nebraska (1992) use the "district plan." In those States, two electors are chosen from the State at-large and the others are picked in each of the State's congressional districts. The district plan was used by several States in the first few presidential elections, but every State except South Carolina had provided for the choice of the electors from the State at large by 1832. Since then, the district plan has been used only by Michigan in 1892 and by Maine and Nebraska.
[24]Article II, Section 1, Clause 4

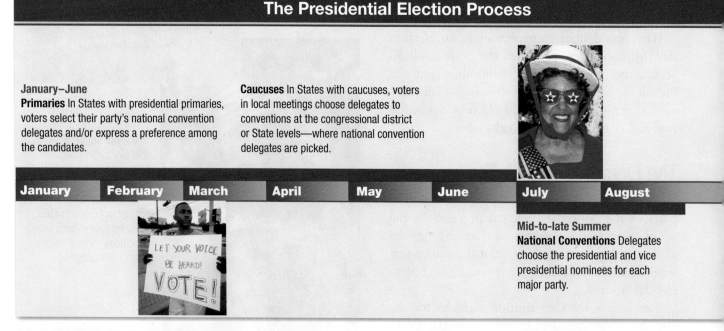

The Presidential Election Process

January–June
Primaries In States with presidential primaries, voters select their party's national convention delegates and/or express a preference among the candidates.

Caucuses In States with caucuses, voters in local meetings choose delegates to conventions at the congressional district or State levels—where national convention delegates are picked.

January	February	March	April	May	June	July	August

Mid-to-late Summer
National Conventions Delegates choose the presidential and vice presidential nominees for each major party.

Interpreting Charts The Framers of the Constitution established the electoral college to allow the most capable citizens in each State to select the President. *Is that how that electoral process works today? Why or why not?* H-SS 12.4.4

formal election of the President and Vice President finally takes place on January 6.[25]

On that date, the president of the Senate opens the electoral votes from each State and counts them before a joint session of Congress. The candidate who receives a majority of the electors' votes for President is declared elected, as is the candidate with a majority of the votes for Vice President.

If no candidate has won a majority—at least 270 of the 538 electoral votes today—the election is thrown into the House of Representatives. This happened in 1800 and again in 1824. The House chooses a President from among the top three candidates in the electoral college. Each State delegation has one vote, and it takes a majority of 26 to elect. If the House fails to choose a President by January 20, the 20th Amendment provides that the newly elected Vice President shall act as President until a choice is made.[26]

If no person receives a majority of votes for Vice President, the Senate decides between the top two candidates. It takes a majority of the whole Senate to elect. The Senate has had to choose a Vice President only once, when it elected Richard M. Johnson in 1837.

Flaws in the Electoral College

The electoral college system is plagued by three major defects: (1) the winner of the popular vote is not guaranteed the presidency; (2) electors are not required to vote in accord with the popular vote; and (3) any election might have to be decided in the House of Representatives.

The First Major Defect

There is the ever-present threat that the winner of the popular vote will not win the presidency. This continuing danger is largely the result of two factors. The most important is the winner-take-all feature of the electoral college system. That is, the winning candidate customarily receives all of a State's electoral votes. Thus in 2004 George W.

---

[25]If that day falls on a Sunday, as it did most recently in 1985 (but will not again until 2013), then the ballot-counting is held the following day.

[26]The 20th Amendment further provides that "the Congress may by law provide for the case wherein neither a President-elect nor a Vice President-elect shall have qualified" by inauguration day. Congress has done so in the Succession Act of 1947; see page 359. The Speaker of the House would "act as President … until a President or Vice President shall have qualified."

January 6 Electoral votes are counted before a joint session of Congress.

January 20 Inauguration Candidate receiving majority of electoral votes is sworn in as President of the United States.

September	October	November	December	January	February	March	April

Tuesday after first Monday in November Election Day Voters cast ballot for a slate of electors pledged to a particular presidential candidate.

Monday after second Wednesday in December Electoral College Vote Winning electors in each State meet in their State capitals to cast votes for President and Vice President. Statement of their vote is sent to Washington, D.C. and opened in early January.

Electoral Votes of Each State, 2004

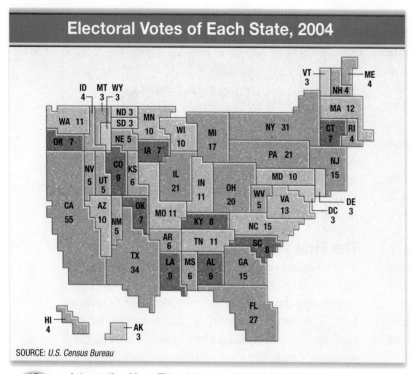

SOURCE: *U.S. Census Bureau*

Interpreting Maps This pictogram shows the number of electoral votes each State had in the 2004 election. *Why are those states in which the election outcome is doubtful called "battleground" States?* H-SS 12.6.6

Bush won 51 percent of the popular vote in Ohio. Still, he won all of that State's 20 electoral votes—despite the fact that some 2.7 million Ohioans voted for his Democratic opponent, John Kerry.

The other major culprit here is the way the electoral votes are distributed among the States. Remember, two of the electors in each State are allotted because of a State's Senate seats, regardless of population. So the allotment of electoral votes does not match the facts of population and voter distribution.

Take the extreme case to illustrate this point: California, the country's most populous State, has 55 electoral votes, one for each 615,848 persons in the State, based on its 2000 population of 33,871,698 residents. Wyoming has three electoral votes, one for each 164,594 persons, based on its 2000 population of 493,782 residents.

The popular vote winner has, in fact, failed to win the presidency four times: in 1824, 1876, 1888, and most recently in 2000. In 1824, Andrew Jackson won the largest share (a plurality, but not a majority) of the popular votes: 151,271, or 41.3 percent of the total. Jackson's nearest rival, John Quincy Adams,

received 113,122 votes, or 30.9 percent. Ninety-nine of the 261 electors then voted for Jackson, again more than any other candidate but far short of a majority. The election thus went to the House and, early in 1825, it elected Adams to the presidency.

In the election of 1876, Republican candidate Rutherford B. Hayes received 4,034,311 popular votes and his Democratic opponent, Samuel J. Tilden, won 4,288,546. Tilden received 184 electoral votes. Hayes won 185 electoral votes and so became President.[27]

In 1888 President Grover Cleveland won 5,534,488 popular votes, 90,596 more than his Republican opponent, Benjamin Harrison. Harrison, however, received 233 electoral votes to Cleveland's 168, and so became the 23rd President.

In the presidential election of 2000, the Democratic candidate, Vice President Al Gore, won 50,992,335 popular votes—537,179 more votes than his Republican opponent, then-Governor of Texas, George W. Bush. However, Mr. Bush received 271 electoral votes—one more than the bare majority in the electoral college, and so he became the nation's 43rd President.

Florida's 25 electoral votes proved to be decisive in the extraordinarily close 2000 election. The popular vote results in several Florida counties were challenged immediately after the polls closed there. The next five weeks were filled with partisan infighting, several recounts, and a number of court disputes. The United States Supreme Court finally brought an end to the bitter contest on December 12. It ruled, in *Bush* v. *Gore*, that the differing ways in which various counties were recounting votes violated the 14th Amendment's Equal Protection Clause. The Court's 5–4 decision ended those recounts. It also

---

[27]The election of 1876 is often called the "Stolen Election." Two conflicting sets of electoral votes were received from Florida (4 votes), Louisiana (8 votes), and South Carolina (7 votes), and the validity of one vote from Oregon was disputed. Congress set up an Electoral Commission with five senators, five representatives, and five Supreme Court justices to decide the matter. The Commissioners, eight Republicans and seven Democrats, voted on strict party lines, awarding all of the disputed votes, and so the presidency, to Hayes.

preserved George W. Bush's 537-vote lead in the Statewide count and, in effect, gave him Florida's 25 electoral votes. The Court's split decision in *Bush* v. *Gore* remains highly controversial.

To this point, 15 Presidents have won the White House with less than a majority of the popular votes cast in their elections. As you have just seen, four of these "minority Presidents" were elected although they, in fact, *lost* the popular vote. The other 11 each won a *plurality* (but less than 50 percent) of the popular vote: James K. Polk (1844), Zachary Taylor (1848), James Buchanan (1856), Abraham Lincoln (1860), James A. Garfield (1880), Grover Cleveland (1884, 1892), Woodrow Wilson (1912, 1916), Harry S Truman (1948), John F. Kennedy (1960), Richard Nixon (1968), and Bill Clinton (1992, 1996).

By now, you see the point: The "winner-take-all" factor produces an electoral vote that is, at best, only a distorted reflection of the popular vote.

The Second Major Defect

Nothing in the Constitution, nor in any federal statute, requires the electors to vote for the candidate favored by the popular vote in their States. Several States do have such laws, but they are of doubtful constitutionality, and none has ever been enforced.

To this point, however, electors have "broken their pledges," or refused to vote for their party's presidential nominee, on only eleven occasions: in 1796, 1820, 1948, 1956, 1960, 1968, 1972, 1976, 1988, 2000, and 2004. Most recently, one Minnesota elector, a Democrat, did not cast his ballot for his party's presidential candidate, John Kerry. He voted, instead, for the Democrats' vice-presidential choice, John Edwards. In fact, he voted for Senator Edwards twice—once for President and then, on his other ballot, once for vice president.

In no case has the vote of a "faithless elector" had a bearing on the outcome of a presidential election. But the potential is certainly there.

The Third Major Defect

In any presidential election, it is possible that the contest will be decided in the House. This has happened only twice, and not since 1824. In several other elections, however—especially in 1912, 1924, 1948, and 1968—a strong third-party bid has threatened to make it impossible for either major party candidate to win a majority in the electoral college.

Look at 1968: George Wallace, the American Independent Party candidate, won five southern States and 46 electoral votes. If Democrat Hubert Humphrey had carried Alaska, Delaware, Missouri, Nevada, and Wisconsin—States where Richard Nixon's margin was thin and in which Wallace also had a substantial vote—Nixon's electoral vote would have been 268, Humphrey's 224. Neither would have had a majority. The House would then have had to decide the election.

Three serious objections can be raised regarding election by the House. First, the voting in such cases is by States, not by individual members. A State with a small population, such as Alaska or Nevada, would have as much weight as the most populous State. Second, if the representatives from a State were so divided that no candidate was favored by a majority, that State would lose its vote. Third, the

Popular Vote vs. Electoral Vote

States	Popular Vote	% Popular Vote	Electoral Vote	% of Total National Electoral Vote
Florida				
Bush	2,912,790	48.85	25	4.6
Gore	2,912,253	48.84		
Nader	97,488	1.63		
Iowa				
Bush	634,373	48.22		
Gore	638,517	48.54	7	1.3
Nader	29,374	2.23		
New Mexico				
Bush	286,417	47.85		
Gore	286,783	47.91	5	.9
Nader	21,251	3.55		
Oregon				
Bush	713,577	46.52		
Gore	720,342	46.96	7	1.3
Nader	77,357	5.04		

SOURCE: Federal Election Commision

Interpreting Tables This table shows the election results in the four States where the 2000 presidential race was the closest. *(a) How do these results illustrate the significance of the "winner-take-all" factor? (b) How did Ralph Nader's third-party candidacy affect these results?*

Constitution requires a majority of the States for election in the House—today, 26 States. If a strong third-party candidate were involved, there is a real possibility that the House could not make a decision by Inauguration Day.[28]

Proposed Reforms

Observers have long recognized the shortcomings of the electoral college system. In fact, constitutional amendments to change the process have been introduced in every term of Congress since 1789. Most of the reforms people have offered fall under three headings: the district plan, the proportional plan, and direct popular election.

The District Plan

Over time, many people have proposed the **district plan,** in which the electors would be chosen in each State in the same way as members of Congress. That is, two electors would be chosen from the State at large, and they would cast their electoral votes in line with the result of the Statewide popular vote. The other electors would be elected, separately, in each of the State's congressional districts. Their votes would be cast in accord with the result of the popular vote in their district.[29]

The district plan would do away with the winner-take-all problem in the present system. Its supporters have argued that it would make the electoral vote a more accurate reflection of the popular returns.

The strongest argument against the plan is that it would not eliminate the possibility that the loser of the popular vote could still win the electoral vote. In fact, had it been in effect in 1960, Richard Nixon would have received 278 electoral votes, and he, not John Kennedy, would have won the presidency. Had the plan

been in place in 2004, George W. Bush would have won 317 electoral votes.

Further, the results under the district plan would depend very much on how the congressional districts were drawn in each State. Its use would be yet another motive for gerrymandering.

The Proportional Plan

Under the **proportional plan,** each presidential candidate would receive the same share of a State's electoral vote as he or she received in the State's popular vote. Thus, if a candidate won 40 percent of the votes cast in a State with 20 electoral votes, he or she would get 8 of that State's electoral votes.

This plan would cure the winner-take-all problem and eliminate faithless electors. It also would yield an electoral vote more in line with the popular vote, at least for each State.

The proportional plan would not necessarily produce the same result nationally, however. Because each of the smaller States is overweighted by its two Senate-based electors, this arrangement would still make it possible for the loser of the popular vote to win the presidency in the electoral vote. In fact, this would have happened in 1896. William Jennings Bryan would have defeated William McKinley, although McKinley had a comfortable popular vote margin of 596,985 (4.3 percent).[30]

Many critics of the proportional plan worry about its effect on the two-party system. Certainly, its adoption would bring an increase in the number and vigor of minor parties. They would no longer need to win entire States in order to get electoral votes. In addition, their candidates would regularly win at least some share of the electoral vote. Then the odds that a presidential election would have to go to the House would be increased.

Most of the plan's backers agree that an increase in minor party clout would mean that the winner of the popular vote would often fail to gain a clear majority of the electoral vote. Hence, advocates of this plan would lower the

---

[28]In such a case, Section 3 of the 20th Amendment states that "the Vice President-elect shall act as President until a President shall have qualified." If no Vice President-elect is available, the Presidential Succession Act would come into play. Note that it is even mathematically possible for the minority party in the House to have control of a majority of the individual State delegations. That party could then elect its candidate, even though he or she may have run second or even third in both the popular and the electoral vote contests.

[29]Maine and Nebraska now use the district plan, as noted earlier. Any other State could do so, but it would take a constitutional amendment to make its use mandatory in all States.

---

[30]In the closest of all presidential elections, Democrat Winfield S. Hancock would have defeated Republican James A. Garfield in 1880, even though Garfield won the popular vote by 10,464 ballots (0.0163 percent). On the other hand, there would have been no "Stolen Election" in 1876, and Cleveland would have defeated Harrison in 1888.

present requirement of a majority of the electoral votes to a plurality of at least 40 percent. If no candidate won 40 percent of the electoral votes, the two frontrunners would face one another in a second, runoff election.

Direct Popular Election

The electoral college reform proposal most often made, and the one most widely supported, is the most obvious one: Do away with the electoral college system altogether and provide for **direct popular election** of the President. The arguments for direct election seem overpowering. The strongest one is that it would support the democratic ideal: Each vote would count equally in the national result. The winner would always be the majority or plurality choice. The dangers and confusions of the present system would be eliminated, replaced by a simple and easily understood process.

The fact that the loser of the popular vote nevertheless won the presidency in the 2000 election has given added weight to the case for direct election. Several obstacles stand in the way of the reform, however.[31]

The constitutional amendment process itself is a major stumbling block. It is time-consuming, difficult, and cumbersome. Second, the smaller States are greatly overrepresented in the electoral college. They would lose that advantage in a direct election. It is likely that enough senators or representatives of small States would oppose a direct election amendment to kill it.

Some opponents argue that direct election would weaken the federal system because the States, as States, would lose their role in the choice of a President. Others believe that direct election would put too great a load on the election process. They say that because every vote cast in each State would count in the national result, the candidates would have to campaign strenuously in every State. The impact that

Interpreting Political Cartoons *What details in the cartoon suggest that the electoral college is one of the most complex parts of the political process?*

would have on campaign time, effort, and finances would be huge and, opponents argue, probably unmanageable.[32]

Some say that direct election would spur ballot-box stuffing and other forms of voting fraud. That, they predict, would lead to lengthy, bitter, highly explosive post-election challenges.

In many States, a State-wide election often hangs on the behavior of some specific group in the **electorate**—the mass of people who can cast votes in an election. The overall result depends on how those voters cast their ballots or, even more importantly, on how heavily they do or do not turn out to vote. Thus, for example, the African American vote in Chicago is often decisive in the presidential election in Illinois. But notice, in a direct election, these groups would not hold the balance of power they now have, so many of them oppose the direct election plan. Given all this, there seems little real chance that the direct election of the President will become fact any time soon.

---

[31]The House of Representatives did approve a direct election amendment by the necessary two-thirds vote in 1969. A Senate filibuster killed the measure in 1970. President Carter championed a similar proposal, but it was rejected by a Senate floor vote in 1979.

[32]In fact, it is possible for a candidate to win the presidency by carrying only the 11 largest States, because they now have a total of 271 electoral votes, one more than the minimum number needed to win the presidency.

The National Bonus Plan

Another and very different plan, called the **national bonus plan,** has recently surfaced. At first glance, the plan seems quite complicated and "off the wall." In fact, it is neither.

The national bonus plan would keep much of the electoral college system intact, especially its winner-take-all feature. It would weight that feature in favor of the winner of the popular vote, however.

Under this plan, a national pool of 102 electoral votes would be awarded, automatically, to the winner of the national popular vote. That is, this bloc of electoral votes would be added to the electoral votes that the candidate won in the election. If all those votes added up to a majority of the electoral college—at least 321—the candidate would win the presidency. In the unlikely event that they did not add up to a majority, a runoff election between the two front runners in the popular vote would then be held.

The advocates of this plan see the electors themselves as unnecessary, and so would do away with them. They say that their plan meets all of the major objections to the present system and all of those raised against the other proposals for its reform. They also claim that their plan would almost guarantee that the winner of the popular vote would always be the winner of the electoral vote.

To date, the national bonus plan has not attracted much public attention. Nor has it attracted much understanding, interest, or support.

Electoral College Supporters

Their case is not often heard, but the present electoral college system does have its defenders. They react to the several proposed reforms by raising the various objections you have just read. Beyond that they argue that critics exaggerate the "dangers" in the present system. Only two elections have ever gone to the House of Representatives and none in more than 180 years. They grant the point that the loser of the popular vote has in fact won the presidency four times. But, they note, that has happened *only* four times over the course of now 55 presidential elections; and they add, it has happened only once in more than a century.

Supporters also say that the present arrangement, whatever its warts, has two major strengths:

1. It is a known process. Each of the proposed, but untried, reforms may very well have defects that could not be known until they appeared in practice.

2. In most cases, it identifies the winner quickly and certainly. With the exception of the 2000 election, the nation does not have to wait for very long to know the outcome.

Section 5 Assessment

Key Terms and Main Ideas

1. How does the way the electoral college functions today differ from the Framers' intentions?
2. What are the three main weaknesses of the electoral college system?
3. Explain the **district plan,** the **proportional plan,** the **direct popular election plan,** and the **national bonus plan** for reforming the electoral college.
4. What are the arguments for and against **direct popular election?**

Critical Thinking

5. **Identifying Alternatives** Suppose you have been asked to draft a plan for reforming the electoral college. Choose one of the methods discussed in this section, or write one of

Standards Monitoring Online
For: Self-quiz with vocabulary practice
Web Code: mqa-4135

your own. Explain how your plan will work and why you think it is superior to other proposed reforms.
6. **Expressing Problems Clearly** Under what circumstances can the winner of the popular vote fail to win the presidency?

Go Online
PHSchool.com

For: An activity on the electoral college today
Web Code: mqd-4135

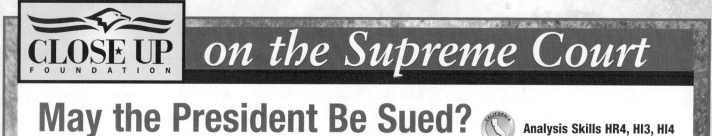
May the President Be Sued?

Analysis Skills HR4, HI3, HI4

The Constitution contains no specific protection of the President against lawsuits. What kind of protection is appropriate for the President? Are all his actions protected, or only those that are taken in good faith and fall within the scope of his official duties?

Nixon v. Fitzgerald (1982)

In November 1968, A. Ernest Fitzgerald, a management analyst with the Department of the Air Force, revealed in testimony before Congress that development of the Air Force's C-5A transport plane would cost about $2 billion more than had been predicted. He also disclosed unexpected technical problems that had developed with the plane.

Just over a year later, in January of 1970, Fitzgerald's department was reorganized and he was laid off, along with some other employees. Fitzgerald complained to the Civil Service Commission, which found that he had been terminated for "purely personal" reasons but not in retaliation for his testimony. Fitzgerald then sued various Defense Department officials and White House aides who, he said, were responsible for his firing.

Fitzgerald later named President Richard M. Nixon as a defendant in his suit because Fitzgerald believed that the President had played a direct role in his firing. Nixon argued that as President, he had absolute immunity—complete protection—against lawsuits over actions he took while in office. The trial court and then the court of appeals both rejected this immunity defense. Nixon then appealed to the Supreme Court, which had never before ruled on the question of how far a President's immunity against lawsuits extended.

Arguments for Nixon

1. The President occupies a unique position under our Constitution, because he serves as chief executive, policymaker, and law enforcement official. For the President to have to deal with private lawsuits as well would harm the effective operation of our government.

2. Judges and prosecutors have received absolute immunity in order to allow them to deal "fearlessly and impartially" with their official duties. The President should receive similar protection.

3. The President's immunity should cover all of his official functions. Otherwise, courts would have to review his motives in each case in order to determine whether particular actions were covered by the immunity.

Arguments for Fitzgerald

1. Past Supreme Court cases have granted governors and Cabinet officials only partial immunity from lawsuits, which protects them only for actions taken in good faith.

2. If the President did in fact order the firing of an employee who was lawfully entitled to retain his job, then he acted outside the boundary of his proper duties and should be subject to a lawsuit for his actions.

3. Absolute immunity would place the President above the law.

Decide for Yourself

1. Review the constitutional grounds on which each side based its arguments and the specific arguments each side presented.

2. Debate the opposing viewpoints presented in this case. Which viewpoint do you favor?

3. Predict the impact of the Court's decision on other situations in which a President might be sued. (To read a summary of the Court's decision, turn to pages 799–806.)

Go Online
PHSchool.com

Use Web Code mqp-4139 to register your vote on this issue and to see how other students voted.

Political Dictionary

chief of state (p. 354), chief executive (p. 354), chief administrator (p. 355), chief diplomat (p. 355), commander in chief (p. 355), chief legislator (p. 355), chief of party (p. 355), chief citizen (p. 355), presidential succession (p. 359), Presidential Succession Act of 1947 (p. 360), balance the ticket (p. 362), presidential electors (p. 365), electoral votes (p. 365), electoral college (p. 366), presidential primary (p. 369), winner-take-all (p. 371), proportional representation (p. 371), national convention (p. 372), platform (p. 373), keynote address (p. 373), district plan (p. 382), proportional plan (p. 382), direct popular election (p. 383), electorate (p. 383), national bonus plan (p. 384)

Standards Review

H-SS 12.4.1 Discuss Article I of the Constitution as it relates to the legislative branch, including eligibility for office and lengths of terms of representatives and senators; election to office; the roles of the House and Senate in impeachment proceedings; the role of the vice president; the enumerated legislative powers; and the process by which a bill becomes a law.

H-SS 12.4.4 Discuss Article II of the Constitution as it relates to the executive branch, including eligibility for office and length of term, election to and removal from office, the oath of office, and the enumerated executive powers.

H-SS 12.6.2 Discuss the history of the nomination process for presidential candidates and the increasing importance of primaries in general elections.

H-SS 12.6.4 Describe the means that citizens use to participate in the political process (e.g., voting, campaigning, lobbying, filing a legal challenge, demonstrating, petitioning, picketing, running for political office).

H-SS 12.6.6 Analyze trends in voter turnout; the causes and effects of reapportionment and redistricting, with special attention to spatial districting and the rights of minorities; and the function of the Electoral College.

H-SS 12.8.2 Describe the roles of broadcast, print, and electronic media, including the Internet, as means of communication in American politics.

Practicing the Vocabulary

Matching *Choose a term from the list above that best matches each description.*

1. The group chosen every four years to make the formal selection of the President and Vice President
2. The role in which the President exercises leadership over his or her political party
3. The role in which the President acts as the main architect of the nation's public policies
4. An election at which a party's voters choose delegates to the party's national convention and/or express a preference for candidates for the party's nomination
5. All the people entitled to vote in a given election

Word Recognition *Replace the underlined definition with the correct term from the list above.*

6. In the past, some presidential primaries were <u>contests in which the winner of the preference vote won the support of all the delegates</u>.
7. As <u>the representative of all the people</u>, the President speaks for the people of the nation and offers important moral leadership.
8. The <u>written declaration of principles and policy decisions</u> of a party is an important product of each national convention.
9. The <u>speech given at a party convention to set the tone for the convention and the campaign to come</u> is usually delivered by one of the party's best orators.

Reviewing Main Ideas

Section 1

10. Explain the significance of each of the following presidential roles: chief executive, chief diplomat, commander in chief.
11. **(a)** What was the origin of the no-third-term tradition? **(b)** Which President broke with this tradition? **(c)** What is the maximum number of terms that a President may now serve?
12. Why do some critics want the 22nd Amendment repealed?

Section 2

13. How does the Constitution ensure a smooth transition of power in the event of a presidential disability?
14. Explain how the Constitution and the Presidential Succession Act of 1947 address the issue of presidential succession.
15. What does the Constitution say about the vice presidency?

Section 3

16. Describe the Framers' plan for the selection of the nation's President.
17. Why did the electoral college cease to function as the Framers had intended?
18. What was the purpose of the 12th Amendment?

Section 4

19. How do presidential primaries differ from the caucus-convention process?
20. For what major purposes do parties hold national conventions?

Section 5

21. **(a)** How are presidential electors chosen? **(b)** How are electoral votes counted?
22. On what grounds is the electoral college system criticized?

Critical Thinking Skills

Analysis Skills HR4, HI1, HI4

23. ***Applying the Chapter Skill*** "Leadership," said Dwight Eisenhower, consists of "getting someone else to do what you want him to do because he wants to do it." Which of the qualifications of a leader described on page 376 do you think the President should possess?

24. ***Distinguishing False from Accurate Images*** The following quotation from John Adams appears earlier in this chapter: "I am Vice President. In this I am nothing, but I may be everything." **(a)** Explain what Adams meant. **(b)** Do you think that a modern Vice President would agree with Adams?

25. ***Identifying Alternatives*** Review the formal qualifications for President in Section 1. **(a)** Why do you think the Framers chose these particular qualifications? **(b)** Do you think that any of these qualifications should be changed?

26. ***Understanding Point of View*** Why do you think that neither major party has, at least to this point, ever nominated a woman or a member of a minority group as its presidential candidate?

Analyzing Political Cartoons

Using your knowledge of American government and this cartoon, answer the questions below.

"Hi there. I'm governor of a large State somewhere out West, and I'm running for President."

27. Why is it significant that the candidate in the cartoon is a governor of a large western state?
28. How accurate is the cartoon in portraying the qualifications necessary for a presidential candidate?

★ You Can Make a Difference

What organizations in your community provide help for children and their families who lack books, food, or clothing? Are these groups privately run or sponsored by government agencies? With your classmates, prepare a guidebook of the resources available in your community, what services they provide, and how they are funded. Organize the guide by services and location. Then look into the volunteer opportunities available for you and your friends.

Participation Activities

Analysis Skills HR1

29. ***Current Events Watch*** Follow news reports of the President's activities and find examples of the President filling any four of the eight roles outlined on pages 354–355. For each of the four roles, hand in a newspaper or magazine clipping or an Internet printout of the report, along with your explanation of which roles the President is filling.

30. ***Chart Activity*** Create a chart showing the advantages and disadvantages of the various plans for reforming the electoral college. Include the advantages and disadvantages of keeping the current system. Which, in your opinion, are the weakest and the strongest plans?

31. ***It's Your Turn*** Draw a political cartoon on one of the following topics: the plight of the Vice President, the flaws of the electoral college, the many roles of the President, the Framers' view of today's election process, or a topic of your own choosing. After you have made a rough sketch, be sure that the point you want to make will be clear to your viewers. Then create a final drawing to display in your classroom. **(Drawing a Cartoon)**

Standards Monitoring *Online*

For: Chapter 13 Self-Test **Visit:** PHSchool.com
Web Code: mqa-4136

As a final review, take the Magruder's Chapter 13 Self-Test and receive immediate feedback on your answers. The test consists of 20 multiple-choice questions designed to test your understanding of the chapter content.

CHAPTER 14

The Presidency in Action

"The President hears a hundred voices telling him that he is the greatest man in the world. He must listen carefully indeed to hear the one voice that tells him he is not."
—Harry S Truman (1964)

Presidents today do have great power—to carry out laws, make policies, choose officials, command the military, and conduct foreign affairs. The Framers gave the President certain "executive powers," which have grown greatly over time. How much power a President actually exercises depends on the person and on the times.

◆ **President Bush in his role as commander in chief**

H-SS 12.1.5 Describe the systems of separated and shared powers, the role of organized interests (*Federalist Paper Number 10*), checks and balances (*Federalist Paper Number 51*), the importance of an independent judiciary (*Federalist Paper Number 78*), enumerated powers, rule of law, federalism, and civilian control of the military.

H-SS 12.4.4 Discuss Article II of the Constitution as it relates to the executive branch, including eligibility for office and length of term, election to and removal from office, the oath of office, and the enumerated executive powers.

H-SS 12.4.6 Explain the processes of selection and confirmation of Supreme Court justices.

H-SS 12.7.5 Explain how public policy is formed, including the setting of the public agenda and implementation of it through regulations and executive orders.

H-SS 12.7.8 Understand the scope of presidential power and decision making through examination of case studies such as the Cuban Missile Crisis, passage of Great Society legislation, War Powers Act, Gulf War, and Bosnia.

SECTION 1

The Growth of Presidential Power
(pp. 390–392)

★ Article II of the Constitution created the presidency and gives the President certain expressed powers.

★ Yet Article II is remarkably brief, leaving Americans to debate whether the Framers intended the presidency to be relatively strong or weak.

★ Since the nation's founding, the power of the presidency has grown significantly.

★ The power a President exercises depends on his views about the office and how he interprets Article II.

SECTION 2

The President's Executive Powers
(pp. 393–397)

★ Article II gives the President the power and responsibility to "execute the laws."

★ This executive power gives the President a great deal of flexibility in deciding how laws are carried out.

★ Among the President's key powers are those to appoint and remove top federal officials.

SECTION 3

Diplomatic and Military Powers (pp. 399–403)

★ The President shares treaty-making and other powers with Congress.

★ Certain diplomatic powers may be carried out without the approval of Congress; increasingly, Presidents have made use of these powers.

★ As commander in chief of the armed forces, the President possesses almost unlimited military power.

SECTION 4

Legislative and Judicial Powers (pp. 405–408)

★ The Constitution gives the President important legislative and judicial powers as part of the system of checks and balances in the Federal Government.

★ The President's key legislative powers are to submit legislation for Congress to consider and to reject legislation that he opposes.

★ The Constitution gives the President several powers of clemency—powers with which he can show mercy to those convicted of federal crimes.

Go Online
PHSchool.com

For: Current Data
Web Code: mqg-4146

For: Close Up Foundation debates
Web Code: mqh-4148

The Growth of Presidential Power

·1·

Section Preview

OBJECTIVES

1. **Explain** why Article II of the Constitution can be described as "an outline."
2. **List** several reasons for the growth of presidential power.
3. **Explain** how Presidents' own views have affected the power of the office.

WHY IT MATTERS

The Constitution establishes the office of the President in Article II. The interpretation of that article continues to be a battleground for people who want a stronger presidency and those who would curb presidential powers.

POLITICAL DICTIONARY

★ **Executive Article**
★ **mass media**
★ **imperial presidency**

The presidency is often called "the most powerful office in the world." Is this what the Framers had in mind when they created the post in 1787? At Philadelphia, they purposely created a single executive with broad powers. But they also agreed with Thomas Jefferson, who wrote in the Declaration of Independence that "a Tyrant is unfit to be the ruler of a free people." So, just as purposely, they constructed a "checked," or limited, presidency.

Article II

Article II, the Constitution's **Executive Article,** begins this way:

> **FROM THE Constitution** *"The executive Power shall be vested in a President of the United States of America."*

With those few words, the Framers established the presidency. The Constitution sets out other, somewhat more specific grants of presidential power as well. Thus, the President is given the power to command the armed forces, to make treaties, to approve or veto acts of Congress, to send and receive diplomatic representatives, to grant pardons and reprieves, and "to take Care that the Laws be faithfully executed."

Still, the Constitution deals with the powers of the presidency in a very sketchy fashion. Article II reads almost as an outline. It has been called "the most loosely drawn chapter" in the nation's fundamental law.[1]

A large part of America's political history has revolved around the struggle over the meaning of the constitutional phrase "executive power." That struggle has pitted those who have argued for a weaker presidency, subordinate to Congress, against those who have pressed for a stronger, independent, co-equal chief executive.

That never-ending contest began at the Philadelphia Convention in 1787. At that time, several Framers agreed with Roger Sherman of Connecticut, who, according to James Madison,

> **PRIMARY Sources** *"considered the executive magistracy as nothing more than an institution for carrying the will of the legislature into effect, that the person or persons [occupying the presidency] ought to be appointed by and accountable to the legislature only, which was the depository of the supreme will of the Society."*
> —*Notes* of Debates in the Federal Convention of 1787, James Madison

▲ President Reagan met with Soviet leader Mikhail Gorbachev in Geneva, Switzerland, in 1985. **H-SS 12.4.4**

---

[1]Edward S. Corwin, *The President: Office and Powers.* Most of the specific grants of presidential power are found in Article II, Sections 2 and 3. A few are elsewhere in the Constitution, such as the veto power, in Article I, Section 7, Clause 2.

★★★★ **390**   Chapter 14 Section 1

Those who argued for a stronger executive carried the day. The convention established a single executive, chosen independently of Congress and with its own distinct powers.

Why Presidential Power Has Grown

The Constitution's formal grants of power to the President have not been changed since 1789. Yet presidential power has grown remarkably over the past 200 years.

That expansion has come, in no small part, because of the unity of the presidency. The office, and its powers, are held by one person. The President is the single, commanding chief executive. In contrast, Congress consists of two houses, and both must agree before Congress can do anything. Moreover, one of those two houses is made up of 100 separately elected members, and the other of 435.

Several other factors have also been at work here. Not least are Presidents themselves, and especially the stronger ones—Abraham Lincoln and the two Roosevelts, for example.

The nation's increasingly complex social and economic life has also had a telling effect. As the country has become more industrialized and technologically advanced, the people have demanded that the Federal Government take a larger role in transportation, communications, health, welfare, employment, education, civil rights, and a host of other fields. And they have looked especially to the President for leadership in those matters.

Clearly, the need for immediate and decisive action in times of crisis, and especially in times of war, has also had a major impact. The ability of the President to act in those situations has done much to strengthen the executive power.

Congress has also been involved, as it has passed the thousands of laws that have been a key part of the historic growth of the Federal Government. Congress has neither the time nor the technical knowledge to provide much more than basic outlines of public policy. Necessarily, it has delegated substantial authority to the executive branch to carry out the laws it has enacted.

The President has a unique ability to attract public attention and build support for policies and actions. Every President since Franklin

Presidents on the Presidency

THOMAS JEFFERSON

1801–1809

"[The presidency] is a place of splendid misery."

WILLIAM H. TAFT

1909–1913

"I'm glad to be going—this is the loneliest place in the world."

THEODORE ROOSEVELT

1901–1909

"I have enjoyed every moment of this so-called arduous and exacting task."

HARRY S TRUMAN

1945–1953

"Being President is like riding a tiger."

Not everyone who occupied the Oval Office has always enjoyed the job. Many former Presidents left the office with mixed emotions or regrets.
H-SS 12.4.4

Roosevelt has used the **mass media**—forms of communication, especially radio, television, and the Internet—to that end.

Still, with all that has just been said, remember: the President has not become all-powerful. In 1952, a labor dispute threatened to shut down the nation's steel industry and imperil the war effort in Korea. To avert a strike, President Harry Truman, acting as commander in chief, ordered the Secretary of Commerce to seize and operate several steel mills. The Supreme Court found that he had overstepped his constitutional authority. It held that only Congress, acting under its commerce power, could authorize the seizure of private property in time of war, *Youngstown Sheet & Tube Co. v. Sawyer*, 1952.

In 2004, the High Court checked the exercise of presidential power again—in two cases involving the detention of "enemy combatants," persons captured in the war against terrorism. President George W. Bush cited his powers as commander in chief to justify their confinement at Guantanamo Bay, Cuba, and elsewhere—indefinitely and without charge or trial. The

Court found that here, too, a President had over-reached. It held that the detainees must be allowed to use the federal courts to challenge the lawfulness of their confinement, *Rasul* v. *Bush*, *Hamdi* v. *Rumsfeld*, 2004.

The Presidential View

Over time, Presidents have taken one of two contrasting views of the presidency and its powers. The stronger, more effective chief executives have seen the office in a broad light—a view that Theodore Roosevelt called "the stewardship theory":

PRIMARY Sources *" My view was that every executive officer . . . in high position, was a steward of the people bound actively and affirmatively to do all that he could for the people. . . . I declined to adopt the view that what was imperatively necessary for the Nation could not be done by the President unless he could find some specific authorization to do it. My belief was that it was not only [a President's] right but his duty to do anything that the needs of the Nation demanded unless such action was forbidden by the Constitution or by the laws. . . . I did not usurp power, but I did greatly broaden the use of executive power. In other words, I acted for the public welfare . . . unless prevented by direct constitutional or legislative prohibition. "*

—Theodore Roosevelt,
Theodore Roosevelt: An Autobiography, 1913

Ironically, the strongest presidential statement of the opposing view came from Roosevelt's handpicked successor in the office, William Howard Taft.

PRIMARY Sources *" My judgment is that the view of Mr. Roosevelt, ascribing an undefined residuum of power to the President, is an unsafe doctrine. . . . The true view of the Executive function is, as I conceive it, that the President can exercise no power which cannot be fairly and reasonably traced to some specific grant of power or justly implied and included within such express grant. . . . Such specific grant must be either in the Federal Constitution or in an act of Congress passed in pursuance thereof. There is no undefined residuum of power which he can exercise because it seems to him to be in the public interest. "*

—William Howard Taft,
Our Chief Magistrate and His Powers, 1916

In recent decades, critics of strong presidential power have condemned what is called the **imperial presidency.** The term paints a picture of the President as emperor, taking strong actions without consulting Congress or seeking its approval—sometimes acting in secrecy to evade or even to deceive Congress. Critics of the imperial presidency worry that Presidents have become isolated policymakers who are unaccountable to the American people through their representatives in Congress. The term *imperial presidency* has been used frequently in reference to President Richard Nixon and the political tactics that brought about his downfall.

Section 1 Assessment

Key Terms and Main Ideas

1. Why is Article II often called the **Executive Article**?
2. Give three reasons for the growth of presidential power.
3. Summarize the two competing views of the constitutional phrase "executive power."
4. Why do some people worry about an **imperial presidency?**

Critical Thinking

5. **Understanding Point of View** Give two examples of how a President might use the mass media to influence public opinion. Do you think there are legitimate reasons for a President to do so? Explain.

Standards Monitoring *Online*
For: Self-quiz with vocabulary practice
Web Code: mqa-4141

6. **Making Comparisons** Compare and contrast the quotations from Presidents Roosevelt and Taft on this page. **(a)** Whose view do you favor? Why? **(b)** Which view do you think most modern-day Presidents have favored? Explain.

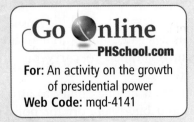

Go Online
PHSchool.com

For: An activity on the growth of presidential power
Web Code: mqd-4141

The President's Executive Powers

Section Preview

OBJECTIVES

1. **Identify** the source of the President's power to execute federal law.
2. **Define** the *ordinance power,* and explain where it comes from.
3. **Explain** how the appointing power works.
4. **Summarize** the historical debate over the removal power.

WHY IT MATTERS

Much of the power of the presidency rests on the discretion the President has in the use of his powers to issue executive orders, to execute the laws, and to appoint key federal officials.

POLITICAL DICTIONARY

★ oath of office
★ executive order
★ ordinance power

Thomas Jefferson wrote this to a friend in 1789: "The execution of the laws is more important than the making of them." Whether Jefferson was altogether right about that or not, in this section you will see that the President's power to execute the law endows him with an enormous amount of authority.

Executing the Law

As chief executive, the President executes (enforces, administers, carries out) the provisions of federal law. The power to do so rests on two brief constitutional provisions. The first of them is the **oath of office** sworn by the President on the day he takes office:

> **FROM THE Constitution** ❝*I do solemnly swear (or affirm) that I will faithfully execute the Office of President of the United States, and will to the best of my Ability, preserve, protect and defend the Constitution of the United States.* ❞
>
> —Article II, Section 1, Clause 8

The other provision is the Constitution's command that "he shall take care that the laws be faithfully executed."[2]

The President's power to execute the law covers all federal laws. Their number, and the different subject matters they cover, nearly boggle

the mind. The armed forces, social security, gun control, minimum wages, affirmative action, environmental protection, air traffic safety, immigration, housing, taxes—these only begin the list. There are scores of others.

The President and his subordinates have much to say about the meaning of the law, as do Congress and the courts. In executing and enforcing law, the executive branch also interprets it. The Constitution requires the President to execute *all* federal laws no matter what the chief executive's own views of any of them may be. Still, the President may, and does, use some discretion as to how vigorously and in what particular way any given law will be applied in practice.

To look at the point more closely: Many laws that Congress passes are written in fairly

▲ President George Washington took the oath of office on this borrowed Bible on April 30, 1789, and so, too, have other Presidents, including George W. Bush.

---

[2]Article II, Section 3; this provision gives the President what is often called the "take care" power.

broad terms. Congress sets out the basic policies and standards. The specific details—much of the fine print necessary to the actual, day-to-day administration of the law—are usually left to be worked out by the executive branch.

For example, immigration laws require that all immigrants seeking permanent admission to this country must be able to "read and understand some dialect or language." But what does this literacy requirement mean in everyday practice? How well must an alien be able to read and write? What words in some language must he or she know, and how many of them? The law does not say. Rather, such answers come from within the executive branch—in this case, from U.S. Citizenship and Immigration Services in the Department of Homeland Security.

The Ordinance Power

From what has just been said, the President clearly deserves the title of chief administrator as well as chief executive. The job of administering and applying most federal law is the day-to-day work of all of the many departments, bureaus, offices, boards, commissions, councils, and other agencies Federal Government. All of the some 2.7 million men and women who staff those agencies are subject to the President's control and direction.

The President has the power to issue executive orders. An **executive order** is a directive, rule, or regulation that has the effect of law. The power to issue these orders, the **ordinance power,** arises from two sources: the Constitution and acts of Congress.

The Constitution does not mention the ordinance power in so many words, but that power is clearly intended. In granting certain powers to the President, the Constitution obviously anticipates their use. In order to exercise those powers, the President must have the power to issue the necessary orders, as well as the power to implement them. The President must also have the power to authorize his subordinates to issue such orders.[3]

The number, the scope, and the complexity of governmental problems has grown over the years. As a result, Congress has found it necessary to delegate more and more discretion to the President and to presidential subordinates to spell out the policies and programs it has passed. Members of Congress are not, and cannot be expected to be, experts in all of the fields in which they must legislate.

▲ During World War II, President Franklin D. Roosevelt issued executive orders requiring gasoline and other strategic war supplies to be rationed—sold in limited quantities. *Critical Thinking Why is it important that the President have such a power, instead of Congress?* H-SS 12.7.5

The Appointment Power

A President cannot hope to succeed without loyal subordinates who support the policies of the President's administration. The Constitution provides that the President

> **FROM THE Constitution** *"by and with the Advice and Consent of the Senate . . . shall appoint Ambassadors, other public Ministers and Consuls, Judges of the Supreme Court, and all other Officers of the United States, whose Appointments are not herein otherwise provided for . . . but the Congress may by Law vest the Appointment of such inferior Officers, as they think proper, in the President alone, in the Courts of Law, or in the Heads of Departments.*"
> —Article II, Section 2, Clause 2

---

[3]All executive orders are published in the *Federal Register,* which appears five times a week. At least once a year, all orders currently in force are published in the *Code of Federal Regulations.* Both of these publications are issued by the National Archives and Records Administration.

Those officers whose appointments are "otherwise provided for" are the Vice President, members of the House and Senate, and presidential electors.

Acting alone, the President names only a handful of the 2.7 million federal civilian employees. Many of that handful fill the top spots in the White House Office, as you shall see shortly.

Appointees

With Senate consent, the President names most of the top-ranking officers of the Federal Government. Among them are:

(1) ambassadors and other diplomats;

(2) Cabinet members and their top aides;

(3) the heads of such independent agencies as the Environmental Protection Agency and the National Aeronautics and Space Administration;

(4) all federal judges, U.S. marshals, and attorneys;

(5) all officers in the armed forces.

When the President makes one of these appointments, the nomination is sent to the Senate. There, the support of a majority of the senators present and voting is needed for confirmation.

The unwritten rule of senatorial courtesy plays an important part in this process. That rule applies to the choice of those federal officers who serve within a State—a federal district judge or a federal marshal, for example. The rule holds that the Senate will approve only those federal appointees acceptable to the senator or senators of the President's party from the State involved. The practical effect of this custom, which is closely followed in the Senate, is to place a meaningful part of the President's appointing power in the hands of particular senators.

Recess Appointments

The Constitution does allow the President to make "recess appointments," that is, appointments "to fill up all Vacancies that may happen during the Recess of the Senate."[4] Any such appointment automatically expires at the end of the congressional term in which it is made.

Recess appointments have often been a matter of contention—in particular, because they make

it possible for the President to bypass the Senate confirmation process. So, as a rule, Presidents have not usually given these appointments to highly controversial personalities or to someone whom the Senate has previously rejected.

The Confirmation Process

For nominees who must be approved by the Senate, a multi-step process leads to their acceptance or rejection. Here are the steps involved in the confirmation of a high-level official nominated by the President, such as a Supreme Court justice.

Nomination
President's staff conducts a thorough search for a competent and acceptable candidate, getting input from key experts inside and outside of government. The President submits his choice to the Senate.

> In 1993, President Clinton nominated Ruth Bader Ginsburg (shown below), a federal Court of Appeals judge for the District of Columbia Circuit, to serve on the Supreme Court.

Senate Committee Hearings
The nomination goes to the appropriate Senate committee. The nominee testifies before the committee—a sometimes grueling process if there is strong opposition to the candidate. The committee calls other experts to testify for and against the nominee. A majority vote is needed to recommend the nominee to the Senate.

> Ginsburg's past doubts about the *Roe* v. *Wade* abortion ruling stirred initial resistance. She had favored a gradual legalization of abortion. But in the hearings she affirmed her support for abortion rights.

Senate Debate
The full Senate considers the nomination. Senators express their views before a floor vote is taken.

> The White House had consulted key senators of both parties before submitting Ginsburg's nomination. Thus, debate was minimal.

Confirmation
If a simple majority votes to approve the nominee, he or she is confirmed.

> On August 3, 1993, by a vote of 97 to 3, the Senate confirmed Ginsburg's nomination. She became the second woman ever to serve on the Supreme Court.

Rejection
If the nominee is rejected, another nomination is made. If strong opposition arises during the process, the President may withdraw the nomination or the nominee may bow out to avoid rejection.

Interpreting Diagrams In recent years, some nominees for top-level jobs have been subjected to bitter, hostile questioning at Senate hearings. Critics worry that the grueling process causes some talented people to shun public service. *Why, do you think, did the Framers create this multi-step process?* H-SS 12.4.6

---

[4] Article II, Section 3. Over time, the words "may happen" have come to mean "may happen to exist" and "the Recess of the Senate" has come to include both the period between regular sessions of Congress and the several short recesses during a session.

Of course, not all executive branch employees are chosen by the President and Senate. Well over half of all the federal civilian work force is selected on the basis of competitive civil service examinations. Today, the Office of Personnel Management examines applicants for some 1.7 million positions.

The Removal Power

The power to remove is the other side of the appointment coin, and it is as critically important to presidential success as the power to appoint. Yet, except for mention of the little-used impeachment process,[5] the Constitution does not say how or by whom appointed officers may be dismissed, whether for incompetence, for opposition to presidential policies, or for any other cause.

The Historical Debate

The question was hotly debated in the first session of Congress in 1789. Several members argued that for those offices for which appointment required Senate approval, Senate consent should also be required for removal. They insisted that this restriction on presiden-

---

[5]Article I, Section 2, Clause 5 and Section 3, Clauses 6 and 7, and Article II, Section 4.

▶ The only removal power specified in the Constitution is that of impeachment, the threat of which prompted Richard Nixon to resign the presidency and brought Gerald Ford to the office in 1974.

tial authority was essential to congressional supervision (oversight) of the executive branch. But others argued that the President could not "take care that the laws be faithfully executed" without a free hand to dismiss those who were incompetent or otherwise undesirable.

The latter view prevailed. The First Congress gave to the President the power to remove any officer he appointed, except federal judges. Over the years since then, Congress has sometimes tried, with little success, to restrict the President's freedom to dismiss.

One notable instance came in 1867. Locked with Andrew Johnson in the fight over Reconstruction, Congress passed the Tenure of Office Act. The law's plain purpose was to prevent President Johnson from removing several top officers in his administration, especially the secretary of war, Edwin M. Stanton. The law provided that any person holding an office by presidential appointment with Senate consent should remain in that office until a successor had been confirmed by the Senate.

The President vetoed the bill, charging that it was an unconstitutional invasion of executive authority. Johnson's veto was overridden, but he ignored Congress and fired Stanton anyway. The veto and Stanton's removal sparked the move for Johnson's impeachment. Ultimately, the President was acquitted, and the law was ignored in practice. It was finally repealed in 1887.

Removal and the Court

The question of the President's removal power did not reach the Supreme Court until *Myers* v. *United States*, 1926. In 1876, Congress had passed a law requiring Senate consent before the President could dismiss any first-class, second-class, or third-class postmaster.

In 1920, without consulting the Senate, President Woodrow Wilson removed Frank Myers as the postmaster at Portland, Oregon. Myers then sued for the salary for the rest of his four-year term. He based his claim on the point that he had been removed in violation of the 1876 law.

The Court found the law unconstitutional. The majority opinion was written by Chief Justice William Howard Taft, himself a former President. The Court held that the power of removal was an essential part of the executive power, clearly necessary to the faithful execution of the laws.

The Supreme Court did place some limits on the President's removal power in 1935, in *Humphrey's Executor* v. *United States*. President Herbert Hoover had appointed William Humphrey to a seven-year term on the Federal Trade Commission (FTC) in 1931. When Franklin D. Roosevelt entered office in 1933, he found Humphrey to be in sharp disagreement with many of his policies. He asked Humphrey to resign, saying that his administration would be better served with someone else on the FTC. When Humphrey refused, Roosevelt removed him. Humphrey soon died, but his heirs filed a suit for back salary.

The Supreme Court upheld the heirs' claim. It based its decision on the act creating the FTC. That law provides that a member of the commission may be removed only for "inefficiency, neglect of duty, or malfeasance in office." The President had given none of these reasons when he removed Humphrey.

The Court further held that Congress does have the power to set the conditions under which a member of the FTC and other such agencies might be removed by the President. It did so because those agencies, the independent regula-

DWANE POWELL
Courtesy News & Observer (N.C.)

Interpreting Political Cartoons President Ronald Reagan's young budget director, David Stockman, cleverly and swiftly pushed through Congress severe budget cuts based on uncertain budget figures. When Stockman admitted as much in a famous magazine interview in 1985, Reagan fired him. ***How does this cartoon reflect this newsmaking episode?***

tory commissions, are not purely executive agencies—a rather complicated point covered in the next chapter.

As a general rule, the President may remove those whom the President appoints. Occasionally, the President does have to remove someone. Most often, however, what was in fact a dismissal is called a "resignation."

Section 2 Assessment

Key Terms and Main Ideas

1. In taking the **oath of office,** what does the President promise to do?
2. How does the President affect the meaning of many of the laws passed by Congress?
3. What is an **executive order,** and in what ways does it give the President great power?
4. What is the **ordinance power,** and where does the President get this power?
5. **(a)** Which officials does the President appoint? **(b)** What is the Senate's role in the appointment process?

Critical Thinking

6. **Making Decisions** Should the President have the sole power to remove all officials he appoints? Or should the Senate have a role in deciding whether to remove officials

Standards Monitoring *Online*
For: Self-quiz with vocabulary practice
Web Code: mqa-4142

that it confirmed? Summarize the arguments on both sides of this debate. Then decide which side you favor, and explain why.

7. **Making Comparisons** Compare and contrast the Supreme Court rulings in *Myers* v. *United States* and *Humphrey's Executor* v. *United States.*

Go Online
PHSchool.com
For: An activity on the President's appointing power
Web Code: mqd-4142

Face the
Issues

President George W. Bush

Executive Powers

Background *A number of the nation's chief executives have argued that the Constitution gives the President the authority to refuse to disclose certain information to Congress or to the federal courts. They have claimed what, since the Eisenhower Administration, has been called "executive privilege." Most often, a claim of executive privilege has been made with regard to conversations and other communications between the President and his closest advisors. When can the President resist congressional or judicial requests or demands for information?*

 **Analysis Skill HR3**

Respect the Need for Confidentiality	Respect for Open Government

Both the doctrine of separation of powers and more than two centuries of practice give the President the right to refuse to disclose certain information to Congress or to the courts. That authority, executive privilege, is absolutely essential to the effective exercise of presidential powers. The Supreme Court first recognized the existence of executive privilege in an historic case, *United States v. Nixon,* in 1974.

The chief executive must rely on the information and advice he receives from key advisors. Clearly, he must be certain that those aides speak to him frankly, honestly, and without reservation. Their ability to do so depends on the confidential nature, the secrecy, of their relationships with the President. Those officials must be certain that what they say to the chief executive will be known publicly only if and when the President chooses to disclose that information.

The system of separation of powers guarantees that Congress' power to make law and the courts' power to decide cases will clash with the President's power to execute the law. Still, Congress and the courts must have access to all of the information necessary to the proper exercise of their constitutional responsibilities.

Too often, executive privilege has been used to cover up some wrongdoing in the executive branch or to shield the President or other official from personal embarrassment. President Nixon claimed executive privilege in an unsuccessful attempt to protect himself from the consequences of the Watergate scandal. More recently, President Bill Clinton sought to contain the fallout from his affair with Monica Lewinsky.

Properly, the President's ability to invoke executive privilege should be limited to the protection of information deemed vital to the security of the United States.

Exploring the Issues

1. Should the executive branch have the right to keep all discussions with advisors private? Why or why not?
2. How serious are concerns about national security when information from Presidential meetings is released to the public? Explain.

For more information about the President's powers, view "President's Powers".

Diactic and Military Powers

3 Diplomatic and Military Powers

Section Preview

OBJECTIVES

1. **Explain** how treaties are made and approved.
2. **Explain** why and how executive agreements are made.
3. **Summarize** for what purposes the power of recognition is used, and give historic examples.
4. **Describe** the powers that the President has in the role of commander in chief.

WHY IT MATTERS

The President shares various diplomatic and military powers with Congress, but in some areas the President's power is almost unlimited.

POLITICAL DICTIONARY

★ treaty
★ executive agreement
★ recognition
★ *persona non grata*

John F. Kennedy once described the pressures of the presidency in these words:

> **PRIMARY Sources** *"When I ran for the presidency . . . I knew the country faced serious challenges, but I could not realize— nor could any man who does not bear the burdens of this office—how heavy and constant would be those burdens."*
>
> —President John F. Kennedy, radio and TV broadcast on the Berlin crisis, July 25, 1961

When President Kennedy made that comment, he had in mind the subject of this section: the President's awesome responsibilities as chief diplomat and as commander in chief.

The Power to Make Treaties

A **treaty** is a formal agreement between two or more sovereign states. The President, usually acting through the secretary of state, negotiates these international agreements. The Senate must give its approval, by a two-thirds vote of the members present, before a treaty made by the President can become effective. Recall, the Constitution makes treaties a part of the "supreme Law of the Land."

Contrary to popular belief, the Senate does not ratify treaties. The Constitution requires the Senate's "Advice and Consent" to a treaty made by the President. Once the Senate has approved a treaty, the President ratifies it by the exchange of formal notifications with the other party or parties to the agreement.

Treaties have the same legal standing as do acts passed by Congress. Congress may abrogate (repeal) a treaty by passing a law contrary to its provisions, and an existing law may be repealed by the terms of a treaty. When a treaty and a federal law conflict, the courts consider the latest enacted to be the law (*The Head Money Cases*, 1884). The terms of a treaty cannot conflict with the higher law of the Constitution (*Missouri* v. *Holland*, 1920), but the Supreme Court has never found a treaty provision to be unconstitutional.

▲ In 1945, the ailing President Franklin D. Roosevelt (right) undertook an ambitious trip to meet at sea with Saudi Arabia's King Ibn Saud, a key ally in the Middle East. *Critical Thinking In what way are the President's diplomatic powers among his strongest?*

Executive Agreements

Many international agreements, especially routine ones, are made as executive agreements. An **executive agreement** is a pact between the President and the head of a foreign state, or between their subordinates. Unlike treaties, executive agreements do not require Senate consent.

Most executive agreements flow out of legislation already passed by Congress or out of treaties to which the Senate has agreed. However, the President can make these executive agreements without any congressional action.[7]

A few executive agreements have been extraordinary—most notably, the destroyers-for-bases deal of 1940. That pact was struck in the first year of World War II, more than a year before the United States became directly involved in the conflict. Under its terms, the United States gave Great Britain 50 "over-age" U.S. destroyers, naval vessels that the British desperately needed to combat German submarine attacks in the North Atlantic. In return, the United States received 99-year leases to a string of air and naval bases extending from Newfoundland to the Caribbean.

The Power of Recognition

When the President receives the diplomatic representatives of another sovereign state, the President exercises the power of **recognition.** That is, the President, acting for the United States, acknowledges the legal existence of that country and its government. The President indicates that the United States accepts that country as an equal in the family of nations. Sovereign states generally recognize one another through the exchange of diplomatic representatives.[8]

Recognition does not mean that one government approves of the character and conduct of another. The United States recognizes several governments about which it has serious misgivings. Among the most notable examples today is the People's Republic of China. The facts of

▲ *The Panama Canal* Former President Jimmy Carter attended the ceremony transferring control of the Panama Canal to Panama on December 14, 1999. **H-SS 12.7.8**

The Framers considered the Senate—with, originally, only 26 members—a suitable council to advise the President in foreign affairs. Secrecy was thought to be necessary and was seen as an impossibility in a body as large as the House.

The two-thirds rule creates the possibility that a relatively small minority in the Senate can kill a treaty. Take one of the most dramatic examples: In 1920 the Senate rejected the Treaty of Versailles, the general peace agreement to end World War I. The treaty included provisions for the League of Nations. Forty-nine senators voted for the pact and 35 against, but the vote was 7 short of the necessary two thirds. More than once a President has been forced to bow to the views of a few senators in order to get a treaty approved, even when this has meant making concessions opposed by the majority.

At times, a President has had to turn to roundabout methods in order to achieve his goals. When a Senate minority defeated a treaty to annex Texas, President Tyler was able to bring about annexation in 1845 by encouraging passage of a joint resolution—a move that required only a majority vote in each house. In 1898 President McKinley used the same tactic to annex Hawaii, again after a treaty his administration had negotiated had failed in the Senate.

---

[7]The Supreme Court has held executive agreements to be as binding as treaties and to be a part of the supreme law of the land, *United States* v. *Belmont,* 1937; *United States* v. *Pink,* 1942.

[8]Recognition may be carried out by other means, such as proposing to negotiate a treaty, since under international law only sovereign states can make such agreements.

life in world politics make relations with these governments necessary.

Recognition is often used as a weapon in foreign relations, too. President Theodore Roosevelt's quick recognition of Panama in 1903 is a classic example of the use of the power as a diplomatic weapon. He recognized the new state less than three days after the Panamanians had begun a revolt against Colombia, of which Panama had been a part. Roosevelt's action guaranteed their success. Similarly, President Truman's recognition of Israel, within hours of its creation in 1948, helped that new state to survive among its hostile Arab neighbors.

The President may show American displeasure with the conduct of another country by asking for the recall of that nation's ambassador or other diplomatic representatives in this country. The official recalled is declared to be *persona non grata,* an unwelcome person. The same point can be made by the recalling of an American diplomat from a post in another country. The withdrawal of recognition is the sharpest diplomatic rebuke one government may give to another and has often been a step on the way to war.

Commander in Chief

The Constitution makes the President the commander in chief of the nation's armed forces.[9] Recall, Congress does have extensive war powers; see pages 301–302. But the President dominates the field of military policy. In fact, the President's powers as commander in chief are almost without limit.

Consider this illustration of the point: In 1907 Theodore Roosevelt sent the Great White Fleet around the world. He did so partly as a training exercise for the Navy, but mostly to impress other nations with America's naval might. Several members of Congress objected to the cost and threatened to block funds for the President's project. To this Roosevelt replied:

"Very well, the existing appropriation will carry the Navy halfway around the world and if Congress chooses to leave it on the other side, all right." Congress was forced to give in.

Presidents delegate much of their command authority to military subordinates. They are not required to do so, however. George Washington actually took command of federal troops and led them into Pennsylvania during the Whiskey Rebellion of 1794. Abraham Lincoln often visited the Army of the Potomac and instructed his generals in the field during the Civil War.

Most Presidents have not become so directly involved in military operations. Still, the President always has the final authority over and responsibility for all military matters, and the most critical decisions are invariably made by the commander in chief.

Making Undeclared War

Does the Constitution give the President the power to make war without a declaration of war by Congress? Although many argue that it does not, 200 years of American history argue otherwise. Presidents have often used the armed forces abroad, in combat, without a declaration of war.[10] In fact, most Presidents have done so, and on several hundred occasions.

John Adams was the first to do so, in 1798. At his command, the Navy fought and won a number of battles with French warships harassing American merchantmen in the Atlantic and the Caribbean. Thomas Jefferson and then James Madison followed that precedent in the war against the Barbary Coast pirates of

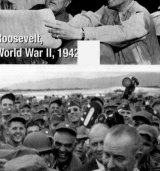

Lincoln, Civil War, 1862

Roosevelt, World War II, 1942

Johnson, Vietnam War, 1967

G.H.W. Bush, pre-Gulf War, 1990

G.W. Bush, War in Iraq, 2003

▲ Presidents have sent the nation's armed forces into combat on hundreds of occasions. *Critical Thinking Why did the Framers choose the President, rather than a military officer, to be commander in chief?* H-SS 12.7.8

[9] Article II, Section 2, Clause 1; see also Chapter 17.

[10] Altogether, Congress has declared war eleven times. It did so against Great Britain in 1812 (the War of 1812); Mexico in 1848 (the Mexican War); Spain in 1898 (the Spanish-American War); Germany and Austria-Hungary in 1917 (World War I); Japan, Germany, and Italy in 1941 and Bulgaria, Hungary, and Romania in 1942 (World War II).

In his second inaugural address in 2005, President **George W. Bush** expressed the values underlying American foreign policy.

❝We are led, by events and common sense, to one conclusion: The survival of liberty in our land increasingly depends on the success of liberty in other lands. The best hope for peace in our world is the expansion of freedom in all the world. . . . Across the generations we have proclaimed the imperative of self-government, because no one is fit to be a master, and no one deserves to be a slave. **❞**

Evaluating the Quotation

How might the President's comments be applied to events in the world today?

North Africa in the early 1800s. There have been a great many other foreign adventures over the past two centuries. The long military conflicts in Korea (from 1950 to 1953) and in Vietnam (from 1965 to 1973) were, at least to this point, the most extensive of those "undeclared wars."

Congressional Resolutions

Congress has not declared war since World War II. On eight occasions since then, however, it has enacted joint resolutions to authorize the President to meet certain international crises with military force:

- President Dwight Eisenhower sought the first of these measures in 1955, to block the designs the People's Republic of China had (and still has) on Taiwan. That show of American resolve, and the presence of American warships, defused the situation.

- In 1957, Congress gave President Eisenhower the authority to use force to check Soviet efforts to gain a foothold in the Middle East. The President dispatched a large contingent of Marines to Lebanon in 1958, to forestall a Soviet-backed coup.

- In 1962, Congress authorized President John F. Kennedy to use the armed forces to deal with the extraordinary dangers posed by installation of Soviet missiles in Cuba.

- In 1962, Congress passed another resolution, to sanction any necessary military response to the erection of the Berlin Wall.

- In 1964, President Lyndon Johnson was directed "to take all necessary steps, including the use of armed force" to defeat communist aggression in Southeast Asia. American forces were not finally withdrawn from Vietnam until 1973.

- In 1991, President George H. W. Bush gained congressional approval for a military campaign to drive Iraq out of Kuwait. Immediately, an international coalition, led by the United States, launched Desert Storm—massive air and then ground attacks on Iraqi troops in Kuwait. The Persian Gulf War ended less than six weeks later, with the liberation of Kuwait and Iraq's defeat.

- In 2001, President George W. Bush was given the authority to use military force against those responsible for the September 11 attacks on the Pentagon and the World Trade Center. That resolution triggered the war in Afghanistan. The Taliban regime, which had sheltered Osama bin Laden and al Qaida terrorists, was eliminated within a few months, but sporadic fighting continues in that country even today. American military units are also engaged in anti-terrorist operations in several other places, including the Philippines, the Republic of Georgia, and Yemen.

- In 2002, Congress agreed that President Bush should take whatever measures were "necessary and appropriate" to eliminate the threat posed by Saddam Hussein and his Iraqi dictatorship. It was widely believed that that regime had amassed huge stores of chemical and biological weapons and was seeking to become a nuclear power—all in direct violation of the Gulf War's cease-fire agreement. In March 2003, a new (but smaller) international coalition, led by the United States, launched Operation Iraqi Freedom—a well-executed military campaign that ousted Saddam Hussein and his government from power. Some 140,000 American troops remain in Iraq today, engaged in the difficult and often dangerous tasks of stabilizing and rebuilding that country.

Other Uses of Military Power

Over the more than 60 years since the end of World War II, there have been many other critical situations in which Presidents have deployed the nation's armed forces—without a congressional resolution to support the action. Certainly, the Korean War stands as the foremost illustration of that fact. Among the other more notable instances:

• The lightning-quick invasion of Grenada, ordered by President Ronald Reagan in 1983, to frustrate a military coup in that Caribbean island nation.

• The invasion of Panama, at the command of President George H.W. Bush in 1989, to oust the dictatorship of General Manuel Noriega and protect American interests there—in particular, the Panama Canal.

• The dispatch of American forces to the Balkans by President Bill Clinton (to Bosnia in 1995 and to Kosovo in 1999) as part of NATO's response to a vicious civil war and the horrific "ethnic cleansing" campaign conducted by the forces of Serbian President Slobodan Milosevic.

The War Powers Resolution

In today's world, no one can doubt that the President must be able to respond rapidly and effectively to threats to this nation's security. Still, many people have long warned of the dangers inherent in the President's power to involve the nation in undeclared wars. They insist that the Constitution never intended the President to have such power.

The nation's frustrations and growing anguish over the war in Vietnam finally moved Congress to pass the War Powers Resolution of 1973. The act is designed to place close limits on the President's war-making powers. President Nixon vetoed the measure, calling it "both unconstitutional and dangerous to the best interest of our nation." Congress overrode the veto.

The resolution's central provisions require that:

(1) Within 48 hours after committing American forces to combat abroad, the President must report to Congress, detailing the circumstances and the scope of his actions.

(2) A commitment of American forces to combat must end within 60 days, unless Congress agrees to a longer period. That 60-day deadline may be extended for up to 30 days, however, to allow for the safe withdrawal of the American forces involved.

(3) Congress may end the combat commitment at any time, by passing a concurrent resolution to that effect.

The constitutionality of the War Powers Resolution remains in dispute. A determination of the question must await a situation in which Congress demands that its provisions be obeyed but the President refuses to do so.

Section 3 Assessment

Key Terms and Main Ideas

1. Summarize the process by which treaties are negotiated and approved.
2. What is the difference between a **treaty** and an **executive agreement**?
3. Explain this statement: *The President's power of recognition can be used positively or negatively.*
4. Under what circumstances might the President declare a country's diplomat to be **persona non grata?**
5. Which of the President's powers is almost unlimited? Why?

Critical Thinking

6. **Making Inferences** Why might a new country eagerly seek diplomatic recognition from the United States?

 **Standards Monitoring *Online***
For: Self-quiz with vocabulary practice
Web Code: mqa-4143

7. **Drawing Conclusions** Framer George Mason said, "The purse and the sword must never be in the same hands." How is this idea reflected in the War Powers Resolution?

Go **Online**
PHSchool.com

For: An activity on presidential agreements
Web Code: mqd-4143

CLOSE UP FOUNDATION *on Primary Sources*

The Monroe Doctrine

Analysis Skills HR4, HI3

In the early 1800s, Spain's Central and South American colonies rebelled and gained their independence. U.S. leaders applauded these successful revolutions, but worried that Spain and its allies would reconquer the region. In 1823, President James Monroe discussed these concerns in a message to Congress. He set out what soon came to be known as the Monroe Doctrine, which became a cornerstone of American foreign policy.

The occasion has been judged proper for asserting, as a principle in which the rights and interests of the United States are involved, that the American continents, by the free and independent condition which they have assumed and maintain, are henceforth not to be considered as subjects for future colonization by any European powers. . . .

United States military might upholds the Monroe Doctrine against European powers in this early twentieth-century cartoon.

In the wars of the European powers, in matters relating to themselves, we have never taken any part, nor does it comport with our policy so to do. It is only when our rights are invaded or seriously menaced that we resent injuries or make preparation for our defense.

With the movements in this hemisphere we are of necessity more immediately connected. . . . The political system of the [European] powers is essentially different . . . from . . . our own, which has been achieved by the loss of so much blood and treasure. . . . We owe it, therefore, to candor and to the amicable [friendly] relations existing between the United States and those powers to declare that we should consider any attempt on their part to extend their system to any portion of this hemisphere as dangerous to our peace and safety.

With the existing colonies or dependencies of any European power we have not interfered and shall not interfere. But with the governments who have declared their independence and maintained it, . . . we could not view any interposition [intervention]

for the purpose of oppressing them . . . in any other light than as the manifestation of an unfriendly disposition [attitude] toward the United States. . . .

Our policy in regard to Europe . . . remains the same, which is, not to interfere in the internal concerns of any of its powers; . . . to cultivate friendly relations with it, and to preserve those relations by a frank, firm, and manly policy. . . . But, in regard to [the American] continents, circumstances are eminently and conspicuously different. It is impossible that the allied powers should extend their political system to any portion of either continent without endangering our peace and happiness; nor can anyone believe that our southern brethren, if left to themselves, would adopt it of their own accord. . . . It is still the true policy of the United States to leave the parties to themselves in the hope that other powers will pursue the same course.

Analyzing Primary Sources

1. According to Monroe, what was the foreign policy of the United States toward the nations of Europe?
2. Why was Monroe concerned about European expansion in Central and South America?
3. Monroe's statement suggests he was most concerned about whose independence, the South American nations or the United States? Explain.

Legislative and Judicial Powers

Section Preview

OBJECTIVES

1. **Describe** the President's two major legislative powers, and explain how these powers are an important part of the system of checks and balances.
2. **Describe** the President's major judicial powers.

WHY IT MATTERS

The Constitution gives the President strong legislative and judicial powers as a part of the system of checks and balances.

POLITICAL DICTIONARY

★ line-item veto
★ reprieve
★ pardon
★ clemency
★ commutation
★ amnesty

As you know, the Federal Government is built on the principles of separation of powers and checks and balances. The Constitution gives to each of the three branches its own powers. It also gives to each of them powers with which to check—to delay or block—actions by the other two branches. As James Madison put it in *The Federalist* No. 51, each branch of the Federal Government has "the necessary constitutional means and personal motives to resist encroachments of the others."

Legislative Powers

With his legislative powers, and the skillful playing of his roles as chief of party and chief citizen, the President can (and often does) have a considerable influence on the actions of Congress. The President is, in effect, the nation's chief legislator.

Recommending Legislation

The Constitution says that the President

> **FROM THE Constitution** *shall from time to time give to the Congress Information on the State of the Union, and recommend to their Consideration such Measures as he shall judge necessary and expedient. . . .*
> —Article II, Section 3

This provision gives the President what is often called the *message power*.

The Chief Executive regularly sends three major messages to Capitol Hill each year. The first is the State of the Union message, a speech he almost always delivers in person to a joint session of Congress. The President's budget message and the annual Economic Report follow that speech soon after. The President often sends the lawmakers a number of other messages on a wide range of topics. In each of them, he calls on Congress to enact those laws he thinks to be necessary to the welfare of the country.

The Veto Power

The Constitution says that "Every Bill" and "Every Order, Resolution, or Vote to which the Concurrence of the Senate and House of Representatives may be necessary (except on a question of Adjournment) shall be presented to the President."[13]

▲ Every year, huge bound volumes of the President's budget plan arrive at the Capitol, where they are distributed for Congress's consideration.

---

[13]Article I, Section 7, Clauses 2 and 3. Recall that, despite these words, joint resolutions proposing constitutional amendments and concurrent resolutions, which do not have the force of law, are not sent to the President.

Remember, the Constitution presents the President with four options when he receives a measure passed by Congress. First, he may sign the bill, making it law. Or he can veto it, and the measure must then be returned to Congress. Of course, Congress can override a presidential veto by a two-thirds vote in each of its two chambers—but it seldom does.

As a third option, the President may allow the bill to become law by not acting on it, neither signing nor vetoing it, within 10 days (not counting Sundays). This rarely happens.

The fourth option, the pocket veto, can be used only at the end of a congressional session. If Congress adjourns within 10 days of sending a bill to the President and the chief executive does not act on it, the measure dies. Most Presidents have used the pocket veto with some frequency, because Congress regularly passes a large number of measures in the closing days of its annual sessions.

The fact that Congress is seldom able to muster the two-thirds majority needed to overturn a presidential veto makes the veto a significant weapon in the Chief Executive's dealings with the legislative branch. The weight that this power has in the executive–legislative relationship is underscored by this important point: The mere threat of a veto is often enough to defeat a bill or to prompt changes in its provisions as it moves through the legislative process. The record of presidential vetoes over the years, and the fact that they are not often overturned, can be seen in the table below.

The Line-Item Veto

If the President decides to veto a bill, he must reject the *entire* measure. He cannot veto only a portion of it.

Since Ulysses S. Grant's day, most Presidents have favored the expansion of the veto power to include a **line-item veto.** That is, they have urged that the President be given the power to cancel specific dollar amounts (line items) in spending bills enacted by Congress. Those Presidents, and the many who have supported their position, have argued over the years that the line-item veto would be a potent weapon against wasteful and unnecessary federal spending.

Over time, opponents of the line-item veto—and there have been many of them—have said that to grant the President such authority would bring a massive and dangerous shift of power to

Presidential Vetoes 1933–2005				
	Regular Vetoes	Pocket Vetoes	Total Vetoes	Vetoes Overridden
Franklin Roosevelt (1933–1945)	372	263	635	9
Harry Truman (1945–1953)	180	70	250	12
Dwight Eisenhower (1953–1961)	73	108	181	2
John Kennedy (1961–1963)	12	9	21	0
Lyndon Johnson (1963–1969)	16	14	30	0
Richard Nixon (1969–1974)	26	14	43	7
Gerald Ford (1974–1977)	48	18	66	12
Jimmy Carter (1977–1981)	13	18	31	2
Ronald Reagan (1981–1989)	39	39	78	9
George H. W. Bush (1989–1993)	29	15	44	1
Bill Clinton (1993–2001)	36	1	37	2
George W. Bush (2001–)	0	0	0	0

SOURCE: Congressional Research Service, Library of Congress

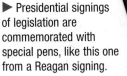

▶ Presidential signings of legislation are commemorated with special pens, like this one from a Reagan signing.

Interpreting Tables Some Presidents have used their veto power more often than others. *(a) What might explain the huge variations in numbers of total vetoes? (b) Why, do you think, did some Presidents have fewer vetoes overridden?*

the executive branch. To this point, efforts to persuade Congress to propose a line-item veto amendment to the Constitution have failed.

In 1996, however, Congress did pass the Line Item Veto Act. That law gave the President the power to reject individual items in spending bills, and to eliminate any provision of a tax bill that benefited fewer than 100 people. President Clinton hailed the statute as a major step against "special interest boondoggles, tax loopholes, and pure pork."

Opponents of the measure challenged it in the courts, and they won their case in *Clinton* v. *New York City*, 1998. There, the Supreme Court struck down the law. By a 6–3 vote, it held that Congress lacked the authority to give the President a line-item veto by statute. If the President is to have such power, said the Court, it must come via an amendment to the Constitution.

Other Legislative Powers

According to Article II, Section 3 of the Constitution, only the President can call Congress into special session. Most recently, President Truman did so in 1948, to have Congress consider post-World War II economic measures. The same constitutional provision also gives the President the power to prorogue (adjourn) Congress whenever the two houses cannot agree on a date for their adjournment—something that has never happened.

Judicial Powers

The Constitution gives the President the power to

 FROM THE Constitution "... *Grant Reprieves and Pardons for Offenses against the United States, except in Cases of Impeachment.* "

—Article II, Section 2, Clause 1

A **reprieve** is the postponement of the execution of a sentence. A **pardon** is legal forgiveness of a crime.

The President's power to grant reprieves and pardons is absolute, except in cases of impeachment, where they may never be granted. These powers of **clemency** (mercy or leniency) may be used only in cases involving federal offenses. The President has no such authority with regard to those who violate State law.

Interpreting Cartoons This cartoon comments on the increasing power of the President—in this case, Harry Truman, who was President from 1945–1953. *According to the cartoonist, who is responsible for this growth in power?* **H-SS 12.1.5**

Presidential pardons are usually granted after a person has been convicted in court. Yet the President may pardon a federal offender before that person is tried, or even before that person has been formally charged.

Pardons in advance of a trial or charge are rare. The most noteworthy pardon, by far, was granted in 1974. In that year, President Gerald Ford gave "a full, free and absolute pardon unto Richard Nixon for all offenses against the United States which he . . . has committed or may have committed or taken part in during the period from January 20, 1969, through August 9, 1974." Of course, that pardon referred to the Watergate scandal—the many and sordid events that ultimately forced Nixon to resign the presidency.

To be effective, a pardon must be accepted by the person to whom it is granted. When one is granted before charge or conviction, as in Nixon's case, its acceptance is regularly seen as an admission of guilt by the person to whom it is given.

Nearly all pardons are accepted, of course, and usually gratefully. A few have been rejected, however. One of the most dramatic refusals led to a Supreme Court case, *Burdick* v. *United States*, 1915. George Burdick, a New York newspaper editor, had refused to testify before a federal grand jury regarding the sources for certain news stories his paper had printed. Those stories

▲ Some men called to serve in the Vietnam War burned their draft cards in protest. Others went into hiding, many fleeing to Canada. In 1977 President Carter pardoned them. *Critical Thinking* **What might have been Carter's motive for using his presidential power to pardon the draft evaders?**

Interestingly, Burdick refused to accept the pardon, and he continued to refuse to testify. With that, the federal judge in that district fined and jailed him for contempt. The judge ruled that (1) the President's pardon was fully effective, with or without Burdick's acceptance and (2) there was, therefore, no basis for Burdick's continued claim of protection against self-incrimination.

The Supreme Court overturned the lower court's action. It unanimously upheld the rule that a pardon must be accepted in order to be effective, and it ordered Burdick's release from jail.

The pardoning power includes the power to grant conditional pardons, provided the conditions are reasonable. It also includes the power of **commutation**—that is, the power to commute (reduce) the length of a sentence or a fine imposed by a court.

The pardoning power also includes the power of **amnesty,** in effect a blanket pardon offered to a group of law violators. Thus, in 1893 President Benjamin Harrison issued a proclamation of amnesty forgiving all Mormons who had violated the antipolygamy (multiple marriage) laws in the federal territories. In 1977 President Jimmy Carter granted amnesty to Vietnam War draft evaders.

reported fraud in the collection of customs duties. He invoked the 5th Amendment, claiming that his testimony could incriminate him. President Woodrow Wilson then granted Burdick "a full and unconditional pardon for all offenses against the United States" that he might have committed in obtaining material for the news stories.

Section 4 Assessment

Key Terms and Main Ideas

1. What are the President's two major legislative powers?
2. What happened to the **line-item veto** law passed by Congress in 1996?
3. Explain how these judicial powers of the President differ: **reprieve, pardon, clemency, commutation, amnesty.**

Critical Thinking

4. **Expressing Problems Clearly** Write two paragraphs summarizing the arguments for and against the line-item veto.
5. **Predicting Consequences** Why, do you think, has no President had to use the power to prorogue Congress?

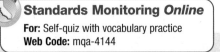

Standards Monitoring *Online*
For: Self-quiz with vocabulary practice
Web Code: mqa-4144

6. **Making Inferences** In giving the President several important judicial powers, what kinds of situations might the Framers have been anticipating?

For: An activity on presidential agreements
Web Code: mqd-4144

When Must the President Reveal Information to a Court?

Analysis Skills HR4, HI3, HI4

Historically, a number of the nation's chief executives have argued that the content of conversations and other communications between the President and his closest aides should not be made public without the President's consent. Does that claim of executive privilege allow a President to withhold information vital to the prosecution of a criminal case?

United States v. Nixon (1974)

During the 1972 presidential campaign, five burglars with links to President Richard Nixon's reelection campaign broke into Democratic headquarters at the Watergate complex in Washington, D.C. Over the next two years, the Nixon administration denied any involvement in what came to be known as the "Watergate scandal." Ultimately, Archibald Cox, the special prosecutor appointed to investigate the criminal aspects of the break-in, brought criminal charges against several of the President's highest ranking advisors, accusing them of conspiring to obstruct justice.

During Senate hearings, a White House aide revealed that the President had secretly taped most of his telephone calls and personal conversations in the Oval Office. When both the special prosecutor and a federal district court ordered Mr. Nixon to release those tapes, he refused. The matter was then carried to the Supreme Court.

Arguments for Nixon

1. In accord with the doctrine of separation of powers, no court has the authority to question a President's claim of executive privilege.
2. The President must have the power to keep his various communications secret. Without that guarantee of confidentiality, presidential aides would not speak as freely as they might, and the President's decision-making ability would be harmed.
3. The forced disclosure of communications between the President and his advisors could pose a threat to the nation's security.

Arguments for the United States

1. Separation of powers does not mean that the three branches of government are absolutely independent of one another. Article III vests "the judicial power of the United States" in the federal courts; their ability to exercise that power would be severely limited without the authority to review acts of the executive branch.
2. The Sixth Amendment guarantees a fair trial to all criminal defendants. If important evidence is withheld from a court, it will be impossible to conduct fair trials.
3. The protection of the secrecy of presidential communications is important, but that protection should be limited to military and diplomatic matters.

Decide for Yourself

1. Review the constitutional grounds on which each side based its arguments and the specific arguments each side presented.
2. Debate the opposing viewpoints presented in this case. Which viewpoint do you favor?
3. Predict the impact of the Court's decision on the way Presidents and their advisors handle damaging information.

Go Online
PHSchool.com

Use Web Code mqp-4149 to register your vote on this issue and to see how other students voted.

Political Dictionary

Executive Article (p. 390), mass media (p. 391), imperial presidency (p. 392), oath of office (p. 393), executive order (p. 394), ordinance power (p. 394), treaty (p. 399), executive agreement (p. 400), recognition (p. 400), *persona non grata* (p. 401), line-item veto (p. 406), reprieve (p. 407), pardon (p. 407), clemency (p. 407), commutation (p. 408), amnesty (p. 408)

Standards Review

H-SS 12.1.5 Describe the systems of separated and shared powers, the role of organized interests (*Federalist Paper Number 10*), checks and balances (*Federalist Paper Number 51*), the importance of an independent judiciary (*Federalist Paper Number 78*), enumerated powers, rule of law, federalism, and civilian control of the military.

H-SS 12.4.4 Discuss Article II of the Constitution as it relates to the executive branch, including eligibility for office and length of term, election to and removal from office, the oath of office, and the enumerated executive powers.

H-SS 12.4.6 Explain the processes of selection and confirmation of Supreme Court justices.

H-SS 12.7.5 Explain how public policy is formed, including the setting of the public agenda and implementation of it through regulations and executive orders.

H-SS 12.7.8 Understand the scope of presidential power and decision making through examination of case studies such as the Cuban Missile Crisis, passage of Great Society legislation, War Powers Act, Gulf War, and Bosnia.

Practicing the Vocabulary

Matching *Choose a term from the list above that best matches each description.*

1. Forms of communication, including printed publications, radio, television, and, most recently, the Internet
2. A formal agreement between two or more nations that requires the approval of two thirds of the Senate
3. The President's power to grant reprieves and pardons in cases involving federal offenses
4. A directive, rule, or regulation from the President that has the effect of law
5. The President's constitutional power to issue executive orders

Fill in the Blanks *Choose a term from the list above that best completes the sentence.*

6. The _____ had been sought by many Presidents, but it was struck down by the Supreme Court as unconstitutional.
7. Unlike a treaty, a _____ does not need congressional approval.
8. The part of the Constitution that establishes the presidency is called the _____.
9. A _____ is the legal forgiveness of a crime, whereas _____ is a general pardon of a group of lawbreakers.
10. _____ can be used as a weapon in foreign relations.

Reviewing Main Ideas

Section 1

11. **(a)** Why has the wording of Article II, Section I produced controversy? **(b)** What differing views did the Framers hold about the power of the presidency?
12. How has the growing complexity of the nation's social and economic life affected presidential power?
13. What opposing views have Presidents had regarding their proper role in the job?

Section 2

14. How does the responsibility for executing the law give the President great power?
15. Why do we know that the Framers intended the President to have ordinance power?
16. Why is it important that the President have the power to appoint officials?
17. What role does senatorial courtesy have in the appointment process?
18. How did the issue of the removal power result in the impeachment of President Andrew Johnson?

Section 3

19. What types of agreements can the President make with foreign countries?
20. Why did the Framers include the Senate, but not the House, in the treaty-making process?
21. What is the power of recognition, and how can the President use it as a diplomatic tool?
22. **(a)** Describe the President's role in military affairs. **(b)** Give examples of presidential use of the power of commander in chief.

Section 4

23. How do the President's legislative and judicial powers illustrate the system of checks and balances?
24. What legislative powers does the President have?
25. How could the line-item veto be added to the President's legislative powers?
26. What judicial powers does the President have?
27. What kind of clemency did President Gerald Ford give to former President Richard Nixon?

Critical Thinking Skills

28. **Face the Issues** When Senator Joseph McCarthy investigated the Army for Communist influences, Dwight Eisenhower ordered Defense Department officials not to talk to him. Describe how you think supporters *and* opponents of executive power might have responded to Eisenhower's order.

29. **Drawing Conclusions** Why, do you think, have so many Presidents decided to make undeclared war?

30. **Predicting Consequences** (a) If the Supreme Court someday were to declare the War Powers Act unconstitutional, on what grounds might the law be struck down? (b) What might be the effect of such a ruling on presidential power?

31. **Drawing Inferences** Article II of the Constitution, which covers the powers of the executive, has been called the most loosely drawn chapter in the Constitution. Why might the Framers have created Article II in this way?

Analyzing Political Cartoons

Using your knowledge of American government and this cartoon, answer the questions below.

32. In the cartoon above, what point is being suggested about how the President and Congress carry out foreign relations? (*Note:* NATO is the North Atlantic Treaty Organization, a 26-member mutual defense group.)

Participation Activities

33. **Current Events Watch** The President often meets with leaders from other countries. Find recent news reports of such a meeting and try to answer these questions: Why did the President meet with that particular dignitary? What topics did they discuss? Why does the President frequently hold such meetings? Can these meetings have any impact on this country's foreign relations? Can they have any impact on politics in this country?

34. **Chart Activity** Create a chart that lists the various powers of the President and the sources of each power. Then write a summary statement contrasting the power of the President today with the power that the Framers intended the President to have when they created the position in 1787.

35. **It's Your Turn** You have completed your first year as President. Write the opening paragraphs of a State of the Union address. Explain how you intend to lead the nation in the year ahead. Open with a statement in which you summarize your beliefs about the role of the President. Explain what you predict will be your greatest upcoming challenge and how you will attempt to address it, using your constitutional powers. **(Writing a Speech)**

Standards Monitoring *Online*

For: Chapter 14 Self-Test **Visit:** PHSchool.com
Web Code: mqa-4145

As a final review, take the Magruder's Chapter 14 Self-Test and receive immediate feedback on your answers. The test consists of 20 multiple-choice questions designed to test your understanding of the chapter content.

CHAPTER 15

Government at Work: The Bureaucracy

"Bureaucracy is not an obstacle to democracy but an inevitable complement to it."

—Joseph A. Schumpeter (1942)

People often criticize and poke fun at the federal bureaucracy. Schumpeter, an economist, knew that it takes millions of bureaucrats to make democratic government work. Americans depend on the civil servants—from accountants to Webmasters—who work in federal agencies throughout the country.

◆ Federal workers sort income tax forms

Standards Preview

H-SS 12.1.4 Explain how the Founding Fathers' realistic view of human nature led directly to the establishment of a constitutional system that limited the power of the governors and the governed as articulated in the *Federalist Papers*.

H-SS 12.1.5 Describe the systems of separated and shared powers, the role of organized interests (*Federalist Paper Number 10*), checks and balances (*Federalist Paper Number 51*), the importance of an independent judiciary (*Federalist Paper Number 78*), enumerated powers, rule of law, federalism, and civilian control of the military.

H-SS 12.2.4 Understand the obligations of civic-mindedness, including voting, being informed on civic issues, volunteering and performing public service, and serving in the military or alternative service.

H-SS 12.4.4 Discuss Article II of the Constitution as it relates to the executive branch, including eligibility for office and length of term, election to and removal from office, the oath of office, and the enumerated executive powers.

H-SS 12.7.5 Explain how public policy is formed, including the setting of the public agenda and implementation of it through regulations and executive orders.

For: Current Data
Web Code: mqg-4157

For: Close Up Foundation debates
Web Code: mqh-4159

SECTION 1

The Federal Bureaucracy (pp. 414–418)

★ The federal bureaucracy is a large, highly organized group that carries out the work of the Federal Government.

★ The names given to agencies, including *commission, administration,* and *corporation,* may indicate an agency's nature.

★ Agencies include line agencies, which operate programs, and staff agencies, which support the line agencies.

SECTION 2

The Executive Office of the President (pp. 419–422)

★ The Executive Office of the President includes several important agencies staffed by the President's closest aides.

★ The White House Office is the "nerve center" of the Executive Office of the President.

★ Other units of the Executive Office advise the President on domestic affairs and foreign policy.

SECTION 3

The Executive Departments (pp. 424–429)

★ Each of the 15 executive departments manages federal policy in a broad field of activity, such as education, labor, or defense.

★ The heads of the departments meet with the President and other advisors in a group called the Cabinet.

★ The President chooses his nominees to lead the executive departments, subject to approval by the Senate.

★ The President decides how often the Cabinet meets.

SECTION 4

Independent Agencies (pp. 430–435)

★ Independent agencies are not part of any of the executive departments.

★ The independent agencies are of three types: independent executive agencies, independent regulatory commissions, and government corporations.

★ Independence gives these agencies some freedom from political pressure.

SECTION 5

The Civil Service (pp. 437–440)

★ The people who work in the federal bureaucracy make up the civil service.

★ Early on, the spoils system infected the civil service.

★ Corruption was a serious problem until reformers began to reshape the civil service in the 1880s.

★ Today, the vast majority of federal employees are hired and promoted on the basis of merit, not party membership.

1 The Federal Bureaucracy

Section Preview

OBJECTIVES

1. **Define** a bureaucracy.
2. **Identify** the major elements of the federal bureaucracy.
3. **Explain** how groups within the federal bureaucracy are named.
4. **Describe** the difference between a staff agency and a line agency.

WHY IT MATTERS

The Federal Government is the nation's largest employer. Nearly 2.7 million men and women work in the federal bureaucracy, and they do nearly all of the day-to-day work of the government.

POLITICAL DICTIONARY

★ **bureaucracy**
★ **bureaucrat**
★ **administration**
★ **staff agency**
★ **line agency**

Think about this for a moment: It is impossible for you to live through a single day without somehow encountering the federal bureaucracy. A **bureaucracy** is a large, complex administrative structure that handles the everyday business of an organization.[1] The Federal Government is the largest organization in the country. Federal employees deliver the mail, regulate business practices, collect taxes, manage the national forests, conduct American foreign policy, administer Social Security programs—the list goes on and on.

▲ Bureaucrats once used red ribbon, called "red tape" in Britain, to hold their files together. Today, people use the phrase "red tape" to describe the delays and paperwork they may face when working with a bureaucracy.

What Is a Bureaucracy?

To many Americans, the word *bureaucracy* suggests such things as waste, red tape, and delay. While that image is not altogether unfounded, it is quite lopsided. Basically, bureaucracy is an efficient and an effective way to organize people to do work.

Bureaucracies are found wherever there are large organizations. They are found in both the public sector and the private sector in this country. Thus, the United States Air Force, McDonald's, the Social Security Administration, MTV, your town or city government, and the Roman Catholic Church are all bureaucracies. Even your school is a bureaucracy.

Three Features of a Bureaucracy

In dictionary terms, a bureaucracy is a system of organization built on these three principles: hierarchical authority, job specialization, and formalized rules.

1. *Hierarchical authority.* The word *hierarchical* describes any organization that is built as a pyramid, with a chain of command running from the top of the pyramid to the bottom. The few officials and units at the top of the organization have authority over those

---

[1]The term *bureaucracy* is a combination of the French word *bureau,* which originally referred to a desk of a government official and later to the place where an official works, and the suffix *–cracy,* signifying a type of governmental structure.

★★★★ **414** Chapter 15 Section 1

officials and units at the larger middle level, who in turn direct the activities of the many at the bottom level.

2. *Job specialization.* Each **bureaucrat,** or person who works for the organization, has certain defined duties and responsibilities. There is a precise division of labor within the organization.

3. *Formalized rules.* The bureaucracy does its work according to a set of established regulations and procedures.

The Benefits of a Bureaucracy

These three features—hierarchical authority, job specialization, and formalized rules—make bureaucracy the most effective way for people to work together on large and complex tasks. The hierarchy can speed action by reducing conflicts over who has the power to make decisions. The higher a person's rank in the organization, the greater the decision-making power he or she has.

Job specialization promotes efficiency because each person in the organization is required to focus on one particular job. Each worker thus gains a set of specialized skills and knowledge.

Formalized rules mean that workers can act with some speed and precision because decisions are based on a set of known standards, not on someone's likes, dislikes, or inclinations. These rules also enable work to continue even as some workers leave an organization and new workers are hired to replace them.

Recognize this very important point about public bureaucracies: their bureaucrats hold appointive offices. Bureaucrats are *unelected* public-policy makers. This is not to say that bureaucracies are undemocratic. However, in a democracy much depends on how effectively the bureaucracy is controlled by those whom the people *do* elect. Listen to James Madison on the point:

 PRIMARY Sources *❝ In framing a government which is to be administered by men over men, the great difficulty lies in this: you must first enable the government to control the governed; and in the next place oblige it to control itself. ❞*

—*The Federalist* No. 51

▲ *The Reagan Building* Second only to the Pentagon in size, the Ronald Reagan Building and International Trade Center houses government offices in downtown Washington, D.C.

Major Elements of the Federal Bureaucracy

The federal bureaucracy is all of the agencies, people, and procedures through which the Federal Government operates. It is the means by which the government makes and administers public policy—the sum of its decisions and actions. As the chart on page 417 shows, nearly all of the federal bureaucracy is located in the executive branch.

The Constitution makes the President the chief administrator of the Federal Government. Article II, Section 3 declares that "he shall take Care that the Laws be faithfully executed." But the Constitution makes only the barest mention of the administrative machinery through which the President is to exercise that power.

Article II does suggest executive departments by giving to the President the power to "require

▲ A federal agency can be called a *commission, bureau, administration,* or one of several other names. **Critical Thinking Why is commission *an appropriate name for the SEC, which oversees stock markets?* H-SS 12.7.5**

the Opinion, in writing, of the principal Officer in each of the executive Departments."[2]

Article II anticipates two departments in particular, one for military and one for foreign affairs. It does so by making the President the "Commander in Chief of the Army and Navy," and by giving him the power to make treaties and to appoint "Ambassadors, other public Ministers, and Consuls."[3]

Beyond those references, the Constitution is silent on the organization of the executive branch. The Framers certainly intended for administrative agencies to be created, however. They understood that no matter how wise the President and the Congress, their decisions still had to be acted upon to be effective. Without an **administration**— the government's many administrators and agencies—even the best policies would amount to just so many words and phrases. The President and Congress need millions of men and women to put policies into action in Washington, D.C., and in offices all around the country.

The chief organizational feature of the federal bureaucracy is its division into areas of specialization. As you can see on page 417, the executive branch is composed of three broad groups of agencies: (1) the Executive Office of the President, (2) the 15 Cabinet departments, and (3) a large number of independent agencies.[4]

The Name Game

The titles given to the many units that make up the executive branch vary a great deal. The name *department* is reserved for agencies of Cabinet rank. Beyond the title of *department,* however, there is little standardized use of titles.

Common titles used in the executive branch include *agency, administration, commission, corporation,* and *authority.*

The term *agency* is often used to refer to any governmental body. It is sometimes used to identify a major unit headed by a single administrator of near-cabinet status, such as the Environmental Protection Agency. But so, too, is the title *administration;* for example, the National Aeronautics and Space Administration and the General Services Administration.

The name *commission* is usually given to agencies charged with the regulation of business activities, such as the Federal Communications Commission and the Securities and Exchange Commission. Top-ranking officers called commissioners head these units. The same title, however, is given to some investigative, advisory, and reporting bodies, including the Civil Rights Commission and the Federal Election Commission.

Either *corporation* or *authority* is the title most often given to those agencies that conduct business-like activities. Corporations and authorities are headed by a board and a manager. Examples include the Federal Deposit Insurance Corporation and the Tennessee Valley Authority.

---

[2]Article II, Section 2, Clause 1. There is also a reference to "Heads of Departments" in Clause 2, and to "any Department or Officer" of the government in Article I, Section 8, Clause 18.

[3]Article II, Section 2, Clauses 1 and 2.

[4]The chart is adapted from the current edition of the *United States Government Manual,* published each year by the Office of the Federal Register in the National Archives and Records Administration. The *Manual* includes a brief description of every agency in each of the three branches of the Federal Government. More than 580 of its now nearly 700 pages are devoted to the executive branch.

The Government of the United States

The Constitution creates three branches of government

THE LEGISLATIVE BRANCH

CONGRESS

Houses of Congress
Senate and House of Representatives

Legislative Agencies
Architect of the Capitol
Government Accountability Office
Government Printing Office
Library of Congress
United States Botanic Garden
Congressional Budget Office
United States Tax Court

THE EXECUTIVE BRANCH

THE PRESIDENT

The Administration

1 Executive Office of the President

2 Executive Departments

3 Independent Agencies

THE JUDICIAL BRANCH

THE SUPREME COURT

Other Courts
Courts of Appeals
District Courts
Federal Claims Court
Court of Appeals for the Federal Circuit
Court of International Trade
Territorial Courts
Court of Appeals for the Armed Forces
Court of Appeals for Veterans Claims
Administrative Office of the
    United States Courts
Federal Judicial Center

---

1 **Executive Office of the President**

White House Office
Office of Management
    and Budget
Council of Economic
    Advisers
National Security Council
Office of the Director of
    National Intelligence
Office of National Drug
    Control Policy
Office of the United States
    Trade Representative
Council on Environmental
    Quality
Office of Science and
    Technology Policy
Office of Administration
Office of the Vice President
Office of Faith-Based and
    Community Initiatives
Office of Homeland Security

2 **Executive Departments**

Department of State
Department of the Treasury
Department of Defense
Department of Justice
Department of the Interior
Department of Agriculture
Department of Commerce
Department of Labor
Department of Health and
    Human Services
Department of Housing and
    Urban Development
Department of Transportation
Department of Energy
Department of Education
Department of Veterans
    Affairs
Department of Homeland
    Security

3 **Independent Agencies***

Central Intelligence Agency
Commission on Civil Rights
Commodity Futures
    Trading Commission
Consumer Product Safety
    Commission
Corporation for National and
    Community Service
Environmental Protection Agency
Equal Employment Opportunity
    Commission
Export-Import Bank of the U.S.
Farm Credit Administration
Federal Communications
    Commission
Federal Deposit Insurance
    Corporation
Federal Election Commission
Federal Housing Finance Board
Federal Maritime Commission
Federal Mediation and Conciliation
    Service

Federal Reserve System
Federal Trade Commission
General Services Administration
Merit Systems Protection Board
National Aeronautics and Space
    Administration
National Archives and Records
    Administration
National Labor Relations Board
National Railroad Passenger
    Corporation
National Transportation Safety Board
Nuclear Regulatory Commission
Office of Personnel Management
Peace Corps
Securities and Exchange Commission
Selective Service System
Small Business Administration
Social Security Administration
Tennessee Valley Authority
U.S. Postal Service

*Altogether, there are some 150 independent agencies in the executive branch.

Interpreting Charts Nearly 90 percent of all of the men and women who work for the Federal Government work outside the Washington, D.C., area. ***According to this chart, which branch makes up the largest share of the federal bureaucracy?*** H-SS 12.1.5

Within each major agency, the same confusing lack of uniformity in the use of names is common. *Bureau* is the name often given to the major elements in a department, but *service, administration, office, branch,* and *division* are often used for the same purpose. For example, the major units within the Department of Justice include the Federal Bureau of Investigation, the United States Marshals Service, the Drug Enforcement Administration, the Office of the Pardon Attorney, and the Criminal Division.

Many federal agencies are often referred to by their initials. The EPA, IRS, FBI, CIA, FCC, and TVA are but a few of the dozens of familiar examples.[5] A few are also known by nicknames. For example, the Government National Mortgage Association is often called "Ginnie Mae," and the National Railroad Passenger Corporation is better known as Amtrak.

Staff and Line Agencies

The several units that make up any administrative organization can be classified as either staff or line agencies. **Staff agencies** serve in a support capacity. They aid the chief executive and other administrators by offering advice and other assistance in the management of the organization. **Line agencies,** on the other hand, actually

---

[5]The use of acronyms can sometimes cause problems. When the old Bureau of the Budget was reorganized in 1970, it was also renamed. It is now the Office of Management and Budget (OMB). However, it was for a time slated to be known as the Bureau of Management and Budget (BOMB).

perform the tasks for which the organization exists. Congress and the President give the line agencies goals to meet, and the staff agencies help the line agencies meet these goals as effectively as possible through advising, budgeting, purchasing, management, and planning.

Two illustrations of this distinction are the several agencies that make up the Executive Office of the President and, in contrast, the Environmental Protection Agency. The agencies that make up the Executive Office of the President (the White House Office, the National Security Council, the Office of Management and Budget, and others, as you will read in the next section) each exist as staff support to the President. Their primary mission is to assist the President in the exercise of the executive power and in the overall management of the executive branch. They are not operating agencies. That is, they do not actually operate, or administer, public programs.

The Environmental Protection Agency (EPA), on the other hand, has a different mission. It is responsible for the day-to-day enforcement of the many federal antipollution laws. The EPA operates "on the line," where "the action" is.

This difference between staff agencies and line agencies can help you find your way through the complex federal bureaucracy. The distinction between the two can be oversimplified, however. For example, most line agencies do have staff units to aid them in their line operations. Thus, the EPA's Office of Civil Rights is a staff unit. Its job is to ensure that the agency's personnel practices do not violate the Federal Government's antidiscrimination policies.

Section 1 Assessment

Key Terms and Main Ideas

1. Describe the three defining features of a **bureaucracy** in your own words.
2. Why does a government need an **administration?**
3. What is the role of a **staff agency?** A **line agency?**

Critical Thinking

4. **Drawing Conclusions** How would you describe the system of naming federal agencies in one word? Explain your answer.
5. **Drawing Inferences** Explain how the three defining characteristics of a bureaucracy can lead to an effective government.

6. **Predicting Consequences** How might a strong, entrenched bureaucracy weaken the power of elected representatives?

2 The Executive Office of the President

Section Preview

OBJECTIVES

1. **Describe** the Executive Office of the President.
2. **Explain** the duties of the White House Office, the National Security Council, and the Office of Homeland Security.
3. **Identify** additional agencies in the Executive Office of the President.

WHY IT MATTERS

The Executive Office of the President is composed of the President's closest advisors and several support agencies. They aid the chief executive in the formation and execution of the nation's public policies.

POLITICAL DICTIONARY

★ **Executive Office of the President**
★ **federal budget**
★ **fiscal year**
★ **domestic affairs**

Thomas Jefferson performed his presidential duties with the help of two aides, one a messenger and the other his secretary. Like other early Presidents, he paid their salaries out of his own pocket. Indeed, Congress did not provide any money for presidential staff until 1857, when it gave President James Buchanan $2,500 for one clerk.

The situation is remarkably different today. President Jefferson presided over an executive branch that employed only some 2,100 people. Now, some 2.7 million men and women work in the Bush administration. Two institutions—the Executive Office of the President and the President's Cabinet—are at the center of today's huge executive branch.

The Executive Office of the President

Every officer, every employee, and every agency in the executive branch of the Federal Government is legally subordinate to the President. They all exist to help the President—the chief executive—in the exercise of the executive power.

The President's right arm, however, is the **Executive Office of the President** (the EOP). The Executive Office of the President is, in fact, an umbrella agency. It is a complex organization of several separate agencies staffed by most of the President's closest advisors and assistants.

The EOP was established by Congress in 1939. It has been reorganized in every administration since then.

The White House Office

The "nerve center" of the Executive Office—in fact, of the entire executive branch—is the White House Office. It houses the President's key personal and political staff.

The two wings on either side of the White House hold the offices of most of the President's staff. These employees occupy most of the crowded West Wing, which the public seldom sees and where the legendary Oval Office and the Cabinet Room are located. Some staff members work in the East Wing, where public tours of the White House

▲ Federal workers in the West Wing **H-SS 12.2.4**

Government at Work: The Bureaucracy 419

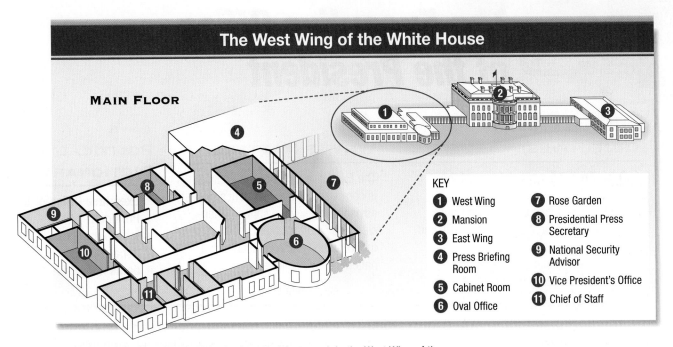

The West Wing of the White House

MAIN FLOOR

KEY

1. West Wing
2. Mansion
3. East Wing
4. Press Briefing Room
5. Cabinet Room
6. Oval Office
7. Rose Garden
8. Presidential Press Secretary
9. National Security Advisor
10. Vice President's Office
11. Chief of Staff

Interpreting Diagrams The President's closest advisors work in the West Wing of the White House, near the Oval Office. *Why do you think the Cabinet Room is so close to the Oval Office?* H-SS 12.7.5

begin. Still others are housed in the historic Old Executive Office Building, across the street from the West Wing.

The chief of staff to the President directs all of the operations of the White House Office and is among the most influential of all the presidential aides. The counselor to the President and a number of senior advisors are also key members of the President's inner circle.

Several other top officials work in the White House Office. Assistants and deputy assistants to the President aid the chief executive in such vital areas as foreign policy, defense, the economy, political affairs, congressional relations, and contacts with the news media and the public.

The staff of the White House Office also includes such other major presidential aides as the press secretary, the counsel (legal advisor) to the President, and the President's physician. The first lady's very visible place in public life today is reflected by the fact that one of the assistants to the President serves as her chief of staff and one of the several deputy assistants is her press secretary. Altogether, the staff of the White House Office now numbers some 400 men and women who, in a very real sense, work for the President.

The National Security Council

Most of the President's major steps in foreign affairs are taken in close consultation with the National Security Council (NSC). It meets at the President's call, often on short notice, to advise him in all domestic, foreign, and military matters that relate to the nation's security.

The President chairs the Council. Its other members are the Vice President and the secretaries of state and defense. The director of the Central Intelligence Agency (CIA) and the chairman of the Joint Chiefs of Staff also attend its meetings.

The NSC has a small staff of foreign and military policy experts. They work under the direction of the President's assistant for national security affairs, who is often called the President's national security advisor. The super-secret Central Intelligence Agency does much of its work at the direction of the NSC.

The National Security Council is a staff agency. That is, its job is to advise the President in all matters affecting the nation's security. However, during the Reagan administration in the 1980s, the NSC's staff actually conducted a number of secret operations. The most spectacular of these involved the sale of arms to Iran, and the use of some of the proceeds (money) from those sales to aid the Contra rebels in

Nicaragua. Congress had prohibited military aid to the Contras, and the disclosure of the NSC's role produced the Iran-Contra scandal of the mid-1980s.

Office of Homeland Security

The Office of Homeland Security is the newest major agency in the EOP. It was created by President Bush immediately after terrorists struck the World Trade Center and the Pentagon on September 11, 2001.

The Office is headed by a director whose primary job is to keep the President fully aware of all ongoing efforts to protect this country against any and all acts of terrorism. The director and his staff work closely with the new Cabinet-level Department of Homeland Security.

Other EOP Agencies

The EOP's umbrella covers several other—and important—agencies. Each of them provides essential staff help to the Chief Executive.

Office of Management and Budget

The Office of Management and Budget (OMB) is the largest and, after the White House Office, the most influential unit in the Executive Office. The OMB is headed by a director who is appointed by the President and confirmed by the Senate. The OMB's major task is the preparation of the federal budget, which the President must submit to Congress in January or February each year.

The **federal budget** is a very detailed estimate of receipts and expenditures, an anticipation of federal income and outgo, during the next **fiscal year.** A fiscal year is the 12-month period used by government and business for record keeping, budgeting, and other financial management purposes. The Federal Government's fiscal year runs from October 1 through September 30.

The budget is more than just a financial document. It is a plan—a carefully drawn, closely detailed work plan for the conduct of government. It is an annual statement of the public policies of the United States, expressed in dollar terms.

The creation of each fiscal year's budget is a lengthy process that begins more than a year before the start of the fiscal year for which the budget is intended. In the first stages, each federal agency prepares detailed estimates of its spending needs for that 12-month period. The OMB reviews those proposals, usually in a series of budget hearings that give agency officials the opportunity to defend their dollar requests. Following that agency-by-agency review, the revised (and usually lowered) spending estimates are fitted into the President's overall program.

The OMB also monitors the spending of the funds Congress appropriates. That is, it oversees the execution of the budget. The President's close control over both the preparation and execution of the budget is a major factor in his ability to command the huge executive branch.

Beyond its budget chores, the OMB is a sort of presidential "handy-man" agency. It makes continuing studies of the organization and management of the executive branch and keeps the President up to date on the work of all its agencies. The OMB checks and clears agency stands on all legislative matters to make certain they agree with the President's policy positions. It also helps the President prepare the hundreds of executive orders he must issue each year and the veto messages he occasionally sends to Congress. In short, the OMB does much to live up to the word *management* in its title.

Office of Faith-Based and Community Initiatives

The Office of Community and Faith-Based Initiatives was created by President Bush in 2001. Much of the best work being done today to combat drug abuse, homelessness, poverty, and similar problems is being done by private groups—by churches and church-related groups and other not-for-profit organizations. The Office of Faith-Based and Community Initiatives is charged with encouraging and expanding these private efforts.

Office of National Drug Control Policy

The Office of National Drug Control Policy was established in 1989. Its existence dramatizes the nation's concern over drugs. The office is headed by a director who is appointed by the President, subject to the Senate's approval.

The news media regularly identify the director as "the nation's drug czar." To this point, the office has operated mostly as an advisory and planning agency, however.

Council of Economic Advisers

Three of the country's leading economists, chosen by the President with the consent of the Senate, make up the Council of Economic Advisers. It is the chief executive's major source of information and advice on the nation's economy. The Council also helps the President prepare his annual Economic Report to Congress, which, together with a presidential message, goes to Capitol Hill in late January or early February each year.

Other Units in the EOP

A number of other agencies in the Executive Office house key presidential aides. These men and women make it possible for the President to meet his many-sided responsibilities.

The Office of Policy Development advises the Chief Executive on all matters relating to the nation's **domestic affairs**—that is, all matters not directly connected to the realm of foreign affairs.

The Council on Environmental Quality aids the President in environmental policy matters and in the writing of the annual "state of the environment" report to Congress. It sees that federal agencies comply with the nation's many environmental laws and with the President's environmental policies.

The council's three members are appointed by the President, with the Senate's consent. They sometimes act as referees in disputes between or among executive branch agencies, such as a conflict between the Environmental Protection Agency and one or more agencies in the Departments of the Agriculture, Interior, or Energy.

The Office of the Vice President houses the Vice President's staff. It now includes more than 50 men and women who make it possible for the Vice President to perform the duties of his office.

The Office of United States Trade Representative advises the chief executive in all matters of foreign trade. The trade representative, appointed by the President and confirmed by the Senate, carries the rank of ambassador and represents the President in foreign trade negotiations.

The Office of Science and Technology Policy is the President's major advisor in all scientific, engineering, and other technological matters relating to national policies and programs. Its director is drawn from the nation's scientific community.

The Office of Administration is the general housekeeping agency for all the other units in the Executive Office. It provides them with the many support services they must have in order to do their jobs, including clerical help, data processing, library services, transportation, and much more.

Section 2 Assessment

Key Terms and Main Ideas

1. List and explain three duties of the agencies that make up the **Executive Office of the President.**
2. Describe an EOP agency that directly relates to **domestic affairs.**
3. Outline the preparation of the **federal budget.**

Critical Thinking

4. **Testing Conclusions** Cite evidence to show that the Executive Office of the President is an essential part of the executive branch.
5. **Drawing Inferences** How does the Office of Management and Budget help the President perform his role of chief administrator?

6. **Understanding Point of View** If you could choose one executive agency for which to work, which would you select? What would you like to accomplish in that agency?

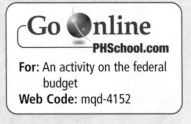

The Making of the Modern Presidency

As he began his second term in 1937, President Franklin D. Roosevelt asked Congress to authorize a major reorganization of the executive branch. Congress responded by creating the Executive Office of the President (EOP), in 1939.

**Analysis Skills
HR4, HI3**

The time has come to set our house in order. . . . The executive structure of the Government is sadly out of date. I am not the first President to report to the Congress that antiquated machinery stands in the way of effective administration and of adequate control by the Congress. . . .

Over a year ago. . . . I appointed a Committee on Administrative Management to examine the whole problem . . . .

*President Franklin D. Roosevelt
1882–1945*

They say what has been common knowledge for 20 years, that the President cannot adequately handle his responsibilities; that he is overworked; that it is humanly impossible under the system which we have, for him to carry out his constitutional duty as Chief Executive, because he is overwhelmed with minor details and needless contacts arising directly from the bad organization and equipment of the Government. I can testify to this. . . .

The Committee includes these major recommendations:

1. Expand the White House staff so that the President may have a sufficient group of able assistants to keep him in closer and easier touch with the widespread affairs of administration. . . .

2. Strengthen and develop the managerial agencies of the Government, particularly those dealing with the budget and efficiency research, with personnel and with planning, as management-arms of the Chief Executive. . . .

In placing this program before you I realize that it will be said that I am recommending the increase of the powers of the Presidency. This is not true. . . . What I am placing before you is not the request for more power, but for the tools of management and authority to distribute the work so that the President can effectively discharge those powers which the Constitution now places upon him. Unless we are prepared to abandon this important part of the Constitution, we must equip the Presidency with authority commensurate with his responsibilities under the Constitution.

Analyzing Primary Sources

1. Why did the executive structure of government become out-of-date, according to Roosevelt?
2. According to Roosevelt, what problem did the existing executive structure create for the President?
3. What did it imply about the Federal Government that Roosevelt had to speak to Congress to reorganize his office?
4. Roosevelt claimed his request would not increase presidential power. Do you agree or disagree? Explain.

③ The Executive Departments

Section Preview

OBJECTIVES

1. **Describe** the origin and work of the executive departments.
2. **Explain** how the members of the Cabinet are chosen.
3. **Identify** the role of the Cabinet in the President's decisions.

WHY IT MATTERS

Fifteen executive departments carry out much of the Federal Government's work. The heads of these departments frequently meet with the President and other officials as the Cabinet.

POLITICAL DICTIONARY

★ **executive departments**
★ **secretary**
★ **attorney general**

I n *The Federalist* No. 76, Alexander Hamilton declared that "the true test of a good government is its aptitude and tendency to produce a good administration." Given that comment, it seems strange that Hamilton and the other Framers of the Constitution spent so little time on the organization of the executive branch of the government they were creating. Instead, the machinery of federal administration has been built over time to meet the changing needs of the country.

Executive Departments

Much of the work of the Federal Government is done by the 15 **executive departments**. Often called the Cabinet departments, they are the traditional units of federal administration, and each of them is built around some broad field of activity.

The First Congress created three of these departments in 1789: the Departments of State, Treasury, and War. As the size and the workload of the Federal Government grew, Congress added new departments. Some of the newer ones took over various duties originally assigned to older departments, and they gradually assumed new functions, as well. Over time, Congress has also created and later combined or abolished some departments.

Chief Officers and Staff

Each department is headed by a **secretary,** except for the Department of Justice, whose work is directed by the **attorney general.** As you will see, these department heads serve in the President's Cabinet. Their duties as the chief officers of their own departments take up most of their time, however.

Each department head is the primary link between presidential policy and his or her own department. Just as importantly, each of them also strives to promote and protect his or her department with the White House, with Congress and its committees, with the rest of the federal bureaucracy, and with the media and the public.

An under secretary or deputy secretary and several assistant secretaries aid the secretary in his or her multidimensional role. These officials are also named by the President and confirmed by the Senate. Staff support for the secretary comes

► President George Washington's (right) first Cabinet included Secretary of State Thomas Jefferson (second left); and Secretary of the Treasury Alexander Hamilton (second right).

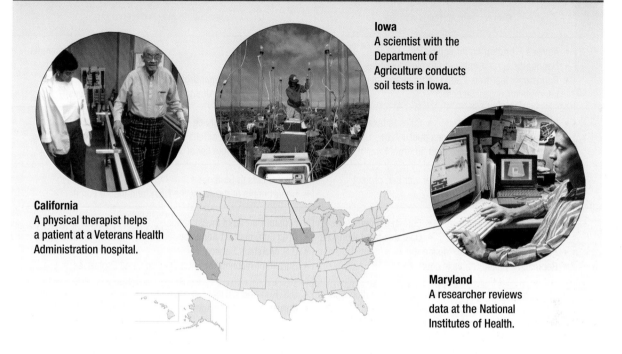

Iowa
A scientist with the Department of Agriculture conducts soil tests in Iowa.

California
A physical therapist helps a patient at a Veterans Health Administration hospital.

Maryland
A researcher reviews data at the National Institutes of Health.

Interpreting Diagrams Federal employees can be found wherever the Federal Government has work to do, including a veterans' hospital in California, a farm in Iowa, or a federal office in Maryland. ***Why do only ten percent of federal employees work in the Washington, D.C., area?*** H-SS 12.7.5

from assistants and aides with a wide range of titles in such areas as personnel, planning, legal advice, budgeting, and public relations.

Subunits

Each department is made up of a number of subunits, both staff and line. Each of these subunits, or agencies, is usually further divided into smaller working units. Thus, the Criminal Division in the Department of Justice is composed of a number of sections, including, for example, the Terrorism and Violent Crime Section and the Narcotics and Dangerous Drugs Section. Approximately 80 percent of the men and women who head the bureaus, divisions, and other major units within each of the executive departments are career people, not political appointees.

Many of the agencies in executive departments are structured geographically. Much of their work is done through regional and/or district offices, which, in turn, direct the activities of the agency's employees in the field. In fact, nearly 90 percent of all of the men and women who work as civilian employees of the Federal

Government are stationed somewhere outside the nation's capital.

Take the Veterans Health Administration, part of the Department of Veterans Affairs, to illustrate the point. It does nearly all of its work providing medical care to eligible veterans at some 150 medical centers, more than 800 outpatient clinics, and a large number of other facilities throughout the country.

The Departments Today

Today, the executive departments vary a great deal in terms of visibility, size, and importance. The Department of State is the oldest and the most prestigious department; but it is also among the smallest, with only about 25,000 employees. The Department of Defense is the largest, with nearly 670,000 civilian workers, and another 1.4 million men and women in uniform.

The Department of Health and Human Services has the largest budget; it accounts for just about a fourth of all federal spending each year. The Department of Homeland Security became the newest of the executive departments when Congress created it in 2002.

The Fifteen Executive Departments

DEPARTMENT (YEAR ESTABLISHED)	PRINCIPAL FUNCTIONS	IMPORTANT AGENCIES	
State (1789)	• Advises President on foreign policy • Negotiates agreements with foreign countries • Represents the United States abroad and in international organizations	• Foreign Service • Regional Bureaus • Bureau of International Organization Affairs • Bureau of Consular Affairs (Office of Passport Services)	• Bureau of Diplomatic Security
Treasury (1789)	• Produces coins and bills • Collects taxes • Borrows money and manages public debt • Enforces alcohol, tobacco, and firearms laws	• Internal Revenue Service • Bureau of the Public Debt • Office of the Comptroller of the Currency	• United States Mint • Bureau of Engraving and Printing
Defense [a] (1789)	• Provides military forces to deter war and protect the nations security	• Joint Chiefs of Staff • Departments of the Army, the Navy, and the Air Force	
Justice [b] (1870)	• Prosecutes those accused • Enforces federal laws of violating federal law • Operates federal prisons • Provides legal advice to President • Represents United States in court	• Federal Bureau of Investigation • Drug Enforcement Administration • U.S. Marshals Service • Bureau of Alcohol, Tobacco, Firearms, and Explosives	• Criminal Division • Civil Rights Division • Bureau of Prisons
Interior (1849)	• Manages public lands, wildlife refuges, and national parks • Operates hydroelectric power plants • Helps Native Americans manage their affairs	• U.S. Fish and Wildlife Service • Bureau of Land Management • Bureau of Indian Affairs	• National Park Service • U.S. Geological Survey • Bureau of Reclamation
Agriculture (1889)	• Manages national forests • Inspects food • Assists farmers and ranchers • Administers food stamp and school lunch programs	• Agricultural Research Service • Food and Nutrition Service • Food Safety and Inspection Service	• Farm Service Agency • Forest Service • Rural Utilities Service
Commerce [c] (1903)	• Conducts census • Grants patents and registers trademarks • Promotes international trade, economic growth, and technological development	• Bureau of the Census • Patent and Trademark Office • International Trade Administration • Economic Development Administration	• National Oceanic and Atmospheric Administration • Minority Business Development Agency
Labor (1913)	• Enforces federal laws on minimum wages, maximum hours, and safe working conditions • Operates job training programs • Administers unemployment insurance and workers' compensation programs	• Employment Standards Administration • Occupational Safety and Health Administration • Employment and Training Administration • Bureau of Labor Statistics	• Employee Benefits Security Administration • Women's Bureau

Interpreting Tables Over the years, Congress created the 15 executive departments to handle the responsibilities of the Federal Government. ***Which three Cabinet departments are the most important? Why?*** H-SS 12.7.5

The 15 departments are profiled in the table on these two pages. The principal functions they perform and the titles of their major agencies provide a useful description of each of them.

The Cabinet

The Cabinet is an informal advisory body brought together by the President to serve his needs. The Constitution makes no mention of it, nor did Congress create it.[6] Instead, the Cabinet is the product of custom and usage.

At its first session in 1789, Congress established four top-level executive posts: secretary of state, secretary of the treasury, secretary of war, and attorney general. By his second term, President George Washington was regularly seeking the advice of the four outstanding people he had named to those offices: Thomas Jefferson in the Department of State, Alexander Hamilton at the Treasury, Henry Knox in the War Department, and Edmund Randolph, the attorney general. So the Cabinet was born.

---

[6]The closest approach to it is in Article II, Section 2, Clause 1, where the President is given the power to "require the Opinion, in writing, of the principal Officer in each of the executive Departments, upon any Subject relating to the duties of their respective Offices." The Cabinet was first mentioned in an act of Congress in 1907, well over a century after its birth.

DEPARTMENT (YEAR ESTABLISHED)	PRINCIPAL FUNCTIONS	IMPORTANT AGENCIES
Health and Human Services [d] **(1953)**	• Funds health care research programs • Conducts programs to prevent and control disease • Enforces pure food and drug laws • Administers Medicare and Medicaid	• Administration for Children and Families • Food and Drug Administration • National Institutes of Health • Centers for Disease Control and Prevention • Centers for Medicare and Medicaid Services
Housing and Urban Development (1965)	• Operates home-financing and public housing programs • Enforces fair housing laws	• Office of Housing • Office of Fair Housing and Equal Opportunity • Government National Mortgage Association
Transportation (1967)	• Administers programs to promote and regulate highways, mass transit, railroads, waterways, air travel, and oil and gas pipelines	• Federal Highway Administration • Federal Railroad • Federal Aviation Administration Administration • Maritime Administration
Energy (1977)	• Promotes production of renewable energy, fossil fuels, and nuclear energy • Transmits and sells hydroelectric power • Conducts nuclear weapons research and production	• Office of Energy Efficiency and Renewable Energy • Office of Nuclear Energy, Science and Technology • Regional Power Administration • Office of Civilian Radioactive Waste Management
Education (1979)	• Administers federal aid to schools • Conducts educational research	• Office of Elementary and Secondary Education • Office of Postsecondary Education
Veterans Affairs (1988)	• Administers benefits, pensions, and medical programs for veterans of the armed forces • Oversees military cemeteries	• Veterans Benefits Administration • Veterans Health Administration • National Cemetery Administration
Homeland Security (2002)	• Border and transportation security • Emergency preparedness and response • Chemical, biological, radiological, nuclear defense • Information analysis and infrastructure protection	• Coast Guard • Secret Service • U.S. Citizenship and Immigration Services • U.S. Immigration and Customs Enforcement • Transportation Security Administration

[a] Congress created the National Military Establishment as an executive department, headed by the Secretary of Defense, in 1947. It was renamed the Department of Defense, in 1949. Since 1947 the department has included the former cabinet-level Departments of War (1789) and the Navy (1798), and the Department of the Air Force.
[b] Congress created the office of Attorney General in 1789 but did not establish the Department of Justice until 1870.

[c] Congress created the Department of Commerce and Labor in 1903; it was replaced by the separate Departments of Commerce and of Labor in 1913.
[d] Congress created the Department of Health, Education, and Welfare in 1953. HEW's education functions were transferred to a new Department of Education in 1979, and HEW was renamed at that time.

By tradition, the heads of the now 15 executive departments form the Cabinet. Each of the last several Presidents has regularly added a number of other top officials to the group, including the director of the Office of Management and Budget and the President's chief domestic policy advisor. The Vice President is a regular participant, and several other major figures usually attend Cabinet meetings—today, in particular, the counselor to the President, the White House chief of staff, the United States trade representative, the director of the Office of National Drug Control Policy, and the administrator of the Environmental Protection Agency.

Choosing Cabinet Members

The President appoints the head of each of the 15 executive departments. Each of these appointments is subject to confirmation by the Senate, but rejections have been exceedingly rare. Of the more than 600 appointments made since 1789, only 12 have been rejected. The most recent rejection occurred in 1989, when the Senate refused to confirm President George H.W. Bush's selection of John Tower as secretary of defense.

Many factors influence the President's Cabinet choices. Party is almost always important. Republican Presidents do not often pick Democrats, and vice versa. One or more of a

▲ **Cabinet Pioneer** In 2005, Alberto Gonzales testified before the Senate committee that would approve his nomination to become the country's first Latino attorney general.

new President's appointees usually come from among those who played a major role in the recent presidential campaign.

Of course, professional qualifications and practical experience are also taken into account in the selection of Cabinet secretaries. Geography also plays a part. In broad terms, each President tries to give some regional balance to the Cabinet. Thus, the secretary of the interior almost always comes from the West, where most of that department's wide-ranging work is carried out. Similarly, the secretary of agriculture usually comes from one of the farm States in the Midwest and the secretary of housing and urban development often comes from one of the nation's major metropolitan centers.

Various interest groups care about Cabinet appointments, and they influence some of the choices. Thus, the secretary of the treasury regularly comes out of the financial world, the secretary of commerce from the ranks of business, the secretary of education from among professional educators, the attorney general from the legal community, and so on.

Other considerations also guide the President's choices. Gender and race, management abilities and experience, and other personal characteristics—these and a host of other factors play a part in selecting Cabinet members.

Women and Minorities

Women and minorities have only gradually become represented in the Cabinet. Franklin Roosevelt appointed the first woman, Frances T. ("Ma") Perkins, who was secretary of labor from 1933 to 1945. Lyndon Johnson named the first African American, Robert C. Weaver, secretary of housing and urban development from 1966 to 1969. Ronald Reagan picked the first Hispanic Cabinet member, Lauro F. Cavazos, who became secretary of education in 1988.

Recent Presidents have regularly tapped women and members of various minority groups for Cabinet posts. Over his eight years in office, Bill Clinton's Cabinet choices included five women, six African Americans, four Hispanics, and the first Asian American: Norman Mineta, secretary of commerce. Madeleine Albright became the first woman to serve as secretary of state and Janet Reno, the first woman to serve as the nation's attorney general.

President George W. Bush's first Cabinet appointments included two African Americans: Secretary of State Colin Powell and Secretary of Education Rod Paige; three women: Secretary of Labor Elaine Chao, Secretary of the Interior Gale Norton, and Secretary of Agriculture Ann Veneman; and one Hispanic, Secretary of Housing and Urban Development Mel Martinez. Secretary Chao was born in China and is the first Chinese American to hold a Cabinet office. Norman Mineta, a Democrat, named Secretary of Transportation, also served in the Clinton Cabinet.

Early in his second term, President Bush added two African Americans to his Cabinet: Secretary of State Condoleezza Rice and Alphonso Johnson, who now heads the Department of Housing and Urban Development. He also picked another woman, Margaret Spellings, to be secretary of education, and named two Hispanics to the Cabinet, Attorney General Alberto Gonzales and Secretary of Commerce Carlos Gutierrez.

The Cabinet's Role

Cabinet members have two major jobs. Individually, each is the administrative head of one of the executive departments. Together, they are advisors to the President.

A number of Presidents have given great weight to the Cabinet and to its advice; others have given it only a secondary role. George H. W. Bush's Cabinet (1989–1993) had more influence with the President than any Cabinet since the Eisenhower presidency in the 1950s. The Cabinet also played a prominent role in the Clinton administration (1993– 2001). On the other hand, John Kennedy saw no need to discuss, say, Defense Department matters with his secretaries of labor and agriculture and found Cabinet meetings "a waste of time."

Kennedy's view notwithstanding, most Presidents have held regular Cabinet meetings—where reports are made and discussed, and advice is offered to the chief executive. That advice need not be taken, of course. Abraham Lincoln once laid a proposition he favored before his seven-member Cabinet. Each member opposed it, whereupon Lincoln declared: "Seven nays, one aye: the ayes have it."

William Howard Taft put the role of the Cabinet in its proper light years ago:

 **PRIMARY Sources** "*The Constitution . . . contains no suggestion of a meeting of all the department heads, in consultation over general governmental matters. The Cabinet is a mere creation of the President's will. . . . It exists only by custom. If the President desired to dispense with it, he could do so.*"
—*Our Chief Magistrate and His Powers*

Interpreting Political Cartoons Many people have criticized the federal bureaucracy as too large and inefficient. *Does the cartoon share this criticism? Do you agree?*

No President has ever suggested eliminating the Cabinet. However, several Presidents have leaned on other, unofficial advisory groups, and sometimes more heavily than on the Cabinet. Andrew Jackson began the practice when he became President in 1829. Several of his close friends often met with him in the kitchen at the White House and, inevitably, came to be known as the Kitchen Cabinet. Franklin Roosevelt's Brain Trust of the 1930s and Harry Truman's Cronies in the late 1940s were in the same mold.

Section 3 Assessment

Key Terms and Main Ideas

1. How were the **executive departments** created?
2. What is the role of the **secretary** of an executive department?
3. Which department does the **attorney general** lead?
4. Who decides how often the **Cabinet** meets?

Critical Thinking

5. **Drawing Conclusions** Why do you think the Framers of the Constitution dealt with the organization of the executive branch of the government they created in such sparse terms?

 **Standards Monitoring** *Online*
For: Self-quiz with vocabulary practice
Web Code: mqa-4153

6. **Drawing Inferences** What does the creation of the Cabinet tell you about the process of constitutional change and development in this country?

 Go **O**nline
PHSchool.com

For: An activity on the executive departments
Web Code: mqd-4153

Section Preview

OBJECTIVES

1. **Explain** why Congress has created independent agencies.
2. **Identify** the characteristics of independent executive agencies and independent regulatory commissions.
3. **Describe** the structure of government corporations.

WHY IT MATTERS

Some 150 executive branch agencies are not located within any of the 15 executive departments. But some of them rival Cabinet departments in the size of their budgets, their functions, and the number of their employees.

POLITICAL DICTIONARY

★ **independent agencies**
★ **independent executive agencies**
★ **independent regulatory commissions**
★ **quasi-legislative**
★ **quasi-judicial**
★ **government corporation**

Until the 1880s, nearly all that the Federal Government did was done through its Cabinet departments. Since then, however, Congress has created a large number of additional agencies—the **independent agencies**—located outside the departments. Today, they number nearly 150. Most of the more important ones are included in the chart on page 417.

Several independent agencies administer programs similar to those of the Cabinet departments. The work of the National Aeronautics and Space Administration (NASA), for example, is similar to that of a number of agencies in the Department of Defense. NASA's responsibilities are also not very far removed from those of the Department of Transportation.

Neither the size of an independent agency's budget nor the number of its employees provides a good way to distinguish between these agencies and the executive departments. The Social Security Administration is the largest of these units today. Only one Cabinet department, Health and Human Services, has a larger budget. The Administration employs some 65,000 people—more than work for several Cabinet agencies.

▲ **NASA** This special envelope celebrates NASA's *Apollo* missions to the moon.

Why Independent Agencies?

The reasons these agencies exist outside of the Cabinet departments are nearly as many as the agencies themselves. A few major reasons stand out, however. Some have been set up outside the regular departmental structure simply because they do not fit well within any department. The General Services Administration (GSA) is a leading example.

The GSA is the Federal Government's major housekeeping agency. Its main chores include the construction and operation of public buildings, purchase and distribution of supplies and equipment, management of real property, and a host of similar services to most other federal agencies. The Office of Personnel Management (OPM) is another example. It is the hiring agency for nearly all other federal agencies.

Congress has given some agencies an independent status to protect them from the influence of both partisan and pressure politics. The OPM stands as a good example here, too. So do the Social Security Administration, the Federal Election Commission, and the Civil Rights Commission. But, notice, this point can be turned on its head: Congress has located some of these agencies outside any of the Cabinet departments because that is exactly where certain pressure groups want them.

Other federal agencies were born as independents largely by accident. No thought was given to the problems of administrative confusion when they were created. Finally, some agencies are independent because of the peculiar and sensitive nature of their functions. This is especially true of the independent regulatory commissions.

The label *independent agency* is a catchall. Most of these agencies are independent only in the sense that they are not located within any of the 15 Cabinet departments. They are not independent of the President and the executive branch. A handful of them are independent in a much more concrete way, however. For most purposes, they do lie outside the executive branch and are largely free of presidential control.

Perhaps the best way to understand all of these independent agencies is to divide them into three main groups: (1) the independent executive agencies, (2) the independent regulatory commissions, and (3) the government corporations.

The Independent Executive Agencies

The **independent executive agencies** include most of the independent agencies. Some are large, with thousands of employees, multimillion-dollar or even billion-dollar budgets, and extremely important public tasks to perform.

The GSA, NASA, and the EPA are, for example, three of the largest independent executive agencies. They are organized much like the Cabinet departments: they are headed by a single administrator with subunits operating on a regional basis, and so on. The most important difference between these independent executive agencies and the 15 executive departments is simply that they do not have Cabinet status.

Some of the agencies in this group are not administrative and policy giants. But they do important work and they sometimes attract public notice. The Civil Rights Commission, the Peace Corps, the Federal Election Commission, and the National Transportation Safety Board all fall into this category.

Most independent executive agencies operate far from the limelight. They have few employees, small budgets, and rarely attract any attention. The American Battle Monuments Commission,

the Citizens' Stamp Advisory Committee, and the Migratory Bird Conservation Commission are typical of the dozens of these seldom seen or heard public bodies.

Independent Regulatory Commissions

The **independent regulatory commissions** stand out among the independent agencies because they are largely beyond the reach of presidential direction and control. There are ten of these agencies today, each created to regulate, or police, important aspects of the nation's economy. Their vital statistics appear in the table on the next page.

Structured for Independence

The independent regulatory commissions' large measure of independence from the White House comes mainly from the way in which Congress has structured them. Each is headed by a board or commission made up of five to

The Independent Regulatory Commissions

Agency	Date Established	Number of Members	Term of Members	Major Functions
Board of Governors, Federal Reserve System (the Fed)	1913	7	14 years	Supervises banking system, practices; regulates money supply, use of credit in economy.
Federal Trade Commission (FTC)	1914	5	7 years	Enforces antitrust, other laws prohibiting unfair competition, price-fixing, false advertising, other unfair business practices.
Securities and Exchange Commission (SEC)	1934	5	5 years	Regulates securities, other financial markets, investment companies, brokers; enforces laws prohibiting fraud, other dishonest investment practices.
Federal Communications Commission (FCC)	1934	5	5 years	Regulates interstate and foreign communications by radio, television, wire, satellite, and cable.
National Labor Relations Board (NLRB)	1935	5	5 years	Administers federal labor-management relations laws; holds collective bargaining elections; prevents, remedies unfair labor practices.
Federal Maritime Commission (FMC)	1936	5	5 years	Regulates waterborne foreign, domestic off-shore commerce of the United States; supervises rates, services.
Consumer Product Safety Commission (CPSC)	1972	5	5 years	Sets, enforces safety standards for consumer products; directs recall of unsafe products; conducts safety research, information programs.
Nuclear Regulatory Commission (NRC)	1974	5	5 years	Licenses, regulates all civilian nuclear facilities and civilian uses of nuclear materials.[a]
Commodity Futures Trading Commission (CFTC)	1974	5	5 years	Regulates commodity exchanges, brokers, futures trading in agricultural, metal, other commodities.
Federal Energy Regulatory Commission (FERC)	1977	5	4 years	Regulates, sets rates for transmission, sale of natural gas, electricity, oil by pipeline; licenses hydroelectric power projects.[b]

[a]These functions performed by the Atomic Energy Commission from 1946 to 1974 (when the AEC was abolished); other AEC functions now performed by agencies in the Energy Department.

[b]These functions performed by the Federal Power Commission (created in 1930) until the FPC was abolished in 1977. The FERC is within the Energy Department, but only for administrative purposes; otherwise it is independent (except the Secretary of Energy may set reasonable deadlines for the FERC action in any matter before it). Under terms of National Energy Act of 1978, the FERC's authority to regulate natural gas prices ended in 1985.

Interpreting Tables Independent regulatory commissions are independent of all three branches of government, and are exceptions to the separation of powers rule. ***How do the functions listed above show that these commissions have legislative and judicial powers?*** H-SS 12.7.5

seven members appointed by the President with Senate consent. However, those officials have terms of such length that it is unlikely a President will gain control over any of these agencies through the appointment process, at least not in a single presidential term.

Several other features of these boards and commissions put them beyond the reach of presidential control. No more than a bare majority of the members of each board or commission may belong to the same political party. Thus, several of those officers must belong to the party out of power.

Moreover, the appointed terms of the members are staggered so that the term of only one member on each board or commission expires in any one year. Finally, the officers of five of these agencies can be removed by the President only for those causes Congress has specified.[7]

As with the other independent agencies, the regulatory commissions are executive bodies. That is, Congress has given them the power to

---

[7]Recall this point from Chapter 14, on page 397. The members of five of these bodies (the SEC, FCC, CPSC, NRC, and CFTC) are exceptions to the rule, however. Congress has provided that any of them may be removed at the President's discretion.

administer the programs for which they were created. However, unlike those other independent agencies, the regulatory commissions are also **quasi-legislative** and **quasi-judicial** bodies.[8] That is, Congress has given them certain legislative-like and judicial-like powers.

These agencies exercise their quasi-legislative powers when they make rules and regulations. Those rules and regulations have the force of law. They implement, spell out the details of, the laws that Congress has directed these regulatory bodies to enforce.

To illustrate the point: Congress has said that those who want to borrow money by issuing stocks, bonds, or other securities must provide a "full and fair disclosure" of all pertinent information to prospective investors. The Securities and Exchange Commission (SEC) makes that requirement effective and indicates how those who offer securities are to meet it by issuing rules and regulations.

The regulatory commissions exercise their quasi-judicial powers when they decide disputes in those fields in which Congress has given them policing authority. For example, if an investor in Iowa thinks a local stockbroker has defrauded (cheated) him, he may file a complaint with the SEC's regional office in Chicago. SEC agents will investigate and report their findings, and the agency will judge the merits of the complaint much as a court would do. Decisions made by the SEC, and by the other independent regulatory bodies, can be appealed to the United States courts of appeals.

In a sense, Congress has created these agencies to act in its place. Congress could hold hearings and set interest rates, license radio and TV stations and nuclear reactors, check on business practices, and do the many other things it has directed the regulatory commissions to do. These activities are complex and time-consuming, however, and they demand constant and expert attention. If Congress did all of this work, it would have no time for its other and important legislative work.

Note that these regulatory bodies possess all three of the basic governmental powers: executive, legislative, and judicial. They are

---

[8]The prefix *quasi* is from the Latin, meaning "in a certain sense, resembling, seemingly."

exceptions to the principle of separation of powers. Technically, they should not be grouped with the other independent agencies. Instead, they should somehow be located somewhere between the executive and legislative branches, and between the executive and judicial branches, too.

Rethinking Regulation

Several authorities, and most recent Presidents, have urged that at least the administrative functions of the independent regulatory commissions be given to executive department agencies. Critics have raised other serious questions about these agencies and proposed to abolish or redesign them.

The most troubling questions are these: Have some of the independent regulatory commissions been captured by the special interests they are expected to regulate? Are all of the many and detailed rules created by these agencies really needed? Do some of these rules have the effect of stifling legitimate competition in the free enterprise system? Do some of them add unreasonably to the costs of doing business and therefore to the prices that consumers must pay?

Congress sets the basic policies of the regulatory agencies, and so it has a major responsibility to answer these questions. It has responded to some questions in recent years, particularly by deregulating much of the nation's transportation

▲ A 1945 map (top) shows one airline's regulated routes in red, while a contemporary map (bottom) lists the routes freely chosen by a different airline. *Critical Thinking Why might the government have decided, under regulation, to require airlines to serve certain cities?*

▲ The government created Amtrak as a corporation to provide passenger train service. After years of losing money and relying on federal subsidies to stay afloat, Amtrak was told that Congress would not cover its losses after 2002. *Critical Thinking* **What advantages might Amtrak enjoy as a government corporation? H-SS 12.7.5**

industry. Airlines, bus companies, truckers, and railroads have greater freedom to operate today than they did only a few years ago. The same trend can be seen in the field of communications, notably with regard to cable television.

Two major regulatory bodies have actually disappeared in recent years. The Civil Aeronautics Board was created in 1938 to oversee commercial air traffic in the United States. For decades it assigned the routes to be flown and the rates charged by airlines and other commercial air carriers, until it was abolished by Congress in 1985.

The Interstate Commerce Commission was the very first of the regulatory commissions to be established by Congress, in 1887. For a century it issued licenses and regulated the rates and routes and most other aspects of commercial transportation by rail, highway, and water. It, too, was abolished by Congress, in 1996.

The Government Corporations

Several of the independent agencies are **government corporations**. Like most of the other independent agencies, government corporations are within the executive branch and subject to the President's direction and control. Unlike the other agencies, however, they were set up by Congress to carry out certain business-like activities.

Congress established the first government corporation when it chartered the Bank of the United States in 1791. Yet government corporations were little used until World War I and the Depression. In both periods Congress set up dozens of corporations to carry out emergency programs. Several still exist—among them, the Federal Deposit Insurance Corporation (FDIC), which insures bank deposits, and the Export-Import Bank of the United States (Eximbank), which makes loans to help the export and sale of American goods abroad.

There are now more than 50 of these corporations. They deliver the mail (the U.S. Postal Service); insure bank deposits (the FDIC); provide intercity rail passenger service (the National Railroad Passenger Corporation, Amtrak); protect pension benefits (the Pension Benefit Guaranty Corporation); and generate, sell, and distribute electric power (the Tennessee Valley Authority).[9]

---

[9]State and local governments maintain their own government corporations, most often called authorities, to operate airports, turnpikes, seaports, power plants, liquor stores, and housing developments, and to conduct many other corporate activities. The Port Authority of New York and New Jersey is one of the best known.

Government v. Private Corporations

The typical government corporation is set up much like a corporation in the private sector. It is run by a board of directors, with a general manager who directs the corporation's operations according to the policies established by that board. Most government corporations produce income that is plowed back into the business.

There are several striking differences between government and private corporations, however. Congress decides the purpose for which the public agencies exist and the functions they can perform. Their officers are public officers; in fact, all who work for these corporations are public employees. The President selects most of the top officers of government corporations with Senate confirmation.

In addition, these public agencies are financed by public funds appropriated by Congress, not private investors. The Federal Government, representing the American people, owns the stock.

The advantage most often claimed for these agencies is their flexibility. It is said that the government corporation, freed from the controls of regular departmental organization, can carry on its activities with the incentive, efficiency, and ability to experiment that make many private concerns successful. Whether that claim is valid is open to question. At the very least, it raises this complex issue: Is a public corporation's need for flexibility compatible with the democratic requirement that all public agencies be held responsible and accountable to the people?

Degrees of Independence

The degree of independence and flexibility government corporations have varies considerably. In fact, some corporations are not independent at all. They are attached to an executive department.

The Commodity Credit Corporation, for example, is the government's major crop-loan and farm-subsidy agency. It is located within the Department of Agriculture, and the secretary of agriculture chairs its seven-member board. The Commodity Credit Corporation carries out most of its functions through a line agency in the Department of Agriculture—the Farm Service Agency—which is also subject to the direct control of the secretary.

Some corporations do have considerable independence, however. The Tennessee Valley Authority (TVA) is a case in point. It operates under a statute that gives it considerable discretion over its own programs. Although its budget is subject to review by the OMB, the President, and Congress, the TVA has a large say in the uses of the income its several operations produce.[10]

---

[10]The TVA is a major example of government in business. Congress established the TVA in the Tennessee Valley Authority Act of 1933. The act called for the coordinated development and use of the natural resources of parts of seven southern States. The TVA has had an extraordinary impact on the Tennessee River Valley and its approximately eight million residents. Its operations include electric power, flood control, reforestation, soil conservation, agricultural research, recreational facilities, and the promotion of industrial growth. The TVA's power program is self-supporting. Much of its other activities are supported by Congress. Still, it generates considerable revenues from sales of electricity and fertilizer and from its ability to issue bonds.

Section 4 Assessment

Key Terms and Main Ideas

1. How do **independent agencies** differ from the other agencies in the executive branch?
2. What is the main purpose of the **independent regulatory commissions**?
3. What is the difference between a legislative body and a **quasi-legislative** body?

Critical Thinking

4. **Drawing Inferences** Name three reasons why independent agencies operate outside the executive departments.
5. **Making Decisions** Economist Milton Friedman called bureaucracy "both a vehicle whereby special interests can achieve their objectives and an important special interest in its own right." What can the government do to minimize the situation Friedman describes?

Gathering Information from Government Sources

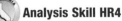 **Analysis Skill HR4**

You might not know it, but if you're a U.S. citizen, you're a co-owner of a treasure-trove of information. The government uses a portion of the tax dollars it collects from its citizens to generate massive amounts of transcripts, research papers, legal records, maps, statistics, studies, videos, facsimiles, manuscripts, and music.

By far the best way to access federal information today is on the Internet. The growth of public and private Web sites containing government information has revolutionized the research process. If you don't have Internet access, however, many of the sources listed at right are available in print at large libraries. To seek out government information, try these steps:

1. Define what information you're seeking. Knowing what you need will help narrow your search. Do you need federal, regional, State, or local information? Are you looking for records, statistics, primary sources, or other media? Decide on a research objective, and write a question that summarizes it.

2. Determine where to search. What agency of the government is responsible for the topic you're researching? Information on water pollution, for example, might come from the Environmental Protection Agency, the Interior Department, the *Congressional Record*, and State and local sites. Using your question from Step 1, identify agencies that might provide relevant information.

3. Gather information. As you collect material, make note of the source: Is it public or private? Is it reliable? Steer clear of anonymous Web sites.

Test for Success

Choose a government-related topic that interests you. Compile a list of at least five good places to search for the information.

Searching Uncle Sam

First Gov is a government Web site that provides the public with easily accessible online U.S. government resources. http://www.firstgov.gov

The National Archives and Records Administration (NARA) manages and provides access to all federal records dating back to the Declaration of Independence —more than 4 billion pieces of paper and 6 million photographs. http://www.nara.gov

The World Factbook is the authoritative source for country-by-country information from the U.S. Central Intelligence Agency (CIA), published annually. http://www.odci.gov/cia/publications/factbook

The Census Bureau tracks where we live, where we work, what we earn, what we eat—you name it. http://www.census.gov

The FedWorld Information Network is a searchable database with links to government agencies. http://www.fedworld.gov

FedStats is a searchable database created by the Federal Interagency Council on Statistical Policy. Get federal, regional, State, and county statistics presented in tables, graphs, and maps. Contains the indispensible Statistical Abstracts. http://www.fedstats.gov

The Library of Congress (LOC), created in 1800, is the world's largest library, the government's official storehouse of more than 115 million multimedia items. Any item ever copyrighted is here. http://www.loc.gov

Thomas, named after President Thomas Jefferson, is the official record of everything that happens in Congress. Thomas contains the *Congressional Record* as well as information on committee hearings and schedules. http://thomas.loc.gov

FindLaw is an online, private source of legal information: Supreme Court decisions, legal issues, news, and other resources. http://www.findlaw.com

5 The Civil Service

Section Preview

OBJECTIVES

1. **Describe** the development of the civil service.
2. **Identify** characteristics of the civil service as it exists today.
3. **Analyze** the restrictions on the political activities of members of the civil service.

WHY IT MATTERS

Most people who work for the Federal Government are members of the civil service. Over time, civil service reformers have worked to reduce corruption and political influence and promote merit in federal employment.

POLITICAL DICTIONARY

★ **civil service**
★ **spoils system**
★ **patronage**
★ **register**
★ **bipartisan**

The **civil service** is composed of those civilian employees who perform the administrative work of government. Some 2.7 million men and women work for the Federal Government today.[11] Only about 300,000 of them work in the Washington area. The rest have jobs in regional, field, and local offices scattered throughout the country and around the world.

The President appoints the people who hold the highest ranking jobs in the executive branch. There are only about 2,500 of those positions—at the top levels of the Executive Office, the Cabinet departments, the independent agencies, and in American embassies and other diplomatic stations. All of the other jobs in the federal bureaucracy are covered by some aspect of the civil service system.

Development of the Civil Service

The Constitution says very little about the staffing of the federal bureaucracy. The only direct reference is in Article II, which says that the President

FROM THE Constitution *"shall nominate, and by and with the Advice and Consent of the Senate, shall appoint Ambassadors, other public Ministers and Consuls, Judges of the supreme Court, and all other Officers of the United States, whose Appointments are not herein otherwise provided for, and which shall be established by Law: but the Congress may by Law vest the Appointment of such inferior Officers, as they think proper, in the President alone, in the Courts of Law, or in the Heads of Departments.* **"**

—Article II, Section 2, Clause 2

◀ The civil service includes people like this ranger who patrols the Grand Canyon National Park in Arizona. **H-SS 12.2.4**

---

[11]Another 1.4 million men and women serve in the armed forces; see Chapter 17. Altogether, there are now some 17.5 million civilian public employees in this country. More than 4 million work for the States, and another 11 million work for local governments (including 6.5 million persons employed by school districts). About 2.5 million of those who work for State and local governments are employed on a part-time basis.

Interpreting Political Cartoons
This cartoon comments on the spoils system under Andrew Jackson.
How does the cartoon illustrate this practice?

The Beginnings

When he became President in 1789, George Washington knew that the success of the new government would depend in large part on those whom he appointed to office. Those to be chosen, he said, would be "such persons alone . . . as shall be the best qualified." Still, he favored members of his own party, the Federalists. So did his successor, John Adams.

In 1801 Thomas Jefferson found most federal posts filled by men politically and personally opposed to him. He agreed with Washington's standard of fitness for office, but he combined it with another: political acceptability. Jefferson dismissed several hundred Federalists and replaced them with members of his own party, the Democratic-Republicans.

The Spoils System

By the late 1820s, the number of federal employees had risen above 10,000. When Andrew Jackson became President in 1829, he dismissed over 200 presidential appointees and nearly 2,000 other officeholders. Jacksonian Democrats replaced them.

Ever since, Andrew Jackson has been called the "father" of the **spoils system**—the practice of giving offices and other favors of government to political supporters and friends. The phrase comes from a statement made on the floor of the Senate in 1832. Senator William Learned Marcy of New York, defending Jackson's appointment of an ambassador, declared: "To the victor belongs the spoils of the enemy."

To call Jackson the father of the spoils system is not altogether fair. Jefferson had laid its foundations at the federal level in 1801. The practice of giving jobs to supporters and friends—also known as **patronage**—was in wide use at the State and local levels long before Jackson's presidency.

Jackson saw his appointing policy as democratic. In his first message to Congress, he defended it on four grounds: (1) Since the duties of public office are simple, any normally intelligent person can fill such office. (2) There should be a "rotation in office" so that many people can have the privilege of serving in government. (3) Long service in office can lead to both tyranny and inefficiency. (4) The people are entitled to have the party they have placed in power control all offices of government, top to bottom.

Whatever Jackson's view, many saw the spoils system as a way to build and hold power. For the next half-century, every change of administration brought a new round of rewards and punishments. As the government's activities, agencies, and payrolls grew, so did the spoils. Many posts were filled by political hacks. Inefficiency and even corruption became the order of the day. Huge profits were made on public contracts at the people's expense. Much of the nation's natural wealth was stolen. Political power was centered in hoards of officeholders and others who owed their livelihoods to the party in power.

The Movement to Reform

Able people, in and out of government, pressed for reforms, but little came of their efforts. Congress did create a Civil Service Commission in 1871, but it soon died away because Congress failed to provide it with enough money.

A tragedy at last brought about fundamental changes in the hiring and other staffing practices of the Federal Government. In 1881, President James Garfield was fatally shot by a disappointed office-seeker, Charles J. Guiteau. Garfield had rejected the mentally unstable Guiteau's request that he be appointed to a high diplomatic post.

The nation was horrified and outraged. Congress, pushed hard by Garfield's successor, Chester Arthur, passed the Pendleton Act—the Civil Service Act of 1883.[12]

---

[12]The Republican convention in 1880 was sharply divided by the civil service question. Its nominee, Garfield, was a strong supporter of reform. To balance the ticket, the convention chose Arthur, a leader of the anti-reform faction, as his running mate. Garfield's assassination brought a dramatic change in Arthur's stance; as President he became a leading champion of reform.

The Pendleton Act

The Pendleton Act laid the foundation of the present federal civil service system. Its main purpose was to make merit—the quality of one's work—the basis for hiring, promotion, and other personnel actions in the federal work force.

The law set up two categories of employment in the executive branch: the classified and the unclassified services. All hiring for positions in the classified service was to be based on merit. That quality was to be measured by "practical" examinations given by an independent agency, the Civil Service Commission.

The Pendleton Act placed only about 10 percent of the Federal Government's then 130,000 employees in the classified service; it did give the President the power to extend that coverage, however. Theodore Roosevelt championed the merit system, and by the end of his term in 1909 the classified umbrella covered two thirds of the 365,000 members of the federal work force. Today, nearly 90 percent of all of the men and women who work for executive branch agencies are covered by the merit system.[13]

The Civil Service Today

The first goal of civil service reform—the elimination of the spoils system—was largely achieved in the early years of the last century. Gradually, a new purpose emerged: recruiting and keeping the best available people in the federal work force.

On the whole, efforts to reach that newer goal have succeeded. Today most federal employees are hired through a competitive process. They are paid and promoted on the basis of written evaluations by their superiors. They are generally protected from disciplinary actions or dismissal for partisan reasons.

Still, the federal civil service is not perfect. Critics often claim that not enough attention is paid to merit in the merit system.

The Office of Personnel Management

The Office of Personnel Management, created in 1978, is now the Federal Government's central personnel agency. Like its predecessor, the old Civil Service Commission, it is an independent agency in the executive branch.

The OPM is headed by a single director appointed by the President and Senate. The agency can best be described as the central clearinghouse in the federal recruiting, examining, and hiring process. It advertises for employees, examines those who apply, and keeps **registers,** lists of those applicants who pass its tests and are qualified for employment. When there is a job opening in an agency, the OPM usually sends that agency the names of the top three persons on its register for that particular type of position.[14]

---

[13]This number does not take into account employees of the United State Postal Service and a few other federal agencies. The Postal Service, with some 750,000 full-time employees, is the largest agency not covered by the civil service system. It is the only federal agency in which employment policies are set by collective bargaining and labor union contracts. The other major agencies not counted in fixing that 90 percent figure are the FBI, CIA, and TVA; each of those agencies has its own merit system.

[14]Each applicant's place on a register is fixed by three factors: (1) date of application, (2) OPM test scores, and (3) veterans' preference points, if any. Some 40 percent of all federal jobs are currently held by veterans, wives of disabled veterans, and unremarried widows of veterans. Some jobs, such as guards and messengers, are reserved especially for veterans.

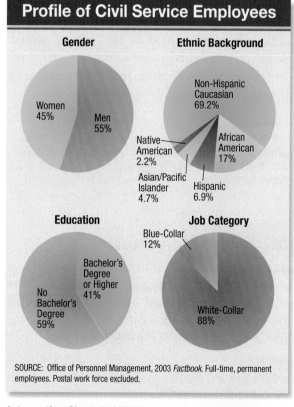

Profile of Civil Service Employees

Gender
Women 45%
Men 55%

Ethnic Background
Non-Hispanic Caucasian 69.2%
Native American 2.2%
Asian/Pacific Islander 4.7%
Hispanic 6.9%
African American 17%

Education
No Bachelor's Degree 59%
Bachelor's Degree or Higher 41%

Job Category
Blue-Collar 12%
White-Collar 88%

SOURCE: Office of Personnel Management, 2003 *Factbook*. Full-time, permanent employees. Postal work force excluded.

Interpreting Charts In 2002 the average civil servant was a 46-year-old man who earned $56,400 a year and had worked for the government for nearly 17 years. *Why might the civil service have a higher proportion of college graduates than the country as a whole?* H-SS 12.2.4

Another independent agency, the Merit Systems Protection Board, enforces the merit principle in the federal bureaucracy. The Board is **bipartisan,** which means it includes members from both parties. It is a three-member panel picked by the President and Senate. It hears appeals from those federal workers who have complaints about personnel actions—for example, denials of pay increases, demotions, or firings.[15]

Pay and Benefits

Equal opportunities for career advancement remain a problem in the federal bureaucracy. Although minority groups and women are well represented in most agencies, they tend to be concentrated in lower-level positions. Women, for example, now hold more than half of all white-collar federal jobs; but they hold only a little more than 10 percent of the highest paid positions.

Congress sets the pay and other job conditions for everyone who works for the Federal Government, except for employees of the United States Postal Service. At the lower and middle levels, civil service pay compares fairly well with salaries paid in the private sector. However, government can never hope to compete dollar for dollar with the upper reaches of private employment.

---

[15]Yet another independent agency, the Federal Labor Relations Authority, handles labor-management relations in federal employment. It, too, is a bipartisan three-member body appointed by the President and Senate.

Political Activities

Several laws and a number of OPM regulations place restrictions on the political activities of federal civil servants. The first of two major laws is the Hatch Act of 1939—the Act to Prevent Pernicious Political Activities. *Pernicious* means "exceedingly harmful." In essence, that law allowed federal workers to vote in elections, but it forbade them to take part in partisan political activities.

Critics of the Hatch Act said it placed unnecessary and unjustifiable limits on the political and civil rights of federal workers. Supporters saw those limits as legitimate ways to prevent the use of civil servants to influence presidential and congressional elections. The Supreme Court has rejected several 1st Amendment challenges to the law; the leading case is *National Association of Letter Carriers* v. *Civil Service Commission,* 1973.

The second major statute is the Federal Employees Political Activities Act of 1993, often called the new Hatch Act, which relaxed many of the older restrictions. Today, a federal worker has the right to vote, help register new voters, contribute money to candidates and parties, participate in campaigns, and even hold office in a political party. The worker may *not* run in partisan elections, engage in party work on government property or while on the job, collect political contributions from subordinates (workers in lower positions) or the general public, or use a government position to influence an election.

Section 5 Assessment

Key Terms and Main Ideas

1. What is the purpose of the **civil service?**
2. How did the **spoils system** develop?
3. What is recorded in the **registers** of the OPM?
4. What is the defining characteristic of a **bipartisan** group?

Critical Thinking

5. **Making Decisions** Why does the government limit the political activities of members of the civil service? Explain whether you would change any of these limits, and why.

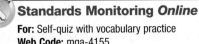
6. **Determining Cause and Effect** Explain how the spoils system was a reflection of corruption in government.

Can States Regulate HMO Claims Reviews?

Analysis Skills HR4, HI3, HI4

When Congress legislates in an area, does it intend to exclude State regulation or can there be shared authority? Many Congressional enactments contain "preemption" provisions, which prevent the States from legislating in the same area. The U.S. Supreme Court has struggled to determine the scope and intent of these preemption clauses.

Rush Prudential HMO v. *Moran* (2002)

In 1996, Debra Moran began having numbness in her right shoulder. Moran belonged to the Rush Prudential HMO (Health Maintenance Organization) through health insurance benefits provided by her husband's employer. Her doctor at Rush tried conventional treatments, but when those did not work he recommended that she go to an outside specialist who had developed an unconventional treatment for her condition. Rush concluded that the special care was not "medically necessary," and instead authorized standard surgery by a Rush doctor.

Moran lived in Illinois, and Illinois law said that HMO members had the right to an independent review when a claim for services was denied. Moran requested an independent medical review, but Rush did not allow her one. She then sued Rush, claiming she was entitled to an independent review under State law and to payment of her claim as medically necessary.

In its defense, Rush argued that the Illinois law was in conflict with the Employee Retirement Income Security Act of 1974 (ERISA). ERISA's preemption provision stipulates that the federal rules "shall supersede any and all State laws insofar as they may now or hereafter relate to any employee benefit plan" except for State laws that regulate "insurance, banking, or securities."

The trial court found that ERISA preempted (superseded) the Illinois law, but the Court of Appeals for the Seventh Circuit reversed on the grounds that the Illinois law regulated insurance. Rush appealed to the U.S. Supreme Court.

Arguments for Rush Prudential HMO

1. ERISA does not allow States to create extra rules for HMOs' workplace health insurance benefits.
2. As an HMO, Rush is a health care provider rather than an insurance company, so the "insurance" exception to preemption does not apply.
3. Subjecting HMOs to varying rules from State to State would violate the national regulatory system that Congress sought to create in ERISA.

Arguments for Moran

1. Rush acts as both an insurance company and a health care provider, so the "insurance" exception to preemption applies.
2. The Illinois "independent opinion" rule does not conflict with any provision of ERISA.
3. ERISA does not prevent States from giving extra rights to HMO-insured employees.

Decide for Yourself

1. Review the constitutional grounds upon which each side based its arguments and the specific arguments each side presented.
2. Debate the opposing viewpoints presented in this case. Which viewpoint did you favor?
3. Predict the impact of the Court's decision on the State supervision of health care services. (To read a summary of the Court's decision, turn to pages 799–806.)

Go Online
PHSchool.com
Use Web Code mqp-4158 to register your vote on this issue and to see how other students voted.

Political Dictionary

bureaucracy (p. 414), bureaucrat (p. 415), administration (p. 416), staff agency (p. 418), line agency (p. 418), Executive Office of the President (p. 419), federal budget (p. 421), fiscal year (p. 421), domestic affairs (p. 422), executive departments (p. 424), secretary (p. 424), attorney general (p. 424), independent agencies (p. 430), independent executive agencies (p. 431), independent regulatory commissions (p. 431), quasi-legislative (p. 433), quasi-judicial (p. 433), government corporation (p. 434), civil service (p. 437), spoils system (p. 438), patronage (p. 438), register (p. 439), bipartisan (p. 440)

Standards Review

H-SS 12.1.4 Explain how the Founding Fathers' realistic view of human nature led directly to the establishment of a constitutional system that limited the power of the governors and the governed as articulated in the *Federalist Papers*.

H-SS 12.1.5 Describe the systems of separated and shared powers, the role of organized interests (*Federalist Paper Number 10*), checks and balances (*Federalist Paper Number 51*), the importance of an independent judiciary (*Federalist Paper Number 78*), enumerated powers, rule of law, federalism, and civilian control of the military.

H-SS 12.2.4 Understand the obligations of civic-mindedness, including voting, being informed on civic issues, volunteering and performing public service, and serving in the military or alternative service.

H-SS 12.4.4 Discuss Article II of the Constitution as it relates to the executive branch, including eligibility for office and length of term, election to and removal from office, the oath of office, and the enumerated executive powers.

H-SS 12.7.5 Explain how public policy is formed, including the setting of the public agenda and implementation of it through regulations and executive orders.

Practicing the Vocabulary

Matching *Choose a term from the list above that best matches each description.*

1. A large, hierarchical organization with job specialization and complex rules
2. A detailed estimate of federal income and spending for a twelve-month period
3. The director of the Department of Justice
4. Describes a group with the power to judge cases outside the court system

Word Relationships *Distinguish between words or phrases in each pair.*

5. staff agency/line agency
6. secretary/bureaucrat
7. Executive Office of the President/Cabinet
8. executive departments/independent agencies
9. administration/patronage

Reviewing Main Ideas

Section 1
10. How did the different components of the bureaucracy in the Federal Government's executive branch develop?
11. What is the "name game" in the context of the federal bureaucracy?2
12. In what ways is a bureaucracy undemocratic?

Section 2
13. What agencies work most directly with the President, providing assistance and advice?
14. Describe the organization of the Executive Office of the President.
15. **(a)** What are the duties of the National Security Council? **(b)** What are the duties of the Office of National Drug Control Policy?

Section 3
16. How was the Cabinet born?
17. In what sense are the executive departments the traditional units of federal administration?

18. What responsibilities do members of the Cabinet have that are not among the duties of the major figures in the Executive Office of the President?

Section 4
19. Explain the major reasons why the independent agencies exist apart from the Cabinet-level departments.
20. **(a)** What are the three types of independent agencies? **(b)** Describe the basic role of each type of agency.
21. What are the major differences between a government corporation and a private corporation?

Section 5
22. Describe the standards for staffing the federal bureaucracy held by Presidents George Washington and Thomas Jefferson.
23. **(a)** What was the spoils system? **(b)** How did the spoils system affect the quality of the public work force?
24. What was the primary objective of the efforts to reform the country's civil service in the late 1800s?

Critical Thinking Skills

Analysis Skill HR4

25. *Applying the Chapter Skill* Use the Internet to find five federal agencies with local offices in your State. What information about your State were you able to find at their Web sites?

26. *Making Comparisons* Consider the following units: executive department, independent executive agency, independent regulatory commission, government corporation. Rank these units from "most independent" to "least independent" of the executive branch, and explain your reasoning.

27. *Expressing Problems Clearly* **(a)** Is an efficient government always an effective government? **(b)** What is the proper relationship between efficiency and effectiveness in government? Give support for your answer.

28. *Drawing Inferences* Thomas Jefferson once said, "When a man accepts a public trust, he should consider himself a public property." **(a)** What do you think this statement means? **(b)** Do you agree or disagree with this statement? **(c)** What values underlie this statement?

Analyzing Political Cartoons

Using your knowledge of American government and this cartoon, answer the questions below.

"First of all, you need to set up a Department of Paperwork. . ."

29. What does this cartoon imply about bureaucracy?

30. Based on your reading, do you agree or disagree with this assessment? Explain.

You Can Make a Difference

Which government agencies or commissions affect your community? For example, is there a clean-up project of the Environmental Protection Agency or a branch of the Federal Emergency Management Agency (FEMA), which gives help after disasters? Consult the "Government" pages in your local telephone book. Choose an agency or department with a local branch office. Arrange an interview with a representative to learn about the role of this bureaucracy in your community. If time allows, invite him or her to speak to your class.

Participation Activities

Analysis Skills CS1, HR1, HR4, HI3

31. *Current Events Watch* Make a photocopy of the chart on page 417. Skim the news section of a newspaper for a week, looking for references to organizations shown on the chart. Highlight or check each organization that is referred to in a news report. At the end of the week, compare your chart with those of your classmates.

32. *Graphing Activity* Research the number of employees of the Federal Government at several points in the nation's history. Create a line graph showing the change in the number of employees over time. Then, create a line graph showing the growth of the United States population over the same period. What conclusions can you draw from your graphs?

33. *It's Your Turn* You are living in the United States in the 1830s. Write a letter to President Jackson offering your views on the spoils system. Before you start, identify three reasons why you think the system is good or bad. Begin the letter by stating your purpose, including your overall opinion of the spoils system. Then devote one paragraph to each of the three reasons you identified to support your argument. Revise the letter, correct any errors, and draft a final copy. **(Writing a Letter)**

Standards Monitoring *Online*

For: Chapter 15 Self-Test **Visit:** PHSchool.com
Web Code: mqa-4156

As a final review, take the Magruder's Chapter 15 Self-Test and receive immediate feedback on your answers.
The test consists of 20 multiple-choice questions designed to test your understanding of the chapter content.

CHAPTER 16

Financing Government

"*The power 'to lay and collect taxes, duties, imposts, and excises' was an indispensable one to...the Federal Government, which without it would possess no means of providing for its own support.*"

—James Polk (1845)

How much money does the Federal Government raise each year, and how does it raise it? How much does it spend each year, and for what? And how much must it borrow each year? The answers to these questions have a real impact on *you*.

◆ The Bureau of Engraving and Printing

SECTION 1

Taxes (pp. 446–452)

★ The Framers put the power to tax first among the expressed powers of Congress.

★ The income taxes paid by individuals and corporations are the largest sources of federal revenue today.

★ Excise taxes, gift and estate taxes, customs duties, and social insurance taxes also support the Federal Government.

★ The power to tax is used, in large part, to raise revenue; however, it is also used to regulate and even discourage some activities.

SECTION 2

Nontax Revenues and Borrowing (pp. 454–456)

★ The Federal Government receives a relatively small amount of revenue from several nontax sources.

★ The Constitution gives Congress the power to borrow, and the Federal Government borrows hundreds of billions of dollars every year.

★ The Federal Government regularly practices deficit financing— that is, in most years it spends more than it takes in and then borrows to make up the difference.

★ The public debt is composed of all of the money the government has borrowed over time and not yet repaid, plus all of the accrued interest on that money.

SECTION 3

Spending and the Budget (pp. 458–462)

★ Federal spending—now some $2 trillion a year—has an enormous impact on the nation's economy.

★ The largest categories of federal spending include entitlements, defense, and interest on the public debt.

★ The federal budget is a major political document—a statement of the public policies of the United States, with dollar signs attached.

·1· Taxes

Section Preview

OBJECTIVES

1. **Explain** how and why the Constitution gives Congress the power to tax.
2. **Describe** the most significant federal taxes collected today.
3. **Summarize** why the Federal Government imposes taxes for nonrevenue purposes.

WHY IT MATTERS

Article I of the Constitution and the 16th Amendment give Congress a very broad—and often very controversial—power to tax. You can see the impact of the exercise of that immense power in nearly every aspect of your daily life.

POLITICAL DICTIONARY

- **progressive tax**
- **tax return**
- **payroll tax**
- **regressive tax**
- **excise tax**
- **estate tax**
- **gift tax**
- **customs duty**

According to Benjamin Franklin's oft-quoted comment, "in this world nothing is certain but death and taxes." In this section, you will consider the second of Franklin's certainties, taxes. More specifically, you will examine those taxes levied by the Federal Government.

During fiscal year 2007, which extends from October 1, 2006, through September 30, 2007, the Federal Government will spend some $2.7

trillion, and it will take in nearly half a trillion less than that stupendous sum. Those mind-boggling numbers tell you that, on average, it now costs every man, woman, and child in this country over $8,000 a year to support the Federal Government. Those figures should also tell you how important the subject of taxes really is.

The Power to Tax

The Constitution underscores the central importance of the power to tax by listing it first among all of the many powers granted to Congress. The Constitution gives to Congress the power

To lay and collect Taxes, Duties, Imposts and Excises, to pay the Debts and provide for the common Defense and general Welfare of the United States. . . .

—Article I, Section 8, Clause 1

First and foremost, Congress exercises the taxing power in order to raise the money needed to operate the Federal Government. However, Congress does levy some taxes for nonrevenue purposes—for reasons other than raising money.

Constitutional Limitations

The power to tax is not unlimited. As with all of its other powers, Congress must exercise the taxing power in accord with the Constitution. Thus,

"So then Tommy Taxpayer said to the big bully, Godzilla government, 'I am unwilling to pay the bill ...'"

JIM BERRY
©NEA

Interpreting Political Cartoons Taxes are essential, but people disagree on how much the Federal Government should tax. ***What is the speaker's attitude toward government?*** H-SS 12.2.3

▲ The Federal Government draws revenue from many sources, including taxes on telephone calls, imported goods, and wages. *Critical Thinking* *Where does the Federal Government get the power to tax imports?* **H-SS 12.2.3**

for example, Congress cannot levy a tax on church services—clearly, such a tax would violate the 1st Amendment.

In more specific terms, the Constitution puts four expressed limits—and one very significant implied limit—on the power to tax.

First, it declares that Congress is given the power to tax in order to "pay the Debts and provide for the common Defense and general welfare of the United States." That is, taxes must be levied *only* for public purposes, not for the benefit of some private interest.

The second expressed limit is the prohibition of export taxes. Article I, Section 9, Clause 5 declares that "No Tax or Duty shall be laid on Articles exported from any State." Thus, customs duties (tariffs) can be applied only to imports—goods brought into the United States. They may not be applied to exports, or goods sent out of the country. This restriction was a part of the Commerce Compromise made by the Framers at Philadelphia in 1787.

While Congress cannot tax exports, it can and does prohibit the export of certain items. It does so under its expressed power to regulate foreign commerce, usually for reasons of national security. For example, Congress has banned the export of computer software that allows people to encrypt files in a code no government can crack.

Thirdly, direct taxes must be equally apportioned, evenly distributed, among the States. The Constitution originally provided that:

FROM THE Constitution ❝No *Capitation, or other direct, Tax shall be laid, unless in Proportion to the Census of Enumeration herein before directed to be taken.* ❞
—Article I, Section 9, Clause 4

This restriction was a part of the Three-Fifths Compromise the Framers made at the Philadelphia Convention. In effect, delegates from the northern States insisted that if slaves were to be counted in the populations of the southern States, then those States would have to pay for them.

Recall that a direct tax is one that must be borne by the person upon whom it is levied. Examples include a tax on land or buildings, which must be paid by the owner of the property; or a capitation tax—a head or poll tax—laid on each person. Other taxes are indirect taxes, or levies that may be shifted to another for payment—as, for example, the federal tax on liquor. That tax, placed initially on the distiller, is ultimately paid by the person who buys the liquor.

The direct tax restriction means, in effect, that any direct tax that Congress levies must be apportioned among the States according to their populations. Thus, a direct tax that raised $1 billion would have to produce just about $120 million in California and $10 million in Mississippi, because California has just about 12 percent of the nation's population and Mississippi 1 percent.

Wealth is not evenly distributed among the States, of course. So, a direct tax laid in proportion to population would be grossly unfair; the

Financing Government **447** ★★★

tax would fall more heavily on the residents of some States than it would on others. As a result, Congress has not imposed a direct tax—except for the income tax—outside the District of Columbia since 1861.

An income tax is a direct tax, but it may be laid without regard to population:

FROM THE Constitution *"The Congress shall have power to lay and collect taxes on incomes, from whatever source derived, without apportionment among the several States, and without regard to any census or enumeration.*"

—16th Amendment

Congress first levied an income tax in 1861, to help finance the Civil War. The tax, which expired in 1873, was later upheld by the Supreme Court in *Springer* v. *United States,* 1881. A unanimous Court found that income tax to be an indirect rather than a direct tax.

However, a later income tax law, enacted in 1894, was declared unconstitutional in *Pollock* v. *Farmers' Loan and Trust Co.,* 1895. There, the Court held that the 1894 law imposed a direct tax that Congress should have apportioned among the several States. The impossibility of taxing incomes fairly in accord with any plan

of apportionment led to the adoption of the 16th Amendment in 1913.

The fourth and final limit, in Article I, Section 8, Clause 1, declares that "all Duties, Imposts and Excises shall be uniform throughout the United States." That is, all of the indirect taxes levied by the Federal Government must be set at the same rate in all parts of the country.

The Implied Limitation

The Federal Government cannot tax the States or any of their local governments in the exercise of their governmental functions. That is, federal taxes cannot be imposed on those governments when they are performing such tasks as providing public education, furnishing health care, or building streets and highways.

Recall, the Supreme Court laid down that rule in *McCulloch* v. *Maryland* in 1819, when it declared that "the power to tax involves the power to destroy." If the Federal Government could tax the governmental activities of the States or their local units, it could conceivably tax them out of existence and so destroy the federal system.

The Federal Government can and does tax those State and local activities that are of a nongovernmental character, however. Thus, in 1893, South Carolina created a State monopoly to sell

The Federal Government's Income (in billions of dollars)						
	1990	**1995**	**2000**	**2005**	**2006***	**2007***
Individual income taxes	$466.9	$590.2	$1,004.5	$927.2	$997.6	$1,096.4
Corporation income taxes	93.5	157.0	207.3	278.3	277.1	260.6
Social insurance taxes and contributions	380.0	484.5	652.9	794.1	841.1	884.1
Excise taxes	35.3	57.5	68.9	73.1	73.5	74.6
Estate and gift taxes	11.5	14.8	29.0	24.8	27.5	23.7
Customs duties	16.7	19.3	19.9	23.4	25.9	28.1
Miscellaneous receipts	27.8	28.6	42.8	33.0	42.8	48.4
Total receipts	$1,032.0	$1,351.8	$2,025.2	$2,153.9	$2,285.5	$2,415.9

*Projected
SOURCE: Office of Management and Budget

 Interpreting Tables Federal revenue comes from several different sources. ***From which of these sources did the revenues collected increase by the greatest percentage from 1990 to 2006?***

liquor, and it claimed that each of its liquor stores was exempt from the federal saloon license tax. But in *South Carolina* v. *United States,* 1905, the Supreme Court held that the State was liable for the tax, because the sale of liquor is not a necessary or usual governmental activity. Today, most States and many local governments are engaged in a variety of business-like enterprises, as you will see in Chapter 25.

Current Federal Taxes

Oliver Wendell Holmes once described taxes as "what we pay for civilized society."[1] Society does not appear to be much more civilized today than it was when Justice Holmes made that observation in 1927. However, "what we pay" has certainly gone up. In 1927, the Federal Government's tax collections came to, altogether, less than $3.4 billion. Compare that figure with the figures in the table on page 448.

The Income Tax

You will recall that the income tax was authorized by the 16th Amendment, in 1913. It is the largest source of federal revenue today. It first became the major source in 1917 and 1918. And, except for a few years during the Depression of the 1930s, it has remained so.

Several features of the income tax fit its dominant role. It is a flexible tax, because its rates can be adjusted to produce whatever amount of money Congress thinks is necessary. The income tax is also easily adapted to the principle of ability to pay. It is a **progressive tax**—that is, the higher one's income, the higher the tax. The tax is levied on the earnings of both individuals and corporations.

The Individual Income Tax

The tax on individuals' incomes regularly produces the largest amount of federal revenue. For fiscal year 2006, the individual income tax was expected to provide nearly $1 trillion.

The tax is levied on each person's taxable income—that is, one's total income in the previous year less certain exemptions and

---

[1]Holmes made this statement in a dissenting opinion in an insurance tax case, *Compania General de Tabacos de Filipinas* v. *Collector of Internal Revenue,* 1927.

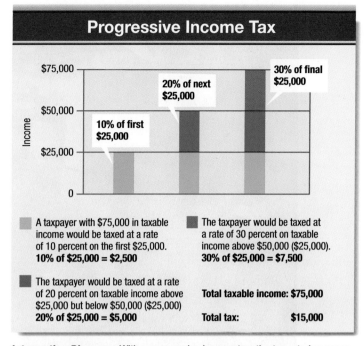

Progressive Income Tax

$75,000

$50,000

$25,000

0

Income

10% of first $25,000

20% of next $25,000

30% of final $25,000

■ A taxpayer with $75,000 in taxable income would be taxed at a rate of 10 percent on the first $25,000.
10% of $25,000 = $2,500

■ The taxpayer would be taxed at a rate of 20 percent on taxable income above $25,000 but below $50,000 ($25,000)
20% of $25,000 = $5,000

■ The taxpayer would be taxed at a rate of 30 percent on taxable income above $50,000 ($25,000).
30% of $25,000 = $7,500

Total taxable income: $75,000

Total tax: $15,000

Interpreting Diagrams With a progressive income tax, the tax rate increases as total income increases. Today, federal income tax rates range from 10% to 35%. *How much would this taxpayer owe with a taxable income of $37,500, which is exactly half the income in the example?* H-SS 12.2.3

deductions. On returns filed in 2006, covering income received in 2005, most taxpayers had a personal exemption of $3,150, and another of the same amount for each dependent. The personal exemption is adjusted to account for inflation each year. Deductions are allowed for a number of things, including the cost of some medical care, most State and local taxes (except sales taxes), interest paid on home mortgages, and charitable contributions.

By April 15 of any given year, everyone who earned taxable income in the preceding calendar year must file a **tax return**—a declaration of that income and of the exemptions and deductions he or she claims. The returns are filed, by mail or online, with the Internal Revenue Service. The IRS now receives more than 120 million returns each year, more than 50 million of them e-filed.

At President Bush's urging, Congress passed major tax-cut legislation in 2001, 2002, and again in 2003. As a result, all taxable income earned in 2005 was taxed (in 2006) at one of six rates (brackets). Those rates range from 10 percent in the lowest bracket on up to 35 percent on the highest incomes. Thus, in the lowest bracket

▲ **Social Security** If they have paid OASDI taxes for several years, Americans can retire at age 65 and receive financial support from OASDI taxes paid by people still in the work force.

such as churches and charitable foundations are not subject to the corporation income tax.

For 2006, the corporate tax rates ran from 15 percent on the first $50,000 of taxable earnings up to a top rate of 35 percent on taxable incomes of more than $10 million.

Social Insurance Taxes

The Federal Government collects huge sums to finance three major social welfare programs: (1) the Old-Age, Survivors, and Disability Insurance (OASDI) program—the basic Social Security program, established by the Social Security Act of 1935; (2) Medicare—health care for the elderly, added to the Social Security program in 1965; and (3) the unemployment compensation program—benefits paid to jobless workers, a program also established by the Social Security Act in 1935.

OASDI and Medicare are supported by taxes imposed on nearly all employers and their employees, and on self-employed persons. These levies are often called **payroll taxes** because the amounts owed by employees are withheld from their paychecks. For 2006, employees paid an OASDI tax of 6.2 percent on the first $94,300 of their salary or wages for the year, and their employers had to match that amount. The self-employed were taxed at 12.4 percent on the first $94,300 of their income.

For Medicare, employees pay a 1.45 percent tax on their total annual income. Employers must match the amounts withheld from their employees' paychecks. The self-employed pay a 2.9 percent Medicare tax on their annual incomes.

The unemployment insurance program is a joint federal-State operation that makes payments to workers who lose their jobs for reasons beyond their control. The program now covers most workers in this country. Each State and the District of Columbia, Puerto Rico, and the Virgin Islands has its own unemployment compensation law. The amount of a worker's weekly benefits, and how many weeks they last, are determined by State law.

The unemployment compensation program is financed by both federal and State taxes. The federal tax is 6.2 percent of the first $7,000 an employer pays to each employee in a year. Each employer is given a credit of up to 5.4 percent against that tax for unemployment taxes that the

in 2006, a married couple paid 10 percent on their taxable income up to $14,600. Taxpayers in the highest bracket sent the IRS 35 percent of their taxable income above $323,000.

Most people who pay income taxes do so through withholding, a pay-as-you-go plan. Employers are required to withhold a certain amount from each employee's paycheck and send that money to the IRS. When the employee files a tax return, he or she receives a refund if the employer withheld more money than the employee owed in taxes, or must pay an additional amount if too little was withheld. Those who earn income from sources not subject to withholding (for example, rent or royalties) must estimate the tax they will owe and make quarterly payments on that amount throughout the year.

The Corporation Income Tax

Each corporation must pay a tax on its net income, that is, on all of its earnings above the costs of doing business. The corporate tax is the most complicated of all federal taxes because of the many deductions allowed. Nonprofit organizations employer pays to the State. So, the federal tax usually amounts to 0.8 percent on taxable wages.

Notice that these social insurance taxes for OASDI, Medicare, and unemployment compensation are not progressive taxes. They are, instead, **regressive taxes**—taxes levied at a flat rate, without regard to the level of a taxpayer's income or his or her ability to pay them. In fact, the regressive OASDI and Medicare taxes now take more money out of the paychecks of many low- and middle-income workers than does the progressive federal income tax.

The IRS collects social insurance taxes. The money is then credited to trust accounts maintained by the Treasury, and Congress appropriates funds for the social insurance programs as they are needed.

Excise Taxes

An **excise tax** is a tax laid on the manufacture, sale, or consumption of goods and/or the performance of services. The Federal Government has imposed and collected excise taxes since Congress acquired its taxing power in 1789.

Today, federal excise taxes are imposed on a long list of things, including gasoline, oil, tires, tobacco, liquor, wine, beer, firearms, telephone services, airline tickets, and more. Many excise taxes are called "hidden taxes" because they are collected from producers who then figure them into the price that the retail customer finally pays. Some are called "luxury taxes" because they are imposed on goods not usually considered necessities. And some excise taxes are known as "sin taxes," particularly those laid on tobacco, beer, wine, liquor, and gambling.

Estate and Gift Taxes

An **estate tax** is a levy imposed on the assets (the estate) of one who dies.[3] A **gift tax** is one imposed on the making of a gift by a living person. Congress first provided for the estate tax in 1916. It added the gift tax in 1932 to plug a loophole in the estate tax that allowed people to avoid the estate tax by giving away money or other property before death.

The first $2 million of an estate is exempt from the federal tax in 2006, 2007, and 2008. So, in fact, most estates are not subject to the federal levy. Deductions are allowed for such things as State death taxes and bequests to religious and charitable groups. Anything a husband or wife leaves to the other is taxed, if at all, only when the surviving spouse dies.

Any person may now make up to $11,000 in tax-free gifts to any other person in any one year. Gifts that husbands/wives make to one another are not taxed, regardless of value.

The estate and gift taxes are separate federal taxes, but they are levied at the same rates. For 2006, those rates range from 18 percent on an estate or gift with a net value of under $20,000, on up to a maximum of 46 percent on an estate or gift worth more than $3 million.

Customs Duties

Customs duties are taxes laid on goods brought into the United States from abroad. Customs duties are also known as tariffs, import duties, or imposts. Congress decides which imports will be dutied and at what rates. Most imports, some 30,000 different items, are dutied; but some are not—for example, Bibles, coffee, bananas, and up to $800 of a tourist's purchases abroad.

Customs duties were the major source of income for the Federal Government for more than a century. Now, they produce just over 1 percent of all of the money the government takes in each year.

▲ Duck hunters must buy a duck stamp from the Federal Government each year. The money is used for wildlife conservation programs. *Critical Thinking Explain why, other than to raise revenue, the Federal Government might require duck hunters to pay an annual fee.* H-SS 12.2.3

---

[3]An inheritance tax is another form of the so-called death tax. It is not levied on the entire net estate but, instead, on each portion inherited by each heir. Most States impose inheritance, not estate, taxes; most States also levy gift taxes.

Taxing for Nonrevenue Purposes

Remember, the power to tax can be, and often is, used for purposes other than the raising of revenue. Usually, that other purpose is to regulate and even discourage some activity that Congress thinks is harmful or dangerous to the public.

Thus, much of the Federal Government's regulation of narcotics is based on the taxing power. Federal law provides that only those who hold a valid license may legally manufacture, sell, or otherwise deal in those drugs—and licensing is a form of taxation. The government also regulates a number of other things by licensing, including, for example, certain firearms, prospecting on public lands, and the hunting of migratory birds. The federal excise tax on gas-guzzling cars is intended to discourage their purchase.

The Supreme Court first upheld the use of the taxing power for nonrevenue purposes in *Veazie Bank* v. *Fenno* in 1869. In 1861, Congress created a national paper money system to provide a single, sound currency for the country. Private bank notes, which also circulated as paper money, soon interfered with the government's new "greenbacks." So, in 1865, Congress imposed a 10 percent tax on the issuing of those private notes, and they soon disappeared. In upholding the tax, the Court declared:

PRIMARY Sources *"Having thus, in the exercise of undisputed constitutional powers, undertaken to provide a currency for the whole country, it cannot be questioned that Congress may, constitutionally, secure the benefit of it to the people by appropriate legislation."*

—*Veazie Bank* v. *Fenno*, Opinion of the Court

In 1912, Congress used its taxing power to destroy a part of the domestic match industry. It levied a tax of two cents per hundred on matches made with white or yellow phosphorus. These highly poisonous substances harmed workers who produced the matches. Matches made from other substances commonly sold for a penny a hundred. Thus, the two-cent tax drove the phosphorus matches from the market.

Congress cannot use its taxing power in any manner it wishes, however. As in all else, Congress is bound by the Constitution. Consider a 1951 tax law aimed at professional gamblers. The law imposed a $50-a-year license tax on bookies, and required them to register with and submit detailed reports to the IRS. The law did produce a small amount of income, but its real purpose was to force gamblers into the open for the benefit of State and local police. It also set a federal tax evasion trap for those who failed to comply.

The Supreme Court overturned the antigambling provisions in *Marchetti* v. *United States*, 1968. The Court did not hold that the taxes had been set for improper purposes, but that the tax, registration, and reporting provisions forced gamblers to give evidence against themselves, violating the 5th Amendment's protection against self-incrimination.

Section 1 Assessment

Key Terms and Main Ideas

1. Describe how tax rates are set under a **progressive tax.**
2. What is the purpose of a **tax return?**
3. What items are subject to **customs duties?**
4. What is the difference between a **gift tax** and an **estate tax?**

Critical Thinking

5. **Identifying Central Issues** List two distinct reasons why the Federal Government imposes taxes.
6. **Demonstrating Reasoned Judgment** Why do you think the Federal Government directs employers to withhold tax money from each paycheck, instead of requiring taxpayers to pay a full year's taxes all at once?

Standards Monitoring *Online*

For: Self-quiz with vocabulary practice
Web Code: mqa-4161

7. **Expressing Problems Clearly** Why do some people claim that the federal income tax amounts to "forced labor" for the government? Explain the thinking behind this comparison, and why you agree or disagree.

Go Online PHSchool.com

For: An activity on taxation
Web Code: mqd-4161

Face the
Issues

Taxes

Background *A cost-benefit analysis is a useful tool for determining whether it makes sense to spend money in a certain way. When it comes to taxes, economists have long debated the cost of tax cuts compared to their potential benefit to the economy. Recent tax cuts, war, and a sluggish economy have led to record federal deficits—a cost that is passed on to tomorrow's taxpayers. Read the arguments. What do you think?*

Analysis Skill HI6

Cut Taxes to Improve America

Rich and poor, young and old, most Americans hate taxes. This country has a long-running tradition of opposition to taxes, dating back to the American Revolution: "No taxation without representation."

Truth be told, even with representation, most Americans are not very happy with taxation. No credible poll has ever found that a majority have said that their taxes were too low, says Karlyn H. Bowman of the American Enterprise Institute. Solid majorities regularly complain that they are too high.

"They don't feel they get good value for their tax dollars," Bowman argues. "They say around 50 cents of every dollar that Washington collects in taxes is wasted."

Tax cuts can stimulate the economy. When people keep more of the money they earn, they tend to spend more and invest more. The Reagan tax cuts of the 1980s ignited an economic boom. A robust economy generates more jobs, higher living standards, and more tax revenues. Over time, those increased revenues will close the deficit.

Don't Borrow Against the Future

Yes, the American people dislike taxes. But, just as certainly, they do like the public services those taxes (plus borrowing) can buy.

The Federal Government will spend at least $400 billion more than it will take in this year. It must borrow to cover that gap between spending and income. That is, it will have to add at least another $400 billion to the nation's already record-high public debt.

The Bush Administration has pushed and Congress has passed several measures to reduce taxes over the past several years. The resulting tax cuts have been heavily weighted in favor of larger corporations and the nation's wealthiest people.

Clearly, all of this means that the bill for hefty tax cuts and spending programs today is being passed on to the taxpayers of the future, the young people of today—and, probably to their children, and even to their children's children.

Enough is enough! Indeed, it is too much. The continuation of what amounts to fiscal lunacy at the federal level can only lead to economic disaster.

Exploring the Issues

1. Identify two arguments for tax cuts and two arguments for increasing taxes.
2. Why do you think many people dislike paying taxes?

To learn more about the debate over raising or lowering taxes, view "Taxes."

Nontax Revenues and Borrowing

Section Preview

OBJECTIVES

1. **List** the nontax sources of Federal Government revenues.
2. **Describe** federal borrowing.
3. **Analyze** the causes and effects of the public debt.

WHY IT MATTERS

When the government spends more money than it takes in, it must borrow money from investors. Over time, government borrowing has created a public debt of nearly $8 trillion.

POLITICAL DICTIONARY

★ **interest**
★ **deficit**
★ **surplus**
★ **public debt**

In *Hamlet,* Shakespeare wrote: "Neither a borrower nor a lender be." That may be good advice in some situations. However, it certainly has not been followed by the government of the United States.

Nontax Revenues

Large sums of money reach the federal treasury from a multitude of nontax sources. As the table on page 448 shows, these miscellaneous receipts now come to over $40 billion a year.

These monies come from dozens of places. A large portion comes from the earnings of the Federal Reserve System, mostly in interest charges. **Interest** is a charge for borrowed money, generally a percentage of the amount borrowed. The interest on loans made by several other federal agencies, canal tolls, and fees for such items as passports, copyrights, patents, and trademarks also generate large sums. So do the premiums on veterans' life

insurance policies, the sale or lease of public lands, the sale of surplus property, and such other items as the fines imposed by the federal courts.

The Treasury Department maintains a "conscience fund" for the several thousands of dollars a year that people send in to ease their minds over their past taxpaying mistakes. Another little-known source of nontax money is *seigniorage*—the profit the United States Mint makes in the production of coins. That profit is the difference between the value of the metals along with other costs of production and the monetary value of the minted coins. The Mint can produce a quarter for less than 25 cents and then "sell" the quarter at its face value. The difference adds up to more than $2 billion in most years.

The Philatelic Sales Branch of the United States Postal Service sells more than $100 million in mint-condition stamps to collectors each year. Stamp collectors spend untold millions more at local post offices. Most of the stamps they buy are never used on mail.

▶ The United States Postal Service earns millions of dollars each year by selling commemorative stamps.

Borrowing

Congress has the power "[t]o borrow Money on the credit of the United States" (Article I, Section 8, Clause 2). Historically, the power to borrow has been viewed as a way for the government (1) to meet the costs of short- and long-term crisis situations and (2) to finance large-scale projects that could not be paid for out of current income. Thus, the Federal Government borrowed huge sums to finance World War I, to combat the

Great Depression of the 1930s, and again during World War II.

Over recent decades, the Federal Government has borrowed for yet another reason: deficit financing. In most years, it purposely spent more money than it collected in tax revenue. That is, it ran up an annual **deficit**—the yearly shortfall between income and outgo; and it borrowed heavily to make up the difference.

Indeed, the government's financial books did not show a **surplus,** more income than outgo, in any year from 1969 until 1998.[4] The Treasury did realize a surplus in the four years 1998–2001, mostly because of a robust economy in the 1990s. But tax cuts and an economic downturn, aggravated by the terrorist strikes of September 11, 2001, brought a return to deficit spending beginning in 2002.

Congress must authorize all federal borrowing. The borrowing itself is done by the Treasury Department, which issues various kinds of securities to investors. These investors are principally individuals and banks, investment companies, and other financial institutions. Securities usually take the form of Treasury notes or bills (T-bills) issued for short-term borrowing, or bonds for long-term purposes. They are, in effect, IOUs, promissory notes in which the government agrees to repay a certain sum, with interest, on a certain date.

The government is able to borrow money at lower rates of interest than those paid by private borrowers. This is true largely because investors can find no safer securities than those issued by the United States. If the United States could not pay its debts, no one else would be able to, either. Federal securities are also attractive because the interest they earn cannot be taxed by the States or their local governments.

Voices on Government

Economist **Alan Greenspan,** one of the most powerful voices in America, has held several government positions. Since 1987 he has been chairman of the Federal Reserve Board, which controls the country's monetary policy. In a lecture, Greenspan gave his view of the American economy:

"The extraordinarily complex machine that we call the economy of the United States is, in the end, made up of human beings struggling to improve their lives. The individual values of those Americans . . . will continue to influence the structure of the institutions that support market transactions, as they have throughout our history. Without mutual trust and market participants abiding by a rule of law, no economy can prosper. Our system works fundamentally on individual fair dealing."

Evaluating the Quotation

How do Greenspan's thoughts about "mutual trust" and "fair dealing" apply to what you have learned about taxes in this chapter?

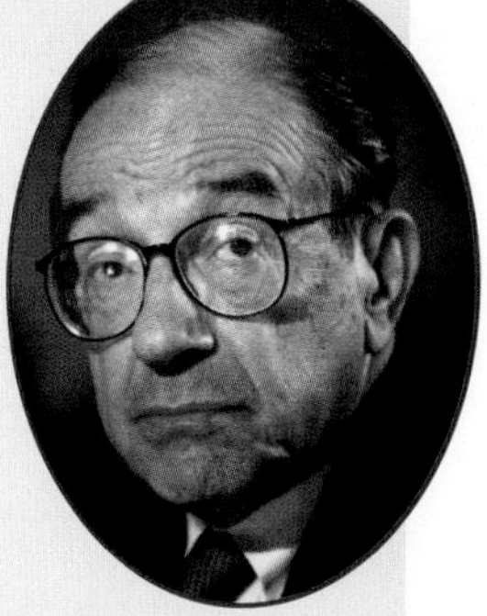

The Public Debt

Borrowing money produces a debt, of course. The public debt is the result of the Federal Government's borrowing over many years. More precisely, the **public debt** is the government's total outstanding indebtedness. It includes all of the money borrowed and not yet repaid, plus the accrued (accumulated) interest.[5]

The Federal Government has built up a huge debt over time. As you can see in the graphs on page 456, the nation's debt more than doubled in the years 1981 through 1985 because of deficit financing. Continued deficit spending had quadrupled the debt by 1992.

The amounts involved here are absolutely mind-boggling. In 1981, when the debt was approaching $1 trillion, President Ronald Reagan said that he found "such a figure—a trillion dollars—incomprehensible." He then drew this verbal picture: "[I]f you had a stack of $1,000 bills in your hand only four inches high, you would be a millionaire. A trillion dollars would be a stack 67 miles high." Mr. Reagan's stack would have to be more than 500 miles high to equal the national debt today!

[4]From 1930 to 2005, the Federal Government ended only 11 fiscal years "in the black"—that is, with a surplus: fiscal years 1947, 1948, 1951, 1956, 1957, 1960, 1969, 1998, 1999, 2000, and 2001.

[5]The Treasury Department's Bureau of the Public Debt acts as the Federal Government's borrowing agent. It issues Treasury bills, notes, and bonds and manages the U.S. Savings Bond Program.

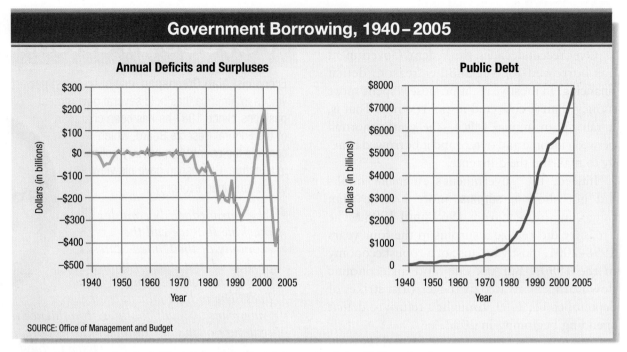

Government Borrowing, 1940–2005

Annual Deficits and Surpluses

Dollars (in billions)

$300 / $200 / $100 / $0 / –$100 / –$200 / –$300 / –$400 / –$500

Year: 1940 1950 1960 1970 1980 1990 2000 2005

Public Debt

Dollars (in billions)

$8000 / $7000 / $6000 / $5000 / $4000 / $3000 / $2000 / $1000 / 0

Year: 1940 1950 1960 1970 1980 1990 2000 2005

SOURCE: Office of Management and Budget

Interpreting Graphs Public debt swelled with deficit spending in the 1980s and early 1990s. **Why is the debt so much larger than the deficit?** H-SS 12.7.5

There is no constitutional limit on the amount that may be borrowed, and so there is no constitutional limit on the public debt. Congress has put a statutory ceiling on the debt, but simply adjusts the ceiling upward whenever fiscal realities seem to call for it.

The debt has always been controversial, and its rapid rise in recent years has fueled the fire. The annual interest on the debt is the amount that must be paid each year to those from whom the government has borrowed. That interest came to

some $200 billion in 2005 and will be even higher for 2006. Approximately one in every ten dollars the Federal Government now spends goes just to service—pay the interest on—the debt.

Most of those who are concerned about the size of the debt are worried about its impact on future generations of Americans. They say that years of short-sightedness and failure to operate government on a pay-as-you-go basis has produced huge debt and interest obligations that will have to be met by tomorrow's taxpayers.

Section 2 Assessment

Key Terms and Main Ideas

1. What is **interest** on a debt?
2. What must a government do to have a budget **surplus?**
3. Explain the difference between an annual budget **deficit** and the **public debt.**

Critical Thinking

4. **Drawing Conclusions** Compare the Federal Government's annual nontax revenues with its annual tax revenues discussed in Section 1. How important are nontax revenues in funding the government?
5. **Drawing Inferences** Based on the graph above, what decade saw the most rapid growth in the public debt? What led to the sharp increase in the debt in that period?

Standards Monitoring *Online*

For: Self-quiz with vocabulary practice
Web Code: mqa-4162

6. **Making Decisions** Borrowing money enables the government to spend more in the present without having to make up the difference until years later. Why do you think that for many years Congress and the President have chosen to borrow money rather than to balance the federal budget?

Go Online
PHSchool.com

For: An activity on the national debt
Web Code: mqd-4162

Budgets in Crisis

Analysis Skills HR4, HI3

The Concord Coalition brings together Democrats and Republicans who wish to balance the budget while protecting major programs such as Social Security, Medicare, and Medicaid. A recent Concord Coalition report issued warnings on the future of the Federal Government's budget deficit.

The Federal Government faces years of budget deficits.

The budget deficit continues to ratchet upward, and there is no consensus on what, if anything, to do about it. At best, Washington policymakers seem content to tread water in the rising tide of red ink. At worst, they are cynically professing concern about the deficit, while pursuing tax and spending policies they know will only dig the fiscal hole deeper. One thing is clear: specific plans to actually reduce the deficit are not on the agenda. . . .

Unfortunately, fiscal policy this year has featured wishful thinking and creative accounting rather than actions to control the deficit. In Congress, deficit reduction talk has produced actions that only make it more difficult to close the gap. . . .

The deficit cannot be dismissed as a self-correcting problem. Even assuming strong economic growth, plausible projections for the 10-year outlook show deficits of about $5 trillion. The longer-term outlook is worse. If policymakers want to get out of this hole, they are going to have to stop digging and start climbing. Deficits matter.

By most projections, the deficit will peak . . . and then decline [for two years]. . . . Yet the desire of many policymakers to extend expiring tax cuts, with or without offsets, and the need to fund military operations abroad and security needs at home will likely keep the deficit at unusually high levels. . . .

Policymakers . . . seem willing to let the economy do all the heavy lifting. It is a strategy with limited potential. While the economy can probably be counted on to produce a budgetary boost in the short-term, this alone will not be nearly enough to close the gap—particularly if policymakers use the proceeds of a growing economy to raise spending and cut taxes. Meanwhile, not a single piece of legislation has been enacted this year that makes any hard choices designed to cut the deficit. . . .

Circumstances have changed dramatically since 2001. The tax cuts can no longer be justified as "refunding a surplus" and whatever short-term stimulus the tax cuts provided has already helped the economy grow out of the recession. The country now faces endless deficit spending that, if left unchecked, will reduce national savings and private sector investment, potentially suppressing future economic growth.

Analyzing Primary Sources

1. Whom does the Concord Coalition criticize for ongoing budget deficits?
2. According to the report, what is the current plan in Congress for budget deficits? How does the Concord Coalition rate this response?
3. Do you agree with the Concord Coalition's priorities? Why or why not?

Section Preview

OBJECTIVES

1. **Identify** the key elements of federal spending.
2. **Explain** how the President and Congress work together to create the federal budget.

WHY IT MATTERS

Federal spending has a huge effect on the economy. In the budget-making process, the President and Congress determine how the wide-ranging activities of the Federal Government will be financed.

POLITICAL DICTIONARY

★ **entitlement**
★ **controllable spending**
★ **uncontrollable spending**
★ **continuing resolution**

The Federal Government will spend more than $2.7 trillion in fiscal year 2006. If you placed 2.7 trillion dollar bills end to end, they would stretch some 230 million miles, more than the distance from Earth to the sun and back again. In this section, you will see how the government spends all that money, and how it plans for that spending through the budget process.

Federal Spending

For more than half of our national history— from independence in 1776 to the mid-1930s —the Government's income and spending were so comparatively small that they had little real impact on the nation's economy. That situation changed dramatically with the coming of the Great Depression of the 1930s and then World War II in the early 1940s.

Today, the Federal Government takes tens of billions of dollars from some segments of the national economy. It then pumps those billions back into other segments of the economy—all, of course, with huge effects on the economy as a whole.

Spending Priorities

Look at the table on page 460. As you can see, the Department of Health and Human Services now spends more money than any other federal agency—well over $600 billion a year. Most of its spending goes for Medicare, Medicaid, and other entitlement programs.

Entitlements are benefits that federal law says *must* be paid to all those who meet the eligibility requirements, such as being above a certain age or below a certain income level. OASDI (the Old Age, Survivors, and Disability Insurance program)—often called "social security"—is the largest entitlement program today. Other major examples include Medicare, Medicaid, food stamps, unemployment insurance, and veterans' pensions and benefits. The Government guarantees assistance for all those who qualify. In effect, the law says that the people who receive those benefits are *entitled* (have a right) to them.

OASDI is administered by an independent agency, the Social Security Administration—

▲ The government-run Food Stamp program provides coupons that recipients can exchange for food.

▲ The three largest categories of federal spending are entitlements, interest on the public debt, and defense. *Critical Thinking* *Which of these three categories is an example of controllable spending?* H-SS 12.7.5

and OASDI's expenditures make SSA the second largest spender in the Federal Government.

Outlays for defense now account for a much larger share of the budget than they have over the past decade. The Defense Department spent more than $440 billion in 2005. It will likely spend over $500 billion in 2006—and DOD spending will continue to grow as the war on global terrorism wears on.

Note that the defense spending figures in the table are somewhat misleading. They do not include the defense-related expenditures of other federal agencies, notably the extensive nuclear weapons research and development work of the Department of Energy, and many of the functions of the Department of Homeland Security.

Interest on the public debt is now the fourth largest category of federal spending. Stoked by years of deficit financing, it has consumed a larger and still larger part of the federal budget over the last several years. In the table on page 460, interest on the debt is included in the Treasury Department's spending. For fiscal year 2006, the net interest on the debt came to more than $220 billion.

Controllable and Uncontrollable Spending

What the Federal Government spends can be described in terms of **controllable** and **uncontrollable spending.** Most specific items in the federal budget are controllable. That is, Congress and the President can decide each year just how much will be spent on many of the things that the government does—for example, for national parks, highway projects, aid to education, military hardware, civil service pay, and so on. Economists often use the term "discretionary spending" to describe spending on those budget items about which Congress and the President can make choices.

Much federal spending is uncontrollable, however. It is because "mandatory spending" was built into many public programs when Congress created them. The Office of Management and Budget estimates that nearly 80 percent of all federal spending today falls into the uncontrollable category.

Take interest on the public debt as a leading example of uncontrollable spending. Paying the interest due cannot be avoided. That interest amounts to a fixed charge; once

Federal Spending (in billions of dollars)

Category	1995	2000	2001	2004	2005	2006*
Legislative Branch	$2.1	$2.9	$3.0	$3.9	$4.0	$4.4
Judicial Branch	2.9	4.1	4.4	5.4	5.6	6.1
Executive Office of the President	0.2	0.3	0.2	3.3	7.7	7.4
Department of Agriculture	56.7	75.7	68.1	71.8	85.3	95.7
Department of Commerce	3.4	7.8	5.0	5.8	6.2	6.5
Department of Defense–Military	259.6	281.2	291.0	437.1	474.4	512.1
Department of Defense–Other	31.7	37.2	38.9	46.5	46.6	53.1
Department of Education	31.3	33.9	35.7	62.8	72.9	84.0
Department of Energy	11.8	15.0	16.4	20.0	21.3	21.7
Department of Health and Human Services	303.1	382.6	426.4	543.4	581.5	641.5
Department of Homeland Security	—	—	—	26.5	39.3	66.8
Department of Housing and Urban Development	29.0	30.8	33.9	45.0	42.5	46.8
Department of the Interior	7.4	8.0	8.0	8.9	9.1	9.1
Department of Justice	10.8	19.6	20.8	29.0	22.7	22.3
Department of Labor	32.1	31.4	39.3	56.7	47.0	51.4
Department of State	5.3	6.8	7.4	10.9	12.8	13.6
Department of Transportation	38.8	46.0	54.1	54.5	57.0	61.3
Department of the Treasury	348.5	391.2	389.9	374.8	408.7	452.1
Department of Veterans Affairs	37.8	47.1	45.0	59.6	70.0	70.4
International Assistance Programs	11.2	7.2	7.4	13.7	15.0	16.3
Environmental Protection Agency	6.3	13.4	14.1	8.3	7.9	7.9
National Aeronautics and Space Administration	13.4	12.1	11.8	15.2	15.6	15.6
Social Security Administration	362.2	441.8	461.8	530.2	561.3	592.5
All Other Independent Agencies	–0.1	69.8	72.2	77.1	82.3	87.7
Deductions (undistributed offsetting receipts)	–137.6	–172.8	–191.1	–212.5	–226.2	–237.9
Total Outlays	**$1,515.4**	**$1,788.8**	**$1,863.9**	**$2,292.2**	**$2,472.2**	**$2,708.7**
Surplus (+) or Deficit (–)	–163.9	+236.4	+127.1	–412.1	–318.3	–423.2

SOURCES: Office of Management and Budget and Financial Management Service, Department of the Treasury.   *Projected

Interpreting Tables *(a) Which of the executive departments now spends the largest amount of money each year? (b) Which executive department spends the least?* H-SS 12.7.5

the Federal Government borrows the money, the interest on that loan must be paid when it comes due—and at the rate the government promised to pay.

Social Security benefits, food stamps, and most other entitlements are also largely uncontrollable—because once Congress has set the standards of eligibility for those programs, it has no control over how many people will meet those standards. Thus, Congress does not—really cannot—determine how many people covered by Social Security will become eligible for retirement benefits each year.

Those expenditures are not completely uncontrollable, however. Congress could redefine eligibility standards, or it could reduce the amount of money each beneficiary is to receive. But clearly those actions would be politically difficult.

In general, the percentage of federal spending that is uncontrollable has grown in recent years, while the percentage of controllable spending has decreased. These trends cause concern to those officials who are responsible for maintaining control of the budget.

The Federal Budget

The Constitution gives to Congress the fabled "power of the purse"—the very significant power to control the financing of the Federal Government and all of its operations:

 ❝ *No Money shall be drawn from the Treasury, but in Consequence of Appropriations made by Law. . . .* **❞**

—Article I, Section 9, Clause 7

Congress—and only Congress—has the power to provide the huge sums that the government consumes each year. In short, it is Congress that decides *how much* the government can spend and, just as importantly, for exactly *what* it can spend that money.

Still, despite the fact that Congress holds the power of the purse, it is the President who initiates the process by which the Federal Government spends its money. He does so by submitting (proposing) a budget to Congress soon after that body begins each of its yearly sessions.[6]

Remember, the federal budget is a hugely important document. It is, of course, a financial statement—a lengthy and detailed estimate of federal income and proposed outgo for the upcoming fiscal year. But it is also much more than that, and much more than a dry listing of so many dollars from here and so many dollars for that. The budget is a major political statement, a declaration of the public policies of the United States. Put another way, the federal budget is the President's work plan for the conduct of the government and the execution of its public policies.

The annual budget-making process is a joint effort of the President and both houses of Congress. The President prepares the budget and submits it to Congress. Congress then reacts to the President's budget proposals, over a period of several months. It usually enacts most of those proposals, many of them in some altered form, in a number of appropriations measures.

The President and the Budget

The process of building the budget is a lengthy one. In fact, it begins some eighteen months before the start of the fiscal year for which the budget is intended. First, each federal agency prepares detailed estimates of its spending needs for that twelve-month period. Each agency then submits its spending plans to the President's budget-making agency, the Office of Management and Budget.

The OMB reviews all of the many agency proposals, often in budget hearings at which agency officials must defend their dollar requests. Following the OMB's review, revised and usually lowered spending plans for all of the agencies in the executive branch are fitted into the President's overall program. They become a part of the budget document—a part of the political statement—that the President sends to Capitol Hill.[7]

Congress and the Budget

Remember that Congress depends upon and works through its standing committees. The President's budget is referred to the Budget Committee in each chamber. There, in both committees, the budget is studied and dissected with the help of the Congressional Budget Office.

The CBO is a staff agency created by Congress in 1974. It provides both houses of Congress and their committees with basic budget and economic data and analyses. The information that the CBO supplies is independent of the information provided by the OMB, which, recall, is the President's budget agency.

The President's budget is also sent to the House and Senate Appropriations Committees.[8] Their subcommittees hold extensive hearings in which they examine agency requests, quiz agency officials, and take testimony from a

---

[6]The word *budget* comes from the French *bougette,* meaning a small pouch or bag with its contents. In the eighteenth century, the budget was the bag in which the British Chancellor of the Exchequer carried financial documents.

[7]Congress enacts a separate budget for its own expenses. The spending requests for the judicial branch, prepared by the Administrative Office of the United States Courts, are included in the President's budget without OMB review.

[8]Those tax proposals included in the budget are referred to the House Ways and Means Committee and to the Senate's Finance Committee.

FUTURE SOCIAL SECURITY BENEFITS FOR RETIRING BABY BOOMERS:

THEY'VE GIVEN US JUST ENOUGH TO PAY FOR OUR MOVE BACK IN WITH THE KIDS

BEATTIE Copley News Service
©'98 Daytona Beach News-Journal/N-Jcenter.com

Interpreting Political Cartoons The Social Security Administration accounts for the largest segment of the federal budget. *What is the cartoonist's view of the future of Social Security?*

wide range of interested parties. Lobbyists for most of the interest groups discussed earlier (in Chapter 9) are actively involved in those hearings. They testify, bring grass roots pressures to bear, and otherwise work to promote the interests of the organizations they represent. (And campaign contributions often find their way to members of those subcommittees—in particular, to their chairmen and ranking members.)

The two Appropriations Committees fashion measures that later are reported to the floor of each house. Those measures are the bills that actually appropriate the funds on which the government will operate.

The two Budget Committees propose a concurrent resolution on the budget to their respective chambers. That measure, which must be passed by both houses by May 15, sets overall targets for federal receipts and spending in the upcoming fiscal year. The estimates are intended to guide the committees in both houses as they continue to work on the budget.

The two Budget Committees propose a second budget resolution in early September. Congress must pass that resolution by September 15, just two weeks before the beginning of the next fiscal year. The second budget resolution sets binding expenditure limits for all federal agencies in that upcoming year. No appropriations measure can provide for any spending that exceeds those limits.

Congress passes thirteen major appropriations bills each year. Recall, each of these measures must go to the White House for the President's action. Every year, Congress hopes to pass all thirteen of the appropriations measures by October 1 —that is, by the beginning of the fiscal year.

It seldom does so, however. Congress must then pass emergency spending legislation to avoid a shutdown of those agencies for which appropriations have not yet been signed into law. That legislation takes the form of a **continuing resolution.** When signed by the President, this measure allows the affected agencies to continue to function on the basis of the previous year's appropriations. Should Congress and the President fail to act, many agencies of the Federal Government would have to suspend their operations.

Section 3 Assessment

Key Terms and Main Ideas

1. How are **entitlements** different from other types of benefits?
2. List two examples of **controllable spending** in the federal budget.
3. What is the purpose of a **continuing resolution?**

Critical Thinking

4. **Drawing Inferences** Why is the term "uncontrollable spending" not completely accurate for some entitlements?
5. **Predicting Consequences** What might happen if the OMB accepted all requests for funding without holding hearings? How would this affect the budget?

Standards Monitoring *Online*
For: Self-quiz with vocabulary practice
Web Code: mqa-4163

6. **Making Comparisons** What is the President's role in the budget-making process? What is the role of Congress in the budget-making process?

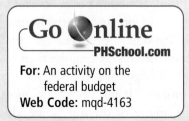

Go Online
PHSchool.com

For: An activity on the federal budget
Web Code: mqd-4163

Can Federal Funds Be Used to Help Religious School Students?

Analysis Skills HR4, HI3, HI4

The 1st Amendment prohibits government from establishing religion or interfering with the free exercise of religion. Because many students attend parochial (religious) schools, States have tried to help with the secular (non-religious) parts of their education without violating the 1st Amendment. To what extent may government funds be used to support secular programs in religious schools?

Agostini v. *Felton* (1997)

In the 1985 case *Aguilar* v. *Felton*, the Supreme Court ruled that New York City public school teachers could not provide extra instruction to disadvantaged students at religious schools during regular school hours. Such instruction, the Court declared, violated the Establishment Clause of the 1st Amendment. Following that decision, the city's board of education used other methods to help religious school students, mostly by busing the students to public school buildings or other (rented) facilities after regular school hours.

In the years after *Aguilar*, the Supreme Court decided other cases involving government support of special education in religious schools. In a case from Arizona, *Zobrest* v. *Catalina Foothills School District* (1993), for example, the Court allowed a sign-language interpreter, paid for with public funds, to help a deaf student with his class work at a parochial high school.

Twelve years after *Aguilar* v. *Felton*, New York City officials returned to court to ask that the decision in that case be reconsidered and reversed in light of the more-recent Supreme Court cases. The district court and court of appeals declined to do so, and the case then went to the Supreme Court.

Arguments for Agostini

1. Government funding of secular instruction in religious schools violates the Establishment Clause by promoting religion. Because the instruction takes place in religious schools, the public school teachers might tailor their teaching to conform to the school's religious beliefs, whether intentionally or not.
2. Government funding of secular instruction in religious schools entangles church and state because the government has to monitor the ways in which the funds are used.

Arguments for Felton

1. The board of education's program does not promote religion because the skills on which students will be helped are not related to students' religious beliefs or where they go to school. Therefore, recipients of aid have no incentive to change their religious beliefs or practices in order to obtain assistance.
2. The program requires only very limited government supervision of the ways in which funds are used, and thus does not result in excessive entanglement with religion.

Decide for Yourself

1. Review the constitutional grounds on which each side based its arguments and the specific arguments each side presented.
2. Debate the opposing viewpoints presented in this case. Which viewpoint do you favor?
3. Predict the impact of the Court's decision on government-funded programs in religious schools. (To read a summary of the Court's decision, turn to pages 799–806.)

Go Online
PHSchool.com

Use Web Code mqp-4166 to register your vote on this issue and to see how other students voted.

Political Dictionary

progressive tax (p. 449), tax return (p. 449), payroll tax (p. 450), regressive tax (p. 451), excise tax (p. 451), estate tax (p. 451), gift tax (p. 451), customs duty (p. 451), interest (p. 454), deficit (p. 455), surplus (p. 455), public debt (p. 455), entitlement (p. 458), controllable spending (p. 459), uncontrollable spending (p. 459), continuing resolution (p. 462)

Standards Review

H-SS 12.2.3 Discuss the individual's legal obligations to obey the law, serve as a juror, and pay taxes.

H-SS 12.4.1 Discuss Article I of the Constitution as it relates to the legislative branch, including eligibility for office and lengths of terms of representatives and senators; election to office; the roles of the House and Senate in impeachment proceedings; the role of the vice president; the enumerated legislative powers; and the process by which a bill becomes a law.

H-SS 12.7.1 Explain how conflicts between levels of government and branches of government are resolved.

H-SS 12.7.5 Explain how public policy is formed, including the setting of the public agenda and implementation of it through regulations and executive orders.

Practicing the Vocabulary

Matching *Choose a term from the list above that best matches each description.*

1. Tax imposed on the assets of one who dies
2. Tax that falls most heavily on those who are least able to pay
3. The total amount of money owed by the United States, plus all interest
4. Payments that federal law says must be paid to all those who meet the eligibility requirements
5. Sometimes called tariffs, import duties, or imposts

Fill in the Blank *Choose a term from the list above that best completes the sentence.*

6. The Federal Government creates a budget _____ when it spends more money in one year than it takes in.
7. Congress passes a _____ to fund government agencies during long budget negotiations.
8. Employers withhold a(n) _____ from each paycheck.
9. Congress can decide how much money to spend each year on programs that are considered _____ (s).
10. The government lays a(n) _____ on the manufacture, sale, or consumption of goods.

Reviewing Main Ideas

Section 1

11. What are the four expressed limitations on the Federal Government's power to tax?
12. What is the one implied limitation on the power to tax?
13. Identify the several different taxes by which the Federal Government raises revenue.
14. Are excise taxes regressive or progressive taxes? Explain your answer.
15. **(a)** Which federal tax raises the largest amount of money each year? **(b)** How did the Federal Government gain the power to levy that tax?

Section 2

16. Identify five of the Federal Government's nontax sources of revenue.
17. **(a)** Describe the different methods the Federal Government can use to borrow money. **(b)** Why does the Federal Government find it fairly easy to borrow money?
18. **(a)** Over the past seventy years, has the Federal Government most often ended a fiscal year with a surplus or a deficit? **(b)** Describe trends in the federal budget deficit since 2000.

19. According to the critics of deficit financing, who will pay the costs of that practice?

Section 3

20. What two major events marked a dramatic change in the amount of federal spending and its impact on the nation's economy?
21. What is the largest item on which the Federal Government spends the money it raises?
22. **(a)** Approximately what percentage of federal spending now goes to pay the interest on the public debt? **(b)** If the government continues to run a deficit each year, what effect will that have on that percentage figure?
23. **(a)** What is the difference between uncontrollable and controllable spending? **(b)** About what percentage of the annual budget is controllable?
24. What are the roles of the Budget Committees and the Appropriations Committees in the budget process?

Critical Thinking Skills

Analysis Skills CS1, HR4, HI6

25. *Face the Issues* Think about different reasons for changing the tax rate and how those changes affect the government and individuals. Identify three factors that a State or the Federal Government should consider when debating a tax cut. Which factor do you believe is most important, and why?

26. *Drawing Inferences* Consider the discussion of the purposes for which Congress can levy taxes. Do you think that the Framers of the Constitution intended Congress to use its power to tax as a way of regulating or destroying certain activities? Explain your answer.

27. *Making Decisions* **(a)** Do you think the Constitution should be amended to require a balanced federal budget each year? **(b)** What might be the consequences of such an amendment?

28. *Drawing Conclusions* The text says that "the federal budget is a hugely important political document." Cite evidence from the chapter to support and/or explain this statement.

Analyzing Political Cartoons

Using your knowledge of American government and this cartoon, answer the questions below.

29. (a) What is the subject of this cartoon? **(b)** Why is the size of the deficit a source of controversy and concern?

30. Does the cartoon accurately portray the ease with which the deficit can be "taken care of"? Why or why not?

Participation Activities

Analysis Skills HR4, HI6

31. *Current Events Watch* Examine one week's issues of a local newspaper and a national paper. Find articles that mention taxes and their impact on the economy. How many of these stories refer to federal taxes? Which federal taxes are discussed? How many articles refer to State or to local taxes? Which State or local taxes are discussed?

32. *Graphing Activity* Choose one country from each of the following continents: Africa, Asia, Europe, and South America. Research the population, national budget, and national debt for each country and for the United States. Calculate national spending per person by dividing the national budget of each country by its population. Next, calculate the national debt per person by dividing the national debt by its population. Create a bar graph showing the population, national spending per person, and national debt per person for all five countries. Which country spends the most per person? Which country owes the most money per person? How does the United States compare to the other countries you chose?

33. *It's Your Turn* You are an editorial writer for a major newspaper. Your boss, the editor of the editorial page, has asked you to write a comment on Justice Oliver Wendell Holmes' famous remark: "Taxes are what we pay for civilized society." Look again at page 449 as you think about what you will write. Will your editorial agree with or take exception to Justice Holmes' view? **(Writing an Editorial)**

Standards Monitoring *Online*

For: Chapter 16 Self-Test **Visit:** PHSchool.com
Web Code: mqa-4164

As a final review, take the Magruder's Chapter 16 Self-Test and receive immediate feedback on your answers.
The test consists of 20 multiple-choice questions designed to test your understanding of the chapter content.

CHAPTER 17

Foreign Policy and National Defense

"A successful foreign policy in a nation where informed citizens have a free vote must be based on a public consensus."

—Representative Millicent Fenwick (1975)

American foreign policy is actually many different policies on many different matters. It is made up of all of this nation's positions and actions in every aspect of its dealings with the rest of the world—diplomatic, military, commercial, and all others.

◆ Americans show patriotism and a united front to the world

H-SS 12.1.5 Describe the systems of separated and shared powers, the role of organized interests (*Federalist Paper Number 10*), checks and balances (*Federalist Paper Number 51*), the importance of an independent judiciary (*Federalist Paper Number 78*), enumerated powers, rule of law, federalism, and civilian control of the military.

H-SS 12.2.4 Understand the obligations of civic-mindedness, including voting, being informed on civic issues, volunteering and performing public service, and serving in the military or alternative service.

H-SS 12.4.1 Discuss Article I of the Constitution as it relates to the legislative branch, including eligibility for office and lengths of terms of representatives and senators; election to office; the roles of the House and Senate in impeachment proceedings; the role of the vice president; the enumerated legislative powers; and the process by which a bill becomes a law.

H-SS 12.7.8 Understand the scope of presidential power and decision making through examination of case studies such as the Cuban Missile Crisis, passage of Great Society legislation, War Powers Act, Gulf War, and Bosnia.

H-SS 12.9.8 Identify the successes of relatively new democracies in Africa, Asia, and Latin America and the ideas, leaders, and general societal conditions that have launched and sustained, or failed to sustain, them.

Go Online
PHSchool.com

For: Current Data
Web Code: mqg-4176

For: Close Up Foundation debates
Web Code: mqh-4179

SECTION 1

Foreign Affairs and National Security
(pp. 468–475)

★ Foreign policy is all the actions and stands that a nation takes in its relations with other nations.

★ With World War II, the United States abandoned isolationism and became a full participant in world affairs.

★ The State Department, headed by the secretary of state, advises the President on foreign policy matters and carries out his policies through its diplomats abroad.

★ The secretary of defense is the President's chief aide and advisor on military matters and the head of the Defense Department.

SECTION 2

Other Foreign and Defense Agencies
(pp. 477–480)

★ The CIA conducts worldwide intelligence operations.

★ The Department of Homeland Security is charged with protecting the nation against terrorist activities.

★ NASA runs the nation's space program. The Selective Service System is on standby.

SECTION 3

American Foreign Policy Overview (pp. 481–489)

★ The Monroe Doctrine and Manifest Destiny shaped American foreign policy through World War I. During that time, the nation expanded and became a colonial power.

★ The two world wars ended America's traditional policy of isolationism and led to a policy of internationalism.

★ Victory in World War II made the United States one of two world superpowers, and led to the policies of collective security and deterrence.

★ U.S. policy during the cold war focused on resisting Soviet aggression through containment.

★ Although the cold war has ended, the world is still a dangerous place requiring continued vigilance.

SECTION 4

Foreign Aid and Defense Alliances (pp. 491–498)

★ Both economic and military foreign aid are usually sent to countries regarded as most critical to this country's interests.

★ The United States belongs to a number of regional security alliances of which NATO is the most important.

★ Although the United States has no alliances in the Middle East, American administrations have worked hard to promote peace in this important region.

★ The purpose of the United Nations is to promote peace among nations, and to improve living conditions around the world.

Foreign Affairs and National Security

Section Preview

OBJECTIVES

1. **Define** foreign policy, and understand the difference between isolationism and internationalism.
2. **Explain** the functions, components, and organization of the Department of State.
3. **Summarize** the functions, components, and organization of the Department of Defense and the military departments.

WHY IT MATTERS

Foreign policy includes all the stands and actions a nation takes in its relationships with other nations. The State Department carries out the President's diplomatic policies. The armed forces provide the nation's defense, but are under civilian control of the President.

POLITICAL DICTIONARY

★ domestic affairs
★ foreign affairs
★ isolationism
★ foreign policy
★ right of legation
★ ambassador
★ diplomatic immunity

In *The Federalist* No. 72, Alexander Hamilton noted that the "actual conduct" of America's foreign affairs would be in the hands of "the assistants or deputies of the chief magistrate," the President. Today, most of the President's "assistants or deputies" in the field of foreign affairs are in the State Department. Those presidential aides in the closely related field of military affairs are located in the Department of Defense.

Foreign affairs have been of prime importance from the nation's very beginnings, more than a dozen years before Hamilton penned his comment in *The Federalist*. Indeed, it is important to remember that the United States would have been hard pressed to win its independence without the aid of its ally, France.

Isolationism to Internationalism

With the coming of independence, and then for more than 150 years, the American people were chiefly concerned with **domestic affairs**—with events at home. **Foreign affairs**, the nation's relationships with other nations, were of little or no concern to them. Through that period, America's foreign relations were very largely shaped by a policy of **isolationism**—a purposeful refusal to become generally involved in the affairs of the rest of the world.

The past 60 years have been marked by a profound change in the place of the United States in world affairs, however. World War II finally convinced the American people that neither they nor anyone else can live in isolation— that, in many ways, and whether we like it or not, the world of today is indeed "one world." The well-being of everyone in this country—in fact, the very survival of the United States—is affected by much that happens elsewhere on the globe. If nothing else, the realities of ultra-rapid travel and instantaneous communications make it clear that we now live in a "global village."

Wars and other political upheavals abroad have an impact on the United States and on the daily lives of the American people. Four times over the past century the United States fought

▲ Benjamin Franklin (center), the first American diplomat, is received at the French court in 1778. Louis XVI and Marie Antoinette are seated at right.

major wars abroad; and in several other instances the nation committed its armed forces to lesser, but significant, foreign conflicts. The nation's security has also been threatened by terrorists in Europe and Asia, as well as at home, by racial strife in southern Africa, by Arab-Israeli conflicts in the Middle East, and by other events in many other places around the globe.

Economic conditions elsewhere also have a direct effect on and in this country. Japanese automobiles, European steel, oil from the Middle East, coffee from Brazil, Italian shoes, and expanding trade with China underscore the fact that every day Americans buy from other countries. American companies also sell their products in foreign markets, and often manufacture them abroad, as well. The American economy has become part of a truly global economy, linked by international banking, multinational corporations, and worldwide investments that transcend national boundaries.

Clearly, today's world cannot be described as "one world" in all respects, however. It remains, in many ways, a very fractured and dangerous place. Acts of international terrorism; civil wars in Sri Lanka, Colombia, Morocco, and the Congo; unrest in what was once the Soviet Union; drug cartels in Latin America and in Southeast Asia; the behavior of North Korea and other "rogue states"; the emerging dangers of chemical and of biological weapons—all of this, and more, make the point abundantly clear. In the interconnected yet divided world of today, only those polices that protect and promote the security of *all* nations can assure the security and the well-being of the United States.

Foreign Policy Defined

Every nation's **foreign policy** is actually many different policies on many different topics. It is made up of all of the stands and actions that a nation takes in every aspect of its relationships with other countries—diplomatic, military, commercial, and all others. To put the point another way, a nation's foreign policy is made up of all of its many foreign policies. In short, it includes everything that that nation's government says and everything that it does in world affairs.

Thus, American foreign policy consists of all of the Federal Government's official statements

▲ *Osama bin Laden* Anti-American sentiment is common in Muslim and Arab nations today. Here, Pakistani Islamists carry a poster of bin Laden during a rally in the province of Baluchistan.

and all of its actions as it conducts this nation's foreign relations. It involves treaties and alliances, international trade, the defense budget, foreign economic and military aid, the United Nations, nuclear weapons testing, and disarmament negotiations. It also includes the American position on oil imports, grain exports, immigration, space exploration, fishing rights in the Atlantic and Pacific oceans, cultural exchange programs, economic sanctions, computer technology exports, and a great many other matters.

Some aspects of foreign policy remain largely unchanged over time. For example, an insistence on freedom of the seas has been a basic part of American policy from the nation's beginnings. Other policies are more flexible. Little more than a decade ago, resisting the ambitions of the Soviet Union was a basic part of American foreign policy. Today, the United States and much of the former Soviet Union are seeking ever closer political, military, and economic ties.

The President is both the nation's chief diplomat and the commander in chief of its armed forces. Constitutionally and by tradition, the President bears the major responsibility for both the making and the conduct of foreign policy. The President depends on a number of officials and agencies—Hamilton's "assistants or deputies"—to meet the immense responsibilities that come with this dual role.

The State Department

The State Department, headed by the secretary of state, is the President's right arm in foreign affairs. The President names the secretary of state, subject to confirmation by the Senate. It is to the secretary of state and to the Department of State that the President looks for advice on both the formulation and the conduct of the nation's foreign policy.

The Secretary of State

The secretary of state ranks first among the members of the President's Cabinet. This ranking speaks to the importance of the office, and also to the fact that the State Department was the first of the now 15 executive departments to be created by Congress.

The Department of Foreign Affairs had first been created in 1781 under the Articles of Confederation. It was re-created by Congress in 1789 as the first major unit in the executive branch under the Constitution. Later that year, its name was changed to the Department of State.

President Washington appointed Thomas Jefferson as the nation's first secretary of state. The first woman to hold the post, Madeleine Albright, was appointed by President Clinton in 1997. Colin Powell, secretary of state under President George W. Bush, became the first African American to hold the office. Today, the duties of the secretary relate almost solely to foreign affairs: to the making and conduct of policy and to managing the work of the department, its many overseas posts, and some 25,000 employees.[1]

Some Presidents have relied heavily on the secretary of state; others have chosen to keep foreign policy more tightly in their own hands. In either case, the secretary has been an important and influential officer in every administration.

Organization and Components

The Department of State is organized along both geographic and functional lines. Some of its agencies, such as the Bureau of African Affairs and the Bureau of Near East Affairs, deal with matters involving particular regions of the world.

Other agencies have broader responsibilities—for example, the Bureau of International Narcotics and Law Enforcement, sometimes called "Drugs 'n' Thugs." Most bureaus are headed by an assistant secretary and include several "offices." Thus, both the Office of Passport Services and the Office of Visa Services are found in the Bureau of Consular Affairs.

The Foreign Service

Some 6,000 men and women now represent the United States abroad as members of the Foreign Service. Under international law every nation has the **right of legation**—the right to send and receive diplomatic representatives.[2] The right of

---

[1] The secretary does have some domestic responsibilities. Thus, when Richard Nixon resigned the presidency on August 9, 1974, his formal, legal announcement of that fact had to be submitted to Secretary of State Henry Kissinger. Over the years, the secretary and the department have had (and been relieved of) various domestic functions—including publishing the nation's laws, issuing patents, and supervising the decennial census.

[2] International law consists of those rules and principles that guide sovereign states in their dealings with one another and in their treatment of foreign nationals (private persons and groups). Its sources include treaties, decisions of international courts, and custom. Treaties are the most important source today.

legation is an ancient practice. Its history can be traced back to the Egyptian civilization of 6,000 years ago.

The Second Continental Congress named this nation's first foreign service officer in 1778. That year, it chose Benjamin Franklin to be America's minister to France.

Ambassadors

An **ambassador** is an official representative of the United States appointed by the President to represent the nation in matters of diplomacy. Today, the United States is represented by an ambassador stationed at the capital of each state the United States recognizes.[3] American embassies are found in more than 180 countries around the world today.

The United States also has some 120 consular offices abroad. There, Foreign Service officers promote American interests in a multitude of ways—for example, encouraging trade, gathering intelligence data, advising persons who seek to enter this country, and aiding American citizens who are abroad and in need of legal advice or other help.

Some ambassadorships are much desired political plums. Too often, Presidents have appointed people to ambassadorships and other major diplomatic posts as a reward for their support—financial and otherwise—of the President's election to office.

President Truman named the first woman as an ambassador, to Denmark, in 1949. President Johnson appointed the first African American (also a woman), as ambassador to Luxembourg in 1965. Today, a large number of women, African Americans, and other minority persons hold high rank in the Foreign Service.

Special Diplomats

Those persons whom the President names to certain other top diplomatic posts also carry the rank of ambassador—for example, the United States representative to the UN and the American member of the North Atlantic Treaty Council.

▲ *From Here to There* Americans usually need passports to travel abroad. Nepal, shown here, is one nation that requires foreign visitors to have visas.

The President also gives the personal rank of ambassador to those diplomats who take on special assignments abroad—for example, representing the United States at an international conference on arms limitations.

Passports

A passport is a certificate issued by a government to its citizens who travel or live abroad. Passports entitle their holders to the privileges accorded to them by international custom and treaties. Few countries will admit persons who do not hold valid passports. Legally, no American citizen may leave the United States without a passport, except for trips to Canada, Mexico, and a few other nearby places.

The State Department's Office of Passport Services issues some eight million passports to Americans each year. Do not confuse passports with visas. A visa is a permit to enter another state and must be obtained from the country one wishes to enter. Trips to most foreign countries require visas. Most visas to enter this country are issued at American consulates abroad.

Diplomatic Immunity

In international law, every sovereign state is supreme within its own boundaries. All persons or things found within that state's territory are subject to its jurisdiction.

As a major exception to that rule, ambassadors are regularly granted **diplomatic immunity.**

---

[3]See page 400. An ambassador's official title is Ambassador Extraordinary and Plenipotentiary. When the office is vacant or the ambassador is absent, the post is usually filled by a next-ranking Foreign Service officer in the embassy. That officer, temporarily in charge of embassy affairs, is known as the chargé d'affaires.

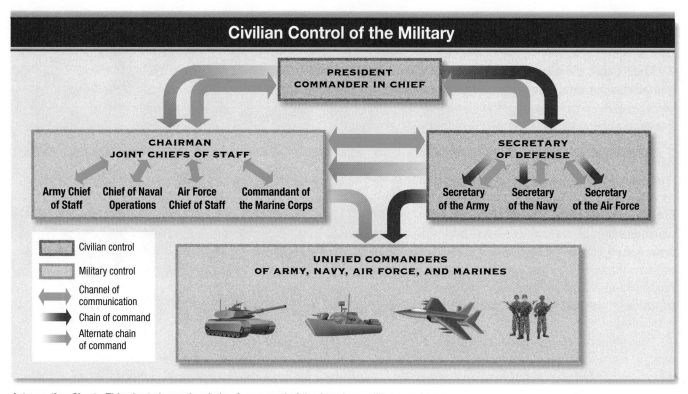

Civilian Control of the Military

PRESIDENT COMMANDER IN CHIEF

CHAIRMAN JOINT CHIEFS OF STAFF

- Army Chief of Staff
- Chief of Naval Operations
- Air Force Chief of Staff
- Commandant of the Marine Corps

SECRETARY OF DEFENSE

- Secretary of the Army
- Secretary of the Navy
- Secretary of the Air Force

UNIFIED COMMANDERS OF ARMY, NAVY, AIR FORCE, AND MARINES

- Civilian control
- Military control
- Channel of communication
- Chain of command
- Alternate chain of command

Interpreting Charts This chart shows the chain of command of the American military services.
Who advises the president on military matters? H-SS 12.1.5

That is, they are not subject to the laws of the state to which they are accredited. They cannot be arrested, sued, or taxed. Their official residences (embassies) cannot be entered or searched without their consent, and their official communications, papers, and other properties are protected. All other embassy personnel and their families normally receive this same immunity.

Diplomatic immunity is essential to the ability of every nation to conduct its foreign relations. The practice assumes that diplomats will not abuse their privileged status. If a host government finds a diplomat's conduct unacceptable, that official may be declared *persona non grata* and expelled from the country. The mistreatment of diplomats is considered a major breach of international law.

Diplomatic immunity is a generally accepted practice. There are exceptions, however. The most serious breach in modern times occurred in Iran in late 1979. Militant followers of the Ayatollah Khomeini seized the American embassy in Teheran on November 4 of that year; 53 Americans were taken hostage and held for 444 days. The Iranians finally released the hostages moments after Ronald Reagan became President on January 20, 1981.

The Defense Department

Congress established what is today called the Department of Defense in the National Security Act of 1947. It is the present-day successor to two historic Cabinet-level agencies: the War Department, created by Congress in 1789, and the Navy Department, created in 1798.

Congress created the Defense Department in order to unify the nation's armed forces. It wished to bring the then-separate army (including the air force) and the navy under the control of a single Cabinet department. Today, there are more than 1.4 million men and women in uniform, and nearly 700,000 civilians also work for the Defense Department.

Civil Control of the Military

The authors of the Constitution understood the importance of the nation's defense. They emphasized that fact clearly in the Preamble, and they underscored it in the body of the Constitution by mentioning defense more frequently than any other governmental function.

The Framers also recognized the dangers inherent in military power. They knew that its very existence can pose a threat to free government. And so the Constitution is studded with provisions to make sure that the military is always subject to the control of the nation's civilian authorities.

Thus, the Constitution makes the elected President the commander in chief of the armed forces. To the same end, it gives wide military powers to Congress—that is, to the elected representatives of the people.[4]

The principle of civilian control has always been a major factor in the making of defense policy, and in the creation and the staffing of the various agencies responsible for the execution of that policy. The importance of civilian control is clearly illustrated by this fact: The National Security Act of 1947 provides that the secretary of defense cannot have served on active duty in any of the armed forces for at least 10 years before being named to that post.

The Secretary of Defense

The Department of Defense is headed by the secretary of defense, whose appointment by the President is subject to Senate confirmation. The secretary, who serves at the President's pleasure, has two major responsibilities. He is (1) the President's chief aide and advisor in making and carrying out defense policy, and (2) the operating head of the Defense Department.

The secretary's huge domain is often called the Pentagon—because of its massive five-sided headquarters building in Virginia, across the Potomac River from the Capitol. Year in and year out, its

operations take a large slice of the federal budget—today, in fact, nearly a fourth of all federal spending. The war on global terrorism has forced increased military outlays; total spending for the nation's defense will run very close to $500 billion in fiscal year 2005.

Chief Military Aides

The five members of the Joint Chiefs of Staff serve as the principal military advisors to the secretary of defense, and to the President and the National Security Council. They are the chairman of the Joint Chiefs, the army chief of staff, the chief of naval operations, the commandant of the Marine Corps, and the air force chief of staff. The highest ranking uniformed officers in the armed services, the members of the Joint Chiefs are named by the President, subject to Senate approval.

The Military Departments

The three military departments—the Departments of the Army, the Navy, and the Air Force—are major units and sub-Cabinet departments within the Department of Defense.[5] Each is headed by a civilian secretary, named by the

---

[4]Recall that the Constitution makes defense a national function and practically excludes the States from that field. Each State does have a militia, which it may use to keep the peace within its own borders. Today, the organized portion of the militia is the National Guard. Congress has the power (Article I, Section 8, Clauses 15 and 16) to "provide for calling forth the Militia" and to provide for organizing, arming, and disciplining it. Congress first delegated to the President the power to call the militia into federal service in 1795, and the commander in chief has had that authority ever since. Today, the governor of each State is the commander in chief of that State's units of the Army and the Air National Guard, except when the President orders those units into federal service.

[5]The United States Marine Corps is a separate branch of the armed forces, but, for organizational purposes, it is located within the Navy Department. The Coast Guard is also a branch of the armed forces. It is organized as a military service, with a present strength of some 35,000 commissioned officers and enlisted personnel. Since 2003, the Coast Guard has been part of the Department of Homeland Security. In time of war or at any other time the President directs, the Coast Guard becomes a part of the United States Navy.

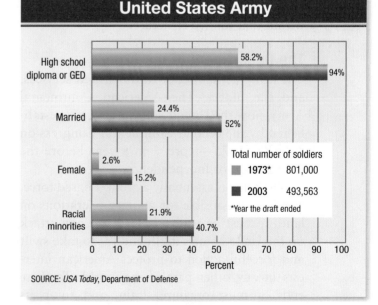

The Changing Face of the United States Army

	Percent
High school diploma or GED	58.2% / 94%
Married	24.4% / 52%
Female	2.6% / 15.2%
Racial minorities	21.9% / 40.7%

Total number of soldiers
1973* 801,000
2003 493,563
*Year the draft ended

SOURCE: *USA Today*, Department of Defense

Interpreting Graphs The make-up of the U.S. Army has changed since the draft ended and it became an all-volunteer force. ***In what ways has the army become more diverse?*** H-SS 12.2.4

"Wisht I could stand up an git some sleep."

Interpreting Political Cartoons Bill Mauldin, who served in the U.S. Army during World War II, drew cartoons "for and about the soldiers because I knew what their life was like." His work appeared in the military newspaper *Stars and Stripes*. **According to this cartoon, what was it like to be a combat soldier? H-SS 12.2.4**

President and directly responsible to the secretary of defense. The nation's armed forces—the army, the navy, and the air force—operate within that unified structure.

The Department of the Army

The army is the largest of the armed services, and the oldest. The American Continental Army, now the United States Army, was established by the Second Continental Congress on June 14, 1775—more than a year before the Declaration of Independence.

The army is essentially a ground-based force, and it is responsible for military operations on land. It must be ready (1) to defeat any attack on the United States itself, and (2) to take swift and forceful action to protect American interests in any other part of the world. To these ends, it must organize, train, and equip its active duty forces—the Regular Army, the Army National Guard, and the Army Reserve. Some 200,000 Army Guard soldiers and

reservists have been called to active duty since September 11, 2001, many of them for service in Afghanistan and Iraq. All of the army's active duty forces are under the direct command of the army's highest ranking officer, the army chief of staff.

The Regular Army is the nation's standing army, the heart of its land forces. There are now some 435,000 men and more than 75,000 women on active duty—officers and enlisted personnel, professional soldiers, and volunteers. The army has been downsized dramatically in the post–cold war era. There were more than 700,000 men and women on active duty when the Soviet Union collapsed in 1991.

Women now serve in all Regular Army units, except the Special Forces. Over recent years, their roles have come to include many combat-related duties in the army and in each of the other armed services, as well.

The army's combat units are trained and equipped to fight enemy forces. The infantry takes, holds, and defends land areas. The artillery supports the infantry, seeks to destroy enemy concentrations with its heavier guns, and gives anti-aircraft cover. The armored cavalry also supports the infantry, using armored vehicles and helicopters to spearhead assaults and oppose enemy counteroffensives.

The other units of the army provide the many services and supplies in support of combat troops. Combat soldiers could not fight without the help of members of the engineer, quartermaster, signal, ordnance, transportation, chemical, military police, finance, and medical corps.

The Department of the Navy

The United States Navy was first formed as the Continental Navy—a fledgling naval force created by the Second Continental Congress on October 13, 1775. From that day to this, its major responsibility has been sea warfare and defense.

The chief of naval operations is the navy's highest ranking officer and is responsible for its preparations and readiness for war and for its use in combat. The navy's ranks also have been thinned in the post–cold war period. Today, some 385,000 officers and enlisted personnel, including some 50,000 women, serve in the navy.

The Second Continental Congress established the United States Marine Corps on November 10, 1775. Today, it operates as a separate armed service within the Navy Department, but it is not under the control of the chief of naval operations. Its commandant answers directly to the secretary of the navy.

The marines are a combat-ready land force for the navy. They have two major combat missions: (1) to seize or defend land bases from which the ships of the fleet and the air power of the navy and marines can operate, and (2) to carry out other land operations essential to a naval campaign. Today, some 160,000 men and 10,000 women serve in the USMC.

Department of the Air Force

The air force is the youngest of the military services. Congress established the United States Air Force and made it a separate branch of the armed forces in the National Security Act of 1947. However, its history dates back to 1907, when the army assigned an officer and two enlisted men to a new unit called the Aeronautical Division of the Army Signal Corps. These three men were ordered to take "charge of all matters pertaining to military ballooning, air machines and all kindred subjects."

Today, the USAF is the nation's first line of defense. It has primary responsibility for military air and aerospace operations. In time of war, its major duties are to defend the United

▲ These Navy fighter pilots serve on the aircraft carrier USS *Dwight D. Eisenhower. Critical Thinking Do you think women should fly combat missions in wartime? Explain your answer.*

States; attack and defeat enemy air, ground, and sea forces; strike military and other war-related targets in enemy territory; and provide transport and combat support for land and naval operations.

The air force now has about 360,000 officers and enlisted personnel, including more than 65,000 women—all under the direct command of the chief of staff of the air force. The authorized strength of the USAF has been cut by more than 150,000 men and women since 1991.

Section 1 Assessment

Key Terms and Main Ideas

1. What is the difference between **foreign affairs** and **domestic affairs**?
2. (a) What was the policy of **isolationism**? (b) During what period was this policy favored by most Americans?
3. Name five kinds of policies that are a part of United States **foreign policy**.
4. How does an **ambassador** reflect the **right of legation**?

Critical Thinking

5. **Drawing Conclusions (a)** Explain how tyranny might result when the military is not kept under civilian control.
   (b) Name one nation where such a situation occurred.

Standards Monitoring Online
For: Self-quiz with vocabulary practice
Web Code: mqa-4171

6. **Analyzing Information** Why do you think the right of legation has been honored by nations for thousands of years?

Go Online
PHSchool.com
For: An activity on foreign affairs
Web Code: mqd-4171

CLOSE UP FOUNDATION
on Primary Sources

Our Obligation as Patriots

Analysis Skills HR4, HI3

Former Secretary of State Colin Powell was awarded the Philadelphia Liberty Medal at Philadelphia's Independence Hall on July 4, 2002, the first Independence Day after the September 11 terrorist attacks. In his acceptance speech, he shared his thoughts on the meaning and importance of patriotism.

Secretary of State Colin Powell receives the Philadelphia Liberty Medal.

Much has happened since we gathered last year to mark the Fourth of July. We were savagely attacked on our own soil. We endured a great national trauma. And we have emerged from it with new strength and a deeper sense of who we are as a people, and who we are as a nation. We showed the world that this nation and this people has a spine of steel, a gallant heart, and a fierce love of liberty. And our enemies now know without doubt that we will not rest until they have been defeated and brought to justice—each and every one of them.

Yes, September 11th brought us back to the fundamentals, the same fundamentals that have defined our nation since its birth, the fundamentals captured in Thomas Jefferson's timeless cadences and the Declaration of Independence. . . .

We stand here today because Jefferson penned those words, and then he and the others assembled here were willing to sign away everything, everything they had, to bring those words to life. As Jefferson did in his time, so too must we recognize that America is not yet perfect. If we would be faithful to that Declaration and we would be faithful to our legacy, we must recognize there is still more to be done. . . .

But what gives us hope and faith in the future is that we also know that our system of government, by the people, is designed to correct injustices and make ours an ever more perfect union.

And our obligation as patriots is to constantly work to reach the goal that was set for us here on that day 226 years ago. Each of us has the duty to stand up not only for our rights, but for the rights of all of our fellow citizens, and to help secure the blessings of liberty for all. . . .

And so on this Fourth of July, in this beautiful place, in this precious moment, my red, white and blue message to you is this: It is up to every one of us to make the words of the Declaration of Independence speak to the men, women and children of our time. It is up to each of us to make America beautiful, to ensure that our country remains the land of liberty and opportunity. It is for us to keep the American Dream alive for our children and for our children's children. And it is for America, the Land of the Free and the Home of the Brave, to help freedom ring across the globe, unto all the peoples thereof. That is our solemn obligation, and we will not fail.

Analyzing Primary Sources

1. Explain Powell's statement that "September 11th brought us back to the fundamentals."
2. Why was the first Independence Day after the September 11 terrorist attacks of special significance?
3. Do you agree that "it is for America . . . to help freedom ring across the globe"? Explain your answer.

Other Foreign and Defense Agencies

Section Preview

OBJECTIVES

1. **Describe** a number of government agencies, besides the Departments of State and Defense, that are involved in foreign and defense policy.
2. **Explain** how the CIA, the Department of Homeland Security, NASA, and the Selective Service System contribute to the nation's security.

WHY IT MATTERS

Besides the Departments of State and Defense, several other government agencies are closely involved with foreign policy. These agencies oversee such tasks as gathering and analyzing intelligence information, supervising the draft, exploring space, and strengthening homeland security.

POLITICAL DICTIONARY

★ **espionage**
★ **terrorism**
★ **draft**

How many federal agencies, in addition to the Departments of State and Defense, are involved with the nation's foreign affairs? Dozens of them. Thus, the FBI combats terrorism and espionage here and abroad. The Public Health Service works with the United Nations and foreign governments to conquer diseases and meet other health problems in many parts of the world. And the Coast Guard keeps an iceberg patrol in the North Atlantic to protect the shipping of all nations.

A recitation of this sort could go on and on. But, as you will see, this section deals with those agencies most directly involved in the areas of foreign and defense policy.

The CIA

The Central Intelligence Agency (CIA) is a key part of the foreign policy establishment. Created by Congress in 1947, the CIA works under the direction of the National Security Council. A director heads "the agency," as it is often called. That director is appointed by the President and confirmed by the Senate.

On paper, the CIA has three major tasks: (1) to coordinate the information-gathering activities of all State, Defense, and other federal agencies involved in the areas of foreign affairs and national defense, (2) to analyze and evaluate all data collected by those agencies, and (3) to

brief the President and the National Security Council— that is, to keep them fully informed of all of that intelligence.

The CIA is far more than a coordinating and reporting body, however. It also conducts its own worldwide intelligence operations. In fact, it is a major "cloak-and-dagger" agency. Much of the information it gathers comes from more or less open sources, such as foreign newspapers and other publications, radio broadcasts, travelers, satellite photos, and the like. Still, a large share of information comes from the CIA's own secret, covert activities. Those operations cover the full range of **espionage,** or spying.

▲ The International Ice Patrol (IIP) of the U.S. Coast Guard tracks icebergs in the North Atlantic to help protect ships of all nations.

▲ **Increased Security** After the September 11, 2001, hijackings and attacks, the National Guard began patrolling airports. These members of the Florida National Guard march through Tampa International Airport. **H-SS 12.2.4**

Much of the CIA's work is shrouded in deepest secrecy. Even Congress has generally shied away from more than a surface check on the agency's activities. Indeed, the CIA's operating funds are disguised in several places in the federal budget each year.

When Congress established the CIA, it recognized the need for such an organization in a trouble-filled world. Most people agree that that need continues today. At the same time, Congress saw the dangers inherent in a super-secret intelligence agency that operates outside the realm of public scrutiny. Therefore, the National Security Act of 1947 expressly denies the CIA the authority to conduct any investigative, surveillance, or other clandestine activities within the United States. However, the agency has not always obeyed that command.

Department of Homeland Security

The Department of Homeland Security is charged with the awesome task of protecting the United States against **terrorism.** Terrorism is the use of violence to intimidate a government or a society, usually for political or ideological reasons.

Congress created the department in 2002 and it became operational in 2003. It is responsible for the coordination and the direction of all anti-terrorist activities of all public agencies operating in the field of domestic security—including thousands of police departments, fire departments, emergency medical and search and rescue units, and other disaster response agencies across the country. The Homeland Security Act of 2002 gives the department major operating responsibilities in five specific areas:

- border and transportation security;
- infrastructure protection;
- emergency preparedness and response;
- chemical, biological, radiological, and nuclear defense; and
- information analysis (intelligence).

The new department is built, in major part, of a number of agencies transferred to it from other Cabinet departments. Those agencies include the Secret Service and the Customs Service (now the U.S. Immigration and Customs Enforcement), from the Treasury Department; the Coast Guard and the Transportation Security Administration, from Transportation; the Immigration and Naturalization Service (now the U.S. Citizenship and Immigration Services), from Justice; and the independent Federal Emergency Management Agency.

The threat of bioterrorism—the use of such biological agents as smallpox or anthrax as weapons—dramatizes the immensity of the problems facing the Department of Homeland Security. So, too, do these facts: There are nearly 600,000 bridges, 170,000 water systems, and more than 2,000 power plants (104 of them nuclear) in the United States. There are also 220,000 miles of railroad, 190,000 miles of natural gas pipelines, 25,000 miles of waterways, and 1,000 harbor channels. And there are 463 skyscrapers (each over 500 feet high), nearly 19,000 airports (including some 300 major facilities), thousands of stadiums and other large gathering places, and nearly 20,000 miles of border.

Add to all that such critical matters as the nation's food supply, its healthcare system, and its communications networks and this point becomes clear: This country cannot be protected—completely and absolutely—against terrorists. Terrorism thrives on unpredictability and uses it as a weapon to foment fear and anxiety.

Quite apparently, the best that can be hoped for in the current circumstances is that (1) most—nearly all—terrorist attacks will be thwarted or their impacts will at least be minimized and (2) those responsible for the attacks will be rooted out and brought to justice.

NASA

The modern space age is only some forty years old. It began on October 4, 1957, when the Soviet Union put its first satellite, *Sputnik I*, in space. The first American satellite, *Explorer I*, was fired into orbit a few months later, on January 31, 1958. From that point on, a great number of space vehicles have been thrust into the heavens, first by the two superpowers and then by other nations as well. The most spectacular of all of those ventures came more than 30 years ago when, on July 20, 1969, two American astronauts, Neil Armstrong and Edwin Aldrin, became the only human beings ever to land on the moon.

The National Aeronautics and Space Administration (NASA) is an independent agency created by Congress in 1958 to handle this nation's space programs. Today, the scope of those programs is truly extraordinary. NASA's work ranges from basic research that focuses on the origin, evolution, and structure of the universe to explorations of outer space.

The military importance of NASA's work can hardly be exaggerated. Nevertheless, Congress has ordered the space agency to bend its efforts "to peaceful purposes for the benefit of all humankind," as well. NASA's research and development efforts have opened new frontiers in several fields: in astronomy, physics, and the environmental sciences; in communications, medicine, and weather forecasting; and in many more areas. Many scientific advances pioneered by NASA have been put to remarkable use in the civilian world both here and abroad.

NASA conducts its operations at a number of flight centers, laboratories, and other installations throughout the country. Among the best known are the Kennedy Space Center at Cape Canaveral in Florida; the Johnson Space Center near Houston, Texas; the Ames Research Center and the Jet Propulsion Laboratory, both in California; and the Goddard Space Flight Center in Greenbelt, Maryland.

▲ A NASA astronaut works on the payload of a space shuttle as that craft orbits the Earth. *Critical Thinking Should the United States continue to fund the exploration of outer space? Why or why not?*

Over the years, NASA's accomplishments were so many, and its programs so successful, that its space flights and other extraterrestrial projects became so seemingly routine that they attracted little continuing public notice. That circumstance changed, dramatically, in 1986, when the space shuttle *Challenger* exploded only moments after liftoff from Cape Canaveral. The entire seven-member crew was lost, including Christa McAuliffe, the first "teacher in space."

NASA, and the nation, recovered from that disaster—but only slowly. No manned space vehicles were launched for nearly three years. The space program did regain its footing over the next decade, however, and once again most people paid scant attention to NASA and its activities.

The nation was jolted by tragedy again, on February 1, 2003 when the shuttle *Columbia* was torn apart as it reentered the Earth's atmosphere. All seven of its astronauts perished. Once again, the space program was put on hold. It will be resumed, however, and, as President Bush put it: "Our journey into space will go on."

A permanently occupied space station ranks first on NASA's to-do list. Russia, Canada, Brazil, Japan, and the ten-nation European Space Center have joined the United States in that venture. Rotating three-member crews have lived aboard the outpost since late 2000. The station, to be completed in a few more years, will become an advanced research laboratory for the exploration of space and all of its untold resources.

The Selective Service System

Through most of American history, the armed forces have depended on voluntary enlistments to fill their ranks. From 1940 to 1973, however, the **draft**—also called conscription, or compulsory military service—was a major source of military manpower.

Conscription has a long history in this country. Several colonies and later nine States required all able-bodied males to serve in their militia. However, in the 1790s, Congress rejected proposals for national compulsory military service.

Both the North and the South did use limited conscription programs during the Civil War. It was not until 1917, however, that a national draft was first used in this country, even in wartime. More than 2.8 million of the 4.7 million men who served in World War I were drafted under the terms of the Selective Service Act of 1917.

The nation's first peacetime draft came with the Selective Service and Training Act of 1940, as World War II raged in Europe but before the United States entered the war. Eventually, more than 10 million of the 16.3 million Americans in uniform in World War II entered the service under that law.

The World War II draft ended in 1947. The crises of the postwar period, however, quickly moved Congress to revive the draft, which was reestablished by the Selective Service Act of 1948. From 1948 to 1973, nearly 5 million young men were drafted.

Mounting criticisms of compulsory military service, fed by opposition to our Vietnam policy, led many Americans to call for an end to the draft in the late 1960s. By 1972, fewer than 30,000 men were being drafted per year, and selective service was suspended in 1973. Nevertheless, the draft law is still on the books.

The draft law places a military obligation on all males in the United States between the ages of $18\frac{1}{2}$ and 26. During the years in which the draft operated, it was largely conducted through hundreds of local selective service boards. All young men had to register for service at age 18. The local boards then selected those who were to enter the armed forces.

As of 1980, the registration requirement was back in place. President Jimmy Carter reactivated it, and his executive order is still in force. All young males are required to sign up soon after they reach their 18th birthday. However, the President's power to order the actual induction of men into the armed forces expired on June 30, 1973. If the draft is ever to be reactivated, Congress must first renew that presidential authority.[6]

---

[6]The Supreme Court first upheld the constitutionality of the draft in the *Selective Draft Law Cases* in 1918. The Court also found its all-male features constitutional in *Rostker* v. *Goldberg* in 1981; see page 499.

Section 2 Assessment

Key Terms and Main Ideas

1. Identify this nation's principle **espionage** agency.
2. What is **terrorism**?
3. When was the **draft** last used to provide manpower for the nation's armed forces?
4. What will be the primary function of the international space station when it is finally completed?

Critical Thinking

5. **Demonstrating Reasoned Judgment** It seems clear that this country cannot be protected—completely and absolutely—against terrorist attacks. Give your reasons for agreeing or disagreeing with this statement.

Standards Monitoring *Online*
For: Self-quiz with vocabulary practice
Web Code: mqa-4172

6. **Checking Consistency (a)** Is an intelligence agency whose actions can be kept secret from the people consistent with the principle of popular sovereignty? Explain. **(b)** Why do you think the CIA is permitted to operate in this way?

Go Online
PHSchool.com

For: An activity on selective service
Web Code: mqd-4172

3 American Foreign Policy Overview

Section Preview

OBJECTIVES

1. **Summarize** American foreign policy from independence through World War I.
2. **Show** how the two World Wars affected America's traditional policy of isolationism.
3. **Explain** the principles of collective security and deterrence and their use during the cold war.
4. **Describe** American foreign policy since the end of the cold war.
5. **Explain** why the world remains a dangerous place.

WHY IT MATTERS

A knowledge of the history of American foreign policy is essential to understanding foreign policy issues today. Over time, the United States changed from an isolationist nation to a world power. Although the United States is the only superpower today, the world remains a dangerous place.

POLITICAL DICTIONARY

★ **collective security**
★ **deterrence**
★ **cold war**
★ **containment**
★ **détente**

The basic purpose of American foreign policy has always been to protect the security of the United States—and so it is today. It would be impossible to present a full-blown history of America's foreign relations in these pages, of course. But we can review its major themes and highlights here.

Why should you know as much as you can about the history of the United States? Because history is not "bunk," as automaker Henry Ford once described it. Let Robert Kelly, a leading historian, tell you what history really is: "History is our social memory. Our memories tell us who we are, where we belong, what has worked and what has not worked, and where we seem to be going."[7]

Foreign Policy From Independence Through WWI

From its beginnings, and for 150 years, American foreign policy was very largely built on a policy of isolationism. Throughout that period, the United States refused to become generally and permanently involved in the affairs of the rest of the world.

Isolationism arose in the earliest years of this nation's history. In his Farewell Address in 1796, George Washington declared that "our true policy" was "to steer clear of permanent alliances with any portion of the foreign world." Our "detached and distant situation," Washington said, made it desirable for us to have "as little political connection as possible" with other nations. In 1801, Thomas Jefferson added his own warning against "entangling alliances."

At the time, and for decades to come, isolationism seemed a wise policy to most Americans. The United States was a new and relatively weak nation with a great many problems, a huge continent to explore and settle, and two oceans to separate us from the rest of the world.

The policy of isolationism did not demand a complete separation from the rest of the world. From the first, the United States developed ties abroad by exchanging diplomatic representatives with other nations, making treaties with many of them, and building an extensive foreign commerce. In fact, isolationism was, over time,

▲ This statue in Washington, D.C., honors the Marquis de Lafayette, a French nobleman who served in the Continental Army during the American Revolution.

---

[7] *The Shaping of the American Past*, 2nd ed.

Foreign Policy and National Defense 481 ★★★★

more a statement of our desire for noninvolvement outside the Western Hemisphere than a description of United States policy within our own hemisphere.

The Monroe Doctrine

James Monroe gave the policy of isolationism a clearer shape in 1823. In a historic message to Congress, he proclaimed what has been known ever since as the Monroe Doctrine.

A wave of revolutions had swept Latin America, destroying the old Spanish and Portuguese empires there. The prospect that other European powers would now help Spain and Portugal to take back their lost possessions was seen as a threat to United States security and a challenge to this country's economic interests.

In his message, President Monroe restated America's intentions to stay out of European affairs. He also warned the nations of Europe—including Russia, then in control of Alaska—to stay out of the affairs of both North and South America. He declared that the United States would look on

PRIMARY Sources *"any attempt on their part to extend their system to any portion of this hemisphere as dangerous to our peace and safety."*

—Speech by President James Monroe to Congress, December 2, 1823

At first, most Latin Americans took little notice of this doctrine. They knew that it was really the Royal Navy and British interest in Latin American trade that protected them from European domination. Later, as the United States became more powerful, many Latin Americans came to view the Monroe Doctrine as a selfish policy designed to protect the political and economic interests of the United States, not the independence of other nations in the Western Hemisphere.

Continental Expansion

The Treaty of Paris officially ended the Revolutionary War in 1783. Under its terms, the United States held title to all of the territory from the Great Lakes in the north to Spanish Florida in the south, and from the Atlantic coast westward to the Mississippi.

The United States began to expand across the continent almost at once. Taking advantage of France's conflict with England in the early 1800s, President Jefferson negotiated the Louisiana Purchase in 1803. At a single stroke, the nation's size was doubled, with territory reaching from the mouth of the Mississippi up to what is now Montana. With the Florida Purchase in 1819, the nation completed its expansion to the south.

Through the second quarter of the nineteenth century, the United States pursued what most Americans believed was this nation's "Manifest Destiny": the mission to expand its boundaries across the continent to the Pacific Ocean. Texas was annexed in 1845. The United States obtained the Oregon Country by treaty with Great Britain in 1846. After its defeat in the Mexican War of 1846–1848, Mexico ceded what today makes up most of the southwestern quarter of the United States.

The Gadsden Purchase in 1853 rounded out the southwestern limits of the nation. By treaty, the United States bought a strip of territory from Mexico. This land in what is now the southern parts of Arizona and New Mexico was acquired to provide the best rail route to the Pacific.

In 1867, the United States bought Alaska from Russia. The treaty of purchase was negotiated by President Andrew Johnson's Secretary of State, William H. Seward. At the time, many Americans criticized the $7.2 million purchase as "Seward's Folly" and called Alaska "Seward's Icebox."

In that same year, the Monroe Doctrine got its first real test. While Americans were immersed in the Civil War, France had invaded Mexico. The French leader, Napoleon III, had installed Prince Maximilian of Austria as Mexico's puppet emperor. In 1867, the United States backed the Mexicans in forcing the French to withdraw, and the Maximilian regime fell.

A World Power

The United States emerged as a first-class power in world politics with the Spanish-American War in 1898. With Spain's decisive defeat, America gained the Philippines and Guam in the Pacific, and Puerto Rico in the Caribbean. Cuba became independent, under American protection. Hawaii was also annexed in 1898.

By 1900, the United States had become a colonial power. Its interests extended across the continent to Alaska, to the tip of Latin America, and across the Pacific to the Philippines.

The Good Neighbor Policy

The threat of European intervention in the Western Hemisphere declined in the second half of the nineteenth century. That threat was replaced by problems within the hemisphere. Political instability, revolutions, unpaid foreign debts, and injuries to citizens and property of other countries plagued Central and South America.

Under what came to be known as the Roosevelt Corollary to the Monroe Doctrine, the United States began to police Latin America in the early 1900s. Several times, the marines were used to quell revolutions and other unrest in Nicaragua, Haiti, Cuba, and elsewhere.

In 1903, Panama revolted and became independent of Colombia, with American blessings. In the same year, the United States gained the right to build a canal across the Isthmus of Panama. In 1917, the United States purchased the Virgin Islands from Denmark to help guard the canal. These and other steps were resented by many in Latin America. They complained of "the Colossus of the North," of "Yankee imperialism," and of "dollar diplomacy"—and many still do.

This country's Latin American policies took an important turn in the 1930s. Theodore Roosevelt's Corollary was replaced by Franklin Roosevelt's Good Neighbor Policy, a conscious attempt to win friends to the south.

Today, the central provision of the Monroe Doctrine—the warning against foreign encroachments in the Western Hemisphere—is set out in the Inter-American Treaty of Reciprocal Assistance (the Rio Pact) of 1947. Still, the United States is, without question, the dominant power in the Western Hemisphere, and the Monroe Doctrine remains a vital part of American foreign policy.

The Open Door in China

Historically, American foreign-policy interests have centered on Europe and on Latin America. But America has also had involvement in the Far East since the mid-1800s.

Interpreting Political Cartoons President Theodore Roosevelt's foreign policy was often described in his own famous statement, "Speak softly and carry a big stick." Here, TR is shown as the policeman of the Western Hemisphere. **Do you think the cartoonist favors this policy or not? Explain your answer. H-SS 12.7.8**

Forty-five years before the United States acquired territory in the far Pacific, the U.S. Navy's Commodore Matthew Perry had opened Japan to American trade.

By the late nineteenth century, however, America's thriving trade in Asia was being seriously threatened. The British, French, Germans, and Japanese were each ready to take slices of the Chinese coast as their own exclusive trading preserves. In 1899, Secretary of State John Hay announced this country's insistence on an Open Door policy in China. That doctrine promoted equal trade access for all nations, and demanded that China's independence and sovereignty over its own territory be preserved.

The other major powers came to accept the American position, however reluctantly. Relations between the United States and Japan worsened from that point on, until the climax at Pearl Harbor in 1941. Over the same period, the United States built increasingly strong ties with China; but those ties were cut when communists won control of the Chinese mainland in 1949. For nearly 30 years, the United States and the People's Republic of China refused diplomatic recognition of one another.

The realities of world politics finally forced a reshaping of American-Chinese relations in the 1970s. President Nixon made a historic visit to Beijing in 1972, and full-fledged diplomatic ties were reestablished in 1979.

Still, the People's Republic is a totalitarian state, and American policy reflects that fact—though many argue that it does not do so strongly enough. The Chinese government's brutal response to pro-democracy demonstrations by thousands of students in Beijing's Tiananmen Square in 1989 has colored American-Chinese relations ever since.

World War I and the Return to Isolationism

Germany's submarine campaign against American shipping in the North Atlantic forced the United States out of its isolationist cocoon in 1917. America entered World War I "to make the world safe for democracy."

With the defeat of Germany and the Central Powers, however, America pulled back from the involvements brought on by the war. The United States refused to join the League of Nations, which had been conceived by President Woodrow Wilson. Many Americans strongly believed that problems in Europe and the rest of the world need not concern them.

The rise of Mussolini in Italy (1922), Hitler in Germany (1933), and the militarists in Japan (1937) cast dark clouds over the world. Yet, for more than 20 years after World War I, an isolationist United States remained aloof, protected by its two oceans.

World War II

America's historic commitment to isolationism was finally ended by World War II. That massive conflict, which began in Europe in 1939, spread to engulf much of the world and lasted for nearly six years. The war involved 61 nations. By the time it ended in 1945, World War II had cost the lives of as many as 75 million people worldwide. The war's other costs, in human suffering and in physical destruction, were at least as appalling.

The United States became directly involved in the war when the Japanese attacked the American naval base at Pearl Harbor in Hawaii on December 7, 1941. From that point on—along with the British, the Russians, the Chinese, and our other Allies—the United States waged an all-out effort to defeat the Axis Powers (Germany, Italy, and Japan).

Under the direction of President Franklin Roosevelt, the United States became the "arsenal of democracy." American resources and industrial capacity supplied most of the armaments and other materials we and our Allies needed to win World War II. Within a very short time, the United States was also transformed into the mightiest military power in the world. American land, naval, and air forces fought and defeated the enemy in the Pacific, the Far East, North Africa, and Europe.

World War II finally ended in the middle of 1945 with the Allies victorious everywhere. In Europe, Germany—which had been devastated by the attacks of American and British forces from the west and by Russian troops from the east—surrendered unconditionally in May. The war in the Pacific came to a sudden end in August. Japan capitulated soon after the United States dropped two atomic bombs, which destroyed the Japanese cities of Hiroshima and Nagasaki.

Two New Principles

World War II brought a historic shift from a position of isolationism to one of internationalism. This nation's foreign policy has been cast in that

▲ *A Hard-Fought Victory* This famous photograph shows U.S. Marines planting the American flag on the Pacific island of Iwo Jima during World War II. **H-SS 12.2.4**

newer direction for more than 60 years now. Even so, the overall objective of that policy remains what it has always been: the protection of the security of the United States. As you will see, the major features of current American foreign policy are all reflections of that overriding goal.

Collective Security

After World War II, the United States and most of the rest of a war-weary world looked to the principle of **collective security** to keep international peace and order. America hoped to forge a world community in which at least most nations would agree to act together against any nation that threatened the peace.

To that end, this country took the lead in creating the United Nations in 1945. The organization's charter declares that the UN was formed to promote international cooperation and so "to save succeeding generations from the scourge of war . . . and to maintain international peace and security" (see pages 494–498).

It soon became clear, however, that the future of the world would not be shaped in the UN. Rather, international security would depend largely on the nature of the relations between the two superpowers, the United States and the Soviet Union. Those relations, never very close, quickly deteriorated—and for the next 40 years American foreign policy was built around that fact.

The United States is the only superpower in today's world. Still, collective security remains a cornerstone of American policy. The United States has supported the United Nations and other efforts to further international cooperation. This country has also taken another path to collective security: building a network of regional security alliances, as you will see.

Deterrence

The principle of deterrence has also been a basic part of American foreign policy since World War II, and it remains a fundamental plank of that policy today. Basically, **deterrence** is the strategy of maintaining the military might of the United States at so great a level that that very strength will deter—discourage, prevent—an attack on this country by any hostile power.

President Harry Truman initiated deterrence as U.S.–Soviet relations worsened after World

Niccoló Machiavelli (1469-1527), Italian statesman, political philosopher Machiavelli was the first to promote the doctrine of national interest in the making and conduct of a nation's foreign policy. In his most famous work, *The Prince* (1513), he advised his sovereign to adopt a "realistic" approach to national affairs and to base foreign policy decisions on *raison d'état* (reason of state). The use of power, he wrote, should be kept separate from moral principles and values. As the concept of national interest has been developed over time, it holds that national security and national advantage must be the paramount focus of a nation's policies; moral considerations, international agreements, and the like should be disregarded if they conflict with a nation's goals. As former Secretary of State Henry Kissinger once put it: "There are times when national interest is more important than the law." *Do you agree with Dr. Kissinger's observation? Why or why not?* **H-SS 12.1.1**

War II. Every President since Truman's day has reaffirmed the strategy; and it was a key factor in the collapse of the Soviet Union.

With the war in Iraq, President George W. Bush expanded the historic policy of deterrence to include the doctrine of preemptive war. That doctrine holds that this nation has the right to conduct a preemptive war—a first-strike war—against any power that it believes poses a significant threat to the security of the United States.

Resisting Soviet Aggression

One cannot hope to understand either recent or current American foreign policy without being familiar with the long years of the **cold war**. The cold war was a period of more than 40 years during which relations between the two superpowers were at least tense and, more often than not, distinctly hostile. It was, for the most part, not a "hot war" of military action, but rather a time of threats, posturing, and military build-up.

Toward the end of World War II, the United States had hoped to work with its wartime ally the Soviet Union, particularly through the UN, to build international cooperation and to keep the peace in the postwar world. Those plans were quickly dashed, however.

At the Yalta Conference in early 1945, Soviet Premier Josef Stalin had agreed with President Franklin Roosevelt and British Prime Minister Winston Churchill that "democratic governments" would be established by "free elections" in the liberated countries of Eastern Europe. Instead, the Soviets imposed dictatorial regimes on those countries. In a famous 1946 speech, Churchill declared that an "iron curtain" had descended across the continent.

As they devoured Eastern Europe, the Soviets also attempted to take over the oil fields of Iran, to the south. At the same time, they supported communist guerrillas in a civil war in Greece. Pursuing the historic Russian dream of a "window to the sea," the Soviet Union also demanded military and naval bases in Turkey.

The Truman Doctrine

The United States began to counter the Soviet Union's aggressive actions in the early months of 1947. The Truman Doctrine marked the first step in that long-standing process. Both Greece and Turkey were in danger of falling under the Soviet Union's control. At President Harry Truman's urgent request, Congress approved a massive program of economic and military aid, and both countries remained free of Soviet control. In his message to Congress, the President declared that it was now

PRIMARY Sources "the policy of the United States to support free peoples who are resisting attempted subjugation by armed minorities or outside pressures. "
—Speech by President Harry S Truman to Congress, March 12, 1947

The Truman Doctrine soon became part of a broader American plan for dealing with the Soviet Union. From mid-1947 through the 1980s, the United States followed the policy of

containment. That policy was rooted in the belief that if communism could be kept within its existing boundaries, it would collapse under the weight of its own internal weaknesses.

The United States and the Soviet Union confronted one another often during the cold war years. Two of those confrontations were of major, near-war proportions: in Berlin in 1948–1949 and in Cuba in 1962. And, during that same period, the United States also fought two hot wars against communist forces in Asia.

The Berlin Blockade

At the end of World War II, the city of Berlin, surrounded by Soviet-occupied East Germany, was divided into four sectors. The Soviet Union controlled one sector, East Berlin. The United States, Britain, and France occupied the other three sectors, which made up West Berlin.

In 1948, the Soviets tried to force their former allies to withdraw from West Berlin. They clamped a land blockade around the city, stopping the shipment of food and supplies to the western sectors. The United States mounted a massive airlift that kept the city alive until the blockade was lifted, nearly a year and a half later.

The Cuban Missile Crisis

The United States and the Soviet Union came perilously close to a nuclear conflict during the Cuban missile crisis in 1962. Cuba had slipped into the Soviet orbit soon after Fidel Castro gained power there in 1959. By mid-1962, huge quantities of Soviet arms and thousands of Soviet "technicians" had been sent to Cuba. Suddenly, in October, the build-up became unmistakably offensive in character. Aerial photographs revealed the presence of several Soviet missiles that were capable of nuclear strikes against this country and much of Latin America.

President John Kennedy immediately ordered a naval blockade of Cuba to prevent the delivery of any more missiles. Cuba and the Soviet Union were warned that the United States would attack Cuba unless the existing Soviet missiles were removed.

After several tense days, the Soviets backed down. Rather than risk all so far from home, they returned the weapons to the Soviet Union.

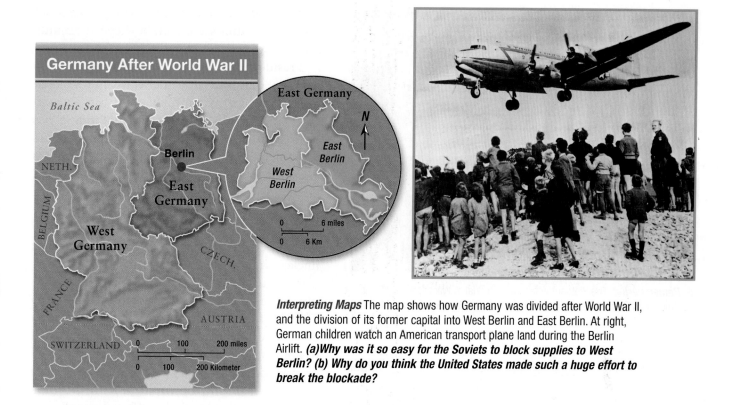

Germany After World War II

Baltic Sea

NETH.

BELGIUM

FRANCE

Berlin

West Germany

East Germany

CZECH.

SWITZERLAND

AUSTRIA

0   100   200 miles

0   100   200 Kilometer

East Germany

N

East Berlin

West Berlin

0   6 miles

0   6 Km

Interpreting Maps The map shows how Germany was divided after World War II, and the division of its former capital into West Berlin and East Berlin. At right, German children watch an American transport plane land during the Berlin Airlift. *(a)Why was it so easy for the Soviets to block supplies to West Berlin? (b) Why do you think the United States made such a huge effort to break the blockade?*

The Korean War

The Korean War began on June 25, 1950. South Korea (the UN-sponsored Republic of Korea) was attacked by communist North Korea (the People's Democratic Republic of Korea). Immediately, the UN's Security Council called on all UN members to help South Korea repel the invasion.

The war lasted for more than three years. It pitted the United Nations Command, largely made up of American and South Korean forces, against Soviet-trained and Soviet-equipped North Korean and communist Chinese troops. Cease-fire negotiations began in July 1951, but fighting continued until an armistice (a cease-fire agreement) was signed on July 27, 1953. Final peace terms have never been agreed to.

The long and bitter Korean conflict did not end in a clear-cut UN victory. The war cost the United States 157,530 casualties, including 33,629 combat dead, and more than $20 billion. South Korea's military and civilian casualties ran into the hundreds of thousands. Much of Korea, north and south, was laid to waste.

Still, the invasion was turned back, and the Republic of Korea remained standing. For the first time in history, armed forces of several nations fought under an international flag

against aggression. There is no telling how far that aggression might have carried had the United States not come to the aid of South Korea.

The War in Vietnam

In the years following World War II, a nationalist movement arose in what is today Vietnam. The Vietnamese nationalists were seeking independence from France. Made up mostly of communist forces led by Ho Chi Minh, the nationalists fought and defeated the French in a lengthy conflict. Under truce agreements signed in Geneva in 1954, what had been French Indochina was divided into two zones: a communist-dominated North Vietnam, with its capital in Hanoi, and an anticommunist South Vietnam, with Saigon as its capital.

Almost at once, communist guerrillas (the Viet Cong), supported by North Vietnamese, began a civil war in South Vietnam. The Eisenhower administration responded with economic and then military aid to Saigon. President Kennedy increased this aid. Even with stepped-up U.S. support to South Vietnam, the Viet Cong—and growing numbers of North Vietnamese supplied with mostly Soviet and

▲ **Remembering** The Vietnam Veterans Memorial in Washington, D.C., is inscribed with the names of Americans killed or missing in action in the Vietnam War.

some Chinese weapons—continued to make major gains.

President Lyndon Johnson committed the United States to full-scale war in early 1965. By 1968, more than 540,000 Americans were involved in a fierce ground and air conflict.

In 1969, President Richard Nixon began what he called the "Vietnamization" of the war. Over the next four years, American troops were gradually pulled out of combat. Finally, a cease-fire agreement was signed in early 1973, and the last American units were withdrawn. (In spite of the cease-fire, the war between North and South Vietnam went on. By 1975, South Vietnam had been overrun, and the two Vietnams became the Socialist Republic of Vietnam.)

The ill-fated war in Vietnam cost the United States a staggering $165 billion and, irreplaceably, more than 58,000 American lives. As the war dragged on, millions of Americans came to oppose American involvement in Southeast Asia—and traces of the divisiveness of that period can still be seen in the politics of today.

Détente and the Return to Containment

As the United States withdrew from Vietnam, the Nixon administration embarked on a policy of **détente**. The term is French, meaning "a relaxation of tensions." In this case, the policy of détente included a purposeful attempt to improve relations with the Soviet Union and, separately, with China.

President Nixon flew to Beijing in 1972 to begin a new era in American-Chinese relations. His visit paved the way for further contacts and, finally, for formal diplomatic ties between the United States and the People's Republic of China. Less than three months later, Mr. Nixon journeyed to Moscow. There, he and Soviet Premier Leonid Brezhnev signed the first Strategic Arms Limitations Talks agreement, SALT I—a five-year pact in which both sides agreed to a measure of control over their nuclear weapons.

Relations with mainland China have improved more or less steadily since the 1970s. Efforts at détente with the Soviets, however, proved less successful. Moscow continued to apply its expansionist pressures and provided economic and military aid to revolutionary movements around the world.

The short-lived period of détente ended altogether when the Soviets invaded Afghanistan in 1979. After that act of aggression, first President Jimmy Carter and then the Reagan administration placed a renewed emphasis on containing Soviet power.

The End of the Cold War

Relations between the United States and the Soviet Union improved remarkably after Mikhail Gorbachev gained power in Moscow in 1985. He and President Ronald Reagan soon met in a series of summit conferences that helped pave the way to the end of the cold war. Those meetings, focused on arms limitations, eased long-standing tensions. George H.W. Bush continued that "summit diplomacy" when he became President in 1989.

Certainly, Mikhail Gorbachev deserves much credit for the fundamental change in the Soviets' approach to world affairs. But, just as certainly, that historic change was prompted by deepening political and economic chaos in Eastern Europe and within the Soviet Union itself—by conditions that ultimately brought the collapse of the Soviet Union in late 1991; see pages 647–648.

The fact that the cold war is now a matter of history should also been seen in this light: The

American policies of deterrence and containment, first put in place in 1947, finally realized their goals. As President Reagan put it, the Soviet Union was left "on the ash heap of history."

The World Remains Dangerous

The sudden collapse of the Soviet Union and, with it, the end of the cold war, did not mean that the world had suddenly become a peaceful place. Far from it. The planet is still plagued by conflicts and it remains a very dangerous place. Osama bin Laden, al Qaida and other terrorist groups, and the global war against them certainly testify to that daunting fact. So, too, do the campaign to root out the last of the Taliban in Afghanistan, the ongoing violence in Iraq, and the efforts to rebuild both of those shattered countries.

Then, too, there is the worrisome fact that North Korea is building a nuclear arsenal, and Iran appears to be headed in the same direction. And there are a number of seemingly endless quarrels elsewhere in today's world—not the least of them Israel's disputes with its Arab neighbors, protracted civil wars in Africa, and repeated clashes between India and Pakistan, both of them nuclear powers.

The situation in Iraq is particularly troubling for the United States. Recall that the dictator Saddam Hussein and his Iraqi forces were soundly defeated in the first Gulf War in 1991; see page 402. At the end of that war, Saddam agreed to destroy his country's stock of chemical and biological weapons and to abandon his efforts to acquire a nuclear capability. He also agreed to allow UN inspectors to monitor his regime's compliance with those commitments.

Convinced that Saddam had not honored those promises and that Iraq had secretly amassed large stores of weapons of mass destruction, President George W. Bush determined to hold Iraq to account in 2002. Efforts to persuade the UN Security Council to support that move proved unsuccessful. But, at his urging, both house of Congress did adopt a joint resolution authorizing the President to take those actions "necessary and appropriate" to eliminate Iraq's "continuing threat to the security of the United States and to international peace."

In March 2003, the United States and Great Britain, supported by a number of smaller nations, launched the second Gulf War, code-named Operation Iraqi Freedom. Iraq was conquered and Saddam Hussein's regime toppled in less than six weeks.

The ongoing efforts to stabilize and rebuild Iraq, and to establish a democratic government there, have proved more than difficult. However, the dramatic capture of Saddam Hussein by American troops in mid-December of 2003 almost certainly boosted prospects for the success of those efforts. It is quite apparent that the United States and Britain—and, it is hoped, the UN and a large number of other countries—will be engaged in the huge task of reconstructing Iraq for some years to come.

Section 3 Assessment

Key Terms and Main Ideas

1. How does the phrase "United we stand, divided we fall" describe the concept of **collective security?**
2. Define **(a)** the historic policy of deterrence, and **(b)** its recent expansion, the doctrine of preemptive war.
3. Explain the policy of **containment**. Was it a success or a failure? Why?
4. **(a)** What was **détente? (b)** What Soviet action ended détente?

Critical Thinking

5. **Identifying Central Issues** Do you think the United States could ever return to isolationism? Why or why not?

6. **Drawing Conclusions** Should the United States actively seek the overthrow of every dictatorial regime in today's world? Why or why not?

Face the Issues

Defending America

Background *For more than 30 years now, the ranks of the nation's armed forces have been filled entirely by volunteers. Today, however, many worry that the continuing demands of wars in Iraq and Afghanistan threaten to stretch the capacities of the armed forces—in particular, the Army—to the breaking point. This has led some people to urge a return to the draft. Neither the President nor the Defense Department has supported that proposal.*

A U.S. soldier returns from Iraq

Analysis Skills CS1, HI1

An All-Volunteer Military

This country has relied on voluntary military forces through much of its history—and for good reason, says noted military sociologist David Segal. "Americans have been willing . . . to volunteer when they felt that national security was threatened. We have been much less comfortable with involuntary servitude."

The American people have always been troubled by compulsory military service. Draft riots erupted during the Civil War and heated resistance to selective service arose during World War I. The existence of an all-volunteer military today is, in no small part, a reaction to the opposition to the draft in the Vietnam era. Gallup polls on the matter have put opposition to the reinstatement of the draft at more than 80 percent.

The stellar performance of the all-volunteer military in both wars in Iraq and in Afghanistan and elsewhere stand as the best evidence of the success of the current system. Volunteers are motivated and dedicated because they choose to serve in uniform, and they deserve the nation's full support.

Crisis Demands a Draft

The draft has served this nation well at various times in our history—most notably during World War II, when more than 10 million of the 16 million Americans who served in the armed forces were draftees.

We are at war again. Because we are, this should be a time of shared sacrifice by all of the people. Those who were in uniform in World War II represented a cross-section of the American people. Today we honor them as "the greatest generation" for their service and patriotism. The burdens of war are not shared generally today, however. They are, instead, borne mostly by the members of the active military and the National Guard and reservists—altogether, some two million people—and by their families.

Senator Chuck Hagel (R., Nebraska) says a draft "may become necessary" in the future. Another decorated combat veteran, Congressman Charles Rangel (D., New York) goes much further. He argues that a draft should be in place today—a move that he says would stimulate genuine patriotism and spread the burdens of military service fairly, across the entire population.

Exploring the Issues

1. Why do you think the Bush Administration has not supported calls for a new draft?

2. What effect might another military conflict—one with, for example, Iran or North Korea—have on the question of a draft?

To learn more about the debate over a draft, view "Defending America."

Face the Issues
Video Collection

Section Preview

OBJECTIVES

1. **Identify** the two types of foreign aid and describe United States foreign aid policy.
2. **Describe** the major security alliances to which the United States belongs, and summarize United States policy in the Middle East.
3. **Examine** the role, structure, and problems that face the United Nations.

WHY IT MATTERS

The United States works with other nations to keep the peace and to ensure political stability around the world. American foreign aid strengthens the economies and security of nations important to the United States. Security alliances deter aggression and the United Nations seeks to promote international peace and security.

POLITICAL DICTIONARY

★ **foreign aid**
★ **regional security alliance**
★ **UN Security Council**

Do you know this ancient saying: "Those who help others help themselves"? You will see that that maxim underlies two basic elements of present-day American foreign policy: foreign aid and security alliances.

Foreign Aid

Foreign aid—economic and military aid to other countries—has been a basic feature of American foreign policy for more than 60 years. It began with the Lend-Lease program of the early 1940s, through which the United States gave nearly $50 billion in food, munitions, and other supplies to its allies in World War II. Since then, this country has sent more than $500 billion in aid to more than 100 countries around the world.

Foreign aid became an important part of the containment policy beginning with American aid to Greece and Turkey in 1947. The United States also helped its European allies rebuild after the devastation of World War II. Under the Marshall Plan, named for its author, Secretary of State George C. Marshall, the United States poured some $12.5 billion into 16 nations in Western Europe between 1948 and 1952.

Foreign aid policy has taken several different directions over the years. Immediately after World War II, American aid was primarily economic. Since that time, however, military assistance has assumed a large role in aid policy. Until the mid-1950s, Europe received the lion's share of American help. Since then, the largest amounts have gone to nations in Asia, the Middle East, and Latin America.

On balance, most aid has been sent to those nations regarded as the most critical to the realization of this country's foreign policy objectives. Over recent years, Israel, Egypt, the Philippines, and various Latin American countries have been the major recipients of American help, both economic and military.

Most foreign aid money must be used to buy American goods and services. So, most of the billions spent for that aid amount to a

◄ The technology to provide clean water to the people in this Moroccan village was provided by foreign aid from the United States.

substantial subsidy to both business and labor in this country. The independent Agency for International Development (AID) administers most of the economic aid programs, in close cooperation with the Departments of State and Agriculture. Most military aid is channeled through the Defense Department.

Security Alliances

Over the past 60 years, the United States has constructed a network of **regional security alliances,** built on mutual defense treaties. In each of those treaties, the United States and the other countries involved have agreed to take collective action to meet aggression in a particular part of the world.

NATO

The North Atlantic Treaty, signed in 1949, established NATO, the North Atlantic Treaty Organization. The alliance was formed initially to promote the collective defense of Western Europe, particularly against the threat of Soviet aggression. Each of the now 19 member countries has agreed that "an armed attack against one or more of them in Europe or in North America shall be considered an attack against them all."

NATO was originally composed of the United States and 11 other countries: Canada, the United Kingdom, France, Italy, Portugal, the Netherlands, Belgium, Luxembourg, Denmark, Norway, and Iceland. Greece and Turkey joined the alliance in 1952, West Germany in 1955, and Spain in 1982. When East and West Germany united in 1990, the new state of Germany became a member of NATO.

With the collapse of the Soviet Union, NATO's mutual security blanket was extended to cover much of Eastern Europe. Poland, Hungary, and the Czech Republic joined NATO in 1999; and seven other one-time Soviet satellites and republics joined in 2004: Bulgaria, Estonia, Latvia, Lithuania, Romania, Slovakia, and Slovenia.

But the collapse of the Soviet Union has also suggested to some observers that NATO's purpose may have collapsed as well. The Secretary General of NATO addressed this perception in a millennium speech:

PRIMARY Sources ❝By the early 1990s, the threat of massive attack on NATO territory was gone, to the great relief of us all. In those circumstances, however, some voices have called NATO's continuing purpose into question. . . . No institution

The NATO Alliance Today

KEY
- Original NATO members
- Joined NATO in 1952
- Joined NATO in 1955
- Joined NATO in 1982
- Unified Germany joined NATO in 1990
- Joined NATO in 1999
- Joined NATO in 2004
- Former Soviet Union

Interpreting Maps This map shows when each NATO member became part of the alliance. *From which part of the world did the newest members come?* **H-SS 12.4.1**

exists for its own sake. If it does not have a useful purpose, it will wither on the vine. And yet, a decade after the end of the Cold War, NATO is more vibrant than ever . . . [and] still plays a crucial role in preserving the safety and security of all of its members. But today, that mission is being accomplished in a very different way. . . .

[A]s we enter the new Millennium, NATO is engaged in a much broader range of activities, all designed with one fundamental goal—to address proactively the security challenges which could, or already do, affect the safety or the interests of its members and their populations. 🙿

—"NATO in the 21st Century"
Secretary General Lord George Robertson

NATO was formed for defensive purposes nearly 60 years ago and—if defense includes military intervention in conflicts that may destabilize Europe and with it the prevention of humanitarian disasters—defense remains its basic charge. The most obvious example of this role is NATO's involvement in the Balkans. First in Bosnia in 1995 and then in Kosovo in 1999, NATO air and ground forces, drawn mostly from the United States, Great Britain, and Canada, brought an end to years of vicious civil war in what was once Yugoslavia. Those military interventions also put an end to the horrific campaigns of "ethnic cleansing," directed by Serbia's President Slobodan Milosevic. NATO troops continue to maintain a fragile peace in the Balkans yet today.

In mid-2003, NATO took command of the International Security Assistance Force (ISAF) in Afghanistan. That multinational force was established in late 2001, in the wake of the American-led war that ousted Afghanistan's Taliban regime. Today, ISAF's military units operate mostly in and around the capital, Kabul, while American forces continue to track down the remnants of Taliban resistance elsewhere in the country. ISAF also has taken a leading role in the rebuilding of war-shattered Afghanistan.

Other Alliances

The Rio Pact, or the Inter-American Treaty of Reciprocal Assistance, was signed in 1947. In this pact, the United States, Canada, and now 32 Latin American countries have agreed "that an

Government Online

Trade Agreements Following World War II, the United States understood that foreign aid alone would not ensure the economic recovery of its allies. They needed to sell their goods in foreign markets. That meant nations had to lower tariffs (taxes on imported goods) and ease trading rules. So, in 1947, the United States helped create the General Agreement on Tariffs and Trade (GATT), a code of conduct for international trade that is now endorsed by more than 90 countries.

The United States has increasingly used trade pacts like GATT to promote free enterprise and political stability around the world. With the backing of the United States, GATT sponsored negotiations in the 1990s that led to the World Trade Organization (WTO), a supreme governing body designed to facilitate global trade and settle international trade disputes. The United States has since extended permanent normal trade relations status to China—a prerequisite to WTO membership—and is encouraging Russia to join, too. Closer to home, the North American Free Trade Agreement (NAFTA) has all but removed tariffs among the United States, Canada, and Mexico.

Go **O**nline
PHSchool.com

Use Web Code mqd-4177 to find out more about trade agreements and organizations and for help in answering the following question: *What are the advantages and disadvantages of trade agreements for both wealthy and for developing nations?*

armed attack by any state against an American state shall be considered as an attack against all the American states." The treaty pledges those countries to the mutual peaceful settlement of all disputes. In effect, the Rio Pact is a restatement of the Monroe Doctrine.

In addition to NATO and the Rio Pact, the United States is party to several other regional security alliances. For example, the ANZUS Pact of 1951 unites Australia, New Zealand, and the United States to ensure their collective security in the Pacific region.

The Japanese Pact also dates from 1951. After six years of American military occupation, the allies of World War II (with the exception of the Soviet Union) signed a peace treaty with Japan. At the same time, the United States and Japan signed a mutual defense treaty. In return for American protection, Japan permitted the United States to maintain land, sea, and air forces in and about its territory.

The Philippines Pact was also signed in 1951. It, too, is a mutual defense agreement. The pact remains in force, but disagreements over its redrafting prompted the withdrawal of all

▲ **Division in the Middle East** In response to terrorist attacks, Israel has begun building a barrier to separate Arab communities in the West Bank from the bulk of the Israeli population.

American military forces from the Philippines in 1992. The Korean Pact, signed in 1953, pledges the United States to come to the aid of South Korea should it be attacked again.

The Taiwan Pact was in effect between the United States and Nationalist China from 1954 to 1980. When the United States and the People's Republic of China established full diplomatic relations in 1979, the United States withdrew its recognition of the Nationalist Chinese government. The United States also served the one-year notice required by the 1954 treaty to abrogate (end) the Taiwan Pact.

The Middle East

The American network of regional alliances is far-reaching, but it does not blanket the entire globe—and, most notably it does not cover the Middle East.

That area of the world is both oil-rich and conflict-ridden. America's foreign policy interests in the Middle East have, for decades, been torn in two quite opposite directions: by its long-standing support of Israel and by the critical importance of Arab oil.

The United Nations created Israel as an independent state on May 14, 1948, and the United States recognized the new Jewish state within a matter of hours. Carved out of what had been British-controlled Palestine, Israel has been in near-constant conflict with most of its Arab neighbors ever since. The day after it was born, Israel was invaded by Egypt, Jordan, Syria, Lebanon, and Iraq. The Israelis won that first Arab-Israeli war, decisively. Over the years since then, they have fought and won three other full-scale wars (in 1956, 1967, and 1973) and been engaged in countless other large and small military skirmishes with various Arab states.

The United States has been Israel's closest friend for nearly 60 years now. At the same time, however, this country has attempted to strengthen its ties with most of the Arab states in the region.

With the active involvement of President Carter, Israel and Egypt negotiated a groundbreaking peace treaty, which became effective in 1979. That agreement, the Camp David Accord, ended more than 30 years of hostilities between those two countries. Israel and Jordan signed a similar pact in 1994.

Israel and the Palestine Liberation Organization (the PLO) took a huge—but so far unfulfilled—step toward peace in 1993. In the Oslo Accords, the PLO at last recognized Israel's right to exist. Israel recognized the PLO as the legitimate agent of the Palestinian people, and it also agreed to limited Palestinian self-rule under an autonomous Palestinian Authority.

To this point, the promise of the Oslo Accords remains to be realized. Both the United States and the United Nations have sought, repeatedly, to bring the two parties together in a continuing dialogue. Despite some recent positive steps, recurring cycles of violence and reprisal continue to characterize the Israeli-Palestinian relationship.

The United Nations

You know that a fundamental change occurred in American foreign policy during and immediately after World War II. The change, a shift from isolationism to internationalism, is strikingly illustrated by this country's participation in the United Nations. Remember, the United States refused to join the League of Nations after World War I. With the end of World War II, however, the American people realized that America was a world power with worldwide interests and responsibilities.

The UN was formed at the United Nations Conference on International Organization, which met in San Francisco from April 25 to June 26, 1945. There, the representatives of 50 nations—the victorious allies of World War II—drafted the United Nations Charter.[7] The charter is a treaty among all of the UN's member-states, and it serves as the body's constitution.

The United States became the first nation to ratify the UN Charter. The Senate approved it by an overwhelming vote, 89–2, on July 24, 1945. The charter was then ratified in quick order by the other states that had taken part in the San Francisco Conference. The charter went into force on October 24, 1945. The UN held the first session of its General Assembly in London on January 10, 1946.

Charter and Organization

The charter is a lengthy document. It opens with an eloquent preamble which declares that the UN was created "to save succeeding generations from the scourge of war." The body of the document begins in Article I with a statement of the organization's purposes: the maintenance of international peace and security, the development of friendly relations between and among all nations, and the promotion of justice and cooperation in the solution of international problems.

Today the UN has 191 members. Under the charter, membership is open to those "peace-loving states" that accept the obligations of the charter and are, in the UN's judgment, able and willing to carry out those obligations. New members may be admitted by a two-thirds vote of the General Assembly, upon recommendation by the Security Council.

The charter sets forth the complicated structure of the UN. It is built around six "principal organs": the General Assembly, the Security Council, the Economic and Social Council, the Trusteeship Council, the International Court of Justice, and the Secretariat.

The General Assembly

The General Assembly has been called "the town meeting of the world." Each of the UN's members has a seat and a vote in the assembly.

The General Assembly meets once a year, normally in September. Sessions are held at the UN's permanent headquarters in New York City. The secretary-general may call special sessions, at the request of either the Security Council or a majority of UN members.

The Assembly may take up and debate any matter within the scope of the charter,[8] and it may make whatever recommendation it chooses to the Security Council, the other UN organs, and any member-state. The recommendations it makes to UN members are not legally binding on them—but these recommendations do carry weight, for they have been approved by a significant number of the governments of the world.

The Assembly elects the 10 nonpermanent members of the Security Council, the 54 members of the Economic and Social Council, and the elective members of the Trusteeship Council. In conjunction with the Security Council, the Assembly also selects the secretary-general and the 15 judges of the International Court of

---

[7]Fifty nations attended the San Francisco conference. Poland did not attend, but it did sign the charter October 15, 1945, and is considered an original member of the UN.

[8]Except those matters currently under consideration by the Security Council.

▲ *Town Meeting of the World* The flags of member nations fly outside the United Nations' headquarters in New York City.

► *Nobel Prize Winner*
Kofi Annan and the UN were awarded the Nobel Peace Prize for 2001. The secretary-general was cited especially for promoting human rights, combating AIDS, and bringing new life to an organization paralyzed by big power struggles through much of its existence.

Justice. The Assembly shares with the Security Council the power to admit, suspend, or expel members. But the Assembly alone may propose amendments to the charter.

The Security Council

The **UN Security Council** is made up of 15 members. Five—the United States, Britain, France, Russia (the Soviet Union's old seat), and China—are permanent members. The 10 non-permanent members are chosen by the General Assembly for two-year terms; they cannot be immediately reelected. The council meets in continuous session.

The Security Council bears the UN's major responsibility for maintaining international peace. It may take up any matter involving a threat to or a breach of that peace. It may adopt measures ranging from calling on the parties to settle their differences peacefully to placing economic and/or military sanctions on an offending nation. The only time the Security Council has undertaken a military operation against an aggressor came in Korea in 1950. It has, however, provided peacekeeping forces in several world trouble spots, with varying degrees of success.

On procedural questions—routine matters—decisions of the Security Council can be made by the affirmative vote of any nine members. On the more important matters—substantive questions—at least nine affirmative votes are also needed. However, a negative vote by any one of the permanent members is enough to kill any substantive resolution. Because of that veto power, the Security Council is effective only when and if the permanent members are willing to cooperate with one another.

The veto does not come into play in a situation in which one or more of the permanent members abstains (does not cast a vote). When, on June 25, 1950, the Security Council called on all UN members to aid South Korea in repelling the North Korean invasion, the Soviet delegate was boycotting sessions of the Security Council and so was not present to veto that action.

Other Important UN Bodies

The UN has several other important bodies:

1. Economic and Social Council (ECOSOC). This council is made up of 54 members elected by the General Assembly to three-year terms. It is responsible to the Assembly for carrying out the UN's many economic, cultural, educational, health, and related activities.

The ECOSOC coordinates the work of the UN's specialized agencies—14 independent international bodies that have a working relationship with the world organization:

• *The World Health Organization (WHO)* combats health problems in underdeveloped countries.

• *The International Labour Organization (ILO)* seeks to improve working conditions worldwide.

• *The International Monetary Fund (IMF)* encourages cooperation among national monetary systems and promotes international trade.

• *The International Bank for Reconstruction and Development (World Bank)* makes loans for projects in developing countries.

• *The International Fund for Agricultural Development (IFAD)* manages funds for rural projects in developing countries.

• *The Food and Agriculture Organization (FAO)* works to increase the output of farms, forests, and fisheries and food distribution and marketing throughout the world.

• *The United Nations Industrial Development Organization (UNIDO)* assists underdeveloped nations in the development of basic industry.

• *The International Civil Aviation Organization (ICAO)* promotes uniform standards for civil air traffic.

• *The International Maritime Organization (IMO)* encourages cooperation in international shipping.

• *The International Telecommunications Union (ITU)* administers international regulations for radio, telephone, and telegraph communications.

• *The Universal Postal Union (UPU)* promotes international postal cooperation.

• *The World Intellectual Property Organization (WIPO)* fosters cooperation among nations to protect literary, scientific, and artistic works.

• *The World Meteorological Organization (WMO)* coordinates national weather-related activities.

• *The United Nations Educational, Scientific, and Cultural Organization (UNESCO)* carries out a large number of programs in dozens of countries.

2. Trusteeship Council. The United Nations Charter requires each member to promote the well-being of the peoples of all "non-self-governing territories" as a "sacred trust."

3. International Court of Justice. The International Court of Justice (ICJ) is the UN's judicial arm. All members of the UN are automatically parties to the ICJ Statute.

Under certain conditions the services of the court are also available to nonmember states. A UN member may agree to accept the court's jurisdiction over cases in which it may be involved either unconditionally or with certain reservations (exceptions that may not conflict with the ICJ Statute).

The ICJ is made up of 15 judges selected for nine-year terms by the General Assembly and the Security Council. It sits in permanent session at the Peace Palace in The Hague, the Netherlands, and handles cases brought to it voluntarily by both members and nonmembers of the UN. The ICJ also advises the other UN bodies on legal questions arising out of their activities. If any party to a dispute fails to obey a judgment of the court, the other party may take that matter to the Security Council.

4. The Secretariat. The Secretariat is the civil service branch of the UN. It is headed by the secretary-general, who is elected to a five-year term by the General Assembly on the recommendation of the Security Council.

The secretary-general heads a staff of some 9,000 persons who conduct the day-to-day work of the UN. Beyond his administrative chores, the charter gives to the secretary-general this hugely important power: He may bring before the

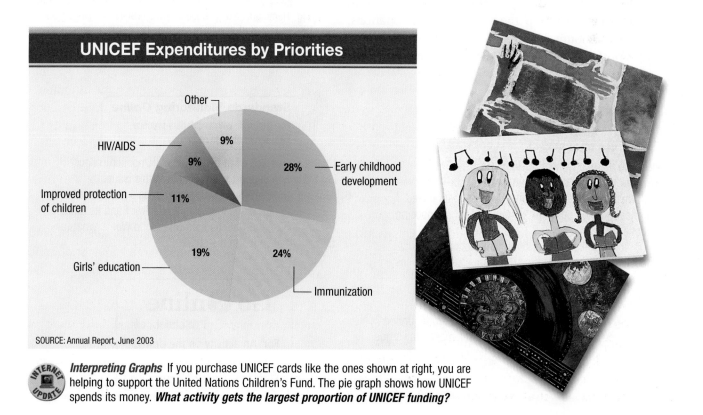

UNICEF Expenditures by Priorities

Other — 9%
HIV/AIDS — 9%
Improved protection of children — 11%
Girls' education — 19%
Immunization — 24%
Early childhood development — 28%

SOURCE: Annual Report, June 2003

Interpreting Graphs If you purchase UNICEF cards like the ones shown at right, you are helping to support the United Nations Children's Fund. The pie graph shows how UNICEF spends its money. *What activity gets the largest proportion of UNICEF funding?*

Security Council any matter he believes poses a threat to international peace and security.

The secretary-general prepares the UN's biennial budget, which must be approved by the General Assembly. For 2005–2006, the world organization's operating budget amounts to slightly more than $2.5 billion. The Assembly apportions the UN's expenses for each two-year period among its member-states.

Early on, the secretary-general was seen as little more than the UN's chief clerk. The post amounts to much more than that, however, because the seven men who have thus far held it transformed the office into a major channel for the negotiated settlement of international disputes.[9]

The Work of the UN

The purpose of the United Nations can be summed up this way: to make the world a better place. To that end, the UN is involved in a wide variety of activities.

Peacekeeping is a primary function of the United Nations. Today, some 67,000 military and civilian personnel provided by more than 100 member countries are engaged in 16 UN peacekeeping operations around the world.

The UN's specialized agencies spend some $4 billion dollars a year for economic and social programs to help the world's poorest nations. That amount does not include the monies loaned by the World Bank and the International Monetary Fund and other UN agencies that further development in poorer countries.

Health is a major concern of UN agencies. A joint program of UNICEF and WHO has immunized 80 percent of the world's children against six killer diseases. It is estimated that this program saves the lives of more than 2 million children a year. The disease smallpox plagued the world for centuries but has now been all but eliminated by a WHO-led campaign. Today, the organization coordinates a massive global effort to control the spread of AIDS.

The health of the environment is also a UN concern. United Nations environmental conventions have helped reduce acid rain, lessen marine pollution, and phase out the production of gases that are destroying the ozone layer.

Human rights has long been a priority for the United Nations. In 1948, the UN drafted the Universal Declaration of Human Rights, and it has sponsored more than 80 treaties that help protect specific rights. Various agencies of the UN work to aid and protect refugees and displaced persons, and the UN raises more than $1 billion annually for assistance to victims of war and natural disaster.

---

[9]The seven secretaries-general: Trigve Lie (Norway, 1946–1953), Dag Hammarskjold (Sweden, 1953–1961), U Thant (Burma, 1962–1972), Kurt Waldheim (Austria, 1972–1982), Javier Perez de Cuellar (Peru, 1982–1992), Boutros Boutros Ghali (Egypt, 1992–1997), and Kofi Annan (Ghana, 1997–).

Section 4 Assessment

Key Terms and Main Ideas

1. Describe the two types of **foreign aid.**
2. What are **regional security alliances?**
3. What two basic considerations have for years pulled American foreign policy in the Middle East in opposing directions?
4. (a) Describe the powers of the United Nations Security Council. (b) In practical terms, what are some limitations on its power?

Critical Thinking

5. **Recognizing Ideologies** Some people say that the United States should not distribute so much foreign aid; they argue that those funds should be spent to help the needy in the

Standards Monitoring *Online*

For: Self-quiz with vocabulary practice
Web Code: mqa-4174

United States. **(a)** What belief does this opinion reflect? **(b)** State and support your opinion on this issue.
6. **Making Comparisons** Compare America's attitude toward the League of Nations following World War I and its attitude toward the United Nations following World War II. What factors might have led to the shift?

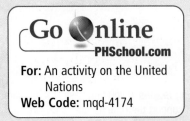

Go Online
PHSchool.com

For: An activity on the United Nations
Web Code: mqd-4174

on the Supreme Court

Should Women Be Drafted?

California — Analysis Skills HR4, HI3, HI4

When you turn 18, you will have to register for the draft—that is, if you are male. The U.S. government has never required women to register for the draft. Though today the armed forces are made up entirely of volunteers (including women as well as men), registration is required by law in case a draft should ever be needed again. Should women be included in any future draft registration?

Rostker v. Goldberg (1981)

In 1971, Robert Goldberg and several other men then subject to the draft challenged the constitutionality of the current draft law, the Military Selective Service Act of 1971. They filed suit in federal district court in Pennsylvania, claiming that the law violated the Due Process Clause of the 5th Amendment. The law unfairly discriminated against men, they argued, by forcing men but not women to register for the draft and to serve in the military.

Congress suspended the draft in 1973, and Goldberg and the others dropped their suit because the issue was no longer relevant. Two years later, the draft registration requirement was suspended altogether. In 1980, however, soon after the Soviet Union invaded Afghanistan, President Carter asked Congress for funds to reinstate draft registration. He also asked that women be included in the registration. Congress agreed to renew registration but did not include women. Goldberg then revived his suit, naming the Selective Service System's director, Bernard Rostker, as defendant.

Three days before registration was to begin, a federal district court ruled in Goldberg's favor. Rostker appealed to the Supreme Court.

Arguments for Rostker

1. Article I, Section 8 of the Constitution gives Congress the power "to raise and support armies" and "to provide and maintain a navy." Congress has broad authority to decide how to accomplish these tasks.
2. The only purpose of registration is to prepare for a possible draft of combat troops. Women, however, are excluded from combat, both by law (in the case of the navy and air force) and by military policy (in the case of the army). Thus there is no military need to include them in registration.
3. Congress decided to exclude women only after careful consideration and on the basis of military need rather than any beliefs about women's roles in society.

Arguments for Goldberg

1. The fact that a single group of people, such as men, is large enough to meet the nation's military needs does not give Congress the right to single it out for duty.
2. Women have served ably in the armed forces for decades. Since women are not excluded from the armed forces, they should not be excluded from registering for military service.
3. Excluding women from the draft reflects the outdated belief that women are less competent than men and also helps promote this belief.

Decide for Yourself

1. Review the constitutional grounds on which each side based its arguments and the specific arguments each side presented.
2. Debate the opposing viewpoints presented in this case. Which viewpoint do you favor?
3. Predict the impact of the Court's decision on the state of gender equality in the United States. (To read a summary of the Court's decision, turn to pages 799–806.)

Go Online
PHSchool.com
Use Web Code mqp-4178 to register your vote on this issue and to see how other students voted.

Political Dictionary

domestic affairs (p. 468), foreign affairs (p. 468), isolationism (p. 468), foreign policy (p. 469), right of legation (p. 470), ambassador (p. 471), diplomatic immunity (p. 471), espionage (p. 477), terrorism (p. 478), draft (p. 479), collective security (p. 485), deterrence (p. 485), cold war (p. 485), containment (p. 486), détente (p. 488), foreign aid (p. 491), regional security alliance (p. 492), UN Security Council (p. 496)

Standards Review

H-SS 12.1.5 Describe the systems of separated and shared powers, the role of organized interests (*Federalist Paper Number 10*), checks and balances (*Federalist Paper Number 51*), the importance of an independent judiciary (*Federalist Paper Number 78*), enumerated powers, rule of law, federalism, and civilian control of the military.

H-SS 12.2.4 Understand the obligations of civic-mindedness, including voting, being informed on civic issues, volunteering and performing public service, and serving in the military or alternative service.

H-SS 12.4.1 Discuss Article I of the Constitution as it relates to the legislative branch, including eligibility for office and lengths of terms of representatives and senators; election to office; the roles of the House and Senate in impeachment proceedings; the role of the vice president; the enumerated legislative powers; and the process by which a bill becomes a law.

H-SS 12.7.8 Understand the scope of presidential power and decision making through examination of case studies such as the Cuban Missile Crisis, passage of Great Society legislation, War Powers Act, Gulf War, and Bosnia.

H-SS 12.9.8 Identify the successes of relatively new democracies in Africa, Asia, and Latin America and the ideas, leaders, and general societal conditions that have launched and sustained, or failed to sustain, them.

Practicing the Vocabulary

Matching *Choose a term from the list above that best matches each description.*

1. Everything that a nation's government says and does in world affairs
2. The right to send and receive diplomatic representatives
3. The rule by which ambassadors are not held subject to the laws of the state to which they are accredited
4. The policy of making the United States and its allies so militarily strong that their very strength will discourage any attack
5. An agreement among countries in a particular part of the world to take collective action to defend each other

Word Relationships *Three of the terms in each of the following sets of terms are related. Choose the term that does not belong and explain why it does not belong.*

6. **(a)** right of legation **(b)** ambassador **(c)** diplomatic immunity **(d)** draft
7. **(a)** isolationism **(b)** foreign policy **(c)** domestic affairs **(d)** containment
8. **(a)** détente **(b)** deterrence **(c)** containment **(d)** foreign aid
9. **(a)** regional security alliance **(b)** collective security **(c)** UN Security Council **(d)** espionage

Reviewing Main Ideas

Section 1

10. Summarize how United States foreign policy moved from isolationism to internationalism.
11. Describe the main duties of the secretary of state.
12. **(a)** What is meant by the phrase "global village"? **(b)** How does this concept affect this nation's foreign policy?
13. What are the two main responsibilities of the secretary of defense?
14. Briefly describe the basic military components of the Defense Department.

Section 2

15. What is the primary function of the Central Intelligence Agency?
16. What is terrorism?
17. Give a brief description of the history of the draft in the United States.

Section 3

18. **(a)** What is the Monroe Doctrine? **(b)** How has it affected American policy from 1823 on to the present day?

19. What was the Open Door policy in China?
20. How did the two world wars change the status of the United States in the world?
21. **(a)** What was the cold war? **(b)** How did the principles of containment and deterrence shape American policy during that time?

Section 4

22. **(a)** What basic consideration guides decisions about where the United States sends foreign aid? **(b)** What countries have received the bulk of that aid in recent years?
23. Name and describe three regional security alliances to which the United States belongs. What region is not covered by any security alliance with this country?
24. **(a)** When was the United Nations formed? **(b)** What is the purpose of the UN?
25. Describe the basic organization of the United Nations.
26. **(a)** What are some major accomplishments of the UN? **(b)** What are some problems the UN faces today?

Critical Thinking Skills

Analysis Skills HR4, HI1

27. *Face the Issues* The Army claims that 90 percent of new military recruits have graduated from high school, compared with 75 percent of the general public. What does this indicate about the nature of the volunteer army?

28. *Recognizing Ideologies* The Framers of the Constitution made sure that the military would always be under the control of the nation's civilian authorities. What constitutional provisions ensure this control? What attitudes regarding the military and government does this insistence on civilian control suggest?

29. *Drawing Conclusions* The philosopher George Santayana said, "Those who cannot remember the past are condemned to repeat it." How might that statement be applied to America's return to isolationism after World War I?

30. *Identifying Central Issues* Why does the UN Charter give each of the permanent members of the Security Council the veto power?

Analyzing Political Cartoons

Using your knowledge of American government and this cartoon, answer the questions below.

"No, no. When I say this new secret weapon can slip past their defenses undetected, I'm not referring to the Russians, I'm referring to Congress."

31. What basic constitutional principle is being illustrated in this cartoon?

32. What does this cartoon suggest about the current relationship between the military and Congress, which must approve the military budget?

★ You Can Make a Difference

How much do you know about other nations? Assume that you are a new Foreign Service officer who has been assigned to work at a U.S. embassy abroad. Before you take up your new post, you need to know more about the country. Pick any nation that has been in the news recently. Then prepare a "country study" like those the State Department makes. Include information about that country's people, government, elections, economy, major problems, and political factions. If possible, find a photograph to share with the class.

Participation Activities

Analysis Skills CS1, CS4, HI1

33. *Current Events Watch* Review news reports about foreign affairs for a one-week period, and determine which current issues or events affect the United States in terms of its relationship with China, Russia, Israel, Pakistan, North Korea, and Cuba. Create a chart that lists each country and relevant current issues.

34. *Time Line Activity* Using information from the chapter, create a time line showing the major events of United States efforts to resist Soviet expansion after World War II. Be sure to include events in all parts of the world.

35. *It's Your Turn* In this chapter, you read that the United States refused to join the League of Nations following World War I, but that we did join the United Nations following World War II. Research the debate and the circumstances that surrounded these two decisions. Write a report of your findings, and compare the political climate at the time each decision was made. **(Researching a Political Issue)**

Standards Monitoring *Online*

For: Chapter 17 Self-Test **Visit:** PHSchool.com
Web Code: mqa-4175

As a final review, take the Magruder's Chapter 17 Self-Test and receive immediate feedback on your answers.
The test consists of 20 multiple-choice questions designed to test your understanding of the chapter content.

◆ The Supreme Court, Washington, D.C.

The Judicial Branch

CONSTITUTIONAL PRINCIPLES

Judicial Review The power of the courts to determine the constitutionality of the acts of government makes the Supreme Court the final authority on the meaning of the Constitution.

Limited Government The principle of limited government is often called constitutionalism—the insistence that government must be conducted according to constitutional principles, that government itself must obey the law. All of government, every public official, and every public agency at every level in this country is bound to honor the principle of limited government. The courts, however, stand as the chief defender of that principle.

Checks and Balances The Constitution guarantees the independence of the federal judiciary. Federal judges are appointed by the President, subject to confirmation by the Senate. The Constitution says that they "shall hold their Offices during good Behavior"—in effect, for an unlimited term.

The Impact on You

Have you ever been to court? Do you know what it is like to be tried for a crime, to sue someone, or to be sued by someone? Most court cases are heard in State courts across the country. The federal courts do hear hundreds of thousands of cases—both civil and criminal—each year, however.

CHAPTER 18

The Federal Court System

"It is emphatically the province and duty of the judicial department to say what the law is. . . . If two laws conflict with each other, the courts must decide on the operation of each."

—Chief Justice John Marshall (1803)

The Framers provided for a national system of courts to correct a major weakness in the Articles of Confederation. The Constitution provides for a Supreme Court and for other courts created by Congress. The federal courts operate in a dual court system, alongside the courts of each of the fifty States.

Protesters argue in front of the Supreme Court Building

Standards Preview

Go Online
PHSchool.com

For: Current Data
Web Code: mqg-5186

For: Close Up Foundation debates
Web Code: mqh-5188

SECTION 1

The National Judiciary (pp. 506–511)

★ The Framers created a national judiciary consisting of a Supreme Court and inferior courts to be created by Congress.

★ The federal courts have exclusive or concurrent and original or appellate jurisdiction over the cases they hear.

★ Federal judges are appointed by the President, subject to confirmation by the Senate.

★ Supreme Court and inferior court judges serve for life, removable only by impeachment, while special court judges serve 15-year terms; Congress sets the salaries of federal judges.

★ Federal court officers, such as magistrates, U.S. attorneys, bailiffs, and clerks, serve in administrative and judicial roles.

SECTION 2

The Inferior Courts (pp. 512–515)

★ The 94 U.S. district courts handle about 80 percent of the federal caseload; they have original jurisdiction over most federal criminal and civil cases.

★ The 12 federal appeals courts have appellate jurisdiction only.

★ The Court of International Trade hears tariff and trade cases; the Court of Appeals for the Federal Circuit has nationwide appellate jurisdiction from various federal courts.

SECTION 3

The Supreme Court (pp. 517–522)

★ All federal and most State courts have the power of judicial review, deciding the constitutionality of an act of government.

★ The U.S. Supreme Court has both original and appellate jurisdiction, but usually hears cases on appeal; the Court decides only a handful of cases each year.

★ The Supreme Court is in session from October through June; it hears oral arguments, studies written briefs, meets in conference to discuss the cases, and renders majority, concurring, and dissenting opinions.

SECTION 4

The Special Courts (pp. 524–526)

★ The U.S. government may not be sued without its consent; those who seek damages must take their cases to the U.S. Court of Federal Claims.

★ Congress has created federal courts for U.S. territories, as well as for the District of Columbia.

★ The U.S. Court of Appeals for the Armed Forces is a civilian tribunal that hears appeals of court-martial cases.

★ The U.S. Court of Appeals for Veterans Claims hears claims regarding veterans' benefits.

★ The U.S. Tax Court hears civil cases concerning tax law.

① The National Judiciary

Section Preview

OBJECTIVES

1. **Explain** why the Constitution created a national judiciary, and describe its structure.
2. **Identify** the criteria that determine whether a case is within the jurisdiction of a federal court, and compare the types of federal court jurisdiction.
3. **Outline** the process for appointing federal judges.
4. **List** the terms of office for federal judges and explain how their salaries are determined.
5. **Examine** the roles of federal court officers.

WHY IT MATTERS

The Framers of the Constitution believed in the need for a national judicial system. The Constitution outlines the structure of the federal judiciary, the jurisdiction of the courts, and the functions of federal judges.

POLITICAL DICTIONARY

★ **inferior courts**
★ **jurisdiction**
★ **exclusive jurisdiction**
★ **concurrent jurisdiction**
★ **plaintiff**
★ **defendant**
★ **original jurisdiction**
★ **appellate jurisdiction**

Joe Smith steals a brand-new sports car, a bright red convertible, in Chicago. Two days later, he is stopped for speeding in Atlanta. Where, now, will he be tried for car theft? In Illinois, where he stole the car? In Georgia, where he was caught? In point of fact, Joe may be on the verge of learning something about the federal court system—and about the Dyer Act of 1925, which makes it a federal crime to transport a stolen automobile across a State line.

Creation of a National Judiciary

During the years the Articles of Confederation were in force (1781–1789), there were no national courts and no national judiciary. The laws of the United States were interpreted and applied as each State saw fit, and sometimes not at all. Disputes between States and between persons who lived in different States were decided, if at all, by the courts in one of the States involved. Often, decisions by the courts in one State were ignored by the courts in the other States.

Alexander Hamilton spoke to the point in *The Federalist* No. 22. He described "the want of a judiciary power" as a "circumstance which crowns the defects of the Confederation." Arguing the need for a national court system, he added: "Laws are a dead letter without courts to expound and define their true meaning and operation."

The Framers created a national judiciary for the United States in a single sentence in the Constitution:

> **FROM THE Constitution** ❝*The judicial Power of the United States shall be vested in one supreme Court, and in such inferior Courts as the Congress may from time to time ordain and establish.*❞
>
> —Article III, Section 1

Congress also is given the expressed power "to constitute Tribunals inferior to the supreme Court" in Article I, Section 8, Clause 9.

A Dual Court System

Keep in mind this important point: There are *two* separate court systems in the United States.[1] On one hand, the national judiciary spans the country with its more than 100 courts. On the other hand, each of the 50 States has its own system of courts. Their numbers run well into the thousands. Most of the cases that are heard in court today are heard in State, not federal, courts.

---

[1] Federalism does not require two court systems. Article III provides that Congress "may" establish lower federal courts. At its first session, in 1789, Congress decided to construct a complete set of federal courts to parallel those of the States. In most of the world's other federal systems, the principal courts are those of the states or provinces; typically, the only significant federal court is a national court of last resort, often called the supreme court.

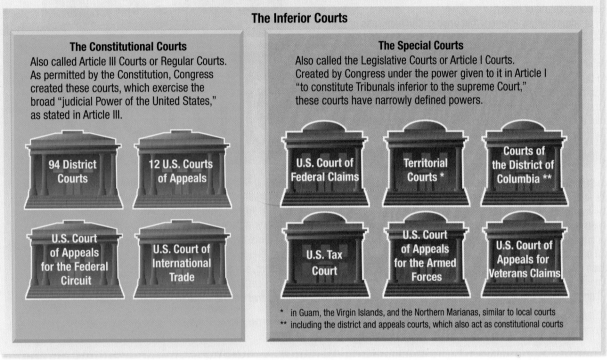

The United States Supreme Court

The Inferior Courts

The Constitutional Courts
Also called Article III Courts or Regular Courts. As permitted by the Constitution, Congress created these courts, which exercise the broad "judicial Power of the United States," as stated in Article III.

94 District Courts

12 U.S. Courts of Appeals

U.S. Court of Appeals for the Federal Circuit

U.S. Court of International Trade

The Special Courts
Also called the Legislative Courts or Article I Courts. Created by Congress under the power given to it in Article I "to constitute Tribunals inferior to the supreme Court," these courts have narrowly defined powers.

U.S. Court of Federal Claims

Territorial Courts *

Courts of the District of Columbia **

U.S. Tax Court

U.S. Court of Appeals for the Armed Forces

U.S. Court of Appeals for Veterans Claims

* in Guam, the Virgin Islands, and the Northern Marianas, similar to local courts
** including the district and appeals courts, which also act as constitutional courts

Interpreting Diagrams The Constitution created only the Supreme Court, giving Congress the power to create any lower, or "inferior," courts, as needed. **Using this diagram, compare and contrast the purpose of the constitutional courts and the special courts, as defined in the Constitution.** H-SS 12.7.7

Two Kinds of Federal Courts

The Constitution creates the Supreme Court and leaves to Congress the creation of the **inferior courts**—the lower federal courts, those beneath the Supreme Court. Over the years, Congress has created two distinct types of federal courts: (1) the constitutional courts and (2) the special courts. The diagram on this page sets out these several federal courts.

The constitutional courts are the federal courts that Congress has formed under Article III to exercise "the judicial Power of the United States." Together with the Supreme Court, they now include the courts of appeals, the district courts, and the U.S. Court of International Trade. The constitutional courts are also called the regular courts or Article III courts.

The special courts do not exercise the broad "judicial Power of the United States." Rather, they have been created by Congress to hear cases arising out of some of the expressed powers given to Congress in Article I. The special courts hear a much narrower range of cases than those that may come before the constitutional courts.

These special courts sometimes are called the legislative courts. Today, they include the U.S. Court of Appeals for the Armed Forces, the U.S. Court of Appeals for Veterans Claims, the U.S. Court of Federal Claims, the U.S. Tax Court, the various territorial courts, and the courts of the District of Columbia. You will look at the unique features of these courts later in this chapter.

Most cases in this country are heard in State courts, not federal courts. Article III, Section 2, Clause I provides that to be heard in a federal court, a case must fall into one of the two categories below.

The Subject Matter of the Case

A case falls within the jurisdiction of the federal courts if it concerns:

(1) the interpretation and application of a provision in the Constitiution or in any federal statute or treaty;

(2) a question of admiralty law (matters that arise on the high seas or navigable U.S. waters)

EXAMPLE collision at sea or crime committed aboard ship

(3) a question of maritime law (matters arising on land but directly relating to the water)

EXAMPLE a contract to deliver a ship's supplies at dockside (The Framers gave the federal courts exclusive jurisdiction in admiralty and maritime cases to ensure national supremacy in the regulation of all waterborne commerce.)

The Parties Involved in the Case

A case falls within the jurisdiction of the federal courts if any of the parties in the case is:

(1) the United States or one of its officers or agencies;

(2) an ambassador, consul, or other official representative of a foreign government;

(3) one of the 50 States suing either another State, a resident of another State, or a foreign government, or one of its subjects;

(4) a citizen of one State suing a citizen of another State;

(5) a U.S. citizen suing a foreign government or one of its subjects;

(6) a citizen of one State suing a citizen of that same State where both claim land under grants from different States.

As the table at left explains, federal courts hear cases involving certain subject matter, such as accidents at sea. (Top photo shows a Norwegian oil tanker ablaze in waters off Galveston, Texas.) Federal cases also may involve certain people, such as foreign diplomats. (Diplomatic license plates, above, are a familiar site in Washington, D.C.) *Critical Thinking Why are such cases heard in federal courts instead of State courts?*

Federal Court Jurisdiction

The constitutional courts hear most of the cases tried in the federal courts. That is, those courts have **jurisdiction** over most federal cases. Jurisdiction is defined as the authority of a court to hear (to *try* and to *decide*) a case. The term means, literally, the power "to say the law."

The Constitution gives the federal courts jurisdiction over certain cases. Article III, Section 2 provides that the federal courts may hear a case because of either (1) the subject matter or (2) the parties involved. The details of this matter are set out in the table above. See, too, the 11th Amendment, page 773.

The criteria for deciding what are federal cases may seem quite complicated, and they are. But the matter is also a reflection of federalism and, so, of the dual system of courts in this country. Stating the whole point of federal court jurisdiction in another way: All cases that are not heard by the federal courts are within the jurisdiction of the States' courts.

Types of Jurisdiction

The federal courts have several different types of jurisdiction, depending on whether or not (1) they share the power to hear the case with State courts and (2) they are the first court to hear the case.

Exclusive and Concurrent Jurisdiction

In some of the cases listed in the table above, the federal courts have **exclusive jurisdiction.** That is, those cases can be heard *only* in the federal courts. For example, a case involving an ambassador or some other official of a foreign government cannot be heard in a State court; it must be tried in a federal court. The trial of a person charged with a federal crime, or a suit involving the infringement of a patent or a copyright, or a case involving any other matter arising out of an act of Congress also falls within the exclusive jurisdiction of the federal courts.

Many cases may be tried in either a federal court or a State court, however. Then the federal and State courts have **concurrent jurisdiction;**

they share the power to hear those cases. Disputes involving citizens of different States are fairly common examples of this type of case. Such cases are known in the law as cases in diverse citizenship.[2]

Congress has provided that the federal district courts may hear cases of diverse citizenship only if the amount of money involved in a case is more than $75,000. In such cases the **plaintiff**—the person who files suit—may bring the case in the proper State or federal court, as he or she chooses. If the case is brought before the State court, the **defendant**—the person whom the complaint is against—can have the trial moved, under certain circumstances, to the federal district court.

Original and Appellate Jurisdiction

A court in which a case is first heard is said to have **original jurisdiction** over that case. A court that hears a case on appeal from a lower court has **appellate jurisdiction** over that case. The higher court—the appellate court—may uphold, overrule, or in some way modify the decision appealed from the lower court.[3]

In the federal court system, the district courts have only original jurisdiction, and the courts of appeals have only appellate jurisdiction. The Supreme Court exercises both original and appellate jurisdiction.

Appointment of Judges

The manner in which federal judges are chosen, the terms for which they serve, and even the salaries they are paid are vital parts of the Constitution's design of an independent judicial branch. The Constitution declares that the President

> **FROM THE Constitution** *shall nominate, and by and with the Advice and Consent of the Senate, shall appoint . . . Judges of the supreme Court . . .*
> —Article II, Section II, Clause 2

---

[2]The major reason that cases of diverse citizenship may be heard in federal courts is to provide a neutral forum to settle the disputes involved. That reason reflects an early fear that State courts (and their juries) might be prejudiced against "foreigners," residents of other States. There seems little likelihood of such bias today.

[3]Appellate comes from the Latin word *appellare*, meaning "to speak to, to call upon, to appeal to."

Congress has provided the same procedure for the selection of all other federal judges.

The Senate has a major part in the selection of all federal judges, and in particular those who sit in the nation's 94 district courts. In effect, the Constitution says that the President can name to the federal bench anyone the Senate will confirm. Recall the practice of senatorial courtesy. It gives great weight to the wishes of the senators from a State in which a federal judge is to serve. In short, that unwritten rule means that the President almost always selects someone the senators from the State recommend.

Most federal judges are drawn from the ranks of leading attorneys, legal scholars and law school professors, former members of Congress, and State court judges. A President applies the same sorts of considerations to his judicial selections as he does to his other appointments.

From George Washington's day, Presidents have looked to their own political party in making judicial appointments. Republican Presidents regularly choose Republicans; Democrats usually pick Democrats. Every President knows that the judges he appoints may serve for decades. So the chief executive regularly looks for judges who tend to agree with his own legal, political, economic, and social views.

The President approaches the selection of a new Supreme Court justice with the greatest care. Commenting on his appointment of the late Chief Justice William Rehnquist in 1971, then President Richard Nixon observed: "Presidents come and go, but the Supreme Court goes on forever. [Its members] make decisions which will affect your lives and the lives of your children for generations to come."

Judicial philosophy—and, in particular, the concepts of judicial restraint and judicial activism—have a major impact on the judicial selection process. All federal judges regularly make decisions in which they must interpret and apply provisions in the Constitution and in acts of Congress. They often decide questions of public policy, and, in doing so, they inevitably shape public policy.

The proponents of *judicial restraint* believe that judges should always try to decide cases on the basis of (1) the original intent of those

The National Judiciary

Court	Created	Number of Courts	Number of Judges	Term of Judges
Supreme Court	1789	1	9	Life
District Court	1789	94	677	Life
Court of Appeals	1891	12	179	Life
Trade Court	1926	1	9	Life
Court of Appeals for the Armed Forces	1950	1	5	15 years
Tax Court	1969	1	19	15 years
Court of Appeals for the Federal Circuit	1982	1	12	Life
Court of Federal Claims	1982	1	16	15 years
Court of Appeals for Veterans Claims	1988	1	7	15 years

Interpreting Tables This table provides key statistics for the major U.S. federal courts. *Why do you think some judgeships are for life and others are for only 15 years?* H-SS 12.4.5

who wrote the Constitution or enacted the statute and (2) precedent—that is, in line with previous decisions in similar cases. They say that elected legislators, not appointed judges, should make law.

Commentators often cite many of the decisions of the Rehnquist Court to illustrate judicial restraint—that is, decisions handed down by the Supreme Court over the years (1986–2005) in which the late William Rehnquist served as Chief Justice.

Those who support *judicial activism* think that judges should act more boldly. They argue that the law should be interpreted and applied in the light of ongoing changes in conditions and values—especially in cases involving civil rights and social welfare issues. Many decisions of the Warren Court, during Chief Justice Earl Warren's tenure (1953–1969) are regularly seen as models of judicial activism.

The President and his closest political and legal aides, especially the attorney general, take the lead in selecting federal judges, of course. Major roles also are played regularly by influential senators (notably those from the nominee's home State); by the President's allies and supporters in the legal profession; and by various other important personalities in the President's political party.

Terms and Pay of Judges

Article III, Section 1 of the Constitution reads, in part: "The Judges, both of the supreme and inferior Courts, shall hold their Offices during good Behavior. . . . " This means that the judges of the constitutional courts are appointed for life—until they resign, retire, or die in office. They may be removed only through the impeachment process. Only 13 federal judges have ever been impeached. Of them, seven were convicted and removed by the Senate, including three in the recent past.[4] The grant of what amounts to life tenure for most judges ensures the independence of the federal judiciary.

The judges who sit in the special courts are not appointed for life. Those who hear cases in the U.S. Court of Federal Claims, the U.S. Court of Appeals for the Armed Forces, the U.S. Tax Court, and the U.S. Court of Appeals for Veterans Claims serve 15-year terms. In the District of Columbia, Superior Court judges are chosen for four-year terms; those who sit on the District's Court of Appeals are chosen for a period of eight years.

The Constitution also declares that federal judges

FROM THE Constitution

"shall, at stated Times, receive for their Services, a Compensation, which shall not be diminished during their Continuance in Office."

—Article III, Section 1

Congress sets the salaries of all federal judges and has provided a generous retirement

---

[4] The judges removed from office were John Pickering of the district court in New Hampshire, for judicial misconduct and drunkenness (1804); West H. Humphreys of the district court in Tennessee, for disloyalty (1862); Robert W. Archbald of the old Commerce Court, for improper relations with litigants (1913); Halsted L. Ritter of the district court in Florida, on several counts of judicial misconduct (1936); Harry E. Claiborne of the district court in Nevada, for filing false income tax returns (1986); Alcee Hastings of the district court in Florida, on charges of bribery and false testimony (1989); and Walter Nixon of the district court in Mississippi, for perjury (1989).

Alcee Hastings was removed in 1989 even though earlier he had been acquitted of the bribery charge. Hastings won election to the House of Representatives in 1992. Four other federal judges were impeached by the House but acquitted in the Senate. Two other district court judges, impeached by the House, resigned and so avoided a Senate trial.

arrangement for them. They may retire at age 70, and if they have served for at least 10 years, receive full salary for the rest of their lives. Or, they may retire at full salary at age 65, after at least 15 years of service. The Chief Justice may call any retired judge back to temporary duty in a lower federal court at any time.

Court Officers

Today, federal judges have little involvement in the day-to-day administrative operations of the courts over which they preside. Their primary mission is to hear and decide cases. The support services they need in order to perform that task are provided by a clerk, several deputy clerks, bailiffs, court reporters and stenographers, probation officers, and other court personnel.

The judges of each of the 94 district courts appoint one or more United States magistrates. There are now more than 400 of these magistrates. They are appointed to eight-year terms and handle a number of legal matters once dealt with by the judges themselves. They issue warrants of arrest and often hear evidence to decide whether or not a person who has been arrested on a federal charge should be held for action by a grand jury. They also set bail in federal criminal cases, and even have the power to try those who are charged with certain minor offenses.

Each federal judicial district also has at least one bankruptcy judge. They handle bankruptcy cases under the direction of the district court to which they are assigned.[5] There are now some 350 bankruptcy judges, all of them appointed to 14-year terms by the judges of each federal court of appeals. The President and the Senate appoint a United States attorney for each federal judicial district. The U.S. attorneys and their many deputies are the government's prosecutors. They work closely with the FBI and other law enforcement agencies, and bring to trial those persons charged with federal crimes. They also represent the United States in all civil actions brought by or against the government in their districts.

The President and Senate also select a United States marshal to serve each of the district courts. These marshals, and their several deputy U.S. marshals, perform duties much like those of a county sheriff. They make arrests in federal criminal cases, hold accused persons in custody, secure jurors, serve legal papers, keep order in courtrooms, and execute court orders and decisions. They also respond to such emergency situations as riots, mob violence, and other civil disturbances, as well as terrorist incidents. All United States attorneys and marshals are appointed to four-year terms—and members of the Senate are usually closely involved in their selections.

---

[5]Recall that bankruptcy is a legal proceeding in which a debtor's assets are distributed among those to whom the bankrupt person, business, or other organization owes money. Although some bankruptcy cases are heard in State courts, nearly all of them fall within the jurisdiction of the federal district courts.

Section 1 Assessment

Key Terms and Main Ideas

1. Why were the **inferior courts** created?
2. (a) What is **jurisdiction**? (b) Explain the difference between **exclusive jurisdiction** and **concurrent jurisdiction**.
3. Describe the roles of **plaintiff** and **defendant**.
4. (a) Contrast **original jurisdiction** and **appellate jurisdiction**. (b) What kind of jurisdiction does the Supreme Court have?

Critical Thinking

5. **Drawing Conclusions** What qualifications do you think the President should consider in the appointment of a federal judge?

6. **Expressing Problems Clearly** Explain why you would favor or oppose constitutional amendments providing for (a) the popular election of federal judges and (b) a fixed term of office for federal judges.

·2· *The Inferior Courts*

Section Preview

OBJECTIVES

1. **Describe** the structure and jurisdiction of the federal district courts.
2. **Describe** the structure and jurisdiction of the federal courts of appeals.
3. **Describe** the structure and jurisdiction of the two other constitutional courts.

WHY IT MATTERS

The inferior courts, those beneath the Supreme Court, are the core of the federal judicial system, hearing nearly all of the cases tried in federal courts. They hear cases, both originally and on appeal, and both criminal and civil cases.

POLITICAL DICTIONARY

★ **criminal case**
★ **civil case**
★ **docket**

You know that the particular meaning of a word often depends on the context—the setting—in which it is used. Thus, *pitch* can be either a baseball or a musical term; or it can refer to the setting up of a tent, or to a high-pressure sales talk.

The word *inferior* has various meanings, as well. Here it describes the lower federal courts, those courts created by Congress to function beneath the Supreme Court. The inferior courts handle most of the cases tried in the federal courts.

The District Courts

The United States district courts are the federal trial courts. Their 677 judges handle more than 300,000 cases a year, about 80 percent of the federal caseload. The district courts were created by Congress in the Judiciary Act of 1789. There are now 94 of them.

Federal Judicial Districts

The fifty States are divided into 89 federal judicial districts, and there are also federal district courts for Washington, D.C., Puerto Rico, the Virgin Islands, Guam, and the Northern Mariana Islands. Each State forms at least one judicial district. Some are divided into two or more districts, however—usually because of the larger amount of judicial business there. At least two judges are assigned to each district, but many districts have several. Thus, New York is divided into four judicial districts; one of them,

the United States Judicial District for Southern New York, now has 28 judges.

Cases tried in the district courts are most often heard by a single judge. However, certain cases may be heard by a three-judge panel.[6]

District Court Jurisdiction

The district courts have original jurisdiction over most cases that are heard in the federal courts (except those few cases that fall within the original jurisdiction of the United States Supreme Court and those cases that are heard by the U.S. Court of International Trade or by one of the special courts). Thus, these district courts are the principal trial courts in the federal court system.

---

[6]Congress has directed that three-judge panels hear certain cases. Chiefly, these are cases that involve congressional districting or State legislative apportionment questions, those arising under the Civil Rights Act of 1964 or the Voting Rights Acts of 1965, 1970, 1975, and 1982, and certain antitrust actions.

Two little-known multi-judge panels play a key role in ongoing efforts to combat terrorism in this country and abroad. Both are shrouded in secrecy. (1) The Foreign Intelligence Surveillance Court, created by Congress in 1978. This tribunal is composed of 11 federal district court judges, appointed to seven-year terms by the Chief Justice of the United States. The court, which meets in secret, has the power to issue secret search warrants—court orders that allow the FBI, the CIA, and other federal law enforcement agencies to conduct covert surveillance of persons suspected of being spies or members of terrorist organizations. (2) The Alien Terrorist Removal Court, created by Congress in 1996. It is made up of five district court judges, appointed by the Chief Justice to five-year terms. This court has the power to decide whether those persons identified as "alien terrorists" by the Attorney General of the United States should be expelled from this country.

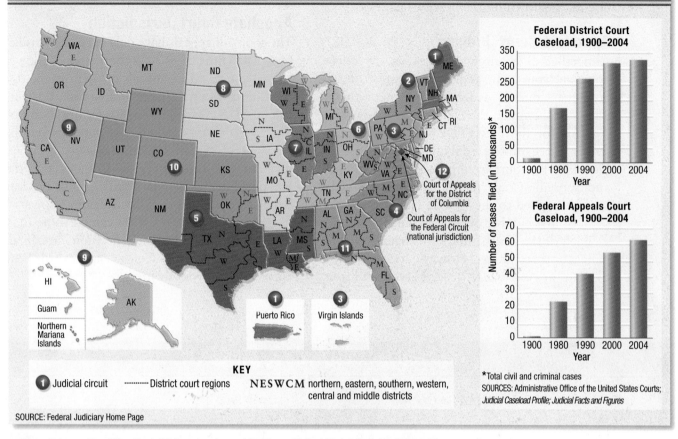

Federal District Court Caseload, 1900–2004

Federal Appeals Court Caseload, 1900–2004

Court of Appeals for the District of Columbia

Court of Appeals for the Federal Circuit (national jurisdiction)

KEY

1 Judicial circuit   ·········· District court regions   **NESWCM** northern, eastern, southern, western, central and middle districts

*Total civil and criminal cases
SOURCES: Administrative Office of the United States Courts; *Judicial Caseload Profile; Judicial Facts and Figures*

SOURCE: Federal Judiciary Home Page

Interpreting Maps Each State comprises at least one United States judicial district. The nation is divided into twelve judicial circuits, as shown on the map. The graphs show increasing federal caseloads. ***Explain how this increase relates to the trend in Congress toward designating more crimes as federal offenses.*** **H-SS 12.7.7**

The district courts hear a wide range of both **criminal cases** and **civil cases.** A criminal case, in the federal courts, is one in which a defendant is tried for committing some action that Congress has declared by law to be a federal crime. A federal civil case involves some noncriminal matter, such as a dispute over the terms of a contract or a claim of patent infringement.[7] The district courts try criminal cases ranging from bank robbery and mail fraud to counterfeiting and tax evasion. They hear civil cases arising under bankruptcy, postal, tax, public lands, civil rights, and other laws of the United States. The district courts are the only federal courts that regularly use grand juries to indict defendants and petit juries to try defendants.

Most of the decisions made in the 94 federal district courts are final. However, some cases are appealed to the court of appeals in that judicial circuit or, in a few instances, directly to the Supreme Court.

The Courts of Appeals

The courts of appeals were created by Congress in 1891. They were established as "gatekeepers" to relieve the Supreme Court of much of the burden of hearing appeals from the district courts. Those appeals had become so numerous that the Supreme Court was then three years behind its **docket**—its list of cases to be heard.

There are now 12 courts of appeals in the judicial system.[8] The United States is divided into

▲ Seal of the U.S. Court of Appeals for the Fifth Circuit

---

[7]The United States is always a party to a federal criminal case, as the prosecutor. Most civil cases involve private parties; but here, too, the United States may be a litigant, as either plaintiff or defendant.

[8]These tribunals were originally known as the circuit courts of appeals. Before 1891, Supreme Court justices "rode circuit" to hear appeals from the district courts. Congress renamed these courts in 1948, but they still are often called the circuit courts.

12 judicial circuits, including the District of Columbia, with one court of appeals for each circuit, as shown on the previous page.

Appellate Court Judges

Altogether, 179 circuit judges sit on these appellate courts. In addition, a justice of the Supreme Court is assigned to each of them. Take, for example, the United States Court of Appeals for the Eleventh Circuit. The circuit covers three States: Alabama, Georgia, and Florida. The court is composed of 12 judges, and Supreme Court Justice Anthony Kennedy is also assigned to the circuit. The judges hold sessions in a number of cities within the circuit.

Each of the courts of appeals usually sits in panels of three judges. However, occasionally, to hear an important case, a court will sit *en banc*—that is, with all of the judges for that circuit participating.

Appellate Court Jurisdiction

The courts of appeals have only appellate jurisdiction. They hear cases on appeal from the lower federal courts. Most appeals come from the district courts within their circuits, but some do come from the U.S. Tax Court and the territorial courts. The courts of appeals also hear appeals from the decisions of several federal regulatory agencies, such as the Federal Trade Commission, the National Labor Relations Board, and the Nuclear Regulatory Commission. (See diagram below.)

The courts of appeals now handle more than 55,000 cases a year. Their decisions are final, unless the Supreme Court chooses to hear appeals taken from them.

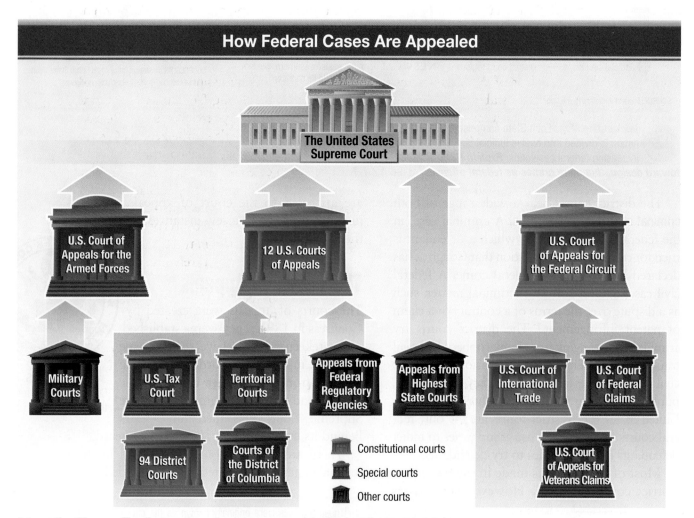

How Federal Cases Are Appealed

The United States Supreme Court

U.S. Court of Appeals for the Armed Forces

12 U.S. Courts of Appeals

U.S. Court of Appeals for the Federal Circuit

Military Courts

U.S. Tax Court

Territorial Courts

Appeals from Federal Regulatory Agencies

Appeals from Highest State Courts

U.S. Court of International Trade

U.S. Court of Federal Claims

94 District Courts

Courts of the District of Columbia

U.S. Court of Appeals for Veterans Claims

Constitutional courts
Special courts
Other courts

Interpreting Diagrams The diagram above shows how cases originating in various courts can be appealed to the U.S. Supreme Court. ***From what you have read so far, what do you think are the two or three inferior courts that handle the largest proportion of cases in the country?*** **H-SS 12.7.7**

Other Constitutional Courts

Congress has created two other Article III courts. They are the U.S. Court of International Trade and the U.S. Court of Appeals for the Federal Circuit.

The Court of International Trade

The Trade Court was created originally in 1890 as the Board of United States General Appraisers. That body became the Court of Customs in 1926, and Congress restructured and renamed that court in 1980.

The Court of International Trade now has nine judges, one of whom is its chief judge. It hears civil cases arising out of tariff and other trade-related laws. The judges of the Trade Court sit in panels of three and often hold trials at such major ports as New Orleans, San Francisco, Boston, and New York. Appeals from decisions of the Trade Court are taken to the Court of Appeals for the Federal Circuit.

The Court of Appeals for the Federal Circuit

Congress created the Court of Appeals for the Federal Circuit in 1982. It established the new court to centralize, and so speed up, the handling of appeals in certain kinds of civil cases. This appellate court, unlike the 12 other federal courts of appeals, hears cases from all across the country. That is, it has a nationwide jurisdiction.

The Court of Appeals for the Federal Circuit hears appeals from several different courts. Many of its cases come from the U.S. Court of International Trade, and others from the U.S. Court of

Interpreting Political Cartoons This 1885 cartoon shows a Supreme Court swamped by appeals. **(a)** *Describe what is going on in this scene.* **(b)** *What is the man in the foreground doing?* **(c)** *What point is the artist making?*

Federal Claims and the U.S. Court of Appeals for Veterans Claims, two of the special courts. It also hears appeals in patent, trademark, and copyright cases coming from the 94 district courts around the country. Then, too, it takes cases that arise out of administrative rulings made by the International Trade Commission, the Patent and Trademark Office in the Department of Commerce, and the Merit Systems Protection Board.

The Court of Appeals for the Federal Circuit has 12 judges. It sits in panels of three or more judges on each case and also may hear or rehear a case *en banc*. The court usually hears cases in Washington, D.C., but it may also do so wherever any of the other federal courts of appeals sits. Appeals from the court may be taken to the Supreme Court, but they rarely are.

Section 2 Assessment

Key Terms and Main Ideas

1. What is the difference between a **criminal case** and a **civil case**?
2. What action did Congress take in the late 1800s to relieve the Supreme Court's overloaded **docket**?
3. Summarize the main purpose of the federal district courts and the federal courts of appeals.

Critical Thinking

4. **Drawing Conclusions** Most of the courts in the federal judiciary are appellate courts. What does this fact suggest about the American judicial process?

Standards Monitoring *Online*
For: Self-quiz with vocabulary practice
Web Code: mqa-5182

5. **Expressing Problems Clearly** What kind of problems might have prompted Congress to create an entirely new type of appellate court in 1982?

Go Online PHSchool.com
For: An activity on political philosophers
Web Code: mqd-5182

Choosing Federal Judges

Analysis Skills HR4, HI3

The Constitution says the President "shall nominate, and by and with the Advice and Consent of the Senate, shall appoint. . . Judges of the supreme Court." Although most Presidents choose judges who agree with their policy viewpoints, Nadine Strossen, President of the American Civil Liberties Union, argues that the Senate should play a more assertive role in the judicial selection process.

The Constitution's appointment clause . . . clearly confers upon the president unfettered [unlimited] discretion to name federal judges of his choosing, subject to the Senate's "advice and consent." It specifies no minimal criteria or essential qualifications for such judges . . . and by failing to set out any limits on that power [to nominate judges], the constitutional text indicates that the president's judicial nominations could also appropriately take the nominees' views into account.

President George W. Bush nominated John Roberts to become the nation's Chief Justice in 2005.

The Constitution is as silent about criteria for the Senate's confirmation decision as it is about those for the president's initial nomination. Accordingly, the text assigns the Senate as open-ended a discretion in the confirmation process as it assigns the president in the nomination process. In exercising that discretion, it is as appropriate for the Senate to consider a candidate's constitutional and judicial philosophy as it is for the president.

The Senate's concurrent role in the judicial selection process is also confirmed by the proceedings at the 1787 Constitutional Convention which led to the adoption of the appointment clause. Indeed, until the final days of the Convention, the proposed constitutional text gave the Senate—or, in some versions, the Senate and the House of Representatives—the sole power to appoint federal judges, including Supreme Court Justices.

In contrast, the delegates roundly rejected all attempts to confer this power on the president alone. Referring to the significant separation of powers concerns implicated by the judicial appointment process, Virginia delegate George Mason said that an exclusively presidential appointment power constituted "a dangerous prerogative" that "might even give him an influence over the Judiciary Department itself."

Only near the end of the Convention did the delegates agree to give the president any role at all in the judicial selection process, by adopting the current appointment clause. The president and the Senate should have a "partnership" relationship in the judicial appointment process. Structural aspects of the Constitution dictate that, in fulfilling their respective roles in the process, each of these partners should consider candidates' constitutional and judicial philosophies.

Analyzing Primary Sources

1. According to the author, how did the Founding Fathers feel about giving the President the power to appoint federal judges?
2. How does the nomination process reflect the principle of separation of powers?
3. Many people believe that a judicial nominee should not be pressured to give his or her opinions on Constitutional issues before the nominee takes a seat as a judge. How would the author respond?

③ The Supreme Court

Section Preview

OBJECTIVES

1. **Define** the concept of judicial review.
2. **Outline** the scope of the Supreme Court's jurisdiction.
3. **Examine** how cases reach the Supreme Court.
4. **Summarize** the way the Court operates.

WHY IT MATTERS

The Supreme Court, the only court created by the Constitution, is the final authority on questions of federal law. It enjoys broad jurisdiction but usually limits its caseload to appeals involving constitutional questions and interpretations of federal law.

POLITICAL DICTIONARY

★ **writ of certiorari**
★ **certificate**
★ **majority opinion**
★ **precedent**
★ **concurring opinion**
★ **dissenting opinion**

The eagle, the flag, Uncle Sam—you almost certainly recognize these symbols. They are used widely to represent the United States. You probably also know the symbol for justice: the blindfolded woman holding a balanced scale. She represents what is perhaps this nation's loftiest goal: equal justice for all. Indeed, those words are chiseled in marble above the entrance to the Supreme Court building in Washington, D.C.

The Supreme Court of the United States is the only court specifically created by the Constitution, in Article III, Section 1. The Court is made up of the Chief Justice of the United States, whose office is also established by the Constitution,[9] and eight associate justices.[10] The Framers quite purposely placed the Court on an equal plane with the President and Congress. As the highest court in the land, the Supreme Court stands as the court of last resort in all questions of federal law. That is, it is the final authority in any case involving any question arising under the Constitution, an act of Congress, or a treaty of the United States.

Judicial Review

Remember, most courts in this country, both federal and State, may exercise the critically important power of judicial review. They have the extraordinary power to decide the constitutionality of an act of government, whether executive, legislative, or judicial. The ultimate exercise of that power rests with the Supreme

Court of the United States. That single fact makes the Supreme Court the final authority on the meaning of the Constitution.

The Constitution does not in so many words provide for the power of judicial review. Still, there is little doubt that the Framers intended

---

[9]Article I, Section 3, Clause 6.
[10]Congress sets the number of associate justices and thus the size of the Supreme Court. The Judiciary Act of 1789 created a Court of six justices, including the Chief Justice. Its size was reduced to five members in 1801 but increased to seven in 1807, to nine in 1837, and to 10 in 1863. It was reduced to seven in 1866 and raised to its present size of nine in 1869.

▲ A scale is often used to represent justice.

that the federal courts—and, in particular, the Supreme Court—should have this power.[11]

Marbury v. Madison

The Court first asserted its power of judicial review in the classic case of *Marbury* v. *Madison* in 1803.[12] The case arose in the aftermath of the stormy elections of 1800. Thomas Jefferson and his Democratic-Republicans had won the presidency and control of both houses of Congress. The outgoing Federalists, stung by their defeat, then tried to pack the judiciary with loyal party members. Congress created several new federal judgeships in the early weeks of 1801; President John Adams quickly filled those posts with Federalists.

William Marbury had been appointed a justice of the peace for the District of Columbia. The Senate had confirmed his appointment and, late on the night of March 3, 1801, President Adams signed the commissions of office for Marbury and for a number of other new judges. The next day Jefferson became the President, and discovered that Marbury's commission and several others had not yet been delivered.

Angered by the Federalists' attempted court-packing, Jefferson at once told James Madison, the new secretary of state, not to deliver those commissions to the "midnight justices." William Marbury then went to the Supreme Court, seeking a writ of mandamus[13] to force delivery.

Marbury based his suit on a provision of the Judiciary Act of 1789, in which Congress had created the federal court system. That law gave the Supreme Court the right to hear such suits in its original jurisdiction (not on appeal from a lower court).

[11]See Article III, Section 2, setting out the Court's jurisdiction, and Article VI, Section 2, the Supremacy Clause.

[12]It is often mistakenly said that the Court first exercised the power in this case, but in fact the Court did so at least as early as *Hylton* v. *United States* in 1796. In that case it upheld the constitutionality of a tax Congress had laid on carriages.

[13]A writ of mandamus is a court order compelling a government officer to perform an act which that officer has a clear legal duty to perform.

An Early Supreme Court Drama: *Marbury* v. *Madison*

The Players

John Adams, outgoing Federalist President of the United States

Thomas Jefferson, incoming Democratic-Republican President of the United States

James Madison, incoming secretary of state

William Marbury, appointed a justice of the peace for the District of Columbia

John Marshall, Chief Justice of the United States Supreme Court

The Case

1. The night before leaving office, Adams signs several judicial commissions.
2. Angered by Adams' actions, Jefferson orders Madison to withhold any commissions not yet delivered.
3. Hoping to force Jefferson to give him the judgeship, Marbury files suit in the Supreme Court. He argues that the Judiciary Act of 1789 allows him to take his case directly to the high court.

The Decision

Marshall, writing for a unanimous court, declares that the Judiciary Act violates Article III, Section 2 and is therefore unconstitutional. Marbury loses, having based his case on an unconstitutional law.

The Impact

The case established the Supreme Court's power of judicial review—its power to determine the constitutionality of a governmental action. The power extends to the actions of all governments in the United States—national, State and local. The Court's decision in *Marbury* assured the place of the judicial branch in the system of separation of powers.

Interpreting Charts In the landmark case *Marbury* v. *Madison,* the Supreme Court ruled against William Marbury because he had based his case on a part of the Judiciary Act of 1789, which was found to be in conflict with the Constitution. ***How did the Court's decision affect the role of the judicial branch in our system of government?*** H-SS 12.5.3

In a unanimous opinion written by Chief Justice John Marshall, the Court refused Marbury's request.[14] It did so because it found the section of the Judiciary Act on which Marbury had based his case to be in conflict with the Constitution and, therefore, void. Specifically, it found the statute in conflict with the section of the Constitution that reads:

 FROM THE Constitution *"In all Cases affecting Ambassadors, other public Ministers and Consuls, and those in which a State shall be Party, the supreme Court shall have original Jurisdiction. In all the other Cases before mentioned, the supreme Court shall have appellate Jurisdiction. . . ."*
—Article III, Section 2, Clause 2

Marshall's powerful opinion was based on three propositions. First, the Constitution is, by its own terms, the supreme law of the land. Second, all legislative acts and other actions of government are subordinate (inferior) to the supreme law and cannot be allowed to conflict with it. Third, judges are sworn to enforce the provisions of the Constitution, and therefore must refuse to enforce any government action they find to be in conflict with it.

The Effects of *Marbury*

The impact of the Court's decision goes far beyond the fate of an obscure individual named William Marbury. In this decision, Chief Justice Marshall claimed for the Supreme Court the right to declare acts of Congress unconstitutional, and so laid the foundation for the judicial branch's key role in the development of the American system of government.

The Court has used its power of judicial review in thousands of cases since 1803. Usually it has upheld the constitutionality of federal and State actions.

The dramatic and often far-reaching effects of the Supreme Court's exercise of the power of

---

[14]Marshall was appointed Chief Justice by President John Adams, and he took office on January 31, 1801. He served in the post for 34 years, until his death on July 6, 1835. He also served as Adams's secretary of state from May 13, 1800, to March 4, 1801. Thus, he served simultaneously as secretary of state and Chief Justice for more than a month at the end of the Adams administration. What is more, he was the secretary of state who had failed to deliver Marbury's commission in a timely fashion.

Voices on Government

David Souter was named a Supreme Court justice by President George H. W. Bush in 1990. From his experience as New Hampshire attorney general and a State court judge, Souter knew that judges' decisions are more than abstract exercises. Here are his thoughtful comments on the point:

Whether we are on a trial court or an appellate court, at the end of our task some human being is going to be affected. . . . If indeed we are going to be trial judges, whose rulings will affect the lives of other people and who are going to change their lives by what we do, we had better use every power of our minds and our hearts and our beings to get those rulings right.

Evaluating the Quotation

Think of an issue that reflects the "human" effects of court decisions that Justice Souter refers to. In what ways did a court decision affect the daily lives of Americans?

---

judicial review tends to overshadow much of its other work. Each year it hears dozens of cases in which questions of constitutionality are not raised, but in which federal law is interpreted and applied. Thus, many of the more important statutes that Congress has passed have been brought to the Supreme Court time and again for decision. So, too, have many of the lesser ones. In interpreting those laws and applying them to specific situations, the Court has had a real impact on both their meaning and their effect.

Supreme Court Jurisdiction

The Supreme Court has both original and appellate jurisdiction. Most of its cases, however, come on appeal—from the lower federal courts and from the highest State courts.

Article III, Section 2 of the Constitution spells out two classes of cases that may be heard by the High Court in its original jurisdiction: (1) those to which a State is a party and (2) those affecting ambassadors, other public ministers, and consuls.

Congress cannot enlarge on this constitutional grant of original jurisdiction. Recall, that

► No Anonymous Tips
In *Florida* v. *J.L.*, 2000, the Supreme Court ruled that under ordinary circumstances, an anonymous tip to police about a concealed firearm was not sufficient to prompt a legal "stop and frisk" search.

is what the Court held in *Marbury*. If Congress could do so, it would in effect be amending the Constitution. Congress can implement the constitutional provision, however, and it has done so. It has provided that the Court shall have original and exclusive jurisdiction over (1) all controversies involving two or more States, and (2) all cases brought against ambassadors or other public ministers, but not consuls.

The Court may choose to take original jurisdiction over any other case covered by the broad wording in Article III, Section 2 of the Constitution. Almost without exception, however, those cases are tried in the lower courts. The Supreme

Court hears only a very small number of cases in its original jurisdiction—in fact, only a case or two each term.

How Cases Reach the Court

Some 8,000 cases are now appealed to the Supreme Court each year. Of these, the Court accepts only a few hundred for decision. In most cases, petitions for review are denied, usually because most of the justices agree with the decision of the lower court or believe that the case involves no significant point of law. The Court selects those cases that it does hear according to "the rule of four": At least four of its nine justices must agree that a case should be put on the Court's docket.

More than half the cases decided by the Court are disposed of in brief orders. For example, an order may remand (return) a case to a lower court for reconsideration in the light of some other recent and related case decided by the High Court. All told, the Court decides, after hearing arguments and with full opinions, fewer than 100 cases a year.

Most cases reach the Supreme Court by **writ of certiorari** (from the Latin, meaning "to be made more certain"). This writ is an order by the Court directing a lower court to send up the record in a given case for its review. Either party

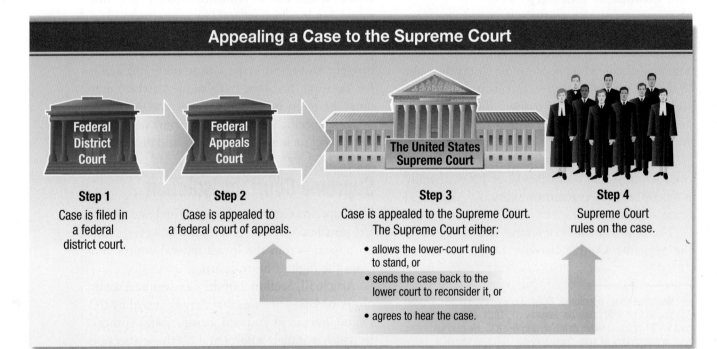

Appealing a Case to the Supreme Court

Federal District Court	Federal Appeals Court	The United States Supreme Court	
Step 1	**Step 2**	**Step 3**	**Step 4**
Case is filed in a federal district court.	Case is appealed to a federal court of appeals.	Case is appealed to the Supreme Court. The Supreme Court either:	Supreme Court rules on the case.

• allows the lower-court ruling to stand, or
• sends the case back to the lower court to reconsider it, or
• agrees to hear the case.

Interpreting Diagrams The diagram above shows the typical route (though not the only one) a case might take to the Supreme Court. *Why do you think this process requires so many steps to reach the Supreme Court—often at great expense and time to the parties involved?* H-SS 12.6.4

to a case can petition the Court to issue a writ. But, again, "cert" is granted in a limited number of instances—typically, only when a petition raises some important constitutional question or a serious problem in the interpretation of a statute.

When certiorari is denied, the decision of the lower court stands in that particular case. Note, however, that the denial of cert is not a decision on the merits of a case. All that a denial means is that, for whatever reason, four or more justices could not agree that the Supreme Court should accept that case for review.

A few cases do reach the Court in yet another way, by **certificate.** This process is used when a lower court is not clear about the procedure or the rule of law that should apply in a case. The lower court asks the Supreme Court to certify the answer to a specific question in the matter.

Most cases that reach the Court do so from the highest State courts and the federal courts of appeals. A few do come, however, from the federal district courts and a very few from the Court of Appeals for the Armed Forces.

How the Court Operates

The Court sits from the first Monday in October to sometime the following June or July. Each term is identified by the year in which it began. Thus, the 2006 term ran from October 2, 2006, into the early summer of 2007.

Oral Arguments

Once the Supreme Court accepts a case, it sets a date on which that case will be heard. As a rule, the justices consider cases in two-week cycles from October to early May. They hear oral arguments in several cases for two weeks; then the justices recess for two weeks to consider those cases and handle other Court business.

While the Supreme Court is hearing oral arguments, it convenes at 10:00 A.M. on Mondays, Tuesdays, Wednesdays, and sometimes Thursdays. At those public sessions, the lawyers make their oral arguments. Their presentations are almost always limited to 30 minutes.[15]

Briefs

Briefs are written documents filed with the Court before oral arguments begin. These detailed statements support one side of a case, presenting arguments built largely on relevant facts and the citation of previous cases. Many briefs run to hundreds of pages.

The Court may also receive *amicus curiae* (friend of the court) briefs. These are briefs filed by persons or groups who are not actual parties to a case but who nonetheless have a substantial interest in its outcome. Thus, for example, cases involving such highly charged matters as abortion or affirmative action regularly attract a large number of amicus briefs. Notice, however, that these briefs can be filed only with the Court's permission or at its request.

The solicitor general, a principal officer in the Department of Justice, is often called the Federal Government's chief lawyer. He—and, certainly, one day she—represents the United States in all cases to which it is party in the Supreme Court and may appear for the government in any federal or State court.[16]

The solicitor general also has another extraordinary responsibility. He or she decides which cases the government should ask the Supreme Court to review and what position the United States should take in those cases it brings before the High Court.

The Court in Conference

On most Wednesdays and Fridays through a term, the justices meet in conference. There, in closest secrecy, they consider the cases in which they have heard oral arguments.[17]

The Chief Justice presides over the conference. He speaks first on each case to be considered and usually indicates how he intends to vote. Then each associate justice summarizes his or her views. Those presentations are made in order of seniority, with the justice most recently named to the Court speaking last. After the justices are "polled," they usually debate the case.

---

[15]The justices usually listen closely to a lawyer's oral arguments and sometimes interrupt them with questions or requests for information. After 25 minutes, a white light comes on at the lectern from which the lawyer addresses the Court; five minutes later a red light signals the end of the presentation, even if the lawyer is in mid-sentence.

[16]The attorney general may argue the government's position before the Supreme Court but rarely does.

[17]At conference, the justices also decide which new cases they will accept for decision.

▲ Front row: Antonin Scalia, John Paul Stevens, Chief Justice William H. Rehnquist, Sandra Day O'Connor, Anthony Kennedy. Back Row: Ruth Bader Ginsburg, David Souter, Clarence Thomas, Stephen Breyer. In 2005, Justice O'Connor announced her retirement and Chief Justice Rehnquist passed away.

About a third of all the Court's decisions are unanimous, but most find the Court divided. The High Court is sometimes criticized for its split decisions. But, notice, its cases pose very difficult questions, and many also present questions on which lower courts have disagreed. In short, most of the Court's cases are controversial ones; the easy cases seldom get that far.

Opinions

If the Chief Justice is in the majority on a case, he assigns the writing of the Court's opinion. When the Chief Justice is in the minority, the assignment is handled by the senior associate justice on the majority side.

The Court's opinion is often called the **majority opinion.** Officially called the Opinion of the Court, it announces the Court's decision in a case and sets out the reasoning on which it is based.[18]

The Court's written opinions are exceedingly valuable. The majority opinions stand as **precedents,** or examples to be followed in similar cases as they arise in the lower courts or reach the Supreme Court.

Often, one or more of the justices who agree with the Court's decision may write a **concurring opinion**—to add or emphasize a point that was not made in the majority opinion. The concurring opinions may bring the Supreme Court to modify its present stand in future cases.

One or more **dissenting opinions** are often written by those justices who do not agree with the Court's majority decision. Chief Justice Charles Evans Hughes once described dissenting opinions as "an appeal to the brooding spirit of the law, to the intelligence of a future day." On rare occasions, the Supreme Court does reverse itself. The minority opinion of today could become the Court's majority position in the future.

---

[18]Most majority opinions, and many concurring and dissenting opinions, run to dozens of pages. Some decisions are accompanied by very brief and unsigned opinions. These *per curiam* (for the court) opinions seldom run more than a paragraph or two and usually dispose of relatively uncomplicated cases.

Section 3 Assessment

Key Terms and Main Ideas

1. **(a)** What does a **writ of certiorari** have in common with a **certificate? (b)** How do the two differ?
2. **(a)** Why are **precedents** important? **(b)** Write a sentence using the word *precedent* in a judicial context.
3. Explain why "easy" cases generally do not reach the Supreme Court.

Critical Thinking

4. **Drawing Conclusions** Why do you think the Supreme Court justices often write concurring and/or dissenting opinions in a case?

5. **Determining Cause and Effect** How does the Court's power of judicial review affect the balance of power in the Federal Government?

Face the
Issues

The Death Penalty

Background *The death penalty has a lengthy history, and so does the controversy surrounding it. The punishment has been a part of American law since the colonial period, and 38 States provide for it today. More than 1,000 persons have been executed in this country since the Supreme Court reinstated capital punishment in 1976. Nearly 3,500 persons sit on death row in American prisons today.*

Young people protest capital punishment

Analysis Skill HR4

End Capital Punishment

The United States is the only western democracy that continues to allow the death penalty. Most executions take place in only a handful of countries, among them China, Iran, Saudi Arabia—and the United States.

"The death penalty is the ultimate cruel, unusual and degrading punishment," says Amnesty International. "It violates the right to life." Clearly, executions cannot be undone in cases of mistaken conviction—and the Death Penalty Information Center reports more than 120 cases in which death row inmates have been exonerated (released with evidence of innocence) over the past 30 years.

Many insist that the death penalty is not administered fairly in this country. Retired Supreme Court Justice Sandra Day O'Connor recently put it this way: "If statistics are any indication, the system may well be allowing some innocent defendants to be executed." Many critics also stress the fact that, of all those who are sentenced to death, a disproportionately large percentage of them are either poor or members of minority groups, or both.

A Legal and Appropriate Penalty

In the American federal system, each State can decide for itself whether to provide for capital punishment or not. The Supreme Court has now several times upheld the constitutionality of State death penalty laws.

Public opinion polls consistently show widespread support for the punishment. Gallup has polled on the question for 70 years and has regularly found that a majority of the people—most recently, 74 percent of them—favor retention of the death penalty. Many support it because they believe that the existence of the penalty is, in itself, a deterrent to crime.

Clearly, the death penalty is the ultimate penalty; and, just as clearly, its use must be very closely restricted to protect the innocent and prevent wrongful convictions. The best remedies for whatever problems exist in the administration of capital punishment should not be found in its abolition. They should be found, instead, in the continuing improvement of the processes by which that ultimate penalty is imposed.

Exploring the Issues

1. Do you agree with the claim that capital punishment "violates the right to life"? Why or why not?

2. Do you agree with the claim that the existence of a death penalty law deters crime? Why or why not?

For more information about capital punishment and the justice system, view "The Death Penalty."

Face the **Issues**
Video Collection

4 *The Special Courts*

Section Preview

OBJECTIVES

1. **Explain** how a citizen may sue the government in the Court of Federal Claims.
2. **Examine** the roles of the territorial courts and of the District of Columbia courts.
3. **Contrast** the functions of the Court of Appeals for the Armed Forces and the Court of Appeals for Veterans Claims.
4. **Explain** what types of cases are brought to the Tax Court.

WHY IT MATTERS

Over time, Congress has enlarged the structure of the federal court system by creating many special courts to handle cases that are outside the mainstream judicial process. Each of these courts has a very narrow jurisdiction.

POLITICAL DICTIONARY

★ **redress**
★ **courts-martial**
★ **civilian tribunal**

Recall that the federal court system is made up of two quite distinct types of courts. They are: (1) the constitutional, or regular courts, which you have read about, and (2) the special courts, which you'll now explore.

The special courts were created by Congress to hear certain cases involving the expressed powers of Congress. These courts, also known as legislative courts, were not established under Article III, so they do not exercise the broad "judicial Power of the United States." Rather, each has a very narrow jurisdiction.

The Court of Federal Claims

The United States government cannot be sued by anyone, in any court, for any reason, without its consent. The government may be taken to court only in cases in which Congress declares that the United States is open to suit.[19] Originally, a person with a claim against the United States could secure **redress**—satisfaction of a claim, payment—only by an act of Congress. In 1855, however, Congress set up the Court of Claims to hear such pleas.[20] That body became the United States Court of Federal Claims in 1993.

The Court of Federal Claims is composed of 16 judges appointed by the President and approved by the Senate for 15-year terms. They

▲ A military commission at Guantanamo Naval Base in Cuba hears the case against David Hicks, an Australian citizen. Classified as an "enemy combatant," Hicks was captured while fighting with the Taliban in Afghanistan against U.S. and coalition troops. **H-SS 12.7.7**

---

[19]The government is shielded from suit by the doctrine of sovereign immunity. The doctrine comes from an ancient principle of English public law summed up by the phrase: "The King can do no wrong." The rule is not intended to protect public officials from charges of corruption or any other wrongdoing. Rather, it is intended to prevent government from being hamstrung in its own courts. Congress has long since agreed to a long list of legitimate court actions against the government.

[20]Congress acted under its expressed power to pay the debts of the United States, Article I, Section 8, Clause 1.

hold trials throughout the country, hearing claims for damages against the Federal Government. Those claims they uphold cannot in fact be paid until Congress appropriates the money, which it does almost as a matter of standard procedure. Appeals from the court's decisions may be carried to the Court of Appeals for the Federal Circuit.

Occasionally, those who lose in the Claims Court still manage to win some compensation. Some years ago, a Puget Sound mink rancher lost a case in which he claimed that low-flying Navy planes had frightened his animals and caused several of the females to become sterile. He asked $100 per mink. He lost, but then his congressman introduced a private bill that eventually paid him $10 for each animal.

The Territorial Courts

Acting under its power to "make all needful Rules and Regulations respecting the Territory . . . belonging to the United States," Congress created courts for the nation's territories. These courts sit in the Virgin Islands, Guam, and the Northern Marianas and function much like the local courts in the 50 States.

The District of Columbia Courts

Acting under its power (Article I, Section 8, Clause 17) to "exercise exclusive Legislation in all Cases whatsoever, over such District . . . as may . . . become the Seat of the Government of the United States," Congress has set up a judicial system for the nation's capital. Both the District Court and the Court of Appeals for the District of Columbia hear many local cases as well as those they try as constitutional courts. Congress has also established two local courts, much like the courts in the States: a superior court, which is the general trial court, and a court of appeals.

The Court of Appeals for the Armed Forces

Beginning in 1789, Congress has created a system of military courts for each branch of the nation's armed forces, as an exercise of its expressed power to "make Rules for the Government and Regulation of the land and naval forces."[21] These military courts—**courts-martial**—serve the special disciplinary needs of the armed forces and are *not* a part of the federal court system. Their judges, prosecutors, defense attorneys, court reporters, and other personnel are all members of the military; most of them are officers. They conduct trials of those members of the military who are accused of violating military law. Today, the proceedings in a court-martial are very much like the trials held in civilian courts across the country.

In 1950, Congress created the Court of Military Appeals, now titled the Court of Appeals for the Armed Forces, to review the more serious court-martial convictions of military personnel. The Court of Appeals for the Armed Forces is a **civilian tribunal,** a court operating as part of the judicial branch, entirely separate from the military establishment. Its five judges—a chief judge and four associate judges—are appointed by the President and Senate to 15-year terms.

Appeals from the court's decisions can, in a limited number of cases, be taken to the Supreme Court. It is, then, the court of last resort in most cases that involve offenses against military law.

Military Commissions

The Defense Department has created several military commissions, courtlike boards of usually five commissioned officers. These tribunals are not a part of the courts-martial system. They are, instead, separate structures set up to try "enemy combatants," including several hundred suspected terrorists captured by American forces in Afghanistan and Iraq.

Most of these suspects are presently held in a military prison at Guantanamo Bay, Cuba, where their trials were begun in 2004 and are expected to continue for at least another year. Their ranks include several hundred alleged

---

[21]Article I, Section 8, Clause 14. This provision allows Congress to provide for the regulation of the conduct of members of the armed forces under a separate, noncivil legal code. The present-day system of military justice has developed over more than 230 years. Today, the Uniform Code of Military Justice, enacted by Congress in 1950, and the Military Justice Acts of 1968 and 1983 are the principal statutes that set out the nation's military law.

members of al Qaida and a number of other foreigners said to have committed violent acts against the United States.

The President provided for the creation of these tribunals by executive order. His power to do so came from (1) his constitutional role as commander in chief and (2) the fact that Congress has authorized him to use "all necessary and appropriate force" to combat global terrorism.

Military tribunals have been established at various times in America's past—most notably during the Mexican-American War, the Civil War, and World War II. Until now, President Franklin Roosevelt had created the most recent one, in 1942. It tried eight Nazi saboteurs, who were landed on the East Coast by German submarines. They had planned various acts of sabotage aimed at the disruption of this nation's war effort. All eight were convicted. Six were executed; the other two, who had turned on their comrades and cooperated with the tribunal, were sentenced to long terms in prison.

The Court of Appeals for Veterans Claims

Acting under its power (Article I, Section 8, Clause 9) to "constitute Tribunals inferior to the supreme Court," Congress created the Court of Veterans Appeals in 1988 and changed its name in 1999 to the Court of Appeals for Veterans Claims. This newest court in the federal judiciary is composed of a chief judge and up to six associate judges, all appointed by the President and approved by the Senate to 15-year terms.

The court has the power to hear appeals from the decisions of an administrative agency, the Board of Veterans Appeals in the Department of Veterans Affairs (VA). Thus, this court hears cases in which individuals claim that the VA has denied or otherwise mishandled valid claims for veterans' benefits. Appeals from the decisions of the Court of Appeals for Veterans Claims can be taken to the Court of Appeals for the Federal Circuit.

The United States Tax Court

Acting under its power to tax, Congress created the United States Tax Court in 1969 as "an independent judicial body" in the legislative branch. It is not, in fact, a part of the federal court system.[22] The Tax Court has 19 judges, one of whom serves as chief judge. Each of these 19 judges is named by the President and Senate for a 15-year term. The Tax Court hears civil but not criminal cases involving disputes over the application of the tax laws. Most of its cases, then, are generated by the Internal Revenue Service and other Treasury Department agencies. Its decisions may be appealed to the federal courts of appeals.

---

[22]Article I, Section 8, Clause 1.

Section 4 Assessment

Key Terms and Main Ideas

1. What does it mean to seek **redress** in a court?
2. What is the difference between military **tribunals** and **courts-martial**?
3. Who created the special courts?

Critical Thinking

4. **Drawing Inferences** Why do you think Congress has seen a need to create special courts instead of sending all federal cases to the regular courts?
5. **Expressing Problems Clearly** Brainstorm a type of case that a citizen might take to the U.S. Court of Federal Claims. Explain your reasoning.

Standards Monitoring Online
For: Self-quiz with vocabulary practice
Web Code: mqa-5184

6. **Drawing Inferences** Why, do you think, did Congress establish a civilian tribunal to hear appeals of serious courts-martial convictions?

Go Online
PHSchool.com

For: An activity on U.S. Court of Appeals for the Armed Forces
Web Code: mqd-5184

Can Groups' Liberties Be Limited During Wartime?

CALIFORNIA Analysis Skills HR4, HI3, HI4

Many difficult questions concerning personal freedoms arise during national emergencies. When the survival of the nation is threatened, strong government action may be necessary to confront the threat. Such action might harm individuals or groups. May government impose limits on civil rights in case of emergencies?

Korematsu v. United States (1944)

Japan's attack on Pearl Harbor, Hawaii, on December 7, 1941, prompted widespread fear that Japan might try to invade the West Coast, and that persons of Japanese ancestry living there might aid the invasion. At that time, about 120,000 persons of Japanese descent lived in the West Coast States; some 70,000 of these were *Nisei* (native-born American citizens).

On February 19, 1942, President Franklin Roosevelt issued Executive Order No. 9066 authorizing the military to designate military areas and to exclude "any or all persons" from them. This order was intended to help protect the country from espionage or sabotage. Congress then passed a law requiring that all persons excluded from those military areas be sent to "war relocation camps" outside the sensitive military areas.

On March 2, 1942, the general in charge of the West Coast Defense Command issued the first of a series of orders that identified the entire Pacific Coast as Military Area No. 1. Soon, all persons of Japanese descent were ordered out of that area.

Fred Korematsu, a native-born American citizen, refused to leave his home in San Leandro, across the bay from San Francisco. He was arrested, charged with failure to report for relocation, and convicted in federal district court. After losing in the court of appeals, he appealed to the Supreme Court.

Arguments for Korematsu

1. Executive Order 9066 denied Korematsu his liberty without due process of law, in violation of the 5th Amendment.

2. The military does not have the authority to regulate civilian conduct, and the President cannot delegate that power to the military when martial law has not been declared.

3. The order of exclusion created a classification based on race, in violation of the Constitution.

Arguments for the United States

1. Although the relocation would not be proper in peacetime, the danger of espionage and sabotage justified this denial of liberty to American citizens under wartime circumstances.

2. Because war had been declared, the President had the authority as commander in chief to issue such orders to the military.

3. The United States had been attacked by Japan, so it was logical that people of Japanese ancestry were suspect. The decision to relocate people from sensitive military areas was based on security concerns and not on racial prejudice.

Decide for Yourself

1. Review the constitutional grounds on which each side based its arguments and the specific arguments each side presented.

2. Debate the opposing viewpoints presented in this case. Which viewpoint do you favor?

3. Predict the impact of the Court's decision on discrimination based on race and national ancestry in the United States. (To read a summary of the Court's decision, turn to pages 799–806.)

Go Online
PHSchool.com

Use Web Code mqp-4147 to register your vote on this issue and to see how other students voted.

inferior courts (p. 507), jurisdiction (p. 508), exclusive jurisdiction (p. 508), concurrent jurisdiction (p. 508), plaintiff (p. 509), defendant (p. 509), original jurisdiction (p. 509), appellate jurisdiction (p. 509), criminal case (p. 513), civil case (p. 513), docket (p. 513), writ of certiorari (p. 520), certificate (p. 521), majority opinion (p. 522), precedent (p. 522), concurring opinion (p. 522), dissenting opinion (p. 522), redress (p. 524), civilian tribunal (p. 525), court-martial (p. 525)

Standards Review

H-SS 12.1.5 Describe the systems of separated and shared powers, the role of organized interests (*Federalist Paper Number 10*), checks and balances (*Federalist Paper Number 51*), the importance of an independent judiciary (*Federalist Paper Number 78*), enumerated powers, rule of law, federalism, and civilian control of the military.

H-SS 12.4.5 Discuss Article III of the Constitution as it relates to judicial power, including the length of terms of judges and the jurisdiction of the Supreme Court.

H-SS 12.4.6 Explain the processes of selection and confirmation of Supreme Court justices.

H-SS 12.5.2 Analyze judicial activism and judicial restraint and the effects of each policy over the decades (e.g., the Warren and Rehnquist courts).

H-SS 12.5.3 Evaluate the effects of the Court's interpretations of the Constitution in *Marbury* v. *Madison, McCulloch* v. *Maryland,* and *United States* v. *Nixon,* with emphasis on the arguments espoused by each side in these cases.

H-SS 12.6.4 Describe the means that citizens use to participate in the political process (e.g., voting, campaigning, lobbying, filing a legal challenge, demonstrating, petitioning, picketing, running for political office).

H-SS 12.7.7 Identify the organization and jurisdiction of federal, state, and local (e.g., California) courts, and the interrelationships among them.

Practicing the Vocabulary

Matching *Choose a term from the list above that best matches each description.*

1. Jurisdiction shared by a State court and a federal court
2. A court made up of non-military judges
3. The Supreme Court's official decision of a case
4. A court's caseload
5. A person who initiated a lawsuit
6. An example to follow in similar cases in the future
7. A court of military personnel, used to try those accused of violating military law

Fill in the Blank *Choose a term from the list above that best completes the sentence.*

8. A _____ would be filed in a claim of patent infringement.
9. Satisfaction of a legal claim is called_____.
10. The Supreme Court issues a _____ when a case relates to the interpretation of law.
11. The Constitution left the creation of the _____ to Congress.
12. A Supreme Court justice may choose to write a _____ if he or she believes that a point in the Court's opinion needs additional emphasis.

Reviewing Main Ideas

Section 1

13. Why did the Framers see a need for a national judiciary?
14. Identify two provisions that the Constitution makes regarding the federal courts and their jurisdictions.
15. Which courts hear most of the cases in this country, the State courts or the federal courts?
16. Describe the process by which most federal judges are nominated and approved.

Section 2

17. **(a)** What jurisdiction do the inferior courts have? **(b)** What kinds of cases do they hear?
18. When the Supreme Court's docket became overloaded in the late 1800s, what did Congress do to ease the burden?
19. In the federal judicial system, what is a circuit?
20. Where do most of the cases that reach the federal courts of appeals come from?
21. How does the Court of Appeals for the Federal Circuit differ from other federal courts of appeals?

Section 3

22. **(a)** Why is it so important for courts to have the power of judicial review? **(b)** What famous court case established the Supreme Court's right to exercise the power of judicial review?
23. **(a)** What kinds of jurisdiction does the Supreme Court have? **(b)** What kind of cases does it usually accept?
24. What is the "rule of four"?
25. If the Supreme Court decides not to hear a case, what then becomes the final result (decision) in that case?
26. Describe how oral arguments are presented before the Supreme Court.

Section 4

27. **(a)** Who creates the special courts? **(b)** Why have they been created?
28. Under what circumstances can an American citizen sue the United States?
29. What kind of claims are heard by the Court of Appeals for Veterans Claims?

Critical Thinking Skills

Analysis Skills CS1, CS2

30. *Face the Issues* On several occasions, courts in some States have ruled that capital punishment is unconstitutional. Do you believe courts have the right to decide this issue, or do you believe voters and the legislature should have the final say on capital punishment? Explain your reasoning.

31. *Drawing Inferences* Why did the Framers create a system of appointing judges that required cooperation between the President and the Senate?

32. *Making Decisions* Occasionally the Supreme Court refuses to hear a certain case, then later agrees to hear a very similar case. Why might the Court decide to hear the later case?

Analyzing Political Cartoons

Using your knowledge of American government and this cartoon, answer the questions below.

THAT COMPASS DOESN'T POINT THE WAY I WANT TO GO. CHANGE IT. NOW!

33. In 1937, President Roosevelt proposed a law that would have allowed him to appoint as many as six new justices to the Supreme Court. He was widely criticized for trying to "pack the court" with judges favorable to his New Deal programs. **(a)** Who is the captain of the ship? **(b)** Who does the smaller sailor represent? **(c)** How is the Supreme Court represented?

34. Does the cartoonist approve of FDR's plan? Explain.

Investigative reporters look into many different kinds of matters, from political scandals to questions of consumer health and safety. Probably you have seen their reports on television or in newspaper articles. Reporters often uncover issues that make people think "something should be done."

Identify a problem or issue involving people whom you think are being treated unfairly. Write a proposal for an investigative report that would track down the truth about this issue. In your proposal, clearly identify the issue. Explain what you expect to find out in your investigation. List the types of people and organizations, governmental or private, you plan to contact, and why. Write a concluding statement suggesting what type of court might hear a case resulting from your investigation.

Participation Activities

Analysis Skills HR4, HI1, HI4

35. *Current Events Watch* Find news reports of a recent major decision by the Supreme Court. Form a mock panel of justices and deliberate on the case, using detailed accounts of the case. When your panel reaches a decision, identify the arguments that most influenced you, and explain why your group agreed or disagreed with the Court.

36. *Graphing Activity* Construct a time line showing the dates when each of the current Supreme Court justices was appointed to the bench. Make a second time line showing the Presidents during that time span. Compare the two to see which President appointed each justice and who appointed the majority of the present-day Court.

37. *It's Your Turn* A justice of the Supreme Court has announced her retirement, giving you, the President, the opportunity to nominate someone to fill that seat. List five factors that might influence your choice of a nominee.

Standards Monitoring *Online*

For: Chapter 18 Self-Test **Visit:** PHSchool.com
Web Code: mqa-5185

As a final review, take the Magruder's Chapter 18 Self-Test and receive immediate feedback on your answers. The test consists of 20 multiple-choice questions designed to test your understanding of the chapter content.

CHAPTER 19

Civil Liberties: First Amendment Freedoms

"All through the years we have had to fight for civil liberty, and we know that there are times when the light grows rather dim, and every time that happens democracy is in danger."
—Eleanor Roosevelt (1940)

Democracy cannot exist without civil liberty—that is, without individual freedom. But, notice, democracy also cannot exist without some degree of authority—that is, without government. Striking the proper balance between freedom and authority is democracy's constant challenge.

◆ Americans enjoying their freedom of religion

Standards Preview

H-SS 12.1.2 Discuss the character of American democracy and its promise and perils as articulated by Alexis de Tocqueville.

H-SS 12.1.6 Understand that the Bill of Rights limits the powers of the federal government and state governments.

H-SS 12.2.1 Discuss the meaning and importance of each of the rights guaranteed under the Bill of Rights and how each is secured (e.g., freedom of religion, speech, press, assembly, petition, privacy).

H-SS 12.2.5 Describe the reciprocity between rights and obligations; that is, why enjoyment of one's rights entails respect for the rights of others.

H-SS 12.3.1 Explain how civil society provides opportunities for individuals to associate for social, cultural, religious, economic, and political purposes.

H-SS 12.3.3 Discuss the historical role of religion and religious diversity.

H-SS 12.5.1 Understand the changing interpretations of the Bill of Rights over time, including interpretations of the basic freedoms (religion, speech, press, petition, and assembly) articulated in the First Amendment and the due process and equal protection-of-the-law clauses of the Fourteenth Amendment.

H-SS 12.6.4 Describe the means that citizens use to participate in the political process (e.g., voting, campaigning, lobbying, filing a legal challenge, demonstrating, petitioning, picketing, running for political office).

H-SS 12.7.4 Discuss the Ninth and Tenth Amendments and interpretations of the extent of the federal government's power.

H-SS 12.8.1 Discuss the meaning and importance of a free and responsible press.

H-SS 12.10 Students formulate questions about and defend their analyses of tensions within our constitutional democracy and the importance of maintaining a balance between the following concepts: majority rule and individual rights; liberty and equality; state and national authority in a federal system; civil disobedience and the rule of law; freedom of the press and the right to a fair trial; the relationship of religion and government.

Go Online
PHSchool.com

For: Current Data
Web Code: mqg-5196

For: Close Up Foundation debates
Web Code: mqh-5198

SECTION 1

The Unalienable Rights (pp. 532–536)

★ The guarantees in the Bill of Rights reflect Americans' long-held commitment to personal freedom as well as the principle of limited government.

★ Individual rights are not absolute; they can be restricted when they come into conflict with the rights of others.

★ The Bill of Rights restricts only the National Government, but the Due Process Clause of the 14th Amendment "nationalizes" most of those guarantees.

SECTION 2

Freedom of Religion (pp. 537–544)

★ Free expression, including freedom of religion, is necessary to a free society.

★ The Establishment Clause sets up what Thomas Jefferson called "a wall of separation between church and state." The nature of this "wall," particularly as it applies to education, has been a matter of continuing controversy.

★ The Free Exercise Clause protects individuals' right to believe—but not to do—whatever they wish.

SECTION 3

Freedom of Speech and Press (pp. 546–553)

★ The 1st and 14th amendments' guarantees of free speech and press protect a person's right to speak freely and to hear what others have to say.

★ These freedoms are not absolute: the Supreme Court has limited such expressions as seditious speech and obscenity, but seldom allows prior restraint of spoken or written words.

★ The media also can be limited: Reporters do not have an unlimited right of confidentiality, and radio and television are subject to more regulation because they use the public airwaves.

★ Symbolic and commercial speech enjoy constitutional protection but can be limited under certain circumstances.

SECTION 4

Freedom of Assembly and Petition (pp. 555–558)

★ The 1st Amendment guarantees the right to assemble peaceably and to petition the government for a redress of grievances.

★ Government can reasonably regulate the time, place, and manner of assembly, but those regulations must be "content neutral."

★ The right of assembly does not give demonstrators a right to trespass on private property.

★ The guarantee of freedom of assembly and petition carries with it a right of association.

Section Preview

OBJECTIVES

1. **Explain** how Americans' commitment to freedom led to the creation of the Bill of Rights.
2. **Understand** that the rights guaranteed by limited government are not absolute.
3. **Show** how federalism affects individual rights.
4. **Describe** how the 9th Amendment helps guarantee individual rights.

WHY IT MATTERS

The United States was founded, in part, to ensure individual rights against the power of government. However, these rights can be restricted when they come into conflict with the rights of others. The Due Process Clause of the 14th Amendment prevents the States from abridging rights guaranteed in the Constitution's Bill of Rights.

POLITICAL DICTIONARY

★ **Bill of Rights**
★ **civil liberties**
★ **civil rights**
★ **alien**
★ **Due Process Clause**
★ **process of incorporation**

Have you ever heard of Walter Barnette? Probably not. How about Toyosaburo Korematsu? Dollree Mapp? Clarence Earl Gideon? Almost certainly, you have the same answer: No.

Walter Barnette was a Jehovah's Witness who told his children not to salute the flag or to recite the Pledge of Allegiance. Toyosaburo Korematsu was a citizen of the United States interned by the Federal Government during World War II. Dollree Mapp was sentenced to prison for possessing "lewd and lascivious books." Finally, Clarence Earl Gideon was jailed for breaking into and entering a poolroom.

You will encounter these names again over the next few pages. Each of them played an important part in building and protecting the rights of all Americans.

A Commitment to Freedom

A commitment to personal freedom is deeply rooted in America's colonial past. Over many centuries, the English people had waged a continuing struggle for individual rights, and the early colonists brought a dedication to that cause with them to America.

Their commitment to freedom took root here, and it flourished. The Revolutionary War was fought to preserve and expand these very rights:

the rights of the individual against government. In proclaiming the independence of the new United States, the founders of this country declared:

PRIMARY Sources *"We hold these truths to be self-evident, that all men are created equal, that they are endowed by their Creator with certain unalienable Rights, that among these are Life, Liberty and the pursuit of Happiness. That to secure these rights, Governments are instituted among Men. . . ."*
—Declaration of Independence

The Framers of the Constitution repeated that justification for the existence of government in the Preamble to the Constitution.

The Constitution, as it was written in Philadelphia, contained a number of important guarantees. The most notable of these can be found in Article I, Sections 9 and 10, and in Article III. Unlike many of the first State constitutions, however, the United States Constitution did not include a general listing of the rights of the people.

That omission raised an outcry. The objections were so strong that several States ratified the Constitution only with the understanding that such a listing would be added immediately. The first session of the new Congress met that demand with a series of proposed amendments. Ten of them, known as the **Bill of Rights,** were ratified by the States and became a part of the Constitution on December 15, 1791. Later amendments, especially the 13th and the 14th, have added to the Constitution's guarantees of personal freedom.

The national Constitution guarantees both rights and liberties to the American people. The distinction between civil rights and civil liberties is at best murky. Legal scholars often disagree on the matter, and the two terms are quite often used interchangeably.

However, you can think of the distinction this way: In general, **civil liberties** are protections *against government*. They are guarantees of the safety of persons, opinions, and property from arbitrary acts of government. Leading examples of civil liberties include freedom of religion, freedom of speech and press, and the guarantee of a fair trial.

The term **civil rights** is sometimes reserved for those *positive acts of government* that seek to make constitutional guarantees a reality for all people. From this perspective, examples of civil rights include the prohibitions of discrimination on the basis of race, sex, religious belief, or national origin set out in the Civil Rights Act of 1964.

Limited Government

Government in the United States is *limited* government. The Constitution is filled with examples of this fact. Chief among them are its many guarantees of personal freedom. Each one of those guarantees is either an outright prohibition or a restriction on the power of government to do something.

All governments have and use authority over individuals. The all-important difference between a democratic government and a dictatorial one lies in the *extent* of that authority. In a dictatorial regime, the government's powers are practically unlimited. The government regularly suppresses dissent, often harshly. In the United States, however, governmental authority is strictly limited. As Justice Robert H. Jackson once put the point:

▲ *Celebrating the Bill of Rights* A crowd gathers for Bill of Rights Day in New York City, December 15, 1941—eight days after the attack on Pearl Harbor.

❝ *If there is any fixed star in our constitutional constellation, it is that no official, high or petty, can prescribe what shall be orthodox in politics, nationalism, religion, or any other matter of opinion or force citizens to confess by word or act their faith therein.* ❞

—*West Virginia Board of Education v. Barnette, 1943*

Rights Are Relative, Not Absolute

The Constitution guarantees many different rights to *everyone* in the United States. Still, *no one* has the right to do anything he or she pleases. Rather, all persons have the right to do as they please as long as they do not infringe on the rights of others. That is, each person's rights are relative to the rights of every other person.

To illustrate the point: Everyone in the United States has a right of free speech, but no one enjoys absolute freedom of speech. A person can be punished for using obscene language, or for using words in a way that causes another person to commit a crime—for example, to riot or to desert from the military. The Supreme Court dealt with this point in a recent case, *ApolloMedia Corporation* v. *United States*, 1999. There, it unanimously upheld a federal law that makes it illegal for anyone to send obscene and intentionally annoying e-mail via the Internet.

Justice Oliver Wendell Holmes put the relative nature of each person's rights this way:

Civil Liberties: First Amendment Freedoms **533** ★★★

"The most stringent [strict] protection of free speech would not protect a man in falsely shouting fire in a theatre and causing a panic."
—*Schenck v. United States, 1919*

When Rights Conflict

Sometimes different guarantees of rights come into conflict with one another. One common example: freedom of the press versus the right to a fair trial.

In one famous case, Dr. Samuel Sheppard of Cleveland, Ohio, had been convicted of murdering his wife. His lengthy trial was widely covered in the national media. On appeal, Sheppard claimed that the highly sensational coverage had denied him a fair trial. The Supreme Court agreed. In *Sheppard* v. *Maxwell,* 1966, the Court rejected the free press argument, overturned Sheppard's conviction, and ordered a new trial.

To Whom Are Rights Guaranteed?

Most constitutional rights are extended to all persons. The Supreme Court has often held that "persons" covers **aliens** as well as citizens. Aliens are people who are not citizens of the country in which they live. Not all rights are given to aliens, however. Thus, the right to travel freely throughout the country is guaranteed to all citizens.[1] But the travel of aliens can be restricted.

After the bombing of Pearl Harbor by Japan, all persons of Japanese descent living on the Pacific Coast were evacuated—forcibly moved—

▲ **The Fugitive** *Sheppard* v. *Maxwell* gave rise to a popular movie, starring Tommy Lee Jones (above) as a police officer who relentlessly pursues an escaped prisoner and former surgeon (played by Harrison Ford) accused of murdering his wife. The story of Dr. Sheppard also inspired an action-adventure television series during the 1960s.

inland. Many suffered economic and other hardships. In 1944 the Supreme Court reluctantly upheld the forced evacuation as a reasonable wartime emergency measure.[2] Still, the relocation was strongly criticized over the years. In 1988 the Federal Government admitted that the wartime relocation had been both unnecessary and unjust. Congress voted to pay $20,000 to each living internee. It also declared: "On behalf of the nation, the Congress apologizes."

Today's war on terrorism has created a political climate not unlike that of the early days of World War II. Did the treatment of Japanese Americans then teach us something for today? Will the rights of Muslims and others of Middle Eastern descent be respected by government as it fights terrorism here and abroad?

Federalism and Individual Rights

Federalism is a complicated governmental arrangement. It produces any number of problems—including a very complex pattern of guarantees of individual rights in the United States.

The Bill of Rights

Remember, the first ten amendments were originally intended as restrictions on the new National Government, not on the already existing States. And that remains the fact of the matter today.[3]

To illustrate this important point: The 5th Amendment says that no person can be charged with "a capital, or otherwise infamous crime" except by a grand jury. As a part of the Bill of Rights, this provision applies only to the National Government. The States are free to use the grand jury to bring accusations of serious crime—or, if they prefer, they can use some other process for that purpose. In fact, the grand jury is a part of the criminal

---

[1] See the two Privileges and Immunities clauses, in Article IV, Section 2, and the 14th Amendment. The guarantee does not extend to citizens under some form of legal restraint—for example, in jail or out on bail awaiting trial.

[2] *Korematsu* v. *United States,* 1944. However, on the same day the Court held, in *Ex parte Endo,* that once the loyalty of any citizen internee had been established, no restriction could be placed on that person's freedom to travel that was not legally imposed on all other citizens.

[3] The Supreme Court first held that the provisions of the Bill of Rights restrict only the National Government in *Barron* v. *Baltimore,* 1833. This was the first case in which the point was raised. The Court has followed that holding (precedent) ever since.

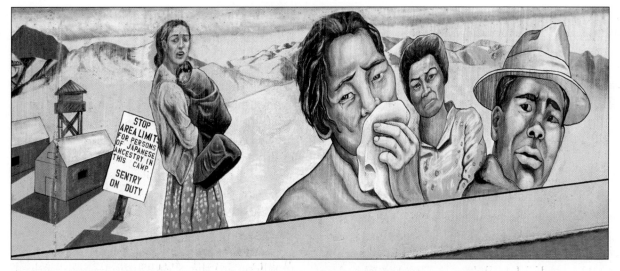

▲ This part of *The Great Wall of Los Angeles,* a half-mile-long mural, depicts Japanese internment during World War II. ***Critical Thinking How does the artist convey the conditions and feelings of the internees?*** **H-SS 12.10**

justice system in only about half of the States today; see pages 577–578 and 704.

The Modifying Effect of the 14th Amendment

Again, the provisions of the Bill of Rights apply against the National Government, not against the States. This does *not* mean, however, that the States can deny basic rights to the people.

In part, the States cannot do so because each of their own constitutions contains a bill of rights. In addition, they cannot deny these basic rights because of the 14th Amendment's **Due Process Clause.** It says:

> FROM THE *Constitution* ❝*No State shall . . . deprive any person of life, liberty, or property, without due process of law. . . .*❞
> —United States Constitution

The Supreme Court has often said that the 14th Amendment's Due Process Clause means this: No State can deny to any person any right that is "basic or essential to the American concept of ordered liberty."

But what specific rights are "basic or essential"? The Court has answered that question in a long series of cases in which it has held that most (but not all) of the protections in the Bill of Rights are also covered by the 14th Amendment's Due Process Clause, and so apply against the States. In deciding those cases, the Court has engaged in what has come to be called the **process of incorporation.** It has incor-

porated—merged, combined—most of the guarantees in the Bill of Rights into the 14th Amendment's Due Process Clause.

The Court began that historic process in *Gitlow* v. *New York* in 1925. That landmark case involved Benjamin Gitlow, a communist, who had been convicted in the State courts of criminal anarchy. He had made several speeches and published a pamphlet calling for the violent overthrow of government in this country.

On appeal, the Supreme Court upheld Gitlow's conviction and the State law under which he had been tried. In deciding the case, however, the Court made this crucial point: Freedom of speech and press, which the 1st Amendment says cannot be denied by the National Government, are also "among the fundamental personal rights and liberties protected by the Due Process Clause of the 14th Amendment from impairment by the States."

Soon after *Gitlow,* the Court held each of the 1st Amendment's guarantees to be covered by the 14th Amendment. It struck down State laws involving speech (*Fiske* v. *Kansas,* 1927; *Stromberg* v. *California,* 1931), the press (*Near* v. *Minnesota,* 1931), assembly and petition (*DeJonge* v. *Oregon,* 1937), and religion (*Cantwell* v. *Connecticut,* 1940). In each of those cases, the Court declared a State law unconstitutional as a violation of the 14th Amendment's Due Process Clause.

In the 1960s, the Court extended the scope of the 14th Amendment's Due Process Clause even

Process of Incorporation

Provisions of the Bill of Rights Incorporated into the 14th Amendment's Due Process Clause

Year	Amendment	Provision	Case
1925	1st	Freedom of speech	*Gitlow* v. *New York*
1931	1st	Freedom of the press	*Near* v. *Minnesota*
1937	1st	Freedom of assembly, petition	*DeJonge* v. *Oregon*
1940	1st	Free Exercise Clause	*Cantwell* v. *Connecticut*
1947	1st	Establishment Clause	*Everson* v. *Board of Education*
1961	4th	Unreasonable searches, seizures	*Mapp* v. *Ohio*
1962	8th	Cruel, unusual punishments	*Robinson* v. *California*
1963	6th	Right to counsel	*Gideon* v. *Wainwright*
1964	5th	Self-incrimination	*Malloy* v. *Hogan*
1965	6th	Confront witnesses	*Pointer* v. *Texas*
1967	6th	Speedy trial	*Klopfer* v. *North Carolina*
1967	6th	Obtain witnesses	*Washington* v. *Texas*
1968	6th	Trial by jury in criminal cases	*Duncan* v. *Louisiana*
1969	5th	Double jeopardy	*Benton* v. *Maryland*

Provisions NOT Incorporated into the 14th Amendment's Due Process Clause

Amendment	Provision
2nd	Right to keep, bear arms
3rd	Quartering of troops
5th	Grand jury
7th	Trial by jury in civil cases

Interpreting Tables This table shows which rights the Supreme Court has "nationalized," by incorporating them into the Due Process Clause of the 14th Amendment. ***Do you think any of the rights "NOT incorporated" should be nationalized in the future? Why or why not?*** **H-SS 12.5.1, 12.1.6**

further. The key cases are set out in the table at left. Due Process now covers nearly all of the guarantees set out in the Bill of Rights. In effect, the Supreme Court has "nationalized" them by holding that the Constitution guarantees them against the States through the 14th Amendment. You will look at each of the guarantees that are involved here shortly—the 1st Amendment rights in this chapter and the others in Chapter 20.

The 9th Amendment

As you know, the Constitution contains many guarantees of individual rights. However, nowhere in the Constitution—and, indeed, nowhere else—will you find a complete catalog of all of the rights held by the American people.

The little-noted 9th Amendment declares that there are rights beyond those set out in so many words in the Constitution:

 **❝** *The enumeration in the Constitution, of certain rights, shall not be construed to deny or disparage others retained by the people.* **❞**
—United States Constitution

Over the years, the Supreme Court has found that there are, in fact, a number of other rights "retained by the people." They include the guarantee that an accused person will not be tried on the basis of evidence unlawfully gained, and the right of a woman to have an abortion without undue interference by government.

Section 1 Assessment

Key Terms and Main Ideas

1. What is the difference between **civil rights** and **civil liberties**?
2. What is the **Bill of Rights**, and how did it come to be added to the Constitution?
3. How does federalism affect the guarantees of individual rights?
4. What is the **process of incorporation**? What guarantees in the Bill of Rights are not now covered by the 14th Amendment's **Due Process Clause**?

Critical Thinking

5. **Identifying Assumptions** For what reason(s) do you think the Supreme Court found that the right to a fair trial outweighed freedom of the press in *Sheppard*? Do you agree with this decision? Why or why not?

 **Standards Monitoring** *Online*
For: Self-quiz with vocabulary practice
Web Code: mqa-5191

6. **Predicting Consequences** How do you think the United States might be different today if the Supreme Court had not applied the process of incorporation to the Due Process Clause?

 **Go** **Online**
PHSchool.com
For: An activity on 1st Amendment rights
Web Code: mqd-5191

Section Preview

OBJECTIVES

1. **Examine** why a free society cannot exist without free expression.
2. **Describe** the "wall of separation between church and state" set up by the Establishment Clause of the 1st Amendment.
3. **Summarize** the Supreme Court rulings on religion and education as well as other Establishment Clause cases.
4. **Explain** how the Supreme Court has interpreted and limited the Free Exercise Clause.

WHY IT MATTERS

Freedom of religion is one component of the constitutional guarantee of free expression. The Establishment Clause sets up what Thomas Jefferson called "a wall of separation between church and state," but the nature of that separation is still being argued in American society and in the courts. The Free Exercise Clause protects Americans' right to believe—though not to do—whatever they wish.

POLITICAL DICTIONARY

★ **Establishment Clause**
★ **parochial**
★ **Free Exercise Clause**

In the early 1830s, a Frenchman, Alexis de Tocqueville, came to this country to observe life in the young United States. He later wrote that he had searched for the greatness of America in many places: in its large harbors and its deep rivers, in its fertile fields and its boundless forests, in its rich mines and its vast world commerce, in its public schools and its institutions of higher learning, and in its democratic legislature and its matchless Constitution. Yet it was not until he went into the churches of America, that Tocqueville said he came to understand the genius and the power of this country.

Freedom of Expression

A free society cannot exist without rights of free expression, without what has been called a "free trade in ideas." Freedom of expression is protected in the 1st Amendment:

> FROM THE
> *Constitution*
> **❝***Congress shall make no law respecting an establishment of religion, or prohibiting the free exercise thereof; or abridging the freedom of speech, or of the press; or the right of the people peaceably to assemble, and to petition the Government for a redress of grievances.* **❞**
> —United States Constitution

Additionally, as you know, the 14th Amendment's Due Process Clause protects these freedoms from the arbitrary acts of States or their local governments.

It is not surprising that the Bill of Rights provides first for the protection of religious liberty. Religion has always played a large and important role in American life. Many of the early colonists, and many later immigrants, came here to escape persecution for their religious beliefs.

▲ Alexis de Tocqueville, author of *Democracy in America* **H-SS 12.1.2**

The 1st and 14th amendments set out two guarantees of religious freedom. These guarantees prohibit (1) an "establishment of religion" (the **Establishment Clause**), and (2) any arbitrary interference by government in "the free exercise" of religion (the Free Exercise Clause).[4]

---

[4] Also, Article VI, Section 3 provides that "no religious Test shall ever be required as a Qualification to any Office or public Trust under the United States." In *Torcaso* v. *Watkins,* 1961, the Supreme Court held that the 14th Amendment puts the same restriction on the States.

▲ **Religious Freedom** Like all Americans, these church-goers are free to practice whatever religion they choose.

Separation of Church and State

The Establishment Clause sets up, in Thomas Jefferson's words, "a wall of separation between church and state." That wall is not infinitely high, however, and it is not impenetrable. Church and government are constitutionally separated in this country, but that does not make them enemies or even strangers to one another.

Government has done much to encourage churches and religion in the United States. Nearly all property of and contributions to religious sects are free from federal, State, and local taxation. Chaplains serve with each branch of the armed forces. Most public officials take an oath of office in the name of God. Sessions of both houses of Congress, most State legislatures, and many city councils open with prayer. The nation's anthem and its coins and currency make reference to God.

The meaning of the Establishment Clause cannot be pinned down in precise terms. The exact nature of the wall of separation—how high it really is—remains a matter of continuing and often heated controversy.

The Supreme Court did not hear its first Establishment Clause case until 1947. A few earlier cases did involve government and religion, but none of them involved a direct consideration of the "wall of separation."

The most important of those earlier cases was *Pierce* v. *Society of Sisters,* 1925. There, the Court held an Oregon compulsory school attendance law unconstitutional. That law required parents to send their children to public schools. It was purposely intended to eliminate private and especially **parochial** (church-related) schools.

In striking down the law, the Court did not address the Establishment Clause question. Instead, it found the law to be an unreasonable interference with the liberty of parents to direct the upbringing of their children—and so in conflict with the Due Process Clause of the 14th Amendment.

Religion and Education

The High Court's first direct ruling on the Establishment Clause came in *Everson* v. *Board of Education,* a 1947 case often called the *New Jersey School Bus Case.* There the Court upheld a State law that provided for the public, tax-supported busing of students attending any school in the State, including parochial schools.

Critics had attacked the law as a support of religion. They maintained that it relieved parochial schools of the need to pay for busing and so freed their money for other, including religious, purposes. The Court disagreed; it found the law to be a safety measure intended to benefit children, no matter what schools they might attend. Since that decision, the largest number of the Court's Establishment Clause cases have involved, in one way or another, religion and education.

Released Time

"Released time" programs allow public schools to release students during school hours to attend religious classes. In *McCollum* v. *Board of Education,* 1948, the Court struck down the released time program in Champaign, Illinois, because the program used public facilities for religious purposes.

In *Zorach* v. *Clauson,* 1952, however, the Court upheld New York City's released time program. It did so because the New York program required that the religious classes be held in private places, for example, in private homes.

Prayers and the Bible

The Court has now decided seven major cases involving the recitation of prayers and the reading of the Bible in public schools. In *Engel v. Vitale*, 1962, the Court outlawed the use, even on a voluntary basis, of a prayer written by the New York State Board of Regents. The prayer read:

PRIMARY Sources *"Almighty God, we acknowledge our dependence upon Thee, and we beg Thy blessings upon us, our parents, our teachers, and our country."*
—Regents' prayer

In striking down the prayer, the Supreme Court held that:

PRIMARY Sources *"[T]he constitutional prohibition against laws respecting an establishment of religion must at least mean that, in this country, it is no part of the business of government to compose official prayers for any group of the American people to recite as part of a religious program carried on by government."*
—Justice Hugo L. Black, Opinion of the Court

The High Court extended that holding in two 1963 cases. In *Abington School District v. Schempp*, it struck down a Pennsylvania law requiring that each school day begin with readings from the Bible and a recitation of the Lord's Prayer. In *Murray v. Curlett*, the Court erased a similar rule in the city of Baltimore. In both of these cases, the Court found violations of "the command of the 1st Amendment that the government maintain strict neutrality, neither aiding nor opposing religion."

Since then, the Supreme Court has found unconstitutional:

• a Kentucky law that ordered the posting of the Ten Commandments in all public school classrooms, *Stone v. Graham*, 1980;

• Alabama's "moment of silence" law, *Wallace v. Jaffree*, 1985, which provided for a one-minute period of silence for "meditation or voluntary prayer" at the beginning of each school day;

• the offering of prayer as part of a public

school graduation ceremony, in a Rhode Island case, *Lee v. Weisman*, 1992;

• a Texas school district's policy that permitted student-led prayer at high school football games, *Santa Fe Independent School District v. Doe*, 2000.

To sum up these rulings, the Court has held that public schools cannot sponsor religious exercises. It has not held that individuals cannot pray when and as they choose in schools or in any other place. Nor has it held that students cannot study the Bible in a literary or historical context in the schools.

These rulings have stirred strong criticism. Many individuals and groups have long proposed that the Constitution be amended to allow voluntary prayer in the public schools. Despite these decisions, both organized prayer and Bible readings are found in a great many public school classrooms today.

Student Religious Groups

The Equal Access Act of 1984 declares that any public high school that receives federal funds (nearly all do) must allow student religious groups to meet in the school on the same terms that it sets for other student organizations.

The Supreme Court found that the law does not violate the Establishment Clause in a case from Nebraska, *Westside Community Schools v. Mergens*, 1990. There, several students had tried to form a Christian club at Omaha's Westside High School. The students had to fight the school board in the federal courts in order to win their point.

The High Court has recently gone much further than it did in *Mergens*—in a case from New York, *Good News Club v. Milford Central School*, 2001. There, a school board had refused to allow a group of grade-school students to meet, after school, to sing, pray, memorize scriptures, and hear Bible lessons. The school board based its action on the Establishment Clause. The Court, however, held that the board had violated Good News Club members' 1st and 14th amendment rights to free speech.

Evolution

In *Epperson v. Arkansas*, 1968, the Court struck down a State law forbidding the teaching of the

▲ *Prayer and the Public Schools* The Supreme Court has ruled that public schools cannot sponsor prayer either in school or at school-related events.

scientific theory of evolution. The Court held that the Constitution

PRIMARY Sources "*forbids alike the preference of a religious doctrine or the prohibition of theory which is deemed antagonistic to a particular dogma. . . . 'The State has no legitimate interest in protecting any or all religions from views distasteful to them.'*"

—Justice Abe Fortas, Opinion of the Court

The Court found a similar law to be unconstitutional in 1987. In *Edwards* v. *Aguillard*, it voided a 1981 Louisiana law that provided that whenever teachers taught the theory of evolution, they also had to offer instruction in "creation science."

Aid to Parochial Schools

Most recent Establishment Clause cases have centered on this highly controversial question: What forms of State aid to parochial schools are constitutional? Several States give help to private schools, including schools run by church organizations, for transportation, textbooks, laboratory equipment, standardized testing, and much else.

Those who support this kind of aid argue that parochial schools enroll large numbers of students who would otherwise have to be educated at public expense. They also point out that the Supreme Court has held that parents have a legal right to send their children to those schools (*Pierce* v. *Society of Sisters*).

To give that right real meaning, they say, the State must give some aid to parochial schools in order to relieve parents of some of the double burden they carry because they must pay taxes to support the public schools their children do not attend. Many advocates also insist that schools run by religious organizations pose no real church-state problems because they devote most of their time to secular (nonreligious) subjects rather than to sectarian (religious) ones.

Opponents of aid to parochial schools argue that parents who choose to send their children to parochial schools should accept the financial consequences of that choice. Many of these critics also insist that it is impossible to draw clear lines between secular and sectarian courses in parochial schools. They say that religious beliefs are bound to have an effect on the teaching of nonreligious subjects in church-run schools.

The *Lemon* Test

The Supreme Court has been picking its way through cases involving State aid to parochial schools for several years. In most of these cases, the Court now applies a three-pronged standard, the *Lemon* test: (1) The purpose of the aid must be clearly secular, not religious; (2) its primary effect must neither advance nor inhibit religion; and (3) it must avoid an "excessive entanglement of government with religion."

The test stems from *Lemon* v. *Kurtzman*, 1971. There, the Supreme Court held that the Establishment Clause is designed to prevent three main evils: "sponsorship, financial support, and active involvement of the sovereign in religious activity." In *Lemon*, the Court struck down a Pennsylvania law that provided for reimbursements (financial payments) to private schools to cover their costs for teachers' salaries, textbooks, and other teaching materials in nonreligious courses.

The Court held that the State program was of direct benefit to the parochial schools, and so to the churches sponsoring them. It also found that the Pennsylvania program required such close State supervision that it produced an excessive entanglement of government with religion.

On the other hand, a number of State aid programs have passed the *Lemon* test over the past 30 years. Thus, the Court has held that a State can pay church-related schools what it costs them to administer the State's standardized tests, *Committee for Public Education and Religious Liberty* v. *Regan*, 1980.

Public funds cannot be used to pay any part of the salaries of parochial school teachers, however, including those who teach only secular courses. In *Grand Rapids School District* v. *Ball*, 1985, the Court said that the way a teacher presents a course cannot easily be checked.

In *Bowen* v. *Kendrick*, 1988, the Court upheld a controversial federal statute, the Adolescent Family Life Act of 1981. That law provides for grants to both public and private agencies dealing with the problems of adolescent sex and pregnancy. Some of the grants were made to religious groups that oppose abortion, prompting the argument that those groups use federal money to teach religious doctrine.

The Supreme Court found the law's purpose—curbing "the social and economic problems caused by teenage sexuality, pregnancy, and parenthood"—to be a legitimate one. Even though some grants pay for counseling that "happens to coincide with the religious views" of some groups, this does not by itself mean that the federal funds are being used with "a primary effect of advancing religion," according to the Court.

Additional *Lemon* Test Cases

In a 1993 Arizona case, *Zobrest* v. *Catalina Foothills School District*, the Court said that the use of public money to provide an interpreter for a deaf student who attends a Catholic high school does not violate the Establishment Clause. The Constitution, said the Court, does not lay down an absolute barrier to placing a public employee in a religious school.

In another recent case, from Louisiana, *Mitchell* v. *Helms*, 2000, the Supreme Court upheld a federal law under which some material and equipment, including computer hardware and software, are loaned to public and private schools. Two facts were key to the Court's ruling: that those items (1) are loaned, not given to parochial schools, and (2) can be used only in "secular, neutral, and nonideological" programs.

In 1973, the Court struck down a New York law that reimbursed parents for the tuition they paid to religious schools, *Committee for Public Education and Religious Liberty* v. *Nyquist*. But in *Mueller* v. *Allen*, 1983, the court upheld a Minnesota tax law that really accomplishes the same end.

The Minnesota law gives parents a State income tax deduction for the costs of tuition, textbooks, and transportation. Most public school parents pay little or nothing for those items, so the law is of particular benefit to parents with children in private, mostly parochial, schools. The Court found that the law meets the *Lemon* test, and it relied on this point: The tax deduction is available to *all* parents with children in school, and they are free to decide which type of school their children attend.

The High Court went much further in *Zelman* v. *Simmons-Harris* in 2002. There, it upheld Ohio's experimental "school choice" plan. Under that plan, parents in Cleveland can receive vouchers (grants for tuition payments) from the State and use them to send their children to private schools. Nearly all families who take the vouchers send their children to parochial schools. The Court found, 5–4, that the Ohio program is not intended to promote religion but, rather, to help children from low-income families.

Other Establishment Clause Cases

Most church-state controversies have involved public education. Some Establishment Clause cases have arisen elsewhere, however.

Seasonal Displays

Many public organizations sponsor celebrations of the holiday season with street decorations, programs in public schools, and the like. Can these publicly sponsored observances properly include expressions of religious belief?

In *Lynch* v. *Donnelly*, 1984, the Court held that the city of Pawtucket, Rhode Island, could include the Christian nativity scene in its holiday display, which also featured nonreligious objects such as candy canes and Santa's sleigh and reindeer. That ruling, however, left open this question: What about a public display made up *only* of a religious symbol?

The Court faced that question in 1989. In *County of Allegheny* v. *ACLU,* it held that the county's seasonal display "endorsed Christian doctrine," and so violated the 1st and 14th amendments. The county had placed a large display celebrating the birth of Jesus on the grand stairway in the county courthouse, with a banner proclaiming "Glory to God in the Highest."

At the same time, the Court upheld another holiday display in *Pittsburgh* v. *ACLU.* The city's display consisted of a large Christmas tree, an 18-foot menorah, and a sign declaring the city's dedication to freedom.

Chaplains

Daily sessions of both houses of Congress and most of the State legislatures begin with prayer. In Congress, and in many States, a chaplain paid with public funds offers the opening prayer.

The Supreme Court has ruled that this practice, unlike prayers in the public schools, is constitutionally permissible. The ruling was made in a case involving Nebraska's one-house legislature, *Marsh* v. *Chambers,* 1983.

The Court rested its distinction between school prayers and legislative prayers on two points.

First, prayers have been offered in the nation's legislative bodies "from colonial times through the founding of the Republic and ever since." Second, legislators, unlike schoolchildren, are not "susceptible to religious indoctrination or peer pressure."

The Ten Commandments

Public displays of the Ten Commandments have ignited controversy in several places in recent years. As you know, the High Court decided its first case on the matter, *Stone* v. *Graham,* in 1980. It ruled on two other similar cases in 2005.

In *Van Orden* v. *Perry,* the Court held that the Ten Commandments monument located on the grounds of the Texas State Capitol in Austin does not violate the 1st and 14th Amendments. The Court's 5–4 majority found that the monument (1) was erected in 1961 as part of a private group's campaign against juvenile delinquency, (2) is set among 37 other historical and cultural markers, and (3) had gone unchallenged for some 40 years. In short, the Court found the monument's overall message to be secular rather than religious and therefore acceptable.

In *McCreary County* v. *ACLU of Kentucky,* a differently divided 5–4 majority ruled that the display of the Ten Commandments in Kentucky county courthouses was unacceptable. They were, said the Court, an impermissible endorsement of religion by government. Framed copies of the Commandments were first posted in county courthouses in 1991. Copies of other nonreligious documents, including the Bill of Rights, were added to the displays some years later, but only after the original display's content had been challenged. The Supreme Court found that the original displays had a clear religious purpose. The later additions were merely "a sham," an attempt to mask that unconstitutional religious purpose.

The Free Exercise Clause

The second part of the constitutional guarantee of religious freedom is set out in the Constitution's **Free Exercise Clause,** which guarantees to each person the right to believe whatever he or she chooses to believe in matters of religion. No law and no other action by any government can violate that absolute constitutional right. It is protected by both the 1st and the 14th amendments.

▲ This Christian nativity scene was displayed in front of the Massachusetts State House. *Critical Thinking Does this seasonal display violate the separation of church and state?* H-SS 12.10

No person has an absolute right to act as he or she chooses, however. The Free Exercise Clause does *not* give anyone the right to violate criminal laws, offend public morals, or otherwise threaten the safety of the community.

The Supreme Court laid down the basic shape of the Free Exercise Clause in the first case it heard on the issue, *Reynolds* v. *United States,* 1879. Reynolds, a Mormon, had two wives. That practice, polygamy, was allowed by the teachings of his church, but it was prohibited by a federal law banning polygamy in any territory of the United States.

Reynolds was convicted under the law. On appeal, he argued that the law violated his right to the free exercise of his religious beliefs. The Supreme Court disagreed. It held that the 1st Amendment does not forbid Congress the power to punish those actions that are "violations of social duties or subversive of good order."

Limits on Free Exercise

Over the years, the Court has approved many regulations of human conduct in the face of free exercise challenges. For example, it has upheld laws that require the vaccination of schoolchildren, *Jacobson* v. *Massachusetts,* 1905; laws that forbid the use of poisonous snakes in religious rites, *Bunn* v. *North Carolina,* 1949; and laws that require businesses to be closed on Sundays ("blue laws"), *McGowan* v. *Maryland,* 1961.

A State can require religious groups to have a permit to hold a parade on the public streets, *Cox* v. *New Hampshire,* 1941; and organizations that enlist children to sell religious literature must obey child labor laws, *Prince* v. *Massachusetts,* 1944. The Federal Government can draft those who have religious objections to military service, *Welsh* v. *United States,* 1970.

The Court has also held that the Air Force can deny an Orthodox Jew the right to wear his yarmulke (skull cap) while on active duty, *Goldman* v. *Weinberger,* 1986. The U.S. Forest Service can allow private companies to build roads and cut timber in national forests that Native Americans have traditionally used for religious purposes, *Lyng* v. *Northwest Indian Cemetery Protective Association,* 1988.

In addition, a State can deny unemployment benefits to a man fired by a private drug

▲ The rabbi at right, a Jewish chaplain at the U.S. Naval Academy, helps a midshipman study the Torah. *Critical Thinking Do you think military chaplains, especially at the service academies, violate the separation of church and state?*

counseling group because he used peyote in violation of the State's drug laws. The Court made that finding even though the man ingested the hallucinogenic drug as part of a ceremony of his Native American Church, *Oregon* v. *Smith,* 1990.

Most recently, the High Court has said that a State that provides financial aid to students who attend its public colleges and universities does not have to make that help available to those students who are studying to become ministers, *Locke* v. *Davey,* 2004.

Free Exercise Upheld

Over time, however, the Court has also found many actions by governments to be incompatible with the free exercise guarantee. The Court did so for the first time in one of the landmark Due Process cases cited earlier in this chapter, *Cantwell* v. *Connecticut,* 1940. In that case, the Court struck down a law requiring a person to obtain a license before soliciting money for a religious cause. The Court reaffirmed that holding in an Ohio case, *Watchtower Bible and Tract Society* v. *Village of Stratton,* 2002.

The Supreme Court has decided a number of other cases in a similar way. Thus, Amish children cannot be forced to attend school beyond the 8th grade, because that sect's centuries-old "self-sufficient agrarian lifestyle essential to their religious faith is threatened by modern education," *Wisconsin* v. *Yoder,* 1972. On the other hand, the Amish, who provide support for their own people, must pay Social Security taxes, as all other employers do, *United States* v. *Lee,* 1982.

A State cannot forbid ministers to hold elected public offices, *McDaniel* v. *Paty,* 1978. Nor can it deny unemployment compensation benefits to a worker who quit a job because it involved a conflict with his or her religious beliefs, *Sherbert* v. *Verner,* 1963; *Thomas* v. *Indiana,* 1981; *Hobbie* v. *Florida,* 1987; *Frazee* v. *Illinois,* 1989.

The Court has often held that "only those beliefs rooted in religion are protected by the Free Exercise Clause," *Sherbert* v. *Verner,* 1963. This leaves open the perplexing question of what beliefs are "rooted in religion"? Clearly, religions that seem strange or even bizarre to most Americans are as entitled to constitutional protection as are the more traditional ones. For example, in *Lukumi Babalu Aye* v. *City of Hialeah,* 1993, the High Court struck down a Florida city's ordinance that outlawed animal sacrifices as part of any church services.

The Jehovah's Witnesses have carried several important religious freedom cases to the Supreme Court. Perhaps the stormiest controversy resulting from these cases arose out of the Witnesses' refusal to salute the flag.

The Witnesses refuse to salute the flag because they see such conduct as a violation of the Bible's commandment against idolatry. In *Minersville School District* v. *Gobitis,* 1940, the Court upheld a Pennsylvania school board regulation requiring students to salute the flag at the beginning of each school day. Walter Gobitis instructed his children not to do so, and the school expelled them. He went to court, basing his case on the constitutional guarantee.

Gobitis finally lost in the Supreme Court, which declared that the board's rule was not an infringement of religious liberty. Rather, the Court held that the rule was a lawful attempt to promote patriotism and national unity.

Three years later, the Court reversed that decision. In *West Virginia Board of Education* v. *Barnette,* 1943, it held a compulsory flag-salute law unconstitutional. Justice Robert H. Jackson's words on page 533 are from the Court's powerful opinion in that case. So are these:

PRIMARY Sources *"To believe that patriotism will not flourish if patriotic ceremonies are voluntary and spontaneous, instead of a compulsory routine, is to make an unflattering estimate of the appeal of our institutions to free minds."*

—Opinion of the Court

Section 2 Assessment

Key Terms and Main Ideas

1. Explain the **Establishment Clause.** Give one example of an Establishment Clause issue that does not involve education.
2. Why does aid to **parochial** schools often pose a constitutional problem?
3. What is the *Lemon* test?
4. Explain the **Free Exercise Clause.** Give one example of a Supreme Court ruling that limits free exercise of religion.

Critical Thinking

5. **Predicting Consequences** How do you think the guarantees of religious freedom ratified in 1791 affected the growth and development of the United States? In other words, how do you think the nation might be different today without these protections?

Standards Monitoring *Online*
For: Self-quiz with vocabulary practice
Web Code: mqa-5192

6. **Recognizing Ideologies** The 1st Amendment protects freedom of religion in two ways. What does this approach reveal about the beliefs and experiences of those Americans who insisted on these guarantees?

Go Online
PHSchool.com
For: An activity on freedom of religion
Web Code: mqd-5192

Religious Freedom in a Diverse Nation

The Freedom Forum is a nonpartisan foundation dedicated to a free press, free speech, and other freedoms for people around the world. In 1999, the foundation completed a study of the status of 1st Amendment rights in the United States. Here, the foundation's report expresses concern for religious freedom in the United States.

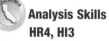

Analysis Skills
HR4, HI3

Religious and ethnic diversity, as shown in this Los Angeles classroom, gives 1st Amendment discussions a new urgency.

The 1st Amendment guarantee of religious freedom has been a binding force in this country for more than two centuries. It is a key element of the boldest political experiment the world has ever known. Today, however, there are disturbing signs in the United States that religious liberty—the freedom to believe or not to believe and to practice one's faith openly and freely without government interference—is in danger. People undermining religious liberty include both those who seek to establish in law a "Christian America" and those who seek to exclude religion from public life entirely.

. . . Religion has become a source of divisiveness as people spar and sometimes resort to violence over issues of conscience and belief like abortion, school prayer, and public school curricula. . . . The situation is made more complicated by the fact that the religious composition of the United States is becoming more diverse than ever. Along with many groups of Christians and Jews, this country is now home to growing numbers of Muslims, Hindus, Buddhists, and other believers. . . . Religious diversity was made possible by the 1st Amendment. Now, ironically, religious diversity makes the 1st Amendment more necessary and urgent than at any time in our history. . . .

As [scholar] Charles Haynes notes: ". . . An American is not defined by race or ethnicity, but by a commitment to the democratic first principles in our framing documents. Because of our exploding religious diversity, there is an urgent need for all citizens to rethink our shared commitment to the guiding principles of religious liberty. These principles of the 1st Amendment provide a civic framework for living with our deepest differences. . . ."

Religious freedom is at the heart of this country's experiment with democracy. The continuing controversies are proof of continued passion for liberty of conscience, even as debates rage about whether religion receives sufficient attention from the media, educators, and the government. Disputes involving religious liberty reflect America's ambivalence about the limits of individual liberty. At present, the country's internationally recognized commitment to tolerance of all cultures and faiths is being tested and torn. The question to be answered is whether we can sustain this commitment into the next century.

Analyzing Primary Sources

1. What defines an American, according to this report?
2. Describe recent changes in the nation's religious makeup identified in this report.
3. What benefit do the authors see in disputes that involve "issues of conscience"? What potential dangers do they see in such disputes?

Freedom of Speech and Press

Section Preview

OBJECTIVES

1. **Explain** the importance of the two basic purposes of the guarantees of free expression.
2. **Summarize** how the Supreme Court has limited seditious speech and obscenity.
3. **Examine** the issues of prior restraint and press confidentiality, and describe the limits the Court has placed on the media.
4. **Define** symbolic and commercial speech; describe the limits on their exercise.

WHY IT MATTERS

The freedom to express ideas freely and to hear the ideas of others is fundamental to American democracy. However, some limitations on freedom of expression have been upheld by the Supreme Court. These include restrictions on certain kinds of speech, such as sedition and obscenity, and on speech in certain circumstances, such as when broadcast over the public airwaves.

POLITICAL DICTIONARY

★ **libel**
★ **slander**
★ **sedition**
★ **seditious speech**
★ **prior restraint**
★ **shield law**
★ **symbolic speech**
★ **picketing**

▲ Free speech is essential to these anti-tax protestors. **H-SS 12.6.4**

Think about this children's verse for a moment: "Sticks and stones may break my bones, but names will never hurt me." That rhyme says, in effect, that acts and words are separate things, and that acts can harm but words cannot.

Is that really true? Certainly not. You know that words can and do have consequences, sometimes powerful consequences. Words, spoken or written, can make you happy, sad, bored, informed, or entertained. They can also expose you to danger, deny you a job, or lead to other serious consequences.

Free Expression

The guarantees of free speech and press in the 1st and 14th amendments serve two fundamentally important purposes:

(1) to guarantee to *each* person a right of free expression, in the spoken and the written word, and by all other means of communication, as well; and

(2) to guarantee to *all* persons a full, wide-ranging discussion of public affairs.

That is, the 1st and 14th amendments give to all people the right to have their say and the right to hear what others have to say.

The American system of government depends on the ability of the people to make sound, reasoned judgments on matters of public concern. Clearly, people can best make such judgments when they know all the facts and can hear all the available interpretations of those facts.

As you examine the Constitution's 1st and 14th amendments here, keep two other key points in mind: First, the guarantees of free speech and press are intended to protect the expression of unpopular views. Clearly, the opinions of the majority need little or no constitutional protection. These guarantees seek to ensure, as Justice Oliver Wendell Holmes put it, "freedom for the thought that we hate," (Dissenting Opinion, *Schwimmer* v. *United States*, 1929).

Second, some forms of expression are not protected by the Constitution. No person has an unbridled right of free speech or free press. Many reasonable restrictions can be placed on those rights. Think about Justice Holmes's comment about restricting the right to shout "Fire!" in a crowded theater. Or consider this restriction: No person has the right to libel or slander another. **Libel** is the false and malicious use of printed words; **slander** is the false and malicious use of spoken words.[6]

Similarly, the law prohibits the use of obscene words, the printing and distributing of obscene materials, and false advertising. It also condemns the use of words to prompt others to commit a crime—for example, to riot or to attempt to overthrow the government by force.

Seditious Speech

Sedition is the crime of attempting to overthrow the government by force or to disrupt its lawful activities by violent acts.[7] **Seditious speech** is the advocating, or urging, of such conduct. It is not protected by the 1st Amendment.

The Alien and Sedition Acts

Congress first acted to curb opposition to government in the Alien and Sedition Acts of 1798. Those acts gave the President the power to deport undesirable aliens and made "any false, scandalous, and malicious" criticism of the government a crime. These laws were meant to stifle the opponents of President John Adams and the Federalists.

The Alien and Sedition Acts were undoubtedly unconstitutional, but that point was never tested in the courts. Some 25 persons were arrested for violating them; of those, ten were convicted. The Alien and Sedition Acts expired before Thomas Jefferson became President in 1801, and he soon pardoned those who had run afoul of them.

The Sedition Act of 1917

Congress passed another sedition law during World War I, as part of the Espionage Act of 1917. That law made it a crime to encourage disloyalty, interfere with the draft, obstruct recruiting, incite insubordination in the armed forces, or hinder the sale of government bonds.

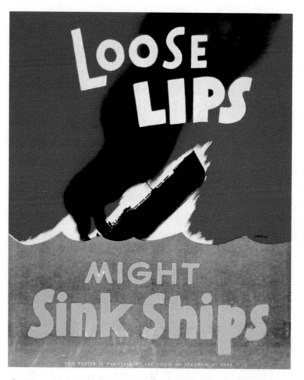

▲ This poster warned of the dangers of careless talk and espionage during World War II. *Critical Thinking How might careless conversation endanger ships during wartime?*

The act also made it a crime to "willfully utter, print, write, or publish any disloyal, profane, scurrilous, or abusive language about the form of government of the United States."

More than 2,000 persons were convicted for violating the Espionage Act. The constitutionality of the law was upheld several times, most importantly in *Schenck* v. *United States*, 1919. Charles Schenck, an officer of the Socialist Party, had been found guilty of obstructing the war effort. He had sent fiery leaflets to some 15,000 men who had been drafted, urging them to resist the call to military service.

The Supreme Court upheld Schenck's conviction. The case is particularly noteworthy because the Court's opinion, written by Justice Oliver Wendell Holmes, established the "clear and present danger" rule.

> **PRIMARY Sources** *"Words can be weapons. . . . The question in every case is whether the words used are used in such circumstances and are of such nature as to create a clear and present danger that they will bring about the substantive evils that Congress has a right to prevent."*
>
> —Opinion of the Court

---

[6] Both libel and slander involve the use of words maliciously—with vicious purpose—to injure a person's character or reputation or expose that person to public contempt, ridicule, or hatred. Truth is generally an absolute defense against a libel or slander claim.

[7] Espionage, sabotage, and treason are often confused with sedition. Espionage is spying for a foreign power. Sabotage involves an act of destruction intended to hinder a nation's war or defense effort. Treason can be committed only in time of war and can consist only of levying war against the United States or giving aid and comfort to its enemies.

In short, the rule says that words can be outlawed. Those who utter them can be punished when the words they use trigger an immediate danger that criminal acts will follow.

The Smith Act of 1940

Congress passed the Smith Act in 1940, just over a year before the United States entered World War II. That law is still on the books. It makes it a crime for anyone to advocate the violent overthrow of the government of the United States, to distribute any material that teaches or advises violent overthrow, or to knowingly belong to any group with such an aim.

The Court upheld the Smith Act in *Dennis* v. *United States*, in 1951. Eleven Communist Party leaders had been convicted of advocating the overthrow of the Federal Government. On appeal, they argued that the law violated the 1st Amendment's guarantees of freedom of speech and press. They also claimed that no act of theirs constituted a clear and present danger to this country. The Court disagreed, and modified Justice Holmes's doctrine as it did so:

PRIMARY Sources *❝An attempt to overthrow the government by force, even though doomed from the outset because of inadequate numbers or power of the revolutionists, is a sufficient evil for Congress to prevent. . . .❞*
—Chief Justice Fred M. Vinson, Opinion of the Court

Later, however, the Court modified that holding in several cases. In *Yates* v. *United States*, 1957, for example, the Court overturned the Smith Act convictions of several Communist Party leaders. It held that merely to urge someone to *believe* something, in contrast to urging that person to do something, cannot be made illegal. In *Yates* and other Smith Act cases, the Court upheld the constitutionality of the law, but interpreted its provisions so that their enforcement became practically impossible.

Obscenity

The 1st and 14th amendments do not protect obscenity, but in recent years the Court has had to wrestle with these questions: What language and images in printed matter, films, and other materials are, in fact, obscene? What restrictions can be properly placed on such materials?

Congress passed the first of a series of laws to prevent the mailing of obscene matter in 1872. The current law, upheld by the Court in *Roth* v. *United States,* 1957, excludes "every obscene, lewd, lascivious, or filthy" piece of material from the mails. The Court found the law a proper exercise of the postal power (Article I, Section 8, Clause 7), and so not prohibited by the 1st Amendment. *Roth* marked the Court's first attempt to define obscenity.

Today, the leading case is *Miller* v. *California,* 1973. There, the Court laid down a three-part test to determine what material is obscene and what is not.

A book, film, recording, or other piece of material is legally obscene if (1) "the average person applying contemporary [local] community standards" finds that the work, taken as a whole, "appeals to the prurient interest"—that is, tends to excite lust; (2) "the work depicts or describes, in a patently offensive way," a form of sexual conduct specifically dealt with in an antiobscenity law; and (3) "the work, taken as a whole, lacks serious literary, artistic, political, or scientific value."

A sampling of Supreme Court decisions involving local attempts to regulate so-called adult book stores and similar places shows how thorny the problem can be. Most of what those stores sell cannot be mailed, sent across State lines, or imported—at least not legally. Still, those shops are usually well-stocked.

The 1st and 14th amendments do not prevent a city from regulating the location of "adult entertainment establishments," said the Court in

IT'S YOUR SON WHO BELIEVES IN FREE SPEECH.

HE'S CALLING COLLECT.

Yates - BRICKMAN

"The Small Society," by Yates-Brickman. Washington Star Syndicate, Inc.

Interpreting Political Cartoons This kind of "free speech" is clearly not what is covered by the 1st Amendment. ***What other kinds of speech are not protected by the Constitution?***

Young v. *American Mini Theaters*, 1976. In *City of Renton* v. *Playtimes Theaters, Inc.*, 1986, the Court ruled that a city can decide to bar the location of such places within 1,000 feet of a residential zone, church, park, or school. But a city cannot prohibit live entertainment in any and all commercial establishments, according to *Schad* v. *Borough of Mount Ephraim*, 1981 (a case that involved nude dancing in adult book stores).

In *City of Erie* v. *Pap's A&M*, 2000, the Court upheld the power of cities to ban taverns, bars, and similar places that feature nude dancing. It found Erie's city ordinance constitutional because that law is not aimed at limiting free expression; instead, it limits the *means* of expression—that is, nude (as distinguished from other forms of) dancing.

In the most recent case in this area of the law, the High Court upheld a federal statute concerned with public libraries and the Internet. That law, the Children's Internet Protection Act, says that those public libraries that receive federal money—nearly all of them do—must use filters to block their computers' access to pornographic sites on the Internet, *United States* v. *American Library Association*, 2003.

Prior Restraint

The Constitution allows government to punish some utterances *after* they are made. But, with almost no exceptions, government cannot place any **prior restraint** on spoken or written words. Except in the most extreme situations, government cannot curb ideas *before* they are expressed.

Near v. *Minnesota*, 1931, is a leading case in point. The Supreme Court struck down a State law that prohibited the publication of any "malicious, scandalous, and defamatory" periodical. Acting under that law, a local court had issued an order forbidding the publication of the *Saturday Press*. That Minneapolis paper had printed several articles charging public corruption and attacking "grafters" and "Jewish gangsters."

The Court held that the guarantee of a free press does not allow a prior restraint on publication, except in such extreme cases as wartime, or when a publication is obscene or incites its readers to violence. The Court said

that even "miscreant purveyors of scandal" and anti-Semitism enjoy this constitutional protection.

The Constitution does not forbid any and all forms of prior censorship, but "a prior restraint on expression comes to this Court with a 'heavy presumption' against its constitutionality," *Nebraska Press Association* v. *Stuart*, 1976.[8] The Court has used that general rule several times—for example, in the famous Pentagon Papers Case, *New York Times* v. *United States*, 1971.

In that case, several newspapers had obtained copies of a set of classified documents, widely known as the Pentagon Papers. Officially titled *History of U.S. Decision-Making Process on Viet Nam Policy*, these documents had been stolen from the Defense Department and then leaked to the press.

---

[8]In this case a judge had ordered the media not to report certain details of a murder trial. The Court held the judge's gag order to be unconstitutional.

► These teenagers should not be admitted to R-rated movies. *Critical Thinking Does the 1st Amendment protect their right to see whatever movie they wish? Why or why not?*

The government sought a court order to bar their publication. The Court, however, held that the government had not shown that printing the Pentagon Papers would endanger the nation's security. The government thus had not overcome the "heavy presumption" against prior censorship.

The few prior restraints the Court has approved include:

• regulations prohibiting the distribution of political literature on military bases without the approval of military authorities, *Greer* v. *Spock*, 1976;

• a CIA rule that agents must agree never to publish anything about the agency without the CIA's permission, *Snepp* v. *United States*, 1980;

• a federal prison rule that allows officials to prevent an inmate from receiving publications considered "detrimental to the security, good order, or discipline" of the prison, *Thornburgh* v. *Abbott*, 1989.

The Court has also said that public school officials have a broad power to censor school newspapers and plays, as well as other "school-sponsored expressive activities." In *Hazelwood School District* v. *Kuhlmeier*, 1988, it held that educators can exercise "editorial control over the style and content of student speech in school-sponsored expressive activities so long as their actions are reasonably related to legitimate pedagogical concerns."

The Media

The 1st Amendment stands as a monument to the central importance of the media in a free society. That raises this question: To what extent can the media—both print and electronic—be regulated by government?

Confidentiality

Can news reporters be forced to testify before a grand jury in court, or before a legislative committee? Can these government bodies require journalists to name their sources and reveal other confidential information? Many reporters and news organizations insist that they must have the right to refuse to testify, the right to protect their sources. They argue that without this right they cannot assure confidentiality, and therefore many sources will not reveal information needed to keep the public informed.

Both State and federal courts have generally rejected the news media argument. In recent years several reporters have refused to obey court orders directing them to give information, and they have gone to jail, thus testifying to the importance of these issues.

In the leading case, *Branzburg* v. *Hayes*, 1972, the Supreme Court held that reporters, "like other citizens, [must] respond to relevant questions put to them in the course of a valid grand jury investigation or criminal trial." If the media are to receive any special exemptions, said the Court, they must come from Congress and the State legislatures.

To date, Congress has not acted on the Court's suggestion, but some 30 States have passed so-called **shield laws.** These laws give reporters some protection against having to disclose their sources or reveal other confidential information in legal proceedings in those States.

Motion Pictures

The Supreme Court took its first look at motion pictures early in the history of the movie industry. In 1915, in *Mutual Film Corporation* v. *Ohio*, the Court upheld a State law that barred the showing of any film that was not of a "moral, educational, or harmless and amusing character." The Court declared that "the exhibition of moving pictures is a business, pure and simple," and "not . . . part of the press of the country." With that decision, nearly every State and thousands of communities set up movie review (really movie censorship) programs.

The Court reversed itself in 1952, however. In *Burstyn* v. *Wilson*, a New York censorship case, it found that "liberty of expression by means of motion pictures is guaranteed by the 1st and 14th amendments."

Very few local movie review boards still exist. Most movie-goers now depend on the film industry's own rating system and on the comments of movie critics.

Radio and Television

Both radio and television broadcasting are subject to extensive federal regulation. Most of this regulation is based on the often-amended Federal Communications Act of 1934, which is administered by the Federal Communications Commission. As the Supreme Court noted in *Red Lion Broadcasting Co.* v. *FCC*, 1969: "Of all forms of communication, it is broadcasting that has received the most limited 1st Amendment protection."

The Court has several times upheld this wide-ranging federal regulation as a proper exercise of the commerce power. Unlike newspapers and other print media, radio and television use the public's property—the public airwaves—to distribute their materials. They have no right to do so without the public's permission in the form of a proper license, said the Court in *National Broadcasting Co.* v. *United States*, 1943.

The Court has regularly rejected the argument that the 1st Amendment prohibits such regulations. Instead, it has said that regulation of this industry actually implements the constitutional guarantee. In *Red Lion Broadcasting Co.* v. *FCC*, 1969, the Court held that there is no "unabridgeable 1st Amendment right to broadcast comparable to the right of every individual to speak, write, or publish." However, "this is not to say that the 1st Amendment is irrelevant to broadcasting. But . . . it is the right of the viewers and the listeners, not the right of the broadcasters, which is paramount."

Congress has forbidden the FCC to censor the content of programs before they are broadcast. However, the FCC can prohibit the use of indecent language, and it can take violations of this ban into account when a station applies for the renewal of its operating license, according to *FCC* v. *Pacifica Foundation*, 1978.

In several recent decisions, the Supreme Court has given the growing cable television industry broader 1st Amendment freedoms than those enjoyed by traditional television.

United States v. *Playboy Entertainment Group*, 2000, is fairly typical. There, the Court struck down an attempt by Congress to force many cable systems to limit sexually explicit channels to late night hours. The Court agreed that shielding children from such programming is a worthy goal; nevertheless, it found the 1996 law to be a violation of the 1st Amendment.

Symbolic Speech

People also communicate ideas by conduct, by the way they do a particular thing. Thus, a person can "say" something with a facial expression or a shrug of the shoulders, or by carrying a sign or wearing an armband. This expression by conduct is known as **symbolic speech.**

Clearly, not all conduct amounts to symbolic speech. If it did, murder or robbery or any other crime could be excused on grounds that the person who committed the act meant to say something by doing so.

Just as clearly, however, some conduct does express opinion. Take picketing in a labor dispute as an example. **Picketing** involves patrolling of a business site by workers who are on strike. By their conduct, picketers attempt to inform the public of the controversy, and to persuade others not to deal with the firm involved. Picketing is, then, a form of expression. If peaceful, it is protected by the 1st and 14th amendments.

The leading case on the point is *Thornhill* v. *Alabama*, 1940. There, the Court struck down a State law that made it a crime to loiter about or to picket a place of business in order to influence others not to trade or work there. Picketing that is "set in a background of violence," however, can be prevented. Even peaceful picketing can be restricted if it is conducted for an illegal purpose, such as forcing someone to do something that is itself illegal.

▲ These demonstrators were protesting the Vietnam War in 1971. *Critical Thinking* *Was this demonstration protected by the 1st Amendment? Why or why not?* H-SS 12.6.4

Other Symbolic Speech Cases

The Supreme Court has been sympathetic to the symbolic speech argument, but it has not given blanket 1st Amendment protection to that means of expression. As a sampling, note these cases:

United States v. *O'Brien,* 1968, involved four young men who had burned their draft cards to protest the war in Vietnam. A court convicted them of violating a federal law that makes that act a crime. O'Brien appealed, arguing that the 1st Amendment protects "all modes of communication of ideas by conduct." The Supreme Court disagreed. Said the Court: "We cannot accept the view that an apparently limitless variety of conduct can be labeled 'speech' whenever the person engaging in the conduct intends thereby to express an idea."

The Court also held that acts of dissent by conduct can be punished if: (1) the object of the protest (here, the war and the draft) is within the constitutional powers of the government; (2) whatever restriction is placed on expression is no greater than necessary in the circumstances; and (3) the government's real interest in the matter is not to squelch dissent.

Using that three-part test, the Court has sometimes denied claims of symbolic speech. Thus, in *Virginia* v. *Black,* 2003, it upheld a State law that prohibits the burning of a cross as an act of intimidation—as a threat that can make a person fear for his or her safety. But the Court also made this point: Those who burn crosses at rallies or parades as acts of political

expression (acts not aimed at a particular person) cannot be prosecuted under the law.

Tinker v. *Des Moines School District,* 1969, on the other hand, is one of several cases in which the Court has come down on the side of symbolic speech. A small group of students in the Des Moines public schools had worn black armbands to publicize their opposition to the war in Vietnam. The school suspended them for it.

The Court ruled that school officials had overstepped their authority and violated the Constitution. Said the Court: "It can hardly be argued that either students or teachers shed their constitutional rights to freedom of speech or expression at the schoolhouse gate."[9]

In *Buckley* v. *Valeo,* 1976, the Court found that campaign contributions are "a symbolic expression of support" for candidates, and therefore the making of those contributions is entitled to constitutional protection. Both federal and State laws regulate campaign contributions, but the fact that in politics "money is speech" greatly complicates the whole matter of campaign finance regulation (see Chapter 7).

Flag Burning

Burning the American flag as an act of political protest is expressive conduct protected by the 1st and 14th amendments—so a sharply divided Court has twice held. In *Texas* v. *Johnson,* 1989, a 5–4 majority ruled that State authorities had violated a protester's rights by prosecuting him under a law that forbids the "desecration of a venerated object." Johnson had set fire to an American flag during an anti-Reagan demonstration at the Republican National Convention in Dallas in 1984. Said the Court:

> PRIMARY *Sources* **❝***If there is a bedrock principle underlying the 1st Amendment, it is that the government may not prohibit the expression of an idea simply because society finds the idea itself offensive. . . . We do not consecrate the flag by punishing its desecration, for in doing so we dilute the*

---

[9]Do not read too much into this, for the Court added, it "has repeatedly affirmed the comprehensive authority of the States and of school authorities, consistent with fundamental constitutional safeguards, to prescribe and control conduct in the schools." The fact that in *Tinker* the students' conduct did not cause a substantial disruption of normal school activities was an important factor in the Court's decision.

freedom that this cherished emblem represents. "

—Justice William J. Brennan, Jr.

The Court's decision in *Johnson* set off a firestorm of criticism around the country and prompted Congress to pass the Flag Protection Act of 1989. It, too, was struck down by the Court, 5 to 4, in *United States* v. *Eichman*, 1990. The Court based its decision on the same grounds as those set out a year earlier in *Johnson*.

Commercial Speech

Commercial speech is speech for business purposes; the term refers most often to advertising. Until the mid-1970s, it was thought that the 1st and 14th amendments did not protect such speech. In *Bigelow* v. *Virginia*, 1975, however, the Supreme Court held unconstitutional a State law that prohibited the newspaper advertising of abortion services. The following year, in *Virginia State Board of Pharmacy* v. *Virginia Citizens Consumer Council*, it struck down another Virginia law forbidding the advertisement of prescription drug prices.

Not all commercial speech is protected, however. Thus, government can and does prohibit false and misleading advertisements, and the advertising of illegal goods or services.

In fact, government can even forbid advertising that is neither false nor misleading. Thus, in 1970, Congress banned cigarette ads on radio and television. In 1986, it extended the ban to include chewing tobacco and snuff.

In most of its commercial speech cases, the Court has struck down arbitrary restrictions on advertising. Thus, in *44 Liquormart, Inc.* v. *Rhode Island*, 1996, the Court voided a State law that prohibited ads in which liquor prices were listed. In *Greater New Orleans Broadcasting Ass'n* v. *United States*, 1999, it struck down a federal law that prohibited casino advertising on radio or television.

Most recently, the Court dealt with limits on smokeless tobacco and cigar advertising. Massachusetts had barred outdoor ads for these commodities within 1000 feet of any school or playground. The Court held that limit a violation of the 1st and 14th amendments' guarantee of free speech, *P. Lorillard Co.* v. *Reilly*, 2001.

One of the Court's first commercial speech cases had an interesting twist. In *Wooley* v. *Maynard*, 1977, the Court held that a State cannot force its citizens to act as "mobile billboards." At least, a State cannot do so when the words used conflict with its citizens' religious or moral beliefs. The Maynards, who were Jehovah's Witnesses, objected to the New Hampshire State motto on their automobile license plates. The words *Live Free or Die* clashed with their belief in everlasting life, and so they covered those words with tape. For this, Maynard was arrested three times. On appeal, the Supreme Court sided with Maynard.

Section 3 Assessment

Key Terms and Main Ideas

1. Compare **libel** with **slander**.
2. Why does the government restrict **seditious speech**?
3. (a) Define **prior restraint**. (b) How has the Supreme Court usually dealt with prior restraint cases?
4. In what way is **picketing symbolic speech**?

Critical Thinking

5. **Identifying Alternatives** Do you think journalists should have the right to protect their sources? Describe one instance where this right would benefit society and one instance where it might be harmful.
6. **Identifying Central Issues** The Constitution makes a particular effort to protect the expression of unpopular views.

(a) Why is this important? (b) Do you think even racist or sexist speech and publications should be protected? (c) Explain your answer.

Face the
Issues

The Patriot Act

Background *In the wake of 9/11, a united Congress passed the USA Patriot Act, which gave the Justice Department broader powers to track down and prosecute suspected terrorists. From its inception, however, the Patriot Act has generated controversy. Critics warn that it has eroded the Bill of Rights. Law enforcement officials counter that it has merely updated the law in response to new technologies and new threats. Several years after the attack on the World Trade Center, the Patriot Act continues to spark debate.*

Attorney General Alberto Gonzales

Analysis Skills CS1, HI1

Renew the Patriot Act	Let the Patriot Act Expire

One lesson of 9/11 is that Americans must be vigilant about terrorists within our country's borders. The Patriot Act gives law enforcement the tools it needs to root out a sophisticated, mobile enemy. A Justice Department representative says the Patriot Act "has played a key part—and often a leading role—in a number of successful operations to protect Americans from the deadly plans of terrorists."

The Patriot Act levels the battlefield in the war on terrorism. Federal agents were once barred from using certain investigative "tools" that were available in drug-trafficking investigations for counterterrorism cases. Now agents can request a so-called "roving wiretap" on a particular suspect in a terrorism case, rather than on a particular phone or place.

Before, intelligence agencies were not allowed to share information with law enforcement agencies. This rule explains in part why the United States failed to detect certain terrorists before they struck on 9/11. Now, these agencies can share information, enhancing our security.

No one disagrees with the goal of protecting Americans. However, the Patriot Act exacts too great a price in loss of privacy and other freedoms.

The 300-page act was passed nearly without debate and without a clear understanding of its effects. Now, the FBI no longer needs a search warrant or even probable cause to get into your medical records, your student records, and your library records—and it can stop anyone from telling you about it.

The Patriot Act is increasingly being used against ordinary crime, not just terrorism. By removing judicial oversight and longstanding checks and balances, it gives federal agencies a virtually free hand to investigate Americans.

The Patriot Act threatens constitutional safeguards against unlawful search and seizure. Americans have to hope and trust that the government uses these expanded powers to protect Americans from terrorism only. However, hope and trust are not always enough. That is why four States have passed resolutions opposing the Patriot Act.

Exploring the Issues

1. Why might the government need special powers to combat modern terrorism?
2. What are the drawbacks of passing a law without much debate?

For more information about the challenge of confronting terrorism, view "The Patriot Act."

Face the **Issues** Video Collection

Freedom of Assembly and Petition

Section Preview

OBJECTIVES

1. **Explain** the Constitution's guarantees of assembly and petition.
2. **Summarize** how the government can limit the time, place, and manner of assembly.
3. **Compare and contrast** the freedom-of-assembly issues that arise on public versus private property.
4. **Explore** how the Supreme Court has interpreted freedom of association.

WHY IT MATTERS

The constitutional guarantees of assembly and petition protect Americans' rights to gather peacefully in order to express their views and to influence public policy, by such means as demonstrations and written petitions. There are place, time, and manner limitations on these freedoms, however.

POLITICAL DICTIONARY

★ **assemble**
★ **content neutral**
★ **right of association**

A noisy street demonstration by gay rights activists, or by neo-Nazis, or by any number of other groups; a candlelight vigil of opponents of the death penalty; the pro-life faithful singing hymns as they picket an abortion clinic; prochoice partisans gathered on the steps of the State capitol . . . these are commonplace events today. They are also everyday manifestations of freedom of assembly and petition.

The Constitution's Guarantees

The 1st Amendment guarantees

> **FROM THE Constitution** " . . . the right of the people peaceably to assemble, and to petition the Government for a redress of grievances. "
> —United States Constitution

The 14th Amendment's Due Process Clause also protects those rights of assembly and petition against actions by the States or their local governments.

The Constitution protects the right of the people to **assemble**—to gather with one another—to express their views on public matters. It protects their right to organize to influence public policy, whether in political parties, interest groups, or other organizations. It also protects the people's right to bring their views to the attention of public officials by such varied means as written petitions, letters, or advertisements; lobbying; or parades, marches, or other demonstrations.

Notice, however, the 1st and 14th amendments protect the rights of *peaceable* assembly and petition. The Constitution does not give people the right to incite others to violence, to block a public street, to close a school, or otherwise to endanger life, property, or public order

But notice this important point as well: a significant part of the history of this country can be told in terms of *civil disobedience*. That is to say that much of our history has been built out of incidents in which people have purposely violated the law, nonviolently but nonetheless deliberately, as a means of expressing their opposition to some particular law or public policy.

Do the 1st and 14th Amendment guarantees of freedom of assembly and petition include a right of civil disobedience? That thorny question cannot be answered absolutely or without qualification, because of the nature of acts of civil disobedience. Such acts are basically expressions of opinion on some public matter.

Still, courts have consistently held that, as a general rule, civil disobedience is not a constitutionally protected right. And those take part in such activities are most often quite aware of that fact.

Time-Place-Manner Regulations

Government can make and enforce reasonable rules covering the time, place, and manner of assemblies. Thus, in *Grayned* v. *City of Rockford,* 1972, the Supreme Court has upheld a city ordinance that prohibits making a noise or causing any other diversion near a school if that action disrupts school activities. It has also upheld a State law that forbids parades near a courthouse when they are intended to influence court proceedings, in *Cox* v. *Louisiana,* 1965.

Rules for keeping the public peace must be more than reasonable, however. They must also be precisely drawn and fairly administered. In *Coates* v. *Cincinnati,* 1971, the Court struck down a city ordinance that made it a crime for "three or more persons to assemble" on a sidewalk or street corner "and there conduct themselves in a manner annoying to persons passing by, or to occupants of adjacent buildings." The Court found the ordinance much too vague.

Government's rules must be **content neutral.** That is, while government can regulate assemblies on the basis of time, place, and manner, it cannot regulate assemblies on the basis of what might be said there. Thus, in *Forsyth County* v. *Nationalist Movement,* 1992, the Court threw out a Georgia county's ordinance that levied a fee of up to $1,000 for public demonstrations.

The law was contested by a white supremacist group seeking to protest the creation of a holiday to honor Martin Luther King, Jr. The Court found the ordinance not to be content neutral, particularly because county officials had unlimited power to set the exact fee to be paid by any group.

Notice that the power to control traffic or keep a protest rally from becoming a riot *can* be used as an excuse to prevent speech. The line between crowd control and thought control can be very thin, indeed.

Public Property

Over the past several years, most of the Court's freedom of assembly cases have involved organized demonstrations. Demonstrations are, of course, assemblies.

Most demonstrations take place in public places, on streets and sidewalks, in parks or public buildings, and so on. Demonstrations take place in these locations because it is the public the demonstrators want to reach.

Demonstrations almost always involve some degree of conflict. Most often, they are held to protest something, and so there is an inherent clash of ideas. Many times there is also a conflict with the normal use of streets or other public facilities. It is hardly surprising, then, that the tension can sometimes rise to a serious level.

Given all this, the Supreme Court has often upheld laws that require advance notice and permits for demonstrations in public places. In an early leading case, *Cox* v. *New Hampshire,* 1941, it unanimously approved a State law that required a license to hold a parade or other procession on a public street.

Right-to-demonstrate cases raise many basic and thorny questions. How and to what extent can government regulate demonstrators and their demonstrations? Does the Constitution require that police officers allow an unpopular group to continue to demonstrate when its activities have excited others to violence? When, in the name of public peace and safety, can police properly order demonstrators to disband?

Gregory v. Chicago

Gregory v. *Chicago,* 1969, is an illustrative case. While under police protection, Dick Gregory and others had marched, while singing, chanting, and carrying placards, from city hall to the mayor's home some five miles away. Marching in the streets around the mayor's house, they demanded the firing of the city's school superintendent and an end to de facto segregation in the city's schools.

A crowd of several hundred people, including many residents of the all-white neighborhood, quickly gathered. Soon, the bystanders began throwing insults and threats, as well as rocks, eggs, and other objects. The police tried to keep order, but after about an hour, they decided that serious violence was about to break out. At that point, they ordered the demonstrators to leave the area. When Gregory and the others failed to do so, the police arrested them and charged them with disorderly conduct.

The convictions of the demonstrators were unanimously overturned by the High Court. The Court noted that the marchers had done no

▲ **Peaceful Protest** These demonstrators have gathered in front of the White House to rally against war maneuvers and bomb storage on the Puerto Rican island of Vieques, located in the Caribbean to the east of the main island of Puerto Rico. **H-SS 12.2.1**

more than exercise their constitutional rights of assembly and petition. Neighborhood residents and others, not the demonstrators, had caused the disorder. So long as the demonstrators acted peacefully, they could not be punished for disorderly conduct.

Recent Cases

Over recent years, many of the most controversial demonstrations have been those held by Operation Rescue and other anti-abortion groups. For the most part, the efforts of those groups have been aimed at discouraging women from seeking the services of abortion clinics, and those efforts have generated many lawsuits.

There have been two particularly notable cases to date. In the first one, *Madsen* v. *Women's Health Services, Inc.*, 1994, the Supreme Court upheld a Florida judge's order directing protesters not to block access to an abortion clinic. The judge's order had drawn a 36-foot buffer zone around the clinic. The High Court found that to be a reasonable limit on the demonstrators' activities.

The other major case is a more recent one, *Hill* v. *Colorado*, 2000. There, the Court upheld, 5–4, a State law that limits "sidewalk counseling" at clinics where abortions are performed. That statute creates an eight-foot buffer zone around anyone who is within 100 feet of the entrance to a health-care facility and wants to enter. No one may make an "unwanted approach" (invade that buffer zone) to talk or do such other things as hand out a leaflet or wave a sign.

The Court found that the Colorado law does not deal with the content of abortion protestors' speech. Instead it is aimed at where, when, and how their message is delivered.

Private Property

What of demonstrations on private property— for example, at shopping centers? The Court has heard only a few cases raising this question. However, at least this much can be said: The rights of assembly and petition do not give people a right to trespass on private property, even if they wish to express political views.

Privately owned shopping centers are not public streets, sidewalks, parks, and other "places of public assembly." Thus, no one has a constitutional right to do such things as hand out political leaflets or ask people to sign petitions in those places.

These comments are based on the leading case here, *Lloyd Corporation* v. *Tanner*, 1972. However, since that case the Court has held this: A State supreme court may interpret the provisions of that State's constitution in such a way as to require the owners of shopping centers to allow the reasonable exercise of the right of petition on their private property.

In that event, there is no violation of the property owners' rights under any provision in the federal Constitution, *PruneYard Shopping Center* v. *Robins*, 1980. In that case, several California high school students had set up a card table in the shopping center. They passed out

Interpreting Political Cartoons *How do you think the Supreme Court might rule in a case like this: for the boys (freedom of association) or for the girl (anti-discrimination)? Explain your answer.* H-SS 12.5.1

pro-Israeli pamphlets and asked passersby to sign petitions to be sent to the President and Congress.

Freedom of Association

The guarantees of freedom of assembly and petition include a **right of association.** That is, those guarantees include the right to associate with others to promote political, economic, and other social causes. That right is not set out in so many words in the Constitution. However, in *National Association for the Advancement of Colored People* v. *Alabama,* 1958, the Supreme Court said "it is beyond doubt that freedom to engage in association for the advancement of

beliefs and ideas is an inseparable aspect" of the Constitution's guarantees of free expression.

The case just cited is one of the early right-to-associate cases. There, a State law required the Alabama branch of the NAACP to disclose the names of all its members in that State. When the organization refused a court's order to do so, it was found in contempt of court and fined $100,000.

The Supreme Court overturned the contempt conviction. It said that it could find no legitimate reason why the State should have the NAACP's membership list.

A more recent case bearing on freedom of association involved the Boy Scouts of America. In *Boy Scouts of America* v. *Dale,* 2000, it held that the Boy Scouts have a constitutional right to exclude gays from their organization. The High Court made that decision in a New Jersey case, noting that opposition to homosexuality is a part of the Boy Scout organization's "expressive conduct"—that is, what they stand for.

The decision overturned a ruling by the New Jersey Supreme Court. That court had applied the State's anti-discrimination law against the Scouts; it ordered a New Jersey troop to readmit James Dale, an Eagle Scout, whom the troop had dismissed when it learned he was gay.

The Court ruled that the Constitution's guarantee of freedom of association means that a State cannot force an organization like the Boy Scouts to accept members when that action would contradict what the organization professes to believe.

Section 4 Assessment

Key Terms and Main Ideas

1. What does the right to **assemble** peaceably mean? Give two examples of peaceful assembly for political purposes.
2. Summarize briefly how the Supreme Court has limited the time, place, and manner of assembly.
3. How does the **right of association** extend the right of assembly?

Critical Thinking

4. **Identifying Central Issues** Why are the freedom to assemble peacefully and the freedom of association central to an open, democratic society?
5. **Formulating Questions** Not all assembly is protected by the 1st Amendment. Suppose you are helping to organize

Standards Monitoring *Online*
For: Self-quiz with vocabulary practice
Web Code: mqa-5194

a demonstration for a political cause. Make up three to five questions you should ask in order to determine if your demonstration would be considered constitutional by the Supreme Court.

Go Online
PHSchool.com

For: An activity on freedom of assembly and petition
Web Code: mqd-5194

May Schools Ban Political Protests?

In order to educate students and also to ensure their safety, school officials need broad authority to control what goes on in schools. Recognizing this fact, the courts have granted schools flexibility in certain areas, such as censorship. Can schools prevent students from peacefully expressing opinions on controversial political issues?

Analysis Skills
HR4, HI3, HI4

Tinker v. *Des Moines School District* (1969)

In December 1965, a group of students and adults in Des Moines, Iowa, met to discuss ways of publicizing their opposition to the war in Vietnam and their support for a truce in the fighting. The group included 15-year-old high school student John Tinker, his sister Mary Beth Tinker, and his friend Christopher Eckhardt. The three students decided to wear black armbands through the end of the holiday season and to fast on two days.

The principals of the Des Moines schools learned of the plans to wear armbands. They met on December 14 and adopted a policy that any student wearing an armband would be asked to remove it. Anyone refusing to comply would be suspended.

On December 16, Mary Beth and Christopher wore their armbands to school. John wore his the following day. All were sent home and were suspended until they returned without the armbands. They did not return to school until January, when the planned time for wearing the armbands had expired. The students' fathers filed suit in federal district court, seeking a court order to prevent enforcement of the school district's ban on armbands. They also asked that the school district not be allowed to discipline the students for wearing them. The court found that the school authorities' actions did not violate the Constitution. The court of appeals agreed with the district court, and the Tinkers appealed to the Supreme Court.

Arguments for Tinker

1. Wearing an armband to express an opinion is symbolic speech that is protected under the Free Speech Clause of the 1st Amendment.

2. Students do not lose their 1st Amendment rights when they are in school. School authorities may restrict speech or action that interferes with the work of the school but may not prohibit silent, passive expressions of opinion that create no such interference.

3. Schools may not limit expressions of opinion to avoid confrontation or disagreement among students over politically sensitive issues.

Arguments for Des Moines School District

1. States and school officials must have complete authority to control conduct in public schools in order to maintain discipline and good order.

2. The ban on armbands was reasonable because it was based upon fear of a disturbance in school.

3. The plaintiffs' wearing of armbands distracted other students from their classwork and diverted them to the highly emotional subject of the Vietnam War. Schools have the right to adopt reasonable regulations to keep students focused on school subjects.

Decide for Yourself

1. Review the constitutional grounds on which each side based its arguments and the specific arguments each side presented.

2. Debate the opposing viewpoints presented in this case. Which viewpoint do you favor?

3. Predict the impact of the Court's decision on other issues relating to students' rights. (To read a summary of the Court's decision, turn to pages 799–806.)

Go Online
PHSchool.com

Use Web Code mqp-5197 to register your vote on this issue and to see how other students voted.

Political Dictionary

Bill of Rights (p. 532), civil liberties (p. 533), civil rights (p. 533), alien (p. 534), Due Process Clause (p. 535), process of incorporation (p. 535), Establishment Clause (p. 537), parochial (p. 538), Free Exercise Clause (p. 542), libel (p. 546), slander (p. 547), sedition (p. 547), seditious speech (p. 547), prior restraint (p. 549), shield law (p. 550), symbolic speech (p. 551), picketing (p. 551), assemble (p. 555), content neutral (p. 556), right of association (p. 558)

Standards Review

H-SS 12.1.2 Discuss the character of American democracy and its promise and perils as articulated by Alexis de Tocqueville.

H-SS 12.1.6 Understand that the Bill of Rights limits the powers of the federal government and state governments.

H-SS 12.2.1 Discuss the meaning and importance of each of the rights guaranteed under the Bill of Rights and how each is secured (e.g., freedom of religion, speech, press, assembly, petition, privacy).

H-SS 12.2.5 Describe the reciprocity between rights and obligations; that is, why enjoyment of one's rights entails respect for the rights of others.

H-SS 12.3.1 Explain how civil society provides opportunities for individuals to associate for social, cultural, religious, economic, and political purposes.

H-SS 12.3.3 Discuss the historical role of religion and religious diversity.

H-SS 12.5.1 Understand the changing interpretations of the Bill of Rights over time, including interpretations of the basic freedoms (religion, speech, press, petition, and assembly) articulated in the First Amendment and the due process and equal protection-of-the-law clauses of the Fourteenth Amendment.

H-SS 12.6.4 Describe the means that citizens use to participate in the political process (e.g., voting, campaigning, lobbying, filing a legal challenge, demonstrating, petitioning, picketing, running for political office).

H-SS 12.7.4 Discuss the Ninth and Tenth Amendments and interpretations of the extent of the federal government's power.

H-SS 12.8.1 Discuss the meaning and importance of a free and responsible press.

H-SS 12.10 Students formulate questions about and defend their analyses of tensions within our constitutional democracy and the importance of maintaining a balance between the following concepts: majority rule and individual rights; liberty and equality; state and national authority in a federal system; civil disobedience and the rule of law; freedom of the press and the right to a fair trial; the relationship of religion and government.

Practicing the Vocabulary

Using Terms in Context *For each of the terms below, write a sentence that shows how it relates to this chapter.*

1. Bill of Rights
2. civil liberties
3. Due Process Clause
4. process of incorporation
5. Establishment Clause
6. Free Exercise Clause
7. prior restraint
8. right of association

Word Relationships *Three of the terms in each of the following sets of terms are related. Choose the term that does not belong and explain why it does not.*

9. (a) libel (b) slander (c) symbolic speech (d) seditious speech
10. (a) civil liberties (b) shield law (c) civil rights (d) right of association
11. (a) Bill of Rights (b) Free Exercise Clause (c) Establishment Clause (d) prior restraint
12. (a) parochial (b) picketing (c) assemble (d) symbolic speech

Reviewing Main Ideas

Section 1

13. (a) Why was there an outcry when the Constitution did not originally contain a general listing of the rights of the people? (b) How was this remedied?
14. How does federalism affect the guarantees of individual rights?
15. (a) Explain this statement: Rights are relative, not absolute. (b) What happens when rights conflict?

Section 2

16. What does the Establishment Clause say that the government cannot do?
17. What are the three elements of the *Lemon* test?
18. Identify three ways in which government may restrict the exercise of religious belief.

Section 3

19. What two basic purposes do the guarantees of free expression serve?
20. What has generally been the Supreme Court's attitude toward prior restraint?
21. Describe briefly one case in which the Supreme Court upheld a restriction on symbolic speech and one case where it struck down a restriction.

Section 4

22. Describe the time, place, and manner limits that government can put on freedom of assembly.
23. (a) What is the right of association? (b) The right of association is "an inseparable aspect" of what constitutional guarantees?

Critical Thinking Skills

Analysis Skills HR4, HI1

24. ***Face the Issues*** Former Representative Bob Barr has said, "The Fourth Amendment is a nuisance to the administration, but the amendment protects citizens and legal immigrants from the government's monitoring them whenever it wants, without good cause—and if that happens, it's the end of personal liberty." **(a)** Explain how the Fourth Amendment is related to the Patriot Act. **(b)** How might supporters of the Patriot Act respond to Barr?

25. ***Determining Relevance*** According to Justice Holmes, one of the most important protections offered by the Bill of Rights is protection of "thought that we hate." **(a)** Explain briefly what this protection means, and why it is so important. **(b)** Then, from your knowledge of history or current affairs, discuss one example of a repressive government suppressing speech that it hates, and the repercussions of that repression.

26. ***Drawing Conclusions*** Your school newspaper wants to publish an article critical of one board member's speech at a school board meeting. The principal has forbidden publication of the article because it is disrespectful, misquotes the board member, and states a position that the school administration does not agree with. What constitutional issues does the principal's action raise? Explain how you think the Supreme Court would rule on each of these issues.

Analyzing Political Cartoons

Using your knowledge of American government and this cartoon,

"Since you have already been convicted by the media, I imagine we can wrap this up pretty quickly."

answer the questions below.

27. **(a)** In the caption of this cartoon, what does "convicted by the media" mean? **(b)** How can this kind of conviction affect a trial?

28. What do you think the cartoonist feels about the right of a free press versus the right to a fair trial?

Participation Activities

Analysis Skills CS4, HR4, HI3

29. ***Current Events Watch*** "Speech" on the Internet is unlike expression in other media. Find recent news articles on this topic. List the sorts of Internet speech some people think should be regulated, the practical difficulties of regulating them, and the 1st Amendment issues they raise.

30. ***Table Activity*** Make a table of the important Supreme Court cases involving freedom of assembly. Include a very brief description of each case; indicate whether the issue was time, place, or manner of assembly; and give the Supreme Court's ruling.

31. ***It's Your Turn*** Choose one of the controversial Supreme Court cases discussed in this chapter, and take a position on the issue. Prepare an argument (speech) that you would present to the Supreme Court—for the government or for the other party to the suit. Your argument should not only state and defend your position on the issue but also answer the opposing arguments. **(Writing a Speech)**

Standards Monitoring *Online*

For: Chapter 19 Self-Test **Visit:** PHSchool.com
Web Code: mqa-5195

As a final review, take the Magruder's Chapter 19 Self-Test and receive immediate feedback on your answers. The test consists of 20 multiple-choice questions designed to test your understanding of the chapter content.

Civil Liberties: Protecting Individual Rights

"Most of all, we have got to remember that the law is people. . . . What we are trying to do is solve people's problems and protect their freedoms and protect their interests."

—Janet Reno (1995)

As Attorney General Reno pointed out, the goal of the law is to serve people, to protect both the rights of individuals and the rights of those accused of crimes. Judges and lawmakers thus constantly debate the spirit of the law and how it applies in real life.

◆ Courtroom with a trial in session

Go Online
PHSchool.com

For: Current Data
Web Code: mqg-5206

For: Close Up Foundation debates
Web Code: mqh-5209

SECTION 1

Due Process of Law (pp. 564–568)

★ The 5th and 14th amendments guarantee that the government cannot deprive a person of "life, liberty, or property, without due process of law."

★ The States' reserved powers include the police power—the power to protect and promote public health, public safety, public morals, and the general welfare.

★ The exercise of the police power can produce conflicts with individual rights.

★ The constitutional guarantees of due process create a right of privacy.

★ The most controversial applications of the right of privacy involve abortion.

SECTION 2

Freedom and Security of the Person (pp. 569–574)

★ The 13th Amendment was added to the Constitution in 1865 to end slavery and involuntary servitude.

★ The 2nd Amendment was added to the Constitution to preserve the right of States to keep a militia.

★ The 4th Amendment prohibits unreasonable searches and seizures, not those which are reasonable. The amendment has given rise to the controversial Exclusionary Rule.

SECTION 3

Rights of the Accused (pp. 576–583)

★ Rights of the accused include the writ of habeas corpus and a constitutional ban on bills of attainder and ex post facto laws.

★ The 5th Amendment says that one may be accused of a serious federal crime only by grand jury indictment.

★ Accused persons are guaranteed a speedy and public trial. They cannot, however, be tried twice for the same crime.

★ The accused also have the right to a trial by jury.

★ The right to an adequate defense and the guarantee against self-incrimination help safeguard the rights of the accused.

SECTION 4

Punishment (pp. 585–588)

★ A person accused of a crime is presumed innocent until proven guilty.

★ The accused must not face excessive bail or fines.

★ The Constitution prohibits cruel and unusual punishment.

★ The Supreme Court has consistently held that the death penalty is constitutional if it is applied fairly.

★ The crime of treason is specifically defined in the Constitution to prevent its use for political purposes.

① Due Process of Law

OBJECTIVES

1. **Explain** the meaning of due process of law as set out in the 5th and 14th amendments.
2. **Define** police power and understand its relationship to civil rights.
3. **Describe** the right of privacy and its origins in constitutional law.

WHY IT MATTERS

The guarantees of due process mean that government must act fairly and in accordance with established rules. The States possess the power to safeguard the well-being of their people through the police power. But in doing so, they must observe due process rights, including the right of privacy.

POLITICAL DICTIONARY

★ **due process**
★ **substantive due process**
★ **procedural due process**
★ **police power**
★ **search warrant**

Are you familiar with the riots that took place in Tulsa, Oklahoma, on May 31–June 1, 1921? Are you aware of the conduct of some officers in the Ramparts Division of the Los Angeles police department much more recently? Both of these matters have been the subject of extensive and ongoing news coverage. Learn what happened in Tulsa in 1921 and what some LAPD officers did much more recently, and you will understand why the concept of due process of law is so very important to you and to everyone in this country.

▲ *A Failure of Due Process* Injured and wounded prisoners are taken to the hospital by the National Guard in the aftermath of the 1921 Tulsa riots.

The Meaning of Due Process

The Constitution contains two **due process** clauses. The 5th Amendment declares that the Federal Government cannot deprive any person of "life, liberty, or property, without due process of law." The 14th Amendment places that same restriction on the States, and, very importantly, on their local governments, as well. A thorough grasp of the meaning of these provisions is absolutely essential to an understanding of the American concept of civil rights.

It is impossible to define the two due process guarantees in exact and complete terms. The Supreme Court has consistently and purposely refused to give them an exact definition. Instead, it has relied on finding the meaning of due process on a case-by-case basis. The Court first described that approach in *Davidson* v. *New Orleans,* 1878, as the "gradual process of inclusion and exclusion, as the cases presented for decision require."

Fundamentally, however, the Constitution's guarantee of due process means this: In whatever it does, government must act fairly and in accord with established rules. It may not act unfairly, arbitrarily, capriciously, or unreasonably.

The concept of due process began and developed in English and then in American law as a procedural concept. That is, it first developed as a requirement that government act fairly, use fair procedures.

Fair procedures are of little value, however, if they are used to administer unfair laws. The Supreme Court recognized this fact toward the end of the nineteenth century. It began to hold that due process requires that both the ways in which government acts *and* the laws under which it acts must be fair. Thus, the Court added the idea of **substantive due process** to the original notion of **procedural due process.**

In short, procedural due process has to do with the *how* (the procedures, the methods) of governmental action. Substantive due process involves the *what* (the substance, the policies) of governmental action.

Examples of Due Process

Any number of cases may be used to illustrate these two elements of due process. Take a classic case, *Rochin v. California*, 1952, to exemplify procedural due process.

Rochin was a suspected narcotics dealer. Acting on a tip, three Los Angeles County deputy sheriffs went to his rooming house. They forced their way into Rochin's room. There the deputies found him sitting on a bed, and spotted two capsules on a nightstand. When one of the deputies asked, "Whose stuff is this?" Rochin popped the capsules into his mouth. Although all three officers jumped him, Rochin managed to swallow them.

The deputies took Rochin to a hospital, where his stomach was pumped. The capsules were recovered and found to contain morphine. The State then prosecuted and convicted Rochin for violating the State's narcotics laws.

The Supreme Court held that the deputies had violated the 14th Amendment's guarantee of procedural due process. Said the Court:

> **PRIMARY Sources** ❝This is conduct that shocks the conscience. Illegally breaking into the privacy of the petitioner, the struggle to open his mouth and remove what was there, the forcible extraction of his stomach's contents—this course of proceeding by agents of government to obtain evidence is bound to offend even hardened sensibilities. They are methods too close to the rack and the screw. . . . ❞
> —Justice Felix Frankfurter,
> Opinion of the Court

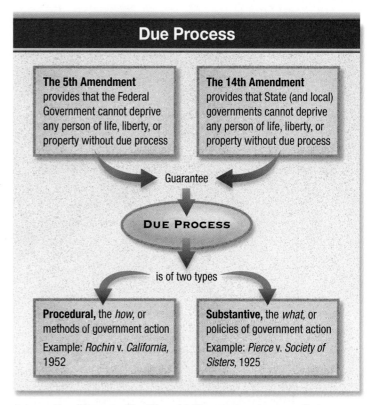

Due Process

The 5th Amendment provides that the Federal Government cannot deprive any person of life, liberty, or property without due process

The 14th Amendment provides that State (and local) governments cannot deprive any person of life, liberty, or property without due process

Guarantee

DUE PROCESS

is of two types

Procedural, the *how,* or methods of government action
Example: *Rochin v. California,* 1952

Substantive, the *what,* or policies of government action
Example: *Pierce v. Society of Sisters,* 1925

Interpreting Diagrams The 5th and 14th amendments ensure that neither the Federal nor State and local governments can deprive any person of "life, liberty, or property, without due process of law." *Why are procedural and substantive due process both necessary?* H-SS 12.5.1

Take *Pierce v. Society of Sisters*, 1925, to illustrate substantive due process. In 1922, Oregon's voters had adopted a new compulsory school-attendance law that required all persons between the ages of 8 and 16 to attend public schools. The law was purposely drawn to destroy private, especially parochial, schools in the State.

A Roman Catholic order challenged the law's constitutionality, and the Supreme Court held that the law violated the 14th Amendment's Due Process Clause. The Court did not find that the State had enforced the law unfairly. In fact, the State's courts had found the law unconstitutional, and it had never been put into effect. Rather, the Court held that the law itself, in its contents, "unreasonably interferes with the liberty of parents to direct the upbringing and education of children under their control."

The 14th Amendment and the Bill of Rights

Recall these crucial points from Chapter 19:

1. The provisions of the Bill of Rights apply against the National Government *only.*

"What's so great about due process? Due process got me ten years."

Interpreting Political Cartoons *Can you assume that the prisoner's complaint is justified? Explain your answer.* **H-SS 12.10**

2. However, the Supreme Court has held that the 14th Amendment's Due Process Clause includes within its meaning most of the protections set out in the Bill of Rights.

In a long series of decisions dating from 1925, the Court extended the protections of the Bill of Rights against the States through the 14th Amendment's Due Process Clause. The landmark cases in which this occurred are set out in the table on page 536—and with them the few (four) provisions in the Bill of Rights that have *not* been incorporated.

The key 1st Amendment cases were discussed in Chapter 19. Those involving the 4th through the 8th amendments are treated in Sections 2–4 of this chapter.

The Police Power

In the federal system, the reserved powers of the States include the broad and important **police power.** The police power is the authority of each State to act to protect and promote the public health, safety, morals, and general welfare. In other words, it is the power of each State to safeguard the well-being of its people.

The use of the police power often produces conflicts with civil rights protections. When

it does, courts must strike a balance between the needs of society, on the one hand, and of individual freedoms on the other. Any number of cases can be used to illustrate the conflict between police power and individual rights. Take as an example a matter often involved in drunk-driving cases.

Every State's laws allow the use of one or more tests to determine whether a person arrested and charged with drunk driving was in fact drunk at the time of the incident. Some of those tests are simple: walking a straight line or touching the tip of one's nose, for example. Some are more sophisticated, however, notably the breathalyzer test and the drawing of a blood sample.

Does the requirement that a person submit to such a test violate his or her rights under the 14th Amendment? Does the test involve an unconstitutional search for and seizure of evidence? Does it amount to forcing a person to testify against himself or herself (unconstitutional compulsory self-incrimination)? Or is the requirement a proper use of the police power?

Time after time, State and federal courts have come down on the side of the police power. They have upheld the right of society to protect itself against drunk drivers and rejected the individual rights argument.

The leading case is *Schmerber* v. *California,* 1966. The Court found no objection to a situation in which a police officer had directed a doctor to draw blood from a drunk-driving suspect. The Court emphasized these points: The blood sample was drawn in accord with accepted medical practice. The officer had reasonable grounds to believe that the suspect was drunk. Further, had the officer taken time to secure a **search warrant**—a court order authorizing a search— the evidence could have disappeared from the suspect's system.

Legislators and judges have often found the public's health, safety, morals, and/or welfare to be of overriding importance. For example:

1. To promote health, States can limit the sale of alcoholic beverages and tobacco, make laws to combat pollution, and require the vaccination of school children.

2. To promote safety, States can regulate the carrying of concealed weapons, require the use of seat belts, and punish drunk drivers.

3. To promote morals, States can regulate gambling and outlaw the sale of obscene materials and the practice of prostitution.

4. To promote the general welfare, States can enact compulsory education laws, provide help to the medically needy, and limit the profits of public utilities.

Clearly, governments cannot use the police power in an unreasonable or unfair way, however. In short, they cannot violate the 14th Amendment's Due Process Clause.

The Right of Privacy

The constitutional guarantees of due process create a right of privacy—"the right to be free, except in very limited circumstances, from unwanted governmental intrusions into one's privacy," *Stanley v. Georgia*, 1969.[1] It is, in short, "the right to be let alone."[2]

The Constitution makes no specific mention of the right of privacy, but the Supreme Court declared its existence in *Griswold v. Connecticut*, 1965. That case centered on a State law that outlawed birth-control counseling and prohibited all use of birth-control devices. The Court held the law to be a violation of the 14th Amendment's Due Process Clause—and noted that the State had no business policing the marital bedroom.

Roe v. Wade

The most controversial applications of the right of privacy have come in cases that raise this question: To what extent can a State limit a woman's right to an abortion? The leading case is *Roe v. Wade*, 1973. There, the Supreme Court struck down a Texas law that made abortion a crime except when necessary to save the life of the mother.

In *Roe*, the Court held that the 14th Amendment's right of privacy "encompass[es] a woman's decision whether or not to terminate her pregnancy." More specifically, the Court ruled that:

1. In the first trimester of pregnancy (about three months), a State must recognize a

---

[1] *Stanley* involved the possession of obscene materials in one's own home. In the most recent right to privacy case, the Court struck down a Texas law that made sexual relations between consenting gay adults a crime, *Lawrence v. Texas*, 2003.

[2] Justice Louis D. Brandeis, dissenting in *Olmstead v. United States*, 1928.

woman's right to an abortion—and cannot interfere with medical judgments in that matter.

2. In the second trimester a State, acting in the interest of women who undergo abortions, can make reasonable regulations about how, when, and where abortions can be performed, but cannot prohibit the procedure.

3. In the final trimester a State, acting to protect the unborn child, can choose to prohibit all abortions except those necessary to preserve the life or health of the mother.

Later Reproductive Rights Cases

In several later cases, the Court rejected a number of challenges to its basic holding in *Roe*. As the composition of the Court has changed, however, so has the Court's position on abortion. That shift can be seen in the Court's decisions in recent cases on the matter.

In *Webster v. Reproductive Health Services*, 1989, the Court upheld two key parts of a Missouri law. Those provisions prohibit abortions, except those to preserve the mother's life or health, (1) in any public hospital or clinic in that State, and (2) when the mother is 20 or more weeks pregnant and tests show that the fetus is viable (capable of sustaining life outside the mother's body).

Two cases in 1990 addressed the issue of minors and abortion. In those cases, the Court said that a State may require a minor (1) to inform at least one parent before she can obtain an abortion, *Ohio* v. *Akron Center for Reproductive Health,* 1990, and (2) to tell both parents of her plans, except in cases where a judge gives permission for an abortion without parental knowledge, *Hodgson* v. *Minnesota,* 1990.

The Court's most important decision on the issue since *Roe* v. *Wade* came in *Planned Parenthood of Southeastern Pennsylvania* v. *Casey* in 1992. There the Court announced this rule: A State may place reasonable limits on a woman's right to have an abortion, but these restrictions cannot impose an "undue burden" on her choice of that procedure.

In *Casey,* the Court applied that new standard to Pennsylvania's Abortion Control Act. It upheld sections of that law that say:

• A woman who seeks an abortion must be given professional counseling intended to persuade her to change her mind.

• A woman must delay an abortion for at least 24 hours after that counseling.

• An unmarried female under 18 must have the consent of a parent, or the permission of a judge, before an abortion.

• Doctors and clinics must keep detailed records of all abortions they perform.

Those four requirements do not, said the Court, place "a substantial obstacle in the path of a woman seeking an abortion of a nonviable fetus." That is, they do not impose an "undue burden" on a woman.

The Court did strike down another key part of the Pennsylvania law, however. That provision required that a married woman tell her husband of her plan to have an abortion.

To this point, the Court has decided only one abortion law case since 1992. In *Stenberg* v. *Carhart,* 2000, it applied *Casey's* "undue burden" rule to a Nebraska law and found that statute unconstitutional. The Nebraska law prohibited an operation that the opponents of abortion call "partial birth abortion." That procedure is one that doctors use only infrequently to terminate pregnancies after about 16 weeks.

The Court's 5–4 majority found the Nebraska law to be flawed because it (1) was too loosely drawn, (2) banned a procedure that may in fact be the most medically appropriate way to end some pregnancies, and (3) allowed an exception to protect the life, but not the health, of a pregnant woman. Thirty other States have passed similar laws in recent years, and the Court's decision in *Stenberg* apparently destroyed those statutes, as well.

Section 1 Assessment

Key Terms and Main Ideas

1. Explain what is meant by **due process**.
2. How do **procedural due process** and **substantive due process** differ?
3. **(a)** Define **police power**. **(b)** How have State and federal courts usually ruled on cases involving the police power and drunk driving suspects?
4. **(a)** What is the right of privacy? **(b)** The most controversial application of the right occurs in cases involving what?

Critical Thinking

5. **Checking Consistency** Considering the constitutional right of privacy, do you think it is proper for a State to use its police power to protect and promote morals among its citizens? Explain your answer.

Standards Monitoring Online

For: Self-quiz with vocabulary practice
Web Code: mqa-5201

6. **Identifying Central Issues** Why do you think the Supreme Court has refused to offer an exact definition of due process?
7. **Drawing Conclusions** What would you reply to someone who argues that the use of seat belts is a matter of individual choice?

Go Online
PHSchool.com

For: An activity on the right to privacy
Web Code: mqd-5201

Freedom and Security of the Person

2

Section Preview

OBJECTIVES

1. **Outline** Supreme Court decisions regarding slavery and involuntary servitude.
2. **Explain** the intent and application of the 2nd Amendment's protection of the right to keep and bear arms.
3. **Summarize** the constitutional provisions designed to guarantee security of home and person.

WHY IT MATTERS

Various constitutional provisions protect Americans' right to live in freedom. The 13th Amendment and subsequent civil rights laws prohibit slavery and involuntary servitude. The 2nd Amendment aims to preserve the concept of the citizen-soldier, while the 3rd and 4th amendments protect the security of home and person.

POLITICAL DICTIONARY

★ **involuntary servitude**
★ **discrimination**
★ **writs of assistance**
★ **probable cause**
★ **exclusionary rule**

Several of the Constitution's guarantees are intended to protect the right of every American to live in freedom. This means that the Constitution protects your right to be free from physical restraints, to be secure in your person, and to be secure in your home.

Slavery and Involuntary Servitude

The 13th Amendment was added to the Constitution in 1865, ending over 200 years of slavery in this country. Section 1 of the amendment declares, "Neither slavery nor involuntary servitude, . . . shall exist within the United States, or any place subject to their jurisdiction." Importantly, Section 2 of this amendment gives Congress the expressed power "to enforce this article by appropriate legislation."

Until 1865, each State could decide for itself whether to allow slavery. With the 13th Amendment, that power was denied to them, and to the National Government, as well.

---

[3] *Selective Draft Law Cases (Arver v. United States),* 1918.

The 13th Amendment: Section 1

As a widespread practice, slavery disappeared in this country more than 140 years ago. There are still occasional cases of it, however. Most often, those cases have involved **involuntary servitude**—that is, forced labor.

The 13th Amendment does not forbid all forms of involuntary servitude, however. Thus, in 1918, the Court drew a distinction between "involuntary servitude" and "duty" in upholding the constitutionality of the selective service system (the draft).[3] Nor does imprisonment for crime violate the amendment. Finally, note this important point: Unlike any other provision in the Constitution, the 13th Amendment covers the conduct of private individuals as well as the behavior of government.

▶ Slave tags serve as a reminder of a time before the passage of the 13th Amendment. **H-SS 12.10**

The 13th Amendment: Section 2

Shortly after the Civil War, Congress passed several civil rights laws based on the 13th Amendment. The Supreme Court, however, sharply narrowed the scope of federal authority in several cases, especially the *Civil Rights Cases*, 1883. In effect, the Court held that racial **discrimination** (bias, unfairness) against African Americans by private individuals did not place the "badge of slavery" on them nor keep them in servitude.

Congress soon repealed most of the laws based on the 13th Amendment. The enforcement of the few that remained was, at best, unimpressive. For years it was generally thought that Congress did not have the power, under either the 13th or 14th Amendment, to act against private parties who practice race-based discrimination.

In *Jones* v. *Mayer*, 1968, however, the Supreme Court breathed new life into the 13th Amendment. The case centered on one of the post-Civil War acts Congress had not repealed. Passed in 1866, that almost-forgotten law provided in part that

> **PRIMARY Sources** *[All] citizens of the United States, . . . of every race and color, . . . shall have the same right, in every State and Territory of the United States, . . . to inherit, purchase, lease, sell, hold, and convey real and personal property . . . as is enjoyed by white citizens. . . .*
>
> —Civil Rights Act of 1866

Jones, an African American, had sued because Mayer had refused to sell him a home, solely because of his race. Mayer contended that the 1866 law was unconstitutional, since it sought to prohibit private racial discrimination.

The Court upheld the law, declaring that the 13th Amendment abolished slavery and gave Congress the power to abolish "the badges and incidents of slavery." Said the Court:

> **PRIMARY Sources** *At the very least, the freedom that Congress is empowered to secure under the 13th Amendment includes the freedom to buy whatever a white man can buy, the right to live wherever a white man can live.*
>
> — Justice Potter Stewart, Opinion of the Court

The Court affirmed that decision in several later cases. Thus, in *Runyon* v. *McCrary*, 1976, two private schools had refused to admit two African American students. By doing so, the schools had refused to enter into a contract of admission—a contract they had advertised to the general public. The Court found that the schools had violated another provision of the 1866 law:

> **PRIMARY Sources** *[All] citizens of the United States, . . . of every race and color, . . . shall have the same right, . . . to make and enforce contracts . . . as is enjoyed by white citizens. . . .*
>
> —Civil Rights Act of 1866

The Court has also ruled that the Civil Rights Act of 1866 protects all "identifiable groups who are subject to intentional discrimination solely because of their ancestry or ethnic characteristics"—for example Jews (*Shaare Tefila Congregation* v. *Cobb*, 1987) and Arabs (*St. Francis College* v. *Al-Khazraji*, 1987).

More recently the Court has backed off a bit. In *Patterson* v. *McLean Credit Union*, 1989, it declared that while the 1866 law does prohibit racial discrimination in a contract of employment, any on-the-job discrimination should be handled in accord with the Civil Rights Act of 1964 (see Chapter 21). Nevertheless, the Court has several times held that the 13th Amendment gives Congress significant power to attack "the badges and incidents of slavery," from whatever source they may come.

The Right to Keep and Bear Arms

The 2nd Amendment reads this way:

> **FROM THE Constitution** *A well regulated Militia, being necessary to the security of a free State, the right of the people to keep and bear Arms, shall not be infringed.*
>
> —United States Constitution

These words excite as much controversy as any words in all of the Constitution. The 2nd Amendment was added to the Constitution to protect the right of each State to keep a militia. The Amendment's aim was to preserve the concept of the citizen-soldier.

Many—including the Bush administration today—insist that the 2nd Amendment also sets out an individual right. They say that it guarantees a right to keep and bear arms just as, for example, the 1st Amendment guarantees freedom of speech.

The Supreme Court has never accepted that interpretation of the 2nd Amendment. The only important 2nd Amendment case is *United States* v. *Miller,* 1939. There, the Court upheld a section of the National Firearms Act of 1934. That section made it a crime to ship sawed-off shotguns, machine guns, or silencers across State lines, unless the shipper had registered the weapons with the Treasury Department and paid a $200 license tax. The Court could find no valid link between the sawed-off shotgun involved in the case and "the preservation . . . of a well-regulated militia."

The 2nd Amendment is not covered by the 14th Amendment's Due Process Clause. Thus, each State can limit the right to keep and bear arms—and all of the States do so, in various ways.

Security of Home and Person

The 3rd and 4th amendments say that government cannot violate the home or person of anyone in this country without just cause.

The 3rd Amendment

This amendment forbids the quartering (housing) of soldiers in private homes in peacetime without the owner's consent and not in wartime but "in a manner to be prescribed by law." The guarantee was added to prevent what had been British practice in colonial days. The 3rd Amendment has had little importance since 1791 and has never been the subject of a Supreme Court case.

The 4th Amendment

The 4th Amendment also grew out of colonial practice. It was designed to prevent the use of **writs of assistance**—blanket search warrants with which British customs officials had invaded private homes to search for smuggled goods.

Each State constitution contains a similar provision. The guarantee also applies to the States through the 14th Amendment's Due Process Clause. Unlike the 3rd Amendment, the 4th Amendment has proved a highly important

guarantee. The text of the 4th Amendment reads:

FROM THE Constitution *"The right of the people to be secure in their persons, houses, papers, and effects, against unreasonable searches and seizures, shall not be violated, and no Warrants shall issue, but upon probable cause, supported by Oath or affirmation, and particularly describing the place to be searched, and the persons or things to be seized. "*
—United States Constitution

Probable Cause

The basic rule laid down by the 4th Amendment is this: Police officers have no general right to search for evidence or to seize either evidence or persons. Except in special circumstances, they must have a proper warrant (a court order). Also, the warrant must be obtained with **probable cause**—that is, a reasonable suspicion of crime.

Florida v. *J. L.,* 2000, illustrates the rule. There, Miami police had received a tip that a teenager was carrying a concealed weapon. Immediately, two officers went to the bus stop where the tipster said the young man could be found. The police located him, searched him, pulled a gun from his pocket, and arrested him.

The Supreme Court held that the police acted illegally because they did not have a proper warrant. All they had was an anonymous tip, unsupported by any other evidence. Their conduct amounted to just the sort of thing the 4th Amendment was intended to prevent.

Police do not always need a warrant, however—for example, when evidence is "in plain view." Thus, the Court recently upheld a search and seizure involving two men who were in a friend's apartment bagging cocaine. A policeman spotted them through an open window, entered the apartment, seized the cocaine, and arrested them. The Court rejected their claim to 4th Amendment protection, *Minnesota* v. *Carter,* 1999.

Many 4th amendment cases are complicated. In *Lidster* v. *Illinois,* 2004, for example, the Court upheld the use of so-called "informational roadblocks." In 1997, police had set up one of those barriers on a busy highway near Chicago, hoping to find witnesses to a recent hit-and-run accident.

Voices on Government

Ruth Bader Ginsburg joined the Supreme Court in 1993. Earlier in her career, she had appeared before the Court several times in cases involving women's rights. She was also a law professor and then a federal judge. When asked about America's greatest challenge, Justice Ginsburg had this answer:

❝ *I thought of Justice Thurgood Marshall's praise of the evolution of the concept 'We the People' to include once excluded, ignored, or undervalued people, then of our nation's motto: E Pluribus Unum ("of many, one"). The challenge, I responded, is to make and keep our communities places where we can tolerate, even celebrate, our differences, while pulling together for the common good. 'Of many, one' is the main challenge, I believe; it is my hope for our country and world.* ❞

Evaluating the Quotation

How might Justice Ginsburg's feelings about inclusion and tolerance affect her decisions on cases involving individual rights and civil liberties? **H-SS 12.10**

When Robert Lidster was stopped, an officer smelled alcohol on him. Lidster failed several sobriety tests and was arrested on a drunk-driving charge. Lidster's attorney filed a motion to quash (set aside) that arrest. The lawyer argued that Lidster was forced to stop by officers who, before they stopped him, had no reason (probable cause) to believe that he had committed any crime.

Lidster lost that argument. The Court upheld both his conviction and the use of informational roadblocks. In short, Lidster had simply run afoul of the long arm of coincidence.

Arrests

An arrest is the seizure of a person. When officers make a lawful arrest, they do not need a warrant to search "the area within which [the suspect] might gain possession of a weapon or destructible evidence."[4] In fact, most arrests take place without a warrant. Police can arrest a person in a public place without one, provided they have probable cause to believe that person has committed or is about to commit a crime.[5]

Illinois v. *Wardlow,* 2000, illustrates this point. There, four police cars were patrolling a high-crime area in Chicago. When Wardlow spotted them, he ran. An officer chased him down an alley, caught him, and found that Wardlow was carrying a loaded pistol. The Court held, 5–4, that Wardlow's behavior—his flight—gave the police "common sense" grounds on which to believe that he was involved in some criminal activity. (Note, however, that the Court did not hold that police have a blanket power to stop anyone who flees at the sight of a police officer.)

When, exactly, does the 4th Amendment protection come into play? The Court has several times held that this point is reached "only when the officer, by means of physical force or show of authority, has in some way restrained the liberty of a citizen," *Terry* v. *Ohio,* 1968.

Automobiles

The Court has long had difficulty applying the 4th Amendment to automobiles. It has several times held that an officer needs no warrant to search an automobile, a boat, an airplane, or some other vehicle, when there is probable cause to believe that it is involved in illegal activities. This is because such a "movable scene of crime" could disappear while a warrant was being sought.

Carroll v. *United States,* 1925, is an early leading case on the point. There, the Court emphasized that "where the securing of a warrant is reasonably practicable it must be used. . . . In cases where seizure is impossible except without a warrant, the seizing officer acts unlawfully and at his peril unless he can show the court probable cause."

The Court overturned a long string of automobile search cases in 1991. Before then, it had several times held that a warrant was usually needed to search a glove compartment, a paper bag, luggage, or other "closed containers" in an automobile. But, in *California* v. *Acevedo,* 1991, the Court set out what it called "one clear-cut rule to govern automobile searches." Whenever

---

[4]This rule was first laid down in *Chimel* v. *California,* 1969.

[5]A person arrested without a warrant must be brought promptly before a judge for a probable cause hearing. In *County of Riverside* v. *McLaughlin,* 1991, the Court held that "promptly" means within 48 hours.

police lawfully stop a car, they do not need a warrant to search anything in that vehicle that they have reason to believe holds evidence of a crime. "Anything" includes a passenger's belongings, *Wyoming* v. *Houghton*, 1999.

Most recently, the Court has held that after police make a routine traffic stop, they do not need a warrant when they use a trained dog to sniff around (search) the outside of a car for narcotics. Police may proceed without a warrant even if, before they made the stop, they had no reason to believe that there was anything illegal in the vehicle, *Illinois* v. *Caballes*, 2005.

The Exclusionary Rule

The heart of the guarantee against unreasonable searches and seizures lies in this question: If an unlawful search or seizure does occur, can that "tainted evidence" be used in court? If so, the 4th Amendment offers no real protection to a person accused of crime.

To meet that problem, the Court adopted, and is still refining, the **exclusionary rule.** Essentially, the rule is this: Evidence gained as the result of an illegal act by police cannot be used at the trial of the person from whom it was seized.

The rule was first laid down in *Weeks* v. *United States*, 1914. In that narcotics case, the Court held that evidence obtained illegally by federal officers could not be used in the federal courts. For decades, however, the Court left questions of the use of such evidence in State courts for each State to decide for itself.

Mapp v. *Ohio*

The exclusionary rule was finally extended to the States in *Mapp* v. *Ohio*, 1961. There, the Court held that the 14th Amendment forbids unreasonable searches and seizures by State and local officers just as the 4th Amendment bars such actions by federal officers. It also held that the fruits of an unlawful search or seizure cannot be used in the State courts, just as they cannot be used in the federal courts.

In *Mapp*, Cleveland police had gone to Dollree Mapp's home to search for gambling evidence. They entered her home forcibly, and without a warrant. Their very extensive search failed to turn up any gambling evidence, but they did find some obscene books. Mapp was convicted of possession of obscene materials and sentenced to jail. The Court overturned her conviction, holding that the evidence against her had been found and seized without a warrant.

Cases Narrowing the Rule

The exclusionary rule has always been controversial. It was intended to put teeth into the 4th Amendment, and it has. It says to police: As you enforce the law, obey the law. The rule seeks to prevent, or at least deter, police misconduct.

Critics of the rule say that it means that some persons who are clearly guilty nonetheless go free. Why, they ask, should criminals be able to "beat the rap" on "a technicality"?

The High Court has narrowed the scope of the rule somewhat over the years—most notably in four cases.

• In *Nix* v. *Williams*, 1984, it found an "inevitable discovery" exception to the rule. The Court ruled that tainted evidence can be used in court if that evidence would have turned up no matter what—"ultimately or inevitably would have been discovered by lawful means."

• In *United States* v. *Leon*, 1984, the Court found a "good faith" exception to the rule. There, federal agents in Los Angeles had used what they thought was a proper warrant to seize illicit drugs. Their warrant was later shown to be faulty, however. The Court upheld their actions nonetheless. It said: "When an officer acting with objective good faith has obtained a search warrant . . . and acted within its scope . . . there is nothing to deter."

• In *Arizona* v. *Evans*, 1995, the Court held that the good faith exception applied in a case where evidence of a crime was seized by police who acted on the basis of a computer printout that later proved to be erroneous. The printout indicated an outstanding arrest warrant against the defendant in the case. In fact, there was no warrant. The computer error was made by court clerks, not the police—who, the Court said, acted in good faith.

• In *Maryland* v. *Garrison*, 1987, the Court gave police room for "honest mistakes." There, it allowed the use of evidence seized in the mistaken search of an apartment in Baltimore. Officers had a warrant to search for drugs in an apartment on the third floor of a building. Not realizing that there were two apartments there, they entered and found drugs in the wrong apartment—the one for which they did not have a warrant.

Drug Testing

Federal drug-testing programs involve searches of persons and so are covered by the 4th Amendment. To date, the Court has held that they can be conducted without either warrants or even any indication of drug use by those who must take them. It did so in two 1989 cases. They involved mandatory drug testing for (1) drug enforcement officers of the United States Customs Service who carry firearms, *National Treasury Employees Union* v. *Von Raab,* and (2) railroad workers following a train accident, *Skinner* v. *Federal Railway Labor Executives Association.*

The Court has also upheld an Oregon school district's drug-testing program, *Vernonia School District* v. *Acton,* 1995. The program required all students who take part in school sports to agree to be tested for drugs. That ruling was extended in *Board of Education of Pottowatomie County* v. *Earls* in 2002. There, the court upheld the random testing of students who want to participate in any competitive extracurricular activity.

Wiretapping

Wiretapping, electronic eavesdropping, videotaping, and other more sophisticated means of "bugging" are now quite widely used in the United States. They present difficult search and seizure questions that the authors of the 4th Amendment could not have begun to foresee.

The Supreme Court decided its first wiretap case in 1928. In *Olmstead* v. *United States,* federal agents had tapped a Seattle bootlegger's telephone calls. Their bugs produced evidence that led to Olmstead's conviction. The High Court upheld that conviction. It found that although the agents had not had a warrant, there had been no "actual physical invasion" of Olmstead's home or office—because the phone lines had been tapped *outside* those places.

The leading case today is *Katz* v. *United States,* 1967. There, the Court expressly overruled *Olmstead.* Katz had been convicted of transmitting gambling information across State lines. He had used a public phone booth in Los Angeles to call his contacts in Boston and Miami. Much of the evidence against him had come from an electronic tap planted on the roof—outside—the phone booth.

The Court held that the bugging evidence could not be used against Katz. Despite the fact that Katz was in a public, glass-enclosed phone booth, he was entitled to make a *private* call. Said the Court: the 4th Amendment protects "persons, not just places." It did go on to say, however, that the 4th Amendment can be satisfied in such situations if police obtain a proper warrant before they install a listening device.

Section 2 Assessment

Key Terms and Main Ideas

1. In what sense has the Supreme Court "breathed new life" into the 13th Amendment?
2. Why was the 2nd Amendment added to the Constitution?
3. Define **probable cause.**
4. **(a)** What is the **exclusionary rule? (b)** What is its basic purpose?

Critical Thinking

5. **Expressing Problems Clearly** Consider this question: Does the exclusionary rule serve the interests of justice? Explain how you might answer this question if you were **(a)** the defendant in a criminal trial; **(b)** a police officer.

Standards Monitoring Online
For: Self-quiz with vocabulary practice
Web Code: mqa-5202

6. **Identifying Assumptions** In 1918, the Court ruled that the 13th Amendment's prohibition of involuntary servitude does not prevent Congress from launching a military draft. What assumptions about the importance of individual rights and civic duty lie behind that decision?

Go Online
PHSchool.com

For: An activity on the security of home and person
Web Code: mqd-5202

Skills for Life

Serving on a Jury

Someday you may receive a notice ordering you to appear for jury duty. This is a rare opportunity to observe the United States justice system at work. That system relies on the participation of ordinary citizens in the judicial process.

Potential jurors are most often selected from voting lists and summoned to appear at court. How long they must serve varies from place to place. People with certain hardships, such as health, language, or job problems, may be excused from jury duty.

When you arrive at the courthouse, you might be dismissed without having served at all. Or you might be chosen to appear for jury selection. In this phase, lawyers for both sides question potential jurors and select those they think will be favorable to their side. Many people are rejected at this stage.

If you are chosen for a jury, you and the other jurors will receive instructions prior to the start of trial. The following steps are adapted from those instructions:

1. Do not be influenced by bias. Your decision should not be affected by any sympathies or dislikes you might have for either side in the case. How might you avoid biased thinking?

2. Follow the law as it is explained to you. Your job is to determine whether or not someone broke the law, regardless of whether you approve of the law. Would you find this requirement difficult? Explain.

3. Remember that the defendant is presumed innocent. The government has the burden of proving a defendant guilty beyond a "reasonable doubt." If it fails to do so, the jury verdict must be "not guilty." What does "reasonable doubt" mean to you?

4. Keep an open mind. Do not form or state any opinion about the case until you have heard all the evidence, the closing arguments of the lawyers, and the judge's instructions on the applicable law. Why is it important for jurors to base their opinions on evidence and testimony alone?

5. During the trial, do not discuss the case. Do not permit anyone to talk about the case with you or in your presence, except your fellow jurors in the secrecy of the jury room. Avoid media coverage of the case once the trial has begun. What is the reason for this rule?

Test for Success

Under "three strikes" laws in several States, a person who commits a third felony can be jailed for 25 years to life. Such laws are aimed to keep violent, habitual criminals behind bars. But the laws are also being applied to nonviolent crimes, such as stealing a bicycle. Some juries have resisted convicting people they know are guilty because the possible penalties are so harsh. If you were a juror on such a case, would you vote to convict? Consider the instructions to jurors given on this page.

Rights of the Accused

Section Preview

OBJECTIVES

1. **Define** the writ of habeas corpus, bills of attainder, and ex post facto laws.
2. **Outline** how the right to a grand jury and the guarantee against double jeopardy help ensure the rights of the accused.
3. **Describe** issues that arise from the guarantee of a speedy and public trial.
4. **Determine** what constitutes a fair trial by jury.
5. **Examine** the right to an adequate defense and the guarantee against self-incrimination.

WHY IT MATTERS

In the American judicial system, any person who is accused of a crime must be presumed to be innocent until proven guilty. The Constitution, especially in the 5th, 6th, and 14th amendments, contains a number of provisions guaranteeing rights to people accused of a crime.

POLITICAL DICTIONARY

★ **writ of habeas corpus**
★ **bill of attainder**
★ **ex post facto law**
★ **grand jury**
★ **indictment**
★ **double jeopardy**
★ **bench trial**
★ **Miranda Rule**

Think about this statement for a moment: "It is better that ten guilty persons go free than that one innocent person be punished." That maxim expresses one of the bedrock principles of the American legal system.

Of course, society must punish criminals in order to preserve itself. However, the law intends that any person who is suspected or accused of a crime must be presumed innocent until proven guilty by fair and lawful means.

Habeas Corpus

The **writ of habeas corpus,** sometimes called the writ of liberty, is intended to prevent unjust arrests and imprisonments.[6] It is a court order directed to an officer holding a prisoner. It commands that the prisoner be brought before the court and that the officer show cause—explain, with good reason—why the prisoner should not be released.

The right to seek a writ of habeas corpus is protected against the National Government in Article I, Section 9 of the Constitution. That right is guaranteed against the States in each of their own constitutions.

The Constitution says that the right to the writ cannot be suspended, "unless when in Cases of Rebellion or Invasion the public Safety may require it." President Abraham Lincoln suspended the writ in 1861. His order covered various parts of the country, including several areas in which war was not then being waged. Chief Justice Roger B. Taney,

WARDEMACRACY

UNION

GREELY   LINCOLN   SUMNER   CHASE   WELLES   SEWAR

THE GRAVE OF THE UNION.
OR MAJOR JACK DOWNING'S DREAM. DRAWN BY ZEKE.

Interpreting Political Cartoons This detail from an 1860s cartoon is critical of President Lincoln's 1861 suspension of the writ of habeas corpus. *Why is a coffin labeled "Constitution" being lowered into the ground?*

---

[6]The phrase *habeas corpus* comes from the Latin, meaning "you should have the body," and those are the opening words of the writ.

sitting as a circuit judge, held Lincoln's action unconstitutional.

Taney ruled that the Constitution gives the power to suspend the writ to Congress alone. Congress then passed the Habeas Corpus Act of 1863. It gave the President the power to suspend the writ when and where, in his judgment, that action was necessary. In *Ex parte Milligan*, 1866, the Supreme Court ruled that neither Congress nor the President can legally suspend the writ where there is no actual fighting nor the likelihood of any.

The right to the writ has been suspended only once since the Civil War and the Reconstruction Period that followed it. The territorial governor of Hawaii suspended the writ following the Japanese attack on Pearl Harbor, December 7, 1941. The Supreme Court later ruled that the governor did not have the power to take that action, *Duncan* v. *Kahanamoku,* 1946.

Bills of Attainder

A **bill of attainder** is a legislative act that inflicts punishment without a court trial. Neither Congress nor the States can pass such a measure (Article I, Sections 9 and 10).

The ban on bills of attainder is both a protection of individual freedom and part of the system of separation of powers. A legislative body can pass laws that define crime and set the penalties for violation of those laws. It cannot, however, pass a law that declares a person guilty of a crime and provides for the punishment of that person.

The Supreme Court has held that this prohibition is aimed at all legislative acts that apply "to named individuals or to easily ascertainable members of a group in such a way as to inflict punishment on them without a judicial trial," *United States* v. *Lovett*, 1946.

The Framers wrote the ban on bills of attainder into the Constitution because both Parliament and the colonial legislatures had passed many such bills. Bills of attainder have been rare in our national history, however.

United States v. *Brown*, 1965, is one of the few cases in which the Court has struck down a law as a bill of attainder. There it overturned a provision of the Landrum-Griffin Act of 1959. That provision made it a federal crime for a member of the Communist Party to serve as an officer of a labor union.

Ex Post Facto Laws

An **ex post facto law** (a law passed after the fact) has three features. It (1) is a criminal law, one defining a crime or providing for its punishment; (2) applies to an act committed before its passage; and (3) works to the disadvantage of the accused. Neither Congress nor the State legislatures may pass such laws.[7]

For example, a law making it a crime to sell marijuana cannot be applied to someone who sold it before that law was passed. Or, a law that changed the penalty for murder from life in prison to death could not be applied to a person who committed a murder before the punishment was changed.

Ex post facto cases do not come along very often. The Court decided its most recent one, *Carmell* v. *Texas*, in 2000. There, the Court overturned a man's sexual abuse conviction because of a change in State law. That change had made it easier for the prosecution to prove its charge than was the case when the abuse was committed.

Retroactive civil laws are *not* forbidden. Thus, a law raising income tax rates could be passed in November and applied to income earned through the whole year.

Grand Jury

The Constitution provides that:

> FROM THE **Constitution** **"** *No person shall be held to answer for a capital, or otherwise infamous crime, unless on a presentment or indictment of a Grand Jury. . . .* **"**
> —5th Amendment

The **grand jury** is the formal device by which a person can be accused of a serious crime.[8] In federal cases, it is a body of from 16 to 23 persons drawn from the area of the federal district court that it serves. The votes of at least 12 of the

---

[7]Article I, Sections 9 and 10. The phrase *ex post facto* is from the Latin, meaning "after the fact."

[8]The 5th Amendment provides that the guarantee of grand jury does not extend to "cases arising in the land or naval forces." The conduct of members of the armed forces is regulated under a code of military law enacted by Congress.

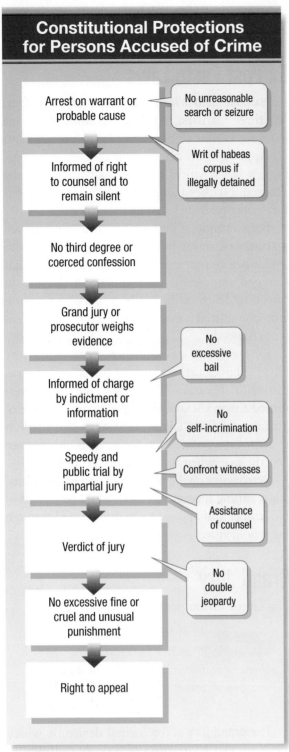

Constitutional Protections for Persons Accused of Crime

Arrest on warrant or probable cause

No unreasonable search or seizure

Writ of habeas corpus if illegally detained

Informed of right to counsel and to remain silent

No third degree or coerced confession

Grand jury or prosecutor weighs evidence

No excessive bail

Informed of charge by indictment or information

No self-incrimination

Speedy and public trial by impartial jury

Confront witnesses

Assistance of counsel

Verdict of jury

No double jeopardy

No excessive fine or cruel and unusual punishment

Right to appeal

Interpreting Charts . What protections does the Constitution extend to those convicted of crime?
H-SS 12.1.6

grand jurors are needed to return an indictment or to make a presentment.

An **indictment** is a formal complaint that the prosecutor lays before a grand jury. It charges the accused with one or more crimes. If the grand jury finds that there is enough evidence

for a trial, it returns a "true bill of indictment." The accused is then held for prosecution. If the grand jury does not make such a finding, the charge is dropped.

A presentment is a formal accusation brought by the grand jury on its own motion, rather than that of the prosecutor. It is little used in federal courts.

A grand jury's proceedings are not a trial. Since unfair harm could come if they were public, its sessions are secret. They are also one-sided—in the law, *ex parte*. That is, only the prosecution, not the defense, is present.

The right to grand jury is intended as a protection against overzealous prosecutors. Critics say that it is too time-consuming, too expensive, and too likely to follow the dictates of the prosecutor.

The 5th Amendment's grand jury provision is the only part of the Bill of Rights relating to criminal prosecution that the Supreme Court has not brought within the coverage of the 14th Amendment's Due Process Clause. In most States today, most criminal charges are not brought by grand jury indictment. They are brought, instead, by an information, an affidavit in which the prosecutor swears that there is enough evidence to justify a trial (see Chapter 24).

Double Jeopardy

The 5th Amendment's guarantee against double jeopardy is the first of several protections in the Bill of Rights especially intended to ensure fair trial in the federal courts.[9] Fair trials are guaranteed in State courts by each State's own constitution and by the 14th Amendment's Due Process Clause.

The 5th Amendment says in part that no person can be "twice put in jeopardy of life or limb." Today, this prohibition against **double jeopardy** means that once a person has been tried for a crime, he or she cannot be tried again for that same crime.

A person can violate both a federal *and* a State law in a single act, however—for example, by selling narcotics. That person can then be

---

[9] See the 5th, 6th, 7th, and 8th amendments and Article III, Section 2, Clause 3. The practice of excluding evidence obtained in violation of the 4th Amendment is also intended to guarantee a fair trial.

tried for the federal crime in a federal court and for the State crime in a State court. A single act can also result in the commission of several crimes. A person who breaks into a store, steals liquor, and sells it can be tried for illegal entry, theft, and selling liquor without a license.

In a trial in which a jury cannot agree on a verdict, there is no jeopardy. It is as though no trial had been held. Nor is double jeopardy involved when a case is appealed to a higher court.[10] Recall that the Supreme Court has held that the 5th Amendment's ban on double jeopardy applies against the States through the 14th Amendment, *Benton* v. *Maryland*, 1969.

Several States allow the continued confinement of violent sex predators after they have completed a prison term. The Court has twice held that that confinement is not punishment—and so does not involve double jeopardy. Rather, the practice is intended to protect the public from harm, *Kansas* v. *Hendrick*, 1987, and *Seling* v. *Young*, 2001.

Speedy and Public Trial

The Constitution commands

> **FROM THE Constitution** **"** *In all criminal prosecutions, the accused shall enjoy the right to a speedy and public trial....* **"**
>
> —6th Amendment

Speedy Trial

The guarantee of a speedy trial is meant to ensure that the government will try a person accused of crime within a reasonable time and without undue delay. But how long a delay is too long? The Supreme Court has long recognized that each case must be judged on its own merits.

In a leading case, *Barker* v. *Wingo*, 1972, the Court listed four criteria for determining if a delay has violated the constitutional protection. They are (1) the length of the delay, (2) the reasons for it, (3) whether the delay has in fact harmed the defendant, and (4) whether the defendant asked for a prompt trial.

---

[10]The Organized Crime Control Act of 1970 allows federal prosecutors to appeal sentences they believe to be too lenient. The Supreme Court has held that such appeals do not violate the double jeopardy guarantee, *United States* v. *Di Francesco*, 1980.

Interpreting Political Cartoons The term "media circus" applies to trials that generate a great deal of publicity. **What are the dangers of a trial becoming too public?**

The Speedy Trial Act of 1974 says that the time between a person's arrest and the beginning of his or her federal criminal trial cannot be more than 100 days. The law does allow for some exceptions, however—for example, when the defendant must undergo extensive mental tests, or when the defendant or a key witness is ill.

The 6th Amendment guarantees a prompt trial in *federal* cases. The Supreme Court first declared that this right applies against the States as part of the 14th Amendment's Due Process Clause in *Klopfer* v. *North Carolina*, 1967.

Public Trial

The 6th Amendment says that a trial must also be public. The right to be tried in public is also part of the 14th Amendment's guarantee of procedural due process.

A trial must not be *too* speedy or *too* public, however. The Supreme Court threw out an Arkansas murder conviction in 1923 on just those grounds. The trial had taken only 45 minutes, and it had been held in a courtroom packed by a threatening mob.

Within reason, a judge can limit both the number and the kinds of spectators who may be present at a trial. Those who seek to disrupt a courtroom can be barred from it. A judge can order a courtroom cleared when the expected

▲ **Cameras in the Courtroom?** Friends and family watch the televised trial (above) of nanny Louise Woodward for the murder of a child in her care. In trials in which cameras are not allowed in the courtroom, lawyers and the public may "view" the trial through courtroom sketches (right).

testimony can embarrass a witness or someone not a party to the case.

Many of the questions about how public a trial should be involve the media—especially newspapers and television. The guarantees of fair trial and free press, however, often collide in the courts. On the one hand, a courtroom is a public place where the media have a right to be present. On the other hand, media coverage can jeopardize the right to a fair trial.

Champions of the public's right to know hold that the courts must allow the broadest possible press coverage of a trial. The Supreme Court has often held, however, that the media have only the same right as the general public to be present in a courtroom. The right to a public trial belongs to the defendant, not to the media.

What of televised trials? Television cameras are barred from all federal courtrooms. Most States do allow some form of in-court television reporting, however. Does televising a criminal trial violate a defendant's rights?

In an early major case, *Estes* v. *Texas*, 1965, the Supreme Court reversed the conviction of an oil man charged with swindling billions of dollars. Radio and television coverage of his trial had been allowed from within the courtroom, over his objection. The Court found that the media coverage had been so

"circus-like" and so disruptive that Estes had been denied his right to a fair trial.

Sixteen years later, the Court held in *Chandler* v. *Florida*, 1981, that nothing in the Constitution prevents a State from allowing the televising of a criminal trial. At least, televising is not prohibited as long as steps are taken to avoid too much publicity and to protect the defendant's rights.

Trial by Jury

The 6th Amendment also says that a person accused of a federal crime must be tried "by an impartial jury." This guarantee reinforces an earlier one set out in Article III, Section 2. The right to trial by jury is also binding on the States through the 14th Amendment's Due Process Clause, but only in cases involving "serious" crimes, *Duncan* v. *Louisiana*, 1968.[11] The trial jury is often called the petit jury. *Petit* is the French word for "small."

The 6th Amendment adds that the members of the federal court jury must be drawn from "the State and district wherein the crime shall have been committed, which district shall have been previously ascertained by law." This clause gives the defendant any benefit there might be in having a court and jury familiar with the people and problems of the area.

A defendant may ask to be tried in another place—seek a "change of venue"—on grounds that the people of the locality are so prejudiced in the case that an impartial jury cannot be drawn. The judge must decide whether a change of venue is justified.

A defendant may also waive (put aside or relinquish) the right to a jury trial. However, he or she can do so only if the judge is satisfied that the defendant is fully aware of his or her rights and understands what that action means. In fact, a judge can order a jury trial even when a defendant does not want one, *One Lot Emerald Cut Stones and One Ring* v. *United States*, 1972. If a defendant waives

---

[11]In *Baldwin* v. *New York*, 1970, the Court defined serious crimes as those for which imprisonment for more than six months is possible.

the right, a **bench trial** is held. That is, a judge alone hears the case. (Of course, a defendant can plead guilty and so avoid a trial of any kind.)

In federal practice, the jury that hears a criminal case must have 12 members. Some federal civil cases are tried before juries of as few as six members, however. Several States now provide for smaller juries, often of six members, in both criminal and civil cases.

In the federal courts, the jury that hears a criminal case can convict the accused only by a unanimous vote. Most States follow the same rule.[12]

In a long series of cases, dating from *Strauder v. West Virginia,* 1880, the Supreme Court has held that a jury must be "drawn from a fair cross section of the community." A person is denied the right to an impartial jury if he or she is tried by a jury from which members of any groups "playing major roles in the community" have been excluded, *Taylor v. Louisiana,* 1975.

In short, no person can be kept off a jury on such grounds as race, color, religion, national origin, or sex. As the Court has put it in several recent decisions on the point: Both the 5th and the 14th amendments mean that jury service cannot be determined by "the pigmentation of skin, the accident of birth, or the choice of religion," *Miller-El v. Dretke,* 2005.

Right to an Adequate Defense

Every person accused of a crime has the right to the best possible defense that circumstances will allow. The 6th Amendment says that a defendant has the right (1) "to be informed of the nature and cause of the accusation," (2) "to be confronted with the witnesses against him" and question them in open court, (3) "to have compulsory process for obtaining witnesses in his favor" (that is, favorable witnesses can be subpoenaed, or forced to attend), and (4) "to have the Assistance of Counsel for his defense."

These key safeguards apply in the federal courts. Still, if a State fails to honor any of them, the accused can appeal a conviction on grounds

that the 14th Amendment's Due Process Clause has been violated. Recall from Chapter 19 that the Supreme Court protected the right to counsel in *Gideon v. Wainwright,* 1963; the right of confrontation in *Pointer v. Texas,* 1965; and the right to call witnesses in *Washington v. Texas,* 1967.

These guarantees are intended to prevent the cards from being stacked in favor of the prosecution. One of the leading right-to-counsel cases, *Escobedo v. Illinois,* 1964, illustrates this point.

Chicago police picked up Danny Escobedo for questioning in the death of his brother-in-law. On the way to the police station, and then while he was being questioned there, he asked several times to see his lawyer. The police denied these requests. They did so even though his lawyer was in the police station and was trying to see him, and the police knew the lawyer was there. Through a long night of questioning, Escobedo made several damaging statements. Prosecutors later used those statements in court as a major part of the evidence that led to his murder conviction.

The Supreme Court ordered Escobedo freed from prison four years later. It held that he had been improperly denied his right to counsel.

In *Gideon v. Wainwright,* 1963, the Court held that an attorney must be furnished to a defendant who cannot afford one. In many places, a judge still assigns a lawyer from the local community, or a private legal aid association provides counsel.

Interpreting Political Cartoons *Would a poll of friends and neighbors produce a fair verdict? Explain your answer.* H-SS 12.10

---

[12]The 14th Amendment does not say that there cannot be juries of fewer than 12 persons, *Williams v. Florida,* 1970, but it does not allow juries of fewer than six members, *Ballew v. Georgia,* 1978. Nor does it prevent a State from providing for a conviction on a less than unanimous jury vote, *Apodaca v. Oregon,* 1972. But if a jury has only six members, it may convict only by a unanimous vote, *Burch v. Louisiana,* 1979.

Since *Gideon*, however, a growing number of States, and many local governments, have established tax-supported public defender offices. In 1970, Congress authorized the appointment of federal public defenders or, as an alternative, the creation of community legal service organizations financed by federal grants.

Self-Incrimination

The guarantee against self-incrimination is among the protections set out in the Fifth Amendment. That provision declares that no person can be "compelled in any criminal case to be a witness against himself." This protection must be honored in both the federal and State courts, *Malloy* v. *Hogan*, 1964.

In a criminal case, the burden of proof is always on the prosecution. The defendant does not have to prove his or her innocence. The ban on self-incrimination prevents the prosecution from shifting the burden of proof to the defendant. As the Court put it in *Malloy* v. *Hogan*, the prosecution cannot force the accused to "prove the charge against" him "out of his own mouth."

Applying the Guarantee

The language of the 5th Amendment suggests that the guarantee against self-incrimination applies only to criminal cases. In fact, the guarantee covers any governmental proceeding in which a person is legally compelled to answer any question that could lead to a criminal charge. Thus, a person may claim the right ("take the Fifth") in a variety of situations: in a divorce proceeding (which is a civil matter), before a legislative committee, at a school board's disciplinary hearing, and so on.

The courts, not the individuals who claim it, decide when the right can be properly invoked. If the plea of self-incrimination is pushed too far, a person can be held in contempt of court.

The guarantee against self-incrimination is a personal right. One can claim it only for oneself.[13] It cannot be invoked in someone else's behalf; a person *can* be forced to "rat" on another.

The privilege does not protect a person from being fingerprinted or photographed, submitting a handwriting sample, or appearing in a police lineup. And, recall, it does not mean that a person does not have to submit to a blood test in a drunk driving situation, *Schmerber* v. *California*, 1966.

A person cannot, however, be forced to confess to a crime under duress, that is, as a result of torture or other physical or psychological pressure. In *Ashcraft* v. *Tennessee*, 1944, for example, the Supreme Court threw out the conviction of a man accused of hiring another person to murder his wife. The confession on which his conviction rested had been secured only after some 36 hours of continuous, threatening interrogation. The questioning was conducted by officers who worked in shifts because, they said, they became so tired that they had to rest.

The gulf between what the Constitution says and what goes on in some police stations can be wide indeed. For that reason, the Supreme Court has come down hard in favor of the defendant in many cases involving the protection against self-incrimination and the closely related right to counsel.

Recall, for example, the Court's decision in *Escobedo* v. *Illinois*, 1964. There it held that a confession cannot be used against a defendant if it was obtained by police who refused to allow the defendant to see his attorney and did not tell him that he had a right to refuse to answer their questions.

Miranda v. Arizona

In a truly historic decision, the Court refined the *Escobedo* holding in *Miranda* v. *Arizona*, 1966. A mentally retarded man, Ernesto Miranda, had been convicted of kidnapping and rape. Ten days after the crime, the victim picked Miranda out of a police lineup. After two hours of questioning, during which the police did not tell him of his rights, Miranda confessed.

The Supreme Court struck down Miranda's conviction. More importantly, the Court said that it would no longer uphold convictions in any cases in which suspects had not been told of their constitutional rights before police questioning. It thus laid down the **Miranda Rule.** Under the rule, before police may question a suspect, that person must be

---

[13]With this major exception: A husband cannot be forced to testify against his wife, or a wife against her husband, *Trammel* v. *United States,* 1980. One can testify against the other voluntarily, however.

(1) told of his or her right to remain silent;

(2) warned that anything he or she says can be used in court;

(3) informed of the right to have an attorney present during questioning;

(4) told that if he or she is unable to hire an attorney, one will be provided at public expense;

(5) told that he or she may bring police questioning to an end at any time.

The Miranda Rule has been in force for 40 years now (and made famous by countless television dramas over that period). As the Court put it in *Dickerson* v. *United States*, 2000, the rule "has become embedded in routine police practice to the point where the warnings have become part of our national culture."

The Supreme Court is still refining the rule on a case-by-case basis. Most often the rule is closely followed. But there are exceptions. Thus, the Court has held that an undercover police officer posing as a prisoner does not have to tell a cell mate of his Miranda rights before prompting him to talk about a murder, *Illinois* v. *Perkins*, 1990.

Missouri v. *Seibert*, 2004, centered on what lately had become fairly common police practice: two-step interrogations, also known as "rehearsed confessions." Here, police officers had questioned Patrice Seibert, drawing out details of the fire she had set to cover up the murder of her son. *Then*, she was told of her Miranda rights—and questioned again. That second round was taped, and she was asked questions based on the incriminating statements

▲ In 1966, the Court struck down the conviction of Ernesto Miranda (right), who had confessed to a crime without being told of his rights. *Critical Thinking* *What were the long-term effects of the Miranda decision on police procedures?* H-SS 12.5.4

she had made in the first—untaped, unwarned—round. She confessed again.

The Supreme Court found that her confession had been coerced and so was invalid. It struck down the two-step practice, saying that it threatened the very purpose of Miranda.

The Miranda rule has always been controversial. Critics say that it "puts criminals back on the streets." Others applaud the rule, however. They hold that criminal law enforcement is most effective when it relies on independently secured evidence, rather than on confessions gained by questionable tactics from defendants who do not have the help of a lawyer.

Section 3 Assessment

Key Terms and Main Ideas

1. What does the **writ of habeas corpus** seek to prevent?
2. Why are **bills of attainder** and **ex post facto laws** forbidden?
3. What guarantees does the 5th Amendment offer to the accused?
4. List the provisions of the 6th Amendment concerning the rights of the accused.

Critical Thinking

5. **Drawing Inferences** The Constitution denies to both Congress and the State legislatures the power to enact bills of attainder. How does this fact illustrate the principle of separation of powers?

6. **Expressing Problems Clearly** Should television cameras be allowed in the courtroom? Why or why not?
7. **Predicting Consequences** If the ban on double jeopardy were removed from the Constitution, what might be the effect on the criminal justice system?

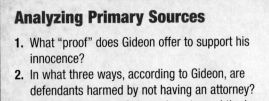
on Primary Sources

The Right to an Attorney

Analysis Skills HR4, HI3

Clarence Gideon was an uneducated man who had to defend himself in a Florida court because he could not afford an attorney and the trial judge refused to provide one at public expense. Here, Gideon writes from prison to the attorney assigned to handle his Supreme Court appeal. Fourteen months after this letter, the Court ruled in Gideon v. Wainwright *that every defendant has a right to an attorney.*

Clarence Gideon
1910–1972

On June 3rd 1961 I was arrested for the crime I am now doing time on. I was charged with Breaking & Entering to comitt a misdemeanor and was convicted in a trial August 4th 1961 [and] sentenced to State Prison August 27th 1961.

This charge growed out of gambling. . . . I worked in this place and did run a Poker game there. . . . I did not break into this building nor did I have to [because] I had the keys to the building. . . . The State witness Cook who was supposed to identify me. Had a bad police record and the Court would not let me bring that out. Nor that one time I had at the point of a pistal made him stop beating a girl[.]

I always believed that the primarily reason of a trial in a court of law was to reach the truth. My trial was far from the truth. One day when I was being arraigned [brought to court to be formally charged] I seen two trials of two different men tried without attorneys. One hour from the time they started they had two juries out and fifteen minutes later they were found guilty and sentenced. Is this a fair trial? This is common practiced through most of this state. . . . I am an electrician here [in prison] and one of my fellow workers has two years for drunk and resisting arrest. Most city Police courts would give a citizen a twenty-five dollar fine for the same charge he was tried without an attorney and convicted. . . .

There was not a crime committed in my case and I don't feel like I had a fair trial. If I had a

attorney[,] he could brought out all these things in my trial.

When I was arrested I was put in solitary confinement and I was not allowed the papers not to use the telephone or write to everyone I should. I did get a speedy arraignment and . . . was allow more time to try and obtain a attorney[,] which I could not do. You know about the rest of my trial. . . .

I hope that [this letter] may help you in preparing this case. I am sorry I could not write better[.] I have done the best I could.

I have no illusions about the law and courts or the people who are involved in them. I have read the complete history of law ever since the Romans first started writing them down and[,] before[,] of the laws of religions. I believe that each era finds a improvement in the law[.] Each year brings something new for the benefit of mankind. Maybe this will be one of those small steps forward. . . .

Analyzing Primary Sources

1. What "proof" does Gideon offer to support his innocence?
2. In what three ways, according to Gideon, are defendants harmed by not having an attorney?
3. What attitude does Gideon show toward the law and the legal system?
4. What point is Gideon trying to make in the last paragraph of his letter?

4 Punishment

Section Preview

OBJECTIVES

1. **Explain** the purpose of bail and preventive detention.
2. **Describe** the Court's interpretation of cruel and unusual punishment.
3. **Outline** the history of the Court's decisions on capital punishment.
4. **Define** the crime of treason.

WHY IT MATTERS

The 8th Amendment addresses the issue of punishment for crime. It bans excessive bail and cruel and unusual punishment. The Court has ruled that the death penalty does not constitute cruel and unusual punishment, although the question of capital punishment continues to be hotly debated.

POLITICAL DICTIONARY

★ bail
★ preventive detention
★ capital punishment
★ treason

Once again, think about this statement: "It is better that ten guilty persons go free than that one innocent person be punished." What do you think of that notion after reading the previous section? Turn now to those guilty persons who do not go free but are instead punished. How should they be treated? The Constitution gives its most specific answers to that question in the 8th Amendment.

Bail and Preventative Detention

The 8th Amendment says, in part:

FROM THE Constitution

❝*Excessive bail shall not be required, nor excessive fines imposed. . . .*❞
—United States Constitution

Each State constitution sets out similar restrictions. The general rule is that the bail or fine in a case must bear a reasonable relationship to the seriousness of the crime involved.

Bail

Bail is a sum of money that the accused may be required to post (deposit with the court) as a guarantee that he or she will appear in court at the proper time. The use of bail is justified on two grounds: (1) A person should not be jailed until his or her guilt is established. (2) A defendant is better able to prepare for trial outside of a jail.

Note that the Constitution does not say that all persons accused of a crime are automatically entitled to bail. Rather, it guarantees that, where bail is set, the amount will not be excessive.

The leading case on bail in the federal courts is *Stack* v. *Boyle*, 1951. There the Court ruled that "bail set at a figure higher than the amount reasonably calculated" to assure a defendant's appearance at a trial "is 'excessive' under the 8th Amendment."

A defendant can appeal the denial of release on bail or the amount of bail. Bail is usually set in accordance with the severity of the crime

Interpreting Political Cartoons *Under what circumstances may bail actually be denied?* **H-SS 12.1.6**

▶ Supporters for (right) and against (left) capital punishment make their views known. *Critical Thinking Briefly summarize arguments for and against the death penalty.* **H-SS 12.2.1**

charged and with the reputation and financial resources of the accused. People with little or no income often have trouble raising bail. The federal and most State courts thus release many defendants "on their own recognizance," that is, on their honor. Failure to appear for trial—"jumping bail"—is itself a punishable crime.

Preventive Detention

In 1984, Congress provided for the **preventive detention** of some people accused of federal crimes. A federal judge can order that the accused be held, without bail, when there is good reason to believe that he or she will commit another serious crime before trial.

Critics of the law claim that preventive detention amounts to punishment before trial. They say it undercuts the presumption of innocence to which defendants are entitled.

The Supreme Court upheld the 1984 law, 6–3, in *United States* v. *Salerno*, 1987. The majority rejected the argument that preventive detention is punishment. Rather, it found the practice a legitimate response to a "pressing societal problem." The Court held that, "There is no doubt that preventing danger to the community is a legitimate regulatory goal." More than half the States have recently adopted preventive detention laws.

Cruel and Unusual Punishment

The 8th Amendment also forbids "cruel and unusual punishment." The 14th Amendment extends that prohibition against the States, *Robinson* v. *California*, 1962.

The Supreme Court decided its first cruel and unusual case in *Wilkerson* v. *Utah*, 1879. There a territorial court had sentenced a convicted murderer to death by a firing squad. The Court held that this punishment was not forbidden by the Constitution. The kinds of penalties the Constitution intended to prevent, said the Court, were such barbaric tortures as burning at the stake, crucifixion, drawing and quartering, "and all others in the same line of unnecessary cruelty." The Court took the same position a few years later when, for the first time, it upheld the electrocution of a convicted murderer, *In re Kemmler*, 1890.

Since then, the Court has heard only a handful of cruel and unusual cases, except for those relating to capital punishment. More often than not, the Court has rejected the cruel and unusual punishment argument.[14] *Louisiana* v. *Resweber*, 1947, is fairly typical. There the Court found that it was not unconstitutional to subject a convicted murderer to a second electrocution after the chair had failed to work properly on the first occasion.

The Court also denied the cruel and unusual claim in a recent case involving California's "three strikes" law, *Lockyer* v. *Andrade*, 2003. That law provides that any person convicted of a crime for a third time must be sent to prison for at least 25 years. Leonard Andrade had received 50 years for stealing $153.54 worth of children's

---

[14]The prohibition of cruel and unusual punishment is limited to criminal matters. It does not forbid paddling or similar punishments in the public schools, *Ingraham* v. *Wright*, 1977.

videos from two K-Mart stores. The K-Mart thefts were treated as separate offenses and he had an earlier burglary conviction on his record.

However, the Court has held some punishments to be cruel and unusual, although only a few. It did so for the first time in *Weems* v. *United States,* 1910. There, the Court overturned the conviction of a Coast Guard official convicted of falsifying government pay records. He had been sentenced to 15 years at hard labor, constantly chained at ankle and wrist. In *Robinson* v. *California,* 1962, the Court held that a State law defining narcotics addiction as a crime to be punished, rather than an illness to be treated, violated the 8th and 14th amendments.[15] In *Estelle* v. *Gamble,* 1976, it ruled that a Texas prison inmate could not properly be denied needed medical care.

Capital Punishment

Is **capital punishment**—punishment by death—cruel and unusual and therefore unconstitutional?[16] For years, the Supreme Court was reluctant to face that highly charged issue.[17]

The Court met the issue more or less directly in *Furman* v. *Georgia,* 1972. There it struck down all of the then existing State laws allowing the death penalty, but not because that penalty as such was cruel and unusual. Rather, the Court voided those laws because they gave too much discretion to judges or juries in deciding whether to impose the death penalty. The Court noted that out of all the people convicted of capital crimes, only "a random few," most of them African American or poor or both, were "capriciously selected" for execution.

Since that decision, Congress and 38 States have passed new capital punishment laws. At first, those laws took one of two forms. Several States made the death penalty mandatory for certain crimes, such as killing a police officer or

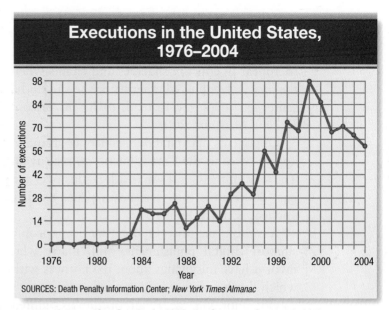

Executions in the United States, 1976–2004

SOURCES: Death Penalty Information Center; *New York Times Almanac*

Interpreting Graphs In 1976, the Supreme Court upheld the constitutionality of the death penalty. ***Summarize the data shown on the graph.***

murder committed during a rape, kidnapping, or arson. Other States provided for a two-stage process in capital cases: first, a trial to settle the issue of guilt or innocence; then, for those convicted, a second hearing to decide whether the circumstances justify a sentence of death.

In considering the scores of challenges to those State laws, the Supreme Court found the mandatory death penalty laws unconstitutional. In *Woodson* v. *North Carolina,* 1976, it ruled that such laws were "unduly harsh and rigidly unworkable." It saw the laws as attempts simply to "paper over" the decision in *Furman.*

The two-stage approach to capital punishment *is* constitutional, however. In *Gregg* v. *Georgia,* 1976, the Court held, for the first time, that the "punishment of death does not invariably violate the Constitution." It ruled that well-drawn two-stage laws can practically eliminate "the risk that [the death penalty] will be inflicted in an arbitrary or capricious manner."

The death penalty can be imposed only for "crimes resulting in the death of the victim," *Coker* v. *Georgia,* 1977. That penalty cannot be imposed on those who are mentally challenged, *Atkins* v. *Virginia,* 2002, or on those who were under the age of 18 when their crimes were committed, *Roper* v. *Simmons,* 2005.

The question of whether the death penalty is to be imposed in a case must be decided by the

---

[15]But, notice, that does not mean that buying, selling, or possessing narcotics cannot be made a crime. Such criminal laws are designed to punish persons for their behavior, not for being ill.

[16]The phrase "capital punishment" comes from the Latin *caput,* meaning "head"; in many cultures, the historically preferred method for executing criminals was beheading (decapitation).

[17]The Court did hold that neither death by firing squad (*Wilkerson* v. *Utah,* 1878) nor by a second electrocution (*Louisiana* v. *Resweber,* 1947) is unconstitutional. But in neither of those cases, nor in others, did it deal with the question of the death penalty as such.

jury that convicted the defendant, not the judge who presided at the trial, *Ring* v. *Arizona*, 2002. A convicted defendant cannot be forced to appear in court in shackles and chains when the jury is deciding whether he or she should be sentenced to die or, instead, to life in prison, *Deck* v. *Missouri*, 2005.

Opponents of capital punishment continue to appeal cases to the Court, but to no real avail. The sum of the Court's many decisions over the past 30 years is this: The death penalty, fairly applied, is constitutional.

A sizable majority of the American people support capital punishment. Still, many who favor it have misgivings about the fairness with which death sentences are applied.

Governor George Ryan of Illinois ignited controversy when he ordered a suspension of executions in his State in 2000. He did so, he said, because the death penalty process is "fraught with error." From 1977 to 2000, 285 people were sentenced to die in Illinois. By 2000, 12 of them had been executed, but 13 others had been released from prison because they had been wrongly convicted.

In 2003, Governor Ryan commuted the sentences of all the inmates then on death row in Illinois. He justified that extraordinary action by citing a State investigation that uncovered corruption and racial bias in the State's death penalty process. The legislature has since passed several reform measures, but current governor Rod Blagojevich has refused to lift the suspension. He says the State's problems continue.

The death penalty statutes in New York and Kansas were held unconstitutional by those States' highest courts in 2004. Efforts to revive those laws continue.

Treason

Treason against the United States is the only crime that is defined in the Constitution. The Framers provided a specific definition of the crime because they knew that the charge of treason is a favorite weapon in the hands of tyrants.

Treason, says Article III, Section 3, can consist of only two things: either (1) levying war against the United States or (2) "adhering to their Enemies, giving them Aid and Comfort." No person can be convicted of the crime "unless on the Testimony of two Witnesses to the same overt Act, or on Confession in open Court."

Congress has set death as the maximum penalty for treason against the United States, but no one has ever been executed for the crime. Note that a person can commit treason only in wartime. However, Congress has made it a crime, during times of either peace or war, to commit espionage or sabotage, to attempt to overthrow the government by force, or to conspire to do any of these things.

Most of the State constitutions also provide for treason. John Brown was hanged as a traitor to Virginia after his raid on Harpers Ferry in 1859. He is believed to be the only person ever to be executed for treason against a State.

Section 4 Assessment

Key Terms and Main Ideas

1. What constitutes excessive **bail**?
2. In cases involving cruel and unusual punishment, how has the Court generally ruled?
3. What is the Supreme Court's view of **capital punishment**?
4. Why does the Constitution specifically define **treason**?

Critical Thinking

5. **Demonstrating Reasoned Judgment (a)** What two forms did State laws allowing capital punishment take after the Court's decision in *Furman* v. *Georgia*? **(b)** Why did the Court find one of those forms "unduly harsh and rigidly unworkable"?

6. **Identifying Assumptions** What assumptions underlie the Court's decision that preventive detention is constitutional?

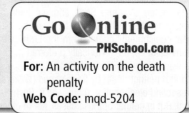

Does a Suspect's Flight From Police Justify a Stop and Search?

Analysis Skills HR4, HI3, HI4

The 4th Amendment prohibits "unreasonable searches and seizures," but it does not define the term "unreasonable." In a leading case, **Terry v. Ohio, 1968,** *the Supreme Court held that police officers may stop and frisk a person when they have good reason to believe that that person is armed and dangerous. May police stop and search a person simply because that person flees when the police approach?*

Illinois v. Wardlow (2000)

William Wardlow was holding a white bag while in an area of Chicago known for heavy drug trafficking when he saw a caravan of police cars approaching. He fled, and the police pursued. When they caught up with him, one of the officers conducted a "pat-down" search for weapons. (In the police officer's experience, weapons were usually found in the vicinity of narcotics transactions.) The officer squeezed the bag Wardlow was carrying and felt a heavy, hard object shaped like a gun. He opened the bag and discovered a .38-caliber handgun with five live rounds of ammunition.

At his trial, Wardlow argued that he should not be prosecuted for possession of the gun because the officer did not have reasonable suspicion to stop and search him. The Illinois trial court ruled against him, and he was convicted of unlawful use of a weapon by a felon. The Illinois Appellate Court then reversed his conviction. The Illinois Supreme Court affirmed that ruling, holding that both the stop and the arrest violated the 4th Amendment. The case then went to the Supreme Court.

Arguments for Illinois

1. The fact that a person fled from a police officer strongly indicates criminal behavior and provides reasonable grounds for stopping the suspect in order to conduct a brief investigation.
2. Even if flight alone is not sufficient to justify stopping and searching a suspect, the fact that the suspect was in a high-crime area, combined with the fact that the suspect fled upon the arrival of the police, provide reasonable grounds for stopping the suspect.
3. The standard that must be met to justify stopping a suspect, "reasonable suspicion," is less demanding than the standard of "probable cause" that must be met to justify arresting a suspect.

Arguments for Wardlow

1. There can be many reasons for fleeing from police; the fact that a person fled does not by itself mean that he is guilty of a crime.
2. Even the combined circumstances of being in a high-crime area, carrying a white bag, and running from the police do not create reasonable suspicion to justify a search.
3. An individual has the right to ignore the police unless and until the police have sufficient grounds under the Constitution to detain or arrest him. No one is required to cooperate with the police.

Decide for Yourself

1. Review the constitutional grounds on which each side based its arguments and the specific arguments each side presented.
2. Debate the opposing viewpoints presented in this case. Which viewpoint do you favor?
3. Predict the impact of the Court's decision on the conduct of police investigations and on relations between minority groups and the police. (To read a summary of the Court's decision, turn to pages 799–806.)

Go Online
PHSchool.com
Use Web Code mqp-5208 to register your vote on this issue and to see how other students voted.

CHAPTER 20 Assessment

Political Dictionary

due process (p. 564), substantive due process (p. 565), procedural due process (p. 565), police power (p. 566), search warrant (p. 566), involuntary servitude (p. 569), discrimination (p. 570), writs of assistance (p. 571), probable cause (p. 571), exclusionary rule (p. 573), writ of habeas corpus (p. 576), bill of attainder (p. 577), ex post facto law (p. 577), grand jury (p. 577), indictment (p. 578), double jeopardy (p. 578), bench trial (p. 580), Miranda Rule (p. 582), bail (p. 585), preventive detention (p. 586), capital punishment (p. 587), treason (p. 588)

Standards Review

H-SS 12.1.6 Understand that the Bill of Rights limits the powers of the federal government and state governments.

H-SS 12.2.1 Discuss the meaning and importance of each of the rights guaranteed under the Bill of Rights and how each is secured (e.g., freedom of religion, speech, press, assembly, petition, privacy).

H-SS 12.2.3 Discuss the individual's legal obligations to obey the law, serve as a juror, and pay taxes.

H-SS 12.5.1 Understand the changing interpretations of the Bill of Rights over time, including interpretations of the basic freedoms (religion, speech, press, petition, and assembly) articulated in the First Amendment and the due process and equal protection-of-the-law clauses of the Fourteenth Amendment.

H-SS 12.5.4 Explain the controversies that have resulted over changing interpretations of civil rights, including those in *Plessy* v. *Ferguson, Brown* v. *Board of Education, Miranda* v. *Arizona, Regents of the University of California* v. *Bakke, Adarand Constructors, Inc.* v. *Pena,* and *United States* v. *Virginia (VMI).*

H-SS 12.10 Students formulate questions about and defend their analyses of tensions within our constitutional democracy and the importance of maintaining a balance between the following concepts: majority rule and individual rights; liberty and equality; state and national authority in a federal system; civil disobedience and the rule of law; freedom of the press and the right to a fair trial; the relationship of religion and government.

Practicing the Vocabulary

Matching *Choose a term from the list above that best matches each description.*

1. A group convened by a court to determine whether or not there is enough evidence against a person to justify a trial
2. A constitutional guarantee that a government will not deprive any person of life, liberty, or property by any unfair, arbitrary, or unreasonable action
3. The power of each State to act to protect and promote the public health, safety, morals, and general welfare
4. A sum of money that an accused person may be required to post as a guarantee that he or she will appear in court at the proper time

Fill in the Blank *Choose a term from the list above that best completes the sentence.*

5. During colonial times, British officials used _____ in order to search private homes for smuggled goods.
6. According to the _____, suspects must be advised of their rights before police questioning.
7. If a person is tried twice for the same crime, he or she may have been subjected to _____.
8. Police generally need a _____ in order search someone's house.
9. An _____ is a law applied to acts performed before the law was passed.

Reviewing Main Ideas

Section 1

10. What is the difference between procedural and substantive due process?
11. Describe the relationship between the States' police power and due process of law.
12. The States may exercise the police power to protect and promote what?
13. What right did the Court first articulate in *Griswold* v. *Connecticut,* 1965?

Section 2

14. Use the examples of the *Civil Rights Cases,* 1883, and *Jones* v. *Mayer,* 1968, to illustrate how the Court's interpretation of the 13th Amendment changed over the years.
15. What are the roots of the 3rd Amendment, and why is it not significant today?
16. What is the aim of the 4th Amendment?
17. What does the exclusionary rule exclude?

Section 3

18. For what reason does the Constitution protect the rights of those accused of a crime?
19. In what ways does the Constitution protect the rights of the accused?
20. What are the key constitutional guarantees of a fair trial?
21. What is the Miranda Rule?

Section 4

22. What are the key constitutional guarantees regarding punishment of the guilty?
23. Under what circumstances has the Supreme Court found death penalty laws to be unconstitutional?
24. What was the significance of *Furman* v. *Georgia,* 1972, in the history of the Supreme Court's rulings regarding capital punishment?
25. (a) What is the only crime defined in the Constitution?
    (b) What requirements must be met in order for a person to be convicted of this crime?

Critical Thinking Skills

Analysis Skills HR4, HI1

26. ***Applying the Chapter Skill*** If you are summoned for jury duty, would you rather serve on a grand jury or a trial jury? Why? On a jury that hears a civil or a criminal case? Why?

27. ***Checking Consistency*** Recall that an accused person can be held without bail when there is good reason to believe that he or she will commit another crime. In your opinion, does this rule violate the principle of presumed innocence until proven guilty? Does it violate the guarantee of due process?

28. ***Identifying Assumptions*** What assumptions underlie the Miranda Rule and its warnings?

29. ***Determining Relevance*** Why may it be said that the 2nd, 3rd, and 4th amendments are a reflection of colonial experience?

30. ***Identifying Central Issues*** **(a)** Why did the Supreme Court adopt the exclusionary rule? **(b)** Do you think the rule should be retained or abandoned?

Analyzing Political Cartoons

Use your knowledge of American history and government and this cartoon to answer the questions below.

"That was fun. What time does the next trial of the century start?"

31. **(a)** Who are the people in the cartoon? **(b)** What are they watching on television?

32. What does the cartoon suggest about television cameras in the courtroom?

Participation Activities

Analysis Skills CS1, HR4

33. ***Current Events Watch*** Scan the newspaper for stories concerning any guarantees of the rights of the accused shown on the chart on page 578. Be prepared to give an oral report of your findings.

34. ***Time Line Activity*** Choose an issue discussed in this chapter (for example, the constitutionality of the death penalty or abortion). Based on both the information in this chapter and your own research, make a list of the key Supreme Court decisions regarding the issue. Present these decisions in a time line that demonstrates the development of the Court's position on this issue.

35. ***It's Your Turn*** Create a survey to gauge opinions on the Constitution's protections of individual rights. First, list the several rights discussed in this chapter. Then note some of the controversies associated with some of those rights. Construct a list of questions designed to prompt the expression of opinions on those matters. Ask a number of people to respond to your survey and compile the results. **(Conducting a Survey)**

Standards Monitoring *Online*

For: Chapter 20 Self-Test **Visit:** PHSchool.com
Web Code: mqa-5205

As a final review, take the Magruder's Chapter 20 Self-Test and receive immediate feedback on your answers.
The test consists of 20 multiple-choice questions designed to test your understanding of the chapter content.

CHAPTER 21

Civil Rights: Equal Justice Under Law

"Our Constitution is color-blind, and neither knows nor tolerates classes among citizens. In respect of civil rights, all citizens are equal before the law."

—Justice John Marshall Harlan, dissenting in *Plessy* v. *Ferguson*, 1896

Justice Harlan objected to the High Court's decision in the case that laid the foundation for some 60 years of legal race-based discrimination in this country. His dissenting view became the majority position when, in 1954, the Court finally, and unanimously, outlawed segregation in public schools.

◆ Demonstrators protest discrimination against African Americans at Woolworth's lunch counters, 1960

H-SS 12.2.2 Explain how economic rights are secured and their importance to the individual and to society (e.g., the right to acquire, use, transfer, and dispose of property; right to choose one's work; right to join or not join labor unions; copyright and patent).

H-SS 12.2.6 Explain how one becomes a citizen of the United States, including the process of naturalization (e.g., literacy, language, and other requirements).

H-SS 12.5.1 Understand the changing interpretations of the Bill of Rights over time, including interpretations of the basic freedoms (religion, speech, press, petition, and assembly) articulated in the First Amendment and the due process and equal protection-of-the-law clauses of the Fourteenth Amendment.

H-SS 12.5.4 Explain the controversies that have resulted over changing interpretations of civil rights, including those in *Plessy* v. *Ferguson*, *Brown* v. *Board of Education*, *Miranda* v. *Arizona*, *Regents of the University of California* v. *Bakke*, *Adarand Constructors, Inc.* v. *Pena*, and *United States* v. *Virginia* (VMI).

H-SS 12.6.4 Describe the means that citizens use to participate in the political process (e.g., voting, campaigning, lobbying, filing a legal challenge, demonstrating, petitioning, picketing, running for political office).

H-SS 12.7.5 Explain how public policy is formed, including the setting of the public agenda and implementation of it through regulations and executive orders.

SECTION 1

Diversity and Discrimination in American Society *(pp. 594–599)*

★ The United States is a diverse nation made up of people from many different backgrounds and communities.

★ African Americans, Native Americans, Hispanic Americans, Asian Americans, and other minority groups have suffered from discrimination at the hands of government and private individuals.

★ Women of all backgrounds experience discrimination in much the same way as members of racial and ethnic minorities.

SECTION 2

Equality Before the Law *(pp. 601–606)*

★ The 14th Amendment guaranteed "equal protection of the law" to all Americans in 1868, yet most States adopted laws allowing race- and gender-based discrimination.

★ The Supreme Court overturned many of these laws—and its own past decisions—during the 1950s and 1960s.

★ De facto segregation persists in public schools and housing.

★ Since 1971, most laws that treat women differently from men have been successfully challenged in court.

SECTION 3

Federal Civil Rights Laws *(pp. 608–612)*

★ Congress passed several acts in the 1960s to guarantee the civil rights of African Americans, other minorities, and women.

★ Affirmative action policies require the Federal Government and those who do business with the Federal Government to take positive steps to remedy past discrimination and prevent its recurrence.

★ Supporters and critics of affirmative action have taken their debate to the Supreme Court, Congress, State legislatures, and the voting booth.

SECTION 4

American Citizenship *(pp. 613–618)*

★ The vast majority of people living in the United States are American citizens who were born in this country or born abroad to parents with citizenship.

★ Several million Americans have become citizens through a difficult process called naturalization.

★ Americans can lose their citizenship by choice or, in rare cases, through a court order.

★ Most immigrants to the United States have come through official channels, but many arrive illegally and face special challenges to stay in this country.

Go Online
PHSchool.com

For: Current Data
Web Code: mqg-5216

For: Close Up Foundation debates
Web Code: mqh-5219

Diversity and Discrimination in American Society

1

Section Preview

OBJECTIVES

1. **Understand** what it means to live in a heterogeneous society.
2. **Summarize** the history of race-based discrimination in the United States.
3. **Examine** discrimination against women in the past and present.

WHY IT MATTERS

The Declaration of Independence declares that "all men are created equal," but this nation still struggles to meet that ideal. Race-based and gender-based discrimination have declined in this country, but they certainly have not disappeared.

POLITICAL DICTIONARY

★ heterogeneous
★ immigrant
★ reservation
★ refugee
★ assimilation

Have you read George Orwell's classic, *Animal Farm?* Even if you have not, you may have heard its most oft-quoted line: "All animals are created equal, but some animals are more equal than others." You might keep Orwell's words in mind as you read the pages in this chapter.

A Heterogeneous Society

The term **heterogeneous** is a compound of two Greek words: *hetero,* meaning "other or different," and *genos,* meaning "race, family, or kind." Something that is heterogeneous is composed of a mix of ingredients. "We the People of

▶ **A Diverse Nation**
Individuals like this attorney (right) have enjoyed great success, despite the fact that women and Native Americans have often been targets of discrimination.

the United States" are a heterogeneous lot, and we are becoming more so, year to year.

The population of the United States is predominantly white. It is today and, as you can see in the table on page 595, it has been historically. The first census in 1790 reported that there were 3,929,214 people living in this country. Four out of every five of them were white. African Americans made up the remaining 20 percent of the population counted in the census. As the nation's population grew over the decades, so, too, did the proportion of the American people who were white—until recently.

Today, the ethnic composition of the population is strikingly different from what it was only a generation ago. **Immigrants**—that is, those aliens legally admitted as permanent residents—have arrived in near-record numbers every year since the mid-1960s. Over that period, the nation's African American, Hispanic American, and Asian American populations have grown at rates several times that of the white population.

A look at gender balance in the population reveals that females are more numerous than males. This has been the case for more than half a century now.

As a result of these changes in the American population, the United States is more heterogeneous today than ever before in its history. That fact is certain to have a profound effect on the American social, political, and economic landscape on through the twenty-first century.

Ethnic Composition of the United States

Ethnic Composition of the Population, 1790 – 2050*

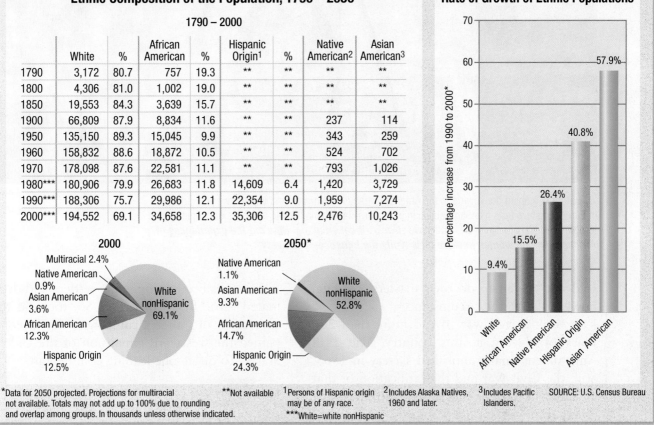

1790 – 2000

	White	%	African American	%	Hispanic Origin[1]	%	Native American[2]	Asian American[3]
1790	3,172	80.7	757	19.3	**	**	**	**
1800	4,306	81.0	1,002	19.0	**	**	**	**
1850	19,553	84.3	3,639	15.7	**	**	**	**
1900	66,809	87.9	8,834	11.6	**	**	237	114
1950	135,150	89.3	15,045	9.9	**	**	343	259
1960	158,832	88.6	18,872	10.5	**	**	524	702
1970	178,098	87.6	22,581	11.1	**	**	793	1,026
1980***	180,906	79.9	26,683	11.8	14,609	6.4	1,420	3,729
1990***	188,306	75.7	29,986	12.1	22,354	9.0	1,959	7,274
2000***	194,552	69.1	34,658	12.3	35,306	12.5	2,476	10,243

2000

Multiracial 2.4%
Native American 0.9%
Asian American 3.6%
African American 12.3%
Hispanic Origin 12.5%
White nonHispanic 69.1%

2050*

Native American 1.1%
Asian American 9.3%
African American 14.7%
Hispanic Origin 24.3%
White nonHispanic 52.8%

Rate of Growth of Ethnic Populations

Percentage increase from 1990 to 2000*

White 9.4%
African American 15.5%
Native American 26.4%
Hispanic Origin 40.8%
Asian American 57.9%

*Data for 2050 projected. Projections for multiracial not available. Totals may not add up to 100% due to rounding and overlap among groups. In thousands unless otherwise indicated.

**Not available

[1] Persons of Hispanic origin may be of any race.

[2] Includes Alaska Natives, 1960 and later.

[3] Includes Pacific Islanders.

***White=white nonHispanic

SOURCE: U.S. Census Bureau

Interpreting Charts Although the population of the United States remains predominantly white, minority populations are growing at a faster rate than the majority population. The 2000 census showed that more and more Americans trace their heritage to multiple groups or choose not to identify themselves by race. ***According to the data, which group will be the largest minority group in 2050?***

Race-Based Discrimination

White Americans have been historically reluctant to yield to nonwhite Americans a full and equal place in the social, economic, and political life of this nation. Over time, the principal targets of that ethnic prejudice have been African Americans, Native Americans, Asian Americans, and Hispanic Americans. The white-male-dominated power structure has also been slow to recognize the claims of women to a full and equal place in American society.

African Americans

Much of what you will read in these pages focuses on discrimination against African Americans. There are three reasons for this focus:

1. African Americans constitute the second largest minority group in the United States. They number more than 40 million today, over 13 percent of all the American people.

2. African Americans have been the victims of consistent and deliberate unjust treatment for a longer time than perhaps any other group of Americans.[1] The ancestors of most African Americans came to this country in chains. Tens of thousands of Africans were kidnapped, crammed aboard sailing vessels, brought to America, and then sold in slave markets. As slaves, they could be bought and

---

[1] Slavery first came to what was to become the United States in 1619; in August of that year, 20 Africans were sold to white settlers at Jamestown in colonial Virginia.

▲ Before beginning the voyage to the Americas, many African men and women were imprisoned in European slave forts like San Sebastian in modern-day Ghana. Untold numbers of people died in terrible conditions in slave forts and slave ships. *Critical Thinking* ***How did the experiences of African men and women in slave forts typify the injustices of slavery?***

sold and forced to do their masters' bidding, however harsh the circumstances.

It took a civil war to end more than 200 years of slavery in this country. The 13th Amendment finally abolished slavery in 1865. Still, the Civil War and the ratification of that amendment did not end widespread racial discrimination in the United States.

3. Most of the gains the nation has made in translating the Constitution's guarantees of equality into a reality for all persons have come out of efforts made by and on behalf of African Americans. For example, the struggles of Martin Luther King, Jr., and others resulted in the Civil Rights Act of 1964 and then the Voting Rights Act of 1965; see pages 159–163.

America is now an inescapably multiracial society. Still, unlike whites, African Americans live with the consequences of America's history of racial discrimination every day of their lives. Of course, this is not to say that other groups of Americans have not also suffered the effects of discrimination. Clearly, many have.

Native Americans

White settlers first began to arrive in America in relatively large numbers in the early middle years of the 17th century. At the time, some one million Native Americans were living in territory that was to become the United States.[2] By 1900, however, their number had fallen to less than 250,000.

Diseases brought by white settlers had decimated those first Americans. So, too, did the succession of military campaigns that accompanied the westward expansion of the United States. To quote one leading commentator:

PRIMARY Sources *"'The only good Indian is a dead Indian' is not simply a hackneyed expression from cowboy movies. It was part of the strategy of westward expansion, as settlers and U.S. troops mercilessly drove the eastern Indians from their ancestral lands to the Great Plains and then took those lands too."*

—Thomas E. Patterson, *The American Democracy*

Today, more than 2.8 million Native Americans live in this country. More than a third of them live on or near **reservations,** which are public lands set aside by a government for use by Native American tribes.

Like African Americans, Native Americans have been the victims of overwhelming discrimination. The consequences of that bias have been truly appalling, and they remain all too evident today. Poverty, joblessness, and alcoholism plague many reservations. The life expectancy of Native Americans living on reservations today is

---

[2]An estimated 8 to 10 million Native Americans lived in all of North and South America in the mid-1600s.

10 years less than the national average, and the Native American infant mortality rate is three times that for white Americans.

Hispanic Americans

Hispanic Americans are those in this country who have a Spanish-speaking background; many prefer to be called Latinos. Hispanics may be of any race. According to the Bilateral Commission on the Future of United States-Mexican Relations, Hispanic Americans "are among the world's most complex groupings of human beings. [The largest number] are white, millions . . . are mestizo, nearly half a million in the United States are black or mulatto."[3]

Hispanic Americans number more than 42 million. They now constitute the largest minority group of Americans. Hispanics replaced African Americans as the largest minority group in the United States around the year 2000.

Hispanic Americans can generally be divided into four main groups:

1. *Mexican Americans.* More than half of all Hispanics in the United States, at least 24 million persons, were either born in Mexico or trace their ancestry there. Those who were born in this country of Mexican parents are often called Chicanos.

The largest part of the Mexican American population lives in the States of California, Arizona, New Mexico, and Texas. Large cities such as Los Angeles and San Antonio, Texas, have Hispanic pluralities or majorities, and smaller border cities such as Laredo and Brownsville, Texas, are over 90 percent Latino.

2. *Puerto Ricans.* Another large group of Hispanics has come to the mainland from the island of Puerto Rico. The population of the United States now includes some three million Puerto Ricans. Most of them have settled in New York, New Jersey, and in other parts of the Northeast.

3. *Cuban Americans.* The Hispanic population also includes some one million Cuban Americans. They are mostly people who fled the Castro dictatorship in Cuba, and their descendants. A majority of Cuban Americans have settled in Miami and elsewhere in South Florida.

4. *Central and South Americans.* The fourth major subgroup of Hispanic Americans came here from Central and South America, many as **refugees.** A refugee is one who seeks protection (refuge) from war, persecution, or some other danger. More than three million persons have emigrated to the United States from Central and South American countries over the past 25 years; they have come in the largest numbers from Nicaragua, El Salvador, Guatemala, Colombia, and Chile. Many have also come from the Dominican Republic, an island nation in the Caribbean.

Asian Americans

The story of white America's mistreatment of Asians is a lengthy one, too. They have faced discrimination from the first day they arrived in this country. As with all immigrant groups, assimilation into the white-dominated population has been difficult. **Assimilation** is the process by which people of one culture merge into and become part of another culture.

Chinese laborers were the first Asians to come to the United States in large numbers. They were brought here in the 1850s to 1860s as contract laborers to work in the mines and to

▲ Many Asian Americans, like this Vietnamese storeowner in Seattle, Washington, came to the United States from Southeast Asia in the 1970s and 1980s. People fled the turmoil of the Vietnam War and the Communist conquest of South Vietnam that followed. *Critical Thinking Did Vietnamese immigrants come to the United States for the same reasons as Chinese immigrants did a century earlier? Explain.* H-SS 12.2.2

---

[3]A mestizo is a person with both Spanish or Portuguese and Native American ancestry. A mulatto is a person with African and white ancestry.

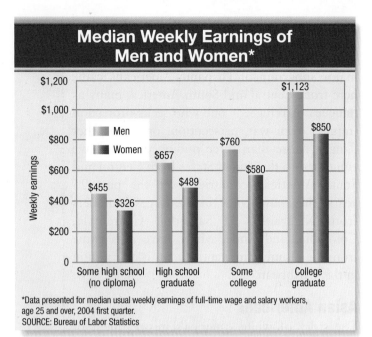

Median Weekly Earnings of Men and Women*

Legend:
- Men
- Women

Education level	Men	Women
Some high school (no diploma)	$455	$326
High school graduate	$657	$489
Some college	$760	$580
College graduate	$1,123	$850

*Data presented for median usual weekly earnings of full-time wage and salary workers, age 25 and over, 2004 first quarter.
SOURCE: Bureau of Labor Statistics

Interpreting Graphs This graph illustrates how much money working men and women earned each week in 2004. **What does the graph show about equality in the workplace today?**

build railroads in the West. Many white Americans, native-born and immigrants, resented the competition of "coolie labor." Their resentments were frequently expressed in violence toward Asians.

Congress brought Chinese immigration nearly to a halt with the Chinese Exclusion Act of 1882. Because of this and other government actions, only a very small number of Chinese, Japanese, and other Asians were permitted to enter the United States for more than 80 years.

Early in World War II, the Federal Government ordered the evacuation of all persons of Japanese descent from the Pacific Coast. Some 120,000 people, two thirds of them native-born American citizens, were forcibly removed to inland "war relocation camps." Years later, the Government conceded that that action had been both unnecessary and unjust.

Congress made dramatic changes in American immigration policies in 1965. Since then, some eight million Asian immigrants have come to this country, mostly from the Philippines, China, Korea, Vietnam, and India. The term "Asian American" describes an ever more diverse population. Asian Americans represent a tremendous variety of languages, religions, and cultures, and many recent immigrants from Asia have little in common with one another.

Today, the Asian American population exceeds 14 million, and it is the nation's fastest growing minority group. Asian Americans now live in every part of the United States. They are a majority of the population in Hawaii and more than 10 percent of that of California. New York City boasts the largest Chinese community outside of China itself.

Discrimination Against Women

Unlike the several ethnic groups described here, women are not a minority in the United States. They are, in fact, a majority group. Still, traditionally in many instances in American law and public policy, women have not enjoyed the same rights as men. Their status was even lower, in many instances, than men who were themselves the target of virulent discrimination. Women have been treated as less than equal in a great many matters—including, for example, property rights, education, and employment opportunities.

Organized efforts to improve the place of women in American society date from July 19, 1848. On that date, a convention on women's rights, meeting in Seneca Falls, New York, adopted a set of resolutions that deliberately echoed the words of the Declaration of Independence. It began:

> **PRIMARY Sources** **❝**When, in the course of human events, it becomes necessary for one portion of the family of man to assume among the people of the earth a position different from that which they have hitherto occupied. . . . We hold these truths to be self-evident: that all men and women are created equal. . . .**❞**
>
> —Declaration of Sentiments

Those who fought and finally won the long struggle for woman suffrage believed that, with the vote, women would soon achieve other basic rights. That assumption proved to be false. Although more than 51 percent of the population is female, women have held only a fraction of one percent of the nation's top public offices since 1789.

Even today, women hold little more than 15 percent of the 535 seats in Congress and little more than 20 percent of the 7,382 seats in the 50 State legislatures. Only eight of the 50 State governors today are female. Women are also hugely underrepresented at the upper levels of corporate management and other power groups in the private sector. Fewer than 20 percent of the nation's doctors, lawyers, and college professors are women.

It is illegal to pay women less than men for the same work. The Equal Pay Act of 1963 requires employers to pay men and women the same wages if they perform the same jobs in the same establishment under the same working conditions. The Civil Rights Act of 1964 also prohibits job discrimination based on sex. Yet, more than 40 years after Congress passed those laws, working women earn, on the average, less than 80 cents for every dollar earned by working men. See the graph on page 598.

Women earn less than men for a number of reasons—including the fact that the male work force is, over all, better educated and has more job experience than the female work force. (Note that these factors themselves can often be traced to discrimination.) In addition, some blame the so-called "Mommy track," in which women put their careers on hold to have children or work reduced hours to juggle child-care responsibilities. Others claim that a "glass ceiling" of discrimination in the corporate world and elsewhere, invisible but impenetrable, prevents women from rising to their full potential.

Certainly it is true that until quite recently women were limited to a fairly narrow range of jobs. In many cases, women were encouraged not to work outside the home once they were

▲ **Women's Work** Very few careers were open to women before the 1960s. Women with college degrees often took jobs as typists or secretaries, hoping for a rare opportunity to move up to better-paying jobs usually reserved for men. **H-SS 12.2.2**

married. Even now, more than three fourths of all jobs held by women are in low-paying clerical and service occupations. The Bureau of Labor Statistics reports that 98 percent of all secretaries today are women; so too are 96 percent of all child-care workers, 93 percent of all registered nurses, 93 percent of all bookkeepers and auditing clerks, 90 percent of all hairdressers and cosmetologists, and 86 percent of all dieticians.

Efforts on behalf of equal rights for women have gained significant ground in recent years. But, recall, that ground has not included an Equal Rights Amendment to the Constitution.

Section 1 Assessment

Key Terms and Main Ideas

1. What defines a **heterogeneous** nation?
2. Name one factor that can lead a **refugee** to leave his or her country.
3. Who are **immigrants?**
4. What is the purpose of a **reservation?**

Critical Thinking

5. **Understanding Point of View** In what sense are women a unique group among those who have suffered discrimination?
6. **Drawing Inferences** Assimilation is a controversial issue for members of minority groups. List two reasons why a recent immigrant to the United States might try to assimilate. Then, list two reasons why an immigrant might choose to retain as much of his or her native land's culture as possible.

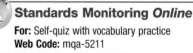

Standards Monitoring *Online*
For: Self-quiz with vocabulary practice
Web Code: mqa-5211

For: An activity on diversity and discrimination
Web Code: mqd-5211

Face the
Issues

Equality in Sports

Analysis Skill CS1

Background *The law known as Title IX, enacted in 1972, ensures women equal treatment in all aspects of education. Since then, Title IX has left its greatest mark on college sports, dramatically expanding opportunities for female athletes by requiring equal opportunity and funding. Critics say the law has unfairly forced cuts to men's teams to accommodate women. Read the arguments. What do you think?*

Women's basketball: a beneficiary of Title IX

Renew Title IX

Some of the best arguments for Title IX could be seen at the 2004 Summer Olympics—in the medal-winning performances of the U.S. women's teams. "Title IX got me where I am today," said Siri Millinix, goalkeeper for the soccer team. Of course, an even better argument for Title IX is the legion of women playing college varsity sports—an estimated 157,000, compared with 30,000 in 1972.

If not for Title IX, most women would never have had this chance. In the past, officials downplayed women's sports. Women did not get the money or opportunity to compete, so few women athletes were visible. People assumed that women didn't want to play sports, so schools did not budget money. Title IX broke this cycle. Given equal opportunities, girls and women joined sports teams by the millions.

Consider: girls and women who play sports are more likely to get better grades. They have more confidence, greater self-esteem, and better body images. Thanks to Title IX, women gain skills to compete and succeed in the workplace *and* on the field.

Equal Access for Athletes

Title IX provided the right medicine for schools in the early 1970s. But the United States has come a long way since then, and we no longer need Title IX to encourage girls and women to compete in sports. Instead, Title IX has become a clumsy tool that penalizes men more than it helps women. The tragic flaw of Title IX is that it requires that both sexes take part in sports at roughly equal rates.

If women make up, say, 50 percent of the general student population, they get half the slots in the school's sports programs and half the budget for athletic scholarships. To meet this test, colleges have had to eliminate 300 men's teams since 1993. Men's sports that don't draw a huge audience, like gymnastics, are unfairly targeted for elimination.

The fact is that money for athletics is limited. Funding should go to the most dedicated athletes of both sexes. If more men than women want to play sports, it is unfair and artificial to divide funding fifty-fifty by sex. Athletes should be judged by their performance and hard work above all else.

Exploring the Issues

1. Do you think women's sports would be popular today if Title IX had never required equal funding? Explain.
2. How might participation in team sports prepare young people for the workplace?

For more information about Title IX funding, view "Equality in Sports."

Face the **Issues**
Video Collection

Section Preview

OBJECTIVES

1. **Explain** the importance of the Equal Protection Clause.
2. **Describe** the history of segregation in America.
3. **Examine** how classification by sex relates to discrimination.

WHY IT MATTERS

The law includes safeguards to protect Americans from unfair discrimination on the basis of race or sex. The most important protections lie in the 5th and 14th amendments and the Civil Rights Act of 1964.

POLITICAL DICTIONARY

★ segregation
★ Jim Crow law
★ separate-but-equal doctrine
★ integration
★ de jure segregation
★ de facto segregation

Records recently unearthed by the Architect of the Capitol show that at least 400 slaves worked on the building's construction from 1792 through 1800, and they likely did for several years thereafter. Those records also indicate payments to a number of local slave owners—for example, "To Joseph Forest, for the hire of the Negro Charles." The slave owners were paid $5 a month for each laborer. Slaves even cast the bronze statue of *Freedom* and hoisted it atop the Capitol in 1800.

Equal Protection Clause

Nothing, not even a constitutional command, can *make* people equal in a literal sense. Individuals differ in strength, intelligence, height, and countless other ways. Still, the democratic ideal demands that government must treat all persons alike.

The equality of all persons, so boldly set out in the Declaration of Independence, is not proclaimed in so many words in the Constitution. Still, that concept pervades the document.

The closest approach to a literal statement of equality is to be found in the 14th Amendment's Equal Protection Clause. It declares:

FROM THE *Constitution*

❝*No State shall . . . deny to any person within its jurisdiction the equal protection of the laws.*❞
—United States Constitution

Those words were originally meant to benefit newly freed slaves. Over time, they have come to mean that the States and their local governments cannot draw unreasonable distinctions between any classes of persons. The Supreme Court has often held that the 5th Amendment's Due Process Clause puts the same restriction on the Federal Government.

Reasonable Classification

Government must have the power to classify, to draw distinctions between persons and groups. Otherwise, it could not possibly regulate human behavior. That is to say, government must be able to discriminate—and it does. Thus, those who rob banks fall into a special class, and they receive special treatment by the law. That sort of discrimination is clearly reasonable.

Government may not discriminate *unreasonably*, however. Every State taxes the sale of cigarettes, and so taxes smokers but not nonsmokers. No State can tax only blonde smokers, however, or only male smokers.

Over time, the Supreme Court has rejected many equal protection challenges to the actions of government. More often than not, the Supreme

▶ *Freedom* atop the Capitol

In 1955, **Rosa Parks** refused to give her seat to a white man on a bus in Montgomery, Alabama, and was subsequently arrested. That simple act led to a bus boycott by African Americans and helped the civil rights movement grow into a national cause. Parks, who had long worked for civil rights, later explained her brave action:

"For half of my life there were laws and customs in the South that kept African Americans segregated from Caucasians and allowed white people to treat black people without any respect. I never thought this was fair, and from the time I was a child, I tried to protest against disrespectful treatment. But it was very hard to do anything about segregation and racism when white people had the power of the law behind them. Somehow we had to change the laws. **"**

Evaluating the Quotation

From what you have read, how did court decisions combine with changes in the law to move the nation toward protecting civil rights?

Court has found that what those governments have done is, in fact, constitutional.[4]

The Rational Basis Test

The Supreme Court most often decides equal protection cases by applying a standard known as the rational basis test. This test asks: Does the classification in question bear a reasonable relationship to the achievement of some proper governmental purpose?

A California case, *Michael M.* v. *Superior Court*, 1981, illustrates that test. California law says that a man who has sexual relations with a girl under 18 to whom he is not married can be prosecuted for statutory rape. However, the girl

---

[4]The Court has voided a number of those actions on equal protection grounds, however. You will consider several of those cases in a moment, and you have encountered many others previously—for example, with regard to lengthy residence requirements for voting purposes and gerrymandering on the basis of race.

cannot be charged with that crime, even if she is a willing partner. The Court found the law to bear a reasonable relationship to a proper public policy goal: preventing teenage pregnancies.

The Strict Scrutiny Test

The Court imposes a higher standard in some equal protection cases, however. This is especially true when a case deals with (1) such "fundamental rights" as the right to vote, the right to travel between the States, or 1st Amendment rights; or (2) such "suspect classifications" as those based on race, sex, or national origin.

In these instances, the Court has said that a law must meet a higher standard than the rational basis test: the strict scrutiny test. The State must be able to show that some "compelling governmental interest" justifies the distinctions it has drawn between classes of people.

An alimony case, *Orr* v. *Orr*, 1979, involved the use of that stricter test. An Alabama law that made women but not men eligible for alimony was held unconstitutional, as a denial of equal protection—because the law's distinction between men and women did not serve a compelling governmental interest.

Segregation in America

Beginning in the late 1800s, nearly half of the States passed racial segregation laws. **Segregation** means the separation of one group from another. Most of those **Jim Crow laws**—laws that separate people on the basis of race—were aimed at African Americans. Some were also drawn to affect Mexican Americans, Asians, and Native Americans. These laws required segregation by race in the use of both public and private facilities: schools, parks and playgrounds, hotels and restaurants, streetcars, even public restrooms and drinking fountains.

Separate-but-Equal Doctrine

In 1896, the Supreme Court provided a constitutional basis for Jim Crow laws by creating the **separate-but-equal doctrine.** In *Plessy* v. *Ferguson*, it upheld a Louisiana law requiring segregation in rail coaches. The Court held that the law did not violate the Equal Protection Clause because the separate facilities provided for African Americans were equal to those provided for whites.

The separate-but-equal doctrine was soon applied in several other fields, and it stood for nearly 60 years. Indeed, until the late 1930s, little effort was made by any arm of government even to see that the separate accommodations for African Americans were, in fact, equal to those reserved to whites. More often than not, they were not.

Brown v. Board of Education

The Supreme Court first began to chip away at the separate-but-equal doctrine in *Missouri ex rel. Gaines* v. *Canada* in 1938. Lloyd Gaines, an African American, was denied admission to the law school at the all-white University of Missouri. Gaines was fully qualified for admission—except for his race. The State did not have a separate law school for African Americans. However, it did offer to pay his tuition at a public law school in any of the four neighboring States which did not discriminate by race. But Gaines insisted on a legal education in his home State.

The Court held that the separate-but-equal doctrine left Missouri with only two choices: It could either admit Gaines to the State's law school or establish a separate-but-equal school for him. The State gave in and admitted Gaines.

Over the next several years, the Court took an increasingly rigorous attitude toward the requirement of equal facilities. It began to insist on equality *in fact* between separate facilities.

Thus, in 1950 the Court decided two major cases in line with its holding in Gaines, *Sweatt* v. *Painter* and *McLaurin* v. *Oklahoma*. G.W. McLaurin was admitted to the University of Oklahoma's graduate school, but "on a segregated basis." Both cases involved African American university students for whom the State had provided separate educational facilities. The Court held that, in both cases, the separate facilities were far from equal. Still, in neither case did the Court go so far as to reexamine the validity of the separate-but-equal doctrine.

Finally, in an historic decision in 1954, the Court reversed *Plessy* v. *Ferguson*. In *Brown* v. *Board of Education of Topeka*, it struck down the laws of four States requiring or allowing separate public schools for white and African American students.[5]

Unanimously, the Court held segregation by race in public education is invalid:

▲ *The Migrants* Beginning early in the last century, many African Americans left the South for jobs in northern cities. Artist Jacob Lawrence captured the lives of African Americans in works such as *The Migrants Cast Their Ballots*. **H-SS 12.6.4**

PRIMARY Sources "*Does segregation of children in public schools solely on the basis of race, even though the physical facilities and other 'tangible' factors may be equal, deprive the children of the minority group of equal educational opportunities? We believe that it does.*

. . . To separate them from others of similar age and qualifications solely because of their race generates a feeling of inferiority as to their status in the community that may affect their hearts and minds in a way unlikely ever to be undone. . . . Separate educational facilities are inherently unequal."
—Chief Justice Earl Warren, Opinion of the Court

The Court in 1955 directed the States to make "a prompt and reasonable start" and to end segregation "with all deliberate speed."

A "reasonable start" was made in Baltimore, Louisville, St. Louis, and elsewhere. In most of the Deep South, however, "massive resistance" soon developed. State legislatures passed laws and school boards worked to block **integration** —the process of bringing a group into the mainstream of society. Most of these steps were clearly

[5]Kansas, Delaware, South Carolina, and Virginia. On the same day, it also struck down racially segregated public schools in the District of Columbia, under the 5th Amendment, *Bolling* v. *Sharpe,* 1954.

unconstitutional, but challenging them in court was both costly and slow.

The pace of desegregation quickened after Congress passed the Civil Rights Act of 1964. That act forbids the use of federal funds to aid any State or local activity in which racial segregation is practiced. It directed the Justice Department to file suits to prompt desegregation actions.

The Supreme Court quickened the pace in 1969. In a case from Mississippi, *Alexander* v. *Holmes County Board of Education,* it ruled that, after 15 years, the time for "all deliberate speed" had ended. Said a unanimous Court: "The continued operation of segregated schools under a standard allowing for 'all deliberate speed' . . . is no longer constitutionally permissible."

De Jure, De Facto Segregation

By fall 1970, school systems characterized by **de jure segregation** had been abolished. De jure segregation is segregation by law, with legal sanction. That is not to say that desegregation had been fully accomplished—far from it.[6]

Many recent integration controversies have come in places where the schools have never been segregated by law. They have occurred, instead, in communities in which **de facto segregation** has long been present, and continues. De facto segregation is segregation in fact, even if no law requires

it. Housing patterns have most often been its major cause. The concentration of African Americans in certain sections of cities inevitably led to local school systems in which some schools are largely African American. That condition is apparent in many northern as well as southern communities.

Efforts to desegregate those school systems have taken several forms. School district lines have been redrawn and the busing of students out of racially segregated neighborhoods has been tried. These efforts have brought strong protests in many places and violence in some.

The Supreme Court first sanctioned busing in a North Carolina case, *Swann* v. *Charlotte-Mecklenburg Board of Education,* 1971. There it held that "desegregation plans cannot be limited to walk-in schools." Since then, busing has been used to increase the racial mix in many school districts across the country—in some by court order, in others, voluntarily.

Segregation in Other Fields

This nation has not yet achieved a complete integration of the public schools, but legally enforced racial segregation in all other areas of life has

---

[6]Some States, several school districts, and many parents and private groups have sought to avoid integrated schools through established or, often, newly created private schools. On the point, see the Court's rulings in *Runyon* v. *McCrary,* 1976, page 570.

The Enduring Constitution

The Supreme Court and Equal Rights

1900

The Constitution describes equal rights only in general terms. As the time line entries show, some Court decisions have supported and broadened equal rights, while other decisions have restricted them.

Go Online
PHSchool.com
Use Web Code mqp-5217 for an interactive time line.

Analysis Skills CS1, CS2, HI1

1883 In the *Civil Rights Cases,* the Court rules that the 14th Amendment does not ban racial discrimination by private individuals or businesses.

1896 In *Plessy* v. *Ferguson,* the Court rules that "separate but equal" facilities for different races are acceptable.

been eliminated. Many State and local laws have been repealed or struck down by the courts.

The Supreme Court has found segregation by race to be as unconstitutional in other areas as it is in public education. It has held that the Equal Protection Clause forbids segregation in: public swimming pools or other recreational facilities, *Baltimore* v. *Dawson,* 1955; local transportation, *Gayle* v. *Browder,* 1956; and State prisons and local jails, *Lee* v. *Washington,* 1968. The High Court struck down all State miscegenation laws (laws that forbid interracial marriages) in *Loving* v. *Virginia,* 1967. And it has held that race cannot be the basis for a child custody decision, *Palmore* v. *Sidoti,* 1984.

Classification by Sex

The Constitution speaks of the civil rights of "the people," "persons," and "citizens." Nowhere does it make its guarantees only to "men" or separately to "women." The only reference to sex is in the 19th Amendment, which forbids denial of the right to vote "on account of sex."

Gender has long been used as a basis of classification in the law, however. By and large, that practice reflected society's historic view of the "proper" role of women. Most often, laws that treated men and women differently were intended to protect "the weaker sex." Over the years, the Supreme Court read that view into the 14th Amendment. It did not find *any* sex-based classification to be unconstitutional until 1971.

In the first case to challenge sex discrimination, *Bradwell* v. *Illinois,* 1873, the Court upheld a State law barring women from the practice of law. In that case, Justice Joseph P. Bradley wrote that:

> **PRIMARY Sources** *The civil law, as well as nature itself, has always recognized a wide difference in the respective spheres and destinies of man and woman. Man is, or should be, woman's protector and defender. The natural and proper timidity and delicacy of the female sex evidently unfits it for many of the occupations of civil life.*
>
> —Concurring Opinion

Even as late as 1961, in *Hoyt* v. *Florida,* the Court could find no constitutional fault with a law that required men to serve on juries, but gave women the choice of serving or not.

Matters are far different today. The Court now takes a very close look at cases involving claims of sex discrimination. It first did so in *Reed* v. *Reed,* 1971; there, the Court struck down an Idaho law that gave fathers preference over mothers in the administration of their children's estates.

Since then, the Supreme Court has found a number of sex-based distinctions to be unconsti-

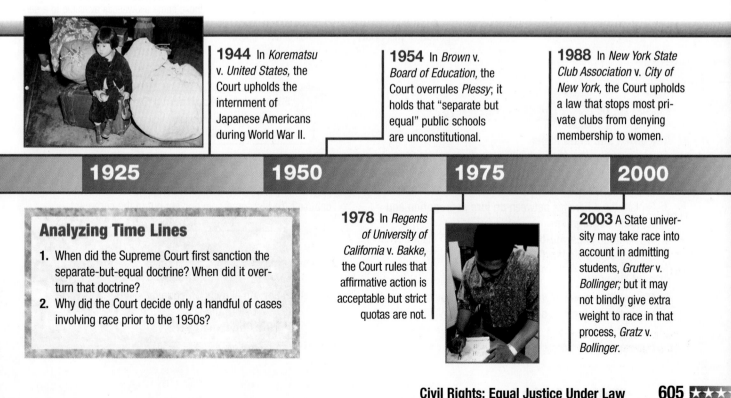

1944 In *Korematsu* v. *United States,* the Court upholds the internment of Japanese Americans during World War II.

1954 In *Brown* v. *Board of Education,* the Court overrules *Plessy;* it holds that "separate but equal" public schools are unconstitutional.

1988 In *New York State Club Association* v. *City of New York,* the Court upholds a law that stops most private clubs from denying membership to women.

1925   **1950**   **1975**   **2000**

Analyzing Time Lines

1. When did the Supreme Court first sanction the separate-but-equal doctrine? When did it overturn that doctrine?
2. Why did the Court decide only a handful of cases involving race prior to the 1950s?

1978 In *Regents of University of California* v. *Bakke,* the Court rules that affirmative action is acceptable but strict quotas are not.

2003 A State university may take race into account in admitting students, *Grutter* v. *Bollinger;* but it may not blindly give extra weight to race in that process, *Gratz* v. *Bollinger.*

tutional. In *Taylor v. Louisiana,* 1975, the Court held that the Equal Protection Clause forbids the States to exclude women from jury service. Among other examples, it has also struck down an Oklahoma law that prohibited the sale of beer to males under 21 and to females under 18, *Craig v. Boren,* 1976. Also unconstitutional is the practice of refusing to admit women to the rigorous citizen-soldier program offered by a public institution, Virginia Military Institute, *United States v. Virginia,* 1996.

In the same vein, the Supreme Court has upheld a California law that prohibits community service clubs from excluding women from membership, *Rotary International v. Rotary Club of Duarte,* 1987. It also upheld a New York City ordinance that forbids sex discrimination in any place of public accommodation, including large private-membership clubs used by their members for business purposes, *New York State Club Association, Inc. v. City of New York,* 1988.

The Court's present attitude was put this way in *Frontiero v. Richardson,* 1973:

 ❝There can be no doubt that our nation has had a long and unfortunate history of sex discrimination. Traditionally, such discrimination was rationalized by an attitude of 'romantic paternalism' which, in practical effect, put women, not on a pedestal, but in a cage. **❞**[7]

—Justice William J. Brennan, Jr.,
Opinion of the Court

Not all sex-based distinctions are unconstitutional, however. The Supreme Court has upheld some of them in several cases. You saw one example of this in *Michael M. v. Superior Court,* 1981. Similarly, the Court has upheld a Florida law that gives an extra property tax exemption to widows, but not to widowers, *Kahn v. Shevin,* 1974; an Alabama law forbidding women to serve as prison guards in all-male penitentiaries, *Dothard v. Rawlinson,* 1977; and the federal selective service law that requires only men to register for the draft and excludes women from any future draft, *Rostker v. Goldberg,* 1981.

In effect, these cases say this: Classification by sex is not in and of itself unconstitutional. However, laws that treat men and women differently will be overturned by the courts unless (1) they are intended to serve an "important governmental objective" and (2) they are "substantially related" to achieving that goal.

In upholding the all-male draft, the Court found that Congress did in fact have an important governmental objective: to raise and support armies and, if necessary, to do so by "a draft of combat troops." "Since women are excluded from combat," said the Supreme Court, they may properly be excluded from the draft.

---

[7]In this case the Court, for the first time, struck down a federal law providing for sex-based discrimination, as a violation of the 5th Amendment's Due Process Clause. That law gave various housing, medical, and other allowances to a serviceman for his wife and other dependents, but it made those same allowances available to a servicewoman only if her husband was dependent on her for more than half of his support.

Section 2 Assessment

Key Terms and Main Ideas

1. What was the purpose of **Jim Crow laws?**
2. Which important Supreme Court case led to school **integration?**
3. Explain the difference between **de jure segregation** and **de facto segregation.**
4. Who put the **separate-but-equal doctrine** in place? What did that doctrine uphold?

Critical Thinking

5. **Making Decisions** In your opinion, which would be harder to combat, de facto or de jure segregation? Why?

Standards Monitoring *Online*
For: Self-quiz with vocabulary practice
Web Code: mqa-5212

6. **Recognizing Bias** Reread Justice Bradley's comment on page 605. **(a)** Which part of that comment is fact, not opinion? **(b)** List three opinions set out in the comment.

Go Online
PHSchool.com

For: An activity on equality before the law
Web Code: mqd-5212

on Primary Sources

Breaking Down Barriers

Analysis Skills HR4, HI3

Ernest Green was the first black student to graduate from Central High School in Little Rock, Arkansas. Mr. Green recalls the historic days in 1957 when, as one of the "Little Rock Nine," he helped bring an end to school segregation in the United States.

When the U.S. Supreme Court handed down its historic *Brown* v. *Board of Education of Topeka, Kansas,* decision in 1954, I was a student in Little Rock, Arkansas, finishing the eighth grade. Little Rock had one high school for blacks . . . and one for whites, Little Rock Central High School. . . .

The *Brown* decision made me feel that the U.S. Constitution was finally working for me. . . . I could believe I was a full citizen, not a second-class citizen as segregation had made me feel.

In the spring of 1957, I was asked, along with other black students in Little Rock, to consider attending Central High School the following fall. Initially, a number of students signed up to enroll, but when fall came, only nine of us had survived the pressure to quit. . . .

During the summer, rumors began to circulate that there might be violence if the "Little Rock Nine," as we became known, tried to attend school in the fall. I didn't pay much attention to what was going on. . . .

But when we tried to attend school, we were met by an angry white mob and armed soldiers. Arkansas Governor Orval Faubus had called out the National Guard to prevent us from enrolling, defying a federal court order to integrate Little Rock schools. Governor Faubus said he was doing this to protect the peace and tranquility of the community; obviously, my rights were secondary. . . .

Finally, President Dwight Eisenhower called out the U.S. Army's famous 101st Airborne Division to protect us and enforce the federal court's integration order. . . .

When we tried to attend school again, about 1,000 paratroopers were there to protect us. We rode to school in an army station wagon, surrounded by army jeeps that were loaded with soldiers holding machine guns and drawn bayonets. It was an exciting ride to school!

Once we got inside, it was like being in a war zone. We were harassed, our books were destroyed, and our lockers were broken into several times a day. . . .

I was a senior that year. As graduation neared, I was surprised at the number of students who signed my yearbook, saying they admired my courage in sticking it out. But on the night of graduation, there was an eerie silence when my name was called. I didn't care that no one clapped for me. I knew that not only had I achieved something for myself, but I had broken a barrier as well.

Ernest Green shows his textbooks to children in Little Rock.

Analyzing Primary Sources

1. Why did Ernest Green decide to enroll in Central High School?
2. What resistance did the "Little Rock Nine" encounter when they tried to attend the school?
3. How was Mr. Green finally able to attend?
4. Why did attending Central High School make Mr. Green feel that he was no longer a "second-class citizen"?

Section Preview

OBJECTIVES

1. **Outline** the history of civil rights legislation from Reconstruction to today.
2. **Explore** the issues surrounding affirmative action.

WHY IT MATTERS

Little more than a generation ago, race-based discrimination was not only widespread in this country, much of it was legal—and evidences of that fact are with us yet today.

POLITICAL DICTIONARY

★ **affirmative action**
★ **quota**
★ **reverse discrimination**

You may have heard this oft-made argument: "You can't legislate morality." That is, racism, sexism, and other forms of discrimination cannot be eliminated merely with laws.

Martin Luther King, Jr., replied to that contention this way: "Laws," he said, "may not change the heart, but they can restrain the heartless." Congress has agreed with Dr. King—as it has enacted a number of civil rights laws over the past 40 years.

Civil Rights: Reconstruction to Today

From the 1870s to the late 1950s, Congress did not pass a single piece of meaningful civil rights legislation. Several factors contributed to that sorry fact. Among the major ones: Through that period the nation's predominantly white population was generally unaware of or little concerned with the plight of African Americans, Native Americans, or other nonwhites in this country. And, southern white Democrats, bolstered by such devices as the seniority system and the filibuster, held many of the most strategic posts in Congress.

◀ Martin Luther King, Jr.

That historic logjam was broken in 1957, very largely as a result of the pressures brought to bear by the civil rights movement led by Dr. King (see Chapter 6, pages 159–163). Beginning in that year, Congress passed a number of civil rights laws—notably, the Civil Rights Acts of 1957, 1960, 1964, and 1968 and the Voting Rights Acts of 1965, 1970, 1975, and 1982.[8]

The Civil Rights Act of 1964

The 1964 law is the most far-reaching of these statutes. It passed after the longest debate in the Senate's history (83 days), and only after the Senate had invoked cloture to kill a filibuster.

Beyond its voting rights provisions, the 1964 law outlaws discrimination in a number of areas. With its several later amendments, the law's major sections now:

(1) provide that no person may be denied access to or refused service in various "public accommodations" because of race, color, religion, national origin, or physical disability (Title II).[9]

---

[8]The 1957 and 1960 laws set up modest safeguards for the right to vote. You considered the voting rights provision in these statutes in Chapter 6. See pages 160–163. The 1957 law created the U.S. Civil Rights Commission. The commission is an independent eight-member agency that is supposed to monitor the enforcement of the various civil rights laws, investigate cases of alleged discrimination, and report its findings to the President, Congress, and the public.

[9]Congress based this section of the law on its commerce power; see Chapter 11, pages 294–300. Title II covers those places in which lodgings are offered to transient guests and those where a significant portion of the items sold have moved in interstate commerce. The Supreme Court upheld Title II and the use of the Commerce Clause as a basis for civil rights legislation in *Heart of Atlanta Motel, Inc.* v. *United States,* 1964.

(2) prohibit discrimination against any person on grounds of race, color, religion, national origin, sex, or physical disability in any program that receives any federal funding; require the cut-off of federal funds to any program that practices such discrimination (Title VI).

(3) forbid employers and labor unions to discriminate against any person on grounds of race, color, religion, sex, physical disability, or age in job-related matters (Title VII).[10]

The Civil Rights Act of 1968

The Civil Rights Act of 1968 is often called the Open Housing Act. With minor exceptions, it forbids anyone to refuse to sell or rent a dwelling to any person on grounds of race, color, religion, national origin, sex, or disability. It also forbids refusal to sell or rent to a family with children. At first, the burden of enforcing the law fell on those persons who claimed to be victims of housing discrimination; they could seek damages from alleged offenders. Congress finally strengthened the law in 1988, to allow the Justice Department to bring criminal charges against those who violate its terms. Still, housing remains among the most segregated areas of American life today.

Affirmative Action

These several civil rights statutes all come down to this: Discriminatory practices based on such factors as race, color, national origin, sex, or disability are illegal. But what about the effects of *past* discrimination? Consider an African American who, for no reason of his or her own making, did not get a decent education and so today cannot get a decent job. Of what real help to that person are all of those laws that make illegal today what was done years ago?

So far, the Federal Government's chief answer to this troubling question has been a policy of **affirmative action.** That policy requires that most employers take positive steps (affirmative action) to remedy the effects of past discriminations. The policy applies to all the agencies of the Federal Government, to all the States and their local

---

[10]The five-member Equal Employment Opportunity Commission is responsible for the enforcement of Title VII.

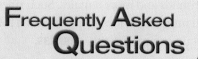

Frequently Asked Questions

Civil Rights

Equal Rights

Civil Rights

What was the Equal Rights Amendment?

The Equal Rights Amendment (ERA) was approved by Congress in 1972, with a seven-year deadline set for its ratification. ERA would have added these words to the Constitution: "Equality of rights under the law shall not be denied or abridged by the United States or any State on account of sex."

ERA was first introduced in Congress in 1923, but it found little public support until the mid-1960s. By 1972, however, ERA was widely supported. Twenty-two States approved it almost immediately and its ratification seemed a near certainty.

Stout opposition soon surfaced, however, and as its seven-year deadline approached, ERA had been approved by only 35 States—three short of the required 38. Congress attempted to save the measure by extending that deadline to June 30, 1982, but to no avail. ERA remained three States shy of ratification as its time ran out. Subsequent efforts to revive the measure proved unsuccessful.

Any Questions?

What would you like to know about civil rights? Brainstorm two new questions and exchange them with a classmate. What did you learn?

---

governments, and to all those private employers who sell goods or services to any agency of the Federal Government.

The Federal Government began to demand the adoption of affirmative action programs in 1965. Some programs are simply plans that call for the wide advertisement of job openings. Most, however, establish guidelines and timetables to overcome past discriminations and/or prevent their recurrence.

To illustrate the policy, take the case of a company that does business with the Federal Government. That private business must adopt an affirmative action plan designed to make its work force reflect the general makeup of the population in its locale. The company's program must also include steps to correct or prevent inequalities in such matters as pay, promotions, and fringe benefits.

For many employers this has meant that they must hire and/or promote more workers with minority backgrounds and more females. Such rules requiring certain numbers of jobs or promotions for members of certain groups are called **quotas.**

Reverse Discrimination?

Affirmative action programs necessarily involve race-based and/or sex-based classifications. Are such programs constitutional?

Critics of the policy say that affirmative action amounts to **reverse discrimination,** or discrimination against the majority group. Affirmative action demands that preference be given to females and/or nonwhites solely on the basis of sex or race. Critics insist that the Constitution requires that all public policies be "color blind."

The Bakke Case

The Supreme Court has been wrestling with affirmative action cases for over two decades now. The Court's first major case, *Regents of the University of California* v. *Bakke,* was decided in 1978.

Allan Bakke, a white male, had been denied admission to that university's medical school at Davis. The school had set aside 16 of the 100 seats in each year's entering class for nonwhite students. He sued, charging the university with reverse discrimination and, so, a violation of the 14th Amendment's Equal

▲ Allan Bakke (left) successfully challenged the admissions policies of the University of California. *Critical Thinking How did the* **Bakke** *case leave the legal status of affirmative action unsettled?* **H-SS 12.5.4**

Protection Clause. By a 5–4 majority, the Court held that Bakke had been denied equal protection and should be admitted to the medical school.

A differently composed 5–4 majority made the more far-reaching ruling in the case, however. Although the Constitution does not allow race to be used as the *only* factor in the making of affirmative action decisions, both the Constitution and the 1964 Civil Rights Act do allow its use as one among several factors in such situations.

Later Cases

The Supreme Court has decided several affirmative action cases since *Bakke.* In some of them it has upheld quotas, especially when longstanding, flagrant discrimination was involved.

In *United Steelworkers* v. *Weber,* 1979, the Kaiser Aluminum Company had created training programs intended to increase the number of skilled African Americans in its work force. Trainees were chosen on the basis of race and seniority. Brian Weber, a white worker, was rejected for training three times. Each time, however, a number of African Americans with less seniority were picked.

Weber went to court. The Court found that the training programs, although built on quotas, did not violate the 1964 law. That law, it said, Congress had purposely designed to "overcome manifest racial imbalances."

Fullilove v. *Klutznick,* 1980, was another case in which the Court upheld quotas. That case centered on a law Congress had passed that provided $4 billion in grants to State and local governments for public works projects. It also contained a "minority set-aside" provision. The provision required that at least 10 percent of each grant had to be set aside for minority-owned businesses.

A white contractor challenged the set-asides. He argued that they were quotas and therefore unconstitutional—because they did not give white contractors an equal chance to compete for all of the available funds. The Court held the law to be a permissible attempt to overcome the effects of blatant and longstanding bias in the construction industry.

Note, however, that quotas can be used in only the most extreme situations. Thus, the Court rejected a city's minority set-aside policy in *Richmond* v. *Croson,* 1989. There the Court held, 6–3, that the city of Richmond, Virginia, had not shown that its ordinance was justified by past discrimination. Therefore, it had denied white contractors their right to equal protection.

Johnson v. *Transportation Agency of Santa Clara County,* 1987, marked the first time the Court decided a case of preferential treatment on the basis of sex. By a 6–3 vote, the justices held that neither the Equal Protection Clause nor Title VII of the 1964 law forbids the promotion of a woman rather than a man, even though he had scored higher on a qualifying interview than she did. The case arose in California, when a woman was promoted to a job that until then had always been held by a man.

The current Supreme Court's conservative bent can be seen in its most recent affirmative action decisions. Thus, the Court's decision in *Adarand Constructors* v. *Pena,* 1995, marked a major departure from its previous rulings in such cases. Until *Adarand,* the Court had regularly upheld affirmative action laws, regulations, and programs as "benign" instances of "race-conscious policymaking." By this, the Court meant that it considered them to be mild but necessary restraints on behavior.

In *Adarand,* however, the Court held that henceforth all affirmative action cases will be reviewed under strict scrutiny—that is, affirmative action programs will be upheld only if it can be shown that they serve some "compelling government interest"; see page 602. "The Constitution protects persons, not groups," wrote Justice Sandra Day O'Connor. "Whenever the government treats any person unequally because of his or her race, that person has suffered an injury" covered by "the Constitution's guarantee of equal treatment." Government can conduct affirmative action programs, said the Court, but only when those programs are "narrowly tailored" to overcome specific cases of discrimination.

Adarand arose when a white-owned Colorado company, Adarand Constructors, Inc., challenged an affirmative action policy of the

▲ *Title IX* Title IX of the Educational Amendments of 1972 requires near-equal funding for men's and women's athletic teams at public schools and universities. This decision dramatically increased opportunities for women to participate in sports. **H-SS 12.7.5**

Federal Highway Administration (FHA). Under that policy, the FHA gave bonuses to highway contractors if 10 percent or more of their construction work was subcontracted to "socially and economically disadvantaged" businesses, including those owned by racial minorities.

The Michigan Cases

Two cases, *Gratz* v. *Bollinger* and *Grutter* v. *Bollinger,* both involving the admissions policies of the University of Michigan, were combined for decision by the Supreme Court in 2003. The resolution of those two cases marked the High Court's most important statement on affirmative action since its decision in *Bakke* in 1978.

In deciding the two cases, a majority of the Court found—definitely and unambiguously— that the State of Michigan (and so all of the States) has a compelling interest in the diversity of the student bodies of its public educational institutions. That compelling interest justifies the narrowly tailored use of race as one factor in the student admissions policies of those institutions.

Jennifer Gratz applied for admission to the University as a freshman in 1997, and Barbara Grutter sought to enter the University's law school that same year. Both women are white, and both were rejected in favor of minority applicants with lower grade point averages and lower entry test scores. Both women sued the University and its chief admissions officer, Lee

▲ Students at the University of California marched to defend affirmative action at their school. *Critical Thinking Did high school and college students have much say in the decision to end state-sponsored affirmative action in California?*

school. The means to this end was the individualized review of each applicant's file and did not include the automatic award of any credit for any characteristic an applicant might possess.

Affirmative Action on the Ballot

The controversy surrounding affirmative action continues. In 1996, California's voters gave overwhelming approval to an initiative measure that eliminated nearly all of the affirmative action programs conducted by public agencies in that State.

The measure, Proposition 209, amended the State's constitution. It forbids all State and local agencies (including public schools, colleges, and universities) to discriminate against or give preferential treatment to any person or group on the basis of race, sex, color, ethnicity, or national origin. The measure covers matters of employment, education, or contracting. It only allows exceptions where necessary to satisfy some federal requirement.

A federal district court found Proposition 209 unconstitutional in late 1996. It held that the measure violated both the 14th Amendment's Equal Protection Clause and the Supremacy Clause in Article VI. That decision was overturned by the Court of Appeals for the 9th Circuit in 1997. The Supreme Court refused to hear an appeal of the Circuit Court's ruling.

In 1998, Washington's voters adopted an initiative measure almost identical to California's Proposition 209. Encouraged by their successes in California and Washington, opponents of affirmative action have launched campaigns to put similar measures on the ballot in other States.

Bollinger, seeking court orders to prevent the University from using race as a factor in the making of admissions decisions. They lost in the lower courts and both appealed to the Supreme Court.

The Supreme Court held, 6–3, that Gratz' rejection was the result of a race-based quota policy prohibited by the 14th Amendment's Equal Protection Clause. The majority found that policy fatally flawed because it included the automatic award of twenty points (out of 100 needed for admission) to any applicant from a minority group underrepresented in the University's undergraduate student body.

Grutter's rejection was upheld, however, 5–4, because the law school employed a much more flexible process in making its admissions decisions. That process was carefully designed to achieve a "critical mass" of otherwise underrepresented minority students in the law

Section 3 Assessment

Key Terms and Main Ideas

1. What is the purpose of **affirmative action**?
2. Under what circumstances has the Supreme Court allowed **quotas**?
3. Who, in a general sense, is disadvantaged by **reverse discrimination**?

Critical Thinking

4. **Expressing Problems Clearly** In your opinion, is it society's responsibility to rectify the harm suffered by a group of people as a result of discrimination in the past?

Standards Monitoring *Online*
For: Self-quiz with vocabulary practice
Web Code: mqa-5213

5. **Making Decisions** Universities often extend preferences to "legacies"—students whose parents attended that school. How do these policies support or weaken the case for affirmative action?

Go Online
PHSchool.com
For: An activity on federal civil rights laws
Web Code: mqd-5213

A re you an American **citizen**—one who owes allegiance to the United States and is entitled to its protection? Very likely you are; more than 90 percent of all the people who live in this country are citizens of the United States. And many of those who are not citizens are actively seeking that distinction.

The Question of Citizenship

As it was originally written, the Constitution mentioned both "citizens of the United States" and "citizens of the States." It did not define either of those phrases, however. Through much of America's early history, it was generally agreed that national citizenship followed that of the States.

The coming of the Civil War and the adoption of the 13th Amendment in 1865 raised the need for a constitutional definition.[11] That need was finally met in 1868 by the 14th Amendment, which begins with these words:

 FROM THE *Constitution*   **"** *All persons born or naturalized in the United States and*

---

[11] In the Dred Scott case (*Scott* v. *Sandford*) in 1857, the Supreme Court had ruled that neither the States nor the National Government had the power to confer citizenship on African Americans—slave or free. The dispute over that issue was one of the several causes of the Civil War.

subject to the jurisdiction thereof, are citizens of the United States and of the State wherein they reside. **"**

—United States Constitution

Thus, the 14th Amendment declares that a person can become an American citizen either by birth or by naturalization. The chart on page 615 summarizes the means by which American citizenship can be acquired.

Citizenship by Birth

Some 260 million Americans—nearly 90 percent of us—are American citizens because we were born in the United States. Another several million are also citizens by birth, even though they were born abroad. Citizenship by birth is determined by either **jus soli** or **jus sanguinis.**

Jus soli is the law of the soil, or where one is born. The 14th Amendment confers citizenship according to the location of a person's birth: "All persons born . . . in the United States. . . ." Congress has defined the United States to include, for purposes of citizenship, the 50 States, the District of Columbia, Puerto Rico, Guam, the Virgin Islands, and the Northern Mariana Islands. It also includes American embassies and American public vessels anywhere in the world.

Until 1924, Native Americans born to tribal members living on reservations were not citizens,

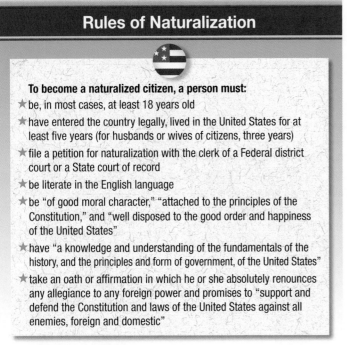

Rules of Naturalization

To become a naturalized citizen, a person must:

★ be, in most cases, at least 18 years old

★ have entered the country legally, lived in the United States for at least five years (for husbands or wives of citizens, three years)

★ file a petition for naturalization with the clerk of a Federal district court or a State court of record

★ be literate in the English language

★ be "of good moral character," "attached to the principles of the Constitution," and "well disposed to the good order and happiness of the United States"

★ have "a knowledge and understanding of the fundamentals of the history, and the principles and form of government, of the United States"

★ take an oath or affirmation in which he or she absolutely renounces any allegiance to any foreign power and promises to "support and defend the Constitution and laws of the United States against all enemies, foreign and domestic"

Interpreting Charts *Which of these requirements do you think is the most difficult to evaluate?* **H-SS 12.2.6**

but wards, persons under the legal guardianship, of the government. In that year, Congress granted citizenship to all Native Americans who did not already possess it.

Jus sanguinis is the law of the blood, or to whom one is born. A child born abroad can become an American citizen at birth under certain circumstances described in the chart on page 615. The child must be born to at least one parent who is a citizen, and who has at some time lived in the United States.

The 14th Amendment does not provide for jus sanguinis, but Congress has included it as a part of American citizenship law since 1790. The constitutionality of the rule has never been challenged.

Citizenship by Naturalization

Naturalization is the legal process by which a person becomes a citizen of another country at some time after birth. Congress has the exclusive power to provide for naturalization. No State may do so.[12]

Individual Naturalization

Naturalization is most often an individual process, conducted by a court. More than 800,000 aliens now become naturalized American citizens each

year. An **alien** is a citizen or national of a foreign state living in this country.

Generally, any person who has come to the United States as an immigrant can be naturalized. The chart on page 615 describes the different ways that people can become American citizens.

The U.S. Citizenship and Immigration Services in the Department of Homeland Security investigates each applicant, and then reports to the judge of the federal or State court overseeing the petition for naturalization. If the judge is satisfied, the oath or affirmation is administered in open court, and the new citizen receives a certificate of naturalization.

Collective Naturalization

At various times entire groups have been naturalized *en masse*. This has most often happened when the United States has acquired new territory. As the chart on the next page indicates, those living in the areas involved were naturalized by a treaty or by an act or a joint resolution passed by Congress.

The largest single instance of collective naturalization came with the ratification of the 14th Amendment, however. The most recent instance occurred in 1977, when Congress gave citizenship to the more than 16,000 native-born residents of the Northern Mariana Islands.

Loss of Citizenship

Although it rarely happens, every American citizen, whether native-born or naturalized, has the right to renounce—voluntarily abandon—his or her citizenship. **Expatriation** is the legal process by which a loss of citizenship occurs.

The Supreme Court has several times held that the Constitution prohibits automatic expatriation. That is, Congress cannot take away a person's citizenship for something he or she has done. Thus, actions such as committing a crime, voting in a foreign election, or serving in the armed forces of another country are not grounds for automatic expatriation.[13]

---

[12]Article I, Section 8, Clause 4.

[13]A person convicted of a federal or a State crime may lose some of the privileges of citizenship, however, either temporarily or permanently—for example, the right to travel freely or to vote or hold public office.

Naturalization

Individually

★ Naturalization of both parents (one parent if divorced or the other is dead) automatically naturalizes children under 16 who reside in the United States. Adopted children born abroad are automatically naturalized if under 18 when adoption becomes final.

★ Federal Courts: Any United States district court

★ State and Territorial Courts: Any general trial court

Collectively

Treaties:
★ Louisiana (1803)
★ Florida (1819)
★ Alaska (1867)

Joint Resolution of Congress:
★ Texas (1845)

Acts of Congress:
★ Hawaii (1898), Puerto Rico (1917), Native Americans (1924), Virgin Islands (1927), Guam (1950), Northern Mariana Islands (1977)

Constitutional Amendment:
★ African Americans and others by 14th Amendment (1868)

Birth

Jus Sanguinis

A child born to an American citizen on foreign soil becomes a citizen if:

★ both parents are American citizens, and at least one has lived in the United States or an American territory at some time

★ one parent is an American citizen who has lived in the United States for at least 10 years, 5 of them after age 14, and the child has lived in the United States continuously for at least 5 years between the ages of 14 and 28

Jus Soli

A child becomes an American citizen if born in the United States, Puerto Rico, Guam, Virgin Islands, Northern Mariana Islands, any United States embassy, or aboard a United States public vessel anywhere in the world

Interpreting Charts Most Americans acquire citizenship at birth. **Name two additional ways that people can acquire American citizenship.** H-SS 12.2.6

Naturalized citizens can lose their citizenship involuntarily. However, this process—**denaturalization**—can occur only by court order and only after it has been shown that the person became a citizen by fraud or deception.

A person can neither gain nor lose American citizenship by marriage. The only significant effect that marriage has is to shorten the time required for the naturalization of an alien who marries an American citizen.

A Nation of Immigrants

We are a nation of immigrants. Except for Native Americans—and even they may be the descendants of earlier immigrants—all of us have come here from abroad or are descended from those who did.

There were only some 2.5 million persons in the United States in 1776. Since then the population has grown more than a hundredfold, to more than 290 million people today. That extraordinary population growth has come from two sources: births and immigration. Some 70 million immigrants have come here since 1820, when figures were first recorded.

Regulation of Immigration

Congress has the exclusive power to regulate immigration. It alone has the power to decide who may be admitted to the United States and under what conditions. The power to control the nation's borders is an inherent power (see page 91). In an early leading case on the point, the Court ruled that the power of the United States to "exclude aliens from its territory . . . is not open to controversy," *Chae Chan Ping* v. *United States*, 1889. The States have no power in the field, *The Passenger Cases*, 1849.

Congress made no serious attempt to regulate immigration for more than a century after independence. As long as land was plentiful and expanding industry demanded more and still more workers, immigration was encouraged.

By 1890, however, the open frontier was a thing of the past, and labor was no longer in short supply. Then, too, the major source of immigration had shifted. Until the 1880s, most immigrants had come from the countries of northern and western Europe. The "new immigration" from the 1880s onward came mostly from southern and eastern Europe. All these factors combined to bring major changes in the traditional policy of encouraging immigration.

Congress placed the first major restrictions on immigration with the passage of the Chinese Exclusion Act in 1882. At the same time, it barred the entry of convicts, "lunatics," paupers, and others likely to become public charges.

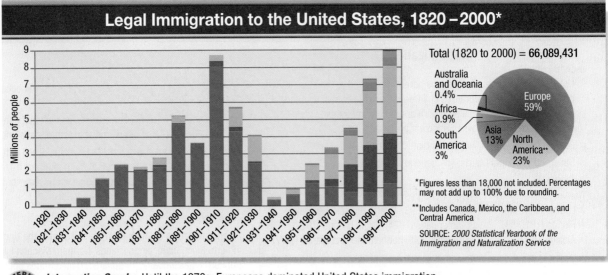

Legal Immigration to the United States, 1820–2000*

Total (1820 to 2000) = 66,089,431

Australia and Oceania 0.4%
Africa 0.9%
South America 3%
Asia 13%
North America** 23%
Europe 59%

*Figures less than 18,000 not included. Percentages may not add up to 100% due to rounding.

**Includes Canada, Mexico, the Caribbean, and Central America

SOURCE: *2000 Statistical Yearbook of the Immigration and Naturalization Service*

Interpreting Graphs Until the 1970s, Europeans dominated United States immigration figures. **Where do the two largest groups of immigrants come from now?**

Over the next several years a long list of "undesirables" was added to the law. Thus, contract laborers were excluded in 1885, immoral persons and anarchists in 1903, and illiterates in 1917. By 1920 more than 30 groups were denied admission on the basis of personal traits.

The tide of newcomers continued to mount, however. In the 10 years from 1905 through 1914, an average of more than a million persons, most of them from southern and eastern Europe, came to this country each year.

Congress responded to pressure for tighter regulation by adding quantitative limits (numerical ceilings) to the qualitative restrictions (personal characteristics) already in place. The Immigration Acts of 1921 and 1924 and the National Origins Act of 1929 assigned each country in Europe a quota—a limit on the number of immigrants who could enter the United States from that country each year. Altogether, only 150,000 quota immigrants could be admitted in any one year. The quotas were purposely drawn to favor northern and western Europe. The quota system was not applied to the Western Hemisphere, but immigration from Asia, Africa, and elsewhere was generally prohibited.

In 1952, Congress passed yet another basic law, the Immigration and Nationality Act. That statute modified the quota system to cover every country outside the Western Hemisphere.

Congress finally eliminated the country-based quota system in the Immigration Act of 1965. That law allowed as many as 270,000 immigrants to enter the United States each year, without regard to race, nationality, or country of origin. The 1965 law gave special preference to immediate relatives of American citizens or of aliens legally residing in this country.

Present Immigration Policies

Today, the Immigration Act of 1990 governs the admission of aliens to the United States. Like its predecessors, it was adopted only after years of intense debate, and many of its provisions are the subject of continuing controversy.

The 1990 law provided for a substantial increase in the number of immigrants who may enter the United States each year. The annual ceiling is now set at 675,000. It also continues the family-preference policy first put in place in 1965; at least one third of those persons admitted under its terms must be the close relatives of American citizens or resident aliens. Those immigrants who have occupational talents in short supply in the United States (notably, highly skilled researchers, engineers, and scientists) also receive special preference.

Only those aliens who can qualify for citizenship can be admitted as immigrants. The law's list of "excludable aliens"—those barred because of some personal characteristic—is extensive. Among those excluded are: criminals (including suspected terrorists), persons with communicable diseases, drug abusers and addicts, illiterates, and mentally disturbed persons who might pose a threat to the safety of others.

Some 20 million nonimmigrants also come here each year for temporary stays. They are mostly tourists, students, and people traveling for business reasons.

Deportation

Most of the civil rights set out in the Constitution are guaranteed to "persons." That term covers aliens as well as citizens. In one important respect, however, the status of aliens is altogether unlike that of citizens: Aliens may be subject to **deportation,** a legal process in which aliens are legally required to leave the United States.

The Supreme Court has long held that the United States has the same almost-unlimited power to deport aliens as it has to exclude them. In an early major case, the Court ruled that (1) deportation is an inherent power, arising out of the sovereignty of the United States, and (2) deportation is not criminal punishment, and so does not require a criminal trial, *Fong Yue Ting v. United States*, 1893.

An alien may be deported on any one of several grounds. The most common today is illegal entry. Thousands of aliens who enter with false papers, sneak in by ship or plane, or slip across the border at night are caught each year and are deported. Many of those who are turned away are repeat offenders who will soon make yet another attempt to cross the border.

Conviction of any serious crime, federal or State, usually leads to a deportation order. In recent years, several thousand aliens have been expelled on the basis of their criminal records, especially narcotics violators. The war on terrorism has also quickened the pace of deportations.

Because deportation is a civil, not a criminal, matter, several constitutional safeguards do not apply—for example, bail and ex post facto laws. Thus, in *Delmore* v. *Kim*, 2003, the Court held that a legal immigrant who faces deportation because of a criminal conviction can be jailed and held without bail, and even without a court hearing to determine whether he or she is either dangerous or a flight risk.

Undocumented Aliens

No one knows how many undocumented aliens reside in the United States today. The Census Bureau now puts their number at about nine million—more than double the Bureau's estimate of a decade ago.

The number of undocumented aliens is increasing by at least half a million a year. Most of these "undocumented persons" enter the country by slipping across the Mexican or Canadian borders, usually at night. Some come with forged papers. Many are aliens who entered legally, as nonimmigrants, but overstayed their legal welcomes.

Well over half of all undocumented aliens have come from Mexico; most of the others come from other Latin American countries and from Asia. A majority of the Mexicans stay here only four to six months a year, working on farms or in other seasonal jobs. Most other illegal aliens hope to remain permanently.

A Troublesome Situation

Once here, most undocumented aliens find it easy to become "invisible," especially in larger cities, and law-enforcement agencies find it very difficult to locate them. Even so, immigration officials have apprehended more than a million undocumented aliens in each of the last several years. Nearly all are sent home. Most go voluntarily, but some leave only as the result of formal deportation proceedings.

The presence of so many undocumented persons has raised a number of difficult problems. Those problems have grown worse over the past several years and, until recently, not much had been done to meet them.

▲ This sign near the California-Mexican border warns drivers that undocumented aliens may try to cross the busy highway. *Prohibido*—prohibited— warns would-be illegal immigrants not to take that risk.

By Don Wright, © 1980: Miami News. New York Times Syndicate.

Interpreting Political Cartoons Newcomers are greeted with suspicion by most cultures. *Why is this cartoon particularly effective?*

One example: Until 1987, it was legal to hire undocumented aliens. As a result, approximately 3.5 million persons who now hold jobs in this country came here illegally. Some employers have been more than willing to hire undocumented aliens, many of whom will work for substandard wages and under substandard conditions.

Hundreds of thousands of undocumented aliens have taken jobs on farms, often as laborers; thousands more have become janitors and dishwashers, or seamstresses in sweatshops, or found other menial work. The increase in population has also placed added stress on the public schools and welfare services of several States, notably California, Arizona, Texas, and Florida.

Current Law

Many groups have been troubled and divided by the problem of undocumented aliens. Those concerned include labor, farm, business, religious, ethnic, civil rights, and other groups. After wrestling with the issue for years, Congress passed the Immigration Reform and Control Act of 1986. Then, after another decade of debate and struggle, Congress passed the Illegal Immigration Restrictions Act of 1996.

The 1986 law did two major things. First, it established a one-year amnesty program under which many undocumented aliens could become legal residents. More than two million aliens used it to legalize their status here. Secondly, that law made it a crime to hire any person who is in this country illegally. An employer who knowingly hires an undocumented alien can be fined from $250 to $10,000. A repeat offender can be jailed for up to six months.

The 1996 law made it easier to deport illegal aliens by streamlining the deportation process. It also toughened the penalties for smuggling aliens into this country, prevented undocumented aliens from claiming Social Security benefits or public housing, and allowed State welfare workers to check the legal status of any alien who applies for any welfare benefit. The new law also doubled the size of the Border Patrol; it now has more than 10,000 uniformed officers on duty.

Section 4 Assessment

Key Terms and Main Ideas

1. How does a person become a citizen through **jus sanguinis**?
2. What is the main difference between a **citizen** and an **alien**?
3. What is the purpose of the **naturalization** process?
4. Members of which group can be threatened by **deportation**?

Critical Thinking

5. **Understanding Point of View** Should employers be punished for hiring undocumented aliens? Why or why not?
6. **Drawing Conclusions** Why do you think the current immigration law gives special preference to immigrants who have certain occupational skills?

Standards Monitoring *Online*
For: Self-quiz with vocabulary practice
Web Code: mqa-5214

7. **Decision Making** Review the chart on page 614. In your opinion, should citizens "by birth" be required to meet the same requirements as naturalized citizens? Why or why not?

Go **Online**
PHSchool.com
For: An activity on American citizenship
Web Code: mqd-5214

May Public Universities Consider Race in Admissions?

Analysis Skills
HR4, HI3, HI4

When selecting students for admission, colleges and universities consider a number of factors, such as test scores and participation in extracurricular activities. Should they also be allowed to consider the race or ethnicity of the applicant?

Grutter v. *Bollinger*; *Gratz* v. *Bollinger* (2003)

Barbara Grutter, a white Michigan resident, applied for admission to the University of Michigan's law school. After placing her on the waiting list, the law school rejected her application.

Jennifer Gratz, a white student, applied to the University of Michigan for undergraduate studies. The University denied her application, even though it considered her "well qualified."

The law school's admissions policy emphasized admitting not only applicants with strong academic credentials, but also students with diverse life experiences and backgrounds. The policy gave special consideration to racial and ethnic diversity to ensure that minorities would have a meaningful presence in the student body. Race was given no specific weight, but was to be considered along with the applicants' other unique qualities and achievements. The undergraduate school simply gave twenty points (out of 100 needed for admission) to "underrepresented minorities."

Both Grutter and Gratz sued the University and chief admissions officer, Lee Bollinger. They sought court orders to force the University to stop considering race in its admissions decisions. The Supreme Court took the two cases together.

Arguments for Grutter and Gratz

1. The 14th Amendment forbids the States, including public universities, from denying any person "the equal protection of the laws." Giving preferential consideration to minorities amounts to unequal treatment of applicants not included in the favored groups.

2. Affirmative action policies favoring minority students actually harm them by suggesting that they are unable to gain admission based on their own accomplishments.

3. Minorities can rely on the law to prevent discrimination against them, but the law should not give them special advantages.

Arguments for Bollinger

1. Having a significant minority presence in universities and law schools is important to enable minorities to assume leadership positions in society.

2. Diversity is essential to the mission of higher education, because students learn as much from each other as they do from their classes.

3. Equal protection should prevent any person from being harmed or burdened because of their race, but it should not prohibit policies intended to create equality for disadvantaged minorities.

Decide for Yourself

1. Review the constitutional grounds on which each side based its arguments and the specific arguments each side presented.

2. Debate the opposing viewpoints presented in this case. Which viewpoint do you favor?

3. How will the Court's decision affect college and graduate school admissions and the job market for graduates? (To read a summary of the Court's decision, turn to pages 799–806.)

Go Online
PHSchool.com
Use Web Code mqp-5218 to register your vote on this issue and to see how other students voted.

Political Dictionary

heterogeneous (p. 594), immigrant (p. 594), reservation (p. 596), refugee (p. 597), assimilation (p. 597), segregation (p. 602), Jim Crow law (p. 602), separate-but-equal doctrine (p. 602), integration (p. 603), de jure segregation (p. 604), de facto segregation (p. 604), affirmative action (p. 609), quota (p. 610), reverse discrimination (p. 610), citizen (p. 613), jus soli (p. 613), jus sanguinis (p. 613), naturalization (p. 614), alien (p. 614), expatriation (p. 614), denaturalization (p. 615), deportation (p. 617)

Standards Review

H-SS 12.2.2 Explain how economic rights are secured and their importance to the individual and to society (e.g., the right to acquire, use, transfer, and dispose of property; right to choose one's work; right to join or not join labor unions; copyright and patent).

H-SS 12.2.6 Explain how one becomes a citizen of the United States, including the process of naturalization (e.g., literacy, language, and other requirements).

H-SS 12.5.1 Understand the changing interpretations of the Bill of Rights over time, including interpretations of the basic freedoms (religion, speech, press, petition, and assembly) articulated in the First Amendment and the due process and equal protection-of-the-law clauses of the Fourteenth Amendment.

H-SS 12.5.4 Explain the controversies that have resulted over changing interpretations of civil rights, including those in *Plessy* v. *Ferguson, Brown* v. *Board of Education, Miranda* v. *Arizona, Regents of the University of California* v. *Bakke, Adarand Constructors, Inc.* v. *Pena*, and *United States* v. *Virginia* (VMI).

H-SS 12.6.4 Describe the means that citizens use to participate in the political process (e.g., voting, campaigning, lobbying, filing a legal challenge, demonstrating, petitioning, picketing, running for political office).

H-SS 12.7.5 Explain how public policy is formed, including the setting of the public agenda and implementation of it through regulations and executive orders.

Practicing the Vocabulary

Matching *Choose a term from the list above that best matches each description.*

1. A person who leaves his or her home in order to escape the dangers of war, political persecution, or other causes
2. The law of the soil; a means by which one acquires citizenship
3. Type of law that required separate facilities for African Americans and whites
4. An act by which one voluntarily forfeits citizenship
5. Segregation as a result of laws
6. Rule that sets a minimum or maximum number of promotions, hires, or acceptances for members of a specific group

Word Recognition *Replace the underlined definition with the correct term from the list above.*

7. Some immigrants and members of minority groups try <u>to merge into and become part of the dominant culture of a country.</u>
8. A person who gains citizenship through fraud or deception can suffer <u>the loss of citizenship through a court order.</u>
9. *Brown* v. *Board of Education* brought an end to <u>separation of one group from another</u> in public schools.
10. The United States can be described as <u>including a mix of different people.</u>

Reviewing Main Ideas

Section 1

11. Briefly describe the trends in the composition of the population over the course of American history.
12. Briefly describe the historical treatment of minority groups in the United States.
13. List two ways that Latin American communities in the United States differ from one another.
14. Do women as a group resemble minority groups?

Section 2

15. What kind of equality does the Constitution guarantee?
16. According to the Supreme Court, what standards must laws that discriminate between groups meet?
17. Briefly describe the history of racial segregation from the late 1800s to today.
18. On what grounds will the present-day Supreme Court uphold a law that treats women differently from men?

Section 3

19. Briefly describe the history of civil rights legislation between the 1870s and today.
20. **(a)** What was the major piece of civil rights legislation enacted during the 1960s? **(b)** What are its major features?
21. Summarize the reasoning behind affirmative action programs. What is the main criticism of these programs?
22. Under what circumstances have affirmative action programs generally been allowed by the courts?

Section 4

23. Describe the ways in which people can become citizens of the United States.
24. Describe the ways in which people can lose citizenship.
25. Briefly describe immigration in the United States today.
26. Identify two controversies involving undocumented aliens.

Critical Thinking Skills

Analysis Skills CS2, HR4

27. *Face the Issues* A supporter of changing Title IX has asked, "Why use the total number of students on campus . . . as your baseline for fairness to begin with? Doesn't it make more sense to only use students who are actually interested in playing sports?" How would supporters of Title IX answer these questions?

28. *Making Comparisons* Recall what you read in Section 2 regarding the Supreme Court's attitude toward women. **(a)** How has this attitude changed since the 1960s? **(b)** Does sex-based discrimination still exist?

29. *Drawing Inferences* Consider the separate-but-equal doctrine. **(a)** Do you think it is possible for facilities to be segregated on the basis of race or gender and be truly equal? **(b)** Why or why not?

30. *Making Decisions* Consider the process by which aliens can become naturalized American citizens. **(a)** In your opinion, should this process be made easier or more difficult? Why? **(b)** What standards, if any, should be added or removed? Why?

Analyzing Political Cartoons

Using your knowledge of American government and this cartoon, answer the questions below.

I'M TELLIN' YA... THERE'S A GLASS CEILING IN THIS BUSINESS! HAVE YOU EVER HEARD OF A **KING** BEE? NO! IT'S A REAL PROBLEM IN OUR CULTURE!

31. (a) What form of discrimination is referenced by this cartoon? **(b)** How does this cartoon reverse the usual situation?

32. Why is "glass ceiling" an appropriate metaphor for this form of discrimination?

Participation Activities

Analysis Skills CS3, HR4, HI1

33. *Current Events Watch* Find a recent news article dealing with affirmative action. Then compose two editorials, one in favor of affirmative action and one opposed to it. Begin each editorial with a reference to the news article and explain how this article relates to your argument. When you have finished both editorials, have a classmate read them and rate your thoroughness and objectivity.

34. *Graphing Activity* Use a library or the Internet to find recent data on per capita income for African American men, African American women, white men, and white women. Create a line graph showing how per capita income has changed over time for all four categories. Then write a paragraph describing your conclusions.

35. *It's Your Turn* Interview a relative or a family friend who moved to the United States from another country or who experienced the civil rights struggles of the 1950s and 1960s. Do they have any personal stories that capture a sense of the time? Do they believe their experiences were typical? How do they feel about television and film portrayals of immigrants' lives or the civil rights struggle? What lessons would they like to convey to members of your generation? Use your interview to write a personal history written from the point of view of that person. **(Interviewing a Relative)**

CALIFORNIA Standards Monitoring *Online*

For: Chapter 21 Self-Test **Visit:** PHSchool.com
Web Code: mqa-5215

As a final review, take the Magruder's Chapter 21 Self-Test and receive immediate feedback on your answers.
The test consists of 20 multiple-choice questions designed to test your understanding of the chapter content.

◆ Celebrating China's 50th anniversary, Tiananmen Square, Beijing, China

Comparative Political and Economic Systems

CONSTITUTIONAL PRINCIPLES

Limited Government In many countries, some people are more equal than others. That is, some governments are more limited than others. The gap between what a constitution says and what exists in practice can be wide, indeed.

Federalism Only a handful of all of the states in the world today divide governmental powers between a central government and a number of regional or local units—Russia and Mexico among them.

Separation of Powers Most national governmental systems are both unitary and parliamentary—the British and the Japanese systems among them. In a parliamentary system, the executive and legislative powers are not separated (as they are in a presidential system) between the different branches of the government.

The Impact on You

A country's political and economic systems play a major role in determining its citizens' lifestyles. For example, a country with a representative government and a market-driven economy would be more open than one with a dictatorship and a state-run economy.

Comparative Political Systems

"No one pretends that democracy is perfect or all-wise. Indeed, it has been said that democracy is the worst form of government except all those other forms that have been tried from time to time."

—Winston Churchill (1947)

Although Americans would agree with Churchill that democracy is the best system available, democratic governments vary greatly. Differences include how power is divided and how leaders are chosen. Many nations, of course, are not democracies at all, but authoritarian systems.

◆ Britain's Houses of Parliament

CALIFORNIA

Standards Preview

H-SS 12.3.4 Compare the relationship of government and civil society in constitutional democracies to the relationship of government and civil society in authoritarian and totalitarian regimes.

H-SS 12.9.1 Explain how the different philosophies and structures of feudalism, mercantilism, socialism, fascism, communism, monarchies, parliamentary systems, and constitutional liberal democracies influence economic policies, social welfare policies, and human rights practices.

H-SS 12.9.2 Compare the various ways in which power is distributed, shared, and limited in systems of shared powers and in parliamentary systems, including the influence and role of parliamentary leaders (e.g., William Gladstone, Margaret Thatcher).

H-SS 12.9.4 Describe for at least two countries the consequences of conditions that gave rise to tyrannies during certain periods (e.g., Italy, Japan, Haiti, Nigeria, Cambodia).

H-SS 12.9.5 Identify the forms of illegitimate power that twentieth-century African, Asian, and Latin American dictators used to gain and hold office and the conditions and interests that supported them.

H-SS 12.9.6 Identify the ideologies, causes, stages, and outcomes of major Mexican, Central American, and South American revolutions in the nineteenth and twentieth centuries.

H-SS 12.9.7 Describe the ideologies that give rise to Communism, methods of maintaining control, and the movements to overthrow such governments in Czechoslovakia, Hungary, and Poland, including the roles of individuals (e.g., Alexander Solzhenitsyn, Pope John Paul II, Lech Walesa, Vaclav Havel).

H-SS 12.9.8 Identify the successes of relatively new democracies in Africa, Asia, and Latin America and the ideas, leaders, and general societal conditions that have launched and sustained, or failed to sustain, them.

Keep It Current

Items marked with this logo are periodically updated on the Internet.

- **Use Web Code mqg-7227 to access this chapter's updated data.**

- **Use Web Code mqh-6220 to access debates from the Close Up Foundation's** *Current Issues* **online.**

Go Online
PHSchool.com

SECTION 1

Historical Political Systems (pp. 626–630)

★ The feudal system, based on a series of relationships between rulers and subjects, was the first step toward modern government.

★ In the 17th century, sovereignty became the defining trait of European countries.

★ Kings and queens gained power and wealth by controlling trade within their borders and with foreign countries.

★ European monarchs sent people, goods, and ideas about government to other parts of the world through colonialism.

SECTION 2

Ideas and Revolutions (pp. 631–638)

★ Popular sovereignty is the idea that governments can rule only because the people agree to respect the government.

★ Governments can give power to the people through a slow, gradual approach that protects institutions or through a revolution that sweeps away the past.

★ Countries that have been colonized face many obstacles to democratic government.

★ Fascist and communist governments pretend to govern with the consent of the people, but they control society and oppress those who disagree with them.

SECTION 3

Transitions to Democracy (pp. 640–645)

★ Tyrannies often collapse because of disagreements within the government, as in communist Poland.

★ A wave of democratization led to the Soviet Union's fall in 1991.

★ Holding free elections is a first step, but countries must build strong democratic institutions if they are to consolidate their democracies.

★ Some countries never successfully transition to democracy and fall back into dictatorship or civil war.

SECTION 4

World Democracies Today (pp. 647–652)

★ Britain's unitary government is based on an unwritten constitution.

★ Britain's bicameral Parliament holds judicial and legislative power.

★ Mexico's government includes an executive branch headed by the president, a bicameral legislature, and a national judiciary.

Section Preview

OBJECTIVES

1. **Identify** the main elements of the feudal society.
2. **Analyze** the rise of sovereign states and the decline of feudalism.
3. **Explain** different ways that governments may become legitimate.
4. **Describe** the impact of mercantilism on European colonies.

WHY IT MATTERS

The modern state has its roots in the feudal system of the early Middle Ages. The development of clear ideas of sovereignty, and economic growth, led to new forms of government that extended to all parts of the world.

POLITICAL DICTIONARY

★ feudalism
★ vassal
★ serf
★ monarch
★ legitimacy
★ mercantilism
★ colonialism

Throughout history, governments have developed as a way for societies to face political and economic challenges. As old challenges faded and new problems arose, governments changed and took new forms. Economic growth, religious movements, and new ways of thinking drove this transformation in Europe, Asia, Africa, and the Americas.

Today, we inhabit a world filled with democracies, like the United States, and dictatorships, like China. Many other countries mix traits of democracy and dictatorship. Some countries are moving toward one form of government and away from the other.

The road to modern democracy began in Europe with the fall of the Roman Empire and the effort to create order out of the chaos that followed. In this section, you will follow the development of governments from those difficult times to the current era of modern states.

The Feudal Society

After the Roman Empire fell in the 5th century A.D., much of Europe slipped into chaos. There were no governments in the modern sense of the word.

Feudal Structures

Feudalism arose in the wake of the fall of Rome and held sway over much of Europe from the 9th on to the 17th century. It was a loosely-organized system of rule in which powerful lords divided up their lands among other, lesser lords. Those with land and power agreed to protect others in exchange for their loyalty, work, and a share of their food and other goods. Thus, feudalism was based on a series of relationships between the more powerful and the less powerful.

The basic relationship in the chain was that between the lord and his **vassals**, the lesser lords who pledged their loyalty to him. The lord ruled, and the vassal watched over his lands.

The lord held some of the responsibilities held by the modern state today. He protected his vassals from attack and administered justice. In return, the vassals supported the lord's decisions and served under the lord's military command when needed. A lord-vassal relationship was just one part of a much larger network of relationship; a vassal was usually lord to other, less powerful vassals, and the lord often served as a vassal under a more powerful lord.

Only individuals at the very top of the system had a say in how the system worked. **Serfs**, workers bound to the land they farmed, made up the bulk of the population. The serfs gave their lords a share of what they grew, and in return, received protection in times of war.

Serfs led hard lives. The serf could not leave the land without the permission of his lord, and the serf's children inherited their ties and responsibilities to the lord. Most serfs died young and never set foot on land beyond a few miles of their lord's manor.

Weaknesses of Feudalism

The feudal system was, in effect, a collection of fiefdoms (the lands held by various lords) governed by a **monarch.** At least in theory, the monarch was the supreme ruler of all the people (lords, vassals, and serfs) within a given region. Most monarchs were, in fact, relatively weak, however. Borders were unclear or irrelevant, and lords and vassals often held competing claims to the same piece of land.

In Western Europe, the Roman Catholic Church functioned outside the feudal system, under the nominal control of the Pope. Officials of the church enjoyed their own power over common people and kings alike.

Feudalism emerged in a primitive time when violence was common, money was rarely used, and most people traded only in goods, food, and their own work. The feudal system served the basic purpose of the state by protecting people from harm. As a more sophisticated economy developed, feudal "governments" had to adapt to a changing world.

Rise of Sovereignty

Feudalism developed slowly and unevenly across Europe. It was, at best, a loose and makeshift basis for government. As cracks emerged in the system—between Catholics and Protestants, the feudal manor and the marketplace—people needed a stronger, more stable arrangement. The outlines of the present-day sovereign state began to emerge.

Economic Growth and Crisis

In the Middle Ages, a Commercial Revolution took place that changed the way people lived and conducted business. As you have read, feudalism relied on personal relationships and agreements in which people exchanged work and food for security and justice. Over time, the rising costs of war and laws required lords to draw in more money from their landholdings. They had to find new ways to collect money.

Some lords accepted money from their vassals in place of military service. Other lords allowed free people to set up towns on their land for a fee under a royal charter. In this way, towns began to spring up across Europe. Those towns

▲ Castles offered protection against attack and demonstrated the strength of a lord in his region. *Critical Thinking Describe two features of the castle that indicated its defensive purpose in the feudal era.* H-SS 12.9.1

were centers of trade and freedom that tested the limits of feudalism.

The liveliest of these towns were found in northern Italy, northern Germany, and the Netherlands. Their income came from foreign trade with Central Europe and the East. The merchants in the towns had an uneasy relationship with the lords. Although the merchants were freer than serfs, they had to pay money to lords for protection and for the right to use roads, rivers, and bridges. Many lords tried to extend their system of justice to the towns. They often failed, because merchants and bankers in the towns faced new problems and disputes not seen in feudalism. Traditional feudal laws designed for the countryside could not resolve such trade disputes as broken contracts.

Two events shocked the feudal system and undermined its claim to power—its ability to protect people from harm. First, in the 1340s, the Black Plague killed over one third of the population in Western Europe. The Black Plague itself did not destroy feudalism, but its effects changed the economic situation that supported it.

After the plague, lords demanded the same amount of work from the smaller numbers of serfs who'd survived. Serfs and free peasants found strength in the high value of their

▶ The increasing use of money, such as this 13th century gold coin from the Italian city of Florence, undermined the feudal system and increased trade.

individual labor and began to demand higher wages and better working conditions. In England, Wat Tyler led a peasant's revolt in 1381, in opposition to a new poll tax levied by the king to pay for war. The uprising was quashed, brutally, but the tax was soon repealed- and Tyler's rebellion stands as one of several events that signaled the coming end of feudalism.

The second shock was the Protestant Reformation in the early 1500s. The Roman Catholic Church coexisted with the feudal system and enjoyed its own sovereignty centered on the Pope. But the Protestant Reformation challenged the authority of the Pope and shook the existing order in Europe. Fighting broke out between Catholics and Protestants and among different Protestant sects. The absence of clear, powerful sovereigns in Western Europe meant there was no authoritative source of decision making to resolve religious disagreements. Lords aligned themselves with different religious groups. Neighboring towns and regions chose opposite sides and went to war.

Peace of Westphalia

The religious violence reached its peak in the Thirty Years' War (1618–48), centered in modern-day Germany. The war ended with a series of treaties collectively known as the Peace of Westphalia. Those landmark agreements, made by most of Europe's political and religious leaders of the time, marked the end of feudalism and the beginning of the modern nation-state system.

In effect, the Peace of Westphalia established the concept of state sovereignty. That is, it put in place the idea that the world is divided into basic political units, or states. Each of these states occupies a definite territory, has an organized government, and has supreme and absolute power (sovereignty) to determine its own domestic and foreign policies.

The idea that a state is sovereign over a given territory was new. Throughout history, most societies either moved from place to place, built empires with ill-defined borders, or looked to divine supervision and so placed sovereignty somewhere outside its territory.

For example, the nomadic San of the Kalahari desert never thought of ruling a defined territory. Everything they possessed had to be portable. Ancient empires such as the Moghul in India or Aztecs in Mexico tolerated political and cultural diversity in the far reaches of their holdings. And the ancient Greeks would often travel to the oracle at Delphi for prophetic guidance in everything from annual crop selections to decisions of war. From the 17th century onward, sovereignty would be identified with the leaders of states with clearly-defined boundaries.

Legitimate Government

The development of sovereignty was useful to creating political organization, but it alone did not establish modern government. The Treaty of Westphalia settled the dispute over decision making, so unclear in the feudal system, by putting that responsibility in the hands of a sovereign leader. While this provided a sound basis for countries to deal with each other, it raised new questions of how governments should treat the people living within their borders.

Leaders might use force against their own people to keep power. But force is difficult to use and expensive over time. Rulers have strong reasons to seek consent for their rule. This consent is known as **legitimacy**, the belief that a government has the right to make public policy. A legitimate government is one that is accepted by the people and recognized by other governments as the sovereign authority of that nation.

Forms of Legitimacy

Governments may gain legitimacy in several ways. One is by tradition. Here, people accept a certain form of government because their society has always been governed that way and people expect their institutions and traditions to be carried on into the future.

Another way for a government, and in particular, one leader, to win legitimacy is through the power of personality. A charismatic person with strong leadership skills can often win the public's support.

The final and most durable form of legitimacy is for governments to bind themselves to rules guided by sound decision-making principles. The rules must be seen as fair and effective for people to trust their government. Constitutional government is an excellent example of this type of legitimacy,

Many countries blend different forms of legitimacy. In an informal sense, the Federal Government of the United States draws legitimacy from the leadership demonstrated by the President and other national leaders and from more than 200 years of continuous government. But more importantly, the Federal Government derives its legitimacy from the rules set out by the Constitution. Legitimacy based on a set of rules, like a Constitution, is one of the most stable forms of that trait.

Legitimacy in Sovereign States

As the feudal system gave way to sovereign states, national leaders such as kings and queens became the leaders of legitimate government. Monarchy suggested security and long-term stability.

Because monarchs already existed within the feudal system, they enjoyed the benefits and respect of tradition. Monarchs were recognized as the strongest individuals who could best govern a state and protect the people from harm. The Peace of Westphalia confirmed this centralization of power when outsiders agreed to recognize a monarch as the sovereign of a state.

Before, the monarch had held the right to *apply* law in accord with tradition. Now, with sovereignty, he gained the right to *make* law.

Mercantilism

By the 1700s, the primitive rural economy of the Middle Ages had developed into a more efficient, sophisticated system supporting hundreds of small cities and towns as centers of trade. Where once most people ate local food and dressed in clothes made locally, they could now choose to buy goods from abroad.

Trade and wealth brought new-found power to merchants and landowners, and monarchies adopted **mercantilism** to control and profit from that situation. Mercantilism was an economic and political theory emphasizing money as the chief source of wealth. The policy stressed the accumulation of precious metals, like gold and silver, through foreign trade. It also called for the establishing of colonies and a merchant marine and the development of industry and mining to attain a favorable balance of trade with other countries.

Mercantilist policies brought the state deep into the economy. Imports were heavily taxed to protect locally produced goods. Foreigners were required to buy licenses from the state in order to trade with local merchants. Local crafts and industries were subsidized in order to build supplies of goods that could be traded abroad. In these and a number of other ways, monarchs sought to fatten their treasuries and enhance their country's power.

The New World

The mercantilist system expanded when European explorers reached the Western Hemisphere. Their explorations opened new opportunities for trade and farming, but few merchants had the power or the

▶ *The Magna Carta* In 1215, merchants joined with England's nobles to demand that King John sign the Magna Carta and grant them a say in ruling the land. The Magna Carta is considered the founding document of Great Britain's constitutional monarchy today.

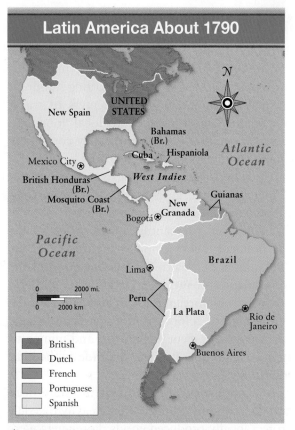

Latin America About 1790

New Spain
UNITED STATES
Mexico City ⊕
Bahamas (Br.)
Cuba
Hispaniola
Atlantic Ocean
British Honduras (Br.)
West Indies
Mosquito Coast (Br.)
Bogotá ⊕
New Granada
Guianas
Pacific Ocean
Lima ⊕
Brazil
Peru
La Plata
Rio de Janeiro ⊕
Buenos Aires ⊕

N

0   2000 mi.
0   2000 km

- British
- Dutch
- French
- Portuguese
- Spanish

▲ *Interpreting Maps* At the time the United States won its independence, European countries still controlled all of Central America and the Caribbean and most of South America. *Critical Thinking Which two countries ruled the largest share of the Americas?* H-SS 12.9.6

money to take advantage of the new circumstances. Only kings had the power to bring soldiers and money to places like Mexico and the Caribbean in order to conquer and control.

The high cost of exploration allowed monarchs to control overseas commerce by setting up companies to monopolize trade with the new regions. The company system allowed monarchs to tap new sources of wealth from distant gold and silver mines and from far-flung trade. The companies set up permanent settlements in Asia, Africa, and the Americas. Thus, Great Britain colonized present-day Ghana, calling it "the Gold Coast," to secure its precious metals. Spain colonized much of the Americas, and used native labor to work the gold and silver mines of Mexico and Peru.

Colonialism

Beginning in the late 1500s, several European monarchies embarked on a policy of **colonialism**—a policy by which nations establish administrative control over foreign lands. European settlers, laws, and religious beliefs spread to areas around the world. As you know, Spain, France, Portugal, the Netherlands, and Great Britain colonized much of the Americas. They established colonies out of a mix of motives, notably, for economic, religious, and military reasons. Whatever their motives, the effect was to strengthen monarchs and extend European power into new regions of the world.

European colonization brought great change to the people of the Americas. Britain's colonial efforts led to the War for Independence and the creation of the United States and its stable constitutional government of today. The experiences of other countries originally colonized by Spain, France, Portugal, and even Great Britain, however, differed in many ways from the American experience.

Section 1 Assessment

Key Terms and Main Ideas

1. What were the main elements of **feudalism?**
2. What was the role of **serfs** in the feudal system?
3. Was the **monarch,** in fact, a supreme ruler in every feudal society? Why or why not?
4. Monarchies adopted mercantilism to exploit what situation?

Critical Thinking

5. **Understanding Cause and Effect** How did the rise of towns and the Commercial Revolution contribute to the fall of the feudal system?

6. **Drawing Inferences** Why is it important for governments to be viewed as legitimate by their subjects?

Standards Monitoring *Online*
For: Self-quiz with vocabulary practice
Web Code: mqa-7221

Go Online
PHSchool.com
For: An activity on comparative government
Web Code: mqd-7221

Section Preview

OBJECTIVES

1. **Understand** the importance of popular sovereignty and how the governments of Britain and France changed to include it.
2. **Analyze** the role of popular sovereignty in Latin America in the 19th century and in the rise of dictatorships around the world.
3. **Describe** key events in the Mexican Revolution and in the modern history of Latin America.
4. **Examine** how fascism and communism distort the idea of popular sovereignty.

WHY IT MATTERS

Popular sovereignty, the idea that government should be based on the consent of the governed, transformed states such as Britain and France in the 1700s and 1800s. Regimes in Latin America, Africa, Asia, and Europe have addressed the question of popular sovereignty in many ways, leading to both democracies and dictatorships.

POLITICAL DICTIONARY

★ divine right of kings
★ encomienda
★ hacienda
★ counter-revolutionary
★ guerilla warfare
★ fascism

In the previous section, you read about the development of governments in Europe from the feudal system to the introduction of the sovereign state. In addition, you learned how states came to be viewed as legitimate by their people. Recall that legitimacy refers to the respect that people give to a state and their recognition of its right to speak on their behalf and govern their lives.

In this section, you will see how legitimacy leads to stable government. You will also discover how governments without legitimacy can fall to revolutions and tyranny.

Popular Sovereignty

One path to legitimacy was known as the **divine right of kings**. Many kings argued that they had a right to rule because God granted them the authority to govern. To disobey a king was to fight the natural order of society and to commit a sin against God. Kings who ruled by divine right did not have to answer to parliaments or to the people, only to God. The divine right of kings was a form of traditional legitimacy because it drew strength from Europe's deep Christian values.

In the 17th and 18th centuries, as religious views grew more diverse and scientific discoveries changed how many people viewed their world, people began to question the divine right of kings. If scientists like Galileo and Copernicus could overturn the Catholic Church's view that the Sun revolved around the Earth, could not reason also challenge the belief in the divine right of kings? After all, many kings who claimed to rule on behalf of God acted in ways that many people could criticize. Economists including Adam Smith and David Ricardo pointed to the fact that mercantilist policies, which helped kings grow wealthier, made most of their subjects poorer and less free. Other philosophers began to speak about the rights of individuals to control their own fate and to have a say in their government.

▲ Angels place a crown of victory on the head of Louis XIII, King of France, following the capture of a rebellious French city.
Critical Thinking How does this painting illustrate the divine right of kings? H-SS 12.9.1

▲ *A Modern Monarchy* Queen Elizabeth II (right) is the sovereign ruler of Great Britain, but over time the monarchy has given up nearly all of its powers to govern.

As monarchs lost some of their legitimacy, their sovereignty also came into question. Popular sovereignty became an increasingly important alternative to monarchical rule. Recall that popular sovereignty is the idea that governments can exist only with the consent of the governed.

Popular sovereignty would eventually form the basis for the many republics and democracies in the world today. Since the 18th century, almost every government on Earth has had to deal with popular sovereignty in one way or another.

Two leading monarchies in 18th century Western Europe, Britain and France, demonstrate two very different approaches to the acceptance of popular sovereignty. Great Britain gradually brought popular sovereignty into its political system. As one of the first countries to allow the common people to have a say in their government, Britain blended this principle with deep-seated cultural traditions. Meanwhile, France took a revolutionary route to popular sovereignty, and rejected many longstanding traditions.

Democracy in Britain

Great Britain is a monarchy led by a queen. Yet Great Britain is a democracy much like the United States. Britons elect a government that is responsible to them and draws its legitimacy from their votes and support. Britain wasn't always democratic. How did a country once ruled by George III and other powerful kings become a vibrant democracy?

Great Britain's history is marked by the steady transfer of sovereignty from the monarchy to the people. The Magna Carta signaled the first move toward a constitutional monarchy. The Petition of Right of 1628 and the Bill of Rights of 1689 took more authority from the King and gave it to the Parliament, which claimed to represent the people. Parliament controlled "the power of the purse," the right to tax people in order to fund the government.

Britain's conception of "the people" has also evolved. Well into the 19th century, only males who owned property could vote, and only those who belonged to officially recognized Protestant churches could hold office. Some of the largest cities in Britain had no representation in Parliament at all.

Far-sighted members of Parliament recognized the need for change. In the 1800s, Parliament passed several laws to expand the right to vote to more and more people. A law passed in 1829 allowed Catholics to hold public office, and landmark parliamentary acts in 1832, 1867, and 1885 lowered and then removed property restrictions on the right to vote. Women gained the vote in 1918.

By adapting its government to embrace popular sovereignty, Britain protected many of its institutions, including the monarchy, Parliament, its legal system, and the Church of England. These institutions have changed to meet the needs of a modern economy and diverse society, but they preserve a link to Britain's past.

Revolution in France

France took a very different route toward popular sovereignty. While the British monarchy compromised with nobles and granted rights to Parliament, the French monarchy expanded and centralized its authority. Royal power reached its peak under Louis XIV (1643–1715), who famously, and correctly, proclaimed, "L'état, c'est moi" ("I am the state"). The continuing concentration of power in the monarchy set the stage for a violent reaction led by those who pushed the concepts of popular sovereignty and rule based on reason as opposed to an insensitive devotion to tradition.

The French Revolution of 1789 would see the end of the French monarchy, followed by a period of confusion and terror, which included the rise of Napoleon and war with the rest of Europe. Historic institutions like the monarchy, nobility, church, and law were destroyed and replaced by new ones. France has undergone a number of revolutions and changes in government since the Revolution of 1789.

Which country serves as a better model for those countries currently challenged by popular sovereignty? The British example seems to offer great stability, but at the cost of flexibility and open-mindedness. Sometimes custom and tradition lead one to reject changes that may, in fact, be good for the country.

On the other hand, the instability of a revolution as in the French model can lead to an abuse of power. In 1959, many cheered when Fidel Castro overthrew the corrupt dictatorship of Fulgencio Batista in Cuba. But the destruction of Cuba's old political system created a vacuum that Castro then filled with his own absolute authority, and Cuba is today as far from a democracy as ever.

Latin America in the 19th Century

Political events in Europe significantly influenced the course of political development in Latin America. However, the region would take a turn very different from that of the European states or its neighbor to the north, the United States. Spain had left Latin America with a difficult legacy. As the *conquistadores,* or conquerors, settled the region, the Spanish monarchy looked on with suspicion. So far from Spain and with access to gold and silver, the conquistadors might come to rival the monarchy for power. In response, the monarchy created a feudal system in Latin America with the *encomienda* system. The monarch announced that all the indigenous peoples of Spanish America—who numbered in the millions—were the property of the crown. The monarchy then entrusted up to several hundred Indians to each settler who promised to protect them and teach them Christianity.

Adopting Popular Sovereignty

Great Britain	France
Reform	Revolution
Legislature passes laws giving more people the right to vote	Government loses control of reform process; people rebel and overthrow government
Institutions reformed and preserved	Old institutions destroyed, new ones created
Little violence, some protests	Great violence
Changes carried out slowly over decades	Changes happen quickly

Interpreting Tables Britain and France followed two different paths to the adoption of popular sovereignty. *Which country's experiences are closer to those of the United States since the 1770s?*

The *encomienda* system proved to be a double-edged sword for the Spanish monarchy. Local landowners found it easy to treat their indigenous laborers as slaves. The *encomienda* system set the stage for large **haciendas,** large landholdings, to emerge as nearly self-sufficient centers of political and economic power in Latin America.

Napoleon's invasion of Spain, and the imprisonment of its King Ferdinand VII from 1808 to 1813, had a major impact on Latin America. Many colonial elites rejected Napoleon's replacement on the Spanish throne, his brother Joseph I, and remained loyal to Ferdinand VII. Other colonists, most notably Simón Bolivar, were inspired by the same Enlightenment ideas that gave rise to the French Revolution, and sought to create a new political order in Latin America, based on popular sovereignty.

Independence

The struggle changed when Ferdinand VII regained the crown, and agreed to grant greater power to parliament and place some restrictions on the Church. To his conservative supporters in the colonies, it was now Ferdinand VII who had betrayed the divine right of kings. Thus, in Mexico, Agustín de Iturbide, who had fought to restore the rule of Ferdinand VII, engineered Mexico's independence in 1821 and had himself crowned its emperor. Iturbide soon would be forced to give up his throne, and Mexico, like many of the new states of Latin America, would fall into periods of civil war on through the 19th century.

▲ Simón Bolívar (left) and Emperor Iturbide (right) fought for independence for the nations of northern South America and for Mexico, respectively. *Critical Thinking In what way was Iturbide a more conservative leader than Bolívar?* H-SS 12.9.6

Most of Latin America won independence from Spain and Portugal in the decades after Napoleon conquered Spain and left the country too weak to control its colonies. Leaders, including Simón Bolívar, José de San Martín, and Bernardo O'Higgins fought for independence for the colonies that became Colombia, Venezuela, Argentina, and several other countries.

Obstacles to Stability

The *haciendas* left behind by the *encomienda* system weakened the political systems of the region. In Britain, the upper classes could support traditional institutions like the monarchy and the nobility while giving power to the people through broad-based elections for Parliament. In Latin America, the elite who owned the land and controlled the economy had no monarch or other common institutions to unite them.

Why were the new states of Latin America unable to absorb popular sovereignty, as in the United States, Great Britain, and France? The United States had clear rallying cries for its independence, including "No taxation without representation," or "Give me liberty, or give me death!" It declared its independence on the principles of freedom and self-government. But in Latin America, independence from Spain could mean a desire to reestablish royal authority, to create a democratic republic, or to embrace the reformist program of King Ferdinand VII. Latin

America's political troubles slowed its development as Europe's political stability allowed countries like Britain, France, and Germany to embrace the Industrial Revolution and the economic development that followed.

The *hacienda* landowners enjoyed great wealth and a sense of personal independence through the 19th century, so they had little motivation to help unite their country. The government in the distant capital had little impact on their lives. Government then became something of a prize for *caudillos,* the leaders of armed militias who sought power to enrich themselves. Once in government, they faced new rebellions because they did little to solve the economic problems and underdevelopment of their countries. Another *caudillo* was always on the horizon to grab power, and eventually suffer the same fate. This cycle of political disorder was common throughout Latin America into the twentieth century.

The Mexican Revolution

Through the 1800s, Mexico grappled, often violently, with a number of questions. Should there be a centralized or a federal government? How much power should a single political leader have? How could Mexico remain independent from its powerful neighbor to the north and other major world powers?

Dictatorship of Díaz

Porfirio Díaz brought Mexico its first long period of stability and economic growth, from 1876 to 1910. His economic plan, which benefited few Mexicans, was based on using cheap labor to work the mineral wealth and large farms of Mexico, and inviting large foreign firms to invest in the exploitation of its natural resources. Francisco Madero organized the first important opposition to Díaz, but Madero was no radical. He belonged to the elite and feared that Diaz' harsh rule would lead to a larger social revolt if reforms were not put in place.

As with many revolutions, Madero's struggle began from the top of society, not the bottom. Often, unhappy members of the elite make the first moves against those in power.

Díaz jailed Madero, but more and more Mexicans were growing weary of his rule. Díaz fled the country in 1911, and Madero assumed the presidency, promising gradual reform to Mexico's government and economy. But the flames of revolution had been stoked for many who followed Emiliano Zapata's call to break up large estates and give land to workers. Madero found himself between **counter-revolutionaries,** those who opposed revolutionary change, and revolutionaries who wanted more change than Madero could support. The counter-revolutionary forces of General Victoriano Huerta assassinated Madero in 1913. Civil war followed.

The PRI

In 1917, the *constitutionalistas* won out, and wrote a new constitution in which the government played a more active role in promoting the quality of Mexican social, economic, and cultural life. Though Zapata and then fellow rebel Pancho Villa were assassinated, the new government absorbed their call for revolution in a state-supported political party, the National Revolutionary Party, which would change its name to the Institutional Revolutionary Party (PRI) in 1946. The PRI controlled the government and politics of Mexico for more than 70 years, until the 2000 presidential elections.

The PRI became increasingly the party of business interests and sought to woo the people as a whole. Though it no longer monopolizes power, for some Mexicans it remains the party of the revolution. For others, the PRI was, and remains, a party that never fulfilled expectations.

Latin America in the Modern Era

While Mexico remained under the stable control of the PRI, the 1960s to 1980s proved to be violent times elsewhere in Latin America. Throughout the 19th century and the first half of the 20th century, most countries had experienced cycles of dictatorship and military control, with wealth and land concentrated in the hands of a few. Democracy had sprouted in the region during the 1950s, but continued economic decline and growing inequality fueled demands for a more just society. Many people were inspired by the Cuban Revolution in 1959, which under communist ideology promised to attend to the basic needs of people. These groups often resorted to **guerrilla warfare** in an attempt to topple the government. Guerrilla warfare is fighting carried out by small groups in hit-and-run raids.

The threat that Communist guerillas and others posed in the 1960s and 1970s led the armed forces to take a more active role in several countries. The military also believed that Latin America's continued economic problems stemmed from the endless debate and corruption of politicians. In their view, the political class had to be curbed and the armed forces had to have the power to strengthen the economy and restore political peace. Only then would Latin America prosper. Democracy could come later.

Despite these struggles, the idea of popular sovereignty—government in the name of the people—remained supreme. Every military leader who intervened in a crisis claimed to be working to create a more perfect democracy. Nonetheless, military rule quickly opened the door to abuse. Innocent civilians were caught up in heavy-handed efforts to defeat the guerrilla groups. In Guatemala, the military adopted a "scorched-earth policy" from 1978 to 1985 to root out suspected insurgents from country villages. The campaign left some 75,000 dead, and made one million more into refugees. Such harsh methods often pushed neutral citizens to join the rebels.

Elsewhere, even the defeat of rebels and the end of the crisis could not stop the military from staying in power. Military governments had an interest in preserving the fear of rebels that made so many people support the armed forces. Repression continued because most people simply did not want to believe that the armed forces, one of the few national institutions the people trusted, could commit such horrific acts.

▶ Francisco Madero, President of Mexico (1911-1913)
H-SS 12.9.6

The events that unfolded in Latin America during this time did so with little official criticism from abroad. During the Cold War, the United States was concerned chiefly with the threat of Soviet Communism spreading in the Americas. The end of the Cold War brought new opportunities for democracy in Latin America.

Legacy of Colonialism

Unlike Latin America, where most countries had won independence by 1830, much of Asia and Africa remained under colonial control through the middle of the 20th century. In theory, their European rulers were preparing them for democracy. In practice, they governed with little respect for native cultures and did not provide their colonies the structures they would need to thrive.

The main goal of colonialism was always to control distant lands in order to extract resources and benefit the mother country. At the Conference of Berlin (1884–1885), major European powers carved nearly the entire continent of Africa into colonial holdings, with artificial boundaries that often sliced through ancient cultures or, just as often, crammed diverse groups of people into a single colony. Not infrequently, a colonial power would favor one segment of the population over another to advance its own interests. These "divide and rule" techniques would leave lasting legacies, as in Rwanda, where efforts by the Belgians to play off Hutus against

▲ A worker in the West African nation of Côte D'Ivoire prepares cacao beans that will be exported to make chocolate.
Critical Thinking How has the reliance on single crops like cacao beans hurt many young nations? H-SS 12.9.8

Tutsis created tensions that exploded in the genocide of the 1990s, more than 30 years after independence.

Economically, each colony was directed to produce a few specific goods for export to Europe. After independence, countries often found that reliance on single crops could drive their economies to prosperity or depression from year to year. Thus, a fall in the world price for coffee or cotton could bring real hardship to an entire country.

Another of the major problems facing the former colonies in Africa and Asia was that most won their independence in the 1950s and 1960s, at the height of the Cold War. Many countries were drawn into the Cold War as the Soviet Union and United States provided arms and money to rebels fighting for control of the new countries in the hopes of winning new allies.

Under these conditions, it is not surprising that democracy failed to take hold in many newly independent countries. Countries that combined many ethnic groups had few common traditions to build upon, and conflicts and mistrust made it difficult to adopt a legal system that everyone could generally agree to. The only way for a government to gain legitimacy was to improve the lives of the people and bring peace. Unfortunately, this left governments vulnerable to economic swings and appealing politicians who easily became dictators. Because most former colonies had underdeveloped economies, there was no large middle class to balance the interests of the vast numbers of poor and those of the few elite.

The military often stood as the only true national institution, so soldiers usually intervened in a crisis with the support from many groups in society. But in almost every case, the military gave in to the lure of power and repressed critics of their rule.

Nigeria

Nigeria experienced many of these problems when it gained independence from Great Britain in 1960. Confronting a diverse population speaking some 250 distinct languages and dialects, the British left Nigeria with a strong federalist system that placed power in the hands of three large ethnic groups, the Yorubas to the southwest, the Hausa-Fulani in the north, and the Igbo in the southeast. The Igbo, the smallest of these population groups, stood apart because of their higher rates of education and their acceptance of Christianity in a Muslim-dominated country. Moreover, the Igbo region included the country's vast oil reserves, and, lacking a true sense of Nigerian nationality, they found it difficult to view their oil wealth as a national, Nigerian resource instead of a regional, Igbo resource.

Feeling dominated, the Igbo supported a military coup, an overthrow of the government, in 1966. Muslim officers from northern Nigeria responded with their own coup, leading the Igbo to proclaim an independent state, Biafra, and provoking a civil war that lasted for more than two years and left a million dead.

Another military coup followed in 1975, but this time the military committed itself to democracy and allowed free elections in 1979. The new civilian government suffered from rampant corruption, which gave the military a reason to intervene and create an equally corrupt government. Democracy finally returned to Nigeria in 1999, but ethnic tensions and general mistrust continue to stir the country. Nigeria still has not resolved its most basic question of national identity: What does it mean to be a Nigerian? As long as the country remains divided, Nigeria will face challenges in building a democratic society.

Fascism and Communism

The experience of dictatorship has been common throughout the world. Two of the chief political philosophies that created the most powerful and destructive dictatorships, particularly in Europe and Asia, are communism and **fascism**. Fascism describes a centralized, authoritarian government whose policies glorify the state over the individual. Communism is principally an economic theory, and you will read more about the economics of communist states in Chapter 23. When referring to a government, communism describes a state based on the idea of government control of the economy to serve the interests of workers without regard for individual liberty. Although the two political movements are quite distinct, they share some traits.

Both communist and fascist governments go to great lengths to address the idea of popular sovereignty, though in doing so they distort that concept significantly. As radical movements, they raise some concerns also found in the French Revolution. Most notably, does revolutionary political change open the door for an abuse of power?

Fascist Governments

Historic examples of fascism include Adolf Hitler's Germany, Benito Mussolini's Italy, and Francisco Franco's Spain. These regimes embraced an ultranationalist, extreme ideology that, in Germany, included intense racist elements. Typically, a charismatic leader leads an all-powerful political party that incites violence against all who disagree. The leader also heads a state that assumes control over social and economic policy in the supposed interests of the nation. The "people" is narrowly defined to exclude cultures and ethnic groups outside the national majority, most infamously in Nazi Germany. Democratic processes are viewed with suspicion, as they lead to debate and delay that prevents the government from working to help the "people." Needless to say, fascist governments rarely helped the people as much as they claimed to.

It is not a coincidence that these governments emerged out of the economic depressions of the 1920s and the 1930s. In such difficult times, people often look for scapegoats, and as in Latin America in later decades, they hope for a strong hand to restore order and prosperity. Hence, in Nazi Germany, Hitler pointed to the Jews as the source of German woes, and in Italy, many supported Mussolini because he "made the trains run on time."

Communist Dictatorships

Communist states promote a left-wing ideology that follows the writings of Karl Marx. Marx believed that the workers of the world would overthrow the capitalist free market system and replace it with their own rule. Unlike fascist governments, communist regimes downplay nationalism. But they too promote a strong dictatorial state, which, under communist ideology, will oversee the end of capitalism and allow greater freedom for all. The state, having now lost its usefulness, will simply "wither away."

Like fascism, the tremendous decision making power given to government "in the name of the people" in a communist state regularly leads to abuse and repression. China stands as a leading illustration of that point.

The People's Republic of China came into being in 1949. It emerged from decades of civil war that began in the 1930s and continued even through World War II. That struggle pitted the Nationalist Government, led by Chiang Kai-shek, against the communist rebels led by Mao Zedong. By 1949, Mao's forces had won control of nearly all of China, and the Nationalists had fled the mainland for the island of Taiwan.

Mao was bent on increasing agricultural and industrial production. He turned to central planning and instituted a series of Five-Year Plans. Frequent and often drastic changes in policy produced chaos and regularly thwarted economic development.

By the mid-1960s, Mao was determined to purge China of what he called the "Four Olds"—old thoughts, old culture, old customs, and old habits. In the Cultural Revolution, begun in 1966, Mao's young, dedicated Red Guards attacked and bullied teachers, intellectuals, and anyone else who seemed to lack revolu-

▲ This 1967 poster features Chairman Mao. Demonstrators are holding copies of the "Little Red Book," which contains the basic tenets of Chinese Communism. **H-SS 12.9.5**

tionary fervor. Artists and scholars were sent to farms to be "re-educated"; ancient books and art were destroyed. By 1968, however, the havoc created by the Cultural Revolution persuaded Mao to abandon that effort.

Deng Xiaoping came to power after Mao's death in 1976. Deng's reforms loosened the government's strict controls on the economy and encouraged some forms of private enterprise. Still, the Chinese government tolerated no political dissent. In May 1989, some 100,000 students and workers occupied Beijing's Tiananmen Square, demanding democratic reforms. Chinese troops and tanks moved into the square to crush the demonstration, killing hundreds of protestors and maiming thousands more. World opinion was outraged. Today, China's leaders continue to encourage economic reforms, and the Chinese economy is booming. But they also continue to impose harsh limits on human rights. The Chinese Communist Party remains the only legally recognized political organization. The government is dictatorial, and though the state still controls much of the economy, its economic policies can no longer be described as strictly communist.

Section 2 Assessment

Key Terms and Main Ideas

1. Why did monarchs often claim the **divine right of kings?**
2. What effects did the *encomienda* system have on the newly-independent countries of Latin America?
3. What role do **counter-revolutionaries** play in a revolution?
4. How does **guerilla warfare** often lead to stronger military governments?

Critical Thinking

5. **Expressing Problems Clearly** Why did Mexico face difficulties in creating a successful democracy after independence?

6. **Drawing Inferences** Why do fascist and communist governments claim to govern by the consent of their people?
7. **Making Comparisons** Describe the difference between Britain's reform model and France's revolutionary model in your own words.

on the Supreme Court

May a State's Law Modify American Foreign Policy?

Analysis Skills HR4, HI3

The President has the authority to make executive agreements with other countries, which are less formal than treaties and do not require ratification by the Senate. Can a State law modify the terms of an executive agreement?

American Insurance Association v. *Garamendi* (2003)

In the years leading up to World War II, the government of Nazi Germany seized money and other property belonging to its Jewish residents, including insurance policies. Following the war, Holocaust survivors and the heirs of Jews who did not survive had great difficulty reclaiming their property and collecting on those insurance policies.

Lawsuits against companies that did business in Germany during the war flooded U.S. courts. In response to complaints from foreign companies and their governments, President Clinton negotiated agreements with Germany, France, and Austria. The governments and businesses of these countries agreed to create foundations to repay Holocaust-era claims. In return, the President promised that when lawsuits were brought in American courts, the government would submit a statement declaring that the claim should be settled out of court.

Meanwhile, the State of California passed the Holocaust Victim Insurance Relief Act of 1999. The HVIRA required any insurance company doing business in California to disclose the status of all policies it, or any related company, issued in Europe between 1920 and 1945. Failure to comply would result in suspension of the company's license to do business in California.

Representing the companies subject to the California law, the American Insurance Association sued John Garamendi, California's insurance commissioner. When the Ninth Circuit Court of Appeals upheld the California law, the insurance companies appealed to the Supreme Court.

Arguments for American Insurance

1. The Federal Government, particularly the President, is responsible for making foreign policy. The States may not pass laws that affect the President's foreign policy decisions.
2. Because California's approach conflicts with the President's preference, the approach taken by the President must govern.
3. When the President acts in any area affecting foreign policy, the States may not make laws affecting that area, even if there is no direct conflict.

Arguments for Garamendi

1. The States have an important interest in helping citizens harmed by the Holocaust.
2. The executive agreements do not specifically forbid States from passing laws regarding Holocaust-era insurance claims; therefore, the States are free to act.
3. Because the HVIRA only requires the foreign companies to disclose information, but does not attempt to settle claims, it does not conflict with the executive agreements.

Decide for Yourself

1. Review the constitutional grounds upon which each side based its arguments and the specific arguments each side presented.
2. Debate the opposing viewpoints presented in this case. Which viewpoint did you favor?
3. How will the Court's decision affect the States' ability to address problems that relate to foreign countries? (To read a summary of the Court's decision, turn to pages 799–806.)

Go Online
PHSchool.com

Use Web Code mqp-6220 to register your vote on this issue and to see how other students voted.

Section Preview

OBJECTIVES

1. **Understand** regimes change from dictatorship to democracy.
2. **Describe** the fall of the Soviet Union.
3. **Explain** the importance of democratic consolidation.
4. **Analyze** why some countries experience setbacks or failed transitions to democracy.

WHY IT MATTERS

The transition from dictatorship to free elections is only the first step in creating a democratic society. Countries must develop strong institutions and a peaceful, unified society in order to have a reasonable chance of producing a lasting democracy.

POLITICAL DICTIONARY

★ **hardliners**
★ **softliners**
★ **democratic consolidation**
★ **amnesty**
★ **genocide**
★ **failed states**

The political scientist Samuel Huntington studied the rise of democracy through history. He noticed an interesting pattern: democratization tends to happen in waves across the world.

The good news from Huntington's study is that the number of democracies rises gradually over time. But this news is cooled by his other finding, that not all those countries swept up by a wave make it to the end and form stable democracies. Some fall back into authoritarianism.

How Regimes Change

Democracy takes root when competing groups give up their urge to control a society and agree to compromise and cooperate in order to make government work. In the modern era, democracies have often been born out of toppled dictatorships.

Dictatorships often find themselves on the defensive. The principle of popular sovereignty forces dictators to explain why they put limits on basic freedoms. Some dictators argue that the state must be strong to create a better society in the long run. Others point to foreign enemies or domestic unrest to justify their repression, and some blame economic backwardness.

Internal and/or external pressures can prompt splits and discord within a dictatorial regime. **Hardliners,** who fight to maintain the status quo, may do battle with **softliners,** who would reform governmental policies or procedures.

Interestingly, softliners are not necessarily democrats. Many support reforms to strengthen their hold on power. Nevertheless, the splits they provoke can create opportunities for the opposition. Influential individuals can then lead social movements to bring real reform.

Poland

Poland provides a case study of reforms prompted by hardliner-softliner clashes. That country was ruled by a communist dictatorship, subject to the will of the Soviet Union, for nearly half a century, from 1945 to 1990.

Decades of economic hardship and political unrest came to a head when, in 1980, shipyard workers in the city of Gdansk formed an independent trade union and called a strike. Led by co-worker Lech Walesa, they demanded—and won—several major concessions from the government, including the right to organize and the right to strike.

Solidarity's gains seemed short-lived when, in 1981, Wojciech Jaruzelski, a general in the Soviet Army, became Poland's prime minister. He declared martial law. Walesa and other Solidarity leaders were arrested, and unions and the right to strike were abolished.

Predictably, Jaruzelski's harsh stance only made the nation's political and economic troubles worse, and his government was never able to suppress the increasingly popular Solidarity movement. By the late 1980s, with the reform-minded Mikhail Gorbachev in power in Moscow, Jaruzelski was determined to resolve Poland's economic problems. But, first, he had to overcome the opposition of Communist Party leaders at the local level, and many of them were bent on protecting their own privileged positions.

Walesa realized that that infighting had weakened the communist regime and he pushed even harder for change. The government gave in and, in mid-1989, agreed to several historic reform measures, including free elections.

Candidates endorsed by Solidarity swept the election of a new Parliament. In 1990, Lech Walesa became the nation's democratically chosen president. Events in Poland led to similar movements and the toppling of communist regimes across Eastern Europe.

Leaders in Democracy

Individuals from all walks of life influence democratization. Lech Walesa worked in a shipyard. Vaclav Havel was an intellectual and a playwright, and he, too, led a march to democracy and became president of his country, Czechoslovakia.

Other individuals avoid politics but influence public opinion. Soviet author Alexander Solzhenitsyn wrote *The Gulag Archipelago* to expose the network of prison camps in his country and spur the cause of human rights in the Soviet Union.

Then, too, some individuals are able to encourage democracy from beyond the borders of their country. Pope John Paul II, a native of Poland, inspired the people of his homeland and maintained pressure on Eastern European countries as they moved toward democracy.

Fall of the Soviet Union

The collapse of the communist regimes in Eastern Europe contributed to the fall of the world's first communist superpower, the Soviet Union, the modern successor to the Russian empire. From the Revolution of 1917 until 1990, the Communist Party was the only political party in the Soviet Union.

A new stage of Soviet government began in 1985 when Mikhail Gorbachev became general secretary of the party. As a softliner,

▲ A crowd of Solidarity supporters cheered newly-elected President Lech Walesa in 1990. *Critical Thinking How did Lech Walesa take advantage of splits within the Polish government to help overthrow the communist state?* **H-SS 12.9.7**

Gorbachev undertook a reform program that rested on the principles of *perestroika* and *glasnost*. *Perestroika* called for a wide-ranging restructuring of political and economic life. *Glasnost* was the policy of openness under which the government increased its tolerance of dissent and freedom of expression.

Transition to Democracy

Changes occurred rapidly after Boris Yeltsin was elected president of Russia in 1991. Russia was then still a republic of the Soviet Union, and although it was not independent, Yeltsin used his position to confront Gorbachev, resigning from the Communist Party and declaring the laws of the Russian Republic sovereign over Russia's population and territory. In August 1991, Gorbachev and his wife were vacationing in the Crimea when a group of hard line Communist Party leaders placed him under house arrest. They wanted a return to the policies of the old Soviet government.

When the Soviet public heard of the attempted coup, thousands of protesters took to the streets of Moscow, led by Yeltsin. After several tense days, the conspirators surrendered. The coup had failed. Extraordinary events followed. The three Baltic republics were the first to depart from the Soviet Union. Soon, the remaining 12 republics left the Union as well.

As the elected leader of the dominant Soviet republic, Boris Yeltsin's power overshadowed that of Gorbachev. Recognizing reality, Gorbachev resigned on December 25, 1991. By the end of the year, the Soviet Union was no more.

Independent Russia

A new constitution was approved in a national referendum in late 1993. It proclaims the Russian Federation to be "a democratic federal legally-based state with a republican form of government." It also set out a new government structure and contains an extensive list of individual rights, including guarantees of freedom of speech, press, association, and religious belief. Under the new constitution, the president holds a dominant role.

Boris Yeltsin kept his presidential role under the new constitution, and was reelected in 1996. Soon thereafter, the economy began to spiral downward. Yeltsin suffered serious health problems and was accused of corruption in his inner circle.

In a surprise move, Yeltsin resigned at the end of December 1999, yielding the presidency to his prime minister, Vladimir Putin. Putin won election on his own in 2000, and again in 2004. Though Putin's reputation as a political strongman allowed him to revive the flagging economy, that same reputation drew criticism as he pushed policies that increasingly concentrated power in the presidency and restricted civil liberties.

Democratic Consolidation

So far, you have read about the process of democratic transition, studying examples in Poland and the Soviet Union. Transition refers to the *change* from dictatorship to democracy and is marked by the holding of free and fair elections. What must happen, once change occurs, to ensure that democracy in fact takes root?

Democratic consolidation is a much longer process that takes place as a country firmly establishes all those factors considered necessary for a democracy to succeed. These factors include a free press, a diverse multi-party system, civilian control over the military, a vibrant collection of interest groups, an economic system that offers clear opportunities to advance, and a professional civil service. Some of these elements may not be present in the early stages of transition. Many take time to take root.

Most of all, democratic consolidation occurs when a society establishes a sense of common trust among all citizens. Because many transitions take place following a civil war or a dictatorship that pitted one group against another, mutual trust can be difficult to establish. But when it is achieved, democracy stands on a solid footing.

The Enduring *Constitution*

America's Place in the World

1900

During the first phase of its history, the United States tried to isolate itself from foreign conflicts. In the 1900s, however, the United States participated in two world wars and became a global superpower. The time line lists critical developments concerning war, peace, and trade in the twentieth century.

1898
United States wins the Spanish-American War and acquires foreign territories.

1917
United States abandons neutrality to join the Allies in World War I.

Go Online
PHSchool.com
Use Web Code mqp-6229 for an interactive time line.

 Analysis Skills CS1, CS2, HI1

El Salvador

Many countries in Latin America, Africa, and Asia have made the transition to democracy. The process of democratic consolidation has proved to be more difficult. El Salvador held its first free and fair elections for president in over 50 years in 1982, but the transition to democracy did not bring peace or stability. The country remained bitterly divided as a rebel group, the Farabundo Martí National Liberation Front (FMLN), pressed the demands of the poor and landless. The armed forces remained largely independent under the new civilian government and engaged in widespread violence in the effort to defeat the FMLN.

Civil war raged until 1992, when the United Nations helped negotiate a peace agreement. Under that agreement, the FMLN laid down its arms and re-organized as a political party, while the government agreed to a general **amnesty** (an agreement not to prosecute past crimes), reduced military influence in government, and established a commission to investigate human rights abuses during the civil war. Today, the violence has ended and the FMLN works toward its goals through the political system—a major sign of democratic consolidation.

Haiti

The recent political history of Haiti, an island nation in the Caribbean, has been more troubled. A former French colony, Haiti was one of the first countries in the Americas to win its independence (1804). Yet, as in many other countries, independence was followed by more than a century of dictatorship and civil war. Today, Haiti is the poorest country in the hemisphere.

The longest recent period of dictatorship came to an end in 1986, when the Duvalier family fled the country after 29 years of brutal rule. After four years of provisional governments and preparation, a presidential election was held and Jean-Bertrand Aristide took office. Members of the armed forces still loyal to the dictatorship, and worried that democracy would reduce their influence, promptly overthrew Aristide and established a military government in 1991.

The international community cut off aid to Haiti and called for Aristide's return, but the military refused to step down. The soldiers finally withdrew in 1994 after the United States threatened to invade with the support of the United Nations. In 1996, he handed power to his political ally, René Préval, in Haiti's first ever transition from one elected ruler to another.

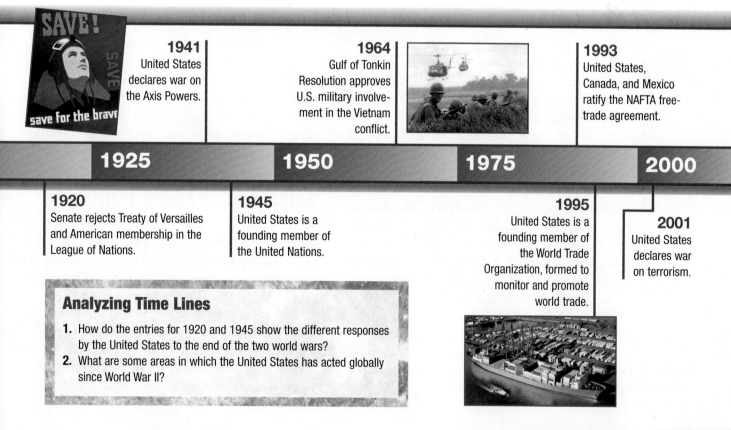

1941
United States declares war on the Axis Powers.

1964
Gulf of Tonkin Resolution approves U.S. military involvement in the Vietnam conflict.

1993
United States, Canada, and Mexico ratify the NAFTA free-trade agreement.

1925   **1950**   **1975**   **2000**

1920
Senate rejects Treaty of Versailles and American membership in the League of Nations.

1945
United States is a founding member of the United Nations.

1995
United States is a founding member of the World Trade Organization, formed to monitor and promote world trade.

2001
United States declares war on terrorism.

Analyzing Time Lines

1. How do the entries for 1920 and 1945 show the different responses by the United States to the end of the two world wars?
2. What are some areas in which the United States has acted globally since World War II?

Voices on Government

The career of **Vaclav Havel**—playwright, essayist, and politician—symbolizes the great changes in world politics in the second half of the twentieth century. When Czechoslovakia was under Soviet domination, Havel went to jail for his dissident views. Then the country peacefully overthrew the Communist regime, and he became the Czech president. On New Year's Day 1990, he spoke about the future:

" *We cannot blame the previous rulers for everything, not only because it would be untrue but also because it could blunt the duty that each of us faces today, namely the obligation to act independently, freely, reasonably, and quickly. Let us not be mistaken: the best government in the world, the best parliament and the best president, cannot achieve much on their own. . . . Freedom and democracy include participation and therefore responsibility from us all.* **"**

Evaluating the Quotation

(a) What do you think Havel means by "participation"? (b) Why might the transition to democracy be difficult for people after 40 years of totalitarian rule? H-SS 12.9.7

But events took a turn for the worse as Aristide and Préval both claimed leadership of their party. Each led large blocs of supporters in parliament and their refusal to work together created gridlock. Both sides were accused of corruption and vote-tampering.

Aristide recaptured the presidency in 2000 in an election that was clearly rigged and widely condemned by foreign observers. The United States and several other countries threatened new sanctions if democratic procedures were not strengthened. Instead, Aristide, once a champion of democracy, became more of a dictator.

An armed revolt in 2004 ousted the government, and Aristide fled into exile. Haiti is now ruled by a provisional government. A small UN peacekeeping force has attempted to maintain order in at least some parts of the country since mid-2004.

René Préval was returned to the presidency in a disputed election in 2006. Poverty and lawlessness have plagued Haiti for decades. There are doubts that a functioning democracy can be established there at any point in the near future.

Iraq

The invasion that toppled Saddam Hussein's brutal dictatorship in Iraq in 2003 was led by the United States. Now, this country is committed to building a democracy in that still strife-torn country. The few instances in which one or more countries have attempted to establish democratic institutions in another country have been filled with difficulties. There have been some spectacular successes, however, notably in Japan and Germany in the years following World War II.

Clearly, the effort to bring democracy to Iraq faces enormous challenges. This land has no history of free institutions upon which a democracy might be built. Nor are there any significant unifying traditions that might help bring the nation's diverse Kurdish, Shia, and Sunni populations together in a tolerant and peaceful whole.

In 2005, Iraqis elected an interim Parliament that drew up a new constitution for the country. Iraqi voters approved the constitution in October 2005, creating the basis for a new democratic government. However, many Sunni Iraqis failed to vote in the first election and voted "no" on the new constitution. The success of Iraqi democracy depends in no small measure on the ability of these three groups to work together and build democratic institutions acceptable to all.

Setbacks and Failed Transitions

While some countries have successfully established democratic governments, and many others have begun the transition to democracy, a third group of countries has not succeeded in joining the world's democracies.

The costs of failure are great. Many countries today find that they must confront new problems previously hidden by dictatorial rule when they attempt to change toward a democracy. Countries that fail to transition to democracy can pose a threat to other countries if they open safe havens for international terrorist groups.

Ethnic Violence

The country of Yugoslavia no longer exists. Founded in 1918, Yugoslavia included people from three major religions and many ethnic groups in one country.

When communist rule began to weaken in the late 1980s, regional political leaders inflamed ethnic differences for their own personal gain. By playing up old battles, they hoped to position themselves as the leaders who would right past wrongs.

The country split apart. Several provinces of Yugoslavia declared independence and went to war with one another for control of land that multiple ethnic groups believed was theirs by right or by history. The province of Bosnia-Herzegovina, peopled with a mix of Muslims, Serbians, and Croatians, was targeted by forces supported by neighboring Serbia and Croatia. The province saw the most intense fighting, and Bosnians suffered a **genocide**, or the attempted extermination of a national group, that killed about 200,000 civilians and sent many more out of the country as refugees. The conflict ended only when NATO intervened to stop the fighting. Instead of leading to democracy, the end of dictatorship in Yugoslavia triggered the bloody break-up of the country into at least five independent states.

Failed States

Other countries remain similarly troubled. Their inability to find stability has even raised security concerns for other states. Countries such as Sudan and Afghanistan include large regions that remain outside the control of their own governments. Somalia, in East Africa, does not have a functioning government and most of the country is ruled by warlords. These countries are known as **failed states**. Security is nonexistent in most places, the economy has collapsed, the health care and school systems are in shambles, and corruption flourishes.

International terrorist groups have found refuge in these lawless lands, and have used them to plan and train for acts of violence. The Soviet Union occupied Afghanistan in the 1980s, and after they withdrew in 1989, they left the country too devastated by war to recover. Afghans who had fought against the Soviets now turned their arms against each other for control of provinces. Foreign countries did not get involved in Afghanistan and few believed anything could be done to end the fighting between warlords. The anarchy provided a haven for Osama Bin Laden and his Al-Qaeda terrorist network to plan their attacks on the United States on September 11, 2001. In response to the attack, U.S. troops moved into Afghanistan and helped establish a democratic government. However, large portions of the country remain outside central authority.

Section 3 Assessment

Key Terms and Main Ideas

1. What role can **softliners** play in a dictatorship?
2. Why is **democratic consolidation** important?
3. Why is an **amnesty** often a positive step in building a democratic state following a rebellion or civil war?

Critical Thinking

4. **Making Comparisons** Explain why El Salvador and Haiti have experienced different outcomes in their transition to democracy.
5. **Drawing Inferences** How might the United States help other countries in the Western Hemisphere to build strong, independent democracies?

Standards Monitoring Online
For: Self-quiz with vocabulary practice
Web Code: mqa-7223

6. **Drawing Conclusions** In what ways do failed states affect their neighbors?

Go Online
PHSchool.com
For: An activity on comparative government
Web Code: mqd-7223

Face the
Issues

Foreign Policy

Background *Several features of American foreign policy, put in place after September 11, 2001, are known as the Bush Doctrine. Essentially, that doctrine declares that this country will make preventive war if necessary to defeat threats to national security, keep America's military the strongest in the world, and promote freedom and democracy everywhere. If cooperative solutions cannot be found, the United States will act alone.*

Coalition troops in Iraq

 **Analysis Skills HR3, HI1**

Support the Bush Doctrine

The United States has arrived at a unique place in its history. Unrivalled economically and militarily, it is the world's only superpower. It has both the right and the duty to protect itself from any threat posed by terrorists or by any rogue state that might possess weapons of mass destruction (WMDs). And it has a golden opportunity to spread freedom and democracy around the globe. These basic concepts drove the invasions of Afghanistan and Iraq.

Most of our old alliances, like NATO, became obsolete with the end of the Cold War. The United Nations is both too weak and too divided to confront many of today's most difficult problems.

New threats call for new thinking and new alliances. America forged "a coalition of the willing" to defeat the Taliban in Afghanistan and to bring Saddam Hussein to justice in Iraq. And it will lead new coalitions to meet new dangers. Those who share our values will rally to the cause of freedom. We cannot afford to be weighed down by old allies who do not share those values.

Rebuild Historic Alliances

The United States must defend itself and its values against all threats. Our traditional allies have been essential to that end over the more than 60 years since the end of World War II.

The Bush Doctrine's "coalition of the willing" was built in large part of smaller, poorer countries with little or no military power. Not bound by any formal alliance, many have dropped out of the conflict. This country has had to provided nearly all of the military power and nearly all of the money for the war in Iraq.

In contrast, the first Gulf War (in 1991) was a model of planning and cooperation. Dozens of countries, large and small, joined with the United States to free Kuwait. And other countries paid more than 80 percent of the costs of that conflict.

In the wake of 9/11, America did have a golden opportunity, yes—to unite the world in a war for freedom and security. The Bush Doctrine has, instead, upset many countries once counted among our close allies in this interdependent world. Those divisions must be healed, and soon.

Exploring the Issues

1. Critical Thinking What is the difference between a "coalition of the willing" and an alliance?

2. Critical Thinking How did 9/11 influence U.S. foreign policy?

For more information about foreign policy debates, view "Foreign Policy."

4 *World Democracies Today*

Section Preview

OBJECTIVES

1. **Examine** the elements of Britain's parliamentary democracy.
2. **Describe** regional and local government in Britain.
3. **Analyze** national politics in Mexico.

WHY IT MATTERS

Democracies take many different forms. Britain and Mexico illustrate two different approaches to democratic government.

POLITICAL DICTIONARY

★ **coalition**
★ **minister**
★ **shadow cabinet**
★ **devolution**
★ **North American Free Trade Agreement (NAFTA)**

A majority of the states in the world today are democratic. Each of them has, however, developed its own set of distinctive institutions. Great Britain and Mexico present contrasting approaches to democratic government.

Great Britain

Like the United States, Great Britain is a democracy. Indeed, the roots of American government are buried deep in English political and social history. Yet there are important differences between the two systems of government. Unlike government in the United States, government in Great Britain is unitary and parliamentary in form and rests upon an unwritten constitution.

The British constitution is not entirely unwritten. Parts of the constitution can be found in books and charters. However, no single document serves as the British constitution. The written part includes historic charters, acts of Parliament, and innumerable court decisions. The unwritten part derives from customs and usages—practices that have gained acceptance over time. The written parts are called the law of the constitution, and the unwritten parts are called the conventions of the constitution.

The Constitution

Many historic documents figure in the written parts of Britain's constitution. Especially important are the Magna Carta of 1215 and the Bill of Rights of 1689. Certain acts of Parliament also form a basic part of the British constitution.

Finally, centuries of court decisions have created a body of legal rules covering nearly every aspect of human conduct. Such decisions make up the common law. The truly unwritten part of the British constitution consists of the customs and practices of British politics.

Great Britain

0   75   150 Mile
0   75   150 Kilometer

Shetland Islands

Orkney Islands

Hebrides

North

SCOTLAND

Atlantic Ocean

North Sea

NORTHERN IRELAND

IRELAND   Irish Sea

ENGLAND

WALES   London

Celtic Sea

English Channel

Interpreting Maps Britain's constitutional monarchy is based on a largely unwritten constitution. The Prime Minister is responsible to the House of commons and is the real head of government. **H-SS 12.9**

The Monarchy

Queen Elizabeth II has been Britain's monarch since 1952. In formal terms, all acts of the British government are performed in the name of the queen. However, the prime minister and other high officials exercise the real power of government. The queen appoints the prime minister (traditionally the leader of the majority party in the House of Commons), but her choice is subject to the approval of that house. She has no power to dismiss the prime minister or any other government official. She has no veto over acts of Parliament. In short, today's monarch reigns but does not rule.

The British Parliament

Parliament is the central institution of British government. It is bicameral, comprised of the House of Lords (the upper house) and the House of Commons (the lower house). Of the two, the House of Commons is by far the more powerful body.

House of Lords

Until recently, a majority of the members of the House of Lords were hereditary peers—persons who inherited noble titles. But the upper house underwent a dramatic change under the 1999 House of Lords Act. This act removed most of the hereditary peers, and filled their seats with peers appointed by a special commission.

The House of Lords holds limited legislative power. If they reject a bill passed by the House of Commons, the Commons only has to approve the bill a second time to make it a law. Some argue that this gives the lower house time to weigh political fallout from controversial actions.

In addition to its legislative role, the House of Lords performs an important judicial function. Its law lords serve as the final court of appeals in both civil and criminal cases in Britain's court system.

House of Commons

The House of Commons has 646 members, known as MPs—members of Parliament. They are elected from single-member districts (constituencies) of roughly equal population.

The majority party largely controls the work of the Commons. It chooses the prime minister and the cabinet (who together form "the government"), and introduces most measures. Its several committees are generalists; that is, a bill can be referred to any of its committees. All bills sent to committee must be reported to the floor, where a party-line vote generally follows the will of the government.

The Prime Minister

The prime minister, although formally appointed by the queen, is in fact responsible to the House of Commons. When a single party holds a majority in the House of Commons, as usually happens, that party's leader becomes prime minister. If no single party holds a majority, a **coalition** must be formed. A coalition is a temporary alliance of parties for the purpose of forming a government. Two or more parties must agree on a common choice for prime minister and on a joint slate of cabinet members.

There are no term limits on the post of prime minister. William Gladstone held the position four times from 1868–94. Once a member of the Conservative Party, he broke ranks to create the Liberal Party, and presided over voting

◀ The House of Commons meets in a small chamber within the Parliament building. Members of rival parties sit facing each other. *Critical Thinking How do the responsibilities of the House of Commons differ from the House of Lords?* H-SS 12.9

reforms that expanded the electorate. Winston Churchill was probably the most famous prime minister because of his leadership during WWII. Margaret Thatcher, Britain's first woman prime minister, governed from 1979 to 1990 and oversaw the denationalizing of many of Britain's coal, steel, and other basic industries. The current prime minister, Tony Blair, was first elected in 1997.

The Cabinet

The prime minister selects the members of the cabinet, or **ministers,** from the House of Commons, although a few may sit in the House of Lords. Collectively, the prime minister and the cabinet provide political leadership,both in making and carrying out public policy. Individually, cabinet ministers head the various executive departments, such as defense, treasury, or health.

The opposition parties appoint their own teams of potential cabinet members. Each of these opposition MPs watches, or shadows, one particular member of the cabinet. If an opposition party should succeed in gaining a majority, its so-called **shadow cabinet** would then be ready to run the government.

Calling Elections

In marked contrast to practice in this country, the British law does not set a fixed date for the holding of elections. Instead, it requires only that a general election—an election in which all the seats in the Commons are at stake—be held at least once every five years. If an MP dies or resigns, a special election, called a by-election, is held in that constituency to choose a replacement.

Customarily, the prime minister calls an election when the political climate favors the majority party. Occasionally, an election is triggered by quite different circumstances: When the government falls because it has lost the confidence (the support) of the House of Commons. If the

▲ *Law Lord* British law lords wear traditional dress. The House of Lords is the court of last resort in the British legal system.

government is defeated on some critical vote in the House of Commons, it loses the confidence of Parliament and the government falls. The prime minister must then ask the queen to dissolve Parliament (end its sessions) and call a new general election. The ability to change governments in this way means that a prime minister who becomes either ineffective or unpopular can be removed before his or her actions cause serious damage to the political system.

Political Parties

Two parties have dominated British politics in recent decades: The Conservative Party and the Labour Party. The Conservatives have long drawn support from middle- and upper-class Britons. They tend to favor private economic initiatives over government involvement in the nation's economic life. The Labour Party has regularly found most of its support among working-class voters. Labour tends to favor government involvement in the economic system and a more socially equal society. Historically, the party preached doctrinaire socialism, but under the leadership of Prime Minister Tony Blair, Labour has moderated its views. Most recently, the Liberal Democratic Party has emerged as an alternative that blends left-wing and moderate views without the Labour Party's ties to unions.

British parties are more highly organized and centrally directed than the major parties in American politics. High levels of party loyalty and party discipline characterize the British party system. Voters regularly select candidates for the House of Commons on the basis of their party labels, not their individual qualifications.

Regional and Local Government

Great Britain has a unitary government. There is no constitutional division of powers between the national government and regional or local governments, as in the American federal system.

All power belongs to the central government. To whatever extent these governments deliver services or do anything else, they can do so only because the central government has created them, given them powers, and financed them.

Regional Government

Great Britain is composed of four separate nations with different histories, cultures, and traditions. In order to provide for the distinctive governmental needs of the people of Scotland, Wales, and Northern Ireland, the Britain has recently undergone a process of **devolution**—the delegation of authority from the central government to regional governments.

Although Parliament has assigned many responsibilities to the devolved bodies, it has reserved for itself the exclusive power to legislate on several matters that affect the whole of the United Kingdom (UK). These include defense, foreign policy, and macroeconomic policy. The British Parliament also continues to legislate more broadly for England, which does not have a devolved assembly.

Local Government

Local government bodies have been a feature of the British political landscape for much longer than have the recently established regional assemblies. Today, there are some 470 local authorities of varying types in the UK. Much as in the United States, local government in the United Kingdom perform a broad range of functions, from running local schools and libraries to collecting trash and maintaining roads.

The Courts

The UK has three separate court systems—one in England and Wales, one in Northern Ireland, and one in Scotland. In England and Wales, most civil cases are tried in county courts. Serious (indictable) criminal cases are tired in the Crown Court, and less serious criminal cases in the magistrates' courts.

Judges and juries try the more serious criminal cases in the Crown Court, while judges or magistrates alone hear the majority of civil disputes and less serious criminal cases. The House of Lords serves as the final court of appeal in a hierarchy of appellate courts. The court system

in Northern Ireland is similar to the system in England and Wales, but the Scottish system is simpler, with fewer hierarchical layers.

Courts in the United Kingdom decide cases based primarily on parliamentary legislation and common law, or on the standards established by judicial precedent. They are not bound to uphold a constitution or bill of rights that stands higher than parliamentary law. Unlike the United States, the courts and judges in the UK, including the law lords, do not possess the power of judicial review. They can never overrule Parliament.

Mexico

Mexico has a political system similar in form to the United States. In operation, however, it is the product of a unique combination of Mexico's history and the cultural makeup of its people.

Three Branches of Government

Mexico's Constitution of 1917 establishes a national government with three independent branches. The executive branch is headed by the president, the legislature is bicameral, and the judiciary in an independent entity. While this may sound like the US political system, perhaps the greatest distinction is the greater strength of the presidency in the Mexican system.

The president of Mexico is popularly elected and serves a single six-year term. The one-term limit is intended to prevent a popular leader from becoming a dictator by winning several reelections.

The president selects the members of the council of ministers (the cabinet) and other top civilian officers of government. He also appoints the senior officers of the armed forces and all federal judges.

In addition to the power usually held by a nation's chief executive, Mexico's president has the power to propose amendments to the constitution. Those amendments must be ratified at both the national and state levels, by a two-thirds vote in each house of Congress, and by a majority (at least 16) of state legislatures. The president also has power to enact laws through executive decree on certain economic issues.

The national legislature, called the General Congress, is composed of the Senate and the

Chamber of Deputies. There are 64 senators, two from each of the 31 Mexican states and two from the Federal District, which includes Mexico City. Senators are elected to six-year terms. Half are elected at the time of the presidential election and half at a mid-term election three years later.

The Chamber's 500 members are elected to three-year terms and cannot be reelected. Three hundred are directly elected from districts of over 300,000 people. The other seats are filled from the ranks of the various political parties, based on their share of the total vote in the national election. Thus, the Chamber is elected in a mixed system of direct and proportional representation.

The Congress meets from September 1 to December 31 each year. The combination of term limits and a short session work to give the General Congress a far less significant role than that played by the Congress in the United States. Moreover, a lack of resources limits the ability of the Mexican Congress to exercise its powers. Its committees are poorly funded and understaffed, which also contributes to the dominant position of the presidency in the governmental system.

The Court System

Mexico's independent judicial system is very similar to that of the United States. But one difference of note is that in most criminal cases trial is by judge, rather than by jury. Two systems of courts—state and federal—operate within the Mexican federal system. Each has its own jurisdiction.

The federal judiciary is built of district and circuit courts that function under the Supreme Court. These tribunals hear all cases that arise under federal law, including those that raise constitutional issues. The 31 separate state court systems are composed of trial and appellate courts. They hear civil and criminal cases in a structure headed by a state Supreme Court of Justice.

National Politics in Mexico

Mexico has a multi-party system. However, it was dominated for decades by the PRI, which won every presidential election from 1929 until the presidential election of 2000. In fact,

Mexico

Interpreting Maps In the federal republic of Mexico, the president is both chief of state and head of government. *How did the PRI maintain control of the government of Mexico for more than 70 years?* H-SS 12.9.5

because the PRI retained its position through patronage and opposition movements were often repressed, Mexico was not generally considered to be democratic until 2000.

The PRI

The PRI's dominant role was seriously threatened in the 1980s. The government had borrowed heavily from foreign lenders during the 1970s, expecting that oil prices would remain at their then-high levels. When oil prices declined sharply worldwide, the country plunged into economic chaos. Debt problems led to severe cutbacks in government programs, and undermined the PRI's patronage system. Prices soared and investment capital fled the country.

The political consequences of that economic calamity were apparent in the elections of 1988, when the PRI made its worst showing ever. The party barely maintained control of government as presidential candidate Carlos Salinas de Gortari won. Allegations of fraud were widespread.

President Salinas pursued broad-based economic, social, and electoral reforms. He also backed the **North American Free Trade Agreement (NAFTA)**. This agreement, promoted by the United States, removed trade and investment restrictions among the United States, Canada, and Mexico. In the 1994 national elections, the

▲ **National Palace, Mexico City** Built on the site where the Aztec emperor Montezuma's palace once stood, the National Palace houses the presidential and other executive offices of Mexican government.

PRI's presidential candidate, Ernesto Zedillo, won 48.8 percent of the total vote, and the PRI kept control of the legislature.

The 2000 Election

By 2000 the PRI faced what only a few years earlier had seemed a complete impossibility: the loss of the presidency. Over recent years, candidates from the conservative National Action Party (PAN) and leftist Democratic Revolutionary Party (PRD) had won increasing numbers of federal, state, and local offices. Now both parties took dead aim at the nation's highest office.

Public opinion, and world attention, forced the PRI to guarantee a fraud-free presidential contest in 2000. When all the votes had been counted, the PAN candidate, Vicente Fox, won

with 45% of the vote. President Fox was inaugurated on December 1, 2000. Lacking a majority in the General Congress, he and his party have always had to work with the PRI and PRD.

Fox initially held approval ratings of over 70%, but has since seen those ratings dip below 50%. President Fox may be a victim of unmet, or even unrealistic expectations. His political rise marked a dramatic event in Mexican politics, but for many Mexicans, their socioeconomic conditions did not improve under his tenure. As a sign of the growing discontent, the PRI may be making a resurgence. Off-year elections allowed it to shore up its majority in the Senate, and to almost gain a majority in the Chamber of Deputies. Moreover, the PRI now lays claim to the most popular politician in the country, Mexico City governor Andrés Manuel López Obrador. He is expected to be the PRI candidate in the 2006 presidential elections.

Regional and Local Government

Mexico is divided into 31 states and one Federal District. The Federal District includes Mexico City and is administered by a governor appointed by the president. Each of the 31 state constitutions provide for a governor, and unicameral legislature, and state courts. Each governor is elected to a six-year term. Legislators hold three-year terms. The governors appoint judges. The states have the power to legislate on local matters and to levy taxes, but most of their funding comes from the national level.

Section 4 Assessment

Key Terms and Main Ideas

1. Under what circumstances would a **coalition** government be formed in Britain?
2. In what major ways are the three branches of Mexican government similar to those in the United States?
3. What is the significance of the **North American Free Trade Agreement (NAFTA)?**

Critical Thinking

4. **Making Comparisons** What are the major differences between the British Parliament and the U.S. Congress? Between the Prime Minister and the President?

Standards Monitoring Online

For: Self-quiz with vocabulary practice
Web Code: mqa-7224

5. **Drawing Inferences** Which do you think is preferable: the Mexican model, a single six-year presidential term, or the American model, a four-year term with the possibility of a second term? Explain your reasoning.
6. **Drawing Conclusions** How was the 2000 election a reflection of Mexican democracy?

For: An activity on Mexican government
Web Code: mqd-6223

A New China

Analysis Skills HR4, HI3

Premier Wen Jiabao of China rose to power in 2003 to help lead a nation undergoing dramatic change. Wen described China's challenges to Americans in a speech that combined free-market principles with the older revolutionary language of the Communist Party.

China and the United States are far apart, and they differ greatly in the level of economic development and cultural background. I hope my speech will help increase our mutual understanding.

In order to understand the true China—a changing society full of promises—it is necessary to get to know her yesterday, her today, and her tomorrow. . . .

From Confucius to Dr. Sun Yat-sen, the traditional Chinese culture presents many precious ideas and qualities, which are essentially populist and democratic. For example, they lay stress on the importance of kindness and love in human relations, on the interest of the community, on seeking harmony without uniformity and on the idea that the world is for all . . . . China today is a country in reform and opening-up and a rising power dedicated to peace . . . . A large population and underdevelopment are the two facts China has to face. . . .

For quite some time in the past, China had a structure of [a] highly-centralized planned economy. With deepening restructuring . . . there was gradual lifting of the former improper restrictions, visible and invisible, on people's freedom in choice of occupation, mobility, enterprise, investment, information, travel, faith, and lifestyles. This has brought extensive and profound changes never seen before in China's history. . . .

The tremendous wealth created by China in the past quarter of a century has not only enabled our

Premier Wen Jiabao

1.3 billion countrymen to meet their basic needs for food, clothing and shelter, and basically realize a well-off standard of living, but also contributed to world development.

The Chinese Government is committed to protecting (1) the fundamental rights of all workers and (2) the right to property, both public and private. . . . This has been explicitly provided for in China's law and put into practice. . . . China tomorrow will continue to be a major country that loves peace and has a great deal to look forward to. . . .

China has laid down her three-step strategy toward modernization. From now to 2020, China will complete the building of a well-off society in an all-round way. By 2049, the year the People's Republic will celebrate its [100th anniversary], we will have reached the level of a medium-developed country. We have no illusions, but believe that on our way forward we shall encounter many foreseeable and unpredictable difficulties and face all kinds of tough challenges.

Analyzing Primary Sources

1. What are Premier Wen's goals for China's future?
2. Why does Wen discuss China's history and culture when talking about its future?
3. Why do you think Wen spoke about peace when describing China to an American audience?

Political Dictionary

feudalism (p. 626), vassal (p. 626), monarch (p. 627), serf (p. 626), legitimacy (p. 628), mercantilism (p. 629), colonialism (p. 630), divine right of kings (p. 631), *encomienda* (p. 633), *hacienda* (p. 633), counter-revolutionary (p. 635), guerilla warfare (p. 635), fascism (p. 637), hardliner (p. 640), softliner (p. 640), democratic consolidation (p. 645), genocide (p. 645), failed state (p. 645), coalition (p. 648), minister (p. 649), shadow cabinet (p. 649), devolution (p. 650), North American Free Trade Agreement (NAFTA) (p. 651)

Standards Review

H-SS 12.3.4 Compare the relationship of government and civil society in constitutional democracies to the relationship of government and civil society in authoritarian and totalitarian regimes.

H-SS 12.9.1 Explain how the different philosophies and structures of feudalism, mercantilism, socialism, fascism, communism, monarchies, parliamentary systems, and constitutional liberal democracies influence economic policies, social welfare policies, and human rights practices.

H-SS 12.9.4 Describe for at least two countries the consequences of conditions that gave rise to tyrannies during certain periods (e.g., Italy, Japan, Haiti, Nigeria, Cambodia).

H-SS 12.9.5 Identify the forms of illegitimate power that twentieth-century African, Asian, and Latin American dictators used to gain and hold office and the conditions and interests that supported them.

H-SS 12.9.6 Identify the ideologies, causes, stages, and outcomes of major Mexican, Central American, and South American revolutions in the nineteenth and twentieth centuries.

H-SS 12.9.7 Describe the ideologies that give rise to Communism, methods of maintaining control, and the movements to overthrow such governments in Czechoslovakia, Hungary, and Poland, including the roles of individuals (e.g., Alexander Solzhenitsyn, Pope John Paul II, Lech Walesa, Vaclav Havel).

H-SS 12.9.8 Identify the successes of relatively new democracies in Africa, Asia, and Latin America and the ideas, leaders, and general societal conditions that have launched and sustained, or failed to sustain, them.

Practicing the Vocabulary

Matching *Choose a term from the list above that best matches each description.*

1. Attempted extermination of a national group
2. Belief that God grants kings the right to govern
3. Lord who pledged his loyalty to a more powerful lord
4. Agreement which removed trade restrictions among the United States, Canada, and Mexico
5. Fighting carried out by small groups in hit-and-run raids

Word Relationships *Distinguish between the words in each pair.*

6. *encomienda/hacienda*
7. mercantilism/colonialism
8. hardliner/softliner
9. monarch/serf
10. coalition/devolution

Reviewing Main Ideas

Section 1

11. **(a)** Why did the feudal system develop? **(b)** Why was feudalism only a "makeshift basis for governance"?
12. How did sovereignty change the way that European countries interacted with one another?
13. Describe mercantilism in your own words.
14. How did mercantilism lead European countries to the founding of colonies in the Americas and elsewhere?

Section 2

15. What are the benefits of Britain's way of changing its government to adopt popular sovereignty?
16. **(a)** Why were Latin American countries unable to found stable democracies when they gained their independence? **(b)** How did the role of *haciendas* change with independence from Spain?
17. Many countries gained their independence in the 1950s and 1960s. List the major problems these countries inherited from their colonial period.
18. How do fascist governments win power?

Section 3

19. Why are most transitions to democracy begun by leaders already inside the government?
20. Identify three different ways that individuals outside of the government can help encourage democratization.
21. Describe the difference between a democratic transition and democratic consolidation.

Section 4

22. In what ways does Great Britain's constitution differ from the United States Constitution?
23. How are Britain's prime minister and cabinet members chosen?
24. **(a)** What was the role of the PRI in the Mexican political system in the 1990s? **(b)** Who won the presidency in 2000?

Critical Thinking Skills

25. *Face the Issues* In 1821, John Quincy Adams declared that America "goes not abroad, in search of monsters to destroy." **(a)** Express Adams' views in your own words. **(b)** How might Adams feel about the Bush Doctrine? Explain.

26. *Making Decisions* Consider the conditions that led to the feudal system. Why is it unlikely that a modern democracy could have succeeded under those conditions?

27. *Making Comparisons* Following the overthrow of Saddam Hussein, the United States worked to establish a democratic government in Iraq. **(a)** In what ways might the United States contribute to democratic consolidation in Iraq? **(b)** Which parts of democratic consolidation would be most difficult for a foreign country, like the United States, to advance?

28. *Drawing Conclusions* Why can it be said that the Peace of Westphalia "marked the end of feudalism and the beginning of the modern nation-state system"?

Analyzing Political Cartoons

Using your knowledge of comparative government and this cartoon, answer the questions below.

29. Dragons have figured prominently in Chinese culture for centuries. What is the significance of the dragon in this cartoon?

30. To what political situation does the cartoon refer?

Participation Activities

31. *Current Events Watch* Choose one of the countries covered in this chapter. Scan magazines and newspapers for articles about recent political events in that country. Then prepare an oral update on your chosen country's government and politics to present to your classmates. Use charts, graphs, or copies of photos to accompany your update if you choose.

32. *Time Line Activity* Create a time line that traces the events in the former Soviet Union and Russia from 1985 to the present. Illustrate your time line with drawings and copies of newspaper and magazine photos.

33. *It's Your Turn* Interview a recent immigrant from one of the countries covered in the chapter or another country of your choice. Find out the ways (if any) that this person participated in politics there and how he or she views the government of that country today. Why did he or she come to the United States? How does he or she view government in the United States? Write up your interview and share it with the class. **(Conducting an Interview)**

★ Standards Monitoring *Online*

For: Chapter 22 Self-Test **Visit:** PHSchool.com
Web Code: mqa-7226

As a final review, take the Magruder's Chapter 22 Self-Test and receive immediate feedback on your answers.
The test consists of 20 multiple-choice questions designed to test your understanding of the chapter content.

CHAPTER 23

Comparative Economic Systems

"You do not like communism. We do not like capitalism. There is only one way out—peaceful coexistence."

—Nikita Khrushchev (1956)

Capitalism, socialism, and communism are the main types of economic systems, and they have often come into conflict. Which of those systems a nation follows has a major impact on its political system and many other aspects of people's lives. Many real-world economic systems include some elements of the other two types.

◆ Stock traders and runners on the floor of the Chicago Mercantile Exchange

SECTION 1

Capitalism (pp. 658–664)

★ Capitalism is another name for the free enterprise system.

★ Entrepreneurs use land, labor, brain power, and capital to produce goods and services.

★ Private ownership, individual initiative, profit, and competition are the fundamental elements of capitalism.

★ A mixed economy is one in which the government intervenes to promote and regulate the economy.

★ Businesses may be organized as sole proprietorships, partnerships, or corporations.

SECTION 2

Socialism (pp. 666–670)

★ In a socialist economy, the government strives for social and economic equality for all members of society.

★ Karl Marx (1818–1883) and his collaborator Friedrich Engels (1820–1895) laid out the basic tenets of modern-day socialism.

★ The British Labour Party and other "Social Democratic Parties" in Europe believe that the ends of socialism can be gained by peaceful, democratic means.

★ Socialist economies feature government ownership of industry, high taxes, and generous public welfare programs.

★ Although socialism began in industrial countries, many developing nations were attracted to socialism by the promise of equality and economic growth.

SECTION 3

Communism (pp. 672–676)

★ Karl Marx predicted that the final stage in human history would be a world of peaceful, democratic communes.

★ No country has ever created a political/economic system that even remotely resembles Marx's ideal.

★ Communist economies depend on a strong central government that owns all industry and farmland and plans all parts of the national economy.

★ In the Soviet Union, Lenin and Stalin created a communist dictatorship that controlled all aspects of life.

★ China, Cuba, North Korea, Vietnam, and other countries have also experimented with communism.

Go Online
PHSchool.com

For: Current Data
Web Code: mqg-6235

For: Close Up Foundation debates
Web Code: mqh-6237

1 Capitalism

Section Preview

OBJECTIVES

1. **Identify** the factors of production.
2. **Describe** the free enterprise system and laissez-faire theory.
3. **Analyze** the role of government in a mixed economy.
4. **Compare and contrast** three types of business organizations.
5. **Explain** the role of profit and loss in a free enterprise system.

WHY IT MATTERS

Although the American free enterprise system is rooted in classic laissez-faire theory, government plays a major role in the nation's economic life—and so in the economic life of every person in this country.

POLITICAL DICTIONARY

★ **factors of production**
★ **capital**
★ **capitalist**
★ **entrepreneur**
★ **free enterprise system**
★ **laws of supply and demand**
★ **monopoly**
★ **trust**
★ **laissez-faire theory**

You have confronted these questions several times in this book: What should a government have the power to do? What should it not be allowed to do? Certainly these questions can be asked of just about all areas of human activity, but they are raised very significantly in the realm of economic affairs.

Questions of politics and economics are inseparable. The most important economic questions faced by a nation are also political questions. For example: Who should decide what goods will be produced? How should goods and services be distributed and exchanged within a nation? What types of income or property ought to be taxed? What social services should a government provide?

Capitalism provides one response to all of these questions. Many aspects of capitalism will be familiar to you because the United States (along with countries such as Japan) follows this system.

Factors of Production

Certain resources are necessary to any nation's economy, no matter what economic system it follows. Economists call these basic resources, which are used to make all goods and services, the **factors of production.**

Land

One factor of production is land, which in economic terms includes all natural resources. Land has a variety of economic uses, such as agriculture, mining, and forestry. Along with farms and property, economists consider the water in rivers and lakes and the coal, iron, and petroleum found beneath the ground to be part of the land.

▲ In a capitalist system, prices are determined by decisions in the market.
H-SS 12.2.2

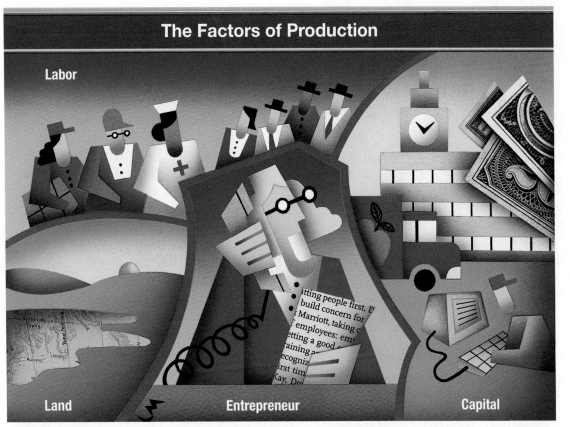

The Factors of Production

Labor

Land

Entrepreneur

Capital

Interpreting Diagrams Land, labor, and capital are the building blocks of the economy. An entrepreneur uses all three factors to create goods and offer services. *Give specific examples of land, labor, and capital involved in producing a jacket.* H-SS 12.9.1

Labor

A second factor of production is a human resource —labor. Men and women who work in mines, factories, offices, hospitals, and other places all provide labor that is an essential part of a nation's economy. In a free market economy, individuals "own" their labor and can sell it to any employer.

Capital

The third factor of production is **capital**—all the human-made resources that are used to produce goods and services. Physical capital (also called "capital goods") includes money, but it also describes the buildings, machines, and computers workers need to turn labor and land into goods and services. Human capital includes knowledge and skills that workers gain from their work experience—an investment in themselves. Note that capital is a product of the economy that is then put back, or reinvested, into the economy.

Someone who owns capital and puts it to productive use is called a **capitalist.** The term is most often applied to people who own large businesses or factories, but can apply to smaller investors as well. The United States economy is called capitalistic because it depends on the energy and drive of thousands of individual capitalists.

The Role of the Entrepreneur

To actually produce goods and services, someone must bring together and organize the factors of production. An **entrepreneur**—literally, an "enterpriser"—is an individual with the drive and ambition to combine land, labor, and capital resources to produce goods or offer services. Entrepreneurs start businesses and make them grow, driving the economic growth that contributes to the high standard of living of modern capitalistic societies.

Free Enterprise System

Capitalism is often called a **free enterprise system.** This is an economic system characterized by private or corporate ownership of capital goods (physical capital) and investments that

▲ **Renewal and Rebirth** In a free enterprise system, entrepreneurs try to put land, labor, and/or capital to the best possible (most profitable) use. Through this process, resources can be put to better use. These unused port buildings in New York City's South Street Seaport have reopened as shops.

are determined by private decision rather than by state control. This system operates in a free market.

A free enterprise system lets consumers, entrepreneurs, and workers enjoy freedom of choice. Consumers can choose from a variety of products and services. Entrepreneurs can switch from one business to another. Workers can quit their jobs and seek new ones.

There are four fundamental factors in a free enterprise system: private ownership, individual initiative, profit, and competition.

Private Ownership

One distinctive characteristic of capitalism is that private individuals and companies own most of the means of production—that is, the resources used to produce goods and services. They decide how this productive property will be used—for example, individuals may use capital to build a business or invest in technology. What the property produces is theirs, as well. The owners of productive property are sometimes individuals, but often are groups of people who share ownership of a company.

In a free enterprise system, individuals also own the right to their labor. Individuals sell their labor by taking a job, and the pay they receive represents the price of their work. In other economic systems, workers may have little choice about what kinds of work they will do and little opportunity to change jobs.

Along with private ownership, the protection of people's property rights is also important. The 5th and 14th amendments to the Constitution declare that no person may be deprived "of life, liberty, or property, without due process of law." The 5th amendment also says that "just compensation" must be paid to owners when private property is taken for public use.

Individual Initiative

In our economy, entrepreneurs are an essential factor in the production of goods and services. Under a free enterprise system, all individuals are free to start and run their own businesses (their own enterprises). They are also free to dissolve those businesses.

That is not necessarily true in other kinds of economic systems. In some places, government officials and public planners make economic decisions about what to produce and how to produce it. There, centralized decision making, not individual initiative, controls the production and distribution of goods and services.

Profit

Just as individuals are free to choose how they will spend or invest their capital under a free enterprise system, they are also entitled to benefit from whatever their investment or enterprise earns or gains in value. The "profit motive" is the desire to gain from business dealings. It is one reason that entrepreneurs are willing to take risks.

Competition

The freedom to enter or start a new business at any time leads to competition. Competition is a situation in which a number of companies offer the same product or service. They then must compete against one another for customers. In a free enterprise system, competition often helps to hold down prices and keep quality high. This is because customers are likely to buy from the company with the best product at the lowest price. Competition thus promotes efficiency; the producer has the incentive (more sales) to keep costs low.

Under competitive conditions, the laws of supply and demand determine prices. Supply is the quantity of goods or services for sale. Demand is the desire of potential buyers for those goods and services. According to the **laws of supply and demand,** when supplies become more plentiful, prices tend to drop. As supplies become scarcer, prices tend to rise. By the same token, if demand drops (that is, if there are fewer buyers), sellers will probably lower their prices in order to make a sale. If demand rises, sellers can raise prices.

Competition does not always work smoothly. Sometimes a single business becomes so successful that all of its rivals go out of business. A firm that is the only source of a product or service is called a **monopoly.** Monopolies can be very powerful in the marketplace. Practically speaking, they can charge as much as they want for a product. Since there is no other supplier of that good or service, the consumer must pay the monopoly price or do without.

Political leaders in the United States decided late in the nineteenth century that monopolies were dangerous. American leaders were especially concerned about a type of monopoly called a **trust**. A trust is a device by which several corporations in the same line of business combine to eliminate competition and regulate prices. By the latter part of the nineteenth century, trusts had gained tight-fisted control over the markets for petroleum, steel, coal, beef, sugar, and a number of other commodities.

In response, Congress passed the Sherman Anti-Trust Act of 1890, which remains the basic law against monopolies today. It prohibits "every contract, combination in the form of a trust or otherwise, or conspiracy in restraint of trade or commerce among the several States, or with foreign nations."

The Anti-Trust Division in the Department of Justice watches business activities to determine whether competition within an industry is threatened. It can, for example, stop the sale or merger of a company if that move threatens competition in a particular market. On rare occasions, the Department has acted to break up a monopoly and restore competition. Thus, in 1911, it won an historic Supreme Court case—*Standard Oil of New Jersey* v. *United States.* The Court's decision dissolved John D. Rockefeller's Standard Oil Trust and, with it, his near-complete control of the petroleum industry. Similarly, it waged a 13-year court battle that forced the break-up of American Telephone & Telegraph (AT&T) in 1982 and so spurred rigorous competition in the long-distance phone market.

In 2000, a federal district court agreed with the Department that Microsoft Corporation had violated the Sherman Anti-Trust Act in its efforts to control the new market for its browser. The trial court ordered that the computer giant be split into at least two competing companies. Microsoft appealed that ruling and, in 2001, it both won and lost in the Court of Appeals for the District of Columbia. The appellate court found that Microsoft had violated the Anti-Trust Act; at the same time, however, it reversed the lower court's break-up order. Following that decision, Microsoft and the Justice Department negotiated a settlement of the government's complaints about the company's business practices.

Laissez-Faire Theory

Early capitalist philosophers believed that, if only government did not interfere, the free enterprise system could work automatically. Adam Smith presented the classic expression of that view in his book, *The Wealth of Nations,* in 1776. Smith wrote that when all individuals are free to pursue their own private interests, an "invisible hand"

Interpreting Political Cartoons The Federal Government sued Microsoft Corporation in the 1990s to restore competition to the software industry. *How does the absence of competition hurt consumers?*

Sadako Ogata of Japan headed the United Nations High Commission for Refugees (UNHCR) from 1991 to 2000. This agency works to help the thousands of people uprooted by political and economic conflicts around the world. Ogata sees a direct link between the living conditions of the world's individual communities and the welfare of the global community as a whole.

❝It is essential that political leaders and the civil society in developed countries—including in the United States—be visionary enough to provide support to social and economic reconstruction and to the reconciliation between divided communities, even in countries and regions which are of less immediate strategic interest to them. Only by putting an end to the recurrence of conflicts, and of refugee flows everywhere, will global security be ensured.❞

Evaluating the Quotation

How might the plight of refugees in some distant land be disruptive to the peace and security of powerful nations like the United States? Do you agree with Ogata that developed nations should help other countries in need? Why or why not?

works to promote the general welfare. In short, Smith preached laissez-faire capitalism.[1]

Laissez-faire theory holds that government should play a very limited, hands-off role in society. Governmental activity should be confined to: (1) foreign relations and national defense, (2) the maintenance of police and courts to protect private property and the health, safety, and morals of the people, and (3) those few other functions that cannot be performed by private enterprise at a profit. The proper role of government in economic affairs should be restricted to functions intended to promote and protect the free play of competition and the operation of the laws of supply and demand.

Laissez-faire capitalism has never in fact operated in this country. Nevertheless, the concept

---

[1]The term *laissez-faire* comes from a French idiom meaning "to let alone."

had, and still has, a profound effect on the structure of the American economic system.

A Mixed Economy

Although the American economic system is essentially private in character, government has always played a large part in it. Economists usually describe an economy in which private enterprise and governmental participation coexist as a mixed economy.

Governments at every level regulate many aspects of American economic life. For example, the government prohibits trusts, protects the environment, and ensures the quality of food.

In addition, government promotes many aspects of American economic life. For example, the government constructs public roads and highways, provides such services as the postal system, the census, and weather reports, operates the Social Security system and other insurance programs, and offers many kinds of subsidies and loan programs that help entrepreneurs and businesses to prosper.

Government also conducts some enterprises that might well be operated privately—for example, public education, the postal system, and municipal water and power systems. And it has assumed some functions that have proved unprofitable to private enterprise—for example, many local transit systems and recycling projects. This latter process is sometimes called "ash-can socialism."

Mixed economies are common in Europe and in former communist countries. In Britain, the government provides free medical care to all. The government of the People's Republic of China owns steel mills and factories. Germany's federal government requires large companies to give workers representation on managing boards and France forbids most companies from asking employees to work more than 35 hours a week. In each of these mixed economies, government intervention co-exists with independent companies and market forces.

Types of Business Organizations

The United States economy contains a number of gigantic companies with thousands of employees and with factories or offices all over the world.

▲ An American firm can organize as a sole proprietorship (left), a partnership (center), or a corporation (right). As a company grows and leaders take on new responsibilities, the company may change from one form to another. *Critical Thinking* **Why is a large manufacturer like Ford unlikely to succeed as a sole proprietorship?**

Still, most businesses in the United States are relatively small. Some 80 percent of businesses employ fewer than 20 people.

There are three basic types of business organizations: sole proprietorships, partnerships, and corporations. Each has advantages and disadvantages.

Sole Proprietorships

Businesses owned by a single individual are sole proprietorships. Typical of businesses in this category might be a hair salon, a garage, or an ice cream shop. Three quarters of businesses in the United States are sole proprietorships. However, because most sole proprietorships are small, they produce only a small fraction of annual sales in the United States.

Sole proprietorships are the most flexible form of business organization. A major advantage of sole proprietorships is that the single owner can make decisions quickly. The owner enjoys full control of the company, and can draw a salary or close the business without needing the approval of others. A major disadvantage is that the owner is personally liable for debts the business might build up. Sole proprietorships

are also limited by the owner's ability to contribute resources and manage the business.

Partnerships

Businesses owned by two or more individuals, called partners, are partnerships. Lawyers and architects are some professionals who often work in partnerships.

An advantage of a partnership is that it can draw on the resources of more than one person for capital to start or expand the business. Different people bring different strengths and perspectives to a business, and a partnership can provide the best framework for entrepreneurs to use their skills to create a small business. A disadvantage is that these differences can also lead to conflict among partners. In addition, partnerships may end if one partner leaves or dies.

Corporations

Corporations include both small companies and large national firms that people encounter every day. Unlike partnerships, corporations have many owners, called shareholders. A share is a fraction of ownership in the corporation. A corporation can continue indefinitely because a shareholder's

Intel's Revenue Will Miss Expectations

News Triggers Tech Sell-Off And Raises Uncertainty About Demand for PCs

By MOLLY WILLIAMS

CMGI Posts Loss Of $633.7 Million On Market Fizzle

By WILLIAM M. BULK

ING & MEDIA

Dial Is Considering Sale of Company; Profit to Fall Short

By EDUARDO PORTER

▲ Financial losses are an unavoidable element of the free market system.

death does not affect the legal status of the corporation. In other words, the corporation exists as its own legal entity, independent from the existence of any stockholders. Under the Supreme Court's interpretation of the 14th Amendment, a corporation enjoys the same legal status as a person.

Corporations can draw their capital from hundreds and even thousands of investors. This enables them to finance such costly projects as putting an earth satellite in orbit or building an oil pipeline. Shareholders are responsible only for the amount of money they have invested. If the business fails, they can lose that amount, but no more. Shareholders have limited liability and are not held responsible for any debts the corporation might have.

One disadvantage of corporations is that their income is taxed twice. First, the corporation pays a tax on its profits. Then, individual shareholders pay a tax on the dividends they are paid.

Profit and Loss

What drives the capitalist economy? The best answer, most often, is profit.

To understand what profit is, you must first understand the idea of investment. An investment is a sum of money, or capital, that is put into a business enterprise. For example, if you buy a car to start a business delivering groceries, what you pay for the car is an investment.

The profit will be the amount of money you earn from the business, after you have subtracted the costs associated with earning that money—in this case, the purchase of the car and the costs of operating it, plus whatever you pay yourself. If earnings are less than the costs, the business has not made a profit; instead, it has taken a loss.

Taking risks and making investments, therefore, are an essential part of the capitalist system. Every year, many businesses fail for lack of profit. Businesses that survive tend to be those that have learned to make the most efficient use of the factors of production.

Section 1 Assessment

Key Terms and Main Ideas

1. What is the difference between physical and human **capital?**
2. Why are **entrepreneurs** important to a **free enterprise system?**
3. How many companies control a market in a **monopoly?**
4. What is the proper role of government according to **laissez-faire theory?**

Critical Thinking

5. **Making Comparisons** Of the factors of production, which do you believe is the most difficult to measure? Why?

Standards Monitoring *Online*
For: Self-quiz with vocabulary practice
Web Code: mqa-6231

6. **Drawing Conclusions** Identify two arguments that can be made for and two against government participation in a free enterprise economy.

Go Online
PHSchool.com
For: An activity on the Economic Freedom Index
Web Code: mqd-6231

Face the
Issues

The Minimum Wage

Background *Currently, the federal minimum wage is set at $5.15 an hour. Only some seven million persons are actually paid that meager amount today. Several million more hold jobs that do not pay much more than that, however. The federal minimum wage does not increase automatically to keep pace with the cost of living. Instead, Congress must act to raise the minimum wage, and it has not done so since 1997.*

Retail workers hold many minimum-wage jobs

Analysis Skill HI6

Raise the Minimum Wage

Inflation has robbed the current minimum wage of a significant share of its value. If that wage had kept pace with the cost of living since 1997, it would now be set at about $6.35 an hour. Raising the minimum wage would greatly help the poorest households. And an increase would ripple through the workforce, benefiting not only minimum-wage workers, but millions more who are paid at only slightly higher rates.

The benefits of higher wages far outweigh the cost of jobs that might be lost. Some recent studies show that higher wages may actually boost employment, if only slightly. Many economists now reject the view that minimum wage hikes have an adverse effect on the rate of employment.

Raising the minimum wage would stimulate the economy, because most low-income workers spend, immediately, any extra money they receive. Any State can set a minimum wage above that established by Congress. Twelve now do so, and the amounts range from $6.15 an hour in Delaware to $7.35 (adjusted annually for inflation) in the State of Washington.

Let the Market Decide

The market is the best mechanism for setting wage levels. In a free market economy, employers pay workers based on the value of their work. Minimum wage laws force some employers to pay people more than their work is actually worth. Sometimes, when employers must pay out more in wages, they must cut jobs to make ends meet.

Raising the minimum wage could mean fewer jobs for those who are most in need. Teenagers who earn low wages really need the training and the experience offered by entry-level jobs more than they need a higher wage.

Less than a majority of lowest income workers now hold full-time jobs. So, raising the minimum wage would have little impact on poverty. The wage hikes would go to workers with family incomes above the poverty level.

Minimum wage laws provide for what amounts to "a one-size-fits-all" approach. Workers should have the freedom to negotiate with their employers.

Exploring the Issues

1. Suppose a fast-food restaurant has to increase workers' pay from $8 an hour to $12.50. How might the manager respond to the hike in labor costs?

2. Why do you think several States now set a higher minimum wage than that required by federal law?

For more information about the minimum wage, view "The Minimum Wage."

Face the
Issues
Video Collection

·2· *Socialism*

OBJECTIVES

1. **Define** socialism and explain how its growth was spurred by the Industrial Revolution.
2. **Identify** important characteristics of socialist economies.
3. **Describe** socialism in developing countries.
4. **Evaluate** the pros and cons of socialism.

WHY IT MATTERS

Industrial countries in Western Europe and agricultural countries around the world have developed socialist economies. In these countries, the government plays a major role in managing the economy and protecting the rights and benefits of individual workers.

POLITICAL DICTIONARY

★ **socialism**
★ **proletariat**
★ **bourgeoisie**
★ **welfare state**
★ **market economy**
★ **centrally planned economy**

You know that in the United States all people are entitled to equal protection under the law. Political equality, of course, is not the same as economic equality. The capitalistic system of the United States enables some to achieve greater financial rewards than others. One economic system, socialism, does seek to distribute wealth equitably throughout society, however.

▶ Britain's Labour Party won control of the government of the UK in the parliamentary elections of 1997. It has remained in power since then by winning the elections held in 2001 and 2005. The Labour Party created a universal health care system and took over key industries when it governed Britain in the late 1940s.
H-SS 12.9.1

What Is Socialism?

Socialism is an economic and political philosophy based on the idea that the benefits of economic activity—wealth—should be equitably distributed throughout a society. This fairness is achieved through the principle of collective (that is, public) ownership of the most important means by which goods and services are produced and distributed. Socialist nations are often democratic; still, they must rely on centralized planning to achieve their goals.

Socialists reject the strong emphasis on individualism and competition for profit that lie at the heart of capitalistic thought and practice. Instead, they emphasize cooperation and social responsibility as ways to achieve a more equitable distribution of both income and opportunity, thus reducing great differences between rich and poor. Real equality, they say, requires that political equality and economic equality go hand in hand. Economic equality can come only when the public controls the centers of economic power.

The roots of socialism lie deep in history. Almost from the beginning there have been those who have dreamed of a society built on socialist doctrine. Most earlier socialists foresaw a collective economy that would arise out of, and then be managed by, voluntary private action, without government action. Thus early socialist doctrine is often called "private socialism."

The Industrial Revolution

Much of present-day socialism was born in the 19th century. It developed out of the Industrial Revolution—the great social changes that swept western nations as they moved from an agricultural to an industrial economy.

The Industrial Revolution was well under way in Great Britain by the late eighteenth century and spread through Western Europe and to the United States in the nineteenth century. Cities expanded rapidly, and large factories replaced smaller, home-based industry.

Many observers of nineteenth-century British factories and cities were appalled by the conditions they found. Men and women often worked 14- to 16-hour days in filthy, noisy, and unsafe conditions for low pay. Small children regularly worked alongside their parents, for even less pay. Most factory workers and their families lived in dank, crowded, and unhealthful slums.

These conditions led many to seek social and economic reforms. Some argued for much more radical change.

Karl Marx

Karl Marx (1818–1883), the father of modern-day socialism, was the most significant critic of capitalism to emerge in the nineteenth century. Much of his work and most of his extensive writings were done in collaboration with Friedrich Engels (1820–1895).

In 1848, Marx and Engels wrote *The Communist Manifesto,* "to do for history," Engels later said, "what Darwin's theory has done for biology." This political document condemned the miseries caused by the Industrial Revolution. It called upon oppressed workers across Europe to free themselves from "capitalist enslavement."

Marx believed that capitalism was fatally flawed. The **proletariat**—the workers—were being so badly abused by the **bourgeoisie**—the capitalists—that they were certain to rise up and overthrow the capitalistic system. The pamphlet ended with this rallying cry:

Sources **❝***The proletarians have nothing to lose but their chains. They have a world to win. Workingmen of all countries, unite!* **❞**

—Friedrich Engels and Karl Marx
The Communist Manifesto

▲ Thousands left the British countryside in the 1800s to live and work in dirty, overcrowded cities like Newcastle (above). Their experiences inspired Karl Marx (right) and Friedrich Engels to write of a new "working class." *Critical Thinking According to Marx, how would workers eventually react to their working conditions?*

Socialists and Communists

A powerful socialist movement took shape among European workers and thinkers during the middle and late nineteenth century. Almost all socialists accepted Marx's criticism of capitalism. The movement was deeply split, however, by the question of how best to achieve socialism. Some argued that a socialist society could come only out of a "violent and bloody revolution." Over time, those who took that view came to be called communists.

Others argued that socialism could be attained by peaceful means through the democratic process. Today, the terms *socialism* and *socialist* are usually used to identify those evolutionary socialists.

The British Labour Party and the major "social democratic" parties in Europe are leading examples of that brand of socialism. At various times in recent history, those parties have controlled their governments and have instituted many socialist programs through democratic means. In the 1997 elections, however, Labour Party leaders deliberately chose to follow a "third way," moving away from socialism. Socialist parties in France and Germany have also reconsidered some of the socialist objectives that have become too expensive to maintain.

Characteristics of Socialist Economies

Countries with a socialist government typically enact one or more of these public policies to achieve the aims of socialism: nationalization, broadening of public services, high taxation, and a centrally planned economy.

Nationalization

Placing enterprises under governmental control, often by taking over privately owned industries, is called nationalization. In the last chapter you read about the nationalization of the oil industry in Mexico in the 1930s. In a democratic country such as Britain, a government may nationalize an enterprise and pay the former owners what it considers a fair price. Often, however, governments have nationalized industries without paying any compensation.

Nationalization under socialism rarely includes all businesses in a country. Socialist governments usually want to control certain sectors

▲ The French government owns most of that country's largest airline, Air France. *Critical Thinking As voters, what power do workers in nationalized companies have over their employer?* H-SS 12.2.2

with many workers and a few dominant firms, such as utilities, transportation, and steel. They allow many smaller companies to remain in private hands. Also, the government may want industries that are based on newly emerging technologies to remain private. This is because individual initiative and entrepreneurial risk-taking are so important during the early phases of a business.

A goal of many socialist governments is to give each company's workers a say in deciding how the company is run. Sweden's Social Democratic Party, for example, has a plan for gradually transferring ownership of private companies to their workers. Elected worker representatives now sit on many companies' boards of directors.

Public Welfare

Socialists place great importance on assuring that everyone in a society is decently housed and fed. Stated another way, socialists aim to guarantee the public welfare by providing for the equal distribution of necessities and services—including retirement pensions, inexpensive health care, free university education, and housing for the poor.

Countries that provide extensive social services at little or no cost to the users are often called **welfare states.** In such countries, medical and dental services may be provided free or for a small charge. People who lose their jobs or who are physically unable to work receive government payments that are nearly as high as their former wages. All people above retirement age receive government pensions. Parents may receive government payments for each child until the child reaches the age of 18. Workers in Europe receive paid maternity leave and several weeks of paid vacation each year—benefits rarely matched in other countries.

Taxation

All governments in capitalist and socialist states get their funds from taxation. Because social welfare services are quite expensive, however, taxes in socialist countries tend to be high. Taxes may take 50 or 60 percent of an individual's total income.

Socialists tend to place most of the burden on the upper and middle classes, consistent with their philosophy of achieving a more equal distribution of wealth. Tax rates can amount to 90 percent of a wealthy person's income.

Centrally Planned Economy

Economies can be divided into several categories, depending on how basic economic decisions are made. Under capitalism, key decisions are made by thousands of private individuals and companies through the give and take of the marketplace. For that reason, a capitalist economy is also called a **market economy.**

Under socialism, economic decision making is more centralized. In a **centrally planned economy,** government bureaucrats plan how an economy will develop over a period of years. They set targets for production and direct investment into specific industries. Because the government, to varying degrees, controls the economy, this is also called a "command economy."

A democratic socialist country may or may not have strict central planning. Market conditions and private businesses are likely to play a role as well as government planning. With a few exceptions, most modern economies are such mixed economies.

Socialism in Developing Countries

Socialism has won a large following in developing countries. There, public ownership and centralized planning are common.

One reason for socialism's appeal is that most developing countries are starting from scratch at building industry. They have no tradition of locally controlled, large-scale industry. Large existing industries are often owned by foreign companies. By nationalizing a foreign-owned company and placing local people in charge, a political leader can win broad public support.

Socialism also appeals to leaders who want to mobilize an entire nation behind a program of industrial growth. Through central planning, leaders can channel investment into the parts of the economy they think are most essential.

Often, however, guided growth of this sort requires painful sacrifices by a nation's people. High taxes skim off a large part of people's income. The government may devote so much attention to one or two basic industries that the

production of food or consumer goods may be neglected. Then public unrest may develop.

Political instability is a persistent problem in developing nations. In such nations, this instability is one reason that socialist and other governments often turn to authoritarian methods. Few developing nations have succeeded in establishing the democratic versions of socialism found in parts of the industrial world.

Pros and Cons

Both capitalistic and socialistic economies have their strengths and weaknesses. For supporters of capitalism, it is easy to see weaknesses in the theory and practice of socialism. For supporters of socialism, on the other hand, capitalism seems filled with faults.

Critics say socialist countries have a tendency to develop too many layers of bureaucracy. They say this complicates decision making and has a

Unemployment in Selected Countries, 1995–2005

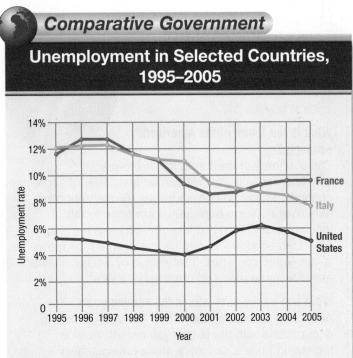

SOURCE: *OECD Quarterly Labour Force Statistics*

Interpreting Graphs Compared to Americans, workers in France and Italy enjoy more vacation days, less expensive health care, and greater legal protection against losing their jobs. One unintended result is that companies hire fewer new workers to avoid paying the high cost of these benefits. ***Although France, Italy, and the United States all enjoyed strong economic growth in the 1990s, how did unemployment rates respond differently in these three countries?***

unpredictable events are involved, and too many clashing interests are at stake. For all its faults, they argue, the invisible hand of the market economy works more efficiently than the visible hand of central planning.

Another criticism is that socialism deprives people of the freedom to decide for themselves how to use their income. Since workers get to keep only a part of their earnings after taxes, they have little incentive to work harder and earn more. Why work hard when your basic needs will be taken care of anyway?

In response, socialists reply that it is fairer to supply everyone with basic needs, such as medical care. They point to the inequalities of wealth and power that exist under capitalism. Socialists argue that socialism is morally superior to capitalism because it evens out inequalities. In their view, socialism makes political democracy work more smoothly by supplementing it with economic democracy.

Defenders of socialism also argue that it gives workers and ordinary citizens more control over their daily lives. Under capitalism, they say, a company's management can abruptly decide to close an unprofitable factory. The company has no obligation to ask its workers' opinions, even though such a decision can throw thousands out of work and disrupt an entire community. This could not happen under socialism, the argument goes. Workers and community leaders would sit on the company's board. They would help decide what was best for the entire work force and community—not just for the company's investors and shareholders.

deadening effect on individual initiative. As a result, critics say, socialist economies are slower to take advantage of new technologies.

In the eyes of socialism's critics, the smooth running of an economy is too complex to be directed by central planners. Too many

Section 2 Assessment

Standards Monitoring *Online*

For: Self-quiz with vocabulary practice
Web Code: mqa-6232

Key Terms and Main Ideas

1. Who is considered the father of **socialism**?
2. According to socialist theory, what is the relationship between the **proletariat** and the **bourgeoisie**?
3. Describe a **welfare state** in your own words.
4. What role does the government play in a **centrally planned economy**?

Critical Thinking

5. **Making Comparisons** How might a socialist and a capitalist government differ in treatment of the problem of unemployment?

6. **Making Decisions** Should the government have the responsibility of providing health care for every citizen? Why or why not?

For: An activity on the Industrial Revolution
Web Code: mqd-6232

The Third Way

Analysis Skills HR4, HI3

After losing four consecutive elections to Britain's Conservative Party, the British Labour Party moved away from its socialist roots to embrace a "third way" between socialism and a free market economy. Party leader Tony Blair issued this statement of party beliefs before the 1997 election. The Labour Party went on to win a landslide victory and has been in power since that time.

I want a country in which people get on, do well, make a success of their lives. I have no time for the politics of envy. We need more successful entrepreneurs, not fewer of them. But these life-chances should be for all the people. And I want a society in which ambition and compassion are seen as partners not opposites—where we value public service as well as material wealth.

New Labour believes in a society where we do not simply pursue our own individual aims but where we hold many aims in common and work together to achieve them. How we build the industry and employment opportunities of the future; how we tackle the division and inequality in our society; how we care for and enhance our environment and quality of life; how we develop modern education and health services; how we create communities that are safe, where mutual respect and tolerance are the order of the day. These are things we must achieve together as a country.

The vision is one of national renewal, a country with drive, purpose and energy. A Britain equipped to prosper in a global economy of technological change; with a modern welfare state; its politics more accountable; and confident of its place in the world.

. . . a new and distinctive approach has been mapped out, one that differs from the solutions of the old left and those of the Conservative right. This is why new Labour is new. . . .

Prime Minister Tony Blair

The old left would have sought state control of industry. The Conservative right is content to leave all to the market. We reject both approaches. Government and industry must work together to achieve key objectives aimed at enhancing the dynamism of the market, not undermining it.

In industrial relations, we make it clear that there will be no return to [the aggressive labor tactics] of the 1970s. There will instead be basic minimum rights for the individual at the workplace, where our aim is partnership not conflict between employers and employees.

In economic management, we accept the global economy as a reality and reject the isolationism and "go-it-alone" policies of the extremes of right or left.

Analyzing Primary Sources

1. Describe Tony Blair's vision for a new Britain in your own words.
2. How does Tony Blair try to distance the Labour Party from its past socialist policies? Why did he do so?
3. What is the Labour Party's view of the global economy and world trade?
4. Do you believe Blair's Third Way between socialism and free market capitalism is practical? Explain.

3 Communism

Section Preview

OBJECTIVES

1. **Summarize** the theories of Karl Marx.
2. **Outline** the characteristics of communist economies.
3. **Describe** communism in the Soviet Union, China, and other nations.

WHY IT MATTERS

Karl Marx once predicted that the workers of the world would overthrow capitalism and create an ideal communist society. Although communist governments emerged in Russia and China in the last century, the reality of communism rarely matched Marx's theory.

POLITICAL DICTIONARY

- **communism**
- **five-year plan**
- **collectivization**
- **Gosplan**
- **privatization**
- **Great Leap Forward**
- **commune**

M odern communism is a political, economic, and social theory developed by Karl Marx in the mid-1800s.[2] Nearly one third of the world's people once lived under communism, but since the collapse of the Soviet Union, it is the guiding economic principle in only a handful of countries. Almost every one of those countries, in fact, is taking steps toward a free market system.

Karl Marx's Theory

Communism is often called a collectivist ideology, which calls for the collective, or state, ownership of land and other productive property. Karl Marx

▲ *May Day Parade* On the first of May, people in the Soviet Union celebrated the workers of their country and the world. The banner depicts the revolutionary founder of the Soviet Union, V. I. Lenin (left), as well as Friedrich Engels (center) and Karl Marx (right). **H-SS 12.9.7**

and Friedrich Engels first set out its basic concepts in *The Communist Manifesto* (1848).

In his major work, *Das Kapital* (1867), Marx analyzed the workings of capitalism. He based the work on four closely related concepts: his theory of history, the labor theory of value, the nature of the state, and the dictatorship of the proletariat.

1. *Marx's View of History.* To Marx, all of history was a story of class struggle—of social classes competing for the control of labor and productive property. One class was the oppressors; the other, the oppressed. In the Middle Ages, the struggle was between the nobility and their serfs. In the modern world, the bourgeoisie oppressed the proletariat.

According to Marx, the class struggle in the modern era would become so intense that the masses would revolt and bring down the bourgeoisie. The communists' political role was to hasten the revolution, by violence if necessary.

2. *The Labor Theory of Value.* Marx rejected the free enterprise ideas of profit and competition. In his view, the value of a commodity was set by the amount of labor put into it. A pair of shoes or a rebuilt bicycle is worth a certain

---

[2]The word *communism* comes from the Latin *communis,* meaning "common, belonging to all." The idea of communal property dates back at least to the early Greeks. In the fourth century B.C., Plato proposed a system of communal property in *The Republic.*

amount because it takes that much labor to produce it. Therefore, communists say, the laborer should receive that value in full.

3. *The Nature of the State.* Marx saw the state and its government as the tools by which the capitalists maintained their power and privileges. Other social institutions also played a role in enforcing capitalist control over the masses. Marx described religion as "the opiate of the people"—a sort of drug that persuades workers to tolerate their harsh lot in this life in the hope that someday they will gain what Marx called a "fictional afterlife."

4. *The Dictatorship of the Proletariat.* Marx did not believe that revolution would bring the final form of communism—the classless society. First, he predicted a transitional phase during which an authoritarian state would represent and enforce the interests of the masses. This he called the "dictatorship of the proletariat." Once the goal of classlessness was realized, the state would "wither away."

Based on these four concepts, Marx envisioned a "free, classless society." Social classes would vanish and the people in common would own all property. Exploitation of labor and unemployment would disappear. Abundant goods would be available to all according to their needs.

Marx also expected that workers in different countries—for example, France and Germany—would share a bond far stronger than national loyalties. Thus, communism would also end nationalism, a major cause of European wars.

Characteristics of Communist Economies

Marx believed that the revolution would come first in industrialized countries with large working-class populations—in particular, France, Germany, Great Britain, and then the United States. Ironically, the revolution occurred first in Russia, then a backward, mainly agricultural nation, in 1917, and later in largely agricultural nations in Asia.[3]

Marx's theories did not provide even a rough blueprint for the formation of a communist society. Communism has taken different forms in different places, but certain characteristics are common.

▲ When northern Vietnam became a communist state, most people lived in the countryside and worked on farms, as they still do today. *Critical Thinking How well did Vietnam fit Karl Marx's description of a country ready for communism?* **H-SS 12.9.1**

1. *Role of the Communist Party.* In any communist-run nation, the Communist Party holds the decision-making power in both the government and the economy. Party leaders also hold the top government positions. From top to bottom, the two institutions run parallel to each other. Inevitably, such centralized political and economic control means control over social, intellectual, and religious life as well.

2. *Central Planning.* Because government makes all the economic decisions, bureaucrats must plan and supervise production in factories, farms, and stores. Typically, a **five-year plan** plays a key role in this economy. The plan shows how leaders want the economy to develop over the next five years. It sets economic goals that dictate where to emphasize growth in industry or agriculture and what each individual factory and farm must produce. The plan also sets prices and decides how goods and services will be distributed.

---

[3]In his later years, Marx did recognize the possibility that his theories might first be tested in Russia. Lenin also took the Russia-first view, in the early 1900s. He thought that less advanced countries, with their comparatively small industrial populations, offered certain advantages to a revolutionary movement—notably, the effectiveness with which workers could be organized and controlled.

▲ Typical of Soviet art, *Builders of Communism* glorifies Soviet workers, including a farmer, a welder, a miner, and an architect. *Critical Thinking According to this picture, what were some roles of women in the Soviet Union?*

3. *Collectivization.* Collective or state ownership of the means of production is one pillar of communism. One major step in creating a communist economy is the merger of small private farms into large government-owned agricultural enterprises. This process of **collectivization** may be voluntary in theory, but in many countries peasant farmers have been coerced into giving up land. Millions died while resisting collectivization in the Soviet Union.

4. *State Ownership.* Industrial enterprises, transportation, and other parts of the economy are also state-owned. This part of the system varies greatly from country to country. In China, for example, provincial and municipal governments, not a central government ministry, own enterprises such as housing, banks, hospitals, and stores.

The Soviet Union

Lenin and his followers took power in Russia in 1917 and began immediately to build a communist state. After a difficult transition, the Soviet Union became a one-party state, with communists in control of the country's social, political, and economic institutions by the time of Lenin's death in 1924. Lenin's successor, Josef Stalin, tightened that control into an authoritarian dictatorship.

The Five-Year Plans

Stalin introduced centralized planning, run by a large agency, **Gosplan.** The First Five-Year Plan (1928–1933) demanded collectivization of agriculture and higher production of chemicals, petroleum, and steel. Later five-year plans also emphasized heavy industry, and the Soviet Union achieved rapid, if uneven, industrialization. Unfortunately, those advances came at the cost of scarce consumer goods, housing, and urban services. Housing, food, and goods were rationed, and sewers, water systems, and other needs lagged behind a dramatic growth in urban population.[4]

Social Policies

The Soviet Union gave its citizens free education, medical care, and even youth summer camps. It was far from a classless society, however. To spur production, economic incentives, cars, and vacation homes went to party officials, bureaucrats, and factory managers. Artists, musicians, and athletes also were rewarded with special privileges. Thus, Stalin created an elite class that owed its privileged status to the Communist Party. He also corrupted the Marxian ideal of economic and social equality.

Gorbachev's Reforms

When Mikhail Gorbachev became Soviet leader in 1985, he inherited an economic system that had changed little since the Stalin years. Economic growth and productivity had declined sharply.

Under *perestroika*, leaders gave more authority to local farm and factory managers, loosened price controls, linked salaries to performance, and allowed some profit incentives. *Perestroika* raised expectations, but it did not increase output. Bureaucrats resisted change, and poor harvests, strikes, and shortages of food and consumer goods made conditions worse. Gorbachev and the Communist Party gave up their leadership of the economy when the Soviet Union collapsed in 1991.

---

[4]The First Five-Year Plan, launched in 1928, was declared completed in 1932, nine months ahead of schedule. The second plan ran from 1932 to 1937 and the third from 1937 until it was interrupted by the German invasion of the Soviet Union in 1941. The Twelfth Five-Year Plan was in place when the Soviet Union collapsed in late 1991.

Transition to a Free Market

Clearly, Russia's transition to a free market system and its moves toward democracy were closely linked. The economic plans that Russian President Boris Yeltsin put in place in 1991 and 1992 called for radical changes, including the lifting of price controls and the privatization of farms and factories. **Privatization** is the process of returning nationalized enterprises to private ownership.

The transition to a market economy has not been easy. Thousands of enterprises were put into private hands, sometimes by giving shares or vouchers to workers, but many are still badly run.

A new elite class of entrepreneurs has made a fortune in today's Russian economy. At the same time, many ordinary Russians have suffered the effects of high inflation, a fall in the value of Russian currency, and the loss of their state pensions. Corruption is rampant, and most people have grown poorer. A complete transition to a market economy awaits strong leadership willing to enforce laws and thoroughly reform the system.

China

Mao Zedong, the founder of the People's Republic of China, was a Marxist. Mao departed from Marx's theory that a workers' revolt would lead to communism. He believed the peasantry would be the key to a communist revolution in China.

After Mao took control of the country in 1949, China developed its own version of a planned economy. Despite its huge population, it lacked skilled workers. The government improved technical and scientific education and then assigned workers to jobs in the state sector. Government regulated the labor market, giving workers little choice about where they worked.

The Great Leap Forward

The five-year plan for 1958, the **Great Leap Forward,** was a drastic attempt to modernize China quickly. All elements of free enterprise, such as rural markets, were eliminated. Collective farms were brought together into a larger unit, the **commune.**

Communes grew into self-sufficient bodies run by party officials. These officials oversaw farms, industries, and government in a region as well as managed social policy. Workers received the same rewards no matter how much they produced, so there were few incentives to work hard. The Great Leap Forward was a disastrous failure, followed by severe famine.

Deng Xiaoping's Reforms

A new leader, Deng Xiaoping, came to power in 1977 and made great changes in the economy. Deng's program of the "Four Modernizations" aimed to improve agriculture, industry, science and technology, and defense. He wanted "socialism with Chinese characteristics."

Deng was more practical and far less ideological than Mao and his dedicated followers. He began to move China from central planning to a market economy and invited foreign investors into China.

Today, China's economic system is a maze of different levels of government bodies and economic units. The state-owned sector is shrinking, while collective enterprises owned and managed by the people of a workplace or residential unit are growing. Private enterprises—mostly small shops and businesses—are also flourishing, as is investment from other countries.

▲ American cultural and economic influence can be seen throughout the world, including in Russia and China. *Critical Thinking (a) How does this photo show the influence of the American free market system? (b) How does it show American cultural influence? (c) In your opinion, are these influences good or bad?*

▲ Fidel Castro watches a May Day parade in Havana, Cuba. Cuba remains the only communist country in the Americas. Castro has ruled Cuba as a personal dictatorship for over 40 years.

Other Communist Nations

Several other countries, mainly in Asia, have centrally planned economies. Most, however, are bringing in some free market elements. Other communist economies have not lasted. Those in the Soviet satellites of Eastern Europe disappeared in the upheavals of 1989–1990.

In Cuba, Fidel Castro led a revolution that overthrew the corrupt rule of Fulgencio Batista in 1959. After Castro nationalized American holdings, the United States broke with him. The Soviet Union supported Castro, and in 1961, he declared himself a Marxist.

Cuba depended heavily on Soviet economic aid. As a result, the fall of the Soviet Union caused an economic crisis in Cuba. In response, the government relaxed economic controls, encouraging tourism and some small businesses.

Communism also took root in Southeast Asia. At the end of World War II, Ho Chi Minh, a communist who had studied in Moscow, fought for Vietnam's independence from French colonial rule. Two wars—one against the French, one against the United States—left the communists in control. Vietnam's government uses five-year plans to guide the economy, and like China, it has made market-oriented reforms.

Communist influence spilled over from Vietnam into neighboring Laos and Cambodia. Laos adopted communism in 1975, and Cambodia had a communist government under Vietnamese control from 1979 to 1993.

One of the last communist countries is North Korea. At the end of World War II, the Korean peninsula was divided between a Soviet-backed regime in the north and an American-backed government in the south. After the Korean War (1950–1953), the peninsula remained divided, and North Korea retreated into isolation.

North Korea's centrally planned economy has not achieved much growth. Agriculture was collectivized in the 1950s, although small private plots can grow food for rural markets. Severe food shortages plague the country today. Recently, North Korea thrust itself onto the international scene and shocked world leaders by announcing that it possesses "several" nuclear weapons.

Section 3 Assessment

Key Terms and Main Ideas

1. Describe **communism** in your own words.
2. What was the purpose of **Gosplan**?
3. What happens during **collectivization**?
4. Which country experienced the **Great Leap Forward**?

Critical Thinking

5. **Drawing Inferences** How well did Soviet communism follow the communist ideal of economic and social equality?

Standards Monitoring *Online*
For: Self-quiz with vocabulary practice
Web Code: mqa-6233

6. **Drawing Conclusions** Is a dictatorship necessary to the existence of a communist society? Why or why not?

Go Online
PHSchool.com
For: An activity on the Russian Economy
Web Code: mqd-6233

May Courts Enforce Discriminatory Private Agreements?

The Equal Protection Clause of the 14th Amendment bars States from discriminating against people based on their race or color. What happens if private individuals make an agreement that discriminates, and one of them later breaks that agreement? Should a court enforce the agreement?

Shelley v. *Kraemer* (1948)

In 1911, thirty property owners in St. Louis, Missouri, signed a restrictive covenant (an agreement limiting the ways in which a piece of property can be used). In this agreement, the property owners promised not to sell their property to non-whites during the next 50 years. The agreement did not restrict the use of the property in any other way.

In 1945, a black family, the Shelleys, bought one of the properties that was subject to the covenant. Kraemer and other property owners governed by the covenant brought suit in the circuit court, seeking to block the Shelleys from taking possession of the property and to reverse the sale. The trial court refused to do so. It concluded that the agreement was not intended to become effective until signed by all the property owners in the district, and that some owners had never signed.

The Missouri Supreme Court reversed the trial court opinion, ruling that the agreement was effective and that it did not violate the Shelleys' constitutional rights. The Shelleys then appealed to the United States Supreme Court.

Arguments for Shelley

1. It would be unconstitutional for States to pass laws or ordinances restricting property ownership or occupancy based on race or color. Therefore, the courts should not enforce any agreement that imposes such restrictions.
2. Although the Equal Protection Clause of the 14th Amendment applies only to "State action" and does not restrict actions by private individuals, judicial enforcement of private

agreements is "State action" within the meaning of the 14th Amendment.
3. The purpose of the 14th Amendment was to establish equality of basic rights and to preserve those rights from discrimination by the States based on race and color. For the courts to enforce the restrictive covenant would not be consistent with that purpose.

Arguments for Kraemer

1. This case does not involve action by State legislators or city councils. Private individuals entered into the agreement at issue.
2. The Equal Protection Clause of the 14th Amendment applies only to "State action" and does not restrict actions by private individuals. Judicial enforcement of private agreements does not amount to "State action" within the meaning of the 14th Amendment.
3. There is no discrimination because the Missouri courts would equally enforce covenants that exclude white people from property ownership.

Decide for Yourself

1. Review the constitutional grounds on which each side based its arguments and the specific arguments each side presented.
2. Debate the opposing viewpoints presented in this case. Which viewpoint do you favor?
3. Predict the impact of the Court's decision on discrimination. (To read a summary of the Court's decision, turn to pages 799–806.)

Go Online
PHSchool.com

Use Web Code mqp-6236 to register your vote on this issue and to see how other students voted.

Political Dictionary

factors of production (p. 658), capital (p. 659), capitalist (p. 659), entrepreneur (p. 659), free enterprise system (p. 659), laws of supply and demand (p. 661), monopoly (p. 661), trust (p. 661), laissez-faire theory (p. 662), socialism (p. 666), proletariat (p. 667), bourgeoisie (p. 667), welfare state (p. 668), market economy (p. 669), centrally planned economy (p. 669), communism (p. 672), five-year plan (p. 673), collectivization (p. 674), Gosplan (p. 674), privatization (p. 675), Great Leap Forward (p. 675), commune (p. 675)

Standards Review

H-SS 12.2.2 Explain how economic rights are secured and their importance to the individual and to society (e.g., the right to acquire, use, transfer, and dispose of property; right to choose one's work; right to join or not join labor unions; copyright and patent).

H-SS 12.3.4 Compare the relationship of government and civil society in constitutional democracies to the relationship of government and civil society in authoritarian and totalitarian regimes.

H-SS 12.9.1 Explain how the different philosophies and structures of feudalism, mercantilism, socialism, fascism, communism, monarchies, parliamentary systems, and constitutional liberal democracies influence economic policies, social welfare policies, and human rights practices.

H-SS 12.9.7 Describe the ideologies that give rise to Communism, methods of maintaining control, and the movements to overthrow such governments in Czechoslovakia, Hungary, and Poland, including the roles of individuals (e.g., Alexander Solzhenitsyn, Pope John Paul II, Lech Walesa, Vaclav Havel).

Practicing the Vocabulary

Matching *Choose a term from the list above that best matches each description.*

1. An organization of several firms that controls the only source of a product or service
2. In Marxist terms, the capitalists
3. Economic system in which individuals are free to start and run their own businesses
4. A government that assumes the role of promoter of citizen welfare through programs that provide health care, education, and pensions
5. Central institution that planned the economy of the Soviet Union

Fill in the Blank *Choose a term from the list above that best completes the sentence.*

6. Marx believed the _____ would one day rise up and overthrow the capitalist system.
7. An economy in which the government directs factories and farms and decides what to produce and how much is a _____.
8. _____ consists of the wealth and tools used to produce goods and services.
9. During _____, many individual farms are combined to create one giant farm.
10. If existing companies do not see and meet demand, a(n) _____ may start a new business and do so.
11. _____ recommends that government play a very small role in the economy.

Reviewing Main Ideas

Section 1

12. **(a)** What are the factors of production? **(b)** What role do the factors of production play in an economy?
13. What are the hallmarks of a free enterprise economy?
14. **(a)** Why is competition important to a free enterprise economy? **(b)** What will happen to a market without competition?
15. According to laissez-faire theory, what are the three duties of government?
16. **(a)** What are the advantages of a sole proprietorship? **(b)** What are the advantages of a corporation?

Section 2

17. **(a)** What is the purpose of socialism? **(b)** How did events in the 19th century contribute to socialism's popularity?
18. **(a)** Briefly describe Karl Marx's basic ideas about the capitalist system. **(b)** What is the major difference between socialism and communism?

19. Describe three characteristics commonly found in socialist countries.
20. **(a)** Why has socialism been popular in developing countries? **(b)** How successful has socialism been in these countries?
21. What are the major criticisms of socialism?

Section 3

22. Briefly describe Marx's view of history and the labor theory of value.
23. Describe four characteristics of communist countries.
24. In what ways did the Soviet Union fail to meet Marx's predictions?
25. Describe the problems facing the Soviet economy under Gorbachev and the Russian economy today.
26. **(a)** What changes did Mao make as leader of the People's Republic of China? **(b)** How did Deng Xiaoping differ from Mao?

Critical Thinking Skills

Analysis Skills CS1, HR4, HI6

27. *Face the Issues* Consider a clothing store in your community. In your opinion, would the store hire more sales people if the minimum wage were abolished? Why or why not?

28. *Recognizing Propaganda* Mao Zedong renamed his country the "People's Republic of China" after the communist takeover in 1949. **(a)** How did this new name reflect the theories of Karl Marx? **(b)** Based on your reading in this chapter, is this an appropriate name for a communist state? Explain your answer.

29. *Drawing Inferences* Consider the common criticism of socialism on the grounds that it discourages individual initiative. **(a)** What assumption about initiative underlies this criticism? **(b)** Is this assumption valid? Why or why not? **(c)** How does a free enterprise system differ from socialism in its treatment of individuals?

Analyzing Political Cartoons

Using your knowledge of economic systems and this cartoon, answer the questions below.

30. What does this cartoon imply about Russia's experiences since the end of communism?

31. How do "Russian communism" and "Russian capitalism" compare with ideal forms of communism and capitalism?

★ You Can Make a Difference

Help educate your classmates about child-labor laws. Contact the U.S. Department of Labor or your State's department of labor to learn more about current U.S. child-labor laws. Then create a poster or display sheet that could be posted in the school guidance office, outlining the hours children are allowed to work and any types of jobs they are not allowed to perform. Your poster should also note whether the hours and types of jobs vary depending on the age of the child.

Participation Activities

Analysis Skills CS4, HR4, HI3

32. *Current Events Watch* Review newspapers and magazines from the past month and find articles that discuss businesses or the economy in China, Russia, and Germany. Are these countries described as communist, socialist, capitalist, or a combination? Based on your reading in this chapter, how would you categorize these three economies?

33. *Graphing Activity* Choose one country from each of the following continents: Africa, Asia, Europe, and South America. Research how much the United States and those four countries spend on health care per capita and as a share of Gross Domestic Product (GDP). Using this data, create a bar graph. Which country spends the most on health care per person? Which country spends the most on health care as a share of GDP? Which country spends the least per person?

34. *It's Your Turn* It is 1932. The world is in the midst of the Great Depression, and you are a young politician running for office. You must convince people that you have the best solution for the country's economic problems. Write a speech in which you explain why you have chosen your particular party and describe the goals of your party. What legislation will you support? Why should people vote for your party instead of the alternatives? After you have written your speech, present it to your class. **(Writing a Speech)**

Standards Monitoring *Online*

For: Chapter 23 Self-Test **Visit:** PHSchool.com
Web Code: mqa-6234

As a final review, take the Magruder's Chapter 23 Self-Test and receive immediate feedback on your answers. The test consists of 20 multiple-choice questions designed to test your understanding of the chapter content.

◆ **State Capitol, Sacramento, California**

Participating in California State and Local Government

CONSTITUTIONAL PRINCIPLES

Federalism The Constitution of the United States creates a federal system in which the powers of government are divided between the National Government and the 50 States. The California constitution creates the structure and the processes by which California is governed.

Limited Government The 50 State constitutions vary in many of their details. However, all of them, including the California constitution, authorize the exercise of governmental power and, at the same time, limit the exercise of governmental power.

Judicial Review The primary function of California State courts is to settle disputes between private persons and between private persons and government. Those courts also all exercise the power of judicial review, which allows them to check the exercise of power by the State and its local governments.

The Impact on You

As a resident of California, you must obey its laws. That means, for example, that you must attend school and that you must be at least a certain age before you can legally do such things as drive a car. Those two illustrations only begin to suggest "the impact on you."

CHAPTER 24

Governing the State of California

"The problems facing us are large but they are no match for our determination. With power from the people and courage in our elected leaders I know that absolutely everything is possible. Together we can keep California moving forward and restore the great promise of our state."

—California Governor Arnold Schwarzenegger (2005)

California is unique in its geography, size, and history; but it is quite similar to the other 49 States in the structure of its government. All States have written constitutions. Like the Federal Government, each has an executive, a legislative, and a judicial branch.

◆ **The California State Assembly**

SECTION 1

The California State Constitution (pp. 684–688)

★ The first State constitutions were based on popular sovereignty and limited government, and they provided for a separation of powers, checks and balances, and protection of individual rights.

★ The California State constitution retains those basic principles; it also sets out the structure, powers, and processes of government, and details method of constitutional change.

SECTION 2

The California State Legislature (pp. 689–693)

★ The legislature is the lawmaking branch of State government. It has the power to pass any law that does not conflict with the State constitution or with federal law.

★ State legislators are chosen by popular vote.

★ State legislatures are organized much like Congress.

★ The legislative process is also similar to that of Congress. California and some other states, however, allow voters to participate directly through the initiative and referendum.

SECTION 3

The Governor and State Administration
(pp. 694–700)

★ The governor is the chief executive officer of the State.

★ In addition to executive powers, a governor has some legislative and judicial powers.

★ The governor of California shares executive powers with other executive officers, who are also popularly elected.

SECTION 4

In the Courtroom (pp. 702–705)

★ The law is the code of conduct by which society is governed. State courts apply constitutional, statutory, and administrative law as well as common law and equity.

★ The law can also be classified as either criminal or civil law.

★ There are two kinds of juries: the grand jury, which brings indictments, and the petit jury, which decides the facts in trials.

SECTION 5

The Courts and Their Judges (pp. 707–712)

★ The California State judicial system has three levels: superior courts, courts of appeal, and a supreme court.

★ Judges in California are selected by a mix of appointment and popular election.

Go Online
PHSchool.com

For: Current Data
Web Code: mqg-7247

For: Close Up Foundation debates
Web Code: mqh-7240

The California State Constitution

Section Preview

OBJECTIVES

1. **Examine** the history, contents, and importance of the first State constitutions.
2. **Describe** the history of the California constitution.
3. **Examine** today's California constitution.
4. **Explain** the process for constitutional change.
5. **Analyze** the need for reform of State constitutions.

WHY IT MATTERS

The constitution of California is the supreme law of the State. It sets out the way the State is governed. Like all State constitutions, the California constitution is based on popular sovereignty and limited government. It includes a Declaration of Rights that guarantees basic human rights to Californians.

POLITICAL DICTIONARY

★ **popular sovereignty**
★ **limited government**
★ **fundamental law**
★ **initiative**
★ **statutory law**

The Constitution of California is the supreme law of California, just as the United States Constitution is the supreme law of the country. It sets out the ways in which the government of California is organized, and it distributes power among the various branches of State government. It authorizes the exercise of power by the government but also places limits on the exercise of that power. As the supreme law of California, the State's constitution is superior to all other State and local laws within California.

Each State's constitution, however, is subordinate to the Constitution of the United States. (See Article VI, Section 2, the Supremacy Clause.) Because of this, no provision in the California constitution may conflict with any form of federal law.

The First State Constitutions

Each of the 50 States has a *written* constitution. That fact, in itself, is very important. From the beginning, government in this country has been based on written constitutions. In fact, the United States has sometimes been described as "a land of constitutions."

Our experience with such documents dates from 1606, when King James I granted a charter to the Virginia Company. That act led to the settlement at Jamestown in the following year and, with it, the first government in British North America. Later, each of the other English colonies was also established and governed on the basis of a written charter.

When the 13 colonies became independent, each faced the problem of establishing a new government. On May 15, 1776, the Second Continental Congress advised each of the new States to adopt

PRIMARY Sources *"such governments as shall, in the opinion of the representatives of the people, best conduce to the happiness and safety of their constituents in particular, and America in general."*
—Second Continental Congress

▲ The settlement of Jamestown, Virginia, in 1607

Most of the colonial charters served as models for the first State constitutions. Indeed, in Connecticut and Rhode Island, the old charters seemed so well suited to the needs of the day that they were carried over as constitutions almost without change.[1]

The earliest State constitutions were adopted in a variety of ways. However, the people played no direct part in the process in any State until 1780. That year, a popularly elected convention prepared a new constitution for Massachusetts. It was then ratified by a vote of the people. Thus, Massachusetts set the pattern of popular participation in the constitution-making process, a pattern generally followed among the States ever since.[2]

Because the first State constitutions came out of the same Revolutionary ferment, they shared many basic features. The doctrines of separation of powers and checks and balances were built into each of the new constitutions. Each proclaimed the principles of **popular sovereignty** and **limited government.** That is, in each of them the people were recognized as the sole source of authority for government. And in each constitution, the powers given to the new government were closely limited. Seven constitutions began with a lengthy bill of rights. All of them made it clear that the sovereign people held "certain unalienable rights" that government must respect.

For their time, the early State constitutions were fairly democratic. Each had, however, several provisions (and some important omissions) that, by today's standards, were quite undemocratic. No constitution provided for full religious freedom. Each one set rigid qualifications for voting and for officeholding, and all gave property owners a highly favored standing.

History of the California Constitution

California has had two constitutions. The first was written in 1849 at the request of the military governor, General Bennett Riley. Following the war with Mexico and the Treaty of Guadalupe Hidalgo, many Californians objected to military rule. Also, gold strikes had brought tens of thousands of new settlers to California, and lawless-

"Now you try to get a fire started while I draft a constitution."

▲ **Interpreting Political Cartoons** **(a) How important does the cartoonist think a written constitution is? How do you know? (b) Do you agree? Explain.**

ness abounded. Riley hoped to stem the anarchy by establishing a civil government. On June 3, 1849, he called for the election of delegates to a constitutional convention.

The Constitution of 1849

The convention began in Monterey on September 1. The 48 delegates who shaped California's first civil government represented a cross-section of their society. This mix of ranchers, lawyers, merchants, and others came mainly from the United States, but six were native Californians and a similar number were Europeans. Some of them did not speak English, so each resolution was translated into Spanish before being voted on.

The Constitution of 1849 was brief. It contained the same basic characteristics that are provided for in the United States Constitution and Bill of Rights. It separated governmental powers into the legislative, executive, and judicial branches, and it created checks and balances among the branches.

The delegates also relied for guidance on existing State constitutions, especially those of

---

[1]Connecticut did not write a new document until 1818, and Rhode Island not until 1842.

[2]As noted in Chapter 2, with independence Massachusetts relied on the colonial charter in force prior to 1691 as its first State constitution. New Hampshire adopted its second and present constitution in 1784. It followed the Massachusetts pattern of popular convention and popular ratification.

California State Constitution of 1849

create the lengthiest constitution (with the possible exception of Louisiana's) of all the states.

The Constitution of 1879 contained several major changes, however, including the creation of a Board of Equalization to equalize the property tax, an elected Railroad Commission, and new restrictions on the power of the legislature and the governor. It also banned the public employment of Chinese immigrants and limited their rights in other ways. The Supreme Court of the United States declared most of the document's anti-Chinese provisions unconstitutional. Many more changes to the constitution came about through amendments. The result is the constitution Californians have today.

The California Constitution Today

Like all State constitutions, the Constitution of California can be described in terms of six general categories: basic principles, civil rights, governmental structure, governmental powers, processes for change, and miscellaneous provisions.

1. *Basic Principles.* Every State's fundamental law is built on the principles of popular sovereignty and limited government. That is, each State constitution recognizes that government exists only with the consent of the people, and that it must operate within certain, often closely defined bounds.

2. *Protections of Civil Rights.* All State constitutions include a bill of rights, a listing of the rights that individuals hold against the State and its officers and agencies. These guarantees often mirror those set out in the first 10 amendments to the Constitution of the United States. This is true of the California constitution, whose first article is a Declaration of Rights. However, the California bill of rights, like those of several other states, goes beyond the national Constitution. For example, it protects against employment discrimination, upholds property rights, and gives specific rights to the victims of crime.

3. *Governmental Structure.* Every State constitution deals with the structure of government at both the State and the local levels. A few follow the national pattern, providing only a broad outline. Most, however, including California's, cover the subject at length and in great detail.

4. *Governmental Powers and Processes.* All State constitutions list in detail the powers vested

Iowa and New York, as they debated and resolved several thorny issues. They decided to skip the usual period as a territory in favor of moving directly toward statehood. For geographical and defensive reasons, they established the eastern boundary of California at the Sierra Nevada range. They unanimously agreed to outlaw slavery, and they granted married women the right to own property in their own names. The first capital, they decided, would be San José.

The convention adopted the constitution without dissent on October 10, 1849, and it won popular approval in a November 13 referendum. Eager to begin governing themselves, the new legislature met for the first time on December 15, 1849, in San José—before California was even a State. It would not officially become the thirty-first State until September 9, 1850.

The Constitution of 1879

During its first decades of statehood, social unrest built up as the government failed to deal with pressing problems. These problems included taxation, the banks, big business, land monopolization, the railroads, and increasing resentment at the immigration of Chinese workers. In 1877, voters approved a proposal for a new constitutional convention.

A group of 145 delegates met on September 28, 1878, in Sacramento, where they made an honest effort to solve the problems that faced the rapidly growing state. Nevertheless, experts agree that they accomplished little more than in the executive branch (the governor and other executive officers), the legislature, the courts, and the units of local government. The powers to tax, spend, borrow, and provide for education are very prominent. So, too, are such processes as elections, legislation, and intergovernmental (State-local) relations.

5. *Constitutional Change.* Each State constitution, including California's, sets out the means by which it may be revised or amended. Since constitutions are **fundamental laws**—laws of basic and lasting importance—they cannot be changed as ordinary law is changed. Constitutional changes are more difficult to bring about, as you will see.

6. *Miscellaneous Provisions.* Most State constitutions begin with a preamble, which has no legal force but does set out the purposes of those who drafted and adopted the document. The California constitution's preamble reads: "We, the People of the State of California, grateful to Almighty God for our freedom, in order to secure and perpetuate its blessings, do establish this Constitution."

Constitutional Change

The national Constitution has been changed over time by formal amendment and by such other processes as court decisions and custom. Constitutional development at the State level has come about mainly through formal amendment.

Two kinds of formal changes have been used: amendments, which usually deal with one or a few provisions in a constitution; and revisions, which are large-scale changes that affect the constitution more broadly. Most of the formal changes that have been made in State constitutions have been made by amendment.

The process of formal change involves two basic steps: proposal and then ratification. In California, the legislature may propose constitutional amendments. If two thirds of the members of each house approve, the proposed amendment will be submitted to the voters. In California, as in 16 other States, voters themselves may also propose constitutional amendments through the **initiative,** a process in which a certain number of qualified voters sign petitions in favor of a proposal.

Procedures for proposing amendments to the constitution vary from state to state, as shown in

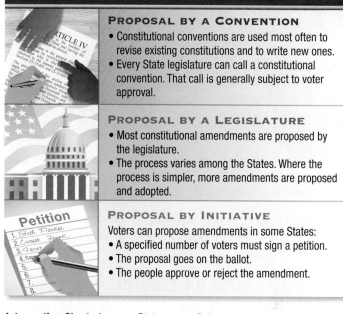

How to Propose Changes to a State Constitution

PROPOSAL BY A CONVENTION
- Constitutional conventions are used most often to revise existing constitutions and to write new ones.
- Every State legislature can call a constitutional convention. That call is generally subject to voter approval.

PROPOSAL BY A LEGISLATURE
- Most constitutional amendments are proposed by the legislature.
- The process varies among the States. Where the process is simpler, more amendments are proposed and adopted.

PROPOSAL BY INITIATIVE
Voters can propose amendments in some States:
- A specified number of voters must sign a petition.
- The proposal goes on the ballot.
- The people approve or reject the amendment.

Interpreting Charts In every State except Delaware, those changes which are proposed must be ratified by the voters. *Which method of proposing constitutional changes gives voters the most input?* H-SS 12.6.4

the chart above. In many States, amendments can be proposed by conventions. However, because they are costly and time consuming, conventions are most often used for the broader purpose of revision. This is true in California, where if two thirds of the members of each house approve, the legislature may propose to call a convention to revise the constitution. A majority of the voters must then vote to accept the call for a convention.

In California, proposed changes to the constitution go directly to the ballot, for approval or rejection by the people. Such ratification by popular vote is required in every State except Delaware.[3] A majority of the California voters must approve a proposed amendment or revision for it to take effect.

The process of changing the constitution is fairly simple in California. Not surprisingly, more amendments are proposed (and ratified) in those States with simpler processes. The

[3]In Delaware, if an amendment is approved by a two-thirds vote in each house of the legislature at two successive sessions, it then becomes effective. In South Carolina, final ratification, after a favorable vote by the people, depends on a majority vote in both houses of the legislature. Both the Alabama and South Carolina constitutions provide that amendments only of local, as opposed to Statewide, application need be approved only by the voters in the affected locale.

▲ *A State Constitutional Convention* James Madison addresses the Virginia Constitutional Convention of 1829–1830.

California constitution, which dates from 1879, has been amended more than 500 times.

The Need for Reform

Almost all State constitutions would benefit from some degree of reform. The typical document is cluttered with unnecessary details, burdensome restrictions, and obsolete sections. It also carries much repetitious, even contradictory, material. Moreover, it fails to deal with many of the pressing problems that the States and their local governments currently face. Even the newest and most recently rewritten constitutions tend to carry over a great deal of material from earlier documents and suffer from these same faults.

Length was not a problem for the first State constitutions. They were quite short, ranging from New Jersey's 1776 constitution (2,500 words) to the 1780 Massachusetts constitution (12,000 words). These early State constitutions were meant simply to be statements of basic principle and organization. Purposely, they left to the legislature—as well as to time and practice—the task of filling in the details as they became necessary.

Through the years, however, State constitutions have grown and grown. The Constitution of the United States, with some 8,700 words, is short compared with State constitutions, which average 26,000 words. The longest constitution is that of Alabama, with more than 310,000 words. In 1961, the California constitution contained about 80,000 words, but through the work of a Constitution Revision Commission, California managed to cut some 40,000 words from its constitution by 1976. Today, California's constitution has some 55,000 words.

Most State constitutions would be improved if the legislatures and the voters separated fundamental law, which should properly be in the constitution, from more routine **statutory law,** which refers to laws passed by the legislature. The line separating fundamental and statutory law may be blurry in some cases. But many provisions clearly do not need to go in the State constitution. For example, California's constitution contains a ban on taxing fruit and nut trees planted within the past four years. Putting such statutory provisions in the constitution makes the document unnecessarily long and complex and obscures the important points of fundamental law that the constitution should showcase. It also makes it harder to make routine changes in governing law when they are needed.

Section 1 Assessment

Key Terms and Main Ideas

1. Explain the concept of **popular sovereignty.**
2. **(a)** List and explain three ways changes to State constitutions can be proposed. **(b)** How may the California constitution be amended and ratified?
3. What is the difference between **fundamental law** and **statutory law?**

Critical Thinking

4. **Predicting Consequences** Do you think the governments of the English colonies or the early States would have developed differently if they had not had written charters or constitutions? Why?

5. **Drawing Inferences** Why do you think many State constitutions have been allowed to become so lengthy, repetitive, and full of outdated provisions?

The California State Legislature

Section Preview

OBJECTIVES

1. **Compare** the structure and size of the California State government with those of the federal system.
2. **Describe** the election process, terms, and compensation of California State legislators.
3. **Explain** the powers and organization of the California State legislature.
4. **Summarize** the legislative process at the State level.

WHY IT MATTERS

At what age can you get married? What are the speed limits on the highways in California? How, and how well, is your school funded? Do you have to pay a sales tax or an income tax, or both? These are but a few examples of the many, many ways your State legislators impact every day of your life.

POLITICAL DICTIONARY

★ police power
★ constituent power
★ referendum

Each State constitution establishes a legislative body that is, in effect, the powerhouse of that State's government. The size of a legislature, the details of its organization and procedures, the frequency and length of its sessions, and even its official name vary among the States. However, the 50 State legislatures do share a fundamental feature with one another: they are lawmaking bodies.

not be so small that the many views and interests within the State cannot be represented adequately.

The California senate has 40 members, representing 40 districts of nearly equal population. The California assembly has 80 members, elected from 80 districts that are all about equal in population.

▲ The California State Seal

The Legislature: Structure and Size

In every State, the legislature is the lawmaking branch of State government. Its basic function goes to the heart of democratic government: The legislature is responsible for translating the public will into the State's public policy.

The California legislature carries out that responsibility as a bicameral body modeled after the Congress of the United States. California's upper house is called the senate, and its lower house is called the assembly. In fact, all State legislatures but one are bicameral. The exception is Nebraska, which calls its single chamber the Legislature.

While there is no ideal size for a legislative body, two basic considerations are important. First, a legislature, and each of its houses, should not be so large as to hamper the orderly conduct of the people's business. Second, it should

The State Legislators

Today, there are 7,382 State legislators—5,411 representatives and 1,971 senators—among the 50 States. Nearly all of them are Republicans or Democrats; fewer than 20 belong to minor parties or are independents. Only one in five of them are women.

Qualifications

Every State's constitution sets out formal requirements of age, citizenship, and residence for legislators. In California, legislators in both the assembly and the senate must be at least 18 years old and qualified to vote. They must have been a United States citizen and a legal resident of California for at least three years, and a legal resident of their voting district for at least one year preceding their election.

In California and in the rest of the States, the realities of politics add informal qualifications, which are harder to meet than the formal ones. They have to do with a candidate's vote-getting abilities, and are based on such characteristics as occupation, name recognition, party identification, race, religion, national origin, and the like.

Election

Legislators are chosen by popular vote in every State. In California and in nearly every other State, candidates for the legislature are nominated at party primaries. Opposing candidates face one another in a partisan general election. Legislative nominees are picked by conventions in only a few States—New York, for example. In only one State, Nebraska, are the candidates nominated in nonpartisan primaries, and they are not identified by party in the general election.

In California, as in most States, the lawmakers are elected in November of even-numbered years. In four States—Mississippi, New Jersey, Virginia, and Louisiana—legislative elections are held in the odd-numbered years, in the hope of separating State and local issues from national politics.

Terms

In California, senators are elected to serve a term of four years. The constitution limits senators to two terms. Members of the assembly are elected for two-year terms, and they may serve a maximum of three terms.

The rate of turnover in legislative seats is fairly high. In a given year, more than one fourth of State legislators around the country are serving their first terms.

Compensation

Far too often, capable men and women refuse to run for seats in State legislatures because of the financial sacrifices that service usually entails.

Legislative pay varies widely among the fifty States. For decades now, New Hampshire has paid the members of its General Court only $200 a year. The other 49 States do somewhat better, however. A handful of States pay their lawmakers less than $20,000 a year, but in most the salary figure is between $25,000 to $50,000 a year. All but a few States also add an expense allowance to the salary.

California's legislators are the best paid in the nation. They now receive $110,800 a year, and an

The Enduring *Constitution*

Defining Federalism

1800

The Framers of the Constitution sought to balance the rights of the States and the powers of the new National Government. Conflicts over States' rights and national power have arisen throughout this nation's history, as the Supreme Court cases in this time line testify.

Go Online
PHSchool.com

Use Web Code mqp-7248 to register your vote on this issue and to see how other students voted.

 Analysis Skills CS1, CS2.HI1

1810
In *Fletcher* v. *Peck,* a case from Georgia, the Court for the first time holds a State law to be unconstitutional.

1819
In *McCulloch* v. *Maryland,* the Court rules that a State cannot tax the Federal Government.

1824
In *Gibbons* v. *Ogden,* the Court affirms the Federal Government's right to regulate interstate trade.

expense allowance of $153 for each day the legislature is in session.

Legislative Sessions

Forty-three State legislatures now hold annual sessions, and the California legislature meets in a continuous two-year session. Only Arkansas, Montana, Nevada, North Dakota, Oregon, and Texas still meet every other year.

Since the 1960s, most States have turned to annual sessions, as it has become increasingly apparent that legislators cannot otherwise handle their workload. Generally, regular sessions are becoming longer and longer. California's legislature, for example, meets in a continious two-year session. In addition, the governor has the power to call special sessions to allow the lawmakers to take up urgent matters between their regularly scheduled meetings.

Powers of the California Legislature

In California, as in every State, the legislature has all of those powers that (1) the State constitution does not grant exclusively to the executive or judicial branches of the State's government or to its local units, and (2) neither the State constitution nor the United States Constitution denies to the legislature.

Legislative Powers

The California legislature can pass any law that does not conflict with federal law or with any part of the State constitution. Therefore, it is impossible to list all its powers. However, the constitution does list several of the legislature's more important powers. These include the powers to tax, spend, borrow, establish courts, and maintain public schools.

As in every State, the California legislature possesses the **police power**—the extraordinarily important power to protect and promote the public health, public safety, public morals, and the general welfare. In short, it is the power to safeguard the well-being of the people of the State. This broad power is the basis for much of what State legislatures do. (See page 566.)

Nonlegislative Powers

Many powers of the California legislature have nothing to do with the making of law. These are the nonlegislative powers:

1. *Executive powers* Some of the nonlegislative powers are executive in nature. The

1925
In *Gitlow* v. *New York*, the Court rules that the protections of the 1st Amendment apply against actions by State governments.

1997 In *Printz* v. *United States*, the Court strikes down the provision of the federal Brady Act requiring States to check the background of handgun buyers.

| 1850 | 1900 | 1950 | 2000 |

1886
In *Wabash, St. Louis & Pacific Railway Co.* v. *Illinois*, the Court rules that States cannot regulate railroad rates on the parts of interstate journeys that fall within their borders.

1964
In *Wesberry* v. *Sanders*, the Court holds that States must draw congressional districts of nearly equal populations.

1972
In *Furman* v. *Georgia*, the Court rules that all existing State death penalty laws violate the Constitution.

2003
In *Nevada* v. *Hibbs*, the Court holds that a State worker can sue the State for money damages for its failure to obey the federal Family and Medical Leave Act of 1993.

Analyzing Time Lines

1. When did the Court first decide that State authorities must observe the civil rights protected by the Bill of Rights?
2. What trend can you see in the Supreme Court decisions in the 1900s?

▲ **State Assembly** Assemblymembers Rebecca Cohn (left) and Sally Lieber (right) meet with Assembly Speaker Fabian Nuñez. **H-SS 12.7.6**

California senate must approve the governor's appointment of State officials, for example. In some States the legislature itself appoints certain executive officeholders.

2. *Judicial powers* The chief illustration of the California legislature's judicial powers is the power of impeachment. Through impeachment by the assembly and trial by the senate, the legislature can remove any elected official in either the executive or judicial branch.

3. **Constituent power** The legislature plays a role in constitution making and the amendment process. Since this does not involve the making of statutes, this function—the constituent power—is a nonlegislative one.

Organization of the Legislature

The California State legislature is organized in much the same manner as Congress. It has presiding officers and a committee system.

The Presiding Officers

Those who preside over the sessions of the State legislative chambers are usually powerful political figures, not only in the legislature itself but elsewhere in State politics.

The California assembly elects its own presiding officer, known as the speaker. The president of the senate, according to the California constitution, is the lieutenant governor—an elected member of the executive branch. By law and custom, however, the lieutenant governor's role in the senate is limited to a few ceremonial visits and the casting of tie-breaking votes. The senate elects

a president *pro tempore* to serve as its actual leader, with all the duties of a presiding officer.

The chief duties of those presiding officers center on the conduct of the legislature's floor business. These duties are also a major source of their power. The presiding officers refer bills to committee, recognize members who seek the floor, and interpret and apply the rules of their chamber to its proceedings.

Unlike the Speaker of the House in Congress, the speaker in the California assembly appoints the chairperson and members of all standing committees. The senate's president *pro tempore* chairs the rules committee in the upper house. This committee has the power to appoint the members and chairs of all the other senate committees.

The Committee System

The committee system in the California legislature works much as it does in Congress. Committee members do much of the work of the legislature when they determine which bills will reach the floor and inform the full chamber on measures they have handled. For the 2005–2006 session, the California legislature has 23 standing committees in the senate and 29 in the assembly.

The standing committees in each house are generally set up by subject matter, such as committees on highways, education, and so on. A bill may be amended or even very largely rewritten in committee. Often, it is ignored altogether.

Other committees also play a prominent role in the California legislature. Conference committees made up of members of both houses resolve the differences in senate and assembly versions of a bill, which can then be sent to the governor. Joint committees, also consisting of members of both houses, conduct investigations, hold hearings, and recommend legislation. Select committees may be created by either house. Their charge is to research a problem and determine whether or not a new law might be needed.

The Legislative Process

The major steps in the legislative process in the California legislature are much like those in Congress. You can review the process in Congress by studying the diagram on page 345.

Sources of Bills

Legally, only a member may introduce a bill in either house in any State legislature. So, in the strictest sense, legislators themselves are the source of all measures introduced. In broader terms, however, the lawmakers are the authors of only a handful of bills.

A large number of bills come from public sources, from officers and agencies of State and local government. Every governor has a legislative program, and often an extensive and ambitious one.

Bills also come from a wide range of private sources. The largest single source for proposed State laws appears to be interest groups. Those groups and their lobbyists have one overriding purpose: to influence public policy to benefit their own particular interests. In California, pressure groups and lobbyists are often referred to as the "third house" of the legislature. Of course, some bills do originate with private individuals—business people, labor union members, and other citizens—who, for one reason or another, think that "there ought to be a law...."

Direct Legislation

The California constitution allows voters to take part directly in lawmaking. The main vehicles for this participation are the initiative and the referendum.

1. *The Initiative.* Through the initiative process, voters in California can propose constitutional amendments and they can also propose ordinary statutes. California uses the more common direct initiative rather than the little-used indirect initiative. The State's initiative proposals, therefore, go directly to the ballot rather than indirectly, through the legislature.

In California's direct initiative, the secretary of state receives a petition setting forth the proposed amendment or statute and containing the signatures of a certain number of qualified voters. If all is in order, the secretary of state submits the proposed measure in the next general election. If the voters approve the measure, it becomes law. If not, it dies.

Proposition 13, approved by an overwhelming vote in 1978, has had extraordinary and lasting consequences in California. It cut local property taxes by 30 percent and placed a limit on all future property tax increases.

2. *The Referendum.* A **referendum** is a process by which a legislative measure is referred to the State's voters for final approval or rejection. California has both mandatory and popular referendums. A *mandatory referendum* requires that the legislature refer a measure to the voters. In California, measures that result in a mandatory referendum include proposed constitutional amendments and the borrowing of money.

Under the *popular referendum,* the people may demand via petition that a statute passed by the California legislature be referred to them for final action. Popular referendums are rare, and most attempts to use them fail, usually for lack of signatures on the petition. In California, since 1912, there have been 52 attempts to qualify referendums for the ballot. Of these, 39 made it to the ballot and 25 of those were approved by the voters.

Section 2 Assessment

Key Terms and Main Ideas

1. The **police power** is used for what purposes?
2. What three kinds of nonlegislative powers does the California legislature have?
3. What are the three usual sources of bills?
4. What is the difference between the initiative and **referendum** in California?

Critical Thinking

5. **Making Comparisons** Consider what you know about Congress and the California legislature. **(a)** In what areas are they most alike? **(b)** In what areas are they most different?

Standards Monitoring *Online*
For: Self-quiz with vocabulary practice
Web Code: mqa-8242

6. **Analyzing Information** Would you support an amendment to your State's constitution that would provide for a unicameral legislature? Why or why not? (See the discussion of bicameralism in Congress in Chapter 10, Section 1 as you think about this question.)

Go Online
PHSchool.com

For: An activity on State legislative processes
Web Code: mqd-8242

Section Preview

OBJECTIVES

1. **Describe** the governorship of California.
2. **Summarize** the governor's many roles, including the powers, duties, and limitations of the office.
3. **Examine** the duties and powers of the lieutenant governor of California.
4. **List** and describe the other State executive offices.

WHY IT MATTERS

The governor is the chief executive of California. Although his or her executive powers are limited in several important ways, the people of the State look to the governor for leadership in State affairs. The governor and other important State executive officers are elected directly by the people.

POLITICAL DICTIONARY

★ **recall**
★ **item veto**
★ **clemency**
★ **pardon**
★ **commutation**
★ **reprieve**
★ **parole**

The governor is the principal executive officer in California. He or she is always a central figure in State politics and is often a well-known national personality as well. The governor of California, like all governors today, holds an office that is the direct descendant of the earliest public office in American politics, the colonial governorship, established in Virginia in 1607.

The Governorship

In colonial America, the actions of the royal governors inspired much of the resentment that fueled the Revolution. That attitude was carried over into the first State constitutions. Most of the powers of government were given to the legislatures; the new State governors, for the most part, had little real authority. In every State except Massachusetts and New York, the governor was chosen by the legislature, and in most of them only for a one-year term.

That original separation of powers soon proved unsatisfactory. Many of the State legislatures abused their powers. Several fell prey to special interests, and the governors were unable to respond. So, as new constitutions were written, and the older ones revised, the powers of the legislatures were curbed and the powers of the governors increased.

Through the early 1800s, the power to choose the governor was taken from the legislature and given to the people. The veto power was vested in the governor, and the gubernatorial powers of appointment and removal were strengthened as well.

Beginning with Illinois in 1917, most States have reorganized and strengthened the executive branch to make the governor the State's chief executive in more than name. To a greater or lesser degree, governors are much more powerful figures today than in decades past.

Qualifications

Anyone who wants to become the governor of a State must be able to satisfy a set of formal qualifications. In California a candidate must be a qualified voter, at least 18 years old, who has been an American citizen and a State resident for at least five years.

Clearly, these formal qualifications are not very difficult to meet. It is the *informal* qualifications that have real meaning. To become a governor, a person must have those characteristics that will first attract a party's nomination, and then attract the voters in the general election.

Those characteristics vary from State to State, and even from election to election within a State. Race, sex, religion, name recognition, personality, party identification, experience, ideology, the ability to use television effectively—these and several other factors are all part of the mix.

Over time, more than 2,500 persons have served as governors of the various States. To this point (2006), only 26 have been women. Eight of them are in office today: Ruth Ann Minner (D., Delaware), first elected in 2000 and re-elected in 2004; Janet Napolitano (D., Arizona), Linda Lingle (R., Hawaii), Kathleen Sebelius (D., Kansas), and Jennifer Granholm (D., Michigan), elected in 2002; Kathleen Blanco (D., Louisiana), elected in 2003; M. Jodi Rell (R., Connecticut), who succeeded to the office from the post of lieutenant governor in 2004; and Christine Gregoire (D., Washington), elected in 2004. The overall total of 26 includes 18 Democrats and 8 Republicans.[4]

Selection

The governor is chosen by popular vote in every State. In California, as in all but a few States, gubernatorial candidates are picked in a primary election. Nearly half the States now provide for the joint election of the governor and the lieutenant governor. In those States, each party's candidates for those offices run as a team, and the voter casts one vote to fill both posts. In California, however, voters elect the governor and lieutenant governor independently.

Term

Governors are elected to four-year terms nearly everywhere today. Only New Hampshire and Vermont still provide for two-year terms. More than half the States, including California, limit the number of terms a governor may serve. California's chief executive can hold the office for, at most, two four-year terms.[5] Only one State, Virginia, now has a single-term limit.

---

[4]All told, 18 other women have served as governors. Fifteen of them were elected to office: Nellie Ross (D., Wyoming, 1925–1927), Miriam Ferguson (D., Texas, 1925–1927, 1933–1935), Lurleen Wallace (D., Alabama, 1967–1968), Ella Grasso (D., Connecticut, 1975–1980), Dixy Lee Ray (D., Washington, 1977–1981), Martha Layne Collins (D., Kentucky, 1984–1987), Madeleine Kunin (D., Vermont, 1985–1991), Kay Orr (R., Nebraska,1987–1991), Joan Finney (D., Kansas, 1991–1995), Barbara Roberts (D., Oregon, 1991–1995), Ann Richards (D., Texas, 1991–1995), Christine Todd Whitman (R., New Jersey, 1994–2001), Jeanne Shaheen (D., New Hampshire, 1997–2003), Jane D. Hull (R., Arizona, 1997–2003), who as secretary of state succeeded to the office in 1997 and was subsequently elected in 1999, and Judy Martz (R., Montana, 2001–2005). Three other women have succeeded to a governorship: Rose Mofford (D., Arizona, 1988–1991), from the post of secretary of state, and Jane Swift (R., Massachusetts, 2001–2003) and Olene Walker (R., Utah, 2003–2005), both from the post of lieutenant governor.

▲ *Recall* Arnold Schwarzenegger announced his candidacy for the California governorship on Jay Leno's Tonight Show in 2003. He won the office at an election in which the incumbent governor, Democrat Gray Davis, was recalled by the voters. **H-SS 12.6.5**

Succession

Governors are mortal. Occasionally, one of them dies in office. Many of them are also politically ambitious. Every so often, one resigns in midterm—to become a United States senator or to accept a presidential appointment, for example.

When a vacancy does occur, it sets off a game of political musical chairs in the State. The political plans and timetables of a number of public personalities are affected by the event. No matter what causes a vacancy, every State's constitution provides for a successor. The California constitution puts the lieutenant governor first in the line of succession. It also makes the lieutenant governor the State's acting governor whenever the duly elected chief executive travels outside the State.

Removal

In California the governor may be removed through the impeachment process. According to the constitution, the assembly votes to impeach and the senate conducts any trial. No California governor has ever been impeached.

California is also one of 18 states in which the governor may be recalled by the voters.[6] The

---

[5]The all-time record for both gubernatorial service and electoral success belongs to George Clinton of New York. He sought and won seven three-year terms as governor and held the office from 1777 to 1795 and again from 1801 to 1804. Clinton was later Vice President of the United States, from 1805 to 1812.

▲ **Governor Schwarzenegger** Joined by legislators and First Lady Maria Shriver, Governor Arnold Schwarzenegger signs a law creating a California Museum for History and Arts. ***Critical Thinking Lawmakers must cope with big demands on available money. What should their priorities be?*** H-SS 12.7.2

recall is a procedure by which voters may remove an elected State official from office before the completion of his or her regular term. The process in California, like initiative and referendum, involves gathering a certain number of signatures on a petition and filing it with the secretary of state. Once sufficient signatures are certified, the governor calls a special election. If a majority votes to recall, the State official is removed from office.

Only two of the nation's governors have ever been recalled—North Dakota's Lynn J. Frazier, a Republican, in 1921 and California's Gray Davis, a Democrat, in 2003. Mr. Davis, whom voters blamed for the State's economic woes and a record budget deficit, was ousted in an election in which 55 percent of the electorate favored his removal. The voters picked Arnold Schwarzenegger as California's 38th chief executive in that same election.

Compensation

California's governor earns $175,000 a year. He is also provided with an expense account and other benefits.

To a governor's salary and other material compensation must be added the intangibles of honor and prestige that go along with the office. It is this

---

6Alaska, Arizona, California, Colorado, Georgia, Idaho, Kansas, Louisiana, Michigan, Minnesota, Montana, Nevada, New Jersey, North Dakota, Oregon, Rhode Island, Washington, and Wisconsin.

factor, along with a sense of public duty, that often brings many of our better citizens to seek the office. Several Presidents were governors before entering the White House, including, since 1900, William McKinley, Theodore Roosevelt, Woodrow Wilson, Calvin Coolidge, Franklin Roosevelt, Jimmy Carter, Ronald Reagan, Bill Clinton, and George W. Bush.

A Governor's Many Roles

Much like the President, a governor plays a number of different roles. He or she is, at the same time, an executive, an administrator, a legislator, a party leader, an opinion leader, and a ceremonial figure. What any State's governorship amounts to depends on how well the particular governor plays these roles.

Many of a governor's formal powers are hedged with constitutional and other legal restrictions. Nonetheless, the powers a governor does have, together with the prestige of the office, make it quite possible for a capable, dynamic person to be a "strong governor," one who can accomplish much for the State and for the public good.

One noted authority on State politics insists that the powers of all governors rest very largely on their talents of persuasion:

PRIMARY Sources ❝ *Their power depends on their ability to persuade administrators over whom they have little authority, legislators who are jealous of their own powers, party leaders who are selected by local constituents, federal officials over whom governors have little authority, and a public that thinks governors have more authority than they really have. Thus, the role of governors is, above all, that of a persuader—of their own administrators, State legislators, federal officials, party leaders, the press, and the public.* ❞

—Thomas R. Dye, *Politics in States and Communities*, 4th ed.

Executive Powers

The presidency and the governorships are similar in several ways, but the comparison can be pushed too far. Remember, the Constitution of the United States makes the President *the* executive in the National

Government. State constitutions, on the other hand, regularly describe the governor as the *chief* executive in the State's government. The distinction here, between *the* executive and the *chief* executive, is a critical one. The executive authority is fragmented in most States, but it is not at the national level.

In the States, the executive authority is shared by a number of "executive officers." California's executive officers include a lieutenant governor, attorney general, controller, secretary of state, and treasurer. All these executive officers are popularly elected, and for that reason, they are very largely beyond the governor's direct control.

In short, most State constitutions so divide the executive authority that the governor can best be described as a "first among equals." Yet, whatever the realities of the distribution of power, the people of California look to their governor for leadership in State affairs. It is also the governor whom they hold responsible for the conduct of those affairs and for the overall condition of the State.

The governor's basic legal responsibility is regularly found in a constitutional provision that directs the chief executive "to take care that the laws be faithfully executed." Though the executive power may be divided, the governor is given a number of specific powers with which to accomplish that task.

1. *Appointment and Removal.* The governor can best execute—enforce and administer—the law with subordinates of his or her own choosing. Hence, the powers of appointment and removal are, or should be, among the most important in the governor's arsenal.

A leading test of any administrator is his or her ability to select loyal and able assistants. Two major factors work against the governor's effectiveness here, however. First is the existence of those other elected executives; the people choose them and the governor cannot remove them.

Second, California's constitution and statutes place restrictions on the governor's power to hire and fire. The governor can, by law, make some 2,000 appointments, including nearly all department directors and high-ranking policy makers. Nevertheless, the senate must confirm about 170 of those appointments. When the governor fills a vacancy among the executive officers, a majority of the senate and assembly must confirm this

Party Control of Governorships, 2006

KEY
■ Republican ■ Democrat

SOURCE: National Governors' Association

Interpreting Maps **Which party controls the governorships of the most populous states?**

nomination. The governor also appoints hundreds of members of State boards and commissions. Even these often have restrictions, such as the need for senate confirmation or the requirement that a certain number of members be licensed professionals or public representatives.

2. *Supervisory Powers.* The governor of California is empowered to supervise the work of thousands of men and women who staff the State's executive branch. Here again, the constitution and statutes of the State often limit the governor's authority. Many State agencies are subject to the governor's direct control, but many are not. The governor's powers of persuasion and ability to operate through informal channels (such as party leadership and appeals to the public) can therefore make a significant difference in his or her ability to supervise the executive branch.

3. *Budget-Making Power.* The California constitution requires the governor to submit a proposed budget each January with an estimate of the State's expenditures and revenues for the fiscal year starting the following July 1. The proposed budget must be balanced; that is, expenditures must not exceed revenues. As a result of a constitutional amendment in 2004, the legislature must be sure that the budget it finally enacts

▲ **California National Guard troops** patrol the Golden Gate Bridge to prevent acts of terrorism. Many members of the California National Guard are serving in Iraq and Afghanistan. **Critical Thinking When does the National Guard perform military functions?**.

five months later, in June, is also balanced. After the bill is enacted, if the governor anticipates a budget imbalance, he or she can proclaim a fiscal emergency, which forces the legislature into special session to address the problem.

4. *Military Powers.* The constitution of California makes the governor the commander in chief of the State militia—in effect, of the State's units of the National Guard. The National Guard is the organized part of the State militia. In a national emergency, the National Guard may be "called up"—ordered into federal service by the President. Today, California National Guard units are on duty in Iraq, Afghanistan, Bosnia, and other foreign lands.

When the State's Guard units are not in federal service (which is most of the time), they are commanded by the governor. On occasion, governors find it necessary to call out the Guard to deal with emergencies such as prison riots, to help fight a dangerous forest fire, to aid in relief and evacuation after a flood, to prevent looting during and after some other natural disaster, and so on.

Legislative Powers

The State's principal executive officer has important formal legislative powers. These powers, together with the governor's own political clout, often make the governor in effect the State's chief legislator.

1. *The Message Power.* This is really the power to recommend legislation, and a strong governor can do much with it.

Much of what the legislature does centers on the governor's program for legislative action. That program is given to the lawmakers in a yearly State of the State address, in the budget, and in several special messages. The most effective governors regularly push their programs by using the formal message power together with a number of informal tactics, such as appeals to the people and close contacts with key legislators.

2. *Special Sessions.* The governor has the power to call the legislature into special session. The basic purpose of this power is to permit the State to meet extraordinary situations, such as a fiscal emergency. Note, however, that the power can also be an important part of the governor's legislative arsenal. On occasion, a governor has persuaded reluctant legislators to pass a bill by threatening to call them back in a special session, if they adjourn the regular session without having passed it.

3. *The Veto Power.* The governor has the power to veto measures passed by the legislature. This power—and even just the threat to use it—is often the most potent power the governor has in influencing the work of the legislature.

Unlike the President, the governor of California does not have the pocket veto. That is, those bills the governor neither signs nor vetoes after the legislature adjourns become law without his or her signature.[7]

In California, however, the governor's veto power does include the **item veto,** or the power to veto of one or more items in a bill without rejecting the entire measure. Using the item veto, the California governor can reduce or eliminate any item of appropriation—money made available for a specific purpose—in any bill, including the budget.

The vote needed to override the governor's veto is two thirds of the full membership of the assembly and the senate. In actual practice, recent governors have rejected less than 10 percent of the measures passed by the legislature.

---

[7]The governor has the pocket veto in only 13 States: Alabama, Delaware, Hawaii, Massachusetts, Michigan, Minnesota, New Hampshire, New Mexico, New York, North Carolina, Oklahoma, Vermont, Virginia.

However, when the veto power is used, it is quite effective. Since 1946, the California legislature has successfully overridden a governor's veto just seven times.

Judicial Powers

In every State the governor has several judicial powers. Most of them are powers of executive **clemency,** or powers of mercy that may be shown toward those convicted of a crime.

With the power to **pardon,** a governor may release a person from the legal consequences of a crime. A pardon may be full or conditional, and it can be granted only after conviction. With the power of **commutation,** a governor may reduce the sentence imposed by a court. Thus a death sentence may be commuted to life imprisonment. The power to **reprieve** postpones the execution of a sentence. The power to **parole** allows the release of a prisoner short of the completion of the original sentence.[8]

In California these judicial powers, except for parole, belong to the governor alone. The governor, however, typically relies on the Board of Prison Terms to investigate applications for reprieves, pardons, and commutations and make recommendations. As for parole, the Board of Prison Terms creates a panel to decide whether and when to release a prisoner on parole. The constitution allows the governor to affirm, modify, or reverse decisions made by the parole panel.

Miscellaneous Duties

Every governor must perform many other, often time-consuming, duties. To list a few: The governor receives official visitors and welcomes other distinguished persons to the State, dedicates new buildings and parks, opens the State fair, and addresses many organizations and public gatherings. In addition, the governor is often called on to help settle labor disputes, to travel elsewhere in the country and sometimes abroad to promote the State and its trade interests, and to endorse worthy causes. The list is endless.

Other Executive Officers

In California, as in nearly every State, the governor must share control of his or her administration with a number of other executive officers.

Recall that most of those officials are, like the governor, chosen by the voters. And those elected executive officers all serve four-year terms concurrently with the governor.

The Lieutenant Governor

The lieutenant governor of California, as president of the senate, is the only State government official who has powers in both the executive and the legislative branches. As the official presiding officer in the senate, the lieutenant governor can cast the tie-breaking vote when necessary.

As in most States, the lieutenant governor in California assumes the powers and duties of the governor when the governor is unable to serve or is absent from the State.[9] He or she can then sign or veto legislation and even make political appointments. California's lieutenant governor also serves on various boards and commissions and can use those positions to support or initiate legislation. Throughout the country, the trend is for lieutenant governors to be given more power and responsibility.

Recall that the governor and lieutenant governor are elected independently in California. Thus, the two can be members of different political parties, with different agendas. In fact, since 1978, California has had a Republican and a Democrat serving in these positions, concurrently, six times.

The office of lieutenant governor is often regarded as a stepping-stone to the governorship. Seven of California's lieutenant governors have succeeded to the office of governor as a result of a governor's death or resignation. Two other lieutenant governors have been elected governor on their own.

The Secretary of State

The secretary of state serves as California's chief elections officer, administering the election laws, monitoring campaign and lobbyist financial reports, and developing programs to educate voters. The secretary of state is also the State's chief clerk and record-keeper. He or she has

---

[8]An extradition request from another State also puts the governor in a judicial role.

[9]The office does not exist in Arizona, Maine, New Hampshire, New Jersey, Oregon, and Wyoming. In Tennessee and West Virginia, the presiding officer of the Senate is also, by statute, the lieutenant governor.

charge of a great variety of public documents and is responsible for recording the official acts of the governor and the legislature. As with most of the other elected State executive officers, the secretary of state has little real discretionary power or authority.

The State Controller

California's controller is the chief financial officer of the State, serving as the State's accountant and bookkeeper. The controller's office reports on the financial operation of State and local government, accounts for and disburses State money, and administers the State's payroll system. He or she is a member of many boards and commissions, including the Board of Equalization.

The State Treasurer

The treasurer serves as banker for the State. His or her main job is to make payments out of the State treasury, as authorized by the controller. The treasurer is also the State's custodian of securities, seller of state bonds, and investment officer for most state funds.

The State Attorney General

The attorney general is the chief lawyer and law-enforcement officer of the State. He or she ensures that laws are properly and uniformly enforced, oversees the work of local district attorneys as they prosecute cases on behalf of the State, and advises State officers and agencies about legal matters.

Much of the power of the office centers on the attorney general's formal written interpretations of constitutional and statutory law. These interpretations, called opinions, are issued to answer questions raised by the governor, other executive officers, legislators, and local officials regarding the lawfulness of their actions or proposed actions. In most States these opinions have the force of law. In California they do not, although State courts have found that the attorney general's opinions are "entitled to great weight."

The State Board of Equalization

California's elected State executive officers include the five members of the Board of Equalization. This board represents the nation's only elected tax commission. One member is elected from each of the State's four Equalization Districts. Recall that the State controller serves as the fifth member.

The board's original mission, outlined in an 1879 amendment to the State constitution, was to ensure statewide equality and uniformity in county property tax assessment practices. The agency still has responsibility for administering property taxes. However, its role has expanded into other areas, including business taxes and income taxes. The Board of Equalization serves to connect State and local governments by distributing money to California's cities, counties, and special tax districts.

Section 3 Assessment

Key Terms and Main Ideas

1. What are the formal qualifications for the office of California governor?
2. What are the executive powers of the California governor?
3. What are the duties of the lieutenant governor of California?
4. Briefly explain these judicial powers of a governor: **clemency, pardon, commutation, reprieve,** and **parole.**

Critical Thinking

5. **Demonstrating Reasoned Judgment** Should the governor of California be able to appoint those other executive officers now chosen by the voters? Why or why not?

6. **Making Comparisons** Compare and contrast the usual powers of the governor with those of the President.

The New Breed of State Legislator

Analysis Skills HR4, HI3

The movement for term limits in the 1990s helped give rise to a new type of State legislator. Newcomers are challenging the traditional leadership and long-established ways of legislatures in several States, including California, Michigan, Ohio, and Florida. This analysis from State Legislatures *magazine examines these trends.*

There was a time when new members came to the legislature, were assigned seats in the back row and made to understand that for a couple of years they should keep quiet and watch. But times have changed. . . . Kathleen A. Stevens is a perfect example. Elected to the Maine House of Representatives when she was only 22 years old, she's . . . perfectly comfortable challenging the powers that be and the way things traditionally have been done.

Kathleen A. Stevens

And because of Maine's term limits, Stevens, who is now 27 and the ranking member of the House Appropriations Committee, is at the end of her career in the House. . . . According to futurist Ed Barlow, . . . state legislatures across the land are increasingly caught up in a subtle interplay between the new kind of lawmaker and the term limits trend, which has both spurred and then suddenly halted their public careers. . . . "History walks out the door when term-limited members have to leave," Barlow says. "These are the people who know . . . how government works, why things have been done the way they [have]." . . .

[The new breed] want to get things done in a hurry. In Michigan such a lawmaker is Mark Jansen, elected to the House only three years ago. . . . "Term limits are good because they give a person like me a chance to take on a real position of leadership," says Jansen. . . . "There are going to be more and more people around here who are less interested in saying that we have to do things a certain way just because

that's the way it has always been done. Instead you are going to see a new generation of people just simply looking for a better way." . . .

The new breed is going to make it harder for legislative leaders to achieve consensus . . . That the newer members are more likely to go find their own sources of information and background for bill research also weakens the leadership. "I can get on line and talk to someone in China in a couple of minutes," says [Tom] Davidson in Maine. "The Internet has . . . given new, mostly younger legislators a powerful tool for making their own connections." . . .

As the nation's legislatures swim into the new millennium, the new breed of legislators will not only become more numerous, but prominent as well. . . . "They are going to change the statehouses as we know them very substantially," says Barlow. "In many ways nothing will be the same as it was before."

Analyzing Primary Sources

1. How does this author describe the "new breed" of State legislators?
2. How has the Internet changed State legislatures, in the author's opinion?
3. How do term limits enable young legislators to rise to leadership positions?
4. Why would term limits make these new legislators impatient with the old ways of governing?

4 In the Courtroom

Section Preview

OBJECTIVES

1. **Identify** and define the kinds of law applied in California State courts.
2. **Compare and contrast** civil law and criminal law.
3. **Describe** the jury system in California.

WHY IT MATTERS

Have you ever been to court—as a plaintiff or as a defendant? If so, you do not need to be told why courts matter. If courts did not exist, we would most certainly have to invent them, for they are indispensable to a civilized society.

POLITICAL DICTIONARY

★ **common law**
★ **precedent**
★ **criminal law**
★ **felony**
★ **misdemeanor**
★ **infraction**
★ **civil law**
★ **jury**
★ **information**
★ **bench trial**

The principal function of the California State courts, as for all the State courts, is to decide disputes between private parties and between private parties and government. In addition, because nearly all of these courts can exercise the power of judicial review, they act as potent checks on the conduct of all of the other agencies of both State and local government.

Kinds of Law Applied in California State Courts

The law is the code of conduct by which society is governed.[10] It is made up of several different forms including constitutional law, statutory law, administrative law, common law, and equity.

1. *Constitutional Law.* The highest form of law in this country is based on the United States Constitution and the State constitutions and on judicial interpretations of these documents.

2. *Statutory Law.* This form of law consists of the statutes (laws) enacted by

◄ Colonial courts, like this one, were patterned after those in Great Britain.

legislative bodies, including the United States Congress, the California legislature, the people (through the initiative or referendum), and city councils and other local legislative bodies.

3. *Administrative Law.* This form of law is composed of the rules, orders, and regulations issued by federal, State, or local executive officers, acting under proper constitutional and/or statutory authority.

4. *Common Law.* The common law makes up a large part of the law of each State except Louisiana.[11] **Common law** is unwritten, judge-made law that has developed over centuries from those generally accepted ideas of right and wrong that have gained judicial recognition. It covers nearly all aspects of human conduct. State courts apply common law except when it is in conflict with written law.

The common law originated in England. It grew out of the decisions made by the king's judges on the basis of local customs. It developed as judges, coming upon situations similar

---

[10] In its overall sense, the term *law* may be defined as the whole body of "rules and principles of conduct which the governing power in a community recognizes as those which it will enforce or sanction, and according to which it will regulate, limit, or protect the conduct of its members"; *Bouvier's Law Dictionary,* 3rd revision, Vol. II.

[11] Because of an early French influence, Louisiana's legal system is largely based on French legal concepts, derived from Roman law. Nevertheless, the common law has worked its way into Louisiana law.

to those found in earlier cases, applied and reapplied the rulings from those earlier cases. Thus, little by little, the law of these cases became *common* throughout England and, in time, the English-speaking world. That is, the common law developed as judges followed earlier decisions and applied the rule of *stare decisis*, "let the decision stand."

American courts generally follow that same rule. A decision, once made, becomes a **precedent,** or a guide to be followed in all later, similar cases, unless compelling reasons call for either an exception or its abandonment and the setting of a new precedent.

The common law is *not* a rigidly fixed body of rules controlled in every case by a clear line of precedents that can be easily found and applied. Judges are regularly called on to interpret and reinterpret the existing rules in the light of changing times and circumstances.

In other words, most legal disputes in American courts are fought out largely over the application of precedents. The opposing lawyers try to persuade the court that the precedents support their side of the case or that the general line of precedents should not, for some reason, be followed.

The importance of the common law in the American legal system cannot be overstated. Statutory law does override common law, but many statutes are based on the common law. A great many statutes are, in effect, common law translated into written law.

5. *Equity*. This branch of the law supplements common law. It developed in England to provide equity—"fairness, justice, and right"—when remedies under the common law fell short of that goal.

Over the years, English common law became somewhat rigid. Remedies were available only through various writs—orders—issued by the courts. If no writ covered the relief sought in a case, the courts could not act.

Those who were thus barred from the courts—for whom there was no adequate remedy at common law—appealed to the king for justice. These appeals were usually referred to the chancellor, a member of the king's council. By the middle of the fourteenth century, a special court of chancery, or equity, was set up.

▲ Some people feel that trial juries should be abolished. *Critical Thinking Do you agree, or do you feel that juries are an important part of our legal system? Explain your answer.* H-SS 12.1.5

Over time, a system of rules developed in the chancery court, and equity assumed a permanent place in the English legal system.

Today, the most important difference between common law and equity is this: The common law is mostly remedial, while equity is preventative. Thus, the common law applies to or provides a remedy for matters *after* they have happened; equity seeks to stop wrongs *before* they occur.

To illustrate this point, suppose your neighbors plan to add a room to their house. You think that a part of the planned addition will be on your land and will destroy your rose garden. You can prevent the construction by getting an injunction, which is a court order prohibiting a specified action by the party named in the order.

A court is likely to grant the injunction for two reasons: (1) the immediacy of the threat to your property, and (2) the fact that the law can offer no fully satisfactory remedy once your garden has been destroyed. It is true that money damages might be assessed under common law, but no amount of money can give back the pride or the pleasure your roses now give you.

The early colonists brought both equity and the common law to America. At first, different courts administered the two forms of law. In time, though, most States provided for the administration of both forms by the same courts, and the procedural differences between the two are disappearing.

Interpreting Political Cartoons According to this cartoon, what kinds of decisions do juries make? Is that an accurate interpretation of the jury system?

"He's big, all right, and he's definitely a wolf, but it'll be up to a jury to decide whether or not he's bad."

Criminal and Civil Law

You have probably heard reference to criminal law and civil law. These are two other categories into which the law is commonly classified.

That portion of the law that defines public wrongs—offenses against the public order—and provides for their punishment is the **criminal law.** A criminal case is brought by the State against a person accused of committing a crime. The State, as the prosecution, is always a party in a criminal case.

California recognizes three kinds of crimes: A **felony** is the worst kind of crime, and it may be punished by a heavy fine and/or imprisonment or even death. A **misdemeanor** is a lesser offense, punishable by a fine and/or a jail term of less than a year. An **infraction,** such as speeding or failing to stop for a red light, is a minor crime punishable by a fine but not incarceration.

The **civil law** relates to human conduct, to disputes between private parties, and to disputes between private parties and government not covered by criminal law. Civil cases are usually referred to as suits, or lawsuits, and often lead to the award of money or a fine. Civil law can involve a wide range of issues, including divorce and custody disputes, torts (private wrongs against a person or property), and contracts.

The Jury System

A **jury** is a body of persons selected according to law who hear evidence and decide questions of fact in a court case. There are two basic types of juries in the American legal system: (1) the grand jury and (2) the petit jury.

The Grand Jury

In California the grand jury has three main functions: (1) to serve as a "watchdog," investigating and reporting on local government issues; (2) to inquire into the misconduct in office of public officials and, if it finds wrongdoing, to file an accusation leading to a trial; (3) to decide whether a crime has been committed and if sufficient evidence exists to indict, or bring formal written charges, against a specific person. This last function reveals the grand jury's historical role as a buffer between citizens and overeager prosecutors.

Grand juries vary greatly in size from State to State and even within States. California grand juries in counties with a population greater than 4 million have 23 jurors. Fifteen of them must agree that an accused person is probably guilty in order to file an accusation or bring an indictment. In counties with 20,000 or fewer people, grand juries have 11 jurors (of whom 8 must agree). All other counties have 19 jurors (of whom 12 must agree).

The grand jury meets in secret. In California the judge appoints one of the jurors to serve as the foreman or forewoman. The prosecuting attorney presents witnesses and evidence against persons suspected of crime. The jurors may question those witnesses and may also summon others to testify against a suspect.

After receiving the evidence and hearing witnesses, the grand jury deliberates alone and in secret. They then move to the courtroom where their report, including any indictments they may have returned or accusations they may have presented, is read in their presence.

The grand jury is expensive, cumbersome, and time-consuming. Therefore, most of the States today depend more heavily on a much simpler process of accusation: the information.

The Information

An **information** is a formal charge filed by the prosecutor, without the action of a grand jury. It is now used for most minor offenses. California also uses it to initiate the vast majority of all criminal prosecutions. In the place of a grand jury's judgment that the evidence is sufficient to proceed, a judge determines probable cause through a preliminary hearing.

The use of an information has much to recommend it. It is far less costly and time-consuming. Also, since grand juries most often follow the prosecutor's recommendations, many argue that a grand jury is really unnecessary.

The chief objection to abandoning the grand jury appears to be the fear that some prosecutors may abuse their powers and be overzealous at the expense of both defendants and justice.

The Petit Jury

Anyone who is indicted on a criminal charge is entitled to a jury trial, as is the defendant in a civil case. The petit jury, or trial jury, hears the evidence in a case and decides the disputed facts.

The number of trial jurors may vary. As it developed in England, the jury consisted of "12 men good and true." As a rule, California petit juries have 12 jurors. In misdemeanor criminal trials and in civil trials, fewer jurors may be seated if both sides agree. Today, in all States, both men and women may serve on juries.

In a criminal case in California, the jury's verdict must be unanimous in order to convict. In a civil case, three fourths of the jurors must agree. If a jury cannot agree on a verdict (a so-called hung jury), either another trial with a new jury takes place or the matter is dropped.

Misdemeanor cases and civil proceedings in which only minor sums are involved are often heard without a jury, in a **bench trial,** by the judge alone. In several States, even the most serious crimes may be heard without a jury if the accused, fully informed of his or her rights, waives the right to trial by jury.

Selection of Jurors

Petit jurors in California are chosen mainly from lists of registered voters and licensed drivers. All jurors in California must meet the same qualifications. They must be U.S. citizens, at least 18 years old, able to understand English enough to discuss the case, and residents of the county that sent them the jury summons. Persons convicted of any felony or wrongdoing in public office cannot serve unless their civil rights have been restored. Persons over the age of 70, with serious health problems, may be excused from jury duty.

As with the grand jury, the States are moving away from the use of the trial jury. Leading reasons are the greater time and cost of jury trials. The competence of the average jury and the impulses that may lead it to a verdict are often questioned, as well. Much criticism of the jury system is directed not so much at the system itself as at its operation.

Several things should be said in favor of the jury system, however. It has a long and honorable place in the development of Anglo-American law. Its high purpose is to promote a fair trial, by providing an impartial body to hear the charges. A jury tends to bring the common sense of the community to bear on the law and its application. The jury system gives citizens a chance to take part in the administration of justice, and it fosters a greater confidence in the judicial system.

Section 4 Assessment

Key Terms and Main Ideas

1. Define **common law, criminal law,** and **civil law.**
2. What is the difference between a **felony** and a **misdemeanor?**
3. Name two kinds of **juries,** and tell what they do.
4. What does it mean when a judge follows a legal **precedent?**

Critical Thinking

5. **Checking Consistency** Most processes of government in this country must be open to public scrutiny, but a grand jury works in secret. **(a)** Why do you think this is so? **(b)** Do you think this secrecy is a good idea? Why or why not?

Standards Monitoring *Online*

For: Self-quiz with vocabulary practice
Web Code: mqa-8244

6. **Identifying Alternatives** Describe a situation in which someone might seek an injunction. Then write a brief argument in favor of granting the injunction and a brief argument against granting this remedy.

Go Online
PHSchool.com

For: An activity on grand juries
Visit: PHSchool.com
Web Code: mqd-8244

Skills for Life

Filing a Consumer Complaint

One of the functions of American government is to protect consumers. If you believe you're the victim of a money scam, an unsafe product, shoddy repair work, false advertising, or a warranty that was not honored, you can file a consumer complaint. The box below lists federal and private sources of consumer help. For State help, try the attorney general's office. To file a complaint, follow these steps:

1. Keep all records of transactions. Get estimates in writing. If a company representative gives you promises over the telephone, ask for them in writing. Get the name of the representative you're speaking with, the time of the call, and take notes from the conversation. What kinds of paper work should you save?

2. If you do not get satisfaction, file a complaint. Many disagreements can be worked out between you and the individual or company involved. But if

that doesn't work, determine what government agency handles your type of problem and file your complaint in writing. Using these letter-writing tips, write a sample first sentence of a complaint letter:

- Include specific facts, such as the date and place of your purchase and a serial or model number. If you are complaining about a service you received, describe the service and who performed it.
- Include <u>copies</u> of all relevant documents.
- Your tone should be firm, but polite—not angry, sarcastic, or threatening. The person reading your letter probably was not responsible for your problem, but may be helpful in fixing it.

3. File the complaint promptly. Some complaints must be made within a certain amount of time, so don't delay. What should you do if you get no response?

Help for Consumers

Consumer Product Safety Commission The CPSC is an independent federal regulatory agency that identifies unsafe consumer products and has the authority to ban the sale of them. CPSC responds to consumer complaints.
http://www.cpsc.gov

Consumer Information Center The CIC, based in Pueblo, Colorado, is perhaps the best-known source of federal consumer information. The CIC publishes a free catalog of more than 200 free and low-cost publications.
http://www.pueblo.gsa.gov/backgrnd.htm

ConsumerWorld This is a nonprofit Web site with links to federal, State, local, and private consumer resources. Read about the latest money scams, file a complaint, learn about your consumer rights, find the wholesale price of a car, or look up product reviews.
http://www.consumerworld.org

Test for Success

Write a fictional letter to a State consumer protection agency to complain about a defective product you bought. Briefly describe problems you had in getting the manufacturer to fix or replace the product.

Section Preview

OBJECTIVES

1. **Explain** how California State courts are organized, and describe the work of each kind of California State court.
2. **Examine** and evaluate the different ways that judges are selected.

WHY IT MATTERS

Millions of cases are filed each year in the California State courts, and thousands of them go to trial. Many of those criminal and civil cases involve only minor offenses or routine disputes. Others involve horrific crimes or quarrels with millions of dollars at stake.

POLITICAL DICTIONARY

★ warrant
★ appellate jurisdiction
★ retention election

They deal with everything from traffic tickets to murder, from disputes over nickels and dimes to settlements involving millions. They are the State courts and the judges who sit in them. In this section you will read about the way the California courts are organized and how they conduct their business. You will also evaluate the procedures for selecting judges.

You will find that the California State judicial system consists of three tiers of courts. The State supreme court and the courts of appeal are appellate courts, whose main task is to review decisions made by the third tier of courts, the superior courts.

California Superior Courts

The California constitution establishes 58 superior courts, one in each county, to serve as the State's trial courts. They handle all criminal cases, including felony and misdemeanor proceedings and motor vehicle matters. They also have jurisdiction over all civil cases, including family law, juvenile, small claims, and probate matters.

History of Trial Courts

Before the mid-1900s, California had a hodgepodge of inferior trial courts, below the superior court level. They included district courts, county courts, city courts, recorders' courts, and police courts, each with its own jurisdiction. The State had no centralized control over these courts, so deficient rules and procedures went unrevised.

In 1950, a constitutional amendment went into effect that consolidated the inferior courts into two types: municipal courts and justice courts. These court systems had uniform qualifications and salaries for judges. Each county was divided into judicial districts. Districts with more than 40,000 people would be served by a municipal court. Districts with fewer than 40,000 people would be served by a justice court.

► Judge Roy Bean (seated at table, at left) tries an accused horse thief in Langtry, Texas, in 1900. In the West of that time, JP's often *were* "the law" in their communities. *Critical Thinking How much confidence would you have had in the justice dispensed in this "courtroom"? Why?*

The law is the code of conduct by which a society is governed. No society, no community of people can possibly survive, let alone flourish, if that legal code is not accepted and obeyed by those who belong to that community. In the community that we call the United States, we honor the concept of freedom for the individual. At the same time, we insist that the law be obeyed.

President **Theodore Roosevelt**, the youngest person ever to sit in the White House, put the point this way in a message to Congress in 1903:

"No man is above the law and no man is below it; nor do we ask any man's permission when we require him to obey it. Obedience to the law is demanded as a right; not asked as a favor.**"**

Evaluating the Quotation

Who, according to Roosevelt, has the right to demand that the law be obeyed?   H-SS 12.2.3

The streamlining did not stop there. In 1994, voters passed Proposition 191, which eliminated the distinction between municipal courts and justice courts. Now the municipal courts handled all misdemeanor cases and infraction cases as well as civil matters involving claims for $25,000 or less. Their jurisdiction also included small claims cases that did not exceed $5,000. At the time, superior courts handled the remaining cases.

Finally, in 1998, voters passed Proposition 220, a constitutional amendment that permitted municipal and superior courts to merge their operations. The goal of this merger, like the earlier streamlining, was to improve services to the public. By 2001, trial judges in all 58 counties had voted to subsume their municipal courts within the superior court system.

Departments of the Superior Courts

Today, each of the superior courts hears those cases arising within its county. Criminal cases dominate the superior courts, with some 7 million cases filed each year. Another 1.5 million civil cases are filed. In every case a judge and sometimes a jury listen to the testimony of witnesses, determine the relevant facts, and base their decision on those facts and the applicable law. Special departments of the court handle family, juvenile, probate, small claims, and traffic cases.

1. *Family Court.* This department of the superior court hears family law matters, including divorce, child custody, child support, and domestic violence. It can issue temporary or permanent restraining orders as well as orders concerning child custody and visitation, spousal support, and other matters.

2. *Juvenile Court.* Individuals under 18 years of age who violate the law are known as juvenile delinquents. They generally are not subject to the justice of the courts in which adults are tried. Instead they are tried in juvenile court. The juvenile justice system is designed to address the special needs and problems of young people. This system generally emphasizes rehabilitation more than punishment. However, under certain circumstances juvenile courts do refer certain offenders to an adult criminal court for trial.

Recently, most States have responded to the rise in juvenile delinquency with tougher laws. Often these statutes make it easier to try juveniles as adults. As of March 2000, based on a law passed by California voters every county's district attorney has the authority to file a case directly in adult criminal court against children aged 14 or older who commit certain serious crimes.

3. *Probate Court.* The probate court supervises the transfer of assets from the estate of a person who has died to his or her legal beneficiaries. The probate process usually involves validating a will, appraising property, paying all debts, and distributing the remaining assets according to the will.

4. *Small Claims Court.* Many people cannot afford the costs of suing for the collection of a small debt. In California, people 18 years or older can go to small claims court to settle disputes in which the money damages are $5,000 or less. The plaintiff may consult a lawyer outside of court but must argue his or her case in person in front of the judge. Not all cases heard here concern money. A person who cannot persuade a neighbor to return her ladder, for example, or a land-

lord seeking back rent from a tenant can settle the dispute in small claims court.

5. *Traffic Court.* Traffic violations are criminal offenses. Most of them are infractions, which in California are not punishable by incarceration and are not subject to a jury trial. For an infraction, such as speeding or running a stop sign, the court can set a fine as high as $200 or more. If a driver fails to pay the fine by the date set, the court can issue a warrant for his or her arrest. A **warrant** is a court order authorizing, or making legal, some official action.

More serious traffic offenses are misdemeanors or felonies. The court can punish a misdemeanor, such as driving under the influence of alcohol or drugs, by a fine of more than $2,000 and up to a year in jail. A felony, like leaving the scene of an accident that causes injury or death, can result in a much higher fine and longer prison sentence.

California Courts of Appeal

Most States now have one or more intermediate appellate courts that stand between the trial courts and the State's highest court. There are six of these tribunals—six courts of appeal—in California today. The State is divided into six appellate districts, and in each of them a court of appeal hears cases brought to it from the superior courts within that district.

The main job of these courts is to review cases decided by the trial courts. When either a plaintiff or a defendant is not satisfied with a decision made in a superior court, he or she can appeal that outcome to the court of appeal for that district. As their title suggests, the six courts of appeal exercise mostly **appellate jurisdiction**. Their original jurisdiction is limited to a narrow class of cases—those involving claims of wrongful arrest (habeas corpus), for example.

In exercising their appellate jurisdiction, these courts do not hold trials. Rather, they hear oral arguments from attorneys, study the briefs (written arguments) that attorneys submit, and review the record of the case in the lower court. Ordinarily, an appellate court does not concern itself with the facts in a case. Rather its decision turns on whether the law was correctly interpreted and applied in the court below.

In California courts of appeal, the attorneys present their legal arguments to a three-judge

Interpreting Political Cartoons (a) What does the cartoon suggest about the use of the appeals process in this country? (b) Should those convicted of crime have an unlimited right to appeal their convictions? Explain your answer. H-SS 12.7.2

panel, consisting of a presiding justice and two associate justices. Besides listening to arguments and reading briefs, the judges may spend a considerable amount of time questioning the attorneys to get a full understanding of the issues. To decide a case, at least two of the three judges must agree.

The governor appoints the 105 judges who sit in the six courts of appeal. They serve 12-year terms. Vacancies are filled by the governor, but selections are subject to the approval of the Commission on Judicial Appointments. That body is composed of the State's chief justice, the attorney general, and the senior presiding judge of the court of appeal in the district in which the vacancy occurred.

The voters decide whether court of appeal judges will serve more than one term. They do so in elections in which judges run on their records, not against opposing candidates, in retain-reject elections patterned on the Missouri Plan.

California courts of appeal hear and dispose of around 25,000 cases a year. The decision by a California court of appeal may be reviewed by the State's supreme court, but its disposition of the case is usually final.

California Supreme Court

The State's supreme court is the highest court in its judicial system. The major function of the

Frequently Asked Questions

The Courts

What is an out-of-court settlement?

Most civil cases never in fact come to trial. They do not because the opposing parties often agree to resolve their dispute at some point before their case is to be heard by a court. In this circumstance, they reach what is regularly called an "out-of-court settlement." When one occurs, the complaint the plaintiff filed against the defendant is dismissed by the court.

Many out-of-court settlements are last-ditch affairs. That is, they happen only a matter of days, sometimes hours, before a court date. To put it another way, many out-of-court settlements are the result of a legal game of "chicken"—a contest in which one party or the other is, for one reason or another, forced to yield.

Again, civil cases are frequently resolved by out-of-court settlements. Criminal cases, however, are *never* resolved in this way.

Any Questions?

What would you like to know about crime or law in the United States? Brainstorm two new questions and exchange them with a classmate. What did you learn?

---

supreme court is to review the decisions of lower courts in those cases that are appealed to it.[23]

The size of the California supreme court is fixed by the State constitution. Seven justices sit on the high bench, including the chief justice. To render a judgment, four of these judges must concur.

The governor appoints justices to the California supreme court, and they are confirmed in the same manner as members of the courts of appeal. They, too, must face the voters at the end of a 12-year term.

The State supreme court is the court of last resort in the California judicial system. Remember, however, many cases also raise questions of federal law. So the United States Supreme Court may review some State supreme court decisions. But not very many State decisions actually go to the federal Supreme Court.[24] Recall that an appeal from a State's high court will be heard in the federal Supreme Court only if (1) a "federal question," meaning some matter of federal law, is involved in the case and (2) the Supreme Court agrees to hear that appeal.

In short, most State supreme court decisions are final. The oft-heard claim, "I'll fight this case all the way to the United States Supreme Court," is almost always just so much hot air.[25]

Unified Court Systems

The typical State court system is organized geographically rather than by types of cases. Thus, the general trial courts are most often organized so that each hears those cases arising within its own district, circuit, or county, no matter what the subject matter may be.

In these map-based systems, a judge must hear cases in nearly all areas of the law. A backlog of cases can and often does build up in some courts while judges sit with little to do in others. Moreover, uneven interpretations and applications of the law may and sometimes do occur from one part of the State to another.

To overcome these difficulties, a number of States have begun to abandon geographical organization. These States, including California, have turned instead to a unified court system, one that is organized on a functional, or case-type, basis.

In a completely unified court system, there is technically only one court for the entire State. It is presided over by a chief judge or judicial council. In California the Judicial Council is the governing body of the State's courts. The State constitution defines the council's role, directing it to provide policy guidelines to the courts, make yearly recommendations to the governor and the legislature, and adopt rules concerning court administration, practice, and procedure. Established in 1926, the

---

[23]The State's highest court is known as the Supreme Court in 45 States. But in Maine and Massachusetts it is called the Supreme Judicial Court; in Maryland and New York, the Court of Appeals; and in West Virginia, the Supreme Court of Appeals. Two States actually have two high courts. In Oklahoma and in Texas, the Supreme Court is the highest court in civil cases, and a separate Court of Criminal Appeals is the court of last resort in criminal cases.

[24]Many of the cases that reach the Supreme Court involve the 14th Amendment's Due Process and Equal Protection clauses.

[25]State law regularly gives its lower courts final jurisdiction over many types of minor cases. That is, review cannot be sought in a higher State court. In those cases, the lower court is the State's court of last resort. If any review is to be had, it can be only in the United States Supreme Court. Such reviews are extremely rare.

Judicial Council is the group that pushed for the streamlining that led to the merger of all inferior courts into the superior court system.

In a typical unified court system, there are a number of levels within the single court, such as California's supreme, intermediate appellate, and trial courts. At each level, departments are established to hear cases in certain specialized or heavy-caseload areas of the law—criminal, juvenile, family relations, and other areas that need special attention.

In such an arrangement, a judge can be assigned to that section or division to which his or her talents and interests seem best suited. To relieve overcrowded dockets, judges may be moved from one section or division to another. In short, the unified court system is a modern response to the old common law adage: "Justice delayed is justice denied."

Selection of Judges

More than 15,000 judges sit in the State trial and appellate courts today. They are most often chosen in one of three ways: (1) by popular election, (2) by appointment by the governor, or (3) by appointment by the legislature.[26]

Popular election is by far the most widely used method by which judges are selected. In fact, in 12 States popular election is the only method for choosing judges.[27] (The exception is that vacancies caused by deaths or by midterm resignations are usually filled by appointments made by the governor.)

The governor appoints nearly a fourth of all State judges today. In three States—Delaware, Massachusetts, and New Hampshire—the governor names all judges. In California, as you have read, the governor appoints justices to the courts of appeal and the supreme court, after which they stand for election in a yes or no vote, also known as a **retention election.** California's superior court justices, however, are chosen exclusively through popular vote for six-year terms in contested, nonpartisan elections. The winning candidate serves a term of six years.

Selection by the legislature is used least often. The legislature now chooses all or at least most judges in only two States: South Carolina and Virginia.

How Should Judges Be Selected?

Most people believe that judges should be independent, that they should "stay out of politics." Whatever method of selection is used should be designed with that goal in mind.

Nearly all authorities agree that selection by the legislature is the most political of all the

---

[26]Some judges are selected by other means in some States. In Ohio, for example, all judges, except those of the Court of Claims, are elected by the voters; the judges of the Court of Claims are appointed by the Chief Justice of the State Supreme Court. In Alabama, Michigan, Mississippi, Oregon, Texas, and Washington, all judges are popularly elected except for municipal court judges, who are chosen in accord with city charter provisions, usually by the city council.

[27] Arkansas, Georgia, Illinois, Kentucky, Louisiana, Minnesota, Montana, Nevada, North Carolina, North Dakota, West Virginia, and Wisconsin.

▲ California superior court judges are elected and campaign along with others running for office (at left). Superior Court Judge Michael Brenner issues a ruling concerning write-in ballots in a contested San Diego mayoral race (right).
Critical Thinking What are the pros and cons for each method of selecting judges? H-SS 12.6.4

methods of choice. Few favor it. So the question really is this: Which is better, popular election of judges or appointment by the governor?

Those who favor popular election generally make the democratic argument. Because judges "say the law," interpret and apply it, they should be chosen by and answer directly to the people. Some also argue that the concept of separation of powers is undercut if the executive (the governor) has the power to name the members of the judicial branch.

Those who favor appointment by the governor argue that the judicial function should be carried out only by those who are well qualified. The fact that a person has the support of a political party or is a good vote-getter does not mean that person has the capacity to be a good judge. Proponents of executive appointment insist that it is the best way to ensure that those persons who preside in courts will have the qualities most needed in that role: absolute honesty and integrity, fairness, and the necessary training and ability in the law.

At best, deciding between these two positions is difficult. The people have often made excellent choices, and governors have not always made wise and nonpolitical ones. Still, most authorities come down on the side of gubernatorial appointment, largely because those characteristics that make a good judge and those that make a good candidate are not often found in the same person.

Popular election is both widely used and widely supported. Moves to abandon it have been strongly opposed by party organizations. So, most moves to revise the method of judicial selection have kept at least some element of voter choice.

The Missouri Plan

For more than 80 years now, the American Bar Association (ABA) has sponsored an approach that combines the election and appointment processes. Because its adoption in Missouri in 1940 involved much political drama and attracted wide attention, the method is often called the Missouri Plan. Some form of the Missouri Plan is now in place in just over half of the States.

Missouri's version is still more or less representative of how the plan is implemented in the other States that use it. The governor appoints the seven justices of the State's supreme court, the 32 judges of the court of appeals, and all judges who sit in certain of the State's trial courts. The governor must make each appointment from a panel, or list, of three candidates recommended by a judicial nominating commission. The commission is made up of a sitting judge, several members of the bar, and private citizens.

Each judge named by the governor serves until the first general election after he or she has been in office for at least a year. The judge's name then appears on the ballot—without opposition. The voters decide whether or not that judge should be kept in office.

If the vote is favorable, the judge then serves a regular term: six years for a trial court judge and 12 years for one who sits on a higher court in Missouri. Thereafter, the judge may seek further terms in future retention elections. Should the voters reject a sitting judge, the process begins again.

Section 5 Assessment

Key Terms and Main Ideas

1. (a) Which level of California court might issue a **warrant** through its traffic court? (b) Why are warrants important?
2. (a) What is **appellate jurisdiction**? (b) Which State courts have this jurisdiction?
3. Describe the work of California's trial courts.
4. How does a contested election differ from a **retention election**?

Critical Thinking

5. **Demonstrating Reasoned Judgment** How do you think judges should be selected? Choose one of the methods described in this section, and "make a case for it" by creating a strong, well-supported argument in its favor.

Standards Monitoring *Online*

For: Self-quiz with vocabulary practice
Web Code: mqa-8245

6. **Drawing Inferences** What qualifications do you think a good judge should possess? Write a "want ad" for the position.

Go Online PHSchool.com

For: An activity on the State judicial system
Visit: PHSchool.com
Web Code: mqd-8245

Must Voting Districts Be Equal in Population?

 Analysis Skills HR4, HI3, HI4

If two voting districts have the same number of representatives in the State legislature but contain unequal numbers of voters, each voter in the more populous district has less influence than each voter in the less populous district. Does the Constitution require States to ensure that all voting districts are roughly equal in population?

Baker v. Carr (1962)

Tennessee's constitution required that the seats in that State's legislature be distributed among the State's 95 counties on the basis of the number of qualified voters in each county. A 1901 law directed that those seats be redistributed, in line with new census figures, every ten years. No reapportionments were made over the next sixty years, however.

Charles W. Baker, the mayor of Nashville, and several others went to the federal courts with a suit against Tennessee's chief election officer, Secretary of State Joe C. Carr. They claimed that the apportionment made in 1901 had been faulty, and they insisted that population changes over the years since had made it even more unfair. They argued that the inequalities produced by that unfair distribution of seats amounted to a violation of the equal protection of the laws guaranteed by the 14th Amendment to the federal Constitution.

The federal district court dismissed the suit, ruling that State apportionment was an issue for the elected branches and could not be reviewed by the courts. The plaintiffs appealed to the Supreme Court.

Arguments for Baker

1. The federal courts have the authority to consider this case because they have the power to prevent States from depriving people of their constitutional rights (in this case, the right to equal protection of the laws).
2. Although the States are responsible for electing their own officials and structuring their own governments, they must do so in ways that do not deprive their citizens of their constitutional rights.
3. The Tennessee apportionment harms voters in more-populous districts and thus violates the Equal Protection Clause of the 14th Amendment.

Arguments for Carr

1. The Constitution does not authorize the Federal Government to interfere in the States' election of their own officials.
2. The States have great flexibility to structure their own governments, and the Federal Government may not override the States' choices in this matter.
3. The Tennessee apportionment was created by the Tennessee legislature. The manner of electing officials is a political question, one not subject to review by the federal courts.

Decide for Yourself

1. Review the constitutional grounds on which each side based its arguments and the specific arguments each side presented.
2. Debate the opposing viewpoints presented in this case. Which viewpoint do you favor?
3. Predict the impact of the Court's decision on State elections and on the composition of State legislatures. (To read a summary of the Court's decision, turn to pages 799–806.)

Go Online
PHSchool.com
Use Web Code mqp-7249 to register your vote on this issue and to see how other students voted.

popular sovereignty (p. 685), limited government (p. 685), fundamental law (p. 686), initiative (p. 687), statutory law (p. 688), police power (p. 691), constituent power (p. 692), referendum (p. 693), recall (p. 696), item veto (p. 699), clemency (p. 699), pardon (p. 699), commutation (p. 699), reprieve (p. 699), parole (p. 699), common law (p. 702), precedent (p. 703), criminal law (p. 704), felony (p. 704), misdemeanor (p. 704), infraction (p. 704), civil law (p. 704), jury (p. 704), information (p. 704), bench trial (p. 705), warrant (p. 708), appellate jurisdiction (p. 709), retention election (p. 711)

Standards Review

H-SS 12.1.5 Describe the systems of separated and shared powers, the role of organized interests (Federalist Paper Number 10), checks and balances (Federalist Paper Number 51), the importance of an independent judiciary (Federalist Paper Number 78), enumerated powers, rule of law, federalism, and civilian control of the military.

H-SS 12.2.3 Discuss the individual's legal obligations to obey the law, serve as a juror, and pay taxes.

H-SS 12.6.4 Describe the means that citizens use to participate in the political process (e.g., voting, campaigning, lobbying, filing a legal challenge, demonstrating, petitioning, picketing, running for political office).

H-SS 12.6.5 Discuss the features of direct democracy in numerous states (e.g., the process of referendums, recall elections).

H-SS 12.7.2 Identify the major responsibilities and sources of revenue for state and local governments.

H-SS 12.7.6 Compare the processes of lawmaking at each of the three levels of government, including the role of lobbying and the media.

H-SS 12.7.7 Identify the organization and jurisdiction of federal, state, and local (e.g., California) courts and the interrelationships among them

Practicing the Vocabulary

Using Words in Context *For each of the terms below, write a sentence that shows how it relates to this chapter.*

1. popular sovereignty
2. reprieve
3. referendum
4. item veto
5. police power
6. civil law
7. bench trial
8. appellate jurisdiction
9. warrant

Fill in the Blank *Choose a term from the list above that best completes each sentence.*

10. The power of executive _____ includes the power to pardon or parole a convicted criminal.
11. Laws passed by the legislature are called _____.
12. A _____ is a more serious offense than a misdemeanor.
13. The _____ is a process by which voters can petition to propose constitutional amendments and legislation.
14. The basis of much American law is the unwritten, judge-made law called _____ which developed in England.

Reviewing Main Ideas

Section 1
15. What are the basic principles on which all State constitutions are based?
16. Briefly trace the history of the California constitution.
17. Describe the two basic steps of constitutional change.

Section 2
18. What powers does the California State legislature have?
19. How are California State legislators chosen?
20. How do the California initiative and referendum processes affect lawmaking in the State?

Section 3
21. List the powers of the governor of California.
22. What is the role of the lieutenant governor of California?

23. Name three other executive officers in State government and describe what they do.

Section 4
24. Name and describe the four kinds of law applied in California State courts.
25. What is the difference between criminal law and civil law?
26. (a) What are the two most common kinds of juries?
    (b) Describe the basic function performed by each of them.

Section 5
27. What are the functions of California's trial courts, intermediate appellate courts, and supreme court?
28. What are the three ways by which State judges are selected today?

Critical Thinking

Analysis Skills HR3, HR4

29. ***Applying the Chapter Skill*** A local jewelry store insists on charging you for fixing your watch, although it is still under warranty. Write a brief consumer complaint letter to a State agency. Describe the documents you have copied and attached to support your claim.

30. ***Identifying Central Issues*** Describe how the system of checks and balances works in State government. What limits does each branch of government place on the other two? Then compare these checks and balances with those in the federal system.

31. ***Recognizing Ideologies*** The idea that "a jury of one's peers" should seek the truth (decide the facts at issue) in a court case has a long history in this country. What does this fact tell you about traditional American views of the proper role of **(a)** ordinary citizens and **(b)** officers of government in the judicial process? **(c)** What does the trend away from the jury process suggest about current American attitudes?

32. ***Checking Consistency*** The governor is both the chief executive and, very often, the chief legislator in most States. Do you think that this circumstance violates the principle of separation of powers? Why or why not?.

Analyzing Political Cartoons

Using your knowledge of American government and this cartoon, answer the questions below.

"We all make mistakes, as Your Honor knows, having been twice reprimanded by the New York State Commission on Judicial Conduct."

33. What does this cartoon suggest about checks and balances in State government?
34. Do you think this cartoonist favors more or less control of the judiciary by other branches of government or by the voters? Explain your answer.

★ You Can Make a Difference

If you were talking with visitors about the history of your own State, what could you tell them? What native peoples lived where you live now? Do you know who the first European or Asian settlers of your area were? Why did they choose to live here? Use resources from your local historical society and from the State historical society to prepare a display and map of the early history of your State. If possible, use copies of drawings or photographs of the native peoples and of the settlers and their settlements.

Participation Activities

Analysis Skills HR3, HR4

35. ***Current Events Watch*** Write a biographical sketch of the governor of California. Trace his or her life from childhood to the governorship. Attempt to find the major factors—family, school, other experiences—that most influenced the shaping of the governor's character and abilities. Review the governor's political career, and try to discover why he or she entered politics. Assess the ways in which the governor uses the powers of the office, and his or her powers of persuasion. Include comments on the relationships between the governor and the media, special interests, and the voters of your State.

36. ***Diagraming Activity*** Using the information in this chapter and additional research, make a diagram of the major steps in changing the California State constitution. Include both the revision and the amendment processes.

37. ***It's Your Turn*** Suppose California were considering the Missouri Plan for selecting judges. Take a position for or against the plan, and write a speech on the subject. State your position clearly, and support it with reasons and facts. Remember, your audience will be listening to—not reading—your testimony. **(Writing a Speech)**

Standards Monitoring *Online*

For: Chapter 24 Self-Test **Visit:** PHSchool.com
Web Code: mqa-8246

As a final review, take the Magruder's Chapter 24 Self-Test and receive immediate feedback on your answers.
The test consists of 20 multiple-choice questions designed to test your understanding of the chapter content.

CHAPTER 25

California Local Government and Finance

"*In a great city, City Hall must be a beacon to the people's aspirations, not a barrier.*"
—Los Angeles Mayor Thomas Bradley, (1973–1993)

People everywhere have the same needs, many of which are fulfilled by local governments. Indeed, it is to local government that most people look for help and services.

◆ City Hall, Fillmore, California

Standards Preview

H-SS 12.6.4 Describe the means that citizens use to participate in the political process (e.g., voting, campaigning, lobbying, filing a legal challenge, demonstrating, petitioning, picketing, running for political office).

H-SS 12.7.2 Identify the major responsibilities and sources of revenue for state and local governments.

H-SS 12.7.5 Explain how public policy is formed, including the setting of the public agenda and implementation of it through regulations and executive orders.

H-SS 12.7.6 Compare the processes of lawmaking at each of the three levels of government, including the role of lobbying and the media.

Go Online
PHSchool.com

For: Current Data
Web Code: mqg-7256

For: Close Up Foundation debates
Web Code: mqh-7259

SECTION 1

California Counties, Special Districts, and Regional Bodies (pp. 718–723)

★ Counties or their equivalents exist in all but two States. Their functions vary depending on region.
★ County government affects the daily lives of all Californians.
★ Special districts provide a wide variety of services, including water and sewage, police and fire, and airport and park services.
★ Towns and townships are forms of local government that exist in certain parts of the country.

SECTION 2

Cities and Metropolitan Areas in California and the Nation (pp. 725–732)

★ Most Americans today live in urban areas.
★ City governments take one of three forms: mayor-council, commission, or council-manager.
★ Population shifts from cities to suburbs have left cities with fewer resources. One response has been the creation of metropolitan districts.

SECTION 3

Providing Important Services (pp. 733–737)

★ Under the federal system, States and their local governments have many powers and provide many important services.
★ California State and local governments provide education, help ensure public welfare and safety, and build and maintain highways.

SECTION 4

Financing State and Local Government (pp. 739–744)

★ The federal Constitution, the 14th Amendment, and the California State constitution restrict State and local taxing powers.
★ Most tax experts agree with Scottish economist Adam Smith that there are four principles of sound taxation.
★ California State and local governments rely on a variety of tax and nontax sources of revenue.
★ The State budget is the means by which California plans the control and use of public money.

California Counties, Special Districts, and Regional Bodies

Section Preview

OBJECTIVES

1. **Compare and contrast** the nation's counties.
2. **Analyze** the structure and functions of county governments in California.
3. **Explain** the reasons behind the formation of special districts and regional bodies.
4. **Describe** the functions of California school districts.
5. **Identify** two forms of local government used outside California.

WHY IT MATTERS

What county do you live in? What school district? Do you have any special districts or regional bodies in your local area? Your life is affected every day by the decisions of these local governments.

POLITICAL DICTIONARY

★ county
★ township
★ charter
★ ordinance
★ special district
★ regional body

The nation has the magnificent Capitol in Washington, D.C., and California has its own impressive capitol in Sacramento. These structures serve as centers for Federal and State governments. In most communities, however, local government has no grand dome. Government in these places is visible mainly in the form of the day-to-day services that keep communities going.

In spite of its humble appearance, local government is vitally important in the lives of every American. As one measure of this fact, recall that of the 87,525 units of government across the nation, 87,474 of them are local.

Counties, Towns, and Townships

A **county** is a major unit of local government in most States. Like all local governments, it is created by the State.[1] There are 3,034 counties in the United States. No close relationship exists between the size of a State and the number of counties it has. The number of counties in a given State runs from none in Connecticut and Rhode Island to as many as 254 in Texas.

In Louisiana, units of government known elsewhere as counties are called parishes. In Alaska, they are known as boroughs. In addition to Connecticut and Rhode Island, several other places across the country have no organized county government. Almost 10 percent of the nation's population lives in those areas today.

In terms of physical size, North Slope Borough, Alaska, is the largest county in the nation, covering 88,817 square miles. Kalawao County in Hawaii is the smallest, covering only 13 square miles. Counties within each State can vary widely in area.

Counties also differ greatly in terms of population. More than 10 million people now live in Los Angeles County in California, but census-takers could find only 67 residents of

---

[1]Recall that whether they are providing services, regulating activities, collecting taxes, or doing anything else, local governments can only act because the State has established them and has given them power to do so.

▲ Homer, Alaska, is just one of the nation's 87,474 units of local government.

Loving County, in West Texas, in 2000. Most counties—in fact nearly three fourths of them—serve populations of fewer than 50,000.

The function of counties varies from region to region. In the South and the West, including California, counties are the major units of government in rural areas. However, counties serve almost solely as judicial districts in the New England States. There, towns carry out most of the local government functions undertaken by counties elsewhere.

Except for a few major cities, each of the six States of New England is divided into towns. Each town generally includes all of the rural and the urban areas within its boundaries. The town delivers most of the services that are the responsibility of cities and counties elsewhere in the country.

At least in form, much of town government today is little changed from colonial times. The main feature is the town meeting, long praised as the ideal vehicle of direct democracy. The town meeting is an assembly open to all the town's eligible voters. It meets yearly, and sometimes more often, to levy taxes, make spending and other policy decisions, and elect officers for the next year. Between town meetings, the board of selectmen/selectwomen chosen at the annual meeting manages the town's business.

The ideal of direct democracy is still alive in many smaller New England towns. It has given way, however, to the pressures of time, population, and the complexities of public problems in many larger towns. There, representative government has largely replaced it.

In many Mid-Atlantic and Midwestern States, counties are divided into subdivisions called **townships**. In these States, from New York and New Jersey west to North and South Dakota, Nebraska, and Kansas, counties and townships share the functions of rural local government. About half of these States provide for annual township meetings, like those held in New England towns. Otherwise, the governing body is a three- or five-member board, generally called the board of trustees or board of supervisors.

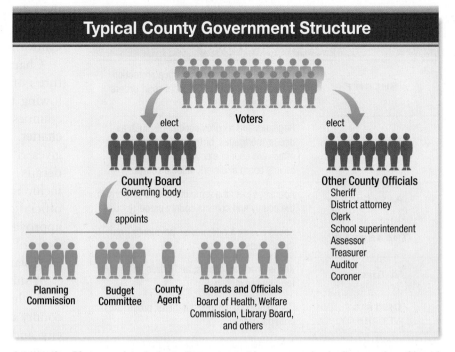

Typical County Government Structure

Voters

elect → **County Board** Governing body

appoints →

Planning Commission

Budget Committee

County Agent

Boards and Officials Board of Health, Welfare Commission, Library Board, and others

elect → **Other County Officials**
Sheriff
District attorney
Clerk
School superintendent
Assessor
Treasurer
Auditor
Coroner

Interpreting Diagrams A typical county government has a governing body, a number of boards or commissions, appointed bureaucrats, and elected officials. ***Why might the fact that the county governing body shares its powers with other elected officials lead to confusion?*** **H-SS 12.7.6**

A municipality (urban political unit) within a township—especially if it is large—usually exists as a separate governmental entity. Thus, township functions tend to be rural. They involve such matters as roads, cemeteries, drainage, and minor law enforcement. In some States, however, the township is also the basic unit of public school administration.

County Governments in California

Like counties throughout the nation, California's 58 counties vary greatly in size, geography, and population. San Bernardino County has the greatest area at 20,062 square miles, much of which is desert. In terms of population, the smallest county in California is mountainous Alpine County, with some 1,190 people. More than 8,000 times that number now live in highly urbanized Los Angeles County. As a result of such differences, the demands on California's county governments can vary considerably.

The State legislature gives each county the powers necessary to provide for the people living within its borders. County services usually include public works, the county road system, voter registration, health and welfare programs,

Typical Elected County Officials and Their Duties

SHERIFF	Runs county jail; provides police protection in rural areas; carries out local court orders; often collects taxes
CLERK	Registers and records documents such as deeds, mortgages, birth/death certificates; often runs county elections; is secretary to county board and clerk of local courts
ASSESSOR	Appraises (sets the value of) taxable property in the county and collects county property taxes
TREASURER	Keeps county funds; makes payments from these funds
AUDITOR	Keeps financial records; authorizes payments for county expenses
DISTRICT ATTORNEY	Conducts criminal investigations; prosecutes criminal cases
SCHOOL SUPERINTENDENT	Administers public elementary and secondary schools in the county
CORONER	Investigates violent deaths; certifies causes of deaths not attended by a physician

Interpreting Tables Elected county officials include people with a wide range of responsibilities that affect local communities. For example, surveyors like the woman pictured here help map local property accurately. **Which of these officials might affect your own daily life?** H-SS 12.7.2

and the recording of official documents, including real estate transactions and vital statistics such as births and deaths. These services cover the entire county, including all cities within the county.

Types of County Government

The California constitution provides for two types of counties: general law counties and charter counties. General law counties follow State law concerning the number of elected officials,

their duties, and other elements of governing the county. Three fourths of the counties in California are general law counties.

Charter counties have accepted the legislature's offer of home rule. Instead of strictly following the government code of laws, these 14 counties have chosen to be governed under a **charter**. A charter is, in effect, a basic law that gives a county some leeway in deciding the details of its own governmental structure, including the powers and duties of county officials. A county may adopt a charter with the approval of the majority of voters. The provisions of a charter have the same force of law as a legislative statute.

A subcategory of charter counties can be created when a city—especially a large city—and its county consolidate into what is called a charter city and county. Each entity retains its charter status, but the city's charter city powers supersede conflicting charter county powers. At present, San Francisco is the only charter city and county in California. You will read more about charter cities in Section 2.

The Board of Supervisors

General law counties and charter counties are both governed by a board of supervisors. The board has legislative powers within the county. It can levy taxes, subject to approval by the voters. It can create police, sanitary, or other **ordinances**, or local laws, as long as they do not conflict with the State's general laws.

Despite the American tradition of separation of powers, the board of supervisors also has executive powers. It can make sure that the taxes that it levies are collected and that the ordinances that it creates are enforced. Its other executive powers include planning for the county's future, overseeing county departments and approving their budgets, and appropriating and spending money on programs designed to meet the needs of county residents.

Generally, the board of supervisors consists of five elected members, each of whom represents one of the five supervisorial districts into which the county is divided. The California constitution, however, allows that in charter counties, more than five members may be elected, either by district or at-large. In district elections a candidate must live in and be a registered voter of the district.

Board members serve four-year, overlapping terms. This assures that there are always experienced members in office. The board's meetings must be open and public, and to pass any act, a majority of the board's members must concur.

Other County Officials

The California constitution calls for the election of at least three other county officials, each to a four-year term. Those elected officers, and their principal duties, are:

1. The county sheriff keeps the county jail and its prisoners, furnishes police protection in rural areas, investigates crimes, and carries out the orders of the local courts.

2. The district attorney prepares indictments and informations, conducts prosecutions, renders legal services to the county and other public entities, and defends all suits brought against the State in his or her county.

3. The county assessor assesses (estimates the value of) all taxable property in the county.

Other county officers in California include a county clerk, a tax collector, a superintendent of schools, a coroner, a surveyor, a fish and game warden, a veterinarian, and a road commissioner. In general law counties the board of supervisors appoints these other officers. In charter counties, the board may choose to provide for the election of some of them.

Special Districts

Tens of thousands of special districts now blanket the country. A **special district** is an independent unit created to perform one or more related governmental functions at the local level. These districts are found in almost mind-boggling variety and in every State.

California has more than 4,800 special districts. Among the most common types are airport districts, irrigation districts, transit districts, water districts, sanitation districts, utility districts, hospital districts, and cemetery districts. Nationally, school districts are by far the most widely found examples of special districts. California law, however, considers school districts as separate from special districts.

A leading reason for the creation of special districts has been the need to provide a particu-

▲ The tradition of the town meeting is still alive in many small New England towns. *Critical Thinking How does the town meeting reflect the ideal of direct democracy?* **H-SS 12.6.4**

lar service in a wider or a smaller area than that covered by a county or a city. For example, a special water pollution district might be needed to handle the stream pollution in the several counties through which a river flows. A fire protection district might be set up to protect an out-of-the-way locale from fires. In many cases, special districts have been formed because other local governments could not or would not provide the services desired.

In California, about half the special districts are dependent, meaning that they depend on another legislative body, such as a board of supervisors, to govern them. The rest are independent, meaning that they are governed by an independent board of directors. These directors may either be elected by the voters within the district's boundaries or appointed by the county's board of supervisors or, in a city, by that city council.

California residents or landowners who want new services and are willing to pay for them may form an independent special district by applying to a commission established for this purpose. Some of these independent special districts operate more like a business. Called enterprise districts, they charge customers for their services. Hospital districts, for example, charge room fees to patients, and water districts charge customers by the amount of water they use. Non-enterprise districts, like library and park districts, are not set up to charge individual users. They rely almost entirely on property taxes.

School Districts

California has more than 1,000 school districts, serving well over 6 million students in about 9,000 schools. There are three main types of school district: elementary (K–8), high (9-12), and unified (K–12). A publicly elected school board is the primary local organization responsible for governing each school district.

According to California law, every school district must have a governing board elected at-large by voters in the district. These school boards generally have five members, although some may have three or seven members, depending in part on the number of students in the district. Each member serves for four years.

Elections for district school boards are often among the most hotly contested local races. These contests can play a major part in determining the books students will use and the subject matter they will be taught. These are critical issues for many parents, and voter turnout for school board elections can be heavy.

A district's school board works with the school district administration to adopt budgets, negotiate with employee unions, and set many instructional and student-related policies. It acts through a majority vote of its members. A school board has the power to hire teachers, prescribe their duties, and fire them for good cause. It can also hire (and fire) a district superintendent of schools. Among other duties, the superintendent makes an annual report to the county superintendent of schools.

As the need to make this report suggests, school governance does not stop at the district level. Each county, too, has its own board of education, with five to seven elected members. The county superintendent of schools is responsible for fiscal oversight of each school district in the county and is also expected to visit each school to observe its operation and report back to the county board.

The State government also plays a role, some would say a major role, in California's schools. The passage of Proposition 13 in 1978 gave the governor and legislature control over education funding. The governor appoints the 11 members of the State Board of Education, the governing body of the California Department of Education. One of the board's members is a public high school student. Through the State superintendent of public instruction, the board establishes policies related to academic standards, instructional materials, assessment, and accountability. It adopts textbooks for grades K–8 and it provides for the administration of all relevant State laws.

Regional Bodies

The Californian legislature provides for the establishment of regional bodies. **Regional bodies** are local government entities designed to address problems that extend beyond the boundaries of any single county or city. The State creates them by statute to achieve a State goal, such as preserving air quality in a particular region.

Some regional bodies are strictly advisory in nature. For example, the San Luis Obispo Council of Governments (SLOCOG) is a State-designated agency responsible for developing a comprehensive transportation planning process and submitting a Regional Transportation Plan to the California Transportation Commission. This non-binding plan, updated by SLOCOG every three years, guides transportation policy for the region by making recommendations of ways to improve

▲ School districts are the most common special districts. *Critical Thinking (a) In what special districts do you live? (b) Why were these districts created?*

the network of highway, transit, air and water, rail, bicycle, and pedestrian facilities.

Other regional bodies have genuine regulatory powers. For example, the South Coast Air Quality Management District (AQMD) draws up comprehensive plans for improving air quality in Orange County and in the urban parts of Los Angeles, Riverside, and San Bernardino counties. But it also regulates and monitors businesses and activities that pollute the air. It has the power to enforce compliance with State and federal air quality standards by assessing fines and other penalties.

Most regional bodies have appointed boards whose members are elected officials from the cities and counties within the designated region. This can present a conflict of interest for board members. Should they make decisions that serve their own city's or county's interests or decisions that promote the best interests of the entire region? The reason for forming these bodies is to deal more effectively with regional issues, and experts in this area tend to agree that members of these boards must think regionally.

Tribal Government

Like all Native Americans, California Indians have survived a series of historical upheavals and injustices. Today, the federal and State governments recognize the sovereign status of 109 California tribes that reside mainly on reservations and rancherias, which are smaller reservations. These Indian groups are working to restore their right to self-determination through tribal government.

Traditional tribal government is organized hierarchically. At the top of the hierarchy, a tribal council serves as a link to federal and State government, provides services to the community, and makes all economic and legal decisions in the best interests of the tribe.

Since 2000, tribal fortunes have been changing, largely as a result of the development of Indian gaming revenues. More than 40 California tribes, exercising their sovereign right to tribal government gaming, now host some form of gambling business. Indian tribal enterprises generally pay no federal or State income taxes on profits.

The billions of dollars in revenue generated by Indian gaming have contributed to California Indians' goal of economic self-sufficiency. This revenue has also brought new energy to tribal governments, better enabling them to provide health care, housing, education, and other basic services to their people. California tribal governments are also pursuing their goals by constructively engaging local, State, and federal governments and by working together on legislative, legal, and regulatory actions.

Section 1 Assessment

Key Terms and Main Ideas

1. What is a **county**?
2. How does a **township** differ from a **special district**?
3. **(a)** What are the two main types of county in California?
   (b) List three elected officials commonly found in county government.
4. What is the primary function of a district's school board?

Critical Thinking

5. **Comparing** How are the reasons for forming special districts similar to the reasons for forming regional bodies?
6. **Drawing Inferences** Review the functions of county government and special districts in California. List and describe at least three examples of how these governing bodies affect the day-to-day lives of people in your community.

Standards Monitoring *Online*
For: Self-quiz with vocabulary practice
Web Code: mqa-8251

Go Online
PHSchool.com
For: An activity on local government
Web Code: mqd-8251

on Primary Sources

Seeing the Regional Future

Analysis Skills CS3, HR4, HI3

Urban planner William Fulton is a senior research fellow at Claremont Graduate University Research Institute. In this selection, he argues that the future of economic development lies in the growth of large regions, not individual cities and towns.

California State University at Chico

Not long ago, I sat down to lunch with all of the planning directors and economic development specialists in Redding, California. . . . The Redding area has suffered from sluggish economic growth in recent years, and for close to two hours these local officials took turns telling me about the troubles their community faced and the "assets" they had to work with in confronting them. . . .

"And, of course, we have a state university with a good reputation," one of the planning directors said. "That's a great help." All the others nodded in agreement.

. . . I had spent the better part of two days touring Redding, and I had seen no educational institution more substantial than a community college. "Where?" I asked. "What university?" And then they explained. The school they were referring to was the California State University campus in Chico . . . 75 miles away.

It had never occurred to me before that a college in one city might be part of the economic foundation of another city. But in fact, it makes perfect sense. As a smaller town located in a rural area, Redding will probably never have all the big-ticket items a city needs if it is going to compete effectively in the modern economy. But it's not really Redding that's competing. It's the whole northern part of the Sacramento Valley: Redding, Chico and a whole string of other towns that are interrelated economically. We live in the age of the region, not the age of the city. . . . If regions are the new building blocks of the world economy—if it is the region that matters,

not the nation or the city or the state—then it is the region that should also be the locus of economic development policy. . . .

You have to swallow a lot of pride in order to think this way and understand what role your community might really play in creating a strong regional economy. After all, this nation is filled with Chicos that don't want to associate with Redding, and Seattles that want nothing to do with Boise. And going against that territorial instinct can sound like political suicide to a lot of local officials. But any successful business owner will tell you that if you want to get rich, you can't be too haughty [overly proud] about what your product is or the customers you sell it to. The future belongs to the politicians who understand that Chico is a part of Redding and Seattle is a part of Boise—and all these combinations are part of regional economies that will be rich at home only to the extent that they can sell successfully to the rest of the world.

Analyzing Primary Sources

1. What did Fulton realize during his meeting with Redding city officials, and how did he arrive at this point of view?
2. What does Fulton mean when he says, "Chico is a part of Redding and Seattle is a part of Boise"?
3. Why might political leaders have trouble accepting the approach to economic development that Fulton suggests?

Section Preview

OBJECTIVES

1. **Examine** reasons for America's shift from a rural to an urban society.
2. **Contrast** the major forms of city government.
3. **Evaluate** the need for city planning and list some municipal functions.
4. **Outline** the challenges that face suburbs and metropolitan areas.
5. **Describe** efforts toward cooperation among local governments.

WHY IT MATTERS

The vast majority of Californians live in urban areas. The larger the urban population, the more extensive the need for services, efficient and responsive government, and creative solutions to problems.

POLITICAL DICTIONARY

★ **incorporation**
★ **mayor-council government**
★ **strong-mayor government**
★ **weak-mayor government**
★ **council-manager government**
★ **commission government**
★ **zoning**
★ **metropolitan area**

We are fast becoming a nation of city dwellers. Where once our population was small, mostly rural, and agricultural, it is now large, mostly urban, and dominated by technology, manufacturing, and service industries. In 1790, a mere 5 percent of the population lived in the nation's few cities. Today, America's cities and their surrounding communities are home to 4 of every 5 persons.[2]

America's Rural-Urban Shift

When the first census was taken in 1790, only 3,929,214 people were living in the United States. Of these, only 201,655 people—5.1 percent —lived in the nation's few cities. Philadelphia was then the largest city, with a population of 42,000; 33,000 people lived in New York and 18,000 in Boston.

Nine years before the first census, James Watt had patented his double-acting steam engine, making large-scale manufacturing possible. Robert Fulton patented his steamboat in 1809, and George Stephenson his locomotive in 1829. These inventions made possible the transportation

of raw materials to factories and, in turn, the wide distribution of manufactured goods.

Almost overnight, home manufacturing gave way to industrial factories, and populations began to concentrate in the new industrial and transportation centers. Cities began to grow rapidly.

At the same time, the invention of several mechanical farm implements reduced the labor needed on farms. Fewer people grew more food, and the surplus farm population began to move to the cities. By 1860, the nation's population had increased more than sevenfold. The urban population had multiplied thirty times. By 1900, nearly two fifths of Americans lived in urban areas, and by 1920, more than half of the population were urban dwellers.

▲ The Riverwalk in San Antonio, Texas, is an excellent example of urban renewal and city planning.

Today, some 240 million people—more than 80 percent of the population—live in the nation's cities and their surrounding suburbs. The figure is much higher for California, where 97 percent of the people live in urban areas. For

---

[2]Depending on local custom and State law, municipalities may be known as cities, towns, boroughs, or villages. The use and meaning of these terms vary among the States. The larger municipalities are known everywhere as cities, and the usual practice is to use that title only for those communities with a significant population.

▲ If you compare this 1878 print (top) with the recent photograph (bottom) of San Francisco, California, you can clearly see the city's growth. *Critical Thinking* *What is the impact of the growth of the nation's cities on local governments?*

local governments in California, as in every State, America's rural-urban shift has had dramatic consequences.

When large numbers of people live close to one another, there is much more strain on local governments. They must provide water, police and fire protection, sewers, waste removal, traffic regulation, public health facilities, schools, and recreation. The larger the population, the more extensive—and expensive—these services become.

Forms of City Government

California's cities, like its counties, were created by the State, receive their powers from the State,

and are subject to a variety of limitations imposed by the State. The process by which a State establishes a city as a legal body is called **incorporation**.[3] In California an unincorporated community can incorporate in either of two ways. (1) The county board of supervisors can resolve to incorporate the area or (2) 25 percent of registered voters within the area of the proposed city can petition for incorporation. A majority of voters must then approve the step.

California recognizes three categories of city: general law, charter, and charter city and county. Of California's 478 incorporated cities, 108 have charters. (As you have read, San Francisco is the only charter city and county.) Like charter counties, charter cities have more freedom to pass ordinances and otherwise take actions to meet local needs. Because California's legislature has tended to give general law cities similarly broadened powers, differences in authority exercised by the two types of city have diminished.

Although variations exist, each city in California has either a mayor-council or a council-manager form of government.

The Mayor-Council Form

Nationally, the **mayor-council government** is the oldest and still the most widely used type of city government. In California, mainly small general law cities and very large cities use the mayor-council form. This form features an elected mayor as the chief executive and an elected council as its legislative body.

The council. The members of all California city councils are popularly elected on a nonpartisan basis. They serve either two- or four-year terms. In general law cities, the council has five, seven, or nine members. Charter cities exhibit great variety in how their councils are organized and how they distribute duties and powers.

The mayor. In most California cities with the mayor-council form of government, the council chooses one of its members to serve as mayor. The mayor, whether elected by the city council or by a vote of the people, presides at council meetings and otherwise has all of the powers and duties of a member of the council.

Mayor-council governments are often described as either the strong-mayor type or the

---

[3]The term *incorporation* comes from Latin *in* (into) *corpus* (body).

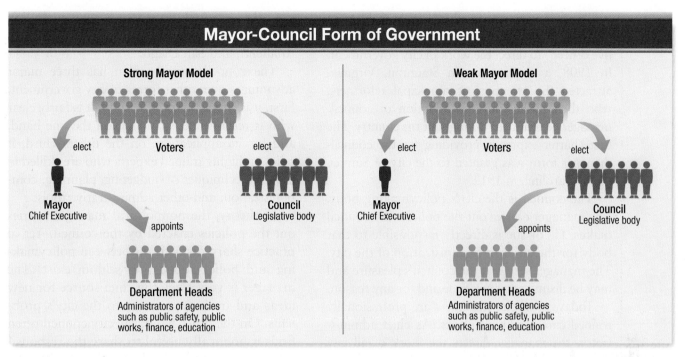

Mayor-Council Form of Government

Strong Mayor Model

Voters

elect → **Mayor** Chief Executive

elect → **Council** Legislative body

appoints →

Department Heads
Administrators of agencies such as public safety, public works, finance, education

Weak Mayor Model

Voters

elect → **Mayor** Chief Executive

elect → **Council** Legislative body

appoints →

Department Heads
Administrators of agencies such as public safety, public works, finance, education

Interpreting Diagrams This diagram compares and contrasts the two basic forms of mayor-council governments. *(a) What are the major differences between these two forms of city government? (b) Which is the better system for a large city? Explain your answer.* H-SS 12.7.2

weak-mayor type, depending on the powers given to the mayor. Most mayor-council cities operate under the weak-mayor plan. The strong-mayor form is generally found in larger cities, such as Los Angeles.

In a **strong-mayor government** the mayor is the chief administrative officer of the city. The mayor of Los Angeles, for example, has the power to veto ordinances passed by the 15-member city council, to hire and fire city officials, and to prepare the city's annual budget. Typically, a strong mayor is able to exercise vigorous leadership in making city policy and running the city's affairs.

In a **weak-mayor government,** the mayor has much less formal power. Executive duties are shared with other council members and elected officials, such as the clerk, treasurer, city engineer, and police chief. All department heads report not to the mayor but directly to the council. Powers of appointment, removal, and budget are shared with the council or exercised by that body alone. The mayor serves mainly as the council's presiding officer and the city's ceremonial head.

The success of the mayor-council form depends in very large measure on the power, ability, and influence of the mayor. In weak-mayor

cities, responsibility for action or inaction is hard to assign. The strong-mayor plan helps solve the problems of leadership and responsibility.

Still, the mayor-council form has these three large defects: (1) It depends heavily on the capacities of the mayor. (2) A major dispute between the mayor and the council can stall the workings of city government. (3) It is quite complicated and so is often little understood by the average citizen.

The Council-Manager Form

It takes special skills to get elected to public office. It takes different skills, however, to administer a fairly large city. Rarely are both sets of skills found in the same individual. As a result, the voters in many cities have adopted the council-manager form of government.

The **council-manager government,** a modification of the mayor-council form, is the most common form of government in California. Its main features are (1) a strong council of five, seven, or nine members elected to four-year terms on a nonpartisan ballot; (2) a weak mayor chosen from among the council members or elected by the voters to a two- or four-year term; (3) a manager, the city's chief administrative officer, named by the council.

The form first appeared in Ukiah, California. In 1904, that city's council appointed an "executive officer" to direct the work of city government. In 1908, a similar step in Staunton, Virginia, attracted the attention of municipal reformers, who then pushed for the adoption of council-manager government throughout the country. The first charter expressly providing for the council-manager form was granted to the city of Sumter, South Carolina, in 1912.

The council is the city's policymaking body. The manager carries out the policies the council makes. He or she is directly responsible to that body for the efficient administration of the city. The manager serves at the council's pleasure and may be dismissed at any time and for any reason.

Today, most city managers are professionally trained career administrators. As chief administrator, the manager directs the work of all city departments and has the power to hire and fire all city employees. The manager also prepares the budget for council consideration and controls the spending of the funds the council appropriates.

The council-manager plan has the backing of nearly every expert on municipal affairs, and its use has spread widely. It is now found in most cities with populations between 25,000 and 250,000. Three fourths of California cities now use the council-manager form, including Sacramento, Oakland, San José, Long Beach, Anaheim, and San Diego.

The council-manager plan has three major advantages over other forms of city government. First, it is simple in form. Second, it is fairly clear who is responsible for policy, on the one hand, and for its application, on the other. Third, it relies on highly trained experts who are skilled in modern techniques of budgeting, planning, computerization, and other administrative tools.

In theory, the nonpolitical manager carries out the policies enacted by the council. Yet in practice sharp distinctions between policymaking and policy-application seldom exist. The manager is very often the chief source for new ideas and fresh approaches to the city's problems. On the other hand, the city council often finds it politically useful to share the responsibility for controversial decisions with the "expendable" city manager.

Some critics of council-manager government hold that it is undemocratic because the chief executive is not popularly elected. Others say that it does not offer strong political leadership. This is a particular shortcoming, they argue, in larger cities, where the population is often quite diverse and has competing interests. Support for this view can be seen in the fact that only three cities with more than a million residents have a council-manager form of government today: Dallas and San Antonio, Texas, and Phoenix, Arizona. The form's shortcomings have led to agitation for change. After years of debate, San Diego voters amended the city's charter in 2004 to convert to a strong-mayor government beginning in 2006.

The Commission Form

The **commission government** is simple in structure. Three to nine, but usually five, commissioners are popularly elected. Together, they form the city council, pass ordinances, and control the purse strings. Individually, they head the different departments of city government: police, fire, public works, finance, parks, and so on. Thus, both legislative and executive powers are centered in one body.

The commission form was born in Galveston, Texas, in 1901. A tidal surge had swept the island city the year before, killing thousands and destroying much of the city. The old

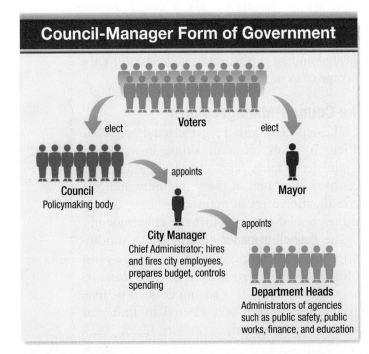

Council-Manager Form of Government

Voters — elect → Council (Policymaking body)
Voters — elect → Mayor
Council — appoints → City Manager (Chief Administrator; hires and fires city employees, prepares budget, controls spending)
City Manager — appoints → Department Heads (Administrators of agencies such as public safety, public works, finance, and education)

Interpreting Diagrams In the council-manager form of government, a professional manager sees that necessary services are performed for city residents. *What are the advantages of the council-manager system over the other forms of city government?* H-SS 12.7.6

mayor-council regime was unable to cope with the emergency. The Texas legislature gave Galveston a new charter, providing for five commissioners to make and enforce the law in the stricken city. Intended to be temporary, the arrangement proved so effective that it soon spread to other Texas cities and then elsewhere in the country. A number of cities in California established commission governments.

Depending on the city, either the voters or the commissioners themselves choose a commissioner to serve as the mayor. Like the other commissioners, the mayor heads one of the city's departments. He or she also presides at council meetings and represents the city at ceremonies. The mayor generally has no more authority than the other commissioners and rarely has veto power.

The simplicity of the commission form, and especially its short ballot, won the support of municipal reformers in the first few decades of the twentieth century. However, experience pointed up serious defects, and its popularity fell off rapidly. Only a few American cities have a commission form of government today, and none of them are in California.

The commission form has three chief defects:

1. The lack of a single chief executive (or, the presence of several chiefs among equals) makes it difficult to assign responsibility. This can also mean that the city has no effective political leadership.

2. A built-in tendency toward "empire building" often surfaces. Each commissioner tries to draw as much of the city's money and influence as possible to his or her own department.

3. A lack of coordination plagues the topmost levels of policymaking and administration. Each commissioner is likely to equate the citywide public good with the particular interests and functions of his or her department.

City Planning

Most American cities developed haphazardly, without a plan or an eye to the future. The results of this shortsightedness can be seen in what is often called the core area or the inner city. These are the older and usually overcrowded central sections of larger cities.

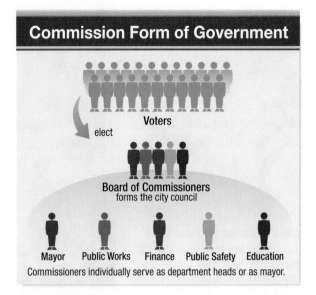

Commission Form of Government

Voters
elect

Board of Commissioners
forms the city council

Mayor   Public Works   Finance   Public Safety   Education

Commissioners individually serve as department heads or as mayor.

Interpreting Diagrams The commission form of government is one of the most uncomplicated systems for a city. ***Does a system of checks and balances exist in this form of government?***

Factories were placed anywhere their owners chose to build them. Rail lines were run through the heart of the community. Towering buildings shut out the sunlight from the narrow streets below. Schools, police and fire stations, and other public buildings were squeezed onto cheap land or put where the political organization could make a profit. Examples are endless.

Planning Growth

Fortunately, many cities have seen the need to create order out of their random growth. Most have established some sort of planning agency. This agency usually consists of a planning commission, supported by a trained professional staff.

A number of factors have prompted this step. The need to correct past mistakes has often been a compelling reason, of course. Then, too, many cities have recognized both the advantages that can result, and the pitfalls that can be avoided, through well-planned and orderly development. Importantly, the Federal Government has spurred cities on. Most federal grant and loan programs require that cities that seek aid must first have a master plan as a guide to future growth.

City Zoning

The practice of dividing a city into a number of districts, or zones, and regulating the uses to which property in each of them may be put is called **zoning**. Generally, a zoning ordinance

▲ Pierre-Charles L'Enfant laid out a plan for Washington, D.C. (above) before a single building was erected. His plan included wide streets running parallel east to west and large areas reserved for public buildings. *Critical Thinking Examine the photo of Washington, D.C. today (right). How is L'Enfant's plan still in evidence?*

places each parcel of land in the city into one of three zones: residential, commercial, or industrial.

Each of these zones is then divided into subzones. For example, each of several residential zones may be broken down into several areas. One may be just for single-family residences. Another may allow both one-family and two-family dwellings. In still another, apartment houses and other multifamily units may be allowed.

Most zoning ordinances also prescribe limits on the height and area of buildings, determine how much of a lot may be occupied by a structure, and set out several other such restrictions on land use. They often have "setback" requirements, which state that structures must be placed at least a certain distance from the street and from other property lines.

Zoning is really a phase of city planning, and an important means for ensuring orderly growth. Zoning still meets opposition from many who object to this interference with their right to use their property as they choose. Even so, nearly every city of any size in the United States is zoned today. The city of Houston, where zoning was turned down twice by popular vote, remained the only major exception until the early 1990s. At that point, the city council finally decided to adopt a zoning code.

Zoning ordinances must be reasonable. Remember that the 14th Amendment prohibits any State, and thus its cities, from depriving any person of life, liberty, or property without due process of law. Each of the 50 State constitutions contains a similar provision.

Clearly, zoning does deprive a person of the right to use his or her property for certain purposes. Thus, if an area is zoned only for single-family dwellings, you cannot build an apartment house or a service station on your property in that zone. Zoning can also reduce the value of a particular piece of property. A choice corner lot, for example, may be much more valuable with a drive-in restaurant on the property than a house.[7]

While zoning may at times deprive a person of liberty or property, the key question always is this: Does it do so without due process? That is, does it do so unreasonably?

The question of reasonableness is one for the courts to decide. The Supreme Court first upheld zoning as a proper use of police power in *Euclid* v. *Amber Realty Co.*, 1926, a case involving an ordinance enacted by the city council of Euclid, Ohio.

Municipal Functions

The services a city provides day in and day out are so extensive that it is almost impossible

---

[7]Nonconforming uses in existence before a zoning ordinance is passed are almost always allowed to continue. Most ordinances give the city council the right to grant exceptions, called variances, in cases where property owners might suffer undue hardships.

★★★ **730** **Chapter 25 Section 2**

to catalog them. Most larger cities, and many smaller ones, issue annual reports on the city's condition. These are often book-length publications.

Consider just a few of the many things that most or all cities do. They provide police and fire protection. They build and maintain streets, sidewalks, bridges, street lights, parks and playgrounds, swimming pools, golf courses, libraries, hospitals, schools, correctional institutions, day-care centers, airports, public markets, parking facilities, auditoriums, and sports arenas. They furnish public health and sanitation services, such as sewers and wastewater treatment, garbage collection and disposal, and disease prevention and eradication programs.

▲ In 2005, Antonio Villaraigosa became the first Latino mayor of Los Angeles in more than 130 years.

Cities operate water, gas, light, and transportation systems. They regulate traffic, building codes, pollution, and public utilities. Many cities also build and manage public housing projects, provide summer youth camps, build and operate docks and other harbor facilities, and maintain tourist attractions.

Suburbs and Metropolitan Areas

The growth of urban areas has raised many problems for city dwellers. Urban growth also affects residents of nearby suburbs.

The Suburban Boom

About half of all Americans live in suburbs today. The nation's suburbs began to grow rapidly in the years immediately after World War II, and then on through the 1950s and 1960s. The suburban growth rate slowed somewhat in the 1970s, but it rebounded in the 1980s and 1990s, especially around the Sunbelt cities of the South and West. Suburban growth in California followed the nationwide pattern.

This dramatic population shift stemmed from Americans' desire for more room, cheaper land, greater privacy, and less smoke, dirt, noise, and congestion. People also sought less crime, newer and better schools, safer streets

and playing conditions, lower taxes, and higher social status. The car and the freeway turned millions of rooted city dwellers into mobile suburbanites.

Businesses followed customers to the suburbs, often clustering in shopping centers or malls. Many industries moved from the central city in search of cheaper land, lower taxes, and a more stable labor supply. Industries also sought an escape from city building codes, health inspectors, and other regulations. These developments stimulated growth.

This "suburbanitis," as some call it, has added to city-dwellers' woes. As high-income families have moved out, they have taken their civic, financial, and social resources with them. They have left behind center cities with high percentages of older people, low-income families, and minorities. Inevitably, both the need for and the stress on city services have multiplied.

Metropolitan Areas

Suburbanites face their share of problems, too, including the need for water supplies, sewage disposal, police and fire protection, transportation, and traffic control. Duplication of such functions by city and suburb or by city and county can be wasteful, even dangerous. More than one fire has raged while neighboring fire departments quibbled over who was responsible for fighting it.

Attempts to meet the needs of **metropolitan areas**—cities and the areas around them—have taken several forms. Over the years, annexation has been the standard means. Outlying areas have simply been brought within a city's boundaries. Many suburbanites resist annexation, however. Cities, too, have often been hesitant to take on the burdens involved.

Another approach has been to create special districts designed to meet the problems of heavily populated urban areas. Their boundaries frequently cut across county and city lines to include an entire metropolitan area. They often are called metropolitan districts.

Interpreting Political Cartoons (a) What is meant by the State of Alabama becoming a suburb of the city of Atlanta, Georgia? (b) What does the cartoon suggest about urban sprawl?

These metropolitan districts are generally set up for a single purpose—for example, parks, as in the Cleveland Metropolitan Park Development District. In some cases, however, these districts can also handle a number of functions.

Yet another approach to the challenges facing metropolitan areas is increasing the authority of counties. Among local governments around the country, counties are generally the largest in area and are most likely to include those places demanding new and increased services.

Cooperation Among Local Governments

Like other areas of the country, California recognizes the need for coordination and cooperation among local governments. One way in which the State has met this need, as you have read, is to establish regional bodies with advisory responsibilities. The councils of governments (COGs) are a prominent example. COGs consist of city councilors, county supervisors, and sometimes representatives of other local and regional agencies. They are created through joint-powers agreements, which are legal arrangements that allow two or more governmental units to cooperate in order to share costs or avoid duplicate efforts while achieving mutually beneficial goals.

COGs work to assist local governments in a variety of ways. Their primary function is to coordinate planning and development of local services, such as public transportation. COGs may also be called on by the State and Federal governments to help evaluate local requests for State or federal funds.

Of the nearly 700 COGs in the country, the largest is the Southern California Association of Governments. This group of local governments is responsible for addressing and resolving regional issues and planning for six counties, 187 cities, and 14 subregions.

Section 2 Assessment

Key Terms and Main Ideas

1. (a) What are the two major forms of city government in California? (b) How are they different?
2. What are the key differences between a **strong-mayor government** and a **weak-mayor government**?
3. List at least five functions of municipal governments.
4. What is the difference between a city and a **metropolitan area**?

Critical Thinking

5. **Making Comparisons** Create a chart comparing the advantages and disadvantages of these types of city government: (a) the mayor-council form; (b) the commission form; (c) the council-manager form.
6. **Determining Cause and Effect** Trace the history of American population shifts, first to the cities and then to the suburbs. Include economic and social reasons for the trends.

3 Providing Important Services

Section Preview

OBJECTIVES

1. **Explain** why State governments have a major role in providing important services.
2. **Identify** the types of services that California's State and local governments provide.
3. **Analyze** why the amount and types of services available to citizens vary greatly from State to State.

WHY IT MATTERS

People are often unaware of the vast array of services provided by State and local governments. The cost of these services has become a huge burden to many States, including California, which struggle to keep up with the expenses of growing populations.

POLITICAL DICTIONARY

★ **Medicaid**
★ **welfare**
★ **entitlement**

California State government, you may by now have noticed, is quite similar in form to the Federal Government. Each has three branches of government, a bicameral legislature, its own constitution, and so on. Given these similarities, it is easy to overlook the many unique features and functions of California State government, and the many services it provides to its citizens.

State Government's Role

In this book, you have read many times about the key role of the States in the American federal system. Recall that among the Framers there was a widespread distrust of a strong, central government. As a result, they created a system in which the States held many important powers. The Constitution reserves to the States all those powers not expressly delegated to Congress and not specifically denied to the States.

The reserved powers are so many and so broad that they really cannot be catalogued. And the ways in which they are exercised vary greatly from one State to the next. Again, that fact reflects the conscious aim of the Framers and the federal system they created.

Along with the powers reserved to the States come some important responsibilities. Like the Federal Government, State governments generally aim to fulfill the lofty purposes set forward in the Preamble to the Constitution; that is, they seek to "establish Justice, ensure domestic Tranquility, provide for the common defense,

promote the general Welfare, and secure the Blessings of Liberty. . . . "

Services That California Provides

California provides services to its citizens in two ways: (1) directly, through State agencies and programs, and (2) through the local govments that they establish. California and its local units provide many services to those who live within their borders. The services that they provide fall into a number of broad categories.

Education

The education of California residents is one of the most important responsibilities that the State

◀ **University of California, Berkeley** The State of California plays a major role in funding the University of California system.

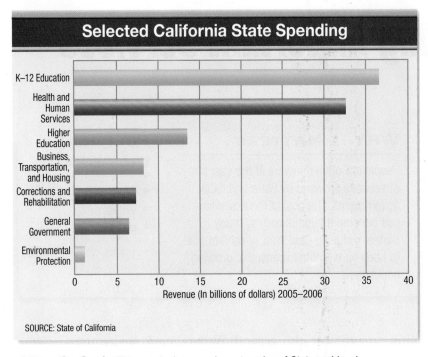

Selected California State Spending

Revenue (In billions of dollars) 2005–2006

SOURCE: State of California

Interpreting Graphs This graph shows major categories of State and local spending. *What do these categories suggest about the role of State and local spending in Americans' daily lives?* **H-SS 12.7.6**

has assumed. It is also the most expensive entry in the State budget. At more than $36 billion, education represents more than 40 percent of all State government expenditures.

The cost of providing education has risen sharply in recent decades and continues to increase year to year. Elementary and secondary public school education is largely the responsibility of State and local governments. Local taxes, especially property taxes, provide a significant proportion of funding for schools. After California's Proposition 13 slashed property taxes, the burden of school funding shifted more to State government. Other States followed California's lead. The total budgeted for California public elementary and secondary schools rose to $50 billion for the period 2005–2006. That represented an average expenditure of about $7,400 per student.

In addition, States set guidelines in order to maintain high quality in the schools. For example, State laws establish teacher qualifications, curricula, quality standards for educational materials, and the length of the school year.

State interest and involvement in such matters have intensified in recent years. California and other States have developed curriculum frameworks and content standards outlining the

material that must be covered in core subjects. Every State now has an extensive state-wide testing program, fueled by the No Child Left Behind Act signed by President Bush in 2002. The California Standards Tests assess progress in English-language arts, mathematics, science, and history-social science.

At the college and university levels, the States likewise play a major role. States understand that for businesses to succeed in the State, a ready supply of highly trained college graduates is key.

Every State also has a public higher education system. California's higher education system is the nation's largest. The University of California alone has 10 campuses, and California State University has 23. In addition, the State has an extensive system of community colleges, which offer two-year programs.

Education at State universities and colleges is generally much less expensive than at private institutions. On average, tuition at four-year public colleges and universities is about one fifth that of private four-year schools. Nevertheless, many State universities, such as the University of California at Berkeley, are ranked among the world's finest schools.

Public Welfare

California takes an active role in promoting the health and welfare of its citizens. The State pursues this goal by a variety of means. The California Health and Human Services Agency supports programs that promote the physical, mental, and financial health of children, adolescents, and adults. Health and human services ranks as the second-largest expenditure in California, after education, and makes up some 30 percent of the State's budget.

1. *Public health.* California funds ambitious public health programs. Most states operate their own public hospitals, but California relies on county-supported public hospitals backed up by private hospitals. Together, these hospitals form a network that cares for more than 12 million Californians. With the Federal Government, California administers such programs as **Medicaid**, which provides medical insurance to low-income families.

Recent soaring costs in the health-care industry have placed a great strain on State budgets. Many governors, State legislators, mayors, and other public officials, including those in California, are among the leading advocates of reform of the nation's health-care system.

2. *Cash assistance.* Another major area in which States contribute to the well-being of their citizens is cash assistance to the poor, commonly called **welfare.** The States, California among them, are now taking a leading role in this area.

Between 1936 and 1996, the Federal Government provided cash assistance to needy families through the Aid to Families with Dependent Children (AFDC) program.[8] AFDC was an **entitlement** program, which means that anyone who met the eligibility requirements was entitled to receive benefits.

The Federal Government and the States shared the costs of providing AFDC benefits. Critics of AFDC pointed to its soaring costs and expanding caseloads as signs of serious problems with the program. They also saw the lack of a limit on the number of months a person could receive AFDC benefits as a serious omission. Because of these issues, critics argued that the program encouraged people to depend on government assistance rather than become self-supporting.

In 1996, Congress responded to these concerns by passing the Personal Responsibility and Work Opportunity Reconciliation Act. This act replaced AFDC with a new and strikingly different program, Temporary Assistance to Needy Families (TANF).

Unlike AFDC, TANF is a block grant: The Federal Government gives States a fixed amount of money each year, regardless of whether the number of TANF recipients rises or falls. States are then free to use the federal grant, plus the State funds that they are obliged to contribute, to design and implement their own welfare programs.

TANF limits recipients to a total of five years of assistance during the course of their lifetime. It also requires recipients to work or participate in some form of vocational training or community service.

California serves its TANF recipients through a program called CalWORKs. The program supports recipients in their job search and provides job readiness skills when needed. In California the time limit for adults matches the federal limit of five years. Children, however, can continue to receive benefits beyond that period.

The number of people on welfare had in fact begun to decline before the creation of the TANF program. It has plunged since then in most States. California experienced a 45 percent drop in its TANF caseload by 2003. Since then the number of recipients has stabilized.

3. *Other efforts.* States do much more to promote their citizens' health and welfare. They enforce antipollution laws to protect the environment; they inspect factories and other workplaces to protect worker safety; they license health-care practitioners to ensure quality care. The list of public welfare services goes on and on.

Voices on Government

Juan Arambula began work as a farm laborer at the age of five, picking cotton and fruit with other family members. This early experience taught him that "education empowers." Later, he earned a law degree. In 1997, he was elected to the Fresno County, California, Board of Supervisors. Before his 2004 election to the State legislature, Mr. Arambula discussed the challenges of serving in local government.

❝*Serving as a County Supervisor is both exciting and exhausting. It is exciting because we are close to the people we serve, and because we have such a wide range of responsibilities, from agriculture to zoning and everything in between. It is exhausting because we are constantly being asked to do more with less. I hope a fundamental restructuring of local government financing takes place soon, so local government has the resources needed to provide essential services.*❞

Evaluating the Quotation

For what reason(s) does Mr. Arambula believe a restructuring of local government is needed?

---

[8]AFDC was authorized by Title IV of the Social Security Act of 1935. Until 1962, the program was named Aid to Dependent Children, as the 1935 act was aimed simply at needy dependent children.

| Issuing Permits | Inspecting | Licensing |

▲ **Promoting Public Welfare** State and local governments work to ensure citizens' health and welfare in a variety of ways. These include issuing construction permits (left), inspecting restaurant kitchens (center), and licensing health-care practitioners (right). **H-SS 12.7.5**

Public Safety

One of the oldest law enforcement groups, the legendary Texas Rangers, was established in 1835. Today, a variety of police forces, from the local sheriff to academy-trained State police operate in every State to preserve law and order.

The California Highway Patrol is perhaps the most visible public-safety group in the State, since its officers patrol the State's roads and highways. State law-enforcement forces perform other vital services as well. They may function as the primary police force in rural communities. They investigate crimes. They provide centralized files for fingerprints and other information. They also provide training to local law enforcement.

Each State has its own corrections system for those convicted of committing State crimes. Thus the California Department of Corrections and Rehabilitation, through its Division of Adult Operations and its Division of Youth Operations, runs more than 30 State prisons and some 50 additional camps and other correctional facilities, including those for juvenile offenders.

Operating these corrections systems is a growing burden for States. During the 1990s, the number of persons held in State prisons increased by more than 70 percent. In California since 1980, the number of prison inmates has increased by more than 550 percent. At the start of 2004, more than 2.2 million people were incarcerated in the United States, well over half of them in State prisons. California, with 164,000 inmates, and Texas, with 167,000, together held more than a quarter of the total.

Two causes of booming prison populations are (1) increases in the number of people sentenced for violent crimes and (2) the increasing length of the average prison sentence. One result is prison overcrowding. Twenty-two State corrections systems are operating at 100 percent or more of their capacity. In California, ongoing prison expansion has kept the State's offender population slightly under capacity.

Another result has been a rise in State corrections spending, which has more than doubled over the past 15 years. States now spend more than $40 billion each year to build, staff, and maintain prisons and to house prisoners. The budget for California's Department of Corrections and Rehabilitation reached $7.4 billion in 2005. Yet while prison spending grows, it is worth noting that, on average, State and local governments still spend ten times as much on education as they do on corrections.

In an effort to expand prison capacity more affordably, many States have hired private contractors to operate some of their prisons. More than 5 percent of all State prisoners are now held in these private facilities.

Highways

Building and maintaining roads and highways is an enormous job. It regularly ranks among the most expensive items in State budgets.

Again, the Federal Government is a partner with the States in funding highways. The most impressive example is the interstate highway system, a network of high-speed roadways that spans the length and breadth of the continental United States. Construction of the system began with the 1956 Federal-Aid Highway Act and continues to this day.

The Interstate Highway System, officially called the Dwight D. Eisenhower System of Interstate and Defense Highways, is now 99 percent finished. The Federal Government has paid roughly 90 percent of its cost. When complete, the interstate highway system will total some 45,000 miles, with at least 2,311 miles of it in California. The longest interstate highway in California is I-5, which runs from the Mexican border to the Oregon State line, a distance of 797 miles.

While the Interstate system is a magnificent achievement, it constitutes only a tiny fraction of the nation's 4 million miles of roads. Many roadways are built with State, not federal, funds.

Once the roads are built, the State has further responsibilities. It must look after the physical safety of the roads and make repairs as needed. In California the Department of Transportation (Caltrans) oversees these activities. In addition, as in all States, California licenses drivers to ensure their competence. The State sets speed limits and requires the periodic inspection of vehicles to ensure their safety.

Regulatory Agencies

Among the many other services that California provides to its residents are those involving the regulation of businesses and commerce. State agencies such as the Department of Consumer Affairs and the Department of Industrial Relations work to promote and protect the interests of Californians.

California regulatory agencies have much in common with their federal counterparts. The agencies are created by the legislature, and agency heads are appointed by the governor. They have executive powers; that is, they administer the programs for which they were created. Like federal regulatory commissions, they also have quasi-legislative and quasi-judicial powers. For example, California's Occupational Safety and Health Standards Board has the power to adopt health standards. The State's Department of Pesticide Regulation has the power to assess fines for noncompliance with its regulations. No less important, however, are functions such as setting aside public lands for conservation and recreation; regulating businesses and the commerce they conduct within the State; and protecting consumers from a variety of dangers and inconveniences.

Section 3 Assessment

Key Terms and Main Ideas

1. What is typically the most expensive item in the California State budget?
2. **(a)** Name three main categories of services that State and local governments provide. **(b)** For each category, describe a specific program or service.
3. For whom does the **Medicaid** program provide benefits?

Critical Thinking

4. **Drawing Inferences** Why do you think many States lobbied the Federal Government to give them block grants that they could use to create and manage their own welfare programs?
5. **Predicting Consequences** Turn to the bar graph on State and Local Spending, on page 734. Choose two categories

Standards Monitoring *Online*
For: Self-quiz with vocabulary practice
Web Code: mqa-8253

and suggest a way to reduce rising costs in each category. What might be the results of such reductions?
6. **Expessing Problems Clearly** What challenges do State and local governments face in providing for public welfare and safety? How are governments meeting these challenges?

For: An activity on local government
Web Code: mqd-8253

Face the Issues

Funding Education

Background *In most places, public schools are largely financed by local property taxes collected from homeowners and businesses in the community. Less-wealthy districts often have less money for education, per student, than wealthier communities. A growing number of States have tried to equalize funding by shifting costs to the State level. The State share of spending for education varies from 98 percent in Hawaii to 8.3 percent in New Hampshire. Which level of government should bear the cost?*

New school construction

Analysis Skills CS4, HI6

State Funding Is More Equitable

States have the responsibility to provide a free education to all of their young people. Students need to complete their education in order to participate in a democracy and succeed in the work world. Yet many States hand off this responsibility to towns and cities that may not have the money to carry it out. States must provide the money to educate students if local districts cannot.

Many districts are based in older towns with special challenges. An urban school built in 1935 will be more expensive to heat, maintain, and repair than a new suburban school. Yet districts with old buildings have to make do with less money. Because property values and incomes are lower in these districts, residents must be taxed at a higher rate. Try the math: a 1% property tax on a $500,000 house raises more money than a 4% property tax on a $100,000 house. Forced to pay a larger share of their income to support schools, people move away, making the problem worse. Sharing resources between towns at a State level can solve this crisis.

Schools Are a Local Responsibility

The problem with American public schools is not a lack of money. The United States spends a higher share of its national income on K–12 education than most industrialized countries.

The single biggest challenge for American schools is effective oversight. Schools need parental involvement and the active participation of the entire community to succeed. Experience has shown that decisions about education are best made at the local level. Communities should have the right to decide how much money they want to raise from citizens to spend on local schools.

Local funding insures greater control of educational quality. Communities paying higher taxes have more incentive to monitor schools and see that they are providing a top-notch education. Even homeowners without school-age children will benefit from increasing property values if schools succeed.

When the burden of school funding shifts to statewide taxes, voters rebel. Local governments must take responsibility for local schools.

Exploring the Issues

1. If public education is a basic right, does it follow that a certain level of funding is a basic right? How should States decide that level of funding?

2. How can local officials work to make schools succeed?

For more information about state and local funding disputes, view "Funding Education."

Face the **Issues** Video Collection

Financing State and Local Government

Section Preview

OBJECTIVES

1. **Describe** the major Federal and State limits on raising revenue.
2. **List** the four principles of sound taxation.
3. **Identify** major tax and nontax sources of California State and local revenue.
4. **Explain** the State budget process.

WHY IT MATTERS

You pay State and local taxes—indeed, you cannot avoid them. Like most of us, you probably find them to be at least inconvenient, but they are also quite necessary—and, by and large, a bargain.

POLITICAL DICTIONARY

★ sales tax
★ use tax
★ regressive tax
★ income tax
★ progressive tax
★ property tax
★ assessment
★ inheritance tax
★ estate tax
★ budget

Altogether, the 50 States and their thousands of local governments now take in and spend nearly $2 trillion a year. How does the State of California gather all the money it needs, and how do its officials decide what to spend it on?

Limits on Raising Revenue

This year the State of California will take in more than $100 billion in revenue. Nearly 90 percent of it will come from taxes and fees, and the rest will come from a number of nontax and federal sources. Recall that taxes are charges made to raise money for public purposes.

The power to tax is one of the major powers of the States in the federal system. In a strictly legal sense, then, California's taxing power is limited only by the restrictions imposed by the federal Constitution and those imposed by California's own fundamental law. [9]

Federal Limitations

The Federal Constitution does place some restrictions on the taxing abilities of State and local governments. Although few in number, those limits have a major impact on the States and their local governments.

1. *Interstate and Foreign Commerce.* The Constitution denies the States the power to "lay any Imposts or Duties on Imports or Exports" and "any Duty of Tonnage." [10] In effect, the States are prohibited from taxing interstate and foreign commerce. The Supreme Court has often held that because the Constitution gives Congress the power to regulate that trade, the States are generally forbidden to do so.

2. *The Federal Government and Its Agencies.* The Supreme Court's decision in *McCulloch v. Maryland*, 1819, bars States from taxing the Federal Government or any of its agencies or functions. They are forbidden to do so because,

---

[9] Remember, a State's power to tax is also limited by any number of practical considerations, such as economic and political factors.
[10] Article I, Section 10, Clauses 2 and 3.

▲ Property taxes, including those on houses such as these, are a major source of local revenue. **H-SS 12.7.2**

as Chief Justice Marshall put it in *McCulloch*: "The power to tax involves the power to destroy." (See page 95.)

3. *Fourteenth Amendment Limitations* The Due Process and Equal Protection clauses place limits on the power to tax at the State and local levels. Essentially, the Due Process Clause requires that taxes (1) be imposed and administered fairly, (2) be not so heavy as to actually confiscate property, and (3) be imposed only for public purposes.

The Equal Protection Clause forbids the making of unreasonable classifications for the purpose of taxation. The clause thus forbids tax classifications made on the basis of race, religion, nationality, political party membership, or any other factors that are deemed to be unreasonable.

State Limitations

Each State's constitution limits the taxing powers of that State. For example, the California constitutional initiative known as Proposition 13 limited local property taxes to 1 percent of the assessed value of all real and personal property. State constitutions also limit the taxing powers of their local governments. As local units have no independent powers, the only taxes they can impose are those the State allows them to levy.

Most States create tax exemptions for various nonprofit groups. The California constitution and statutes exempt the properties of nonprofit

organizations operated exclusively for religious, charitable, scientific, or hospital purposes. California also exempts from sales taxes some basic products, such as food, and some sales by nonprofit groups, such as religious and educational organizations.

The Principles of Sound Taxation

Any tax, if taken by itself, can be shown to be unfair. If a government's total revenues were to come from one tax—say, a sales, an income, or a property tax—its tax system would be very unfair. Some people would bear a much greater burden than others, and some would bear little or none. Each tax should thus be defensible as part of a tax system.

In his classic 1776 book *The Wealth of Nations*, Scottish economist Adam Smith laid out four principles of a sound tax system, which most tax experts still cite today:

PRIMARY Sources *"1. The subjects of every state ought to contribute towards the support of the government as nearly as possible, in proportion to their respective abilities; that is, in proportion to the revenue which they respectively enjoy under the protection of the state.*
2. The tax which each individual is bound to pay ought to be certain, and not arbitrary.
3. Every tax ought to be levied at the time, or in the manner, in which it is most likely to be convenient for the contributor to pay it.
4. Every tax ought to be so contrived as to take out and to keep out of the pockets of the people as little as possible over and above what it brings into the public treasury. . . . "

Shaping a tax system that meets these standards of equality, certainty, convenience, and economy is just about impossible. Still, that goal should be pursued.

Sources of California Revenue

Beyond the limits noted, the State of California can levy taxes as it chooses. The legislature decides what taxes the State will levy, and at what rates. In most States, the legislature also decides what taxes local governments can levy.

▲ In 1978, a California ballot measure known as Proposition 13 touched off a series of State and local initiatives to limit property taxes. Here a family shows support for that measure (left). At the same time, teachers rallied to express their concern about tax cuts (right). *Critical Thinking* **(a) Why might teachers be concerned about tax cuts? (b) What other groups might have similar concerns?** H-SS 12.7.5

In California, however, cities have historically exercised significant local control over fiscal matters. By statute, they may impose any local tax that State law does not prohibit. Nonetheless, the trend in California is toward greater State control over local finances.

The Sales and Use Tax

In California the sales and use tax accounts for nearly 30 percent of all State revenue. A **sales tax** is a tax placed on the sale of various commodities; the seller, who is obliged to pay the sales tax to the State, collects the tax from the purchaser. The sales tax may be either general or selective in form. A general sales tax is one applied to the sale of most commodities. A selective sales tax is one placed only on the sale of certain commodities, such as cigarettes, liquor, or gasoline.

A **use tax** is imposed on transactions in which no sales tax is collected; the purchaser is obliged to pay it to the State. California levies a use tax on products purchased outside the State for storage, use, or consumption within the State.

Today, 45 States levy a general sales tax.[12] California's general sales and use tax rate of 7.25 percent, the highest in the nation, includes a statewide local tax of 1 percent. California now levies a selective sales tax on vehicle fuels, cigarettes, alcoholic beverages, and insurance policies. Many local governments in California support the activities of cities, counties, and special districts through additional sales and use taxes, ranging from 0.25 percent to 1.25 percent.

Sales taxes are widely used for two major reasons: They are easy to collect, and they are dependable revenue producers. Yet a sales tax is a **regressive tax**—that is, it is not levied according to a person's ability to pay. Everyone in a certain State who buys, say, a hammer has to pay the same amount of sales tax on it. Therefore, to a poor person who buys the hammer the tax is a heavier burden than it is to a wealthy person. Critics of regressive taxes say that States should not raise so much of their revenue from citizens least able to pay.

The Income Tax

The **income tax,** which is levied on the income of individuals and/or corporations, yields almost one third of State tax revenues nationwide.

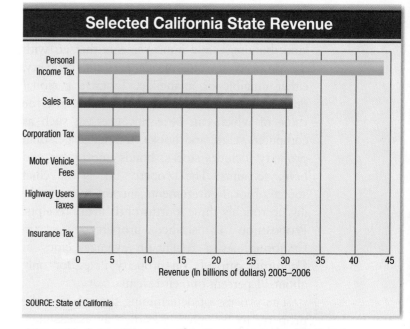

Selected California State Revenue

Revenue (In billions of dollars) 2005–2006

SOURCE: State of California

Interpreting Graphs This graph shows the major sources of State and local revenue in California. *Are the types of taxes shown on the graph the fairest ways for California and its local governments to pay for services? Explain your answer.*

Forty-three States levy an individual income tax; forty-six have some form of corporate income tax.[13] Individual and corporate income taxes in California produce nearly half of the State's total revenue.

The individual income tax is usually a **progressive tax**—that is, the higher your income, the more tax you pay. Income tax rates vary among the States. In California the lowest incomes are taxed at 1 percent. From there, rates rise to 9.3 percent, with an additional 1 percent surcharge on the highest incomes. Taxpayers receive various exemptions and deductions in calculating taxable income.

Corporate income tax rates in California, as in most States, are a uniform, fixed percentage of income. Only a few States set the rates on a graduated, or progressive, basis.

The progressive income tax is held by many to be the fairest—or the least unfair—form of taxation, because it can be geared to a person's ability to pay. If the rates are too high, however, the tax can discourage individual enterprise.

[12]Alaska, Delaware, Montana, New Hampshire, and Oregon have no general sales tax, but each imposes selective sales taxes.

[13]Nevada, Texas, Washington, and Wyoming levy neither type of income tax. Alaska, Florida, and South Dakota impose only the corporate tax.

The Property Tax

A **property tax** is a levy on (1) real property, such as land, buildings, and improvements that go with the property if sold; or (2) personal property, either tangible or intangible. Tangible personal property is movable wealth that is visible and the value of which can be easily assessed, such as computers, cars, and books. Intangible personal property includes stocks, bonds, mortgages and bank accounts. The property tax is the chief source of local governments' income today, making up roughly three fourths of their tax receipts. Proposition 13 slashed property taxes in California. As a result, on average, cities in California can rely on property taxes for only about 11 percent of their revenue.

The process of determining the value of the property to be taxed is known as **assessment**. The task is carried out in California by the county tax assessor. Monitored by the Board of Equalization, the county tax assessor annually determines the full taxable value of each property in his or her county. The county assessor must list all taxable property and enroll the property on the local assessment roll. The county tax collector collects the property taxes, and the county auditor allocates the revenue, according to State law, to the county and its cities, special districts, and school districts.

Property is usually assessed at less than its true market value. Most property owners seem better satisfied if the assessment is set at, say, one-half of its real value. Thus, a house assessed at $300,000 may actually be worth $600,000. If the tax rate is set at 2 percent, the tax will be $6,000. In reality, this result is the same as a 1 percent tax on the $600,000 house.

Supporters of the property tax argue that because government protects property and often enhances its value, a tax on property can properly be required to support the government. Critics note that the property tax is not truly progressive. Although the amount of real property one owns may have been a fair measure of one's wealth in earlier times, it is not today. (You might inherit a valuable home, for instance, but not be wealthy enough to pay the property tax on it.) Second, it is all but impossible to assess all taxable property on a fair and equal basis.

Inheritance or Estate Taxes

Every State has some form of inheritance or estate tax, sometimes called the "death tax." An **inheritance tax** is levied on the beneficiary's (heir's) share of an estate. California's inheritance tax was repealed in 1982. It was replaced by an **estate tax**, one that is levied on the full estate itself.

Business Taxes

A variety of business taxes, in addition to the corporate income tax, are important sources of revenue in most States. More than half the States, California among them, impose severance taxes. These are levies on commercial producers who sever, or remove, natural resources from the soil or water, including timber, minerals, and fish. Unlike other States with fossil fuel reserves, however, California has no statewide severance tax on oil and gas. Oil and gas producers do pay a small statewide assessment of around five cents per barrel of oil and five cents per each 10,000 cubic feet of natural gas produced. This revenue goes to support the Department of Conservation's Division of Oil, Gas, and Geothermal Resources.

California also requires that corporations be licensed to do business in the State. For this they

"It was just a sapling when we moved in."

Interpreting Political Cartoons You might have heard the expression, "Prices have gone through the roof." **What point is the cartoon making about property taxes?**

pay license fees. Certain other kinds of businesses, such as horse-racing tracks, transportation lines, and bars and taverns, must also pay license, permit, or registration fees to operate. Then, too, California requires the licensing of doctors, dentists, funeral directors, barbers, plumbers, architects, electricians, and others.

Other Taxes

California and its local governments also impose a number of other taxes. For example, the State collects payroll taxes. Money generated by these taxes is held in trust funds for social welfare programs, such as unemployment, job training, and disability insurance. Some local governments tax utility users and guests at hotels and motels. Some also collect a tax on general admissions to certain amusements, such as movies and sporting events.

Nontax Sources

State and local governments now take in over $1 trillion a year from a wide range of nontax sources. Much of that huge amount comes in grants from the Federal Government each year. For example, annual federal grants to California now total more than $50 billion.

The States and many of their local governments also make money from a number of publicly operated business enterprises. Toll bridges and toll roads are popular in the East. Several States, notably Washington, are in the ferry business. North Dakota markets a flour sold under the brand name Dakota-Maid and is in the commercial banking business. California operates a short railway line in San Francisco.

Eighteen States are in the liquor business, selling alcohol in State-operated stores.[14] For years, Washington and Oregon jointly owned a distillery in Kentucky and sold its product in their outlets.

Many cities throughout the country own and operate their water, electric power, and bus transportation systems. Some cities operate farmers' markets; rent space in their office buildings, warehouses, and housing projects; and

---

Tax Rebellions Throughout our history, taxes have been a favorite subject of political cartoons and political speeches. It's a popular subject because few people love to pay their taxes. "Taxation without representation" was one reason the colonists revolted against England. Almost two centuries later, California taxpayers led another rebellion against taxes—one that triggered what the *Washington Times* called "a tectonic shift in American politics."

During the late 1970s, double-digit inflation was pushing property taxes through California roofs. In 1978, voters passed the controversial Proposition 13, slashing the State's property taxes by 30 percent and capping the rate of future increases. Critics feared these massive cuts would permanently hobble public education and public safety. But within two years, 43 states had followed suit and passed some kind of property tax cuts or limits. Fifteen states had lowered their income tax rates, and ten others had indexed them to the inflation rate.

In 1980, the tax revolt helped usher Ronald Reagan into the White House. The next year, he pushed through what was then the largest tax cut in U.S. history. The ensuing years saw a legion of tax-cutting Republicans swept into office at all levels of government.

Go Online
PHSchool.com

Use Web Code mqd-7257 to find out more about State and local taxes and taxpayers' rebellions and for help in answering the following question: *(a) Does your State have a tax cap? (b) If so, what has been its effect? (c) Describe any citizen movements in your State or local community today that seek to raise or lower taxes.*

---

operate dams and wharves. Receipts from such businesses support the local governments that own them. Other nontax sources include court fines, sales and lease of public lands, and interest from loans, investments, and late tax payments.

California and many other States have relaxed their once-strict antigambling laws, hoping to attract dollars, jobs, and tourists. State-run lotteries now bring in some $12 billion a year for 41 States and the District of Columbia and Puerto Rico.[15] In California, by law, 34 percent of State lottery revenues must go to public education. In 2004, the California State Lottery provided more than $1 billion to the State's public schools.

Borrowing

California and its local governments regularly borrow money for unusually large undertakings, such as the construction of public buildings, bridges, and highways, that cannot be paid for out of current income. That borrowing is often

---

[14]Those states are Alabama, Idaho, Iowa, Maine, Michigan, Mississippi, Montana, New Hampshire, North Carolina, Ohio, Oregon, Pennsylvania, Utah, Vermont, Virginia, Washington, West Virginia, Wyoming. North Carolina's stores are operated by the counties; Wyoming's liquor monopoly operates only at the wholesale level.

[15]States that do not have lotteries are Alabama, Alaska, Arkansas, Hawaii, Mississippi, Nevada, South Carolina, Utah, and Wyoming.

done by issuing bonds, much as the Federal Government does. California State and local (or municipal) bonds are easy to market because the interest from them is generally not taxed by the Federal Government-or by the State if the bonds are purchased by California residents.

In the past, many State and local governments have defaulted on their debts. Thus, most State constitutions now place detailed limits on the power to borrow. States' debts now exceed $550 billion, and local governments owe more than $900 billion. California's State and local government debt in 2005 was nearly $90 billion.

The Budget Process

A **budget** is a financial plan for the use of public money, personnel, and property. It is also a political document, a statement of public policy. In its budget, the State sets its priorities and decides who gets what and how much.

Until the 1920s, State budgets were the result of haphazard and uncoordinated steps centered in the legislature. Thus, various State agencies appeared regularly before legislative appropriations committees, each seeking its own funding, often in bitter competition with one another. Their chances of success depended far less on need or merit than on their political muscle. When the legislature adjourned, no one had any real idea of how much it had appropriated or for what.

State budgets are very different today. They remain highly charged political documents, but they are by and large the products of an orderly, planned process.

California and 46 other States have now adopted the executive budget, which gives the governor two vital powers: (1) to prepare the State budget, and (2) to administer the funds the legislature appropriates. In most States, the governor has the help of a budget agency, appointed by and answering to the governor. The Department of Finance serves this purpose in California.

California's budget is developed and enacted through the following process:

1. Department directors and agency heads prepare estimates of their needs and expenditures for the coming fiscal year.

2. The Department of Finance reviews these requests and resolves any issues, with input from the governor.

3. By January 10, the governor sends the proposed budget to the legislature.

4. The legislature considers the budget part by part, appropriates funds, and enacts any necessary revenue measures in order to pass the finished budget bill to the governor by June 15.

5. The governor may reduce or eliminate any appropriation through the line-item veto. By July 1, the start of the fiscal year, the governor signs or vetoes the budget bill.

Section 4 Assessment

Key Terms and Main Ideas

1. Explain whether the following taxes are either **regressive** or **progressive: (a) sales tax; (b) income tax.**
2. What limits does the Federal Constitution put on the States' ability to tax?
3. What is the difference between an **inheritance tax** and an **estate tax**?
4. In what ways do States tax businesses?

Critical Thinking

5. **Determining Relevance (a)** Restate in your own words Adam Smith's four principles of sound taxation. **(b)** What do you think makes each of them important?

6. **Identifying Alternatives** What might be the advantages and disadvantages of raising revenue through **(a)** a State-run lottery? **(b)** a State-run business? **(c)** a State-wide property tax?

Must Local Government Follow the "One Person, One Vote" Rule?

Analysis Skills HR4, HI3, HI4

As the Supreme Court ruled in **Baker** *v.* **Carr** *(1962), State legislatures must be apportioned according to population so that each person's vote has roughly equal weight. Should this principle apply to local government as well?*

Board of Estimate of City of New York v. Morris (1989)

New York City's Board of Estimate manages all city property, sets salaries of city employees, grants all city contracts, and shares authority with the City Council over the city budget. The Board has eight members: the mayor, comptroller, and president of the city council (chosen by citywide election), and the presidents of New York's five boroughs (chosen by borough election). The three citywide members each have two votes on the Board, while the borough representatives have one.

Beverly Morris and others who lived and voted in Brooklyn, the most populous borough, filed suit in 1981. They argued that the vote of each person in the less-populous boroughs counted more than each vote in Brooklyn, because all boroughs had equal representation on the Board despite great differences in population.

A federal district court dismissed the case, concluding that the Board was a "nonelective, nonlegislative body." Therefore, past Supreme Court decisions regarding apportionment did not apply to the Board. A court of appeals reversed that decision. It concluded that the Board really is an elective body, and ordered the district court to decide whether the Board's selection process met the "one person, one vote" standard. The district court ruled that it did not meet this standard, the court of appeals agreed with that ruling, and the City appealed to the Supreme Court.

Arguments for the Board of Estimate

1. The Board is a unique political body with non-legislative powers. Thus it should not have to meet the "one person, one vote" standard that legislatures must meet.
2. The Board has proven itself effective in the past and should not be disturbed. It is essential to the governing of New York City.
3. The fact that boroughs of unequal population have equal representation on the Board is not critical, because the three citywide members have double votes and can outvote the five borough members. Thus citywide interests predominate on the Board.

Arguments for Morris

1. In order for all citizens to have fair and effective representation in government, all votes must carry approximately equal weight. The Board's structure is inconsistent with this principle.
2. The principle of "one person, one vote" applies to local governments as well as to State legislatures. The Board is sufficiently legislative in its powers and must follow this principle.
3. The at-large members do not always vote together, so their majority is only theoretical.

Decide for Yourself

1. Review the constitutional grounds on which each side based its arguments and the specific arguments each side presented.
2. Debate the opposing viewpoints presented in this case. Which viewpoint do you favor?
3. Predict the impact of the Court's decision on local elections and local politics. (To read a summary of the Court's decision, turn to pages 799–806.)

Go Online
PHSchool.com

Use Web Code mqp-7258 to register your vote on this issue and to see how other students voted.

Political Dictionary

county (p. 718), township (p. 718), charter (p. 720), ordinance (p. 720), special district (p. 722), regional body (p. 722), incorporation (p. 726), mayor-council government (p. 726), strong-mayor government (p. 727), weak-mayor government (p. 727), council-manager government (p. 727), commission government (p. 728), zoning (p. 729), metropolitan area (p. 731), Medicaid (p. 734), welfare (p. 735), entitlement (p. 735), sales tax (p. 741), use tax (p. 741), regressive tax (p. 741), income tax (p. 741), progressive tax (p. 742), property tax (p. 742), assessment (p. 742), inheritance tax (p. 742), estate tax (p. 742), budget (p. 744)

Standards Review

H-SS 12.6.4 Describe the means that citizens use to participate in the political process (e.g., voting, campaigning, lobbying, filing a legal challenge, demonstrating, petitioning, picketing, running for political office).

H-SS 12.7.2 Identify the major responsibilities and sources of revenue for state and local governments.

H-SS 12.7.5 Explain how public policy is formed, including the setting of the public agenda and implementation of it through regulations and executive orders.

H-SS 12.7.6 Compare the processes of lawmaking at each of the three levels of government, including the role of lobbying and the media.

Practicing the Vocabulary

Matching *Choose a term from the list above that best matches each description.*

1. The major unit of local government in most States except Rhode Island and Connecticut
2. A form of city government consisting of three to nine popularly elected commissioners who form a city council
3. A form of government in which the mayor heads the city administration, prepares the budget, and generally exercises strong leadership
4. A tax on individual and corporate income
5. A tax that is based on a person's ability to pay

Using Words in Context *For each of the terms below, write a sentence that shows how it relates to this chapter.*

6. incorporation
7. charter
8. entitlement
9. special district
10. estate tax
11. metropolitan area
12. zoning

Reviewing Main Ideas

Section 1

13. What are the main forms of local government in California?
14. How do California's two types of county government differ?
15. What is the main reason for the creation of special districts?
16. What is the purpose of the New England town meeting?

Section 2

17. **(a)** What are the basic forms of city government? **(b)** Which form is most common in California?
18. Briefly describe how most cities in the United States developed.
19. Describe the impact of "suburbanitis."
20. How are the councils of government an example of regional cooperation in California?

Section 3

21. Briefly describe the major categories of services that California provides to its residents.

22. Why was Aid to Families with Dependent Children replaced by the Temporary Assistance to Needy Families program?
23. Why do the amount and types of government services vary from State to State?
24. **(a)** In what ways do States try to ensure the public safety of their citizens? **(b)** What challenges do States face in ensuring public safety?

Section 4

25. What are the general limits on the ability of State and local governments to tax?
26. List the major categories of taxes that are levied at the State and local levels in this country.
27. What are the major sources of nontax revenue available to the States?
28. Who are the main officials involved in the budget process in California?

Critical Thinking Skills

Analysis Skill HI1

29. *Face the Issues* In some States, wealthier school districts are allowed to raise money through higher property taxes only if they turn over a certain share of the increased revenue to poorer districts in the State. What are some potential advantages and disadvantages of this system?

30.. *Predicting Consequences* The decision by Houston voters to reject zoning until the early 1990s had noticeable results. **(a)** What do you think those results were? **(b)** What effects might a lack of zoning have on homeowners?

31. *Understanding Point of View* Many elderly property owners in California still strongly support Proposition 13, the initiative that cut property taxes. Many younger residents with families oppose it. Why? Explain the points of view that might be involved in this situation.

32. *Formulating Questions* What questions might you ask the mayor or other public officials in your community to discover how they think your local government could be improved?

Analyzing Political Cartoons

Using your knowledge of American government and this cartoon, answer the questions below.

"As for me, I believe in no taxation, with or without representation."

33. Describe the situation depicted in the cartoon.
34. What would be the impact on government and the services it provides if there were no taxes?

Participation Activities

35. *Current Events Watch* Find a news report on a proposal to improve the amount or type of funding for schools in California. Analyze the proposal. What impact would it have on State and local governments and on school administrators? Would you support or oppose the proposal? Why?

36. *Chart Activity* How is the government of your county organized? The government of your city? What officials hold the key positions in those governments? How are they chosen? Summarize your findings in charts like those on pages 727–729.

37. *It's Your Turn* You are the governor of a State that does not impose a general sales tax; it relies, instead, on an income tax, which is levied at comparatively high rates. You believe that the tax system would be more fair if the State adopted a sales tax and if, at the same time, income tax rates were reduced. Write a speech in which you urge the State legislature to adopt your plan. **(Writing a Speech)**

 Standards Monitoring *Online*

For: Chapter 25 Self-Test **Visit:** PHSchool.com
Web Code: mqa-8255

As a final review, take the Magruder's Chapter 25 Self-Test and receive immediate feedback on your answers. The test consists of 20 multiple-choice questions designed to test your understanding of the chapter content.

"A LIVE JACKASS KICKING A DEAD LION."

Reference Section

Databank

Outline of the Constitution

United States Constitution

Historical Documents

Supreme Court Glossary

Glossary

Spanish Glossary

Index

Acknowledgments

Stop the Presses

Databank

The United States: A Statistical Profile

State	Capital	Population (in thousands) 2000	Population (in thousands) 1990	% Change	Land Area in Sq. Mi.	% Land Federally Owned	Population per Sq. Mi.
United States	**Washington, D.C.**	**281,422**	**248,710**	**13.2**	**3,536,278**	**28.8**	**79.6**
Alabama	Montgomery	4,447	4,041	10.1	50,750	3.4	87.6
Alaska	Juneau	627	550	14.0	570,374	67.9	1.1
Arizona	Phoenix	5,131	3,665	40.0	113,642	45.6	45.2
Arkansas	Little Rock	2,673	2,351	13.7	52,075	10.2	51.3
California	Sacramento	33,872	29,760	13.8	155,973	44.9	217.2
Colorado	Denver	4,301	3,294	30.6	103,729	36.4	41.5
Connecticut	Hartford	3,406	3,287	3.6	4,845	0.5	703.0
Delaware	Dover	784	666	17.6	1,955	2.1	401.0
Florida	Tallahassee	15,982	12,938	23.5	53,937	8.3	296.3
Georgia	Atlanta	8,186	6,478	26.4	57,919	5.6	141.3
Hawaii	Honolulu	1,212	1,108	9.3	6,423	14.7	188.7
Idaho	Boise	1,294	1,007	28.5	82,751	62.5	15.6
Illinois	Springfield	12,419	11,431	8.6	55,593	1.8	223.4
Indiana	Indianapolis	6,080	5,544	9.7	35,870	2.2	169.5
Iowa	Des Moines	2,926	2,777	5.4	55,875	0.7	52.4
Kansas	Topeka	2,688	2,478	8.5	81,823	1.3	32.9
Kentucky	Frankfort	4,042	3,685	9.7	39,732	4.8	101.7
Louisiana	Baton Rouge	4,469	4,220	5.9	43,566	4.5	102.6
Maine	Augusta	1,275	1,228	3.8	30,865	1.0	41.3
Maryland	Annapolis	5,296	4,781	10.8	9,775	3.2	541.8
Massachusetts	Boston	6,349	6,016	5.5	7,838	1.6	810.0
Michigan	Lansing	9,938	9,295	6.9	56,809	11.2	174.9
Minnesota	St. Paul	4,919	4,375	12.4	79,617	8.7	61.8
Mississippi	Jackson	2,845	2,573	10.5	46,914	5.9	60.6
Missouri	Jefferson City	5,595	5,117	9.3	68,898	4.8	81.2
Montana	Helena	902	799	12.9	145,556	28.0	6.2
Nebraska	Lincoln	1,711	1,578	8.4	76,878	1.5	22.3
Nevada	Carson City	1,998	1,202	66.3	109,806	83.1	18.2
New Hampshire	Concord	1,236	1,109	11.4	8,969	13.2	137.8
New Jersey	Trenton	8,414	7,730	8.9	7,419	3.4	1,134.1
New Mexico	Santa Fe	1,819	1,515	20.1	121,364	34.2	15.0
New York	Albany	18,976	17,990	5.5	47,224	0.4	401.8
North Carolina	Raleigh	8,049	6,629	21.4	48,718	8.0	165.2
North Dakota	Bismarck	642	639	0.5	68,994	4.2	9.3
Ohio	Columbus	11,353	10,847	4.7	40,953	1.5	277.2
Oklahoma	Oklahoma City	3,451	3,146	9.7	68,679	2.9	50.2
Oregon	Salem	3,421	2,842	20.4	96,002	52.6	35.6
Pennsylvania	Harrisburg	12,281	11,882	3.4	44,820	2.4	274.0
Rhode Island	Providence	1,048	1,003	4.5	1,045	0.6	1,002.9
South Carolina	Columbia	4,012	3,487	15.1	30,111	6.1	133.2
South Dakota	Pierre	755	696	8.5	75,896	5.6	9.9
Tennessee	Nashville	5,689	4,877	16.7	41,219	6.1	138.0
Texas	Austin	20,852	16,987	22.8	261,914	1.7	79.6
Utah	Salt Lake City	2,233	1,723	29.6	82,168	64.5	27.2
Vermont	Montpelier	609	563	8.2	9,249	6.3	65.8
Virginia	Richmond	7,079	6,187	14.4	39,598	9.0	178.8
Washington	Olympia	5,894	4,867	21.1	66,581	28.5	88.5
West Virginia	Charleston	1,808	1,793	0.8	24,087	7.6	75.1
Wisconsin	Madison	5,364	4,892	9.6	54,314	5.6	98.8
Wyoming	Cheyenne	494	454	8.9	97,105	49.9	5.1
Washington, D.C.		572	607	-5.7	61	23.4	9,377.0

Sources: Bureau of the Census; Federal Election Commission

State	Population (in thousands)				Popular Vote, 2004 Presidential Election					
	% Urban	African American	Hispanic† Origin	% Foreign Born	George W. Bush (Republican)	%	John Kerry (Democrat)	%	All Others	%
United States	**80.1**	**34,862**	**31,337**	**7.9**	**62,040,610**	**50.7**	**59,028,444**	**48.3**	**1,226,291**	**1.0**
Alabama	70.1	1,139	45	1.1	1,176,394	62.5	693,933	36.8	13,122	0.7
Alaska	41.5	24	25	4.5	190,889	61.1	111,025	35.5	10,684	3.4
Arizona	87.8	176	1,084	7.6	1,104,294	54.9	893,524	44.4	14,767	0.7
Arkansas	48.6	411	54	1.1	572,898	54.3	469,953	44.6	12,094	1.2
California	96.7	2,487	10,460	21.7	5,509,826	44.4	6,745,485	54.3	166,541	1.3
Colorado	84.0	176	604	4.3	1,101,255	51.7	1,001,732	47.0	27,343	1.3
Connecticut	95.6	309	279	8.5	693,826	44.0	857,488	54.3	27,455	1.7
Delaware	81.6	149	28	3.3	171,660	45.8	200,152	53.4	3,378	0.9
Florida	93.0	2,333	2,334	12.9	3,964,522	52.1	3,583,544	47.1	61,744	0.8
Georgia	68.9	2,236	240	2.7	1,914,254	58.0	1,366,149	41.4	21,472	0.7
Hawaii	73.1	34	95	14.7	194,191	45.3	231,708	54.0	3,114	0.7
Idaho	38.3	8	93	2.9	409,235	68.4	181,098	30.3	8,114	1.4
Illinois	84.5	1,854	1,276	8.3	2,345,946	44.5	2,891,550	54.8	36,826	0.7
Indiana	71.7	498	154	1.7	1,479,438	60.0	969,011	39.3	19,553	0.8
Iowa	44.6	58	62	1.6	751,957	49.9	741,898	49.2	13,053	0.9
Kansas	56.4	157	148	2.5	736,456	62.0	434,993	36.6	16,307	1.4
Kentucky	48.3	288	35	0.9	1,069,439	59.6	712,733	39.7	13,710	0.8
Louisiana	75.2	1,415	119	2.1	1,102,169	56.7	820,299	42.2	20,638	1.1
Maine	35.8	6	9	3.0	330,201	44.6	396,842	53.6	13,709	1.9
Maryland	92.7	1,454	199	6.6	1,024,703	42.9	1,334,493	55.9	27,482	1.2
Massachusetts	96.1	405	391	9.5	1,071,109	36.8	1,803,800	61.9	37,479	1.3
Michigan	82.6	1,415	276	3.8	2,313,746	47.8	2,479,183	51.2	46,323	1.0
Minnesota	70.1	149	93	2.6	1,346,695	47.6	1,445,014	51.1	36,678	1.3
Mississippi	35.9	1,010	24	0.8	684,981	59.5	458,094	39.8	9,070	0.8
Missouri	68.0	617	91	1.6	1,455,713	53.3	1,259,171	46.1	16,480	0.6
Montana	33.4	3	16	1.7	266,063	59.1	173,710	38.6	10,672	2.4
Nebraska	51.8	68	77	1.8	512,814	65.9	254,328	32.7	11,044	1.4
Nevada	86.1	140	304	8.7	418,690	50.5	397,190	47.9	13,707	1.7
New Hampshire	60.2	9	20	3.7	331,237	48.9	340,511	50.2	5,990	0.9
New Jersey	100.0	1,197	1,027	12.5	1,670,003	46.2	1,911,430	52.9	30,258	0.8
New Mexico	57.0	46	708	5.3	376,930	49.8	370,942	49.0	8,432	1.1
New York	91.9	3,222	2,661	15.9	2,962,567	40.1	4,314,280	58.4	114,189	1.5
North Carolina	67.1	1,686	176	1.7	1,961,166	56.0	1,525,849	43.6	13,992	0.4
North Dakota	43.1	4	7	1.5	196,651	62.9	111,052	35.5	5,130	1.6
Ohio	81.0	1,304	185	2.4	2,859,768	50.8	2,741,167	48.7	26,973	0.5
Oklahoma	60.5	262	137	2.1	959,792	65.6	503,966	34.4	0	0
Oregon	72.7	62	213	4.9	866,831	47.2	943,163	51.4	26,788	1.5
Pennsylvania	84.5	1,170	326	3.1	2,793,847	48.4	2,938,095	50.9	37,648	0.7
Rhode Island	93.8	50	69	9.5	169,046	38.7	259,765	59.4	8,323	1.9
South Carolina	70.0	1,157	54	1.4	937,974	58.0	661,699	40.9	18,057	1.1
South Dakota	34.0	5	9	1.1	232,584	59.9	149,244	38.4	6,387	1.7
Tennessee	67.8	913	67	1.2	1,384,375	56.8	1,036,477	42.5	16,467	0.7
Texas	84.5	2,470	6,045	9.0	4,526,917	61.1	2,832,704	38.2	51,144	0.7
Utah	76.7	19	151	3.4	663,742	71.5	241,199	26.0	22,903	2.5
Vermont	27.9	3	5	3.1	121,180	38.8	184,067	58.9	7,062	2.3
Virginia	78.1	1,385	266	5.0	1,716,959	53.7	1,454,742	45.5	26,666	0.8
Washington	82.9	204	377	6.6	1,304,894	45.6	1,510,201	52.8	43,989	1.5
West Virgina	41.9	56	10	0.9	423,778	56.1	326,541	43.2	5,568	0.7
Wisconsin	67.8	293	140	2.5	1,478,120	49.3	1,489,504	49.7	29,383	1.0
Wyoming	29.6	4	29	1.7	167,629	68.9	70,776	29.1	5,023	2.0
Washington, D.C.	100.0	319	38	9.7	21,256	9.3	202,970	89.2	3,360	1.5

† Persons of Hispanic origin may be of any race.

Political Map of the United States

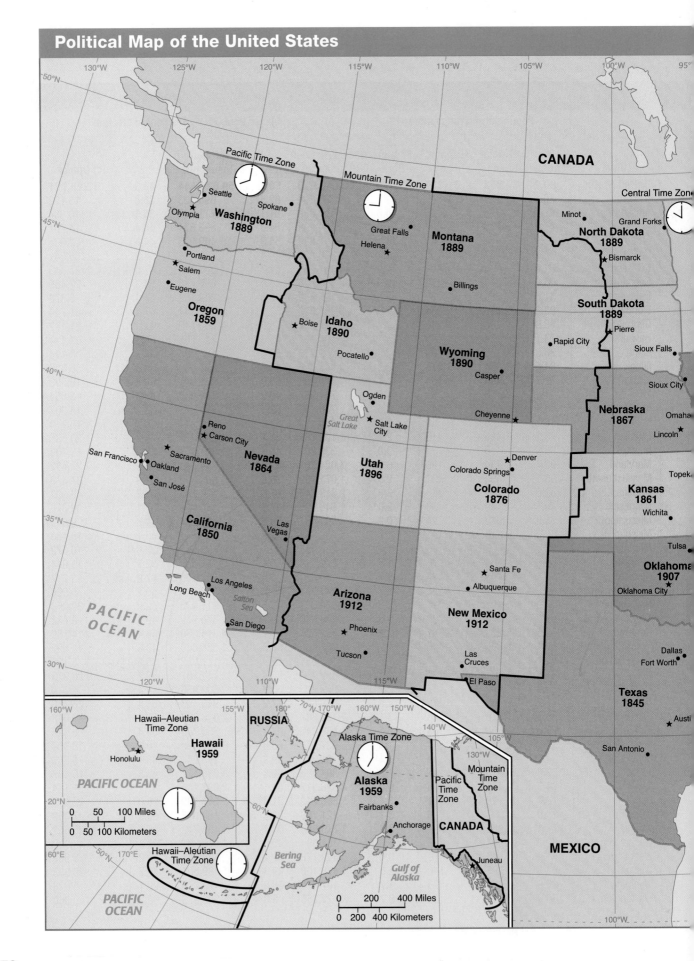

CANADA

Pacific Time Zone

Mountain Time Zone

Central Time Zone

Seattle
Spokane
Olympia
Washington 1889

Montana 1889
Great Falls
Helena

Minot
Grand Forks
North Dakota 1889
Bismarck

Portland
Salem
Eugene

Oregon 1859

Boise
Idaho 1890
Pocatello

Billings

South Dakota 1889
Rapid City
Pierre
Sioux Falls

Sioux City

Wyoming 1890
Casper

Reno
Carson City

San Francisco
Sacramento
Oakland
San José

Nevada 1864

Ogden
Great Salt Lake
Salt Lake City

Cheyenne

Nebraska 1867
Omaha
Lincoln

Utah 1896

Denver
Colorado Springs
Colorado 1876

Topeka
Kansas 1861
Wichita

California 1850

Las Vegas

Long Beach
Los Angeles
Salton Sea
San Diego

PACIFIC OCEAN

Arizona 1912
Phoenix
Tucson

Santa Fe
Albuquerque

New Mexico 1912

Las Cruces
El Paso

Tulsa
Oklahoma 1907
Oklahoma City

Dallas
Fort Worth

Texas 1845

Austin
San Antonio

MEXICO

160°W
Hawaii–Aleutian Time Zone
Hawaii 1959
Honolulu
PACIFIC OCEAN

0   50   100 Miles
0   50 100 Kilometers

Hawaii–Aleutian Time Zone

PACIFIC OCEAN

RUSSIA

Alaska Time Zone

Alaska 1959
Fairbanks
Anchorage

Pacific Time Zone

Mountain Time Zone

CANADA

Juneau

Bering Sea

Gulf of Alaska

0   200   400 Miles
0   200   400 Kilometers

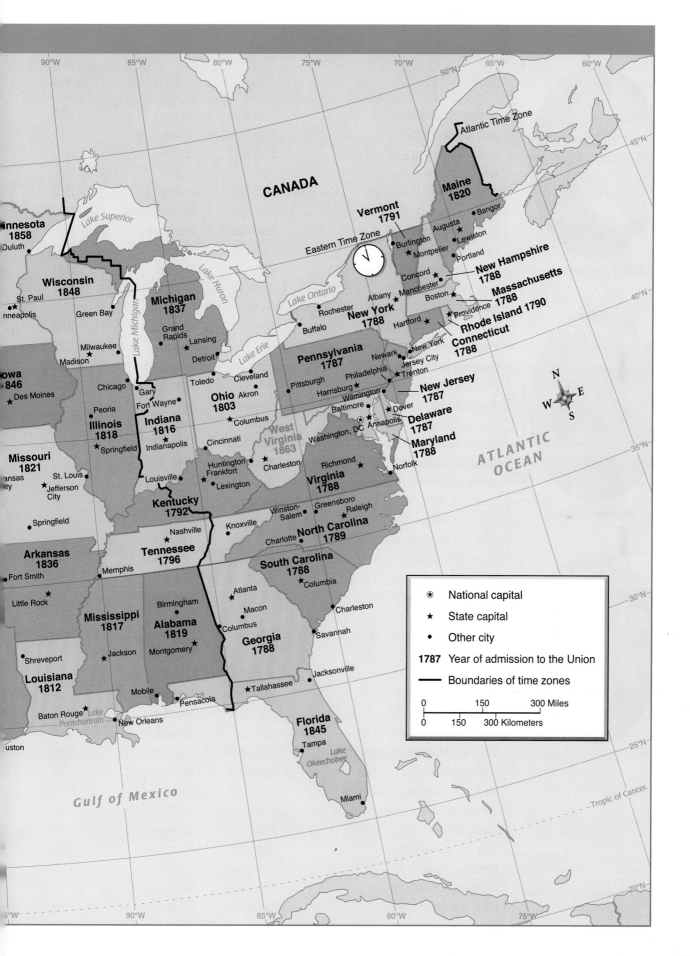

CANADA

Atlantic Time Zone

Maine
1820

• Bangor

Minnesota
1858

• Duluth

Lake Superior

Vermont
1791

Augusta
★

• Lewiston

Eastern Time Zone

• Burlington

Portland

Wisconsin
1848

Lake Huron

• Montpelier

New Hampshire
1788

St. Paul

Concord ★

Michigan
1837

Manchester

Massachusetts
1788

Minneapolis

Green Bay

Lake Ontario

Albany ★

Boston ★

Grand
Rapids

Rochester

New York
1788

Hartford ★

Providence ★

Rhode Island 1790

Iowa
1846

Milwaukee
★

Lansing
★

• Buffalo

Connecticut
1788

Madison
★

Detroit

Lake Erie

New York

Chicago

Toledo

Cleveland

Pennsylvania
1787

Newark

Des Moines
★

Gary

Peoria

Fort Wayne

Ohio
1803

Akron

Pittsburgh

Harrisburg ★

Philadelphia

Jersey City

Trenton ★

New Jersey
1787

Illinois
1818

Indiana
1816

Wilmington

Springfield
★

Indianapolis

Columbus

West
Virginia
1863

Baltimore

Dover •

Delaware
1787

Missouri
1821

Cincinnati

Charleston ★

Washington, DC

Annapolis ★

Maryland
1788

Kansas
City

St. Louis •

Louisville

Frankfort
★

Huntington

ATLANTIC
OCEAN

Jefferson
City
★

Lexington

Richmond
★

Norfolk •

Springfield •

Kentucky
1792

Knoxville •

Virginia
1788

Nashville
★

Winston-
Salem

Greensboro

Raleigh
★

Arkansas
1836

Tennessee
1796

Charlotte •

North Carolina
1789

Fort Smith •

Memphis •

South Carolina
1788

Little Rock
★

Atlanta
★

Columbia
★

Mississippi
1817

Birmingham •

Macon •

Charleston •

Alabama
1819

Columbus

Georgia
1788

Savannah •

Jackson
★

Montgomery
★

Shreveport •

Jacksonville •

Louisiana
1812

Mobile •

Baton Rouge ★

Pensacola •

★ Tallahassee

Lake
Pontchartrain

New Orleans

Houston

Florida
1845

Gulf of Mexico

Tampa •

Lake
Okeechobee

Tropic of Cancer

Miami •

N
W   E
S

⊛	National capital
★	State capital
•	Other city
1787	Year of admission to the Union
—	Boundaries of time zones

0   150   300 Miles
0   150   300 Kilometers

Presidents of the United States

NAME	PARTY	STATE [a]	ENTERED OFFICE
George Washington (1732–1799)	Federalist	Virginia	1789
John Adams (1735–1826)	Federalist	Massachusetts	1797
Thomas Jefferson (1743–1826)	Dem-Rep [b]	Virginia	1801
James Madison (1751–1836)	Dem-Rep	Virginia	1809
James Monroe (1758–1831)	Dem-Rep	Virginia	1817
John Q. Adams (1767–1848)	Dem-Rep	Massachusetts	1825
Andrew Jackson (1767–1845)	Democrat	Tennessee (SC)	1829
Martin Van Buren (1782–1862)	Democrat	New York	1837
William H. Harrison (1773–1841)	Whig	Ohio (VA)	1841
John Tyler (1790–1862)	Democrat	Virginia	1841
James K. Polk (1795–1849)	Democrat	Tennessee (NC)	1845
Zachary Taylor (1784–1850)	Whig	Louisiana (VA)	1849
Millard Fillmore (1800–1874)	Whig	New York	1850
Franklin Pierce (1804–1869)	Democrat	New Hampshire	1853
James Buchanan (1791–1868)	Democrat	Pennsylvania	1857
Abraham Lincoln (1809–1865)	Republican	Illinois (KY)	1861
Andrew Johnson (1808–1875)	Democrat [c]	Tennessee (NC)	1865
Ulysses S. Grant (1822–1885)	Republican	Illinois (OH)	1869
Rutherford B. Hayes (1822–1893)	Republican	Ohio	1877
James A. Garfield (1831–1881)	Republican	Ohio	1881
Chester A. Arthur (1829–1896)	Republican	New York (VT)	1881
Grover Cleveland (1837–1908)	Democrat	New York (NJ)	1885
Benjamin Harrison (1833–1901)	Republican	Indiana (OH)	1889
Grover Cleveland (1837–1908)	Democrat	New York (NJ)	1893
William McKinley (1843–1901)	Republican	Ohio	1897
Theodore Roosevelt (1858–1919)	Republican	New York	1901
William H. Taft (1857–1930)	Republican	Ohio	1909
Woodrow Wilson (1856–1924)	Democrat	New Jersey (VA)	1913
Warren G. Harding (1865–1923)	Republican	Ohio	1921
Calvin Coolidge (1872–1933)	Republican	Massachusetts (VT)	1923
Herbert Hoover (1874–1964)	Republican	California (IA)	1929
Franklin Roosevelt (1882–1945)	Democrat	New York	1933
Harry S Truman (1884–1972)	Democrat	Missouri	1945
Dwight D. Eisenhower (1890–1969)	Republican	New York (TX)	1953
John F. Kennedy (1917–1963)	Democrat	Massachusetts	1961
Lyndon B. Johnson (1908–1973)	Democrat	Texas	1963
Richard M. Nixon (1913–1994)	Republican	New York (CA)	1969
Gerald R. Ford (1913–)	Republican	Michigan (NE)	1974
James E. Carter (1924–)	Democrat	Georgia	1977
Ronald W. Reagan (1911–2004)	Republican	California (IL)	1981
George H.W. Bush (1924–)	Republican	Texas (MA)	1989
William J. Clinton (1946–)	Democrat	Arkansas	1993
George W. Bush (1946–)	Republican	Texas	2001

George Washington

Abraham Lincoln

Theodore Roosevelt

[a] State of residence when elected; if born in another State, that State in parentheses.
[b] Democratic-Republican
[c] Johnson, a War Democrat, was elected Vice-President on the coalition Union Party ticket.
[d] Resigned October 10, 1973.
[e] Nominated by Nixon, confirmed by Congress on December 6, 1973.
[f] Nominated by Ford, confirmed by Congress on December 19, 1974.

Age On Taking Office	Religion	Ancestry	Vice President(s)
57	Episcopalian	English	John Adams
61	Unitarian	English	Thomas Jefferson
57	————	Welsh	Aaron Burr/George Clinton
57	Episcopalian	English	George Clinton/Elbridge Gerry
58	Episcopalian	Scottish	Daniel D. Tompkins
57	Unitarian	English	John C. Calhoun
61	Presbyterian	Scots-Irish	John C. Calhoun/Martin Van Buren
54	Dutch Reformed	Dutch	Richard M. Johnson
68	Episcopalian	English	John Tyler
51	Episcopalian	English	none
49	Presbyterian	Scots-Irish	George M. Dallas
64	Episcopalian	English	Millard Fillmore
50	Unitarian	English	none
48	Episcopalian	English	William R. King
65	Presbyterian	Scots-Irish	John C. Breckinridge
52	————	English	Hannibal Hamlin/Andrew Johnson
56	————	English	none
46	Methodist	English-Scottish	Schuyler Colfax/Henry Wilson
54	Methodist	Scottish	William A. Wheeler
49	Disciples of Christ	English	Chester A. Arthur
51	Episcopalian	Scots-Irish	none
47	Presbyterian	English-Irish	Thomas A. Hendricks
55	Presbyterian	English	Levi P. Morton
55	Presbyterian	English-Irish	Adlai E. Stevenson
54	Methodist	Scots-Irish	Garret A. Hobart/Theodore Roosevelt
42	Dutch Reformed	Dutch	Charles W. Fairbanks
51	Unitarian	English	James S. Sherman
56	Presbyterian	Scots-Irish	Thomas R. Marshall
55	Baptist	English-Scottish-Irish	Calvin Coolidge
51	Congregationalist	English	Charles G. Dawes
54	Quaker	Swiss-German	Charles Curtis
51	Episcopalian	Dutch	John N. Garner/Henry A. Wallace/Harry S Truman
60	Baptist	English-Scottish-Irish	Alben W. Barkley
62	Presbyterian	Swiss-German	Richard M. Nixon
43	Roman Catholic	Irish	Lyndon B. Johnson
55	Disciples of Christ	English	Hubert H. Humphrey
56	Quaker	Scots-Irish	Spiro T. Agnew [d]/Gerald R. Ford [e]
61	Episcopalian	English	Nelson A. Rockefeller [f]
52	Baptist	English-Scottish-Irish	Walter F. Mondale
69	Episcopalian	English-Scottish-Irish	George H. W. Bush
64	Episcopalian	English	J. Danforth Quayle
46	Baptist	English	Albert Gore, Jr.
54	Episcopalian	English	Richard B. Cheney

Woodrow Wilson

Franklin Roosevelt

Ronald Reagan

Political Map of the World

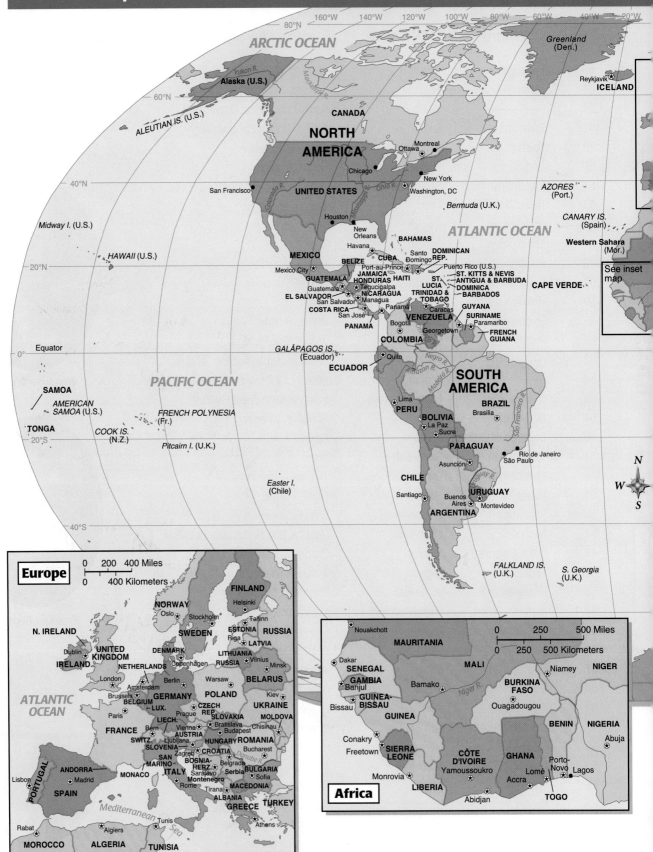

ARCTIC OCEAN

Greenland (Den.)

Alaska (U.S.)

ALEUTIAN IS. (U.S.)

Reykjavik
ICELAND

CANADA

NORTH AMERICA

Montreal
Ottawa

Chicago

New York

San Francisco

UNITED STATES

Washington, DC

Bermuda (U.K.)

AZORES (Port.)

ATLANTIC OCEAN

CANARY IS. (Spain)

Midway I. (U.S.)

Houston

Western Sahara (Mor.)

BAHAMAS

Havana

HAWAII (U.S.)

New Orleans

MEXICO

Mexico City

CUBA

BELIZE

Port-au-Prince

Santo Domingo

DOMINICAN REP.

JAMAICA

HAITI

Puerto Rico (U.S.)

ST. KITTS & NEVIS

See inset map

GUATEMALA

Guatemala

HONDURAS

Tegucigalpa

ST. LUCIA

ANTIGUA & BARBUDA

DOMINICA

CAPE VERDE

EL SALVADOR

NICARAGUA

TRINIDAD & TOBAGO

BARBADOS

San Salvador

Managua

COSTA RICA

Panama

Caracas

GUYANA

SURINAME

San José

Bogotá

Georgetown

Paramaribo

FRENCH GUIANA

PANAMA

VENEZUELA

COLOMBIA

GALÁPAGOS IS. (Ecuador)

Quito

Negro R.

Equator

ECUADOR

Amazon R.

Madeira R.

SOUTH AMERICA

PACIFIC OCEAN

SAMOA

Lima

PERU

BRAZIL

Brasília

São Francisco R.

AMERICAN SAMOA (U.S.)

BOLIVIA

La Paz

Sucre

TONGA

FRENCH POLYNESIA (Fr.)

COOK IS. (N.Z.)

PARAGUAY

Rio de Janeiro

São Paulo

Pitcairn I. (U.K.)

Asunción

Uruguay R.

N

Easter I. (Chile)

CHILE

URUGUAY

W E

Santiago

Buenos Aires

Montevideo

S

ARGENTINA

FALKLAND IS. (U.K.)

S. Georgia (U.K.)

Europe

0   200   400 Miles

0   400 Kilometers

FINLAND

Helsinki

NORWAY

Oslo   Stockholm

Tallinn

N. IRELAND

SWEDEN

ESTONIA

RUSSIA

Riga

Dublin

UNITED KINGDOM

DENMARK

LATVIA

LITHUANIA

IRELAND

NETHERLANDS

Copenhagen

RUSSIA

Vilnius

Minsk

London   Amsterdam

Berlin

Warsaw

BELARUS

ATLANTIC OCEAN

Brussels

GERMANY

POLAND

Kiev

BELGIUM

LUX.

CZECH REP.

UKRAINE

Paris

LIECH.

Prague

SLOVAKIA

MOLDOVA

FRANCE

Bern

Vienna

Bratislava

Chisinau

SWITZ.

AUSTRIA

Budapest

Ljubljana

HUNGARY

ROMANIA

SLOVENIA

Zagreb

CROATIA

Bucharest

SAN MARINO

BOSNIA-HERZ.

Belgrade

PORTUGAL

ANDORRA

MONACO

Sarajevo

Serbia

BULGARIA

Lisbon

Madrid

ITALY

Montenegro

Sofia

SPAIN

Rome

Tirana

MACEDONIA

ALBANIA

GREECE

TURKEY

Mediterranean Sea

Tunis

Rabat

Algiers

Athens

MOROCCO

ALGERIA

TUNISIA

Africa

0   250   500 Miles

0   250   500 Kilometers

Nouakchott

MAURITANIA

Dakar

MALI

Niamey

NIGER

SENEGAL

Bamako

GAMBIA

Banjul

BURKINA FASO

Bissau

GUINEA-BISSAU

Niger R.

Ouagadougou

GUINEA

BENIN

NIGERIA

Conakry

Abuja

Freetown

SIERRA LEONE

CÔTE D'IVOIRE

GHANA

Porto-Novo

Lagos

Yamoussoukro

Lomé

Monrovia

Accra

LIBERIA

TOGO

Abidjan

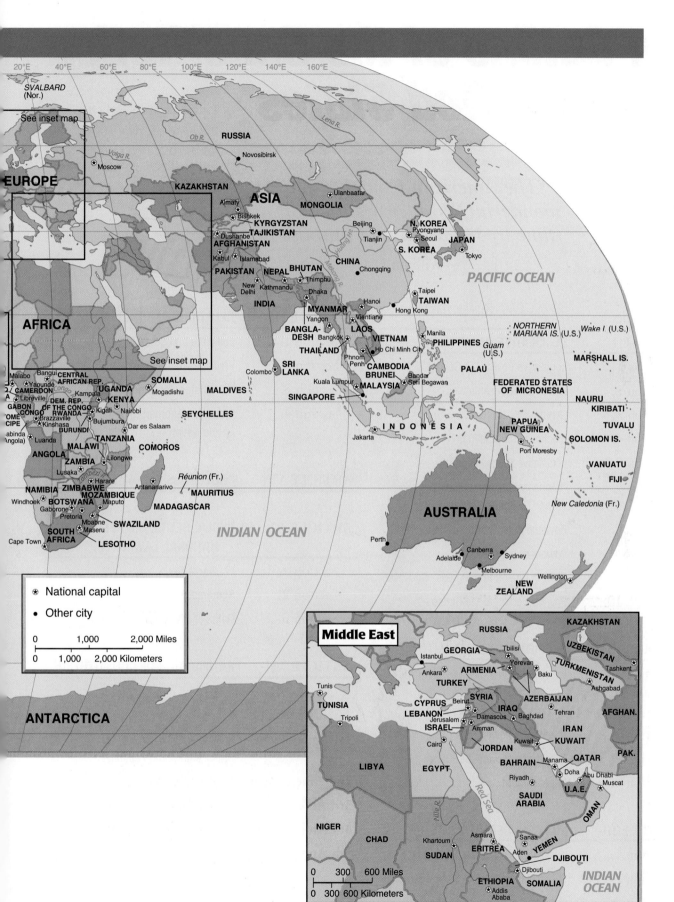

National capital
Other city

0	1,000	2,000 Miles
0	1,000	2,000 Kilometers

Middle East

0	300	600 Miles
0	300	600 Kilometers

An Outline of the Constitution of the United States

"The American Constitution is the most wonderful Work ever struck off at a given time by the brain and purpose of man."

—William E. Gladstone

6th Amendment	Criminal Proceedings
7th Amendment	Jury Trials in Civil Cases
8th Amendment	Bail; Cruel, Unusual Punishment
9th Amendment	Unenumerated Rights
10th Amendment	Powers Reserved to the States
11th Amendment	Suits Against the States
12th Amendment	Election of President and Vice President
13th Amendment	Slavery and Involuntary Servitude
Section 1.	Slavery and Involuntary Servitude Prohibited
Section 2.	Power of Congress
14th Amendment	Rights of Citizens
Section 1.	Citizenship; Privileges and Immunities; Due Process; Equal Protection
Section 2.	Apportionment of Representation
Section 3.	Disqualification of Officers
Section 4.	Public Debt
Section 5.	Powers of Congress
15th Amendment	Right to Vote—Race, Color, Servitude
Section 1.	Suffrage Not to Be Abridged
Section 2.	Power of Congress
16th Amendment	Income Tax
17th Amendment	Popular Election of Senators
Section 1.	Popular Election of Senators
Section 2.	Senate Vacancies
Section 3.	Inapplicable to Senators Previously Chosen
18th Amendment	Prohibition of Intoxicating Liquors
Section 1.	Intoxicating Liquors Prohibited
Section 2.	Concurrent Power to Enforce
Section 3.	Time Limit on Ratification
19th Amendment	Equal Suffrage—Sex
Section 1.	Suffrage Not to Be Abridged
Section 2.	Power of Congress

20th Amendment	Commencement of Terms; Sessions of Congress; Death or Disqualification of President-Elect
Section 1.	Terms of President, Vice President, members of Congress
Section 2.	Sessions of Congress
Section 3.	Death or Disqualification of President-Elect
Section 4.	Congress to Provide for Certain Successors
Section 5.	Effective Date
Section 6.	Time Limit on Ratification
21st Amendment	Repeal of 18th Amendment
Section 1.	Repeal of Prohibition
Section 2.	Transportation, Importation of Intoxicating Liquors
Section 3.	Time Limit on Ratification
22nd Amendment	Presidential Tenure
Section 1.	Restriction on Number of Terms
Section 2.	Time Limit on Ratification
23rd Amendment	Inclusion of District of Columbia in Presidential Election Systems
Section 1.	Presidential Electors for District
Section 2.	Power of Congress
24th Amendment	Right to Vote in Federal Elections—Tax Payment
Section 1.	Suffrage Not to Be Abridged
Section 2.	Power of Congress
25th Amendment	Presidential Succession; Vice Presidential Vacancy; Presidential Inability
Section 1.	Presidential Succession
Section 2.	Vice Presidential Vacancy
Section 3.	Presidential Inability
26th Amendment	Right to Vote—Age
Section 1.	Suffrage Not to Be Abridged
Section 2.	Power of Congress
27th Amendment	Congressional Pay

Outline of the Constitution

The Preamble states the broad purposes the Constitution is intended to serve—to establish a government that provides for greater cooperation among the States, ensures justice and peace, provides for defense against foreign enemies, promotes the general well-being of the people, and secures liberty now and in the future. The phrase *We the People* emphasizes the twin concepts of popular sovereignty and of representative government.

LEGISLATIVE DEPARTMENT

Section 1. Legislative power; Congress

Congress, the nation's lawmaking body, is bicameral in form; that is, it is composed of two houses: the Senate and the House of Representatives. The Framers of the Constitution purposely separated the lawmaking power from the power to enforce the laws (Article II, the Executive Branch) and the power to interpret them (Article III, the Judicial Branch). This system of separation of powers is supplemented by a system of checks and balances; that is, in several provisions the Constitution gives to each of the three branches various powers with which it may restrain the actions of the other two branches.

Section 2. House of Representatives

Clause 1. Election Electors means voters. Members of the House of Representatives are elected every two years. Each State must permit the same persons to vote for United States representatives as it permits to vote for the members of the larger house of its own legislature. The 17th Amendment (1913) extends this requirement to the qualification of voters for United States senators.

Clause 2. Qualifications A member of the House of Representatives must be at least 25 years old, an American citizen for seven years, and a resident of the State he or she represents. In addition, political custom requires that a representative also reside in the district from which he or she is elected.

Clause 3. Apportionment The number of representatives each State is entitled to is based on its population, which is counted every 10 years in the census. Congress reapportions the seats among the States after each census. In the Reapportionment Act of 1929, Congress fixed the permanent size of the House at 435 members with each State having at least one representative. Today there is one House seat for approximately every 650,000 persons in the population.

The words "three-fifths of all other persons" referred to slaves and reflected the Three-Fifths Compromise reached by the Framers at Philadelphia in 1787; the phrase was made obsolete, was in effect repealed, by the 13th Amendment in 1865.

Clause 4. Vacancies The executive authority refers to the governor of a State. If a member leaves office or dies before the expiration of his or her term, the governor is to call a special election to fill the vacancy.

PREAMBLE

We the People of the United States, in Order to form a more perfect Union, establish Justice, insure domestic Tranquility, provide for the common defence, promote the general Welfare, and secure the Blessings of Liberty to ourselves and our Posterity, do ordain and establish this Constitution for the United States of America.

Article I.

Section 1.

All legislative Powers herein granted shall be vested in a Congress of the United States, which shall consist of a Senate and House of Representatives.

Section 2.

1. The House of Representatives shall be composed of Members chosen every second Year by the People of the several States, and the Electors in each State shall have the Qualifications requisite for Electors of the most numerous Branch of the State Legislature.

2. No Person shall be a Representative who shall not have attained to the age of twenty-five Years, and been seven Years a Citizen of the United States, and who shall not, when elected, be an Inhabitant of that State in which he shall be chosen.

3. Representatives ~~and direct Taxes~~* shall be apportioned among the several States which may be included within this Union, according to their respective Numbers, ~~which shall be determined by adding to the whole Number of free Persons, including those bound to Service for a Term of Years and excluding Indians not taxed, three fifths of all other Persons.~~ The actual Enumeration shall be made within three Years after the first Meeting of the Congress of the United States, and within every subsequent term of ten Years, in such Manner as they shall by Law direct. The Number of Representatives shall not exceed one for every thirty Thousand, but each State shall have at Least one Representative; and, until such enumeration shall be made, the State of New Hampshire shall be entitled to choose three, Massachusetts eight, Rhode Island and Providence Plantations one, Connecticut five, New York six, New Jersey four, Pennsylvania eight, Delaware one, Maryland six, Virginia ten, North Carolina five, South Carolina five, and Georgia three.

4. When vacancies happen in the Representation from any State, the Executive Authority thereof shall issue Writs of Election to fill such Vacancies.

---

*The black lines indicate portions of the Constitution altered by subsequent amendments to the document.

5. The House of Representatives shall choose their Speaker and other Officers; and shall have the sole Power of Impeachment.

Section 3.

1. The Senate of the United States shall be composed of two Senators from each State ~~chosen by the Legislature thereof~~ for six Years; and each Senator shall have one Vote.

2. Immediately after they shall be assembled in Consequences of the first Election, they shall be divided, as equally as may be, into three Classes. The Seats of the Senators of the first Class shall be vacated at the Expiration of the second Year; of the second Class, at the Expiration of the fourth Year; and of the third Class, at the Expiration of the sixth Year; so that one-third may be chosen every second Year; ~~and if Vacancies happen by Resignation, or otherwise, during the Recess of the Legislature of any State, the Executive thereof may make temporary Appointments until the next Meeting of the Legislature, which shall then fill such Vacancies.~~

3. No Person shall be a Senator who shall not have attained to the Age of thirty Years, and been nine Years a Citizen of the United States, and who shall not, when elected, be an Inhabitant of that State for which he shall be chosen.

4. The Vice President of the United States shall be President of the Senate but shall have no Vote, unless they be equally divided.

5. The Senate shall choose their other Officers, and also a President pro tempore, in the Absence of the Vice President, or when he shall exercise the Office of President of the United States.

6. The Senate shall have the sole Power to try all Impeachments. When sitting for that Purpose, they shall be on Oath or Affirmation. When the President of the United States is tried, the Chief Justice shall preside: And no Person shall be convicted without the Concurrence of two thirds of the Members present.

7. Judgment in Cases of Impeachment shall not extend further than to removal from Office, and disqualification to hold and enjoy any Office of honor, Trust, or Profit under the United States: but the Party convicted shall nevertheless be liable and subject to Indictment, Trial, Judgment and Punishment, according to Law.

Clause 5. Officers; impeachment The House elects a Speaker, customarily chosen from the majority party in the House. Impeachment means accusation. The House has the exclusive power to impeach, or accuse, civil officers; the Senate (Article I, Section 3, Clause 6) has the exclusive power to try those impeached by the House.

Section 3. Senate

Clause 1. Composition, election, term Each State has two senators. Each serves for six years and has one vote. Originally, senators were not elected directly by the people, but by each State's legislature. The 17th Amendment, added in 1913, provides for the popular election of senators.

Clause 2. Classification The senators elected in 1788 were divided into three groups so that the Senate could become a "continuing body." One-third of the Senate's seats are up for election every two years.

The 17th Amendment provides that a Senate vacancy is to be filled at a special election called by the governor; State law may also permit the governor to appoint a successor to serve until that election is held.

Clause 3. Qualifications A senator must be at least 30 years old, a citizen for at least nine years, and must live in the State from which elected.

Clause 4. Presiding officer The Vice President presides over the Senate, but may vote only to break a tie.

Clause 5. Other officers The Senate chooses its own officers, including a president pro tempore to preside when the Vice President is not there.

Clause 6. Impeachment trials The Senate conducts the trials of those officials impeached by the House. The Vice President presides unless the President is on trial, in which case the Chief Justice of the United States does so. A conviction requires the votes of two-thirds of the senators present.

No President has ever been convicted. In 1868 the House voted eleven articles of impeachment against President Andrew Johnson, but the Senate fell one vote short of convicting him. In 1974 President Richard M. Nixon resigned the presidency in the face of almost certain impeachment by the House. The House brought two articles of impeachment against President Bill Clinton in late 1998. Neither charge was supported by even a simple majority vote in the Senate, on February 12, 1999.

Clause 7. Penalty on conviction The punishment of an official convicted in an impeachment case has always been removal from office. The Senate can also bar a convicted person from ever holding any federal office, but it is not required to do so. A convicted person can also be tried and punished in a regular court for any crime involved in the impeachment case.

Section 4. Elections and Meetings

Clause 1. Election In 1842 Congress required that representatives be elected from districts within each State with more than one seat in the House. The districts in each State are drawn by that State's legislature. Seven States now have only one seat in the House: Alaska, Delaware, Montana, North Dakota, South Dakota, Vermont, and Wyoming. The 1842 law also directed that representatives be elected in each State on the same day: the Tuesday after the first Monday in November of every even-numbered year. In 1914 Congress also set that same date for the election of senators.

Clause 2. Sessions Congress must meet at least once a year. The 20th Amendment (1933) changed the opening date to January 3.

Section 5. Legislative Proceedings

Clause 1. Admission of members; quorum In 1969 the Supreme Court held that the House cannot exclude any member-elect who satisfies the qualifications set out in Article I, Section 2, Clause 2.

A majority in the House (218 members) or Senate (51) constitutes a quorum. In practice, both houses often proceed with less than a quorum present. However, any member may raise a point of order (demand a "quorum call"). If a roll call then reveals less than a majority of the members present, that chamber must either adjourn or the sergeant at arms must be ordered to round up absent members.

Clause 2. Rules Each house has adopted detailed rules to guide its proceedings. Each house may discipline members for unacceptable conduct; expulsion requires a two-thirds vote.

Clause 3. Record Each house must keep and publish a record of its meetings. The *Congressional Record* is published for every day that either house of Congress is in session, and provides a written record of all that is said and done on the floor of each house each session.

Clause 4. Adjournment Once in session, neither house may suspend (recess) its work for more than three days without the approval of the other house. Both houses must always meet in the same location.

Section 6. Compensation, Immunities, and Disabilities of Members

Clause 1. Salaries; immunities Each house sets its members' salaries, paid by the United States; the 27th Amendment (1992) modified this pay-setting power. This provision establishes "legislative immunity." The purpose of this immunity is to allow members to speak and debate freely in Congress itself. Treason is strictly defined in Article III, Section 3. A felony is any serious crime. A breach of the peace is any indictable offense less than treason or a felony; this exemption from arrest is of little real importance today.

Clause 2. Restrictions on office holding No sitting member of either house may be appointed to an office in the executive or in the judicial branch if that position was created or its salary was increased during that member's current elected term. The second

---

Section 4.

1. The Times, Places and Manner of holding Elections for Senators and Representatives, shall be prescribed in each State by the Legislature thereof; but the Congress may at any time by law make or alter such Regulations, except as to the Places of choosing Senators.

2. The Congress shall assemble at least once in every Year, and such Meeting shall be on the first Monday in December, unless they shall by Law appoint a different Day.

Section 5.

1. Each House shall be the Judge of the Elections, Returns and Qualifications of its own Members, and a Majority of each shall constitute a Quorum to do Business; but a smaller Number may adjourn from day to day, and may be authorized to compel the Attendance of absent Members, in such Manner, and under such Penalties, as each House may provide.

2. Each House may determine the Rules of its Proceedings, punish its Members for disorderly Behavior, and, with the Concurrence of two thirds, expel a Member.

3. Each House shall keep a Journal of its Proceedings, and from time to time publish the same, excepting such Parts as may in their Judgment require Secrecy; and the Yeas and Nays of the Members of either House on any question shall, at the Desire of one fifth of those Present, be entered on the Journal.

4. Neither House, during the Session of Congress, shall, without the Consent of the other, adjourn for more than three days, nor to any other Place than that in which the two Houses shall be sitting.

Section 6.

1. The Senators and Representatives shall receive a Compensation for their Services, to be ascertained by Law, and paid out of the Treasury of the United States. They shall in all Cases, except Treason, Felony, and Breach of the Peace, be privileged from Arrest during their Attendance at the Session of their respective Houses, and in going to and returning from the same; and for any Speech or Debate in either House, they shall not be questioned in any other Place.

2. No Senator or Representative shall, during the Time for which he was elected, be appointed to any civil Office under the Authority of the United States, which shall have been created, or the Emoluments whereof shall have been increased during such time; and no Person holding any Office under the United States, shall be a Member of either House during his Continuance in Office.

Section 7.

1. All Bills for raising Revenue shall originate in the House of Representatives; but the Senate may propose or concur with amendments as on other Bills.

2. Every Bill which shall have passed the House of Representatives and the Senate, shall, before it become a law, be presented to the President of the United States: If he approve, he shall sign it, but if not he shall return it, with his Objections to that House in which it shall have originated, who shall enter the Objections at large on their Journal, and proceed to reconsider it. If after such Reconsideration two thirds of the House shall agree to pass the Bill, it shall be sent, together with the Objections, to the other House, by which it shall likewise be reconsidered, and if approved by two thirds of that House, it shall become a Law. But in all such Cases the Votes of both Houses shall be determined by Yeas and Nays, and the Names of the Persons voting for and against the Bill shall be entered on the Journal of each House respectively. If any Bill shall not be returned by the President within ten Days (Sunday excepted) after it shall have been presented to him, the Same shall be a law, in like Manner as if he had signed it, unless the Congress by their Adjournment, prevent its Return, in which Case it shall not be a Law.

3. Every Order, Resolution, or Vote to which the Concurrence of the Senate and House of Representatives may be necessary (except on a question of adjournment) shall be presented to the President of the United States; and before the Same shall take Effect, shall be approved by him, or, being disapproved by him, shall be repassed by two thirds of the Senate and House of Representatives, according to the Rules and Limitations prescribed in the Case of a Bill.

Section 8.

The Congress shall have Power

1. To lay and collect Taxes, Duties, Imposts and Excises to pay the Debts and provide for the common Defence and general Welfare of the United States; but all Duties, Imposts and Excises, shall be uniform throughout the United States;

2. To borrow Money on the credit of the United States;

3. To regulate Commerce with foreign Nations, and among the several States, and with the Indian Tribes;

part of this clause—forbidding any person serving in either the executive or the judicial branch from also serving in Congress—reinforces the principle of separation of powers.

Section 7. Revenue Bills, President's Veto

Clause 1. Revenue bills All bills that raise money must originate in the House. However, the Senate has the power to amend any revenue bill sent to it from the lower house.

Clause 2. Enactment of laws; veto Once both houses have passed a bill, it must be sent to the President. The President may (1) sign the bill, thus making it law; (2) veto the bill, whereupon it must be returned to the house in which it originated; or (3) allow the bill to become law without signature, by not acting upon it within 10 days of its receipt from Congress, not counting Sundays. The President has a fourth option at the end of a congressional session: If he does not act on a measure within 10 days, and Congress adjourns during that period, the bill dies; the "pocket veto" has been applied to it. A presidential veto may be overridden by a two-thirds vote in each house.

Clause 3. Other measures This clause refers to joint resolutions, measures Congress often passes to deal with unusual, temporary, or ceremonial matters. A joint resolution passed by Congress and signed by the President has the force of law, just as a bill does. As a matter of custom, a joint resolution proposing an amendment to the Constitution is not submitted to the President for signature or veto. Concurrent and simple resolutions do not have the force of law and, therefore, are not submitted to the President.

Section 8. Powers of Congress

Clause 1. The 18 separate clauses in this section set out 27 of the many expressed powers the Constitution grants to Congress. In this clause Congress is given the power to levy and provide for the collection of various kinds of taxes, in order to finance the operations of the government. All federal taxes must be levied at the same rates throughout the country.

Clause 2. Congress has power to borrow money to help finance the government. Federal borrowing is most often done through the sale of bonds on which interest is paid. The Constitution does not limit the amount the government may borrow.

Clause 3. This clause, the Commerce Clause, gives Congress the power to regulate both foreign and interstate trade. Much of what Congress does, it does on the basis of its commerce power.

Clause 4. Congress has the exclusive power to determine how aliens may become citizens of the United States. Congress may also pass laws relating to bankruptcy.

Clause 5. Congress has the power to establish and require the use of uniform gauges of time, distance, weight, volume, area, and the like.

Clause 6. Congress has the power to make it a federal crime to falsify the coins, paper money, bonds, stamps, and the like of the United States.

Clause 7. Congress has the power to provide for and regulate the transportation and delivery of mail; "post offices" are those buildings and other places where mail is deposited for dispatch; "post roads" include all routes over or upon which mail is carried.

Clause 8. Congress has the power to provide for copyrights and patents. A copyright gives an author or composer the exclusive right to control the reproduction, publication, and sale of literary, musical, or other creative work. A patent gives a person the exclusive right to control the manufacture or sale of his or her invention.

Clause 9. Congress has the power to create the lower federal courts, all of the several federal courts that function beneath the Supreme Court.

Clause 10. Congress has the power to prohibit, as a federal crime: (1) certain acts committed outside the territorial jurisdiction of the United States, and (2) the commission within the United States of any wrong against any nation with which we are at peace.

Clause 11. Only Congress can declare war. However, the President, as commander in chief of the armed forces (Article II, Section 2, Clause 1), can make war without such a formal declaration. Letters of marque and reprisal are commissions authorizing private persons to outfit vessels (privateers) to capture and destroy enemy ships in time of war; they were forbidden in international law by the Declaration of Paris of 1856, and the United States has honored the ban since the Civil War.

Clauses 12 and 13. Congress has the power to provide for and maintain the nation's armed forces. It established the air force as an independent element of the armed forces in 1947, an exercise of its inherent powers in foreign relations and national defense. The two-year limit on spending for the army insures civilian control of the military.

Clause 14. Today these rules are set out in a lengthy, oft-amended law, the Uniform Code of Military Justice, passed by Congress in 1950.

Clauses 15 and 16. In the National Defense Act of 1916, Congress made each State's militia (volunteer army) a part of the National Guard. Today, Congress and the States cooperate in its maintenance. Ordinarily, each State's National Guard is under the command of that State's governor; but Congress has given the President the power to call any or all of those units into federal service when necessary.

Clause 17. In 1791 Congress accepted land grants from Maryland and Virginia and established the District of Columbia for the nation's capital. Assuming Virginia's grant would never be needed, Congress returned it in 1846. Today, the elected government of the District's 69 square miles operates under

4. To establish an uniform Rule of Naturalization, and uniform Laws on the subject of Bankruptcies throughout the United States;

5. To coin Money, regulate the Value thereof, and of foreign Coin, and fix the Standard of Weights and Measures;

6. To provide for the Punishment of counterfeiting the Securities and current Coin of the United States;

7. To establish Post Offices and post Roads;

8. To promote the Progress of Science and useful Arts, by securing, for limited Times to Authors and Inventors the exclusive Right to their respective Writings and Discoveries;

9. To constitute Tribunals inferior to the supreme Court;

10. To define and punish Piracies and Felonies committed on the high Seas, and Offences against the Law of nations;

11. To declare War, grant Letters of Marque and Reprisal, and make Rules concerning Captures on Land and Water;

12. To raise and support Armies; but no Appropriation of Money to that Use shall be for a longer Term than two Years;

13. To provide and maintain a Navy;

14. To make Rules for the Government and Regulation of the land and naval Forces;

15. To provide for calling forth the Militia to execute the Laws of the Union, suppress Insurrections and repel Invasions;

16. To provide for organizing, arming, and disciplining the Militia, and for governing such Part of them as may be employed in the Service of the United States, reserving to the States respectively the Appointment of the Officers, and the Authority of training the Militia according to the discipline prescribed by Congress;

17. To exercise exclusive Legislation in all Cases whatsoever, over such District (not exceeding ten Miles square) as may, by Cession of Particular States, and the Acceptance of Congress, become the Seat of the Government of the United States, and to exercise like

Authority over all Places purchased by the Consent of the Legislature of the State in which the Same shall be, for the Erection of Forts, Magazines, Arsenals, Dockyards and other needful Buildings;—And

18. To make all Laws which shall be necessary and proper for carrying into Execution the foregoing Powers and all other Powers vested by this Constitution in the Government of the United States, or in any Department or Officer thereof.

Section 9.

1. The Migration or Importation of such Persons as any of the States now existing shall think proper to admit, shall not be prohibited by the Congress prior to the Year one thousand eight hundred and eight, but a Tax or duty may be imposed on such Importation, not exceeding ten dollars for each Person.

2. The Privilege of the Writ of Habeas Corpus shall not be suspended, unless when in Cases of Rebellion or Invasion the public safety may require it.

3. No Bill of Attainder or ex post facto Law shall be passed.

4. No Capitation, ~~or other direct, Tax~~ shall be laid, unless in Proportion to the Census of Enumeration here-inbefore directed to be taken.

5. No Tax or Duty shall be laid on Articles exported from any State.

6. No Preference shall be given by any Regulation of Commerce or Revenue to the Ports of one State over those of another: nor shall Vessels bound to, or from, one State, be obliged to enter, clear or pay Duties in another.

7. No Money shall be drawn from the Treasury, but in Consequence of Appropriations made by Law; and a regular Statement and Account of the Receipts and Expenditures of all public Money shall be published from time to time.

8. No Title of Nobility shall be granted by the United States: And no Person holding any Office of Profit or Trust under them, shall, without the Consent of the Congress, accept of any present, Emolument, Office, or Title, of any kind whatever, from any King, Prince, or foreign State.

Section 10.

1. No State shall enter into any Treaty, Alliance, or Confederation; grant Letters of Marque and Reprisal; coin Money; emit Bills of Credit; make any Thing but

---

the authority of Congress. Congress also has the power to acquire other lands from the States for various federal purposes.

Clause 18. This is the Necessary and Proper Clause, also often called the Elastic Clause. It is the constitutional basis for the many and far-reaching implied powers of the Federal Government.

Section 9. Powers Denied to Congress

Clause 1. The phrase "such persons" referred to slaves. This provision was part of the Commerce Compromise, one of the bargains struck in the writing of the Constitution. Congress outlawed the slave trade in 1808.

Clause 2. A writ of habeas corpus, the "great writ of liberty," is a court order directing a sheriff, warden, or other public officer, or a private person, who is detaining another to "produce the body" of the one being held in order that the legality of the detention may be determined by the court.

Clause 3. A bill of attainder is a legislative act that inflicts punishment without a judicial trial. See Article I, Section 10, and Article III, Section 3, Clause 2. An *ex post facto* law is any criminal law that operates retroactively to the disadvantage of the accused. See Article I, Section 10.

Clause 4. A capitation tax is literally a "head tax," a tax levied on each person in the population. A direct tax is one paid directly to the government by the taxpayer—for example, an income or a property tax; an indirect tax is one paid to another private party who then pays it to the government—for example, a sales tax. This provision was modified by the 16th Amendment (1913), giving Congress the power to levy "taxes on incomes, from whatever source derived."

Clause 5. This provision was a part of the Commerce Compromise made by the Framers in 1787. Congress has the power to tax imported goods, however.

Clause 6. All ports within the United States must be treated alike by Congress as it exercises its taxing and commerce powers. Congress cannot tax goods sent by water from one State to another, nor may it give the ports of one State any legal advantage over those of another.

Clause 7. This clause gives Congress its vastly important "power of the purse," a major check on presidential power. Federal money can be spent only in those amounts and for those purposes expressly authorized by an act of Congress. All federal income and spending must be accounted for, regularly and publicly.

Clause 8. This provision, preventing the establishment of a nobility, reflects the principle that "all men are created equal." It was also intended to discourage foreign attempts to bribe or otherwise corrupt officers of the government.

Section 10. Powers Denied to the States

Clause 1. The States are not sovereign governments and so cannot make agreements or otherwise negotiate with foreign states; the power to conduct foreign relations is an exclusive power of the National Government. The power to coin money is also an exclusive power of the National Government. Several powers forbidden to the National Government are here also forbidden to the States.

Clause 2. This provision relates to foreign, not interstate, commerce. Only Congress, not the States, can tax imports; and the States are, like Congress, forbidden the power to tax exports.

Clause 3. A duty of tonnage is a tax laid on ships according to their cargo capacity. Each State has a constitutional right to provide for and maintain a militia; but no State may keep a standing army or navy. The several restrictions here prevent the States from assuming powers that the Constitution elsewhere grants to the National Government.

EXECUTIVE DEPARTMENT
Section 1. President and Vice President

Clause 1. Executive power, term This clause gives to the President the very broad "executive power," the power to enforce the laws and otherwise administer the public policies of the United States. It also sets the length of the presidential (and vice-presidential) term of office; see the 22nd Amendment (1951), which places a limit on presidential (but not vice-presidential) tenure.

Clause 2. Electoral college This clause establishes the "electoral college," although the Constitution does not use that term. It is a body of presidential electors chosen in each State, and it selects the President and Vice President every four years. The number of electors chosen in each State equals the number of senators and representatives that State has in Congress.

Clause 3. Election of President and Vice President This clause was replaced by the 12th Amendment in 1804.

gold and silver Coin a Tender in Payment of Debts; pass any Bill of Attainder, ex post facto Law, or Law impairing the Obligation of Contracts, or grant any Title of Nobility.

2. No State shall, without the Consent of the Congress, lay any Imposts or Duties on Imports or Exports, except what may be absolutely necessary for executing its inspection Laws; and the net Produce of all Duties and Imposts, laid by any State on Imports or Exports, shall be for the Use of the Treasury of the United States; and all such Laws shall be subject to the Revision and Control of the Congress.

3. No State shall, without the Consent of Congress, lay any Duty of Tonnage, keep Troops, or Ships of War in time of Peace, enter into any Agreement or Compact with another State, or with a foreign Power, or engage in War, unless actually invaded, or in such imminent Danger as will not admit of delay.

Article II
Section 1.

1. The executive Power shall be vested in a President of the United States of America. He shall hold his Office during the Term of four Years, and, together with the Vice President, chosen for the same Term, be elected as follows:

2. Each State shall appoint, in such Manner as the Legislature thereof may direct, a Number of Electors, equal to the whole Number of Senators and Representatives to which the State may be entitled in the Congress: but no Senator or Representative, or Person holding an Office of Trust or Profit, under the United States, shall be appointed an Elector.

3. ~~The Electors shall meet in their respective States, and vote by Ballot for two Persons, of whom one at least shall not be an Inhabitant of the same State with themselves. And they shall make a List of all the Persons voted for, and of the Number of Votes for each; which List they shall sign and certify, and transmit sealed to the Seat of the Government of the United States, directed to the President of the Senate. The President of the Senate shall, in the Presence of the Senate and House of Representatives, open all the Certificates, and the Votes shall then be counted. The Person having the greatest Number of Votes shall be the President, if such Number be a majority of the whole Number of Electors appointed; and if there be more than one who have such Majority, and have an equal Number of Votes, then, the House of Representatives shall immediately choose by Ballot one of them for President; and if no Person have a Majority, then from the five highest on the List the said House shall in like Manner choose the President. But in choosing the President, the Votes shall be taken by States, the Representatives from each State having one Vote; a quorum for this Purpose shall consist of a Member or Members from two thirds of the States, and a Majority of~~

~~all the States shall be necessary to a Choice. In every Case, after the Choice of the President, the Person having the greatest Number of Votes of the Electors shall be the Vice President. But if there should remain two or more who have equal Votes, the Senate shall choose from them by Ballot the Vice President.~~

4. The Congress may determine the Time of choosing the Electors, and the Day on which they shall give their Votes; which Day shall be the same throughout the United States.

5. No Person except a natural born Citizen, or a Citizen of the United States, at the time of the Adoption of this Constitution, shall be eligible to the Office of President; neither shall any person be eligible to that Office who shall not have attained to the Age of thirty-five Years, and been fourteen Years a Resident within the United States.

6. ~~In Case of the Removal of the President from Office, or of his Death, Resignation, or Inability to discharge the Powers and Duties of the said Office, the Same shall devolve on the Vice President,~~ and the Congress may by Law provide for the Case of Removal, Death, Resignation or Inability, both of the President and Vice President, declaring what Officer shall then act as President, and such Officer shall act accordingly, until the Disability be removed, or a President shall be elected.

7. The President shall, at stated Times, receive for his Services, a Compensation, which shall neither be increased nor diminished during the Period for which he shall have been elected, and he shall not receive within that Period any other Emolument from the United States, or any of them.

8. Before he enter on the Execution of his Office, he shall take the following Oath or Affirmation:
"I do solemnly swear (or affirm) that I will faithfully execute the Office of President of the United States, and will to the best of my Ability, preserve, protect and defend the Constitution of the United States."

Section 2.

1. The President shall be Commander in Chief of the Army and Navy of the United States, and of the Militia of the several States, when called into the actual Service of the United States; he may require the Opinion, in writing, of the principal Officer in each of the executive Departments, upon any Subject relating to the Duties of their respective Offices, and he shall have Power to Grant Reprieves and Pardons for Offences against the United States, except in Cases of Impeachment.

2. He shall have Power, by and with the Advice and Consent of the Senate, to make Treaties, provided two thirds of the Senators present concur; and he shall nominate, and by and with the Advice and Consent of the Senate, shall appoint Ambassadors, other public Ministers

Clause 4. Date Congress has set the date for the choosing of electors as the Tuesday after the first Monday in November every fourth year, and for the casting of electoral votes as the Monday after the second Wednesday in December of that year.

Clause 5. Qualifications The President must have been born a citizen of the United States, be at least 35 years old, and have been a resident of the United States for at least 14 years.

Clause 6. Vacancy This clause was modified by the 25th Amendment (1967), which provides expressly for the succession of the Vice President, for the filling of a vacancy in the Vice Presidency, and for the determination of presidential inability.

Clause 7. Compensation The President now receives a salary of $400,000 and a taxable expense account of $50,000 a year. Those amounts cannot be changed during a presidential term; thus, Congress cannot use the President's compensation as a bargaining tool to influence executive decisions. The phrase "any other emolument" means, in effect, any valuable gift; it does not mean that the President cannot be provided with such benefits of office as the White House, extensive staff assistance, and much else.

Clause 8. Oath of office The Chief Justice of the United States regularly administers this oath or affirmation, but any judicial officer may do so. Thus, Calvin Coolidge was sworn into office in 1923 by his father, a justice of the peace in Vermont.

Section 2. President's Powers and Duties

Clause 1. Military, civil powers The President, a civilian, heads the nation's armed forces, a key element in the Constitution's insistence on civilian control of the military. The President's power to "require the opinion, in writing" provides the constitutional basis for the Cabinet. The President's power to grant reprieves and pardons, the power of clemency, extends only to federal cases.

Clause 2. Treaties, appointments The President has the sole power to make treaties; to become effective, a treaty must be approved by a two-thirds vote in the Senate. In practice, the President can also make executive agreements with foreign governments; these pacts, which are frequently made and usually deal with routine matters, do not require Senate consent. The President appoints the principal officers of the executive branch and all federal judges; the "inferior officers" are those who hold lesser posts.

Clause 3. Recess appointments When the Senate is not in session, appointments that require Senate consent can be made by the President on a temporary basis, as "recess appointments."

Section 3. President's Powers and Duties

The President delivers a State of the Union Message to Congress soon after that body convenes each year. That message is delivered to the nation's lawmakers and, importantly, to the American people, as well. It is shortly followed by the proposed federal budget and an economic report; and the President may send special messages to Congress at any time. In all of these communications, Congress is urged to take those actions the Chief Executive finds to be in the national interest. The President also has the power: to call special sessions of Congress; to adjourn Congress if its two houses cannot agree for that purpose; to receive the diplomatic representatives of other governments; to insure the proper execution of all federal laws; and to empower federal officers to hold their posts and perform their duties.

Section 4. Impeachment

The Constitution outlines the impeachment process in Article I, Section 2, Clause 5 and in Section 3, Clauses 6 and 7.

JUDICIAL DEPARTMENT
Section 1. Courts, Terms of Office

The judicial power conferred here is the power of federal courts to hear and decide cases, disputes between the government and individuals and between private persons (parties). The Constitution creates only the Supreme Court of the United States; it gives to Congress the power to establish other, lower federal courts (Article I, Section 8, Clause 9) and to fix the size of the Supreme Court. The words "during good behavior" mean, in effect, for life.

Section 2. Jurisdiction

Clause 1. Cases to be heard This clause sets out the jurisdiction of the federal courts; that is, it identifies those cases that may be tried in those courts. The federal courts can hear and decide—have jurisdiction over—a case depending on either the subject matter or the parties involved in that case. The jurisdiction of the federal courts in cases involving States was substantially restricted by the 11th Amendment in 1795.

and Consuls, Judges of the supreme Court, and all other Officers of the United States, whose Appointments are not herein otherwise provided for, and which shall be established by Law: but the Congress may by Law vest the Appointment of such inferior Officers, as they think proper, in the President alone, in the Courts of Law, or in the Heads of Departments.

3. The President shall have Power to fill up all Vacancies that may happen during the Recess of the Senate, by granting Commissions which shall expire at the End of their next Session.

Section 3.

He shall from time to time give to the Congress Information of the State of the Union, and recommend to their Consideration such Measures as he shall judge necessary and expedient; he may, on extraordinary Occasions, convene both Houses, or either of them, and in Case of Disagreement between them, with Respect to the Time of Adjournment, he may adjourn them to such Time as he shall think proper; he shall receive Ambassadors and other public Ministers; he shall take Care that the Laws be faithfully executed, and shall Commission all the Officers of the United States.

Section 4.

The President, Vice President and all Civil Officers of the United States, shall be removed from Office on Impeachment for and Conviction of, Treason, Bribery, or other high Crimes and Misdemeanors.

Article III
Section 1.

The judicial Power of the United States, shall be vested in one supreme Court, and in such inferior Courts as the Congress may from time to time ordain and establish. The Judges, both of the supreme and inferior Courts, shall hold their Offices during good Behavior, and shall, at stated Times, receive for their Services, a Compensation, which shall not be diminished during their Continuance in Office.

Section 2.

1. The judicial Power shall extend to all Cases, in Law and Equity, arising under this Constitution, the Laws of the United States, and Treaties made, or which shall be made, under their Authority;— to all Cases affecting Ambassadors, other public ministers, and Consuls;— to all Cases of Admiralty and maritime Jurisdiction;— to Controversies to which the United States shall be a Party;— to Controversies between two or more States;— between a State and Citizens of another State;— between Citizens of different States;— between Citizens of the same State claiming Lands under Grants of different States, and between a State, or the Citizens thereof, and foreign States, Citizens, or Subjects.

2. In all Cases affecting Ambassadors, other public Ministers and Consuls, and those in which a State shall be a Party, the supreme Court shall have original Jurisdiction. In all the other Cases before mentioned, the supreme Court shall have appellate Jurisdiction, both as to Law and Fact, with such Exceptions, and under such Regulations as the Congress shall make.

3. The trial of all Crimes, except in Cases of Impeachment, shall be by Jury; and such Trial shall be held in the State where the said Crimes shall have been committed; but when not committed within any State, the Trial shall be at such Place or Places as the Congress may by Law have directed.

Section 3.

1. Treason against the United States shall consist only in levying War against them, or in adhering to their Enemies, giving them Aid and Comfort. No Person shall be convicted of Treason unless on the Testimony of two Witnesses to the same overt Act, or on Confession in open Court.

2. The Congress shall have Power to declare the Punishment of Treason, but no Attainder of Treason shall work Corruption of Blood, or Forfeiture except during the Life of the Person attainted.

Article IV
Section 1.

Full Faith and Credit shall be given in each State to the public Acts, Records, and judicial Proceedings of every other State. And the Congress may by general Laws prescribe the Manner in which such Acts, Records and Proceedings shall be proved, and the Effect thereof.

Section 2.

1. The Citizens of each State shall be entitled to all Privileges and Immunities of Citizens in the several States.

2. A Person charged in any State with Treason, Felony, or other Crime, who shall flee from justice, and be found in another State, shall on Demand of the executive Authority of the State from which he fled, be delivered up, to be removed to the State having Jurisdiction of the Crime.

3. ~~No Person held to Service or Labor in one State, under the Laws thereof, escaping into another, shall, in Consequence of any Law or Regulation therein, be discharged from Service or Labor, but shall be delivered up on Claim of the Party to whom such Service or Labor may be due.~~

Clause 2. Supreme Court jurisdiction Original jurisdiction refers to the power of a court to hear a case in the first instance, not on appeal from a lower court. Appellate jurisdiction refers to a court's power to hear a case on appeal from a lower court, from the court in which the case was originally tried. This clause gives the Supreme Court both original and appellate jurisdiction. However, nearly all of the cases the High Court hears are brought to it on appeal from the lower federal courts and the highest State courts.

Clause 3. Jury trial in criminal cases A person accused of a federal crime is guaranteed the right to trial by jury in a federal court in the State where the crime was committed; see the 5th and 6th amendments. The right to trial by jury in serious criminal cases in the State courts is guaranteed by the 6th and 14th amendments.

Section 3. Treason

Clause 1. Definition Treason is the only crime defined in the Constitution. The Framers intended the very specific definition here to prevent the loose use of the charge of treason—for example, against persons who criticize the government. Treason can be committed only in time of war and only by a citizen or a resident alien.

Clause 2. Punishment Congress has provided that the punishment that a federal court may impose on a convicted traitor may range from a minimum of five years in prison and/or a $10,000 fine to a maximum of death; no person convicted of treason has ever been executed by the United States. No legal punishment can be imposed on the family or descendants of a convicted traitor. Congress has also made it a crime for any person (in either peace or wartime) to commit espionage or sabotage, to attempt to overthrow the government by force, or to conspire to do any of these things.

RELATIONS AMONG STATES
Section 1. Full Faith and Credit

Each State must recognize the validity of the laws, public records, and court decisions of every other State.

Section 2. Privileges and Immunities of Citizens

Clause 1. Residents of other States In effect, this clause means that no State may discriminate against the residents of other States; that is, a State's laws cannot draw unreasonable distinctions between its own residents and those of any of the other States. See Section 1 of the 14th Amendment.

Clause 2. Extradition The process of returning a fugitive to another State is known as "interstate rendition" or, more commonly, "extradition." Usually, that process works routinely; some extradition requests are contested however—especially in cases with racial or political overtones. A governor may refuse to extradite a fugitive; but the federal courts can compel an unwilling governor to obey this constitutional command.

Clause 3. Fugitive slaves This clause was nullified by the 13th Amendment, which abolished slavery in 1865.

Section 3. New States; Territories

Clause 1. New States Only Congress can admit new States to the Union. A new State may not be created by taking territory from an existing State without the consent of that State's legislature. Congress has admitted 37 States since the original 13 formed the Union. Five States—Vermont, Kentucky, Tennessee, Maine, and West Virginia—were created from parts of existing States. Texas was an independent republic before admission. California was admitted after being ceded to the United States by Mexico. Each of the other 30 States entered the Union only after a period of time as an organized territory of the United States.

Clause 2. Territory, property Congress has the power to make laws concerning the territories, other public lands, and all other property of the United States.

Section 4. Protection Afforded to States by the Nation

The Constitution does not define "a republican form of government," but the phrase is generally understood to mean a representative government. The Federal Government must also defend each State against attacks from outside its border and, at the request of a State's legislature or its governor, aid its efforts to put down internal disorders.

PROVISIONS FOR AMENDMENT

This section provides for the methods by which formal changes can be made in the Constitution. An amendment may be proposed in one of two ways: by a two-thirds vote in each house of Congress, or by a national convention called by Congress at the request of two-thirds of the State legislatures. A proposed amendment may be ratified in one of two ways: by three-fourths of the State legislatures, or by three-fourths of the States in conventions called for that purpose. Congress has the power to determine the method by which a proposed amendment may be ratified. The amendment process cannot be used to deny any State its equal representation in the United States Senate. To this point, 27 amendments have been adopted. To date, all of the amendments except the 21st Amendment were proposed by Congress and ratified by the State legislatures. Only the 21st Amendment was ratified by the convention method.

NATIONAL DEBTS, SUPREMACY OF NATIONAL LAW, OATH

Section 1. Validity of Debts

Congress had borrowed large sums of money during the Revolution and later during the Critical Period of the 1780s. This provision, a pledge that the new government would honor those debts, did much to create confidence in that government.

Section 2. Supremacy of National Law

This section sets out the Supremacy Clause, a specific declaration of the supremacy of federal law over any and all forms of State law. No State, including its local governments, may make or enforce any law that conflicts with any provision in the Constitution, an act of Congress, a treaty, or an order, rule, or regulation properly issued by the President or his subordinates in the executive branch.

Section 3.

1. New States may be admitted by the Congress into this Union; but no new State shall be formed or erected within the Jurisdiction of any other State; nor any State be formed by the Junction of two or more States, or Parts of States, without the Consent of the Legislatures of the States concerned as well as of the Congress.

2. The Congress shall have Power to dispose of and make all needful Rules and Regulations respecting the Territory or other Property belonging to the United States; and nothing in this Constitution shall be so construed as to Prejudice any Claims of the United States, or of any particular State.

Section 4.

The United States shall guarantee to every State in this Union a Republican Form of Government, and shall protect each of them against Invasion; and on Application of the Legislature, or of the Executive (when the Legislature cannot be convened) against domestic Violence.

Article V

The Congress, whenever two thirds of both Houses shall deem it necessary, shall propose Amendments to this Constitution, or, on the Application of the Legislatures of two thirds of the several States, shall call a Convention for proposing Amendments, which, in either Case, shall be valid to all Intents and Purposes, as Part of this Constitution, when ratified by the Legislatures of three fourths of the several States, or by Conventions in three fourths thereof, as the one or the other Mode of Ratification may be proposed by the Congress; Provided ~~that no Amendment which may be made prior to the Year One thousand eight hundred and eight shall in any Manner affect the first and fourth Clauses in the Ninth section of the first Article; and~~ that no State, without its Consent, shall be deprived of its equal Suffrage in the Senate.

Article VI

Section 1.

All Debts contracted and Engagements entered into, before the Adoption of this Constitution, shall be as valid against the United States under this Constitution, as under the Confederation.

Section 2.

This Constitution, and the Laws of the United States which shall be made in Pursuance thereof; and all Treaties made, or which shall be made, under the Authority of the United States, shall be the supreme Law of the Land; and the Judges in every State shall be bound thereby, anything in the constitution or Laws of any State to the Contrary notwithstanding.

Section 3.

The Senators and Representatives before mentioned, and the Members of the several State legislatures, and all executive and judicial Officers, both of the United States and of the several States, shall be bound by Oath or Affirmation, to support this Constitution; but no religious Test shall ever be required as a Qualification to any Office or public Trust under the United States.

Article VII

The ratification of the Conventions of nine States, shall be sufficient for the Establishment of this Constitution between the States so ratifying the same.

Done in Convention by the Unanimous Consent of the States present the Seventeenth Day of September in the Year of our Lord one thousand seven hundred and Eighty-seven and of the Independence of the United States of America the twelfth. In witness whereof We have hereunto subscribed our Names.

Attest: William Jackson,
　SECRETARY
George Washington,
　PRESIDENT AND
　DEPUTY FROM
　VIRGINIA
NEW HAMPSHIRE
　John Langdon
　Nicholas Gilman
MASSACHUSETTS
　Nathaniel Gorham
　Rufus King
CONNECTICUT
　William Samuel Johnson
　Roger Sherman

NEW YORK
　Alexander Hamilton
NEW JERSEY
　William Livingston
　David Brearley
　William Paterson
　Jonathan Dayton
PENNSYLVANIA
　Benjamin Franklin
　Thomas Mifflin
　Robert Morris
　George Clymer
　Thomas Fitzsimons
　Jared Ingersoll
　James Wilson
　Gouverneur Morris

DELAWARE
　George Read
　Gunning Bedford, Jr.
　John Dickinson
　Richard Bassett
　Jacob Broom
MARYLAND
　James McHenry
　Dan of St. Thomas Jennifer
　Daniel Carroll
VIRGINIA
　John Blair
　James Madison, Jr.

NORTH CAROLINA
　William Blount
　Richard Dobbs Spaight
　Hugh Williamson
SOUTH CAROLINA
　John Rutledge
　Charles Cotesworth
　　Pinckney
　Charles Pinckney
　Pierce Butler
GEORGIA
　William Few
　Abraham Baldwin

AMENDMENTS

1st Amendment.

Congress shall make no law respecting an establishment of religion, or prohibiting the free exercise thereof, or abridging the freedom of speech, or of the press; or the right of the people peaceably to assemble, and to petition the Government for a redress of grievances.

Section 3. Oaths of Office

This provision reinforces the Supremacy Clause; all public officers, at every level in the United States, owe their first allegiance to the Constitution of the United States. No religious qualification can be imposed as a condition for holding any public office.

RATIFICATION OF CONSTITUTION

The proposed Constitution was signed by George Washington and 37 of his fellow Framers on September 17, 1787. (George Read of Delaware signed for himself and also for his absent colleague, John Dickinson.)

The first 10 amendments, the Bill of Rights, were each proposed by Congress on September 25, 1789, and ratified by the necessary three-fourths of the States on December 15, 1791. These amendments were originally intended to restrict the National Government—not the States. However, the Supreme Court has several times held that most of their provisions also apply to the States, through the 14th Amendment's Due Process Clause.

1st Amendment. Freedom of Religion, Speech, Press, Assembly, and Petition

The 1st Amendment sets out five basic liberties: The guarantee of freedom of religion is both a protection of religious thought and practice and a command of separation of church and state. The guarantees of freedom of speech and press assure to all persons a right to speak, publish, and otherwise express their views. The guarantees of the rights of assembly and petition protect the right to join with others in public meetings, political parties, interest groups, and other associations to discuss public affairs and influence public policy. None of these rights is guaranteed in absolute terms, however; like all other civil rights guarantees, each of them may be exercised only with regard to the rights of all other persons.

2nd Amendment. Bearing Arms

Each State has the right to maintain a militia, an armed force for its own protection—today, the National Guard. The National Government and the States can and do regulate the private possession and use of firearms.

3rd Amendment. Quartering of Troops

This amendment was intended to prevent what had been common British practice in the colonial period; see the Declaration of Independence. This provision is of virtually no importance today.

4th Amendment. Searches and Seizures

The basic rule laid down by the 4th Amendment is this: Police officers have no general right to search for or seize evidence or seize (arrest) persons. Except in particular circumstances, they must have a proper warrant (a court order) obtained with probable cause (on reasonable grounds). This guarantee is reinforced by the exclusionary rule, developed by the Supreme Court: Evidence gained as the result of an unlawful search or seizure cannot be used at the court trial of the person from whom it was seized.

5th Amendment. Criminal Proceedings; Due Process; Eminent Domain

A person can be tried for a serious federal crime only if he or she has been indicted (charged, accused of that crime) by a grand jury. No one may be subjected to double jeopardy—that is, tried twice for the same crime. All persons are protected against self-incrimination; no person can be legally compelled to answer any question in any governmental proceeding if that answer could lead to that person's prosecution. The 5th Amendment's Due Process Clause prohibits unfair, arbitrary actions by the Federal Government; a like prohibition is set out against the States in the 14th Amendment. Government may take private property for a legitimate public purpose; but when it exercises that power of eminent domain, it must pay a fair price for the property seized.

6th Amendment. Criminal Proceedings

A person accused of crime has the right to be tried in court without undue delay and by an impartial jury; see Article III, Section 2, Clause 3. The defendant must be informed of the charge upon which he or she is to be tried, has the right to cross-examine hostile witnesses, and has the right to require the testimony of favorable witnesses. The defendant also has the right to be represented by an attorney at every stage in the criminal process.

7th Amendment. Civil Trials

This amendment applies only to civil cases heard in federal courts. A civil case does not involve criminal matters; it is a dispute between private parties or between the government and a private party. The right to trial by jury is guaranteed in any civil case in a federal court if the amount of money involved in that case exceeds $20 (most cases today involve a much larger sum); that right may be waived (relinquished, put aside) if both parties agree to a bench trial (a trial by a judge, without a jury).

8th Amendment. Punishment for Crimes

Bail is the sum of money that a person accused of crime may be required to post (deposit with the court) as a guarantee that he or she will appear in court at the proper time. The amount of bail required and/or a fine imposed as punishment must

United States Constitution

2nd Amendment.

A well-regulated Militia being necessary to the security of a free State, the right of the people to keep and bear Arms, shall not be infringed.

3rd Amendment.

No Soldier shall, in time of peace be quartered in any house, without the consent of the Owner, nor, in time of war, but in a manner to be prescribed by law.

4th Amendment.

The right of the people to be secure in their persons, houses, papers, and effects, against unreasonable searches and seizures, shall not be violated, and no Warrants shall issue, but upon probable cause, supported by Oath or affirmation, and particularly describing the place to be searched, and the persons or things to be seized.

5th Amendment.

No person shall be held to answer for a capital, or otherwise infamous crime, unless on a presentment or indictment of a Grand Jury, except in cases arising in the land or naval forces, or in the Militia, when in actual service in time of War, or public danger; nor shall any person be subject for the same offence to be twice put in jeopardy of life or limb; nor shall be compelled in any criminal case to be a witness against himself, nor be deprived of life, liberty, or property, without due process of law; nor shall private property be taken for public use, without just compensation.

6th Amendment.

In all criminal prosecutions, the accused shall enjoy the right to a speedy and public trial, by an impartial jury of the State and district wherein the crime shall have been committed, which district shall have been previously ascertained by law, and to be informed of the nature and cause of the accusation; to be confronted with the witnesses against him; to have compulsory process for obtaining witnesses in his favor, and to have the Assistance of Counsel for his defence.

7th Amendment.

In Suits at common law, where the value in controversy shall exceed twenty dollars, the right of trial by jury shall be preserved, and no fact tried by a jury, shall be otherwise re-examined in any Court of the United States, than according to the rules of the common law.

8th Amendment.

Excessive bail shall not be required, nor excessive fines imposed, nor cruel and unusual punishment inflicted.

9th Amendment.

The enumeration in the Constitution, of certain rights, shall not be construed to deny or disparage others retained by the people.

10th Amendment.

The powers not delegated to the United States by the Constitution, nor prohibited by it to the States, are reserved to the States respectively, or to the people.

11th Amendment.

The Judicial power of the United States shall not be construed to extend to any suit in law or equity, commenced or prosecuted against one of the United States by Citizens of another State, or by Citizens or Subjects of any Foreign State.

12th Amendment.

The Electors shall meet in their respective States and vote by ballot for President and Vice President, one of whom, at least, shall not be an inhabitant of the same State with themselves; they shall name in their ballots the person voted for as President, and in distinct ballots the person voted for as Vice President, and they shall make distinct lists of all persons voted for as President, and of all persons voted for as Vice President, and of the number of votes for each, which lists they shall sign and certify, and transmit sealed to the seat of the government of the United States, directed to the President of the Senate;— The President of the Senate shall, in the presence of the Senate and the House of Representatives, open all the certificates and the votes shall then be counted;— the person having the greatest Number of votes for President shall be the President, if such number be a majority of the whole number of Electors appointed; and if no person have such a majority, then, from the persons having the highest numbers not exceeding three on the list of those voted for as President, the House of Representatives shall choose immediately, by ballot, the President. But in choosing the President, the votes shall be taken by States, the representation from each State having one vote; a quorum for this purpose shall consist of a member or members from two thirds of the States, and a majority of all the States shall be necessary to a choice. And if the House of Representatives shall not choose a President whenever the right of choice shall devolve upon them, before the fourth day of March next following, then the Vice President shall act as President, as in case of death or other constitutional disability of the President. The person having the greatest number of votes as Vice President, shall be the

---

bear a reasonable relationship to the seriousness of the crime involved in the case. The prohibition of cruel and unusual punishment forbids any punishment judged to be too harsh, too severe for the crime for which it is imposed.

9th Amendment. Unenumerated Rights

The fact that the Constitution sets out many civil rights guarantees, expressly provides for many protections against government, does not mean that there are not other rights also held by the people.

10th Amendment. Powers Reserved to the States

This amendment identifies the area of power that may be exercised by the States. All of those powers the Constitution does not grant to the National Government, and at the same time does not forbid to the States, belong to each of the States, or to the people of each State.

11th Amendment. Suits Against States

Proposed by Congress March 4, 1794; ratified February 7, 1795, but official announcement of the ratification was delayed until January 8, 1798. This amendment repealed part of Article III, Section 2, Clause 1. No State may be sued in a federal court by a resident of another State or of a foreign country; the Supreme Court has long held that this provision also means that a State cannot be sued in a federal court by a foreign country or, more importantly, even by one of its own residents.

12th Amendment. Election of President and Vice President

Proposed by Congress December 9, 1803; ratified June 15, 1804. This amendment replaced Article II, Section 1, Clause 3. Originally, each elector cast two ballots, each for a different person for President. The person with the largest number of electoral votes, provided that number was a majority of the electors, was to become President; the person with the second highest number was to become Vice President. This arrangement produced an electoral vote tie between Thomas Jefferson and Aaron Burr in 1800; the House finally chose Jefferson as President in 1801. The 12th Amendment separated the balloting for President and Vice President; each elector now casts one ballot for someone as President and a second ballot for another person as Vice President. Note that the 20th Amendment changed the date set here (March 4) to January 20, and that the 23rd Amendment (1961) provides for electors from the District of Columbia. This amendment also provides that the Vice President must meet the same qualifications as those set out for the President in Article II, Section 1, Clause 5.

United States Constitution

Vice President, if such number be a majority of the whole number of Electors appointed, and if no person have a majority, then from the two highest numbers on the list, the Senate shall choose the Vice President; a quorum for the purpose shall consist of two thirds of the whole number of Senators, a majority of the whole number shall be necessary to a choice. But no person constitutionally ineligible to the office of President shall be eligible to that of Vice-President of the United States.

13th Amendment. Slavery and Involuntary Servitude

Proposed by Congress January 31, 1865; ratified December 6, 1865. This amendment forbids slavery in the United States and in any area under its control. It also forbids other forms of forced labor, except punishments for crime; but some forms of compulsory service are not prohibited—for example, service on juries or in the armed forces. Section 2 gives to Congress the power to carry out the provisions of Section 1 of this amendment.

13th Amendment.

Section 1. Neither slavery nor involuntary servitude, except as a punishment for crime whereof the party shall have been duly convicted, shall exist within the United States, or any place subject to their jurisdiction.

Section 2. Congress shall have power to enforce this article by appropriate legislation.

14th Amendment. Rights of Citizens

Proposed by Congress June 13, 1866; ratified July 9, 1868. Section 1 defines citizenship. It provides for the acquisition of United States citizenship by birth or by naturalization. Citizenship at birth is determined according to the principle of *jus soli*— "the law of the soil," where born; naturalization is the legal process by which one acquires a new citizenship at some time after birth. Under certain circumstances, citizenship can also be gained at birth abroad, according to the principle of *jus sanguinis*—"the law of the blood," to whom born. This section also contains two major civil rights provisions: the Due Process Clause forbids a State (and its local governments) to act in any unfair or arbitrary way; the Equal Protection Clause forbids a State (and its local governments) to discriminate against, draw unreasonable distinctions between, persons.

Most of the rights set out against the National Government in the first eight amendments have been extended against the States (and their local governments) through Supreme Court decisions involving the 14th Amendment's Due Process Clause.

The first sentence here replaced Article I, Section 2, Clause 3, the Three-Fifths Compromise provision. Essentially, all persons in the United States are counted in each decennial census, the basis for the distribution of House seats. The balance of this section has never been enforced and is generally thought to be obsolete.

14th Amendment.

Section 1. All persons born or naturalized in the United States and subject to the jurisdiction thereof, are citizens of the United States and of the State wherein they reside. No State shall make or enforce any law which shall abridge the privileges or immunities of citizens of the United States; nor shall any State deprive any person of life, liberty, or property, without due process of law; nor deny to any person within its jurisdiction the equal protection of the laws.

Section 2. Representatives shall be apportioned among the several States according to their respective numbers, counting the whole number of persons in each State, excluding Indians not taxed. But when the right to vote at any election for the choice of electors for President and Vice President of the United States, Representatives in Congress, the Executive and Judicial officers of a State, or the members of the Legislature thereof, is denied to any of the male inhabitants of such State, being twenty-one years of age and citizens of the United States, or in any way abridged, except for participation in rebellion, or other crime, the basis of representation therein shall be reduced in the proportion which the number of such male citizens shall bear to the whole number of male citizens twenty-one years of age in such State.

Section 3. No person shall be a Senator or Representative in Congress, or elector of President and Vice President, or hold any office, civil or military, under the United States, or under any State, who, having previously taken an oath, as a member of Congress, or as an officer of the United States, or as a member of any State legislature, or as an executive or judicial officer of any State, to support the Constitution of the United States, shall have engaged in insurrection or rebellion against the same, or given aid or comfort to the enemies thereof. But Congress may, by a vote of two thirds of each House, remove such disability.

This section limited the President's power to pardon those persons who had led the Confederacy during the Civil War. Congress finally removed this disability in 1898.

Section 4. The validity of the public debt of the United States, authorized by law, including debts incurred for payment of pensions and bounties for services in suppressing insurrection or rebellion, shall not be questioned. But neither the United States nor any State shall assume or pay any debt or obligation incurred in aid of insurrection or rebellion against the United States, or any claim for the loss or emancipation of any slave; but all such debts, obligations and claims shall be held illegal and void.

Section 4 also dealt with matters directly related to the Civil War. It reaffirmed the public debt of the United States; but it invalidated, prohibited payment of, any debt contracted by the Confederate States and also prohibited any compensation of former slave owners.

Section 5. The Congress shall have power to enforce, by appropriate legislation, the provisions of this article.

15th Amendment.

Section 1. The right of citizens of the United States to vote shall not be denied or abridged by the United States or by any State on account of race, color, or previous condition of servitude.

Section 2. The Congress shall have power to enforce this article by appropriate legislation.

15th Amendment. Right to Vote— Race, Color, Servitude

Proposed by Congress February 26, 1869; ratified February 3, 1870. The phrase "previous condition of servitude" refers to slavery. Note that this amendment does not guarantee the right to vote to African Americans, or to anyone else. Instead, it forbids the States from discriminating against any person on the grounds of his "race, color, or previous condition of servitude" in the setting of suffrage qualifications.

16th Amendment.

The Congress shall have power to lay and collect taxes on incomes, from whatever source derived, without apportionment among the several States, and without regard to any census or enumeration.

16th Amendment. Income Tax

Proposed by Congress July 12, 1909; ratified February 3, 1913. This amendment modified two provisions in Article I, Section 2, Clause 3, and Section 9, Clause 4. It gives to Congress the power to levy an income tax, a direct tax, without regard to the populations of any of the States.

17th Amendment.

The Senate of the United States shall be composed of two Senators from each State, elected by the people thereof, for six years; and each Senator shall have one vote. The electors in each State shall have the qualifications requisite for electors of the most numerous branch of the State legislatures.

When vacancies happen in the representation of any State in the Senate, the executive authority of such State shall issue writs of election to fill such vacancies: *Provided,* That the legislature of any State may empower the executive thereof to make temporary appointments until the people fill the vacancies by election as the legislature may direct.

This amendment shall not be so construed as to affect the election or term of any Senator chosen before it becomes valid as part of the Constitution.

17th Amendment. Popular Election of Senators

Proposed by Congress May 13, 1912; ratified April 8, 1913. This amendment repealed those portions of Article I, Section 3, Clauses 1 and 2 relating to the election of senators. Senators are now elected by the voters in each State. If a vacancy occurs, the governor of the State involved must call an election to fill the seat; the governor may appoint a senator to serve until the next election, if the State's legislature has authorized that step.

18th Amendment. Prohibition of Intoxicating Liquors

Proposed by Congress December 18, 1917; ratified January 16, 1919. This amendment outlawed the making, selling, transporting, importing, or exporting of alcoholic beverages in the United States. It was repealed in its entirety by the 21st Amendment in 1933.

19th Amendment. Equal Suffrage—Sex

Proposed by Congress June 4, 1919; ratified August 18, 1920. No person can be denied the right to vote in any election in the United States on account of his or her sex.

20th Amendment. Commencement of Terms; Sessions of Congress; Death or Disqualification of President-Elect

Proposed by Congress March 2, 1932; ratified January 23, 1933. The provisions of Sections 1 and 2 relating to Congress modified Article I, Section 4, Clause 2, and those provisions relating to the President, the 12th Amendment. The date on which the President and Vice President now take office was moved from March 4 to January 20. Similarly, the members of Congress now begin their terms on January 3. The 20th Amendment is sometimes called the "Lame Duck Amendment" because it shortened the period of time a member of Congress who was defeated for reelection (a "lame duck") remains in office.

This section deals with certain possibilities that were not covered by the presidential selection provisions of either Article II or the 12th Amendment. To this point, none of these situations has occurred. Note that there is neither a President-elect nor a Vice President-elect until the electoral votes have been counted by Congress, or, if the electoral college cannot decide the matter, the House has chosen a President or the Senate has chosen a Vice President.

Congress has not in fact ever passed such a law. See Section 2 of the 25th Amendment, regarding a vacancy in the vice presidency; that provision could some day have an impact here.

18th Amendment.

Section 1. After one year from the ratification of this article the manufacture, sale, or transportation of intoxicating liquors within, the importation thereof into, or the exportation thereof from the United States and all territory subject to the jurisdiction thereof for beverage purposes is hereby prohibited.

Section 2. The Congress and the several States shall have concurrent power to enforce this article by appropriate legislation.

Section 3. This article shall be inoperative unless it shall have been ratified as an amendment to the Constitution by the legislatures of the several States, as provided in the Constitution, within seven years of the date of the submission hereof to the States by Congress.

19th Amendment.

The right of citizens of the United States to vote shall not be denied or abridged by the United States or by any State on account of sex.

Congress shall have power to enforce this article by appropriate legislation.

20th Amendment.

Section 1. The terms of the President and Vice President shall end at noon on the 20th day of January, and the terms of Senators and Representatives at noon on the 3d day of January, of the years in which such terms would have ended if this article had not been ratified; and the terms of their successors shall then begin.

Section 2. The Congress shall assemble at least once in every year, and such meeting shall begin at noon on the 3d day of January, unless they shall by law appoint a different day.

Section 3. If, at the time fixed for the beginning of the term of the President, the President elect shall have died, the Vice President elect shall become President. If a President shall not have been chosen before the time fixed for the beginning of his term, or if the President-elect shall have failed to qualify, then the Vice President elect shall act as President until a President shall have qualified; and the Congress may by law provide for the case wherein neither a President elect nor a Vice President elect shall have qualified, declaring who shall then act as President, or the manner in which one who is to act shall be selected, and such person shall act accordingly until a President or Vice President shall have qualified.

Section 4. The Congress may by law provide for the case of the death of any of the persons from whom the House of Representatives may choose a President whenever the right of choice shall have devolved upon them, and for the case of the death of any of the persons from whom the Senate may choose a Vice President whenever the right of choice shall have devolved upon them.

Section 5. Sections 1 and 2 shall take effect on the 15th day of October following the ratification of this article.

Section 6. This article shall be inoperative unless it shall have been ratified as an amendment to the Constitution by the legislatures of three fourths of the several States within seven years from the date of its submission.

Section 5 set the date on which this amendment came into force.

Section 6 placed a time limit on the ratification process; note that a similar provision was written into the 18th, 21st, and 22nd amendments.

21st Amendment.

Section 1. The eighteenth article of amendment to the Constitution of the United States is hereby repealed.

Section 2. The transportation or importation into any State, Territory, or possession of the United States for delivery or use therein of intoxicating liquors, in violation of the laws thereof, is hereby prohibited.

Section 3. This article shall be inoperative unless it shall have been ratified as an amendment to the Constitution by conventions in the several States, as provided in the Constitution, within seven years from the date of the submission hereof to the States by the Congress.

21st Amendment. Repeal of 18th Amendment

Proposed by Congress February 20, 1933; ratified December 5, 1933. This amendment repealed all of the 18th Amendment. Section 2 modifies the scope of the Federal Government's commerce power set out in Article I, Section 8, Clause 3; it gives to each State the power to regulate the transportation or importation and the distribution or use of intoxicating liquors in ways that would be unconstitutional in the case of any other commodity. The 21st Amendment is the only amendment Congress has thus far submitted to the States for ratification by conventions.

22nd Amendment.

Section 1. No person shall be elected to the office of the President more than twice, and no person who has held the office of President, or acted as President, for more than two years of a term to which some other person was elected President shall be elected to the office of the President more than once. But this Article shall not apply to any person holding the office of President, when this Article was proposed by the Congress, and shall not prevent any person who may be holding the office of President, or acting as President, during the term within which this Article becomes operative from holding the office of President or acting as President during the remainder of such term.

Section 2. This article shall be inoperative unless it shall have been ratified as an amendment to the Constitution by the legislatures of three fourths of the several states within seven years from the date of its submission to the States by the Congress.

22nd Amendment. Presidential Tenure

Proposed by Congress March 24, 1947; ratified February 27, 1951. This amendment modified Article II, Section I, Clause 1. It stipulates that no President may serve more than two elected terms. But a President who has succeeded to the office beyond the midpoint in a term to which another President was originally elected may serve for more than eight years. In any case, however, a President may not serve more than 10 years. Prior to Franklin Roosevelt, who was elected to four terms, no President had served more than two full terms in office.

23rd Amendment.

Section 1. The District constituting the seat of Government of the United States shall appoint in such manner as the Congress may direct:

A number of electors of President and Vice President equal to the whole number of Senators and Representatives in Congress to which the District would be entitled if it were a State, but in no event more than the least populous State; they shall be in addition to those appointed by the States, they shall be considered, for the purposes of

23rd Amendment. Presidential Electors for the District of Columbia

Proposed by Congress June 16, 1960; ratified March 29, 1961. This amendment modified Article II, Section I, Clause 2 and the 12th Amendment. It included the voters of the District of Columbia in the presidential electorate; and provides that the District is to have the same number of electors as the least populous State—three electors—but no more than that number.

the election of President and Vice President, to be electors appointed by a State; and they shall meet in the District and perform such duties as provided by the twelfth article of amendment.

Section 2. The Congress shall have power to enforce this article by appropriate legislation.

24th Amendment. Right to Vote in Federal Elections—Tax Payment

Proposed by Congress September 14, 1962; ratified January 23, 1964. This amendment outlawed the payment of any tax as a condition for taking part in the nomination or election of any federal officeholder.

24th Amendment.

Section 1. The right of citizens of the United States to vote in any primary or other election for President or Vice President, for electors for President or Vice President, or for Senator or Representative in Congress, shall not be denied or abridged by the United States or any State by reason of failure to pay any poll tax or other tax.

Section 2. The Congress shall have power to enforce this article by appropriate legislation.

25th Amendment. Presidential Succession, Vice Presidential Vacancy, Presidential Inability

Proposed by Congress July 6, 1965; ratified February 10, 1967. Section 1 revised the imprecise provision on presidential succession in Article II, Section 1, Clause 6. It wrote into the Constitution the precedent set by Vice President John Tyler, who became President on the death of William Henry Harrison in 1841.

Section 2 provides for the filling of a vacancy in the office of Vice President. Prior to its adoption, the office had been vacant on 16 occasions and had remained unfilled for the remainder of each term involved. When Spiro Agnew resigned the office in 1973, President Nixon selected Gerald Ford in accord with this provision; and, when President Nixon resigned in 1974, Gerald Ford became President and then chose Nelson Rockefeller as Vice President.

This section created a procedure for determining if a President is so incapacitated that he cannot perform the powers and duties of his office.

25th Amendment.

Section 1. In case of the removal of the President from office or of his death or resignation, the Vice President shall become President.

Section 2. Whenever there is a vacancy in the office of the Vice President, the President shall nominate a Vice President who shall take office upon confirmation by a majority vote of both Houses of Congress.

Section 3. Whenever the President transmits to the President *pro tempore* of the Senate and the Speaker of the House of Representatives his written declaration that he is unable to discharge the powers and duties of his office, and until he transmits to them a written declaration to the contrary, such powers and duties shall be discharged by the Vice President as Acting President.

United States Constitution

Section 4. Whenever the Vice President and a majority of either the principal officers of the executive departments or of such other body as Congress may by law provide, transmit to the President *pro tempore* of the Senate and the Speaker of the House of Representatives their written declaration that the President is unable to discharge the powers and duties of his office, the Vice President shall immediately assume the powers and duties of the office as Acting President.

Thereafter, when the President transmits to the President *pro tempore* of the Senate and the Speaker of the House of Representatives his written declaration that no inability exists, he shall resume the powers and duties of his office unless the Vice President and a majority of either the principal officers of the executive department or of such other body as Congress may by law provide, transmit within four days to the President *pro tempore* of the Senate and the Speaker of the House of Representatives their written declaration that the President is unable to discharge the powers and duties of his office. Thereupon Congress shall decide the issue, assembling within forty-eight hours for that purpose if not in session. If the Congress, within twenty-one days after receipt of the latter written declaration, or, if Congress is not in session, within twenty-one days after Congress is required to assemble, determines by two-thirds vote of both Houses that the President is unable to discharge the powers and duties of his office, the Vice President shall continue to discharge the same as Acting President; otherwise, the President shall resume the powers and duties of his office.

26th Amendment.

Section 1. The right of citizens of the United States, who are eighteen years of age or older, to vote shall not be denied or abridged by the United States or by any State on account of age.

Section 2. The Congress shall have the power to enforce this article by appropriate legislation.

27th Amendment.

No law varying the compensation for the services of the Senators and Representatives, shall take effect, until an election of Representatives shall have intervened.

Section 4 deals with the circumstance in which a President will not be able to determine the fact of incapacity. To this point, Congress has not established the "such other body" referred to here. This section contains the only typographical error in the Constitution; in its second paragraph, the word "department" should in fact read "departments."

26th Amendment. Right to Vote—Age

Proposed by Congress March 23, 1971; ratified July 1, 1971. This amendment provides that the minimum age for voting in any election in the United States cannot be more than 18 years. (A State may set a minimum voting age of less than 18, however.)

27th Amendment. Congressional Pay

Proposed by Congress September 25, 1789; ratified May 7, 1992. This amendment modified Article I, Section 6, Clause 1. It limits Congress's power to fix the salaries of its members— by delaying the effectiveness of any increase in that pay until after the next regular congressional election.

United States Constitution

Historical Documents

The Code of Hammurabi

The Code of Hammurabi, believed to date before 1750 B.C., is a series of laws decreed by Hammurabi, the ruler of the city of Babylon when that ancient city was at the peak of its power. Inscribed on stone columns over seven feet high, these laws were intended to inform the people of what they could and could not do. They were written down and codified so that judges and administrators would have a uniform set of rules to follow in deciding disputes and imposing penalties for crimes. The Code consists of 280 sections that deal with such matters as land tenure, property rights, trade and commerce, family relations, and the administration of justice. Selected sections of the Code are excerpted below:

If a man practice (robbery) and be captured, that man shall be put to death. . . .

If a man has come forward in a lawsuit for the witnessing of false things, and has not proved the thing that he said, if that lawsuit is a capital case, that man shall be put to death. If he came forward for witnessing about corn or silver, he shall bear the penalty (which applies to) that case.

If a man has concealed in his house a lost slave or slave-girl belonging to the Palace or to a subject, and has not brought him (or her) out at the proclamation of the Crier, the owner of the house shall be put to death.

If a fire has broken out in a man's house, and a man who has gone to extinguish it has cast his eye on the property of the owner of the house and has taken the property of the owner of the house, that man shall be thrown into the fire.

If a man is subject to a debt bearing interest, and Adad (the Weather-god) has saturated his field or a high flood has carried (its crop) away, or because of lack of water he has not produced corn in that field, in that year he shall not return any corn to (his) creditor. He shall . . . not pay interest for that year.

If a man has donated field, orchard or house to his favourite heir and has written a sealed document for him (confirming this), after the father has gone to his doom, when the brothers share he (the favorite heir) shall take the gift that his father gave him, and apart from that they shall share equally in the property of the paternal estate.

If an artisan has taken a child for bringing up, and has taught him his manual skill, (the child) shall not be (re)claimed. If he has not taught him his manual skill, that pupil may return to his father's house.

If a man aid a male or female slave . . . to escape from the city gates, he shall be put to death. . . .

If a man be in debt and sell his wife, son, or daughter, or bind them over to service, for three years they shall work in the house of the purchaser or master; in the fourth year they shall be given their freedom. . . .

If a builder has made a house for a man but has not made his work strong, so that the house he made falls down and causes the death of the owner of the house, that builder shall be put to death. If it causes the death of the son of the owner of the house, they shall kill the son of the builder.

If a man would put away [divorce] his wife who has not borne him children, he shall give her money to the amount of her marriage settlement and he shall make good to her the dowry which she brought from her father's house and then he may put her away.

If a son has struck his father, they shall cut off his hand.

If a man has destroyed the eye of a man of the "gentleman" class, they shall destroy his eye. If he has broken a gentleman's bone, they shall break his bone. If he has destroyed the eye of a commoner or broken a bone of a commoner, he shall pay one mina (about $300) of silver. If he has destroyed the eye of a gentleman's slave, he shall pay half the slave's price.

If a gentleman's slave strikes the cheek of a man of the "gentleman" class, they shall cut off (the slave's) ear.

If a gentleman strikes a gentleman in a free fight and inflicts an injury on him, that man shall swear "I did not strike him deliberately," and he shall pay the surgeon.

Madison's *Notes:* Debate of June 6 on the Virginia Plan

James Madison's Notes *enable readers today to gain a glimpse of the debates that took place behind closed doors at the Constitutional Convention held in Philadelphia in the summer of 1787. Excerpted here are portions of Madison's* Notes *on the debate of June 6 on the Virginia Plan's call for a bicameral (two house) legislature.*

MR. PINCKNEY [S.C.], according to previous notice and rule obtained, moved "that the first branch of the national legislature be elected by the state legislatures, and not by the people," contending that the people were less fit judges in such a case, and that the legislatures would be less likely to promote the adoption of the new government if they were to be excluded from all share in it.

MR. RUTLEDGE [S.C.] seconded the motion.

MR. GERRY [MASS.]: Much depends on the mode of election. In England the people will probably lose their liberty from the smallness of the proportion having a right of suffrage. Our danger arises from the opposite extreme; hence in Massachusetts the worst men get into the legislature. Several members of that body had lately been convicted of infamous crimes. Men of indigence, ignorance, and baseness spare no pains, however dirty, to carry their point against men who are superior to the artifices practised. He was not disposed to run into extremes. He was as much principled as ever against aristocracy and monarchy. It was necessary, on the one hand, that the people should appoint one branch of the government in order to inspire them with the necessary confidence. . . . His idea was that the people should nominate certain persons in certain districts, out of whom the state legislatures should make the appointment.

MR. WILSON [PA.]: He wished for vigor in the government, but he wished that vigorous authority to flow immediately from the legitimate source of all authority. The government ought to possess not only, first, the *force* but, second, the *mind or sense* of the people at large. The legislature ought to be the most exact transcript of the whole society. Representation is made necessary only because it is impossible for the people to act collectively. . . .

MR. SHERMAN [CONN.]: If it were in view to abolish the state governments, the elections ought to be by the people. If the state governments are to be continued, it is necessary, in order to preserve harmony between the national and state governments, that the elections to the former should be made by the latter. The right of participating in the national government would be sufficiently secured to the people by their election of the state legislatures. The objects of the Union, he thought, were few: (1) defense against foreign danger; (2) against internal disputes and a resort to force; (3) treaties with foreign nations; (4) regulating foreign commerce and drawing revenue from it. These, and perhaps a few lesser objects, alone rendered a confederation of the states necessary. All other matters, civil and criminal, would be much better in the hands of the states. . . .

COLONEL MASON [VA.]: Under the existing Confederacy, Congress represent the *states,* not the *people* of the states; their acts operate on the *states,* not on the individuals. The case will be changed in the new plan of government. The people will be represented; they ought therefore to choose the representatives. The requisites in actual representation are that the representatives should sympathize with their constituents, should think as they think and feel as they feel, and that, for these purposes, [they] should even be residents among them. Much, he said, had been alleged against democratic elections. He admitted that much might be said; but it was to be considered that no government was free from imperfections and evils and that improper elections, in many instances, were inseparable from republican governments. . . .

MR. MADISON [VA.] considered an election of one branch, at least, of the legislature by the people immediately as a clear principle of free government, and that this mode, under proper regulations, had the additional advantage of securing better representatives as well as of avoiding too great an agency of the state governments in the general one. He differed from the member from Connecticut (Mr. Sherman) in thinking the objects mentioned to be all the principal ones that required a national government. Those were certainly important and necessary objects; but he combined with them the necessity of providing more effectually for the security of private rights and the steady dispensation of justice.

Interferences with these were evils which had more, perhaps, than anything else produced this Convention. Was it to be supposed that republican liberty could long exist under the abuses of it practised in some of the states? . . .

All civilized societies would be divided into different sects, factions, and interests, as they happened to consist of rich and poor, debtors and creditors, the landed, the manufacturing, the commercial interests, the inhabitants of this district or that district, the followers of this political leader or that political leader, the disciples of this religious sect or that religious sect. In all cases where a majority are united by a common interest or passion, the rights of the minority are in danger. What motives are to restrain them? . . .

Conscience, the only remaining tie, is known to be inadequate in individuals; in large numbers, little is to be expected from it. . . .

What has been the source of those unjust laws complained of among ourselves? Has it not been the real or supposed interest of the major number? Debtors have defrauded their creditors. The landed interest has borne hard on the mercantile interest. The holders of one species of property have thrown a disproportion of taxes on the holders of another species.

The lesson we are to draw from the whole is that where a majority are united by a common sentiment, and have an opportunity, the rights of the minor party become insecure. In a republican government the majority, if united, have always an opportunity. . . .

MR. DICKINSON [DEL.] considered it as essential that one branch of the legislature should be drawn immediately from the people and as expedient that the other should be chosen by the legislatures of the states. This combination of the state governments with the national government was as politic as it was unavoidable. In the formation of the Senate, we ought to carry it through such a refining process as will assimilate it as near as may be to the House of Lords in England. He repeated his warm eulogiums on the British constitution. He was for a strong national government but for leaving the states a considerable agency in the system. The objection against making the former dependent on the latter might be obviated by giving to the Senate an authority permanent and irrevocable for three, five, or seven years. Being thus independent, they will speak and decide with becoming freedom.

MR. READ [DEL.]: Too much attachment is betrayed to the state governments. We must look beyond their continuance. A national government must soon of necessity swallow all of them up. They will soon be reduced to the mere office of electing the national Senate. He was against patching up the old federal system; he hoped the idea would be dismissed. It would be like putting new cloth on an old garment. The Confederation was founded on temporary principles. It cannot last; it cannot be amended. If we do not establish a good government on new principles, we must either go to ruin or have the work to do over again. . . .

MR. PIERCE [GA.] was for an election by the people as to the first branch and by the states as to the second branch, by which means the citizens of the states would be represented both *individually* and *collectively.*

GENERAL PINCKNEY wished to have a good national government and at the same time to leave a considerable share of power in the states. An election of either branch by the people, scattered as they are in many states, particularly in South Carolina, was totally impracticable. He differed from gentlemen who thought that a choice by the people would be a better guard against bad measures than by the legislatures. . . .

The state legislatures also, he said, would be more jealous and more ready to thwart the national government if excluded from a participation in it. The idea of abolishing these legislatures would never go down.

MR. WILSON would not have spoken again but for what had fallen from Mr. Read; namely, that the idea of preserving the state governments ought to be abandoned. He saw no incompatibility between the national and state governments, provided the latter were restrained to certain local purposes; nor any probability of their being devoured by the former. . . .

On the question for electing the first branch by the state legislatures as moved by Mr. Pinckney, it was negatived.

Pledge of Allegiance

By FRANCIS BELLAMY

The Pledge of Allegiance first appeared in 1892 in a magazine called The Youth's Companion. *The original Pledge, attributed to Francis Bellamy, stated: "I pledge allegiance to my Flag and the Republic for which it stands; one Nation indivisible with liberty and justice for all." In 1924, "my Flag" was changed to "the Flag of the United States of America." Congress officially recognized the Pledge in 1942 and added the words "under God" in 1954.*

I pledge allegiance to the Flag of the United States of America, and to the Republic for which it stands, one nation under God, indivisible, with liberty and justice for all.

The Federalist No. 10 (James Madison)

*One of the 29 essays believed to have been written by James Madison, the tenth of
The Federalist papers presents Madison's observations on dealing with the "mischiefs
of faction" and the advantages of a republican (representative) form of government
over that of a pure democracy. This essay was first published on November 23, 1787.*

Among the numerous advantages promised by a well-constructed Union, none deserves to be more accurately developed than its tendency to break and control the violence of faction. The friend of popular governments never finds himself so much alarmed for their character and fate as when he contemplates their propensity to this dangerous vice. He will not fail, therefore, to set a due value on any plan which, without violating the principles to which he is attached, provides a proper cure for it. The instability, injustice, and confusion introduced into the public councils have, in truth, been the mortal diseases under which popular governments have everywhere perished; as they continue to be the favorite and fruitful topics from which the adversaries to liberty derive their most specious declamations.

The valuable improvements made by the American constitutions on the popular models, both ancient and modern, cannot certainly be too much admired; but it would be an unwarrantable partiality to contend that they have as effectually obviated the danger on this side, as was wished and expected. Complaints are everywhere heard from our most considerate and virtuous citizens, equally the friends of public and private faith, and of public and personal liberty, that our governments are too unstable, that the public good is disregarded in the conflicts of rival parties, and that measures are too often decided, not according to the rules of justice and the rights of the minor party, but by the superior force of an interested and overbearing majority. However anxiously we may wish that these complaints had no foundation, the evidence of known facts will not permit us to deny that they are in some degree true.

It will be found, indeed, on a candid review of our situation, that some of the distresses under which we labor have been erroneously charged on the operation of our governments; but it will be found, at the same time, that other causes will not alone account for many of our heaviest misfortunes; and, particularly, for that prevailing and increasing distrust of public engagements, and alarm for private rights, which are echoed from one end of the continent to the other. These must be chiefly, if not wholly, effects of the unsteadiness and injustice with which a factious spirit has tainted our public administrations.

By a faction, I understand a number of citizens, whether amounting to a majority or minority of the whole, who are united and actuated by some common impulse of passion, or of interest, adversed to the rights of other citizens, or to the permanent and aggregate interests of the community.

There are two methods of curing the mischiefs of faction: the one, by removing its causes; the other, by controlling its effects.

There are again two methods of removing the causes of faction: the one, by destroying the liberty which is essential to its existence; the other, by giving to every citizen the same opinions, the same passions, and the same interests.

It could never be more truly said than of the first remedy that it was worse than the disease. Liberty is to faction what air is to fire, an ailment without which it instantly expires. But it could not be less folly to abolish liberty, which is essential to political life, because it nourishes faction, than it would be to wish the annihilation of air, which is essential to animal life, because it imparts to fire its destructive agency.

The second expedient is as impracticable as the first would be unwise. As long as the reason of man continues fallible, and he is at liberty to exercise it, different opinions will be formed. As long as the connection subsists between his reason and his self-love, his opinions and his passions will have a reciprocal influence on each other; and the former will be objects to which the latter will attach themselves. The diversity in the faculties of men, from which the rights of property originate, is not less an insuperable obstacle to a uniformity of interests. The protection of these faculties is the first object of government. From the protection of different and unequal faculties of acquiring property, the possession of different degrees and kinds of property immediately results; and from the influence of these on the sentiments and views of the respective proprietors ensues a division of the society into different interests and parties.

The latent causes of faction are thus sown in the nature of man; and we see them everywhere brought into different degrees of activity, according to the different circumstances of civil society. A zeal for different opinions concerning religion, concerning government, and many other points, as well of speculation as of practice; an attachment of different leaders ambitiously contending for preeminence and power; or to persons of other descriptions whose fortunes have been interesting to the human passions, have, in turn, divided mankind into parties, inflamed them with mutual animosity, and rendered them much more disposed to vex and oppress each other than to cooperate for their common good. So strong is this propensity of mankind to fall into mutual animosities that, where no substantial occasion presents itself, the most frivolous and fanciful distinctions have been sufficient to kindle their unfriendly passions and excite their most violent conflicts. But the most common and durable source of factions has been the various and unequal distribution of property.

Those who hold and those who are without property have ever formed distinct interests in society. Those who are creditors and those who are debtors fall under a like discrimination. A landed interest, a manufacturing interest, a mercantile interest, a moneyed interest, with many lesser interests, grow up of necessity in civilized nations and divide them into different classes, actuated by different sentiments and views. The regulation of these various and interfering interests forms the principal task of modern legislation and involves the spirit of party and faction in the necessary and ordinary operations of the government.

No man is allowed to be a judge in his own cause, because his interest would certainly bias his judgment and, not improbably, corrupt his integrity. With equal, nay, with greater reason, a body of men are unfit to be both judges and parties at the same time; yet what are many of the most important acts of legislation but so many judicial determinations, not indeed concerning the rights of single persons, but concerning the rights of large bodies of citizens? And what are the different classes of legislators but advocates and parties to the causes which they determine? Is a law proposed concerning private debts? It is a question to which the creditors are parties on one side and the debtors on the other. Justice ought to hold the balance between them. Yet the parties are, and must be, themselves the judges; and the most numerous party or, in other words, the most powerful faction must be expected to prevail.

Shall domestic manufactures be encouraged, and in what degree, by restrictions on foreign manufactures? [These] are questions which would be differently decided by the landed and the manufacturing classes, and probably by neither with a sole regard to justice and the public good. The apportionment of taxes on the various descriptions of property is an act which seems to require the most exact impartiality; yet there is, perhaps, no legislative act in which greater opportunity and temptation are given to a predominant party to trample on the rules of justice. Every shilling with which they overburden the inferior number is a shilling saved to their own pockets.

It is in vain to say that enlightened statesmen will be able to adjust these clashing interests and render them all subservient to the public good. Enlightened statesmen will not always be at the helm. Nor, in many cases, can such an adjustment be made at all without taking into view indirect and remote considerations, which will rarely prevail over the immediate interest which one party may find in disregarding the rights of another or the good of the whole. The inference to which we are brought is that the *causes* of faction cannot be removed and that relief is only to be sought in the means of controlling its *effects*.

If a faction consists of less than a majority, relief is supplied by the republican principle, which enables the majority to defeat its sinister views by regular vote. It may clog the administration, it may convulse the society; but it will be unable to execute and mask its violence under the forms of the Constitution. When a majority is included in a faction, the form of popular government, on the other hand, enables it to sacrifice to its ruling passion or interest both the public good and the rights of other citizens. To secure the public good and private rights against the danger of such a faction, and at the same time to preserve the spirit and the form of popular government, is then the great object to which our inquiries are directed. Let me add that it is the great desideratum by which this form of government can be rescued from the opprobrium under which it has so long labored and be recommended to the esteem and adoption of mankind.

By what means is this object attainable? Evidently by one of two only. Either the existence of the same passion or interest in a majority at the same time must be prevented, or the majority, having such coexistent passion or interest, must be rendered, by their number and local situation, unable to concert and carry into effect schemes of oppression. If the impulse and the opportunity be suffered to coincide, we well know that neither moral nor religious motives can be relied on as an adequate control. They are

not found to be such on the injustice and violence of individuals and lose their efficacy in proportion to the number combined together, that is, in proportion as their efficacy becomes needful.

From this view of the subject it may be concluded that a pure democracy, by which I mean a society consisting of a small number of citizens who assemble and administer the government in person, can admit of no cure for the mischiefs of faction. A common passion or interest will, in almost every case, be felt by a majority of the whole; a communication and concert result from the form of government itself; and there is nothing to check the inducements to sacrifice the weaker party or an obnoxious individual. Hence it is that such democracies have ever been spectacles of turbulence and contention; have ever been found incompatible with personal security or the rights of property; and have in general been as short in their lives as they have been violent in their deaths. Theoretic politicians, who have patronized this species of government, have erroneously supposed that by reducing mankind to a perfect equality in their political rights, they would, at the same time, be perfectly equalized and assimilated in their possessions, their opinions, and their passions.

A republic, by which I mean a government in which the scheme of representation takes place, opens a different prospect and promises the cure for which we are seeking. Let us examine the points in which it varies from pure democracy, and we shall comprehend both the nature of the cure and the efficacy which it must derive from the Union.

The two great points of difference between a democracy and a republic are: first, the delegation of the government, in the latter, to a small number of citizens elected by the rest; secondly, the greater number of citizens, and greater sphere of country, over which the latter may be extended.

The effect of the first difference is, on the one hand, to refine and enlarge the public views by passing them through the medium of a chosen body of citizens, whose wisdom may best discern the true interest of their country, and whose patriotism and love of justice will be least likely to sacrifice it to temporary or partial considerations. Under such a regulation, it may well happen that the public voice, pronounced by the representatives of the people, will be more consonant to the public good than if pronounced by the people themselves, convened for the purpose. On the other hand, the effect may be inverted. Men of factious tempers, of local prejudices, or of sinister designs may, by intrigue, by corruption, or by other means, first obtain the suffrages, and then betray the interests of the people. The question resulting is, whether small or extensive republics are more favorable to the election of proper guardians of the public weal; and it is clearly decided in favor of the latter by two obvious considerations:

In the first place, it is to be remarked that, however small the republic may be, the representatives must be raised to a certain number, in order to guard against the cabals of a few; and that, however large it may be, they must be limited to a certain number, in order to guard against the confusion of a multitude. Hence, the number of representatives in the two cases not being in proportion to that of the two constituents, and being proportionally greater in the small republic, it follows that, if the proportion of fit characters be not less in the large than in the small republic, the former will present a greater option, and consequently a greater probability of a fit choice.

In the next place, as each representative will be chosen by a greater number of citizens in the large than in the small republic, it will be more difficult for unworthy candidates to practice with success the vicious arts by which elections are too often carried; and the suffrages of the people being more free, will be more likely to center in men who possess the most attractive merit and the most diffusive and established character.

It must be confessed that in this, as in most other cases, there is a mean, on both sides of which inconveniences will be found to lie. By enlarging too much the number of electors, you render the representative too little acquainted with all their local circumstances and lesser interests; as by reducing it too much, you render him unduly attached to these and too little fit to comprehend and pursue great and national objects. The federal Constitution forms a happy combination in this respect: the great and aggregate interests being referred to the national, the local and particular to the state legislatures.

The other point of difference is the greater number of citizens and extent of territory which may be brought within the compass of republican than of democratic government; and it is this circumstance principally which renders factious combinations less to be dreaded in the former than in the latter. The smaller the society, the fewer probably will be the distinct parties and interests composing it; the fewer the distinct parties and interests, the more frequently will a majority be found of the same party; and the smaller the number of individuals composing a majority, and the smaller the compass within which they are placed, the more easily will they concert and execute their plans of oppression. Extend the sphere and you take in a greater variety of parties and interests; you make it less probable that a majority of the whole will have a common motive to invade the rights of other citizens; or if such a common motive exists, it will be more difficult for all who feel it to discover their own strength and to act in unison with each other. Besides other impediments, it may be remarked that, where there is a consciousness of unjust or dishonorable purposes, communication is always checked by distrust in proportion to the number whose concurrence is necessary.

Hence, it clearly appears that the same advantage which a republic has over a democracy, in controlling the effects of factions, is enjoyed by a large over a small republic—is enjoyed by the Union over the States composing it. Does the advantage consist in the substitution of representatives whose enlightened views and virtuous sentiments render them superior to local prejudices and to schemes of injustice? It will not be denied that the representation of the Union will be most likely to possess these requisite endowments. Does it consist in the greater security afforded by a greater variety of parties, against the event of any one party being able to outnumber and oppress the rest? In an equal degree does the increased variety of parties comprised within the Union increase this security? Does it, in fine, consist in the greater obstacles opposed to the concert and accomplishment of the secret wishes of an unjust and interested majority? Here, again, the extent of the Union gives it the most palpable advantage.

The influence of factious leaders may kindle a flame within their particular States but will be unable to spread a general conflagration through the other States. . . . A rage for paper money, for an abolition of debts, for an equal division of property, or for any other improper or wicked project will be less apt to pervade the whole body of the Union than a particular member of it; in the same proportion as such a malady is more likely to taint a particular county or district than an entire State.

In the extent, and proper structure of the Union, therefore, we behold a republican remedy for the diseases most incident to republican government. And according to the degree of pleasure and pride we feel in being republicans, ought to be our zeal in cherishing the spirit and supporting the character of Federalists.

The Federalist No. 51 (James Madison)

Here Madison discusses the need for a system of checks and balances to guard against "a gradual concentration of the same powers [of the new government] in the same department." First published February 8, 1788.

To what expedient, then, shall we finally resort, for maintaining in practice the necessary partition of power among the several departments as laid down in the Constitution? The only answer that can be given is that as all these exterior provisions are found to be inadequate the defect must be supplied, by so contriving the interior structure of the government as that its several constituent parts may, by their mutual relations, be the means of keeping each other in their proper places. Without presuming to undertake a full development of this important idea, I will hazard a few general observations which may perhaps place it in a clearer light, and enable us to form a more correct judgment of the principles and structure of the government planned by the convention.

In order to lay a due foundation for that separate and distinct exercise of the different powers of government, which to a certain extent is admitted on all hands to be essential to the preservation of liberty, it is evident that each department should have a will of its own; and consequently should be so constituted that the members of each should have as little agency as possible in the appointment of the members of the others. Were this principle rigorously adhered to, it would require that all the appointments for the supreme executive, legislative, and judiciary magistracies should be drawn from the same fountain of authority, the people, through channels having no communication whatever with one another. Perhaps such a plan of constructing the several departments would be less difficult in practice than it may in contemplation appear. Some difficulties, however, and some additional expense would attend the execution of it. Some deviations, therefore, from the principle must be admitted. In the constitution of the judiciary department in particular, it might be inexpedient to insist rigorously on the principle; first, because peculiar qualifications being essential in the members, the primary consideration ought to be to select that mode of choice which best secures these qualifications; secondly, because the permanent tenure by which the appointments are held in that department must soon destroy all sense of dependence on the authority conferring them.

It is equally evident that the members of each department should be as little dependent as possible on those of the others for the emoluments annexed to their offices. Were the executive magistrate, or the judges, not independent of the legislature in this particular, their independence in every other would be merely nominal.

But the great security against a gradual concentration of the several powers in the same department consists in giving to those who administer each department the necessary constitutional means and personal motives to resist encroachments of the others. The provision for defense must in this, as in all other cases, be made commensurate to the danger of attack. Ambition must be made to counteract ambition. The interest of the man must be connected with the constitutional rights of the place. It may be a reflection on human nature that such devices should be necessary to control the abuses of government. But what is government itself but the greatest of all reflections on human nature? If men were angels, no government would be necessary. If angels were to govern men, neither external nor internal controls on government would be necessary. In framing a government which is to be administered by men over men, the great difficulty lies in this: You must first enable the government to control the governed; and in the next place, oblige it to control itself. A dependence on the people is, no doubt, the primary control on the government; but experience has taught mankind the necessity of auxiliary precautions.

This policy of supplying, by opposite and rival interests, the defect of better motives might be traced through the whole system of human affairs, private as well as public. We see it particularly displayed in all the subordinate distributions of power; where the constant aim is to divide and arrange the several offices in such a manner as that each may be a check on the other—that the private interest of every individual may be a sentinel over the public rights. These inventions of prudence cannot be less requisite in the distribution of the supreme powers of the State.

But it is not possible to give to each department an equal power of self-defense. In republican government, the legislative authority necessarily predominates. The remedy for this inconveniency is to divide the legislature into different branches; and to render them, by different modes of election, and different principles of action, as little connected with each other as the nature of their common functions and their common dependence on the society will admit. It may even be necessary to guard against dangerous encroachments by still further precautions. As the weight of the legislative authority requires that it should be thus divided, the weakness of the executive may require, on the other hand, that it should be fortified. An absolute negative on the legislature appears, at first view, to be the natural defense with which the executive magistrate should be armed. But perhaps it would be neither altogether safe nor alone sufficient. On ordinary occasions it might not be exerted with the requisite firmness, and on extraordinary occasions it might be perfidiously abused. May not this defect of an absolute negative be supplied by some qualified connection between this weaker department and the weaker branch of the stronger department, by which

the latter may be led to support the constitutional rights of the former, without being too much detached from the rights of its own department?

If the principles on which these observations are founded be just, as I persuade myself they are, and they be applied as a criterion to the several State constitutions, and to the federal Constitution, it will be found that if the latter does not perfectly correspond with them, the former are infinitely less able to bear such a test.

There are, moreover, two considerations particularly applicable to the federal system of America, which place that system in a very interesting point of view.

First. In a single republic, all the power surrendered by the people is submitted to the administration of a single government; and the usurpations are guarded against by a division of the government into distinct and separate departments. In the compound republic of America, the power surrendered by the people is first divided between two distinct governments, and then the portion allotted to each subdivided among distinct and separate departments. Hence a double security arises to the rights of the people. The different governments will control each other, at the same time that each will be controlled by itself.

Second. It is of great importance in a republic not only to guard the society against the oppression of its rulers, but to guard one part of the society against the injustice of the other part. Different interests necessarily exist in different classes of citizens. If a majority be united by a common interest, the rights of the minority will be insecure. There are but two methods of providing against this evil: The one by creating a will in the community independent of the majority—that is, of the society itself; the other, by comprehending in the society so many separate descriptions of citizens as will render an unjust combination of a majority of the whole very improbable, if not impracticable. The first method prevails in all governments possessing an hereditary or self appointed authority. This, at best, is but a precarious security; because a power independent of the society may as well espouse the unjust views of the major as the rightful interests of the minor party, and may possibly be turned against both parties. The second method will be exemplified in the federal republic of the United States. Whilst all authority in it will be derived from and dependent on the society, the society itself will be broken into so many parts, interests, and classes of citizens, that the rights of individuals, or of the minority, will be in little danger from interested combinations of the majority. In a free government the security for civil rights must be the same as that for religious rights. It consists in the one case in the multiplicity of interests, and in the other in the multiplicity of sects. The degree of security in both cases will depend on the number of interests and sects; and this may be presumed to depend on the extent of country and number of people comprehended under the same government. This view of the subject must particularly recommend a proper federal system to all the sincere and considerate friends of republican government, since it shows that in exact proportion as the territory of the Union may be formed into more circumscribed Confederacies, or States, oppressive combinations of a majority will be facilitated: the best security, under the republican forms, for the rights of every class of citizens, will be diminished; and consequently, the stability and independence of some member of the government, the only other security, must be proportionally increased. Justice is the end of government.

It is the end of civil society. It ever has been and ever will be pursued until it be obtained, or until liberty be lost in the pursuit. In a society under the forms of which the stronger faction can readily unite and oppress the weaker, anarchy may as truly be said to reign as in a state of nature, where the weaker individual is not secured against the violence of the stronger: And as, in the latter state, even the stronger individuals are prompted by the uncertainty of their condition to submit to a government which may protect the weak as well as themselves. So, in the former state, will the more powerful factions or parties be gradually induced, by a like motive, to wish for a government which will protect all parties, the weaker as well as the more powerful. It can be little doubted that if the State of Rhode Island was separated from the Confederacy and left to itself, the insecurity of rights under the popular form of government within such narrow limits would be displayed by such reiterated oppressions of factious majorities that some power altogether independent of the people would soon be called for by the voice of the very factions whose misrule had proved the necessity of it. In the extended republic of the United States, and among the great variety of interests, parties, and sects which it embraces, a coalition of a majority of the whole society could seldom take place on any other principles than those of justice and the general good; whilst there being thus less danger to a minor from the will of the major party, there must be less pretext, also, to provide for the security of the former, by introducing into the government a will not dependent on the latter; or, in other words, a will independent of the society itself. It is no less certain that it is important, notwithstanding the contrary opinions which have been entertained, that the larger the society, provided it lie within a practicable sphere, the more duly capable it will be of self-government. And happily for the *republican cause*, the practicable sphere may be carried to a very great extent by a judicious modification and mixture of the *federal principle*.

The Federalist No. 78 (Alexander Hamilton)

The Federalist *papers were the brainchild of Alexander Hamilton, who conceived them and recruited James Madison and John Jay to the project. He then arranged for their publication. Hamilton is usually credited as the author of 51 of the 85 essays in the collection. Here, he discusses the national judiciary to be established by Article III in the proposed Consitution. He emphasizes the vital need for an independent judiciary and its role in the interpretation of laws and the determination of their constitutionality. First published April 11, 1788.*

We proceed now to an examination of the judiciary department of the proposed government. In unfolding the defects of the existing Confederation, the utility and necessity of a federal judicature have been clearly pointed out. It is the less necessary to recapitulate the considerations there urged as the propriety of the institution in the abstract is not disputed; the only questions which have been raised being relative to the manner of constituting it, and to its extent. To these points, therefore, our observations shall be confined.

The manner of constituting it seems to embrace these several objects: 1st. The mode of appointing the judges. 2nd. The tenure by which they are to hold their places. 3rd. The partition of the judiciary authority between different courts and their relations to each other.

First. As to the mode of appointing the judges: this is the same with that of appointing the officers of the Union in general and has been so fully discussed in the two last numbers that nothing can be said here which would not be useless repetition.

Second. As to the tenure by which the judges are to hold their places: this chiefly concerns their duration in office, the provisions for their support, the precautions for their responsibility.

According to the plan of the convention, all judges who may be appointed by the United States are to hold their offices *during good behavior*; which is conformable to the most approved of the State constitutions, and among the rest, to that of this State. Its propriety having been drawn into question by the adversaries of that plan is no light symptom of the rage for objection which disorders their imaginations and judgments. The standard of good behavior for the continuance in office of the judicial magistracy is certainly one of the most valuable of the modern improvements in the practice of government. In a monarchy it is an excellent barrier to the despotism of the prince; in a republic it is a no less excellent barrier to the encroachments and oppressions of the representative body. And it is the best expedient which can be devised in any government to secure a steady, upright, and impartial administration of the laws.

Whoever attentively considers the different departments of power must perceive that, in a government in which they are separated from each other, the judiciary, from the nature of its functions, will always be the least dangerous to the political rights of the Constitution; because it will be least in a capacity to annoy or injure them. The executive not only dispenses the honors but holds the sword of the community. The legislature not only commands the purse but prescribes the rules by which the duties and rights of every citizen are to be regulated. The judiciary, on the contrary, has no influence over either the sword or the purse; no direction either of the strength or of the wealth of the society, and can take no active resolution whatever.

This simple view of the matter suggests several important consequences. It proves incontestably that the judiciary is beyond comparison the weakest of the three departments of power; that it can never attack with success either of the other two; and that all possible care is requisite to enable it to defend itself against their attacks. It equally proves that though individual oppression may now and then proceed from the courts of justice, the general liberty of the people can never be endangered from that quarter; I mean so long as the judiciary remains truly distinct from both the legislature and the executive. For I agree that "there is no liberty if the power of judging be not separated from the legislative and executive powers." And it proves, in the last place, that as liberty can have nothing to fear from the judiciary alone, but would have everything to fear from its union with either of the other departments; that as all the effects of such a union must ensue from a dependence of the former on the latter, notwithstanding a nominal and apparent separation; that as, from the natural feebleness of the judiciary, it is in continual jeopardy of being overpowered, awed, or influenced by its coordinate branches; and that as nothing can contribute so much to its firmness and independence as permanency in office, this quality may therefore be justly regarded as an indispensable ingredient in its constitution, and, in a great measure, as the citadel of the public justice and the public security.

The complete independence of the courts of justice is peculiarly essential in a limited Constitution. By a limited Constitution, I understand one which contains certain specified exceptions to the legislative authority; such, for instance, as that it shall pass no bills of attainder, no *ex post facto* laws, and the like. Limitations of this kind can be preserved in practice no other way than through the medium of courts of justice, whose duty it must be to declare all acts contrary to the manifest tenor of the Constitution void. Without this, all the reservations of particular rights or privileges would amount to nothing.

Some perplexity respecting the rights of the courts to pronounce legislative acts void, because contrary to the Constitution, has arisen from an imagination that the doctrine would imply a superiority of the judiciary to the legislative power. It is urged that the authority which can declare the acts of another void must necessarily be superior to the one whose acts may be declared void. As this doctrine is of great importance in all the American constitutions, a brief discussion of the grounds on which it rests cannot be unacceptable.

There is no position which depends on clearer principles than that every act of a delegated authority, contrary to the tenor of the commission under which it is exercised, is void. No legislative act, therefore, contrary to the Constitution, can be valid. To deny this would be to affirm that the deputy is greater than his principal; that the servant is above his master; that the representatives of the people are superior to the people themselves; that men acting by virtue of powers may do not only what their powers do not authorize, but what they forbid.

If it be said that the legislative body are themselves the constitutional judges of their own powers and that the construction they put upon them is conclusive upon the other departments, it may be answered that this cannot be the natural presumption where it is not to be collected from any particular provisions in the Constitution. It is not otherwise to be supposed that the Constitution could intend to enable the representatives of the people to substitute their *will* to that of their constituents. It is far more rational to suppose that the courts were designed to be an intermediate body between the people and the legislature in order, among other things, to keep the latter within the limits assigned to their authority. The interpretation of the laws is the proper and peculiar province of the courts. A constitution is, in fact, and must be regarded by the judges as, a fundamental law. It therefore belongs to them to ascertain its meaning as well as the meaning of any particular act proceeding from the legislative body. If there should happen to be an irreconcilable variance between the two, that which has the superior obligation and validity ought, of course, to be preferred; or, in other words, the Constitution ought to be preferred to the statute, the intention of the people to the intention of their agents.

Nor does this conclusion by any means suppose a superiority of the judicial to the legislative power. It only supposes that the power of the people is superior to both, and that where the will of the legislature, declared in its statutes, stands in opposition to that of the people, declared in the Constitution, the judges ought to be governed by the latter rather than the former. They ought to regulate their decisions by the fundamental laws rather than by those which are not fundamental.

This exercise of judicial discretion in determining between two contradictory laws is exemplified in a familiar instance. It not uncommonly happens that there are two statutes existing at one time, clashing in whole or in part with each other and neither of them containing any repealing clause or expression. In such a case, it is the province of the courts to liquidate and fix their meaning and operation. So far as they can, by any fair construction, be reconciled to each other, reason and law conspire to dictate that this should be done; where this is impracticable, it becomes a matter of necessity to give effect to one in exclusion of the other. The rule which has obtained in the courts for determining their relative validity is that the last in order of time shall be preferred to the first. But this is a mere rule of construction, not derived from any positive law but from the nature and reason of the thing. It is a rule not enjoined upon the courts by legislative provision but adopted by themselves, as consonant to truth and propriety, for the direction of their conduct as interpreters of the law. They thought it reasonable that between the interfering acts of an *equal* authority that which was the last indication of its will should have the preference.

But in regard to the interfering acts of a superior and subordinate authority of an original and derivative power, the nature and reason of the thing indicate the converse of that rule as proper to be followed. They teach us that the prior act of a superior ought to be preferred to the subsequent act of an inferior and subordinate authority; and that accordingly, whenever a particular statute contravenes the Constitution, it will be the duty of the judicial tribunals to adhere to the latter and disregard the former.

Historical Documents

It can be of no weight to say that the courts, on the pretense of a repugnancy, may substitute their own pleasure to the constitutional intentions of the legislature. This might as well happen in the case of two contradictory statutes; or it might as well happen in every adjudication upon any single statute. The courts must declare the sense of the law; and if they should be disposed to exercise *will* instead of *judgment,* the consequence would equally be the substitution of their pleasure to that of the legislative body. The observation, if it prove anything, would prove that there ought to be no judges distinct from that body.

If, then, the courts of justice are to be considered as the bulwarks of a limited Constitution against legislative encroachments, this consideration will afford a strong argument for the permanent tenure of judicial offices, since nothing will contribute so much as this to that independent spirit in the judges which must be essential to the faithful performance of so arduous a duty.

This independence of the judges is equally requisite to guard the Constitution and the rights of individuals from the effects of those ill humors which the arts of designing men, or the influence of particular conjunctures, sometimes disseminate among the people themselves, and which, though they speedily give place to better information, and more deliberate reflection, have a tendency, in the meantime, to occasion dangerous innovations in the government, and serious oppressions of the minor party in the community. Though I trust the friends of the proposed Constitution will never concur with its enemies in questioning that fundamental principle of Republican government which admits the right of the people to alter or abolish the established Constitution whenever they find it inconsistent with their happiness; yet it is not to be inferred from this principle that the representatives of the people, whenever a momentary inclination happens to lay hold of a majority of their constituents incompatible with the provisions in the existing Constitution would, on that account, be justifiable in a violation of those provisions; or that the courts would be under a greater obligation to connive at infractions in this shape than when they had proceeded wholly from the cabals of the representative body. Until the people have, by some solemn and authoritative act, annulled or changed the established form, it is binding upon themselves collectively, as well as individually; and no presumption, or even knowledge of their sentiments, can warrant their representatives in a departure from it prior to such an act. But it is easy to see that it would require an uncommon portion of fortitude in the judges to do their duty as faithful guardians of the Constitution, where legislative invasions of it had been instigated by the major voice of the community.

But it is not with a view to infractions of the Constitution only that the independence of the judges may be an essential safeguard against the effects of occasional ill humors in the society. These sometimes extend no farther than to the injury of the private rights of particular classes of citizens, by unjust and partial laws. Here also the firmness of the judicial magistracy is of vast importance in mitigating the severity and confining the operation of such laws. It not only serves to moderate the immediate mischiefs of those which may have been passed but it operates as a check upon the legislative body in passing them; who, perceiving that obstacles to the success of iniquitous intention are to be expected from the scruples of the courts, are in a manner compelled, by the very motives of the injustice they mediate, to qualify their attempts. This is a circumstance calculated to have more influence upon the character of our governments than but few may be aware of. The benefits of the integrity and moderation of the judiciary have already been felt in more States than one; and though they may have displeased those whose sinister expectations they may have disappointed, they must have commanded the esteem and applause of all the virtuous and disinterested. Considerate men of every description ought to prize whatever will tend to beget or fortify that temper in the courts; as no man can be sure that he may not be tomorrow the victim of a spirit of injustice, by which he may be a gainer today. And every man must now feel that the inevitable tendency of such a spirit is to sap the foundations of public and private confidence and to introduce in its stead universal distrust and distress.

That inflexible and uniform adherence to the rights of the Constitution, and of individuals, which we perceive to be indispensable in the courts of justice, can certainly not be expected from judges who hold their offices by a temporary commission. Periodical appointments, however regulated, or by whomsoever made, would, in some way or other, be fatal to their necessary independence. If the power of making them was committed either to the executive or legislature there would be danger of an improper complaisance to the branch which possessed it; if to both, there would be an unwillingness to hazard the displeasure of either; if to the people, or to persons chosen by them for the special purpose, there would be too great a disposition to consult popularity to justify a reliance that nothing would be consulted but the Constitution and the laws.

There is yet a further and a weighty reason for the permanency of the judicial offices which is deducible from the nature of the qualifications they require. It has been frequently remarked with great propriety that a voluminous code of laws is one of the inconveniences necessarily connected with the advantages of a free government. To avoid an arbitrary discretion in the courts, it is indispensable that they should be bound down by strict rules and precedents which serve to define and point out their duty in every particular case that comes before them; and it will readily be conceived from the variety of controversies which grow out of the folly and wickedness of mankind that the records of those precedents must unavoidably swell to a very considerable bulk and must demand long and laborious study to acquire a competent knowledge of them. Hence it is that there can be but few men in the society who will have sufficient skill in the laws to qualify them for the stations of judges. And making the proper deductions for the ordinary depravity of human nature, the number must be still smaller of those who unite the requisite integrity with the requisite knowledge. These considerations apprise us that the government can have no great option between fit characters; and that a temporary duration in office which would naturally discourage such characters from quitting a lucrative line of practice to accept a seat on the bench would have a tendency to throw the administration of justice into hands less able and less well qualified to conduct it with utility and dignity. In the present circumstances of this country and in those in which it is likely to be for a long time to come, the disadvantages on this score would be greater than they may at first sight appear; but it must be confessed that they are far inferior to those which present themselves under the other aspects of the subject.

Upon the whole, there can be no room to doubt that the convention acted wisely in copying from the models of those constitutions which have established *good behavior* as the tenure of their judicial offices, in point of duration; and that so far from being blamable on this account, their plan would have been inexcusably defective if it had wanted this important feature of good government. The experience of Great Britain affords an illustrious comment on the excellence of the institution.

Anti-Federalist Responses
Arguments Against the Adoption of the Constitution

When the Constitutional Convention of 1787 produced the new Constitution, many thoughtful, patriotic people from all over the country opposed its adoption. These Anti-Federalists, as they were known, had a number of objections to the Constitution. Five of their most significant objections were these: (1) The new Constitution was a document written by and for the primary benefit of a wealthy and powerful aristocracy. (2) The Constitution lacked a bill of rights. (3) The Constitutional Convention was not authorized to do anything but amend the Articles of Confederation; therefore, the Constitution was an illegal document. (4) States would be wholly subordinate to the new National Government and lose their sovereignty. (5) The powers given to the new United States Government were so extensive as to lead inevitably to tyranny and despotism. The following documents provide a sampling of Anti-Federalist arguments.

Richard Henry Lee

Lee from Virginia wrote the best-known Anti-Federalist essays of the time, "Letters from the Federal Farmer to the Republican." These excerpts are from these letters written in October 1787.

The present moment discovers a new face in our affairs. Our object has been all along to reform our federal system and to strengthen our governments—to establish peace, order, and justice in the community—but a new object now presents. The plan of government now proposed is evidently calculated totally to change, in time, our condition as a people. Instead of being thirteen republics under a federal head, it is clearly designed to make us one consolidated government. . . . This consolidation of the states has been the object of several men in this country for some time past. Whether such a change can ever be effected, in any manner; whether it can be effected without convulsions and civil wars; whether such a change will not totally destroy the liberties of this country, time only can determine. . . .

The Confederation was formed when great confidence was placed in the voluntary exertions of individuals and of the respective states; and the framers of it, to guard against usurpation, so limited and checked the powers that, in many respects, they are inadequate to the exigencies of the Union. We find, therefore, members of Congress urging alterations in the federal system almost as soon as it was adopted. . . .

We expected too much from the return of peace, and, of course, we have been disappointed. Our governments have been new and unsettled; and several legislature, [by their actions] . . . have given just cause of uneasiness. . . .

The conduct of several legislatures touching paper-money and tender laws has prepared many honest men for changes in government, which otherwise they would not have thought of—when by the evils, on the one hand, and by the secret instigations of artful men, on the other, the minds of men were become sufficiently uneasy, a bold step was taken, which is usually followed by a revolution or a civil war. A general convention for mere commercial purposes was moved for—the authors of this measure saw that the people's attention was turned solely to the amendment of the federal system; and that, had the idea of a total change been started, probably no state would have appointed members to the Convention. The idea of destroying, ultimately, the state government and forming one consolidated system could not have been admitted. A convention, therefore, merely for vesting in Congress power to regulate trade was proposed. . . .

The plan proposed appears to be partly federal, but principally, however, calculated ultimately to make the states one consolidated government.

The first interesting question therefore suggested is how far the states can be consolidated into one entire government on free principles. In considering this question, extensive objects are to be taken into view, and important changes in the forms of government to be carefully attended to in all their consequences. The happiness of the people at large must be the great object with every honest statesman, and he will direct every movement to this point. If we are so situated as a people as not to be able to enjoy equal happiness and advantages under one government, the consolidation of the states cannot be admitted.

* * *

There are certain unalienable and fundamental rights, which in forming the social compact ought to be explicitly ascertained and fixed. A free and enlightened people, in forming this compact, will not resign all their rights to those who govern, and they will fix limits [a bill of rights] to their legislators and rulers, which will soon be plainly seen by those who are governed, as well as by those who govern; and the latter will know they cannot be passed unperceived by the former and without giving a general alarm. These rights should be made the basis of every constitution; and if a people be so situated, or have such different opinions, that they cannot agree in ascertaining and fixing them, it is a very strong argument against their attempting to form one entire society, to live under one system of laws only.

* * *

It may also be worthy our examination how far the provision for amending this plan, when it shall be adopted, is of any importance. No measures can be taken toward amendments unless two-thirds of the Congress, or two-thirds of the legislature of the several states, shall agree. While power is in the hands of the people, or democratic part of the community, more especially as at present, it is easy, according to the general course of human affairs, for the few influential men in the community to obtain conventions, alterations in government, and to persuade the common people that they may change for the better, and to get from them a part of the power. But when power is once transferred from the many to the few, all changes become extremely difficult; the government in this case being beneficial to the few, they will be exceedingly artful and adroit in preventing any measures which may lead to a change; and nothing will produce it but great exertions and severe struggles on the part of the common people. Every man of reflection must see that the change now proposed is a transfer of power from the many to the few, and the probability is the artful and ever active aristocracy will prevent all peaceful measures for changes, unless when they shall discover some favorable moment to increase their own influence.

* * *

It is true there may be danger in delay; but there is danger in adopting the system in its present form. And I see the danger in either case will arise principally from the conduct and views of two very unprincipled parties in the United States—two fires, between which the honest and substantial people have long found themselves situated. One party is composed of little insurgents, men in debt, who want no law and who want a share of the property of others—these are called levelers, Shayites, etc. The other party is composed

of a few but more dangerous men, with their servile dependents; these avariciously grasp at all power and property. You may discover in all the actions of these men an evident dislike to free and equal government, and they will go systematically to work to change, essentially, the forms of government in this country—these are called aristocrats. . . .

. . . The fact is, these aristocrats support and hasten the adoption of the proposed Constitution merely because they think it is a stepping-stone to their favorite object. I think I am well-founded in this idea; I think the general politics of these men support it, as well as the common observation among them that the proffered plan is the best that can be got at present; it will do for a few years, and lead to something better. . . .

Luther Martin

Martin, the leading Anti-Federalist from Maryland, attended the Constitutional Convention as a delegate. In this excerpt from a speech before the Maryland State legislature on November 29, 1787, he defends his decision to leave the Convention before its work was finished.

It was the states as states, by their representatives in Congress, that formed the Articles of Confederation; it was the states as states, by their legislatures, who ratified those Articles; and it was there established and provided that the states as states (that is, by their legislatures) should agree to any alterations that should hereafter be proposed in the federal government, before they should be binding; and any alterations agreed to in any other manner cannot release the states from the obligation they are under to each other by virtue of the original Articles of Confederation. The people of the different states never made any objection to the manner in which the Articles of Confederation were formed or ratified, or to the mode by which alterations were to be made in that government—with the rights of their respective states they wished not to interfere. Nor do I believe the people, in their individual capacity, would ever have expected or desired to have been appealed to on the present occasion, in violation of the rights of their respective states, if the favorers of the proposed Constitution, imagining they had a better chance of forcing it to be adopted by a hasty appeal to the people at large (who could not be so good judges of the dangerous consequence), had not insisted upon this mode . . . .

It was also my opinion that, upon principles of sound policy, the agreement or disagreement to the proposed system ought to have been by the state legislatures; in which case, let the event have been what it would, there would have been but little prospect of the public peace being disturbed thereby; whereas the attempt to force down this system, although Congress and the respective state legislatures should disapprove, by appealing to the people and to procure its establishment in a manner totally unconstitutional, has a tendency to set the state governments and their subjects at variance with each other, to lessen the obligations of government, to weaken the bands of society, to introduce anarchy and confusion, and to light the torch of discord and civil war throughout this continent. All these considerations weighed with me most forcibly against giving my assent to the mode by which it is resolved that this system is to be ratified, and were urged by me in opposition to the measure.

. . . [A] great portion of that time which ought to have been devoted calmly and impartially to consider what alterations in our federal government would be most likely to procure and preserve the happiness of the Union was employed in a violent struggle on the one side to obtain all power and dominion in their own hands, and on the other to prevent it; and that the aggrandizement of particular states, and particular individuals, appears to have been much more the subject sought after than the welfare of our country . . . .

When I took my seat in the Convention, I found them attempting to bring forward a system which, I was sure, never had entered into the contemplation of those I had the honor to represent, and which, upon the fullest consideration, I considered not only injurious to the interest and rights of this state but also incompatible with the political happiness and freedom of the states in general. From that time until my business compelled me to leave the Convention, I gave it every possible opposition, in every stage of its progression. I opposed the system there with the same explicit frankness with which I have here given you a history of our proceedings, an account of my own conduct, which in a particular manner I consider you as having a right to know. While there, I endeavored to act as became a free-man and the delegate of a free state. Should my conduct obtain the approbation of those who appointed me, I will not deny it would afford me satisfaction; but to me that approbation was at most no more than a secondary consideration—my first was to deserve it. Left to myself to act according to the best of my discretion, my conduct should have been the same had I been even sure your censure would have been my only reward, since I hold it sacredly my duty to dash the cup of poison, if possible, from the hand of a state or an individual, however anxious the one or the other might be to swallow it . . . .

William Findley, Robert Whitehill, and John Smilie

Findley, Whitehill, and Smilie—who were delegates to the Pennsylvania State convention—believed that they and other opponents of the Constitution were prevented from expressing their views because of the political maneuverings of the Federalists. This excerpt is from "The Address and Reasons of Dissent of the Minority of the Convention of the State of Pennsylvania to their Constituents," which the three men published in the Pennsylvania Packet and Daily Advertiser *on December 18, 1787.*

The Continental Convention met in the city of Philadelphia at the time appointed. It was composed of some men of excellent character; of others who were more remarkable for their ambition and cunning than their patriotism; and of some who had been opponents to the independence of the United States. The delegates from Pennsylvania were, six of them, uniform and decided opponents to the constitution of the commonwealth [the Articles of Confederation]. The convention sat upward of four months. The doors were kept shut, and the members brought under the most solemn engagements of secrecy. Some of those who opposed their going so far beyond their powers, retired, hopeless, from the convention; others had the firmness to refuse signing the plan altogether; and many who did sign it, did it not as a system they wholly approved but as the best that could be then obtained; and notwithstanding the time spent on this subject, it is agreed on all hands to be a work of haste and accommodation. . . .

Our objections are comprised under three general heads of dissent, viz.:

We dissent, first, because it is the opinion of the most celebrated writers on government, and confirmed by uniform experience, that a very extensive territory cannot be governed on the principles of freedom otherwise than by a confederation of republics, possessing all the powers of internal government but united in the management of their general and foreign concerns. . . .

We dissent, secondly, because the powers vested in Congress by this Constitution must necessarily annihilate and absorb the legislative, executive, and judicial powers of the several states, and produce from their ruins one consolidated government, which from the nature of things will be *an iron-handed despotism*, as nothing short of the supremacy of despotic sway could connect and govern these United States under one government.

As the truth of this position is of such decisive importance, it ought to be fully investigated, and if it is founded, to be clearly ascertained; for, should it be demonstrated that the powers vested by this Constitution in Congress will have such an effect as necessarily to produce one consolidated government, the question then will be reduced to this short issue, viz.: whether satiated with the blessings of liberty, whether repenting of the folly of so recently asserting their unalienable rights against foreign despots at the expense of so much blood and treasure, and such painful and arduous struggles, the people of America are now willing to resign every privilege of freemen, and submit to the dominion of an absolute government that will embrace all America in one chain of despotism; or whether they will, with virtuous indignation, spurn at the shackles prepared for them, and confirm their liberties by a conduct becoming freemen. . . .

We dissent, thirdly, because if it were practicable to govern so extensive a territory as these United States include, on the plan of a consolidated government, consistent with the principles of liberty and the happiness of the people, yet the construction of this Constitution is not calculated to attain the object; for independent of the nature of the case, it would of itself necessarily produce a despotism, and that not by the usual gradations but with the celerity that has hitherto only attended revolutions effected by the sword.

To establish the truth of this position, a cursory investigation of the principles and form of this Constitution will suffice.

The first consideration that this review suggests is the omission of a Bill of Rights ascertaining and fundamentally establishing those unalienable and personal rights of men, without the full, free, and secure enjoyment of which there can be no liberty, and over which it is not necessary for a good government to have the control— the principal of which are the rights of conscience, personal liberty by the clear and unequivocal establishment of the writ of habeas corpus, jury trial in criminal and civil cases, by an impartial jury of the vicinage or county, with the common law proceedings for the safety of the accused in criminal prosecutions; and the liberty of the press, that scourge of tyrants, and the grand bulwark of every other liberty and privilege. The stipulations heretofore made in favor of them in the state constitutions are entirely superseded by this Constitution. . . .

Articles of Confederation

In force from March 1, 1781 to March 4, 1789

To all to whom these Presents shall come, we the undersigned Delegates of the States affixed to our Names send greeting. Whereas the Delegates of the United States of America in Congress assembled did on the fifteenth day of November in the Year of our Lord One Thousand Seven Hundred and Seventy seven, and in the Second Year of the Independence of America agree to certain articles of Confederation and perpetual Union between the States of New Hampshire, Massachusetts Bay, Rhode Island and Providence Plantations, Connecticut, New York, New Jersey, Pennsylvania, Delaware, Maryland, Virginia, North Carolina, South Carolina and Georgia in the Words following, viz. "Articles of Confederation and perpetual Union between the states of New Hampshire, Massachusetts Bay, Rhode Island and Providence Plantations, Connecticut, New York, New Jersey, Pennsylvania, Delaware, Maryland, Virginia, North Carolina, South Carolina and Georgia.

[ART. I.] The Stile of this confederacy shall be "The United States of America."

[ART. II.] Each state retains its sovereignty, freedom and independence, and every Power, Jurisdiction and right, which is not by this confederation expressly delegated to the United States, in Congress assembled.

[ART. III.] The said states hereby severally enter into a firm league of friendship with each other, for their common defence, the security of their Liberties, and their mutual and general welfare, binding themselves to assist each other, against all force offered to, or attacks made upon them, or any of them, on account of religion, sovereignty, trade, or any other pretence whatever.

[ART. IV.] The better to secure and perpetuate mutual friendship and intercourse among the people of the different states in this union, the free inhabitants of each of these states, paupers, vagabonds and fugitives from Justice excepted, shall be entitled to all privileges and immunities of free citizens in the several states; and the people of each state shall have free ingress and regress to and from any other state, and shall enjoy therein all the privileges of trade and commerce, subject to the same duties, impositions and restrictions as the inhabitants thereof respectively, provided that such restriction shall not extend so far as to prevent the removal of property imported into any state, to any other state of which the Owner is an inhabitant; provided also that no imposition, duties or restriction shall be laid by any state, on the property of the united states, or either of them.

If any Person guilty of, or charged with treason, felony, or other high misdemeanor in any state, shall flee from Justice, and be found in any of the united states, he shall upon demand of the Governor or executive power, of the state from which he fled, be delivered up and removed to the state having jurisdiction of his offence.

Full faith and credit shall be given in each of these states to the records, acts and judicial proceedings of the courts and magistrates of every other state.

[ART. V.] For the more convenient management of the general interests of the united states, delegates shall be annually appointed in such manner as the legislature of each state shall direct, to meet in Congress on the first Monday in November, in every year, with a power reserved to each state, to recall its delegates, or any of them, at any time within the year, and to send others in their stead, for the remainder of the Year.

No state shall be represented in Congress by less than two, nor by more than seven Members; and no person shall be capable of being a delegate for more than three years in any term of six years; nor shall any person, being a delegate, be capable of holding any office under the united states, for which he, or another for his benefit receives any salary, fees or emolument of any kind.

Each state shall maintain its own delegates in a meeting of the states, and while they act as members of the committee of the states.

In determining questions in the united states, in Congress assembled, each state shall have one vote.

Freedom of speech and debate in Congress shall not be impeached or questioned in any Court, or place out of Congress, and the members of congress shall be protected in their persons from arrests and imprisonments, during the time of their going to and from, and attendance on congress, except for treason, felony, or breach of the peace.

[ART. VI.] No state without the Consent of the united states in congress assembled, shall send any embassy to, or receive any embassy from, or enter into any conference, agreement, or alliance or treaty with any King, prince or state; nor shall any person holding any office of profit or trust under the united states, or any of them, accept of any present, emolument, office or title of any kind whatever from any king, prince or foreign state; nor shall the united states in congress assembled, or any of them, grant any title of nobility.

No two or more states shall enter into any treaty, confederation or alliance whatever between them, without the consent of the united states in congress assembled, specifying accurately the purposes for which the same is to be entered into, and how long it shall continue.

No state shall lay any imposts or duties, which may interfere with any stipulations in treaties, entered into by the united states in congress assembled, with any king, prince or state, in pursuance of any treaties already proposed by congress, to the courts of France and Spain.

No vessels of war shall be kept up in time of peace by any state, except such number only, as shall be deemed necessary by the united states in congress assembled, for the defence of such state, or its trade; nor shall any body of forces be kept up by any state, in time of peace, except such number only, as in the judgment of the united states, in congress assembled, shall be deemed requisite to garrison the forts necessary for the defence of such state; but every state shall always keep up a well regulated and disciplined militia, sufficiently armed and accounted, and shall provide and constantly have ready for use, in public stores, a due number of field pieces and tents, and a proper quantity of arms, ammunition and camp equipage.

No state shall engage in any war without the consent of the united states in congress assembled, unless such state be actually invaded by enemies, or shall have received certain advice of a resolution being formed by some nation of Indians to invade such state and the danger is so imminent as not to admit of a delay, till the united states in congress assembled can be consulted: nor shall any state grant commissions to any ships or vessels of war, nor letters of marque or reprisal, except it be after a declaration of war by the united states in congress assembled, and then only against the kingdom or state and the subjects thereof, against which war has been so declared, and under such regulations as shall be established by the united states in congress assembled, unless such state be infested by pirates, in which case vessels of war may be fitted out for that occasion, and kept so long as the danger shall continue, or until the united states in congress assembled shall determine otherwise.

[ART. VII.] When land-forces are raised by any state for the common defence, all officers of or under the rank of colonel, shall be appointed by the legislature of each state respectively by whom such forces shall be raised, or in such manner as such state shall direct, and all vacancies shall be filled up by the state which first made the appointment.

[ART. VIII.] All charges of war, and all other expences that shall be incurred for the common defence or general welfare, and allowed by the united states in congress assembled, shall be defrayed out of a common treasury, which shall be supplied by the several states, in proportion to the value of all land within each state, granted to or surveyed for any Person, as such land and the buildings and improvements thereon shall be estimated according to such mode as the united states in congress assembled, shall from time to time direct and appoint. The taxes for paying that proportion shall be laid and levied by the authority and direction of the legislatures of the several states within the time agreed upon by the united states in congress assembled.

[ART. IX.] The united states in congress assembled, shall have the sole and exclusive right and power of determining on peace and war, except in the cases mentioned in the sixth article—of sending and receiving ambassadors—entering into treaties and alliances, provided that no treaty of commerce shall be made whereby the legislative power of the respective states shall be restrained from imposing such imposts and duties on foreigners, as their own people are subjected to, or from prohibiting the exportation or importation of any

species of goods or commodities whatsoever—of establishing rules for deciding in all cases, what captures on land or water shall be legal, and in what manner prizes taken by land or naval forces in the service of the united states shall be divided or appropriated—of granting letters of marque and reprisal in times of peace—appointing courts for the trial of piracies and felonies committed on the high seas and establishing courts for receiving and determining finally appeals in all cases of captures, provided that no member of congress shall be appointed a judge of any of the said courts.

The united states in congress assembled shall also be the last resort on appeal in all disputes and differences now subsisting or that hereafter may arise between two or more states concerning boundary, jurisdiction or any other cause whatever; which authority shall always be exercised in the manner following. Whenever the legislative or executive authority or lawful agent [of any] state in controversy with another shall present a petition to congress stating the matter in question and praying for a hearing, notice thereof shall be given by order of congress to the legislative or executive authority of the other state in controversy, and a day assigned for the appearance of the parties by their lawful agents, who shall then be directed to appoint by joint consent, commissioners or judges to constitute a court for hearing and determining the matter in question; but if they cannot agree, congress shall name three persons out of each of the united states, and from the list of such persons each party shall alternately strike out one, the petitioners beginning, until the number shall be reduced to thirteen; and from that number not less than seven, nor more than nine names as congress shall direct, shall in the presence of congress be drawn out by lot, and the persons whose names shall be so drawn or any five of them, shall be commissioners or judges, to hear and finally determine the controversy, so always as a major part of the judges who shall hear the cause shall agree in the determination: and if either party shall neglect to attend at the day appointed, without shewing reasons, which congress shall judge sufficient, or being present shall refuse to strike, the congress shall proceed to nominate three persons out of each state, and the secretary of congress shall strike in behalf of such party absent or refusing; and the judgment and sentence of the court to be appointed, in the manner before prescribed, shall be final and conclusive; and if any of the parties shall refuse to submit to the authority of such court, or to appear to defend their claim or cause, the court shall nevertheless proceed to pronounce sentence, or judgment, which shall in like manner be final and decisive, the judgment or sentence and other proceedings being in either case transmitted to congress, and lodged among the acts of congress for the security of the parties concerned: provided that every commissioner, before he sits in judgment, shall take an oath to be administered by one of the judges of the supreme or superior court of the state, where the cause shall be tried, "well and truly to hear and determine the matter in question, according to the best of his judgment, without favour, affection or hope of reward;" provided also that no state shall be deprived of territory for the benefit of the united states.

All controversies concerning the private right of soil claimed under different grants of two or more states, whose jurisdictions as they may respect such lands, and the states which passed such grants are adjusted, the said grants or either of them being at the same time claimed to have originated antecedent to such settlement of jurisdiction, shall on the petition of either party to the congress of the united states, be finally determined as near as may be in the same manner as is before prescribed for deciding disputes respecting territorial jurisdiction between different states.

The united states in congress assembled shall also have the sole and exclusive right and power of regulating the alloy and value of coin struck by their own authority, or by that of the respective states—fixing the standard of weights and measures throughout the united states—regulating the trade and managing all affairs with the Indians, not members of any of the states, provided that the legislative right of any state within its own limits be not infringed or violated—establishing and regulating post-offices from one state to another, throughout all the united states, and exacting such postage on the papers passing thro' the same as may be requisite to defray the expences of the said office—appointing all officers of the land forces, in the service of the united states, excepting regimental officers—appointing all the officers of the naval forces, and commissioning all officers whatever in the service of the united states—making rules for the government and regulation of the said land and naval forces, and directing their operations.

The united states in congress assembled shall have authority to appoint a committee, to sit in the recess of congress, to be denominated "A Committee of the States," and to consist of one delegate from each state; and to appoint such other committees and civil officers as may be necessary for managing the general affairs of the united states under their direction—to appoint one of their number to preside, provided that no person be allowed to serve in the office of president more than one year in any term of three years; to ascertain the necessary sums of Money to be raised for the service of the united states, and to appropriate and apply the same for defraying the public expences—to borrow money, or emit bills on the credit of the united states, transmitting every half year to the respective states an account of the sums of money so borrowed or emitted—to build and equip a navy—to agree upon the number of land forces, and to make requisitions from each state for its quota, in proportion to the number of white inhabitants in such state; which requisition shall be binding, and thereupon the legislature of each state shall appoint the regimental officers, raise the men and clothe, arm and equip them in a soldier like manner, at the expence of the united states, and the officers and men so clothed, armed and equipped shall march to the place appointed, and within the time agreed on by the united states in congress assembled. But if the united states in congress assembled shall, on consideration of circumstances judge proper that any state should not raise men, or should raise a smaller number than its quota, and that any other state should raise a greater number of men than the quota thereof, such extra number shall be raised, officered, clothed, armed and equipped in the same manner as the quota of such state, unless the legislature of such state shall judge that such extra number cannot be safely spared out of the same, in which case they shall raise, officer, clothe, arm and equip as many of such extra number as they judge can be safely spared. And the officers and men so clothed, armed and equipped, shall march to the place appointed, and within the time agreed on by the united states in congress assembled.

The united states in congress assembled shall never engage in a war, nor grant letters of marque and reprisal in time of peace, nor enter into any treaties or alliances, nor coin money, nor regulate the value thereof, nor ascertain the sums and expences necessary for the defence and welfare of the united states, or any of them, nor emit bills, nor borrow money on the credit of the united states, nor appropriate money, nor agree upon the number of vessels of war, to be built or purchased, or the number of land or sea forces to be raised, nor appoint a commander in chief of the army or navy, unless nine states assent to the same: nor shall a question on any other point, except for adjourning from day to day be determined, unless by the votes of a majority of the united states in congress assembled.

The congress of the united states shall have power to adjourn to any time within the year, and to any place within the united states, so that no period of adjournment be for a longer duration than the space of six Months, and shall publish the Journal of their proceedings monthly, except such parts thereof relating to treaties, alliances or military operations as in their judgment require secrecy; and the yeas and nays of the delegates of each state on any question shall be entered on the Journal, when it is desired by any delegate; and the delegates of a state, or any of them, at his or their request shall be furnished with a transcript of the said Journal, except such parts as are above excepted, to lay before the legislatures of the several states.

[Art. X.] The committee of the states, or any nine of them, shall be authorised to execute, in the recess of congress, such of the powers of congress as the united states in congress assembled, by the consent of nine states, shall from time to time think expedient to vest them with; provided that no power be delegated to the said committee, for the exercise of which, by the articles of confederation, the voice of nine states in the congress of the united states assembled is requisite.

[Art. XI.] Canada acceding to this confederation, and joining in the measures of the united states, shall be admitted into, and entitled to all the advantages of this union: but no other colony shall be admitted into the same, unless such admission be agreed to by nine states.

[Art. XII.] All bills of credit emitted, monies borrowed and debts contracted by, or under the authority of congress, before the assembling of the united states, in pursuance of the present confederation, shall be deemed and considered as a charge against the united states, for payment and satisfaction whereof the said united states, and the public faith are hereby solemnly pledged.

[ART. XIII.] Every state shall abide by the determinations of the united states in congress assembled, on all questions which by this confederation are submitted to them. And the Articles of this confederation shall be inviolably observed by every state, and the union shall be perpetual; nor shall any alteration at any time hereafter be made in any of them; unless such alteration be agreed to in a congress of the united states, and be afterwards confirmed by the legislatures of every state.

And whereas it hath pleased the Great Governor of the World to incline the hearts of the legislatures we respectively represent in congress, to approve of, and to authorize us to ratify the said articles of confederation and perpetual union. Know ye that we the undersigned delegates, by virtue of the power and authority to us given for that purpose, do by these presents, in the name and in behalf of our respective constituents, fully and entirely ratify and confirm each and every of the said articles of confederation and perpetual union, and all and singular the matters and things therein contained: And we do further solemnly plight and engage the faith of our respective constituents, that they shall abide by the determinations of the united states in congress assembled, on all questions, which by the said confederation are submitted to them. And that the articles thereof shall be inviolably observed by the states we respectively represent, and that the union shall be perpetual. In Witness whereof we have hereunto set our hands in Congress. Done at Philadelphia in the state of Pennsylvania the ninth Day of July in the Year of our Lord one Thousand seven Hundred and Seventy-eight, and in the third year of the independence of America.

JOSIAH BARTLETT
JOHN WENTWORTH Junr
August 8th 1778
On the part & behalf of
the State of New Hampshire

JOHN HANCOCK
SAMUEL ADAMS
ELBRIDGE GERRY
FRANCIS DANA
JAMES LOVELL
SAMUEL HOLTEN
On the part and behalf of
the State of Massachusetts Bay

WILLIAM ELLERY
HENRY MARCHANT
JOHN COLLINS
On the part and behalf
of the State of Rhode Island
and Providence Plantations

ROGER SHERMAN
SAMUEL HUNTINGTON
OLIVER WOLCOTT
TITUS HOSMER
ANDREW ADAMS
On the part and behalf of
the State of Connecticut

JA^S DUANE
FRA^S LEWIS
W^M DUER.
GOUV MORRIS

On the Part and Behalf of
the State of New York

JNO WITHERSPOON
NATH^L SCUDDER
On the Part and in Behalf of
the State of New Jersey.
Novr 26, 1778.—

ROB^T MORRIS
DANIEL ROBERDEAU
JON^A BAYARD SMITH.
WILLIAM CLINGAN
JOSEPH REED
22^d July 1778
On the part and behalf of
the State of Pennsylvania

THO M:KEAN
Feby 12 1779
JOHN DICKINSON
May 5th 1779
NICHOLAS VAN DYKE,
On the part & behalf of
the State of Delaware

JOHN HANSON
March 1 1781
DANIEL CARROLL d^o
On the part and behalf
of the State of Maryland

RICHARD HENRY LEE
JOHN BANISTER
THOMAS ADAMS

JN^O HARVIE
FRANCIS LIGHTFOOT LEE
On the Part and Behalf of
the State of Virginia

JOHN PENN
July 21st 1778
CORN^S HARNETT
JN^O WILLIAMS
On the part and Behalf
of the State of N^O Carolina

HENRY LAURENS
WILLIAM HENRY DRAYTON
JN^O MATHEWS
RICH^D HUTSON.
THO^S HEYWARD Junr
On the part & behalf of
the State of South Carolina

JN^O WALTON
24th July 1778
EDW^D TELFAIR.
EDW^D LANGWORTHY
On the part and behalf of
the State of Georgia

Gettysburg Address

Abraham Lincoln delivered the following address on November 19, 1863, at the dedication of the National Cemetery in Gettysburg, Pennsylvania, site of a major Civil War battle. The eloquent speech, which took only two minutes to deliver, soon became one of the world's most-quoted orations.

Four score and seven years ago our fathers brought forth on this continent, a new nation, conceived in Liberty, and dedicated to the proposition that all men are created equal.

Now we are engaged in a great civil war, testing whether that nation, or any nation so conceived and so dedicated, can long endure. We are met on a great battle-field of that war. We have come to dedicate a portion of that field, as a final resting place for those who here gave their lives that that nation might live. It is altogether fitting and proper that we should do this.

But, in a larger sense, we can not dedicate—we can not consecrate—we can not hallow—this ground. The brave men, living and dead, who struggled here, have consecrated it, far above our poor power to add or detract. The world will little note, nor long remember what we say here, but it can never forget what they did here. It is for us the living, rather, to be dedicated here to the unfinished work which they who fought here have thus far so nobly advanced. It is rather for us to be here dedicated to the great task remaining before us—that from these honored dead we take increased devotion to that cause for which they gave the last full measure of devotion—that we here highly resolve that these dead shall not have died in vain—that this nation, under God, shall have a new birth of freedom—and that government of the people, by the people, for the people, shall not perish from the earth.

The Emancipation Proclamation
Issued by President Abraham Lincoln on January 1, 1863

Whereas on the 22d day of September, A.D. 1862, a proclamation was issued by the President of the United States, containing, among other things, the following, to wit:

"That on the 1st day of January, A.D. 1863, all persons held as slaves within any State or designated part of a State the people whereof shall then be in rebellion against the United States shall be then, thenceforward, and forever free; and the Executive Government of the United States, including the military and naval authority thereof, will recognize and maintain the freedom of such persons and will do no act or acts to repress such persons, or any of them, in any efforts they may make for their actual freedom.

"That the executive will on the 1st day of January aforesaid, by proclamation, designate the States and parts of States, if any, in which the people thereof, respectively, shall then be in rebellion against the United States; and the fact that any State or the people thereof shall on that day be in good faith represented in the Congress of the United States by members chosen thereto at elections wherein a majority of the qualified voters of such States shall have participated shall, in the absence of strong countervailing testimony, be deemed conclusive evidence that such State and the people thereof are not then in rebellion against the United States."

Now, therefore, I, Abraham Lincoln, President of the United States, by virtue of the power in me vested as Commander-in-Chief of the Army and Navy of the United States in time of actual armed rebellion against the authority and government of the United States, and as a fit and necessary war measure for suppressing said rebellion, do, on this 1st day of January, A.D. 1863, and in accordance with my purpose so to do, publicly proclaimed for the full period of one hundred days from the first day above mentioned, order and designate as the States and parts of States wherein the people thereof, respectively, are this day in rebellion against the United States the following, to wit:

Arkansas, Texas, Louisiana (except the parishes of St. Bernard, Plaquemines, Jefferson, St. John, St. Charles, St. James, Ascension, Assumption, Terrebonne, Lafourche, St. Mary, St. Martin, and Orleans, including the city of New Orleans), Mississippi, Alabama, Florida, Georgia, South Carolina, North Carolina, and Virginia (except the forty-eight counties designated as West Virginia, and also the counties of Berkeley, Accomac, Northhampton, Elizabeth City, York, Princess Anne, and Norfolk, including the cities of Norfolk and Portsmouth), and which excepted parts are for the present left precisely as if this proclamation were not issued.

And by virtue of the power and for the purpose aforesaid, I do order and declare that all persons held as slaves within said designated States and parts of States are, and henceforward shall be, free; and that the Executive Government of the United States, including the military and naval authorities thereof, will recognize and maintain the freedom of said persons.

And I hereby enjoin upon the people so declared to be free to abstain from all violence, unless in necessary self-defense; and I recommend to them that, in all cases when allowed, they labor faithfully for reasonable wages.

And I further declare and make known that such persons of suitable condition will be received into the armed service of the United States to garrison forts, positions, stations, and other places, and to man vessels of all sorts in said service.

And upon this act, sincerely believed to be an act of justice, warranted by the Constitution upon military necessity, I invoke the considerate judgment of mankind and the gracious favor of Almighty God.

Over the course of the Civil War, nearly 180,000 African Americans wore the Union uniform.

Supreme Court Glossary

Agostini v. Felton (1997)

Decision: The Court decided that it was appropriate to reconsider *Aguilar* v. *Felton* as subsequent cases had undermined several of the assumptions, for example that public employees placed at parochial schools would "inevitably inculcate religion," upon which the decision was based. The Court then found that New York City's Title I Program did not violate any of the criteria used "to evaluate whether government aid has the effect of advancing religion: it does not result in governmental indoctrination; define its recipients by reference to religion; or create an excessive entanglement." As a result, the Court concluded that "a federally funded program providing supplemental, remedial instruction to disadvantaged children on a neutral basis is not invalid under the Establishment Clause when such instruction is given on the premises of sectarian schools by government employees pursuant to a program containing safeguards" against excessive entanglement between government and religion.

American Insurance Association v. Garamendi (2003)

Decision: California's Holocaust Victim Insurance Relief Act interferes with the President's conduct of the nation's foreign policy and is therefore unconstitutional. Although the executive agreements do not specifically prohibit State action, they do pre-empt (override) the State's authority to act on the same subject matter, even in the absence of any direct conflict.

Bethel School District #403 v. Fraser (1986)

(1st Amendment, freedom of speech) A high school student gave a sexually suggestive political speech at a high school assembly to elect student officers. The school administration strongly disciplined the student, Fraser, who argued that school rules unfairly limited his freedom of political speech. Fraser's view was upheld in State court. Washington appealed to the Supreme Court, which found that "it does not follow. . . that simply because the use of an offensive form of expression may not be prohibited to adults making what the speaker considers a political point, the same latitude must be permitted to children in a public school."

Board of Estimate of City of New York v. Morris (1989)

Decision: The reapportionment requirement of "one-person, one-vote" applies to the Board of Estimate. The Board has sufficient legislative functions that its composition must fairly represent city voters on an approximately equal basis. The fact that some members are elected citywide is one factor to be considered in evaluating the fairness of the electoral structure, but it is not determinative. The City's expressed interests—that the Board be effective and that it accommodate natural and political boundaries as well as local interests—does not justify the size of the deviation from the "one-person, one-vote" ideal. The City

could structure the Board in other ways that would further these interests while minimizing the discrimination in voting power.

Bob Jones University v. United States (1983)

(14th Amendment in conflict with 1st Amendment) Bob Jones University, a private school, denied admission to applicants in an interracial marriage or who "espouse" interracial marriage or dating. The Internal Revenue Service then denied tax exempt status to the school because of racial discrimination. The university appealed, claiming their policy was based on the Bible. The Court upheld the IRS ruling, stating that ". . . Government has a fundamental overriding interest in eradicating racial discrimination in education."

Brown v. Board of Education of Topeka (1954)

(14th Amendment, Equal Protection Clause) Probably no twentieth century Supreme Court decision so deeply stirred and changed life in the United States as Brown. A 10-year-old Topeka girl, Linda Brown, was not permitted to attend her neighborhood school because she was an African American. The Court heard arguments about whether segregation itself was a violation of the Equal Protection Clause and found that it was, commenting that "in the field of public education the doctrine of 'separate but equal' has no place. . . . Segregation is a denial of the equal protection of the laws." The decision overturned *Plessy* v. *Ferguson*, 1896.

The Civil Rights Cases (1883)

(14th Amendment, Equal Protection Clause) The Civil Rights Act of 1875 included punishments of businesses that practiced discrimination. The Court ruled on a number of cases involving the Acts in 1883, finding that the Constitution, "while prohibiting discrimination by governments, made no provisions . . . for acts of racial discrimination by private individuals." The decision limited the impact of the Equal Protection Clause, giving tacit approval for segregation in the private sector.

Cruzan v. Missouri (1990)

(14th Amendment, Due Process Clause) After Nancy Beth Cruzan was left in a "persistent vegetative state" by a car accident, Missouri officials refused to comply with her parents' request that the hospital terminate life-support. The Court upheld the State policy under which officials refused to withdraw treatment, rejecting the argument that the Due Process Clause of the 14th Amendment gave the parents the right to refuse treatment on their daughter's behalf. Although individuals have the right to refuse medical treatment, "incompetent" persons are not able to exercise this right; without "clear and convincing" evidence that Cruzan desired the withdrawal of treatment, the State could legally act to preserve her life.

Dennis v. United States (1951)

(1st Amendment, freedom of speech) The Smith Act of 1940 made it a crime for any person to work for the violent overthrow of the United States in peacetime or war. Eleven Communist party leaders, including Dennis, had been convicted of violating the Smith Act, and they appealed. The Court upheld the Act.

Dred Scott v. Sandford (1857)

(5th Amendment, individual rights) This decision upheld property rights over human rights by saying that Dred Scott, a slave, could not become a free man just because he had traveled in "free soil" States with his master. A badly divided nation was further fragmented by the decision. "Free soil" federal laws and the Missouri Compromise line of 1820 were held unconstitutional because they deprived a slave owner of the right to his "property" without just compensation. This narrow reading of the Constitution, a landmark case of the Court, was most clearly stated by Chief Justice Roger B. Taney, a States' rights advocate.

Engel v. Vitale (1962)

(1st Amendment, Establishment Clause) The State Board of Regents of New York required the recitation of a 22-word nonsectarian prayer at the beginning of each school day. A group of parents filed suit against the required prayer, claiming it violated their 1st Amendment rights. The Court found New York's action to be unconstitutional, observing, "There can be no doubt that. . . religious beliefs [are] embodied in the Regent's prayer."

Edwards v. South Carolina (1963)

(1st Amendment, freedom of speech and assembly) A group of mostly African American civil rights activists held a rally at the South Carolina State Capitol, protesting segregation. A hostile crowd gathered and the rally leaders were arrested and convicted for "breach of the peace." The Court overturned the convictions, saying, "The Fourteenth Amendment does not permit a State to make criminal the peaceful expression of unpopular views."

Escobedo v. Illinois (1964)

(6th Amendment, right to counsel) In a case involving a murder confession by a person known to Chicago-area police who was not afforded counsel while under interrogation, the Court extended the "exclusionary rule" to illegal confessions in State court proceedings. Carefully defining an "Escobedo Rule," the Court said, "where. . . the investigation is no longer a general inquiry . . . but has begun to focus on a particular suspect . . . (and where) the suspect has been taken into custody . . . the suspect has requested . . . his lawyer, and the police have not . . . warned him of his right to remain silent, the accused has been denied . . . counsel in violation of the Sixth Amendment."

Ex parte Milligan (1866)

(Article II, executive powers) An Indiana man was arrested, treated as a prisoner of war, and imprisoned by a military court during the Civil War under presidential order. He claimed that his rights to a fair trial were interfered with and that military courts had no authority outside of "conquered territory." He was released because, "the Constitution . . . is a law for rulers and people, equally in war and peace, and covers . . . all . . . men, at all times, and under all circumstances." The Court held that presidential powers to suspend the writ of *habeas corpus* in time of war did not extend to creating another court system run by the military.

Flast v. Cohen (1968)

Decision: The Supreme Court concluded that the rule announced in *Frothingham* v. *Mellon* expressed a practical policy of judicial self-restraint rather than an absolute constitutional limitation on the power of federal courts to hear taxpayer suits. While mere status as a federal taxpayer ordinarily will not give sufficient "standing" to allow a person to challenge the constitutionality of a federal law, there may be times when taxpayers are appropriate plaintiffs. *Flast* v. *Cohen*, in which plaintiffs argued that the First Amendment specifically prohibited taxing them in order to support religious activities, was one in which their role as taxpayers was well suited to the challenge they sought to assert. The Court ruled that they had standing to sue, and allowed them to proceed with their case.

Furman v. Georgia (1972)

(8th Amendment, capital punishment) Three different death penalty cases, including *Furman*, raised the question of racial imbalances in the use of death sentences by State courts. Furman had been convicted and sentenced to death in Georgia. In deciding to overturn existing State death-penalty laws, the Court noted that there was an "apparent arbitrariness of the use of the sentence. . . ." Many States rewrote their death-penalty statutes and these were generally upheld in *Gregg* v. *Georgia*, 1976.

Gibbons v. Ogden (1824)

(Supremacy Clause) This decision involved a careful examination of the power of Congress to "regulate interstate commerce." Aaron Ogden's exclusive New York ferry license gave him the right to operate steamboats to and from New York. He said that Thomas Gibbons's federal "coasting license" did not include "landing rights" in New York City. The Court invalidated the New York licensing regulations, holding that federal regulations should take precedence under the Supremacy Clause. The decision strengthened the power of the United States to regulate any interstate business relationship. Federal regulation of the broadcasting industry, oil pipelines, and banking are all based on *Gibbons*.

Gideon v. Wainwright (1963)

(6th Amendment, right to counsel) In 1961 a Florida court found Clarence Earl Gideon guilty of breaking and entering and sentenced him to five years in prison. Gideon appealed his case to the Supreme Court on the basis that he had been unconstitutionally denied counsel during his trial due to Florida's policy of only providing appointed counsel in capital cases. The Court granted Gideon a new trial, and he was found not guilty with the help of a court-appointed attorney. The "Gideon Rule" upheld the 6th Amendment's guarantee of counsel of all poor persons facing a felony charge, a further incorporation of Bill of Rights guarantees into State constitutions.

Gitlow v. New York (1925)

(1st Amendment, freedom of speech) A New York socialist, Gitlow, was convicted under a State law on "criminal anarchy" for distributing copies of a "left-wing manifesto." For the first time, the Court considered whether the 1st Amendment applied to State laws. The case helped to establish what came to be known as the "incorporation" doctrine, under which, it was argued, the provisions of the 1st Amendment were "incorporated" by the 14th Amendment, thus applying to State as well as federal laws. Although New York law was not overruled in this case, the decision clearly indicated that the Supreme Court could make such a ruling. See also *Powell v. Alabama*, 1932.

Goss v. Lopez (1975)

(14th Amendment, Due Process Clause) Ten Ohio students were suspended from their schools without hearings. The students challenged the suspensions, claiming that the absence of a preliminary hearing violated their 14th Amendment right to due process. The Court agreed with the students, holding that "having chosen to extend the right to an education. . . Ohio may not withdraw that right on grounds of misconduct, absent fundamentally fair procedures to determine whether the misconduct has occurred, and must recognize a student's legitimate entitlement to a public education as a property interest that is protected by the Due Process Clause."

Gregg v. Georgia (1976)

(8th Amendment, cruel and unusual punishment) A Georgia jury sentenced Troy Gregg to death after finding him guilty on two counts each of murder and armed robbery. Gregg appealed the sentence, claiming that it violated the "cruel and unusual punishment" clause of the 8th Amendment and citing *Furman v. Georgia*, 1972, in which the court held that Georgia's application of the death penalty was unfair and arbitrary. However, the Court upheld Gregg's sentence, stating for the first time that "punishment of death does not invariably violate the Constitution."

Griswold v. Connecticut (1965)

(14th Amendment, Due Process Clause) A Connecticut law forbade the use of "any drug, medicinal article, or instrument for the purpose of preventing conception." Griswold, director of Planned Parenthood in New Haven, was arrested for counseling married persons and, after conviction, appealed. The Court overturned the Connecticut law, saying that "various guarantees (of the Constitution) create zones of privacy. . ." and questioning, ". . .would we allow the police to search the sacred precincts of marital bedrooms. . . ?" The decision is significant for raising for more careful inspection the concept of "unenumerated rights" in the 9th Amendment, later central to *Roe v. Wade*, 1973.

Grutter v. Bollinger; Gratz v. Bollinger (2003)

Decision: *(Gratz)* The policy of the University of Michigan, giving undergraduate applicants twenty points just for being a member of a racial or ethnic group, violates the Equal Protection Clause of the 14th Amendment. The policy discriminates on the basis of race, but is not narrowly tailored to create a diverse student body. *(Grutter)* The

policy of the University of Michigan's law school, considering an applicant's racial or ethnic background as just one factor in attempting to admit a diverse student body, is constitutional. Because the law school considers each applicant individually, and does not assign an inflexible value for race, the policy creates a diverse student body without discriminating on the basis of race.

Hazelwood School District v. Kuhlmeier (1988)

(1st Amendment, freedom of speech) In 1983, the principal of Hazelwood East High School in Missouri removed two articles from the upcoming issue of the student newspaper, deeming their content "inappropriate, personal, sensitive, and unsuitable for student readers." Several students sued the school district, claiming that their 1st Amendment right to freedom of expression had been violated. The Court upheld the principal's action, stating that "a school need not tolerate student speech that is inconsistent with its basic educational mission, even though the government could not censor similar speech outside the school." School officials had full control over school-sponsored activities "so long as their actions are reasonably related to legitimate pedagogical concerns. . . ."

Heart of Atlanta Motel, Inc. v. United States (1964)

Decision: The Court ruled that Congress could outlaw racial segregation of private facilities that are engaged in interstate commerce. The Court's decision stated, "If it is interstate commerce that feels the pinch, it does not matter how 'local' the operation which applies the squeeze. . . . The power of Congress to promote interstate commerce also includes the power to regulate the local incidents thereof, including local activities. . . which have a substantial and harmful effect upon that commerce."

Hutchinson v. Proxmire (1979)

Decision: The Court held that the Speech or Debate Clause gives members of Congress immunity from suit for defamatory statements made within the legislative chambers, but the privilege does not extend to comments made in other locations, even if they merely repeat what was said in Congress. The newsletters and press release were not within the deliberative process nor were they essential to the deliberation of the Senate. They also were not part of the "informing function" of members of Congress, since they were not a part of legislative function or process. The comments were merely designed to convey information on the Senator's individual positions and beliefs. Finally, although Hutchinson had received extensive attention in the media as a result of his receipt of the Golden Fleece Award, he was not a public figure prior to that controversy and thus is entitled to the greater protection against defamation that is extended to non-public figures. The fact that the public may have an interest in governmental expenditures does not make Hutchinson himself a public figure.

Illinois v. Wardlow (2000)

Decision: The Supreme Court refused to say that flight from the police will always justify a stop or that it will never do so. Instead, the Court ruled that flight can be an important factor in determining whether police have "reasonable suspicion" to stop a suspect. The trial court will have to determine in each case whether the information available to the police officers, including the fact of a suspect's flight, was sufficient to support the stop.

In Re Gault (1966)

(14th Amendment, Due Process Clause) Prior to the Gault case, proceedings against juvenile offenders were generally handled as "family law," not "criminal law" and provided few due process guarantees. Gerald Gault was assigned to six years in a State juvenile detention facility for an alleged obscene phone call. He was not provided counsel and not permitted to confront or cross-examine the principal witness. The Court overturned the juvenile proceedings and required that States provide juveniles "some of the due process guarantees of adults," including a right to a phone call, to counsel, to cross-examine, to confront their accuser, and to be advised of their right to silence.

Johnson v. Santa Clara Transportation Agency (1987)

(Discrimination) Under their affirmative action plan, the Transportation Agency in Santa Clara, California, was authorized to "consider as one factor the sex of a qualified applicant" in an effort to combat the significant under-representation of women in certain job classifications. When the Agency promoted Diane Joyce, a qualified woman, over Paul Johnson, a qualified man, for the job of road dispatcher, Johnson sued, claiming that the Agency's consideration of the sex of the applicants violated Title VII of the Civil Rights Act of 1964. The Court upheld the Agency's promotion policy, arguing that the affirmative action plan created no "absolute bar" to the advancement of men but rather represented "a moderate, flexible, case-by-case approach to effecting a gradual improvement in the representation of minorities and women . . . in the Agency's work force, and [was] fully consistent with Title VII."

Korematsu v. United States (1944)

Decision: The Court upheld the military order in light of the circumstances presented by World War II. "Pressing public necessity may sometimes justify the existence of restrictions which curtail the civil rights of a single racial group." The Court noted, however, that racial antagonism itself could never form a legitimate basis for the restrictions.

Lemon v. Kurtzman (1971)

(1st Amendment, Establishment Clause) In overturning State laws regarding aid to church-supported schools in this and a similar Rhode Island case, the Court created the *Lemon* test limiting ". . . excessive government entanglement with religion." The Court noted that any State law about aid to religion must meet three criteria: (1) purpose of the aid must be clearly secular, (2) its primary effect must neither advance nor inhibit religion, and (3) it must avoid "excessive entanglement of government with religion."

Mapp v. Ohio (1962)

(4th and 14th Amendments, illegal evidence and Due Process Clause) Admitting evidence gained by illegal searches was permitted by some States before *Mapp*. Cleveland police raided Dollree Mapp's home without a warrant and found obscene materials. She appealed her conviction, saying that the 4th and 14th Amendments protected her against improper police behavior. The Court agreed, extending "exclusionary rule" protections to citizens in State courts, saying that the prohibition against unreasonable searches would be "meaningless" unless evidence gained in such searches was "excluded." *Mapp* developed the concept of "incorporation" begun in *Gitlow* v. *New York,* 1925.

Marbury v. Madison (1803)

(Article III, judicial powers) After defeat in the 1800 election, President Adams appointed many Federalists to the federal courts, but James Madison, the new secretary of state, refused to deliver the commissions. William Marbury, one of the appointees, asked the Supreme Court to enforce the delivery of his commission based on a provision of the Judiciary Act of 1789 that allowed the Court to hear such cases on original jurisdiction. The Court refused Marbury's request, finding that the relevant portion of the Judiciary Act was in conflict with the Constitution. This decision, written by Chief Justice Marshall, established the evaluation of federal laws' constitutionality, or "judicial review," as a power of the Supreme Court.

McCulloch v. Maryland (1819)

(Article I, Section 8, Necessary and Proper Clause) Called the "Bank of the United States" case. A Maryland law required federally chartered banks to use only a special paper to print paper money, which amounted to a tax. James McCulloch, the cashier of the Baltimore branch of the bank, refused to use the paper, claiming that States could not tax the Federal Government. The Court declared the Maryland law unconstitutional, commenting ". . . the power to tax implies the power to destroy."

Miranda v. Arizona (1966)

(5th, 6th, and 14th Amendments, rights of the accused) Arrested for kidnapping and sexual assault, Ernesto Miranda signed a confession including a statement that he had "full knowledge of [his] legal rights. . . ." After conviction, he appealed, claiming that without counsel and without warnings, the confession was illegally gained. The Court agreed with Miranda that "he must be warned prior to any questioning that he has the right to remain silent, that anything he says can be used against him in a court of law, that he has the right to. . . an attorney and that if he cannot afford an attorney one will be appointed for him. . . ." Although later modified by *Nix* v. *Williams,* 1984, and other cases, *Miranda* firmly upheld citizen rights to fair trials in State courts.

New Jersey v. T.L.O. (1985)

(4th and 14th Amendments) After T.L.O., a New Jersey high school student, denied an accusation that she had been smoking in the school lavatory, a vice-principal searched her purse and found cigarettes, marijuana, and evidence that T.L.O. had been involved in marijuana dealing at the school. T.L.O. was then sentenced to probation by a juvenile court, but appealed on the grounds that the evidence against her had been obtained by an "unreasonable" search. The Court rejected T.L.O.'s arguments, stating that the school had a "legitimate need to maintain an environment in which learning can take place," and that to do this "requires some easing of the restrictions to which searches by public authorities are ordinarily subject. . ." The Court thus created a "reasonable suspicion" rule for school searches, a change from the "probable cause" requirement in the wider society.

New York Times v. United States (1971)

(1st Amendment, freedom of the press) In 1971 *The New York Times* obtained copies of classified Defense Department documents, later known as the "Pentagon Papers," which revealed instances in which the Johnson Administration had deceived Congress and the American people regarding U.S. policies during the Vietnam War. A U.S. district court issued an injunction against the publication of the documents, claiming that it might endanger national security. On appeal, the Supreme Court cited the 1st Amendment guarantee of a free press and refused to uphold the injunction against publication, observing that it is the obligation of the government to prove that actual harm to the nation's security would be caused by the publication. The decision limited "prior restraint" of the press.

Nixon v. Fitzgerald (1982)

Decision: The Court ruled that a President or former President is entitled to absolute immunity from liability based on his official acts. The President must be able to act forcefully and independently, without fear of liability. Diverting the President's energies with concerns about private lawsuits could impair the effective functioning of government. The President's absolute immunity extends to all acts within the "outer perimeter" of his duties of office, since otherwise he would be required to litigate over the nature of the acts and the scope of his duties in each case. The remedy of impeachment, the vigilant scrutiny of the press, the Congress, and the public, and presidential desire to earn reelection and concern with historical legacy all protect against presidential wrongdoing.

Nixon v. Shrink Missouri Government PAC (2000)

Decision: In *Buckley v. Valeo*, 1976, the Supreme Court had upheld a $1000 limit on contributions by individuals to candidates for federal office. In *Nixon v. Shrink Missouri Government PAC*, the Court concluded that large contributions will sometimes create actual corruption, and that voters will be suspicious of the fairness of a political process that allows wealthy donors to contribute large amounts. The Court concluded that the Missouri contribution limits were appropriate to correct this problem and did not impair the ability of candidates to communicate their messages to the voters and to mount an effective campaign.

Olmstead v. United States (1928)

(4th Amendment, electronic surveillance) Olmstead was engaged in the illegal sale of alcohol. Much of the evidence against him was gained through a wiretap made without a warrant. Olmstead argued that he had "a reasonable expectation of privacy," and that the *Weeks v. United States* decision of 1914 should be applied to exclude the evidence gained by the wiretap. The Court disagreed, saying that Olmstead intended "to project his voice to those quite outside . . . and that . . . nothing tangible was taken." Reversed by subsequent decisions, this case contains the first usage of the concept of "reasonable expectation of privacy" that would mark later 4th Amendment decisions.

Oregon v. Mitchell (1970)

Decision: The Supreme Court was unable to issue a single opinion of the Court supported by a majority of the justices. However, in a series of separate opinions, differing majority groups agreed that (1) the 18-year-old minimum-age requirement of the Voting Rights Act Amendments is valid for national elections but not for State and local elections; (2) the literacy test provision is valid in order to remedy discrimination against minorities; and (3) the residency and absentee balloting provisions are a valid Congressional regulation of presidential elections.

Plessy v. Ferguson (1896)

(14th Amendment, Equal Protection Clause) A Louisiana law required separate seating for white and African American citizens on public railroads, a form of segregation. Homer Plessy argued that his right to "equal protection of the laws" was violated. The Court held that segregation was permitted if facilities were equal. The Court interpreted the 14th Amendment as "not intended to give Negroes social equality but only political and civil equality. . . ." The Louisiana law was seen as a "reasonable exercise of (State) police power. . ." Segregated public facilities were permitted until *Plessy* was overturned by the *Brown v. Board of Education* case of 1954.

Powell v. Alabama (1932)

(6th Amendment, right to counsel) The case involved the "Scottsboro boys," seven African American men accused of sexual assault. This case was a landmark in the development of a "fundamentals of fairness" doctrine of the Court over the next 40 years. The Scottsboro boys were quickly prosecuted without the benefit of counsel and sentenced to death. The Court overturned the decision, stating that poor people facing the death penalty in State courts must be provided counsel, and commenting, ". . . there are certain principles of Justice which adhere to the very idea of free government, which no [State] may disregard." The case was another step toward incorporation of the Bill of Rights into State constitutions.

Printz v. United States (1997)

Decision: The Court ruled that the Brady Act's interim provision requiring certain State or local law enforcement agents to perform background checks on prospective handgun purchasers was unconstitutional. Although no provision of the Constitution deals explicitly with federal authority to compel State officials to execute federal law, a review of the Constitution's structure and of prior Supreme Court decisions leads to the conclusion that Congress does not have this power.

Reno v. Condon (2000)

Decision: The Court upheld the federal law that forbids States from selling addresses, telephone numbers, and other information that drivers put on license applications. They agreed with the Federal Government that information, including motor vehicle license information, is an "article of commerce" in the interstate stream of business and therefore is subject to regulation by Congress. The Court emphasized that the statute did not impose on the States any obligation to pass particular laws or policies and thus did not interfere with the States' sovereign functions.

Republican Party of Minnesota v. White (2002)

Decision: The Supreme Court decided that the State prohibition on "announcing" a judicial candidate's views violates the 1st Amendment. It unduly restricts the candidates' rights of free speech without adequately furthering the expressed goal of improving judicial impartiality and the appearance of impartiality. The government may not restrict speech based on its content, as this rule does. In addition, the government may not restrict speech about candidates' qualifications for office, which the rule also does. In addition, the rule is not well designed to preserve impartiality, since it has no effect on the candidate's beliefs. Finally, the lack of any longstanding tradition of such a rule shows there is no historical presumption of constitutionality.

Roe v. Wade (1973)

(9th Amendment, right to privacy) A Texas woman challenged a State law forbidding the artificial termination of a pregnancy, saying that she "had a fundamental right to privacy." The Court upheld a woman's right to choose in this case, noting that the State's "important and legitimate interest in protecting the potentiality of human life" became "compelling" at the end of the first trimester, and that before then, ". . . the attending physician, in consultation with his patient, is free to determine, without regulation by the State, that . . . the patient's pregnancy should be terminated." The decision struck down the State regulation of abortion in the first three months of pregnancy and was modified by *Planned Parenthood of Southeastern PA v. Casey*, 1992.

Rostker v. Goldberg (1981)

Decision: The Court ruled that women did not have to be included in the draft registration. The purpose of having draft registration was to prepare for the actual draft of combat troops if they should be needed. Since Congress and the President had both consistently decided not to use women in combat positions, it was not necessary for women to register either. The Court also noted that the role of women in the armed services had been debated extensively in the Congress, and concluded that the legislature had reached a thoughtful, reasoned conclusion on this issue.

Roth v. United States (1951)

(1st Amendment, freedom of the press) A New York man named Roth operated a business that used the mail to invite people to buy materials considered obscene by postal inspectors. The Court, in its first consideration of censorship of obscenity, created the "prevailing community standards" rule, which required a consideration of the work as a whole. In its decision, the Court defined as obscene that which offended "the average person, applying contemporary community standards." In a case decided the same day, the Court applied the same "test" to State obscenity laws.

Rush Prudential HMO, Inc. v. Moran (2002)

Decision: The Supreme Court decided that ERISA does not preempt the Illinois medical-review statute. The statute regulates insurance, which is one of the functions HMOs perform. Although HMOs provide healthcare as well as insurance, the statute does not require choosing a single or primary function of an HMO. Congress has long recognized that HMOs are risk-bearing organizations subject to state regulation. Finally, allowing States to regulate the insurance aspects of HMOs will not interfere with the desire of Congress for uniform national standards under ERISA.

Schenck v. United States (1919)

(1st Amendment, freedom of speech) Charles Schenck was an officer of an antiwar political group who was arrested for alleged violations of the Espionage Act of 1917, which made active opposition to the war a crime. He had urged thousands of young men called to service by the draft act to resist and to avoid induction. The Court limited free speech in time of war, stating that Schenck's words, under the circumstances, presented a "clear and present danger. . . ." Although later decisions modified the decision, the Schenck case created a precedent that 1st Amendment guarantees were not absolute.

School District of Abington Township, Pennsylvania v. Schempp (1963)

(1st Amendment, Establishment Clause) A Pennsylvania State law required reading from the Bible each day at school as an all-school activity. Some parents objected and sought legal remedy. When the case reached the Court, it agreed with the parents, saying that the Establishment Clause and Free Exercise Clause both forbade States from engaging in religious activity. The Court created a rule holding that if the purpose and effect of a law "is the advancement or inhibition of religion," it "exceeds the scope of legal power."

Shelley v. Kraemer (1948)

Decision: The Court ruled that "in granting judicial enforcement of the restrictive agreements . . . the States have denied petitioners the equal protection of the laws. . . ." No individual has the right under the Constitution to demand that a State take action that would result in the denial of equal protection to other individuals. The Court rejected the respondents' argument that, since state courts would also enforce restrictive covenants against white owners, enforcement of covenants against black owners did not constitute a denial of equal protection. "Equal protection of the laws is not achieved through indiscriminate imposition of inequalities."

Sheppard v. Maxwell (1966)

(14th Amendment, Due Process Clause) Dr. Samuel Sheppard was convicted of murdering his wife in a trial widely covered by national news media. Sheppard appealed his conviction, claiming that the pretrial publicity had made it impossible to get a fair trial. The Court rejected the arguments about "press freedom," overturned his conviction, and ordered a new trial. As a result of the Sheppard decision, some judges have issued "gag" orders limiting pretrial publicity.

Tahoe-Sierra Preservation Council v. Tahoe Regional Planning Agency (2002)

Decision: The 32-month moratorium imposed by the Tahoe Regional Planning Agency on development in the Lake Tahoe Basin between Nevada and California is not a taking of property for which compensation is required. It is impossible in the abstract to say how long a restriction would be permissible. Although 32 months is a long moratorium, it is not unreasonable in this case and does not restrict the property owners' economic use of their property sufficiently to amount to a taking for which compensation must be paid.

Tennessee Valley Authority v. Hill (1978)

(Article I, Section 8, Necessary and Proper Clause) In 1975 the secretary of the interior found that the Tennessee Valley Authority's work on the Tellico Dam would destroy the endangered snail darter's habitat in violation of the Endangered Species Act of 1975. When the TVA refused to stop work on the project, local residents sued and won an injunction against completion of the dam from the federal court of appeals. The TVA appealed, arguing that the project should be completed since it had already been underway when the Endangered Species Act had passed and, with full knowledge of the circumstances of the endangered fish, Congress had continued to appropriate money for the dam in every year since the Act's passage. However, the Supreme Court found the injunction against the TVA's completion of the dam to be proper, stating "examination of the language, history, and structure of the legislation. . . indicates beyond doubt that Congress intended endangered species to be afforded the highest of priorities."

Tinker v. Des Moines School District (1969)

Decision: The Court upheld the students' First Amendment rights. Because students do not "shed their constitutional rights to freedom of speech or expression at the schoolhouse gate," schools must show a possibility of "substantial disruption" before free speech can be limited at school. Students may express personal opinions as long as they do not materially disrupt classwork, create substantial disorder, or interfere with the rights of others. In this case, the wearing of black armbands was a "silent, passive expression of opinion" without these side effects and thus constitutionally could not be prohibited by the school.

U.S. Term Limits, Inc. v. Thornton (1995)

Decision: The Arkansas amendment preventing any person who had already served three terms as U.S. representative or two terms as U.S. senator from being listed on the ballot violates Article I, Section 2, Clause 2 and Section 3, Clause 3 of the Federal Constitution. The Arkansas law in effect established term limits for members of Congress, but the Constitution is the sole source of qualifications for membership. Such limits can only be set by an amendment to the Federal Constitution.

United States v. American Library Association (2003)

Decision: Requiring public libraries to install filters to block obscene or pornographic Internet sites as a condition for obtaining federal funds for Internet access does not violate the 1st Amendment. Congress' substantial interest in protecting children from harmful materials justifies the minimal interference with free speech caused when library users are forced to request access to a specific site.

United States v. Amistad (1841)

In 1839 two Spaniards purchased a group of kidnapped Africans and put them aboard the schooner *Amistad* for a journey from Cuba to Principe. The Africans overpowered the ship's crew, killing two men, and ordered the Spaniards to steer towards Africa. The crew steered instead toward the United States coast, where the U.S. brig *Washington* seized the ship, freeing the Spaniards and imprisoning the Africans. A series of petitions to the courts ensued, in which the Spaniards claimed the Africans as their property, and the Americans who had seized the ship claimed a share of the cargo, including the Africans, as their lawful salvage. The Court, however, declared that the Africans were not property and issued a decree that the unlawfully kidnapped Africans "be and are hereby declared to be free."

United States v. Eichman (1990)

Decision: The Court agreed with the trial courts' rulings that the Flag Protection Act violated the 1st Amendment. Flag-burning constitutes expressive conduct, and thus is entitled to constitutional protection. The Act prevents protesters from using the flag to express their opposition to governmental policies and activities. Although the protesters' ideas may be offensive or disagreeable to many people, the government may not prohibit them from expressing those ideas.

United States v. General Dynamics Corp. (1974)

A deep-mining coal producer, General Dynamics Corp., acquired control of a strip-mining coal producer, United Electric Coal Companies. The Government filed suit against the company, claiming that the acquisition violated the Clayton Act by limiting competition in coal sales and production. The Court rejected the Government's argument, finding that, although the acquisition may have increased concentration of ownership, it did not threaten to substantially lessen competition and was therefore not in violation of the Clayton Act.

United States v. Leon (1984)

(4th Amendment, exclusionary rule) Police in Burbank, California, gathered evidence in a drug-trafficking investigation using a search warrant issued by a state court judge. Later a District Court found that the warrant had been improperly issued and granted a motion to suppress the evidence gathered under the warrant. The Government appealed the decision, claiming that the exclusionary rule should not apply in cases where law enforcement officers acted in good faith, believing the warrant to be valid. The Court agreed and established the "good-faith exception" to the exclusionary rule, finding that the rule should not be applied to bar evidence "obtained by officers acting in reasonable reliance on a search warrant issued by a detached and neutral magistrate but ultimately found to be invalid."

United States v. Lopez (1990)

(Article I, Section 8, Commerce Clause) Alfonzo Lopez, a Texas high school student, was convicted of carrying a weapon in a school zone under the Gun-Free School Zones Act of 1990. He appealed his conviction on the basis that the Act, which forbids "any individual knowingly to possess a firearm at a place that [he] knows. . . is a school zone," exceeded Congress's legislative power under the Commerce Clause. The Court agreed that the Act was unconstitutional, stating that to uphold the legislation would "bid fair to convert congressional Commerce Clause authority to a general police power of the sort held only by the States."

United States v. Nixon (1974)

(Separation of powers) During the investigation of the Watergate scandal, in which members of President Nixon's administration were accused of participating in various illegal activities, a special prosecutor subpoenaed tapes of conversations between Nixon and his advisors. Nixon refused to release the tapes but was overruled by the Court, which ordered him to surrender the tapes, rejecting his arguments that they were protected by "executive privilege." The President's "generalized interest in confidentiality" was subordinate to "the fundamental demands of due process of law in the fair administration of criminal justice."

Wallace v. Jaffree (1985)

(1st Amendment, Establishment Clause) An Alabama law authorized a one-minute period of silence in all public schools "for meditation or voluntary prayer." A group of parents, including Jaffree, challenged the constitutionality of the statute, claiming it violated the Establishment Clause of the 1st Amendment. The Court agreed with Jaffree and struck down the Alabama law, determining that "the State's endorsement. . . of prayer activities at the beginning of each schoolday is not consistent with the established principle that the government must pursue a course of complete neutrality toward religion."

Walz v. Tax Commission of the City of New York (1970)

(1st Amendment, Establishment Clause) State and local governments routinely exempt church property from taxes. Walz claimed that such exemptions were a "support of religion," a subsidy by government. The Court disagreed, noting that such exemptions were just an example of a "benevolent neutrality" between government and churches, not a support of religion. Governments must avoid taxing churches because taxation would give government a "control" over religion, prohibited by the "wall of separation of church and state" noted in *Everson* v. *Board of Education*, 1947.

Watchtower Bible & Tract Society v. Village of Stratton (2001)

Decision: The Court ruled the Village's ordinance requiring canvassers to get a permit to be unconstitutional. Although a municipality may have a legitimate interest in regulating door-to-door solicitation, there must be a balance between furthering that interest and restricting 1st Amendment rights. The ordinance restricts religious or political speech, and thus needs strong justification to be valid. Because the ordinance is not restricted to commercial activities, it is broader than necessary to protect fraud. Residents have other ways to protect their privacy—they can post "no solicitation" signs or refuse to talk with unwelcome visitors. Finally, the 1st Amendment protects the right to anonymous expressions of religious or political belief.

Watkins v. United States (1957)

Decision: The Court held that Watkins was not given a fair opportunity to determine whether he was within his rights in refusing to answer the Committee's questions. Congress has no authority to expose the private affairs of individuals unless justified by a specific function of Congress. Congress's investigative powers are broad but not unlimited, and must not infringe on 1st Amendment rights of speech, political belief, or association. When witnesses are forced by subpoena to testify, the subject of Congressional inquiry must be articulated in the Committee's charter or explained at the time of testimony if 1st Amendment rights are in jeopardy.

West Virginia Board of Education v. Barnette (1943)

(1st Amendment, freedom of religion) During World War II the West Virginia Board of Education required all students to take part in a daily flag saluting ceremony or else face expulsion. Jehovah's Witnesses objected to the compulsory salute, which they felt would force them to break their religion's doctrine against the worship of any "graven image." The Court struck down the rule, agreeing that a compulsory flag salute violated the 1st Amendment's exercise of religion clause and stating "no official, high or petty, can prescribe what shall be orthodox in politics, nationalism, religion, or other matters of opinion. . . ."

Board of Education of Westside Community Schools v. Mergens (1990)

(1st Amendment, Establishment Clause) A request by Bridget Mergens to form a student Christian religious group at school was denied by an Omaha high school principal. Mergens took legal action, claiming that a 1984 federal law required "equal access" for student religious groups. The Court ordered the school to permit the club, stating, "a high school does not have to permit any extracurricular activities, but when it does, the school is bound by the . . . [Equal Access] Act of 1984. Allowing students to meet on campus and discuss religion is constitutional because it does not amount to 'State sponsorship of a religion.'"

Wisconsin v. Yoder (1972)

(1st Amendment, Free Exercise Clause) Members of the Amish religious sect in Wisconsin objected to sending their children to public schools after the eighth grade, claiming that such exposure of the children to another culture would endanger the group's self-sufficient agrarian lifestyle essential to their religious faith. The Court agreed with the Amish, while noting that the Court must move carefully to weigh the State's "legitimate social concern when faced with religious claim for exemption from generally applicable educational requirements."

Glossary

Absentee voting Provisions made for those unable to get to their regular polling places on election day. p. 189

Acquit Find not guilty of a charge. p. 311

Act of admission A congressional act admitting a new State to the Union. p. 100

Adjourn Suspend, as in a session of Congress. p. 264

Administration The officials in the executive branch of a government and their policies and principles. p. 416

Affirmative action A policy that requires most employers take positive steps to remedy the effects of past discriminations. p. 609

Albany Plan of Union Plan proposed by Benjamin Franklin in 1754 that aimed to unite the 13 colonies for trade, military, and other purposes; the plan was turned down by the colonies and the Crown. pp. 35–36

Alien Foreign-born resident, or noncitizen. pp. 534, 614

Ambassador An official representative of the United States appointed by the President to represent the nation in matters of diplomacy. p. 471

Amendment A change in, or addition to, a constitution or law. p. 72

Amnesty A blanket pardon offered to a group of law violators. p. 408

Anti-Federalists Those persons who opposed the ratification of the Constitution in 1787–1788. p. 56

Appellate jurisdiction The authority of a court to review decisions of inferior (lower) courts; *see* original jurisdiction. pp. 509, 709

Apportion Distribute, as in seats in a legislative body. p. 267

Appropriate Assign to a particular use. p. 305

Articles Numbered sections of a document. The unamended Constitution is divided into seven articles. p. 65

Articles of Confederation Plan of government adopted by the Continental Congress after the American Revolution; established "a firm league of friendship" among the States, but allowed few important powers to the central government. p. 44

Assemble To gather with one another in order to express views on public matters. p. 555

Assessment The process of determining the value of property to be taxed. p. 742

Assimilation The process by which people of one culture merge into, and become part of, another culture. p. 597

At-large election Election of an officeholder by the voters of an entire governmental unit (e.g. a State or country) rather than by the voters of a district or subdivision. p. 270

Attorney General The head of the Department of Justice. p. 424

Authoritarian A form of government in which those in power hold absolute and unchallengeable authority over the people. All dictatorships are authoritarian. p. 13

Autocracy A form of government in which a single person holds unlimited political power. p. 13

Bail A sum of money that the accused may be required to post (deposit with the court) as a guarantee that he or she will appear in court at the proper time. p. 585

Balance the ticket When a presidential candidate chooses a running mate who can strengthen his chance of being elected by virtue of certain ideological, geographic, racial, ethnic, gender, or other characteristics. p. 362

Ballot The device voters use to register a choice in an election. p. 190

Bankruptcy The legal proceeding by which a bankrupt person's assets are distributed among those to whom he or she owes debts. p. 300

Bench trial A trial in which the judge alone hears the case. pp. 580, 705

Bicameral An adjective describing a legislative body composed of two chambers. p. 31

Bill A proposed law presented to a legislative body for consideration. p. 334

Bill of Attainder A legislative act that inflicts punishment without a court trial. p. 577

Bill of Rights The first ten amendments to the Constitution. pp. 76, 532

Bipartisan Supported by two parties. pp. 120, 440

Blanket primary A voting process in which voters receive a long ballot containing the names of all contenders, regardless of party, and can vote however they choose. p. 183

Block grant One type of federal grants-in-aid for some particular but broadly defined area of public policy; *see* grants-in-aid. p. 103

Bourgeoisie The social class between the aristocracy and the proletariat class; the middle class. p. 667

Boycott Refusal to buy or sell certain products or services. p. 36

Budget A financial plan for the use of money, personnel, and property. p. 744

Bureaucracy A large, complex administrative structure that handles the everyday business of an organization. p. 414

Bureaucrat A person who works for a bureaucratic organization; *see* bureaucracy. p. 415

Cabinet Presidential advisory body, traditionally made up of the heads of the executive departments and other officers. p. 81

Capital All the human-made resources that are used to produce goods and services. p. 659

Capitalist Someone who owns capital and puts it to productive use; often applied to people who own large businesses. p. 659

Capital punishment The death penalty. p. 587

Categorical grant One type of federal grants-in-aid; made for some specific, closely defined, purpose; *see* grants-in-aid. p. 102

Caucus As a nominating device, a group of like-minded people who meet to select the candidates they will support in an upcoming election. p. 180

Censure Issue a formal condemnation. p. 312

Centrally planned economy A system in which government bureaucrats plan how an economy will develop over a period of years. p. 669

Certificate A method of putting a case before the Supreme Court; used when a lower court is not clear about the procedure or rule of law that should apply in a case and asks the Supreme Court to certify the answer to a specific question. p. 521

Charter A city's basic law, its constitution; a written grant of authority from the king. pp. 31, 720

Checks and balances System of overlapping the powers of the legislative, executive, and judicial branches to permit each branch to check the actions of the others; *see* separation of powers. p. 67

Chief administrator Term for the President as head of the administration of the Federal Government. p. 355

Chief citizen Term for the President as the representative of the people, working for the public interest. p. 355

Chief diplomat Term for the President as the main architect of foreign policy and spokesperson to other countries. p. 355

Chief executive Term for the President as vested with the executive power of the United States. p. 354

Chief legislator Term for the President as architect of public policy and the one who sets the agenda for Congress. p. 355

Chief of party Term for the President as the leader of his or her political party. p. 355

Chief of state Term for the President as the ceremonial head of the United States, the symbol of all the people of the nation. p. 354

Citizen A member of a state or nation who owes allegiance to it by birth or naturalization and is entitled to full civil rights. p. 613

Civil case A case involving a noncriminal matter such as a contract dispute or a claim of patent infringement. p. 513

Civil law The portion of the law relating to human conduct, to disputes between private parties, and to disputes between private parties and government not covered by criminal law. p. 704

Civil liberties The guarantees of the safety of persons, opinions, and property from the arbitrary acts of government, including freedom of speech and freedom of religion. p. 533

Civil rights A term used for those positive acts of government that seek to make constitutional guarantees a reality for all people, e.g., prohibitions of discrimination. p. 533

Civil service Those civilian employees who perform the administrative work of government. p. 437

Civilian tribunal A court operating as part of the judicial branch, entirely separate from the military establishment. p. 525

Clemency Mercy or leniency granted to an offender by a chief executive; *see* pardon and reprieve. pp. 407, 699

Closed primary A party nominating election in which only declared party members can vote. p. 182

Cloture Procedure that may be used to limit or end floor debate in a legislative body. p. 344

Coalition A temporary alliance of several groups who come together to form a working majority and so to control a government. pp. 122, 648

Coattail effect The effect of a strong candidate running for an office at the top of a ballot helping to attract voters to other candidates on the party's ticket. p. 190

Cold war A period of more than 40 years during which relations between the two superpowers were at least tense, and often hostile. A time of threats and military build up. p. 485

Collective security The keeping of international peace and order. p. 485

Collectivization Collective or state ownership of the means of production. p. 674

Colonialism Administrative control over foreign lands. p. 630

Commander in chief Term for the President as commander of the nation's armed forces. p. 355

Commerce and Slave Trade Compromise An agreement during the Constitutional Convention protecting slave holders; denied Congress the power to tax the export of goods from any State, and, for 20 years, the power to act on the slave trade. p. 53

Commerce power Exclusive power of Congress to regulate interstate and foreign trade. p. 297

Commission government A government formed by commissioners, heads of different departments of city government, who are popularly elected to form the city council and thus center both legislative and executive powers in one body. p. 728

Committee chairman Member who heads a standing committee in a legislative body. p. 325

Committee of the Whole A committee that consists of an entire legislative body; used for a procedure in which a legislative body expedites its business by resolving itself into a committee of itself. p. 339

Common law An unwritten law made by a judge that has developed over centuries from those generally accepted ideas of right and wrong that have gained judicial recognition. p. 702

Commune A large grouping of several collective farms. p. 675

Communism An ideology which calls for the collective, or state, ownership of land and other productive property. p. 672

Commutation The power to reduce (commute) the length of a sentence or fine for a crime. pp. 408, 699

Compromise An adjustment of opposing principles or systems by modifying some aspect of each. p. 20

Concurrent jurisdiction Power shared by federal and State courts to hear certain cases. p. 508

Concurrent powers Those powers that both the National Government and the States possess and exercise. p. 93

Concurrent resolution A statement of position on an issue used by the House and Senate acting jointly; does not have the force of law and does not require the President's signature. p. 335

Concurring opinion Written explanation of the views of one or more judges who support a decision reached by a majority of the court, but wish to add or emphasize a point that was not made in the majority decision. p. 522

Confederation A joining of several groups for a common purpose. pp. 15, 35

Conference committee Temporary joint committee created to reconcile any differences between the two houses' versions of a bill. p. 333

Connecticut Compromise Agreement during the Constitutional Convention that Congress should be composed of a Senate, in which States would be represented equally, and a House, in which representation would be based on a State's population. p. 52

Consensus General agreement among various groups on fundamental matters; broad agreement on public questions. pp. 121, 292

Constituency The people and interests that an elected official represents. p. 277

Constituent power The non-legislative power of Constitution-making and the constitutional amendment process. p. 692

Constitution The body of fundamental laws setting out the principles, structures, and processes of a government. p. 4

Constitutionalism Basic principle that government and those who govern must obey the law; the rule of law; *see* limited government. p. 65

Containment A policy based in the belief that if communism could be kept within its existing boundaries, it would collapse under the weight of its internal weaknesses. p. 486

Content neutral The government may not regulate assemblies on the basis on what might be said. p. 556

Continuing resolution A measure which allows agencies to continue working based on the previous year's appropriations. p. 462

Continuous body Governing unit (e.g. the United States Senate) whose seats are never all up for election at the same time. p. 277

Controllable spending An amount decided upon by Congress and the President to determine how much will be spent each year on many individual government expenditures, including environment protection programs, aid to education, and so on. p. 459

Copyright The exclusive, legal right of a person to reproduce, publish, and sell his or her own literary, musical, or artistic creations. p. 302

Council-manager government A modification of the mayor-council government, it consists of a strong council of members elected on a non-partisan ballot, a weak mayor, elected by the people, and a manager, named by the council; *see* mayor-council government; *see* also weak mayor government. p. 727

Counter-revolutionary Those who oppose revolutionary change. p. 635

County A major unit of local government in most States. p. 718

Court-martial A court composed of military personnel, for the trial of those accused of violating military law. p. 525

Criminal case A case in which a defendant is tried for committing a crime as defined by the law. p. 513

Criminal law The portion of the law that defines public wrongs and provides for their punishment. p. 704

Customs duty A tax laid on goods brought into the United States from abroad, also known as tariffs, import duties, or imposts. p. 451

De facto segregation Segregation even if no law requires it, e.g., housing patterns. p. 604

De jure segregation Segregation by law, with legal sanction. p. 604

Defendant In a civil suit, the person against whom a court action is brought by the plaintiff; in a criminal case, the person charged with the crime. p. 509

Deficit The yearly shortfall between revenue and spending. p. 455

Deficit financing Funding government by borrowing to make up the difference between spending and revenue. p. 296

Delegated powers Those powers, expressed, implied, or inherent, granted to the National Government by the Constitution. p. 89

Democracy A form of government in which the supreme authority rests with the people. p. 5

Denaturalization The process through which naturalized citizens may involuntarily lose their citizenship. p. 615

Deportation A legal process in which aliens are legally required to leave the United States. p. 617

Détente A relaxation of tensions. p. 488

Deterrence The policy of making America and its allies so militarily strong that their very strength will discourage, or prevent, any attack. p. 485

Devolution The delegation of authority from the central government to regional governments. p. 650

Dictatorship A form of government in which the leader has absolute power and authority. p. 5

Diplomatic immunity When an ambassador is not subject to the laws of the state to which they are accredited. p. 471

Direct popular election Proposal to do away with the electoral college and allow the people to vote directly for President and Vice President. p. 383

Direct primary An election held within a party to pick that party's candidates for the general election. p. 182

Direct tax A tax that must be paid by the person on whom it is levied; *see* indirect tax. p. 296

Discharge petition A procedure enabling members to force a bill stuck in committee onto the floor for consideration. p. 336

Discrimination Bias, unfairness. p. 570

Dissenting opinion Written explanation of the views of one or more judges who disagree with (dissent from) a decision reached by a majority of the court; *see* majority opinion. p. 522

District plan Proposal for choosing presidential electors by which two electors would be selected in each State according to the Statewide popular vote and the other electors would be selected separately in each of the State's congressional districts. p. 382

Divine right of kings The belief that God grants kings the right to govern. p. 631

Division of powers Basic principle of federalism; the constitutional provisions by which governmental powers are divided on a geographic basis (in the United States, between the National Government and the States). pp. 14, 89

Docket A court's list of cases to be heard. p. 513

Doctrine Principle or fundamental policy. p. 308

Domestic affairs All matters not directly connected to the realm of foreign affairs. pp. 422, 468

Double jeopardy Part of the 5th Amendment which says that no person can be put in jeopardy of life or limb twice. Once a person has been tried for a crime, he or she cannot be tried again for the same crime. p. 578

Draft Conscription, or compulsory military service. p. 480

Due process The government must act fairly and in accord with established rules in all that it does. p. 564

Due Process Clause Part of the 14th Amendment which guarantees that no state deny basic rights to its people. p. 535

Economic protest parties Parties rooted in poor economic times, lacking a clear ideological base, dissatisfied with current conditions and demanding better times. p. 133

Electoral college Group of persons chosen in each State and the District of Columbia every four years who make a formal selection of the President and Vice President. pp. 81, 366

Electoral votes Votes cast by electors in the electoral college. p. 365

Electorate All of the people entitled to vote in a given election. pp. 129, 148, 383

Eminent domain Power of a government to take private property for public use. p. 304

Enabling act A congressional act directing the people of a United States territory to frame a proposed State constitution as a step towards admission to the Union. p. 99

Encomienda Feudal system in Latin America. p. 633

English Bill of Rights Document written by Parliament and agreed on by William and Mary of England in 1689, designed to prevent abuse of power by English monarchs; forms the basis for much in American government and politics today. p. 30

Engross To print a bill in its final form. p. 340

Entitlement A benefit that federal law says must be paid to all those who meet the eligibility requirements, e.g., Medicare, food stamps, and veterans' pension. pp. 458, 735

Entrepreneur An individual with the drive and ambition to combine land, labor, and capital resources to produce goods or offer services. p. 659

Espionage Spying. p. 477

Establishment Clause Separates church and state. p. 537

Estate tax A levy imposed on the assets of one who dies. pp. 451, 742

Ex post facto law A law applied to an act committed before its passage. p. 577

Excise tax A tax laid on the manufacture, sale, or consumption of goods and/or the performance of services. p. 451

Exclusionary rule Evidence gained as the result of an illegal act by police cannot be used against the person from whom it was seized. p. 573

Exclusive jurisdiction Power of the federal courts alone to hear certain cases. p. 508

Exclusive powers Those powers that can be exercised by the National Government alone. p. 93

Executive agreement A pact made by the President directly with the head of a foreign state; a binding international agreement with the force of law but which (unlike a treaty) does not require Senate consent. pp. 80, 400

Executive Article Article II of the Constitution. Establishes the presidency and gives the executive power of the Federal Government to the President. p. 390

Executive departments Often called the Cabinet departments, they are the traditional units of federal administration. p. 424

Executive Office of the President An organization of several agencies staffed by the President's closest advisors. p. 419

Executive order Directive, rule, or regulation issued by a chief executive or subordinates, based upon constitutional or statutory authority and having the force of law. p. 394

Executive power The power to execute, enforce, and administer law. p. 4

Expatriation The legal process by which a loss of citizenship occurs. p. 614

Expressed powers Those delegated powers of the National Government that are spelled out, expressly, in the Constitution; also called the "enumerated powers." pp. 89, 290

Extradition The legal process by which a fugitive from justice in one State is returned to that State. p. 107

Faction A conflicting group. p. 127

Factors of production Basic resources which are used to make all goods and services. p. 658

Failed state Countries without functioning governments. p. 645

Fascism A philosophy supporting a centralized, authoritarian government whose policies glorify the state over the individual. p. 637

Federal budget A detailed financial document containing estimates of federal income and spending during the coming fiscal year. p. 421

Federal government A form of government in which powers are divided between a central government and several local governments. p. 14

Federalism A system of government in which a written constitution divides power between a central, or national, government and several regional governments. pp. 70, 88

Federalists Those persons who supported the ratification of the Constitution in 1787–1788. p. 56

Felony A serious crime which may be punished by a heavy fine and/or imprisonment or even death. p. 704

Feudalism A loosely-organized system of rule in which powerful lords divided up their land among other, lesser lords. p. 626

Filibuster Various tactics (usually long speeches) aimed at defeating a bill in a legislative body by preventing a final vote; associated with the U.S. Senate; *see* cloture. p. 343

Fiscal year The 12-month period used by a government and the business world for its record-keeping, budgeting, revenue-collecting, and other financial management purposes. p. 421

Five-year plan A plan which projects economic development over the next five years. p. 673

Floor leaders Members of the House and Senate picked by their parties to carry out party decisions and steer legislative action to meet party goals. p. 324

Foreign affairs A nation's relationships with other countries. p. 468

Foreign aid Economic and military aid to other countries. p. 491

Foreign policy A group of policies made up of all the stands and actions that a nation takes in every aspect of its relationships with other countries; everything a nation's government says and does in world affairs. p. 469

Formal amendment Change or addition that becomes part of the written language of the Constitution itself through one of four methods set forth in the Constitution. p. 73

Framers Group of delegates who drafted the United States Constitution at the Philadelphia Convention in 1787. p. 48

Franchise The right to vote. p. 148

Franking privilege Benefit allowing members of Congress to mail letters and other materials postage-free. p. 283

Free enterprise system An economic system characterized by private or corporate ownership of capital goods; investments that are determined by private decision rather than by state control, and determined in a free market. pp. 20, 659

Free Exercise Clause The second part of the constitutional guarantee of religious freedom, which guarantees to each person the right to believe whatever he or she chooses to believe in matters of religion. p. 542

Full Faith and Credit Clause Constitution's requirement that each State accept the public acts, records, and judicial proceedings of every other State. p. 106

Fundamental law Laws of basic and lasting importance which may not easily be changed. p. 687

Gender gap Measurable differences between the partisan choices of men and women today. p. 169

General election The regularly scheduled election at which voters make a final selection of officeholders. p. 179

Genocide Attempted extermination of a national group. p. 645

Gerrymandering The drawing of electoral district lines to the advantage of a party or group. pp. 159, 271

Gift tax A tax on a gift by a living person. p. 451

Gosplan A large agency in the Soviet Union, introduced by Stalin, to run centralized planning. p. 674

Government The institution through which a society makes and enforces its public policies. p. 4

Government corporation Corporations within the executive branch subject to the President's direction and control, set up by Congress to carry out certain business-like activities. p. 434

Grand jury The formal device by which a person can be accused of a serious crime. p. 577

Grants-in-aid program Grants of federal money or other resources to States, cities, counties, and other local units. p. 101

Grass roots Of or from the people, the average voters. p. 253

Great Leap Forward The five-year plan for 1958 which was an attempt to quickly modernize China. p. 675

Guerilla warfare Fighting carried out by small groups in hit-and-run raids. p. 635

Hacienda Large landholdings in Latin America. p. 633

Hardliner A powerful figure in a tyrannical government who wants to maintain the status quo. p. 640

Hard money Campaign money that is subject to regulations by the FEC. p. 202

Heterogeneous Of another or different race, family or kind; composed of a mix of elements. p. 594

Ideological parties Parties based on a particular set of beliefs, a comprehensive view of social, economic, and political matters. p. 132

Immigrant Those people legally admitted as permanent residents of a country. p. 594

Impeach To bring formal charges against a public official; the House of Representatives has the sole power to impeach civil officers of the United States. p. 311

Imperial presidency Term used to describe a President as an "emperor" who acts without consulting Congress or acts in secrecy to evade or deceive Congress; often used in reference to Richard Nixon's presidency. p. 392

Implied powers Those delegated powers of the National Government that are suggested by the expressed powers set out in the Constitution; those "necessary and proper" to carry out the expressed powers; *see* delegated powers, expressed powers. pp. 90, 290

Income tax A tax levied on the income of individuals and/or corporations. p. 741

Incorporation The process by which a State establishes a city as a legal body. p. 726

Incumbent The current officeholder. p. 127

Independent agencies Additional agencies created by Congress located outside the Cabinet departments. p. 430

Independent executive agencies Agencies headed by a single administrator with regional subunits, but lacking Cabinet status. p. 431

Independent regulatory commissions Independent agencies created by Congress, designed to regulate important aspects of the nation's economy, largely beyond the reach of presidential control. p. 431

Independents A term used to describe people who have no party affiliation. p. 171

Indictment A formal complaint before a grand jury which charges the accused with one or more crimes. p. 578

Indirect tax A tax levied on one party but passed on to another for payment. p. 296

Inferior courts The lower federal courts, beneath the Supreme Court. p. 507

Infraction A minor crime punishable by a fine but not incarceration. p. 704

Information A formal charge filed by a prosecutor without the action of a grand jury. p. 704

Inherent powers Powers the Constitution is presumed to have delegated to the National Government because it is the government of a sovereign state within the world community. pp. 91, 290

Inheritance tax A tax levied on the beneficiary's share of an estate. p. 742

Initiative A process in which a certain number of qualified voters sign petitions in favor of a proposed statute or constitutional amendment, which then goes directly to the ballot. p. 687

Injunction A court order that forces or limits the performance of some act by a private individual or by a public official. p. 161

Integration The process of bringing a group into equal membership in society. p. 603

Interest A charge for borrowed money, generally a percentage of the amount borrowed. p. 454

Interest group Private organizations whose members share certain views and work to shape public policy. p. 216

Interstate compact Formal agreement entered into with the consent of Congress, between or among States, or between a State and a foreign state. p. 105

Involuntary servitude Forced labor. p. 569

Isolationism A purposeful refusal to become generally involved in the affairs of the rest of the world. p. 468

Item veto A governor may veto one or more items in a bill without rejecting the entire measure. p. 698

Jim Crow law A law that separates people on the basis of race, aimed primarily at African Americans. p. 602

Joint committee Legislative committee composed of members of both houses. p. 333

Joint resolution A proposal for action that has the force of law when passed; usually deals with special circumstances or temporary matters. p. 335

Judicial power The power to interpret laws, to determine their meaning, and to settle disputes within the society. p. 4

Judicial review The power of a court to determine the constitutionality of a governmental action. p. 69

Jurisdiction The authority of a court to hear a case. p. 508

Jury A body of persons selected according to law who hear evidence and decide questions of fact in a court case. p. 704

Jus sanguinis The law of blood, which determines citizenship based on one's parents' citizenship. p. 613

Jus soli The law of soil, which determines citizenship based on where a person is born. p. 613

Keynote address Speech given at a party convention to set the tone for the convention and the campaign to come. p. 373

Labor union An organization of workers who share the same type of job, or who work in the same industry, and press for government policies that will benefit their members. p. 244

Laissez-faire theory A theory which suggests that government should play a very limited role in society. p. 662

Law of supply and demand A law which states that when supplies of goods and services become plentiful, prices tend to drop. When supplies become scarcer, prices tend to rise. pp. 21, 661

Legal tender Any kind of money that a creditor must, by law, accept in payment for debts. p. 299

Legislative power The power to make a law and to frame public policies. p. 4

Legitimacy The belief that a government has the right to make public policy. P. 628

Libel False and malicious use of printed words. p. 546

Liberal constructionist One who argues a broad interpretation of the provisions of the Constitution, particularly those granting powers to the Federal Government. p. 291

Limited government Basic principle of American government which states that government is restricted in what it may do, and each individual has rights that government cannot take away; *see* constitutionalism, popular sovereignty. pp. 29, 685

Line agency An agency which performs the tasks for which the organization exists. p. 418

Line-item veto A President's cancellation of specific dollar amounts (line items) from a congressional spending bill; instituted by a 1996 congressional act, but struck down by a 1998 Supreme Court decision. p. 406

Literacy A person's ability to read or write. p. 156

Lobbying Activities by which group pressures are brought to bear on legislators, the legislative process, and all aspects of the public-policy-making process. p. 251

Magna Carta Great Charter forced upon King John of England by his barons in 1215; established that the power of the monarchy was not absolute and guaranteed trial by jury and due process of law to the nobility. p. 29

Major parties In American politics, the Republican and the Democratic parties. p. 116

Majority opinion Officially called the Opinion of the Court; announces the Court's decision in a case and sets out the reasoning upon which it is based. p. 522

Mandate The instructions or commands a constituency gives to its elected officials. p. 216

Market economy Economic system in which decisions on production and consumption of goods and services are based on voluntary exchange of markets. p. 669

Mass media Those means of communication that reach large audiences, especially television, radio, printed publications, and the Internet. pp. 211, 391

Mayor-council government The oldest and most widely used type of city government—an elected mayor as the chief executive and an elected council as its legislative body. p. 726

Medicaid A program administered by the State to provide medical insurance to low-income families. p. 734

Medium A means of communication; something which transmits information. p. 223

Mercantilism An economic policy designed to maximize the inflow of precious metals, like gold and silver, through trade, and to make the national economy independent of other countries. P. 629

Metropolitan area A city and the area around it. p. 731

Minister Cabinet members, most commonly of the House of Commons. p. 649

Minor party One of the political parties not widely supported. p. 119

Miranda Rule The constitutional rights which police must read to a suspect before questioning can occur. p. 582

Misdemeanor A lesser offense, punishable by a small fine and/or a short jail term. p. 704

Mixed economy An economy in which private enterprise exists in combination with a considerable amount of government regulation and promotion. p. 21

Monarch A hereditary ruler. p. 627

Monopoly A firm that is the only source of a product or service. p. 661

Multiparty A system in which several major and many lesser parties exist, seriously compete for, and actually win, public offices. p. 122

National bonus plan Proposal for electing a President by which the winner of the popular vote would receive a bonus of 102 electoral votes in addition to his or her State-based electoral college votes. If no one received at least 321 electoral votes, a run-off election would be held. p. 384

National convention Meeting at which a party's delegates vote to pick their presidential and vice-presidential candidates. p. 372

Naturalization The legal process by which citizens of one country become citizens of another. pp. 302, 614

Necessary and Proper Clause Constitutional clause that gives Congress the power to make all laws "necessary and proper" for executing its powers; *see* implied powers. p. 305

New Jersey Plan Plan presented as an alternative to the Virginia Plan at the Constitutional Convention; called for a unicameral legislature in which each State would be equally represented. p. 51

Nomination The process of candidate selection in an electoral system. p. 178

Nonpartisan election Elections in which candidates are not identified by party labels. p. 184

North American Free Trade Agreement An agreement which removed trade restrictions among the United States, Canada, and Mexico, thus increasing cross-border trade. p. 651

Oath of office Oath taken by the President on the day he takes office, pledging to "faithfully execute" the office and "preserve, protect, and defend" the Constitution. p. 393

Off-year election Congressional election that occurs between presidential election years. pp. 164, 269

Oligarchy A form of government in which the power to rule is held by a small, usually self-appointed elite. p. 13

One-party system A political system in which only one party exists. p. 123

Open primary A party-nominating election in which any qualified voter can take part. p. 183

Opinion leader Any person who, for any reason, has an unusually strong influence on the views of others. p. 212

Ordinance A local law. p. 720

Ordinance power Power of the President to issue executive orders; originates from the Constitution and acts of Congress. p. 394

Original jurisdiction The power of a court to hear a case first, before any other court. p. 509

Oversight function Review by legislative committees of the policies and programs of the executive branch. p. 281

Pardon Release from the punishment or legal consequences of a crime, by the President (in a federal case) or a governor (in a State case). pp. 407, 699

Parliamentary government A form of government in which the executive branch is made up of the prime minister, or premier, and that official's cabinet. p. 16

Parochial Church-related, as in a parochial school. p. 538

Parole The release of a prisoner short of the complete term of the original sentence. p. 699

Partisan Lawmaker who owes his/her first allegiance to his/her political party and votes according to the party line. p. 281

Partisanship Government action based on firm allegiance to a political party. p. 117

Party caucus A closed meeting of a party's House or Senate members; also called a party conference. p. 324

Party identification Loyalty of people to a political party. p. 171

Party in power In American politics, the party in power is the party that controls the executive branch of government—i.e., the presidency at the national level, or the governorship at the State level. p. 118

Patent A license issued to an inventor granting the exclusive right to manufacture, use, or sell his or her invention for a limited period of time. p. 303

Patronage The practice of giving jobs to supporters and friends. p. 438

Payroll tax A tax imposed on nearly all employers and their employees, and on self-employed persons—the amounts owed by employees withheld from their paychecks. p. 450

Peer group People with whom one regularly associates, including friends, classmates, neighbors, and co-workers. p. 212

Perjury The act of lying under oath. p. 311

Persona non grata An unwelcome person; used to describe recalled diplomatic officials. p. 401

Petition of Right Document prepared by Parliament and signed by King Charles I of England in 1628; challenged the idea of the divine right of kings and declared that even the monarch was subject to the laws of the land. p. 30

Picketing Patrolling of a business site by workers who are on strike. p. 551

Plaintiff In civil law, the party who brings a suit or some other legal action against another (the defendant) in court. p. 509

Platform A political party's formal statement of basic principles, stands on major issues, and objectives. p. 373

Pluralistic society A society which consists of several distinct cultures and groups. p. 121

Plurality In an election, the number of votes that the leading candidate obtains over the next highest candidate. p. 120

Pocket veto Type of veto a chief executive may use after a legislature has adjourned; when the chief executive does not sign or reject a bill within the time allowed to do so; *see* veto. p. 346

Police power The authority of each State to act to protect and promote the public health, safety, morals, and general welfare of its people. pp. 566, 691

Political Action Committee The political extension of special-interest groups which have a major stake in public policy. p. 197

Political efficacy One's own influence or effectiveness on politics. p. 166

Political party A group of persons who seek to control government through the winning of elections and the holding of public office. p. 116

Political socialization The process by which people gain their political attitudes and opinions. p. 168

Politico Lawmaker who attempts to balance the basic elements of the trustee, delegate, and partisan roles; see trustee, delegate, partisan. p. 281

Poll book List of all registered voters in each precinct. p. 155

Poll tax A special tax, demanded by States, as a condition of voting. p. 157

Polling place The place where the voters who live in a certain precinct go to vote. p. 190

Popular sovereignty Basic principle of the American system of government which asserts that the people are the source of any and all governmental power, and government can exist only with the consent of the governed. pp. 39, 685

Preamble Introduction. p. 65

Precedent Court decision that stands as an example to be followed in future, similar cases. pp. 522, 703

Precinct The smallest unit of election administration; a voting district. pp. 140, 190

Preclearance Mandated by the Voting Rights Act of 1965, the prior approval by the Justice Department of changes to or new election laws by certain States. p. 162

President of the Senate The presiding officer of a senate; in Congress, the Vice President of the United States; in a State's legislature, either the lieutenant governor or a senator. p. 323

President *pro tempore* The member of the United States Senate, or of the upper house of a State's legislature, chosen to preside in the absence of the president of the Senate. p. 323

Presidential elector A person elected by the voters to represent them in making a formal selection of the Vice President and President. p. 365

Presidential government A form of government in which the executive and legislative branches of the government are separate, independent, and coequal. p. 15

Presidential primary An election in which a party's voters (1) choose State party organization's delegates to their party's national convention, and/or (2) express a preference for their party's presidential nomination. p. 369

Presidential succession Scheme by which a presidential vacancy is filled. p. 359

Presidential Succession Act of 1947 Law specifying the order of presidential succession following the Vice President. p. 360

Presiding officer Chair. p. 45

Preventive detention A law which allows federal judges to order that an accused felon be held, without bail, when there is good reason to believe that he or she will commit yet another serious crime before trial. p. 586

Prior restraint The government cannot curb ideas before they are expressed. p. 549

Privatization The process of returning national enterprises to private ownership. p. 675

Privileges and Immunities Clause Constitution's stipulation (Article IV, Section 2) that all citizens are entitled to certain "privileges and immunities," regardless of their State of residence; no State can draw unreasonable distinctions between its own residents and those persons who happen to live in other States. p. 107

Probable Cause Reasonable grounds, a reasonable suspicion of crime. p. 571

Procedural due process The government must employ fair procedures and methods. p. 565

Process of incorporation The process of incorporating, or including, most of the guarantees in the Bill of Rights into the 14th Amendment's Due Process Clause. p. 535

Progressive tax A type of tax proportionate to income. pp. 449, 741

Project grant One type of federal grants-in-aid; made for specific projects to States, localities, and private agencies who apply for them. p. 103

Proletariat The working class. p. 667

Propaganda A technique of persuasion aimed at influencing individual or group behaviors to create a particular belief, regardless of its validity. p. 249

Property tax A tax levied on real and personal property. p. 742

Proportional plan Proposal by which each presidential candidate would receive the same share of a State's electoral vote as he or she received in the State's popular vote. p. 382

Proportional representation rule Rule applied in Democratic primaries whereby any candidate who wins at least 15 percent of the votes gets the number of State Democratic convention delegates based on his or her share of that primary vote. p. 371

Proprietary Organized by a proprietor (a person to whom the king had made a grant of land). p. 32

Prorogue Adjourn, as in a legislative session. p. 265

Public affairs Those events and issues that concern the people at large, e.g., politics, public issues, and the making of public policies. pp. 208, 239

Public agenda The public issues on which the people's attention is focused. p. 228

Public debt All of the money borrowed by the government and not yet repaid, plus the accrued interest on that money; also called the national debt or federal debt. pp. 296, 455

Public-interest group An interest group that seeks to institute certain public policies of benefit to all or most people in this country, whether or not they belong to or support that organization. p. 247

Public opinion The complex collection of the opinions of many different people; the sum of all their views. p. 209

Public opinion poll Devices that attempt to collect information by asking people questions. p. 217

Public policy All of the many goals that a government pursues in all of the many areas of human affairs in which it is involved. pp. 4, 236

Quasi-judicial Having to do with powers that are to some extent judicial. p. 433

Quasi-legislative Having to do with powers that are to some extent legislative. p. 433

Quorum Least number of members who must be present for a legislative body to conduct business; majority. pp. 58, 339

Quota A rule requiring certain numbers of jobs or promotions for members of certain groups. p. 610

Quota sample A sample deliberately constructed to reflect several of the major characteristics of a given population. p. 219

Random sample A certain number of randomly selected people who live in a certain number of randomly selected places. p. 218

Ratification Formal approval, final consent to the effectiveness of a constitution, constitutional amendment, or treaty. p. 44

Reapportion Redistribute, as in seats in a legislative body. p. 267

Recall A petition procedure by which voters may remove an elected official from office before the completion of his or her regular term. p. 696

Recognition The exclusive power of a President to recognize (establish formal diplomatic relations with) foreign states. p. 400

Redress Satisfaction of a claim payment. p. 524

Referendum A process by which a legislative measure is referred to the State's voters for final approval or rejection. p. 693

Refugee One who leaves his or her home to seek protection from war, persecution, or some other danger. p. 597

Regional body Local government entity designed to address problems that extend beyond a single county or city. p. 722

Regional security alliances Treaties in which the U.S. and other countries involved have agreed to take collective action to meet aggression in a particular part of the world. p. 492

Register A record or list of names, often kept by an official appointed to do so. p. 439

Registration A procedure of voter identification intended to prevent fraudulent voting. p. 154

Regressive tax A tax levied at a flat rate, without regard to the level of a taxpayer's income or ability to pay them. pp. 451, 741

Repeal Recall. p. 37

Representative government System of government in which public policies are made by officials selected by the voters and held accountable in periodic elections; *see* democracy. p. 29

Reprieve An official postponement of the execution of a sentence; *see* pardon. pp. 407, 699

Reservation Public land set aside by a government for use by Native American tribes. p. 596

Reserved powers Those powers that the Constitution does not grant to the National Government and does not, at the same time, deny to the States. p. 92

Resolution A measure relating to the business of either house,

or expressing an opinion; does not have the force of law and does not require the President's signature. p. 335

Retention election A yes or no vote to renew the term of an appointed judge. p. 711

Revenue sharing Form of federal monetary aid under which Congress gave a share of federal tax revenue, with virtually no restrictions, to the States, cities, counties, and townships. p. 102

Reverse discrimination Discrimination against the majority group. p. 610

Right of association The right to associate with others to promote political, economic, and other social causes. p. 558

Right of legation The right to send and receive diplomatic representatives. p. 470

Rider Unpopular provision added to an important bill certain to pass so that it will "ride" through the legislative process. p. 335

Rule of law Concept that holds that government and its officers are always subject to the law. p. 66

Runoff primary A primary in which the top two vote-getters in the first direct primary face one another. p. 184

Sales tax A tax placed on the sale of various commodities, paid by the purchaser. p. 741

Sample A representative slice of the public. p. 218

Search warrant A court order authorizing a search. p. 566

Secretary An official in charge of a department of government. p. 424

Sectionalism A narrow-minded concern for, or devotion to, the interests of one section of a country. p. 129

Sedition The crime of attempting to overthrow the government by force, or to disrupt its lawful activities by violent acts. p. 547

Seditious speech The advocating, or urging, of an attempt to overthrow the government by force, or to disrupt its lawful activities with violence. p. 547

Segregation The separation of one group from another. p. 602

Select committee Legislative committee created for a limited time and for some specific purpose; also known as a special committee. p. 331

Senatorial courtesy Custom that the Senate will not approve a presidential appointment opposed by a majority party senator from the State in which the appointee would serve. p. 81

Seniority rule Unwritten rule in both houses of Congress reserving the top posts in each chamber, particularly committee chairmanships, for members with the longest records of service. p. 326

Separate-but-equal doctrine A constitutional basis for laws that separate one group from another on the basis of race. (Jim Crow Laws.) p. 602

Separation of powers Basic principle of American system of government, that the executive, legislative, and judicial powers are divided among three independent and coequal branches of government; *see* checks and balances. p. 66

Serf Worker bound to the land he or she farmed. p. 626

Session Period of time during which, each year, Congress assembles and conducts business. p. 264

Shadow cabinet Members of opposition parties who watch, or shadow, particular Cabinet members, and would be ready to run the government. p. 649

Shield law A law which gives reporters some protection against having to disclose their sources or reveal other confidential information in legal proceedings. p. 550

Single-interest group Political action committees that concentrate their efforts exclusively on one issue. p. 251

Single-issue parties Parties that concentrate on only one public policy matter. p. 132

Single-member district Electoral district from which one person is chosen by the voters for each elected office. pp. 120, 270

Slander False and malicious use of spoken words. p. 547

Socialism A philosophy based on the idea that the benefits of economic activity should be fairly distributed. p. 666

Softliner A powerful figure in a tyrannical government who wants reform. p. 640

Soft money Money given to State and local party organizations for voting-related activities. p. 201

Sound bite Short, sharply focused reports that can be aired in 30 or 45 seconds. p. 229

Sovereign Having supreme power within its own territory; neither subordinate nor responsible to any other authority. p. 6

Speaker of the House The presiding officer of the House of Representatives, chosen by and from the majority party in the House. p. 322

Special district An independent unit created to perform one or more related governmental functions at the local level. p. 721

Special session An extraordinary session of a legislative body, called to deal with an emergency situation. p. 265

Splinter parties Parties that have split away from one of the major parties. p. 133

Split-ticket voting Voting for candidates of different parties for different offices at the same election. pp. 141, 171

Spoils system The practice of giving offices and other favors of government to political supporters and friends. p. 438

Staff agency An agency which supports the chief executive and other administrators by offering advice and other assistance in the management of the organization. p. 418

Standing committee Permanent committee in a legislative body to which bills in a specified subject-matter area are referred; *see* select committee. p. 329

State A body of people living in a defined territory who have a government with the power to make and enforce law without the consent of any higher authority. p. 5

Statutory law A law passed by the legislature. p. 688

Straight-ticket voting The practice of voting for candidates of only one party in an election. p. 171

Straw vote Polls that seek to read the public's mind simply by asking the same question of a large number of people. p. 217

Strict constructionist One who argues a narrow interpretation of the Constitution's provisions, in particular those granting powers to the Federal Government. p. 291

Strong-mayor government A type of government in which the mayor heads the city's administration. p. 727

Subcommittee Division of existing committee that is formed to address specific issues. p. 337

Subpoena An order for a person to appear and to produce documents or other requested materials. p. 313

Subsidy A grant of money, usually from a government. p. 197

Substantive due process The government must create fair policies and laws. p. 565

Successor A person who inherits a title or office. p. 311

Suffrage The right to vote. p. 148

Surplus More income than spending. p. 455

Symbolic speech Expression by conduct; communicating ideas through facial expressions, body language, or by carrying a sign or wearing an arm band. p. 551

Tax A charge levied by government on persons or property to meet public needs. p. 295

Tax return A declaration of taxable income and of the exemptions and deductions claimed. p. 449

Term Two-year period of time during which Congress meets.

Terrorism The use of violence to intimidate a government or society. p. 478

Three-Fifths Compromise An agreement at the Constitutional Convention to count a slave as three-fifths of a person when determining the population of a State. p. 52

Township A subdivision of a county. p. 719

Trade association Interest groups within the business community. p. 244

Transient Person living in a State for only a short time, without legal residence. p. 153

Treason Betrayal of one's country; in the Constitution, by levying war against the United States or offering comfort or aid to its enemies. p. 588

Treaty A formal agreement between two or more sovereign states. pp. 80, 399

Trust A device by which several corporations in the same business work to eliminate competition and regulate prices. p. 661

Trustee Lawmaker who votes based on his or her conscience and judgment, not the views of his or her constituents. p. 281

Two-party system A political system dominated by two major parties. p. 119

UN Security Council A 15-member panel which bears the UN's major responsibility for keeping international peace. p. 496

Unconstitutional Contrary to constitutional provision and so illegal, null and void, of no force and effect. p. 69

Uncontrollable spending Spending that Congress and the President have no power to change directly. p. 459

Unicameral An adjective describing a legislative body with one chamber; *see* bicameral. p. 32

Unitary government A centralized government in which all government powers belong to a single, central agency. p. 14

Use Tax A tax imposed on transactions in which no sales tax is collected. p. 741

Vassal A lord who pledged his loyalty to a more powerful lord. p. 626

Veto Chief executive's power to reject a bill passed by a legislature; literally (Latin) "I forbid"; see pocket veto. pp. 67, 346

Virginia Plan Plan presented by delegates from Virginia at the Constitutional Convention; called for a three-branch government with a bicameral legislature in which each State's membership would be determined by its population or its financial support for the central government. p. 51

Ward A unit into which cities are often divided for the election of city council members. p. 140

Warrant A court order authorizing, or making legal, some official action, such as a search warrant or an arrest warrant. p. 709

Weak-mayor government A type of government in which the mayor shares his or her executive duties with other elected officials. p. 727

Welfare Cash assistance to the poor. p. 735

Welfare state Countries that provide extensive social services at little or no cost to the users. p. 668

Whips Assistants to the floor leaders in the House and Senate, responsible for monitoring and marshalling votes. p. 325

Winner-take-all An almost obsolete system whereby a presidential aspirant who won the preference vote in a primary automatically won all the delegates chosen in the primary. p. 371

Writ of assistance Blanket search warrant with which British custom officials had invaded private homes to search for smuggled goods. p. 571

Writ of certiorari An order by a higher court directing a lower court to send up the record in a given case for review; from the Latin meaning "to be more certain." p. 520

Writ of habeas corpus A court order which prevents unjust arrests and imprisonments. p. 576

Zoning The practice of dividing a city into a number of districts and regulating the uses to which property in each of them may be put. p. 727

Spanish Glossary

Number(s) after each definition refer to page(s) where the term is defined.

Absentee voting/Voto en Ausencia Medidas para que voten, en el día de la elección, aquellas personas que no puedan hacerlo en su lugar habitual de votación. Pág. 189

Acquit/Absolver Determinar que no se es culpable de un delito. Pág. 311

Act of admission/Decreto de Admisión Una ley del Congreso mediante la cual se admite a un nuevo estado dentro de la Unión. Pág. 100

Adjourn/Aplazamiento Suspender, por ejemplo, una sesión del Congreso. Pág. 264

Administration/Administración Los funcionarios de la rama ejecutiva de un gobierno, así como sus políticas y sus directores. Pág. 416

Affirmative action/Acción afirmativa Una política que exige que la mayoría de los empleados lleve a cabo ciertas acciones para remediar los efectos de discriminaciones pasadas. Pág. 609

Albany Plan of Union/Plan de Unión Albany Proyecto propuesto por Benjamin Franklin en 1754 cuyo objetivo era unir a las 13 colonias respecto a asuntos comerciales, militares, así como para otros propósitos; las colonias y la Corona rechazaron el plan. Págs. 35–36

Alien/Extranjero residente Nacido en otro país, o persona que no es ciudadano. Págs. 534, 614

Ambassador/Embajador Delegado oficial designado por el Presidente para que represente a la nación en asuntos diplomáticos. Pág. 471

Amendment/Enmienda Cambio o adición a la Constitución o a las leyes. Pág. 72

Amnesty/Amnistía Perdón general que se brinda a un grupo de violadores de la ley. Pág. 408

Anti-Federalists/Anti-federalistas Aquellas personas que se opusieron a la ratificación de la Constitución en 1787–1788. Pág. 56

Appellate jurisdiction/Tribunal de apelación Autoridad de una corte para revisar decisiones de cortes inferiores; *ver* original jurisdiction/jurisdicción original. Págs. 509, 709

Apportion/Prorrateo Distribuir, como los escaños de un cuerpo legislativo. Pág. 267

Appropriate/Asignar Destinar a un uso particular. Pág. 305

Articles/Artículos Secciones numeradas de un documento. La Constitución, sin enmiendas, está dividida en siete artículos. Pág. 65

Articles of Confederation/Artículos de la Confederación Plan de gobierno adoptado por el Congreso Continental, después de la Independencia de los Estados Unidos; se enunciaron como "un vínculo firme de amistad" entre los estados; no obstante, delegaron unos cuantos poderes importantes al gobierno central. Pág. 44

Assemble/Congregar Reunirse con otras personas para expresar puntos de vista sobre asuntos públicos. Pág. 555

Assessment/Valuación Proceso para determinar el valor de una propiedad que será gravada. Pág. 742

Assimilation/Asimilación Proceso mediante el cual las personas de una cultura se fusionan con otra y se convierten en parte de ella. Pág. 597

At-large election/Elección general Elección de un funcionario público por los votantes de una unidad gubernamental completa (por ejemplo, un estado o país), en vez de por los votantes de un distrito o subdivisión. Pág. 270

Attorney General/Procurador general El titular del Departamento de Justicia. Pág. 424

Authoritarian/Autoritario Forma de gobierno en donde aquellos que ejercen el poder imponen un poder absoluto e inapelable sobre el pueblo. Todas las dictaduras son autoritarias. Pág. 13

Autocracy/Autocracia Forma de gobierno en la que una sola persona ejerce un poder político ilimitado. Pág. 13

Bail/Fianza Suma de dinero que se exige que el acusado desembolse (es decir, que deposite en la corte) como garantía de que se presentará en dicha corte en el momento apropiado. Pág. 585

Balance the ticket/Designar al compañero de fórmula Cuando un candidato presidencial elige al candidato a la vicepresidencia que reforzará sus oportunidades de ser triunfador, gracias a las características ideológicas, geográficas, raciales, étnicas, de género, o debido a otras virtudes. Pág. 362

Ballot/Papeleta electoral Medio que los votantes utilizan para señalar su preferencia en una elección. Pág. 190

Bankruptcy/Bancarrota Procedimiento mediante el cual los bienes de una persona declarada en bancarrota se distribuyen entre las personas con las que tiene deudas. Pág. 300

Bench trial/Juicio ante judicatura Proceso en donde sólo el juez escucha el caso. Págs. 580, 705

Bicameral/Bicameral Adjetivo que describe un cuerpo legislativo compuesto por dos cámaras. Pág. 31

Bill/Proyecto de ley Ley propuesta que se presenta a un cuerpo legislativo para su consideración. Pág. 334

Bill of Attainder/Escrito de proscripción y confiscación Acto legislativo que inflige un castigo sin que haya un juicio ante jurado de por medio. Pág. 577

Bill of Rights/Declaración de derechos Las primeras diez enmiendas a la Constitución. Págs. 76, 532

Bipartisan/Bipartidista Apoyado por dos partidos. Págs. 120, 440

Blanket primary/Elecciones primarias generales Proceso de elección en el que los votantes reciben una papeleta electoral grande que contiene los nombres de todos los contendientes, sin importar el partido, y en el cual pueden elegir como lo deseen. Pág. 183

Block grant/Subsidio en conjunto Tipo de subsidio público federal; proporcionado para alguna área particular pero ampliamente definida; *ver* grants-in-aid program/programa de subvención de fondos públicos. Pág. 103

Bourgeoisie/Burguesía Clase social ubicada entre la aristocracia y la clase media; la clase trabajadora. Pág. 667

Boycott/Boicot Rechazo a vender o a comprar determinados productos o servicios. Pág. 36

Budget/Presupuesto Plan financiero para la utilización del dinero, el personal y la propiedad. Pág. 744

Bureaucracy/Burocracia Estructura administrativa grande y compleja que gobierna los negocios cotidianos de una organización. Pág. 414

Bureaucrat/Burócrata Persona que trabaja en una organización burocrática; *ver* bureaucracy/burocracia. Pág. 415

Cabinet/Gabinete Cuerpo consultivo del Presidente que tradicionalmente está compuesto por los titulares de los departamentos ejecutivos y otros funcionarios. Pág. 81

Capital/Capital Todos los recursos hechos por el hombre que se utilizan para producir bienes y servicios. Pág. 659

Capitalist/Capitalista Persona que posee capital y le da un uso productivo; término que en la mayor parte de los casos se aplica a las personas que poseen grandes negocios o fábricas. Pág. 659

Capital punishment/Pena capital La pena de muerte. Pág. 587

Categorical grant/Subsidio categórico Tipo de subsidio público; proporcionado para algún propósito específico y rigurosamente definido; *ver* grants-in-aid program/programa de subvenciÛn de fondos públicos. Pág. 102

Caucus/Junta de dirigentes En función de instrumento nominativo, grupo de personas con ideología similar que se reúne para seleccionar a los candidatos que apoyarán en una elección venidera. Pág. 180

Censure/Censurar Emitir una condena formal. Pág. 312

Centrally planned economy/Economía centralmente planificada Sistema en el que burócratas gubernamentales planean la forma en que la economía se desarrollará durante determinados años. Pág. 669

Certificate/Certificación Método de remitir un caso a la Corte Suprema; se utiliza cuando una corte inferior no está segura de qué procedimiento o regla deberá aplicar en un caso y consulta a la Corte Suprema para que certifique una respuesta a una pregunta específica. Pág. 521

Charter/Carta constitucional Ley básica de una ciudad, su constitución; concesión escrita de autoridad por parte del rey. Págs. 31, 720

Checks and balances/Sistema de pesos y contrapesos Mecanismo en el que se traslapan los poderes de las ramas legislativas, ejecutivas y judiciales para permitir que cada rama verifique las acciones de las otras dos; *ver* separation of powers/separación de poderes. Pág. 67

Chief administrator/Administrador en jefe Nombre que se da al Presidente en cuanto a que es el jefe de la administración del gobierno federal. Pág. 355

Chief citizen/Primer ciudadano Nombre que se da al Presidente, en cuanto a que es representante del pueblo y trabaja para el interés público. Pág. 355

Chief diplomat/Diplomático titular Nombre que se da al Presidente en cuanto a que es el arquitecto principal de la política exterior y el vocero ante otros países. Pág. 355

Chief executive/Primer mandatario Nombre que se da al Presidente, en cuanto a que está investido con el poder ejecutivo de los Estados Unidos. Pág. 354

Chief legislator/Legislador en jefe Nombre que se da al Presidente en cuanto a que es arquitecto de la política pública y uno de los que determina la agenda del Congreso. Pág. 355

Chief of party/Jefe del partido Nombre que se da al Presidente en cuanto a que es líder de su partido político. Pág. 355

Chief of state/Jefe de estado Nombre que se da al Presidente en cuanto a que es titular ceremonial de los Estados Unidos, el símbolo de toda la gente de la nación. Pág. 354

Citizen/Ciudadano Miembro de un estado o nación a la cual le debe lealtad por nacimiento o naturalización y al que se le acreditan todos los derechos civiles. Pág. 613

Civil case/Caso civil Caso que involucra un asunto no criminal, como un litigio por contrato, o una demanda por violación de patentes. Pág. 513

Civil law/Ley civil Área de la ley que se relaciona con la conducta humana, con litigios entre partes privadas, así como entre partes privadas y el gobierno, la cual no abarca la ley penal. Pág. 704

Civil liberties/Libertades civiles Garantías concernientes a la seguridad, opiniones y propiedad de las personas en contra de actos arbitrarios del gobierno; también incluyen la libertad de expresión y de religión. Pág. 533

Civil rights/Derechos civiles Término utilizado para aquellos actos positivos del gobierno que pretenden hacer realidad las garantías constitucionales para todo el pueblo, por ejemplo la prohibición de la discriminación. Pág. 533

Civil service/Servicio Civil Grupo de empleados públicos desempeñan el trabajo administrativo del gobierno. Pág. 437

Civilian tribunal/Tribunal civil Corte que funciona como parte de la rama judicial, el cual está separado por completo de la institución militar. Pág. 525

Clemency/Indulgencia Misericordia o piedad que dispensa el Presidente a un delincuente; *ver* pardon/perdón y rep/reprieve/suspensión de la ejecución. Págs. 407, 699

Closed primary/Elección primaria cerrada Elección para una nominación partidista en la que sólo los miembros declarados del partido pueden votar. Pág. 182

Cloture/Limitación del debate Procedimiento que puede utilizarse para restringir o terminar un debate verbal de un cuerpo legislativo. Pág. 344

Coalition/Coalición Una alianza temporal de varios grupos que se agrupan para alcanzar el poder mayoritario y controlar el gobierno. Págs. 122, 648

Coattail effect/Efecto de refilón Efecto que produce un fuerte candidato a un puesto de elección, situado en primer sitio, mediante el cual ayuda a atraer votantes hacia otros candidatos de su mismo partido. Pág. 190

Cold war/Guerra Fría Periodo de más de 40 años de duración en el que las relaciones entre las dos superpotencias fueron por lo menos tensas, y a menudo hostiles. Época de amenazas y de desarrollo militar. Pág. 485

Collective security/Seguridad colectiva Conservación de la paz y el orden internacionales. Pág. 485

Collectivization/Colectivización Hacer colectivos o propiedad del estado los medios de producción. Pág. 674

Colonialism/Colonialismo Control administrativo de territorios extranjeros. p. 630

Commander in chief/Comandante en jefe Nombre que se da al Presidente en cuanto a que es el comandante de las fuerzas armadas de la nación. Pág. 355

Commerce and Slave Trade Compromise/Avenencia de comercio y trata de esclavos Acuerdo durante la Convención Constitucional que protegió los intereses de los dueños de esclavos, al negarle al Congreso el poder de gravar la exportación de bienes desde cualquier estado, así como el poder de actuar, durante 20 años, en contra de la trata de esclavos. Pág. 53

Commerce power/Poder mercantil Poder exclusivo del Congreso para regular el comercio interestatal e internacional. Pág. 297

Commission government/Junta municipal Gobierno formado por comisionados, titulares de distintos departamentos del gobierno de la ciudad, que se eligen por voto popular para formar el Consejo de la ciudad y, por consiguiente, reúnen los poderes legislativos y ejecutivos en un solo cuerpo. Pág. 728

Committee chairman/Presidente de comisión Miembro que encabeza una comisión permanente en un cuerpo legislativo. Pág. 325

Committee of the Whole/Comité Plenario Comité que consiste en la totalidad de un cuerpo legislativo; utilizado para un procedimiento mediante el cual un cuerpo legislativo da curso a sus asuntos transformándose en un comité en sí. Pág. 339

Common law/Derecho consuetudinario Ley no escrita sancionada por un juez y que se ha desarrollado a lo largo de los siglos con base a aquellas ideas generalmente aceptadas de lo bueno y lo malo que se han ganado un reconocimiento judicial. Pág. 702

Commune/Comuna Un grupo grande de diversas granjas colectivas. Pág. 675

Communism/Comunismo Ideología que exige la propiedad colectiva, o estatal, de la tierra y de otros medios de producción. Pág. 672

Commutation/Conmutación El poder de reducir (conmutar) la duración de una sentencia o el monto de la multa de un crimen. Págs. 408, 699

Compromise/Compromiso Avenencia entre principios o sistemas opuestos, mediante la modificación de algún aspecto de cada uno de ellos. Pág. 20

Concurrent jurisdiction/Jurisdicción coincidente Poder compartido por cortes federales y estatales para atender ciertos casos. Pág. 508

Concurrent powers/Poderes concurrentes Aquellos poderes que el gobierno nacional y los estados poseen y ejercen. Pág. 93

Concurrent resolution/Resolución conjunta Enunciado de una posición sobre un asunto utilizado por la Cámara de Representantes y el Senado al actuar conjuntamente; no tiene la fuerza de la ley y no requiere la firma del Presidente. Pág. 335

Concurring opinión/Opinion coincidente Explicación escrita de los puntos de vista de uno o más jueces que apoyan una decisión alcanzada por una mayoría de la corte, pero en la que se desea añadir o recalcar un punto que no se remarcó en la decisión mayoritaria. Pág. 522

Confederation/Confederación Unión de diversos grupos para un propósito común. Págs. 15, 35

Conference committee/Comité de Consulta Comité conjunto temporal creado para reconciliar cualquier diferencia entre las versiones de las dos cámaras legislativas sobre una propuesta de ley. Pág. 333

Connecticut Compromise/Acuerdo de Connecticut Acuerdo alcanzado durante la Convención Constitucional respecto a que el Congreso debería estar integrado por un Senado en donde cada estado estuviera representado de manera igualitaria, y una Cámara de Representantes en la que la representación estuviera basada en la población de cada estado. Pág. 52

Consensus/Consenso Acuerdo general entre diversos grupos respecto a temas fundamentales; amplio acuerdo sobre temas varios. Págs. 121, 292

Constituency/Distrito electoral Las personas e intereses que un funcionario elegido representa. Pág. 277

Constituent power/Poder constituyente Poder no legislativo de la elaboración de la Constitución y del proceso de enmiendas constitucionales. Pág. 692

Constitution/Constitución Cuerpo de leyes fundamentales que delinean los principios, las estructuras y los procesos de gobierno. Pág. 4

Constitutionalism/Constitucionalismo Principio básico que establece que el gobierno y los gobernantes deben obedecer la ley; el gobierno de la ley; *ver* limited government/gobierno limitado. Pág. 65

Containment/Contención Política basada en la creencia de que si el comunismo se pudiera limitar dentro de sus fronteras existentes, se derrumbaría bajo el peso de sus debilidades internas. Pág. 486

Content neutral/Voto neutral El gobierno no regulará a las asambleas en lo concerniente a lo que se expresará en ellas. Pág. 556

Continuing resolution/Resolución ininterrumpida Medida que permite que las agencies continúen funcionando sobre la base de las asignaciones del año anterior. Pág. 462

Continuous body/Cuerpo legislativo ininterrumpido Unidad gubernamental (por ejemplo, el Senado de Estados Unidos) cuya totalidad de escaños nunca se elige al mismo tiempo. Pág. 277

Controllable spending/Gasto controlable Cantidad de dinero decidida entre el Congreso y el Presidente y que señala el monto anual de muchos gastos gubernamentales individuales, como programas para protección del ambiente, ayuda a la educación, etcétera. Pág. 459

Copyright/Derechos de autor Derechos legales y exclusivos de una persona para reproducir, publicar y vender su trabajo creativo literario, artístico, o musical. Pág. 302

Council-manager government/Gobierno de consejo-superintendente Una modificación del gobierno de consejo-alcalde, que consiste en un vigoroso consejo de miembros elegido mediante un sufragio no partidista; un alcalde débil, elegido por el pueblo y un superintendente nombrado por el consejo; *ver* mayor-council government/gobierno de consejo-alcalde; *ver también* weak-mayor government/gobierno de alcalde débil. Pág. 727

Counter-revolutionary/Contrarrevolucionario Quien se opone al cambio revolucionario. Pág. 635

County/Condado Una unidad importante de gobierno local en la gran parte de los estados. Pág. 718

Court-martial/Corte marcial Corte compuesta por personal militar para juzgar a los que están acusados de violar la ley militar. Pág. 525

Criminal case/Caso criminal Caso en el que se juzga al acusado por cometer un crimen, tal y como éste se define en la ley. Pág. 513

Criminal law/Derecho penal Área de la ley que define los agravios públicos y que establece su castigo. Pág. 704

Customs Duty/Derecho de aduana Impuesto gravado sobre los bienes traídos a los Estados Unidos desde el exterior, también se conoce como arancel, impuesto sobre importaciones o tasa sobre importaciones. Pág. 451

De facto segregation/Discriminación de facto o de hecho Segregación, incluso si la ley no lo exige, por ejemplo en la asignación de vivienda. Pág. 604

De jure segregation/Discriminación de jure o de ley Segregación con base en la ley, que implica una sanción legal. Pág. 604

Defendant/Acusado En un juicio civil, es la persona en contra de quien el demandante pide ejecutar una acción judicial; en un caso criminal, es la persona acusada de un crimen. Pág. 509

Deficit/Déficit La diferencia anual entre los ingresos y los egresos. Pág. 455

Deficit financing/Déficit financiero Práctica de subvencionar al gobierno mediante préstamos, a fin de compensar la diferencia entre los gastos y los ingresos gubernamentales. Pág. 296

Delegated powers/Poderes delegados Poderes explícitos, implícitos o inherentes que la Constitución transfiere al gobierno nacional. Pág. 89

Democracy/Democracia Forma de gobierno en donde la autoridad suprema reside en el pueblo. Pág. 5

Denaturalization/Desnaturalización Proceso en el que los ciudadanos naturalizados pueden perder su ciudadanía de manera involuntaria. Pág. 615

Deportation/Deportación Proceso legal mediante el que se les exige a los extranjeros que abandonen los Estados Unidos. Pág. 617

Détente/Relajamiento Disminución de las tensiones. Pág. 488

Deterrence/Disuasión Política de convertir a los Estados Unidos y sus aliados en una fuerza militar tan poderosa que su fortaleza desaliente, o prevenga, cualquier ataque. Pág. 485

Devolution/Delegación Transferencia de la autoridad del gobierno central a los gobiernos regionales. Pág. 650

Dictatorship/Dictadura Forma de gobierno en la que el líder ejerce poder y autoridad absolutos. Pág. 5

Diplomatic immunity/Inmunidad diplomática Cuando un embajador no está sujeto a las leyes del estado en el que se le acredita como tal. Pág. 471

Direct popular election/Elección popular directa Propuesta para abolir el colegio electoral y permitir que la gente elija de manera directa al Presidente y al Vicepresidente. Pág. 383

Direct primary/Elección primaria directa Elección realizada dentro de un partido para escoger a los candidatos del partido para una elección general. Pág. 182

Direct tax/Impuesto directo Gravamen que debe pagar la persona a la que se le impone; *ver* indirect tax/impuesto indirecto. Pág. 296

Discharge petition/Petición de exoneración Procedimiento que permite a los miembros autorizar una propuesta de ley que se ha estancado en una comisión de debate para su consideración. Pág. 336

Discrimination/Discriminación Prejuicio, injusticia. Pág. 570

Dissenting opinión/Opinión disidente Explicación escrita de los puntos de vista de uno o más jueces, que está(n) en desacuerdo con una decisión tomada por la mayoría de la corte; *ver* majority opinion/opinión mayoritaria. Pág. 522

District Plan/Plan de Distrito Propuesta para elegir a los electores presidenciales, mediante la cual se seleccionarían dos electores en cada estado, de acuerdo con el voto popular de todo ese estado, y los otros electores se elegirían de manera separada en cada uno de los distritos del Congreso de ese estado. Pág. 382

Divine right of kings/Derecho divino de los reyes Creencia de que Dios daba a los reyes el derecho de gobernar. p. 631

Division of powers/División de poderes Principio básico del federalismo; las estipulaciones constitucionales que establecen que los poderes gubernamentales están separados de acuerdo con bases geográficas. Págs. 15, 89

Docket/Agenda Lista de casos de una corte por atender. Pág. 513

Doctrine/Doctrina Principio de política fundamental. Pág. 308

Domestic affairs/Asuntos internos Todas cuestiones no conectadas al campo de los asuntos exteriores. Págs. 422, 468

Double jeopardy/Doble juicio Parte de la 5ª enmienda que establece que una vez que se ha juzgado por un crimen a una persona, no puede volvérsele a juzgar por el mismo delito. Pág. 578

Draft/Reclutamiento Conscripción o servicio militar obligatorio. Pág. 480

Due process/Proceso legal establecido El gobierno debe actuar con justicia y de acuerdo con las reglas establecidas en todo lo que hace. Pág. 564

Due Process Clause/Cláusula del proceso legal establecido Parte de la 14ª enmienda que garantiza que ningún estado negará los derechos básicos a su pueblo. Pág. 535

Economic protest parties/Partidos de protesta económica Partidos surgidos en tiempos de descontento económico, los cuales carecen de una base ideológica bien definida, están insatisfechos por las condiciones presentes y exigen mejores épocas. Pág. 133

Electoral college/Colegio electoral Grupo de personas (electores presidenciales) elegidos cada cuatro años en todos los estados y en el Distrito de Columbia a fin de hacer una elección formal del Presidente y Vicepresidente. Págs. 81, 366

Electoral votes/Votos electorales Votos emitidos por los electores en el Colegio electoral. Pág. 365

Electorate/Electorado Todas las personas que tienen derecho a votar en una elección determinada. Págs. 129, 148, 383

Eminent domain/Dominio supremo Poder de un gobierno de expropiar la propiedad privada para uso público. Pág. 304

Enabling act/Ley de habilitación Una ley del Congreso que orienta al pueblo de un territorio de los Estados Unidos para que redacte una constitución propuesta para el estado, como un paso hacia la admisión de dicho estado dentro de la Unión. Pág. 99

Encomienda/Encomienda Sistema feudal en América Latina. p. 633

English Bill of Rights/Declaración inglesa de los derechos Documento redactado por el Parlamento y aceptado por William y Mary de Inglaterra en 1689, elaborado para evitar el abuso del poder por parte de los monarcas ingleses; constituye la base de muchas cosas del gobierno y la política estadounidenses actuales. Pág. 30

Engross/Transcribir Imprimir un proyecto de ley en su forma final. Pág. 340

Entitlement/Derecho Beneficio que la ley federal establece que se debe pagar a todos los que cumplan los requisitos para ser elegibles, por ejemplo: el seguro médico, bonos de comida y pensión para los veteranos. Pág. 458, 735

Entrepreneur/Empresario Individuo con el impulso y la ambición de combinar los recursos de la tierra, la mano de obra y el capital para producir bienes u ofrecer servicios. Pág. 659

Espionage/Espionaje Acto de espiar. Pág. 477

Establishment Clause/Cláusula del establecimiento Separa a la iglesia del estado. Pág. 537

Estate tax/Impuesto testamentario Gravamen sobre los bienes de una persona que muere. Págs. 451, 742

Ex post facto law/Ley ex post facto Ley que se aplica a un acto cometido con anterioridad a la aprobación de la ley. Pág. 577

Excise tax/Impuesto al consumo Gravamen sobre la manufactura, venta o consumo de bienes y/o al suministro de servicios. Pág. 451

Exclusionary rule/Regla de exclusión Evidencia obtenida como resultado de una acción ilegal de la policía y que no puede utilizarse contra la persona arrestada. Pág. 573

Exclusive jurisdiction/Jurisdicción exclusiva Poder exclusivo de las cortes federales para atender ciertos casos. Pág. 508

Exclusive powers/Poderes exclusivos Poderes que pueden ejercerse sólo por el gobierno nacional. Pág. 93

Executive agreement/Acuerdo ejecutivo Pacto hecho de manera directa por el Presidente con otro jefe de un estado extranjero; un pacto internacional obligatorio con la fuerza de la ley pero que no requiere (a diferencia de un tratado) de la aprobación del Senado. Págs. 80, 400

Executive Article/Artículo del ejecutivo El segundo artículo de la Constitución. Define la presidencia y le otorga el poder ejecutivo del gobierno federal al Presidente. Pág. 390

Executive departments/Oficinas del poder ejecutivo A menudo llamadas oficinas del gabinete; son las unidades tradicionales de la administración federal. Pág. 424

Executive Office of the President/Oficina ejecutiva del Presidente Una organización compleja, que abarca diversas oficinas separadas, cuyo personal está compuesto por los consejeros y asistentes más cercanos al Presidente. Pág. 419

Executive order/Orden ejecutiva Directiva, regla o reglamento expedida por un primer mandatario o por sus subordinados, con base en su autoridad estatutaria o constitucional y la cual tiene fuerza de ley. Pág. 394

Executive power/Poder ejecutivo Poder para ejecutar, administrar y obligar al cumplimiento de la ley. Pág. 4

Expatriation/Expatriación Proceso legal mediante el cual ocurre la pérdida de ciudadanía. Pág. 614

Expressed powers/Poderes explícitos Aquellos poderes delegados del gobierno nacional que se señalan explícitamente en la Constitución; también se conocen como los "poderes enumerados." Págs. 89, 290

Extradition/Extradición Proceso legal a través del cual un fugitivo de la justicia en un estado se envía a ese estado. Pág. 107

Faction/Facción Un grupo disidente. Pág. 127

Factors of production/Factores de producción Recursos básicos que se utilizan para elaborar todos los bienes y servicios. Pág. 658

Failed state/Estado en proceso de desestructuración País sin un gobierno que funciona. p. 645

Fascism/Fascismo Filosofía que apoya un gobierno centralizado y autoritario, cuyas políticas glorifican el estado por sobre el individuo. p. 637

Federal budget/Presupuesto federal Documento financiero detallado que contienen las estimaciones de las recaudaciones y gastos que anticipan los ingresos y egresos federales durante el año fiscal venidero. Pág. 421

Spanish Glossary

Federal government/Gobierno federal Forma de gobierno en la que los poderes están divididos entre un gobierno central y diversos gobiernos locales. Pág. 14

Federalism/Federalismo Sistema de gobierno en el que una constitución escrita divide los poderes del gobierno, sobre una base territorial, entre un gobierno central (o nacional) y diversos gobiernos regionales. Págs. 70, 88

Federalists/Federalistas Personas que apoyaron la ratificación de la Constitución en 1787–1788. Pág. 56

Felony/Felonía Un crimen grave que puede castigarse con una gran multa, la prisión o incluso la muerte. Pág. 704

Feudalism/Feudalismo Sistema de gobierno poco organizado en el que los señores feudales poderosos dividían sus tierras entre otros señores con menos poder. p. 626

Filibuster/Obstrucción Diversas tácticas (por lo general, prolongar el debate verbal) dirigidas a derrotar una propuesta de ley en un cuerpo legislativo, evitando así que se tenga un voto final; a menudo se asocia con el Senado de los Estados Unidos; *ver* cloture/limitación del debate. Pág. 343

Fiscal year/Año fiscal Periodo de 12 meses utilizado por el gobierno y el mundo de los negocios para su contabilidad, presupuesto, recaudación de ingresos y otros propósitos financieros. Pág. 421

Five-year plan/Plan quinquenal Plan que hace proyecciones sobre el desarrollo económico durante los siguientes cinco años. Pág. 673

Floor leaders/Líderes de fracciones partidistas Miembros de la Cámara de Representantes y del Senado elegidos por sus partidos con el objeto de llevar a cabo las decisiones partidistas e impulsar la acción legislativa a fin de que cumplan con los propósitos partidistas. Pág. 324

Foreign Affairs/Asuntos exteriores Relaciones de una nación con otros países. Pág. 468

Foreign aid/Ayuda extranjera Auxilio militar y económico a otros países. Pág. 491

Foreign policy/Política exterior Conjunto de políticas conformado por todas las posturas y acciones que una nación asume en cada uno de los aspectos de sus relaciones con otros países; todo lo que el gobierno de una nación expresa y hace respecto a los asuntos mundiales. Pág. 469

Formal amendment/Enmienda formal Cambio o adición que se convierte en parte del lenguaje escrito de la Constitución misma, mediante uno de los cuatro métodos enunciados de la Constitución. Pág. 73

Framers/Redactores Grupo de delegados que esbozaron la Constitución de los Estados Unidos en la Convención de Filadelfia en 1787. Pág. 48

Franchise/Sufragio Derecho a votar. Pág. 148

Franking privilege/Exención de franquicia Beneficio otorgado a los miembros del Congreso que les permite enviar por correo cartas y otros materiales sin pagar los derechos del correo. Pág. 283

Free enterprise system/Sistema de libre empresa Sistema económico caracterizado por la propiedad privada o corporativa de los bienes de capital; inversiones que están determinadas por una decisión privada, en vez del control estatal, y están sujetas a un mercado libre. Págs. 20, 659

Free Exercise Clause/Cláusula de la libertad de cultos Segunda parte de la garantía constitucional de libertad religiosa, que garantiza a todo mundo el derecho de creer en lo que ella escoja en materia de religión. Pág. 542

Full Faith and Credit Clause/Cláusula de fe y crédito cabal Requisito constitucional (Artículo IV, Sección 1) según el cual cada estado acepta (da "fe y crédito cabal") los actos públicos, documentos y procedimientos judiciales de cualquier otro estado. Pág. 106

Fundamental law/Ley fundamental Leyes de importancia primordial y duradera que no se cambiarán con facilidad. Pág. 687

Gender gap/Brecha de género Diferencias medibles entre las elecciones partidistas actuales de hombres y mujeres. Pág. 169

General election/Elección general Elección programada regularmente en la que los votantes hacen una selección final de los funcionarios públicos. Pág. 179

Genocide/Genocidio Intento de exterminio de un grupo nacional. p. 645

Gerrymandering/Demarcación arbitraria Establecimiento de los límites de los distritos electorales de modo que den ventaja a un partido. Págs. 159, 271

Gift tax/Impuesto a los regalos Gravamen sobre los regalos dados por una persona viva. Pág. 451

Gosplan/Gosplán Importante oficina de la Unión Soviética, creada por Stalin, para llevar a cabo la planificación centralizada. Pág. 674

Government/Gobierno Institución mediante la cual una sociedad lleva a cabo y hace cumplir sus políticas públicas. Está compuesto por aquellas personas que ejercen sus poderes, aquellos que tienen autoridad y control sobre el pueblo. Pág. 4

Government corporation/Corporación gubernamental Instituciones dentro de la rama ejecutiva que están sujetas a la dirección y control del Presidente, formadas por el Congreso para que realicen determinadas actividades de tipo empresarial. Pág. 434

Grand jury/Gran Jurado El dispositivo formal a través del cual puede acusarse a una persona de un crimen serio. Pág. 577

Grants-in-aid program/Programa de subvención de fondos públicos Subvenciones de dinero federal o de otros recursos para los estados y/o sus ciudades, condados y otras unidades locales. Pág. 101

Grass roots/Fundamentos De extracción popular, los votantes promedio. Pág. 253

Great Leap Forward/Gran salto hacia adelante Plan quinquenal de 1958 que fue un intento de modernizar rápidamente a China. Pág. 675

Guerilla warfare/Guerra de guerrillas Lucha armada realizada por pequeños grupos en ataques relámpago. p. 635

Hacienda/Hacienda Propiedad de gran extensión en América Latina. p. 633

Hardliner/Partidario de la línea dura Figura poderosa en un gobierno tirano, que quiere mantener el statu quo. p. 640

Hard money/Fondos fiscalizados Dinero de campaña que está sujeto a las regulaciones de la FEC. Pág. 202

Heterogeneous/Hetereogéneo De diferente raza, familia o especie; compuesto por una mezcla de elementos. Pág. 594

Ideological parties/Partidos ideológicos Partidos basados en un conjunto determinado de creencias, un punto de vista comprehensivo sobre asuntos sociales, económicos y políticos. Pág. 132

Immigrant/Inmigrante Persona que es admitida legalmente en calidad de residente permanente de un país. Pág. 594

Impeach/Impugnar Fincar cargos formales en contra de un funcionario público; la Cámara de Representantes tienen el exclusivo poder de impugnar a los funcionarios públicos de los Estados Unidos. Pág. 311

Imperial presidency/Presidencia imperial Término utilizado para describir a un Presidente como "emperador", quien actúa sin consultar al Congreso o de manera secreta para evadir o engañarlo. Pág. 392

Implied powers/Poderes implícitos Aquellos poderes delegados del gobierno nacional que se sugieren o están implícitos por los poderes explícitos; aquellos que son "necesarios y apropiados" para realizar los poderes explícitos; *ver* delegated powers/poderes delegados, expressed powers/poderes explícitos. Págs. 90, 290

Income tax/Impuesto sobre el ingreso Gravamen sobre el ingreso de los individuos y/o corporaciones. Pág. 741

Incorporation/Incorporación Proceso mediante el cual un estado establece a una ciudad como un cuerpo legal. Pág. 726

Incumbent/Titular El funcionario público actual. Pág. 127

Independent agencies/Oficinas independientes Agencias adicionales creadas por el Congreso y que se ubican fuera de los departamentos del gabinete. Pág. 430

Independent executive agencies/Oficinas ejecutivas independientes Agencias que incluyen a la mayor parte de las agencias independientes, que están organizadas de una forma muy similar a los departamentos del gabinete y cuyo titular es un administrador que tiene subunidades operativas regionales pero que carece del estatus del gabinete. Pág. 431

Independent regulatory commissions/Comisiones regulatorias independientes Agencias independientes cuya función es regular aspectos importantes de la economía de la nación, en su mayoría fuera del control y dirección del Presidente. Pág. 431

Independents/Independientes Término usado para describir a las personas que carecen de filiación partidista. Pág. 171

Indictment/Denuncia Queja formal que el fiscal expone ante un gran jurado, que incluye cargos al acusado por uno o más crímenes. Pág. 578

Indirect tax/Impuesto indirecto Gravamen a una parte pero transferido a otra para su pago. Pág. 296

Inferior courts/Cortes inferiores Las cortes federales menores, que están por debajo de la Corte Suprema. Pág. 507

Information/Información Acusación oficial presentada por un acusador sin acción de parte del jurado. Pág. 704

Infraction/Infracción Crimen menor penado con una multa, pero no con cárcel. p. 704

Inherent powers/Poderes inherentes Aquellos poderes delegados del gobierno nacional que le pertenecen de manera inherente, debido a que es el gobierno de un estado soberano de la comunidad mundial. Págs. 91, 290

Inheritance tax/Impuesto sobre la herencia Gravamen sobre la parte de la herencia del beneficiario. Pág. 742

Initiative/Iniciativa Proceso en el que determinado número de votantes calificados firman peticiones a favor de una propuesta, la cual se pasa después directamente a la cédula de votación. Pág. 687

Injunction/Mandato Orden judicial que fuerza o limita el desempeño de determinado acto, mediante la intervención de un individuo privado o un funcionario público. Pág. 161

Integration/Integración El proceso de ofrecer a un grupo una pertenencia igualitaria dentro de la sociedad. Pág. 603

Interest/Interés Cargo que se hace por el dinero prestado, por lo general es un porcentaje de la cantidad prestada. Pág. 454

Interest group/Grupo de interés Organizaciones privadas cuyos miembros comparten determinados puntos de vista y trabajan para dar forma a las políticas públicas. Pág. 216

Interstate compact/Pacto interestatal Acuerdo formal suscrito con el consentimiento del Congreso, entre dos estados o entre un estado y un estado extranjero, el cual está autorizado por la Constitución. (Artículo I, Sección 10). Pág. 105

Involuntary servitude/Servidumbre involuntaria Trabajo forzado. Pág. 569

Isolationism/Aislacionismo Rechazo voluntario a verse involucrado, de manera general, en los asuntos del resto del mundo. Pág. 468

Item veto/Veto de artículo Un gobernador puede vetar uno o más artículos de una propuesta de ley, sin que rechace toda la medida. Pág. 698

Jim Crow law/Ley Jim Crow Tipo de ley que separa a un grupo de personas del resto de la gente, con base en la raza, dirigido principalmente a los afroamericanos. Pág. 602

Joint committee/Comité conjunto Comité legislativo compuesto por miembros de ambas cámaras. Pág. 333

Joint resolution/Resolución conjunta Propuesta de acción que tiene la fuerza de ley cuando se aprueba; a menudo tiene que ver con circunstancias especiales o asuntos temporales. Pág. 335

Judicial power/Poder judicial Poder para interpretar las leyes, determinar su significado y resolver las disputas que surgen dentro de la sociedad. Pág. 4

Judicial review/Revisión judicial Poder de una corte para determinar la constitucionalidad de una acción gubernamental. Pág. 69

Jurisdiction/Jurisdicción Autoridad de una corte para atender (juzgar y decidir) un caso. Pág 508

Jury/Jurado Conjunto de personas seleccionadas de acuerdo con la ley para que escuchan la evidencia y deciden cuestiones de hechos en un caso de la corte. Pág. 704

Jus sanguinis/*Jus sanguinis* Ley de la sangre que define la ciudadanía con base en la ciudadanía de los padres. Pág. 613

Jus soli/*Jus soli* Ley del territorio que determina la ciudadanía con base en el lugar de nacimiento de la persona. Pág. 613

Keynote address/Discurso de apertura Alocución dada en una convención de partido para establecer el tono de la convención y de la futura campaña. Pág. 373

Labor union/Sindicato laboral Organización de trabajadores que comparten el mismo tipo de trabajo, o que laboran en la misma industria y que presiona por lograr políticas gubernamentales que beneficien a sus miembros. Pág. 244

Laissez-faire theory/Teoría del dejar hacer Teoría que sugiere que el gobierno debería desempeñar un papel limitado dentro de la sociedad. Pág. 662

Law of supply and demand/Ley de la oferta y la demanda Ley que establece que cuando los suministros de bienes y servicios son abundantes, entonces los precios tienden a bajar. Cuando los suministros escasean, entonces los precios tienden a subir. Págs. 21, 661

Legal tender/Moneda de curso legal Cualquier moneda que un acreedor debe aceptar, por ley, como pago de deudas. Pág. 299

Legislative power/Poder legislativo Poder para hacer una ley y redactar políticas públicas. Pág. 4

Legitimacy/Legitimidad Creencia de que un gobierno tiene el derecho de establecer las leyes públicas. p. 628

Libel/Libelo Utilización falsa y maliciosa de las palabras impresas. Pág. 546

Liberal constructionist/Construccionista liberal Aquel que argumenta una amplia interpretación de las estipulaciones de la Constitución, en particular las que otorgan poderes al gobierno federal. Pág. 291

Limited government/Gobierno limitado Principio básico del sistema estadounidense de gobierno que establece que el gobierno está restringido en cuanto a lo que puede hacer, y en donde el individuo tiene ciertos derechos que el gobierno no puede enajenar; *ver* constitutionalism/constitucionalismo, popular sovereignty/soberanía popular. Págs. 29, 685

Line agency/Agencia del ramo Oficina que desempeña las tareas para las que la organización existe. Pág. 418

Line-item veto/Veto de partida Cancelación presidencial de ciertas cantidades de dólares (partidas) de una cuenta de gastos del Congreso; este veto se instituyó en 1996 mediante una ley del Congreso, pero la Suprema Corte lo derogó en 1998. Pág. 406

Literacy/Alfabetismo Capacidad de una persona para leer o escribir. Pág. 156

Lobbying/Cabildeo Actividades mediante las que las presiones de un grupo se aplican a los legisladores y al proceso legislativo, incluyendo todos los métodos utilizados por el grupo para dirigir las presiones hacia todos los aspectos del proceso de creación de políticas públicas. Pág. 251

Magna Carta/Carta Magna Constitución que los barones impusieron al rey John de Inglaterra en 1215; estableció el principio de que el poder del monarca no era absoluto y garantizó los derechos fundamentales, como el de un juicio con jurado y procesos establecidos legales para la nobleza. Pág. 29

Major parties/Partidos principales En la política estadounidense, los partidos Demócrata y Republicano. Pág. 116

Majority opinion/Opinión mayoritaria Llamada oficialmente Opinión de la Corte; anuncia la decisión de la Corte sobre el caso y describe el razonamiento sobre el que ésta se basa. Pág. 522

Mandate/Mandato Las intrucciones u órdenes que un grupo de votantnes da a sus funcionarios electos. Pág. 216

Market economy/Economía de mercado Un sistema económico en el que se basa las decisiones de la producción y el consumo de bienes en el intercambio voluntario de mercados. Pág. 669

Mass media/Medios masivos de comunicación Aquellos medios de comunicación que llegan a grandes audiencias, sobre todo la radio, televisión, publicaciones impresas e Internet. Págs. 211, 391

Mayor-council government/Gobierno de consejo-alcalde El más antiguo y más utilizado tipo de gobierno municipal: un alcalde electo como Presidente y un consejo electo como su cuerpo legislativo. Pág. 726

Medicaid/*Medicaid* Programa administrado por el Senado para proporcionar seguro médico a las familias de bajos ingresos. Pág. 735

Medium/Medio Un medio de comunicación; algo que transmite información. Pág. 223

Mercantilism/Mercantilismo Política económica diseñada para potenciar la entrada de metales preciosos, como oro y plata, a través del comercio, y hacer que la economía nacional sea independiente de la de otros países. p. 629

Metropolitan area/Área metropolitana La ciudad y el área que le circunda. Pág. 731

Minister/Ministro Miembro del gabinete, y más frecuentemente de la Cámara de los Comunes. Pág. 649

Minor party/Partido minoritario Partido político que no cuenta con gran apoyo. Pág. 119

Miranda Rule/Regla Miranda Derechos constitucionales que la policía debe especificar a un sospechoso antes de que pueda hacérsele una interrogación. Pág. 582

Misdemeanor/Falta leve Delito menor que se castiga mediante una pequeña multa o un breve período de encarcelamiento. Pág. 704

Mixed economy/Economía mixta Sistema económico en donde la iniciativa privada existe en combinación con una considerable regulación y promoción gubernamental. Pág. 21

Monarch/Monarca Un gobernante hereditario. Pág. 627

Monopoly/Monopolio Empresa que es la única fuente de un producto o servicio. Pág. 661

Multiparty/Multipartidista Sistema en el que varios partidos importantes y muchos secundarios existen, compiten seriamente y en realidad ganan puestos de elección popular. Pág. 122

National Bonus Plan/Plan de bono nacional Propuesta para elegir al Presidente y Vicepresidente, mediante el cual se le otorgaría una suma nacional de 102 votos electorales al ganador del voto popular, además de los votos del colegio electoral de su estado. Si ningún candidato recibe al menos 321 votos electorales, se llevaría a cabo una elección complementaria. Pág. 384

National convention/Convención nacional Reunión en la que los delegados de un partido votan para elegir a sus candidatos a la presidencia y vicepresidencia. Pág. 372

Naturalization/Naturalización Proceso legal mediante el cual los ciudadanos de un país se convierten en ciudadanos de otro. Págs. 302, 614

Necessary and Proper Clause/Cláusula de necesidad y conveniencia Cláusula constitucional que otorga al Congreso el poder de expedir leyes "necesarias y convenientes" para el ejercicio de sus poderes; *ver* implied powers/poderes implícitos. Pág. 305

New Jersey Plan/Plan Nueva Jersey Plan presentado en la Convención Constitucional como una alternativa al Plan Virginia; proponía una legislatura unicameral en la que cada estado estuviera representado de forma equitativa. Pág. 51

Nomination/Nominación Proceso de selección de candidatos en una democracia. Pág. 178

Nonpartisan election/Elección no partidista Elección en la que los candidatos no están identificados por membretes de partidos. Pág. 184

North American Free Trade Agreement/Tratado de Libre Comercio de Norteamérica Acuerdo que elimina las restricciones comerciales entre los Estados Unidos, Canadá y México, con lo cual se incrementa el comercio transfronterizo. Pág. 651

Oath of office/Juramento al asumir un cargo Juramento que hace el Presidente el día que asume la presidencia, jurando "cumplir fielmente" con sus responsabilidades, así como "preservar, proteger y defender" la Constitución. Pág. 393

Off-year election/Elección intermedia Elección del Congreso que ocurre entre las elecciones presidenciales. Págs. 164, 269

Oligarchy/Oligarquía Forma de gobierno en la que el poder de gobernar lo ejerce una elite pequeña y por lo general autonombrada. Pág. 13

One-party system/Sistema unipartidista Sistema político en el que sólo existe un partido. Pág. 123

Open primary/Elección primaria abierta Elección partidista de nominación en la que cualquier votante calificado puede tomar parte. Pág. 183

Opinion leader/Líder de opinión Cualquier persona que por alguna razón tiene una poderosa influencia en los puntos de vista de otras. Pág. 212

Ordinance/Ordenanza Ley local. p. 720

Ordinance power/Poder de decreto Poder del Presidente de emitir órdenes ejecutivas; se fundamenta en la Constitución y en los actos del Congreso. Pág. 394

Original jurisdiction/Jurisdicción original Poder de una corte de atender un caso antes que otra corte. Pág. 509

Oversight function/Función de vigilancia Revisión de las políticas y los programas de la rama ejecutiva por parte de los comités legislativos. Pág. 281

Pardon/Perdón Exoneración del castigo o de las consecuencias legales de un crimen que lleva a cabo el Presidente (en el caso federal) o el gobernador (en el caso estatal). Págs. 407, 699

Parliamentary government/Gobierno parlamentario Forma de gobierno en la que la rama ejecutiva está conformada por el primer ministro, o premier, y el gabinete oficial. Pág. 16

Parochial/Parroquial Relacionado con la iglesia, como las escuelas parroquiales. Pág. 538

Parole/Liberación bajo palabra Libertad condicional de un prisionero poco antes de que termine el lapso de su sentencia original. Pág. 699

Partisan/Partidista Legislador que le debe fidelidad, en primer lugar, a su partido político, por lo que vota de acuerdo con la línea del partido. Pág. 281

Partisanship/Partidarismo Acción gubernamental basada en la vigorosa fidelidad a un partido político. Pág. 117

Party caucus/Junta de dirigentes de partido Reunión cerrada de los miembros de la Cámara de Representantes o del Senado; también se conoce como Conferencia de partido. Pág. 324

Party identification/Identificación con el partido Lealtad de la gente hacia un partido político. Pág. 171

Party in power/Partido en el poder En la política estadounidense, el partido en el poder es aquel que controla la rama ejecutiva; es decir la presidencia, a nivel nacional, o la gubernatura, a nivel estatal. Pág. 118

Patent/Patente Licencia expedida a un inventor para garantizar el derecho exclusivo de manufactura, uso o venta de su invento, durante un tiempo limitado. Pág. 303

Patronage/Patrocinio Práctica de dar trabajo a los simpatizantes y amigos. Pág. 438

Payroll tax/Impuesto sobre la nómina Gravamen tasado a casi todos los empleadores y sus empleados, así como a las personas autoempleadas; cantidad debida por los empleados que se les descuenta de su salario. Pág. 450

Peer group/Grupo de camaradas Gente con la que uno se asocia regularmente y que incluye a socios, amigos, compañeros de clase, vecinos y compañeros de trabajo. Pág. 212

Perjury/Perjurio El hecho de mentir bajo juramento. Pág. 311

Persona non grata/Persona *non grata* Una persona que no es bienvenida; se utiliza para describir a los funcionarios diplomáticos destituidos. Pag. 401

Petition of Right/Solicitud de Derecho Documento preparado por el Parlamento y firmado por el rey Charles I de Inglaterra en 1628; cuestionó la idea del derecho divino de los reyes y declaró que incluso el monarca está sujeto a las leyes de la tierra. Pág. 30

Picketing/Vigilancia Manifestación de los trabajadores en el sitio donde están en huelga. Pág. 551

Plaintiff/Demandante En el derecho civil, la parte que entabla un juicio u otra acción legal contra otra (el demandado) en una corte. Pág. 509

Platform/Plataforma Un enunciado formal por parte de un partido político respecto a sus principios básicos, opiniones sobre cuestiones políticas importantes y objetivos. Pág. 373

Pluralistic society/Sociedad pluralista Sociedad que está formada por distintos grupos y culturas. Pág. 121

Plurality/Mayoría En una elección, el número de votos que el candidato que va a la punta tiene de ventaja sobre su competidor más cercano. Pág. 120

Pocket veto/Veto indirecto Tipo de veto que el Presidente puede utilizar después de que una legislatura se suspende; se aplica cuando un Presidente no firma formalmente o rechaza una propuesta de ley, dentro del tiempo comprendido para eso; *ver* Veto. Pág. 346

Police power/Facultad policial Autoridad de cada estado para proteger y promover la salud pública, la seguridad, la moral y el bienestar general de su pueblo. Págs. 566, 691

Political Action Committee/Comité de acción política Extensión política de grupos de interés especiales, los cuales tienen un gran interés en la política pública. Pág. 197

Political efficacy/Eficacia política La influencia o eficacia individual en la política. Pág. 166

Political party/Partido político Grupo de personas que buscan controlar el gobierno mediante el triunfo en las elecciones y la conservación de los puestos públicos. Pág. 116

Political socialization/Socialización política Proceso mediante el que la gente obtiene sus actitudes y opiniones políticas. Pág. 168

Politico/Político Legislador que intenta equilibrar los elementos básicos de los miembros del directorio, los delegados y los roles partidistas; *ver* trustee/independiente, delegate/delegado, partisan/partidista. Pág. 281

Poll book/Padrón electoral Lista de todos los votantes registrados en cada distrito. Pág. 155

Poll tax/Impuesto sobre el padrón electoral Gravamen especial, exigido por los estados como una condición para votar. Pág. 157

Polling place/Casilla electoral Lugar donde los votantes que viven en cierto distrito acuden a votar. Pág. 190

Popular sovereignty/Soberanía popular Principio básico del sistema estadounidense de gobierno que establece que el pueblo es la fuente de todos los poderes gubernamentales, y que el gobierno sólo puede existir con el consentimiento de los gobernados. Págs. 39, 685

Preamble/Preámbulo Introducción. Pág. 65

Precedent/Precedente Decisión judicial que se toma como un ejemplo a seguir en el futuro para casos similares. Págs. 522, 703

Precinct/Distrito Unidad mínima de la administración electoral; distrito de votación. Págs. 140, 190

Preclearance/Preautorización Ordenada por la Ley de Derechos de Votos de 1965, respecto a la aprobación anterior, por parte del Departamento de Justicia, de los cambios en las leyes electorales existentes o nuevas en ciertos estados. Pág. 162

President of the Senate/Presidente del Senado Funcionario que preside un Senado; en el Congreso es el Vicepresidente de los Estados Unidos; en la legislatura estatal, cualquier vicegobernador o un senador. Pág. 323

President *pro tempore*/Presidente *pro tempore* Miembro del Senado de Estados Unidos, o de la cámara superior de la legislatura estatal, elegido para ser Presidente, en caso de ausencia del Presidente del Senado. Pág. 323

Presidential elector/Elector presidencial Persona elegida por los votantes para representarlos en la selección formal del Presidente y Vicepresidente. Pág. 365

Presidential government/Gobierno presidencial Forma de gobierno en la que las ramas ejecutivas y legislativas del gobierno están separadas, son independientes y están en la misma jerarquía. Pág. 15

Presidential primary/Elección presidencial primaria Elección en la que los votantes de un partido: (1) eligen a varios o a todos los delegados de la organización partidista estatal para la convención nacional de su partido, y/o (2) expresan una preferencia por alguno de los distintos contendientes para la nominación presidencial de su partido. Pág. 369

Presidential succession/Sucesión presidencial Plan mediante el cual se resuelve la vacante presidencial. Pág. 359

Presidential Succession Act of 1947/Ley para la sucesión presidencial de 1947 Ley que especifica el orden para la sucesión presidencial, después del Vicepresidente. Pág. 360

Presiding officer/Primer funcionario Presidente. Pág. 45

Preventive detention/Arresto preventivo Ley que permite a los jueces federales ordenar que un acusado de felonía sea arrestado, sin derecho a fianza, cuando existen buenas razones para creer que cometerá otro crimen grave antes del juicio. Pág. 586

Prior restraint/Prohibición anticipada El gobierno no puede reprimir las ideas antes de que se expresen. Pág. 549

Privatization/Privatización Regresar las empresas nacionales a la iniciativa privada. Pág. 675

Privileges and Immunities Clause/Cláusula de privilegios e inmunidades Estipulación constitucional (Artículo IV, Sección 2), en que se conceden ciertos "privilegios e inmunidades" a los ciudadanos, sin importar su estado de residencia; ningún estado puede hacer distinciones no razonables entre sus propios residentes y aquellas personas que vivan en otros estados. Pág. 107

Probable Cause/Causa probable Fundamentos razonables, sospecha razonable de un crimen. Pág. 571

Procedural due process/Procesos legales establecidos El gobierno debe emplear procedimientos y métodos justos. Pág. 565

Process of incorporation/Proceso de incorporación Proceso de integrar, o incluir, la mayor parte de las garantías de la

Declaración de los derechos en la Cláusula de proceso legal establecido de la 14a enmienda. Pág. 535

Progressive tax/Impuesto progresivo Tipo de impuesto que es proporcional con el ingreso. Págs. 449, 742

Project grant/Subvención de proyecto Tipo de subvención de fondos públicos; proporcionada para proyectos específicos de los estados, las localidades y las oficinas privadas que la solicitan. Pág. 103

Proletariat/Proletariado La clase trabajadora. Pág. 667

Propaganda/Propaganda Una técnica inmoral de persuasión orientada a influir en los comportamientos individuales o colectivos con el objeto de originar una creencia particular, independientemente de su validez. Pág. 249

Property tax/Impuesto a la propiedad Gravamen sobre los bienes raíces y la propiedad personal. Pág. 742

Proportional plan/Plan proporcional Propuesta para seleccionar electores presidenciales, mediante la cual cada candidato recibiría la misma cantidad de votos electorales de un estado que recibió durante la votación popular del estado. Pág. 382

Proportional representation rule/Regla de la representación proporcional Procedimiento aplicado en las elecciones primarias del partido Demócrata, en el cual cualquier candidato que gane al menos el 15% de los votos emitidos en una elección primaria, obtienen el número de delegados a la convención estatal demócrata, que le corresponda a esa proporción de las primarias. Pág. 371

Proprietary/Propiedad Organizada por un dueño (persona a quien el rey le ha otorgado tierras). Pág. 32

Prorogue/Prórroga Aplazamiento, como en la sesión legislativa. Pág. 265

Public affairs/Asuntos públicos Aquellos acontecimientos y asuntos que importan al público en general, por ejemplo: la política, los temas públicos y la determinación de las políticas públicas. Págs. 208, 239

Public agenda/Agenda pública Asuntos públicos sobre los cuales está enfocada la atención de las personas. Pág. 228

Public debt/Deuda pública Todo el dinero que ha pedido prestado el gobierno a lo largo de los años y que todavía no paga, además del interés acumulado sobre ese capital; también se conoce como deuda nacional o deuda federal. Págs. 296, 455

Public-interest group/Grupo de interés público Grupo de interés que busca instituir determinadas políticas públicas de beneficio para la mayoría de las personas de su país, sin importar si pertenecen o apoyan a la organización. Pág. 247

Public opinion/Opinión pública Colección compleja de opiniones de diversas personas; la suma de todos sus puntos de vista. Pág. 209

Public opinion poll/Encuestas de opinión pública Dispositivos que intentan recolectar información al hacerle preguntas a las personas. Pág. 217

Public policy/Políticas públicas Todas las metas que un gobierno se fija, así como los distintos cursos de acción que toma en sus intentos por llevar a cabo esos objetivos. Págs. 4, 236

Quasi-judicial/Cuasi-judicial Que tiene que ver con los poderes que en alguna forma son judiciales. Pág. 433

Quasi-legislative/Cuasi-legislativo Que tiene que ver con poderes que son legislativos en cierta medida. Pág. 433

Quorum/Quórum Mínimo número de miembros que debe estar presente para que un cuerpo legislativo funcione; mayoría. Págs. 58, 339

Quota/Cuota Regla que requiere que determinado número de trabajos o ascensos se den en miembros de ciertos grupos. Pág. 610

Quota sample/Muestra de cuota Muestra deliberadamente hecha para reflejar ciertas características importantes de una determinada población. Pág. 219

Random sample/Muestra aleatoria Determinado número de gente seleccionada al azar y que vive en ciertos lugares seleccionados de manera aleatoria. Pág. 218

Ratification/Ratificación Aprobación formal, consentimiento definitivo de la eficacia de una constitución, de una enmienda constitucional o de un tratado. Pág. 44

Reapportion/Reasignación Redistribución, como los escaños en un cuerpo legislativo. Pág. 267

Recall/Retirada inesperada Procedimiento de petición por el que los votantes puedan destituir a un funcionario oficial antes de terminar su mandato. Pág. 696

Recognition/Reconocimiento El poder exclusivo de un Presidente para reconocer (establecer relaciones diplomáticas) a estados extranjeros. Pág. 400

Redress/Resarcir Satisfacer una queja, por lo general mediante un pago. Pág. 524

Referendum/Referendo Proceso mediante el cual una medida legislativa se consulta con los votantes de los estados para su aprobación o rechazo final. Pág. 693

Refugee/Refugiado Persona que abandona su hogar para buscar protección contra la guerra, la persecución o algún otro peligro. Pág. 597

Regional body/Cuerpo regional Entidad de gobierno local diseñada para atender problemas que traspasan las fronteras de un condado o ciudad. p. 722

Regional security alliances/Alianzas regionales de seguridad Tratados mediante los cuales los Estados Unidos y otros países han acordado actuar colectivamente para enfrentar una agresión en una determinada parte del mundo. Pág. 492

Register/Padrón Registro o lista de nombres, a menudo bajo el cuidado de un funcionario asignado para esa labor. Pág. 439

Registration/Registro Procedimiento de identificación del voto pensado para evitar votaciones fraudulentas. Pág. 154

Regressive tax/Impuesto regresivo Gravamen con una tasa semejante, sin considerar el nivel de ingreso de los contribuyentes o su capacidad para pagarlo. Págs. 451, 741

Repeal/Revocación Derogación. Pág. 37

Representative government/Gobierno representativo Sistema de gobierno en el que las políticas públicas están elaboradas por funcionarios elegidos por los votantes y que rinden cuentas en elecciones periódicas; *ver* democracy/democracia. Pág. 29

Reprieve/Suspensión Un aplazamiento oficial de la ejecución de una sentencia; *ver* pardon/perdón. Págs. 407, 699

Reservation/Reservación Terrenos públicos que un gobierno reserva para el uso de las tribus nativas estadounidenses. Pág. 596

Reserved powers/Poderes reservados Aquellos poderes que la Constitución no otorga al gobierno nacional, pero que tampoco niega, al mismo tiempo a los estados. Pág. 92

Resolution/Resolución Medida relativa al funcionamiento de cualquier Cámara, o una expresión de opinión sobre un asunto; no tiene la fuerza de una ley y no requiere la firma del Presidente. Pág. 335

Retention election/Elección de retención Voto de sí o no para renovar el período en el cargo de un juez designado. p. 711

Revenue sharing/Participación en los ingresos Forma de ayuda monetaria federal, vigente de 1972 a 1987, bajo la cual el Congreso daba una participación anual de los ingresos tributarios, sin que virtualmente hubiera ninguna restricción en su uso, a los estados y sus ciudades, condados y villas. Pág. 102

Reverse discrimination/Discriminación inversa Segregación en contra del grupo mayoritario. Pág. 610

Right of association/Derecho de asociación Derecho de asociarse con otros para promover causas políticas, sociales, económicas y de otra índole. Pág. 558

Right of legation/Derecho de legación Derecho a enviar y recibir representantes diplomáticos. Pág. 470

Rider/Cláusula adicional Provisión poco probable de ser aprobada por méritos propios, que se agrega a un proyecto de ley importante que se tiene la seguridad que será aprobado, así que dicha cláusula "cabalga" por todo ese proceso legislativo. Pág. 335

Rule of law/Gobierno de la ley *ver* constitutionalism/constitucionalismo. Pág. 66.

Runoff primary/Elección primaria complementaria Elección primaria en la que los dos candidatos con más votos en la elección primaria directa se enfrentan; el ganador de esa votación se convierte en el nominado. Pág. 184

Sales tax/Impuesto a las ventas Gravamen sobre las ventas de distintos bienes, el cual paga el comprador. Pág. 741

Sample/Muestra Una porción representativa del público. Pág. 218

Search warrant/Orden de allanamiento Autorización judicial para hacer registros. Pág. 566

Secretary/Secretario Funcionario a cargo de un departamento de gobierno. Pág. 424

Sectionalism/Regionalismo Preocupación estrecha, o devoción por los intereses de una región del país. Pág. 129

Sedition/Sedición Crimen de intentar derrocar al gobierno mediante la fuerza, o de interrumpir las actividades legales por medio de actos violentos. Pág. 547

Seditious speech/Discurso sedicioso El llamado o el apoyo a un intento de derrocar al gobierno mediante la fuerza, o a la interrupción de actividades legales por medio de la violencia. Pág. 547

Segregation/Segregación Separación de un grupo respecto a otro. Pág. 602

Select committee/Comité selecto Comité legislativo creado por un tiempo limitado y para algún propósito específico; también se conoce como comité especial. Pág. 331

Senatorial courtesy/Cortesía senatorial Costumbre de que el Senado no aprobará una nominación presidencial, si esa designación no es aprobada por el senador del partido mayoritario de ese estado, en donde la persona designada habría de servir. Pág. 81

Seniority rule/Regla de antigüedad Regla no escrita de ambas Cámaras del Congreso, de acuerdo con la cual, los puestos más altos de cada una de ellas los ocuparán aquellos miembros que tengan un historial de servicio más antiguo; se aplica de forma más estricta a las presidencias de los comités. Pág. 326

Separate-but-equal doctrine/Doctrina de iguales pero separados Base constitucional para leyes que segregan a un grupo respecto a otro, con base en la raza. (Leyes Jim Crow.) Pág. 602.

Separation of powers/Separación de poderes Principio básico del sistema de gobierno estadounidense, según el cual los poderes ejecutivo, legislativo y judicial están divididos en tres ramas independientes e iguales; *ver* checks and balances/pesos y contrapesos. Pág. 66

Serf/Siervo Trabajador unido a la tierra que cultivaba. p. 626

Session/Sesión Período regular durante el cual reune el Congreso para atender a asuntos oficiales. Pág. 264

Shadow cabinet/Gabinete alterno Miembros de los partidos de oposición que vigilan, o supervisan, a un miembro particular del gabinete, y que estarían listos para ejercer el gobierno. Pág. 649

Shield law/Ley Escudo Ley que ofrece a los reporteros cierta protección contra la revelación de sus fuentes o la publicación de otra información confidencial durante los procedimientos legales. Pág. 550

Single-interest group/Grupos de un único interés Comités de acción política que concentran sus esfuerzos exclusivamente en un solo asunto. Pág. 251

Single-issue parties/Partidos de un único asunto Partidos que se concentran en un solo aspecto de la política pública. Pág. 132

Single-member district/Distrito de un solo miembro Distrito electoral en donde los votantes eligen, en la papeleta electoral, una sola persona para cada cargo. Págs. 120, 270

Slander/Calumnia Utilización falsa y maliciosa del discurso hablado. Pág. 547

Socialism/Socialismo Filosofía económica y política basada en la idea de que los beneficios de la actividad económica deberían distribuirse de manera equitativa a toda la sociedad. Pág. 666

Softliner/Partidario de la línea blanda Figura poderosa en un gobierno tirano partidario de reformas. p. 640

Soft money/Fondos no fiscalizados Fondos otorgados al estado y a organizaciones partidistas locales para actividades relacionadas con el voto, por ejemplo: registro de votantes, envío de propaganda por correo, anuncios. Pág. 201

Sound bite/Informe sucinto Informaciones breves y concisas que pueden despacharse en 30 ó 45 segundos. Pág. 229

Sovereign/Soberano Tener poder supremo y absoluto dentro de su propio territorio; no estar subordinado ni ser responsable ante ninguna otra autoridad. Pág. 6

Speaker of the House/Vocero de la Cámara Funcionario que preside la Cámara de Representantes y que es electo por el partido mayoritario en la Cámara, al cual pertenece. Pág. 322

Special district/Distrito especial Unidad independiente creada para llevar a cabo una o más funciones gubernamentales relacionadas a nivel local. Pág. 721

Special session/Sesión especial Sesión extraordinaria de un cuerpo legislativo, convocada para tratar una situación de emergencia. Pág. 265

Splinter parties/Partidos de escisión Partidos formados por la fractura de uno de los principales partidos; la mayor parte de los partidos pequeños importantes en el ámbito político estadounidense son partidos de escisión. Pág. 133

Split-ticket voting/Voto diferenciado Votar, en la misma elección, por candidatos de distintos partidos, para puestos diferentes. Págs. 141, 171

Spoils system/Sistema de prebendas Práctica de ofrecer cargos y otros favores gubernamentales a los simpatizantes y amigos políticos. Pág. 438

Staff agency/Oficina de apoyo Tipo de agencia cuya función es dar respaldo al Presidente y a otros administradores, ofreciendo consejos y otro tipo de asistencia en la administración de la organización. Pág. 418

Standing committee/Comisión permanente Comité permanente de un cuerpo legislativo a quien se presentan las propuestas de ley sobre una materia específica; *ver* comité selecto. Pág. 329

State/Estado Conjunto de personas que viven en un territorio definido y que tienen un gobierno con el poder de legislar y de hacer cumplir la ley, sin tener el consentimiento de una autoridad superior. Pág. 5

Statutory law/Ley estatuida Ley aprobada por los legisladores. Pág. 688

Straight-ticket voting/Voto duro Práctica de votar en una elección por los candidatos de un solo partido. Pág. 171

Straw vote/Encuesta pre-electoral Encuestas que pretenden conocer la opinión de la gente haciendo simplemente la misma pregunta a una gran cantidad de personas. Pág. 217

Strict constructionist/Construccionista estricto Persona que defiende una interpretación estrecha de las estipulaciones de la Constitución, en particular las referentes al otorgamiento de poderes al gobierno federal. Pág. 291

Strong-mayor government/Gobierno de alcalde vigoroso Tipo de gobierno en el que el alcalde encabeza la administración de la ciudad. Pág. 727

Subcommittee/Subcomité División de un comité existente que se forma para atender asuntos específicos. Pág. 337

Subpoena/Citación Orden para que se presente una persona o para que se elaboren documentos u otros materiales solicitados. Pág. 313

Subsidy/Subsidio Una subvención de dinero, por lo general por un gobierno. Pág. 197

Substantive due process/Proceso legal duradero El gobierno debe crear políticas y leyes justas. Pág. 565

Successor/Sucesor Persona que hereda un título o un cargo. Pág. 311

Suffrage/Sufragio El derecho de votar. Pág. 148

Surplus/Superávit Cuando hay más ingresos que gastos. Pág. 455

Symbolic speech/Discurso simbólico Expresión mediante la conducta; comunicación de ideas a través de expresiones faciales, lenguaje corporal o mediante el uso de un signo o portando una banda en el brazo. Pág. 551

Tax/Impuesto Cargo gravado por el gobierno a las personas o propiedades, con el objeto de satisfacer las necesidades públicas. Pág. 295

Tax return/Declaración de impuestos Declaración del ingreso gravable y de las exenciones y deducciones exigidas. Pág. 449

Term/Término Lapso especificado durante el cual se desempeñará en el cargo un funcionario elegido. Pág. 264

Terrorism/Terrorismo El uso de violencia para intimidar a un gobierno o sociedad. Pág. 478

Three-Fifths Compromise/Avenencia de las tres quintas partes Acuerdo logrado en la Convención Constitucional respecto a que un esclavo debería contarse como tres quintas partes de una persona, para propósitos de determinar la población de un estado. Pág. 52

Totalitarian/Totalitario Gobierno que ejerce un poder (autoridad) dictatorial en casi todos los aspectos de los asuntos humanos. Pág. 14

Township/Municipio División de un condado. Pág. 719

Trade association/Asociación comercial Grupos de interés dentro de la comunidad de los negocios. Pág. 244

Transient/Transeúnte Persona que vive en un estado sólo por un breve tiempo, sin residencia legal. Pág. 153

Treason/Alta traición Deslealtad hacia el país propio; en la Constitución, librar una guerra en contra de los Estados Unidos, proporcionar aliento u ofrecer ayuda a sus enemigos. Pág. 588

Treaty/Tratado Acuerdo formal entre dos o más estados soberanos. Págs. 80, 399

Trust/Cartel Mecanismo mediante el cual diversas corporaciones de la misma línea de negocios se ponen de acuerdo para eliminar a la competencia y regular los precios. Pág. 661

Trustee/Independiente Legislador que vota en cada asunto de acuerdo con su conciencia y su juicio independiente, sin considerar las opiniones de sus electores o de otros grupos. Pág. 281

Two-party system/Sistema bipartidista Sistema político dominado por dos partidos importantes. Pág. 119

UN Security Council/Consejo de Seguridad de la ONU Panel de 15 miembros que tiene la máxima responsabilidad de la ONU para la conservación de la paz internacional. Pág. 496

Unconstitutional/Inconstitucional Contrario a las estipulaciones constitucionales y, por lo tanto, ilegal, nulo e inválido, que no tiene fuerza ni efecto. Pág. 69

Uncontrollable spending/Gasto incontrolable Gastos que ni el Congreso ni el Presidente tienen el poder de cambiar de manera directa, incluyendo los intereses de la deuda. Pág. 459

Unicameral/Unicameral Adjetivo que describe un cuerpo legislativo con una sola Cámara; *ver* bicameral. Pág. 32

Unitary government/Gobierno unitario Gobierno centralizado en el que los poderes ejercidos por el gobierno pertenecen a una única oficina central. Pág. 14

Use Tax/Impuesto por uso Impuesto a las transacciones en las que no se recaudan impuestos a las ventas. p. 741

Vassal/Vasallo Señor que jura lealtad a una señor más poderoso. p. 626

Veto/Veto Poder del Presidente para rechazar un proyecto de ley aprobado por una legislatura; literalmente (latín) "Prohíbo"; *ver* pocket veto/veto indirecto. Págs. 67, 346

Virginia Plan/Plan Virginia Proyecto presentado por los delegados de Virginia en la Convención Constitucional; proponía un gobierno con tres poderes y una legislatura bicameral en la que la representación de cada estado estuviera determinada por su población o por su apoyo financiero al gobierno central. Pág. 51

Ward/Distrito Unidad en la que suelen dividirse las ciudades para la elección de los miembros del consejo municipal. Pág. 140

Warrant/Mandamiento Orden judicial que autoriza o hace legal alguna acción oficial, como la orden de allanamiento o la orden de arresto. Pág. 709

Weak-mayor government/Gobierno de alcalde débil Tipo de gobierno en el que el alcalde comparte las obligaciones ejecutivas con otros funcionarios electos. Pág. 727

Welfare/Beneficencia Ayuda en efectivo a los pobres. Pág. 735

Welfare state/Estado benefactor Países que ofrecen una amplia gama de servicios sociales a un bajo costo o de manera gratuita para los usuarios. Pág. 668

Whips/*Whips* Auxiliares de los líderes de las fracciones partidistas en la Cámara de Representantes y el Senado que son responsables de vigilar y ordenar los votos. Pág. 325

Winner-take-all/El ganador se lleva todo Sistema casi obsoleto en donde un aspirante presidencial que ganaba la preferencia del voto en las elecciones primarias, automáticamente obtenía el apoyo de todos los delegados elegidos en dichas elecciones. Pág. 371

Writ of assistance/Auto de ayuda Orden general de allanamiento con la que los funcionarios aduanales británicos invadían los hogares privados en busca de bienes de contrabando. Pág. 571

Writ of certiorari/Auto de avocación o *certiorari* Orden emitida por una corte superior dirigida a una corte inferior para que remita el expediente de un determinado caso para su revisión; el significado en latín de la expresión es "tener mayor certeza". Pág. 520

Writ of habeas corpus/Auto de *habeas corpus* Orden judicial que evita arrestos y encarcelamientos injustos. Pág. 576

Zoning/Zonificación Práctica de dividir a una ciudad en determinado número de distritos y de regular los usos que se dará a la propiedad en cada uno de ellos. Pág. 729

Index

Note: Entries with a page number followed by an *(c)* denote reference to a chart on that page; those followed by a *(p)* denote a photo; those followed by a *(m)* denote a map; those followed by a *(g)* denote a graph.

Index **827** ★★★

Index

Index

Index **Index** **839** ★★★★

Acknowledgments

Team Credits The people who made up the **Magruder's American Government** team—representing editorial, editorial services, design services, market research, on-line services/multimedia development, product marketing, production services, and publishing processes—are listed below. Bold type denotes core team members.

Joyce Barisano, Todd Christy, Lori-Anne Cohen, Gabriela Perez Fiato, **Paul Gagnon, Mary Hanisco, Lance Hatch, Dotti Marshall, Grace Massey,** Tim McDonald, Judi Pinkham, Lisa Smith-Ruvalcaba, **Luess Sampson-Lizotte,** Emily Soltanoff, Mark Staloff, Merce Wilczek

Cover Design

Sweetlight Creative Partners; Paul Gagnon

Cover Image

Flag, Terry Why/Index Stock Imagery, Inc.; **The White House,** James Lemass/Index Stock Imagery, Inc.

Illustration

Tables and graphs: Accurate Art, Inc., Outlook/ANCO, and Matt Mayerchak **Creative Art:** Steve Artley **20, 145, 185, 201, 240, 349, 383, 558, 579, 585, 621;** Annie Bissett **133;** Jim Bliss **134;** Kathy W. Boake **706;** Doug Bowles **293;** James Bozzini **517;** Ken Condon **344;** Richard Ewing **291, 518;** Leighton & Co./Lisa Manning **6, 659;** MapQuest.com, Inc **72;** Karen Minot **xlii, xliii, xlvii, 16, 31, 57, 73, 101, 128–129,140, 180, 183, 184, 191, 193, 199, 209, 219, 276, 280, 295, 304, 308, 322, 367, 369, 380, 395, 400, 417, 439, 461, 509, 510, 513, 541, 565, 578, 587, 595, 614, 615, 687, 697, 719, 727, 728, 729;** Brucie Rosch **lii, 155;** Neil Stewart **68, 330, 345, 420, 426, 472, 507, 514, 520;** Baker Vail **100, 263, 268, 270, 271, 487, 492, 630, 638, 642, 647, 651, 724;** XNR Productions., Inc. **270, 630, 722**

Picture Research

Paula Wehde, Siri Schwartzman

Photography

Front Matter Page i Flag, Terry Why/Index Stock Imagery, Inc.; **The White House,** James Lemass/Index Stock Imagery, Inc.

Table of Contents Page iv tl, National Portrait Gallery, Smithsonian Institution/Art Resource, NY; **iv m,** H. Armstrong Roberts; **iv bl, bm,** The Granger Collection, New York; **iv br,** AP Photos/Evan Vucci; **v bl,** Russ Lappa; **v tr,** Corbis-Bettman; **v m,** David Young-Wolff/Photo Edit; **v br,** Reuters NewMedia Inc./Corbis; **vi tl,** Jeffery S. Underwood, Ph.D.,United States Air Force Museum Historian; **vi bl,** Collection of Ralph J. Brunke; **vi br,** UPI/Corbis-Bettmann; **vi inset,** Collection of Bette Lane. Photograph ©Rob Huntley/Lightstream; **vii t,** Corbis; **vii tm,** White House Historical Association; **vii bm,** Dennis Brack/Black Star; **vii b,** Brooks Kraft/Corbis; **viii tl,** Corbis; **viii bl,** Sandra Baker/Liaison Agency; **viii bm,** Corbis-Bettmann; **viii br** SuperStock; **ix t,** Corbis-Bettmann; **ix m,** AP/Wide World Photos; **ix b,** Paula Lerner/Woodfin Camp & Associates; **x,** White House Historical Association; **xi,** Richard Bloom/ SABA Press Photos; **xii l,** The Granger Collection, New York; **xii r,** Corbis; **xiii,** The Granger Collection, New York; **xvi t,** Tony Freeman/PhotoEdit; **xvi b,** Art Resource, New York; **xvii tl,** D. Lada/H. Armstrong Roberts; **xvii tm,** H. Armstrong Roberts; **xvii tr,** A.Tovy/H. Armstrong Roberts **xvii ml, mr,** Supreme Court Historical Society; **xvii bl,** Joe Sohm/Visions of America; **xx,** The Granger Collection, New York; **xxiii l,** Tony Freeman/PhotoEdit; **xxiii r,** AP Photo/Pool, Nancee Lewis; **xxv l,** David McNew/Getty Images, Inc.; **xxv r,** AP Photo/Gary Kazanjian; **xxvi l,** Supreme Court Historical Society; **xxvi r,** AP Photo/Charles Dharapak; **xxviii,** Tony Freeman/PhotoEdit; **xxix,** AP Photo/Paul Sakuma; **xxx,** Joe Sohm/Visions of America; **xxxi,** Ron Stroud/Masterfile Corporation; **xxxii,** AP Photo/Stephan Savoia; **xxxiii l,** Bettmann/Corbis; **xxxii r,** AP/Wide World Photos/Kamenko Pajic; **xxxviii,** Pictures Now; **xl,** Skjold Photographs; **xli,** The Grainger Collection, New York; **xlii,** Prentice Hall; **xlv both,** The Grainger Collection, New York; **xlviii,** Russ Lappa; **xlix t,** T. Graham/Corbis Sygma; **xlix b,** James Andanson/Corbis Sygma; **l l,** Dennis Brack/Black Star; **l r,** J.P. Laffont/Corbis Sygma; **liii,** Corbis.

UNIT 1 Page xx–1, Smithsonian Institution; **2–3,** Corbis-Bettman; **4 all,** Visions of America; **5,** Thomas E. Franklin/Bergen Record/Corbis SABA; **7 tl,** The Granger Collection, New York; **7 bl,** Brenda Carter/ National Geographic Society; **7 m,** Erich Lessing/Art Resource; **7 r,** Corbis-Bettmann; **8,** By permission of Johnny Hart and Creators Syndicate, Inc.; **9,** AP Photo/Tim Sharp; **11,** The Granger Collection, New York; **13,** Deb Hebib/Concord Monitor/Impact Visuals; **14 l,** Memorial De Caen/Sygma; **14 r,** Tom Wurl/Stock Boston; **15,** Walter Bibikow/AGE Fotostock; **17,** Kaiser Andree/Sipa Photos; **18,** The Granger Collection, New York; **19,** AP/Wide World Photos/Bill JANSCHA; **21,** Tom & Dee Ann McCarthy/Corbis; **25,** ©The New Yorker Collection 1983 Ed Fisher from cartoonbank.com. All Rights Reserved.; **26–27,** A. Kord/H. Armstrong Roberts; **28,** ©Christie's Images, Ltd. 1999; **29, 33,** The Granger Collection, New York; **34,** Colonial Williamsburg Foundation; **35,** National Portrait Gallery, Smithsonian Institution/Art Resource, New York; **36, 37,** The Granger Collection, New York; **40,** Independence National Historic Park Collection; **41,** SuperStock; **41–42,** Corbis-Bettmann; **42 t,** ©1997 North Wind Pictures; **42 b,** SuperStock; **43,** Corbis; **44, 46,** The Granger Collection, New York; **47,** G. Ahrens/H. Armstrong Roberts; **48,** The Granger Collection, New York; **50,** Art Resource, New York; **52,** Museum of American Textile History, Grant Heilman Photography; **54,** Independence National Historic Park Collection; **55,** AP/Wide World Photos; **56,** American Antiquarian Society; **58 l,** New York State Office of Parks; **58 m,** The Library Company of Philadelphia; **58 r, 61,** The Granger Collection, New York; **62–63,** Art Resource, New York; **64, 64–65,** The Granger Collection, New York; **65,** AP Photos/Evan Vucci; **66,** Hulton Getty; **67,** J.B. Handelsman/cartoonbank.com; **68 l,** D. Lada/H. Armstrong Roberts; **68 m,** H. Armstrong Roberts; **68 r,** A.Tovy/H. Armstrong Roberts; **69,** SuperStock; **69,** Dennis Brack/Black Star; **70,** Kevin Flaming/Corbis; **71,** Bob Strong/Reuters/Corbis; **74,** The Granger Collection, New York; **75 t, 75 bl,** UPI/Corbis-Bettmann; **75 br,** H. Armstrong Roberts; **77,** Dave Schaefer/The Picture; **78,** The Granger Collection, New York; **79,** Wally McNamee/Corbis; **80 t,** Ron Stroud/Masterfile Corporation; **80 b,** Saeed Khan/AFP/Getty Images, Inc.; **81,** The Granger Collection, New York; **82 l,** Russ Lappa; **82 r,** Archive Photos; **85,** Ed Fisher/cartoon bank.com; **86–87,** Joe Sohm/Visions of America; **88,** Tony Freeman/PhotoEdit; **89 t,** Les Stone/Sygma; **89 b,** David R. Frazier Photolibrary/ Photo Researchers; **90 l,** Mark C. Burnett/Stock Boston; **90 m,** Jeff Greenberg/Stock Boston; **90 r,** AP Photo; **91,** Trippet /Sipa Photos; **92,** Dave Lawrence/The Stock Market; **94 ,** Index Stock Imagery; **96,** Stock Boston; **97,** The Granger Collection, New York; **98,** Reuters/Robert Galbraith/Landov; **99,** David McNew/Getty Images, Inc.; **101,** Michael Dwyer/Stock Boston; **102,** Bob Daemmrich/Stock Boston; **104,** Pat O'Hara/Corbis; **105,** David N. Davis/Photo Researchers; **106,** Russ Lappa; **107,** Bob Daemmrich/Stock Boston; **108 l,** Lee Snider/The Image Works; **108 r,** Bob Krist/Corbis; **111,** Frank Cotham/cartoonbank.com.

UNIT 2 Page 112–113, Sipa Press; **114–115,** Richard Ellis/Corbis Sygma; **116 both,** Ian Wagreich/Illustrative Images; **117,** Brooks Kraft/Corbis; **118 l,** Reuters NewMedia Inc./Corbis; **118 m,** AP Photo/Dennis Cook; **119,** Russ Lappa; **120,** Michael Smith/Liaison Agency; **120 r,** Ian Wagreich/Illustrative Images; **121 t,** "Dunagin's People" by Ralph Dunagin, Reprinted with special permission of N.A.S., Inc.; **121 b,** AP Photo/Joe Cavaretta; **122,** EPA-Photo/ANSA/Mario DeRenzis; **123,** National Portrait Gallery, Smithsonian Institution, Art Resource, New York; **125,** Win McNamee/Corbis; **126,** Museum of American Political Life, University of Hartford, West Hartford, CT; **127 both,** The Granger Collection, New York; **128,** Museum of American Political Life, University of Hartford, West Hartford, CT; **132 t,** Museum of American Political Life; **132** Richard Hayes; **134 r,** Corbis; **134 the rest,** The Granger Collection, New York; **136,** AP Photo/J. Scott Applewhite; **137,** Joe Sohm/The Image Works; **139 l,** William Thomas Cain/Getty Images, Inc.; **139 r,** AP Photo/File; **141 t,** AP Photo/Eric Gay Pool; **141b,** ©1991 The *New Yorker* Collection/J.B Handelsman from cartoonbank.com; **146–147,** The Piedmont Library/Art Resource, New York; **148 l,** Joe Griffin/Archive Photos; **148 r,** The Granger Collection, New York; **149 t,** Bob Daemmrich Photography; **149 l,** The Granger Collection, New York; **149 r,** Library of Congress; **151 t,** Bob Daemmrich/Stock Boston; **151 b,** Tony Freeman/Photo Edit; **152,** Bob Daemmrich/The Image Works; **153,** ©1870 Harper's Weekly; **154,**"Taylor"/*Albuquerque Tribune,* N.M./Rothco; **155,** Mauldin/© 1952 *St. Louis Post-Dispatch;* **157,** © 1978 Matt Herron/Take Stock; **158,** ©2000 Mick Stevens from cartoonbank.com. All rights reserved.; **159,** Eve Arnold/Magnum Photos; **160,** The Granger Collection, New York; **161 both,** Corbis-Bettmann; **162,** Charles Moore/Black Star; **163,** Corbis-Bettmann; **165,** "ROB ROGERS" Reprinted by permission of UFS, Inc.; **166,** KAL/*The Baltimore Sun;* **168,** Jane Marinsky/Images.com; **169,** Gordon Hodge/Corbis Sygma; **171,** Tom Vano; **175,** © 1986 *The Philadelphia Inquirer.* Reprinted with permission of Universal Press Syndicate. All rights reserved.; **176–177,** Michael Newman/PhotoEdit; **178,** Spencer Grant/PhotoEdit; **179 l,** ©1968 Burt Glinn/Magnum Photos, Inc.; **179 ml,** Owen Franken/ Stock Boston; **179 mr,** Arthur Grace/Corbis Sygma; **179 r,** ©1992 Matthew McVay/SABA Press Photos; **181 both,** The Museum of American Political Life, University of Hartford, West Hartford, CT; **182,** "Dunagin's People" by Ralph Dunagin. Reprinted with special permission of N.A.S., Inc.; **186,** J. Patrick Forden/Corbis Sygma; **187,** UPI/Corbis-Bettman; **188,** Haviv/ SABA Press Photos; **189,** Courtesy, Office of Senator Maria Cantwell **192,** The Museum of American Political Life, University of Hartford, West Hartford, CT; **194,** Russ Lappa; **195,** Robert H. McGee/Getty Images, Inc.; **196,** Federal Election Commission; **202,** ©The New Yorker Collection, 1997 Mick Stevens from cartoonbank.com. All Rights Reserved.; **205,** Steve Sack; **206–207,** NCSA, University of Illinois/Science Photo Library/Photo Researchers, Inc.; **209,** Booth/cartoonbank.com; **210 l,** Gabe Kirchheimer/Black Star; **210 m,** Bob Daemmrich Photography; **210 r,** Tony Freeman/PhotoEdit; **213,** Detroit News; **214,** AP Photo/Harry Cabluck; **215,** R. Ellis/Corbis Sygma; **216,** David McNew/Getty Images, Inc.; **217 t,** Harris Interactive; **217 b,** Prentice Hall; **218,** Reprinted by permission of United Features Syndicate; **220,** Corbis; **221,** By permission of Mike Luckovich and Creators Syndicate; **222 l,** Dana White/ PhotoEdit; **222 r,** www.gallup.com; **223,** Corbis; **224 l,** Bettmann/Corbis; **224 r,** AP/Wide World Photos/Kamenko Pajic; **225,** (1998 data) Pew Research Center's Biennial Media Consumption Survey;(1999 data) Pew Research Center's 1999 Survey; (2000 data) Pew Internet Project's Fall Tracking Survey; (2001 data) Pew Internet Project's August/September Survey; (2002 data) Pew Internet Project's September/October Survey; (2003 data) Pew Internet Project's August Survey **226,** Sam Saregent/Liaison Agency; **227,** David Young-Wolff/Photo Edit; **228,** Patrick Forestier/Corbis Sygma; **229,** Courtesy of Joseph Turow; **230,** Russ Lappa; **233,** MacNelly/MacNelly.com/ *Chicago Tribune*; **234–235,** ©1999 Thomas Dodge/AGStockUSA; **236,** Russ Lappa; **237 l,** Families USA; **237 m,** P.F. Gyro/Corbis Sygma; **237 r,** Bob Daemmrich/Stock Boston; **238, 239,** David Maung/Impact Visuals; **241,** Paul Scott/Corbis Sygma; **242,** American Medical Association/Courtesy AMA Archives; **243 l,** Courtesy of the Santa Monica Chamber of Commerce; **243 r,** Colin Young-Wolff/PhotoEdit; **244,** AP/Wide World Photos/CHITOSE SUZUKI; **245 l,** Porterfield-Chickering/ Photo Researchers, Inc.; **245 r,** Lianne Enkelis/Stock Boston; **246,** Martin Simon/SABA Press Photos; **248,** AP Photo/Ron Edmonds; **249,** http://www.friendsoftheriver.org; **250,** Kamenko Pajic/Sipa Press; **251,** Mike Keefe/Courtesy *Denver Post;* **252 t,** © 1993 Washington Stock Photo; **252 b,** David Young-Wolff/ PhotoEdit; **253 t,** American Conservative Union; **253 b,** State PIRGs; **253l,** Americans for Decocratic Action; **257,** Schwadron/Rothco.

UNIT 3 Page 258–259, R. Krubner/H. Armstrong Roberts; **260–261,** Ian Wagreich /Illustrative Images; **262 l,** AP Photo/Susan Walsh; **262 r,** AP Photo/Justin Sullivan; **264,** Jose Fuste Raga/AGE Fotostock; **265,** AP Photo/Gary Kazanjian; **266,** Reza Estakhrian/Getty Images, Inc.; **271,** Corbis-Bettmann; **273,** Troy Glasgow/Black Star; **274,** Kevin Siers, *The Charlotte Observer,* King Features Syndicate; **275,** The Granger Collection, New York; **278,** ©1890 Puck; **279,** AP Photo/Ron Edmonds; **281,** Liaison Agency; **282 l and m,** Courtesy of Rep. Ileana Ros-Lehtinen; **282 r,** Ian Wagreich/Illustrative Images; **283,** Joseph Farris/cartoonbank.com; **287,** © 1999 by Herblock in *The Washington Post;* **288–289,** Markel/Liaison Agency; **290,** Library of Congress; **291 t,** Courtesy of Representative Xavier Becerra; **292,** Bob Artley, Courtesy *Washington* (Minn) *Daily Globe;* **294,** Najlah Feanny/Stock Boston; **296,** ©1986 Jim Morin, The Miami Herald. Reprinted with special permission of Cartoonists & Writers Syndicate; **297,** The Granger Collection, New York; **298 l,** Jonathan Nourok/Getty Images, Inc; **298 r,** John Johnston/Grant Heilman

Photography; **299 b,** Courtesy Cybercoin; **299 the rest,** Courtesy of the Federal Reserve Bank of San Francisco; **300,** Andrew Sacks/AGStockUSA; **303 all,** Russ Lappa; **305,** "The Federal Procession in N.Y., 1788" from Lamb's History of the City of N.Y. American Antiquarian Society. Hand-colored by Sandi Rygiel/Picture Research Consultants; **306 l,** Library of Congress; **306 r,** Collection of Ralph J. Brunke; **307 t,** Jeffery S. Underwood, Ph.D.,United States Air Force Museum Historian; **307 b,** Harry Edelman/Black Star; **307 tr,** Ray Stott/The Image Works; **309,** R. Ellis/Corbis Sygma; **310,** UPI/Corbis-Bettmann; **310 inset,** Collection of Bette Lane. Photograph©Rob Huntley/Lightstream; **311 tl,** SuperStock; **311 bl,** Collection of Bill McClenaghan; **311 tr,** Corbis; **311 br,** Terry Ashe/Liaison Agency; **313,** RolandFreeman/ Magnum Photos; **314,** Corbis; **317,** © 2000 by Herblock in the *Washington Post;* **318–319,** Ian Wagreich/Illustrative Images; **320,** United States Congress; **321,** Brad Markel/Liaison Agency; **322,** The New Yorker Collection, 1988 Donald Reilly from cartoonbank.com; **323,** AP Photo/Ron Edmonds **327,** AP Photo/Joe Marquette; **328,** Brad Markel/Liaison Agency; **329,** AP Photos/U.S. Mint; **330,** A.Tovy/H. Armstrong Roberts; **334,** United States House of Representatives; **336,** Corbis; **337,** AP Photo/Saeed Khan, Pool; **338,** Tomaschoff, Rheinische Post, Dusseldorf Germany/ Creators & Writers Syndicate; **339,** Courtesy of the Office of Congresswoman Carolyn Cheeks Kilpatrick; **341,** Royalty-Free/Corbis; **342,** United States Senate; **343,** AP/Wide World Photos; **346,** Susan Sterner/White House/Getty Images, Inc.

UNIT 4 Page 350–351, Peter Gridley/FPG International; **352–353,** Jim Verchio/USAF/Getty Images; **354,** White House Historical Society; **355,** Markel/Liaison Agency; **356 t,** Corbis; **356 b,** The Granger Collection, New York; **357,** The White House; **357 t,** Allan Tannenbaum/Corbis Sygma; **357 b,** Benainous-Hires-Rey/Liaison Agency; **358,** Dennis Brack/Black Star; **359,** AP Photo/White House, Cecil Stoughton; **360,** Martha Bates/Stock Boston; **361 l,** Russ Lappa; **361 r,** Fred Ward/Black Star; **362,** Frank Cotham from cartoonbank.com; **363,** Reuters News Media, Inc./Corbis **364,** Michael Philippot/Corbis Sygma; **365,** Sally Andersen-Bruce/Museum of American Political Life; **365 buttons,** Museum of American Political Life; **366 l,** The Granger Collection, New York; **366 m and r, 370 t,** Corbis; **370,** 2004 John Kerry Campaign; **370 b,** Bush/Cheney 04 Campaign Website; Chris Hondros/Getty Images, Inc.; **371,** AP Photo/Mark Kegans; **372,** Tribune Media Services, Inc. All rights reserved. Reprinted with permission.; **373 t,** Prentice Hall; **373 b,** Jonathan Nourok/Photo Edit; **374,** Robert Galbraith/Corbis; **376,** Jeff Greenberg/New England Stock Photography; **377 t,** Prentice Hall; **377 b,** Bob Mahoney/The Image Works; **378 t,** Joseph Sohm/ChromoSohm/Corbis; **378 b,** Bob Daemmrich/ Corbis Sygma; **379 l,** ©1993 Joseph Sohm/ChromoSohm/Photo Researchers, Inc.; **379 r,** White House; **387,** The New Yorker Collection 1987, Charles Barsotti from cartoonbank.com; **388–389,** AP Photo/Stephan Savoia; **390,** J.L. Atlan/Corbis Sygma; **391 Taft,** Art Resource, New York; **391 the rest,** White House Historical Association; **393,** St. John's Masonic Lodge of New York; **394 tr,** Richard Strauss/Smithsonian Institution; **394 top insets,** Jeff Tinsley/Smithsonian Institution; **395,** Rob Crandall/Stock Boston; **396,** AP/Wide World Photos; **397,** Courtesy *News & Observer* (N.C.) Distributed by L.A. Times Syndicate; **398,** Ron Sachs/Corbis; **399,** Bettmann/Corbis; **400,** AP Photo/Thomas Van Houtryve; **401 t,** The Granger Collection, New York; **401 tm,** Bettmann/Corbis; **401 m,** Fred Ward/Stockphoto.com; **401 bm,** D. Hudson/Corbis Sygma; **401b,** Brooks Kraft/Corbis; **402,** Reuters/Corbis; **404, 405,** Corbis; **406,** Special Collections Bowdoin Library; **407,** Chicago Historical Society; **408,** AP/Wide World Photos; **411,** ©1999 Herblock/*The Washington Post;* **412–413,** AP Photo/Doug Mills; **414,** Russ Lappa; **415,** Corbis Sygma; **416 l,** U.S. Securities and Exchange Commision; **416 m,** Federal Bureau of Investigation; **416 r,** Farm Credit Administration Agency; **417 l,** A.Tovy/H. Armstrong Roberts; **417 m,** H. Armstrong Roberts; **417 r,** D. Lada/H. Armstrong Roberts; **419,** Dirck Halstead/Liaison Agency; **421 l,** Corbis; **421 m,** U.S. Department of Health and Human Services; **421 r,** A. Ramey/PhotoEdit; **423,** The Granger Collection, New York; **424,** The Granger Collection, New York; **425 l,** Paul Conclin/PhotoEdit; **425 m,** Cary Wolinsky/Stock Boston; **425 r,** Rob Crandall/Stock Boston; **428,** Larry Downing/Reuters/Corbis; **429,** Non Sequitur 2003 Wiley Miller. Reprinted with permission of Universal Press Syndicate. All rights reserved*;* **430,** Russ Lappa; **431,** Larry Downing/Corbis Sygma; **433,** Russ Lappa; **434,** Milepost 92 1/2 /Corbis; **436,** Central Intelligence Agency; **437,** Corbis; **438,** Bettmann/Corbis; **443,** Reprinted by permission, Tribune Media Services; **444–445,** AP Photo/Dan Loh; **446,** Jim Berry/NEA, Inc.; **447 l,** Dagmar Ehling/Photo Researchers, Inc.; **447 m,** Sam Saregent/Liaison Agency; **447 r,** Frank Siteman/Photri; **450,** Michael A. Dwyer/Stock Boston; **451,** Prentice Hall; **453,** Joe Heller/Green Bay Press-Gazette; **454,** Russ Lappa; **455,** Brad Markel/Liaison Agency; **457,** AP/Wide World Photos/Ruth Fremson, *New York Times,* POOL; **458,** Corbis; **459 l,** Tom McCarthy/Photri; **459 r,** Eric Horan/Liaison Agency; **459 inset,** Russ Lappa; **462,** Bruce Beattie/©98 *Daytona Beach News-Journal;* **465,** Jeff Stahler 2003. Reprinted with permission of United Media*;* **466–467,** Tim Sharp/AP/Wide World Photos; **468,** The Granger Collection, New York; **469,** Reuters NewMedia Inc./Corbis; **470,** Alex Wong/Getty Images; **471,** Corbis; **474,** From THE BRASS RING, © 1971 by William Mauldin; **475,** Les Stone/Corbis Sygma; **476,** Tim Shaffer/Reuters/Timepix; **477 both,** US Coast Guard; **478,** AP Photo/Chris O'Meara; **479,** Stone; **481,** Julio Etchart/The World Bank; **483,** Library of Congress; **484,** National Archives; **485,** Archivo Iconografico, S.A./Corbis; **487,** Corbis; **488,** Christopher Morris/Black Star; **490,** AP Photo/Bill Haber; **491,** AP Photo/CARE; **494,** Uriel Sinai/Getty Images, Inc.; **495,** Doug Armand/Stone; **496,** Reuters NewMedia, Inc./Corbis; **497,** Russ Lappa; **501,** ©The New Yorker Collection 1985, James Stevensen from cartoonbank.com. All Rights Reserved.

UNIT 5 Page 502–503, P.Costas/Washington Stock Photo; **504–505,** Dennis Breck/Black Star; **508 t,** Sam C. Pierson, Jr. 1990/Photo Researchers, Inc.; **508 b,** Ian Wagreich/ Illustrative Images; **510,** Dennis Brack/Black Star; **513,** Federal Court of Appeals for the 5th Circuit; **515,** Corbis Bettmann; **516,** AP Photo/Charles Dharapak; **519,** US Supreme Court; **520,** Dorothy Littell Greco/Stock Boston; **522,** Supreme Court Historical Society; **523,** Jana Birchum/The Image Works; **524,** Illustration by Art Lein/Handout/Reuters/Corbis; **524 t,** US Claims Court; **524 b,** ©2000 John R. Welch, White Mountain Apache Tribe Historic Preservation Officer; **525 l,** Courtesy Judge Eugene R. Sullivan; **525 r,** U.S. Court of Appeals; **529,** Corbis-Bettmann; **530,** Camerique/H. Armstrong Roberts; **533,** UPI/Corbis-Bettmann; **534,** The Kobal Collection/Warner Bros/Stephen Vaughan; **535,** Tony Freeman/PhotoEdit; **537,** The Granger Collection, New York; **538,** Bob Daemmrich/Stock Boston; **540,** Corbis; **542,** Eunice Harris/Photo Researchers, Inc.; **543,** From the private collection of Rabbi Albert I. Slomovitz, Ph.D.; **545,** A. Ramey/Stock Boston; **546,** AP/Wide World Photos/Mark Humphrey; **547,** National Archives; **548,** Yates-Brickman/King Features Syndicate; **549,** Fred Ward/Black Star; **550,** International Stock; **552,** Michael Abramson/ Black Star; **554,** REUTERS/Daniel Munoz/Landov; **557,** AP/Wide World Photos/Kamenko Pajic; **561,** © The New Yorker Collection 1991, Mischa Richter from cartoonbank.com. All Rights Reserved.; **562–563,** Stone; **564,** Hulton GettyPicture Library; **566,** ©The New Yorker Collection 1970, J.B. Handelsman from cartoonbank.com. All Rights Reserved.; **569,** South Carolina State Museum; **570,** Marc Asnin/SABA Press Photos; **572,** Photo by Ron Sachs/Consolidated News Pictures/Getty Images, Inc.; **575 t,** Russ Lappa; **575 b,** Bob Daemmrich/Stock Boston; **576,** Library of Congress; **580 l,** AP Photo/John Giles; **580 r,** Lauren Greenfield/Corbis Sygma; **581,** Wayne Stayskal/Courtesy *Tampa Tribune;* **583,** Corbis-Bettmann; **584,** Flip Schulke/Black Star; **586 l,** Andrew Lichenstein/Corbis Sygma; **586 r,** Kevin Maloney/Liaison Agency; **591,** ©The New Yorker Collection 1999, Jack Ziegler from cartoonbank.com. All Rights Reserved.; **592–593,** Corbis-Bettmann; **594,** Bob Daemmrich/Stock Boston; **596,** Fabian Falcon/Stock Boston; **597,** Matthew McVay/SABA Press Photos; **599,** Hulton Getty; **600,** Duomo Photography Inc.; **601,** Sandra Baker/Liaison Agency; **602,** Corbis; **603,** The Newark Art Museum/Art Resource, New York; **604,** Library of Congress; **605 l,** Corbis-Bettmann; **605 r,** Stock Boston; **607,** Corbis-Bettmann; **608,** SuperStock; **609,** Jim West/The Image Works; **610,** AP Laser Photo; **611,** David Young-Wolff/PhotoEdit; **612,** Rod Rolle/Liaison Agency; **617,** Bill Aron/PhotoEdit; **618,** ©Don Wright, *The Palm Beach Post.*

UNIT 6 Page 622–623, AP Photo/Greg Baker; **624–625,** Ed Pritchard/Stone; **627,** Peter William Thornton/Lonely Planet Images; **628,** Bildarchiv Preussischer Kulturbesitz/Art Resource, NY; **629,** National Archives; **631,** The Art Archive/Musée des Beaux Arts La Rochelle/Dagli Orti; **632,** AP Photo/Max Nash/Pool; **634 l,** The Art Archive/Mireille Vautier; **634 r, 635,** The Art Archive/National History Museum Mexico City/Dagli Orti; **636,** Michael Dwyer/Alamy; **638,** The Granger Collection, New York; **641,** Maciej Macierzynski/Corbis; **642,** Museum of Flight/Corbis; **643 l,** Woodfin Camp & Associates; **643 tr,** The Image Works; **643 br,** Lester Lefkowitz/The Stock Market; **644,** Jeffrey Mrkowitz/Corbis Sygma; **646,** Thomas Coex/AFP/ Getty Images, Inc.; **648, 649,** Universal Pictorial Press Agency; **652,** Richard During/Stone; **653,** Jessica Rinaldi/Reuters; **655,** Gary Brookins/Courtesy *Richmond Times-Dispatch;* **656–657,** Joseph Sohm/Stock Boston; **658,** Myrleen Ferguson/ PhotoEdit; **660,** Jeff Greenberg/PhotoEdit; **661,** Steve Sack; **662,** Reiss/Action Press/SABA Press Photos; **663 l,** David Young-Wolff/PhotoEdit; **663 m,** Gary Conner/PhotoEdit; **663 r,** Michael L. Abramson/Woodfin Camp & Associates; **664,** Russ Lappa; **665,** Spencer Grant/PhotoEdit; **667 t,** Hulton Corbis; **667 inset,** Corbis; **668,** AP/Wide World Photos; **669,** Images.com/Corbis; **671,** Corbis Sygma; **672,** Sovfoto/Eastfoto; **673,** Owen Franken/Stock Boston; **674,** Sovfoto/Eastfoto; **675,** Christy Bowe/Corbis Sygma **675,** Prentice Hall; **679,** Danziger.

UNIT 7 Page 680–681, Robert Holmes/Corbis; **682–683,** AP Photo/Paul Sakuma; **684,** The Granger Collection, New York; **685,** From the Rotarian, June 1972. By permission of the Publisher.; **686,** California State Archives; **688,** Virginia Historical Society; **689,** California State Library; **690,** The Granger Collection, New York; **691 l,** Corbis; **691 r,** Najlan Feanny/SABA Press Photos; **692,** AP Photo/Rich Pedroncelli; **695,** AP Photo/Kevork Djansezian; **696,** AP Photo/Rich Pedroncelli; **698,** Swift Thor/Gamma; **701,** Joel Page Photo; **702,** North Wind Picture Archives; **703,** Bob Daemmrich/Pictor; **704,** ©The New Yorker Collection 1999, Michael Maslin from cartoonbank.com. All Rights Reserved.; **707,** National Archives; **708,** Art Resource, New York; **709,** ©The New Yorker Collection 1998, Michael Maslin from cartoonbank.com. All Rights Reserved.; **710,** Comstock; **711 l,** Tony Freeman/PhotoEdit; **711 r,** AP Photo/Pool, Nancee Lewis; **715,** © The New Yorker Collection 1981, James Stevenson from cartoonbank.com. All Rights Reserved.; **716–717,** Jeff Greenberg/The Image Works; **718,** Mark C. Burnett/Stock Boston; **720,** Bob Darmmrich/Stock Boston; **721,** Paula Lerner/Woodfin Camp & Associates; **722,** Charles Schoffer/Index Stock Imagery; **724,** Photo by Jeff Teeter. Courtesy of California State University, Chico; **725,** Wolfgang Kaehler/Liaison Agency; **726 t,** The Granger Collection, New York; **726 b,** R. Foulds/Washington Stock Photo; **730 l,** The Granger Collection, New York; **730 r,** R. Foulds/ Washington Stock Photo; **731,** Ted Soqui/Corbis; **732,** By permission of Mike Luckovich and Creator's Syndicate, Inc.; **733,** Robert Holmes/Corbis; **735,** Courtesy of Juan Arambula; **736 l,** Alamy Images; **736 m,** Kevin Horan/Stock Boston; **736r,** Wernher Krutein/Liaison Agency; **738,** AP Photo/Mike Derer; **739,** Catherine Karnow/Woodfin Camp &Associates; **740 l,** Tony Korody/Corbis Sygma; **740 r,** Corbis; **742,** Reprinted with permission from the *Minneapolis Star and Tribune;* **743,** ©Sheryl Schindler/Courtesy of the Office of the Board of Education, San Francisco; **747,** ©The New Yorker Collection 1955, Ed Fisher from cartoonbank.com. All Rights Reserved.

End Matter Page 748 background, P. Costas/Washington Stock; **748 tl, tr,** The Granger Collection, New York; **748 mr,** Rob Crandall/Stock Boston; **748 bl,** UPI/Corbis-Bettmann; **748 br,** AP Photo/Stephan Savoia; **749,** The Granger Collection, New York; **754 all,** Art Resource, New York; **755 t,** White House; **755 the rest,** White House Historical Association; **797,** Library of Congress; **798,** Chicago Historical Society.

Text Acknowledgments

Page 78, "Letters of Liberty" Adapted with permission from the publisher. From THE BILL OF RIGHTS: A USERS GUIDE © 2000. Close-Up Foundation, Alexandria, Virginia; **96,** "More Power To The States" Excerpt from "The New Federalism: Two Views" by Linda Chavez; adapted with permission from the publisher. From PERSPECTIVES: READINGS ON CONTEMPORARY AMERICAN GOVERNMENT © 1989. Close-Up Foundation, Alexandria, Virginia; **158,** "The Dangers of Voter Apathy" By Curtis Gans. Reprinted with permission from the publisher. From PERSPECTIVES: READINGS ON CONTEMPORARY AMERICAN GOVERNMENT © 1989. Close-Up Foundation, Alexandria, Virginia; **214,** "The Latino Media Story" Excerpt from "Demographics Drive the Latino Media Story" by Kim Campbell. This article first appeared in THE CHRISTIAN SCIENCE MONITOR on June 21, 2001 and is reproduced with permission. © 2001 THE CHRISTIAN SCIENCE MONITOR (www.csmonitor.com). All rights reserved.; **274,** "Supreme Court Upholds Congressional District Against Racial Gerrymandering Claim" (by Richard Zitrin) From lexisONE. Copyright © 2001 lexisONE. Used by permission; **607,** "Breaking Down Barriers" Excerpt from "Perspectives on the Constitution" by Ernest Green; adapted with permission from the publisher. From PERSPECTIVES: READINGS ON CONTEMPORARY AMERICAN GOVERNMENT © 1989. Close-Up Foundation, Alexandria, Virginia; **671,** "The Third Way" Excerpt of Tony Blair's speech from The Labour Party Annual Conference 2000. Reprinted by permission of the Labour Party U.K.; **701,** "The New Breed of State Legislator" Excerpt from "Enter The New Breed" by Garry Boulard. Reprinted from STATE LEGISLATURES, July/August 1999, Vol. 25, No. 7. Copyright © 1999 by the National Conference of State Legislatures. Used by permission; **724,** "Seeing The Regional Future" Excerpt from the Economic Development Column by William Fulton in CONGRESSIONAL QUARTERLY. Copyright © 1999 by Congressional Quarterly, Inc. Reproduced with permission of Congressional Quarterly, Inc. via Copyright Clearance Center

NOTE: Every effort has been made to locate the copyright owner of material reprinted in this book. Omissions brought to our attention will be corrected in subsequent editions.

Stop the Presses

Bury me on my face; for in a little while everything will be turned upside down.

—Diogenes

 On this and the following page you will find a number of last-minute items which, for reasons of timing, could not be included in the main body of the text.

Go Online
PHSchool.com

Access Web Code mqc-8261 for further updates.

Deficits and Hurricanes

The federal deficit for fiscal year 2005 (which ended September 30, 2005) came to $318.62 billion—more than $12 billion less than the amount initially reported by the Office of Management and Budget. The shortfall for 2005 is the third largest ever recorded. It is, however, markedly smaller than the all-time record deficit of $412.85 billion set in 2004. Although federal spending in 2005 rose to $2.47 trillion, 7.9 percent above the total for 2004, tax receipts increased by 14.6 percent, to $2.15 trillion.

The Office of Management and Budget has projected deficits of approximately $341 billion for fiscal year 2006 and $233 billion for fiscal 2007. It now appears quite certain that those estimates will prove to be far too low, however. They will in large part because they were made before the advent of hurricanes Katrina and then Rita and then Wilma in September and October of 2005. Those massive storms devastated much of the Gulf Coast region from southeastern Texas through Mississippi and Alabama to Florida.

President Bush requested and Congress quickly provided $62 billion in emergency aid for people in the stricken areas. The President has indicated that he will seek at least $200 billion in additional aid in the coming months. See pages 88–89, 98–99, 296–297, 390–392, 454–456.

Presidential Nominating Process

A study commission appointed by the Democratic National Committee has recommended that at least two other States, and perhaps four, join Iowa and New Hampshire in holding the first contest in the Democratic Party's presidential nominating process in 2008. The proposed increase in the number of early contests is intended to provide for more racial and geographic diversity in that process. Together, Iowa and New Hampshire represent only some 1.5 percent of the nation's population, and the residents of those two States are predominantly white. Needless to say, most Democrats and many others in both Iowa and New Hampshire are staunchly opposed to any such change in the presidential primary-caucus schedule. See pages 369–372.

Also, the DNC has set the dates (but has not yet selected a site) for the Democratic Party's national convention in 2008. The meeting will be held Monday, August 25 through Thursday, August 28. These late-August dates will allow the party's prospective presidential candidate to raise and spend private money for almost a month longer than was the case in 2004.

The DNC will not select a site for the party's next convention until some time after the 2006 midterm elections are held. The Republican National Committee will begin the process of picking a site and setting the dates for the GOP's 2008 convention some time in early 2006. See pages 196–202, 368–370.

The Supreme Court

The Supreme Court, with two new justices including new Chief Justice John Roberts, will hear and decide a number of critically important cases during its current term. Among those cases, these are of particular importance:

• *Gonzales* v. *Oregon* involves a unique State law that authorizes physician-assisted suicide. In 1994 Oregon voters approved an initiative measure, the Death with Dignity Act, to allow medical doctors to prescribe lethal doses of certain prescription drugs to assist in the painless death of competent yet terminally ill persons. The law sets out closely detailed procedures designed to protect vulnerable patients and ensure that their decisions in the matter are both reasoned and voluntary. Oregon's voters reaffirmed their support of the law in 1997, by defeating a ballot measure that sought to repeal the Death with Dignity Act. Over the past ten years, some 200 persons have opted to use that law to end their lives.

In 2001, John Ashcroft, then the Attorney General of the United States, announced what has come to be known as the "Ashcroft Directive." It holds that physician-assisted suicides under the Oregon law violate the federal Controlled Substances Act of

1970, because assisting a suicide is not "a legitimate medical practice" that would justify the dispensing of any controlled substance. Accordingly, any physician who prescribes a controlled substance to assist a suicide can lose his or her federal license to prescribe controlled substances and can also be prosecuted for violating federal law.

In 2002, a doctor, a pharmacist, several terminally ill patients, and the State of Oregon brought this challenge to the Ashcroft Directive. The case does not involve either the wisdom or the ethical foundations of the Oregon law. It centers, instead, on (1) the question of whether Congress intended the Controlled Substances Act to be interpreted and applied as the Ashcroft Directive would have it and (2) the breadth of the reserved power of a State to regulate the practice of medicine within its own borders. See pages 92–93, 94–95, 393–395.

• *Randall* v. *Sorrell*, a case from Vermont, asks the Court to revisit its decision in the landmark campaign finance law case *Buckley* v. *Valeo*, 1976. There, among its many holdings in that case, the Court ruled that, because in politics "money is speech," the several limits that Congress had placed on spending by candidates for federal office were unconstitutional. It has been widely affirmed over the years since then, and both federal and State courts have regularly held that the 1st and 14th Amendments prohibit any caps on spending by candidates for public office.

In 1997, the Vermont legislature adopted a campaign finance law that purposefully challenged that view. That law puts very strict limits on campaign spending; and it does so, Vermont's secretary of state has said, with the "express goal of giving the Supreme Court an opportunity to re-evaluate its decision in *Buckley* v. *Valeo*."

The supporters of the law argue that much has changed over the past 30 years. They say that there are now at least two compelling justifications for limits on campaign spending that did not exist when the Court decided *Buckley*: (1) widespread public cynicism about the impact of money in politics and (2) the fact that unlimited spending often turns elected officeholders into full-time fundraisers who should, instead, devote their time to the public's business. See pages 196–198, 200.

• *Rumsfeld* v. *Forum for Academic and Institutional Rights (FAIR)* centers on the constitutionality of a provision in a 1994 act of Congress appropriating money for the Defense Department. That provision, known as the Solomon Amendment, directs the government to withhold or withdraw federal funds from an institution of higher education if any unit within that college or university denies to military recruiters the same access to its campus and students that it grants to other prospective employers. The Solomon Amendment was prompted by opposition to the Defense Department's "don't ask, don't tell" policy that bars military service by openly gay men and women.

For decades, the American Association of Law Schools, which includes nearly every law school in the country, has had a non-discrimination policy which forbids its members to allow employers who discriminate on the basis of race or gender to use its career placement facilities. In 1990, the organization unanimously voted to include sexual orientation as a protected category in its non-discrimination policy. FAIR, an association of 30 law schools, maintains that the Solomon Amendment violates law schools' 1st Amendment rights of expression. The group also argues that its member schools are being forced to endorse a Defense Department policy ("don't ask, don't tell") which they oppose. See pages 472–476, 546–547, 555, 558.

• *Ayotte* v. *Planned Parenthood of Northern New England* presents a challenge to a New Hampshire abortion law, the Parental Notification Prior to Abortion Act of 2003. That statute makes it unlawful for a physician to perform an abortion on any female less than 18 years of age until at least 48 hours after a parent has received written notice of the pending operation. In certain circumstances, a judge may grant an exception to the parental notification requirement.

Planned Parenthood of Northern New England claims that the New Hampshire law does not meet the "undue burden" standard set out by the Court in *Planned Parenthood of Southeastern Pennsylvania* v. *Casey* in 1992 and is therefore unconstitutional. The group argues that the law fails to meet the "undue burden" standard primarily because it does not contain an explicit exception to the notification requirement aimed at protecting the health of a pregnant minor. See pages 536, 567–568.